Handbooks of Sociol Research

Series Editor

John DeLamater, University of Wisconsin, MADISON, Wisconsin, USA

Each of these Handbooks survey the field in a critical manner, evaluating theoretical models in light of the best available empirical evidence. Distinctively sociological approaches are highlighted by means of explicit comparison to perspectives characterizing related disciplines such as psychology, psychiatry, and anthropology. These seminal works seek to record where the field has been, to identify its current location, and to plot its course for the future. If you are interested in submitting a proposal for this series, please contact the series editor, John DeLamater: delamate@ssc.wisc.edu.

More information about this series at http://www.springer.com/series/6055

Seth Abrutyn
Editor

Handbook of Contemporary Sociological Theory

Editor
Seth Abrutyn
Department of Sociology
The University of Memphis
Memphis, Tennessee, USA

ISSN 1389-6903
Handbooks of Sociology and Social Research
ISBN 978-3-319-61601-8 (PB)
ISBN 978-3-319-32248-3 (HB) ISBN 978-3-319-32250-6 (eBook)
DOI 10.1007/978-3-319-32250-6

Library of Congress Control Number: 2016941062

Printed on acid-free paper

This Springer imprint is published by Springer Nature
The registered company is Springer International Publishing AG Switzerland

In loving memory of my Mom,
Alie

Foreword

In recent decades, large handbooks and even larger encyclopedias on virtually all topics have proliferated in the academic world. Part of this trend is to be explained by the proliferation of knowledge in an ever-more specialized intellectual ecosystem; there is now a market for summaries and reviews because it is virtually impossible to keep up in the ever-expanding subfields within disciplines, to say nothing of new disciplines that continue to emerge. The penetration of the World Wide Web has only accelerated these trends. Yet, if truth be told, another reason that so many handbooks are being published is that it is still one of the few types of books that libraries still feel compelled to buy, although the goose that has been laying this golden egg—i.e., academics willing to write chapters for a little cost and libraries all-too-willing to buy them—may itself be subject to the forces of publishing evolution: the overproduction of handbooks leading to increasing density and competition in a limited resource niche. Indeed, it is entirely conceivable that publishers will soon need to produce Meta-Handbooks to consolidate the knowledge in the proliferating handbooks, or alternatively, the Goose will simply go extinct and be replaced by something more like Wikipedia-type reviews.

Fifteen years ago, when I was asked to edit the first *Handbook of Sociological Theory*, handbooks were only beginning to proliferate. At the time, I was reluctant to take on all of the work because, as I have learned, editing books often resembles trying to herd cats to a deadline in a particular format. As it turned out, this first *Handbook of Sociological Theory* was surprisingly easy because virtually everyone delivered their chapter on time, in the right format, and spot-on in terms of its content. Indeed, I was so impressed that I edited several more books, which did not quite replicate my experience with the first *Handbook of Sociological Theory*. And so, when I was approached to edit another *Handbook of Sociological Theory*, I demurred because the potential amount of work involved but, also, because I felt that a different approach was required. The book should be edited by a younger, rising theorists with a different set of eyes and with a less ossified mind, and it is for this reason that Seth Abrutyn was selected to edit the volume; and the differences between the first and this second handbook are so clearly evident. This book has a better mix of scholars at different stages of their careers; and the book is more focused on key issues and topics rather than being overly encyclopedic. It is, I think, a much tighter and focused book than the one that I edited, even though so many prominent scholars wrote chapters that became necessary "read's" by theorists. I like the whole thrust of the organization in this new *Handbook of Sociological Theory: Re-thinking* and bringing into the twenty-first century classical questions (Part I); rethinking the never-ending macro-micro debate in ways that, in my view, obviate the debate and demonstrate how far sociology has come in resolving the issues (Part II); demonstrating that sociologists do indeed have a coherent view of the basic properties of the social universe (Part III); delineating new forms of micro sociology and the constraints imposed on the micro universe (Part IV); and outlining new models of social change that update those of the past (Part VI). In reading over the specific chapters that Seth Abrutyn reviews in his introduction, including the two chapters that I contributed, there is a very different feel in this handbook. For example, in writing about the macro and meso basis of the micro-social order, I knew that I would be in dialogue with Edward Lawler and his team (Shane Thye and Jeongkoo Yoon), and they appeared to have felt the same way. The result is a much more powerful set of theoretical argument than each of the chapters alone, and one in which we all are trying to address each others' work. Add to his, chapters on networks and fields to rethinking the macro-macro linkage, and the whole section demonstrates *how far* sociology has come. Indeed, I have recently taken to arguing that sociology is the most mature science when it comes to resolving its micro-macro "gap" problems; and I am prepared to defend this, even when the most mature sciences, biology and physics, are considered.

What also emerges in all of the sections is this: The chapters review arguments, to be sure, but they each also try to explain something. This may seem rather odd compliment for a theory volume but, in fact, so much theoretical sociology *does not* explain how anything operates. It does not tell us how and why a process and set of processes operate and unfold; rather, too much theoretical sociology is locked into foundational, ontological, epistemological, and other debates that are, in essence, never ending. I have often derisively called this "talk about talk"—which has earned me a few friends—but the fact is that too many sociologists, and particularly those who see themselves as theorists, do not believe that a science of the social universe is possible, or even desirable. They criticize positivism, proclaim as "pretentious" efforts to develop sociological laws and models of fundamental social processes, and otherwise debunk those who think that there is nothing fundamentally different about the social universe compared to the biotic and physicochemical universes.

Somehow the facts that humans have big brains (totally explicable in terms of biological theory) and, hence, can develop language and culture makes the human universe unique and out of reach of science. Nothing could be further from the truth, and many of the chapters clearly demonstrate that such is the case. The social world of humans is, of course, a different domain of the universe, but it is one that I am confident will be seen as universal across the galaxies, if and when we humans are ever able to contact other life forms with intelligence, language, and culture. I would argue that the same laws and models that we develop here on earth for human beings and their patterns of social organization will look much the same across the universe—which, to some, may seem preposterous. But if we believe that human social organization reveals generic and universal properties that can be explained by theories and models, just like those in physics, then why should social organization created by intelligent, culture-using animals be so different elsewhere in the universe.

I do not want to get too carried away here, but the point is clear: theory should explain why and how humans behave, interact, and organize themselves in all times and places. And while there will always be a "historically" unique aspect to how any given pattern of social organization came to exist, its actual operation can be explained by abstract laws and models. Historical explanations are a very legitimate mode of explanation, and they often yield insights that allow for more nomothetic explanations to be developed—as has been the case with physics where the history of the universe is best explained by the abstract principles of physics. The same is true of any biotic system, or geological system, and so why would we think that such could not be the case for human social systems? And while the case is often made that humans have "agency," and thus the very nature of the universe can be changed, agentic behaviors themselves are understandable by abstract laws and models; and, moreover, agency *cannot* change the laws of social organization. Indeed, agency is often crushed by the reality of social organization whose dynamics change agents often assume they can obviate. Indeed, failed agency is a very good indicator that more fundamental forces are in play, and that perhaps it is a good idea to figure out what these are and to understand their dynamics so that agents do not make the same mistakes over and over again.

Not all who have contributed to this volume will agree with my advocacy, of course, but this handbook provides a very good look at the potential for scientific explanation in sociology. There is less mushing abound in the quagmire of old philosophical debates, relativism, and constructivism; rather, there is more of a feel that scholars can roll up their sleeves and explain how the social world operates. Since the late 1950s, sociology has faced a crisis of confidence, masked by a shrill of unfounded overconfidence that the social world is not amenable to scientific explanations about generic and universal processes in all times and places that humans have organized. There has been a kind of smug cynicism about sociology's assumed failings to explain very much with science. Yet, in fact, if we look back to theoretical sociology 50 years ago, about the time that I became a professional sociologist, the progress in theoretical sociology has been unbelievably rapid. Sociology can explain far more of the social universe than it could back then, and it is now poised to explain even more. And, as much as one book can, this handbook offers a sense for what can be done in the future.

When I entered graduate school in the mid-1960s, there was a real sense that sociology had arrived at the table of science. Sociology would be able to develop testable theories, formally stated, that could explain the operative dynamics of the social universe. Indeed, confidence among some was so great that we were required to read the plethora of "theory construction" books and articles that began to appear in both sociology and philosophy. I always thought that these were incredibly boring—ironical, I guess, because I now write much of this boring formal theory. But my objection to such books is the implicit view the "instructions for constructing theories" where very much like methods textbooks or manual for statistical modeling. But, in fact, theorizing is a creative activity of having insights into the nature and operation of some fundamental social process; formalizing the theory is "mop up work" of trying to find a way to state the relationships among the forces in play in a parsimonious way. Formalization, itself, is not theorizing; having insights in the forces driving the social universe is theorizing. So, while there is a little formal theorizing in this handbook, it is filled with insights into how the social universe operates. Others can build upon these ideas, and once they are well developed, it becomes possible to express them more formally—but, again, that is not what is most important. Ideas over formats and formalization are what will drive sociological theorizing; and this handbook is filled with such ideas.

Finally, I have a dream—most likely never to be realized but a dream nonetheless—that *Handbooks of Sociological Theory* will someday in the near future never be necessary because our discipline's introductory textbooks would, like those in physics, outline most of the basic principles. Gone would be discussion of our classical figures, cartoons, boxes full of color and not much else, diagrams for the sake of graphics, and all of the fluff that is now in a sociology textbook. Physics textbooks have adopted much of this look, but it is not fluff in the manner of sociology textbooks. It is a sincere effort to communicate basic principles, and this is what sociology books of the future should look like. Biology textbooks also have that "four color look" (and expense) but if one reads them closely, this "look" focuses on explaining on generic biological processes. In my dream, there would be no theory handbooks; rather, handbook*s* in sociology would be about the rapidly accumulating knowledge in subfields where empirical research, theoretically informed, could be assembled for a quick review. And such handbooks might be needed every year because a field where data is collected to assess theories advance rapidly. In some ways, the very need for a *Handbook of Sociological Theory* like this one in 2016 tells us that we still have ways to go in separating theory as a goal of science as opposed to social theory that debunks science; that tells us once again the stories of St. Marx, St. Weber, St. Durkheim, and other canonized figures in whose shadows we still stand; that drags in old philosophical debates; and that expresses relativistic, constructivist, and sophistic views about sociology.

The chapters in this book give me some hope that we can avoid a fate dominated by critics. And so, let us dedicate this *Handbook of Sociological Theory* and the others that will be necessary in the near future to obviating, in the future, the need for such *Handbooks of Sociological Theory*. We should look and work for a day when there would be such wide consensus about explanations of how the social universe operates that our introductory textbooks would tell much of the basic theoretical story. Perhaps sociology would have fewer interested students, but they would be students with theoretical knowledge that would be useful in making the social world a better place for all.

Institute for Theoretical Social Science
Santa Barbara, CA, USA

Jonathan H. Turner

Acknowledgements

I would like to first extend a warm thank you to each of the contributors to this volume. You all made the challenge of managing an editorship such as this much easier, and the handbook is a testament to your expertise and the care you put into your respective chapters. In addition, I would like to thank Jonathan Turner, my grad school advisor, good friend, and confidant, for opening doors and giving constant encouragement, advice, and support. Additionally, Jon, Steve Brint, Sandy Maryanski, Chris Chase-Dunn, Jan Stets, and Peter Burke were all instrumental in shaping my eclectic taste in theory, as well as shaping the theorist I have become, and thus have much to do with the vision of this handbook. I also have to thank my collaborator and close colleague, Anna S. Mueller, for tolerating (and encouraging) my forays into the theoretical ether; my graduate theory seminar students who have allowed me to use the class as a laboratory for my ideas; the sociology department at Memphis for being supportive and excellent colleagues; and, finally, my graduate assistant, Taylor M. Binnix, who was instrumental in helping format and proof these chapters. Finally, my wife, Danielle Morad Abrutyn, and son Asa Jonas, deserve a huge thank you: they have done nothing but, inspire me, and encourage and support all of my academic endeavors, including this handbook.

Contents

Part V Modes of Change

Contributors

Seth Abrutyn Department of Sociology, University of Memphis, Memphis, TN, USA

Stephen Benard Department of Sociology, Indiana University, Bloomington, IN, USA

Christof Brandtner Stanford University, Stanford, CA, USA

Michael J. Carter Sociology Department, California State University, Northridge, Northridge, CA, USA

Alicia D. Cast Department of Sociology, University of California, Santa Barbara, Santa Barbara, CA, USA

Nick Crossley University of Manchester, Manchester, UK

Neil Fligstein University of California, Berkeley, CA, USA

Andreas Glaeser Department of Sociology, The University of Chicago, Chicago, IL, USA

Katja M. Guenther University of California, Riverside, Riverside, CA, USA

Matthew M. Hollander Department of Sociology, University of Wisconsin-Madison, Madison, WI, USA

Michael D. Irwin Duquesne University, Pittsburgh, PA, USA

Daniel N. Kluttz University of California, Berkeley, CA, USA

Edward J. Lawler Cornell University, Ithaca, NY, USA

Omar Lizardo Department of Sociology, University of Notre Dame, Notre Dame, IN, USA

Richard Machalek University of Wyoming, Laramie, WY, USA

Matthew C. Mahutga University of California, Riverside, Riverside, CA, USA

Michael W. Martin Adams State University, Alamosa, CO, USA

Douglas W. Maynard Department of Sociology, University of Wisconsin-Madison, Madison, WI, USA

Kevin McCaffree Department of Sociology, Indiana-Purdue University, Fort Wayne, IN, USA

Trenton D. Mize Department of Sociology, Indiana University, Bloomington, IN, USA

Dana M. Moss University of Pittsburgh, Pennsylvania, PA, USA

Simone Polillo The Department of Sociology, University of Virginia, Charlottesville, VA, USA

Walter W. Powell Stanford University, Stanford, CA, USA

Zandria Felice Robinson Rhodes College, Memphis, TN, USA

Christina Simko Department of Anthropology and Sociology, Williams College, Williamstown, MA, USA

Lynn Smith-Lovin Department of Sociology, Duke University, Durham, NC, USA

David A. Snow University of California, Irvine, CA, USA

Jan E. Stets Department of Sociology, University of California, Riverside, Riverside, CA, USA

Erika Summers-Effler University of Notre Dame, Notre Dame, IN, USA

Panu Suppatkul University of California, Riverside, Riverside, CA, USA

Iddo Tavory New York University, New York, NY, USA

Shane R. Thye University of South Carolina, Columbia, SC, USA

Jonathan H. Turner Department of Sociology, University of California, Santa Barbara, CA, USA

Jason Turowetz Department of Sociology, University of Wisconsin-Madison, Madison, WI, USA

Justin Van Ness University of Notre Dame, Notre Dame, IN, USA

Lisa Slattery Walker Department of Sociology, University of North Carolina, Charlotte, Charlotte, NC, USA

Yingyao Wang The Watson Institute for International and Public Affairs, Brown University, Providence, RI, USA

Murray Webster Jr. Department of Sociology, University of North Carolina, Charlotte, Charlotte, NC, USA

Emi A. Weed Department of Sociology, Duke University, Durham, NC, USA

Jeongkoo Yoon Ewha Women's University, Seoul, South Korea

Introduction

1

Seth Abrutyn

1.1 Orienting Ourselves

For several years, I mused "Who now reads Parsons" as a sort of ironic twist of Parsons' famous opening line in the *Structure of Social Action* asking the same question of Herbert Spencer's work. Perhaps it is time to revise this question, to ask "who now reads theory?" On the one hand, this question is preposterous in that every sociology major and graduate student has to read *some* theory on the road to matriculation; there are several folks, such as myself, who label themselves a theorist; and, nearly all work submitted for review and accepted for publication requires a modicum of theoretical import. On the other hand, because theory is treated as a distinct course, apart from methods and statistics, and because we continue to advertise positions for theory professorships, theory remains a de facto specialization; as a specialization, it can be rightfully ignored by those specializing in substantive areas. As Lizardo (2014) has argued, the "theorist" as we all came to know him or her is dead, yet many sociologists continue to imagine the armchair, ivory tower theorist as real. In doing so, they dissociate themselves from having to learn theory as a theorist presumably once did. More importantly, they absolve themselves of having to learn what it means to *theorize*, and how to contribute to a common goal of cumulative knowledge and language. And so, what theory is and how much a sociologist actually reads varies wildly. For the most part, as this essay will show, what the student reads is as much a function of the arbitrary decisions the professor makes, the textbook he or she may employ, and the biases installed by his or her former advisor and/or department culture; while active scholars read what is new in their area and perhaps re-visit the seminal theoretical treatises occasionally. Compounding this, are the endless debates about what theory is or isn't (Turner 1985; Collins 1988; Alexander 1990; Abend 2008), the philosophy of science surrounding epistemology and ontology that pose as theory, and meta-theoretical discourse revolving around potentially unimportant and, perhaps, unsolvable "dilemmas" like the macro-micro link (Knorr-Cetina 1981; Lenski 1988; Fine 1991; Collins 1994).

This essay, and especially this Handbook, does not focus on these issues, though they are the backdrop upon which the various chapters and threads tying them together are built. Instead, this Handbook turns away from these debates, tempting as they may be, and presents a vision of a more coherent theoretical world, and a more optimistic sense of what is possible. The art, craft, and practice of theorizing can be the most rewarding experience a sociologist has, but the

S. Abrutyn (✉)
Department of Sociology, University of Memphis, Memphis, TN, USA
e-mail: sbbrutyn@memphis.edu

S. Abrutyn (ed.), *Handbook of Contemporary Sociological Theory*,
Handbooks of Sociology and Social Research, DOI 10.1007/978-3-319-32250-6_1

discipline's paradoxical reverence and simultaneous distaste for theorists, the crystallized discipline-wide pedagogy, and the residuals from past practices and beliefs have erected artificial barriers that deter people from embracing theory at the level that might best serve sociology and its contribution to knowledge, policy, and everyday experience. These barriers are, at least, weakened, by the chapters presented herein. Indeed, many of the authors are not self-identified theorists, but their command over bodies of knowledge reveal that theory remains the central backbone of the sociological imagination.

Before elucidating the challenges and opportunities present, some definitional work is in order. To begin, I believe sociology is a science and, as such, is rooted in theories that *guide research problems, make sense of data, are tested using the scientific method* (regardless of the specific analytic strategy), and provide *ways of talking, thinking, understanding, and, ultimately, explaining the world.* I realize that there are many types and kinds of theories, and while I see no need to stake out firm ground that propositional, formal analytic theorizing or modeling is the *only* kind of theorizing, I do believe that not everything a scholar calls theory is theory; critical theory, for instance, is not really theory in the sense that it *cannot* be tested, but rather offers normative comparisons between parts of the real world and an idealized world that may or may not be possible or desirable. Hence, theories require some degree of abstraction, or conceptual distance from their subject; they *must* be operationalizable, though how we operationalize them may not always be readily apparent; they must be used to either understand or, even better, explain a phenomenon, process, or other sociological object of study; and, finally, theories that transcend time and space are often superior to those that do not, which calls attention to sociology's continued need for historical and comparative work.

Finally, theory and theories should be cumulative, which means that sociologists should be working *together*, not just on the specific case or substantive problem that brings notoriety, but on the common endeavor of building a language and conceptual world that makes cooperation, interaction, as well as debate and conflict more fruitful. To be sure, I celebrate eclectic and diverse theoretical traditions; I was drawn to graduate work by a master's level theory course in which we had freedom over our coursework. Marcuse was the first seductive theorist for me. Yet, I have also come to recognize the need for a coherent language and, as I have seen from the reaction of students exhausted from being presented one vision of social reality after another from one class to the next, a relatively coherent view of the social universe. It's not that we know everything, but we know quite a bit and it is time theorists and sociologists stopped acting as though we do not. We know, as Collins (1975) noted four decades ago, a lot about stratification and organization; we know a lot about power across levels of social reality, as well as status, identity, and roles. Having a firm theoretical grounding does not deter from novel, creative methods; from studying understudied populations; from discovering new principles, or modifying old ones. Rather, it provides a community of scholars the foundation for pursuing these very endeavors because it provides us with a firmer understanding of the gaps in knowledge, of the fuzzy areas that have been less attended to, and, ultimately, a road map for pursuing social research.

1.2 Three Challenges

Many of the classic statements on theory and its challenges have focused on the political, provincial, and ideological dilemmas preventing our discipline from coalescing and from theory becoming a site of some basic agreement. Having spent 5 years in academia as a professor, I am prepared to chalk these up to constants and deal with the environment as constructed. Hence, there are pragmatic challenges that I believe can be more easily overcome without treading too deeply into the ideological or political battles (perhaps that is naïve). In a perfect world, of course, sociologists would be a *community* or a *society*—the American Sociological Society, as it was once called—and not an *association*; for Weber (1978:40–1), the former is based on "a subjective feeling of the parties…that they belong together," whereas the former "rests on rationally motivated adjustment of interests." But, perhaps we are more like the actors in a Bourdieuian field than in a Marxian primitive communist society: tenure requirements, individual professional goals, elite networks and schools, ego, and the growing scarcity of valued resources flowing to, within, and out from higher education lead to the objectification of sociological relationships. Ironically, however, sociological theory *explains* what has happened: between Collins' (1998) law of small numbers, and, concomitantly, Spencer's (1874–1896) law of differentiation, Durkheim's (1893) law of specialization, and the pressure for effective integrative mechanisms, the state of sociology can be easily explained. But, I digress. In the following three section, I consider three interrelated challenges: the time crunch; the slavish adherence principle; and the conceptual crunch.

1.2.1 The Time Crunch

Elsewhere, I have commented on what I deem the 'time crunch' (Abrutyn 2013; Carter 2013). In short, sociological theory as currently taught and conceptualized, sedimented in textbook after textbook, and contested as well is facing its own internal temporal pressures. Two hundred fifty years of theorists and theory can no longer be adequately taught in two courses (Classic/Contemporary), or worse, in a single blended course. The desire to add more and more minority theorists to the classical canon, for example, further presses against the constraints of time, while the unending march of time adds new sociological theorists, forces us to make choices about old theorists and their viability, makes it difficult to know "all" theory, and raises implicit unanswered questions about what the heck we are even teaching! If there is any challenge that should be signaling we are doing this all wrong, this is it.

In 1960, classical/contemporary classes made sense: pre-Parsons fit the former and Parsons and beyond fit the latter. Today, what constitutes contemporary? Post 1970? 1990? 2000s and beyond? What constitutes classical? Pre-1960? Pre-1980? It is arbitrary either way, and invites arbitrary decision making that elevates one flavor of the period over another: this month it will be DuBois, and then next month it will be Sorokin. But, while we spend time looking for the founders of this or that, for inclusivity, for some unmined theorist who we can write five or six papers about, we are not resolving the pedagogical problem and, ultimately, how we socialize students into what theory is. I cannot tell you how many times I have taught Durkheim or Marx and because they do not formalize their propositions and their works are sprawling, students lose the connection between theory and research. There is not enough time to walk a student through Durkheim's suicide, and the evolution of the sociology of suicide throughout the course of the twentieth and twenty-first century! Not if I need to also lecture on Marx, Weber, DuBois, Martineau, Simmel, Mead, Cooley, and Spencer; and, what about Comte, Park, Sumner, Wirth, Thomas, Znaniecki? Or, if you want to go really deep, what about Tarde, Le Bon, Sorokin, de Tocqueville, *ad infinitum*?

In some ways, this is a function of path dependency: textbooks have been written for several decades now based on these two classes. These textbooks are involved in an arms race focused mainly on presentation and form, but also the content matter; the former two, however, constrain the latter. The one creative space an author has in updating their classical textbook is the "discovery" of some long lost theorist or, better, social/moral philosopher that other textbook authors have neglected. As if sociology students didn't have to learn enough names, now they must tangle with Nietzsche and Ibn Khaldun. One could just as easy go back to Plato or Pliny the Elder, or better yet, the unnamed author(s) of the Epic of Gilgamesh to find recurring ideas that found their way into sociological theory! To be sure, there is value in noting the intellectual heritage of a theorist, as Coser's (1977) classic text did with Durkheim, and Comte/Saint Simon/Diderot/Condorcet, but there is also a point where the principles of the theorist are lost in the vagaries of the philosophical statements of so and so. Who cares? And, more importantly, how is this theory? Indeed, if Durkheim's theoretical statements are only understandable within the context of his intellectual milieu, then they are not worth teaching in a science of society; if they transcend time and space, or at least some principles transcend time and space, then perhaps we should get on with the business of teaching those statements and leaving the rest out? The conflict, for instance, between town and country that underscores Marx's discussion of the inherent problems in the division of labor and the uneven distribution of economic power can be found in Ibn Khaldun, but not surprisingly, also in several Mesopotamian texts that were written from an urban perspective, though still highlight the logic of this divide. So, where do we stop? Because, there are several ethnographies on non-literate philosophers (Radin 1927 [1955]) that are also worth mining if we are indeed interested in going backwards.

In other ways, this is more an indictment of the discipline's inability to create even the most modest scopes around theory or theorizing. Perhaps it is radical to suggest that theories and not theorists be taught. From here, it is a short step to saying theory is about scientific research, and not cult of the personality or deep exegesis of one's favorite theorist. The methods people employ are less important than the rigor surrounding the methods. It is not theory, for instance, to debate whether a method achieves what it sets out to achieve; it is theory that guides the selection of methods as well as their creation. It is an entirely different task to debate the merits of this method or that. Regardless of where one falls ideologically, we can agree on one thing: the time crunch is real and needs fixing. It is untenable to imagine another decade of theorizing and few changes to how we conceptualize the pedagogical dissemination of theory.

1.2.2 The Slavish Adherence Principle

Besides these pedagogical problems, the size and density of theoretical knowledge available ensures that few sociologists have the time to read it all, and that most become versed in more than a small subsection of an already small subsection, and come to rely on textbooks—which are already designed for the lowest common denominator—for quick reviews, refreshers, or rehashing. The consequence is what I call the *slavish adherence principle*, or the tendency for sociologists in their work and in their reviews of others work to believe that: "if [insert your favorite theorist here] wrote "X," then any attempt to update, revise, reinterpret, or synthesize "X" is a violation of all that is holy. This axiom is especially true of the classics, which are jealously guarded by folks who identify as Marxists or as Durkheimians. However, it remains true of Bourdieuians and Foucaltians, and the like. There are numerous flaws that this axiom rests on. First, nearly every theorist—though not all—that is worshipped, is worshipped precisely because their body of work is sprawling, filled with contradictions, and vague in definition. Like the Bible, one can find their favorite quotes for "habitus" and write an article or a book about this conceptualization. (If this first flaw sounds like a violation of the principle, then the reader is aware of the biggest weakness with slavish adherence).

Second, there is a larger set of sociologists who read Durkheim's *Division of Labor* or *Suicide*, or the *German Ideology*, or whatever, 10, 15, or 20 years ago. Time rarely permits us to re-read the classics or much theory once we become professors, because we are busy keeping up with the field we work in and the latest research. Consequently, our understanding of a theory or a concept is crystallized in our graduate school or early professorial days, and the essence often becomes obscured by our specialized focus or by the inevitable decay of memory. Yet, many remain insistent that theorist X said theory A or defined concept B, regardless of its factuality, but insistent on the fact that their interpretation, correct or incorrect, is fact and, thus, the theory cannot be altered. Finally, many sociologists remember the co-opted version of a theory. Merton's (1938) famous paper on *anomie* drew his conceptualization from one section of Durkheim's (1897 [1951]) *Suicide*. Since then, many have employed explicitly or implicitly the Mertonian structural functional conception of anomie in testing Durkheim's hypotheses. Thus, the concept is rarely defined precisely, is often rooted in someone else's interpretation,[1] and, unfortunately, becomes arbitrary in analysis. For instance, a recent paper by Hoffman and Bearman (2015) treats the definition and operationalization of anomie as taken for granted, barely reviewing the debates surrounding its meaning, ignoring Durkheim's own words, all while making important empirical claims about anomie vis-à-vis the consequences of media exposure; claims that, if true, would call into question guidelines media outlets use in reporting celebrity suicides.

Slavish adherence also kills the sociological imagination. It hermetically seals sociological theory, and erects provincial boundaries that make sense, to some degree, for folks protecting their hard fought positions in the discipline, subfield, or substantive area. The number of reviews I have received that continue to adhere to Durkheim's fourfold typology, golden equilibrium of integration/regulation, and macro-level orientation is truly confounding. (Yet, it does make some sense when we consider the time crunch discussion above: there simply isn't enough time to digest all the different theories and theorists available). Without beating a dead horse, let's look a little closer at Durkheim and how some of his works are portrayed slavishly by the discipline.

First, there is the frame we bracket his work in: Durkheim is usually presented to undergraduates and graduate students alike as a structural functionalist. To be sure, in the opening salvos of the *Division of Labor*, he speaks like an organicist, and yes he believed the social body to be greater than its parts. And, we can admit that he was constantly seeking to understand what mechanisms functioned to generate solidarity. But, is functionalism really a bad word? Marxists also assert functional theories, as they try to elucidate the mechanisms that sustain economic power relations. In fact, it is hard to not be a functionalist as a theorist, because part of theorizing is pointing out how the social universe looks and why it tends to continue to look that way (e.g., Bourdieu's structured structures and structuring structures). Nevertheless, Durkheim has the label. How then do we fit in the rest of his career post 1893? How do we make sense of the shift towards emotions in *The Rules*, throughout *Suicide*, and in full force in *The Elementary Forms*? Even the most cursory read of these works would force the reader to question just how functionalist he is; especially compared to, say, Parsons or Merton. In fact, he gradually became a social psychologist who, despite rejecting all of his rival Tarde's ideas, came to embrace ideas like emotional contagion and group identity, and small scale interaction rituals.

A second example can be culled from *Suicide*, which I have already begun referring to above. Nearly all sociology of suicide over the last 100 years has, understandably, been Durkheimian (Stack 2000; Wray et al. 2011). Except, it hasn't really been. As noted above, it generally adheres slavishly to the common interpretations of Durkheim: there are four types of suicide, two of which (egoism/anomic) are present in modernity, two of which (altruism/fatalism) are relics of traditional, ascriptive societies. Therefore, we should only study the former two, because the others ones cannot possibly be located in modernity. In terms of altruism, until recently (Abrutyn and Mueller 2015), a review found only one empirical article (Leenaars 2004). One must reply to the slavish adherents: how can a theory be generalizable when two of its main concepts are denied applicability by its founder, and when they remain understudied? Of course, Durkheim could not have cared that much about at least one of the two "traditional" forms of suicide, fatalism, as it was hastily analyzed in a single paragraph, in a single footnote (1897 [1951]:276), never to be discussed by Durkheim again. How can we even slavishly adhere to a fourfold model when its progenitor was not fully committed to the model?!

The larger point is such: what is gained by not isolating the principles of suicide or rituals, and moving on from Durkheim's sociocultural milieu? Again, if the principles cannot be extracted from the nineteenth century, then the

[1] In this case, Merton, who had a very different idea than Durkheim did (Hilbert 1989), but in other cases, it is one's mentor's interpretation.

theory is not worth keeping and then why are we teaching Durkheim besides the fact that he established the discipline? Clearly, his work has something timeless that inspires contemporary sociologists. Thus, we do not need to debate who belongs in the canon and who does not; we need to extract the ideas, and move them forward with the various methodological tools we have. However, we cannot move on until we arrive at a point where "power," "anomie," or the basic dynamics of organizations or stratification are presented as *sociological knowledge*.

1.2.3 The Conceptual Crunch

The conceptual crunch refers to a set of interrelated dilemmas surrounding theory. First, because of the size of theory and the way we teach it, many scholars invent neologisms for concepts or processes already extant. Sometimes it is because the scholar, such as Bourdieu and habitus, believes extant concepts are inadequate; these maneuvers are not the best for clarity and shared theoretical language, but they are at least defensible. But, often new concepts are the hallmark of young professors trying to create their own theory for professional reasons. Second, some concepts are rejected, not on their empirical or theoretical validity and utility, but for ideological or political reasons—could one imagine a physicist deciding to call "atoms" something else because he or she did not like the term concept or felt they had a "better" metaphor? Third, many of our most cherished concepts have resisted definition, yet continue to be used as if they do have some semblance of shared meaning—e.g., institution (see Chap. 11) or self (see Chap. 17).

One of the casualties of the crunch are good, clear concepts. Take *role* for instance: a concept that stood for the generalized behavioral repertoires and expectation-sets that people meeting certain criteria could occupy is rarely referred to in contemporary parlance. For some it is too functionalist, being connected to Parsons and Merton; for others, it isn't cultural enough or lacks agency; and for others, it is too deterministic and structural. Yet, the arguments against role rests less on empirical grounds that verify or cast doubt on the concept's effects on behavior and attitudes, and more on parochial positions, advisor or department preferences, and the pursuit of sociological fame. A perfectly useful and empirical valid concept is denied its value on non-scientific grounds. The same problems plague seminal concepts like anomie and class, to name two.

It remains frustrating that sociology has avoided some type of common socialization beyond everyone knowing Durkheim, Weber, and Marx! The fact that this is the baseline for becoming a sociologist speaks directly to a constellation of problems surrounding theory itself. And, while I am not trying to advance a political position, I am merely speaking a social fact: communities that do not share a common language, have a hard time sharing a modicum of common reality. Moreover, it supports the (false) idea that sociology does not have any laws or scientific value to solving problems. Indeed, the chapters of this book demonstrate, throughout, common threads that tie sociology together as a discipline and community of scholars. These threads are sometimes made explicit, but other times implicit. The reader is invited to consider the way the social world can be envisioned. In the following section, I lay out the organization of the book and, briefly, the content of each of the three major sections; each section, ultimately, presenting a slightly different pedagogical strategy for teaching a course in sociological theory.

1.3 An Overview

The first handbook of theory is a testament to the sheer diversity and eclectic nature of sociological theory (Turner 2001). Nearly two decades old, most of the perspectives remain used today in various subfields across the discipline. Thus, my vision for this companion, stand-alone volume, was under two distinct pressures: to be unique from the former volume and, as opposed to having authors simply review the theoretical terrain, offer something penetrating and more advanced than is often assumed of handbooks. To resolve the first pressure, my emphasis from the onset was on *commonalities* and *convergence*. The first handbook is notable in its encyclopedic form, whereas I wanted this handbook to present the instructor, the student, and the academic with a way or set of ways for organizing the social universe and the practice of sociology. To that effect, the reader is presented with three major delineations: (1) questions that have been explicit and implicit to sociological theorizing since Comte (and before), but which look and feel different in contemporary sociology today (Chaps. 2, 3, 4, 5, and 6); (2) a vision of the social universe constructed by the various levels of social reality sociologists focus on (Chaps. 7, 8, 9, 10, 11, 12, 13, 14, 15, 16, and 17); and, finally, a set of substantive phenomena, distinct to be sure, but interrelated in their deep inextricable link to the classics (many of which have been long forgotten) and for their tendency towards the cutting edges of sociology (Chaps. 18, 19, 20, 21, 22, 23, 24, 25, and 26).

The second contribution of the handbook was truly out of my hands, and was the responsibility of the author(s) of each chapter. To that effect, I am greatly indebted to each author for accepting the challenge of balancing a review-like expectation with breaking new ground. Several of the chapters present radically unique perspectives, while others synthesize often disparate, far-flung traditions; however, all of them offer fresh, authoritative statements about the social world. What was most rewarding for me was that the authors, in several cases, accidentally weaved threads from other chapters throughout their own, helping make the volume coherent, consistent, and convergent. Below, I briefly consider each section and the vision behind it, as well as the realization made possible by the contributors.

1.3.1 Classic Questions

The late-great Israeli sociologist, Shmuel Eisenstadt (1985, 1987) argued that the entire sociological practice was anchored in three basic questions or problems: integration (Durkheim 1893, 1915 [1995])—or, what mechanisms bring/hold individuals and groups together, regulation (Marx 1845–6 [1972]; Weber 1978)—or, what mechanisms allow individuals and groups to control and coordinate the behavior of other individuals and groups, and legitimation (Weber 1920 [2002], 1946)—or, how is shared meaning constructed and maintained. In terms of the Handbook, the first section is devoted to these three questions (Chaps. 2, 3, 4, and 5) and a fourth question that is implicit in classical sociology, but has become a central question since at least the 1970s as the cultural anthropologies of folks like Geertz (1972), Douglas (1970), and Turner (1974) became increasingly relevant to challenging the rather flat cultural version of Parsonsian (1951) sociology.

Thus, Chaps. 2 and 3 focus on integration and regulation, respectively. Both draw from the traditional well of references, but chart more holistic, unique views on the problem. In Chap. 2, Turner posits a general theory of integration, drawing from structuralism, social psychology, evolutionary biology, and the sociology of emotions. Integration, or the lack there of, has long been cited as a source of various social problems—e.g., Durkheim's *Suicide*; an argument that has received plenty of empirical support (Umberson and Montez 2010; Thoits 2011). In Turner's framework, gone are the old functionalist tropes, replaced by many of the important advances in neuroscience and social psychology. This chapter is followed by Yingyao and Pollilo's (Chap. 3) treatment of regulation. A sophisticated review of the winding threads of Marxian and Weberian theory unfolds into a fascinating consideration of organizational power as the central site of coordination and control in modernity. Hence, while the authors consider the macro- and micro-level dynamics, it is at the meso-level that the true force of power, in modernity, is unleashed, along with the contradictions between distributive power (domination) and social or collective power.

Chapters 4 and 5 turn our attention to the problem of legitimation, first in action and then in interaction. In Glaeser's discussion of action, new theoretical ground is staked out on a very old topic: what is social action? The problem of meaning emerges in the work of Marx, Durkheim, and most explicitly in Weber as they contend with the "ghost," or perhaps specter, of the great utilitarian tradition of Smith and Bentham, but Glaeser's work extends far beyond these old debates, offering a processual, comprehensive action theory. Tavory's examination of interaction is no less inspired: while careful to hew closely to the road mapped out by symbolic interactionists, Tavory's Chap. 5 moves into newer horizons, pushing for more processual notions of interaction and self. Confronting critiques from different sources, Tavory considers the most recent push for inter-situational analyses.

Finally, in Chap. 6, Lizardo's work challenges the reader, and the discipline: (1) is culture really something the classical theorists like Weber and Durkheim thought of, or is it a Parsonian creation and (2) what is the future for the concept and assorted constellation of elements orbiting it in sociology? Lizardo presents a careful analysis of the classics, in particular Durkheim and Weber, and elucidates how "culture" is largely alien to their work, and is really added *post hoc* by Parsons. Lizardo does not leave us with a definitive answer to the second question, though his essay cogently argues that Durkheim, and even Bourdieu, presents sociologists with examples of how to theorize *without* the culture concept, and thus provocatively implies, perhaps, culture is less useful a concept than modern sociology often assumes.

In short, this section offers a new pedagogical direction for theory courses: organizing weeks and readings by major theoretical dilemmas. Integration, for instance, remains as relevant to theorizing and empirical research today as it did for Comte or Durkheim. The first cluster of readings, then, could be centered on the problem of integration, fleshing out the various ways it is studied across levels of social reality. Processes and research at the meso-level look at social capital (Portes 1998, 2014), organizational segmentation (Hannan and Freeman 1977), isomorphism (DiMaggio and Powell 1983), and embedded fields (Chap. 9; also, Fligstein and McAdam 2012) are all interested in integration; likewise, many dynamics at the micro-level, such as rituals and emotions (Chap. 20; also, Collins 2004; Lawler et al. 2009) and exchange (Chap. 18; also, Cook et al. 2006), continue to look hard at integration as a process (as well as the consequences for too much or too little). Likewise, regulation (and, more often, power) remain central to sociological research (Reed 2013), as does the question of action (Swidler 1986; Emirbayer and Mische 1998; Vaisey 2009), interaction and meaning making (Chap. 19; also, Stryker 2008; Burke and Stets 2009), and, of course, cultural processes (Lizardo 2006; Pugh 2009; Abrutyn and Mueller 2015).

1.3.2 Levels of Social Reality

Fresh out of graduate school, the first two theory courses I taught tried to build a coherent sociological world for the students by way of starting at the macro-level and working down to the organizational level. Then, the class shifted to the micro-level and built back up, ending with theories of groups and organizational life. Nearly impossible to do in a 14-week class, this pedagogical strategy did get positive reviews: most specifically, students expressed happiness that a coherent social world emerged over the course of the class as opposed to the eclecticism of substantive courses that move from one level to the next, one theory to the next, and with little commitment to a "this is how sociologists generally see the world" type of orientation. The advantage to this method is clear. Each level or the different phenomena at each level, are embedded and thus have equivalencies to those higher-order levels pressing against them; however, each level reveals distinct, emergent properties and dynamics that force us to study each one as distinct *and* as linked to the above and below. Second, while the levels themselves deserve analysis, the interlinkages between them are of equal importance. How encounters and corporate units interact, for instance, matters because it is in the flow between the two that microdynamics produce, reproduce, and alter the meso-level and, conversely, it is the meso-level that constrains and facilitate the production and reproduction of encounters. Perhaps not radical, it remains important to develop common ways of talking about what sociologists study that matters to creating a society and not an association of sociologists.

Ultimately, this approach allows students to see the diversity of sociological research, and come to understand both the reasons why some scholars are drawn to historical research and others qualitative ethnographies, as well as how both strategies require some semblance of a social world filled within nested or embedded levels. It is true, we don't often talk about the social world this way, and there are always radical positions on both sides (micro and macro) asserting the non-existence of the other, but, the goal of theory is to provide the student with different tools to deal with different research problems. Providing a set of vantage points is as important as the formal and substantive aspects of the theories themselves.

The next set of sections is devoted to this sort of pedagogic approach, beginning with a subsection on macro-micro linkages (Chaps. 7, 8, 9, and 10) and followed by a subsection that considers the major social units across each level of social reality (Chaps. 11, 12, 13, 14, 15, 16, and 17).

1.3.2.1 Rethinking the Macro-Micro Link

The first subsection takes up a question that had gained prominence in the 1980s: how can we link the seemingly wide chasm between the lived, everyday experience and the invisible social structure that so fascinated the young Durkheim. In this section, the reader is presented with four chapters—two that explicitly deal with the problem (the first starting from the top-down (Chap. 7) and the second from the bottom-up (Chap. 8)), and two that offer alternative ways of dealing with the presumed chasm (Chaps. 9 and 10).

In charting a link from the macro to the micro, Turner (2010a, b, 2011) argues that emotions are, ultimately, the thread that runs through the entire system; a point cogently made by Lawler, Thye, and Joon in their exposition of the links flowing up from the micro to the macro; and, importantly, the conclusion that Durkheim (1915 [1995]) eventually reached: emotional forces generated in palpable, recurring interaction continually remade the group while temporarily charging the batteries of those participants and, even, those in the audience. The juxtaposition of the two chapters, and the authors' awareness of each other, presents a unique chance to see how two opposed positions (top-down and bottom-up) often reach similar conclusions about the social world. Macrosociology, which was once the center of the sociological world, is presented from the point of view of a theorist whose career has increasingly sought to integrate neuroscience into sociology, and it thus sensitive to the macro-micro links. Lawler and his colleagues, for their part, begin within the exchange tradition which has structural assumptions built in, and thus the macro already looms over their theorizing. In the end, the reader comes to realize that both approaches can complement each other, rather than be dichotomous positions.

The alternatives, as I see them, are found in field theory and in the network/relational approach that is both a methodological and theoretical perspective. To be sure, fields are meso-level units of analysis, as are networks, and could just as well be placed in the following subsection, yet there is some logic behind seeing them as alternatives to more traditional macro-micro solutions. They both turn away from the overly abstract macro accounts, preferring either real nodal connections or embedded arenas filled with real groups competing against each other. That is, neither gives primacy to the individual or the über macro sphere that acts as an environment for collective action. Instead, they have a sort of Simmelian approach focused on the relationships—exchange-based, competitive, or conflict-oriented—and the structure of these relationships. Where they perhaps differ most, is in their natural affinities with other subfields—and, thus, the theoretical traditions they are most comfortable borrowing from to explain the social world. On the one hand, network theory easily borrows from social psychology, either from the exchange traditions (Coleman 1988; Cook et al. 2006) or from identity-based concepts (Pescosolido 2006; Thoits 2011). On the other hand, field theory is far more comfortable with culture and structure intermingling (Bourdieu 1992, 1993) then network theory is (Emirbayer and Goodwin 1994).

One final note, Fligstein and McAdam's (2012) *strategic action fields* has been, in my perspective, a major advance in field theory in that they consciously sought to expand traditional field analyses by adding social movements theory. Theorizing is a process of building upon existing literatures; rather than reinventing the wheel, it is the essence of extending, synthesizing, and making robust (Turner 2010a, b; Abrutyn and Mueller 2015). Network theory is perhaps ready for that type of revolutionary theorizing. Cultural sociologies have already begun to interact (Lizardo 2006), and my work with Mueller (Abrutyn and Mueller 2014; Mueller and Abrutyn 2015) has advocated for expanding the social psychological "vocabulary" of network applications to include emotions. Both areas seem to me exciting sites of opportunities and challenges, and have already made major inroads in offering new strategies of seeing the macro-micro link. Hence, in a theory course that begins with this question, the actual *art of theorizing* instead of the process of learning theorists could make for an exciting and engaging classroom.

1.3.2.2 From Top to Bottom

The second subsection explore the three major levels of analysis, and the principles units of social reality we study at each level. At the macro-level, we find institutional spheres (Chap. 11) and stratification systems (Chap. 12); at the meso, communities (Chap. 13), organizations (Chap. 14), and categoric units (Chap. 15); and, at the micro, small groups (Chap. 16) and the self (Chap. 17). While each chapter focuses on the specific phenomenon of interest, they each work to contextualize the phenomenon within the higher and lower levels of social reality. Furthermore, each chapter takes serious the way sociologists try to study the unit of analysis, exploring how theory and research work together as opposed to the traditional pedagogy of teaching theory and methods as a separate set of ideas and skills.

My own take on institutions draws from classical sociologists and anthropologists who talked about the world as divided into major social spheres like religion, law, or kinship. Chapter 11 presents these types of discussions in a fresh light, drawing on ecological and evolutionary theory to explore how macro-structural and cultural spheres shape the everyday reality we all encounter. Conversely, in Chap. 12, Guenther and her colleagues take on the macro-level dynamics of stratification. Exploring a range of empirical and theoretical studies, this chapter presents the tools that sociologists use to explore inequalities within nations, comparatively across nations, and between clusters of nations.

Chapters 13 and 14 provide close examinations of two key corporate units: communities and organizations. Communities have always been essential to theory; de Tocqueville, Töennies, Durkheim, and then later the Chicago school's urban ecology and a significant proportion of sociological ethnographies. Irwin presents a sophisticated review and theoretical exposition of what community is, and the potential it has for theorizing about social organization and action. Irwin's inspired writing challenges sociology to embrace a concept that has been repeatedly deemed moribund, but which continues to show resilience. In Chap. 14, Powell and Brandtner offer a wholly original synthesis of the organization literature, presenting a new pathway for integrating advances in other disciplines. Organizations, then, become both things and forces for Powell and Brandtner; sites in which informal groups and selves are produced and reproduced daily, and forces of change in communities and institutional spheres. What makes these two chapters so important—as well as Chaps. 9 (fields) and 10 (networks)—is that the meso-level is the site in which the everyday meets the abstract, invisible forces that facilitate and constrain reality. Threads of integration, regulation, legitimation, and culture abound, as do the questions of macro-micro linkages. These same questions continue to be relevant in Chap. 15, where Webster and Walker consider the other side of the meso-level: categoric units (e.g., sex, race, age) and inequality. A sprawling and erudite review, is followed by a close consideration of the empirical foundations of a cluster of theoretical traditions that consider how certain status characteristics affect the functioning of various types of groups that we all find ourselves in; how these characteristics come to have that effect; and how that shapes the experiences of people across categories. Like its companion chapters, Webster and Walker's chapter presents important ideas that explicitly spillover into Chap. 16 (small groups) and Chap. 18 (microsociologies), but which also touch on numerous other chapters including that of regulation (Chap. 3) and the self (Chap. 17).

Finally, the micro-level is represented by a chapter on groups and one on the self. In the latter, Cast and Stets ambitiously present a synthetic look at the self both as a micro-level phenomenon, and a thing embedded in various other levels of social reality. To talk about the self, as even Mead clearly emphasized, the larger environments must be considered too; though, we often lose sight of the other levels of reality. Cast and Stets push us to consider the many layers that the self interacts with to become our anchor in the social world. In Chap. 16, Benard and Mize present a fresh, comprehensive take on small groups. Once the center of the sociological world (Bales and Slater 1955; Berger 1958), small groups have become peripheralized despite their continued importance to understanding the social world and empirical research (Berger et al. 1998; Benard 2012; Fine 2012). Indeed, it is in small groups that vast majority of our lives are spent, as they mediate our experiences in organizations and communities, institutions and stratification systems. Thus, the self is our personal anchor to the social world while small groups are the social anchor to the larger universe. Integration, regulation, and legitimation *cannot* be understood without considering the anchors that are most visible and known to each person, and thus, these chapters tie the entire section together, and in many ways, serve as a fulcrum to the next major section in which we offer a third strategy to teaching sociological theory.

1.3.3 Theorizing the Social World

The final section of the book takes a third approach to the sociological endeavor that breaks sociology into different thematic areas—two of which are presented herein. To be sure, many of the chapters of the Handbook could fit into this space, but these chapters (and their substance) tend to be less abstract than those in the first cluster (Chaps. 2, 3, 4, 5, and 6) and, in many cases, cut across various levels of analysis instead of being rooted in one or the other.

1.3.3.1 Constraints on the Lived Experience

This section considers many of the questions raised in Chaps. 2, 3, 4, 5, and 6, but does not interrogate them explicitly or as the focus of the chapter. Instead, they present the reader with the varieties of social forces constraining the way we experience the reality in which we are embedded. Picking up where Chaps. 17 on the self, as well as 15 on small groups and 16 on categoric units left off, the first chapter of this section (Chap. 18) further explores the microdynamics of social life. In this chapter, Carter pushes sociologists to revisit the once porous borders between social and psychological social psychology, pulling theoretical strands that supplement insights drawn from various areas of contemporary microsociology that take attribution and evaluation as the central mechanism or process from which theoretical explanations emerge. Chapter 19 offers a fresh take on the field of ethnomethodology. Often marginalized in contemporary sociology, or perhaps forgotten in some ways, this chapter reminds the reader of the roots beyond Garfinkel's groundbreaking work, but quickly turns towards the perspective and method's footprint in contemporary research. Like the chapters on communities and small groups, this chapter reminds sociologists that this area is not frozen, and instead of teaching ethnomethodology as "Garfinkel's theory" or in breaching experiments, Turowetz and his colleagues press us to consider the active research that continues to provide insights into the construction of meaning and action.

Finally, complementing both of these chapters is an exposition on the sociology of emotions (Chap. 20). What distinguishes Weed and Smith-Lovin's chapter from most discussions of emotions is its careful division and clear elucidation of the three dominant strands of emotions in social psychology today: the performative-dramaturgical strand built on Goffman and, most prominently, Hochschild's seminal text; the symbolic interactionist tradition (Kemper 1978; cf. Shott 1979) that has found its expression across a variety of theoretically-driven research programs like Affect Control Theory, Identity Control Theory, and Status Expectations States Theory; and, the interaction ritual tradition (Collins 2004; Summers-Effler 2004). Finding the points of convergence, this chapter collapses many of the unnecessary distinctions across these different perspectives, promoting the commonalities that link the study of emotions. In short, a pathway for a more integrative study of emotions is posited.

The next cluster of chapters follows in the theme of exterior constraints on the lived experience. In Chap. 21, Simko explores a very old idea that has somehow been forgotten, ironically, or simply undertheorized: collective memory. Drawing from Durkheim's *Elementary Forms* and, especially, his forgotten student Halbwachs (1992), this chapter urges readers to consider how the past is a social creation; how it becomes exterior and constraining in monuments and other physical spaces, temporal differentiation, sedimented interaction and ritual, and so on. Memory is the cutting edge, as it draws the Durkheimian sense of integration into dialogue with the Weberian notion of regulation and legitimation: that is, memory is both a force of cohesion and shared meaning, as well as something individuals and groups strive to control for those very same reasons. In Chap. 22, we turn towards, again, an older area of sociology that had lost favor for several decades because of Parsons "flat" treatment: the sociology of morality. Recent years has seen an explosion of research on morality (Hitlin and Vaisey 2013), ranging from cultural-cognitive studies (Vaisey 2009) to social psychological inquiries (Stets and Carter 2012). McCaffree pivots quickly from the roots of the sociology of morality to both consider the many angles sociologists exploit to examine morality, but also offers a compelling new theoretical take on how we can go about studying morality social scientifically. Finally, in Chap. 23, Robinson offers a much needed essay on intersectionality. Not simply content with the conventional ways intersectionality is taught and mobilized in research, this chapter pushes new ground, trying to add new items to the agenda in the study of inequality, stratification, and various subfields like race and gender. Like the previous chapters on memory and morality, this chapter sits on the frontiers of where sociology has been moving, and brings an essential perspective to how lived experience is constrained by those in structurally and culturally disadvantaged positions.

1.3.3.2 Modes of Change

The last three chapters of the Handbook fittingly explore one of the most important and compelling aspects of sociology: change. Here, three important modes of change, found across all of the classical sociologists, also present the frontiers of sociological research, cross-cutting most of the chapters above, and bringing insights from other disciplines. First, Machalek and Martin begin this section by delineating the diverse and ever-growing area of evolutionary sociology. Once a mainstay of sociological theory—found in Comte, Marx, Spencer, Durkheim, and even Weber—evolutionary theory has undergone a renaissance in the last two decades or so. Neuroscience, cognitive science, archaeology, history, and anthropology have found their way into these theories, as have the most up-to-date findings in genetics and evolutionary biology. Evolutionary sociology runs along several different tracks: general theories that reflect the classics, but are far more cautious in their construction; gene-culture interaction; neuroscience and the evolution of the brain; group-level selection; and neo-Darwinian theorizing.

In Chaps. 25 and 26, we present the reader with two complimentary chapters: the first on collective behavior and the second on social movements. In the latter, Moss and Snow deftly delineate the massive body of literature on social movements, offering original insights into the dynamics of social movements. In the former, Van Ness and Summers-Effler revisit another subfield that was once central to sociological inquiry, but which has fallen out of favor to some degree. Of course, the study of social movements was historically embedded in the study of collective behavior, but since the 1960s, social movements have become a distinct and vibrant area in its own right. Hence, like the juxtaposition of macro-micro approaches (Chaps. 7 and 8), these two chapters round the Handbook out by offering two highly interrelated theoretical traditions, but distinct in important ways. In Chap. 25, then, a cogent argument for why collective behavior should join social movements as an important area of research and theory is posited. Drawing from a wide ranging reservoir of insights in cultural sociology and the cognitive sciences, as well as new shifts in social movements' research and theory, this chapter presents a fresh vantage point for thinking about how collectives act, how they engulf individuals, and how they affect social change in ways different and similar to social movements. Moss and Snow, in their treatment of social movements, also goes to the proverbial well to show how social psychology, emotions, and culture have become important elements integrated into the classic ways sociologists have theorized and researched social movements. In short, a set of chapters explore the basic theme of change highlighting the cutting edge, synthetic work being done.

1.4 Conclusion

Ultimately, the discipline is due for a paradigm shift. If theory is a specialization, then we need to resuscitate and support theorists in journals, professorial appointments, and in training; if theory is the backbone of a social science, then we need to begin to teach theory as set of principles that sociologists can deploy in developing research. This Handbook is one small step forward, inspired by the desire to unite sociologists under a common umbrella that *does not* dissuade creativity, the pursuit of understudied problems, or the continued development of theory. Rather, a society or community instead of an association is more likely to cooperate in an effort to push sociology into the twenty-first century and make our discipline one that is consulted when politicians, economic leaders, community organizers, and the like have problems they need help solving.

References

Abend, G. (2008). The meaning of theory. *Sociological Theory, 26*(2), 173–199.

Abrutyn, S. (2013). Teaching sociological theory for a new century: Contending with the time crunch. *The American Sociologist, 44*(2), 132–154.

Abrutyn, S., & Mueller, A. S. (2014). The socioemotional foundations of suicide: A microsociological view of Durkheim's suicide. *Sociological Theory, 32*(4), 327–351.

Abrutyn, S., & Mueller, A. S. (2015). When too much integration and regulation hurt: Re-envisioning Durkheim's Altruistic suicide. *Society and Mental Health*.doi:10.1177/2156869315604346.

Alexander, J. C. (1990). Beyond the epistemological dilemma: General theory in a postpositivist mode. *Sociological Forum, 5*(4), 531–544.

Bales, R. F., & Slater, P. E. (1955). Role differentiation in small, decision making groups. In T. Parsons & R. F. Bales (Eds.), *Family, socialization and interaction process* (pp. 259–306). Glencoe: Free Press.

Benard, S. (2012). Cohesion from conflict does intergroup conflict motivate intragroup norm enforcement and support for centralized leadership? *Social Psychology Quarterly, 75*(2), 107–130.

Berger, J. (1958). *Relations between performance, rewards, and action-opportunities in small groups*. Cambridge: Sociology Department, Harvard University.

Berger, J., Ridgeway, C. L., Fisek, M. H., & Norman, R. Z. (1998). The legitimation and delegitimation of power and prestige orders. *American Sociological Review, 63*, 379–405.

Bourdieu, P. (1992). *The rules of art: Genesis and structure of the literary field*. Stanford: Stanford University Press.

Bourdieu, P. (1993). *The field of cultural production: Essays on art and literature*. New York: Columbia University Press.

Burke, P. J., & Stets, J. E. (2009). *Identity theory*. New York: Oxford University Press.

Carter, M. J. (2013). Comment on Abrutyn's "Time Crunch" problem in teaching classical and contemporary sociological theory: Time for the dichotomy to

become a trichotomy? *American Sociologist, 44*, 302–311.
Coleman, J. S. (1988). Social capital in the creation of human capital. *American Journal of Sociology, 94*(Supplement), S95–S-120.
Collins, R. (1975). *Conflict sociology: Towards an explanatory science*. New York: Academic.
Collins, R. (1988). *Theoretical sociology*. San Diego: Harcourt Brace Jovanovich, Publishers.
Collins, R. (1994). The microinteractionist tradition. In *Four sociological traditions*. New York: Oxford University Press.
Collins, R. (1998). *The sociology of philosophies: A global theory of intellectual change*. Cambridge: The Belknap Press.
Collins, R. (2004). *Interaction ritual chains*. Princeton: Princeton University Press.
Cook, K. S., Cheshire, C., & Gerbasi, A. (2006). Power, dependence, and social exchange. In P. J. Burke (Ed.), *Contemporary social psychological theories* (pp. 194–216). Stanford: Stanford University Press.
Coser, L. A. (1977). *Masters of sociological thought*. Fort Worth: Harcourt Brace Jovanovich College Publishers.
DiMaggio, P., & Powell, W. W. (1983). The iron cage revisited: Institutional isomorphism and collective rationality in organizational fields. *American Sociological Review, 48*(2), 147–160.
Douglas, M. (1970). *Natural symbols: Explorations in cosmology*. New York: Pantheon Books.
Durkheim, E. (1893). *The division of labor in society* (W.D. Halls, Trans.). New York: The Free Press.
Durkheim, E. (1897 [1951]). *Suicide: A study in sociology* (J.A. Spaulding, & G. Simpson, Trans.). Glencoe: Free Press.
Durkheim, E. (1915 [1995]). *The elementary forms of religious life* (K. E. Fields, Trans.). New York: Free Press.
Eisenstadt, S. N. (1985). Macro-societal analysis—Background, development and indications. In S. N. Eisenstadt & H. J. Helle (Eds.), *Macro sociological theory: Perspectives on sociological theory* (pp. 7–24). London: Sage.
Eisenstadt, S. N. (1987). Macrosociology and sociological theory: Some new directions. *Contemporary Sociology, 16*(5), 602–609.
Emirbayer, M., & Goodwin, J. (1994). Network analysis, culture, and the problem of agency. *American Journal of Sociology, 99*, 1141–1154.
Emirbayer, M., & Mische, A. (1998). What is agency? *American Journal of Sociology, 103*, 962–1023.
Fine, G. A. (1991). On the macrofoundations of microsociology: Constraint and the exterior reality of structure. *The Sociological Quarterly, 32*(2), 161–177.
Fine, G. A. (2012). Group culture and the interaction order: Local sociology on the meso-level. *Annual Review of Sociology, 38*, 159–179.
Fligstein, N., & McAdam, D. (2012). *A theory of fields*. New York: Oxford University Press.
Geertz, C. (1972). *The interpretation of cultures*. New York: Basic Books.
Halbwachs, M. (1992). *On collective memory*. Chicago: University of Chicago.
Hannan, M. T., & Freeman, J. (1977). The population ecology of organizations. *American Journal of Sociology, 82*(5), 929–964.
Hilbert, R. A. (1989). Durkheim and Merton on anomie: An unexplored contrast and its deritatives. *Social Problems, 36*(3), 242–250.
Hitlin, S., & Vaisey, S. (2013). The new sociology of morality. *Annual Review of Sociology, 39*, 51–88.
Hoffman, M. A., & Bearman, P. S. (2015). Bringing anomie back in: Exceptional events and excess suicide. *Sociological Science, 2*, 186–210.
Kemper, T. (1978). *A social interactional theory of emotions*. New York: Wiley.
Knorr-Cetina, K. (1981). The micro-sociological challenge of macro-sociology: Toward a reconstruction of social theory and methodology. In K. Knorr-Cetina & A. V. Cicourel (Eds.), *Advances in social theory and methodology: Toward an integration of micro- and macro-sociologies* (pp. 1–46). Boston: Routledge and Kegan Paul.
Lawler, E. J., Thye, S., & Yoon, J. (2009). *Social commitments in a depersonalized world*. New York: Russell Sage.
Leenaars, A. (2004). Altrusitic suicide: A few reflections. *Archives of Suicide Research, 8*(1), 1–7.
Lenski, G. (1988). Rethinking macrosociological theory. *American Sociological Review, 53*(2), 163–171.
Lizardo, O. (2006). How cultural tastes shape personal networks. *American Sociological Review, 71*(5), 778–807.
Lizardo, O. (2014). The end of theorists: The relevance, opportunities, and pitfalls of theorizing in sociology. In *American sociological association*. San Francisco.
Marx, K. (1845–6 [1972]). The German ideology. In R. C. Tucker (Ed.), *The Marx-Engels reader* (pp. 146–202). New York: W.W. Norton & Company.
Merton, R. K. (1938). Social structure and anomie. *American Sociological Review, 3*(5), 672–682.
Mueller, A. S., & Abrutyn, S. (2015). Suicidal disclosures among friends: Using social network data to understand suicide contagion. *Journal of Health and Social Behavior, 56*(1), 131–148.
Parsons, T. (1951). *The social system*. Glencoe: Free Press.
Pescosolido, B. A. (2006). Of pride and prejudice: The role of sociology and social networks in integrating the health sciences. *Journal of Health and Social Behavior, 47*(3), 189–208.
Portes, A. (1998). Social capital: Its origins and applications in modern sociology. *Annual Review of Sociology, 24*, 1–24.
Portes, A. (2014). Downsides of social capital. *PNAS, 111*(52), 18407–18408.
Pugh, A. J. (2009). *Longing and belonging: Parents, children, and consumer culture*. Berkeley: University of California Press.
Radin, P. (1927 [1955]). *Primitive Man as philosopher*. New York: Dover Publications.

Reed, I. A. (2013). Power: Relational, discursive, and performative dimensions. *Sociological Theory, 31*(3), 193–218.

Shott, S. (1979). Emotion and social life: A symbolic interactionist analysis. *American Journal of Sociology, 84*(6), 1317–1334.

Spencer, H. (1874–96). *The principles of sociology*. New York: Appleton.

Stack, S. (2000). Suicide: A 15-year review of the sociological literature Part 1: Cultural and economic factors. *Suicide and Life Threatening Behavior, 30*(2), 145–162.

Stets, J. E., & Carter, M. J. (2012). A theory of the self for the sociology of morality. *American Sociological Review, 77*(1), 120–140.

Stryker, S. (2008). From mead to structural symbolic interactionism and beyond. *Annual Review of Sociology, 34*, 14–31.

Summers-Effler, E. (2004). A theory of the self, emotion, and culture. *Advances in Group Processes, 21*, 273–308.

Swidler, A. (1986). Culture in action: Symbols and strategies. *American Sociological Review, 51*(2), 273–286.

Thoits, P. A. (2011). Mechanisms linking social ties and support to physical and mental health. *Journal of Health and Social Behavior, 52*(2), 145–161.

Turner, V. (1974). *Dramas, fields, and metaphors: Symbolic action in human society*. Ithaca: Cornell University Press.

Turner, J. H. (1985). In defense of positivism. *Sociological Theory, 3*(2), 24–30.

Turner, J. H. (2001). *The handbook of sociological theory*. New York: Kluwer Academic/Plenum Publishers.

Turner, J. H. (2010a). *Theoretical principles of sociology, volume 1: Macrodynamics*. New York: Springer.

Turner, J. H. (2010b). *Theoretical principles of sociology, Volume 2: Microdynamics*. New York: Springer.

Turner, J. H. (2011). *Theoretical principles of sociology, Volume 3: Mesodynamics*. New York: Springer.

Umberson, D., & Montez, J. K. (2010). Social relationships and health: A flashpoint for health policy. *Journal of Health and Social Behavior, 51*(1 suppl), S54–S66.

Vaisey, S. (2009). Motivation and justification: A dual process model of culture in action. *American Journal of Sociology, 114*(+), 1675–1715.

Weber, M. (1920 [2002]). *The protestant ethic and the "Spirit" of capitalism and other writings* (P. Baehr, & G. C. Wells, Trans.). New York: Penguin Books.

Weber, M. (1946). The social psychology of world religions. In H. Gerth & C. W. Mills (Eds.), *From Max Weber: Essays in sociology* (pp. 264–301). New York: Oxford University Press.

Weber, M. (1978). In G. Roth & C. Wittich (Eds.), *Economy and society: An outline of interpretive sociology* (Vol. 1–2). Berkeley: University of California Press.

Wray, M., Colen, C., & Pescosolido, B. A. (2011). The sociology of suicide. *Annual Review of Sociology, 37*, 505–528.

Part I

Classical Questions Contemporalized

2 Integrating and Disintegrating Dynamics in Human Societies

Jonathan H. Turner

2.1 Approaching the Analysis of Integration in Societies

The concept of integration has long been both an implicit and explicit concern of all sociological theorists. Yet, despite this provenance, integration is a topic that has been subject to criticism because evaluative considerations of what is "good" or "pathological" in a society. For example, Marxists see the modes of integration of a societal formations as filled with contradictions and basically as a "necessary evil" in an historical process leading to a "better" form of integration as these contradictions lead to conflict and reform. Early functionalists such as Auguste Comte, Herbert Spencer, Emile Durkheim and, more recently, Talcott Parsons have tended to analyze social structures in terms of meeting functional needs for integration, thereby converting existing structural and cultural arrangements into implicit statements that the status quo is "functional" for a society. Such analyses deliberately or inadvertently moralize what should be a more neutral conception of integration. For my purposes here, I see integration as simply *the modes and mechanisms by which social units and the social activities in and between them are coordinated into coherent patterns of social organization and the potential of these mechanisms to stave off, or to accelerate, the inevitable disintegration of all patterns of social organization*. And so, whether integration is achieved by open markets or high levels of coercion and stratification, it *is* nonetheless integration by the above definition. The point of this chapter is to outline the various forms that integration takes and the degree to which particular forms generate pressures for continued integration or for disintegration. In the long run, disintegration is the fate of societies and their constituent sociocultural formations; the issue then is what modes of integration stave off for how long the inevitable entropy inherent in the social universe. For theorizing about human societies to be complete, it becomes essential to understand both the negative entropic and entropic forces working on human societies.

As I will argue, integration and disintegration operate at all three fundamental levels of human social organization: (1) the micro universe of interaction in face-to-face encounters, (2) the meso world of [a] corporate units (groups, organizations, and communities) revealing divisions of labor and [b] categoric units built from social distinctions based upon criteria such as ethnicity, religion, gender, and age that become that bases for moral evaluations of members of subpopulations in a society, and (3) the macro systems of (a) institutional domains and (b) stratification systems as these become the pillars of (c) societal

J.H. Turner (✉)
Department of Sociology, University of California, Santa Barbara, CA, USA
e-mail: jturner@soc.ucsb.edu

S. Abrutyn (ed.), *Handbook of Contemporary Sociological Theory*, Handbooks of Sociology and Social Research, DOI 10.1007/978-3-319-32250-6_2

and (d) inter-societal systems. Integration is simply the way in which micro, meso, and macro social formations are laced together, but this process is complicated by the fact that integration operates not only between levels of social organization but within each of these three levels. Thus, there are complex causal relations among the micro, meso, and macro bases of integration and, as will become evident, disintegration as well (Turner 2010a). All of the processes by which such connections are generated and sustained constitute the subject matter *of integration* as a fundamental force in the social universe, while the operation of these forces are also the explanation for the disintegrative potential in all sociocultural formations.

Another way to view integration is as connections among the "parts" of the social universe; and the outline below of the three levels of social reality suggests what these part are: individual persons, encounters of individuals in face-to-face interaction, corporate units (groups, organizations, and communities) organizing encounters, categoric units of persons denoted as distinctive and evaluated in terms of their perceived distinctiveness that constrain what transpires in encounters, institutional domains built up from corporate units, stratification systems built around categoric-unit distinctions, and societies as well as inter-societal systems arising from institutional domains and systems of stratification.

To conceptualize integration and also disintegration at the same time, it is necessary to recognize that these parts are connected horizontally within each level of social reality and vertically across the micro, meso, and macro levels of the social universe and that disintegration occurs when these horizontal and vertical linkages break down. For example, at the micro level, when persons enter encounters, horizontal processes revolving around interaction rituals (Collins 2004; Turner 2002) and other interpersonal dynamics operate to integrate chains of interaction over time and space. At the same time, encounters are embedded in corporate and categoric units at the meso level and; in turn, these meso-level units are embedded in macro-level formations, thus assuring the operation of vertical integrative process across levels of social organization. As with the micro-level interaction rituals, horizontal integrative processes operate among also meso-level units. Corporate units differentially distribute resources to persons, which partially determines their categoric unit memberships—at a minimum their social class. Conversely, members of categoric units are located in positions within the divisions of labor of corporate units. And the dynamics revolving around these horizontal connections within the meso level are important to integration not only at this level but also at both the micro and macro levels. Macro structures and cultures are built from meso-level structures, while the corporate and categoric units of the meso-level constrain what transpires in micro encounters. Reciprocally, dynamics of encounters affect the dynamics of integration at the meso level and, at times, even the macro level of social organization.

The arrows moving within and across levels of social organization portrayed in Fig. 2.1 are intended to denote these paths of connection and potential disconnection; and while the processes are complicated, a general theory of integration and disintegration can, it is hoped, make understanding of these connections much simpler than it may seem at first glance. How and where do we get started? I think the best place to start is at the macro level, particularly the societal level of social organization; from there we can move up and down the levels of the figure and begin to fill in the picture of dynamic processes of integration and disintegration in human societies.

2.2 The Macrodynamics of Integration

As outlined above, the macro-level universe is composed of inter-societal systems and societies that are built from institutional domains and stratification systems which, in turn, are built respectively from meso-level corporate and categoric units (Turner 2010a). The dynamics of integration at the macro level of social reality can best be understood by the nature of sociocultural

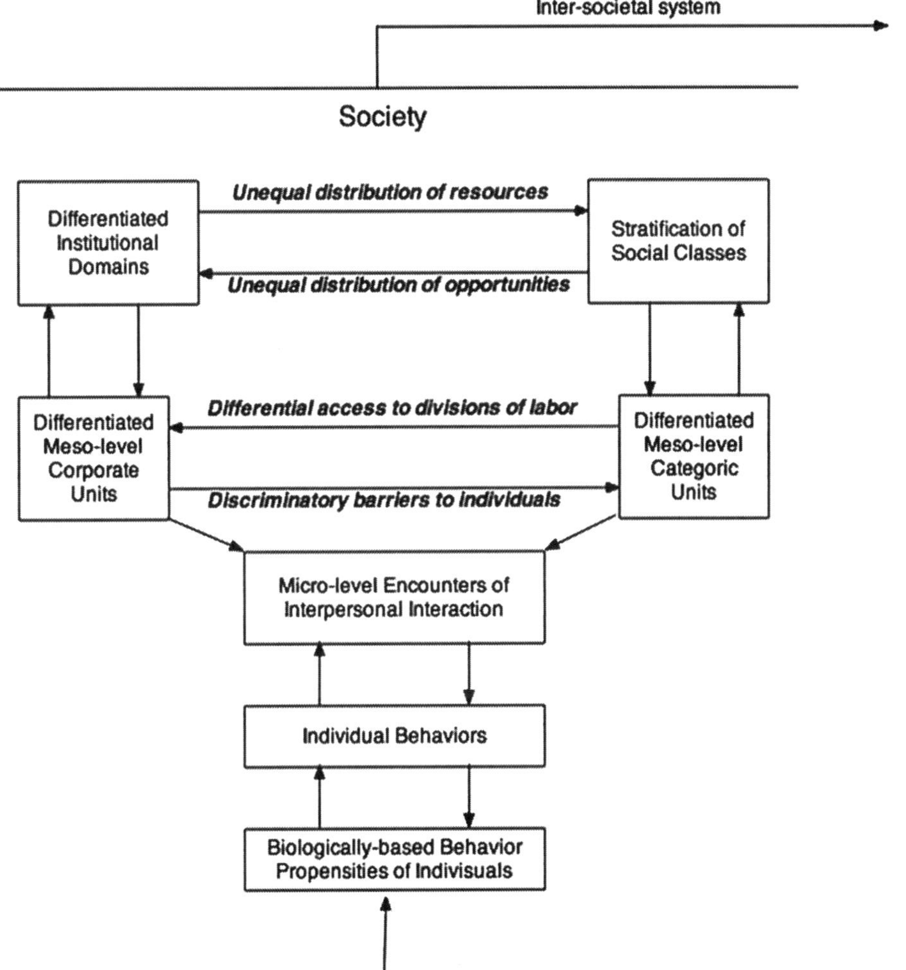

Fig. 2.1 Levels of social reality

formations that organize corporate units and categoric units into institutional domains and stratification systems. There are well-studied *structural mechanisms* by which the macro level of social reality is generated and sustained, including (Turner 2010a): (1) segmentation, (2) differentiation, (3) interdependencies, (4) segregation, (5) domination and stratification, and (6) intersections. While culture is always part of these social structural mechanisms, there are still distinctive *cultural mechanisms* revolving around 2010 (Turner 2010a, b): (1) values, (2) generalized symbolic media, (3) ideologies, (4) meta-ideologies, (5) corporate-unit belief and normative systems, (6) categoric-unit status belief and normative systems, and (7) expectation states in micro-level encounters. Let me begin with an outline of the structural mechanisms of integration.

2.2.1 Structural Mechanisms of Integration

2.2.1.1 Segmentation

Emile Durkheim ([1893] 1963) originally conceptualized the process of segmentation as "mechanism solidarity" (in juxtaposition to "organic solidarity)—a distinctions that he had dropped from his sociology by 1896 in favor of discovering the dynamics of integration common to both simple and complex societies (Durkheim [1912] 1984). Segmentation is the process of producing and reproducing similar corporate units, revealing (a) high levels of structural (regular) equivalence in the network structures of these corporate units (Freeman et al. 1989) and (b) high levels of cultural equivalence in that individuals are guided by the same sets of cultural codes—values, ideologies, meta-ideologies, beliefs, norms, and expectation states. Under these conditions, individuals at locations in similar corporate units experience the social universe in equivalent ways, and thus develop common orientations because they stand in the same relationships to all other positions in the corporate unit and its culture. When human societies first began to grow, segmentation was the principle mechanisms of integration, as new hunter-gather bands and, later, new community structures were spun off of the old, with each new structure revealing the same basic network forms and systems of culture.

Segmentation always continues to operate as an integrative mechanisms even as societies differentiate new kinds of corporate and categoric units. For example, Weber's ([1922] 1968: 956–1004) famous typology on "bureaucracy" is, in essence, an argument about segmentation. Even bureaucratic structures that evolve in different institutional domains evidence some equivalence in their structure and culture. Businesses, schools, churches, government agencies, science organizations, sports teams, and so on are, at a fundamental level, very similar structurally, revealing some cultural equivalences promoting integration, even as persons engage in very different kinds of institutional activities. The result is that individuals diversely situated in seemingly different structures experience a common structural and cultural environment, such as relations of authority and similar norms for impersonality, goal directness, and efficiency. Moreover, segmentation also operates to distinguish axes of differentiation so that those corporate units in the same institutional domain all reveal higher levels of cultural and structural equivalence. Thus, even as institutional sectors differentiate, the corporate units within these sectors converge in their structure and culture, thereby integrating the sector while, at the same time, having sufficient similarities to corporate units in at least some other institutional domains and sectors in these domains to promote some structural and cultural equivalences across larger swaths of the macro realm. And so, even as high levels of differentiation among corporate units are used to build diverse institutional domains—e.g., economy, polity, education, science, religions, etc.—the continuing segmentation of generic types of corporate units within and between institutional domains operates as a powerful integrative force.

Segmentation does, however, eventually generate disintegrative pressures because there are limitations in how far structural and cultural equivalences can link together large numbers of diverse corporate units and individuals in these units. If only segmentation is possible, a society and inter-societal system cannot become very large because segmentation cannot integrate large and diverse (by categoric unit memberships) populations, without the addition of new integrative mechanisms.

2.2.1.2 Differentiation

As Herbert Spencer ([1874–96] 1898) phrased the matter, growth in the social mass –whether in organic or super-organic bodies—will eventually require a more complex skeleton to support the larger mass. That is, structural and cultural differentiation is a function of the size and rate of growth of populations organized into societies and inter-societal systems. Differentiation involves the creation of new types of corporate units, revealing divisions of labor, organized to purse diverse goals within and between institutional domains. While, as emphasized above, some degree of segmentation is retained during differentiation, the process of differentiation still divides up labor and functions so that larger-scale tasks can be performed to sustain a population. If a population grows but cannot differentiate new types of corporate units to build out diverse insti-

tutional domains to
society will disinteg
produce, reproduce,

Differentiation, h
of integrative probl
coordinate relations among differentiated corpo-
rate units and between corporate units and categoric units. And these integrative problems can be aggravated by conflicts of interests, hardening boundaries and divergent cultures of corporate units with sectors of an institutional domain or among domains, and increases in inequalities among class and other categoric units. Thus, differentiation very rapidly generates new integrative problems that, in turn, generate selection pressures for new mechanisms forging interdependencies among differentiated units.

2.2.1.3 Interdependencies

Interdependencies among corporate units reveal a number of distinctive forms, including (Turner 2010a): (a) exchange, (b) embedding and inclusion, (c) overlap, and (d) mobility. Each of these is examined below.

Exchanges Corporate units form many levels and types of exchange relations with each other and with incumbents in their respective divisions of labor. At the macro level, exchanges cannot become extensive without markets and quasi markets (Simmel [1907] 1979; Weber [1922]1968: 635–40; Braudel [1979] 1982, 1977; Turner 1995, 2010a). Markets institutionalize the exchange of one resource for another, typically after some negotiation over the respective values of the resources possessed by the actors. Such exchanges are often "economic" because they involve the flow of a generalized resource like *money* among corporate units and between corporate units and members of categoric units who are incumbent in corporate-unit divisions of labor. In turn, increases in the scope, volume, and types of exchanges force the elaboration of distributive infrastructures for moving people, resources, and information across territorial and sociocultural spaces, thereby providing a new mechanisms of integration. Also, exchanges generate further integrative mechanisms, coinage of money, regulation of

…n of credit, and differen-
exchanges of equities and
nassing capital used in
And, these mechanism all
velocity, and scope of
e same time increasing the
disintegrative potential in markets and, indeed, all economic exchanges (Braudel 1977; Collins 1990; Turner 1995, 2010a).

In addition to these more economic exchanges, the expansion of markets and market infrastructures generate *quasi markets*, thereby increasing the number of social relationships in societies revealing a market-like quality (Simmel [1907] 1979; Turner 1995, 2010a). Quasi markets are, in some ways, a form of loose segmentation because they mimic the basic structure of market exchanges but are not generally explicitly economic. For example, memberships in voluntary corporate units—clubs, churches, sports teams, etc.—take on an exchange character, with the corporate unit "marketing" it resources to potential members and with members joining the corporate unit for non-economic resources, such as religiosity, fun, companionship and love, loyalty, commitments, and philanthropy, aesthethics, competition, prestige, etc. (Hechter 1987). Money may become part of this exchange if dues, fees, and other "price" considerations enter. But, when we speak of a marriage or "dating market," money is not the explicit medium of exchange (Abrutyn 2015), although such markets can be usurped by more economic forces, as is the case in the dating market that is increasingly regulated by corporate units providing match-making services for a fee. Indeed, as critical theorists like Jurgen Habermas ([1973] 1976) have argued, cold symbolic media like money and power may "colonize" social relationships, with quasi markets being especially vulnerable because they already have many properties of economic markets.

The expansion of economic markets and quasi markets dramatically alters that nature of social relationships in societies, as Geog Simmel ([1907]1979) was the first to fully explore. Relations become more instrumental, and individuals begin to have more choice in the resources, including friendships and group affiliations, that they seek. As individuals give up resources—time, energy, commitments, money—they generally do so because they experience an increase in their sense of value, which generates commitments to the macro-level system of market-mediated relations and its institutional supports that allow for a sense of "profit" to be realized in each successive exchange in a market or quasi market. Thus, exchanges not only generate commitments among exchange partners, whether individuals or corporate units, they lead individuals to form commitments to macrostructural systems like institutions and societies as a whole that have enabled them to experience an increase in utilities or profits from exchange activities (Lawler and Yoon 1996; Lawler et al. 2009; Lawler 2001).

But exchange also generates disintegrative pressures. Inherent in all markets—whether economic or quasi markets—are de-stabilizing forces, such as inflation or deflation, fraud and manipulation, oscillations in supplies and demands, exploitation of the disadvantaged, increases in inequalities, pyramiding of meta-markets where the medium of exchange (e.g., money) in a lower market becomes the commodity exchange in higher-level (e.g., money market), speculative markets (equity and futures markets) that are subject of fraud, and over-speculation and collapse. The result is that exchanges force the elaboration of another key integrative mechanisms: the consolidation and centralization of power—to be examined shortly.

Embedding and Inclusion Social structures and their cultures typically become embedded, with smaller units lodged inside of ever-larger corporate units within an institutional domain. In this way, there is a kind of meta-coordination of the divisions of labor of corporate units, their cultures, and their exchange relations, all of which reduce the disintegrative potential of differentiation and exchanges as integrative mechanisms. When there are network ties and relations of authority across embedded structures, when the same generalized symbolic media are employed, and when these media have been used to form institutional ideologies that in turn regulate the formation of beliefs and norms, highly differentiated structures become more integrated.

Embedding thus generates structural inclusion, but such inclusions also generate their own disintegrative pressures. One is rigidity across wide sectors of institutional domains that makes them unable to respond to new environmental exigencies. Another is the problems that always come with complexity of social structure: poor coordination, fraud, exploitation, abuse of authority, and inefficiencies—all of which can become sources of tension and, hence, institutional if not societal and inter-societal disintegration.

Overlaps The divisions of labor of diverse corporate units sometimes overlap within institutional domains, with the result that the network structure and culture of corporate units become more integrated across a larger set of positions and members incumbent in these positions. If members are from diverse categoric units, overlaps also generates intersections, which as I will analyze later, are a critical mechanism integrating societies. And the more individuals, per se, interact, but especially individuals from diverse and differentially-evaluated categoric units, the less salient will categoric-unit memberships or different locations in divisions of labor become (Blau 1977, 1994; Turner 2002, 2010b), and hence the more integrated will be the overlapping corporate units, and the greater will be the positive emotions that individuals feel for the overlapping corporate units.

Overlaps can, however, consolidate members of categoric-unit memberships when each of the overlapping units reveals high levels of homogeneity of memberships, which reduces rates of inter categoric-unit interaction. Moreover, if overlaps reinforce hierarchies in the divisions of labor, with one unit dominating over the other, then the tensions associated with hierarchy will increase the potential for disintegration (see later discussions of hierarchy and domination).

Mobility Mobility across corporate unit within and between institutional domains increases integration by virtue of increasing the connections among individuals across sociocultural space. Individuals bring the culture of one unit to the other, and out of the blending of cultures (ideologies, beliefs, norms, expectations) cultural similarities across a larger swath of corporate-unit positions increases, and hence, so does cultural integration. Moreover, to the extent that mobility also brings members of different categoric units together and increases their rates of interaction, inequalities in the evaluation of categoric-unit memberships decline, thereby making connections less stressful. And, as stress is reduced, positive emotional arousal increases and reduces tensions associated with inequalities.

However, mobility has the ironic consequence of sometimes increasing the sense of relative deprivation among those who are not mobile but who must observe the mobility of others (Merton 1968). Those left behind can be stigmatized by the ideologies of the domains in which they are incumbent in corporate units, thereby increasing their negative emotions and potential for conflict with, or at least resentment of, those who have been mobile. And, if those left behind are disproportionately members of devalued categoric units, while those who have been mobility are members of more valorized categoric units, then the tensions among members of categoric units in a society will increase, thereby raising the potential for disintegration.

2.2.1.4 Segregation

The opposite of interdependencies is segregation. When corporate units and members of categoric units are consistently separated in space and time, segregation exists and, for a time, can promote integration by separating corporate and categoric units that engage in incompatible activities and/or have histories of conflict and other disintegrative relations. There are almost always entrance and exit rules (Luhmann 1982) for entering and leaving corporate units that have been segregated. There will also be highly ritualized forms of interaction among members of populations that have been separated but, still, must have some ties to each other (Goffman 1967). Entrance/exit rules and rituals enable actors to make the transition from one culture and/or social structure to another, without activating disintegrative relations with those who have been segregated.

Yet, segregation per se will typically generates disintegrative pressures over the long run because separation of corporate units or subpopulations, or both, almost always involves the use of power and domination to impose and maintain the separation; and once imposed, the distribution of resources often becomes ever-more unequal. And if segregation of corporate units and subpopulations are consolidated, this consolidation of parameters marking status locations (in divisions of labor) with diffuse status characteristics of incumbents in categoric units generally works to increase tensions between (a) corporate units, (b) divisions within them, and (c) members of valued and devalued categoric units.

While such systems can promote integration (that is, regularized patters of relationships) for considerable periods of time, segregation in the end will increase tensions and the potential for disintegrative conflicts because segregation is typically part of a larger pattern of inequality and stratification in a society or inter-societal system that is created and sustained by domination.

2.2.1.5 Domination and Stratification

Max Weber's ([1922]1968: 212–299) analysis of domination is perhaps the strongest part of his sociology because it views inequalities and stratification as part of a larger process by which power is mobilized to control and regulate; and in so doing, domination provides a central mechanisms of macrostructural integration. As populations grow and differentiate, polity and law as institutional domains differentiate and begin to consolidate power. Other domains can also do so, as is the case with religion and, at times, with powerful economic actors. Consolidation of power occurs along four bases (Mann 1986; Turner 1995, 2010a): (1) physical coercion, (2) administrative control, (3) manipulation of incentives, and (4) use of cultural symbols. And, depending upon the particular combination of bases mobilized, the resulting system of domination will vary. Domination is also part of the broader stratification system in which corporate units in various institutional domains distribute resources unequally by virtue of whether or not they allow individuals to become incumbent in the corporate units of differentiated institutional domains and, if admitted, where they can become incumbent in the division of labor and where they can be mobile within and across corporate units.

Inequality and stratification created by domination can promote integration, even under conditions of very high inequality. Indeed, where inequality is great, where domination is extensive and extends to all social relations within and between corporate units and members of categoric units, and where social strata (class and other hierarchical divisions) are consolidated with memberships in valued and devalued categoric units, integration can be high—albeit in a most oppressive manner. Highly stratified societies are integrated but they also possess high potential for tension and conflict in the longer run, but they can persist for considerable periods of time across large expanses of territory.

In contrast, high degrees of integration will be likely when domination is less pronounced. Under this condition of lower domination, intersection of memberships of categoric units in divisions of labor of corporate units will be higher. And high levels of intersection creates less bounded classes that, in turn, encourage upward mobility across the class system. Thus, societies revealing lower levels of dominations have greater flexibility to deal with tensions and conflicts as they arise. Domination and stratification systems between these two extremes of very high and low domination are the mostly likely to reveal immediate disintegrative potential (Turner 2010a: 186–90). Typically, inequality is high and consolidation of resource-distributing corporate units with high and low evaluations of memberships in categoric units is also high. Yet, at the same time, the consolidation of the coercive, administrative, symbolic bases of power is weak, and the lack of material resources makes consolidation of a material incentive base of power unviable. Under these conditions mobilization for conflict by those denied opportunities to secure valued resources becomes ever-more likely (Turner 2013: 337–74). Indeed, such systems may be in constant cycles of conflict, with the outcome of conflict never leading to a new and stronger system of domination.

2.2.1.6 Intersections

Peter Blau's (1977, 1994) last major theorizing on macrostructures argued that high rates of interaction among diverse types of individuals at different locations of social structures promotes integration. He emphasized that individuals, when viewed from a macro-level perspective, can be arrayed as a series of distributions among subpopulations distinguished by what he termed "parameters." There are two types of parameters: *Graduated parameters* mark individuals location with respect to markers that vary by degree—e.g. amount of income, levels of wealth, years of education, age, etc. *Nominal parameters* mark individuals as members of a discrete social category that is distinct from other categories, or what I am labeling *categoric units*. The key to integration, Blau argued, is *intersection* whereby individuals with high and low locations on graduated parameters and membership marked by high and low evaluations of nominal parameters have *opportunities to interact*: the higher the intersection and rates of interaction among people located in different places on graduated and nominal parameters, the more integrated will be a society.

Conversely, the more *consolidated* are parameters, whereby rates of contact and interaction across graduated and nominal parameters are low, the less integrated will the society be. I would add the caveat that such consolidations is almost always part of a system of domination and stratification and, hence, by my definition, such a system can be highly integrated, at least for a time. But, I think that Blau is essentially correct that intersection of parameters promotes considerable mobility and at time chaos, but it does not lead to the building up of tensions and hostility among subpopulations compared to societies where consolidation of parameters causes the accumulation of tensions and hostilities between subpopulations defined by their categoric-unit memberships. With intersection, tensions can be resolved and conflicts can be frequent and institutionalized by law, thereby promoting a flexible system of integration, whereas consolidation produces a more rigid system held together by (a) high levels of coercive power, especially around its administrative base, (b) high levels of resource inequality, (c) low rates of mobility, and (d) segregation of individuals and families at divergent points of salient graduated and nominal parameters.

2.2.1.7 Cultural Integration

At the macro level of organization *texts* (written and oral), *technologies* (knowledge about how to manipulate the environment), values (general moral imperatives), *ideologies* (moral imperatives for specific institutional domains, and *meta-ideologies* (moral imperative combining ideologies from several institutional domains) are the most important elements of culture when analyzing integration. Ideologies and meta-ideologies provide, respectively, the moral tenets for beliefs of corporate-unit culture and status beliefs about members of categoric units operating as the meso-level of social organization. units tend to be lodged within a particular institutional domain. At times, meta-ideologies can also be involved in corporate units within the set of domains generating a meta-ideology. And so, the culture of any given corporate unit will be highly constrained by the elements of ideologies and, at times, meta-ideologies of the domain(s) in which it is embedded. Meta-ideologies legitimate the inequalities of the stratification system in a society. Status beliefs at the meso level social organization are derived by meta-ideologies, and these beliefs specify the moral worth and other characteristics of members of categoric units. In turn, normative expectations on incumbents in the divisions of labor in corporate units and on members of categoric units are drawn from the dominant beliefs of corporate-unit culture and the status beliefs about the moral worth and characteristics of members of various categoric units. These normative expectations then determine the specific expectation states on individuals in locations in the divisions of labor and on members of categoric units during the course of encounters of face-to-face interaction at the micro-level of social organization (see Webster and Foschi 1988 for literatures on expectation states).

Cultural integration increases in a society when there is *consistency* among the cultural systems outlined above. If texts (e.g., histories, philosophies, stories, folklore, etc.) are consistent with each other and with technologies, values, and ideologies, they provide a firmer cultural platform for the development of beliefs, norms, and expectation states at the meso and micro levels of social organization. In contrast, if these cultural systems reveal contradictions and inconsistencies, integration by culture will be much weaker. When cultural systems are *embedded* inside each other, with less encompassing moral codes lodged inside of, and even derived from, more generalized cultural codes, then another level of cultural integration is achieved. Ideologies, then, are derived from texts, technologies, and values; and in turn, meta-ideologies are built up from ideologies so derived, then beliefs in corporate-unit culture and status beliefs about members of categoric units follow from ideologies and meta-ideologies that regulate and legitimate actions with institutional domains and moral evaluations of those at different places in the class system of a society. Then, if normative systems are taken from the moral codings of beliefs (and ideologies and meta-ideologies at the macro level), then expectation states on individuals will be clear, allowing interactions at the micro level to proceed smoothly.

Consistency, embedding, and successive derivation of lower- from higher- level moral codings thus increase integration, even when they legitimate structural arrangements in institutional domains that generate tension-producing inequalities in the stratification system and the differential moral evaluation of members of categoric units. Yet, under such circumstances, the underlying tensions created by inequalities will work to increase potential pressures for disintegration at a social structural level. And, as social structural level tensions increase, these can work to undermine the level of integration provided by culture as ideologies, meta-ideologies, beliefs, and expectation states are called into question by mobilization for structural (and now cultural as well) conflict (Turner 2013: 337–74; Snow and Soule 2010; Goodwin and Jasper 2006; Goodwin et al. 2000, 2004).

The last element of note are the dynamics revolving around *generalized symbolic media of exchange* (see Table 7.1 Chap. 7 and Table 11.2 in Chap. 11). As actors develop corporate units to deal with adaptive problems, they begin to build culture through discourse about what they are trying to do (Abrutyn 2009, 2014, 2015; Abrutyn and Turner 2011). This discourse is almost always moral, arguing that a particular way of doing things is the most likely to be successful. Emerging from such discourse is the ideology of an institutional domain; and this ideology legitimates and justifies the way corporate units in a domain act and interact to form both the structure and cultural of a domain. These generalized media also can become the valued resource that corporate units distribute unequally to members in different corporate units and at different locations in the divisions of labor of any given corporate unit. Cultural integration increases when there is consensus over the appropriateness of a given generalized symbolic medium as a topic for discourse, text-construction, exchange, and distribution because its moral tenets are used to construct a coherent ideology, the elements of which are consistent with each other and over which there is consensus. The result is that actors see and orient to their environment with a common culture that legitimates their actions and, often, provides valued resources that bring reinforcement. Thus, *money*, *authority/power*, *sacredness-piety*, *love-loyalty*, *imperative coordination/justice*, *aesthetics*, *learning*, *knowledge*, *competition*, etc. are all inherently rewarding, and if individuals agree on the ideologies built from the symbolic part of these medium and can also receive acceptable shares of the resource part of these media (that is, money, authority, love/loyalty, etc.), they will experience positive emotions and make positive attributions to both an institutional domain and the elements of the stratification system created by the inequality distribution of valued resources to individuals at different locations in the divisions of labor of corporate units and in different categoric units.

And, when these dynamics unfold for dominant institutions, then meta-ideologies across these institutional domains form and add further legitimization to the inequalities in the stratification system. Such meta-ideologies moralize a larger social space: many diverse types of corporate units in multiple institutional domains and potentially multiple hierarchies (e.g., class, ethnic, gender, religious) in the stratification system. Meta-ideologies are particularly likely to form when the generalized symbolic media distributed by corporate units in diverse domains are exchanged across institutional domains, leading to their persistent circulation. For example, *money* from the economy flows through most corporate units in virtually all institutional domains in complex societies, as does *authority* to corporate units that has been franchised out by polity and law, as does *learning* and *knowledge* across domains such as economy, polity, law, education, and science. The more generalized symbolic media circulate and the more widely they are distributed to incumbents in corporate units and in categoric units, the more likely are multiple systems of meta-ideologies to form in a society and provide a basis for integration by legitimating inter-institutional activities, by legitimating inequalities and stratification, and by providing positive utilities and rewards for individuals to receive these media as valued resources that lead them, in turn, to develop commitments to corporate units, to institutional domains rewarding them with these media, and even to systems of inequality making up the stratification system in a society.

This complex of cultural integration can sustain a society for long periods of time, but the very interdependencies among cultural elements and between these elements and structural formations makes integration vulnerable, especially if there are high degrees of inequality in the distribution of symbolic media as valued resources and if the moral meanings of some generalized symbolic media are not consistent with each other (e.g., explanations from science in terms of verified knowledge vs. explanations from texts about the sacred/supernatural from religion). And so, if consistency in moral tenets of symbolic media is low, then ideologies and meta-ideologies may come into conflict with each other and with other cultural elements such as (a) texts, technologies, and values at the macro level of social organization, (b) beliefs and status beliefs as they generate normative systems at the meso level, and (c) expectation states at the micro level.

Thus, cultural integration in societies is always problematic because, once structural differentiation occurs, sustaining common texts and values, ideologies and meta-ideologies, beliefs and status beliefs, normative expectations for incumbents in divisions of labor of corporate units and for members in categoric units, and on-the-ground expectations states for individuals in encounters all can become more difficult. Consistency among, embedding of less inclusive codes in more inclusive codes, and deriving moral codes down this ladder of embedding is not easily assured, per se, and often becomes doubly problematic if cultural codes cause societies with high levels of inequality and stratification to emerge, thereby setting up potential disintegrative pressures from the unequal distribution of the very symbolic media from which cultural integration is sustained.

2.3 The Microdynamics of Integration

The macro-level dynamics of integration revolve around structural and cultural systems that give direction and constraint to both individual and collective actions at the meso- and micro-levels of the social universe. Before examining the meso level in more detail, it is useful to skip down to the micro dynamics of societal integration at the level of encounters before turning to meso-level corporate and categoric units. The micro level of social organization generates, or fails to do so, commitments among individuals to meso and macro structures and their cultures (Turner 2002, 2007, 2010b). These commitments are generated by the arousal of positive emotions that are able to break what Edward Lawler (2001) has characterized as the *proximal bias* inherent in emotional arousal in encounters. This concept of proximal bias emphasizes the fact that positive emotional flows tend to circulate in local encounters and, hence, stay at the micro level. Emotions that generate micro commitments can, and often do, generate solidarities and sentiments among individuals in encounters; and often these positive sentiments can emerge among individuals who view meso and macro structures (and their cultures) in negative terms, thereby sustaining micro level integration at the cost of macro-level integration. And so, if this proximal bias is not broken, allowing positive emotions to flow outward beyond the local encounter to meso and macro structures, the commitments to the meso and macro levels of reality so necessary for societal integration cannot emerge.

Moreover, the problems of breaking the proximal bias to positive emotions are aggravated by the *distal bias* for negative emotions which, Lawler (2001) argues, tend to move away from local encounters outward toward meso and macro structures, thus reducing the ability for commitments to form and, indeed, encouraging distancing emotions like alienation from, or even hostility toward, meso and macro structures and their cultures. This distal bias, I argue, is fed by the activation of defense mechanisms protecting persons in local encounters and activating attributions toward safer, less immediate structures and their cultures (Turner 2002, 2007, 2010b).

Thus, the basic problem on micro-level integration revolves around the dual problems of overcoming both the proximal and distal biases of positive and negative emotions. If positive emotions remain local, and negative emotions consistently target meso and macro structures and their cultures, then the potential power of emotions to integrate and connect *all three levels* of the social universe is not realized, causing only micro-level integrations among chains of encounters and small corporate units like groups. And often, as noted above, these encounters and groups sustain their local focus by viewing other groups in negative emotional terms, thus promoting conflict among groups. Gang violence would be a good example of how micro solidarity of the gang is sustained by positive emotions aroused by interactions within the gang, reinforced by negative emotional reactions toward rival gangs. A social universe built from rival gangs will be disintegrated across all three levels of social reality, whereas an integrated society evidences connections within and across all three levels of reality. How, then, are these connections created and sustained in the presence of the proximal and distal biases of, respectively, positive and negative emotions? Some of my answer is given in Chap. 7 of this volume; let's consider some of these arguments.

2.3.1 Basic Conditions of Emotion Arousal

Humans are wired to be highly emotional (Turner 2000, 2002, 2007, 2010b); and emotions are aroused under two basic conditions: (1) expectations and (2) sanctions. When expectations for what should occur in a situation are met, individuals experience mild to potentially more intense positive emotions, whereas when expectations are not realized, the opposite is the case, thereby activating the distal bias that generally takes negative emotions away from the local encounter and targets more remote objects that will not disrupt the encounter and, at the same time, will protect individuals from negative feelings about themselves. When individuals experience positive sanctions, or approving responses from others, they experience positive emotions, whereas when they experience negative sanctions, they experience such negative emotions as anger, fear, shame, guilt, and humiliation, thus activating external attributions as a defense mechanism to protect both self and viability of the local encounter. Thus, I argue that the cognitive-emotional machinery driving the distal bias to negative emotions is, first, repression of negative emotions toward self, second, their transmutation into safer emotions like anger and alienation, and, third, activation of external attributions that push negative emotions outward onto safer objects, away from self and the local encounter (Turner 2007). For there to be integration within and across levels of social reality, it is necessary for individuals to perceive that they have met expectations and that they have received positive sanctioning from others in a situation.

But more is involved; individuals must *consistently experience* this sense of meeting expectations and receiving positive sanctions in encounters iterated over time and in encounters across a large number of *different types of corporate units* (groups, organizations, and communities) *embedded in many differentiated* institutional domains and *across memberships in diverse categoric units* (Turner 2002, 2007). Thus, solidarity at the level of the encounter and across domains of reality is not a "one shot" process, but a consistent experience of meeting expectations in iterated in encounters across corporate units lodged in diverse institutional domains in a society and across encounters where categoric unit memberships have been salient and expectations for treatment and sanctions have activated positive emotions. It is the *repetition of these positive emotional experiences across many contexts* that activates positive emotions to the point where they can break the hold of the proximal bias, and move out from the encounter and, thereby, target meso-level and macro-level structures and their cultures. Persistent positive emotional arousal in many diverse contexts allows individuals to perceived the source of positive emotional as emanating from the structure and culture of meso and macro social units. And as these positive emotions build up, their arousal dampens the effects of the distal bias inhering in negative emotional arousal.

In this way individuals develop commitments to meso and macro structures, seeing them as responsible for their ability to meet expectations and receive positive sanctions. And, the more individuals who can have these experiences and the more often they can have them across many different types of encounters embedded in different types of corporate units within diverse institutional domains, the greater will be their commitments of a population to all levels of social structure and culture outlined in Figs. 7.1 and 7.3. What conditions, then, allow people to meet expectations and receive positive sanctions from others?

2.3.2 The Distribution of Generalized Symbolic Media

In general, the distribution of generalized symbolic media will be highly salient in almost all encounters because these are not just symbolic codings forming moralities (and derived expectation states), they are often *the valued resource* distributed unequally by corporate units (Abrutyn 2015). When people can consistently meet expectations for receipt of generalized symbolic media across many institutional domains, they will typically experience positive emotions, even if their expectations are comparatively low. But, when these expectations are not realized, the negative emotional arousal will be intense and will contribute considerably to the potential undermining of the system of stratification, and particularly so, if there are high levels of intersection among social class and non-class memberships in categoric units.

2.3.3 Meeting Expectations and Receiving Positive Sanctions

When expectations are clear, non-contradictory, consistent, and successively embedded from the most general (texts and values, for example) to increasingly specific moral codes (i.e., ideologies, meta-ideologies, beliefs in corporate units and status beliefs for categoric, norms and situational expectations), it is likely that individuals will, first of all, hold realistic expectations. Secondly, they will be able to behave in ways that allows them to meet these expectations for self and to facilitate others' capacity to meet the expectations.

When expectations are met, the positive emotions aroused feel like positive sanctions, but it is also necessary for persons to perceive that others are actively signaling approval of their behaviors. Thus, the clarity of expectations, as this clarity follows from the conditions enumerated above, is also critical to meeting feelings of being positively sanction by others. And, when clarity, consistency, and successive embedding are not present, individuals are likely to behave in ways that, to some degree, make them feel like they have not met expectations and, moreover, that they have failed in the eyes of others who are perceived to be sanctioning them negatively.

As noted above, when the parameters marking individuals as members of differentially valued categoric units are highly consolidated, meeting expectations that will arouse positive emotions can be difficult and avoiding the sense of being negatively sanctioned can be hard to avoid. For example, if ethnicity in a society is highly correlated with social class memberships, with members of devalued ethnic subpopulations over-represented in lower classes and with members of other, more-valued ethnic subpopulations incumbent in middle-to-higher social classes, then interactions among these different ethnic groups will often be difficult because they will sustain low and high evaluations, and force those who are less valued to meet expectations that stigmatize them and, in so doing, that make it seem like they are being negatively sanctioned by higher-status individuals. Under these conditions, even meeting expectations can be humiliating and shame-provoking, thereby arousing negative emotions that must often be repressed. Given that consolidation also typically involves consolidation of members of higher- and lower-ranked members of different categoric units with particular corporate units, such as neighborhoods, schools, workplaces, and even churches, some of the stigma of inter-categoric unit interactions can be mitigated by *intra*-categoric unit interactions where individuals can meet intra-categoric and corporate-unit expectations and feel as if others are approving of them in giving off positive responses to behaviors. Still, segregation as a macro-level integrative mechanism (as it generates high rates of intra-categoric unit interaction at the micro level or reality) can only go so far because people know they are devalued in the broader society, and as a consequence, they experience the sting of such an evaluation when forced to interact as subordinates with those in higher-ranking positions in divisions of labor and with those in more highly valued, even valorized, categoric units.

Domination and other integrative mechanisms like segregation and even interdependencies can, therefore, make retreat to consolidated and segregated "safe heavens" unfulfilling. Hence, high levels of inequality and discrimination against members of categoric unit sustaining inequality will, eventually, arouse large pools of negative emotions—anger, fear, shame, humiliation, sadness, alienation, and unhappiness in general—among subpopulations where at least some of their interactions in encounters are not gratifying.

Thus, like any other valued resource in a society, positive and negative emotions are distributed unequally (Turner 2014); and when negative emotions are disproportionately consolidated with lower class and other devalued memberships in non-class categoric units, integration will be under duress, eventually shifting into mobilization by members of devalued categoric units against the existing system of integration in various forms of intra- or even inter-society conflict.

Still, at the micro level, even interactions among unequals—whether the inequality stems from different locations in the divisions of labor, memberships in evaluated categoric units, or both (in the case of consolidation)—have a tendency for unequals to honor expectations states. Higher status persons will be allowed to initiate more talk and action and will be given deference by lower status persons; and lower status persons will often sanction their fellow lower-status members who challenge the micro system of inequality (imposed by the meso, and ultimately, macro levels of social organization). For, to challenge the inequality invites negative emotional arousal by higher-status persons and hence negative sanctions that carry the power to make lower-status members of groups feel even more negative emotions. In return for acceptance of the status order, then, higher-status persons treat those in lower positions with respect and dignity, thereby arousing positive emotions within the encounter (Ridgeway 1994). Of course, if a higher-status person fails to honor this implicit bargain, the tension in the encounter will increase, but most people, most of the time, implicitly realize what is at stake: constant tension or mild positive emotional flow, with the latter being more gratifying (Ridgeway 1994; Turner 2002). This dynamic mitigates some of the negative processes unleashed by consolidation of parameters, as discussed above, but does not obviate them. And so, the corrosive emotional effect of prolonged inequalities across many diverse situations on people trapped in consolidated devaluated categoric units will gradually increase the potential for disintegrative conflict, as negative emotions build up to the point where individuals become ever-more willing to engage in conflict.

2.3.4 Transactional Needs and Their Effects on Meeting Expectations and Receiving Positive Sanctions

Many expectations come from what I have labeled *transactional needs* (Turner 1987, 2002, 2007, 2010b), which are motive states that arouse and direct the behaviors of all humans. These are, I believe, hard-wired into human neuroanatomy, with sociocultural elaborations; and in virtually every micro-levels encounter, these transactional needs establish expectations for how a person should be treated by others. If others treat a person as expected, then the person will experience positive emotions just as this person would from expectations from any other source. When not treated as expected by the arousal of need states, the failure to do so will arouse negative emotions, per se, but with a super-charging effect from a sense of being sanctioned by others. This failure to meet expectations arising from need states will thus almost always be seen as a negative sanction by others, thus doubling up on the person's negative emotional arousal. And, if large numbers of individuals in devalued categoric units must consistently fail in meeting their transactional needs, the pool of negative emotional arousal will consolidate with class and other devalued categoric memberships.

While people may lower their expectations when consistently not realized, such is more difficult to do for expectations generated by transactional needs that are *part of the person's sense of who and what they are*, above and beyond their memberships in categoric units. Hence, even as people come to accept a certain consistent level of failure in meeting needs, the corrosive effects of negative emotional arousal, often accompanied by repression, further stock the pool of negative emotions that can undermine societal integration.

Table 2.1 lists the universal transactional needs that drive the behaviors of individuals in virtually every encounter of interpersonal behavior (Turner 1987, 1988, 2002, 2007, 2010b). These needs vary in the relative power, as is captured in the rank-ordering implied by the list in Table 2.1.

As the ranking in the table denotes, *verification of* various levels of i*dentity* is the most powerful transactional need; and the ranking of these various types of selves (from core-self down through social-, group-, and role-identities) indicate their relative power to arouse negative or positive emotions. The second most powerful need is, I believe, the need to feel that one has gained a *profit in exchanges of resources*—both intrinsic and extrinsic—with others. Human calculations of profit are determined by the value of resources received for those given up as costs and investments (accumulated costs), evaluated against various cultural standards of fairness and justice. The third most powerful need is one that I have added in recent work, and it emphasizes achieving a *sense of efficacy* in interaction, or the sense that one has some control over what will occur and what the outcomes will be. The fourth need is a need for *group inclusion*, or the sense that one is part of the ongoing flow of the interaction. The fifth is a *sense of trust* that depends up the predictability of self and others respective actions, the ability to fall into what Collins (2004) rhythmic synchronization in talk and body movements, and the sense that others are being sincere and respective to self. These five transactional needs are the most powerful, and they have the greatest effect on, first, establishing expectations in a situation and on, secondly, the intensity of the emotional reaction, whether positive or negative, for success or failure in

Table 2.1 Transactional needs generating expectation states

1. **Verification of identities**: needs to verify one or more of the four basic identities that individuals present in all encounters
(a) *Core-identity*: the conceptions and emotions that individuals have about themselves as persons that they carry to most encounters
(b) *Social-identity*: the conception that individuals have of themselves by virtual of their membership in categoric units which, depending upon the situation, will vary in salience to self and others; when salient, individuals seek to have others verify their social identity
(c) *Group-identity*: the conception that individuals have about their incumbency in corporate units (groups, organizations, and communities) and/or their identification with the members, structure, and culture of a corporate unit; when individuals have a strong sense of identification with a corporate unit, they seek to have others verify this identity
(d) *Role-identity*: the conception that individuals have about themselves as role players, particularly roles embedded in corporate units nested in institutional domains; the more a role-identity is lodged in a domain, the more likely will individuals need to have this identity verified by others
2. **Making a profit the exchange of resources**: needs to feel that the receipt of resources by persons in encounters exceeds their costs and investments in securing these resources and that their shares of resources are just compared to (a) the shares that others receive in the situation and (b) reference points that are used to establish what is a just share
3. **Efficacy**: needs to feel that one is in control of the situation and has the individual capacity and opportunity to direct ones own conduct, despite sociocultural constraints
4. **Group inclusion**: needs to feel that one is a part of the ongoing flow of interaction in an encounter; and the more focused is the encounter, the more powerful is this need
5. **Trust**: needs to feel that others' are predictable, sincere, respective of self, and capable of rhythmic sustaining synchronization
6. **Facticity**: needs to feel that, for the purposes of the present interaction, individuals share a common inter-subjectivity, that matters in the situation are as they seem, and that the situation has an obdurate character

meeting expectations and perceiving that others are positively or negatively sanctioning a person. The sixth need for *facticity* will arouse highly negative emotions when not met, as when individuals do not achieve the sense that they are experiencing the situation in the same manner, but it is not as powerful as the other need states; and when the sense of facticity is achieved, it does not arouse strong positive emotions.

People in most encounters, even those among unequals, are typically trying to meet each others transactional needs because, to fail to do so, will breach an encounter and often arouse intense negative emotions, especially if an identity or sense of profit is denied by others. Not only are the expectations not realized, but others are likely to be seen as responsible, thus filling the encounter with negative emotions that are difficult for all to endure. And so, if individuals can understand the nature of expectations arising from these needs—and people are very adept at reading these expectations in the gestures of others—they will do so, if they possibly can. And if they cannot get a firm initial reading about each other's expectations, they will tread "interpersonal" water and stay in a highly ritualized mode of conduct until they have a better sense of which identity is most salient in the situation, which resources are in play in exchanges, what will make others feel a sense of efficacy, what is involved in securing a sense of being part of the action, and what is necessary to communicate a sense of trust. This positive bias to most interactions is part of the proximal bias; and it is one reason why people are able to experience positive emotions in most—but, obviously, not all—encounters. This bias thus assures some degree of integration at the micro level, and if sufficiently consistent over encounters and across situations, the positive emotions generated can break the hold of proximal bias and begin to form commitments to meso and macro structures and their cultures in a society.

Yet, when people consistently do not meet the expectations arising from their transactional needs across encounters in an array of corporate units in different institutional domains, the negative emotions will be particularly painful because need states are internal to the individual and, as noted earlier, are part of a person's basic sense of who they are and how they should be treated. So, failing to meet even lowered expectations (from past readjustment downward of these expectations) arouses not only emotions like shame, alienation, and withdrawal from commitments to macrostructures but also proactive emotions like anger and needs for vengeance to strike out at the source of this failure. The distal bias and the use of external attributions toward meso and macrostructures will increase disaffection from social structures, and rapidly erode commitments to all levels of social reality, except those that continue to offer some chance of meeting expectations.

2.4 Mesodynamics of Integration

The macro and micro levels of reality meet in the meso level, composed of corporate and categoric units. Almost every encounter is embedded in a corporate unit revealing a division of labor and several categoric units composed of persons who are placed into variously evaluated social categories. Corporate units are the building blocks of institutional domains, but once these domains are formed, corporate units are also the conduits by which the culture and structure of the macro realm makes its down and imposes expectations—derived from societal-level values, institutional ideologies and the symbolic media used to develop these ideologies, meta-ideologies, corporate units beliefs, norms of the division of labor of corporate units and, finally, expectations states derived from these norms that will guide interaction in micro encounters.

Categoric units are the building blocks of the macro realm, via their effects on the formation of a system of stratification in society, whereby social strata or classes are, to various degrees, consolidated with memberships in non-class categoric units, such as ethnicity/race, religious affiliation, gender, age, national origins, and the like. Stratification systems are created by the unequal distribution of the generalized symbolic media summarized in Table 11.2 as valued resources and legitimated by the meta-ideologies that form from the circulation of generalized symbolic media across sets of institutional domains. As such, the meta-ideologies of the stratification system set up status beliefs and expectations states for individuals in encounters who are members of diverse categoric units that are typically differentially evaluated in terms of their moral worth.

When the conditions outlined for macro-level integration are in place, then the structures of the macro and meso realms are well integrated, and if the culture associated with these structures is also well connected in the patterned outlined above, beliefs and norms at the meso level provide clear expectation states for micro level behaviors among individuals in encounters. Conversely, if there are gaps, inconsistencies, failures to embed or if integration is achieve by segregation and consolidations within and between corporate and categoric units, then expectations may be somewhat clear but they are likely to generate negative emotions at the level of the encounter. In so doing, they erode integration by reducing commitments of persons to meso and the macro structures and cultures built up from meso structures. These dynamics have been discussed in the sections on macro and micro integration, but they can be given additional focus by viewing corporate units as operating within *cultural and structural fields* generated by the institutional domains in which they are lodged and the modes of integrating corporate units with and across institutional domains. Similarly, focus is achieved by examining the dynamics of *consolidation and intersection* of categoric units in cultural and structural fields generated by the structure of the stratification system and the meta-ideology legitimating this system. Let me first take on the fields and niches of corporate units.

2.4.1 Fields and Niches Among Corporate Units

The institutional domains in which corporate units are embedded constitute, on the one hand, a set of resource niches in which corporate units seek resources necessary to function, and on the other, a cultural and structural field. The emergence of organizational ecology (e.g., Hannan and Freeman 1977, 1989) changed the way organizations and, potentially, corporate units more generally are analyzed, whereas, the so-called "new institutionalism" (Powell and DiMaggio 1991; Friedland and Alford 1991; Fligstein and McAdam 2012)) did the same but in a less useful way than organizational ecology. In the new institutionalism, the field of any given organization is other organizations, which is certainly true but misses the critical point that other organizations are part of *emergent* institutional domains with their own macro-level structures and cultures that are sustained by the macro modes of integration examined earlier. Let me first examine what organizational ecology adds to a view of integrative dynamics in societies, and then turn to the notion of field emerging from the new institutionalism.

2.4.1.1 The Ecology of Corporate Units

When attention shifts to the ecology of corporate units, instead of just organizations, the ideas of both urban and organizational ecology become relevant (Turner 2015; Irwin 2015), as does a more micro view of groups as seeking resource niches. Macro-level dynamics of integration organize the environments of corporate units, once they have been built up into institutional domains that distribute resources generating stratification as a macro-level system. These environments can be seen as distributions of various types of resources—demographic, material, cultural, and structural—needed to sustain the operation of a corporate unit. One generalization is that when institutional domains are integrated by differentiation and interdependencies, the number of resource niches dramatically increases, especially as markets and other distributive infrastructures move resources across institutional domains. And, as the number of resource niches increases, the greater will be the pressures for further differentiation within and between the corporate units in diverse institutional domains; and hence, the greater will be the number of corporate units organizing a population. As this number increases, selection pressures build for further mechanisms of macro-level integration outlined earlier relying more upon interdependencies more than domination, and for more equitable distribution of generalized symbolic media as resources within the system of stratification. And as differentiation among corporate unit increases, so will the level of intersection among members of diverse categoric units across the divisions of labor of corporate units in a greater number of institutional domains.

A related set of generalizations arise from a view of corporate units as seeking diverse resources in niches, in which the competition for resources is regulated by markets and quasi markets. Organizations in particular, but other corporate units as well, will compete not just for clients, members, and incumbents but also the additional resources that they may bring to an organization (sales receipts, dues, positive feelings, learning, knowledge, loyalty, competitiveness, etc.). The result will be that generalized symbolic media will tend to flow across different corporate units within and across institutional domains, providing a basis for integration; and if this integration is built up by intersections between corporate and categoric units, these intersections will reduce tensions associated with inequalities and, thereby, increase integration. Further, as both differentiation and resource-seeking efforts of corporate units encourage recruitment of clients, customers, members, and incumbents, individuals in a society will have access to more generalized symbolic media as resources across diverse resource-seeking and resource-giving corporate units across diverse institutional domains, thereby by increasing positive emotional arousal and commitments to macro structures and their cultures and, thus, increasing micro-level integration of macro structures and their cultures.

Differentiation and dynamism of resource-seeking corporate units also increases integration by encouraging such institutional domains as polity and law to rely upon (a) material incentives (thereby creating new resource niches) more than coercive or administrative power, which will decrease resources available to corporate units, and (b) more on positivistic law than traditionalism and rigid systems (e.g., religious) of moral codes to direct corporate-unit activities. The result is that tensions and conflicts among corporate units can be negotiated and resolved in various political and legal forums without resorting to coercive domination. Moreover, when an arena of politics and positivistic law exist as regulatory mechanisms of integration (Luhmann 1982), competition among corporate units will be less likely to evolve into open and potentially violent conflict that would increase the disintegrative potential in a society.

Thus, integrated ecosystems at the societal level require internal capacities to regulate competition for resources. Markets represent one mechanisms for doing so, but the co-evolution of a polity relying more on incentives than coercion and a legal system built around the capacity to adjust legal codes and contracts to new conditions (positivistic law) decrease the likelihood that regulated competition in markets will evolve into coercive dynamics revolving around strategies employing violent conflict to gain access to resources.

Yet, as resource niches become too densely population by corporate units, they can fail (Hannan and Freeman 1977), thereby also failing to meet the expectations of their incumbents. Moreover, systems regulated by markets, even those with political and legal controls, are inherently unstable, often resulting in contractions of the number of corporate units in resource niches, and thus, causing once again a failure of individuals to meet expectations for resources. The result is that even in systems where domination is low-key and revolves around manipulation of material incentive and positivistic law are vulnerable to the vagaries of competition in resource niches, which can increase disintegrative pressures at all levels of social organization.

2.4.1.2 Structural and Cultural Fields

The new institutionalism tended to see the fields of organizations as revealing such properties as "logics" that directed the activities of organizations in their environments. While there is a certain vagueness to terms like "logics," I interpret the underlying idea in the following way: the integration of macro structures and their cultures generate cultural and structural environments to which not only organizations, but also all other types of corporate units must adapt. The modes and mechanisms of structural integration at the macro level of social organization provide create and sustain a system of relationships among corporate units (and categoric units as well) to which any given corporate unit must adapt, and in many cases also adopt as part of its structure and culture. Similarly, the cultural systems of moral coding (see Fig. 7.3 in Chap. 7) attached to institutional domains and the stratification system provide a set of highly moralized instructions in their ideologies and meta-ideologies to all corporate units; and in so doing, this system of moral codings provides beliefs, norms, and expectations directing incumbents in the divisions of labor of corporate units and for members in categoric units. Let me now elaborate on both structural and cultural fields as integrative mechanisms.

Structural Fields A structural field is created by the macro-level integration on corporate units as institutional domains evolve. For example, if segmentation is the dominant mechanism of integration, existing structures and their cultures provide both organizational templates and systems of moral codings that, in essence, need to be copied. Segmentation always generates structural and cultural fields, even as other mechanisms become more prominent. For instance, as differentiation increases and, in turn, as differentiation forces the evolution of new mechanisms of integration revolving around building up interdependencies, the particular configuration mechanisms that emerge provide structural templates for corporate units to built up their structures so as to be able to fit into patterns of interdependencies generated by these mechanisms. If, for example, exchange becomes a dominant mechanism for creating and sustaining interdependencies, then corporate units will develop structures designed to use market forces to secure resources and build up their structures, and they will develop culture codes viewing competition for resources as an acceptable mode of conduct. Conversely, let us say that domination becomes the central mechanisms for ordering relations in a society, coupled with high levels of inequality and segregation among members of different categoric units. The emerging system of relationships among corporate units, and the culture that they develop, will be very different than one based upon market forces guiding exchanges among corporate units. All existing and emergent corporate units in such a system will need to organize themselves so as to fit into this template or, if one prefers, "logic" of social organization at the macro level.

Cultural Fields There are always idiosyncratic elements to the cultural systems that emerge as societies evolve; these elements are shaped by the unique features of a population's history, its geographical location, and its previous modes of integration. Still, there are certain general classes of cultural systems operating in all societies. All societies reveal value systems, all evidence ideologies of existing institutional domains, all reveal meta-ideologies legitimating the stratification system and evaluations of members of categoric units, all generate belief system derived from ideologies and meta-ideologies governing the operation of corporate and categoric unit dynamics, and all impose micro-level expectations states at the level of the encounter drawn from these meso-level belief systems. Thus, cultural fields will always reveal a pattern or logic based upon these invariant dimensions of how culture structures itself in relation to social structures, and vice versa.

The cultural field of any corporate or categoric unit is thus composed of the general value premises of the society, the ideologies and meta-ideologies that evolve to legitimate activities in institutional domains, the beliefs shaping corporate-unit culture derived from ideologies and the status beliefs drawn from meta-ideologies shaping the evaluation of members of categoric, and the expectations states in local encounters constrained by these belief systems. The content of any of these of moral codings will, of course, varying by virtue of unique empirical and historical events (which cannot be so easily theorized) and by the particular configuration of institutional domains that exists and the modes and mechanisms by which these domains and the stratification system are integrated. Once we know these structural fields that have been created, it becomes possible to determine the structure of the cultural fields, and vice versa. For example, if religion becomes a dominant institutional domain and consolidates coercive power and uses this power as a mean of domination, the ideology of religion and the meta-ideology that is built around religion will become the cultural field to which all corporate and categoric units must adapt and adopt. Present day Iran offers a good illustration of such a cultural field. In contrast, if the institutional revolves around economic trade with other populations and within a society, the cultural field that evolves will be very different because it is more likely to be created to justify exchange as a dominant mechanism of integration revolving around interdependencies, and the ideology of this domain will be the center of meta-ideologies from other institutional domains that are used to legitimate the stratification system, and vice versa. This cultural field will then shape the evolution and modes of integration among corporate units that evolve in this society. The emergence of capitalism, as described by Weber ([1905] 1930) and Braudel (1977) provide a good illustration such fields. The differences between these fields cannot always be predicted, but a reasonable hypothesis would be that a population with a history of conflict with neighboring populations would produce a cultural field built more around ideologies of domination than one that does not have such a history or one that has a history of external trade relations rather than warfare with it neighbors. But, the point here is not so much the prediction but the realization that, for whatever reason, the particular configuration of mechanism of integration that evolve in a society at the macro level will shape the configuration of the cultural fields that evolve, and vice versa. And so, in trying to understand how cultural fields integrate societies, it is necessary to understand how they were used during the period when new kinds of corporate units were forming and beginning to build up (a) new and diverse institutional domains and (b) a stratification system composed of categoric units created by the unequal distribution of generalized symbolic media as resources by these new corporate units.

By viewing cultural fields in this way, we can see their effect on meso-level integration. Corporate and categoric units are always being forced to adapt to the more macro-level cultural systems—values, ideologies, and meta-ideologies (as well as texts and technologies)—and as they do so, they implicitly seek to incorporate the logic or the commands of these moral codes. And to the degree that the belief systems evolve around corporate units within institutional domains and around status differences among members of categoric units are consistent with, and follow from, the ideologies, meta-ideologies, and general values of the macro realm, they promote integration at the meso level because they present a coherent cultural field. As they do so, they increase the likelihood that expectations at the micro level will be clear and, thereby, realized at least to some degree, thus promoting integration at the micro level. And, as beliefs and expectations states at the meso and micro level reproduce the cultural field and the structural arrangement that it legitimates, these fields thus reproduce the structures and cultures of the macro realm, thereby promoting integration.

The converse is true if there are dramatic discontinuities and inconsistencies in the moral codes of the macro realm, or if beliefs are not derived from existing ideologies and meta-ideologies but, instead, are evolving on-the-ground as actors seeks to justify new types of sociocultural formations. Such a system will not be integrated and will be likely to experience dramatic change, as ideologies of existing institutional systems come into conflict with new ones that are evolving or with new types of corporate units challenging the existing "logics" of the fields in which corporate units had heretofore operated.

2.4.2 Intersection and Consolidation Among Categoric Units

To the extent that structural and cultural fields, as well as competition for resources by corporate units in various resource niches, increase rates of discrimination against members of devalued categoric units, they promote consolidation of parameters marking categoric unit memberships with differential rates of access to resource-distributing corporate units, with varying rates of mobility up the divisions of labor of such corporate units and, in so doing, with over- or under-representation members of categoric units in the hierarchy of classes in a society. When domination and segregation are prominent mechanisms of integration at the macro level of social organization, consolidation is most likely and severe, but all societies evidence some degree of consolidation of memberships in categoric units with locations in divisions of labor of corporate units, even those relying upon interdependencies regulated by polities relying heavily on the material incentive base of power and by positivistic law. Consolidation also occurs, as is evident in societies like the United States, that evidence egalitarian tenets in value premises and most institutional ideologies and meta-ideologies. Thus, consolidation is a powerful force in all human societies, beginning with the emergence of advanced horticultural forms during societal evolution and continuing well into the post-industrial age and, no doubt, into the future. Thus, all societies reveal disintegrative potential from consolidation, and the higher is the level of consolidation, the greater is this potential.

Even in societies with high rates of intersection, which increase mobility among members of variously evaluated categoric units across corporate units in more institutional domains, and up the hierarchical divisions of labor in these units, there are typically subpopulations that are over-represented in lower social classes and that are subject to prejudicial status beliefs, even in societies with moral codes emphasizing equality among persons and/or equalities of opportunity. Consolidation at the meso level limits rates of interaction between members of valued and devalued categoric units at the micro level and, if interaction occurs, it is structured around inequalities in status, differential stigma imposed by status beliefs and expectation states drawn from meta-ideologies, and often open discrimination. Thus, the persistence of consolidation in human societies assures that there will always be powerful disintegrative pressures working against those promoting integration.

Intersection of memberships of variously valued categoric units across all types of corporate units in all institutional domains, and mobility up and down the divisions of labor of these units, increases rates of interaction at the micro level will all work to reduce the salience of status beliefs at the meso level which, in turn, reduces the power of beliefs that legitimate discrimination. Intersection becomes more likely in societies using differentiation and interdependencies as macro-level mechanisms of integration, and very high rates of intersection reduce the power of stigmatizing and prejudicial status beliefs, which in turn make discrimination and segregation less acceptable and more difficult to legitimate with prejudicial beliefs pulled from meta-ideologies, thereby changing the cultural and structural fields of all meso-level corporate units.

The result is increased integration of a society, albeit sometimes chaotic because of the constant play of conflicting interests and the normal problems with markets regulating corporate-unit competition in resource niches. But this kind of chaos occurs in systems that are more flexible and thus able to adapt to more frequent but less severe disintegrative forces, particularly when compared to societies where coercive domination is the master form of integration. Societies that effectively use domination may appear less chaotic on the surface but the underlying tensions arising from inequalities, discrimination and segregation, and consolidation of membership in categoric unit with access to resource-distribution corporate units bode for disintegrative problems in the future. The breakup of Yugoslavia or the forced dismantling of the Husain regime in Iraq document what happens when cracks in the system of domination appear.

2.5 Conclusion

In this chapter, I have phrased the arguments in the terminology that I have used in recent decades. But the ideas come from all over sociology and from thinkers in both classical and contemporary sociology. In many ways, integration as a force driving the dynamics of human societies has been under-theorized, even as most scholars trying to develop general theory in sociology have proposed at least partial theories of integration. My goal in this chapter has been to bring the pieces of theorizing together into a more unified theory, although many may object to the limitations of my conceptual vocabulary. Yet, if we are to address integration at all levels of social organization, and trace out how it operates within any given level as well as across levels, we need a simplifying vocabulary that retains a focus as analysis shifts from one level to another. There are some aspects of integration than cannot easily be theorized because they occur by virtue of unique historical circumstances, but I think that we can describe what happens in history with a common conceptual vocabulary. And, once we have done this, we can begin to tease out the integrative dynamics that ensue and to see these as part of a more general sociological theory of integration.

At the very least, I have proposed that integration is a multi-level and complex process that cannot be theorized any one level of social organization. We cannot simply pronounce processes—say interaction rituals, self verification, exchange, cultural fields, networks, etc.—as a master mechanism of societal integration. This has been the theoretical tendency, and it has led scholars to abandon the effort to develop a general theory of integration. But once we seek integration as a series of mechanisms operating at distinct levels of social reality, and then, across levels of reality, we place ourselves in a position to develop a more robust theory. This chapter represents my best effort to pull together what are often conflicting strains of theorizing over the last 100 years and place them in one, reasonably coherent, framework for understanding the dynamics of the social universe. What emerges is a composite, but a composite of ideas that are linked conceptually. The result is at a minimum the beginnings of a more robust and unified theory of integration in human societies.

References

Abrutyn, S. (2009). Toward a general theory of institutional autonomy. *Sociological Theory, 27*(4), 449–465.

Abrutyn, S. (2014). *Revisiting institutionalism in sociology: Putting the institution back into institutional analysis*. New York: Routledge.

Abrutyn, S. (2015). Money, love, and sacredness: Generalized symbolic media and the production of instrumental, affectual, and moral reality. *Czech Sociological Review, 51*(3), 445–471.

Abrutyn, S., & Turner, J. H. (2011). The old institutionalism meets the new institutionalism. *Sociological Perspectives, 54*(3), 283–306.

Blau, P. M. (1977). *Inequality and heterogeneity: A primitive theory of social structure*. New York: Free Press.

Blau, P. M. (1994). *Structural contexts of opportunities*. Chicago: University of Chicago Press.

Braudel, F. (1977). In P. M. Ranum (Ed.), *Afterthoughts on material civilization and capitalism*. Baltimore: Johns Hopkins University Press.

Braudel, F. ([1979] 1982). *Wheels of commerce, volume 2: Civilization and capitalism 15th–18th century*. New York: Harper/Collins.

Breiger, R. L., & Mohr, J. W. (2004). Institutional logics from the aggregation of organizational networks: Operational procedures for the analysis of counted data. *Computational & Mathematical Organization Theory, 10*(1), 17–43.

Collins, R. (1990). Market dynamics as the engines of historical change. *Sociological Theory, 8*, 111–135.

Collins, R. (2004). *Interaction ritual chains*. Princeton: Princeton University Press.

Durkheim, E. ([1893] 1963). *The division of labor in society*. New York: Free Press.

Durkheim, E. ([1912] 1984). *The elementary forms of the religious life*. New York: Free Press.

Fligstein, N., & McAdam, D. (2012). *A theory of fields*. New York: Oxford University Press.

Freeman, L., White, D. R., & Romney, A. K. (Eds.). (1989). *Research methods in social network analysis*. Fairfax: George Mason University Press.

Friedland, R., & Alford, R. R. (1991). Bringing society back in: Symbols, practices, and institutional contradictions. In W. Powell & P. DiMaggio (Eds.), *The new institutionalism in organizational analysis* (pp. 232–266). Chicago: The University of Chicago Press.

Goffman, E. (1967). *Interaction ritual*. Garden City, NY: Anchor.

Goodwin, J., Jasper, J., & Polletta, F. (2000). The return of the repressed: The fall and rise of emotions in social movement theory. *Mobilization: An international quarterly, 5*, 65–83.

Goodwin, J., & Jaspers, J. M. (2006). Emotions and social movements. In J. E. Stets & J. H. Turner (Eds.), *Handbook of The Sociology of Emotions* (pp. 611–631). New York: Springer.

Goodwin, J., Jasper, J., & Polletta, F. (2004). Emotional dimensions of social movements. In D. A. Snow, S. A. Soule, & H. Kries (Eds.), *The blackwell companion to social movements*. Malden: Wiley-Blackwell.

Habermas, J. ([1973] 1976). *Legitimation crisis* (T. McCarthy, Trans.). London: Heinemann.

Hannan, M. T., & Freeman, J. H. (1977). The population ecology of organizations. *American Journal of Sociology, 82*, 929–964.

Hannan, M. T., & Freeman, J. H. (1989). *Organizational ecology*. Cambridge, MA: Harvard University Press.

Hechter, M. (1987). *A theory of group solidarity*. Berkeley: University of California Press.

Irwin, M. D. (2015). Evolving communities: Evolutionary analysis in classical and neoclassical human ecology. In J. H. Turner, R. Machalek, & A. Maryanski (Eds.), *Handbook of evolution and society* (pp. 316–332). Boulder: Paradigm Press.

Lawler, E. J. (2001). An affect theory of social exchange. *American Journal of Sociology, 107*, 321–352.

Lawler, E. J., & Yoon, J. (1996). Commitment in exchange relations. *American Sociological Review, 61*, 89–108.

Lawler, E. J., Thye, S. R., & Yoon, J. (2009). *Social commitments in a depersonalized world*. New York: Russell Sage.

Luhmann, N. (1982). *The differentiation of society*. New York: Columbia University Press.

Mann, M. (1986). *The social sources of power. Volume 1 on a history of power from the beginning to a.d. 1760*. Cambridge: Cambridge University Press.

Merton, R. K. (1968). *Social theory and social structure*. New York: Free Press.

Mohr, J. W., & White, H. C. (2008). How to model an institution. *Theory and Society, 37*(5), 485–512.

Powell, W. B., & DiMaggio, P. (1991). *The new institutionalism in organizational analysis*. Chicago: University of Chicago Press.

Ridgeway, C. (1994). Affect. In M. Foschi & E. J. Lawler (Eds.), *Group processes: Sociological analyses*. Chicago: Nelson-Hall.

Simmel, G. ([1907] 1978). *The philosophy of money* (T. Bottomore, & D. Frisby, Trans.). Boston: Routledge and Kegan Paul.

Snow, D., & Soule, S. A. (2010). *A primer on social movements*. New York: Norton.

Spencer, H. ([1894–96]1898). *The principles of sociology*, three volumes. New York: Appleton Century.

Turner, J. H. (1987). Toward a sociological theory of motivation. *American Sociological Review, 52*, 15–25.

Turner, J. H. (1988). *A theory of social interaction*. Stanford: Stanford University Press.

Turner, J. H. (1995). *Macrodynamics: Toward a theory on the organization of human populations*. New Brunswick: Rutgers University Press.

Turner, J. H. (2000). *On the origins of emotions: A sociological inquiry into the evolution of human affect*. Stanford: Stanford University Press.

Turner, J. H. (2002). *Face to face: Toward a theory of interpersonal behavior*. Stanford: Stanford University Press.

Turner, J. H. (2007). *Human emotions: As sociological theory*. Oxford: Routledge.

Turner, J. H. (2010a). *Theoretical principles of sociology: Volume 1 on macrodynamics*. NewYork: Springer.

Turner, J. H. (2010b). *Theoretical principles of sociology: Volume 2 on microdynamics*. New York: Springer.

Turner, J. H. (2013). *Theoretical principles of sociology: Volume 3 on mesodynamics*. New York: Springer.

Turner, J. H. (2014). *Revolt from the middle: Emotional stratification and change in post-industrial societies*. New Brunswick: Transaction Press.

Turner, J. H. (2015). Organizational ecology: Darwinian and non-Darwinian. In J. H. Turner, R. Machalek, & A. Maryanski (Eds.), *Handbook of evolution and society: Toward an evolutionary social science* (pp. 333–349). Boulder: Paradigm Press.

Weber, M. ([1905] 1930). *The protestant ethic and the spirit of capitalism* (T. Parsons, Trans.). Boston: Unwin.

Weber, M. ([1922] 1968). *Economy and society* (G. Roth, Trans.). Berkeley: University of California Press.

Webster, M., & Foschi, M. (1988). *Status generalization: New theory and research*. Stanford: Stanford University Press.

Power in Organizational Society: Macro, Meso and Micro

3

Yingyao Wang and Simone Polillo

3.1 Introduction

What makes the status quo persistent in the face of conflict and inequality, and by the same token, why social change tends to be rare in spite of pervasive injustice, are perennial problems in social theory. The classical founders of sociology—Marx, Weber, and Durkheim—all attempted to grasp the shifting foundations of social order, and the emergence of new forms of conflict, in the context of rapid industrialization. Each of them, of course, focused a different theoretical lens on these problems, each foregrounding different institutional arenas: the economy (Marx), politics and organizations (Weber) and culture/religion (Durkheim). Marx highlighted the revolutionary nature of the capitalist system, and identified the dialectic between the rapidly changing forces of production and the slower moving relations of production as a source of temporary stability—a stability that in the long run would give way to revolution. Weber identified a different determinant of social order, that he believed extended far beyond the economic realm: the intensification of rationalization, giving rise to new forms of authority (rational-legal authority) and social control (formal organization, bureaucracy). With the spread of rationalization, Weber suggested, social conflict would become increasingly institutionalized, attenuated, and ultimately neutralized as the "iron cage" of passionless bureaucracy tightened its grip. Durkheim was the most optimistic among the three—though of course he was very attuned to what he called the anomic effects of industrialization. He argued that the most radical change was in the nature of the division of labor. Unlike in "mechanically" integrated societies, where the division of labor was shallow, and face-to-face, religious rituals were sufficient for the reproduction of a stable normative order, in complex modern society the division of labor exhibited unprecedented levels of interdependence and specialization. This called forth a new form of solidarity, "organic" solidarity as he called it, which would normatively integrate society through values of individual dignity, autonomy, and fairness.

The legacy of Marx, Weber, and Durkheim remains relevant to contemporary discussions of the nature and sources of stability and control in modern society, though the terms of the debate have interpenetrated in new ways. On the one hand, contemporary discussion no longer reflects a simplistic tripartite distinction of the three theorists on the basis of the institutional arena they prioritized (the economy for Marx, organizational

Y. Wang (✉)
The Watson Institute for International and Public Affairs, Brown University, Providence, RI, USA
e-mail: yingyao_wang@brown.edu

S. Polillo
The Department of Sociology, University of Virginia, Charlottesville, VA, USA
e-mail: Sp4ft@virginia.edu

S. Abrutyn (ed.), *Handbook of Contemporary Sociological Theory*,
Handbooks of Sociology and Social Research, DOI 10.1007/978-3-319-32250-6_3

politics for Weber, and culture/religion for Durkheim). Nevertheless, on the other hand, as discussions of control, regulation, and power have crystallized into modern institutional analysis, different ways of combining insights from Marx, Weber, and Durkheim have led to distinctive approaches within that general framework. Marx and Weber have been built upon in what W. Richard Scott (2001) identifies as the "regulative pillar" of modern institutional analysis: a tradition that emphasizes the ways that rules and laws reproduce power systems through the coercive imposition of organizational mandates and standards. A second way Marx and Weber have been jointly drawn from, with substantial borrowings from Durkheim as well, is by focusing on what Scott dubs the "normative pillar" of institutions: the ways in which norms and values invest social life with meanings that in turn embody prescriptions, evaluations, and obligations. Control, from this perspective, is a function of individuals internalizing, and acting on the basis of, normative orientations. A third tradition is more squarely Durkhemeian, with strong Weberian influence as well. In line with Durkheim, it foregrounds the "cognitive-cultural" dimension of institutions, namely, the shared conceptions and schemas that help individuals constitute a meaningful social reality. Following Weber, this tradition emphasizes the disciplinary effect of such systems of cultural regulation. Cutting across these three pillars of institutional analysis is a shared recognition that modern social order is to a large extent an organizational accomplishment. By the same token, the regulative, normative, and cultural-cognitive dimensions are pillars of institutional analysis because they highlight how, under what conditions, and to what extent the attributes and relational properties of organizations contribute to the persistence of the status quo.

In this chapter, we zero in on power as a form of regulation. While we are attentive to all three dimensions of institutions, and their effect on power, regulation and control, we organize our discussion differently, in terms of levels of analysis. We depart from Weber's thesis that rationalization and increased, organization-based control are two defining features of contemporary society. In one respect, we move beyond older theories of power that would tend to define it in terms of coercion, meant to "overcome resistance (of the power subject) in achieving a desired objective or results." (Pfeffer 1981: 2). For if power is as ubiquitous and as coervice a phenomenon as these scholarly works acknowledge, we should be living in a dim world, suffering from ceaseless emotional distress and physical constrains. This is an exaggerated scenario once squared with our actual experiences with power.

More recent scholarship has gone beyond the enterprise of conceptualization to probe the dimensions (Reed 2013), forms (Poggi 2001), or sources (Mann 2012a, b, c, d) of power. In categorizing the workings of power, these lines of research suggest that power is plural and largely "context and relationship specific" (Pfeffer 1981: 3). Therefore power is a concept which we should treat as "sensitizing device" that orients us to "certain forms and contents in a social relationship" (Bacharach and Lawler 1980: 15) or a form of causality (Reed 2013).

This chapter is written in the same spirit of explaining power in terms of how forms and contents of power are constructed. We are interested in understanding how power operates, instead of what power is (in this respect, see Foucault 1980). Unlike Foucault, we do so by focusing on different levels of observation and analysis—respectively the macro, meso, and micro levels. Scale matters as it affects the forms and nature of power. We argue that most existing research implicitly imagines power either as a macro phenomenon shaping large-scale social outcomes or as a parameter of micro-level relations. What it neglects is the meso-level of power relations, manifested and heavily regulated in formal organizations. Distinct from interpersonal or intra-small-group relations, formal organizations are bounded entities that have clearly prescribed rules governing the pattern of interactions among organizational members, and thus possess formal structures. As organizations permeate our social lives, this "organizational society" enables a twin goal, or a "paradox:" organizational members are "freer from coercion through the power of command of superiors than most people have been, yet men in positions of power today probably exercise more control than any tyrant ever has" (Blau and Schenherr 1971: 347).

This chapter sets to synthesize the mechanisms of how this has been achieved. By drawing attention to the distinctive forms and natures of power relations at this meso-level, our end goal is to extend power analysis from the macro and micro-level to analytical interactions among all three levels of analyses. Power flows both upwards and downwards, so that the interaction and conversion of different forms of power at different levels can generate new sets of emergent and interstitial structures and relations.

3.2 The Macro Approach to Power

From a macro perspective, power is a force that shapes large-scale social formations and outcomes. This force derives from macro conceptual entities such as spheres of action, fields or institutions (Abrutyn 2013a).

Michael Mann's voluminous works of the "history of power" are a prominent example of this macro approach to power (Mann 2012a, b, c, d). According to Mann, the constellations of four sources of power—ideological, economic, military, and political, coterminous with four kinds of human needs and spheres of actions, determine the structures of societies in human history. The force of power is causal: power triggers large-scale historical transformations. Different sources of power, imagined as independent causal chains, can join each other in different constellations and sequences, and produce emergent social entities, such as nation states, and mobilize new actors, such as social classes. Nations and classes are examples of macro-outcomes to which Mann's historical analysis draws attention.

The French sociologist Pierre Bourdieu also perceives power as the exertion of forces. He borrows this analytical architecture from field theory (Bourdieu 1980, 1984, 1988, 1996a, b). The term "field," which Bourdieu derives from the physics of electromagnetic forces, refers to "a configuration of objective relations between positions." (Bourdieu and Wacquant 1992: 97) Fields impose causal forces on actors who reside within them, forces that are mediated by the positions they occupy within those fields. The specific expression and measurement of power is capital, with its amount proportional to positions and its types specific to fields. According to Bourdieu, capital varies in volume and can also be of different types, e.g. social, economic, cultural, or symbolic capital; different types of capital can be converted to one another. On account of the logic of conversion, power in Bourdieusian theory is the generalized medium of exchange in fields, similar in this respect to Mann's conceptualization.

Bourdieu's notions of power and field are macro-oriented in that Bourdieusian fields, first, ontologically and causally precede individual actions, and second, they produce macro-outcomes. Chief among these outcomes is the formation of social classes, political elites, and the bureaucracy. The logic of specific fields also determines the value and the exchange rates between different types of capital. Bourdieu's theory is therefore a full-fledged macro-meso theory. The operation of forces in fields shapes the general "topology" and distribution of social spaces by clustering those who occupy similar positions in the fields and generating hierarchies and oppositions among these clusters. Social classes, formed within a field in this fashion, can form alliances with their counterparts across fields, generating oft-unforeseen social repercussions that go well beyond class formation. Recent scholarship, for instance, sets out to illuminate how interactions across fields, involving multi-layered conflicts, and requiring geographical, administrative coordination, generate large-scale change (Gorski 2013). For example, as nineteenth-century German officials left the bureaucratic field in the metropole to manage German colonies, they carried over and localized existing power struggles among them. Colonial officials also vied with one other on the amount of "ethnographic capital" they would hold, which in return fed back into, and intensified, status competition at home (Steinmetz 2007).

Institutional theory shares much with Bourdieu, but instead of fields, institutional theorists attribute the source of power to another high-order entity—institutions. Institutions are "macro-level structural and cultural spheres or domains in which actors, resources, and authority systems are distributed in bounded ecological space" (Abrutyn 2013b). Major examples of institutions are the market, the state, the corporation, the profession, religion, and the family. Institutions are powerful in that they impose overarching "institutional logics" (Thornton et al. 2012). Institutional logics are the "socially constructed, historical patterns of material practices, assumptions, values, beliefs, and rules" which inform and compel actors to "produce and reproduce material subsistence, organize time and space, and provide meaning to their social reality" (Thornton and Ocasio 1999: 804). Empirically, the point where actors cease to bear the influence of such institutional logic is the point where institutions reach their boundaries. Identifying the intensity and boundaries of such institutional power, is a task similar to that of delineating the boundaries of distinct institutions. Various institutional theorists describe these "institutional logics" in different terms and languages. But they all agree that institutions have the capacity to steer individuals to act in a concerted and predictable fashion. This often occurs in the context of dramatic events that capture the attention of a wide public: power can then be considered "performative" (Reed 2013), in the sense of being attached to an organizational capacity to control how events, facts, and ideas are presented to, and perceived by, a larger audience. Power carries an emergent status: it exists prior to, other than in the midst of, any concrete courses of actions, in macro social entities (Thornton and Ocasio 2008).

By imagining power as a set of causal forces shaping societies, macro understandings of power render analytically legible some otherwise unobservable macro entities. This scholarly approach to power as a macro-phenomenon pivots on an understanding of the rise of the most important macro-entities of all—the state. It is no coincidence that the authors who are most explicit in their theorizing of power, such as Michael Mann (2012a, b, c, d), Shmuel N. Eisenstadt (1993), Pierre Bourdieu (1994, 2015), and James Scott (1999), are also meticulous scholars of processes of political centralization, state formation, and governance. According to Eisenstadt, in early periods, power and the state were almost synonymous for good empirical reasons. The formation of the "polity" is the effect of power itself (Eisenstadt 1995; Abrutyn and Lawrence 2010). The emergence of polities from kinship organizations was initiated by a group of non-kin-based leaders who specialized in power possession and generation, using whatever means happened to be available to them. As polities formed, power became a generalized means of control, and then a commodity. Whoever was interested in gaining power, and capable of holding on to it, could bid for it. This new trend built up a perpetual sense of uncertainty among rulers, who responded by seeking to stabilize their relationship with the ruled. "Society", in its opposition to the political center, was called into existence in this fashion.

State-driven projects of making societies more "legible," whereby political and administrative elites would construct policy on the basis of their perception of society, turned out to be catastrophic for local traditions and local knowledge. As James Scott highlights, the recent century of human history has seen no shortage of modernist, technocratic, and destructive programs that are a direct consequence of states "formatting" society and using those maps as blueprints for political control. Scott thus draws our attention to a unique type of epistemic power that the state possesses in the enterprise of "seeing like a state." This proposition is a useful complement and necessary caveat to Weber's emphasis on rationalization and Eisenstadt's focus on centralization: it emphasizes how political control rests on a capacity to gather information, and how the very process of information-gathering is never politically neutral.

This strand of research on state formation grounds empirically the analysis of the formation and institutionalization of power as a macro phenomenon. To an unprecedented scale, states have consolidated and expanded over vast swaths of territories. Geographical expansion has gone hand in hand with macro-social maneuvering on the part of state builders, in their efforts to establish a manageable relationship with an increasingly differentiating society. Over time, state-builders either isolated or incorporated different social groups into the orbit of political decision-making. Sustaining the mammoth institution of the state ultimate rests on the production of "long-range trust and meaning," which gets built into the exercise of power and gears political arrangements towards "broader institutional goals and promises," (Eisenstadt 1995: 360–161) such as economic development, administrative rationality and nation building. The macro approach touches on the genesis of power and also constitutes a wellspring for research on the grand evolution of the nature of power to the present.

3.3 The Micro Approach to Power

Another strand of social theory examines power in micro settings. Micro settings refer to small-scale social interactions ranging from ego-environment relationships, to dyadic interactions and small-group dynamics. A small scope of inquiry is not the sole reason that we call it the micro-approach to power. A micro perspective to power also assumes that the presence of power, the state of being constrained and controlled, is empirically actualized in direct contacts and small-scale interactions, which makes a relational measurement of power relations the most desirable. Conceptualizing power in terms of micro-settings is empirically intuitive, theoretically parsimonious, and has great validity.

A relational understanding of power has inspired and underpinned many of the classical definitions of power. In these definitions, power is manifested in the dynamics of dyadic relationships, driven by asymmetrical possession of resources, capacities or benefits. For example, Weber famously defines power as "the probability that one actor within a social relationship will be in a position to carry out his own will despite resistance" (Weber 1947) Similarly, Lukes concisely states the Weberian position as "A exercises power over B when A affects B in a manner contrary to B's interests" (Lukes 2005: 34). Other power theorists downplay the resistance component in defining power but consistently portray power in terms of A–B relations. For example, Dahl posits that "A has power over B to the extent that he can get B to do something which B would not otherwise do" (Dahl 1957: 202–203). Likewise, according to Bell, Walker and Willer, power is "A's capacity to create change in B's activity based in A's control of sanctions." (Bell et al. 2000).

Social psychology and exchange theory have generated some of the most important insights on how power works at the level of micro-interactions. Focusing on the giving and receiving of valued resources, and often framing exchanges in terms of cost, benefits, and marginal utility—terms imported from economics—this perspective is broadly concerned with an expectation of reciprocity that builds up from repeated exchanges, and of the implications of such expectations when the exchange takes place in a situation of power imbalance. Thus Blau (1964) argues that over time, exchanges of resources produce a normative expectation that current levels of exchange will be sustained over time. Power is exercised through dramaturgical means, when individuals enhance or even exaggerate the value of the resources they can bring to an exchange, manipulating perception and setting up expectations that validate this inflated value down the line. More generally, power derives from the fact the more individuals control resources that are indispensable, hard to procure from alternative sources, and difficult to seize by force, the more they can demand compliance: a surplus amount of allegiance that resource-poor partners must offer to compensate for their weak bargaining position. Over time, Blau argues, escalating demands for compliance generate resentment towards perceived violation of norms of reciprocity, thereby causing conflict.

Emerson (1962, 1964) similarly posits that power is a function of resource dependence, and it is especially salient when it is difficult for partners to the exchange to find alternative ways of obtaining those resources, and especially when those resources are valuable. Power is used when partners to the exchange jockey for better access to resources and better terms of exchange, in turn causing a power imbalance that motivates their counterparts to engage in actions that reduce dependence, actions that Emerson calls "balancing acts." Cook and Emerson (1978) extend this argument by focusing on "commitment" between exchange partners, the tendency of partners to remain in an exchange even when they could potentially get better terms or better resources from others. Commitment is possible because, functioning as a long-term expectation that exchanges will continue over time, it lowers transaction costs, reduces uncertainty, and, more important to our discussion, decreases the likelihood of power being exercised.

As a third party is introduced, a dyad becomes a triad. George Simmel offers an influential thesis on how triads, and small group dynamics by extension, qualitatively transforms power relations, therefore enriching our understanding of the relational sources of power. Simmel explains that the third party can gain tremendous leverage through maneuvering the relationship between the two alters, for instance, by balancing them against each other, or monopolizing information flows between them. In both cases, the third parties derive power from certain structural positions without necessarily possessing resources of their own (Simmel and Wolff 1964).

Simmel's thinking on social relations and power keeps inspiring research on social networks. One of the latter's core analytical mission has been to identify structural positions in networks and explain how these positions can generate power. Particularly influential in this regard is Burt's work on brokerage through the exploitation of "structural holes," network positions that allow individuals to uniquely connect ("bridge") social clusters that would not otherwise communicate (Burt 1992). Structural holes, argues Burt, afford individuals access to unique information, which individuals are then able to recombine in new ways that gives them leverage and advantage. Although the social networks under study in this tradition have become considerably large and appear "macro" in scale, the theoretical assumption about the source and distribution of power in networks is consistent with the micro approach under discussion. In stricter versions of the theory, network ties almost invariably imply direct contacts between agents (in a tradition that harkens back to classical studies of the diffusion of innovations, such as Coleman et al. 1966). A different tradition draws from role theory and specifies power in terms of "structural equivalence," similarities in patterns of relations without implying direct contacts between individuals. Throughout the studies, the power of network positions is not conceived as an attribute derived from preexisting macro-entities. Instead, it is a certain kind of leverage and a range of choices built into constellations of relationships and patterns of interactions among individual entities. The network notion of power tends to be micro also because the transmission of such power, such as in the form of information, resource or reputation is via an on-the-ground construction of relationships.

The last instance of micro settings is small groups. Dalh's celebrated study of power in community politics illustrates this category (Dalh 1961). In his examination of the power structure in New Haven, he developed a pluralist view of power in which power exercise is a competitive process in which different interest groups vied for control over decisions. Dalh's theorization of power has been discussed in several works; few have dubbed it "micro." We group his study together with other micro approaches on account of the way he introduced actors as independent individual entities, and of the way he approached power as relational and interactional dynamics. Additionally, he also isolated a range of historical and institutional factors and narrowed down the focus to particular instances of decision-making settings where conflicts were the most visible and observable and power relations could be directly measurable by decision outcomes. These epistemological and methodological aspects set his study apart from the macro-approach to power we have described.

An important critique to Dahl's pluralist model of decision-making can be derived from Ridgeway and Berger (1986)'s model of power and prestige orders in small-group settings. Ridgeway and Berger argue that small groups, especially those focused on the accomplishment of a task, develop local understandings and expectations of one another's capacity to meaningfully contribute to the task at hand. But they do not do so in a vacuum, as their expectations are based on more diffuse understandings of whose status and whose power should be rewarded, regardless of the relevance of status attributes to the task at hand. Group activities therefore tend to reproduce social hierarchies and reinforce social inequality, in contrast with Dahl's more optimistic view that group's mere access to decision-making arenas is a hallmark and safeguard of democracy.

3.4 Introducing the Meso-Level

The micro and macro notions of power do not exhaust the range of experiences we have with power. We don't constantly live in dyadic conflicts. Our exchanges with society certainly go beyond small group arrangements. We follow instructions and obey authorities, even when orders come from those whom we don't have prior contacts with. Power will be felt most strongly in observable conflicts at the level of interpersonal relations. Yet power exists across a variety of social forms. We are compelled to act in certain ways by more distant forces. The macro-approach to power has strengthened our ability to map out these structural forces. However, important questions remain. A particularly intriguing one has to do with the reach of power relations. For example, those who live in times of rapid social changes, or at the epicenter of a structure undergoing transformation, will feel the impact of power formation and redistribution most directly. But the rest of the population will be affected by power relations only through several degrees of mediation. What micro and macro notions of power leave unexplored, in short, is the meso-level architecture that regularizes micro-exchanges, bears the brunt of macro transformation, and constitutes the more immediate environment within which power is experienced, challenged, and reformatted collectively (Tuner 2012: 25). This is the environment of formal organizations.

Formal organizations are omnipresent, but the analysis of power has not been a prominent issue in organization studies (Pfeffer 1981: 9–10). The vast majority of us are associated with formal organizations in one way or another, by either working for them, learning in them, or relying on them for goods or services. Examples of organizations are numerous. Corporations, parties, schools, clubs, professional associations, and international organizations are organizations devoted to economic, political, educational, recreational, professional, or normative purposes. This meso-level reality is not just an analytical construct. It is such an ingrained part of our empirical routines that we tend to take our organizational environment for granted. Power, as is routinized in careers, budgets, the divisions of labor, and all other standard operating procedures and rules, paradoxically remains hidden in plain sight. In organized purposeful settings, the line between being compelled to do something and being capable of doing something can be blurry and conflated. Uncovering how power operates, hides, and transfers in organizations is therefore a necessary scholarly exercise, especially if we aim to develop a fuller understanding of how our intentions, behaviors, and beliefs are regulated in organizational society.

What are organizations and what are their key features? One of the most widely accepted definitions of formal organizations is offered by W. Richard Scott. Organizations are "collectivities oriented to the pursuit of relatively specific goals and exhibiting relatively highly formalized social structures." (Scott 1992: 23) To elaborate, these collectivities organize social lives such that they sustain long-term visions, aggregate courses of action, and give our existences collective purposes independent of individual choices. Internally, organizations bear formalized structures, of which hierarchies and specialization through an internal division of labor are two most prominent features. One should not underrate the extent to which formal structures construct our social realities, a point to which we will return later. For now, it should suffice to say that formalization entails the abstraction of a large amount of concrete data so that further social action can be governed by that abstraction without having to "go behind it" (Stinchcombe 2001). Formal organizations arrange society by abstraction; they designate roles and positions, and regularize patterns of interactions. Organizations inscribe these designations in binding charts, procedures, and rules so that goals, positions, roles, and patterns of interactions outlive individual participants. In this sense, organizations, once created, achieve an emergent reality of their own. We enter an organization expecting to accept the organizational reality as it is and "socialize" into it (Wanous et al. 1984; Hall 1987).

3.4.1 A Brief History of the Emergence of Organizational Society

Before we delve deeper into the question of how power operates in organizations, a brief history on the emergency of organizational society will be instructive. Various authors have reflected on how the ascendance of organizations have revolutionized pre-modern social structures and changed the power balance between different segments of the populations. James Coleman (1974) provides a revealing account on the rise of corporate actors that changed the distribution of power in societies. This gradual movement commenced from the "incorporation" of churches, landed communities, and kings as these entities acquired the status of unified actors with rights to own, contract, engage in transactions, and collectively embody honor and authority. The corporate form taken by these social entities eventually spread to all sorts of associations, and engulfed also those originally non-purposive social units in which persons were born such as the family, the village and the nation. According to Coleman, this layer of "intermediary entities" emerged between the state and individuals and created much more flexible social structures and mobile persons than those in traditional societies (Coleman 1974: 31). Natural persons can join or leave corporations and can establish its relationship with corporations through various resources invested in them without having to participate physically.

While Coleman argues that the rise of corporate society increased the total sum of power in societies and therefore expanded freedom and liberty, other authors offer mixed assessments. The classical author on bureaucracy, Max Weber, on the one hand, celebrates the effectiveness with which bureaucratic organizations rationalized capitalist production and the administration of the state. According to Weber, formal authority, in combination with specialized professional knowledge inscribed in bureaucratic positions, provides an unprecedented legitimate foundation to domination and ruling. One the other hand, Weber alerts us to the dehumanizing effect of these "iron-cages." Bureaucratic machines can thrive for the mere sake of reproducing themselves (Weber 1978). This is the "bad" kind of formalism that Stinchcombe also refers to, a formalism that does not serve substantial purposes and prevents others from making improvements to the abstraction on which successful formalization rests (Stinchcombe 2001). Put more succinctly, both authors highlight the very real possibility that formal organizations generate a new form of oppressive, even callous control.

In the first half of the twentieth century, the rise of big corporations and the intensified bureaucratization of all spheres of lives prompted new waves of reflection on how organizations have reconfigured political and economic power. Michels observes that how incumbents of powerful organizational structures would become more interested in investing in the reproduction of the structure per se rather than in pursing the goals that the organization was originally set up to achieve (Michels 1959). Michels focuses on political organizations, but this same process can be observed in the conglomeration movement, a historical phase in which corporations begin pursuing growth strategies through diversification and vertical integration. John Galbraith argues that, as large corporations extended the scope of their activities, they became threats to efficiency: as price and wages could be determined through internal planning instead of competition, a Michelsian dynamic set in (1959). Corporations, put differently, began exercising market power, a point Galbraith makes in the context of a larger argument that economic organizations can pursue control and growth at the expense of earnings and efficiency—an argument that in turn is heavily indebted to Veblen (1934). In the production realm, modern technologies such as the assembly line and the practices associated with "scientific management" created a deep cleavage between workers and the managerial class. Clegg has an insightful account of how these new workplace relations, with their new routines and their push towards specialization, facilitated the production of predictable and compliant agency. This causal process of forming collective dispositions of the employees, Clegg argues, paved the "foundation of organization power" (Clegg 2009).

In parallel to these critiques of large organizations, an array of authors emerged as the foundational generation of organization researchers, focused on a mission to dissolve the myth of "scientific management" and to understand the organizational causes of its imperfections. Influentially, James March and Herbert Simon delved into the decision-making process in organizations from a perspective of human cognition. They found that individuals in organizations are subject to bounded rationalities in processing information, elaborating programs, and evaluating outcomes. Cognitive limitation drives the tendency for organizations to routinize and places a sunk cost on organizational innovation (March and Simon 1958). Still another strand of the literature, heralded by Stinchcombe's famous 1965 essay, surveys the "relation of society outside organizations to the internal life of organizations" (1965: 142). Stinchcombe suggests that social structure, comprising "groups, institutions, laws, population characteristics, and sets of social relations that form the environments of the organization" (1965:142) leave imprints on the forms and power relations within the organizations and affect their survival rates. Newly founded organizations in particular suffer from a "liability of newness" in that for social roles and relations to settle into stable patterns to answer to organizational goals, organizations have to go through a risky process of wrestling with employees' existing identities and bonding a group of strangers including with other organizations. Stinchcombe suggests that after a certain threshold, the attenuation of social and cognitive discrepancies paves the way for routinization. This point echoes March and Simon's argument and generates tremendous insights for our understanding of individual-organization relationships.

Organizational forms have continued to evolve in the past half a century. Organization scholars have drawn our attention to at least two directions of development. First of all, it is harder for organizations to be self-sustaining: an increasing amount of organizational decisions must address inter-organizational concerns. With intensified market competition, faster turnover of products, and more volatile technological and financial markets, incumbents find themselves in constant battles with challengers; both also have to react to regulatory attempts of government units and a broader array of stakeholders. This type of "strategic action field" rewards the kind of "social skills" that can secure cooperation from other organizations and forge a new form of collective identity (Fligstein and McAdam 2012). Secondly, scholars also affirm that soft power and a culturally based type of legitimacy have gained more importance in soliciting individual compliance. This is not to say that reward and punishment have ceased to be the bread and butter of organizational sanctions, but "soft power" is assuming a stronger role in shaping both the body and souls of "organizational men" (and women) (William and Nocera 2002; Clegg 2009). Organizations are perceived as being capable of developing personas and embodying "organizational cultures," which employees internalize as their own values (see esp. Selznick 2010). Organization ethnographers disclose that even blue-collar workers engaging the most tedious job find the moral meaning in their work (Burawoy 1982; Lamont 2002). Norms, identities, and moral standards can be both homegrown and imported.

Organizational practices and forms are perceived legitimate simply because other organizations, especially the leading ones, are pursuing them as well. Either way, individual compliance originates not from beliefs in the inherent efficiency of certain organizational structures or production arrangements, but from cultural consensuses and fads (DiMaggio and Powell 1983).

Overall, these reflections on the evolution of organizational power provide historical background to our understanding of their contemporary variations. They also call for systematic efforts at taking stock of the forms of power specific to formal organizations. Let's reiterate here that this task is possible because, regardless of the variations in technologies and management styles, formal organizations share common characteristics and undertake similar activities, such as settings goals, designing bureaucratic structures, delegating authorities, securing stable personnel, utilizing expertise, and identifying organizational boundaries. Theoretical expositions on organization and power are scattered in organization studies and are rarely placed in organic conversations with existing studies of power. Our synthesis below draws inspirations on existing research but also attempts to sharpen and articulate the distinctive operation of power at the meso-level.

3.4.2 Empowering Organizations

We argue that organizations intersect with power in two major ways: First, organizations serve as vehicles to power. Second, organizations shape the nature of power by making it invisible and multiplying the sources from which power springs. In this section, we focus on the first proposition—the "empowering" aspect of organizations, while the next section is devoted to elaborating our second point.

Humans are purposive beings. Power is a means to achieve those purposes, however construed. Organizations are a regularized form of such means. Through coordination, organizations can achieve much more than a mere aggregation of individuals could. This supra-individual power of organizations has two implications.

First, organized collectivities are not simply the sum of individuals' preexisting wills and actions; organizations generate the kind of institutional surplus that reduces the cost of collective action. Both eminent features of organizational structure—hierarchy and the division of labor—have this function. Hierarchies streamline flows of orders and information and reasonably narrow down the orientation of participants to their direct superiors. Divisions of labor encourage patterns of specialization and in general can reduce the cost of training, while creating stronger commitment from those who accumulate human capital specific to the organization. Hierarchical power can certainly be constraining; just as specialization is also a source of alienation. Nevertheless, formal organizations are expected to "get things done" by channeling individuals into clearly designated duties and overcoming intractable collective action problems that any group efforts might encounter. Individuals, irrespective of the extent to which they personally agree with the actions organizations take, potentially benefit from the collective gains that organizations make possible.

Second, in most legal contexts, organizations have the juridical status of persons, so they enjoy rights just as natural persons would but are immune to certain punishments applicable to natural persons. The meso-level reality indeed has a legal infrastructure. Organizations as persons enjoy limited responsibilities and only receive financial rather than corporeal punishments. You certainly cannot ask an organization to serve prison terms. On the other hand, organizations are allowed to conduct many activities that natural persons carry out. They can buy, sell, invest, donate, or even vote. Presently this empowering effect of organizations is an international norm. The existence of robust and diverse organizations is perceived as a sign of strong and healthy civil societies. The absence of them, by contrast, indicates that power is monopolized and centralized in society, probably by single or oligarchic entities.

Both means, erecting formalized routines and conferring legal existences to them, enable organizations to operate on a long-range horizon, and towards relatively long term objectives. Long-term goals compel trust building and suspend short-term domination. Organized methods of obtaining and exercising power also appear much less conspicuous than one-time use of coercive method. They take on evolutionary and routinized features, with attention divided among staged goals and numerous small tasks.

3.4.3 The Nature of Power in Organizations

Organizations are effective means to pursue power; they also shape the nature of power itself. The same features—organizational hierarchies and routines—that are ostensibly means to efficiency also exert power internally on organizational members. Theoretically, power is hierarchical and concentrated in organizations. The pyramid organizational structures are direct reflections of hierarchical power relations. For this reason, Michels warned against the oligarchic tendency of bureaucratic power (Michels 1959). Along the same lines, Rueschemeyer discusses the "disproportionate power" found in organizations, that is, how power concentrated in the hands of individuals and groups with similar interest and preferences is amplified when mobilized through organizational means, partly because organizations justify themselves thorough claims to higher efficiency (Rueschemeyer 1986: 46).

But if hierarchical power were so equivocal and inescapable, organizations would be repressive and emotionally violent environments, constantly threatening the viability of their organizational mandates. In reality, these are aberrant instances rather than the norm. We join organization theorists who submit that power is diffuse in organizations, rather than concentrated (Bacharach and Lawler 1980; Bell et al. 2010). It is not simply that power does not cause tremendous disruptions in organizations because it is based on consent, rather than coercion, or that, as March and Simon put it, because power seems "natural," since "hierarchical ordering fits more general cultural norms for describing social relations in terms of domination and subordination" (1993: 3). Rather, formal organizations transform power dynamics into means-end problems calling for practical solutions. As Rueschemeyer (1986) has most powerfully argued, organizations find legitimacy in their pursuit of efficiency through endless specialization, but in doing so they hide the truth of efficiency: that is it not universally valid criterion independent of the interests of those who decide whose goals should be efficiently pursued.

First, organizations formalize power relationship into positions and ranks; positions and ranks stabilize expectations and embody organization-specific norms and values. Except for organizations in the midst of formative and transformative times (as highlighted by Stinchcombe 1965), organizational positions and ranks are independent of the idiosyncrasies of their occupants. They create stable expectations about the scope of their duties, the structure of rewards, and the schedule of promotions. Weber uses this point to illustrate the merit of bureaucracy in achieving efficiency and impartiality. We are interested in reconnecting formal ordering with the discussion of power. Managing expectations by virtue of creating career ladders plays an instrumental role in translating power into regulations. Patterns of expectations minimize the contingent exercise of coercion. With rules and procedures in place, individuals do not have to negotiate their benefits with organizations individually so that they reduce possible discretions. Signing onto these career expectations amounts to signing onto a social contract in which personal freedom is traded with life security, so that voluntarily, "the social control of one's behavior by others becomes an expected part of organizational life" (Pfeffer 1981: 5). Positions and ranks are also building blocks of the system of organizational norms and values. Sociologists, despite their disagreements on how norms and values are formed, concur that norms and values play an indispensible role in holding society together and stabilizing social interactions. Organizations are the meso-venues where norms are deployed and contextualized.

Second, power is highly depersonalized in organizations, which also tend to generate depersonalized conflicts. Authority is codified in formalized rights and privileges, attached to the hierarchy of jobs in organizations. Positional authorities do not derive from, or die with personal power. Organizational rules and procedures are distributed to new recruits prior to their active duties so that he or she will be assured that rewards and punishment will have an impersonal nature. When a CEO gives his or her employee a routine order, the employee would not be personally offended as he or she understands that the order is made on behalf of an organization and the same order would be made to anyone who were at his or her post. Those in power certainly carry their personal motives and interests. Such personal power, however, is often mistaken as impartiality in the eyes of the powerless. It is because the powerful think and act in terms of positions (those of corporations and public offices) and their personal interests tend to align with organizational ones (Rueschemeyer 1986: 48).

Depersonalizing power is a process in which the source of power is removed from its means (Coleman 1974: 37–39). In relatively large organizations, even the most authoritarian commands at the very power center have to be dispersed throughout myriads of lines and orders and legitimated through layers of superior-subordinate relationships. It is undeniable that at the very apex of the hierarchy, political struggles can be fierce and shot through with "family and patronage relations" (Rueschemeyer 1986: 63). Employees at various points of distances with the power center however do not see and experience these struggles directly. Hierarchy acts as a buffer to "politics at the top."

Depersonalized power by no means prevents all conflicts from rising. Conflicts are the very "power-full" moments where the intention of exerting power is revealed, stakes are acted upon and challenging coalitions are formed. However, depersonalized power likely goes hand in hand with depersonalized conflicts. That is, many intra-organizational conflicts stem from "structural" problems, problems, that is, that inhere to formal organizational structures and that inevitably contain contradictions of responsibilities, overlapping jurisdictions, and goal misalignments. While structural conflicts are tolerated or even institutionalized, personalized conflicts are usually discouraged and stigmatized in organizations.

Third, power in organization is differentiated and generative. Differentiation reduces the number of losers and sometimes renders the question of winning or losing entirely meaningless. Externally, organizations stratify society into "membership society" and subcultures in which "members" of these communities are not readily comparable on a single dimension or along a continuum. Internally, power in organizations creates differences through the following means—the division of labor, the delegation of authorities, and entitlement—where each renders power no longer a zero-sum game but rather the effect of a multivariate structure of incentives. Division of labor in organizational settings generates multiple lines of authority and within them multiple tracks of mobility. This helps reduce conflicts and dependence as participants will not be subject to only one dimension of competition. Delegation transfers authority to subordinates. Subordinates are agents who possess more local information than their principals and can withhold such information to bargain with their superiors. Entitlement is another activity of expanding, if not inflating, the supply of power in organizations without offending the status quo. With differentiation, delegation and entitlement. Overall, precisely because of the generative nature of divided labor and its readiness to be mistaken as reflective of human nature or professionalization, Rueschemeyer calls for exercising a power analysis to uncover the *process* of division of labor, by investigating the political and economic institutions that supported division of labor, the resources mobilized to sustain it, and the special needs they meet (1986).

Lastly, power sources in organizations are diversified, creating multiple ways to control uncertainty. Power in organizations springs from multiple sources. We often equate power with resources, but what counts as resources in organizations is specific to the organizational context, as the micro-approach to power well understands. Resources can be measured by the control over the number of personnel and financial resources, the range of the jurisdiction, or the position of ranking, all of which is imperfectly commensurate with but largely reflected in pay structures. Other types of sources of power are less measurable but nevertheless consequential. These resources include titles, reputations, information, knowledge, etc. The power of this array of resource, we argue, comes from their efficacy in generating or resolving uncertainty, since uncertainty is the common enemy of organizational routines. This power in relation to uncertainty can counter-intuitively afford occupants at non-central locations a great amount of leverage. For example, line workers can create enormous disturbance of routines by striking. Small group leaders can be instrumental in appeasing conflicts and retrieve organizational solidarity by force of reputation. Lower level organizational members have power because they possess a unique set of information, e.g. contacts with clients, or familiarity with the production process, that is hard to be replaced and taken away. Experts' power also ultimately lies in their indispensible solutions to uncertainties and crises (Barnes 1988). In a word, organizational aversion to uncertainty produces power that cannot be deduced purely from hierarchical power. With multiple sources of power crosscutting, balancing and offsetting each other, the diversified source of power generates a more complicated picture of power distribution than an organizational chart would predict, which makes the study of power in organizations all the more intriguing and challenging.

3.5 Connecting the Micro with the Meso Level Analysis of Power

Power in organizations subordinates interpersonal relationships to the mandates of rules and impersonalized authorities. In many circumstances, micro-power in the form of personal power, dyadic conflicts and small group dynamics can also exist and assert their influence in spite of formal structures. This is because formal rules are after all enacted in myriads of behavioral patterns and relationships of exchanges and transactions. Decisions, one of the most important forms of output in organizations, have to flow through the chains and relationships of real people. Organizational legitimacy likewise has both legal and relational components. It is legally supported but also has to be observed and endorsed by organizational members and their mutual acknowledgement of each other's endorsement for that matter. These processes of enacting rules and decisions in interpersonal relationships have opened room for power dynamics in small and informal settings. We will discuss various scenarios in the following space, built on illustrations of existing studies as well as our suggestions for future research.

First of all, it is common to observe that individuals acquire personal power not attributable to organizational authorization and unique to these individuals. One source of such personal power is charisma. Weber defines charisma as power legitimized on the basis of a leader's exceptional personal qualities or the demonstration of extraordinary insight and accomplishment, which inspire loyalty and obedience from followers (Weber 2004). Charisma facilitates effective leadership. The conventional understanding is that charisma, once routinized, gives away to another type of authority—rational-legal authority in Weber's account. However, historical and contemporary attempts to create "charismatic organizations" challenge this characterization of charismatic individuals and bureaucratic organizations as incompatible (Teiwes 1984). Mao's Cultural Revolution called for the rebels to embody and spread his personal charisma until it became the institutional feature of the state bureaucracy. Although the movement ultimately failed catastrophically, the fact that it carried on for nearly a decade offered a rare chance for researchers to investigates the possibility of personification of power at the organizational level. One reason charismatic authority can be sustained for long periods of time lies in the dramaturgical nature of power: as argued by Blau (1956) among others, individuals have incentive to exaggerate the value of the resources they can bring to an exchange, because those perceived initial advantages constitute sources of long-term leverage as expectations about levels of exchange stabilize. Successfully manipulating the perception of one's contribution can therefore have long-term implications.

Dyadic relationships and small exchange networks are the fabrics of organizations. These small groups are bounded by direct and frequent contacts. Close contacts increase the odds that local power dynamics will take root independent of global organizational structures. Non-organizationally-sanctioned traits of individuals, such as strong personalities, or status acquired outside of organizations, will likely interfere with organizationally sanctioned transactions between organizational members. The mere fact that some individuals might be stuck in a long-term relationship creates a strategic opportunity for personalizing it by altering or circumscribing formal organizational rules, as research on the durability of commitment in exchange suggests (see Cook and Emerson 1978). Favors and personally felt obligations can then be utilized towards formal organizational goals. For example, in the most commonplace dyads of organizations—superior/subordinate relationship, order-giving-and-taking rarely characterizes the full range of any organizationally sanctioned relationship. Bosses are often keen to suspend exercise of their formal power, or go out of their way to do a favor for their subordinates beyond any of their official duties. Discretion in terms of when to act and what do compels subordinates to increase compliance (Blau 1956) and develop a feeling of long term obligation (Emerson 1962). Subordinates will chose to work more diligently. The exercise of personalized and patrimonial power can become a tacit pillar of organizational authority. Japanese corporations are understood to thrive on this patrimonial work culture (Rohlen 1979).

Power dynamics in small groups also intersect with formal power. Membership in small groups will allow individuals to defer to, or in other cases ignore, formal organizational boundaries, between positions, subunits, or even ranks. In opposition to the sanctioned organizational groupings, these groups are referred to as "informal" groups, with some of them taking on "clique"-like features, with heavily policed boundaries and strong ties among the members. The relationship between informal and formal power in organizations is an unceasingly fascinating research topic. Unfortunately, the current artificial separation between network analysis and organization studies as two subfields has slowed the study of the cross-fertilization of power resided in networks and organizations. Informal networks can block, co-exist or even facilitate the exercise of formal power. Formal organizations can domesticate, coopt, or develop out of informal networks (Adams 2007). To study the translation between network power and organizational power, we might need to look for common units of analysis. "Position" is an excellent choice, since positions are anchors of power in both networks and organizations. The question then becomes how positional power that derives from structural positions in exchange networks differs from the one that is embedded in organizational hierarchies and divisions of labor. Are they mutually reinforcing or contradictory?

In extreme cases, when informal groupings and coalitions dominate the institutional landscape of formal organizations, power struggles in these organizations might well resemble some kind of free-style bargaining describe by the pluralist model (Bacharach and Lawler 1980). In these cases, our imagery for the ways power is exercised in organizations is less like a flow of commands and more like an exchange of information, resources, and power among different blocks by way of both formal and informal means.

Overall, the interaction between the micro level and meso level power is probably the most intense in times of uncertainty. Founding stages, moments of crisis or periods organizational reforms are times pregnant with uncertainty. Since organizational structure themselves are sediments of historical struggles, they carry imprints of informal influence from these sensitive periods and will continue to change as more uncertainties strike (Johnson 2007).

3.6 Connecting the Macro with the Meso Level Analysis of Power

As group actions increasingly take place in organizational and institutionalized domains, organizations become the major constituents of macro-entities. Previously loosely connected macro-entities, such as fields and markets can also grow their own organizational sinews and cannot be discussed without referring to their organizational infrastructure. The connection between the meso- and macro-level reality is tightened and their interface enlarged. This leaves us with considerable empirical opportunities to examine how organizational and inter-organizational power affect macro forces and how such macro forces in turn impose adaptive pressures on organizational actions (Turner 2010).

Macro-level operation of power hinges on the growth of inter-organizational relations. Organizations that share similar goals or employ similar technologies tend to develop a system of mutual recognition and exchanges among themselves. An institutional sphere, alternatively termed "organizational field," or "industrial sector" in various literatures (Powell and DiMaggio 1991), can develop out of such mutual recognition, exchange, and associations of organizations. Institutional spheres tend to develop explicit institutional architectures of their own, such as annual conventions, professional associations, industrial standards or even legitimating bodies. Power at the institutional level is not a simple aggregation of power of each organization. The distribution of power at the institutional level does not always directly reflect resource distribution at the organizational level. The mightiest organization, measured by either its size or capital might well have the power to lead pricing or set industrial standards. Scholars have also found that institutions disproportionally reward those organizational actors that are blessed with symbolic power, such as regulators, professional associations, or rating agencies (DiMaggio and Powell 1983). These organizations can determine, not the value of material resources, but the exchange value of their resources to other types of power, e.g. reputation, confidence, honor, knowledge, which can all be stored and capitalized in the future. Symbolic power is inherently a field-level property as it exists only in the perception of other organizations.

An organizational bid for symbolic power is often an attempt to shape broader ideological structures. Macro-institutions persist through influence, technology, and ideology rather than coercive power. Symbolic power can act as a generalized medium of exchange, a convertible central currency in institutions. On account of such convertibility, power at the macro level can be very multi-dimensional and open to contestation. Isaac Reed offers an extremely insightful reinterpretation of power as taking causal effect on different dimensions: relational, discursive, and performative (Reed 2013). These dimensions connect macro- and micro-level processes by foregrounding meso-level dynamics: as Reed suggests, gaining power is not only about striving for better and larger resources, it is also about uttering discourses and performing creative events for the purposes of building environmental pressures to one's advantage. Successful discursive and performative actions can enhance the status even of materially disadvantaged organizations. To this effect, Carpenter (2010) shows how the U.S. Food and Drug Administration gained and maintained unparalleled reputation and power (in the context of a historic distrust towards government agencies) by skillfully communicating with multiple audiences.

Inter-organizational relationships bring out emergent power dynamics at the macro level. Such relationships go beyond exchanges of products, resources, and technologies. Inter-organizational transactions can be an organic part of social production, taking place through movements of people, the diffusion of organizational forms, and the traffic of ideas. These inter-organizational movements facilitate large-scale social and cultural formation and integration.

Inter-organizational exchanges do not always transpire on smooth and peaceful terms. Organizations can be incompatible in terms of their goals, values, and technological standards. Inter-organizational incompatibility halts cooperation and exchanges. In some cases, however, ostensible inter-organizational incompatibility also unexpectedly creates strategic positions for power brokers and opportunities for mutual learning and innovation (Padgett and Powell 2012).

In organizational societies, macro entities are increasingly institutionalized, even turning into organizations themselves. The state is a prime example. Previous discussions of the state characterize the power of the state as omnipresent and ideological, radiating from an undifferentiated center. What has not been emphasized sufficiently is the fact that the state has a highly elaborate organizational edifice of its own, with its authority and power divided among ministries, commissions and departments. It is possible that each department might be more committed to developing its constituencies in societies rather than contributing to the bureaucratic unity of the state as a whole. Therefore, what appears to be an administrative decision from a coherent state can be a product of inter-organizational struggles, or a parochial view of a particularly powerful department. These possibilities point to the explanatory necessity of unpacking any macro-entity into its organizational constituents. A minimum knowledge of power relations among these constituent organizations is essential to assessing the source and determinants of how power operates at the macro level.

Macro-categories, such as gender, class and race, intersect with occupational and professional categories of organizations as well (Stainback et al. 2010). Bureaucratic organizations allegedly have a social leveling effect as they tend to recruit and promote on the basis of qualifications and performance. In organizations, classifications are removed from intrinsic personal characteristics and rest on the dimension of occupations, titles, and professions. Still, organizational routines can reproduce social inequality in a systematic fashion. Occupational differentiation often maps onto gender, class, and race boundaries. Precisely because power is hidden and bureaucracies hold meritocratic façades, how organizationally produced power structures affect social inequality can be much less discernible and harder to detect (Tilly 1999).

In conclusion, power does not simply spill over from organizational containers to their environments. Power coalesces, transforms and translates at interstitial organizational spaces, that in turn shape the nature of power at the macro-level. To connect the meso- and macro-level analysis of power requires using an organizational lens to give more concrete characterizations of macro forces. The blurry boundary between macro and meso entities/categories also calls for analytical interpenetration. Macro studies of political power and social inequality should attend to their organizational causes. All in all, macro-entities are made of organizations; how power is formed in organizations and at inter-organizational spaces affects power at the macro level.

3.7 Conclusions

Power is notoriously hard to define, observe and analyze because it is mediated and regulated. Macro theories of power treat it as a causal force that originates within differentiated social spheres, a power that institutions channel into more general frameworks within which this force can be contained and regulated. Micro-level theories, by contrast, understand power as leverage which individuals gain by virtue of occupying particular positions within social relationships and networks. We have argued that, in our present social world, it is organizations that mediate and regulate power. Organization-mediated power is embodied in authorities (such as the state, or professional associations), dispersed in the division of labor among various "parties," jobs, and positions, and organized into collective purposes that privilege routinization and trust building.

In this chapter, we zeroed in on the organizational level of power dynamics, a level that is more aggregate and abstract than interpersonal relations but more concrete than the diffusive notion of power held by macro-theory. Organizations embody and make rules and routines. We sought to reveal how rules, routines, and differentiation obscure the potential for discretion in rule making. Instead, the operation of power in organizations follows a plural, generative, and depersonalized logic so much so that it tends to reduce the perception of domination. With the interstitial spaces and incompatible logics organizations also produce, they create expectations for the exercise of one's creativity and leverage.

The second goal of the paper is to link the meso-approach to power with examinations of power at the macro-level of social formations and the micro-level of exchanges. We argued that even though power at each level acquires distinctive structural and symbolic features, exchanges, translations, and conversions of power across the different levels of social units generates new types of social, institutional, and ideological formations that can not be reduced to power originating from any given level alone. At these emergent spaces between individual decision-makings, meso-regulations, and macro-institutions, informalities can be an important source of power and the powerless can excel by exploiting structural positions. This chapter thus concludes that regulatory power at the meso-level is both empowering and dominating.

Does our focus on organizations as a matrix of power leave out dynamics that affect people outside of organizations? Given the retreat of what Davis (2009) felicitously calls "corporate feudalism"—the golden age of organized capitalism in the US where a generalized expectation of stability and affluence motivated the emerging middle class to join corporate ranks—it may seem anachronistic to emphasize the organized nature of power in a time of post-fordist flexible specialization (see Jessop 1995). Yet here we find it useful to retrieve an important analytical distinction Rueschemeyer (1986) makes by juxtaposing Marx and Durkheim.

There are two types of division of labor: the social division of labor, and the manufacturing division of labor. The social division of labor refers to specialization across all social realms. It is both enabling and constraining: it enhances the potential for individual freedom while increasing individual interdependence. The manufacturing division of labor, by contrast, rests on coercive authority in the workplace through deskilling, or the breaking down of production into simple, mindless steps. The manufacturing division of labor increases the power of those who already are in a position of authority, while it deprives the powerless of even the most basic form of control—control over their labor. Rueschemeyer reminds us that the two types always interpenetrate empirically. As hierarchical organizations multiply, for instance, the experience of the powerless will deteriorate, but individuals with the skills and capital to navigate organizational politics will thrive precisely as authority tightens its grip. Competing sources of legitimacy and control tend to also generate a space for new classes of experts invested with the power to assess and rank (DiMaggio and Powell 1983; see also Espeland and Sauder 2007). What this implies for power in the age of corporate downsizing is that power as efficacy will multiply at the very interstices of organizational boundaries just as power as coercive control intensifies within organizational boundaries. States become more punitive just as allegedly free markets expand (Harcourt 2011). There is tension and contradiction between these two trends, which becomes unsustainable when organizations are no longer able to meet their legitimizing criteria of efficiency in production and delivery of goods and services. When power turns from generative to destructive, organizations regain the upper hand. We believe that organizational power will remain the defining feature of the twenty-first century.

References

Abrutyn, S. (2013a). *Revisiting institutionalism in sociology: Putting the "institution" back in institutional analysis*. New York: Routledge.

Abrutyn, S. (2013b). Reconceptualizing the dynamics of religion as a macro-institutional domain. *Structure and Dynamics, 6*(3), 1–21.

Abrutyn, S., & Lawrence, K. (2010). From chiefdom to state: Toward an integrative theory of the evolution of polity. *Sociological Perspectives, 53*(3), 419–442.

Adams, J. (2007). *The familial state: Ruling families and merchant capitalism in early modern Europe*. Ithaca: Cornell University Press.

Bacharach, S. B., & Lawler, E. (1980). *Power and politics in organizations: The social psychology of conflict, coalitions, and bargaining*. San Francisco: Jossey-Bass Inc Pub.

Barnes, B. (1988). *The nature of power*. Urbana: University of Illinois Press.

Bell, R. S., et al. (2000). Power, influence, and legitimacy in organizations: Implications of three theoretical research programs. In S. Bacharach & E. J. Lawler (Eds.), *Research in the sociology of organizations* (Vol. 17, pp. 131–177). Greenwich: JAI Press.

Blau, P. M. (1956). *Bureaucracy in modern society*. New York: Random House.

Blau, P. M. (1964). *Exchange and power in social life*. New York: Wiley.

Blau, P. M., & Schoenherr, R. A. (1971). *Structure of organizations*. New York: Basic Books.

Bourdieu, P. (1980). *The logic of practice*. Stanford: Stanford University Press.

Bourdieu, P. (1984). *Distinction*. Cambridge: Harvard University Press.

Bourdieu, P. (1988). *Homo academicus*. Stanford: Stanford University Press.

Bourdieu, P. (1996a). *The rules of art: Genesis and structure of the literature field*. Stanford: Stanford University Press.

Bourdieu, P. (1996b). *The state nobility*. Stanford: Stanford University Press.

Bourdieu, P. (2015). *On the state*. Cambridge: Polity.

Bourdieu, P., & Wacquant, L. (1992). *An invitation to reflexive sociology*. Chicago: The University of Chicago Press.

Bourdieu, P., et al. (1994). Rethinking the state: Genesis and structure of the bureaucratic field. *Sociological Theory, 12*(1), 1–18.

Burawoy, M. (1982). *Manufacturing consent: Changes in the labor process under monopoly capitalism*. Chicago: The University of Chicago Press.

Burt, R. S. (1992). *Structural holes*. Cambridge: Harvard University Press.

Carpenter, D. P. (2010). *Reputation and power: Organizational image and pharmaceutical regulation at the FDA*. Princeton: Princeton University Press.

Clegg, S. (2009). Foundations of organization power. *Journal of Power, 2*(1), 35–64.

Coleman, J. S. (1974). *Power and the structure of society*. New York: W. W Norton & Company.

Coleman, J. S., Katz, E., & Menzel, H. (1966). *Medical innovation: A diffusion study*. Indianapolis: The Bobbs-Merrill Company.

Cook, K. S., & Richard, M. E. (1978). Power, equity and commitment in exchange networks. *American Sociological Review, 43*(5), 721–739.

Dahl, R. (1957). The concept of power. *Behavioral Science, 2*(3), 201–208.

Dahl, R. (1961). *Who governs? Democracy and power in an American city*. New Haven: Yale University Press.

Davis, G. F. (2009). *Managed by the markets*. New York: Oxford University Press.

DiMaggio, P., & Powell, W. (1983). The iron cage revisited: Institutional isomorphisms and collective rationality in organizational fields. *American Sociological Review, 48*(2), 147–160.

Eisenstadt, S. N. (1993). *The political systems of empires*. New Brunswick: Transaction Publishers.

Eisenstadt, S. N. (1995). *Power, trust, and meaning: Essays in sociological theory and analysis*. Chicago: University of Chicago Press.

Emerson, R. M. (1962). Power-dependence relations. *American Sociological Review, 27*, 31–41.

Emerson, R. M. (1964). Power-dependence relations: Two experiments. *Sociometry, 27*, 282–298.

Espeland, W., & Sauder, M. (2007). Rankings and reactivity: How public measures recreate social worlds1. *American Journal of Sociology, 113*(1), 1–40.

Fligstein, N., & McAdam, D. (2012). *A theory of fields*. New York: Oxford University Press.

Foucault, M. (1980). *Power/knowledge: Selected interviews and other writings, 1972–1977*. New York: Pantheon.

Galbraith, J. K. (1958). *The affluent society: the economics of the age of opulence-a literate and expert revision of the basic ideas*. Boston: Houghton Mifflin.

Gorski, P. (2013). Bourdieusian theory and historical analysis. In P. Gorski (Ed.), *Bourdieu and historical analysis*. Durham: Duke University Press.

Hall, D. H. (1987). Careers and socialization. *Journal of Management, 13*(2), 301–321.

Harcourt, B. E. (2011). *The illusion of free markets: Punishment and the myth of natural order*. Cambridge: Harvard University Press.

Jessop, B. (1995). The regulation approach, governance and post-Fordism: Alternative perspectives on economic and political change? *Economy and Society, 24*(3), 307–333.

Johnson, V. (2007). What is organizational imprinting: Cultural entrepreneurship in the founding of the Paris opera. *American Journal of Sociology, 113*(1), 97–127.

Lamont, M. (2002). *The dignity of working men: Morality and the boundaries of race, class, and immigration*. New York: Harvard University Press.

Lukes, S. (2005). *Power: A radical view*. Houndmills: Palgrave Macmillan.

Mann, M. (2012a). *The sources of social power: Volume 4, globalizations, 1945–2011*. New York: Cambridge University Press.

Mann, M. (2012b). *The sources of social power: Volume 1, a history of power from the beginning to ad 1760*. New York: Cambridge University Press.

Mann, M. (2012c). *The sources of social power: Volume 2, the rise of classes and nation-states, 1760–1914* (2nd ed.). New York: Cambridge University Press.

Mann, M. (2012d). *The sources of social power: Volume 3, global empires and revolution, 1890–1945*. New York: Cambridge University Press.

Michels, R. (1959). *Political parties: A sociological study of the oligarchical tendencies of modern democracy*. New York: Dover.

Padgett, J. F., & Powell, W. (2012). *The emergence of organizations and markets*. Princeton: Princeton University Press.

Pfeffer, J. (1981). *Power in organizations*. Cambridge: Ballinger Pub Co.

Poggi, G. (2001). *Forms of power*. Cambridge: Polity.

Powell, W., & DiMaggio, P. (Eds.). (1991). *The new institutionalism in organizational analysis*. Chicago: The University of Chicago Press.

Reed, I. (2013). Power: Relational, discursive, and performative dimensions. *Sociological Theory, 31*(3), 193–218.

Ridgeway, C. L., & Berger, J. (1986). Expectations, legitimation, and dominance behavior in groups. *American Sociological Review, 51*, 603–617.

Rohlen, T. P. (1979). *For harmony and strength: Japanese white-collar organization in anthropological perspective*. Berkeley: University of California Press.

Rueschemeyer, D. (1986). *Power and the division of labor*. Stanford: Stanford University Press.

Scott, W. R. (1992). *Organizations: Rational, natural and open systems*. New Jersey: Prentice-Hall.

Scott, J. C. (1999). *Seeing like a state: How certain schemes to improve the human condition have failed*. New Haven: Yale University Press.

Scott, W. R. (2001). *Institutions and organizations*. Thousand Oaks: SAGE Publications.

Selznick, P. (2010). *TVA and the grass roots; a study in the sociology of formal organization*. Charleston, South Carolina: Nabu Press

Simmel, G., & Wolff, K. H. (1964). *The sociology of Georg Simmel*. Glencoe: Free Press.

March, H. A. & Simon, J. G., (1958). *Organizations*. New York: Wiley.

Stainback, K., Tomaskovic-Devey, D., & Skaggs, S. (2010). Organizational approaches to inequality: Inertia, relative power, and environments. *Annual Review of Sociology, 36*, 225–247.

Steinmetz, G. (2007). *The devil's handwriting: Precoloniality and the German colonial state in Qingdao, Samoa, and southwest Africa*. Chicago: University of Chicago Press.

Stinchcomebe, A. L. (1965). Social structure and organizations. In J. G. March (Ed.), *Handbook of organizations*. Chicago: Rand McNally & Company.

Stinchcomebe, A. L. (2001). *When formality works: Authority and abstraction in law and organizations*. Chicago: University of Chicago Press.

Teiwes, F. C. (1984). *Leadership, legitimacy, and conflict in China: From a charismatic Mao to the politics of succession*. London: Palgrave Macmillan.

Thornton, P. H., & Ocasio, W. (1999). Institutional logics and the historical contingency of power in organizations: Executive succession in the higher education publishing industry, 1958–1990. *American Journal of Sociology, 105*(3), 801–843.

Thornton, P. H., & Ocasio, W. (2008). Institutional logic. In R. Greenwood, C. Oliver, K. Sahlin-Andersson, & R. Suddaby (Eds.), *The SAGE handbook of organizational institutionalism* (pp. 99–129). Thousand Oaks: Sage.

Thornton, P. H., Ocasio, W., & Lounsbury, M. (2012). *The institutional logics perspective: A new approach to culture, structure and process*. Oxford: Oxford University Press.

Tilly, C. (1999). *Durable inequality*. Berkeley: University of California Press.

Tuner, J. H. (2012). *Theoretical principles of sociology, volume 3: Mesodynamics*. New York: Springer.

Veblen, T. (1934). *The theory of the leisure class: An economic study in the evolution of institutions*. New York: Modern Library.

Wanous, J. P., Reichers, A. E., & Malik, S. D. (1984). The organizational socialization and group development: Toward an integrative perspective. *Academy of Management Review, 9*(4), 670–683.

Weber, M. (1947). *The theory of social and economic organizations*. New York: Oxford University.

Weber, M. (1978). *Economy and society: An outline of interpretive sociology*. Berkeley: University of California Press.

Weber, M. (2004). *The vocation lectures*. Indianapolis: Hackett Publishing Company.

William, W., Nocera, J. (2002). *The Organizational men*. University of Pennsylvania Press.

Action in Society: Reflexively Conceptualizing Activities

4

Andreas Glaeser

4.1 Sovereignty, Rational Action, and the Puzzles of Modernity

The concept of action transmitted by the Europeanoid tradition into the nineteenth century presupposes a principally autonomous actor whose actions are guided by the lights of reason at the prompting of his or her own free will (Seigel 2005; Taylor 1989; Mauss 1938). That there is nothing "natural" about this understanding can be demonstrated, for example, by analyzing the ways Archaic Greek or Ancient Hebrew texts present causes and consequences, motives and responsibilities for action. Both of these ancient Mediterranean bodies of writing invariably emphasize the role of the community and that of supernatural powers in stipulating, guiding and taking responsibility for action. Since the Europeanoid tradition self-consciously builds on these traditions, it follows that the notion of the free willing, autonomous, and rational actor is the consequence of a long historical development. More specifically, it results from the combined effects of ideas and practices deriving from Roman Law (in particular the notions of personal property and contract (Schiavone 2012)), Christianity (notably ideas about person specific judgment, grace, and the import of free will in theodicy (Siedentop 2014; Dumont 1983)), natural rights philosophy (above all the concept of personal freedom rights), the Enlightenment (especially understandings of reason as personal power, as well as of self-emancipation as goal (Schneewind 1998)) and finally of empiricism and early scientism (with its nominalistic tencencies to see only the particular and individual as real (Daston and Gallison 2010).

In the wake of the Religious Wars of the sixteenth and seventeenth centuries this historically forged notion of willed, individual, and rational action became the foil on which to understand the emergence and maintenance of large scale social orders which until then were seen as divinely chartered. The motivating circumstances prompting this move were thoroughly political. The fact that in most of these religious wars no side could simply vanquish the other, the contenders needed to come to a negotiated peace agreement involving some form of toleration.[1] This made it more plausible to think of order as a consciously sought human achievement—even where it was

A. Glaeser (✉)
Department of Sociology, The University of Chicago, Chicago, IL, USA
e-mail: aglaeser@uchicago.edu

[1] Examples are the Peace of Augsburg of 1555, the Edict of Nantes of 1598, and in a different constellation the English Act of Toleration of 1688. Historically, such agreements were echoing medieval efforts of the church, of the emperor, and of cities to create systems of adjudication with centralized monopolies of violence in lieu of the feuding rights of nobles. Perhaps the most famous one of these is the Old Swiss Confederacy of 1291.

S. Abrutyn (ed.), *Handbook of Contemporary Sociological Theory*,
Handbooks of Sociology and Social Research, DOI 10.1007/978-3-319-32250-6_4

seen as divinely enabled.[2] Accordingly, contract theory (Hobbes 1651; Locke 1689a; Rousseau 1762) proposed to understand societies and states as the intentional product of rational action. In accordance with this view, states were seen as governed by the will of sovereigns, divine and secular; and history became the narration of the deeds of great men (embodying sovereignty rather than the unfolding of Providence). The successful revolutions in England, the United States and France lent credibility to the individual actor/contract model of self and society.

At the same time, and once more prompted by the splitting of the church (and thus authority), the notion of rationality favored by philosophers began to move in the direction of *formalization*. In other words it began to shift towards logics of operations and away from the discovery and articulation of *substantive* norms, motives, and goals. As faith had become in principle open to conversion, norms, motives and goals were seen increasingly as a matter of conscience-induced choice and as such simply personal (Luther 1520; Spinoza 1677; Locke 1689b). That is to say while there was growing awareness that any kind of agreement on substance may be elusive, hope emerged that agreements on *formal* aspects of reason were still possible. The beginning industrial revolution and the expansion of commerce in the 18th and its virtual explosion in the nineteenth century contributed further to the formalization of the concept of rational action (Weber 1920a) which through the idea of self-regulating markets created a second model for association through rational action.

Other historical developments, however, began to raise serious doubts about the rational action model and its expansion into explaining social orders. The stifling over-regulated, calculating and isolating atmosphere of absolutist court life and society (Reddy 2001; Elias 1969) triggered a search for models of personal and social life which gave sensations, feelings and communal belonging a much greater role, leading to the celebration of authenticity (rather than calculation) as favored modality of social relationships on all scales. This holistic critique found expression in literature and philosophy,[3] but also in experimentation with new forms of social association from literary salons to religious revival movements. Holism received unexpected but also confounding nourishment in the descent of the French revolution into terror, dictatorship, and restauration. Further corroboration for supra-rational holistic understandings of social life was provided by the seemingly authorless, unwilled, and in its consequences chaotic, self-accelerating social transformations of the nineteenth century with all the unspeakable human misery they produced in their wake.[4] Both human activities and society appeared to a growing number of theorists ever less like the result of deliberation, reason and will, and ever more like the result of uncontrollable and yet probably law-governed processes. These were seen as unleashing "forces" akin to those of nature in their inevitability, scope, and might. The call of the moment was, then, one for a naturalization of the perspectives on human beings and social life and thus to make sense of the experience that the individual human appears entirely powerless in face of society and that therefore any assumption of individual autonomy is simply preposterous.[5]

[2] What Parsons (1937) characterizes as a universal problem of social order has thus very specific historical roots, which is to say it gets *thematized* as a problem only in particular historically specific circumstances.

[3] What I call here holism was articulated in different countries at around the same time in different ways, to different extents, and with different emphasis, which came to be known under different names. Paradigmatic examples are Sentimentalism in England and Romanticism (with a precursor in "Sturm und Drang") in Germany. Importantly, both were simultaneously literary and philosophical movements.

[4] Earlier critics were Vico (1744; Herder 1784–1991) and the Romantics after them.

[5] This shift in concerns and attention can be nicely brought to the fore by contrasting graphical depictions of supreme power and sovereignty. Whereas medieval and early Renaissance images show the Christian divinity in the guise of an old man who as heavenly puppeteer holds the strings of his own creation, the frontispiece of Hobbes' Leviathan shows the sovereign state made up of all

This ancient sentiment of helplessness that previously led people to join mystery cults, embrace Stoic philosophy, or take refuge in piety found an entirely modern expression in the drive for a science to find new routes to overcome it.

The new times required new concepts. Before discussing the activity concepts (or their studious avoidance) deemed appropriate for the modernizing world, however, I want to disrupt my historical narrative to discuss criteria to adjudicate the *adequacy* of activity concepts. I want to do so because the theories discussed in what follows all still have contemporary resonance.

4.2 Thinking About Appropriate Activity Concepts

Even this very brief introduction makes it quite clear that the ways in which actors and actions are understood vary culturally and historically in rather profound ways. Moreover, these understandings appear to be deeply intertwined with other central aspect of a culture such as notions of self, intentionality, agency, culpability, and in fact politics. As such they appear as a constitutive aspect of the institutional fabric of a particular time that is shaped in part at least by the very activity concepts in use.[6] Moreover, the moral tone with which activity concepts are imbued and the vigor with which they are argued against alternatives suggests that there are often not one but several activity notions in play in any social context. Those articulated by intellectuals may also not be the (often not so explicitly formulated) ones guiding the actions of other people of which there may be once more a plurality. Far from serving merely as tools of the intellectual trade reflecting on social life, then, explicit and implicit activity concepts are a linchpin of that social life scholars want to study. For that reason, emic and etic notions of activity have to be carefully differentiated from each other and a plurality of such concepts has to be considered.[7] Therefore, and this is the first criterion for a good sociological activity concept for our time:

1. Sociological activity concepts need to be such that they can integrate a possibly diverse set of emic notions of action into a multidimensional etic analysis. One could also say then need to be loadable.

This suggests further, that the social sciences must generate two kinds of activity concepts. They need particular ones to model historically specific and where needed domain specific activity concepts. They also require general concepts that can be used to compare local understandings of acting and the differences they make for the institutional fabric within which people live while also supporting an analysis of how people move over time (or across domains) from one set of emic concepts of acting to another.

The import of activity concepts for social life also requires that scholars think about how they are part of a historically specific culture and how their etic musings can become ideologies supporting or undermining particular emic understandings of activities with all the institutional consequences this move may entail. From this consideration follows a second criterion for a social-scientifically adequate activity concept namely:

2. Activity concepts need to enable critical reflection on their own limits while remaining open to change.

Such openness requires that theories are taken to operate as metaphors which can be more or less appropriate in lighting up those aspects of

citizens together in front of the beautiful order they have created together and govern through him in scepter and sword. Nineteenth century depictions are much less flattering. Daumier for example shows Louis Philippe the "citizen king" chained by his own obesity to the throne where he is force-fed the goods of the kingdom while he is at the same time endlessly defecating laws keeping his brown-nosing underlings busy.

[6]This does by no means imply, of course, that the emic notion of activity is in any sense true. It simply means that their employment does have *an* effect on the course of activities.

[7]Emic refers to the study of a cultural phenomenon based on its specific, internal elements and their functioning, in short local use, whereas etic refers to the study of cultural phenomenon by applying general, external for example academic frames.

reality that a researcher is interested in (Glaeser 2015). This immediately raises the question what our interests in creating concepts to analyze social life are or ought to be, for as Weber (1904) has pointed out, self-consciously perspectival concept formation is the only chance we have to get to a meaningful social science in the first place.[8] Historically, the aim has often been to generate impulses and in more ambitious cases even goals and guidance for politics. The third criterion is therefore:

3. Sociological activity concepts need to be politically fecund.

Putting it in this way raises the question *how* activity concepts can become politically relevant. Since politics is, according to the criteria presented here, best understood as any intentional activity to establish, alter, or maintain institutions (Glaeser 2011, 2015), that is to say since as an activity politics is both motivated and enabled by the possibility of alternative states of the world, politically fecund activity concepts need to be linkable to imaginaries which can generate such alternatives. Moreover, since institutions as the proper object of politics are, again to keep with the criteria presented here, most fruitfully understood as self-similar replications of action-reaction webs (Glaeser 2014 and below Sect. 4.4), politically fecund concepts must show how activities can form institutions. And finally, since institutions exist in the coordination of the activities of often very many people politically fecund concepts need to show how the activities of others including very many others can be influenced in desirable directions. This, however, is to say that politicians need reliable guidance for their activities in the world which translates directly into the final demand of a suitable action concept:

4. Sociological activity concepts must be ontically fecund.

In other words, action concepts need to provide useful guidance in the world. Some philosophers of science (e.g. Vaihinger 1922) but also many practicing social scientists (e.g. Friedman 1953) have argued strongly in favor of the predictive power of a social scientific model as a master criterion of goodness that could be interpreted to guarantee both political and ontic fecundity. The advantage of this criterion would be that the problematic notion of correspondence evoking some similitude between conceptual edifices and world could be safely discarded. Yet, prediction has proved to be a most elusive goal, attainable, if at all, only in the most rarified circumstances.[9] Worse, perhaps, even where it works it offers only a narrow range of politically relevant information. Prediction tells at best what state to expect, not how to intervene successfully in the world to get to a particular state. The only viable measure for ontic fecundity is the concept's quality as a metaphor highlighting relevant features of the world to orient and guide action successfully.

Metatheoretically speaking, the four criteria together imply a significant departure from the scientific pretentions that have carried large parts of the social sciences for far too long (Glaeser 2015). Substantively speaking, these criteria in the very least imply a renewed search for integrating models of social analysis that can help to overcome the fragmentation of the social sciences into subject-hyphenated domain specialties and paired oppositions of research perspectives such as the positive and normative, micro-macro,

[8] Historically, efforts to theorize social life emerged at the interstices between cognitive and political interests. In some cases the political element is more obviously in the foreground, as with Machiavelli's *Prince*, Hobbes' *Leviathan*, Smith's *Wealth of Nations*, or with Marx and Engels' *Communist Manifesto*. In other cases, say Mommsen's *Roman History*, or Malinowski's *Argonauts* the description of the lives of people at some other time and place may make it appear as if social inquiry was a content-neutral purveyor of facts of life at some distant place. Yet the political purpose of such writing, often the other as an example to emulate (or to avoid), self-discovery, calls for help, preservation or transformation etc. are everywhere shining through the prefaces, styles, and rhetorical structures of these texts.

[9] Not surprisingly it is rarely used as a criterion to discard beloved concepts notably by its strongest proponents in economics.

structural-cultural, individual-social, diachronic-synchronic etc. What is needed is a framework that allows the exploration of *connections* across such compartmentalization and beyond these oppositions. The urgent political questions of our time such as growing domestic and international inequality, political stalemate, and global political, economic and natural reconfigurations such as climate change require precisely a modality of analysis suitable to fathom the temporal depth and to survey the spatial scope of a wide-range of interconnections. We need concepts to defetishize institutional formations to show whose contributions and manners of contributing are most significant in maintaining these formations to enable ourselves politically.

4.3 Action in Modern Social Thought

The actual course of the French Revolution and the rapid transformations of western European societies during the nineteenth century prompted a complete rethinking of social life and with it a complete reconceptualization of the traditional Europeanoid notion of action. Befitting what became gradually known through this process as modernity, the result was a plurality of models beholden to incompatible ontologies and epistemologies.[10] For the purposes of distinguishing modern activity concepts I will present their conceptual development in stylized form as a tree with two major ontological branching points. The first corresponds to the split between *individualists* who keep the traditional notion of the basic autonomy of persons, and *communalists* who work under the assumption of a fundamental, indissoluble sociality of human beings. I will then show how the communal branch splits once more into structuralists who propose to study society as an emergent phenomenon that is autonomous from the activities giving rise to it, and social activity theorists conceiving action itself as social. All three groups of theoretical traditions have striven to grow out of their philosophical roots to attain the status of an empirical social science (which ended up meaning different things in each case).[11]

4.3.1 Individualism

Utilitarian rationalism (Bentham 1823; Mill 1863) became the dominant form of individualism during the nineteenth century and has maintained this position ever since.[12] In maintaining the idea of the autonomous individual as basis of its models, it has remained heir to traditional notions of rational action. Yet, it has sought scientific rigor by radicalizing the Enlightenment tendency to formalize reason in terms of algorithmic, machine-like operations in the direction of the optimal pursuit of advantage (Menger 1871; Jevons 1871). Eventually this search has led to the adoption and continuous refinement of systems of mathematical representation (e.g. infinitesimal calculus, set theory, game theory) which make its users look every bit as scientific as engineers or theoretical physicists. Resolute formalization has stripped reason of its previously glorified capabilities to discover and judge truth, justice, and beauty.[13] Motives, ends, and

[10]The use of the term modern as adjective reaches back into the Renaissance to denote perceptible temporal breaks with the past. As a noun and further solidified into the term modernity it begins to become an epochal marker during the Enlightenment to reach the significance we attribute to it today in the second half of the nineteenth century. As a contrasting term it always implies plurality. The degree of plurality and fragmentation of authority then comes to be mapped onto "early modern", "modern" as well as more recently onto the "post-modern".

[11]This implies a decisive shift in the overarching project from within which the conceptualization of action was undertaken. The analysis of action for the sake of making it better (more ethical or less sinful) gave way to an interest in understanding it as a feature of the world as it is. Only with this shift did action become an object of theoretization in its own right.

[12]The label utilitarian rationalism is not common in the literature. I use it to emphasize its pronounced differences with traditional models of rational action and contract while also marking its tendency to engage in a priori reasoning.

[13]Advantage of course garnered the attention it did because the calculus developed here was immensely use-

values are seen in these formalized models as matters of private tastes and choices that are, where not explicitly stated, taken to be "revealed" in action (Samuelson 1938). Understood as preferences, they are viewed if not as irrational, then certainly as extra-rational, and as such outside of the purview of proper scientific inquiry. In disemboweling reason of its substantive capabilities, utilitarian rationalism completely breaks with the traditional Europeanoid models of rational action.

For utilitarian rationalists, the social is the result of aggregated individual actions. Where these are mediated by free markets the outcome of this mediation is also thought to show socially optimal characteristics. The market has therefore replaced contract as the central integrating imaginary of this model.

So how does utilitarian rationalism fare vis-à-vis the criteria of goodness I have spelled out in the last section? The most important point to note is that utilitarian rationalism operates with a monothetic model of action which it deems if not as universally valid then certainly as the best available approximation for how humans in fact act. This monism has a number of consequences. First, emic action concepts are either treated as forms of false consciousness or they are simply deemed irrelevant. Second, monothetic models obliterate any space for critical reflections about the performative consequences of the posited action model. In other words, there is no room for what has been called self-reflexivity in the social sciences (Marcus and Fischer 1986; Wacquant and Bourdieu 1992). Third, monothetic action concepts completely obliterate the existential tensions created by the co-existence of a multiplicity of action logics (Weber 1922). Fourth, for the same reason monothetic action concepts reduce the evaluation and thus meaning of action to a single dimension. Thus they forfeit important insights into the dynamics of social life.

In spite of all criticisms, it has to be recognized that utilitarian rationalism has become politically fecund in a number of different ways. The most important of these is that utilitarian rationalism proposes with the idea of positive and negative incentives a very powerful but simple model to shape the behavior of people thus offering a seemingly universally applicable means of directing politics. Unlike much action-distant sociological macro theory, the firm grounding of utilitarian rationalism in a theory of action enables it to make action recommendations. The second reason for its political fecundity lies in the fact that if politicians want to allocate scarce resources in an efficient fashion over competing targets with differential impact on the overall goal, it offers excellent tools of reasoning through this process. And finally, efficiency has become a paramount historically specific criterion for judging action itself.

Ontologically speaking, the action model of utilitarian rationalism is, owing to its commitment to ontological individualism, quite barren. It has no credibility as reasonably good guide for how people actually act in general. The historical and culturally comparative, as well as psychological-experimental evidence speaks against it as much as the following three theoretical arguments aiming to demonstrate the fundamental sociality of internal life above all of reason itself. Reason has two main dimensions. Its basis is the capacity of human beings to be object and subject at the same time, that is to be a self. Humans acquire both, the general capacity and the particular form of self-hood by internalizing their relations to others (Mead 1934; Vygotsky 1986; Stern 1985). The second dimension of reason is to make oneself object of oneself in a systematic fashion which is to say to do so in a rule governed way. The capacity to follow rules mentally, however, as Wittgenstein's private language argument makes clear (1953) is contingent on a self's embeddedness in a community of interpretation in which to follow this rule is a practice. Finally, reflection has to take place in some structured symbolic medium such as ordinary language or mathematics,

ful first in justifying and later also in conducting business. The possibility to formalize the pursuit of advantage, that is pure scientific form mattered as well. There were, needless to say, efforts to formalize the pursuit of truth and justice as well. Yet these have not gone nearly as far as the pursuit of advantage now dubbed "utility".

which is likewise socially derived and requires social relations for its upkeep.

This said, the utilitarian rationalists' model of action is relevant as an etic theory of action wherever something like utility maximization is the desired outcome. It is relevant as an *emic* theory precisely where the model has become performatively relevant because people actually use it consciously or have become habituated to work in accord with it. That is to say because it has been politically so fecund and because in the meantime generations of managers have been trained in its image and workers are supposed to follow it down to their sports activities and even eating habits it is of considerable import as an emic model.

4.3.2 Communalism[14]

For communalists not individuality but sociality has become the basic assumption about human life, if one that has been conceived as varying in form phylogenetically and historically, ontogenetically and biographically. In fact, individuality has been understood by communalists as a particular modality of organizing the relations between human beings and as such the result of a particular historical development (e.g. Simmel 1908; Durkheim 1893). Due to this shift in fundamental ontological assumptions, sociologies felt compelled to break completely with traditional rational action and contract models. This break came in two main varieties, as structuralism feeling compelled to abandon any grounding of social analysis in activity concepts, and as a diverse group of approaches which continued to see activity concepts as central and which I will call here for want of a better term social activity theorists.

4.3.2.1 Emergent Social Facts: Sociology Without Activity Concepts

The scholar who has for the longest time been credited with the honor of having invented the term sociology, Auguste Comte (1844), developed over the second quarter of the nineteenth century a rather influential model that mapped his understanding of a stratified reality onto a system of sciences each addressing itself to one of these strata. For Comte the layers of reality are hierarchically nested in such a way that the more complex higher layers are materially grounded in the lower ones. The layers are separated by thresholds of emergence through which new laws come into effect which must become the object of specialized sciences if progress is to be made in capturing the phenomena as they really are. The most complex layer of reality, social life, forms the top-most layer of being and accordingly requires its own science, sociology.

Emile Durkheim (1895) has adapted this model to justify his design for a truly scientific sociology. He is much concerned, therefore, with establishing the autonomy of sociology as a discipline, and does so in two related steps. The first is to delineate the proper object for sociological research which he designates as social facts. Working on the paradigm of sanctioned norms he characterizes them as exerting force on individual humans as well as by their diffusion, that is their independence from individual acts and modes of thinking which can for that reason also not simply be willed away (1895). In Durkheim's view, these social facts emerge from individual activities as objective characteristics of the world through social organization which can be studied with regards to its particular objective structure. Knowledge of this structure renders an investigation of the underlying individual actions superfluous; worse, attention to action would be as distracting and misleading as attempting to study the evolution of life by aiming to grasp it at the

[14] Proponents of individualism typically denigrate communal perspectives as collectivist playing on not so subtle associations with fascism and socialism. Conversely, communalists of either of the two stripes of discussed below often reciprocate by calling the opposing perspective atomism with likewise not so subtle overtones of confusing the study of social life with the study of dead matter. Although I am in some sense clearly taking sides in the debate I want to avoid such name calling not least because all well-established models discussed in what follows have value if typically in a domain much smaller than the one imagined by their authors.

molecular level.[15] Ancillary to this object definition is an effort to differentiate that new science of social facts, sociology, from that older science of individuals and their actions, psychology. The result of this procedure is a stark contrast between an individualistically conceived psychology and a communally framed sociology.

The second step is taken with the development of methods to measure social facts empirically. This meant turning away from individual actions toward observable manifestations of social facts. Among them are large scale institutions (notably the law and religion), forms of social organization, or otherwise statistical averages minimizing the adulterating effect of an attention to individuals and their idiosyncratic choices. From a study of such indicators of social fact Durkheim is then deriving what in his eyes are laws of macro-social development the most prominent of which is his assertion that societies evolve from simple to more complex forms passing on their way through distinct modes of social organization, and mental composition of people.

Durkheim's sociology is not entirely without attention to activities. At the center of his analysis lies an interest in rituals through which both the social ties of people and their individual life energy are renewed in the experience of actions, feelings and thoughts shared in each other's co-presence (1893; 1912). These moments of "effervescence," and the order they create are existentially meaningful in Durkheim's understanding of social life because they perform the transcendence of individuality towards the point of origin of all human life: society. And it is this contrast between power inducing collective embeddedness and individual isolation that for Durkheim becomes the contrast between the sacred and the profane, the source code of all signification and meaning. Indeed here and in his ethics specifying his own categorical imperative to live a life in perfect attunement to the need of one's society at its present stage of development, lie the roots of Durkheim's vision of sociology as a positive religion in Comte's sense.[16]

The Durkheimian vision of a sociology beyond activities is chiefly responsible for the paradoxical situation with which I started this chapter. The large segments of the discipline that make do without an action concept are often called structuralist or structure functionalist in direct reference to Durkheim's example. Of course from the vantage point of the Comte-Durkheim theory this is only an apparent paradox which disappears as soon as the fact of emergence is taken seriously.

There are, however, two fundamental problems with the argument of emergence in social life. First, it posits the independent pre-existence of the elements from which something is said to emerge. For the social world emergentists must argue, therefore, that the social emerges from individual activities. However, as I have already argued in the last section, the social as it is most fruitfully understood today, has no pre-social to emerge from.[17] As far as sociality is concerned, all that happens is that its forms change both ontogenetically and biographically as children move from their entanglements in smaller (e.g. dyadic) relationships to the mastery of larger (e.g. triadic and onward) and more complexly structured groupings of humans. Much the same holds historically as many sociologist have pointed out, and perhaps even phylogenetically as evolutionary anthropologists and linguists are beginning to speculate (Tomasello 2014). In other words with the social sciences the use of the term emergence in the Comte-Durkheim sense of a "strong" emergence is ontically quite problematic.

[15] This is of course precisely what is done in biology today—a valuable lesson in the half-time of naturalistic metaphors.

[16] The fruitful tradition of looking at nationalisms, notably the American one as a "civic religion" (Bellah 1968) has taken off from here and it has contributed to communitarian thought the only successful normative school of social thought in which American sociology after World War II was represented with important scholars such as Bellah.

[17] The emergentists much quoted examples from nature cannot serve as proper analogies here. While natural scientists can for example observe elements and their properties independently of the molecules of which they can be a part, the same is not true in society.

The second fundamental problem with emergence is that it treats the process of emerging more or less as a black box. Apart from general hints (Durkheim 1895) and a few thought experiments (Archer 1995) which are cited time and again in the literature, there is no systematic attempt to theorize the process of emergence. Its invocation has therefore something mystifying. Rather than pointing to possibilities for political intervention, it effectively obscures processes and it posits the existence of doubtful entities such as a base line of general sharing—Durkheim's collective conscience enabling a fundamental level of mechanical solidarity—for the existence of viable political communities. It is therefore a politically highly problematic concept.

Emergentists (e.g. Bhaskar 1979; Archer et al. 1998; Sawyer 2005; Elder-Vass 2010) often present their own paradigm as the only alternative to individualism. Yet, the sociological phenomena they point to in order to make their case for emergence remain unpersuasive because they can be explained without either taking recourse to the concept of emergence or by relapsing into the individualist reductions favored by utilitarian rationalists. There is indeed a third possibility, namely making sense of social life *dialectically* that is by taking recourse to processes of co-constitution in which parts and whole get reconfigured together—if often through a conflict ridden process of adjustments. Indeed, the three arguments about the social constitution of inner life I have provided in the last section do exactly that. If humans are fundamentally social in the sense in which these theories think sociality, then action is never individual rational action, but the socially embedded action of a person whose very rationality is produced and reproduced through institutionalized social relations. But this also means that we can think of what sociologists like to call structure as fully grounded in activities without having to add to it some mysterious emergent properties. People and their modalities of acting simply change with the social and cultural environment, the institutions and structures.[18]

4.3.2.2 Social Activity Concepts

While the radical political and social transformations during the long nineteenth century prompted and in a sense even demanded a fresh conceptualization of action and social life, the quickly loosening immediate grip of Christianity freed the social imagination and made it more plausible for scholars to develop a whole range of *social* activity concepts. Hegel plays a crucial role as an inspiration for theorists of social action. His *Phenomenology of Spirit* (1807) and later his *Philosophy of Right* (1818–1832) set an example for the idea of historically changing forms of sociality which are configuring and being configured by the actions of people. He also conceives forms of sociality as entangled in a dialectical relationship with changing forms of peoplehood characterized by the differentiation and growth of mental capacities. Hegel thus systematically reinterprets as historical achievements and relationally configured the very characteristics of humans that Enlightenment thinkers have attributed to them as fixed, inalienable patrimony, while insisting that these changing characteristics of humans entail changing possibilities for organizing social life. Ontologically speaking, then, Hegel opposes traditional nominalism by showing how individuals are abstractions from the dialectical processes that constitute them. At the same time he opposes traditional realism by historicizing the forms concepts take. In the *Phenomenology's* account of human development of which the master-slave dialectic is but the best known part, he argues, for example, that self-consciousness, the very basis for rational thinking, is attainable only in the recognition of others. Since property rights are for Hegel the crucible of recognition, this leads to violence and subjugation. In general Hegel assumes that intentional actions inevitably lead to failures or resis-

[18] To say it with the natural metaphors of the emergentists: It is as if the oxygen in water was different from the oxygen in carbondioxide. It is as if there was no oxygen tout court, but only oxygen in something else. It would be pointless then to be puzzled by the fact that the properties of oxygen and hydrogen would not "add up" to form those of water, simply because nobody had ever seen oxygen and hydrogen and carbon by itself. At the level of biology: yes humans are made of cells, but these cells operate differently from mono-cellular beings in spite of very many structural similarities. Humans emerge no more from flagellates than society from individuals.

tance in the sense that they all entail what we now call unintended consequences in nature and society. Thus, the struggle for recognition does not lead to the anticipated death of one of the contenders, but to domination; and once more contrary to the intention, domination stunts the master, but forces the slave to transcend himself and to develop and finally overcome domination etc. Failure and resistance, however, lead human beings to form better concepts about the world and themselves. The formation of these concepts is wrapped up in an ongoing process of revision because they need to be adjusted constantly to the effects that humans have brought about through their past intentions formed on the basis of these concepts. This "history of spirit" as a history of concepts, of social forms, of social organization, will continue to unfold until ideas and world are perfectly aligned and humans have thus realized their potential in harmony between their universality and their particularity. In the Hegelian world action assumes basic subjective meaning because it is driven by intentions, it is existentially meaningful as a step, however minute, in a process of human self-liberation and in its highest form move in the objective drama of self-unfolding sprit in the history of the World.

Marx honed his skills in historical and dialectical reasoning in the encounter with Hegel, and even where Marx' language begins to shed its Hegelian sound in his later writings, the methods remain with him. Yet, in Marx' mind Hegel's work suffered from two fatal conceits. First among these is Hegel's insistence that history had already reached the point where reason had come into its own by having reshaped the world in its image (Marcuse 1941; Avineri 1968). Yet, the dramatic situation of the working classes in Europe indicated that the present order could not possibly be anywhere near the realization of human potential that Hegel had assumed. Second, Marx accused Hegel and his followers of misunderstanding human beings as principally idea driven whereas in his mind they needed to be primarily understood as material beings in need to produce their own livelihood for survival. Following Hegel, he took a deep interest in labor, but now understood not as a vehicle to intellectual growth, but as a material necessity. Activities in the world assume a much greater role in Marx' theory and concept formation takes a back-seat as a super-structural phenomenon. The dialectic that unfolds in his theory is still one of self and other embedded in a wider system of social forms. Yet the main failures, forms of resistance and conflicts (i.e. "contradictions") are no longer lodged between mind and world, but between material interests and within systemic institutional incompatibilities. And as in Hegel there is in Marx' theory the positing of an inevitable development towards a secular paradise; yet it is no longer achieved by state bureaucrats (as a universal class) acting in the interests of all, but by a proletariat universalized by generalized exploitation and suffering which enables them to launch a world revolution.

Marx's theorization of activities is grounded in a reinterpretation of the notion of praxis. For the ancient Greeks, praxis was an integrated and organized set of activities such as shoe-making or lyre-playing that was systematically connected to particular forms of knowing.[19] During the Enlightenment praxis was juxtaposed to theory as modality of engaging with the world, and by emphasizing practice Marx thus signals both his movement from a focus on ideas to one on material production and with it a turn away from naturalized conceptions of intentional action to socially preconfigured activities (1845; Marx and Engels 1846). The early Marx distinguishes between free activity and determinate activity where the former marks only the end point of historical development in communism, the latter the form of human activities take on the path to the final proletarian revolution. Indeed, Marx analyzes determinate activities as standardized forms of operating that integrate knowledge, specific locations where they are performed etc. Most importantly, however, he shows through a discussion of the historicity of the division of labor, of

[19] Aristotle (322BCEa, b) gave praxis the added specific meaning of a set of activities that is not undertaken for the sake of something else that is what he calls poiesis, but completely for its own sake. As central as this distinction is to Aristotelian practical philosophy, it is specific to him and his school.

ownership, of family relations, of forms of commerce, and of government, how a wide variety of practices are interdependent and presuppose each other across society with a particular mode of production at its center. Modalities of producing knowledge, raising children, or doing politics are in this sense dependent on modalities of running commerce, laboring in factories and managing them under conditions of changing markets and ever new technologies.

Closely related to the notion of praxis/practice is that of habitus/habit. Like its cousin's its theoretization began in ancient Greece, where it designated the mental disposition corresponding to practices.[20] Yet, with all the individualizing tendencies I have mentioned above, habit came to be side-tracked as an important component of theorizing actions. Worse, perhaps, it appeared as old-fashioned, anti-modern, as that which resists reason.[21] This changed dramatically in the late nineteenth and early twentieth centuries. Growing psychological empiricism (e.g. James 1890), but even more so a changing social threat scenario cultivated in contemporary imaginaries placed danger to society no longer in the pigheaded farmer resisting scientific innovation and democratic responsibility (as the Enlightenment did), but in the rootless, dissipated individual (e.g. Durkheim 1897; Thomas 1923). In American pragmatism, especially in the work of Dewey (1922) habit is both the vehicle to reintroduce the sociality of action as well a means to eclipse the significance of will and rational planning.[22]

Norbert Elias (1935) brings significant innovations to the concept of habitus by understanding it as a response to particular institutional configurations. At the same time Elias sees in habitus the means for the structural continuation of these configurations. In particular Elias employs habitus to come to an understanding how increasing requirements for coordination in lengthening action chains can be met institutionally. His answer is that this is possible only to the degree that control becomes internalized. In other words, Elias provides us with a way to investigate the co-constituting relationships between institutional arrangements on a larger scale and their presuppositions in the psychological makeup of the persons carrying these institutions. Equipped with this dialectical imaginary, Elias directs our attention to what he calls "mechanisms of interweaving" that is everything that brings human beings into the range of each other's activities allowing on the one hand lengthening chains of interaction requiring on the other new tools of coordination.[23]

Pierre Bourdieu (1972; 1986) follows Elias in seizing upon habitus as the mediating link between the personal and the social. Yet, while Elias' animating questions pertains to large scale historical transformations, Bourdieu's centers around the reproduction of class boundaries. To answer his questions he suggested a productive set of metaphors that described habitus shaped in the struggle for status ("symbolic capital") in which the contestants have to differentiate themselves along several dimensions from other con-

[20] The ancient Greeks saw good habits as a basis for good practice and as such of virtuous behavior. Accordingly, habits became the target of educational efforts. Yet, the Greeks also saw that these habits are the results of practices as much as of direct instruction. Although manifesting themselves as characteristics of persons, then, the Greeks saw habits as the result of a social process of instruction as well as of experience, of repeatedly acting in social context (Aristotle 322BCEa). Politically good habits were seen as the basis of a stable and reliable social order (Aristotle 322BCEb).

[21] It appears that habit was generally suspect to thinkers aspiring to effect changes. Missionizing Christianity is, unsurprisingly, not interested in habit. In the work of Augustine, and this is very significant for the place of habit in Europeanoid social thought after the Reformation, will and choice are emphasized and habit no longer plays a roles as a significant theoretical concept. Of course there are sound theological reasons for this preference as well. Yet, with Christianity firmly established and through the reappropriation of Aristotle's practical philosophy in the thirteenth century, habit once more played a significant, if secondary, role notably in the work of Thomas Aquinas. Subsequent revolutionary movements kept to Augustine rather than Aquinas.

[22] Dewey even collapses will into habit.

[23] Elias is concerned here with processes of colocation (e.g. urbanization) or connection (e.g. trade) following political centralization and expansion as much as in socio-technological means of coordination (e.g. money, standardization, clocks).

testants. Habitus is both the result of this struggle and its animating principle. As among the Greeks, Bourdieusian habitus conveys know how for practices.[24] And it does so—Bourdieu is in agreement here with previous habitus theorists—in form of tacit, embodied knowing which is hard to penetrate for critical reflection.

The notions of practice and habitus belong together; they form two sides of the same coin. The problem with this approach is that most practices do not only build on tacit knowledge, habitus, but they are often shot through with forms of deliberation making use of explicit theories ranging in their degree of sophistication and explicit awareness from sayings to elaborate theories. Yet, it is also important in this context to point out with Wittgenstein's private language argument that systematic reasoning (which inevitably is a form of rule following) needs to be grounded in practices. Moreover, it is clear that praxis/habits as highly institutionalized forms of activity cannot stand on their own and require more basic activity concepts to account for their genesis.

Georg Simmel begins a completely new strand of thinking with the physical sciences inspired notion of interaction (*Wechselwirkung*) (1908). He introduces this term as a metatheoretical activity concept to think through a wide variety of dialectical, co-constituting social processes. The basic imaginary behind the notion of interaction casts two people acting towards each other in mutual orientation. Examples discussed in detail by Simmel are exchange (1900), competition and other forms of conflict, as well as subordination and super-ordination (1908). Interaction for Simmel has especially two intertwining characteristics. It is "sociating", that is to say that it produces particular forms of social relations which mediate the flow of effects in either direction; it also more or less subtly transforms both interacting parties. Moreover, Simmel envisions how several kinds of interactions can dovetail and how objects fit into interaction. Exchange is a good example for how Simmel reasons about these matters and how the notion of interaction can be usefully deployed to better understand social processes of co-constitution (1900). Possession, a form of interaction with objects shapes both, the thing and its proprietor. In giving up a possession in exchange for something else the two objects in play obtain value. All components of this form of interaction can become objectified in repeated exchange; both proprietors are set in relation to each other; and so as are the goods. Now consider how bringing in money changes the entire character of the exchange and all that participates in it.

A very important dimension of the Simmelian theory of interaction is provided by his transcendental reflections on the conditions for the possibility of interaction to take place in the first place. In keeping with Kantian language he calls the conditions aprioris (1908) and points to three necessary aspects of what I would prefer to call a social imaginary. The first is typification of self, other, and situation, the second is an awareness that the types employed fail to exhaust reality, and the third is a kind of general trust that there is a workable place for the interaction in some vaguely conceived larger social whole.[25] Simmel's concept of interaction bore extraordinary fruit in the work of George Herbert Mead's

[24] Elias too was concerned about the habitus generating powers of status competition. Yet, in his work it works as only one kind of interweaving mechanisms among many others. The similarities in both accounts are as interesting as their respective differences. Suffice it to say here that Elias' concept is wide enough to see that cooperation is as powerful a generator of habitus as competition. Bourdieu on the other hand adds a Cartesian precision and level of self-reflective theorizing which is absent in Elias. This depth is particularly useful where Bourdieu provides to tools to study the self-normalizing tendencies of fields and the symbolic violence they exert on participants (1990).

[25] These three aprioris are not reconcilable with caretaker-infant interaction (e.g. Stern 1984) because they presuppose a fully developed self with linguistic abilities. As such they fail as aprioris in the sense intended by Simmel. However, the Simmelian aprioris can be interpreted fruitfully as dimensions of a social imaginary for fully symbolized social interactions. Yet, since early developmental interactional forms make much use of affect attunement and since they do not simply subside it is clear that Simmel's notion of interaction is fundamentally incomplete even for adult interaction.

theory of self-formation discussed above and through him (as well as directly) on the symbolic interactionism (Blumer 1962) of the second Chicago school.

The theory of dialogue as developed by Martin Buber (1923) and significantly expanded by Mikhail Bakhtin (1929; 1938/1939) offers important depth to the notion of interaction.[26] First it emphasizes the import of the emotive and cognitive attitude with which the other is encountered. As dialogic thinkers show, these attitudes have dramatic consequences for processes of self-development of both participants as well as for the course of the interaction. In particular Buber distinguishes between completely open and closed (objectifying) relationships which Bakhtin labels dialogic and monologic.[27] Second, the theory of dialogue opens an important normative perspective on social interaction. Beyond reiterating that most of what we call ethics lies in the manner of engaging with others it produces an attractive positive vision of what ethical interaction should look like.

Max Weber (1922) is the inventor of the very term social action and made it, in his famous definition of sociology, the proper object of sociological research. Action becomes social for Weber when it is oriented in its intended meaning toward the actions of others. According to Weber understanding the subjective meaning imbued in the action is tantamount to understanding the action in its causes and effects, sociology becomes a discipline engaged in a double resolution hermeneutics: that of the actor and that of the wider context of actions.[28] To help with this task Weber develops an ideal typical framework to reconstruct the subjective meaning of actions that urges its user to differentiate between means-ends rational, value-rational, affective, and traditional motives for action. One of the great strengths of this approach is its effort to think together different modalities of acting, different action logics if you will, fathoming the possibility of ambiguities, ambivalences and even contradictions. Not only does Weber's framework make more room again for pre-nineteenth century Europeanoid notions of rationality but he allows for the integration of habitus and emotions into a thoroughly pluralistic, if you will multi-voiced, or polyphonic analysis of action. It is almost secondary in this regard that he has failed to grasp the ways in which precisely the affective and the traditional modalities of acting can be experiences as profoundly meaningful.

Unfortunately Weber's own efforts at developing a methodology to use his scheme have remained sketchy at best. Worse, perhaps, Weber created very unfortunate misunderstandings by recommending instrumental rationality as the primary measuring device against which actual performance should be measured as deviation.[29] Taking Weber as a starting point, few have done more than Alfred Schütz (1932; Schütz and Luckmann 1984) to elucidate both meaning in action and the challenges to understanding subjective meanings. Critical of Weber's understanding of motives as preceding action, Schütz draws

[26] Bakhtin systematically builds on Buber (Friedman 2001). At this point it is unclear to me, however, whether either Buber or Bakhtin had actually read Simmel's apposite texts and whether they saw themselves developing his notion of interaction further. In a certain sense Simmel's work was prolific but was often received in a piecemeal fashion.

[27] Feminism and postcolonial theory (Fabian 1983) have drawn significantly on a dialogic imaginary. On the monologic/objectifying end of these attitutes there has been something of a common thematic focus and intensive cross-fertilization of ideas emerging from dialogism, a reinvigorated interest in Hegel's notion of recognition (Honneth 1992) a postmarxian Lukacs (1923) inspired interest in processes of objectification (Honneth 2005) and a Freud inspired line thinking of processes of fetishization (Kaplan 2006; Böhme 2006).

[28] This of course includes the possibility that that the interpretation given to an action by a sociologist may deviate significantly from the meaning the actor may have connected with it. The point Weber is making is simply that no matter what the actor may have thought he or she was doing, their intended meaning matters to understand the particular course of action they have taken as other meanings would have putatively led to other actions.

[29] In the lack of a more sophisticated understanding of meaning comes to the fore one of the lacunae of Weber's otherwise so stunning erudition: the complete absence of linguistic knowledge of either the classical historical school of linguistics, of the synchronic linguistics of Saussure or of Peirce's semiotics.

attention to the temporal constitution of meaning during, in, and through the process of acting itself.

Starting in the late 1930s, the terms social action and theory of action became closely associated with Talcott Parsons (1937; respectively Parsons and Shils 1951) and his school. Parsons, more than anybody else after Weber, saw in action the very building block of the social and then also of the psychological and finally of the organismic world (1978). Yet he did not share Weber's hermeneutic approach to the social sciences instead endorsing Durkheim's scientistic vision. Not surprisingly, then, Parsons very self-consciously saw his work as integrating a significantly enriched version of Durkheim's functionalism and Weber's focus on action. The hallmark of Parsons' approach is considering action at the crossroads of what he defines as systems, namely the social system, the cultural system, the behavioral system and the personality system. Any concrete action is for Parsons at the same time understandable as the expression of these systems' interaction as well as a functional operation within these systems aiming to either adapt the systems to the environment, and/or to set the systems' goals (or target values); to either coherently harmonize and integrate the system and/or to latently maintain the system as a structure. Parsons thus furnishes the aspiring analyst with a systematic way to think about action in various kinds of contexts (Alexander 1988).

The last social activity concept I want to discuss briefly is performance and with it the related notion of performativity. It is perhaps not surprising that these concept emerged only after WWII when the experience of mass mediation in cinema, radio and press photography had already become mundane. The extensive use of mass media for propaganda in commerce and politics both in authoritarian and liberal-democratic governance significantly contributed to the development of these concepts (Bernays 1928; Lippmann 1926; Dewey 1927). The concepts of performance and performativity were developed to in the intersection of several theoretical innovations. There was Goffman's (1956) employment of theatrical metaphors to describe the efforts of actors to steer the perception of their actions by others in the right direction. At the same time, the "new rhetoric" (Burke 1950; Perelman and Olbrechts-Tyteca 1952) recovered, once more, the ancient idea that speaking is addressed to particular audiences and crafted in relation to them. Wittgenstein-inspired speech act theory (Austin 1962; Searle 1969), finally argued the two closely related points that speaking can be very often fruitfully understood as acting to achieve a particular effect however elusive its actual attainment may be, and that in fact the combination of a particular speech act, following a particular set of rules whereby a 'scertain set of signs are deployed, and its subsequent uptake by others prompted by the very decoding of these signs, may produce, where successful, the very thing the speech act intended. Austin labeled the successful conjuncture of speech intentions and uptake performativity. Three core ideas are present in all of these theoretical departures: addressivity, the deployment of signs in action, and a decoding of these signs in evaluative reaction. In short, successful performance leads to performativity.[30]

4.3.2.3 Weaknesses and Strengths of Established Social Action Theories

The notions of praxis/practice, habitus/habit, interaction, social action, and performance all contribute significant components to the communal coproduction of seemingly individual activities. Yet, it is unclear how these concepts can be

---

[30] The tracing of ideas is of course an endless business. An alternative but crucially incomplete line of reasoning unfolds from Kant's epistemology (together with Aristotle and Plato the terminus a quo par excellence), to Durkheim's (1907, 1912) pioneering work on the importance of socially derived categories operating as systems of classifying the world; then came the acquisition of these ideas by W. I. Thomas (1928) who thus remembered them for a younger American audience, yet without the important layer of a mediating semiotics to then feed into Merton's notion of self-fulfilling prophecy again sens linquitics. These ideas have since then been recycled a number of times (e.g., Butler, Mckenzie). I have highlighted the rhetorical strand here because the symbolic mediation matters here centrally.

thought together. How would we get from social action and interactions to practices? Worse perhaps, how would we get to institutions, and to that level of analysis that is usually at play when scholars invoke the term social structure? Or how do we understand from within these concepts the dynamics, the historical transformations of the forms of practices, habitus, interactions and social actions? There is nothing in the Simmelian theory of interaction, for example, that explains how local interactions congeal into a transposable form while detailing something like the conditions for the form's reproduction. The Bourdieusian notions of practice and habitus are well articulated for multidimensional processes of status competition taking place within what he calls fields. However, the theory offers next to nothing by way of expanding these notions to other kinds of social processes and institutional arrangements, thus leaving the question of the emergence and transformation of field logics and their wider integration into social life mostly unclear.

Parsons' action theory offers an integrative framework that in spite of its enormous reach, remains fixated on systems' maintaining and integrating processes and is of little use in understanding contradictory pluralities of action logics as well as the temporal dynamics of institutionalization and deinstitutionalization.

The notions of performance and performativity open up an imaginary that points in fruitful directions to remedy some of the problems inherent in other activity concepts. Performance brings back the idea of a double mediation in the nexus between actors: a primary mediation through some symbolic medium and then a secondary medium ranging from stages to TV channels through which primary mediation can become effectively disseminated. Yet, phenomena of both primary and secondary mediation are much wider than envisioned in performance theory. Performativity in turn focuses our attention on the dialectical interplay of activities and their transformation of reality, without, however, providing a satisfying answer on how this transformation works.

In sum, while each concept offers a useful partial perspective, none of them offers much that would allow for their mutual integration into a more comprehensive framework and thus they fall short of the criteria enumarated in part two of this chapter. What is needed, then, is a metatheoretical activity concept that can show any of the social activity concepts discussed as special cases of a more general framework, while making up the gaps I have just pointed to, especially the gaps in internal plurality, scalability and historicity while doing the very best possible to avoid blackboxing. I have developed such a concept over the last years (2011, 2014) and will discuss it now in the final section of this chapter.

4.4 Action-Reaction Effect Sequences

It is the aim of this section to craft a general, loadable, reflexive, and politically as well as ontically fecund concept of action that can draw on what is best in extant activitiy concepts while creating a roadmap for empirical research. It proceeds from a basic, consequently processualist and dialectical account of social life.[31] It assumes that the social exists in the complex flow of actions prompting each other in multiply intersecting and spatially and temporally differentiated ways. Within this model, any action is reaction to a number of temporally prior actions of self and others while at the same time giving rise to a multiplicity of other actions by self and others.[32] One

[31] I have elaborated the following sketch of the model in much greater detail in Glaeser 2011 where I also put it to use in interpreting a major "macro-structural" transformation. I have traced the historical roots of this model in the hermeneutic tradition of social thought in Glaeser 2014.

[32] To avoid misunderstandings: Reaction does not mean reactive. Neither does it imply any other kind of mechanistic response. Reactions can be eminently creative, like the clever repartee in a dialogue. Indeed, creativity lies in what is made of the available pieces in the immediate present or in the more distant past, not in a divine creation ex nihilio. And these pieces are even as memories, understandings etc. ultimately traceable to actions, past and present. When Arendt (1958) leaning on Augustine (395) describes creativity as a capacity for new beginnings I

particularly nasty problem of conceptualizing activities, namely finding proper boundaries demarcating an action, is immediately addressed by this formulation, as any activity can become something determinate only in the reaction by others.[33]

It is important to keep in mind that both the antecedent and consequent actions can have taken/could take place at faraway places and distant times. If so, their effects need to be projectively articulated with the help of socio-technological means of storage and transportation for things, and memory and communication for ideas. Under certain circumstances actions and reactions are repeated in a self-similar manner over a certain stretch of time possibly even by a changing cast of participating actors. If this is the case, they have become regularized and common parlance nominalizes (and by implication objectifies) such a complex of intersecting, self-similar action-reaction chains as *an* institution. Institutionalized webs of action-reaction sequences vary in scope, complexity and temporal staying power from family rituals to the papacy. So here is a very simple and in principle researchable way of seeing structure as activity and activity as structured. The question is now how that self-sameness, how that stability comes about?

An answer to the question of institution formation emerges by first wondering how reactions pick up and respond to antecedent actions and how the concrete temporal form of acting itself comes to be ordered. And here the answer is through the mediation of consciously or unconsciously employed understandings which are discursive, emotive, and/or sensory (including kinesthetic) modalities of differentiating and integrating the world.[34] Through understanding, antecedent actions obtain relevant specificity and perlocutionary force, for example when a gesture registers as threat rather than a greeting, a speech as a call for revolution rather than a mere description of grievances etc. The simultaneous use of a number of understandings of several modes can then provide orientation, direction, and where necessary the means for coordinating and justifying courses of action. In other words understandings can systematically guide, that is structure, activities because they themselves are structured.

Evidently, then, stable reactions can be thought of as prompted and guided by the primary mediation of constant understandings. Hence, the next step in solving the puzzle of institutionalization is to wonder how understandings as self/world mediators become stable. The ordering of activities suggested by understanding is first of all a process, an open-ended flow of differentiation and integration that may originally flow from nothing more than acting itself. And yet, where orderings in action become *validated* in agreement with other human beings (I call this form of validation recognition), where they are confirmed or disconfirmed in the ex post assessment of action success (here I speak of corroboration), or where they fit in or are compatible with already objectified understandings (that is when they begin to resonate), they congeal into more rigid, at the far end even objectified forms. Thus, understand*ing* (continuous verb) becomes *an* understanding (gerund) which as memorized exemplar or abstracted schema hence forth allows for its decontextualized application, which is nothing other than what we more commonly call learning.

And yet once more an answer to the question of institutionalization seems to be simply pushed backward to another level of analysis. And indeed so it is, because we now have to puzzle how validations can become regularized. And here the answer can only be that they must issue from institutionalized sources. Recognitions for example may come forth from a constant source, say the stable character of a friend who reliably praises the same sorts of behavior/understandings and disparages others with the same constancy. But that is to say that the friend is an institution in the sense in which it is defined here, and one is thus forced to admit that there is no ending to this process, that there is no stopping

would respond that what looks like the ability to start something new is better understood as the jiu-jitsu-like art to alter trajectories thanks to the artful triangulation of vectors pointing in all sorts of directions.

[33] See Glaeser 2011, introductory chapter for an extended example. The reasoning here is analogous to Bakhtin's delimination of meaning units in speech (Bakhtin 1953).

[34] Subjective means here merely employed by this actor. Understanding therefore does not imply truth in any objective sense of that word.

point, just seemingly infinite deferment. And indeed I have called this endless deferment institutiosis, in adapting the Peirceian concept of semiosis to institutional analysis. What gives society stability then, are either loops, that is recursive patters or, more importantly, the very inertia caused by the friction involved in the interplay of so many processes which are difficult to orchestrate at will by any one participant.

The two notions of projective articulation and of institutions are the central link between what goes traditionally for micro-analysis and for macro-analysis. Both of these notions can be employed systematically to think through the flow of action effects temporally from sources to consequences, as well as spatially to their distribution between people and institutional domains. If one wants to use these terms at all, macro and micro thus become mere labels for more or less temporally, spatially and domain dispersed action effects.[35]

The mundanely observed fact that actions of one and the same person seem to follow different logics in different contexts as well as the discrpancy that may occur between the actors own understanding of her actions and the understanding that an observer suspects is underlying the actual also appear in a new light. The understandings through which we operate do not only have an ordering dimension but also carry with them an accent of validity which distinguishes them into those that are actualized because they appear valid enough for us to act upon and those which do not. Continuously validated understandings become naturalized; we forget that we could understand differently which is to say that we literally embody these understandings. Now, since validation is situationally variant simply because different people present in different situations differentially validate understandings, because the space resonates with some understandings more than with others and because different situations afford different possibilities for corroborating understandings in action, while different contexts may actualize different understandings hence making us act differently. The upshot of this idea is that we can live quite well and in many modern circumstances *need* to live with contradictory understandings which become actualized differentially, leading quite "naturally" to different action patterns in different contexts.[36]

These deliberations immediately shed light on the notorious issue of structure and agency. If agency is the capability to act, than besides the physical preconditions of time, space and energy, the capability to perform particular actions is dependent on particular actualized understandings of the actor, as well as of the actualized understandings of others whose participation is necessary to complete the act (Austin 1962). In other words, anybody's capability to act is deeply enmeshed with the institutionalized activities of others. Conversely, any institution exists in repeatedly enabled action and thus agency. The opposition between agency and structure is therefore entirely misleading.[37]

The problem of agency articulated in this manner leads to a fresh consideration of power and politics. From the perspective of consequent processualism, politics is a very particular and socially most significant form of activity, namely, as I have already indicated above, the intentional effort to form, maintain or alter institutions of various spatial and temporal depths and import. Since institutions are formed by minimally two but potentially millions of people constituting the

[35] From the perspective of the consequently processualist model presented here it is therefore highly misleading to speak of micro and macro as "levels". It makes no sense to talk, as Coleman (1990) does of "social conditions" causing the micro- phenomenon of frustration. What causes frustration are the concrete actions of concrete others, if potentially many of them and repeatedly, for example competing with ego for few goods, creating price hikes, etc. that is the level of action-reaction effects is never left. To say this is of course not to argue that everything is "micro" which would totally overlook the fact that even single actions can be the consequence of a wide variety of spatially and temporally dispersed actions.

[36] This model therefore allows for a much more nuanced approach to the vexing ambiguity in the results of experiments on cognitive dissonance (Festinger 1957; Petty and Cacioppo 1981). Dissonances can only occur if two contexts actualize the same profiles of understandings. As such the model also provides the resources to think through the "tensions" (*Spannungen*) Weber (1920a, b) thematizes as a major driver of innovation in institution formation and ideas.

[37] For further critiques of this opposition see Bourdieu (1972, 1980) and Sewell (2005).

targeted institution through their actions, the elicitation of support from others is the central axis around which politics revolves. And that axis has two poles. The first is rhetoric that is the style and content of addressing others in speech and other kinds of performances to join in the political project. Apart from naked coercion there is no politics, big and small, without rhetoric (Burke 1950).[38] The second pole of the political axis is organization. It comes into play simply because the elicitation of participation in the constitution of institutions on a larger scale requires many helping hands making use of techniques of projective articulation which need to be coordinated and focused to yield the desired institution forming effect. The hitch is, that organizations themselves are institutions, and a very particular kind at that. What distinguishes them from other institutions is that they have become self-conscious through a dedicated staff of people maintaining and or directing them.[39]

Power is the ability to succeed in politics. That is to say power is potentiated agency; beyond the ability to act it includes the ability to deliver on intentions. This can happen by a whole spectrum of different ways structured by the degree to which the involvement of others proceeds dialogically such that they become in fact fully equal co-politicians, or monologically by subjecting others to some form of control (Glaeser 2013).[40] Power is constituted in different ways in different situations. Indeed, different kinds of institution-forming projects require different capabilities and forms of control.[41] Money is power only if money can buy the kinds of actions required for the institutionalizing project under consideration. Neither is knowledge per se power. Indeed it is important to note, that under certain circumstances knowledge may even be detrimental to the exercise of power, for example if it raises doubts thus undermining the trust in understandings that enable acting (Glaeser 2011). However, situationally specific knowledge can become political knowledge, where it enables an imagination of alternative states, provides understandings concerning the action-reaction effect chains central to the particular institution politically targeted, and where it involves knowledge about how to mobilize the people that need to participate in carrying that institution. Knowledge satisfying all three of these requirements is indeed a constitutive aspect of power.

4.5 Conclusion

The aim to create a unitary, monothetic and universal theory of action for the social sciences is highly misguided both in terms of describing and analyzing social life under particular circumstances as well as for political efforts other than blatantly ideological uses. As the brief historical introduction has shown, different historical constellations characterized by different institutional arrangements and existential, political and economic problematiques have given rise to different activity concepts which highlight different aspect of human action at the expense of others. In retrospect these are not simply false if replaced in the course of time by a newer one. Instead they are merely superseded by new concepts answering to new constellations of institutional arrangements, problems, and intentions. Moreover, the pleading tone with which changing conceptualizations of action are introduced and defended indicates that in activity concepts are often argued

[38] It is no accident, therefore, that the art of rhetoric as a self-conscious practice bloomed first in participatory politics of the ancient Greek poleis and in Republican Rome. Accordingly within the Europeanoid tradition Aristotle's *On Rheotoric* and Cicero's *Orator* have become the defining texts.

[39] This has very interesting consequences. As institutions organizations require a self-politics to maintain them for the purposes of engaging in target politics. That creates all sorts of interesting problems concerning the relationship between both kinds of politics. Many of the problems and frustrations commonly seen in politics are closely related to conflicts between target politics and self politics. Pioneers in the field of political organization had to wait for mass-modernity to appear. The most important first generation encompasses Lenin (1902), Michels (1911). and Weber (1922).

[40] Control efforts can have rather interesting ironic effect in that they produce the illusion of power while actually undermining it.

[41] For a discussion of the ironies such control efforts can produce see Glaeser 2013.

against other more or less explicit action logics that is against a plurality of understandings in play within a local context.

If the search for a substantively rich, unitary and monothetic activity concept valid for human beings in all historically extant social configurations is misguided at least for those purposes traditionally avowed in the social sciences, we should instead look for a metatheoretical activity concept which is configurable in many different ways, and that can work as a formidable search tool to develop culturally and historically sensitive notions of action for specific domains of social life while satisfying the four criteria of appropriateness which I have discussed begun this chapter. With the consequently processualist notion of multiply intersecting action-reaction effect chains I have provided such a metatheoretical concept. By comparison with other notions it is low in metaphysical commitments beyond arguing that social world, including institutions, that is the more stable parts, crucially exists in the actions of people; that people act mostly in response to the actions of others and in doing so configure and reconfigure their multi-modal understandings that mediate their relationship with the world by simultaneously integrating and differentiating it from their particular vantage point. There is no commitment in this model to a particular kind of discursivity (and hence rationality), no need to posit emotionality as enactment of universal basic emotions, and no urge to limit sensing to universal schemes. Instead the model asks researchers to tease out the relevant features of the social world by using the model as a guide to ask questions about it. Thus, social thought and empirical research about social life can once more open themselves to the full plasticity of human beings which might have empowering consequences for the political imagination.

References

Alexander, J. (1988). *Action and its environments: Towards a new synthesis*. New York: Columbia University Press.

Archer, M. (1995). *Realist social theory: The morphogenetic approach*. Cambridge: Cambridge University Press.

Archer, M., Bhaskar, R., Collier, A., Lawson, T., & Norrie, A. (1998). *Critical realism: Essential readings*. London: Routledge.

Arendt, H. (1958). *The human condition*. Chicago: University of Chicago Press.

Aristotle. (322BCEa [2011]). *Nicomachean Ethics*. In R. C. Bartlett, & S. Collins (Trans.). Chicago: The University of Chicago Press.

Aristotle. (322BCEb (1998]). *Politics*. In C. D. C. Reeve (Trans.). Indianapolis: Hackett.

Austin, J. L. (1962). *How to do things with words*. Cambridge: Harvard University Press.

Avineri, S. (1968). *The social and political thought of Karl Marx*. Cambridge: Cambridge University Press.

Bakhtin, M. (1929 [1984]). *Problems of Dostoevsky's poetics*. Minneapolis: University of Minnessota Press.

Bakhtin, M. (1929 [1984]). *Problems of Dostoevsky's poetics*. Minneapolis: University of Minnessota Press.

Bentham, J. (1823 [1988]). *An introduction to the principles of morals and legislation*. Amherst: Prometheus Books.

Bernays, E. (1928 [2004]). *Propaganda*. New York: Ig Publishing.

Bhaskar, R. (1979). *The possibility of realism*. Brighton: Harvester Press.

Blumer, G. (1962 [1969]). *Symbolic interactionism*. Englewood Cliffs: Prentice Hall.

Böhme, H. (2006). *Fetischismus und Kultur: Eine Andere Theorie der Moderne*. Berlin: Rowohlt.

Bourdieu, P. (1972 [1977]). *Outline of a theory of practice*. Cambridge: Cambridge University Press.

Bourdieu, P. (1980 [1990]). *The logic of practice*. Stanford: Stanford University Press.

Buber, M. (1923 [1999]). *Ich und Du*. Gütersloh: Gütersloher Verlagshaus.

Burke, K. (1950). *A rhetoric of motives*. Berkeley: University of California Press.

Coleman, J. (1990). *Foundations of social theory*. Cambridge: Harvard University Press.

Comte, A. (1844 [1988]). *Introduction to positive philosophy*. Indianapolis: Hackett.

Daston, L., & Gallison, P. (2010). *Objectivity*. New York: Zone Books.

Dewey, J. (1922). *Human nature and conduct: An introduction to social psychology*. New York: Henry Holt.

Dewey, J. (1927 [1954]). *The Public and its Problems*. Athens: University of Ohio Press.

Dumont, L. (1983 [1986]). *Essays on individualism: Modern ideology in anthropological perspective*. Chicago: University of Chicago Press.

Durkheim, E. (1893 [1997]). *The division of labor in society*. New York: Free Press.

Durkheim, E. (1895 [1982]). *Rules of sociological method*. New York: Free Press.

Durkheim, E. (1897 [1951]). *Suicide: A sociological study*. Glencoe: Free Press.

Elder-Vass, D. (2010). *The causal power of social structures: Emergence, structure and agency*. Cambridge: Cambridge University Press.

Elias, N. (1935 [1976]). *Über den Prozeß der Zivilisation*. Frankfurt: Suhrkamp.

Elias, N. (1969). *Die höfische Gesellschaft*. Frankfurt: Suhrkamp.

Fabian, J. (1983). *Time and the other: How anthropology makes its object*. New York: Columbia University Press.

Friedman, M. (1953). The methodology of positive economics. In *Essays in positive economics* (pp. 3–43). Chicago: University of Chicago Press.

Friedman, M. (2001). Martin Buber and Mikhail Bakhtin: The dialogue of voices and the word that is spoken. *Religion & Literature, 33*(3), 25–36.

Glaeser, A. (2011). *Political epistemics: The secret police, the opposition, and the end of east German socialism*. Chicago: University of Chicago Press.

Glaeser, A. (2014). Hermeneutic institutionalism: Towards a new synthesis. *Qualitative Sociology, 37*(2), 207–241.

Glaeser, A. (2015). Theorizing the present ethnographically. In D. Boyer, J. Faubion, & G. Marcus (Eds.), *Theory can be more than it used to be: Learning anthropology's method in a time of transition*. Ithaca: Cornell University Press.

Goffman, E. (1956 [1959]). *The presentation of self in everyday life*. New York: Anchor Books.

Herder, J. G. (1784–1791 [2002]). *Ideen zu einer Philosophie der Geschichte der Menschheit*. München: Hanser.

Hobbes, T. (1651 [1994]). *Leviathan or the matter, form and power of commonwealth, ecclesiastical and civil*. Indianapolis: Hackett.

Honneth, A. (1992). *Kampf um Anerkennung: Zur moralischen Grammatik sozialer Konflikte*. Frankfurt: Suhrkamp.

Honneth, A. (2005). *Verdinglichung*. Frankfurt: Suhrkamp.

James, W. (1890). *Principles of psychology*. New York: Henry Holt.

Jevons, W. S. (1871 [1956]). The theory of political economy. In J. R. Newman (Ed.), *From the world of mathematics: Volume two* (pp. 1217–1237). New York: Simon and Schuster.

Kaplan, L. (2006). *Cultures of fetishism*. New York: Palgrave Macmillan.

Lenin, V. I. (1902 [1969]). *What is to be done? Burning questions of our movement*. Moscow: International Publishers.

Lippmman, W. (1926 [1997]). *Public opinion*. New York: Free Press.

Locke, J. (1689a [1960]). The second treatise on government. In P. Laslett (Ed.), *Two treatises of government* (pp. 265–428). Cambridge: Cambridge University Press.

Locke, J. (1689b [1983]). In J. H. Tully (Ed.) and (W. Popple, Trans.), *A letter concerning toleration* [Epistola de Toleratia] Indianapolis: Hackett.

Lukacs, G. (1923). Die Verdinglichung und das Bewußtsein des Proletariats. In *Geschichte und Klassenbewußtsein*. Berlin: Malik Verlag.

Luther, M. (1520 [1990]). Von der Freiheit eines Christenmenschen. In K. Bornkamm & G. Ebeling (Eds.), *Schriften*, Frankfurt: Insel.

Marcus, G. E., & Fischer, M. M. J. (1986). *Anthropology as cultural critique: An experimental moment in the human sciences*. Chicago: University of Chicago Press.

Marcuse, H. (1941 [1999]). *Reason and revolution: Hegel and the rise of social theory*. New York: Humanity Books.

Marx, K. (1845 [1973]). Thesen über Feuerbach. In *Marx-Engels Werke, volume three* (pp. 3–7). Berlin: Dietz.

Marx, K., & Engels, F. (1846). Die Deutsche Ideologie. In *Marx-Engels werke: Volume three* (pp. 9–530). Berlin: Dietz.

Mauss, M. (1938 [1985]). The category of the person. In M. Carrithers, S. Collins, & S. Lukes (Eds.), *Essays on Marcel Mauss' the category of the person*. Cambridge: Cambridge University Press.

Mead, G. H. (1934). *Mind, self, and society*. Chicago: University of Chicago Press.

Menger, C. (1871). *Grundsätze der Volkswirtschaftslehre*. Wien: Baumüller.

Michels, R. (1911 [1957]). *Zur Soziologie des Parteiwesens in der modernen Demokratie: Untersuchungen über die oligarchischen Tendenzen des Gruppenlebens*. Stuttgart: Kröner.

Mill, J. S. (1863 [2002]). *Utilitarianism*. Indianapolis: Hackett.

Parsons, T. (1937). *The structure of social action*. New York: Free Press.

Parsons, T. (1978). A paradigm of the human condition. In *Action theory and the human condition* (pp. 352–433). New York: Free Press.

Parsons, T., & Shils, E. (Eds.). (1951 [2008]). *Towards a general theory of action*. New Brunswick: Transaction Publishers.

Perelman, C., & Olbrechts-Tyteca, L. (1952 [1979]). *The new rhetoric: A treatise on argumentation*. South Bend: University of Notre Dame Press.

Petty, R. E., & Cacioppo, J. T. (1981 [1996]). *Attitudes and persuasion: Classic and contemporary approaches*. Boulder: Westview.

Reddy, W. M. (2001). *The navigation of feeling: A framework for the history of emotions*. Cambridge: Cambridge University Press.

Rousseau, J-J. (1762 [1997]). *The social contract and other later political writings*. Cambridge: Cambridge University Press.

Samuelson, P. (1938). A note on the pure theory of consumers' behaviour. *Economica, 5*(17), 61–71.

Sawyer, K. R. (2005). *Social emergence: Societies as complex systems*. Cambridge: Cambridge University Press.

Schiavone, A. (2012). *The invention of the law in the West*. Cambridge: Harvard University Press.

Schneewind, J. B. (1998). *The invention of autonomy: A history of modern moral philosophy*. Cambridge: Cambridge University Press.

Schütz, A. (1932 [1981]). *Der sinnhafte Aufbau der sozialen Welt: Eine Einleitung in die verstehende Soziologie*. Frankfurt: Suhrkamp.

Schütz, A., & Luckmann, T. (1984). *Strukturen der Lebenswelt* (Vol. 2). Suhrkamp: Frankfurt.

Searle, J. (1969). *Speech acts: An essay in the philosophy of language*. Cambridge: Cambridge University Press.

Seigel, J. (2005). *The idea of the self: Thought and experience in western Europe since the seventeenth century*. Cambridge: Cambridge University Press.

Sewell, W. (2005). *The logic of action*. Chicago: University of Chicago Press.

Siedentop, L. (2014). *Inventing the individual: The origins of western liberalism*. Cambridge: Harvard University Press.

Simmel, G. (1900 [1989]). *Philosophie des Geldes*. Gesamtausgabe Band 6. Frankfurt: Suhrkamp.

Simmel, G. (1908 [1988]). *Soziologie*. Frankfurt: Suhrkamp.

Spinoza, B. (1677 [2007]). *Theological-political treatise*. Cambridge: Cambridge University Press.

Stern, D. (1985). *The interpersonal world of the infant. A view from psychoanalysis and developmental psychology*. New York: Basic Books.

Taylor, C. (1989). *Sources of the self: The making of modern identity*. Cambridge: Harvard University Press.

Tomasello, M. (2014). *A natural history of human thinking*. Cambridge: Harvard University Press.

Vaihinger, H. (1922). *Die philosophie des als ob. System der theoretischen, praktischen und religiösen Fiktionen der Menschheit auf Grund eines idealistischen Positivismus. Mit einem Anhang über Kant und Nietzsche*. Leizig: Felix Meiner.

Vico, G. (1999 [1744]). In D. Marsh (Trans.) *New science: Principles of the new science concerning the common nature of nations*. London: Penguin.

Vygotsky, L. (1986). *Thought and language* (Rev. ed. by A. Kozulin). Cambridge: MIT Press.

Wacquant, L., & Bourdieu, P. (1992). *An invitation to reflexive sociology*. Chicago: The University of Chicago Press.

Weber, M. (1904 [1988]). Die Objektivität sozialwissenschaftlicher Erkenntnis. In *Gesammelte Aufsätze zur Wissenschaftslehre* (pp. 146–214). Tübingen: J.C.B. Mohr (Siebeck).

Weber, M. (1920b [1988]). Zwischenbetrachtung. In *Gesammelte Aufsätze zur Religionssoziologie: Volume 1* (pp. 536–573). Tübingen: J.C.B. Mohr (Siebeck).

Weber, M. (1922 [1984]). *Wirtschaft und Gesellschaft*. Tübingen: J.C.B. Mohr (Siebeck).

Weber, M. (1920a [1988]). Vorbemerkung. In *Gesammelte Aufsätze zur Religionssoziologie*: *Volume 1* (pp. 1–16). Tübingen: J.C.B. Mohr (Siebeck).

Wittgenstein, L. (1952 [1984]). Philosophische Untersuchungen. In *Collected works*: *Volume one* (pp. 225–620). Frankfurt: Suhrkamp.

Interactionism: Meaning and Self as Process

5

Iddo Tavory

5.1 Introduction

It is a sociological truism that human reality is shaped socially. While biology surely plays a role in our development and the capacities we have, such capacities are molded by the human world we live in. As Berger and Luckmann (1967) once put it, there is no natural "human world" the way that we can think about the world of mice, bees or zebras. People are shaped by meaning, and this meaning is socially constructed. That much we know. But what does it mean to say that people, and meanings, are socially constructed?

The core insight of symbolic interactionism lies in a deceptively simple point: that both meanings and selves are made through interaction: in the ordinary back and forth of social intercourse with others. What makes this insight radical is thus not so much its assumption that the human world is socially constructed (what sociologist would argue with that?), but the insight that the meanings into which we are inculcated are constantly negotiated in interaction. Rather than a "social" that stands outside and beyond us, meanings are constantly being shaped and reshaped in concrete situational settings.

The philosophical roots of this interactional tradition lie in the pragmatist school of American philosophy. From its very inception in the work of Charles S. Peirce in the late nineteenth century, pragmatists argued that meanings were in constant flux. Rather than the frozen picture of European semiotics (de Saussure [1916] 1986), the American tradition saw that meanings are shaped within actual situations, as actors navigate the challenges of the day to day. Thus, Peirce's work already prefigures two of the most important loci of interactionist theory: the ongoing flux of meaning in ordinary pragmatic action, and way that the situation shapes such ongoing action.

But even more important than Peirce was the work of G. H. Mead, a Chicago philosopher whose posthumous (1934) series of lectures *Mind Self and Society* influenced a generation of sociologists that fashioned interactionism as a discrete intellectual project. Mead's lectures centered around the social sources and development of the human self. As Mead argued, humans come to have a distinct notion of their selves (which cats, for example, just don't have) through the reflexive incorporation of others' perspectives. We are not only socialized into society, but become humans through it. Without others, there cannot be a self.

This process, for Mead, is dynamic. We constantly act and see our actions through the lenses of our socialized self. It is in this back and forth of action and reflexivity that human existence comes into being and through which we shape

I. Tavory (✉)
New York University, New York, NY, USA
e-mail: iddo.tavory@nyu.edu

S. Abrutyn (ed.), *Handbook of Contemporary Sociological Theory*,
Handbooks of Sociology and Social Research, DOI 10.1007/978-3-319-32250-6_5

our world. In this, Mead's philosophy gave theoretical meat to an influential idea that an early Chicago sociologist, Charles Horton Cooley (1902), has called "the looking glass self"—that the way we understand ourselves is always mediated by the way we think others understand us.

As a sociological perspective, however, the study of interaction needed to move beyond philosophical abstractions and into the realm of the empirical. The person who is credited with doing so, and who coined the term "Symbolic Interactionism" was Herbert Blumer, a Chicago-trained sociologist who was Mead's student and research assistant, and who took over his course on Social Psychology when Mead became too ill to teach (see Huebner 2014).

Blumer became, both intellectually and organizationally, the most important figure in the development of interactionism. First, in training cohorts of students at Chicago—where he and his colleague Everett C. Hughes made an indelible impression upon students such as Erving Goffman, Anselm Strauss, Howard Becker, Fred Davis and others. Later, he also built up the department of sociology at Berkeley, which, again, was to become an important intellectual center.

But perhaps the main force of Blumer's symbolic interactionist insight was its theoretical simplicity. Blumer (1937, 1969: 2) set up three tenets of interactionism. First, that "human beings act toward things on the basis of the meanings that the things have for them"; second, that the "meaning of such things is derived from, or arises out of, the social interaction that one has with one's fellows"; and last, that "meanings are handled in, and modified through, an interpretive process used by the person in dealing with the things he encounters." And there you have it, the tenets of interactionism, from which a deluge of research has subsequently emerged.

But, simple as it sounds, there are a few important assumptions and assertions that work their way into this definition. Assumptions that, as I will show throughout this chapter, set up both interactionism's incredible strength, but also its moments of blindness.

First, the symbolic interactionist approach that Blumer crafted centers on interaction as a medium that lies between people. And though this may sound obvious (after all, this is what interaction implies), it means that rather than looking at the personal characteristics of people who enter interaction, it is more important to focus on what actually happens in it. That is, the unit of analysis in interactionism is what Blumer (following another one of his teachers, Robert Park) called "the collective act." Interaction deals with relations, not so much with attributes.

Closely related, a second tenet that emerges from the interactionist definition above is the importance of the situation. People negotiate meaning not in the abstract, but in actual concrete situations. In this, Blumer was harkening back to the early work of D.S. Thomas and W. I. Thomas' (1928), the only sociologists who presented something that others recognized as "a theorem"—"If men [sic] define situations as real, they are real in their consequences." The situation, then, is the key arena for interactionists.

The third is the assumption that works its way into the "symbolic" part of symbolic interactionism. Based on Mead, but also drawing on the work of German sociologist Georg Simmel, Blumer assumed that the relevant facets of communication and self were symbolic—that is, meanings turned into words. Rather than the kind of conversation of gestures that most animals are able to enact, the kinds of meanings that Blumer stressed were those that could be turned into words. The realm of embodiment and emotion did not figure prominently in this vision of interactionism.

Lastly, there is no simple link between method and theory (Meltzer et al. 1973). Interactionism received different interpretations, from postmodernist renditions in which all reality is fluid (Denzin 1992) and selves endlessly shifting and protean (Lifton 1993), to a positivist rendering that used a 20-question personality questionnaire to work through the formation of selves (Kuhn 1964), and social psychological experimentation (e.g. Stets and Burke 2000; Heise 1986). And yet, in the main, theory in this case did select for a method. Following Blumer, most interactionists agree that if we are interested in the ways in which people collectively make meaning in interaction in concrete situations, then it would be a good idea to look at what these interactional moments look like. If we try to take shortcuts through statistical analysis of survey responses, or even through interviews, we would lose the processual nature of meaning. We will take frozen reflections, and substitute them for the fluid realm of emergent meaning. Interactionism, then, became identified with ethnographic methods. If you want to understand the situation, you had better be there.

5.2 Research Projects

While the precepts above provide a general theoretical orientation to symbolic interactionism, the proof is in the pudding. What made interactionism into a prominent intellectual position were the research projects that it engendered. And although there is a vast number of interactionist-inspired empirical projects, we can identify three important paradigmatic research traditions: one focused on patterned transformations of self, one on the patterning of situational outcomes, and one on the emergence and ongoing construction of collectives.

5.2.1 Patterns of Self: "Becoming a..."

Perhaps the best known interactionist research tradition centers on the construction of recognizable social characters—things like "the criminal," "the pothead" or "the bureaucrat." Here, we start from G. H. Mead's idea that the self develops socially, as we learn to take on the perspective of the group we take part in. Seen from this perspective, the self is best thought of as an ongoing process. Since the groups we take part in are constantly changing, the self is never completely congealed. We are never "finished" products, always in the process of becoming. The sociological project that emerges out of this insight asks how we then end up with social types: with people who do not only do certain things, but that also, we think, *are* certain things.

To understand why this was a radical research project it is useful to think about "deviance," the array of unsanctioned behaviors and social types. Take, for example, teenage delinquents. One way to think about delinquency—say, vandalism, some violence and light drug use—is that the people who engage in these activities are "naturally" deviant. That is, that there is something wrong about them, either psychologically, or, who knows, perhaps even biologically.

But if we take an interactionist perspective, the contours of the question radically change. Instead of asking about what these people "are" we ask about the process in which they are defined in such a way. Rather than thinking about deviance and deviants as natural objects, we think about it as an interactionally emergent "career"—not something that naturally happens, but something that is negotiated; rather than a state of being, it become re-conceptualized as an accomplishment.

One of the best examples of this form of research is Howard Becker's (1953) early and celebrated paper on "Becoming a Marijuana User." In an era in which smoking pot was seen as a dangerous criminal activity done by depraved individuals, Becker flipped the question. Rather than asking about personal characteristics, he asked how people become successful pot smokers. His answer, based on research with Jazz musicians and quite a bit of introspection, was that in order to become a smoker one needs to learn three things. The successful pothead needs to learn the techniques (e.g. how long to keep the smoke in; how to roll a joint); they then need to learn to recognize the physical effects as the effects of the drug (e.g. you aren't just very hungry, you have the munchies; you aren't simply confused, you're high); and one needs to learn that these physical effects are actually enjoyable—which isn't completely obvious since the effects themselves are ambiguous.

Each of these phases (especially in pre-internet days) needed to be interactionally negotiated. Smokers learn to smoke from someone, learn about the effects, and are told not to "stress it" and let themselves enjoy the sensations. In Becker's telling, becoming a pothead is an interactionally emergent accomplishment.

This form of sociological explanation has not only intellectual, but also political stakes. Think back, for example, on the example of the "juvenile delinquent." Interactional sociology (under the banner of "labeling theory", see Becker 1963) argued that becoming a juvenile delinquent was not so much about the acts, but about how they were interactionally interpreted and labeled. Thus, when the author of this chapter was caught once upon a time defacing his whole high school with Graffiti, he was told off, given a brush, and told to re-paint the school. He never became a "delinquent." It was considered a youthful folly more than anything else. But, of course, in many schools—especially in disadvantaged neighborhoods—the police would immediately be involved, a criminal record opened, and a definition of the actor as "delinquent" would emerge. The vague "primary deviance" (the actual act) would turn into a definition of the person (see Lemert 1967). The passage from an action to a definition of self is socially negotiated.

Of course, it is not only "deviants" who solidify their identity in interaction. After he was done with Marijuana users Howard Becker's (Becker et al. 1961) next project took him, and a bunch of colleagues, to a medical school. As part of their study they found something that may not surprise students reading this text: that becoming a student is also a negotiated accomplishment. Students, as they show, often came into the school truly wanting to learn. However, they soon found out that what matters for their future residency is mostly their grades, not how much they challenged themselves intellectually. Talking to each other about ways to "game the system," they quickly shift their group perspective. Rather than focusing on what most interested them, they focused on courses that would assure them better grades—courses and professors known as "easy As." Becoming a student, although far from a deviant identity, is a processual accomplishment.

5.2.2 Situational Patterns: Institutional Constraints and Actors' Pragmatics

The second important line of search that emerged through interactionism focuses on the situation itself. Rather than taking the emergence and patterned transformation of selves as its point of departure, it asks how the interactional dynamics of specific situations are patterned. In doing so, this line of research addresses one of the recurrent problems of interactionism, to which we will return below: where do stable patterns come from? If we assume that meanings are fluid and made in specific situations, how can we explain the recurrence of recognizable outcomes? Why do things tend to happen in predictable ways?

In order to answer this question through an interactional perspective, interactional researchers needed to make a few simplifying assumptions. First, as true pragmatists, they assume that people are practical problem-solvers. They usually enter situations with a general idea of what they want to happen in it. On the other hand, for both organizational and historical reasons, the situations are already constructed in ways that predate the actors. Given the management of these two constraints, interactionists show, actors land upon predictable emergent solutions that give these situation their recurrent character (Rock 1979).

A classic example of this interactionist research project can be seen in the work of Fred Davis, one of Herbert Blumer's students at Chicago. In one of his early articles, Davis shows how the interaction between taxi drivers and their clients take on a predictable form. The pragmatics of the situation are quite simple: the taxi driver needs to know what "kind of" client they have. If it is a newcomer to town, they might be able to make an extra buck by taking them for a longer ride than is necessary. The interaction is also very short, and probably never repeated. We don't usually get the same taxi driver again and again. The client, on the other hand, finds herself in a fleeting interaction with a person with whom they are in close proximity, but will probably never see again. And this, too, gives rise to predictable interactional patterns.

On the driver's side, as Davis shows, the situation comes to mean that they—like others in businesses that depend on fleeting interactions—end up with a system of classification that uses superficial traits of the clients to guide their interaction. This is true for drivers, but also for waiters, air hosts, and other such professions. For clients, it was the fleeting nature of the interaction that was of utmost importance. On the one hand, the pragmatics of the situation is such that they might tell the driver secrets that they would perhaps not divulge to even their closest friends. On the other hand, they can engage in behaviors that they would never engage in with someone they would have more than a fleeting interaction with: making out with a partner, or changing clothes. These two negotiated reactions—extreme intimacy and complete disregard—as Davis shows, stem from the same institutional structure: that the interaction is so fleeting that the driver can be seen as a "non-person."

A second, and a bit more morbid, example comes from the research of death and dying. As Glaser and Strauss argued in a series of publications (1964, 1965), people who had terminal illness in America faced predictable circumstances. Doctors, at that time, were not obligated to inform patients of their condition. And, obviously, they had quite a bit of information, whereas the patient had very little to go on. As they show, since doctors wanted to make their treatment as smooth as possible, they wanted to avoid a conversation in which they confronted their patients regarding their impending death. What it amounted to was a coalition of caretakers hiding the situation from the patients. Doctors, nurses, but also often the families of patients, colluded to create a "closed awareness context," in which the patient was not aware of their situations although everyone else around them knew they were dying. As Glaser and Strauss then showed, as the hospitalization and the disease progressed, the parties engaged in a delicate choreography of awareness contexts—in some situations, the reality of impending death would be revealed, but in most cases it wouldn't. And, as not to destroy the fabric of the situation, patients who strongly suspected that they were going to die kept on performing, thus creating a predictable situation in which all parties know of the coming death, but where they all keep a pretense of an optimistic diagnosis.

Sometimes, the institutional structure is manifested even more concretely, physically inscribed in the situation. To see how this works, we can take the case of racial classification, one of the most pernicious recurrences of our times. How does such classification emerge interactionally? Shouldn't we trace it back to people's attitudes and stereotypes? As in the "becoming a…" project outlined above, interactionists tend to be cautious about assuming such attitudes. It isn't that attitudes don't exist, but that there are important elements of the situation that give rise to forms of classification even when the people involved in enacting the classification do not use racial stereotypes.

In a first example, Phil Goodman shows how officers who process inmates end up assigning them to predefined racial groups. As the officers work with documents they need to fill, they need to know where to house the inmates. Thus, ethnicity becomes omni-relevant as a way to organize people's lives in interaction. See the following conversation (Goodman 2008: 759):

Officer:	Race?
Inmate:	Portuguese.
Officer:	Portuguese? [pause] You mean White?
Inmate:	Nah, I'm Portuguese, not White.
Officer:	Sure, but who do you house with?
Inmate:	Usually with the "Others."
Officer:	We don't fuck with that here. It's just Black, White, or Hispanic.
Inmate:	Well, I'm Portuguese.
	Second officer, looking on the whole time: Put him with the Negros, then ["Negro" pronounced in Spanish].
Inmate:	What?!
Second officer:	Oh, now you're serious, huh. So you want to house with the Whites, do you?
Inmate:	Fine, with the Whites.
Officer:	OK, with the Whites it is.

What is going here? Are the officers simply racist? The answer, in an interactional vein, is not so simple. The officers have a practical aim: they need to process people as quickly as possible. After all, there is a long line to prison, especially in California, where Goodman conducted his research. In order to process inmates they need to fill in a form that says where inmates should be housed. At some point, probably because of inter-gang conflict in prison (but maybe also because they held racial stereotypes), someone decided that inmates should be housed according to their race. This decision was then codified into a seemingly small detail of the situation—a box that needs to be checked. But this little box powerfully channels and shapes the meanings that people can craft. In the example above, the inmate doesn't want to be put into a box, he is Portuguese, an "other" in his own self-definition. But in the California prison, there are no "others." And so he must decide between the given categories. And although he might be able to assign himself into multiple categories, the officer pressures him to self classify. Without anyone in the situation being racist, a racist outcome emerges.

Similarly, Kameo and Whalen (2015) show that because 911 call-takers need to send the police a form that includes the suspect's race, the operative ends up putting pressure on the caller to identify the "race" of the suspect, even when the caller didn't use racial classifications as part of their description. Race becomes salient through interaction, as the pragmatics of the situation—here codified in forms—propels the dispatcher to pressure the caller to make race into a salient marker of personhood.

In sum, the "situational pragmatics" project sets out to show how recurrent patterns are built up from the situation. It is not that the wider social structure doesn't matter. The wider historical and institutional context sets up the kinds of constraints and affordances of the situation. But once set up, outcomes tend to become uncannily similar. The world is made predictable one situation at a time.

5.2.3 Patterns of Collectivity

Whereas the first stream of research outlined above begins with the self and the second is primarily about the patterning of situations, the third is primarily about the emergence of collective life in the process. That is, even if we know something about how selves arise, and how situations are structured, we may understand relatively little about how groups take shape. And, for sociologists, this is obviously an important question.

By and large, there are two interactionist attempts to answer this question. The first, led by sociologist Gary Alan Fine (see, e.g. 1979, 1998, 2012), focuses on the emergence of small group cultures, what he called an "idioculture." The insight fueling this agenda is that in order to understand any collectivity, we need to understand how they come to develop and share a symbolic universe. The image that emerges through Fine's work is that of a bottom-up process of emergence. As people hang out together over an extended period of time they begin to share a history, a set of memories, shared future projects, jokes, and even linguistic terms. A collectivity, in this reading, is made of the congealed set of meanings and ties within small aggregations of people. The social world writ large, in this reading, is the sum of these small groups and their relationships.

To understand the utility of this notion, think of the smallest idiocultural unit—the one that emerges between two people, say a dating couple. After a while, the couple does not only share jokes and stories (the common refrain "you should have been there…" may be the first sign of an emerging idioculture), but also ways of being together, and even new terms and shorthand expressions that are completely opaque to others (see also Bernstein 1964). And, like the model of the couple, we can begin thinking of cliques, of the idioculture that congeals when people are engaged in shared work or leisure activities (Fine's first noted example of idioculture-construction was the little-league baseball team).

Importantly, this way to interactionally theorize collectivities is slightly suspicious of any talk of "Society" or of "Culture" if they are thought of in an all-encompassing sense. Meanings do congeal, and aren't completely malleable once they are set. Yet they congeal in specific and concrete interactional contexts. The study of small groups, in this reading, is the study of society in miniature (Stolte et al. 2001).

The second stream of research, spearheaded by writers such as Tamotsu Shibutani, Anselm Strauss and Howard Becker (all students of Blumer from his Chicago days) takes a different approach. Rather than beginning with the small group, it starts with the social organization of activity—with the collective act. As Shibutani (1955) put it in an early and influential article, a social world is "a universe of regularized mutual response." That is, it is a plurality of actors organized around a shared activity, where the actions of one set of actors in this world affects, and is expected to affect, others who are engaged in different aspects of the same activity (see also Strauss 1978).

The image emerging here is perhaps more amenable to a macro-oriented approach. If the idiocultural approach imagines a world made of the intersection and emergence of a multitude of small groups, the social worlds perspective imagines the world as made of a multitude of actors, through whose actions specific arenas of activity emerge. It is a visualization that looks a lot more like a network-image than like the budding idiocultures of Fine's analysis. This is still, however, a deeply interactionist vision. The focus is on the concrete activity and the ways actors practically affect each other's actions, and therefore the way to circumscribe the activity is quite different than the way we usually do so.

Thus, for example, Becker's (1982a) Art Worlds takes a social worlds perspective to the study of art. In doing so, Becker makes a deceptively simple point. Usually when people think about art worlds they imagine a world made by the artists, sometimes the consumers of art. But as Becker begins with the collective act of art, a different set of protagonists emerges—these include the artists, but also include the people who install the art in the museum, those who make and sell the canvases and paints, the guards and cashiers at the museum, etc. By beginning with the concrete activity, then, a social worlds perspective gives one a very different view of life than if we would think about them as "fields" or "professions." Rather than the rarefied few, we must, as Becker puts it (1982a: 34) incorporate "all the people whose activities are necessary to the production of the characteristic works which that world, and perhaps others as well, define as art."

5.3 Interactionism: Challenges and Developments

Like all intellectual traditions, Interactionism has had its challenges. These can be parsed out into different clusters. First, for many sociologists, the focus on the situation seemed to induce blindness to questions of power and inequality. In being locked in an "occasionalist illusion" as Bourdieu (1977: 81) once called it, interactionists (so the argument goes) ignored the weight of structural injustice. In other words, since Blumer's definition of interactionism places its emphasis on what occurs within situations, we could forget both that (a) situations are already set up in uneven ways, and that; (b) actors' ability to navigate these situations may not be evenly distributed.

Closely connected to this critique is what theorists used to think of as "the micro-macro problem." As interactionists think about concrete situations, they seem to necessarily think of micro-contexts of action. What of larger structures that are the bread and butter of sociology—what of the state? What of world capitalism? This micro-macro critique also had an additional correlate: that interactionism is largely blind to culture. In its focus on the construction of meaning in the interactional context, it seems to overlook widely shared sets of meanings and ways of doing things. For many research questions, so the argument goes, specific situations are little more than instantiations of wider patterns of meaning. Looking at the situation, then, is looking at precisely the wrong place.

Lastly, critiques have also arisen from other micro-sociological traditions, with some phenomenologically-inclined sociologists of the body being wary of what seems to be a deep cognitive bias in interactionism. The gist of the argument here is that the *symbolic* in symbolic interactionism elevates deliberation and language as the key sites where meanings are made. What, however, of emotion? What of embodiment? Should sociologists only study purposeful meaningful action, or should they also take careful stock of pre-conceptual, embodied, behaviors that also tend to be socially patterned?

I would like to propose that although interactionism has its share of problems, critics have been usually barking at the wrong tree. Thus, to take the set of studies already outlined above, it already becomes clear that the research traditions that stem from interactionism are far from blind to the ways in which the situation is set up. That 911-call dispatchers need to fill in a box that tells the police what is the suspect's race is crucial; that doctors hold the information and the patient none at all sets up the entire research program on awareness contexts in dying. When laws that mandate disclosure were set the situation deeply changed. Power, in the interactionist tradition, comes from the uneven institutionalization of situations.

Of course, a critic can argue that it is crucial for sociologists to trace how unequal situational footing developed in just these ways. But, interactionists could retort, this is simply not the project they outlined for themselves. Interactionism never claimed that power did not exist on a macro-level, or that tracing the history of power relations wasn't important. What it said was that meaning-making in the situation cannot be completely reduced to these structures, and that to understand both stability and change in macro-regimes requires a close attention to the ways in which people make and reshape meaning in the actual world. In fact, there is a provocative—and humanistic—theory of power at play in interactionism. While the situation may be unevenly set, the capacities of actors is treated as equal. It is for this reason that interactionists are loath to put much emphasis on actors' ingrained bodily habits or culture.

In fact, most ethnographers who draw on interactionism today combine research on the macro-organizational, legal and economic setting of the situation, and the actual interaction they observe—as, in fact, did the early proponents of the Chicago school of sociology from which interactionism emerged. This, for example, is the research strategy used in Forrest Stuart's (2016) book, *Down, Out and Under Arrest*. The book traces the social effects of zero-tolerance policing on the inhabitants of Skid Row, a Los Angeles downtown area that has become the place of last resort for people when they're down on their luck. Stuart documents an intensive form of policing in which people are at risk for arrest for minor infractions and violations (sitting on the sidewalk, jaywalking).

Setting the stage, Stuart delves deeply into the historical emergence of Skid Row as well as the legal structure that underlies the situations he describes. Once he sets up the macro-environment, however, Stuart shows how the interactional situation is set up in predictable ways. In a poignant move, Stuart shows that this form of intense policing results in men and women on the street policing each other's actions. As Stuart writes:

> The constant threat of police interference forced the vendors to adopt the gaze of the police and to act as surrogate officers, thus engendering a perverse mode of privatized enforcement that undermined the commonly theorized benefits of informal control, undercut the possibilities for rehabilitation, and worsened the social and economic marginalization of Skid Row residents. (p. 190)

In effect, Stuart depicts an interactionist mechanism: one of the unforeseen effects of intensive policing is that people who constantly get stopped, frisked and arrested, begin to "see like a cop." That is, as a result of the back and forth between police and Skid Row, citizens change the definition of the situation and assume the perceptive schemas of police officers. Because this reaction is modeled after repeatedly-observed police actions, residents integrate the contextual aspects typical of police modus operandi: if police officers stop someone in your vicinity, they are likely to also ticket you for some infraction, real or imagined. Here, then, emerges a second part of the mechanism Stuart describes, where some men and women begin to themselves enact modes of "third party policing" in order to keep their environment safe from police presence.

The irony is not only that third party policing emerges from fear rather than a spirit of collaboration, but also that these men and women react to perceived infractions. Thus, for example, since white men (unless they are extremely disheveled) seem out of place, residents police them away; since women are assumed to be sex-workers, a few men forcefully removed a man from Skid Row who was trying to keep his drug addicted wife with him. When policing the perceived perceptions of the police, the men on the street ended up replicating some of the most repressive and unjust forms of such policing.

Stuart's work, like that of other leading interactionist ethnographers (e.g. Jerolmack 2009; Lee 2016; Timmermans 1999), moves between the situation and the larger social context. It shows both how interactions are shaped by the macro-processes they are embedded in, but also why it is crucial to look at the interactional situation in order to understand these macro-contexts. Although the way Skid Row citizens interactionally negotiate the meaning of their situation may make sense in hindsight, it is only through paying attention to the situation that some of the most problematic aspects of the policing of Skid Row came to the fore. In sum, then, there is little in interactionism to hinder a macro-analysis of power. Just the opposite seems to be the case, as an analysis of the macro-structure on its own would be blind some of its the most nefarious effects.

Much like the problem of macro-structures and power, aspects of the problem of the body and emotion were somewhat overblown. This is both because, as researchers such as Arlie Hochschild (1979) and Susan Shott (1979) have shown, we learn how to feel in certain situations, and these feelings-rules are mediated by interaction (see also Barbalet 2009). But, more importantly, research into the process of embodiment has shown that emotions very often emerge interactionally. Thus, for example, as Jack Katz (1999) shows in *how emotions work*, laughter emerges as people align their bodies and selves to others. To show that, Katz has videotaped people going to fun-house mirrors. Rather than finding that people laugh as they see themselves distorted, he finds that people laughed much more when they walked together. And, by analyzing the videos in painstaking detail, he showed that in order for laughter to emerge, people walking together took great pains to position themselves so that they saw the same thing. It was when people were together, and managed to sustain a shared perceptual vantage point, that they laughed.

What we get out of these studies, then, is a corrective to some of the usual critiques leveled against interactionism. By taking the prestructured nature of the situation into account, interactionists (both in social psychology and in ethnography) have been able to incorporate the larger macro-context—including contexts of racism or poverty. By looking closely at feeling rules and at the actual processual production of emotion, interactionists have been able to incorporate elements of emotion and embodied behavior into their explanation without making them any less interactionist in the process.

5.3.1 The Tricky Problem of Culture

But not all questions are so easily answerable. Both the question of embodiment and the question of macro-structures contain features that are far trickier to approach from an interactionist perspective. The problem in both cases is quite similar—though coming at it from opposite ends. If we think about the macro-patterning of the social world as the multiplication of structurally pre-set situations, we may be able to capture some elements of power, but we will miss more subtle forms of discursive power (Lukes 1974). In other worlds, by assuming that the only element that skews situations in predictable ways is structural, we miss the whole realm of ideology and discourse. More generally (and less power-centered) we miss the sharedness of culture, as it sets people's anticipations of what they can expect in a given situation, and how to go about muddling through it.

On the other end of culture, the most generative sociological projects that emphasize embodiment argue that what makes the body and emotion so salient is that it precedes the situation and shapes the way that selves are molded over time. Thus, for example, Bourdieu's (e.g. 1977, 2000) notion of habitus focuses on the way in which both our bodies, tastes and modes of perception and cognition are shaped by the conditions of existence in which we grow up. Thus, in any actual situation, we are enacting schemas of action and perception that we arrived with. The challenge that this position implies is that interactionism seems to assume that people generally come into the situation with the same capacities and embodied ways of enacting their selves. If we problematize this assumption, some aspects of symbolic interactionism may be treading on shaky ground.

These criticisms are not new, and classical interactionists were well aware of the problem of culture. And yet, there was something a little too facile about their initial responses to this challenge. Thus for example, Howard Becker tried to provide an interactionist's account of culture by arguing (1982b) that culture was the set of pre-given expectations that actors brought with them into interaction. Taking Jazz musicians as his example, he argued that we can compare "culture" to the shared repertoire of songs and expected variations that musicians come armed with. It's an important part of the situation, no doubt, but the more important aspect of the action is the kind of improvisations and unexpected variations that happen when musicians actually work together. In a different vein, Sheldon Stryker (1980), the most important architect of symbolic interactionist social psychology, attempted to come to terms with larger cultural considerations by producing a structuralist variety of interactionism. In his version, the theorist takes the position of actors seriously, as each position entails different significant others, and thus different conceptions of self.

These attempts, however, fall short of taking either culture or people's embodied positions seriously. For Becker, that people come into the situation with a repertoire of action seems too taken for granted. Rather than thinking about the complex relationship between the cultural repertoire that people come armed with and what happens in the situation, he relegates culture to a background characteristic. For Stryker, selves are structurally located as individuals are socialized to appreciate a different "generalized other" (G. H. Mead's term for the internalization of the social as such), but the mechanism for such different locations is purely cognitive, and a theory of the interaction of shared culture and interaction is lacking.

To answer these challenges, recent interactionists have moved in two complementary directions. Thus, Eliasoph and Lichterman (2003) locate this meeting point in the notion of "group style." As they put it, cultural meanings (such, for example, as "civic action") are ever present. They are a resource that both constrains and enables social action across a wide variety of settings. We all know what civic action means, at least "sort of." However, it is this "sort of" that provides a clue to the relationship between culture and interaction. What something like "civic action" actually means is more ambiguous than cultural theorists often acknowledge. People don't go to the dictionary or to the nearest sociologist to check whether what they are doing is "civic." This, for Eliasoph and Lichterman, is where interaction becomes crucial. As people interact with each other, they invest meaning in general cultural concepts. And although there may be a certain family resemblance between the different ways in which groups breath practical meaning into culture, the actual practices they enact are different at every given case, as actors face different practical problems and different group dynamics.

This position may sound a lot like Fine's "idiocultural" perspective describes above, but there are important theoretical differences between the two. For Fine, the most interesting dynamic is the emergence, from the bottom up, of local forms of meanings. For Eliasoph and Lichterman, the most interesting location is the medium between the interaction and the wider culture.

A complementary attempt to tie wider notions of culture to interactionism takes a different route. Rather than thinking about the availability of general cultural tropes that actors then mold anew, the new generation of interactionists are increasingly trying to see how actors biographies and notions of the future shape the way they interact. In order to do so, these theorists need to account for actors' ingrained habits, and see how actors' locations shape the interaction. This, as we will see, forces us to relax quite a lot of the situational purism of some early interactionists. But it does so without losing sight of the creative potential of the situation as a locus of meaning-making.

To understand the direction taken by these theorists it is useful to think about the notion of time. For classical interactionists, the most relevant temporality is that of the situation. Although they may trace the history that set up the situation in a particular way, once the stage is set the unfolding of the narrative arc of the situation is their primary focus. But if we want to understand how people operate within a wider culture, and why social worlds are structured in predictable ways, it isn't enough to look at this situational unfolding. In any particular situation, people orient themselves towards other temporalities. They are shaped by their pasts through habits of thought and action—often deeply ingrained in their very bodies—and they are anticipating and coordinating their futures. Since actors extend in time, the situation cannot be understood without such extensions.

One current direction, inspired by the work of Jack Katz, lies in the notion of biography. As Michael DeLand (frth) has recently argued, in order to understand a social situation, and especially a recurring social scene, we need to understand where the interaction fits in the biographies of actors. The very same activity—in his example, playing pickup basketball at a local park—is very different depending on whether going to the park is a recurring part of one's everyday life, or whether it is something we do every now and then; whether it is defines our identity in important ways, or considered an appendage to other activities. A scene, in this reading, can be understood as the predictable intertwining of actors' biographies, and their pragmatic and existential concerns.

Rather than holding the situation as the most important element for interactional analysis, it is the situation as it fits into actors' longer terms textures of life. To understand a party, for example, is not only to understand what happens in the situation, but also at what point of the life course of actors it appears. A party held when participants just turned 21 is going to be markedly different than a party held two years later, when drinking is less of a novelty. The tenor of a party will depend on how the specific situation fits the trajectories of actors—whether it is something they do every Friday? Every day? Almost never?

Taking a similar tack, the author of this chapter and others (Snyder 2016; Tavory 2016; Tavory and Eliasoph 2013; Trouille and Tavory frth) have argued that in order to understand both actors and social worlds sociologists need to think inter-situationally. That is, not only within the situation, but in the predictable rhythms of situations that make up the social world. Simply put, we can't completely understand what happens within a situation as an isolated incident, since people live not only in the present situation, but also implicitly compare this situation to other situations that they have experienced, as well as implicitly locating this situation in relation to the situation they expect to find themselves in later. So, from the point of view of actors', the focus only on the here and now of the situation misses much of what makes it what it is. This, then, is all the more true for the study of social worlds: focusing on specific situations and aggregating them into a social world, as do writers in the classic social worlds tradition outlined above, ignores the rhythms and patterns of situations and interaction.

In an ethnography of an Orthodox Jewish neighborhood, Tavory (2016) argues that being an orthodox Jew in that neighborhood was not simply a matter of belief or affiliation. As important as these individual projects were, residents needed to practically learn how to expect the rhythms of their social world. These included the obvious—the recurring moments of synagogue life and religious observances, the structured demands of their children's schools—but also included a host of other predictable rhythms. Thus, for example, Orthodox residents learned to expect comments on the street (usually just questions about their Orthodoxy, but also the rarer anti-Semitic incidents), and had to learn how to transition between their work in the non-Jewish world around them to their seemingly insular Orthodox life at home. To understand both the way in which Orthodox residents' identities were constructed, and the way the social world operated as a whole, the researcher needs to be attentive to the ways these rhythms of situations defined both actors and situations.

Thinking between situations allows the researcher to think about wider temporal horizons, and about the anticipations and skills that people bring into each situation. Paying attention to the rhythm of situations, as Snyder (2016) shows, allow as to gain purchase on what it means, for example, to experience unemployment in the aftermath of the 2008 economic crisis. As he shows, the shock of unemployment in a changing world occurred not only the moment of termination, but as situation after situation shows the job seeker that the world they knew seems to have disappeared. As they meet others who send CV after CV in vain, and their own effort increasingly seems unmoored from the new economic reality, they realize what it means to live in unsettled times. It is in the concatenation of situations and as people try to make sense of them together and piece negotiate the meaning of their world and their own identities that the social world is made.

The recent emphases on inter-situational analysis, futures, rhythms and biographies thus attempts to inject a more complex temporality into the situation. Although the situation, and the interactions of actors within it, is still extremely important, extending the temporality of actors allows us to better theorize their expectations of the situation, their proclivity to act and interpret their world in certain ways, and the way that both change and the etching of identities occur over time. Combined with the theorization of the notion of "group styles," as the negotiation of shared available tropes and their interactional negotiation, it doubly locates the situation in its cultural environment—both "from above" in the form of shared culture, and "from below" in the shape of actors own complex biographies and anticipated futures.

5.4 So Where Does This All Leave Us?

Once upon a time, when first year students walked into an intro class in sociology, they learned that there were three paradigms in sociology—conflict paradigm (Marx was the hero, or villain, depending on instructor), structural functionalism (with Parsons taking the lead), and interactionism. These days are no more. It is questionable if this was ever the true lay of the land, but even if it was, as sociology developed it has fractured into multiple parties, and the battles lines are not as intensely drawn. Interactionism, as others have observed (Fine 1993) has enriched the imagination of sociologists throughout the discipline, but became less and less of a well-defined paradigm.

Interactionism is also not alone in focusing on the realm of everyday life. As other chapters in this volume show, other research traditions have mined these grounds. Erving Goffman was crucially influenced by early interactionism, but went on to craft a more dramaturgical perspective that focused on actors' ongoing performance in social settings; exchange theorists have looked at the interactional situations through the lenses of rational choice; ethnomethodologists and conversation analysts have been theorizing and observing the ongoing emergence of taken for granted social structures in everyday life.

Still, interactionism remains an important theoretical locus. By focusing on the situation, on the collective act and on the malleability of meaning in interaction, interactionists were able to think about both creativity and the patterning of the social world in ways that other theorists simply could not. Rather than assuming that actors acted rationally, they could see how actors practically made sense of their world within the situation; rather than focusing on actors' performances, they looked to the way meaning interactionally emerged. And by remaining with the concreteness of the social, interactionism was able to show the dizzying possibilities of everyday life, as well as its predictable patterns.

Like all important theoretical accounts of the social, interactionism also attracted quite a bit of criticism. These ranged from arguing that it was blind to power and to macro-structures, not being attentive enough to the body, or pointing out that it was insensitive to the workings of culture. As this chapter makes clear, some of these criticisms were based on a misreading of the interactionist project, but others did point to important problems in early interactionists' approach to the social world.

In response, interactionists over the past two decades developed different ways to think about the social world in ways that acknowledged the place of shared meaning and of temporality in a fuller way. They did so, however, without letting go of the crucial importance of concrete social situation, and the ways that actors make their worlds together in them. It is this promise of interactionism that still makes it so exciting and radical as a theoretical perspective.

References

Barbalet, J. (2009). Pragmatism and symbolic interactionism. In B. S. Turner (Ed.), *The new Blackwell companion to social theory* (pp. 199–217). Oxford: Blackwell.

Becker, H. S. (1953). Becoming a marijuana user. *American Journal of Sociology, 59*(3), 235–242.

Becker, H. S. (1963). *Outsiders: Studies in the sociology of deviance*. Glencoe: Free Press.

Becker, H. S. (1982a). *Art worlds*. Berkeley: University of California Press.

Becker, H. S. (1982b). Culture: A sociological view. *Yale Review, 71*, 512–527.

Becker, H. S., Geer, B., Hughes, E. C., & Strauss, A. L. (1961). *Boys in white: Student culture in medical school*. Chicago: University of Chicago Press.

Berger, P. L., & Luckmann, T. (1967). *The social construction of reality: A treatise in the sociology of knowledge*. New York: Anchor Books.

Bernstein, B. (1964). Elaborated and restricted codes: Their social origins and some consequences. *American Anthropology, 66*(6), 55–69.

Blumer, H. (1937). Social psychology. In E. P. Schmidt (Ed.), *Man and society: A substantive introduction to the social sciences* (pp. 144–198). New York: Prentice-Hall.

Blumer, H. (1969). *Symbolic interactionism: Perspective and method*. Engelwood Cliffs: Prentice Hall.

Bourdieu, P. (1977). *Outline of a theory of practice*. Cambridge: Cambridge University Press.

Bourdieu, P. (2000). *Pascalian meditations*. Stanford: Stanford University Press.

Cooley, C. H. (1902). *Human nature and the social order*. New York: Scribner.

de Saussure, F. ([1916] 1986). *Course in general linguistics*. New York: Open Court.

Deland, M. (Frth). The ocean run: Stage, cast, and performance in a public park basketball scene. *Journal of Contemporary Ethnography.*

Denzin, N. K. (1992). *Symbolic interaction and cultural studies*. Oxford: Blackwell.

Eliasoph, N., & Lichterman, P. (2003). Culture in interaction. *American Journal of Sociology, 108*(4), 735–794.

Fine, G. A. (1979). Small groups and culture creation: Idioculture of little league baseball teams. *American Sociological Review, 44*, 733–745.

Fine, G. A. (1993). The sad demise, mysterious disappearance, and glorious triumph of symbolic interactionism. *Annual Review of Sociology, 19*, 61–87.

Fine, G. A. (1998). *Morel tales: The culture of mushrooming*. Harvard: Harvard University Press.

Fine, G. A. (2012). *Tiny publics*. New York: Russell Sage.

Glaser, B. G., & Strauss, A. L. (1964). Awareness contexts. *American Sociological Review, 29*(5), 669–679.

Glaser, B. G., & Strauss, A. L. (1965). *Awareness of dying*. Chicago: Aldine.

Goodman, P. (2008). "It's just Black, White, or Hispanic": An observational study of racializing moves in California's segregated prison reception centers. *Law & Society Review, 42*, 735–770.

Heise, D. R. (1986). Modeling symbolic interaction. In S. Lindenberg, J. S. Coleman, & S. Nowak (Eds.), *Approaches to social theory* (pp. 291–309). New York: Russell Sage.

Hochschild, A. (1979). Emotion work, feeling rules, and social structure. *American Journal of Sociology, 85*(3), 551–575.

Huebner, D. R. (2014). *Becoming Mead: The social process of academic knowledge*. Chicago: University of Chicago Press.

Jerolmack, C. (2009). Primary groups and cosmopolitan ties: The rooftop pigeon flyers of New York. *Ethnography, 10*(2/3), 211–233.

Kameo, N., & Whalen, J. J. (2015). Organizing documents: Standard forms, person production and organizational action. *Qualitative Sociology, 38*(2), 205–229.

Katz, J. (1999). *How emotions work*. Chicago: University of Chicago Press.

Kuhn, M. H. (1964). Major trends in symbolic interaction theory in the past twenty-five years. *Sociological Quarterly, 5*, 61–84.

Lee, J. (2016). *Blowin' up: Rap dreams in South Central*. Chicago: University of Chicago Press.

Lemert, E. (1967). *Human deviance, social problems and social control*. Englewood Cliffs: Prentice-Hall.

Lifton, R. J. (1993). *The protean self: Human resilience in an age of fragmentation*. Chicago: University of Chicago Press.

Lukes, S. (1974). *Power: A radical view*. London: Macmillan.

Mead, G. H. (1934). In C. W. Morris (Ed.), *Mind, self and society: From the standpoint of a social behaviorist*. Chicago: University of Chicago Press.

Meltzer, B. N., Petras, J. W., & Reynolds, L. T. (1973). *Symbolic interactionism: Genesis, varieties, and criticism*. Boston: Routledge.

Rock, P. (1979). *The making of symbolic interactionism*. New Jersey: Rowman and Littlefield.

Shibutani, T. (1955). Reference groups as perspectives. *American Journal of Sociology, 60*(6), 562–569.

Shott, S. (1979). Emotion and social life: A symbolic interactionism analysis. *American Journal of Sociology, 84*(6), 1317–1334.

Snyder, B. H. (2016). *The disrupted workplace: Time and the moral order of flexible capitalism*. Oxford: Oxford University Press.

Stets, J. E., & Burke, P. J. (2000). Identity theory and social identity theory. *Social Psychology Quarterly, 70*, 106–124.

Stolte, J., Fine, G. A., & Cook, K. S. (2001). Sociological miniaturism: Seeing the big through the small in social psychology. *Annual Review of Sociology, 27*, 387–413.

Strauss, A. L. (1978). A social worlds perspective. *Studies in Symbolic Interaction, 1*, 119–128.

Stryker, S. (1980). *Symbolic interactionism: A social structural version*. Menlo Park: Caldwell.

Stuart, F. (2016). *Down, out, and under arrest: Policing and everyday life in Skid Row*. Chicago: University of Chicago Press.

Tavory, I. (2016). *Summoned: Identification and religious life in a Jewish neighborhood*. Chicago: University of Chicago Press.

Tavory, I., & Eliasoph, N. (2013). Coordinating futures: Towards a theory of anticipation. *American Journal of Sociology, 118*(4), 908–942.

Thomas, W. I., & Thomas, D. S. (1928). *The child in America: Behavior problems and programs*. New York: Knopf.

Timmermans, S. (1999). *Sudden death and the myth of CPR*. Philadelphia: Temple University Press.

Trouille, D., & Tavory, I. (Frth). Shadowing: Warrants for inter-situational variation in ethnography. *Sociological Methods & Research*.

Cultural Theory

6

Omar Lizardo

6.1 Introduction

Long abandoned by anthropologists as a foundational concept (e.g. Abu-Lughod 1991), the last two decades have seen a virtual explosion of interest in culture among sociologists, not only as a "topic" of analysis (the "sociology of culture") but most importantly as a "resource" for general sociological explanation ("cultural sociology"). This is exemplified by the fact that, while beginning as a relatively small and largely peripheral intellectual movement in the mid 1980s, today the American Sociological Association's "Section on Culture" is decidedly central, boasting one of the largest rates of membership especially graduate student members. Intellectually, cultural sociologists (or sociologists of culture for that matter) can proclaim with confidence that their work stands "at the crossroads of the discipline" (Jacobs and Spillman 2005), helping to inform the work of social scientists working across essentially every substantive field of research. This includes social science history (e.g. Bonnell and Hunt 1999), cognitive sociology (e.g. DiMaggio 1997), the sociology of religion (e.g. Smilde 2007), organizational studies (e.g. Weber and Dacin 2011), social movement theory (e.g. Polletta 2008), economic sociology (e.g. Bandelj et al. 2015), culture and inequality studies (e.g. Small et al. 2010), and even traditionally "positivist" subfields such as demography (Bachrach 2014). Articles and books dealing with cultural analysis have become field-wide citation classics (e.g. Swidler 1986; Bellah et al. 1985; Lamont 1992; Sewell 1992; DiMaggio 1997; Lareau 2011), handbooks on cultural sociology continue to be published at a rapid pace (e.g. Bennett and Frow 2008; Hall et al. 2010; Alexander et al. 2012), and contemporary debates on foundational issues on the theory of action, the basic parameters of social explanation, and the foundations of social order take place largely under the umbrella of "cultural theory" and "cultural analysis" (e.g. Reed 2011; Vaisey 2009; Swidler 2001; Patterson 2014; Alexander 2003).

Given this, it is uncontroversial to propose that the "concept of culture" has joined the couplet of "structure" and "agency" as one of contemporary sociology's foundational notions. Yet, just like those other foundational ideas, the concept is beset with ambiguity and vagueness (Kroeber and Kluckhohn 1952; Stocking 1966), as well as lingering doubts as to its analytical import and exact relation to other foundational notions in social theory such as "social structure" and "agency" (Alexander 2003; Sewell 1999; Patterson 2014; Archer 1995). As a result, while both "culture and structure" and "culture in action" debates continue to rage, there does not seem to be any immediate resolution to these

O. Lizardo (✉)
Department of Sociology, University of Notre Dame, Notre Dame, IN, USA
e-mail: olizardo@nd.edu

S. Abrutyn (ed.), *Handbook of Contemporary Sociological Theory*, Handbooks of Sociology and Social Research, DOI 10.1007/978-3-319-32250-6_6

perennial problems in sight (e.g. Vaisey 2009; Alexander 2003; Sewell 2005). This unsatisfactory *détente* acquires more importance, when we consider the fact that the basic theoretical debates in the discipline in the American scene—e.g. those inaugurated by Parsons's (1937) problematic interpretation of a selection of European thinkers—now take place largely under the auspices of "cultural theory" and not "theory" in its unqualified form (Swidler 1995).

Whether the culture concept or cultural sociology as a general analytic approach is up to this task remains to be seen. What is not in doubt is that continuing progress (or possible resolutions) to contemporary theoretical impasses will depend on whether "culture" has the potential to serve as such a unifying meta-concept. The basic argument in this chapter is that the contemporary version of the culture concept in sociology is simply not the sort of analytic resource that is up to this task and that "cultural theory" *as currently configured* will not make headway on the relevant analytical issues. The reason for this is that the concept of culture in contemporary sociology melds (in somewhat anachronistic ways) both basic concerns inherited from the classics and post-classical issues inherited from the incorporation of the modern ("analytical") concept of culture developed in anthropology into this classical tradition by Talcott Parsons.[1] As such, the status of cultural sociology as a meta-field unifying other areas of substantive inquiry in the discipline will remain problematic, even as "cultural theory" will continue to serve as a stand in for "theory" in the general sense.

An important, if often unremarked issue, is that the "modern" culture concept had no strict conceptual analogue among the sociological classics (here I restrict my definition of "classics" to the standard canon of Marx, Weber, Durkheim). This means that many of the issues that preoccupy contemporary cultural theorists only have superficial similarity to those that preoccupied Marx, Weber, and Durkheim; this also means that the retroactive recasting of the sociological classics as budding cultural theorists (e.g. Parsons 1951; Swidler 1995) is an anachronism of consequential import. In this sense, contemporary cultural theory inherits a post-classical problematic which has no strict analogue in the classics. Given this, my argument is that it makes little exegetical or analytical sense to project a "concept of culture" to such pre-cultural theorists Marx, Weber, and Durkheim (or even the early Parsons!). Instead, we should go back to the drawing board and dissociate the classics from the contemporary culture concept. All the same, they may also provide a model for how to do social theory without relying on that concept as a central line of support.

The rest of the chapter is organized as follows. In the next section I outline the conceptual armamentarium deployed by Marx, Weber, and Durkheim to deal with theoretical issues that have now been retroactively (and anachronistically) remapped as central problems in cultural theory. The basic argument is that none of the classics had anything close to what can be called a "concept of culture" because they did not need one to deal with the analytical issues that preoccupied them. I will then argue that it is the figure that marks the transition from "classical" to "contemporary" sociological theory namely, Talcott Parsons, who recasts the classics as "cultural theorists" *status nascendi* thus retroactively recruiting them to deal with basic problems that emerge from his own (failed) attempt to link his own version of the anthropological concept of culture to theoretical issues in action theory and normativist functionalism. We will see that Parsons's primary analytic concern in regards to cultural theory has to do mainly with the mechanisms of how persons become "encultured," which for Parsons is essentially a resolution to an unfinished chapter in his own interpretation of Durkheim. Parsons coupled his solution

[1] By the "analytical" concept of culture I mean what used to be called the "anthropological" concept (when that discipline had full ownership of it) and like that concept it should be contrasted with the "classical" or "humanist" (Arnoldian) culture concept along the usual dimensions of the denial of absolutism in favor of relativism, the denial of "progressivism" in favor of homeostatic functionalism, the denial of a hierarchy among "cultures," and the emphasis on the determinism of inherited traditions over conscious reasoning in the shaping of conduct (see Stocking 1966: 868).

(enculturation as "internalization") with a conception of the "cultural system" as a systematic ensemble of ideal elements. Clifford Geertz for his part, takes up the remnants of Weber's "meaning" problematic, but does so from within the constraints of a Parsonian (via Kroeber and Kluckhohn) conceptualization of culture as (external) "system" or "pattern." This is the way in which this particular problem continues to be formulated in contemporary cultural analysis.

In the fourth section, I will review some of the basic issues in contemporary cultural analysis. We will see that contemporary cultural theorists essentially divide themselves into analytic camps depending on their stance vis a vis the Parsonian model of enculturation, such that acceptance or rejection of a conception of culture as either "internal" to the actor or as part of the external environment becomes correlative to acceptance or rejection of a conception of the *nature* of culture as either systematic or fragmented (respectively). A third group of contemporary cultural sociologists abandons the Parsonian problematic of enculturation and internalization in favor of a return to the "problem of meaning" as a defining issue for sociological explanation more generally. This group however, remains wedded to a Parsonian conception of culture as systematic, although reinforced with a more contemporary formulation of systematicity taken from structural linguistics. I close by outlining the implications of this situation for the future of the "concept of culture" as a central analytic resource in sociology.

6.2 The Sociological Classics as Pre-cultural Theorists

Given its current status as a central analytic construct, it might seem impossible to imagine how one can get a conceptual bearing on the central analytic issues of social theory, such as understanding the nature of action or explicating the nature and origins of social change and reproduction *without* a culture concept. Yet, it is well known that the contemporary *analytic* "concept of culture" did not exist until well into the twentieth century, itself being an invention of American anthropologists (themselves reacting against what they saw as an unduly austere British functionalism); most centrally Franz Boas (the innovator), his student Alfred Kroeber (the systematizer), and later on Margaret Mead (the popularizer).[2] That means that none of the sociological classics operated with anything like the modern culture concept yet they undoubtedly dealt with the "central problems in social theory" (Giddens 1979). Accordingly, we may conclude that the culture concept is not necessary for such a task, a claim supported by the fact that the discipline from which sociologists got the concept in the first place (Anthropology) continues to plug along after having renounced it as essentialist and reductive (Abu-Lughod 1991), and one of the major thinkers in twentieth century Sociology, Pierre Bourdieu, largely conducted his work without ever making *analytic* use of the notion (although of course he took it up as "topic" of analysis).[3] How then were the classics ever able to manage without a modern culture concept? The answer is that both used cognate notions available from their native intellectual traditions (Levine 1995). What were these?

6.2.1 The Germanic Tradition

In the case of Marx and Weber, the concept that performed the analytic task is that of ideas (*idee, vorstellung*) inherited from the Kantian-Fichtean-Hegelian tradition of German Idealism in Philosophy. Marx and Weber thus drew on a "German" (in Levine's 1995 sense) sociological tradition in which the "cognitive element" of

[2] See Stocking (1966) for the definitive historical treatment of the central role of Boas in crafting the modern analytical culture concept; see Kuper (1999) for a wider ranging study linking the culture concept to interacting but analytically autonomous traditions in England, France, and Germany; for a lexicographic analysis of the concept as used in standard (non-academic) discourse see Goddard (2005) and Sewell (2005: 169–172) does a masterly job of disambiguating the folk and analytic conceptions of culture.

[3] For more details on Bourdieu as a "non-cultural" or at least "post-cultural" theorist see Lizardo (2011).

action (Warner 1978) was largely thought of in terms of "ideas." The German tradition came in two brands; the first one came from the Hegelian obsession with the "motor forces" of history and basically dealt with a controversy in the so-called Philosophy of History as to which one of the two set of forces was most important in accounting patterns of historical and social change usually conceptualized in teleological "evolutionary" (in the pre-Darwinian "telos of history" sense) terms.

The second flavor is (Neo)Kantian and has a more direct concern with the battle between ideal and material forces *within* the individual in determining conduct and not as macro-social "forces" or "factors" in historical societies. In the (neo) Kantian version of the tradition, ideas are thought of as subjective conceptions of the world held by actors, which may or may not accurately reflect its objective features. Accordingly, ideas are seen as the creative, "active" elements determining action via relations of non-Newtonian, *intentional* (final) causality, counterposed against external "deterministic" elements that push people around via relations of physical (inclusive of the bodily instincts), efficient causation. Ideas were thus thought of as a possible *driver* of action along with other forces, most importantly instinctual (biological) and environmental determinants (which we may refer to as "material" for short). In this respect, this tradition linked "cultural analysis" (with this term being used in an admittedly anachronistic way) with the problematic of "action theory" (another anachronism as this term does not become prevalent until after Parsons).

The distinction between the "societal" and "individual" version of the German "idealist" tradition is important because these two debates tend to be run together and continue to be conflated in contemporary "cultural" analysis. Conceptually however, they are thoroughly independent and rely on very different premises. The Hegelian debate deals with (to use a modern term) "emergent" factors at the level of "societies" conceived in quasi-organismic terms as coherent wholes. The Kantian debate deals with action at the level of the individual. Most of the arguments regarding the Hegelian debate over ideas operated with either no or very rudimentary references to a theory of action; the Kantian version, on the other hand, operated from an *a priori* methodological presumption (somewhat muddily articulated by Max Weber) that there were *no* emergent macro-social "forces" (either "material" or "ideal"), that "society" as an organismic whole was a spurious analytic unit, and that the Hegelian "debate" in the Philosophy of History (of which Marx and Engels's historical materialism was viewed as an entry) was just a useless conceptual muddle. It was only in the twentieth century recuperation of this debate by Parsons that problems of action theory were again linked up to "macrosocial" issues, in so-called structural-functionalism.

6.2.2 Marx and Engels's "Big" Idea

The problematic that was most poignant in the early nineteenth century and that was thus the one inherited by Marx and dealt with primarily in the collaborative writings with Engels from the mid 1840s to the late 1850s[4] was the Hegelian "macrosocial" one (essentially the middle "sociological" period between the philosophical anthropology of the early 1840s and the "political economy" writings of the 1860s). The so-called "materialist conception of history" of Marx and Engels essentially boils down, in between withering satire of the so-called Young Hegelians, Proudhon, utopian socialists or whoever stood in their way, to arguing that *at the macrosocial level* "ideal" factors as conceptualized by *philosophers of history* up to that stage did not matter for explaining historical change as much as the "material" factors of classical political economy (essentially land, labor, and capital, which "technology" being the most important part of the latter). Note that what counts as "ideal factors" in this tradition is essentially mostly the intellectual outputs of symbol producing elites, inclusive of political theory, theology and popu-

[4]These include, most importantly, the set of notes that came to be known as "The German Ideology" (finished approx. 1846) but also the first part of the "Communist Manifesto" (1848) and the programmatic "Preface to a Contribution to the Critique of Political Economy" (1859).

lar religious doctrines, but also "philosophies of history" or even the "philosophies" peddled by the "Young Hegelians."[5]

However, Marx and Engels *also counted* "technical" ideas such as the ideas produced by the classical political economists (e.g. Malthus, Smith and Ricardo) and even radical movement actors (such as syndicalists like Proudhon and anarchists such as Bakunin) as "ideas." Note that from the point of view of modern "cultural theory" this conception of "ideas" would be considered *radically* limited as it ignores the schemas, practices, beliefs and normative commitments of the folk and essentially everything that is not ordered into some expert "system" either "scientific" or "political." Yet, this makes perfect sense for Marx and Engels, as their primary goal had nothing to do with culture as some generic "dimension" of society but with the role of certain "ideological" (meaning systematized and possibly distorting) belief systems in directing social change. Their point was that rather than directing change, transformations at the level of the "infrastructure" (*unterbau*) happen first, and the "ideologues" emerge at the level of the superstructure (*überbau*) to justify those changes by crafting ideas into ideology. The key issue is that Marx and Engels never talk about anything that would be recognized as "culture" today at the level of individual action.

6.2.3 Max Weber's Little Ideas

The theorist who would move the German debate over ideas to the level of the individual was Max Weber. Rivers of ink have been spilled on the issue of whether there is a direct line of continuity between the theoretical tradition initiated by Marx and Engels and that of Max Weber. The position taken here is that the preponderance of evidence suggests a radical incommensurability (in the Kuhnian sense) between Weber and the Marx/Engels's project. In essence, while the latter were radical "reverse-Hegelians" concerned primarily with evolutionist issues that began in the philosophy of history and which they attempted to move to the empirical terrain of "science," (understood mainly as classical political economy) the former is a neo-Kantian concerned with proto-phenomenological issues of the existential determinants of human action as it pertains to the generation of unique historical complexes at given conjunctures (Weber 1946a, b). While the solution of these neo-Kantian concerns had *implications* for our understandings of the origins and trajectory of these unique historical complexes (such as "rational capitalism"). These had no real ontological status (existing only as nominal "ideal types"), and Weber never saw himself theorizing about them as such at a macrosocial level.

Attempts to recast Weber as a macrosocial theorist in the realist mode hinge on extremely partial (and exegetically indefensible) readings of some of the least reliable of his "writings" in English (such as the lectures known as *General Economic History* or excerpts from *Economy and Society*) that downplay the bulk of the work that was actually published in Weber's lifetime and that he gave his living editorial approval to (essentially the writings known as *The Economic Ethics of the World Religions* [*EEWR*]). They also ignore Weber's explicit pronouncements in the methodological writings that pure holistic analysis was a non-starter both substantively and theoretically. As such, there is nothing wrong with Weberian *inspired* macrosociology (e.g. Collins 1986) as long as it is understood to be a fundamental deviation from Weber's own line of thinking. This has implication for modern debates in cultural theory. For instance, while it is perfectly legitimate to claim Weber as a pre-Parsonian forerunner of "culture in action" debates (Swidler 1986), it is madness to think that Weber prefigured (macro) debates about "culture and structure" at the "societal" level.

[5] Sometimes this distinction is lost because Marx and Engels's historical materialism is interpreted as making statements about the balance between ideal and material "forces" at the level of group of individuals or even individual themselves and not historical societies. Yet, there is little evidence that Marx or Engels cared about classes (or individuals) in this sense or predicated theories taken standalone "classes" or "groups" as their referent. It was in fact Max Weber (especially in the writings on religion) who moved the debate to this level. Most of the ideal versus material interest debate in sociology is thus a purely Weberian and not a Marxian debate.

As first noted by Parsons, Weber's fundamental concern was precisely with "the role of ideas in social action" (Parsons 1938) and this approach is distilled in the two "theoretical" essays in *EEWR*.[6] In this respect, Weber targets the historical materialists only secondarily. More directly located in his line of fire were all sort of instinctual psychologies (such as Nietzsche's proto-Freudianism), environmentalism, generic motive theories of the origins of historical complexes (such as Sombart's "acquisitive motive" account), and other assorted biologisms prominent at the time. Because he was working at the level of individual action, Weber is able to develop something pretty close to a modern action-theoretic perspective on the role of "culture" in social action as long as we understand that the Weberian notion of "ideas" is semantically much more restrictive than the modern concept of culture. Weber does this by arguing that "ideas" *as historically constructed conceptions characteristic of given persons* (or in the aggregate groups) have an independent effect on conduct, and that this was noted precisely in those historical cases in which we see persons essentially override, instincts, biology, generic motives and environmental pressures (all swept under the rug of "material interests") in order to fulfill an "ideal interest" (Weber 1946a).

6.2.4 Emile Durkheim's Représentations

One of the most disastrous bits of classical exegeses enacted by Parsons (1937) concerns his classification of Durkheim as an (inconsistent) member of a tradition of (German?) "idealism."[7] We know now, especially after the efflorescence of Durkheimian studies in the 1990s, that this characterization—still repeated as late as Alexander (1982)—is patently non-sensical as there is an even deeper Kuhnian incommensurability gulf separating Durkheim from any representative of the German idealist tradition (properly called because it derives its preoccupations from German Idealism). We also know thanks to the pioneering (and painstaking) work of such scholars as Stephen Turner, W. F. Pickering, Warren Schmaus, Sue Stedman-Jones, Anne Rawls, Robert Alun-Jones and others, that Durkheim actually belonged to a non-German-idealist tradition of *French Neo-Kantianism*, which combined a set of problematics that while derived from *the French reception of* Kant in the early to mid nineteenth century, featured a set of solutions actually derived from Aristotelian, Thomist, and personalist conceptions autochthonous to the French tradition (Schmaus 2004). These conceptual approaches have little if nothing to do (in a substantive sense if not in allusive sense) with German neo-Kantianism.

The French Neo-Kantian tradition, systematized by such thinkers as Renouvier, Maine De Biran, and Victor Cousin, rejected the Kantian problematic of ideas, derided Kant's departure from the Humean skeptical argument as to the problematic origin of general categories as a non-starter, and even questioned the whole notion that "ideas" could be different from or "independent" from a "non-ideal" objective reality. Instead, these thinkers, beginning with Renouvier, developed an ontology of representations (*représentations*) in which the dualistic tendencies typical of the German tradition (in which ideas and material forces fight it out to determine action or history) is renounced in favor of a "naturalistic" conception in which *représentations* exist in the same natural plane as objects in the world (thus Parsons, in his mangled interpretation of

[6] These are the "Social Psychology of the World Religions" (1946a, serving as the "introduction" or *Eilentung*) to the collection and the interlude or "intermediate reflections" (*zwischenbrachtungen*) known in English as "Religious Rejections of the World and their Directions" (1946b).

[7] Durkheim was an inconsistent member of the idealist category because, according to the now thoroughly discredited "two Durkheims" argument in *Structure*, he begins his career as an idealist (in *Division*) but ends it by going "clean over" into "idealism" in *Elementary Forms*. These claims can only be made sense of by accepting Parsons's idiopathic (and exegetically obsolete) understanding of the term "idealism" to encompass any human being who considers the mental component important for explaining action.

Durkheim, confused good old fashioned Aristotelian naturalism with the German bugaboo of "materialism").[8] Contra the German tradition, French thinkers did not see the causality pertaining to *représentations* as different from material or efficient causality (Turner 1984), thought that persons became epistemically acquainted with concrete (e.g. "perceptual") *représentations* in the same way that they became acquainted with "abstract" (e.g. "categorical") ones (Schmaus 2004), and asserted that *représentations* in this sense could *not* fail (unless under pathological conditions) to match reality, since *représentations* (like persons and their consciousness) were natural objects and thus an integral part of that very same reality (Stedman-Jones 2001; see the essays collected in Pickering 2000).

This representationalist ontology is adopted wholesale by Durkheim who sees in this concept the key to the founding of a new "special" science (actually a "special psychology") of a particular kind of object. Because *représentations* were a natural object (as opposed to "ideas" which Kantians held to be non-naturalistic), they could form the foundation of a plain-old science (in the same sense as Physics and Biology) and there was no need to go through all of the tortured hand-wringing (productive of mostly unreadable texts) that German neo-Kantians participating in the *methodenstreit* had to go through in questioning whether scientific methods were proper or not for such non-naturalistic entities as ideas. Instead, having travelled to the laboratories of Wilhelm Wundt as a young representative of the best that the French intelligentsia had to offer after the national humiliation suffered during the Franco-Prussian war, Durkheim had seen concrete institutional proof that *représentations* could be studied scientifically, naturalistically, and objectively.

From the point of view of the nascent science of sociology, the issue had nothing to do with scientific *method* (as with the German neo-Kantian tradition) and everything to do with scientific *object*. Durkheim noted that what sociologists were lacking was not a special method but a special "thing" to study. Durkheim "solved" the problem as follows: While Wundt and the nascent science of German scientific psychology (and even German "social psychology") would be concerned with "individual representations" (*représentations individuelles*) as their natural object, the "new" French science of Sociology was going to re-direct the same scientific bravado to a set of natural objects that had yet to be dealt with in the same vein: collective representations (*représentations collectives*). The only thing left to do (e.g. Durkheim 1893) was to write an anti-philosophical manifesto proclaiming the existence and causal preponderance (in relation to *représentations individuelles*) of this novel scientific object, and their analytic resistance to armchair (read classical philosophical) introspective methods. Collective representations are "things" (and thus a "natural kind" in modern parlance) just like chairs, pains, atoms, and chickens, and can be studied with the same methods and using the same old concepts of causation.

It is hard to overstate, in light of recent discoveries in Durkheim scholarship, how incredibly alien is Durkheim's original conceptual apparatus (Rawls 2005), methodological approach (Schmaus 1994), and set of epistemic and ontological commitments (Stedman-Jones 2001) from contemporary "germanic" cultural sociology in the United States. Most importantly, how alien is the *naturalistic* conception of *représentations* (Pickering 2000) from the (germanic!) Boasian-Parsonian "concept of culture" that continues (to paraphrase a germanic theorist) to weigh heavily upon the brains of living American sociologists.

For instance, it is clear that neither the standard "culture versus structure" nor "culture in action" debate fit the Durkheimian problematic because the notion of *représentations* is not commensurable (once again in the Kuhnian sense) with any modern conception of the culture concept. To wit, (the "early") Durkheim was a "monist" organicist for whom the issue was not,

[8] In what follows, I use the conventional tactic in modern Durkheimian studies of using the untranslated term *représentations* to refer to the original French notion, as the term is not semantically equivalent to the English word "representation" which is beset by Germanic (e.g. Kantian) hangups not applicable to the French notion.

as it was for the dualist organicism of the middle-period Marx or modern "culture and structure" theorists (e.g. Archer 1995), whether there was one "factor" (e.g. the material or "social") that was preponderant upon another factor (the ideal). Interpreting Durkheim in a "germanic" mode (as do Parsons and Alexander) leads to bizarre notions such as "Durkheimian materialism" or the even crazier idea of the "paradigm shift" from the "materialism" of *Division* to the "idealism" of *Elementary Forms* (Schmaus 1994).

For Durkheim, the primary analytic issue was whether the whole "social" organism composed primarily of social facts (inclusive of person to person bonds, institutional facts, traditions, and mores) conceived as *représentations collectives*, held together as a unity or not. This is the sort of formulation that Weber would have rejected as non-sensical mysticism. At this level, the issue was whether different sets of collective representations fit together or not. At the level of the individual Durkheim does not face the action-theoretical problematic of whether "ideal" factors were most important than "material" factors in determining conduct. For Durkheim *all* action had to be driven by *représentations*, (the notion of action without representations is patently non-sensical from the point of view of the Aristotelian neo-Kantianism under which Durkheim was reared). The key issue is thus, *which* kind of representation is preponderant in determining action; *représentations individuelles* or *représentations collectives*. According to Durkheim's "dualist" conception of the individual, when the social organism is whole and healthy action is driven (unproblematically) by the appropriate (for that social type) set of collective representations although these must be of sufficient strength and carry enough authority to subjugate the dissipative force of individual (and thus eogistic, evanescent) representations.

6.3 Enter "Culture": Talcott Parsons

As alluded to above, the biggest theoretical disaster in modern social theory consists of Parsons's shoehorning of Durkheim into a German "ideal/materialist" frame. All modern Durkheim scholars now reject this formulation along with associated non-problems such a the (non-materialist) meaning of "thing" in Durkheim's definition of social facts, along with the related non-shift from "materialism" to "idealism" (Schmaus 2004). In the 1970s there was an entire anti-functionalist movement designed to free Max Weber from the cage of normativist functionalism (e.g "de-Parsonizing Weber"). Yet a movement to "de-Parsonize Durkheim" (e.g. Stedman-Jones 2001) has only been enacted recently among a small cadre of specialty Durkheim scholars having little impact on social and cultural theory writ large. But this matters, because it is my contention that modern cultural theory is the unholy offspring of Parsons's conceptual mixture of German neo-Kantian and post-Hegelian hangups concerning "the role of ideas in social action" and the "balance" between "cultural" and "material" forces at the social level with Durkheim's (as we saw above absolutely incommensurable) conceptual apparatus. The result is a "Germanized Durkheim"; an analytically incoherent conceptual "monster" (in Douglas's 1966 sense) that continues to play havoc on the theoretical imagination of modern cultural theorists.

Parsons's conceptual monster emerges in two steps. From the point of view of modern cultural theory the key conceptual moves occur in two distinct periods; the "action-theoretic" period of "the early essays" and *Structure* (1935–1938) where Parsons still operates with a pre-cultural vocabulary steeped in the nineteenth century germanic neo-Kantian tradition (e.g. voluntarism, ideas, materialism, positivism). At this stage, the "anthropological" (analytic) concept of culture is absent; what we have instead are the twin germanic concepts of "ideas" (Parsons 1938) and "values" (1935; including ultimate values). The second period is the so-called "middle period" of normativist functionalism proper culminating in the publication of *The Social System* (1951), and most importantly for cultural theorists the book co-authored with Parsons and Shils (*Towards a General Theory of Action* (1951)) and the collection of essays, mostly written from the late 1940s to the late 1950s, known as *Social Structure and Personality* (1964). This period is key because it is here that Parsons becomes acquainted with various fledgling versions of the "analytical" culture concept floating around in American anthropology since at least 1911 (Stocking 1966; Bidney 1967) and uses them to develop his own, and ultimately decisive for us, version of the culture concept (Parsons 1972; Kroeber and Parsons 1958).

6.3.1 Parsons Invents "Culture"

We have seen that the classics, in particular Weber and Durkheim, did not have a concept that maps onto the "modern" (anthropological) concept of culture; as such, it is an analytical and exegetical mistake (as well as an embarrassing anachronism) to treat the classics as budding "cultural theorists." However, this is done regularly by both cultural analysts (e.g. Swidler 1995) and by everybody who has been tasked with writing a "classics" question for a qualifying exam on "culture" in a contemporary graduate program in sociology (myself) in the United States. How did we get to this sad point? The answer is that the classics became "cultural theorists" because Talcott Parsons re-read them as such. The story of how this happened is messy, because everybody focuses on the "rewriting" of the classics that Parsons enacted in *Structure of Social Action* (1937) when Parsons still did not have access to the modern culture concept. Everybody forgets, however, that Parsons kept rewriting and re-interpreting the classics throughout his entire career.[9] This was especially true during the highly active (both theoretically and in terms of institution building) middle period that saw the publication of *The Social System* (1951) and various mid-career theoretical essays (1964), when Parsons was fully equipped with a modern (analytic) culture concept (Kuper 1999).[10]

Where did Parsons get an *analytic* version of the culture concept? The short answer, is that he got it from the anthropologists in particular via the influence of Clyde Kluckhohn (the leading, because he was the only, cultural anthropologist at Harvard) and the professional link to one of Franz Boas's most influential student: Alfred Kroeber. The influence of Clyde Kluckhohn's notion of culture as "pattern" and Alfred Kroeber's neo-Spencerian conceptualization of culture as "superorganic" on Parsons's thinking on this score, the equally important influence that Talcott Parsons had on anthropological definitions of the culture concept, as well as the famous disciplinary turf-splitting "deal" enacted by the two *doyens* of American social science—such that Anthropology got to keep the "cultural system" and sociology got "the social system" (e.g. Parsons and Kroeber 1958)—is an unwritten chapter in the history of sociology (but see Kuper 1999 coming to bat for anthropology). For instance, it is clear that Kroeber and Kluckhohn (1952) were spurred to clarify systematize, and update the Tylor-Boas analytic culture concept right after Parsons began to make use of his own (ultimately decisive) twist on this very notion (e.g. Parsons 1951) as one of the central concepts of the middle-period functionalist scheme (with the other two being the "social" and "personality" systems). As Kuper has noted, this is hugely important because the culture concept did not emerge from anthropology as a result of an internal conceptual need within the discipline. Instead, "it was Parsons who created the need for a modern, social scientific conception of culture, and who persuaded the leading anthropologists of the United States that their discipline could flourish only if they took culture in his sense as their particular specialty" (1999: 68).

[9] As we have seen, it is important to note that Parsons kept trying to demonstrate the existence of various "convergence theses" after 1937, including the even more fantastic (and ridiculous) "Freud/Durkheim" convergence thesis around the issue of "cultural internalization."

[10] Of most immediate direct influence was Clyde Kluckhohn the leading anthropologist at Harvard, and via Kluckhohn, Berkeley's Alfred Kroeber who received the first PhD in anthropology awarded at Columbia by Franz Boas.

It is also clear that at that time the disciplinary identity and intellectual coherence of the sociological and anthropological projects hung of the balance of this definitional contest, which was precisely what lay behind the famous Kroeber/ Parsons "truce" (Kroeber and Parsons 1958), one that was no truce at all but essentially the capitulation on the part of Kroeber to give "society" the sociologists (something that would have been, and was, unthinkable for a Malinowski or a Radcliffe-Brown) and keep the desiccated Parsonian version of "culture" as an idealist symbol system made up of "patterns" for the anthropologists. The culture concept is thus as American as apple pie and an inherent (not accidental) outgrowth of normativist functionalism.

The career of the analytic concept of culture within anthropology has been written on extensively both during the heyday of functionalism (e.g. Kroeber and Kluckhohn 1952; Bidney 1967) during the immediate post-functionalist period (e.g. Stocking 1966) and more recently (e.g. Kuper 1999) and as such it is relatively not very obscure, although it is clear that most cultural sociologists are blissfully ignorant about it. However, there is no doubt that there had been an "analytic" concept of culture available to anthropologists since at least the 1870s, when Tylor defined the concept in a sufficiently "value-free" way as to serve the relevant scientific purposes. Yet, Tylor's formulation remained inherently tied to ethnocentric views of cultural evolution that saw something like Victorian era England as the pinnacle of civilization (with "Australians" at the bottom and the "Chinese" in between). As such Tylor's famous "complex whole" rendering of the culture concept, in spite of the largely inaccurate hagiography enacted by Kroeber and Kluckhohn (1952) remained indelibly tied to nineteenth century (racist) version concept. It was in fact Kroeber's teacher Franz Boas, himself drawing on his upbringing in a (liberal, not racist) version of the germanic tradition, who developed something like the modern (fully relativist) culture concept and who used it to vanquish the last remnants of ethnocentric evolutionism and racialism still extant in the American field. This begat the American version of (what later came to be known as) cultural anthropology and then known as "ethnology" (Stocking 1966). In Boas, culture becomes equivalent to the "social heritage" essentially everything from beliefs, values, morals, and technology that is not given by the human biological constitution is learned by novices and is preserved and transmitted from generation to generation.

But the funny thing is that even though Boas developed this concept in early writings before 1920, most anthropologists did not take notice. Instead, a variety of definitions, counter-definitions, and redefinitions of culture began to accrete during the 40 separating Boas's early writings from Kroeber and Kluckhohn's emergency intervention as a reaction to the Parsonian incursion (so much so that they were able to collect about 164 of these in 1952). It is obvious that no anthropologist during this period thought that anything big for the professional status of anthropology actually rode on coming up with a "crisp" consensual definition of the culture concept and that was an entirely correct perception. For once Boas vanquished the bugaboo of racialist biologism, his particular version of the culture concept seem to have done its knowledge-political job and people felt free to ignore and develop their own twists on the idea. Accordingly, other anthropological writers with their own partial and concrete interests began to propose other ideas about what culture might or might not be some (like Sapir and the early Kroeber) even harking back to "normative" or "humanistic" notions of culture. Lines of division (and here I rely on Bidney 1967) began to form those who remained loyal to Boas's more naturalistic "social heritage" notion (which includes artifacts, buildings, habits, techniques, mores, and essentially everything that is learned and "man-made") from those who thought of culture as more restrictive terms as referring exclusively to non-material, non-naturalistic *ideal* or *conceptual* elements.

Most importantly, there were those who thought of culture not as a set of contents (either material or ideal) but as a *pattern* (later on referred to as cybernetic "program" by both Parsons and Geertz) abstracted out from the social behavior of persons (importantly

Kluckhohn was of this persuasion, but both Ruth Benedict and Margaret Mead provide popular versions of this story). This "pattern" was akin to a set of general recipes or abstract guidelines for how to behave but did not reduce to particular bits of behavior or even the symbols via which they are expressed. Patterns could be typed and classified, and therefore the job of the cultural anthropologist was to uncover these and possibly come up with exhaustive list of variants across the world's "cultures." At the time, most anthropologists linked their definitions of culture to the Kroeberian (1917) notion of the "superorganic" (even if they were critical of the details Kroeber's particular formulation they all liked the autonomist implications) in which "culture" was thought to constitute its own emergent level analytically and ontological separate from the biological individual and acting back on persons to constrain their behavior.

It is from these idea bits that Parsons built up his own version of the concept of culture in the 1940s and 1950s. In contrast to the anthropologists, Parsons understood full well the knowledge-political implications of nailing down a culture concept, for he was engaged in his own bit of empire making at Harvard at the time. These were the years (1946 to be exact) when Parsons leveraged an outside offer to finally take down rug down from under Sorokin in Sociology. This would be done by agreeing to lead the formation of the "Social Relations" department that would include a group of like-minded psychologists and sociologists along with Clyde Kluckhohn in anthropology. Because the department was to be a combination of sociology, anthropology, and psychology, each of the branches (in good Durkhemian fashion) was to have its own "object." To sociology would go "the social system" to psychology "the personality system" and to anthropology "the cultural system" (Parsons 1951).

Working analytical definitions of society and personality were already there, but Parsons noted that no such neat definition existed for "culture" and that meant that he needed to provide one. To construct his definition, Parsons combined the notion that the elements of "culture" were ideal (cultural) objects linked to one another to form a system (Parsons 1951; Parsons and Shils 1951); this system contained both the content via which persons expressed their values and constructed their beliefs and the (following Kluckhohn) more generalized "patterns" via which they organized their actions. The cultural system was thus a Kroeberian superorganic addendum to both persons and society, hovering above them while at the same time serving as the storehouse of the system of ultimate values that gave persons their motivations and provided the necessary order to systems of social interaction.[11]

In this way, what was for the anthropologists a substantive proposal used for the pragmatic purpose of arguing against racialist and "primitive mentality" theories (e.g. Boas 1911) became for Parsons a full-fledged analytic abstraction used—for the first time—as a macro-level repository for all of the Germanic elements that had received separate treatment previously (ideas, values, beliefs). It is at this point that Parsons first develops the *essentializing* assumption (Biernacki 2000) with respect to culture as an analytic category installing it as a fundamental component of the full functionalist systems ontology. In Parsons's hands, culture thus goes from a relatively non-committal concept used to refer to certain habitual modes of acting, feeling, and believing along with the requisite set of material objects and know how used by persons to get by in the world (as in the Boasian/Malinowskian tradition) to a set of "substantialized ideal objects" (cultural objects) existing in their own ideal world (in a cultural realm?), expressed in cultural symbols, communicated via symbolic media, and towards which persons may be "oriented" in the same way that they orient themselves in relation to tables, cats, and other people. Culture (while still "expressive" of underlying

[11] The full definition, first previewed in *The Social System* and then fully brought out to the world in the famous "truce" paper with Kroeber is "transmitted and created content and patterns of values, ideas and other symbolic-meaningful systems." Culture in this sense serves as a "factor" in the "shaping of human behavior and the artifacts produced through behavior" (Kroeber and Parsons 1958: 583).

sentiments and value patterns) is now part of the "furniture" of the world.

6.3.2 Culturalizing the Classics

Parsons basic conceit was that while this particular concept "culture" could of course not be found in any of the classics, they somehow had intuited something pretty close to it except that they did not have the right words for it. In Parsons's (fantastic) proposal, "Comte and Spencer, and Weber and Durkheim spoke of society as meaning essentially the same thing Tylor meant by culture" (Kroeber and Parsons 1958: 583). This is a statement that is radically ludicrous in its brazen anachronism and completely inaccurate in every word. We know now for a fact that what Tylor meant by culture had little to do with what Boas meant by culture, which had even less to do with what Parsons meant by culture. Regardless, for Parsons, given that the classics had a concept of culture (except that it was "society" and except that they really did not) then it was perfectly fine to simply project, his own *invented* notion of culture as behaviorally relevant symbolic patterns transmitted from generation to generation to Durkheim and Weber without remainder. By culturalizing the classics, Parsons is able to "demonstrate" that Durkheim and Weber "converge" once again (but the 1950s convergence argument is not quite the same as the 1930s one) because it turns out that they were talking about two sides of the same coin: objective culture (existing as "patterns" in a superorganic system) and subjective culture (existing as internalized norms, values, and ideas about the world inside the person).

The key move in this "middle" period is therefore the integration of Parsons's twist on the anthropological concept of culture into the early action-theoretical problematic (essentially swapping the nineteenth century germanic notion of "ideas" for the his notion of culture), the incorporation of Kroeber's (1917) notion of "superorganic" culture pattern into the functionalist macro-sociology, and the proposal that the (Weberian) action-theoretical level could be joined to the (Durkheimian) macro-social level via the theory of "internalization," a pseudo-Freudian concept that Parsons not only devised whole cloth but which he later went on to claim *Durkheim* had also come up with *independently* from "Freud." Parsons goes on to propose the implausible notion that because Durkheim and Freud had "converged" on the same (bizarre) notion that therefore the convergence spoke (in a perfect circle) to the scientific validity of the notion. The foundational Parsonian moves (essentially defining the basic set of problems of modern cultural theory) have had disastrous conceptual consequences.

In essence, middle-period Parsons replaces Weber's nineteenth century focus on "ideas" (even if he earlier endorsed it; see Parsons 1938) and Durkheim's focus on "representations" in favor of a hyper-inflated and hypostatized version of the culture concept. But we have also seen that Parsons's concept was not the anthropologists's concept; it was an idealist abstraction that separated culture from "society" (or social structure) as a *sui generis* entity. Not even Kluckhohn was ready to go that far for it implied that anthropology was no longer in the business of studying society (although clearly Kroeber was willing to play).

Finally we have also seen that while basic elements from which Parsons cobbled together his version of the concept seems deceptively harmless and all were available in Parsons's *milieu*; but together they generate a powerful conceptual monster. In the Parsonian recasting of the modern anthropological concept, culture becomes a "superorganic" *system* of ideal elements (but most importantly beliefs, norms, and values) expressed in significant symbols and communicated via symbolic media (e.g. language) that act to *constrain* (following Parsons favorite recourse to cybernetic metaphors) via a top-down "pattern maintaining" process both action (for agents) and patterns of interaction (for social systems) (Parsons 1951).[12] Under the middle-period

[12] On the quite non-sensical—in Wittgenstein's sense—status of the very idea that something like "culture" as conceived in the analytic sense can "constrain" see Martin (2015, Chap. 2).

scheme, Durkheim's concern with "collective representations" now comes to be recast as a concern with (institutionalized) elements of the "cultural system," thus taking care of culture's public, external side. Weber's concern with subjective "ideas" then gets recast into a concern with the subjective (internalized) elements of the same pseudo-Durkheimian cultural system.

Durkheim fixes Weber by providing him with a theory explaining why cultural worldviews come to acquire validity and authority, and Weber fixes Durkheim by providing him with a theory explaining how external culture comes to acquire subjectively binding forms for the actor and comes to be directly implicated in driving and motivating action.[13] Properly anthropologized, the classics now provide justification for a "culturalist functionalism" that is "cultural" through and through, in which "culture" had an external order (in terms of the patterning of symbolic elements in the cultural system) and an internal order (in terms of the patterning of internalized norms and value orientations in the personality). The Parsonian problem of external patterning is taken up by Geertz and yields the modern problematic of "interpretation" around the (fuzzy) notion of "cultural system" (Geertz 1973). The problem of internal patterning was taken up by Parsons's more directly (in the middle period work) and resulted in the unwieldy edifice of "socialization theory" in normativist functionalism. Let us take a closer look at this, as it is important for the overall story.

6.3.3 Classical Socialization Theory

Textbook introductions to normativist functionalism usually propose that Parsons thought that social order was accomplished via "socialization" whereby this process reduces to the "internalization of values." This account, while correct in spirit, is actually summarily incorrect in the most consequential details. The problem is that by focusing on "values" as the central element that is allegedly internalized, it ignores a fundamental shift in Parsons's thinking, one that is crucially involved in his incorporation of the anthropological theory of culture into the normativist-functionalist scheme.

As we saw above, the Parsons of the 1930s (up an including the so-called "early essays" (esp. 1935, 1938) and the uber-classic *Structure of Social Action*, is still operating with a "pre-cultural" vocabulary one that still tethers him more or less directly to two nineteenth century germanic sources, one the germanic cultural vocabulary of "ideas" (e.g. 1938) and the Americanized neo-Kantian vocabulary of "values" (e.g. 1935). Both of these terms appear in *Structure*, and provide the first attempt to "update" the nineteenth century classics for Parsons's twentieth century theoretical concerns. Because the Germanic language of ideas and values was already closer to Weber (and Parsons for biographical and intellectual reasons was at this point just an American broker for the transatlantic importation of the Germanic tradition into sociology) Weber does not come off too badly in *Structure*. As we have already seen, the theorist that gets absolutely mangled is Durkheim, because Parsons has to retrofit the awkward vocabulary of "ideas" to a theorist for whom this was a meaningless concept.

However, the more important point is that there is a fundamental shift in Parsons's vocabulary post-structure, so that the classical theory of internalization does not reduce to a "value internalization" account. Instead, the little-discussed Freud/Durkheim convergence (that it was even more exegetically preposterous as the Weber/Durkheim convergence at the center of *Structure* is not important) comes to play a key role. In this respect, few contemporary theorists actually comprehend the radicality of Parsons's proposal at this "middle period" stage, because they still confuse the Parsonian model of enculturation with the value internalization account and dismiss it as a "special" and not a "general" pro-

[13] As Parsons acknowledges in his last published statement in this regard, "Durkheim did not work out a Weberian analysis of the various steps between religious commitment and obligations in the field of social action, especially in what he called the profane sphere, but the congruence with Weber s analysis is quite clear" (Parsons 1972: 259).

posal. The key is to realize that Parsons came to realize that both "values" and the broader "conceptual schemes" through which social actors come to *know* and *classify* the entire world of objects, agents, and situations (essentially what we moderns use the term "culture" to refer to) have to be internalized. Thus, any theory that presupposes that persons internalize the basic categories with which they make sense of the world from the external environment is still essentially consonant with a "Parsonian" model.

Parsons only tweak on Freud consists in his chiding him for not having a ("Durkheimian") theory of cognitive socialization. According to Parsons Freud's mistake was precisely to think that only normative standards externally (e.g. culturally) specified and thus internalized within the personality as the "Superego" but that the organism does need to internalize a cognitive apparatus with which to make sense of the object-environment, relying instead on a pre-social, naturally given (and thus always veridical) system of perception and cognition. For Parsons, (as for most sociologists of culture) this is mistake. In Parsonese, Freud, "failed to take explicitly into account the fact that the frame of reference in terms of which objects are cognized, and therefore adapted to, is cultural and thus cannot be taken for granted as given, but must be internalized" (Parsons 1964: 23).

One ironic consequence of not recognizing that Parsons's theory changes dramatically once the early language of "ideas" and "values" is junked and the theory goes "full cultural" is that even though contemporary cultural sociologists are quick to reject the Parsonian value-internalization account, they continue to abide by the Parsonian model of cognitive socialization. In essence, most sociologists continue to believe that people share cultural contents (e.g. world-views and beliefs) because they *internalize* those contents from the larger culture. Any theory that presupposes that persons introject the basic categories with which they make sense of the world from the external environment is still essentially a "Parsonian" theory of enculturation even if the adjective Parsonian has come to (wrongly) be limited to the "value internalization" account.

Accordingly, the Parsonian theory of culture and cognition is (discouragingly) hard to distinguish from contemporary approaches, especially in presuming the wholesale internalization of entire conceptual schemes by socialized actors. For instance, Jeffrey Alexander chides post-functionalist conflict theory for failing to emphasize "…the power of the symbolic to shape interactions from within, as normative precepts or narratives that carry *internalized moral force*" (Alexander 2003: 16; italics added; see also pp. 152–153 of the same book on the internalization of cultural codes). Eviatar Zerubavel for his part notes, that when it comes to the "logic of classification," by the age of three a child has already "*internalized* conventional outlines of the category 'birthday present' enough to know that, if someone suggests that she bring lima beans as a present he must be kidding" (1999: 77, our italics).

These so-called "contemporary" accounts are simply not conceptually distinguishable in any way from the culturalized Parsonianism of the middle period (which goes to tell you that just because somebody writes something today it does not make contemporary). Thus, rather than being some sort of ancient holdover from functionalism, a model pretty close to Parsons's Durkheimian Freudianism continues to be used by contemporary theorists, *whenever* those theorists wish to make a case for enculturation as a form of mental modification via experience. There do exist a family of contemporary proposals that is truly "post-functionalist" in the sense of recasting the question of culture in action away from issues of "internalization," this leads us to a consideration of "contemporary" cultural theory.

6.4 Contemporary Cultural Theory: Fighting the Parsonian Ghost in the Machine

From this account, it is easy to see that the culturalized functionalism of the middle-period Parsons provides a skeleton key to understand contemporary cultural theory. The classic text is Swidler

(1986) who essentially uses sound pragmatist sensibilities to develop a "negative" (in the photographic sense) theoretical system in which the two basic premises of culturalized functionalism are denied. In Swidler there is no "internal" cultural order (because actors don't "deeply internalize" any culture) nor is there any "external" cultural order because culture does *not* exist outside of people's heads in the form of tightly structured systems. Instead, actors are only lightly touched by culture (learning what they need ignoring the rest) and draw on disorganized external cultural elements in expedient ways. We may refer to this "negative" of culturalized functionalism as the "cultural fragmentation" model. This account is essentially hegemonic in contemporary cultural analysis and heterodox positions today (e.g. Vaisey 2009; Alexander 2003) can only be understood within the context of this hegemony. A good entry into this debate thus is the quasi-functionalist problematic of "cultural depth" opened up by Swidler (1986) and repeatedly revisited by subsequent cultural theorists (e.g. Sewell 1992; Patterson 2014).

6.4.1 The Problem of "cultural depth"

As we have seen, Between the 1930s and 1950s, it was the synthetic work of Parsons (Parsons 1937, 1951; Parsons and Shils 1951) that provided the first fully developed account of how some cultural elements acquire the capacity to become significant in their capacity to direct action. Parsons's centerpiece proposal was that some cultural elements come to play a more significant role in action because they are subject to an internalization process whereby they come to form an integral part of the cognitive and motivational makeup of the actor. This internalization mechanism, as a particularly powerful variant of the learning process, arranges cultural elements according to a gradient of "cultural depth." Cultural elements that are deeply internalized are more crucial in determining an actor's subjective stances towards a wide range of objects across an equally wide range of settings and situations than elements towards which the actor only owes "shallow" allegiance.

Contemporary cultural theory can be read as a repeated attempt to relax the stipulation that cultural power derives from "deep internalization" (Swidler 1986; Sewell 1992). The guiding observation is that individuals do not seem to possess the highly coherent, overly complex and elaborately structured codes, ideologies or value systems that the classical theory expects they should possess (Martin 2010). Instead of regular demonstrations of the possession of coherent cultural systems on the part of "socialized" agents what these newer "toolkit" theories suggest (and what the empirical evidence appears to support) is that persons do not (and cognitively cannot) internalize highly structured symbolic systems in the ways that classical socialization accounts portray. These cultural systems are simply too "cognitively complex" to be deeply internalized; people simply wouldn't be able to remember or keep straight all of the relevant (logical or socio-logical) linkages (Martin 2010).

Instead, as Swidler (2001) has pointed out, much coherence is actually offloaded outside of the social agent and into the external world of established institutional arrangements, objectified cultural codes and current relational commitments. That is, "cultural meanings are organized and brought to bear at the collective and social, not the individual level" (Swidler 2008: 279), and gain whatever minimal coherence they can obtain "out of our minds" through concrete contextual mechanisms-instead of "inside" them. However, this is not a return to functionalism because external culture is also unstructured, acquiring whatever "coherence" it has via extra-cultural (political, economic, institutional) means (Sewell 2005).

This view of internal *and* external culture as "fragmented," "contradictory," "weakly bounded" and "contested" has become the de facto standard in contemporary discussions in cultural sociology (e.g. Sewell 2005: 169–172), cognitive sociology (e.g. DiMaggio 1997) and "post-cultural" anthropology (e.g. Hannerz

1996), the latter of whom have thoroughly rejected the "myth of cultural integration" (Archer 1985) inherited from culturalist functionalism. Contemporary cultural theory thus relies primarily on an unquestioned conception of cultural fragmentation. What is distinctive about the cultural fragmentation model in relation to its Parsonian counterpart is (a) its primary empirical motivation (the failure of persons to display highly structured ideologies), (b) its rejection of any form of a positive account of subjective modification of the actor via cultural transmission, and (c) its theorization of the "power" of culture as located "outside of the head" of the actor.

As Swidler noted in her classic paper, "[p] eople do not build lines of action from scratch, choosing actions one at a time as efficient means to given ends. Instead, they construct chains of action beginning with at least some pre-fabricated links" (1986: 276). This implies a critique of socialization models that operate via the "psychological modification" of actors: "[c]ulture does not influence how groups organize action via enduring psychological proclivities implanted in individuals by their socialization. Instead, publicly available meanings facilitate certain patterns of action, making them readily available, while discouraging others" (Swidler 1986: 283). What is appealing about the fragmentation formulation is that we get to keep the phenomenon of interest (e.g. occasionally systematic patterns of action) without relying on the doubtful assumption than an entire model of the social world or a whole system of values or logically organized conceptual scheme has to be internalized by social agent (Martin 2010).

Contemporary cultural theorists are thus nearly unanimous in proposing a common mechanism that accounts for how "coherence is possible" when the norm is that culture tends toward incoherence; cultural coherence is possible through external structuration. The specific form in which external structuration mechanisms are theorized is less important than the agreement on this basic point. For instance, Sewell (2005: 172–174) points to mechanisms of power and constraint as the source of external structuration. Through the systematic "organization of difference" by powerful institutional actors (and counter-movements) cultures can become (quasi) coherent. DiMaggio (1997: 274), drawing on research from the cognitive sciences (broadly defined), argues that the "sources of stability in our beliefs and representations" should not be sought in the structure of our minds but rather in "cues embedded in the physical and social environment" (see also Shepherd 2011).

The point to keep in mind is that coherence does not exist "inside of people's heads" but instead is offloaded towards "the efforts of central institutions and the acts of organized resistance to such institutions" (Sewell 2005: 174). From this perspective, persons do not need to internalize highly coherent sets of classificatory structures and "value systems" in order for their action to be "systematic" since a lot of the "systematicity" and regularity in human action actually lies outside, in the world of objectified institutions and situational contexts (Swidler 2001). In the contemporary conception, culture is not possessed in a "deep" way, but rather in a "shallow," disorganized fashion that requires structuring and support from the external social environment to produce coherent judgments.

6.4.2 Reactions to the (Over) reaction

If the cultural fragmentation reaction against culturalist functionalism is the contemporary orthodoxy, then it is easy to predict the shape that the heterodoxy has to take (Patterson 2014). Either one tries to bring back some semblance of theorizing the "internal" order of culture as embodied in actors (Vaisey 2009) or one tries to bring back a conception of the strong external patterning of culture. This first route has been followed by contemporary cultural theorists who draw on post (or non)functionalist theoretical traditions (e.g. practice theory) to develop a conception of internalization that is not subject to Swidlerian objections.

The rising appeal of Vaisey's (2009) appropriation of the discursive/practical consciousness distinction (Giddens 1979), and his importation of "dual process" models from moral psychology, in order to suggest that culture can be internalized in both weakly and strongly patterned ways can be traced to this. In the same way, revivals of "strong external patterning" of the "superorganic" element of culture such as Alexander (2003) or Reed (2011) attempt to conceptualize this patterning without relying on the problematic (quasi-organicist) conception of culture as a "system." Instead, these analysts have attempted to revive neo-Saussurean conceptions of patterning as ordered sets of binary codes, which license strong theoretical proclamations as to the coherence of culture, and justify an "interpretative" (textualist) approach to cultural explanation. This is of course a methodological approach that was advocated by Geertz (1973) but which was not quite compatible with the Parsonian notion of the "cultural system" that he was conceptually stuck with (at least in the core essays written in the 1960s). Today these heterodox conceptions of both the internal and external order of culture compete against still hegemonic fragmentation ideas for explanatory hegemony.

6.4.3 Whatever Happened to the Cultural System?

Accordingly, a contradictory aspect of contemporary cultural theory in American sociology is that while some version of the fragmentation model is usually the first thing cultural sociologists trot out of their toolkit when trying to explain something, there has been a simultaneous movement to see strong patterning in cultural systems at a "deep level" and to see cultural fragmentation as a surface mirage. These "strong program" sociologists, tend point to culture as the fundamental dimension of social reality and link a methodological interpretivism to a substantive conception of culture as a "system of signs." This approach, seemingly antithetical to the fragmentation idea, is actually a close cousin of it and emerges from the same set of problematics inherited from Parsons.

Recall that Parsons's main contribution was to develop a culture concept that made robust assumptions about the makeup, nature, of culture as a macro-level ontological category. These were ideas that a lot of anthropologists had played around with (inclusive of the more brilliant Boas students such as Sapir and Kroeber) but which none had systematically laid out (Kuper 1999). It is Parsons that comes clean and offers the notion of the "cultural system" as a *scientific* object of study. However, it was an upstart student in the department of social relations, Clifford Geertz, who runs away with the culture notion of "cultural system" and actually cashes in on the analytic potential of Parsons revolutionary notion. In a series of essays written primarily in the 1960s (collected in 1973 in the classic *Interpretation of Cultures*), Geertz is able to formulate both an evolutionary/naturalistic foundation for the culture concept and a non-naturalistic, "interpretative" methodological manifesto that Geertz seduced everybody into thinking that it *followed* from that foundation. Geertz's approach was masterful in the knowledge political sense; for Geertz sees Parsons "gift" of culture to anthropology and ups the ante by taking this gift and using it to argue into irrelevance the other two denizens of the Parsonian systems ontology (personality and society).

Geertz thus squares the Germanic circle by separating ontology from methodology or more accurately by using ontology to justify methodology. Not surprisingly, this "methodology" is nothing but good old fashioned "interpretation" (*verstehen*) updated with nods to (for Geertz) contemporary anti-naturalistic arguments in the philosophy of action (Gilbert Ryle) and hermeneutics (Ricoeur). In this way, Geertz becomes the conduit via which a host of Parsonian problematics (and associated issues from the Kantian/Hegelian Germanic legacy that Parsons only provide pseudo-solutions to) have been passed along to modern cultural theorists in essentially pristine forms. How did he do it?

Geertz basically used a loophole in the Parsonian charter. For while Parsons was content to define a new object of study for anthropology and even give clues as to its ontological constitution, he said little about *how* to study. The hint, left hanging by Parsons for Geertz to take, was that while an ontology of systems emphasizing the cold scientific language of homeostasis, prerequisites, cybernetic control, and so on was appropriate for the more "physical," or "material" (or biological) of the three systems (society and personality) given the symbolic nature of culture its "systemness" was not to be conceived in the same physicalist terms. Instead, the cultural system was held together by *meaningful* links and its mysteries could only be cracked by mixing a scientistic language that conceived of the cultural system as a sort of "program" or "code" (similar to the genetic code; Parsons 1972) with a humanistic language that cracked that code by relying on the deep interpretation of meaningful action.

The classic text here is the early essay on the "The Impact of the Concept of Culture on the Concept of Man" (Geertz 1973: 33–54; originally published in 1965). Here Geertz takes on Parsons indirectly by attacking Kluckhohn's attempt to pursue a sort of Parsonian "psychological anthropology" aimed at uncovering and typologizing universal cultural patterns across societies. Geertz's point is simple: culture does not exist in dessicated cross-cultural generalities tied to the empty generalizations of psychological science, but in the irreducibly unique configuration that produce the uniqueness of each cultural display in explicit symbolism. These configurations (which may include the shaping of a person's most intimate desires and worldviews) can only be *described* not catalogued; it is thus in the sum total of these time and place specific configurations of cultural elements that "generality" will be found in the anthropological project. While it is true that in *theory* nature of culture can be described as a Parsonian/Kluckhohnian "pattern," "program," or "code," culture does not present itself to the analyst in this form; its concrete reality can only be ascertained in the specific symbolic manifestations by which it shapes even the most exotic patterns of behavior and action.

This attempt to bring together the most abstract of naturalistic generalities (e.g. the notion that culture is a program, like a computer program or a code like the genetic code) with the most specific of humanistic particularities is the key to Geertz's counter-charter; and in this sense the nod to culture as a naturalistic phenomenon that emerges in evolution as an external control system (in the form of programs or models) for human behavior is only a sideshow (as in the much overhyped essay "The Growth of Culture and the Evolution of Mind"; see e.g. Sewell 1997). For what Geertz was after was the foundations for an analytic approach to cultural analysis that justified a purely non-naturalistic understanding of the sources of human action. The naturalistic fact that persons are born incomplete and depend on cultural programming to become "fully formed," leads to an anti-naturalistic conclusion: that these foundational meanings can only be grasped via hermeneutic methods and not by uncovering psychological needs, biological underpinnings, or appeals to the functional prerequisites of social systems (Kuper 1999).

For Geertz, the most important thing is that people *necessarily* become entangled in and external "web of meanings" to give pattern and meaning to their actions; both the social and personality system are just the formless clay upon which the form giving powers of the cultural system work to produce the phenomena available for analytic inspection (see Reed 2011 for an update on this argument). While cultural theorists tend to read the Geertzian "web of meanings" aphorism as a nod to Weber, it is important to understand that this is actually a nod to *Parsons's* "culturalized" Weber and that Geertz understood both the ontological existence of this cultural web and people's entanglement in it in a quite substantive (rather than a heuristic) sense. In this last respect, if Geertz's is supposed to have provided an early preview of the "strong program" in cultural analysis (Alexander 2008), then it is clear that contemporary versions of this approach are a direct outgrowth of the Parsonian notion of culture. It is thus no wonder that is precisely such "recovering functionalists" (e.g. Alexander 2003) who have gone farthest in reviving a neo-Parsonian notion of culture as both an autonomous (substantive) "realm" with an internal structure modelled after language (replacing talk about "programs" with neo-Saussurean talk of "semiotic codes" but keeping the underlying Parsonian definition essentially the same) designed to give "order and meaning" to individual and collective action.

All of this is of much more than purely historical interest; for the Parsonian ghost continues to haunt the sociological appropriation of the cultural concept via the massive influence that the Geertzian inflection has had on practitioners of this approach especially in sociological "cultural studies" (Alexander 2003; Reed 2011) and "cultural history" (Sewell 1997). As Biernacki (2000) notes, two foundational assumptions of Parsons's idiosyncratic rendering of the culture concept (which he blames Geertz for) continue to haunt us to this very day. The first assumption ("the essentializing premise") is the ontological rendering of the cultural system as an addendum to the social and material world manifested as an assemblage of signs and signifying objects and actions. The second assumption ("the formalizing premise") is the endowment of this hypostatized cultural system with an endogenous capacity to generate "meaning" and signification via the internal interplay of signs only in isolation from action, cognition, and social structure. Both of these Biernacki traces to Geertz but as we have seen, Geertz only clarified features of the culture concept that were already explicit in Parsons's radical rendering.[14] Accordingly, when "[c]ultural historians and sociologists followed Geertz in reifying the concept of a sign system as a naturally given dimension of…reality" (Biernacki 2000: 294) they were actually following Parsons without realizing it.

6.5 Conclusion

Contemporary cultural theory is, in its essential aspects, an offshoot of culturalist functionalism. Because of this lineage, it is also ineluctably tethered conceptually, thematically, and ideologically to Parsons's (long known to be misleading) appropriation of the classics and his idiosyncratic but ultimately agenda-setting rendering of the anthropological culture concept. The fragmentation model that has become standard in contemporary cultural theory is for all intents and purposes a "negative image" of the mid-twentieth century Parsonian concoction and more recent reactions to the (over)reaction boil down to trying to "bring back" some of the Parsonian goodies unfairly dismissed by the hegemonic model (e.g. values, internalized culture, strong external structuration) (Patterson 2014).

In addition, contemporary attempts to bring culture as a robust dimension of reality and as key in the explanation of social action are unwitting prey of Geertz's radicalization of the Parsonian rendering and his (successful) knowledge-political attempt to undercut the Parsons-Kroeber compromise by making what would been only one element of the culture-personality-society triad the overarching factor that swallowed up the other two. Analysts peddling hermeneutic approaches to cultural analysis are unwitting scions of Geertz's radical move to remove naturalism from cultural theory by acknowledging the naturalist essence of culture but disallowing access to cultural explanation via naturalist methods in the same breath (Geertz 1973). In all, every single one of the problems of contemporary cultural theory, from those related to enculturation, to the relationship of culture and action, to those of analytical method and the ontological nature of "culture" as a dimension of social reality are problems generated by the mid-twentieth century Parsonian intervention.

Insofar as middle-period functionalism became the model for what "theory" and "theoretical discourse" looks like for sociologists, and insofar as it is Parsons who first formulates and subsequently defines the "hard" problems in social theory, it is no wonder that "cultural theory" has essentially become the stand-in for theory in general in the discipline, at least among (institutionally) young sociologists who do empirical research. But what if the "theoretical" problems that cultural theorists are grappling with are "iatrogenic," self-generated by the

[14] Parsons himself (1972) was quite open to conceptualization the structure of the cultural system using methods from linguistics.

(anachronistic) Parsonian "culturalization" of the classics in the first place? We have seen that there is little exegetical warrant to consider the classics as "cultural theorists" as neither Marx, Weber, nor Durkheim trafficked in notions that have a one-to-one match with the modern "culture concept." Surprisingly (to some), this implies that it is possible to do social theory and attend to its various conundra *without a culture concept* as we conceive of it. In fact, it can be argued that the reason why we seem to go around and around the same Parsonian issues is that, in spite of their self-perceptions, most cultural theorists have not actually moved that far away from culturalist functionalism (as we saw above in the case of cognitive internalization). In fact, it is even more surprising (given the intellectual history) that the culture concept itself is seldom tagged by sociologists as an inherently *functionalist* concept (even though the intellectual history in anthropology says it is; see Kuper 1999). Regardless, there is no question that the culture concept is as closely tied to functionalism as such now "dead" notions such as "latent pattern maintenance," "need dispositions," and "functional prerequisites." It is also very likely that the culture concept, due to its indelible link to functionalism, currently functions as a theoretical trojan horse smuggling other Parsonian (pseudo) issues into the contemporary scene. These "problems" then become the core dividing lines of theoretical argumentation and position-takings among cultural theorists.

Ironically, the classics provide models of how one may be able to have a post-cultural social theory. For instance, Warner (1970), in a now largely forgotten paper, convincingly argued that the whole of Weberian sociology can be made sense of using (a properly refurbished version of) the germanic notion of "ideas" and the new fangled notion of "models" (a notion that ironically has been revived in current "post-cultural" cognitive anthropology (c.f. Shore 1996)). Recent calls to treat "ideas" seriously are consistent with a post-cultural revival of the notion (e.g. Campbell 1998).

But it is clear that the most neglected classic in this regard Durkheim (because he was the one most mangled by the Parsonian germanization). I am not talking about the "culturalized" Durkheim of those who want to recruit him for a project of (germanic, and now obsolete) "cultural studies" (e.g. Alexander 1990). I am talking about the *real* Durkheim that has been unearthed and saved from intellectual oblivion in the recent exegetical and historical intellectual work alluded to above. This Durkheim sees what people now call cultural phenomena from a *naturalistic* perspective and avoids the germanic imbroglio of conceptualizing culture in non-naturalistic terms (thus leading the "method battles"). In fact, this Durkheim points to a coherent post-cultural landscape in which most of the so-called "cultural" phenomena that are thought to be only accessible via non-naturalistic methods (e.g. textual analysis, hermeneutics, phenomenology, etc.) may yield to naturalistic approaches.

Furthermore, this "new" old Durkheim, as some perspicacious analysts have noted (e.g. Schmaus 2004; Turner 2007), is closer to the naturalistic spirit of what has been called "cognitive science" while avoiding the sort of tail-chasing neo-Kantian problematics that come from banishing the cultural and the mental to an incoherent nether-region outside of the natural world (Sperber 1995). It is no wonder that it is the most recent sociological heir of the French strand of naturalistic rationalism (Pierre Bourdieu) who has provided us with the only other coherent theoretical program in sociology that does not make use of the "culture" concept for analytic purposes (Lizardo 2011).

In spite of what the future may hold, it is becoming increasingly clear that "cultural theory" is the only intellectual site in which this future will be resolved if only for the simple reason that it is the only subfield in contemporary sociology within which the "big questions" get asked by empirically oriented scholars. These analysts however, must begin to seriously grapple with the spotty intellectual genealogy of their favorite conceptual tools, since it may be time for us, as Weick (1996) once noted in a different context, to drop those tools and try to run to the safest space.

References

Abu Lughod, L. (1991). Writing against culture. In R. G. Fox (Ed.), *Recapturing anthropology: Working in the present* (pp. 137–162). Santa Fe: School of American Research Press.

Alexander, J. (1982). *Theoretical logic in sociology: The antinomies of classical thought: Marx and Durkheim*. Berkeley: University of California Press.

Alexander, J. C. (1990). *Durkheimian sociology: Cultural studies*. Cambridge/New York: Cambridge University Press.

Alexander, J. C. (2003). *The meanings of social life: A cultural sociology*. Oxford: Oxford University Press.

Alexander, J. C. (2008). Clifford Geertz and the strong program: The human sciences and cultural sociology. *Cultural Sociology, 2*(2), 157–168.

Alexander, J. C., Jacobs, R., & Smith, P. (2012). *The Oxford handbook of cultural sociology*. Oxford: Oxford University Press.

Archer, M. S. (1985). The myth of cultural integration. *British Journal of Sociology, 36*, 333–353.

Archer, M. S. (1995). *Culture and agency: The place of culture in social theory*. Cambridge: Cambridge University Press.

Bachrach, C. A. (2014). Culture and demography: From reluctant bedfellows to committed partners. *Demography, 51*, 3–25.

Bandelj, N., Spillman, L., & Wherry, F. F. (2015). Economic culture in the public sphere: Introduction. *European Journal of Sociology, 56*, 1–10.

Bellah, R. N., Madsen, R., Sullivan, W. M., Swidler, A., & Tipton, S. M. (1985). *Habits of the heart: Individualism and commitment in American life*. Berkeley: University of California Press.

Bennett, T., & John F. (2008). *The Sage handbook of cultural analysis*. Sage Publications.

Bidney, D. (1967). *Theoretical anthropology*. New Brunswick: Transaction Publishers.

Biernacki, R. (2000). Language and the shift from signs to practices in cultural inquiry. *History and Theory, 39*, 289–310.

Boas, F. (1911). *The mind of primitive man*. New York: Macmillan Co.

Bonnell, V. E., & Hunt, L. A. (1999). *Beyond the cultural turn: New directions in the study of society and culture*. Berkeley: University of California Press.

Campbell, J. L. (1998). Institutional analysis and the role of ideas in political economy. *Theory and Society, 27*, 377–409.

Collins, R. (1986). *Weberian sociological theory*. Cambridge: Cambridge University Press.

DiMaggio, P. (1997). Culture and cognition. *Annual Review of Sociology, 23*, 263–287.

Douglas, M. P. (1966). *Purity and Danger: An analysis of concepts of pollution and taboo*. London: Routledge & Kegan Paul.

Durkheim, E. (1893). *The division of labor in society*. New York: Free Press.

Geertz, C. (1973). *The interpretation of cultures: Selected essays*. New York: Basic books.

Giddens, A. (1979). *Central problems in social theory: Action, structure, and contradiction in social analysis*. Berkeley: University of California Press.

Goddard, C. (2005). The lexical semantics of culture. *Language Sciences, 27*(1), 51–73.

Hall, J. R., Grindstaff, L., & Lo, M.-C. (2010). In J. R. Hall, L. Grindstaff, & M.-C. Lo (Eds.) *Handbook of cultural sociology*. Routledge.

Hannerz, U. (1996). *Transnational connections: Culture, people, places*. New York: Taylor & Francis.

Jacobs, M. D., & Spillman, L. (2005). Cultural sociology at the crossroads of the discipline. *Poetics, 33*, 1–14.

Kroeber, A. L. (1917). The superorganic. *American Anthropologist, 19*, 163–213.

Kroeber, A. L., & Kluckhohn, C. (1952). *Culture: A critical review of concepts and definitions. Papers*. Peabody Museum of Archaeology & Ethnology, Harvard University.

Kroeber, A. L., & Parsons, T. (1958). The concepts of culture and of social system. *American Sociological Review, 23*(5), 582–583.

Kuper, A. (1999). *Culture: The anthropologists' account*. London: Harvard University Press.

Lamont, M. (1992). *Money, morals, and manners: The culture of the French and the American upper-middle class*. Chicago: University of Chicago Press.

Lareau, A. (2011). *Unequal childhoods: Class, race, and family life*. Berkeley: University of California Press.

Levine, D. N. (1995). *Visions of the sociological tradition*. Chicago: University of Chicago Press.

Lizardo, O. (2011). Pierre Bourdieu as a post-cultural theorist. *Cultural Sociology, 5*, 25–44.

Martin, J. L. (2010). Life's a beach but you're an ant, and other unwelcome news for the sociology of culture. *Poetics, 38*, 229–244.

Martin, J. L. (2015). *Thinking through theory*. New York: W. W. Norton.

Parsons, T. (1935). The place of ultimate values in sociological theory. *International Journal of Ethics, 45*, 282–316.

Parsons, T. (1937). *The structure of social action*. New York: Free Press.

Parsons, T. (1938). The role of ideas in social action. *American Sociological Review, 3*, 652–664.

Parsons, T. (1951). *The social system*. New York: Free Press.

Parsons, T. (1964). *Social structure and personality*. New York: Free Press.

Parsons, T. (1972). Culture and social systems revisited. *Social Science Quarterly, 53*, 253–266.

Parsons, T., & Shils, E. A. (1951). *Toward a general theory of action*. Cambridge: Cambridge University Press.

Patterson, O. (2014). Making sense of culture. *Annual Review of Sociology, 40*, 1–30.

Pickering, W. S. F. (Ed.). (2000). *Durkheim and representations*. London: Routledge.

Polletta, F. (2008). Culture and movements. *The Annals of the American Academy of Political and Social Science, 619*, 78–96.

Rawls, A. W. (2005). *Epistemology and practice: Durkheim's the elementary forms of the religious life*. Cambridge: Cambridge University Press.

Reed, I. A. (2011). *Interpretation and social knowledge: On the use of theory in the human sciences*. Chicago: University of Chicago Press.

Schmaus, W. (1994). *Durkheim's philosophy of science and the sociology of knowledge: Creating an intellectual niche*. Chicago: University of Chicago Press.

Schmaus, W. (2004). *Rethinking Durkheim and his tradition*. Cambridge: Cambridge University Press.

Sewell, W. H. (1992). A theory of structure: Duality, agency, and transformation. *American Journal of Sociology, 98*(1), 1–29.

Sewell, W. H. (1997). Geertz, cultural systems, and history: From synchrony to transformation. *Representations, 59*, 35–55.

Sewell, W. H. (2005). *Logics of history: Social theory and social transformation*. Chicago: University of Chicago Press.

Shepherd, H. (2011). The cultural context of cognition: What the implicit association test tells us about how culture works. *Sociological Forum, 26*, 121–143.

Shore, B. (1996). *Culture in mind: Cognition, culture, and the problem of meaning*. Oxford: Oxford University Press.

Small, M. L., Harding, D. J., & Lamont, M. (2010). Reconsidering culture and poverty. *The Annals of the American Academy of Political and Social Science, 629*, 6–27.

Smilde, D. (2007). *Reason to believe: Cultural agency in Latin American evangelicalism*. Berkeley: University of California Press.

Sperber, D. (1995). *Explaining culture*. Oxford: Blackwell.

Stedman Jones, S. (2001). *Durkheim reconsidered*. New York: Wiley.

Stocking, G. W. (1966). Franz boas and the culture concept in historical perspective. *American Anthropologist, 68*(4), 867–882.

Swidler, A. (1986). Culture in action: Symbols and strategies. *American Sociological Review, 51*, 273–286.

Swidler, A. (1995). Cultural power and social movements. In H. Johnston & B. Klandermans (Eds.), *Social movements and culture* (pp. 25–40). Minneapolis: University of Minnesota Press.

Swidler, A. (2001). *Talk of love: How culture matters*. Chicago: University of Chicago Press.

Swidler, A. (2008). Comment on Stephen Vaisey's "Socrates, Skinner, and Aristotle: Three ways of thinking about culture in action." *Sociological Forum, 23*, 614–618.

Turner, S. P. (1984). Durkheim as a methodologist: Part II-Collective forces, causation, and probability. *Philosophy of the Social Sciences, 14*(1), 51–71.

Turner, S. (2007). Social theory as a cognitive neuroscience. *European Journal of Social Theory, 10*, 357–374.

Vaisey, S. (2009). Motivation and justification: A dual-process model of culture in action. *American Journal of Sociology, 114*, 1675–1715.

Warner, R. S. (1970). The role of religious ideas and the use of models in Max Weber's comparative studies of non-capitalist societies. *The Journal of Economic History, 30*, 74–99.

Warner, R. S. (1978). Toward a redefinition of action theory: Paying the cognitive element its due. *American Journal of Sociology, 83*, 1317–1349.

Weber, M. (1946a). The social psychology of the world religions. In H. H. G. Mills & C. Wright (Eds.), *From Max Weber: Essays in sociology* (pp. 267–301). Oxford: Oxford University Press.

Weber, M. (1946b). Religious rejections of the world and their directions. In H. H. Gerth & C. W. Mills (Eds.), *From Max Weber: Essays in sociology* (pp. 323–359). Oxford: Oxford University Press.

Weber, K., & Dacin, M. T. (2011). The cultural construction of organizational life: Introduction to the special issue. *Organization Science, 22*, 287–298.

Weick, K. E. (1996). Drop your tools: An allegory for organizational studies. *Administrative Science Quarterly, 41*, 301–313.

Zerubavel, E. (1999). *Social mindscapes: An invitation to cognitive sociology*. Harvard: Harvard University Press.

Part II

Rethinking the Macro-Micro Link

7 The Macro and Meso Basis of the Micro Social Order

Jonathan H. Turner

7.1 Introduction

The Holy Grail of theoretical explanations is to explain connections among all levels of reality in the universe studied by a science. For a long time, anti-scientist critics of sociological theory used the "failure" to close the micro-macro "gap" in theorizing about the social universe as "proof" that scientific theory about the social world is not possible—conveniently ignoring the fact that *no* science has been fully successful, including physics, in so doing. In the last two decades, however, this criticism rings very hollow because theoretical sociology has closed this gap; and I will make what may initially seem like an extreme statement: Of all of the sciences, sociology is the furthest along in theoretically linking the micro, meso, macro realms of the social universe. Sociology has less of a problem than biology, economics, and physics in this regard, even though sociologists often consider explanatory theory in sociology to be inadequate. In a number of places, I have offered my explanation (Turner 2002, 2007, 2010a, b; 2013a, Turner 2013b) of the theoretical connections among levels of social reality, while others have presented very convergent views (e.g., Lawler et al. 2009).

J.H. Turner (✉)
Department of Sociology, University of California, Santa Barbara, CA, USA
e-mail: jturner@soc.ucsb.edu

In this chapter, my charge is to outline one half of the problem: connecting the levels of social reality theoretically, beginning with the macro realm. A complete explanation of the micro-macro problem warrants both a bottom-up and top-down explanation, but sometimes it is useful to focus on one direction—in my case here, the top-down explanation from macro to meso to micro levels of the social universe. I have often termed as "macro chauvinists" those who perform such an exercise because they often assert that this is the only, or at least the most important, way of explaining the social world. I also label as "micro chauvinists" those who say the opposite. My effort in this chapter begins with the recognition that I am telling only *part of the story*, although I will turn to some of the key microdynamics that complete the story at the end of the chapter.

7.2 A Simple Conceptual Scheme

Figure 7.1 represents an outline of the conceptual scheme that I have been using for over a decade to get a handle on the fundamental properties at each level of social organization. This scheme explains nothing about dynamics, but it does lay out the levels of social reality that need to be explained, while the arrows in the figure denote the areas where key dynamics make the connections within and between levels of reality

S. Abrutyn (ed.), *Handbook of Contemporary Sociological Theory*,
Handbooks of Sociology and Social Research, DOI 10.1007/978-3-319-32250-6_7

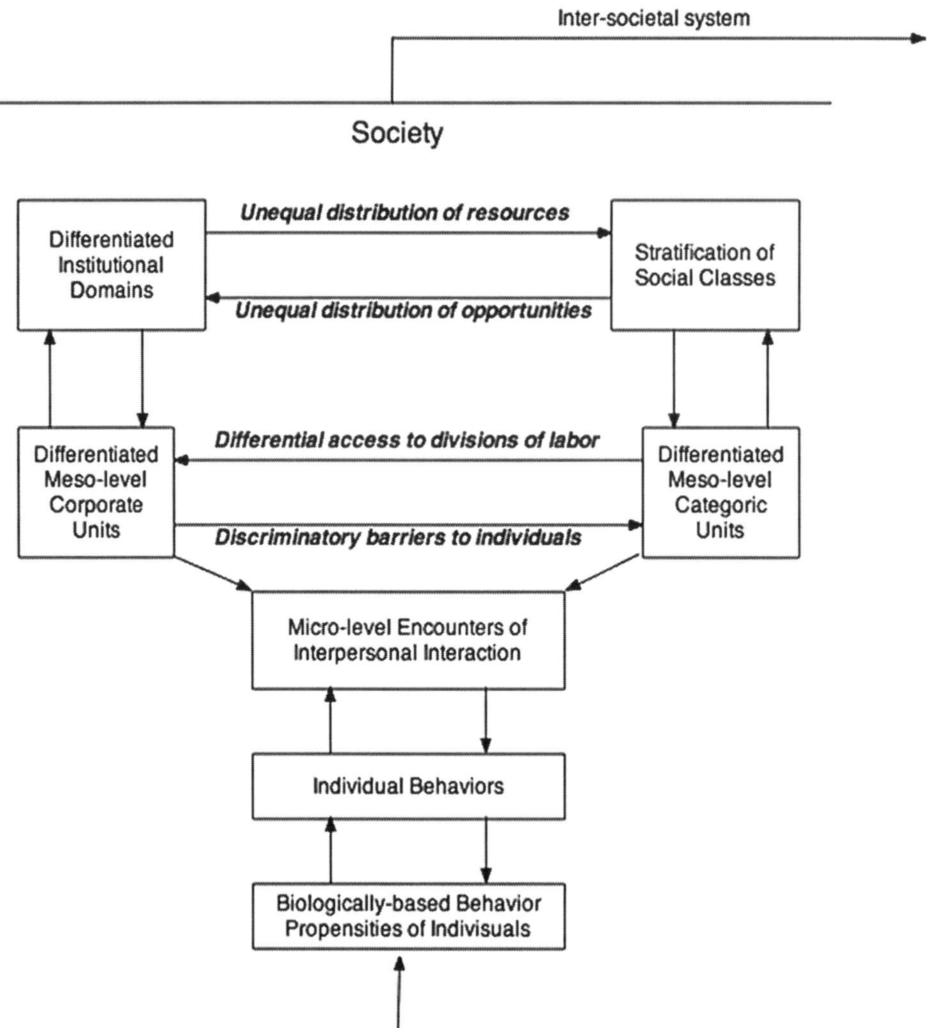

Fig. 7.1 Levels of social reality

delineated in the scheme. Too often scholars as diverse as Talcott Parsons and Anthony Giddens see such schemes as explanatory, but in fact, the theoretical explanation is not to be found in a system of categories but, rather, in abstract models and abstract principles explaining the dynamics within and between the levels denoted in the scheme. Conceptual schemes are only the starting point, not the endpoint, of an explanation.

7.2.1 Levels of Social Reality

As is evident, the scheme is organized around three levels of social reality: (1) the *macro* realm of inter-societal systems, societies, institutional domains, and stratification systems, (2) the meso realm of corporate units and what I term categoric units, and (3) the micro realm of focused and unfocused encounters among individuals.

As is evident in Fig. 7.1, I have added at the micro level of reality behaviors as these are affected by biologically based behavioral propensities of humans as evolved species of ape; and while I have done a great deal of work at this level (e.g., 2013a, b; 2014a, b; 2015a; b; Turner and Maryanski 2012, 2013, 2015), I will confine myself in this chapter to terrain that is more familiar and comfortable for most sociologists. Thus, the most micro-level unit of sociology for my purposes will be what Erving Goffman (1961, 1983) termed *focused* (face-to-face) and *unfocused* (face avoidance) encounters, while the most macro level is inter-societal system but for reasons of space I will emphasize societies and the institutional domains and stratifications from which inter-societal systems are ultimately built. The meso level, which mediates between the macro and micro, is composed of *corporate units* (i.e., groups, organizations, communities) revealing a division of labor to pursue variously defined goals and *categoric units* composed of members defined by traits or characteristics (e.g., gender, class, ethnicity, age, religious affiliation, national origins, etc.). A top-down theory, then, must explain how the dynamics of the macro realm affect the meso realm which, in turn, affects the micro realm of encounters. There are, of course, reciprocal affects from the micro to meso to macro, but these will be underemphasized because of the charge given to me in writing this chapter.

It is certainly true that this conceptualization of levels of reality is a set of analytical distinctions, but it is also *how reality actually unfolds* empirically. Interacting humans create, reproduce, and often change the basic corporate units organizing their activities—in groups, organizations, and communities—and as they do so, they may also change institutional domains, stratification systems, societies, or even inter-societal systems. Similarly interacting individuals create social definitions of individual differences, codifying these in labels and evaluative beliefs that are used, in part, to form stratification systems and, hence, societies and inter-societal systems. Once meso and macro units are in place, however, they *always* constrain what transpires at any given level and between any two levels of reality; and my charge in this chapter is to explain how this constraint operates.

7.2.2 Embedding

This explanation is greatly facilitated by the fact that micro levels of reality are embedded in the meso, and that meso levels of reality are embedded in the macro. Embedding generates conduits by which the more and the less inclusive structures affect each other. Smaller structures and their cultures will always be constrained by the more inclusive structures and their culture in which they are lodged. Of course, as the building blocks of larger structures, the smaller always have the potential to change the structure and operation of those larger-scale units in which they are embedded—which is, of course, the bottom-up side of my story in this chapter. The fact that the social universe is built around micro structures embedded in meso structures, and meso structures lodged in macro structures does, however, greatly facilitate explanation of social reality from a top-down perspective. Still, as the arrows in Fig. 7.1 indicate, there are also important relations occurring *within* each level; that is, focused and unfocused encounters influence each other, as do corporate and categoric units, or institutional domains and stratification systems. Moreover, these within-level dynamics are often mediated by the effects between the structures and their cultures at different levels of social organization—which, of course, adds complications to the explanations.

7.2.3 Structure and Culture

Since Marx's distinction between substructure (the "real" driving structure) and superstructure (the derivative structure and culture), sociologists have had a tendency to visualize structure and culture as "two different things" that have to be snapped together like Lego blocks. Indeed, sociology seems to wax and wane between periods when culture or structure is given priority. The advent of conflict sociology in the 1960s gave emphasis to structure, whereas the new "strong program" in cultural sociology over the last two decades does the opposite (e.g., Alexander and Smith 2001). In my view, it is not useful to slice and dice structure and culture in this way, and then put them back together. Any definition of social structure must include references to the symbol systems inhering in this structure, and vice versa. Here, the analytical separation of culture and structure is just that—an *analytical* distinction that gives us a vantage point for examining structure and culture. Yet, we must put them back together again when theorizing because they are mutually constitutive. Flowing across and down the conduits of embedded structures are symbols that, first of all, make structures possible and meaningful and that, secondly, that drive many of the dynamic properties of social reality within and across levels of social organization.

7.2.4 Evolution of the Social Universe

The cosmos of stars evolved from something—once thought to be a big bang, but now with some doubts and proposed alternative scenarios. The social universe also evolved from something—the agency and actions of individual persons trying to adapt to environments. Thus, part of the explanation of the macro universe will involve an "origins" story of how humans created the levels of social reality outlined in Fig. 7.1, but we do not need to get too involved here. But in understanding how meso and then macro reality evolved, we will gain insight into some of the dynamics that, like the forces of the physical universe, bind the social universe together. I have tried to tell this evolutionary story in more detail (e.g., Turner 2010a), but here my point is only to touch upon evolutionary processes as they provide useful information for developing explanatory theory. The same, by the way, would be true if I were starting from the micro level: I would want to know how humans evolved as a species and how this evolution determined their capacities and behavioral propensities that set into motion the building up of the social universe (and this is why I insert biology and behavior at the bottom of Fig. 7.1). One cannot explain all of meso and macro reality by humans' biological capacities and propensities, but understanding how these drive the micro realm would, if I were engaged in a bottom up explanation, will help explain how and why humans created the meso and macro realms in the manner that they are now constituted. Thus, *evolutionary sociology must be part of our theorizing* at all levels of social reality—despite the reservations of many theorists and sociologists more generally.

7.3 The Macro Level of Social Reality

For most of human existence, social life was lived out in smaller sociocultural formations: (a) group-level corporate units (nuclear kinships units embedded in hunting and gathering band) and (b) basic categoric units denoting gender and age differences. The beginning of a macro realm became evident as soon as bands began to see themselves as part of a larger "people" or population living in a given territory, but these were only loose cultural constructions with variable sociocultural networks. But the potential was there, and it was periodically used to create exchange networks and alliances among members of one set of bands with another set. And, once humans began to settle down into new types of corporate units, such as communities and then organizations (in kin-based complex organizations structured around descent rules), the meso realm expanded and could then be used to build up a more macro realm. Then, around 10,000 years ago, the scale and complexity of human societies began to grow at an increasing rate, leading to the evolution of the macro realm.

7.3.1 Selection Pressures and the Formation of Macro Reality

Sociological theorizing has been reluctant to employ the notion of selection as a driving force because of its connection to Social Darwinism and even evolutionary theory more generally. With a few notable exceptions (Runciman 2015; Abrutyn 2013a, b; Carneiro 2015), selection is not explicitly analyzed but, nonetheless, has implicitly been part of much theoretical sociology. As I have argued, natural selection operates at both the biological and sociocultural levels of reality, but selection at the biological level is different than that at the sociocultural level. Herbert Spencer ([1874–1896] 1898) had the most complete model of selection dynamics among early sociologists who have, in essence, built upon his insights. Unfortunately, Spencer's ideas were converted into functional analysis that de-emphasized the selectionist argument. For Spencer, persons and the corporate units organizing their activities seek to adapt and adjust to their physical, biotic, and sociocultural environments; and as populations grow, they are forced to use their capacities for agency to create new types of social structures and cultural systems to do so. Figure 7.2 outlines the basic argument developed by Spencer.

As populations get larger, they are increasingly under pressure to differentiate new types of sociocultural formations, or suffer the disintegrative consequences. Spencer also emphasized that there are certain universal fault lines along which adaptive problems develop and begin to increase the pressure on members of a population and the units organizing their activities to develop sociocultural formations to deal with these problem. The fault lines are rather familiar: production (of resources needed to sustain life and sociocultural formations), reproduction (of persons and structures organizing their activities), regulation and coordination (with power, interdependencies, and culture), and distribution (through material infrastructures and eventually markets). Unfortunately, these fault lines got converted by subsequent theorists into functional needs or requisites; and while Spencer also emphasized functions, he always remembered the selectionist argument implicit in functionalism but ignored by modern-day functionalists. Sociocultural formations represent a response to adaptive problems in production, reproduction, regulation (coordination, control, and integration of social structures and their cultures), and distribution. If new sociocultural formations prove adaptive, they are retained in the morphology of a society, whereas if they do not, a population can die out, disintegrate into a simpler form, or be conquered by a more adapted population.

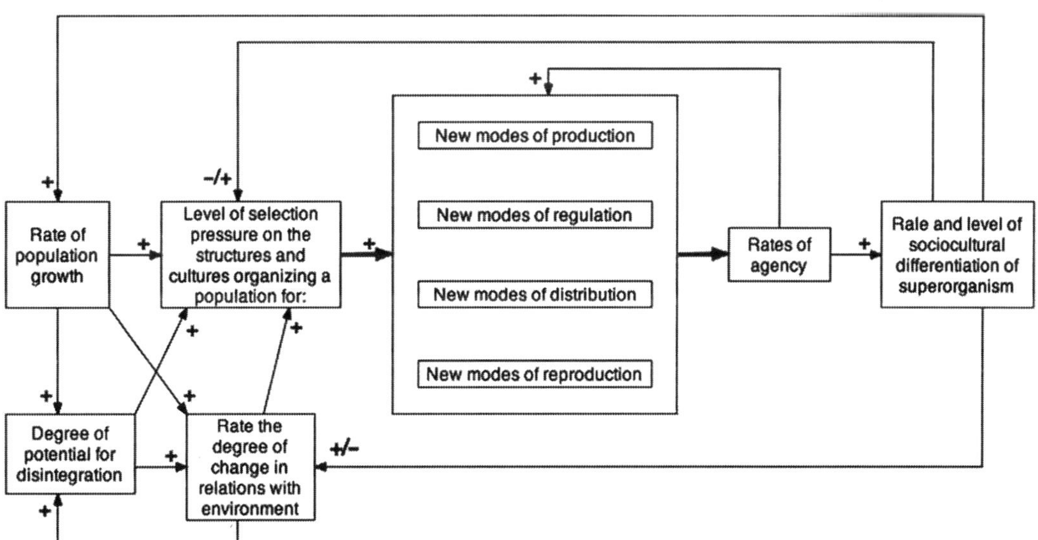

Fig. 7.2 Spencer's model of selection on, and differentiation of, societies

For Spencer and most subsequent sociologists, institutional domains evolve in response to these selection pressures by forcing individual and collective actors to create new types of corporate units and new configurations of relations among such units that can resolve—for a time—the adaptive problems generating selection pressures (see Chap. 11 for more details on institutional domains). Institutions are thus congeries of corporate units responding to the pressures from these universal fault lines; and as they do so, they generate a core set of corporate units and a relatively common culture. As Spencer emphasized, the first societies were very small and simple, meeting all selection pressures with nuclear kinship units organized into bands. With population growth, however, selection pressures increased, forcing populations to develop new kinds of corporate units for dealing with intensifying adaptive problems. Once this process of institutional differentiation was initiated, it became the template for addressing subsequent adaptive problems, with the result that virtually all societies in the world today reveal a more complex set of differentiated institutional domains: kinship, religion, polity, economy, law, education, medicine, science, arts, sport, and perhaps a few others (Turner 1972, 1997, 2003, 2010a; Abrutyn 2009, 2013b). These domains are built from corporate units (groups embedded in organizations located within communities); and societies are, in part, the sum total of institutional domains organizing the activities of members of a population.

As Fig. 7.1 outlines, valued resources are distributed unequally by corporate units within institutional domains; and thus, stratification increases along a number of fronts as institutional domains differentiate. Thus, institutional domains directly provide the structural and cultural backbone of a society and, indirectly, they create the other, less-steady pillar of societies: systems of stratification that can, for a time, integrate a population and thus facilitate regulation but that, over the long run, generate tension and conflict that lead to social change in all societies (see discussion in Chap. 2 on integration and disintegration). The properties and dynamics of societies, therefore, are very much determined by macro-level sociocultural formations—i.e., institutional domains and stratification systems—from which they are constructed, and of course, the corporate and categoric units from which institutions and stratification systems are built.

7.3.2 Properties of the Macro Realm of Reality

Before turning to dynamics of the macro realm as these affect meso and micro reality, it is necessary to outline some critical properties of the macro realm as it is formed in response to selection pressures. By breaking reality apart for analysis, the nature of these properties and the dynamics that inhere in them can be better understood, as long as we remember to put them back together again. Accordingly, I will begin with culture and then isolate some of the key dynamics inhering in these properties of the macro realm when viewed as a distinctive level of sociocultural formation that exerts powerful effects on the meso and, through the meso, the micro level of social reality.

7.3.2.1 Cultural Properties of the Macro Realm

When engaged in general theorizing, we need to embrace a "weak" rather than "strong program" when examining culture. We need to remain detached from the specific empirical and historical contexts in which culture is produced and reproduced in order to examine the fundamental and universal properties of culture of the macro realm as they constrain meso and micro-level social dynamics. This goes against the grain in today's revival of cultural sociology (See Chap. 6), but something has been lost in much recent theorizing that needs to be recaptured. Surprisingly, perhaps, we need to go back to functional theory—for all of its obvious flaws—to see what was thrown out with the bathwater in the rush to kill off functional analysis.

7.3.2.2 The Ordering of Cultural Elements

In Fig. 7.3, I have outlined elements of culture that I believe are most important in understanding macro to micro dynamics. I have arranged these hierarchically, with the arrows denoting the influence of one level of culture on another. True, this figure looks something like Talcott Parsons' long forgotten, or rejected, "cybernetic hierarchy of control," but its only similarity to Parsons' formulation is the recognition that like social structures, cultural systems are embedded in each other.

The culture of any society reveals texts (oral and/or written), technologies (or information about how to manipulate the environment), and values (highly abstract moral codes on rights and wrongs). All of these basic elements have large effects on how the macro world becomes organized; and often, this societal-level organization is influenced by connections to other societies, where texts, technologies, and the ideologies of other societies penetrate the culture of a particular society. Thus, complex or simple texts, high or low levels of technology, and highly charged or lower-key moral codes exert pressures on members of a society and the corporate units organizing their activities. This influence results in the development of more specific codings—ideologies, meta-ideologies, beliefs, and normative

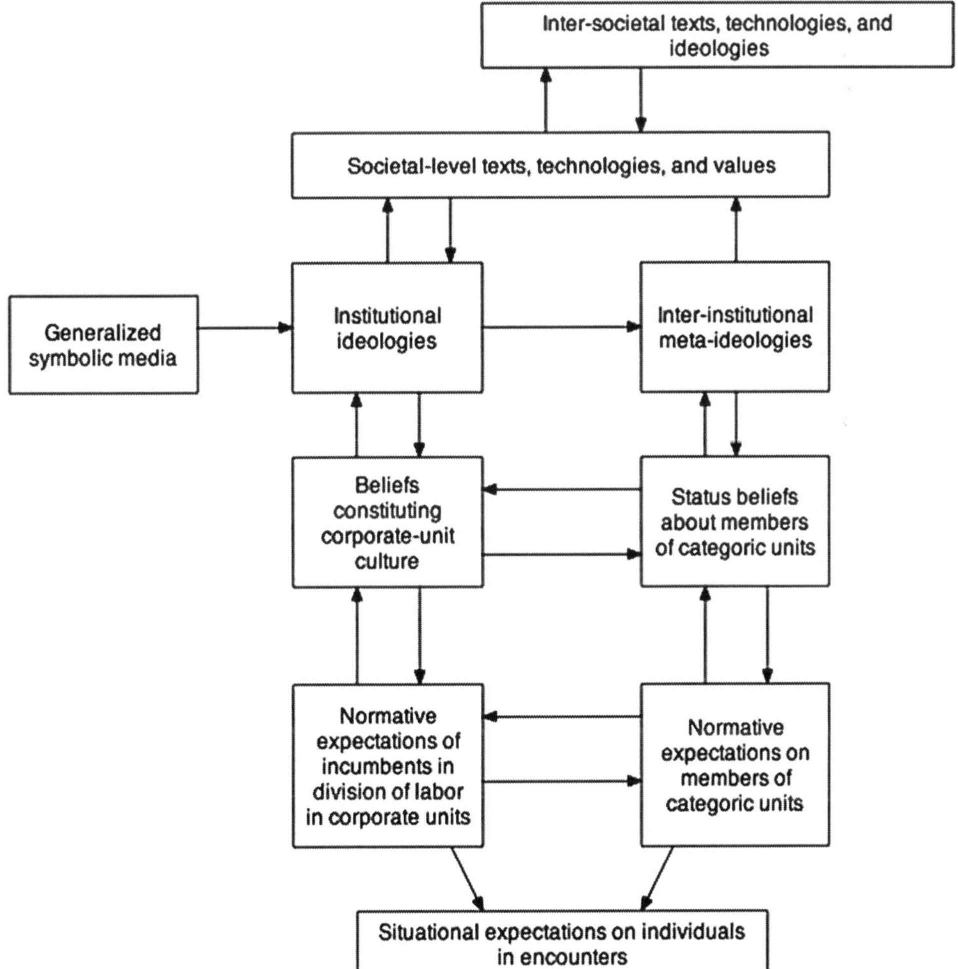

Fig. 7.3 Elements of micro-level culture as they constrain meso- and micro-level culture

expectations—that are at least partially consistent with higher-level moral codes and compatible with existing technologies. This constraint is greatest when there is a high degree of consensus on value premises (about right/wrong, good/bad, appropriate/inappropriate), when these codes reveal high degrees of internal consistency in their mandates, when they embody both official and more general cultural texts, and when they allow for the implementation of technological knowledge.

The Importance of Ideologies and Meta-ideologies The most important cultural codes below these higher-order and abstract codings in a society's culture are *ideologies* and *meta-ideologies*. Ideologies translate value premises into more specific moral codings for what is right/wrong, good/bad, and appropriate/inappropriate within a particular institutional domain, such as kinship, economy, polity, law, religion, or education. They, in essence, translate the highly abstract value premises into more specific sets of moral instructions about conduct and action within any given domain. In turn, ideologies constrain the beliefs that emerge in corporate-unit cultures and the normative expectations for incumbents at different locations in the division of labor of corporate units; and consequently, these normative beliefs and expectations constrain the situational expectation states of individuals in micro-level encounters. Meta-ideologies are blended composite of the ideologies from dominant institutional domains, and like ideologies more generally, they translate abstract value premises and texts into more specific moral premises within and between institutional domains. Like ideologies, meta-ideologies provide the more immediate and specific moral imperatives for meso-level sociocultural formations.

As societies become more complex, the corporate units within diverse institutional domains interact in often complex ways; and as these interactions occur, the respective ideologies of several domains are mixed together to form a composite ideology. As noted above, I term these inter-institutional cultural formations *meta-ideologies*; and the meta-ideology of the dominant institutional domains in a society—say, economy, polity, education, science—reconciles elements in each of the respective ideologies of these institutional domains, but these meta-ideologies do something even more important: they legitimate the unequal distribution of valued resources by corporate units within institutional domains—in the example here, the unequal distribution of *money* by the economy, *power* by the polity, *learning* by education, and *verified knowledge* by science (see discussion and Table 7.1 for a listing of symbolic media as valued resources). Thus, those who possess higher levels of these valued resources are seen as "deserving," while those not receiving large shares of these resources are seen as "undeserving." As a consequence, beliefs valorize the moral worth of those with resources, and conversely, stigmatize those who do not possess resource shares. Stratification systems are thus built up from the unequal distribution of valued resources that are distributed unequally by the divisions of labor in corporate units within institutional domains; and this inequality is legitimated by the ideologies within each domain and, even more importantly, by the meta-ideology that combines and reconciles the individual ideologies of differentiated domains. And, like the ideologies of variously autonomous institutional domains, this meta-ideology constrains the formation of beliefs in the culture of corporate units and the status beliefs about those placed in social categories and receiving different shares of valued resources.

The Importance of Generalized Symbolic Media of Exchange Ideologies and meta-ideologies are built up from *generalized symbolic media of exchange*. As entrepreneurs seek to form corporate units capable of responding to selection pressures, they begin to employ terms of discourse to explain and justify what they are doing; and as some of these actors become the dominant or core players in an evolving institutional domain, this use of a particular generalized symbolic medium is increasingly used by others (Turner 2010a, c; Abrutyn 2013a, b; 2015; Abrutyn and

Table 7.1 Generalized symbolic media of institutional domains

Kinship	**Love/loyalty**, or the use of intense positive affective states to forge and mark commitments to others and groups of others
Economy	**Money**, or the denotation of exchange value for objects, actions, and services by the metrics inhering in money
Polity	**Power**, or the capacity to control the actions of other actors
Law	**Imperative coordination/justice**, or the capacity to adjudicate social relations and render judgments about justice, fairness, and appropriateness of actions
Religion	**Sacredness/Piety**, or the commitment to beliefs about forces and entities inhabiting a non-observable supernatural realm and the propensity to explain events and conditions by references to these sacred forces and beings
Education	**Learning**, or the commitment to acquiring and passing on knowledge
Science	**Knowledge**, or the invocation of standards for gaining verified knowledge about all dimensions of the social, biotic, and physico-chemical universes
Medicine	**Health**, or the concern about and commitment to sustaining the normal functioning of the human body
Sport	**Competitiveness**, or the definition of games that produce winners and losers by virtue of the respective efforts of players
Arts	**Aesthetics**, or the commitment to make and evaluate objects and performances by standards of beauty and pleasure that they give observers

Note: These and other generalized symbolic media are employed in discourse among actors, in articulating themes, and in developing ideologies about what should and ought to transpire in an institutional domain. They tend to circulate within a domain, but all of the symbolic media can circulate in other domains, although some media are more likely to do so than others

Turner 2011). What eventually emerges is an ideology specifying the moral correctness of a particular line of conduct by individuals and corporate-unit organizing individuals' activities within an institutional domain. For example, as *money* is increasingly used to expand economic trade, it is not only the medium by which such trade occurs in emerging markets, its ability to symbolize value also makes it a moral symbol that is incorporated into, for example, the ideology of capitalism emphasizing that profits and accumulation of capital are right, proper, and moral, thereby moralizing and justifying capitalist behaviors and actions. Similarly, as *power* is increasingly used to consolidate control of other institutional domains in an emerging polity, it is not only the resource used to do so, but its mobilization is justified by the symbolic nature of power—that a moral good that is needed to establish control and order in a society.

Generalized symbolic media of exchange thus have several unique properties (Turner 2010b, c, 2014b). They are (a) the terms of discourse within an evolving institutional domains; (b) they are the resource that is used to justify the organization of corporate units to deal with selection pressures; (c) they can often be the actual valued resource that is unequally distributed within and institutional system and thereby one of the resources that leads to the formation of a stratification system in a society; and (d) they are the moral codes that are used to form ideologies and meta-ideologies that constrain all meso and micro level social processes.

In addition to these properties, generalized symbolic media are often reified as "totemized" objects of worship toward which ritualized appeals are often made. For example, people do indeed "worship" *money* and *power*; and such as also the case for other generalized symbolic media such as *love-loyalty* in family and kinship, *imperative coordination* and *justice* in law, *learning* in education, *sacredness-piety* in religion, *verified knowledge* in science, *competition* in sport, and *aesthetics* in arts. As symbols of morality and as valued resources, generalized symbolic media can become totems of worship, thereby reifying them and giving them even more moral power to constrain the emergence of beliefs, normative expectations, and expectations states in meso- and micro-level sociocultural formations.

To some degree these properties of generalized symbolic media were recognized by Gorg Simmel ([1907] 1990) in his early analysis of money, and by more recent theorists such as Talcott Parsons (1963a; b) and Nicklas Luhmann

(1982). Even more recent theorists (Turner 2010a, 2013b; Abrutyn and Turner 2011) have extended the analysis of generalized symbolic media because they are the basis of those cultural coding systems—ideologies and meta-ideologies—that constrain the formation of cultural codes and expectations at the meso and micro levels of social organization. And, from an evolutionary perspective, generalized symbolic media evolved in response to selection pressures as actors seek to cope with adaptive problems arising from selection pressures, and to justify and legitimate their solutions to these problems. Thus, in a sense, generalized symbolic media arise at a more micro and meso level in history, but once institutionalized they become external constraints on the culture of these meso- and micro-level social structures.

7.3.2.3 Structural Properties and Dynamics of the Macro Realm

The macro realm consists of societies, variously embedded in inter-societal systems or, alternatively, in conflict with other societies. The nature of inter-societal relations affects the structure and culture of institutional domains within a society. Societal structures are built on two basic pillars: (a) Institutional domains resolving adaptive problems (see Chap. 11) and (b) stratification systems (see Chap. 12) revealing distinctive strata as a consequence of the unequal distribution of resources by corporate units within institutional domains.

Institutional domains are congeries of corporate units integrated by structural relations with each other and culture (see my discussion on integration in Chap. 2 in this volume) that, as noted above, have evolved to solve adaptive problems facing populations. Each institutional domain distributes through its constituent corporate units its own distinctive generalized symbolic media and, often, the media of other domains; and because most corporate units evidence hierarchical divisions of labor, this distribution of resources is unequal. The unequal distribution of generalized symbolic media and other valued resources like prestige and positive emotions determine the structure and culture of the stratification system (2008, 2014). The degree of stratification in a society is a positive and cumulative function of (Turner 1986): (1) the degree of inequality in the distribution of valued resources, (2) the degree to which configurations of resource shares of persons and families converge, thereby forming a distinctive stratum within the overall stratification system, (3) the linearity and clarity of ranked-ordering of strata by the respective total resource shares of resource of their members, (4) the level of homogeneity in culture and lifestyles of members of distinctive strata, (5) the extent to which meta-ideologies valorize or stigmatize members in high and low social strata, (6) the degree of correlation between membership in strata and other categoric-unit memberships, and (7) the pervasiveness of restrictions on mobility of persons and families across strata.

Inter-societal Structural Properties and Dynamics When societies are embedded in inter-societal systems, it is typically through particular institutional domains, such as the economy (in trade), polity (political alliances), religion (common religious beliefs and structures), education (exchanges of students), kinship (migrations of families), or science (coordination of searches for knowledge), and at times through locations in stratification systems. Thus, much of the influence of inter-societal systems filters into a society through connections among institutions, which, in turn, have large effects on the evolution of the stratification system in a society. And, as corporate and categoric units are, respectively, embedded in institutions and stratification systems, the effects of intersocietal embeddedness eventually filter down through meso structures to micro-level encounters.

It is, of course, an empirical/historical question about such embedding in an inter-societal system, but the more embedded is a society in such a system, the more the nature of the embedding affects the institutional systems and the resulting stratification system of a society. If the embedding involves domination by another society, or its converse, the effects will work primarily through political domains as these influence unbalanced economic exchanges. If the embedding is mutual and among more or less equal societies, then the embedding will be more economic and cultural, revolving around exchanges of symbols and material products as well as high rates of mobility among societies. In these more equal inter-societal relations meta-ideologies are more likely to involve the dominant institutional domains of different societies.

Societal Properties and Dynamics The dynamics of societies at the macro level revolve around (a) the patterns of differentiation among institutional domains, (b) the unequal distribution of valued resources, including generalized symbolic media, by corporate units within domains, (c) the degree of stratification emerging from this unequal distribution and (d) the extent to which memberships in categoric units is correlated with class locations in the stratification system. The ideologies and meta-ideologies are formed from the circulation of generalized symbolic media across domains and legitimate, with varying degrees of success, the inequalities of the stratification system. In general, these meta-ideologies denote the moral worth of individuals and families by virtue of their class locations, with those at upper-, middle-, and lower-class locations having high, medium, and lower moral evaluations. Moreover, to the extent that class locations are correlated with categoric-unit memberships, evaluations of categoric units will follow their location in the class system, although there can be additional evaluations beyond the class system based upon other criteria arising from the history of categoric-unit members in a society.

If a society is part of an inter-societal system or if it is in conflict with other societies, these relationships will always involve economy and polity, and at times other domains such as kinship, religion, education, science, and sport. Yet, the direct effects on individuals at the micro realm of social reality of these inter-societal relations will generally be highly constrained and mediated by the properties and dynamics of institutional domains as they determine the dynamics of the stratification system within a particular society. Thus, analysis at the micro level is somewhat simplified by this fact. For example, if society is at war, polity will centralize power and use this power to regulate other institutional domains and, hence, corporate and categoric units at the meso level and, encounters at the micro level. The effects of war on inequality will similarly be mediated by constraints on corporate units within institutional domains and how these affect stratification dynamics and the meta-ideologies legitimating these dynamics. Similarly, the migration into a society of members of a new religion will affect the internal dynamics of religion as an institutional domain, the meta-ideology of religion, and perhaps a new, differentially evaluated categoric unit based upon religious affiliation and modal location of its members in the class system. It is these effects at the level of institutional domains and stratification that will, as I will outline below, have the greatest impact on micro-level social processes.

Additionally, inequalities always generate tensions in societies, and when inequalities are associated with categoric unit memberships, these tensions can become more intense. In either case, inequalities often lead to the mobilization of subpopulations for conflict; and as conflict unfolds, challenges to meta-ideologies legitimating inequalities will increase, as will challenges to discriminatory practices of corporate units in key resource-distributing domains. And, conflict often begins at the micro level as emotions among individuals in encounters and corporate units are aroused because of discrimination against their memberships in categoric units; and as mobilization around grievances ensues, changes in the structure and culture of institutional domains and the profile and culture of the class system occur, thereby altering the dynamics at the micro level of social organization. Even if a social movement or episode of conflict fails to alter discriminatory patterns that fuel resentments over inequalities, micro level interactions at the level of encounters may be altered because, once challenges to the institutional order occur, new ideologies come into play and begin to circulate across domains;

and as new ideas circulate, they have effects on the beliefs and expectations that guide interactions at the micro level. All of these effects are, however, mediated by the meso level of social reality.

7.4 The Meso Realm of Social Reality

7.4.1 The Cultural Beliefs of Corporate and Categoric Units

7.4.1.1 Beliefs in Corporate Units

Within any corporate unit, a culture specific to that unit can typically be found, especially if the unit endures for a time and is embedded in institutional systems. This corporate-unit culture is constrained by the institution within which it is lodged and, potentially, by several institutional domains in which it may also be partially embedded—thereby invoking meta-ideologies. The moral codes of these ideologies and meta-ideologies provide the moral force of corporate-unit culture, while the specific history, technologies employed, division of labor, distributions of authority, and goals of the organization provide other cultural beliefs that fill in around these moral codes. In this manner beliefs remain isomorphic with what is actually occurring in the corporate unit, but these beliefs are almost always moralized by ideologies and meta-ideologies.

7.4.1.2 Beliefs About Categoric Units

As the literature in social psychology on status beliefs documents, members of categoric units (see Chap. 16) are almost always defined and evaluated by beliefs about their relative worth as defined by locations in the stratification system. These status beliefs generally get their power from the meta-ideologies legitimating the stratification system of a society because once individuals are defined as distinctive and members of a category, they are often treated differentially and thus over-represented at particular points in the class system of a society. And once a correlation exists between class location and categoric-unit memberships, the meta-ideology legitimating the stratification system becomes the moral codings that are drawn upon to formulate status beliefs about, and evaluations of, members of categoric units. Not all status beliefs are connected to the stratification system, but those beliefs carrying moral power to judge and evaluate members of categoric units almost always invoke implicitly the moral standards of meta-ideologies.

Cultural beliefs typically flow down to corporate units from institutional domains, whereas beliefs about members of categoric units—sometimes referred to as *status beliefs* in the social psychological literature (e.g., Webster and Foschi 1988; Berger et al. 1977; Berger and Zelditch 1993) disproportionately come from the meta-ideology legitimating the stratification system. Encounters embedded in corporate and categoric units are, and subsequently, directed by expectation states that are derived from of these status that are often generated "on the ground" as encounters are iterated over time. Beliefs from corporate and categoric units, as well as the expectation states that they engender, are very much influenced by the structure of the meso realm because it is along the conduits provided by patterned relationships within and between structures that culture travels, much like transmission wires in older forms of wired communication. The analogy to a more wireless network is also appropriate, because at times ideologies and the beliefs that they generate are free floating and are picked up in key structural "hot spots" where density of interaction is high. Thus, to understand how culture flows to the encounter from meso and often macro levels of social reality requires that we examine structure relations of corporate and categoric unit to, on the one hand, build up macro structures and their cultures and, on the other, constrain the structure and culture of focused and unfocused encounters.

7.4.2 The Structure of Corporate and Categoric Units

Cultural beliefs vary along a number of dimensions, the most important being (a) the clarity of,

(b) the consensus over, and (c) the regulatory power of these beliefs. In turn, if meso-level cultural beliefs are clear, widely held, and authoritative, the expectations on individuals at the micro level of social organization will also reveal these properties. The question then becomes what structural properties and dynamics increase clarity, consensus, and authoritative influence on meso-level beliefs. Some of the most important for a top-down theory of the micro order are explored below.

7.4.2.1 Successive Embedding

In general, the more embedded are micro-level structures in meso structures, and meso in macro structures, the more integrated is a society and the more likely are expectations at the level of the encounter to be derived from the ideologies and meta-ideologies legitimating, respectively, the particular institutional domains in which an encounter is embedded (via corporate units) and the system of stratification. At the level of corporate units, there can be additional successive embedding because groups are often embedded in organizations and because organizations are located in communities and in a particular institutional domain, such as polity, economy, kinship, religion, law, education, etc. And so, the more there is successive embedding of (a) encounters in groups, (b) groups in organizations, and (c) organizations in communities and institutional domains, the more readily will the culture of the larger units flow down to the level of the encounter and constrain the flow of interaction. Moreover, because embedding imposes structural constraints on culture, this structural embedding increases the likelihood that higher-order cultural formations like ideologies and meta-ideologies will provide the moral underpinnings for lower-order cultural. In so doing, the greater will be the clarity of, consensus over, and power of the expectations derived from beliefs in corporate units on micro-level interpersonal behavior.

For categoric units, embedding is sometimes less linear. Meta-ideologies legitimating the stratification system establish moral evaluations for members of different social classes, with such evaluations moving from high levels of stigma for those in the lowest classes to less stigma, if any, for those in higher classes, unless there exists open class conflict in a society in which case the moral order of the upper classes in general is under assault. Memberships in identifiable categoric units are often correlated with class locations in the stratification system, and the more that such is the case, the more status beliefs will be additive, if not multiplicative, with the combined evaluation of class and categoric unit. However, categoric-unit memberships often reveal an alternative scale of evaluation of moral worth from the ideologies of particular institutional domains. For example, membership in a stigmatized religion within a society can lower evaluations of persons and families, regardless of their class position. The same can be true also of highly stigmatized ethnic subpopulations (for various historical reasons not wholly related to class). But, if members of these categoric units are over-representative in lower social classes, then the effect of this double stigma is more multiplicative than additive. And, if stigmatized memberships in categoric units are correlated with higher class locations, some of the prestige of these higher locations is deducted by virtue of other moral standards. For instance, Jews in Europe and even in the United States are among the most successful of religious/ethnic subpopulations economically but some of the prestige that normally would be associated with upper-middle and upper-class locations is lost because of prejudicial beliefs about Jews. These intersectional dynamics will be discussed in more detail in the next section and in Chap. 2 as well.

Since class locations are the outcome of status locations in resource-distributing corporate units (e.g., organizations), with evaluations of people in lower, middle, and higher locations in divisions of labor of organizations generally correlating with their class locations. However, a number of factors can distort this correlation. One is the particular corporate units from which individuals gain their resources. For example, a higher-level employee in an educational bureaucracy will not earn as much income and, hence, occupy the same class position as a high-level incumbent in law or economy; and so under these conditions, there can be a complex interplay between prestige associated with locations in divisions of labor and class positions. The same might be true of an established artist or musician and a higher-class lawyer or business executive. Again, I will explore the complexity of consolidation and intersection of status shortly, as well as in Chap. 2. Yet, even with these complexities, what is remarkable is that at the level of encounters, individuals are usually able to sort sets of expectations out during the course of the encounter, or even before the encounter because they have had previous experience with reconciling class locations with markers of prestige in the divisions of labor in various types of organizations in diverse institutional domains, since many domains offer highly valued resources that do not always translate into more money and higher class locations.

7.4.2.2 Consolidation and Intersection

An important property of corporate and categoric units that sets into motion important dynamics is the degree of *consolidation* or *intersection* of memberships in categoric units with locations in the divisions of labor in corporate units (Blau 1977; Turner 2002). If the distribution of members across both horizontal and vertical divisions of labor in corporate units is proportionate to their numbers in the general population, and if this proportionate distribution occurs across a wide variety of corporate units in a large number of institutional domains, then the salience of status beliefs about categoric unit members declines, and beliefs about individuals are derived from their status in the division of labor (rather than status beliefs about categoric-unit memberships). Thus, only when the distribution of members of devalued categoric units across all social classes approximates their proportion of the total population will the moral codes, derived by meta-ideologies that stigmatize members of a categoric unit, begin to decline. For example, as women have moved into positions in divisions of labor once held only by men and once they are more proportionately distributed across class levels, the less stigmatizing are the status beliefs directed at them. There may still remain status beliefs that distinguish men from women, but these will carry increasingly less moral evaluation. The same is true of members of ethnic minorities as they gain access to mobility across class lines.

As implied above, the converse of this generalization is also true: The more membership in categoric units is correlated with high, medium, and low positions in hierarchical divisions of labor in corporate units and with distinctive locations in horizontal divisions of labor, the more salient will the evaluative content of status beliefs become. And, the more likely will the evaluative content of status beliefs about memberships in categoric units affect the beliefs about status locations in divisions of labor. As status beliefs about categoric unit have this effect, the power of status beliefs increases within any given corporate unit, as well as in all situational encounters in the broader society.

Thus, while the distribution of resources within corporate units in institutional domains determines the basic structure of the stratification system, the distribution of categoric-unit memberships across divisions of labor also has large effects on the culture of corporate and categoric units. When distributions consolidate memberships in categoric units to particular types and levels of locations in corporate units, categoric-unit memberships and status beliefs about locations in divisions of labor consolidate and harden (Turner 2002); and as a result, a society becomes more stratified. Conversely, when high rates of intersection between memberships in categoric units and status locations in corporate units exists, the salience and evaluative tenor of status beliefs about categoric-unit memberships decline, relative to locational status; and as a result, a society becomes less stratified since resources in general are distributed more proportionately across members of categoric units. Class as a categoric unit, however, may persist even as resources are distributed across other categoric units, but once some intersection of categoric-unit memberships and diverse locations in divisions of labor occurs, social mobility in a society is likely to increase, with class memberships becoming less distinct, except perhaps at the very top and bottom of the stratification system.

In sum, then, (1) the number of distinctive categoric units, (2) the degree to which they are differentially evaluated, and (3) the degree of their consolidation or intersection with locations in corporate units will have large effects on the situational expectations on individuals in micro-level encounters—as I outline below. Moreover, the degree to which categoric-unit membership is correlated or uncorrelated with social class and with locations in the division of labor will have large effects on the level of integration in a society across micro, meso, and macro levels of reality (see Chap. 2).

7.5 The Micro Level of Social Reality

7.5.1 The Culture of Situational Expectations in Micro-level Encounters

Virtually all encounters, both focused and unfocused, are embedded in corporate and categoric units. Hence, the culture of these units sets up normative expectations for individuals. For corporate units, there will always be normative expectations tied to their location in the division of labor, while for members of categoric units, what are termed *expectation states* in the social psychology literature (e.g., Berger and Webster 2006; Berger and Zelditch 2002; Ridgeway 2001; Ridgeway and Correll 2004; Ridgeway and Erickson 2000) will follow from status beliefs, ultimately tied to the stratification system. And, to the degree that categoric-unit memberships correlated with high, medium, and low (in authority, pay, prestige) locations in the division of labor, normative expectations will always carry additional evaluative content—whether stigmatizing or valorizing—of status beliefs and expectation states for members of categoric units. In fact, if the correlation is very high between locations in divisions of labor and categoric-unit memberships, normative expectations at different levels of a corporate unit will be heavily influenced by expectation states tied to categoric-unit memberships. Conversely, if membership in diverse categoric units does not correlate with locations in the division of labor and, hence, intersects with these locations, then the salience of expectation states arising from categoric unit membership will decline relative to normative expectations inhering in status locations within the division of labor of corporate units. Thus, under conditions of high intersection, the default expectations become those of the corporate rather than categoric unit.

Mobility of members of stigmatized categoric units begins with mobility up divisions of labor in corporate units, and the more mobility there is across a wide range of corporate units in diverse institutional domains, the less salient will be expectations states attached to diffuse status characteristics for the mobile members of categoric units. The converse, however, is also true: lack of mobility up a hierarchical division of labor in corporate unit will make even more salient the evaluations attached to categoric-unit memberships, particularly those who must endure stigmatized status beliefs in lower-level positions of the division of labor.

When the corporate-unit in which focused and unfocused encounters occur is ambiguous, individuals will initially rely upon status beliefs and expectation states tied to categoric-unit memberships, but this reliance will generally be tempered by highly ritualized interpersonal diplomacy so as to avoid hostility and potential conflict. Thus, expectations from corporate units and categoric units interact in complex ways, but as a general rule, when embedding of an encounter in categoric units or locations in divisions of labor in meso-level units is not clear, the status with the most clarity will generally become the default reference point in determining initial expectations for micro-level behaviors. But these expectations can change with more information about categoric-unit status or locational status in the divisions of labor of corporate units.

If categoric unit memberships remain salient and are correlated with divisions of labor in corporate units, then divisions in the stratification system will persist and increase the salience of status beliefs and expectation states. As categoric unit memberships increasingly intersect with positions in a broad range of corporate units in an equally diverse number of institutional domains, then the general salience of status beliefs and expectation states in all interactions among members of a population will decline, and if the location in a corporate unit is known, the normative expectations attached to places in the division of labor will become the dominant expectations at the micro level. If the corporate unit locations of participants in an encounter are not known, but the salience of categoric-unit membership has declined in general, then individuals will need to use tact to create new situational expectations to guide the flow of the interaction—often a very stressful process but the price to be paid for a reduction in stratification at the macro level of social organization.

7.5.2 The Structural Properties of Micro Reality

The basic building blocks of social structures are status along with associated roles and expectations. Thus, the nature of how status is organized at the level of the encounter has considerable effect on how expectations affect the actions and interactions of individuals. Some of these key organizational properties of status are reviewed below.

7.5.2.1 The Nature of Status

The most important dimension of status is whether it is tied to corporate units or categoric units (*diffuse status characteristics*). As noted earlier, when high and low moral evaluations of diffuse status characteristics are correlated on a consistent basis with, respectively, higher and lower positions in divisions of labor across resource-bestowing institutional domains, then the effects of diffuse and locational status are consolidated and hence more influential. The opposite is the case with intersection; increasing intersections of locational status with diffuse status characteristics decreases the influence of status beliefs, especially as intersections come from upwardly mobile of previously devalued members of categoric units into new, more resource-giving positions in corporate units. Evaluation of diffuse status becomes more problematic (due to shifting status beliefs), with the result that people in encounters will generally use locational status, if relevant, as the default position and invoke expectations states for differentiated positions in the divisions of labor of corporate units rather than expectations derived from diffuse status characteristics. If neither locational or diffuse status are clear, then individuals will need to do considerable interpersonal work "on the ground" to create or discover relevant expectation states for guiding their conduct.

7.5.2.2 The Nature of the Corporate Units

There have been just three basic types of corporate units invented by humans: groups, organizations, and communities. These units vary in the explicitness and formality of their respective divisions of labor, with organizations the most likely to evidence explicit vertical and horizontal divisions of labor. Thus, expectation states will be more explicit, clear, agreed upon, and authoritative in organizations than in either groups or communities. Such is particularly likely to be the case if an organization has explicit goals, and the division of labor is set up to meet these goals. Of course, if a group is embedded in an organization, then the expectations guiding the division of labor will be very evident to all; but over time, groups tend to develop a more informal and relaxed set of expectations states, unless those in authority push them on subordinates, in which case subordinates may develop their own unique subculture and expectation states (often dedicated to resistance against authority). In communities, if the encounter is part of one of the organizations that make up a community (e.g., police, medical offices, schools, churches, etc.), then the expectations inhering in the division of labor of the organization in which an encounter is embedded will be operative. At other times, in less focused encounters in public, expectations will be ambiguous or will have to evolve if an encounter becomes focused, especially so if the encounter is iterated over time.

7.5.2.3 Boundary Markers and Rituals

The more bounded is a corporate unit in physical space, with explicit entrance and exit rules and rituals (such as entering a Catholic church or a lecture hall), the more explicit will be expectation states (Luhmann 1982). And, the more conscious will individuals be of their respective status locations which, in general, will dominate over diffuse status characteristics in establishing expectations states in encounters.

Situational Ecology
Unfocused encounters occur in an ecology that carries cultural meanings for partitions, props, use spaces, and other physical properties. These meanings will almost always carry rights and privileges associated with status. For example, in the segregated south in the United States, benches, drinking fountains, and partitions were all arrayed to mark the diffuse status characteristics of blacks and whites; and thus, it was not surprising that the mid-twentieth century civil rights movement began and often challenged the traditional meanings of situational ecology (e.g., sit-ins at lunch counters and refusals to go to the back of a bus). But, more generally and less oppressively, situational ecology often carries more benign meanings. Sometimes these increase the salience of status but often they do just the opposite: they become places where status considerations are relaxed, as is the case when highly diverse persons sit on public park benches, or use playground equipment, or gather on the edge of a public fountain.

Nature of the Encounter Encounters are either focused or unfocused, although they can flow between these two poles. Focused encounters almost always force some judgment of relative status, if only to determine its relevance to the situational expectations that are in play. Unfocused encounters are intended to avoid face engagement, but this does not mean that individuals do not assess diffuse and locational status of others as they monitor each others' movements in space. There will almost always be expectations as to the appropriate demeanor in space; and so, individuals will monitor to determine if such proper demeanor is being practiced (Goffman 1963, 1971). If there is deviation from what is expected, the situation will be monitored more carefully to determine if this deviation poses a threat to the public order. Naturally, those wishing to assert their status, especially where higher-status others are not in a position to sanction deviations, can often be a means for chronically lower status persons to gain some sense of efficacy and esteem by forcing higher status people to give way or retreat. Societies with high levels of inequality and with low-levels of monitoring of public places by forces of social control will often see lower-status persons and groups using unfocused encounters as a means to gain some increase in status, or to release hostilities against higher status persons and families. And again, it should not be surprising that when larger-scale uprisings over inequality begin in a society, they often begin with violations of expectations about unfocused encounters in public places. But, most of the time, individuals and groups of individuals tend to abide by the expectations of places where encounters are to be unfocused.

Whether by intent or accident, encounters in places where unfocus is normatively expected, but suddenly become focused lead stereotypical apologies or, alternatively, greeting rituals to signal a basic willingness to abide by expectations of a more focused encounter. Moreover, some situations that are normally unfocused can be become situationally focused among strangers in close proximity, such as standing in line outside an Apple store on launch day for a new product or just standing in line to enter a movie or sport activity. These local breaking of expectations for unfocus are almost always highly animated in very ritualized ways as individuals, without status cues about locations in organizations and without salience of categoric unit expectations, work to sustain a positive emotional flow and, thereby, avoid breaching the focus. Thus, most of the time when unfocus is breached by accident rather than by intent, individuals will work very hard to prevent a breach of the focused encounter in order to avoid the conflict that also accompanies breaches of focused encounters.

7.6 Motivational and Emotional Dynamics in Encounters

Encounters are episodes of interaction among individuals, but I have yet to address fully how individuals respond to the structural locations that they occupy in encounters and the expectations that filter down form the macro through the meso to micro levels of social reality. Humans are always *motivated*, and they react to the cultural expectations that constrain them and the resources that they can derive from status locations in corporate units. And, their reactions determine how an encounter will proceed. But, more is also involved: people's emotional reactions to what transpires at the level of the encounter will also have large effects on the viability of all those structures and their cultures that are built from encounters—which, in essence, means all of the social structures and cultures of a society. The meso and macro levels of reality do, indeed, constrain interaction at the micro level, but the reverse is also true: motivated and emotional humans determine just how viable an encounter is to be and, thus, how viable social structures at all levels of human social organization are to be.

7.6.1 Meeting the Expectations States Generated by Transactional Needs

In Table 7.2, I posit what I see as universal transactional needs that individuals seek to meet in every encounter. These needs are arrayed in their order of salience in most encounters; and thus, verification of various levels of self or identity is the most powerful need that individuals must meet (Burke and Stets 2009; Tajfel and Turner 1986), followed by perceptions of receiving a "profit" in exchanges of resources with others. Experiencing a sense of efficacy, group inclusion, trust, and facticity are also important needs.

Table 7.2 Transactional needs generating expectation states

1. **Verification of identities**: needs to verify one or more of the four basic identities that individuals present in all encounters
(a) *Core-identity*: the conceptions and emotions that individuals have about themselves as persons that they carry to most encounters
(b) *Social-identity*: the conception that individuals have of themselves by virtual of their membership in categoric units which, depending upon the situation, will vary in salience to self and others; when salient, individuals seek to have others verify their social identity
(c) *Group-identity*: the conception that individuals have about their incumbency in corporate units (groups, organizations, and communities) and/or their identification with the members, structure, and culture of a corporate unit; when individuals have a strong sense of identification with a corporate unit, they seek to have others verify this identity
(d) *Role-identity*: the conception that individuals have about themselves as role players, particularly roles embedded in corporate units nested in institutional domains; the more a role-identity is lodged in a domain, the more likely will individuals need to have this identity verified by others
2. **Making a profit the exchange of resources**: needs to feel that the receipt of resources by persons in encounters exceeds their costs and investments in securing these resources and that their shares of resources are just compared to (a) the shares that others receive in the situation and (b) reference points that are used to establish what is a just share
3. **Efficacy**: needs to feel that one is in control of the situation and has the individual capacity and opportunity to direct ones own conduct, despite sociocultural constraints
4. **Group inclusion**: needs to feel that one is a part of the ongoing flow of interaction in an encounter; and the more focused is the encounter, the more powerful is this need
5. **Trust**: needs to feel that others' are predictable, sincere, respective of self, and capable of rhythmic sustaining synchronization
6. **Facticity**: needs to feel that, for the purposes of the present interaction, individuals share a common inter-subjectivity, that matters in the situation are as they seem, and that the situation has an obdurate character

In general, individuals make an implicit calculation of whether or not, as well as to what degree, these needs can be realized within the expectations attached to status, both locational in corporate units and diffuse status characteristics for members of categoric units. There is both an absolute need to meet these needs that generates one level of expectations, which in turn, is qualified by implicit calculations of what is actually possible. The emerging meta-expectation states become the ones that will guide a person through an encounter. Meeting this composite set of expectations for each need state leads to positive emotional arousal at relative low levels, such as satisfaction, contentment, pleasure, whereas not meeting these needs immediately generates more intense negative emotions, such as shame if self is on the line and/or guilt if the situation was defined as highly moral (Turner 2002, 2007, 2010b). These emotions can be repressed, but they will transmute, respectively, into such emotions as diffuse anger and diffuse anxiety, thereby increasing the sense of negative emotional arousal.

Even when individuals can meet expectations of the situation that have filtered down from macro to meso to micro encounters, the failure to meet expectations generated by transactional needs will arouse negative emotions (Kemper 1978b; Kemper and Collins 1990). If negative emotions are aroused, the most likely defense mechanisms to be activated is attribution as to who or what has caused these negative feelings. Attribution operates under both conditions of repression and transmutation, or non-repression and cognitive awareness of the painful emotions being experienced. Furthermore, as Edward Lawler (2001; see Chap. 8) argued, negative emotions reveal a *distal bias* and are pushed out beyond the encounter to local corporate unit, members of categoric units, or even further to institutional domains and the stratification system. People tend not to make self or attributions to immediate others because, to do so, breaches the encounter and invites negative sanctions from others and hence more negative emotional arousal. Only when others in the local situation cannot fight back, as is the case with domestic abusers, will individuals make local attributions for their feelings. The cumulative result of this process is that negative emotions tend to target meso and macro structures, as well as their cultures, in ways that de-legitimate institutional domains and the stratification system. Thus, a society in which there is persistent negative arousal in a wide variety of encounters across a large number of corporate units embedded in institutional domains will be potentially unstable as a result of large pools of negative emotions among members of the population (Turner 2010c, 2014a, b); if, meeting expectations imposed by micro-level culture from corporate and categoric units is difficult or imposes further degradations on individuals, then negative emotional arousal and its targeting of more remote structures will be that much more intense.

In general, then, failure to meet expectations of any sort causes negative emotional arousal. The conflagration of situational expectations filtering down via status to situational expectations states and expectations derived from the relative power and salience of transitional needs represents one of the key dimensions generating emotional arousal among humans. And so, as noted above, failure to meet expectations will activate negative emotions, often made more complex by the activation of defense mechanisms that will also activate attribution processes and thereby the distal bias inherent in negative emotional arousal. In contrast, when expectations are realized, individuals will experience positive emotions but, unlike negative emotions, these reveal a proximal bias, as individuals make self-attributions or display positive feelings to those in the local encounter. The result is that positive emotions have a tendency to stay local, charging of the positive emotional flow in interaction rituals in encounters (Collins 2004; Lawler 2001). The problem that emerges here is that if positive emotions stay local and negative emotions are pushed outward toward macrostructures and their culture, how does a society hold together? What forces break the centripetal hold of the proximate bias and thereby allow positive emotions to flow outward and legitimate macrostructures, while generating commitments to these structures and their culture?

My answer to this question is that when expectation states associated with status and, even more importantly, with meeting transactional needs are (1) consistently realized (2) across a wide variety of encounters embedded in corporate units in (3) a large set of diverse institutional domains, positive emotions begin to filter out to macrostructures via the structural paths provided by successive embedding of encounters in groups, groups in organizations, organizations in communities, and organizations in resource-giving institutional domains that, in turn, are embedded in societal and even inter-societal systems. In particular, I would argue that meeting needs for self verification, exchange payoffs, and efficacy dramatically increase the likelihood that the hold of the proximal bias will be broken and, as a result, positive emotions will begin to legitimate institutional domains and their culture as well as the society as a whole. People will develop commitments to the micro, meso, and macro structures that have rewarded them, and this even includes the meta-ideology of the stratification system that generates inequalities in a society. As these processes of legitimation and commitment develop, the ideologies and meta-ideologies of macrostructures gain in power and salience. Consequently, the culture of macrostructures will filter down to meso-level beliefs about locational and diffuse status characteristics and to sets of clear and powerful expectation states at the level of the encounter. In this way, microdynamics reproduce social structures and their cultures, and as they do so, they also reinforce the culture of structures at all levels of social organization, thereby intensifying the power and clarity of expectation states operating at the micro level of social organization.

7.6.2 Receiving Positive or Negative Sanctions

Beyond the multiple sources of expectation states, the second major dimension affecting emotional arousal is sanctioning. Positive sanctions have the same effect as meeting expectations, and the more these sanctions revolve around positive sanctions for self and identities, the greater will be the emotional arousal and the more will positive emotions flow through an encounter. Conversely, negative sanctions have the same effect as failures to meet expectations, from whatever source. Negative sanctions generate negative emotions that activate defense mechanisms and the external bias driven by attribution dynamics. Thus, societies in which there is a considerable amount of punishment generating anger and shame will generally produce large pools of negative emotional arousal among subpopulations and, as a consequence, make a society less stable. High levels of differentiation of authority in corporate units, large numbers of people in stigmatized categoric units; and high levels of resource inequality as a result of discrimination denying access to resource-bestowing corporate units or to positions in these corporate units for large numbers of persons across a wide spectrum of institutional domains will all increase the rate of negative sanctioning in a society. Even when people have come to expect this fate, the sanctions themselves arouse negative emotions that, if sufficiently widespread and intense, can cause conflict and change in a society.

In contrast, positive emotions when experienced in many encounters embedded in corporate units across a wide range of institutional domains will have the same effects as meeting expectation states in breaking the hold of the proximal bias and leading to legitimation of, and commitment to, macrostructures and their cultures. Indeed, meeting expectations can double up and often be viewed as a positive sanction, thereby increasing the pressure to break out of the centripetal pull of the proximal bias. Additionally, the consequence will be much the same as meeting expectations, especially expectations for self-verification and positive exchange payoffs because sanctions from others are always taken "personally" and seen from the identities being brought to bear by a person in an encounter. Positive sanctioning will thereby increase the power of the culture in macro and meso structures and hence the expectation states on individuals in micro-level encounters. Once the proximal bias is broken, microdynamics become more likely to reproduce the meso and macro structures, along with their cultures, that constrain interactions in encounters. Conversely, if large segments of the population fail to meet expectations or do so only under conditions of high rates of negative sanctioning, then reproduction of the structure and culture of meso and macro structures becomes increasingly problematic, with social control at the level of the encounter revolving around constraint and punishment which, in the long run, will only add fuel to the distal bias of negative emotions and delegitimate meso and macro structures and, thereby, encourage mobilization for conflict by those persistently experiencing negative emotions.

Ironically, there is a vulnerability built in societies where expectations and receipt of positive sanctions have consistently been met over time in the corporate units of wide variety of institutional domains. The vulnerability resides in raised expectations for meeting situational expectation states, especially those from transactional needs, and for raised expectations for receipt of positive sanctions. When these suddenly do not occur, as might be the case, for example in the United States, with dramatically increasing levels of wealth and income inequality, the middle classes may suddenly experience spikes in negative emotions (Turner 2014); and while their commitments to existing institutional arrangements from past experiences may delay their mobilization for conflict, these individuals have resources (some money, organizational affiliations, experience in social movements organizing various causes, and historically high rates of voting) to effectively mobilize once they begin to withdraw commitments to at least some aspect of the institutional order (Turner 2014).

7.7 Comparing Top-Down with Bottom-Up Explanations

For over a decade now, my efforts to build general theory have been shadowed and, more importantly, informed by the work of Edward Lawler and his colleagues (1992, 2001), particularly S. Thye and Y. Yoon (2000, 2008, 2009, 2013, 2014). Lawler's approach has evolved from experimental psychological experiments drawing primarily from Richard Emerson's (1972) seminal insights on exchange networks and power dependence relations, whereas as my work has always been purely theoretical in the often discredited "grand theorizing" tradition. Curiously, our work has increasingly converged over the last 15 years in our respective efforts to explain the connections among micro, meso, and macro levels of social reality. Since Lawler, Thye, and Yoon devoted a section comparing our respective theories, let me do the same from my perspective. There is little that I disagree with in their portrayal of my approach, although there are a couple of misunderstandings that I can resolve here. The similarities in our approaches, especially when taking the bottom-up perspective of Lawler's, Thye's, and Yoon's chapter are more important than our minor differences: Micro interactions generate the emotions and feelings that can be valenced as positive and negative; such emotions are the glue that binds societies together or the explosive fuel that tears them apart; attributions for positive and negative emotional experiences are a critical dynamic of the social universe; these attributions are biased with positive emotions revealing a *proximal bias* of staying in the local encounter or group whereas negative emotions evidence a *distal bias* of targeting meso and macrostructures; and the basic dilemma of the social order is how the distal bias for negative emotions can be overcome by breaking the centripetal force of the proximal bias and thereby allowing positive emotions to flow outward toward meso and macro structures and their respective cultures.

The differences in our respective approaches revolves around the mechanism by which the proximal bias is broken, although some of these are not large differences and, in fact, are highly complementary. As I have emphasized in this chapter, clarity of expectations is one important mechanism because it increases the likelihood that individuals will hold realistic expectations that they can meet and, at the same time, receive positive sanctions from others. Lawler, Thye and Yoon argue that emotions are always generated in interaction, regardless of clarity of expectations and that a sense of efficacy and shared control and responsibility are probably more important in generating positive emotions than clarity of expectations. Moreover, successive embedding of social structures—encounters in groups, groups in organizations, organizations in communities, organizations in institutional domains, etc.—implies hierarchies of authority than can undermine the forces that they posit—productive exchange, efficacy, and shared control and autonomy—to generate positive emotions. For them, positive emotions arise from the nature of shared control, efficacy, and support of higher-level meso structures within which interactions are played out. I do not disagree with their portrayal of the effects of efficacy and shared control/autonomy, but I do need to qualify their portrayal of embedding as equivalent to hierarchies of authority.

I would agree that *if* there are high degrees of authority imposed from macro to meso to micro, this excessive control along with punitive aspects of any authority structure will arouse negative emotions, even as local encounters produce some positive emotions. Thus, they are correct that *the nature of the embedding* is critical in determining whether or not encounters can break the proximal bias and allow positive emotions can migrate out, first, to meso and, then, to macro structures and their cultures. High levels of inequality, consolidations of parameters marking categoric units, and high levels of authoritative control all work against breaking the proximal bias and, in fact, increase the likelihood that the distal bias of negative emotions will de-legitimate meso and macro sociocultural formations. Moreover, the positive emotions arising from encounters at the micro level will often mobilize positive emotions in support of ever-more negative portrayals of meso structures which, in turn, increases the likelihood of conflict in the system on domination.

But embedding across multiple levels of social reality *does not need to involve long chains of domination*, as in a Soviet-style society. Encounters are embedded in groups, which can have varying degrees of autonomy from other groups and the larger meso-level corporate unit in which they are embedded. Similarly, corporate units can have autonomy from other like units and institutional domains in which they are embedded. They importance of embedding is that it places encounters within a delimited culture, within specific institutional domains dealing with delimited range of adaptive problems in a society, and within meso-level corporate and categoric units where expectations are also more delimited and hence clear. The more these connections involve authority in a larger, society-wide system of domination, there more true is Lawler's, Thye's, and Yoon's portrayal: clarity at a very high cost of excessive control, which only aggravates the distal bias (see Chap. 10 where I outline the disintegrative effects of integration based upon a system on domination). And so, they are correct in emphasizing that encounters must involve meeting the transactional needs outlined in Table 7.2, which all converge with the propositions that Lawler et al. develop on mechanisms on non-separability of actions, joint responsibilities, share autonomy, group-level focus.

I am subsuming much of their analysis under motivational need states, basic to humans. Encounters must verify self, at any or all of the four levels portrayed (including both group or corporate-unit identities and social or categoric-unit identities); encounters must yield profitable exchange payoffs where profits exceed costs and investments, measured against cultural standards of justice and fairness; encounters must allow people to achieve a sense of efficacy (an ideas that, once again, I began to include in my theorizing about the time Lawler et al. began to draw out the meso and macro implications of their theory); encounters must allow people to feel a sense of group inclusion, which perhaps I should be broadened to include their emphasis on shared control and autonomy; and encounters must generate a sense of trust or feelings that the actions of others are predictable, that these actions lead to interaction rituals (Collins 2004) that arouse positive emotions about the encounter, that people are sincere and respectful of self and, perhaps I should add, that increase individuals' positive orientations to the group-level structures in which an encounter is embedded.

Thus, what Lawler, Thye, and Yoon characterize as mechanisms are, for me, *motive states* that come from individuals (Turner 2002, 2007, 2010b); they are, in my view, hard-wired biologically; and they are present in each and every encounter; and if they can be realized, these need states will lead to positive emotional arousal, even under structural conditions of meso-level constraint. Perhaps the positive emotions aroused under constraint may not break the proximal bias, but they will make the micro level world of encounters more gratifying and forestall their rejection of the meso and macro worlds constraining their options.

A final clarification along these lines is also in order. When I argue that embedding of the micro in meso, and the meso in the macro, provides conduits by which positive emotions can travel outward when the proximal bias is broken, I have a much more robust conception of how this process works. In complex societies, individuals engage in hundreds and indeed thousands of encounters in a surprisingly short period of time in a wide variety of groups, lodged inside of a wide variety of corporate units and categoric units, in at least 8–12 institutional domains, and within various strata of the larger stratification system. As I argued earlier, the key to the positive emotional arousal that breaks the proximal bias is not experiencing positive emotions in a delimited set of groups and corporate units in one or two institutional domains, but experiencing positive emotions (1) consistently across (2) many groups (3) lodged in many organizations across (4) multiple institutional domains for extended periods of their life course. Under these four conditions, positive emotions—first here and then there—break the hold of the proximal bias and begin to send positive emotions to corporate units and then to most institutional domains and most sectors of the stratification system, thereby legitimating macrostructures and their cultures. My theory is not about particular encounters in a particular organization, although the dynamics that both Lawler et al. and I outline are relevant, but my goal is to explain how positive emotions become the force integrating the three levels of the social universe, as portrayed in Fig. 7.1. This is the same goal as Lawler, Thye, and Yoon, but they are coming at the issue of commitment (for me, one mechanisms of integration) from a micro perspective; I am coming at it as a general theorist and, in this chapter, as a macro-level theorist. Our differences are still surprisingly minor; and I do not find any really large disagreements—although they might not buy into my more psychoanalytic views of emotions (not examined here)—in our theories. My emphasis on expectations and sanctions as generic emotion-arousing mechanisms actually encompasses many of the concepts that they employ. I use these ideas because they are also very well documented dynamics from the experimental literature in social psychology as well as in other theories of emotions (e.g., Kemper 1978a), but there is probably room to expand these in ways that incorporates the mechanisms outlined by Lawler, Thye, and Yoon. We are almost at the same place with overlapping theories which, to me, means that we are all on the right track because we started at such divergent places and have, it appears, arrived a pretty much the same place.

7.8 Conclusion

Humans are born into ongoing patterns of social relations in societies. Each newborn begins to acquire the behavioral capacities that enable them to role take with varieties of others in organized contexts and within common culture. Thus, from a biographical standpoint, it is the person that must first learn how to navigate in the expectations of micro, meso, and eventually macrostructures and, only later, become part of encounters that can reproduce or change meso and, perhaps eventually macrostructures and their cultures. Much depends upon the ratio of positive to negative emotional arousal that individuals experience at the level of the encounters in meso units across a range of institutional domains. As such, a top-down perspective from macro and micro encounters gives us a good look at what all humans must do. Together with the ability to meet or the failure to meet expectations states derived from ideologies and meta-ideologies of institutional stratification systems, expectations generated by transactional needs, coupled with sanctioning experiences, set into motion complicated emotional dynamics that either reproduce and thereby reinforce the power of expectation states and the macro-level cultural beliefs generating these states, or alternatively, undermine the culture (i.e., ideologies, meta-ideologies, status beliefs, and corporate unit beliefs) of meso and macrostructures. As withdrawal of legitimacy proceeds, the expectations at the level of micro-level encounters become less coherent, consensual, and powerful—thereby disrupting encounters even more and causing negative emotional arousal.

Ultimately, the forces of the micro realm of the social universe are constantly feeding back to the meso and macro realms, making them more or less viable. As long as this feedback reinforces commitments to the structures and cultures of the meso and macro realm, a top-down analysis offers a great deal of explanatory power of what is likely to transpire in the micro universe. But, once feedback is driven by negative emotions, then the power of macro and meso structures and cultures declines, and conflict and disintegration of a society become more likely—until, if possible, a new macro and meso order is built up again.

There are now large literatures on social movement organizations; and it is at this meso level that micro-level emotions congeal into organized efforts to change the institutional structures and cultures of a society. If social movements are not possible in a society (because of repression by the state), then more revolutionary protests will eventually begin to erupt; the key to sustaining a society, therefore, is the capacities of persons to meet expectations from all sources on a consistent basis across a wide variety of corporate units in diverse institutional domains. Only in this way can the macro-to-meso-to-micro forces outlined in this chapter be effective; when these forces fail, analysis must shift to how the negative emotions generated at the level of the encounter begin to erode commitments to the structures and culture of the macro realm and to arouse persons to mobilize into various types of organizations to change the structure and culture of particular institutional domains and perhaps the whole society. In short, a top-down analysis tells us only one half of the story about how societies remain integrated, but unlike most other sciences, sociology also has the ability to outline the bottom-up dynamics that allow sociology, as much or more than any other science, to have theories explaining the relations among all levels of the social universe. Lawler's, Thye's, and Yoon's theory demonstrates how far sociology has come and, I hope, so does mine. Sociology is close to doing what *no other* science has done: explain all levels of its operative universe theoretically.

References

Abrutyn, S. (2009). Toward a general theory of institutional autonomy. *Sociological Theory, 27*(4), 449–465.

Abrutyn, S. (2013a). Revisiting and reinvigorating evolutionary sociology: Bringing institutions back to life. *Current Perspectives in Social Theory, 31*, 246–276.

Abrutyn, S. (2013b). *Revisiting Institutionalism in sociology: Putting 'institution' back into institutional analysis*. New York: Routledge.

Abrutyn, S. (2015). Money, sacredness and love: Generalized symbolic media and the production of instrumental, affectual and moral reality. *Czech Sociological Review, 51*(2), 445–471.

Abrutyn, S., & Turner, J. H. (2011). The old institutionalism meets the new institutionalism. *Sociological Perspectives, 54*(5), 283–306.

Alexander, J. C., & Smith, P. (2001). The strong program in cultural theory: Elements of a structural hermeneurtics. In J. H. Turner (Ed.), *Handbook of sociological theory* (pp. 135–150). New York: Klewer Academic/Plenum Publishers.

Berger, J., & Webster, M., Jr. (2006). Expectations, status, and behavior. In P. J. Burke (Ed.), *Contemporary social psychological theories* (pp. 268–300). Stanford: Stanford University Press.

Berger, J., & Zelditch, M., Jr. (Eds.). (1993). *Theoretical research programs: Studies in the growth of theory*. Stanford: Stanford University Press.

Berger, J., & Zelditch, M., Jr. (Eds.). (2002). *New directions in contemporary sociological theory*. New York: Rowman and Littlefield.

Berger, J., Fisek, M. H., Norman, R. Z., & Zelditch, M. (Eds.). (1977). *Status characteristics and social interaction*. New York: Elsevier.

Blau, P. (1977). A macrosociological theory of social structure. *American Journal of Sociology, 83*, 26–54.

Burke, P. J., & Stets, J. E. (2009). *Identity theory*. New York: Oxford University Press.

Carneiro, R. L. (2015). Spencer's conception of evolution and its application to political development of societies. In J. H. Turner, R. Machalek, & A. Maryanski (Eds.), *Handbook of evolution and society: Toward an evolutionary social science* (pp. 215–227). Boulder: Paradigm Press/Routledge.

Collins, R. (2004). *Interaction ritual chains*. Princeton: Princeton University Press.

Emerson, R. (1972). Exchange theory part II: Exchange relations and networks. In J. Berger, M. Zelditch Jr., & B. Anderson (Eds.), *Sociological theories in progress* (pp. 58–87). Boston: Houghton-Mifflin.

Goffman, E. (1961). *Encounters*. Indianapolis: Bobbs-Merril.

Goffman, E. (1963). *Behavior in public places: Notes on the social organization of gatherings*. New York: Free Press.

Goffman, E. (1971). *Relations in public: Microstudies of the public order*. New York: Basic Books.

Goffman, E. (1983). The interaction order. *American Sociological Review, 48*, 1–17.

Kemper, T. D. (1978a). *An interactional theory of emotions*. New York: Wiley.

Kemper, T. D. (1978b). *A social interactional theory of emotions*. New York: Wiley.

Kemper, T. D., & Collins, R. (1990). Dimensions of microinteractionism. *American Journal of Sociology, 96*, 32–68.

Lawler, E. J. (1992). Affective attachments to nested groups: A choice-process theory. *American Sociological Review, 57*, 327–336.

Lawler, E. J. (2001). An affect theory of social exchange. *American Journal of Sociology, 107*, 321–352.

Lawler, E. J., & Yoon, J. (1993). Power and the emergence of commitment behavior in negotiated exchange. *American Sociological Review, 58*, 465–481.

Lawler, E. J., & Yoon, J. (1996). Commitment in exchange relations: Test of a theory of relational cohesion. *American Sociological Review, 61*, 89–108.

Lawler, E. J., & Yoon, J. (1998). Network structure and emotion in exchange relations. *American Sociological Review, 58*, 465–481.

Lawler, E. J., Thye, S. R., & Yoon, J. (2000). Emotion and group cohesion in productive exchange. *American Journal of Sociology, 106*, 616–657.

Lawler, E. J., Thye, S. R., & Yoon, J. (2008). Social exchange and micro social order. *American Sociological Review, 73*, 519–542.

Lawler, E. J., Thye, S. R., & Yoon, J. (2009). *Social commitments in a depersonalized world*. New York: The Russell Sage Foundation.

Lawler, E. J., Thye, S. R., & Yoon, J. (2013). The emergence of collective emotions in social exchange. In C. V. Scheve & M. Salmela (Eds.), *Collective emotions* (pp. 189–203). Oxford: Oxford University Press.

Lawler, E. J., Thye, S. R., & Yoon, J. (2014). Emotions and group ties in social exchange. In J. Stets & J. Turner (Eds.), *Handbook of the sociology of emotions II* (pp. 77–102). New York: Springer.

Luhmann, N. (1982). *The differentiation of society* (S. Holmes, & C. Larmore, Trans.). New York: Columbia University Press.

Parsons, T. (1963a). On the concept of power. *Proceedings of the American Philosophical Society, 107*, 232–262.

Parsons, T. (1963b). On the concept of influence. *Public Opinion Quarterly, 27*, 37–62.

Ridgeway, C. (2001). Inequality, status, and the construction of status beliefs. In J. H. Turner (Ed.), *Handbook of sociological theory* (pp. 323–342). New York: Kuwer Academic/Plenum.

Ridgeway, C., & Correll, S. J. (2004). Unpacking the gender system: A theoretical perspective on cultural beliefs and social relations. *Gender and Society, 18*, 331–350.

Ridgeway, C., & Erickson, K. G. (2000). Creating and spreading status beliefs. *American Journal of Sociology, 106*, 579–615.

Runciman, W. G. (2015). Evolutionary sociology. In J. H. Turner, R. Machalek, & A. Maryanski (Eds.), *Handbook of evolution and society: Toward an evolutionary social science* (pp. 194–214). Boulder: Paradigm Press/Routledge.

Simmel, G. ([1907] 1990). *The philosophy of money* (T. Botomore, & D. Frisby, Trans.). Boston: Routledge.

Spencer, H. ([1874–1896] 1898). *The principles of sociology, three volumes*. New York: Appleton Century.

Tajfel, H., & Turner, J. H. (1986). The social identity theory of intergroup relations. In S. Worchel & W. G. Austin (Eds.), *Psychology of intergroup relations* (pp. 7–24). Chicago: Nelson-Hall.

Thye, S. R., & Yoon, J. (2017). Building organizational commitment in nested groups: Theory and new evidence from South Korea. *Sociological Focus*.

Thye, S. R., Yoon, J., & Lawler, E. J. (2002). The theory of relational cohesion: Review of a research program. In S. R. Thye & E. J. Lawler (Eds.), *Advances in group process* (Vol. 19, pp. 89–102). Oxford: Elsevier.

Thye, S. R., Lawler, E. J., & Yoon, J. (2011). The emergence of embedded relations and group formation in networks of competition. *Social Psychology Quarterly, 74*, 387–413.

Thye, S. R., Vincent, A., Lawler, E. J., & Yoon, J. (2014). Relational cohesion, social commitments and person to group ties: Twenty five years of a theoretical research program. In S. R. Thye & E. J. Lalwer (Eds.), *Advances in group processes* (Vol. 31, pp. 99–138). London: Emerald Press.

Thye, S. R., Lawler, E. J., & Yoon, J. (2015). Affective bases of order in task groups: Testing a new theory of social commitments. An unpublished manuscript.

Turner, J. H. (1972). *Patterns of social organization: A survey of social institutions*. New York: McGraw-Hill.

Turner, J. H. (1986). *Societal stratification: A theoretical analysis*. New York: Columbia University Press.

Turner, J. H. (2000). *On the origins of emotions: A sociological inquiry into the evolution of human affect*. Stanford: Stanford University Press.

Turner, J. H. (1997). *The institutional order*. New York: Longman.

Turner, J. H. (2000). *On the origins of human nature: A sociological inquiry into the evolution of human affect*. Stanford: Stanford University Press.

Turner, J. H. (2002). *Face-to-face: Toward a theory of interpersonal behavior*. Stanford: Stanford University Press.

Turner, J. H. (2003). *Human institutions: A new theory of societal evolution*. Boulder: Rowman and Littlefield.

Turner, J. H. (2007). *Human emotions: A sociological theory*. New York: Routedge.

Turner, J. H. (2010a). *Theoretical principles of sociology, volume 1 on macrodynamics*. New York: Springer.

Turner, J. H. (2010b). *Theoretical principles of sociology, volume 2 on microdynamics*. New York: Springer.

Turner, J. H. (2010c). The stratification of emotions: Some preliminary generalizations. *Sociological Inquiry, 80*, 168–199.

Turner, J. H. (2013a). Neurology and interpersonal behavior: The basic challenge for neurosociology. In D. Franks & J. H. Turner (Eds.), *Neurosociology* (pp. 119–138). New York: Springer.

Turner, J. H. (2013b). *Theoretical principles of sociology, volume 32 on mesodynamics*. New York: Springer.

Turner, J. H. (2014a). The evolution of human emotions. In J. E. Stets & J. H. Turner (Eds.), *Handbook of the sociology of emotions: Volume II* (pp. 11–32). New York: Springer.

Turner, J. H. (2014b). *Revolt from the middle: Emotional stratification and change in post-industrial societies*. New Brunswick: Transaction Publishers.

Turner, J. H. (2015a). The evolutionary biology and sociology of social order on the edge of chaos. In E. J. Lawler, S. Thye, & J. Yoon (Eds.), *Order on the edge of chaos: Social psychology and the problem of order* (pp. 18–42). New York: Cambridge University Press.

Turner, J. H. (2015b). The neurology of human nature: Implications for human happiness and well being. In M. S. Keshavana, L. J. Seidman, & R. K. Schutt (Eds.), *Connecting the brain to the social world*. Cambridge, MA: Harvard University Press.

Turner, J. H., & Maryanski, A. (2012). The biology and neurology of group processes. In W. Kalkhoff, S. R. Thye, & E. J. Lawler (Eds.), *Advances in group processes 29, special issue on biosociology and neurosociology* (pp. 1–37). London: Emerald Press.

Turner, J. H., & Maryanski, A. (2013). The evolution of the neurological basis of the evolution of human sociality. In D. Franks & J. H. Turner (Eds.), *Neurosociology* (pp. 289–310). New York: Springer.

Turner, J. H., & Maryanski, A. (2015). Evolutionary sociology: A cross-species strategy for discovering human nature. In J. H. Turner, R. Machalek, & A. Maryanski (Eds.), *Handbook on evolution and society: Toward an evolutionary social science* (pp. 546–571). Boudler: Paradigm Press/Routledge.

Webster, M., & Foschi, M. (1988). *Status generalization: New theory and research*. Stanford: Stanford University Press.

8 The Problem of Social Order in Nested Group Structures

Edward J. Lawler, Shane R. Thye, and Jeongkoo Yoon

8.1 Introduction

People tend to form commitments to multiple social objects, including activities (volunteer work), specific behaviors (exercise), other people (family and friends), careers (professions), neighborhoods or communities, organizations, and to nations in which they are citizens. Commitments organize action and interaction and make it possible for people to individually or collectively produce outcomes of value to them and to their groups, communities, or organizations. The social world of the twenty-first century, however, is often characterized as a fragmented world in which people and organizations have multiple, often conflicting, commitments, and also a world in which commitments to groups and organizations are in decline (see Putnam 2000). The focus of this paper is the multiple commitments that people form to local groups and the larger ones that often encompass them.

Multiple group commitments pose issues of choice, priority, and identity for individuals and the groups, organizations, or communities of which they are members. In this paper we theorize "nested group commitments" which can be construed as a particular form or manifestation of the multiple commitment phenomenon (Lawler 1992; Lawler et al. 2009). Nested commitments can occur in contexts where people interact with others in a local or immediate group (i.e., a proximal group) that is nested within a larger more removed group, organization, or community (i.e., a distal group). A decentralized or loosely-coupled organizational structure exemplifies a context where nested commitments can be problematic (Orton and Weick 1990). Nested commitments accentuate problems of coordination in a complex differentiated organization and make social dilemmas even more difficult to resolve.

For example, the problem of nested commitments tends to be integral to the daily experience of central administrators in universities, political leaders in federalist political structures, and managers in loosely-coupled organizations. If members form stronger commitments to a local unit or proximal group (e.g., an academic department) than to the larger unit or distal group (e.g., the university), this makes it harder for the larger unit to mobilize collective efforts on behalf of its overarching goals or to sustain them over time. In

Authorship is alphabetical. This paper is based on a program of research that was supported by five grants from the National Science Foundation.

E.J. Lawler (✉)
Cornell University, Ithaca, NY, USA
e-mail: ejl3@cornell.edu

S.R. Thye
University of South Carolina, Columbia, SC, USA
e-mail: srthye@sc.edu

J. Yoon
Ewha Womans University, Seoul, South Korea
e-mail: jkyoon@ewha.ac.kr

S. Abrutyn (ed.), *Handbook of Contemporary Sociological Theory*,
Handbooks of Sociology and Social Research, DOI 10.1007/978-3-319-32250-6_8

this paper we theorize the conditions under which people develop stronger or weaker commitments to the local immediate group versus the larger group within which it is nested and, relatedly when these multiple, nested commitments are mutually reinforcing or in tension.

Our theorizing is cast in highly abstract, fundamental terms such that it might be applied to a wide variety of specific contexts. It bears on questions such as: How and when faculty members develop stronger commitments to their university than their department? When employees develop stronger commitments to a larger corporation than to their local organizational subunit? When citizens have stronger commitments to their ethnic communities than to their larger nation-state? Our aim is to identify common underlying conditions and processes that operate across very different organizational contexts where a local group is nested within a larger, more encompassing group. The proximal group is the locus of core activities (i.e., interaction, performance, production) whereas the distal group is the locus of higher level governing activities (i.e., strategy, management, administration).

A broad orienting premise for us is that "nested commitments" are an important, yet unrecognized, dimension of the Hobbesian problem of social order. In the Hobbesian framework the problem is primarily about individual-level orientations and behavioral propensities (cut-throat competition, mutual avarice, and hostility), and the capacities of central organizational governance systems to control these behaviors. People ostensibly are prepared to cede control to central authority in exchange for the normative regulation and security this authority provides. A person-to-group transaction or exchange, therefore, is the prospective solution to the problem of social order. Much of the contemporary work on rational-choice and social dilemma solutions to problems of coordination and cooperation echoes the Hobbesian solution.

We move beyond this Hobbesian framing by introducing three new ideas: (*i*) the idea that people may form stronger and more resilient ties to smaller more immediate groups instead of to larger groups at the scale of concern to Hobbes and his contemporaries; (*ii*) the idea that person-to-group ties are more stable and resilient if they are affective (emotional) rather than purely transactional in form as Hobbes and others presume (e.g., Hechter 1987; Coleman 1990); and (*iii*) the idea that transactional ties, under some conditions, evolve into affective ties (e.g., Lawler et al. 2014). The locus or scope of the group unit is important as is the form of the prevailing person-to-group tie. Overall, these ideas complicate but also deepen the analysis of the generic problems of social order posed by Hobbes and contemporary rational choice (Hechter 1987; Coleman 1990) and social dilemma theorists (Fehr and Gintis 2007). Our purpose is to take up this theoretical task, building upon a longstanding program of theory and research that has produced a substantial evidentiary basis for these ideas (e.g., Lawler et al. 2014; Thye et al. 2014 for recent reviews).

The central theme in this program of research is that emotions and emotional ties to groups are the foundation for stable, resilient social orders. Groups that are a context for repeated experiences of positive emotions are likely to be the strongest and most affective objects of commitment. We posit that commitments emerge and are sustained through a "bottom up" process in which people who are engaged in task interactions experience positive emotions and feelings. These individual feelings, in turn, shape the form and strength of person-to-group ties or commitments (see also Turner 2007, 2014). We argue that people in interaction tend to attribute positive (individual) emotions to their local immediate group and negative emotions to the larger, more removed or distal group (Lawler 1992; Lawler et al. 2009); this is a fundamental reason that larger groups confront problems of fragmentation and balkanization. Despite this tendency it makes sense that if the larger more removed group is the primary facilitator of the positive emotions, then the larger group unit rather than the local group could conceivably become a stronger object of commitment. The distal group or organization might counteract balkanization tendencies in this way. We theorize some of the basic contingencies or conditions under which nested-group commitments undermine or enhance social order at the smaller or larger levels.

8.2 Theoretical Orientation

This section presents orienting ideas and elaborates the backdrop for this paper, starting with the concept of social order.

8.2.1 Concept of Social Order

Social orders are defined here in simple terms as repetitive, regular, or predictable patterns of behavior and interaction in groups, organizations, communities, and the like (e.g., see Berger and Luckmann 1966; Collins 1981; Wrong 1995). Repetitive interactions in local settings congeal into regularities but also reflect the impact of existing macro-level organizations and institutions. Repeated social interactions constitute the micro-foundation of macro social orders in the sense that order cannot exist or be sustained without affirmation by individuals and their concomitant social interaction processes. Macro structures and cultures likely frame social interactions at the micro level but those interactions represent independent, "agent like" forces that undergird the framing force of macro-level organizational and institutional patterns. We argue that emotions drive this force (see also Turner 2007, 2014).

This simple, micro-based concept of social order is founded on the notion that a semblance of social order is necessary for people to navigate their social worlds, deal with uncertainties in their lives, and produce collective goods, services, or other benefits to individuals. Yet, social orders can take many different forms, unexpectedly change, and often are contested implicitly if not explicitly (Rawls 2010). People impose order and act to affirm and reproduce it in order to make their lives predictable but it is a sociological truism that any social order is tenuous and fragile. What is socially constructed can be socially unraveled or reconstructed in a new form. In fact, history is replete with instances of established orders, seemingly inviolate and permanent, self-destructing unexpectedly and then being reconstructed or reconstituted in a different institutional form. The abrupt and unexpected demise of communism in Eastern Europe is a recent historical example.

Yet, while social orders are inherently fragile, they are not equally so. It is reasonable to suspect that some social orders have more potential than others to decline, self-destruct, or otherwise change radically in a short period of time. One might conceive of many historical and institutional reasons why order in some groups are highly resilient while others are incredibly fragile. We propose that the *form of social tie* between people (members) and their group units (organization, community, or nation) is a key differentiating property of more resilient versus more fragile groups or organizations. Group ties are more fragile if based solely on instrumental (individual) benefits to members, which is the primary focus of Hobbes and social dilemma theorists. With such ties, members commit to a group only as long as that flow of individual benefits continue to outweigh those of alternatives. Continuation of benefit flow is never certain because it requires group level resources that may wax and wane, and groups of whatever scale exercise only limited control over their environments. Thus, instrumentally-based person-to-group ties are likely to be brittle in the face of limited or varying resources. A second form of group tie is affective or emotional. An *affective tie* is a "gut level" positive feeling about the group or organization. The tie entails additional, larger meaning to people beyond the instrumental benefits they receive as members. The group affiliation itself is meaningful, intrinsically pleasurable, and often self-enhancing. Such affective-emotional group ties are non-instrumental in the sense that the group is an end in itself, not just a means to an end as is the case with an instrumental tie.

8.2.2 Emotions and Social Order

The overall implication is clear: *Groups that generate and sustain the commitment of members (employees, citizens) through instrumental incentives are more fragile and less stable than groups that generate and sustain the commitment of members through affective ties.* Affective ties lead members to stay and support the group even if benefits decline significantly because the intrinsic feelings about membership have compensatory effects. The contrast of instrumental and affective ties is probably as old as the discipline of sociology itself (e.g., see Weber 1968; Parsons 1947), and it is central to research on organizational commitments in business organizations (see Mathieu and Zajac 1990). However, the interrelationships of instrumental and affective commitments, as well as the social-interaction foundations of these, have not received much attention (see Johnson et al. 2009).

Over the past two decades we have developed four complementary theories about the bases, interrelationships, and consequences of such commitments. The common focus is on how and when instrumental ties become affective or expressive over time in the context of repeated interactions around joint tasks. The four theories are: nested-group theory (Lawler 1992); relational cohesion theory (Lawler and Yoon 1993, 1996, 1998; Thye et al. 2002); an affect theory of social exchange (Lawler 2001; Lawler et al. 2008); and the theory of social commitments (Lawler et al. 2009; Thye et al. 2015). The common focus of these theories is to understand how emotional aspects of micro-level interactions can generate non-instrumental, affectively-imbued ties to a group, whether it is a small, local one or a broader more encompassing one. Here, we selectively draw upon elements of these theories to build a deeper more comprehensive understanding of the nested-group problem.

Each of the four theories has a distinct emphasis. *Nested-group theory* (Lawler 1992) first proposed the proximal-group bias in attributions of emotions (positive and negative), indicating that people attribute positive emotions and experiences to local (proximal) groups and negative emotions and experiences to the larger more encompassing (distal) groups. The main hypothesis is that people develop stronger affective ties to those groups that provide them a greater sense of efficacy and control, and this is most commonly the local group. *Relational cohesion theory* (Lawler and Yoon 1996; Lawler et al. 2000) specifies an endogenous emotional process through which repeated (instrumental) exchanges produce affective commitments to a relational or group unit. The implication is that the proximal bias is grounded in the emotional byproducts of repeated interactions among actors in the local unit. The *Affect Theory of Social Exchange* (Lawler, 2001; Lawler et al. 2008) keys on the nature of the task or task structure in social exchange contexts. It indicates that the more joint a social exchange task, the more likely it is to foster a sense of shared responsibility among those accomplishing it; a sense of shared responsibility, in turn, promotes social unit attributions of individual feelings from the task interaction. Affective group commitments, therefore, are strongest to groups in which tasks are accomplished jointly with others. *Social Commitments Theory* (Lawler et al. 2009) generalizes the above three theories into a broader explanation regarding the role of affective group commitments in the problem of social order. The proximal bias is weaker here because jointness and a sense of shared responsibility can be generated not only in the local, immediate unit, but also the larger more distal unit. The locus of shared responsibility is contingent on how jointly the task is structured, how collectively it is framed, and whether that framing is by leaders (managers) of the proximal or distal group.

8.2.3 Research Evidence

There is substantial empirical evidence on key principles of the four theories. Most of the evidence is from laboratory experiments in which subjects repeatedly engage in an exchange task with the same others over time (see Lawler and

Yoon 1996; Lawler et al. 2008). In this context, we measure the frequency of exchange, self-reported emotions (pleasure-satisfaction and interest/excitement), as well as perceptions of cohesion and behavioral commitments (see Lawler and Yoon 1996 for the experimental context and measures). Only one study set out to directly test the nested-group formulation (Mueller and Lawler 1999), but several bits of evidence from experimental research on the other theories can be interpreted in terms of the nested-group commitment problem. This cumulative empirical foundation sets the stage for our theoretical analysis of the nested-group problem to follow. Four relevant points that can be extracted from the research.

1. The most direct evidence for the nested group theory comes from a survey study of work attitudes in a decentralized (school system) and centralized (military) organization, both with nested subunits: schools (proximal) in a school district (distal), and a medical center (proximal) in the air force (distal) (Mueller and Lawler 1999). The study indicates that commitments to the local unit were stronger in the decentralized than in the centralized organization. The locus of control and autonomy over work conditions was associated with the locus of organizational commitments. Work conditions controlled locally affect commitments to that local organizational unit, whereas those controlled by the larger unit shape commitments to that larger unit. Importantly, the locus of commitment corresponds with the locus of control (Mueller and Lawler 1999).
2. Turning to our experimental research on dyads, networks, and small groups, when people repeatedly exchange things of value, they experience positive emotions and these feelings, in turn, generate commitment behaviors such as the propensity to (*i*) stay in the relation, (*ii*) give unilateral benefits or gifts to others in the group, and (*iii*) cooperate with members in a social dilemma (Lawler and Yoon 1996; Lawler et al. 2000). Evidence clearly indicates that positive emotions mediate the impact of repetitive exchange on relational or group ties.
3. Relational ties with such an emotional foundation tend to fragment networks of exchange around "pockets of cohesion," based on frequent exchanges and resulting positive emotions; ties are to the local proximal exchange relation not the larger more distal network (Lawler and Yoon 1998). Yet, if networks are high in density and consist primarily of equal power relations, this breakdown around pockets of cohesion does not occur. Under these conditions, networks are transformed into perceived group entities and thus there are group ties to both the relational and more encompassing network unit (Thye et al. 2011).
4. When two or more people undertake joint tasks, they tend to perceive a shared responsibility and, when this occurs, positive feelings from the task interaction are attributed to the group in which the task is accomplished. The result of social unit attributions of individual emotion is affective ties to the group unit (Lawler et al. 2008, 2009; Thye et al. 2015). Tasks that generate greater sense of shared responsibility lead to stronger affective group ties. This research, however, dealt only with a single immediate group (the local or proximal unit). One might hypothesize that if a sense of shared responsibility is produced at a distal group level, as well as the proximal level, the result should be a positive relationship between commitments to the local and larger unit. An important question is when or under what conditions are commitments at the local level in competition with those at the larger level (i.e., a zero sum relation) or positively related (i.e., mutually supportive)?

As a whole, these theories suggest that in analyzing nested-group contexts, three conditions warrant careful attention: (*i*) autonomy and control at the local and larger group level; (*ii*) the frequency or density of interactions within and outside the local unit; (*iii*) the jointness of the task structure and locus of shared responsibility.

A fourth condition is added by theoretical work of Jon Turner (2007) on the proximal bias: (*iv*) the degree that the proximal group unit is embedded in the distal group unit. We introduce Turner's notion here and then return to it later.

Jon Turner's "sociological theory of emotion" (Turner 2007) argues that emotions and emotional processes are the ultimate foundation for macro social orders. These emotions originate in micro level social "encounters." The strength and resilience of a macro order is contingent on micro level encounters that produce positive emotions, and also the spread of those feelings to larger groups, organizations, or communities. The key obstacle is the proximal bias: people tend to attribute positive feelings from encounters to local, micro level units and attribute negative events and feelings to larger (meso or macro) social units. Turner argues that the social-embeddedness of local-unit encounters within the larger unit can counteract the proximal bias, by generating stronger interconnections between behavior in the local group and the larger, distal institutional or organizational grouping. Social embeddedness, therefore, may determine whether emotion attributions stay local or spread to larger units. This has important implications for the nested-group component of the Hobbesian problem of social order and we will compare our approach to Turner's shortly.

8.3 Theoretical Mechanisms

In this section we compare different theoretical formulations for the problem of nested-group commitments. The focus is to identify commonalities and sharpen the conditions, mechanisms, or processes that underlie nested group commitments, including those explicit in Lawler (1992) and Turner (2007) as well as those implicit in other work (e.g., Lawler and Yoon 1996; Lawler 2001; Lawler et al. 2009). We emphasize four specific conditions or processes: (*i*) autonomy and control; (*ii*) interaction frequency; (*iii*) jointness of the task structure; and (*iv*) structural interconnections of proximal and distal groups.

8.3.1 Autonomy and Control

The first formulation of the nested group problem (Lawler 1992) treated the sense of control as the key explanation for social unit attributions of individual feelings. *Sense of control* is conceived as perceptions of how much impact, self-determination, or efficacy people have in a situation (White 1959; Deci 1975). The logic here is based on three ideas. First, when people experience a sense of individual control or efficacy, they tend to feel positive emotions or feelings (e.g., feeling good, satisfied, excited). This idea has substantial empirical support in psychology (see Westcott 1988). Second, people are likely to interpret the source of these positive feelings and, in the process, attribute them to a source such as themselves, others, or relevant social units. Third, interpretations of control are based on the source and balance of "enabling" and "constraining' dimensions of social structure (Giddens 1984). All things being equal, groups that "enable" actions or interactions are objects for positive feelings whereas those that "constrain" actions and interactions are objects for negative emotions. Broadly, this is a way that "freedom" can promote affective ties to a group.

Nested group theory (Lawler 1992) aims to identify structural conditions under which individuals' emotion attributions target local (proximal) groups or overarching (distal) units in which these are nested. The theoretical argument centers on the degree of control (or autonomy) people have in the situation and where they believe that control comes from. In a work organization, local autonomy and control may be high or low, and such conditions may stem from the talents and experiences of individuals in the local unit, collaborative relations in that unit, the past success of the unit, or the value of the proximal group to the larger distal group. To the degree that members of the local group are high in choice, autonomy, and control, more positive feelings are likely to result from task activity and these feelings, in turn, are more likely to be attributed to that proximal group than to the distal group. One important consequence is stronger affective commitments to the local group and greater willingness to sacrifice on behalf of it. Conversely, if members of the local group are low in choice, autonomy, and control, negative feelings ensue and these, in turn, are more likely to be attributed to the distal than the proximal group. In this manner, structures and perceptions of control are the key condition determining whether positive or negative emotions occur and also whether these are attributed to proximal or distal groups (See Lawler 1992; Lawler et al. 2009; Thye and Yoon 2015).

The theory posits a strong tendency for people to attribute positive events, experiences, and emotions to their most local, immediate groups. The rationale is that this is where people interact and define the situation, and these definitions tend to favor the local, proximal group. In contrast, people tend to attribute negative events, experiences, and feelings to a removed, overarching, or distal group (e.g., university, corporation, community), and these perceptions also emerge from interactions in the local group. Attributions of negative emotion to the larger group may be a source of cohesion and solidarity in the local group. Overall, the proximal bias for positive emotions and distal bias for negative emotions captures the fundamental problem of order in nested group structures.

Lawler (1992) and Turner (2007) offer different but complementary explanations for the proximal/distal biases in positive/negative emotion attributions. It is instructive to consider these closely. Lawler (1992) reasons that proximal groups are the locus of interactions with others, and perceptions of control are likely to be developed or socially constructed in these proximal contexts or situations. Local groups essentially have an "interaction advantage" in shaping social definitions of control in the situation (See Collins 1981 for a similar idea); and they are likely to take responsibility for positive indications of control and resulting feelings, while blaming larger, more distant groups for constraints or limits on control. These interpretations and attributions are often revealed in negative or pejorative comments and attitudes by employees toward "higher ups," corporate headquarters, and central administrators. Those more distant structural levels, offices, or individuals often are perceived as clueless, unaware, or mindless when it comes to what is necessary for the core work of the organization which is accomplished at the local group level (for an interesting explanation for why this occurs see Dunning 2015).

Turner (2007) pushes the logic of this argument in several interesting ways. He elaborates the nested group problem by explicitly theorizing that proximal and distal biases protect the local groups which people are dependent on and regularly interact within (*i*) by "internalizing" positive emotions within the local group and thereby building cohesion and solidarity and (*ii*) by "externalizing" negative emotions and blaming larger units or groups. He implies that the micro social orders are stronger to the degree that positive emotions are internalized and negative emotions externalized, but these processes simultaneously tend to weaken order at higher meso or macro levels. Turner (2007) proposes an important qualification of the proximal bias for positive emotions. Positive emotions can "externalize" and essentially spread to larger (distal) group units if people are involved in multiple social interactions (encounters) in multiple groups within that larger, distal group unit. This means that the proximal bias is likely to be stronger if members interact primarily in only one local (proximal) group and the boundaries among local groups in the larger organization are not crossed or bridged regularly. A more fluid or permeable local group structure, therefore, is important to mitigate excessively strong commitments to local groups and facilitate the spread of positive emotions from repeated micro level encounters in multiple groups to meso- or macro-level groups (see Turner 2007). Commitments to proximal and distal groups may not be inversely related if emotions spread upward in this sort of way.

8.3.2 Interaction Frequency

Both Lawler (1992) and Turner (2007) aim to ground macro phenomena in micro-level encounters or interactions (see also Collins 1981). Emotions that can forge affective ties to larger social units emerge here. Thus, it is important to consider how this happens – that is, what are the mechanisms that generate emotions in the first place and then lead people to interpret them in collective, group-based terms. This boils down to a question of "social emergence." The theory of relational cohesion (Lawler and Yoon 1993, 1996) takes up this question for social exchange contexts.

Social exchanges occur because people can receive something they value by giving something in return (Homans 1961; Emerson 1972). By definition, social exchange is purely instrumental as are the relations that emerge from repeated exchanges by the same persons. Lawler and Yoon (1996), however, develop and test a theory that indicates otherwise; repeated exchanges even if instrumentally-driven have unintended social byproducts. The byproducts might entail a reduction of uncertainty from exchanging with the same others or the emergence of trust (Kollock 1994; Cook et al. 2005). Lawler and Yoon (1996) propose that mild positive, everyday emotions (e.g., uplift, pleasure, satisfaction, and excitement) are a distinct class of byproduct with a distinct effect on exchange relations. These emotions create affective ties to the relation itself.

An exchange *relation* is defined as a pattern of repeated exchange by the same actors over time (Emerson 1972). The theory of relational cohesion indicates that repeated exchanges build expressive, non-instrumental relations that people are motivated to sustain and nurture. This occurs through an emotional process: repeated exchanges generate positive emotions and these emotions in turn produce relational cohesion, defined as perceptions of the relation as a unifying social object in the situation. Through the cohesion effects of positive emotion, the relation takes on a "life of its own," becoming salient as an object for actors; and emotions from exchange are associated with that object.

Relational cohesion theory and research does not address the nested-group problem directly, but it does contribute in a couple of ways (Lawler and Yoon 1996, 1998; Lawler et al. 2000; Thye et al. 2011, 2014). First, it elaborates why local units become available and salient targets for individual emotions and feelings, specifically, because positive emotions generated by repeated interactions make the local unit salient. To the degree that interactions of members in an organization are organized in and around local group units, stronger ties may develop to those local groups than to the overarching larger group through the emotion-to-cohesion process. Horizontal differentiation in an organization may generate such effects. Second, relational cohesion theory examines exchange in dyads or triads without making any predictions for higher level units. A study by Thye et al. (2011), however, demonstrates micro-to-macro effects in the following form: relational cohesion in dyads (micro level) within a network has positive effects on perceptions of connectedness and group-ness at the network level. At the network level people perceive a connection even to those that they do not exchange or interact with. In effect this "spread" is not unlike that theorized by Turner (2007), but occurs for different theoretical reasons. In this case the effects are stronger in networks that promote equal power relations and those with greater network density. The overall point is that relational cohesion research points to an interaction-to-emotion-to-cohesion mechanism for nested group commitments and suggests some conditions under which there are positive rather than negative effects on ties to larger, more encompassing social units. The salience of the relevant unit – dyad or network – is central to these emotion-infused processes.

Turner's (2007) theory also suggests that positive emotions constitute the fundamental link between repeated interactions (termed encounters) and integrative ties to larger social units. He argues more specifically that social encounters produce positive emotions if they fulfill or confirm expectations of the actors. Fulfillment of expectations leads to expressions of gratitude and positive sanctions back and forth among those in the encounter; and positive affect tends to build across encounters. Thus, confirmation of expectations plays the same role as exchange frequency does in relational cohesion theory. Turner (2007) uses the "clarity of expectations" to explain how and when emotions at the micro level spread to larger, more encompassing units.

8.3.3 Tasks and Shared Responsibility

The Affect Theory of Social Exchange (Lawler 2001; Lawler et al. 2008) focuses in on the structure of social exchange "tasks," arguing distinct structures have differential effects on group ties (cohesion, commitment, and solidarity). Social Commitments Theory (Lawler et al. 2009, 2014) generalizes and applies principles of the affect theory to how social interactions bear on problems of social order. Here we highlight the broader formulations and the new social mechanism offered by social commitments theory. The orienting assumption is that social interactions inherently entail one or more tasks, implicitly or explicitly; but, tasks as such receive very little attention in sociological analyses of structure and interaction. Social interactions are organized around tasks and, therefore, these can help to understand the interrelationships of social structure and social interaction. Many others (e.g., Homans 1950; Collins 1981, 2004; Wrong 1995; Berger and Luckmann 1966) have theorized how micro level social interactions bear on macro phenomena, but none have seriously considered the role of the interaction task itself.

A *task* is defined as a set of behaviors that enact methods and procedures (means) for producing a desired result (goal, outcome). The methods, procedures, and goals have exogenous (objective) and endogenous (subjective) components; together they focus the attention and behavior of participants. On an objective level, tasks are a component of social structures; they frame and shape how and why people interact in pursuit of instrumental ends in a concrete situation; on a subjective level, elements of a task are cognitively definable or interpretable in varied ways and these definitions are socially constructed (see Lawler et al. 2014). Tasks may be structured in terms of individual or collective behaviors, and the same task may be socially defined in terms of individual behaviors and responsibilities or in terms of collective or joint behaviors and responsibilities. Collective outcomes, for example, may stem from the mere aggregation of individual behaviors (e.g., sales totals in an office or retail department) or from a combined set of behaviors that generate a distinctive joint product (e.g., a team of authors who collaboratively produce a book). This individual-collective responsibility dimension of tasks is fundamental to social commitments theory.

Social commitments theory posits that social interactions in nested group contexts entail tasks likely to vary along an individual-collective responsibility dimension, i.e., how joint or individual is the task activity (Lawler et al. 2009). Tasks, objectively structured or subjectively defined as joint efforts, are a stimulus for social unit attributions of emotion. If people undertake a task collectively or jointly with others and that task activity generates positive feelings, they are likely to attribute those emotions in part to the relevant group unit. Consider a simple example. Having a nice meal at a restaurant is likely to foster positive feelings regardless of whether a person has dinner alone or with a group of friends. However, having dinner with a group of friends may lead them to attribute positive feelings from the meal in part to the friendship group itself, especially if they repeatedly go to dinner together. The result is a stronger and more affective tie to the friendship group. This is the central proposition of the theory. Importantly, it is general enough to apply to work groups or teams in a work organization, local chapters of an environmental group, departments in a university, or regional offices in a corporation.

The individual-collective dimension of a task bears on the degree that group members perceive a shared responsibility, not only for whether it is successfully accomplished, but also for the procedures (means) or processes for undertaking it. The sense of shared responsibility tends to emerge from the process of interacting around the task. Repeated interactions that promote a sense of shared responsibility foster social unit attributions of positive emotions from the task activity which, in turn, increase the affective commitment to the group. The sense of shared responsibility therefore is a contingency (moderator) for social unit attributions, whereas social unit attributions are how (mediator) joint tasks engender the formation or strengthening of affective commitments to the group. Logically the argument specifies a moderator (perceptions of shared responsibility) for a mediator (social unit attributions) of the task-to-commitment process.

Repeated social interactions are central to this process, but individual emotions may be felt but not expressed in ways visible to others. There are at least two ways people in interaction influence and magnify each other's felt emotion. The first way is through emotional contagion, that is, the mere tendency of people to read subtle behavioral cues, synchronize their behaviors, and in the process feel what others are feeling at the moment (see Hatfield et al. 1993). Emotions readily spread across individuals in face to face settings or where there is "bodily co-presence," and this is one reason work teams often have collective affective or emotional tones (Bartel and Saavedra 2000; Barsade 2002). Social commitments theory indicates that the sense of shared responsibility and emotional contagion are reciprocally related, each accentuating the other and in the process generating cycles of positive feeling (See Lawler et al. 2009). The second mode of mutual influence stems from the possibility that those experiencing a given emotion infer that others like them in the same situation are experiencing the same feelings, i.e., inferences of common emotions. Joint tasks make salient the common focus and activity of those interacting and thus are likely to enhance inferences of common emotions. An important implication is that even in purely virtual interactions without bodily co-presence, people mutually infer others are experiencing the same feelings and this boosts perceptions of shared responsibility and the likelihood of social unit attributions (Lawler et al. 2014). In sum, either emotional contagion or emotional inferences are sufficient to strengthen the impact of joint tasks, perceptions of shared responsibility, and social unit attributions on affective group commitments. Emotional contagion effects are limited to contexts of "bodily co-presence" or face-to-face interaction, but emotional inferences can have similar effects in the absence of bodily co-presence (see Lawler et al. 2013).

The nested group problem is touched on in the affect theory of social exchange but social commitments theory develops it further than Lawler (1992). The main points implied by social commitments theory are as follows. First, the strength of affective ties to proximal and distal group depends on the locus of shared responsibility, not the locus of autonomy and control. This shifts the basis of a proximal bias. If joint tasks are enacted and accomplished in local groups, ties to those local units should be stronger than those to the larger, more distal unit, even if the locus of control is the distal unit. Second, while tasks are enacted locally, they may be designed and framed by either proximal or distal groups. If designed and framed locally, then the locus of control and locus of responsibility converge at the proximal group level, and ties to the local group should be strongest here. If tasks are designed and framed by the distal group, the local group could generate a strong a sense of shared responsibility even with little sense of control or autonomy. Third, the larger, more encompassing and removed group is likely to have greater capacity to shape perceptions of responsibility in non-zero sum, collective terms than to shape perceptions of control in such terms. Control and autonomy have an underlying zero-sum structural basis that is not inherently present for shared responsibility. The organizational design of roles and tasks, as well as communications from leaders have the capacity to extend a sense of shared responsibility or "we are all in this together" perceptions beyond the proximal group by embedding joint tasks at the local level into broader or larger organizational tasks and responsibilities. For such reasons, joint tasks and a sense of shared responsibility may prevail in the context of highly variable levels of local control and autonomy.

Thus, in theorizing conditions for proximal or distal group ties, nested group theory (Lawler 1992) and social commitments theory (Lawler et al. 2009) key on different structures and processes. Nested group theory asks: Where is the locus of control and autonomy? With stronger local control and autonomy, proximal groups will become the prime objects of commitment, and the larger distal groups face serious obstacles to collective mobilization around larger group goals. It is not clear how these obstacles can be overcome except through potentially costly instrumental means (e.g., selective incentives) that build instrumental rather than affective commitments to the distal group. In contrast, social commitments theory asks: Where is the locus of a sense of shared responsibility? Joint tasks and perceptions of shared responsibility may exist simultaneously in both proximal and distal groups. To the degree that organizational structures or leaders define tasks as joint and promote a sense of shared responsibility at the larger, distal group level, this should mitigate the nested group problem and make the distal unit a stronger object of affective commitment. An understanding how and when proximal and distal commitments complement and mutually support one another is an important but neglected issue in research on organizational commitments (see for an exception Johnson et al. 2009).

To summarize, the current formulation of social commitments theory (see Lawler et al. 2009) predicts that affective group commitments are strongest if group members perceive both (*i*) a high degree of autonomy and control and (*ii*) joint tasks that promote shared responsibility. The proximal bias remains but it can be mitigated or overturned if local joint tasks are subsumed within or tied directly to joint tasks at the larger group level. There is, nevertheless, an important gap or unanswered question in the theory. At the local proximal level, low control and autonomy may combine with joint tasks and a strong sense of shared responsibility. For this condition nested group and social commitment theories make contradictory predictions based on different mechanisms. One way to address this problem is to more explicitly theorize the nature and degree of interconnections between proximal and distal groups in the group, organization, or society (see Turner 2007).

8.3.4 Interconnections of Proximal and Distal Groups

What structural properties are likely to promote or weaken the proximal bias for affective commitment? We consider two that have been analyzed elsewhere: social embeddedness (Turner 2007) and the degree that the distal group supports the local group (Thye and Yoon forthcoming). Each is discussed in turn below.

For Jon Turner "social-embeddedness" is a fundamental structural condition under which positive emotions in micro (proximal) encounters spread outward and upward to larger group units (meso and macro); and, conversely, macro/meso forces penetrate and permeate the local through ideologies and norms, and other shared cultural elements. When positive emotions spread, the proximal bias is weakened or eliminated. The tighter the structural connections between proximal groups and distal – meso or macro – group units, the more likely are micro-based emotions to have such meso- or macro-level effects. Tighter connections, however, also imply tighter control from the distal unit and thus less autonomy and control at the local level. The theoretical rationale is that with tighter connections, distal groups produce greater "clarity of expectations" for people in proximal level social encounters (interactions). Recall that for Turner, social encounters (micro level) arouse positive emotions when people confirm their expectations in those encounters or groups. Embeddedness, by increasing the clarity of expectations, improves the prospects for satisfying (expectation-confirming) encounters that make people feel good and weakens the proximal bias. Macro level organizations and institutions are the primary source of clear expectations, and the spread of micro level positive emotions upward to the micro level occurs in this context.

Thus, "clarity of expectations" mediates the impact of structural embeddedness on positive emotions in micro level encounters. Implied is the notion that the clarity of expectations is a macro-to-micro ("top down") process, and confirming expectations in encounters initiates a micro-to-macro ("bottom up") process. The bottom up process is contingent on positive emotions from multiple encounters in multiple local groups within the same meso (organizational) or macro (institutional or categorical) group. In sum, there are two primary structural conditions for the micro-to-macro spread of emotions in Turner's (2007) argument: (*i*) The local unit is tightly embedded in the distal unit, meaning that the distal unit conveys clear expectations for behavior in local units, and (*ii*) members interact with others in multiple local units, and experience positive emotions across such unites (Turner 2007, 2014).[1]

Thye and Yoon (2015) take a different approach by using and adapting theory and research on "perceived organizational support" (POS). They set out to test and further specify nested-group theory (Lawler 1992). *Organizational support* refers to the degree that an organization values its members' contributions and cares about their individual well-being (Eisenberger et al. 1986). It is a perceptual phenomenon with a structural foundation, but generally treated in perception terms by research on organizations (see Eisenberger et al. 1986). In brief, the research indicates that if employees perceive organizational support in these ways (i.e., valuing and caring), they reciprocate with attitudes and behaviors that benefit the organization. The employee-employer relationship is conceived as an exchange of valued goods or outcomes, and in this context Thye and Yoon (2015) analyze the identity (or self-definitional) implications of perceived organizational support. The main hypothesis is that if employees perceive organizational support, the organizational identity becomes more salient and meaningful to them, and they "re-categorize" self in terms of not only the local unit but also the larger, distal unit. This then counteracts the proximal bias posited by the nested group theory, and by extension, Turner's (2007) analysis.

[1]Important to note is that emotions from confirming expectations at the micro level have a moral component to the degree that, not only is the micro level tightly connected to or embedded in meso (organizational) level organizations, but the meso level units also are tightly embedded in macro level institutions and culture.

Thye and Yoon (2015) tested this hypothesis in a survey of teams within a large electric company in South Korea. Teams were the local, proximal unit and the larger company was the distal unit. The survey measured job satisfaction (positive feelings about the job), perceived organizational support, affective commitment, and various job characteristics (autonomy, variety, etc.) as well as other controls. There are two findings of particular relevance to the nested group problem. First, job satisfaction had a stronger impact on commitment to the team than to the company, a finding generally consistent with nested group theory and Turner's (2007) proximal bias. Second, the predicted interaction effect of team commitment and perceived organizational support confirmed the study's main hypothesis: team commitment had a stronger positive effect on organizational commitment when employees perceived greater organizational support for employees. This study extends nested group theory by suggesting a general strategy for organizations to overcome the nested group problem and also by pointing to the role of group identities. The overall message to be taken from both Turner (2007) and Thye and Yoon (2015) is that both (*i*) structural and (*ii*) cognitive interconnections of proximal and distal groups must be taken into consideration and analyzed to fully understand how these are intertwined.

8.3.5 Comparing Our Approach to Jon Turner's

There are important similarities and differences between our theorizing and that of Turner (2007). The following ideas represent key similarities. First, micro level social interactions at the person-to-person level are the ultimate source of emotions and feelings, albeit positive or negative. Second, positive emotions constitute the fundamental glue or social adhesive that hold together groups, organizations, communities, and societies; whereas negative emotions threaten to weaken tear apart social units. Third, the impact of positive emotion is contingent on the kinds of attributions (e.g., to people, to units, to which units) that people make in the course of interpreting their emotions and feelings. Finally, people are more likely to attribute positive emotions to proximal social objects (self, other, group) and negative emotions to more removed or larger social objects (organizations, communities, nations). The latter poses a fundamental threat to the stability of those larger units.

There also are key differences between out theorizing and that of Turner, primarily regarding the emotion-generating mechanism and the social context for it. Turner deploys "clarity of expectations" as the central emotion-generating mechanism in his theoretical analysis. When people confirm expectations they feel good and reward each other and this strengthens further those positive feelings. In our research program, interactions generate emotions regardless of how clear expectations are or whether they are necessarily fulfilled. Positive emotions stem from social interaction, task structure, how well individuals work together, and what sort of collective impact such interactions produce. Expectations are not necessarily explicit or clear, in fact, people may perceive greater control and shared responsibility under conditions of ambiguity. One implication or hypothesis, developed in our general theory (Lawler et al. 2009: Chapter 7), is that network-based organizations tend to generate affective commitments whereas hierarchy-based organizations tend to generate instrumental commitments because of a greater sense of shared responsibility in flatter network structures (Lawler et al. 2009). In contrast, Turner's clarity-of-expectations mechanism seems to suggest that hierarchical organizations generate stronger affective ties because the expectations are likely to be clearer in this context.

There is also a subtle difference in the primary social objects to which emotions are attributed. For Turner (2007) the proximal bias entails positive emotions being attributed to social objects within the group – i.e., to self or others – not explicitly to the group itself as an object, although the group benefits from these internal attributions of emotion within the group. By implication, attributions to the group occur through attributions of emotion to self and/or other(s). We presume that the group is a distinct and salient social object, and social unit attributions are directly made to the group itself. Moreover, in Turner's theory, emotions spread upward to meso or macro units to the degree that positive emotions are produced across a variety of encounters in a variety of local groups within the same overarching meso or macro entities. In our theory, the spread of emotions only requires repeated social interaction in a single local group where people demonstrate a capacity to work together. If the local task is undertaken or enacted jointly with others and it fosters a sense of shared responsibility among those doing it, conditions are established for social attributions to proximal, distal, or both types of social units.

Having reviewed these approaches to the nested group problem, there are several unanswered questions that suggest the need for more theoretical work. One concerns the role of control-autonomy (Lawler 1992) and shared-responsibility (Lawler et al. 2009) as the basis for a proximal bias and also for understanding how distal groups or organizations overcome it. A second concerns the role of identities in the ties to proximal and distal groups. The more encompassing distal group may provide individuals a broader context of meaning for enacting roles and identities than the more immediate local group. One condition for this is that the self-enhancing effects of a group identity are stronger for the more encompassing distal group (e.g., a nation) than a smaller proximal unit (e.g., a neighborhood). A third concerns the role of dense interactions in a single local group versus more varied interactions across multiple local groups in a larger social unit. There are good reasons to posit that a proximal bias will be stronger in the single-group case; and if it is countered, the locally-based feelings may forge a stronger affective tie to distal organizations than where group ties diffuse across multiple local groups. Interaction in multiple groups may generate more diffuse or looser local or proximal ties, but they also broaden the range or variety of positive emotional experiences within a larger, distal unit (Turner 2007). Below we suggest some ways to resolve the control-responsibility and single-multiple group issues and build in a stronger role for identities.

8.4 Developing a New Theoretical Formulation

This section does not present a new theory but instead an outline or sketch of a few ideas to explain the strength and interconnections of proximal and distal group ties. The purpose is to look more closely at the *nature of* person-to-group ties and further specify the conditions where a proximal bias is stronger or weaker. We assume a nested group context in which the distal group has an oversight/governing role and the proximal group is the locus of the core tasks or activities of the distal group.[2] In this context proximal and distal ties have the capacity to generate commitment behaviors, such as staying (low exit rates or turnover), prosocial behaviors (donations to the organization, informally helping others), and citizenship behaviors (involvement in or sacrifice of time for the group). These behaviors are directed at local (proximal) or larger encompassing (distal) groups contingent on the strength and resilience of group ties.

Several ideas motivate and orient a new theoretical effort, all of which are implied by previous sections of this paper.

1. When people have purely instrumental ties to others and relevant groups (proximal and distal), social order is highly problematic because of social dilemmas and exit options. This is the classic situation assumed by Hobbes and, more recently, rational choice approaches to cooperation and social order (Hechter 1987; Fehr and Gintas 2007).
2. Affective ties to local, proximal groups make it easier for social dilemma problems to be solved at the micro level, but in the process they generate a fragmented or federated social order with weaker ties to macro group entities than to local entities. This fragmentation is driven by either the control-autonomy or the shared-responsibility mechanisms.
3. Macro social orders become stronger and more resilient if (*i*) affective ties to macro units are strong and those to micro units are weak; or if (*ii*) there are mutually-supportive affective ties at micro and macro levels. The former (*i*) will obtain if the distal, removed group or organization is more salient as the primary locus of control-autonomy or the primary locus of members' sense of shared-responsibility than local units.[3] The latter (*ii*) will obtain if there are tight interconnections between micro level structures or task activities and macro level structures and strategic-level tasks (Turner 2007).

The nested-group problem of social order, therefore, boils down to whether or when group ties have an affective, non-instrumental component, and whether or when the affective component is stronger at one level than at another.

8.4.1 The Argument

The fundamental nature of affective and instrumental person-to-unit bonds have implications for the structural and cognitive interconnections between proximal and distal groups. Theories of group formation are instructive because they tend to fall into non-instrumental and instrumental categories. The non-instrumental class of theories indicates that groups are based on homophily or social similarities (Tajfel and Turner 1986;

[2]This defines the scope of the nested group context as one in which the membership and activities of proximal and distal group are structurally interconnected. Core activities might be teaching in an educational organization, production in a factory, customer service in a retail organization; these locally enacted activities reflect the organization's larger mission, charter, goals, or strategies. Group memberships are also interconnected because to be a member of the local group is by definition also to be a member of the more encompassing or distal group. It is not possible to join the local group without joining the larger group.

[3]As an example, this might occur where local units are not well-defined or fluid, those who work together are spread out geographically, and/or people participate simultaneously in several different work groups, teams, or projects.

McPherson et al. 2001). Common or shared identities are a unifying thread binding people to groups. The rationale is that people tend to associate with and form ties with people like themselves. This could be due to their own preferences or to their structural opportunities for interaction (Blau 1977). In comparison, the instrumental class of group-formation theories indicates that groups are based on the rational choices people make about where they receive the greatest individual benefits or rewards (Hechter 1987). People are profit maximizers and they join groups that are important to their individual rewards, in particular, where they benefit from joint or collective services or goods that they cannot access alone. In sum, groups are instrumental objects if they mediate valued individual rewards or collective outcomes or goods that are the source of those individual rewards or benefits (see Hechter 1987).

The social identity tradition demonstrates that social categories, even those that have little value or extrinsic meaning, are sufficient to generate perceptions of being in a group and promote positive behaviors toward other members (Tajfel and Turner 1986). One rationale for such common identity effects is that being with similar others or being in the same social category is self-defining. Social categories and groups shape how people define themselves and also how others define them, and these self-other definitions are manifest in behavior and interaction. If a group becomes an important part of how people define themselves, the ties to that group becomes at least partly non-instrumental. The result is that positive qualities of the group become positive qualities of self.

This simple characterization of instrumental and non-instrumental ties suggests two conditions for strong person-to-group ties: (*i*) whether or to what degree the group identity is self-defining for members, that is, the group identity is an important aspect of "who they are" or "how they view themselves;" and (*ii*) whether the group mediates the access of people to collective goods that are the basis for valued individual rewards, i.e., the group is a source of collective efficacy. Identities entail shared meanings about self, role, and group membership, whereas, collective goods are the most unique instrumental benefit of group members and an indicator of collective efficacy. Each dimension is elaborated, in turn below.

Group ties are symbolic and expressive because groups can be an important marker for how a person defines themselves and how others also define them. These self-other definitions are shared meanings and often affectively imbued (Burke and Stets 2009; MacKinnon and Heise 2010). If the group is a context in which a person verifies or affirms a self-definition in social interaction with others, it makes sense that they would intrinsically value the group membership and treat the group as an end in itself. A group membership has self-enhancing effects as long as the group identity is an important part of how people define themselves. The implication is that people form stronger affective ties or commitments to groups within which they affirm and verify important self-definitions. Identity verification, therefore, is the principle motivation for group-oriented behavior (Burke and Stets 2009).[4]

Given this logic the implication for nested group contexts is clear. A distal bias for positive emotions should be present if the larger, removed group is more self-defining than the local, immediate group. This is quite plausible for distal group units that are high in status, reputation, or brand-recognition. Examples might be a faculty member for whom their university (e.g., Harvard, Cornell, UC-Berkeley, Stanford) is more self-defining than their college or departmental unit, or an employee who defines self primarily with reference to a corporation's name (e.g., Goldman Sachs, IBM, Apple, Google) rather than their team, department, or division within that corporation. A self-defining larger group is more likely to be subject to the distal bias. Thus, the degree that proximal or distal groups are self-defining may determine the target of social unit attributions either by shaping perceptions of control or the

[4]Some separation of group and personal identity remains except in extreme cases where the group and personal identities are so intertwined as to be inseparable (e.g., in cult memberships). The self-defining link between person and group is variable.

sense of shared responsibility. If positive definitions of self are based on self-efficacy in the situation, perceived control and autonomy will be most important, but if positive definitions are based on collective efficacy, shared responsibility will be most important. Finally, if proximal and distal group identities are highly interwoven, affective ties or commitments to each should be mutually supportive and positively associated (see Thye and Yoon 2005; Yoon and Thye 2002).

Turning to the second condition, groups are of instrumental value especially if they generate collective or joint goods that individuals cannot generate alone or in other groups or groupings (Hechter 1987). This implies that groups may be a source of collective efficacy. Repeated generation of collective goods should promote beliefs in the "collective efficacy" of a group unit because members become more confident that that "together they can make things happen" and have an impact not possible or likely by themselves. Recall that the logic of nested group theory (Lawler 1992) stipulates that the experience of individual self-efficacy is one reason local control and autonomy is so important to affective group ties or commitments. It seems reasonable to infer then that if a group mediates access to collective goods and these goods are instrumental to individuals, perceptions of self-efficacy are likely to be intertwined with perceptions of collective efficacy. Beliefs in the collective efficacy of the group should make it more likely that joints tasks generate a sense of shared responsibility.

More work is needed to flesh out these ideas, but a tentative conclusion is implied: *either proximal or distal groups may be strong objects of commitment contingent on the degree that they (a) are self-defining and (b) generate beliefs in a group's collective efficacy*. The confluence of both conditions generates the strongest and most resilient social orders

The self-defining property of a group is an *exogenous* condition that strengthens the sense of shared responsibility and social unit attributions of emotions that occur. People will do much more for groups that are central to how they define themselves, in part because the fate of those self-definitions are wrapped up with the fate of the group, i.e., self and group are more tightly interconnected. What is positive and enhancing for the group is positive and enhancing for self and vice versa. Similarly, what is negative or diminishing for one is negative or diminishing for the other.

In contrast, beliefs in collective efficacy represent an *endogenous* condition that requires repeated production of collective goods with instrumental value to members. Such beliefs are trans-situational interpretations of situational experiences of shared responsibility and they bear on the group's generalized capacity to produce goods of value to individuals. Stronger beliefs in collective efficacy should produce stronger person-to-group ties but the nature of these ties is primarily instrumental, unless the group is also self-defining. The main principles of social commitments theory help to account for beliefs in collective efficacy, whereas self-defining group identities accentuate positive emotions and likelihood of social unit attributions.

8.5 Conclusion

The problem of person-to-group ties in the context of nested groups is ubiquitous in the contemporary world. A key issue for small businesses, organizations, large corporations, radical social movements, or even nation states is how to foster and encourage group membership, prosocial behavior, sacrifice, and commitment to the agenda of larger, more distant and removed, social units. The theory and research, presented here, suggest that strong commitments to larger units occur, but only to the degree that certain structural and cognitive social conditions are realized. If left unchecked, primary or fundamental interaction processes tend to promote commitment and stable orders in more local or proximal groups while inhibiting or weakening ties to larger, distal groups. This is termed the "proximal bias" in commitment formation. In this paper we have reviewed and identified several sociological mechanisms that promote person-to-unit bonds from the micro-to-macro levels. These can explain the source of the proximal bias but also how larger social units overcome it.

There are three primary micro-social mechanisms that come to the foreground in our theoretical analysis. First, when the *sense of control* is tied to the proximate unit, rather than the more distal unit, it is likely that any positive feelings experienced from social interactions are attributed to and form the basis for stronger affective ties to the more local, nested unit (Lawler 1992). The locus of control creates a structural and cognitive push for positive emotions to be attributed locally, and negative emotions to be attributed to and blamed on the more distal units. Second, Turner (2007) identifies a different social mechanism for the proximal bias – specifically, if social encounters *confirm expectations*, then they produce positive emotions and stronger ties to local groups. Third, the theory of social commitments (Lawler et al. 2009) asserts that ties to proximal and distal social units depend on the locus of *perceptions of shared responsibility*. A proximal bias is likely if local unit generates a sense of shared responsibility, but if interactions are framed and guided by a distal group, affective ties to it will be stronger. We theorize that the structural interconnections of local and larger units determine the prospects for strong ties to larger units and these can be understood in terms of the above three mechanisms.

In closing, the complex, multi-faceted structures of the modern world almost guarantee that nested groups will pose problems of cohesion, commitment and social order. We use select theories from micro-sociology to analyze how, and under what conditions, these problems of social order are likely to be mitigated by local person-to-unit ties that spread and are generalized to larger and more encompassing social units. The theoretical work reviewed here suggests that human interaction – and the emotions, cognitions, and perceptions that are generated by it – can overcome nested group commitments. Fundamental qualities of human social interaction are the source of the nested group problem but they also contain the "seeds" of stable and resilient social orders and stability across sociological levels, ranging from the most proximate or immediate to the most distal, removed, or encompassing.

References

Barsade, S. G. (2002). The ripple effect: Emotional contagion and its influence on group behavior. *Administrative Science Quarterly, 47*, 644–657.

Bartel, C. A., & Saavendra, R. (2000). The collective construction of work group moods. *Administrative Science Quarterly, 45*, 197–231.

Berger, P., & Luckmann, T. (1966). *Social construction of reality*. New York: Anchor Book.

Blau, P. (1977). A macrosociological theory of social structure. *American Journal of Sociology, 83*, 26–54.

Burke, P. J., & Stets, J. E. (2009). *Identity theory*. New York: Oxford University Press.

Coleman, J. S. (1990). *Foundations of social theory*. Cambridge, MA: Harvard University Press.

Collins, R. (1981). On the microfoundations of macrosociology. *American Journal of Sociology, 86*, 984–1014.

Collins, R. (2004). *Interaction ritual chains*. Princeton: Princeton University Press.

Cook, K. S., Yamagish, T., Cheshire, C., Cooper, R., Matsuda, M., & Mashima, R. (2005). Trust building via risk taking: A cross-societal experiment. *Social Psychology Quarterly, 68*, 121–142.

Deci, E. L. (1975). *Intrinsic motivation*. New York: Plenum.

Dunning, D. (2015). On identifying human capital: Flawed knowledge leads to faulty judgements of expertise by individuals and groups. In S. R. Thye & E. J. Lawler (Eds.), *Advances in group processes, 32*. London: Emerald Press.

Eisenberger, R., Hungtington, R., Hutchison, S., & Sowa, D. (1986). Perceived organizational support. *Journal of Applied Psychology, 71*, 500–507.

Emerson, R. (1972). Exchange theory part II: Exchange relations and networks. In J. Berger, M. Zelditch, & B. Anderson (Eds.), *Sociological theories in progress* (pp. 58–87). Boston: Houghton-Mifflin.

Fehr, E., & Gintis, H. (2007). Human motivation and social cooperation: Experimental and analytical foundations. *Annual Review of Sociology, 33*, 43–64.

Giddens, A. (1984). *The constitution of society: Outline of the theory of structuration*. Berkeley: University of California Press.

Hatfield, E., Cacioppo, J. T., & Rapson, R. L. (1993). Emotional contagion. *Current Directions in Psychological Science, 2*, 96–99.

Hechter, M. (1987). *Principles of group solidarity*. Berkeley: University of California Press.

Homans, G. C. (1950). *The human group*. New Brunswick: Transaction Publishers.

Homans, G. C. (1961). *Social behavior: Its elementary forms*. New York: Harcourt Brace and Jovanovich.

Johnson, R. E., Groff, K. W., & Taing, M. U. (2009). Nature of the interactions among organizational commitments: Complementary, competitive, or synergistic? *British Journal of Management, 20*, 431–447.

Kollock, P. (1994). The emergence of exchange structures: An experimental study of uncertainty, commitment, and trust. *American Journal of Sociology, 100*, 315–345.

Lawler, E. J. (1992). Affective attachments to nested groups: A choice-process theory. *American Sociological Review, 57*, 327–336.

Lawler, E. J. (2001). An affect theory of social exchange. *American Journal of Sociology, 107*, 321–352.

Lawler, E. J., & Yoon, J. (1993). Power and the emergence of commitment behavior in negotiated exchange. *American Sociological Review, 58*, 465–481.

Lawler, E. J., & Yoon, J. (1996). Commitment in exchange relations: Test of a theory of relational cohesion. *American Sociological Review, 61*, 89–108.

Lawler, E. J., & Yoon, J. (1998). Network structure and emotion in exchange relations. *American Sociological Review, 58*, 465–481.

Lawler, E. J., Thye, S. R., & Yoon, J. (2000). Emotion and group cohesion in productive exchange. *American Journal of Sociology, 106*, 616–657.

Lawler, E. J., Thye, S. R., & Yoon, J. (2008). Social exchange and micro social order. *American Sociological Review, 73*, 519–542.

Lawler, E. J., Thye, S. R., & Yoon, J. (2009). *Social commitments in a depersonalized world*. New York: The Russell Sage Foundation.

Lawler, E. J., Thye, S. R., & Yoon, J. (2013). The emergence of collective emotions in social exchange. In C. V. Scheve & M. Salmela (Eds.), *Collective emotions* (pp. 189–203). Oxford: Oxford University Press.

Lawler, E. J., Thye, S. R., & Yoon, J. (2014). Emotions and group ties in social exchange. In J. Stets & J. Turner (Eds.), *Handbook of the sociology of emotions II* (pp. 77–102). New York: Springer.

MacKinnon, N. J., & Heise, D. R. (2010). *Self, identity, and social institutions*. New York: Palgrave Macmillan.

Mathieu, J., & Zajac, D. M. (1990). A review and meta-analysis of the antecedents, correlates, and consequences of organizational commitment. *Psychological Bulletin, 108*, 171–194.

McPherson, M., Smith-Lovin, L., & Cook, J. M. (2001). Birds of a feather: Homophily in social networks. *Annual Review of Sociology, 27*, 415–444.

Mueller, C. W., & Lawler, E. J. (1999). Commitment to nested organizational units: Some basic principles and preliminary findings. *Social Psychology Quarterly, 62*, 325–346.

Orton, J. D., & Weick, K. E. (1990). Loosely coupled systems: A reconceptualization. *Academy of Management Review, 15*, 203–223.

Parsons, T. (1947). *The structure of social action*. New York: The Free Press.

Putnam, R. D. (2000). *Bowling alone: The collapse and revival of American community*. New York: Simon and Schuster.

Rawls, A. W. (2010). Social order as moral order. In S. Hitlin & S. Vasey (Eds.), *Handbook of the sociology of morality* (pp. 95–121). New York: Springer.

Tajfel, H., & Turner, J. H. (1986). The social identity theory of intergroup relations. In S. Worchel & W. G. Austin (Eds.), *Psychology of intergroup relations* (pp. 7–24). Chicago: Nelson-Hall.

Thye, S. R., & Yoon, J. (2015). Building organizational commitment in nested groups: Theory and new evidence from South Korea. *Sociological Focus, 48*, 249–270.

Thye, S. R., Yoon, J., & Lawler, E. J. (2002). The theory of relational cohesion: Review of a research program. In S. R. Thye & E. J. Lawler (Eds.), *Advances in group process* (Vol. 19, pp. 89–102). Oxford: Elsevier.

Thye, S. R., Lawler, E. J., & Yoon, J. (2011). The emergence of embedded relations and group formation in networks of competition. *Social Psychology Quarterly, 74*, 387–413.

Thye, S. R., Vincent, A., Lawler, E. J., & Yoon, J. (2014). Relational cohesion, social commitments and person to group ties: Twenty five years of a theoretical research program. In S. R. Thye & E. J. Lawler (Eds.), *Advances in group processes, 31* (pp. 99–138). London: Emerald Press.

Thye, S. R., Lawler, E. J., & Yoon, J. (2015). Affective bases of order in task groups: Testing a new theory of social commitments. An unpublished manuscript.

Turner, J. H. (2007). *Human emotions: A sociological theory*. New York: Routledge.

Turner, J. H. (2014). The evolution of human emotions. In J. E. Stets & J. H. Turner (Eds.), *Handbook of the sociology of emotions: Volume II* (pp. 11–32). New York: Springer.

Weber, M. (1968). *Economy and society: An outline of interpretive sociology*. New York: Bedminster Press.

Westcott, M. R. (1988). *The psychology of human freedom: A human science perspective and critique*. New York: Springer.

White, R. W. (1959). Motivation reconsidered: The concept of competence. *Psychological Review, 66*, 297–333.

Wrong, D. (1995). *Power: Its forms, bases, and uses*. New York: Harper and Row.

Yoon, J., & Thye, S. R. (2002). A dual process model of organizational commitment. *Work and Occupations, 29*, 97–124.

Social Networks and Relational Sociology

9

Nick Crossley

9.1 Introduction

In recent years a number of writers, myself included, have made the case for a 'relational' approach to sociology (Crossley 2011, 2013, 2015a, b; Depelteau and Powell 2013a, b; Donati 2011; Emirbayer 1997; Mische 2011). In my own case, which I elaborate here, relational sociology posits that the basic focus of sociology should be interaction, ties and networks between social (human and corporate) actors. The social world is not a mere aggregate of actors, from this point of view, but rather entails their connection. Furthermore, though interaction, ties and networks presuppose actors involved in them the actor is as much the product as the producer of these structures from the relational perspective.

These ideas are not new. One can identify approximations of them in the work of many of sociology's founding thinkers, including Durkheim, Simmel, Marx and Mead. Indeed, I draw upon these thinkers in my version of relational sociology. It is my contention, however, that the insights of these thinkers were forgotten, to some extent, in the second half of the twentieth century, as sociologists turned, firstly, to a variety of forms of holism which hypostatized and reified 'society', replacing a focus upon actors and their relations with a focus upon systems and their institutionalized 'parts'; secondly, to various forms of individualism which sought to bring the actor back into focus but gave insufficient attention and weight to the interactions, ties and networks in which actors are both formed and embedded. The purpose of my own call for relational sociology is to tackle these theoretical blind alleys and bring interactions, ties and networks back into focus.

This is not only a matter of theory. In a series of important publications Andrew Abbott (1997, 2001) has pointed to the mismatch between sociological theory, on one side, and research methods and methodologies on the other. The main discrepancy, for him, is that sociological theory stresses the importance of the actor and her actions, whereas our research methods typically focus upon variables. It is not actors who act and interact in much sociological research, he notes, but rather variables, a problem which we must redress. I agree and wish to develop this argument. A relational rethink in sociology cannot be restricted to theory. It must extend to methodology and methods. If we theorize the social world in relational terms then we must analyze it in those terms too. Currently, in most cases, we do not. The survey methods which Abbott criticizes, and which are involved in a large proportion of our research, utilize statistical models which require a random sample of unconnected

N. Crossley (✉)
University of Manchester, Manchester, UK
e-mail: nick.crossley@manchester.ac.uk

S. Abrutyn (ed.), *Handbook of Contemporary Sociological Theory*,
Handbooks of Sociology and Social Research, DOI 10.1007/978-3-319-32250-6_9

respondents (case-wise independence). They design relations out of consideration. This is clearly problematic from the perspective of relational sociology. And our other main method of sociological research, analysis of qualitative interviews, is seldom much better. It is very often focused upon the experiences and perceptions of 'the individual', again failing to consider interaction, ties, networks and, by default, rendering experiences and perceptions as properties of the individual rather than interactional accomplishments and positions (see Billig 1991). Relational sociology must address this. It must employ and develop ways of analyzing interaction, ties and interactions.

A number of methods do already exist. In my work to date I have focused upon one such method, social network analysis (SNA). In this chapter I reflect upon this methodological choice, showing how SNA facilitates genuinely relational work in sociology.

The largest part of the chapter will be an elaboration and justification of these opening remarks. I begin by reflecting upon the holism/individualism debate. I then discuss the key concepts of relational sociology, considering how networks, in particular, can be researched by way of SNA. Having done this, however, I turn to two further dualisms which have troubled sociology in recent years: structure/agency and micro/macro. Whilst these dualisms point to issues which relational sociologists will always need to be sensitive to, it is my contention that the approach is well prepared to deal with them and I explain how.

9.2 Holism and Individualism

During the 1940s and 1950s functionalism, a variety of holism, was the dominant paradigm within sociology and Talcott Parsons (1951) was its key point of reference. Notwithstanding Parsons' own reticence regarding the problematic teleological form of 'functional explanations' (advocated, for example, by Radcliffe-Brown 1952), and that of Merton (1957), whom he cites approvingly, 'social facts' were explained by reference to the functions which they serve within social systems. The 'parts' of the system were explained by reference to the whole and more specifically its 'functional pre-requisites'. Having argued for the importance of the actor in his earlier works (Parsons 1937), moreover, Parsons (1951) shifted them out of focus in his later, more holistic works. Actors were assumed but only as incumbents of roles and it was the roles, along with norms and other institutionalized 'social facts' that comprised the 'parts' of the systems he sought to analyze.

During the 1960s functionalism's dominance began to wane. It was subject to extensive challenges. In some cases, however, most notably certain varieties of Neo-Marxism which themselves achieved a degree of dominance within the discipline, the primacy of the whole and this same way of theorizing it were retained. Marxists adopted their own version of functional explanation, explaining social institutions by showing that and how they serve capitalism and referring morphology and changes in society's 'superstructure' to the needs of its 'economic base'. Furthermore, the Marxist approach to history was, as Karl Popper (2002) observed, 'historicist'; referencing 'laws' and a telos to which the process of social life would inevitably succumb (see also Merleau-Ponty's (1973) critique). In the work of Althusser (1969) in particular, moreover, the apparent break marking Marx's later work, where (according to Althusser) all reference to 'man' was removed in favor of such structural concepts as 'mode of production' and 'social formation', was celebrated. Althusserian Marxism, like Parsonian functionalism, removed human actors from the picture, identifying institutions as the relevant parts of the capitalist system for analysis and critique (although Althusser (1971) later reintroduced 'the subject' in his theory of ideology).

I am simplifying but this way of thinking about 'wholes' persists within sociology and it is deeply problematic. The concept of 'functions' is legitimate and often useful but the problems of functional explanation are well-documented (Hollis 1994), even, in some cases, by writers from within the functionalist camp (esp. Merton 1957). To explain a social fact, such as a role, norm or convention by reference to the function which it serves within a system, especially when any reference to the actor who executes it is removed, is to explain it by reference to its effect. The causal arrow runs backwards, effect becoming cause, without any explanation being offered as to how such a counter-intuitive chain of events is possible. And a similar problem is evident in relation to historicism; the end of history, its telos, is identified as the cause of those actions which bring it about –again without any explanation of how such 'backwards causation' is possible.

The whole is hypostatized and reified in this form of holism. It is not only more than the sum of its parts but more than the sum of their relations too; a metaphysical essence separate from and determining both parts and their relations. Society is not constituted through the interaction and ties of its members but is rather something 'above' or 'behind' such praxes, steering them. The sociological holist, or at least this type of holist, commits what Gilbert Ryle (1949) calls a 'category error', imagining a separate substance of 'society' behind all manifestations of it, which explains those manifestations. Society is conceived as a thing, a substance. Relational sociology offers an alternative to this. Before I outline the relational approach, however, I want to briefly consider the other side of this coin.

A number of Parsons' critics called for 'men' (sic) to be brought back into sociological theory, arguing that 'systems' and the 'social facts' which form their parts do not *do* anything and possess no causal power; that they are mere patterns of human activity, *done* by *social actors* (Homans 1973; Wrong 1961). Actors 'do' the social world and everything in it from this perspective. They, not systems or social facts, have causal powers and should be the focus of our analysis.

In some versions of this argument 'actor' means 'human actor'. Other versions, however, admit of 'corporate actors', such as trade unions, political parties, economic firms and national governments (Coleman 1990; Axelrod 1997). Hindess (1988) offers a good argument in favor of the idea of corporate actors, suggesting that a collective of human actors form a corporate actor where they have a means of making decisions which are irreducible to those of their members, and of acting upon those decisions. An economic firm, for example, typically has a means of making decisions (e.g. a ballot of shareholders), which are then binding upon its members, who are both empowered and compelled to execute this decision. The decisions of such corporate actors can be shown to be irreducible to those of their human participants, Hindess argues, because different procedures of collective decision making (e.g. different voting systems) give different outputs for the same individual inputs. In addition, the actions of a corporate actor are often irreducible to those of the human actors who staff it in virtue of its legal status, power and resources. Only a national government can declare war or a state of emergency, for example, and only a trade union can call a strike. The human individuals who act on the corporate actor's behalf in such cases act in the name of the corporate actor, drawing upon its (not their individual) resources and its (not their individual) legal status.

A focus upon actors and their causal powers is important and affords a robust response and rebuttal to those forms of holism which invoke 'society' or 'the system' as a mysterious ordering principle of social life. However, this position is often couched in terms of individualism, and this is problematic.

In some cases individualism is ontological. The theorist claims that social facts and practices are merely shorthand ways of referring to the actions of individuals. For the ontological individualist 'there is no such thing as society, only individuals …',[1] to cite ex-British Prime Minister, Margaret Thatcher. Or rather society is a mere aggregate of individuals. Many sociological advocates claim to be methodological rather than ontological individualists, however. What this means is not always clear but I will suggest two variants.

[1] Actually she said '… individuals and families …' but her politics was a clear manifestation of this individualism. The quote is from an interview in *Women's Own* magazine 31/10/87.

In some cases it means that the sociologist acknowledges the existence of 'emergent properties' in social life; that is to say, they accept the existence of 'social facts' which can only exist in the context of collective life and which are irreducible to individuals or aggregates of individuals; but they maintain that such properties must be oriented to by individuals to enjoy any effect and that sociology should therefore remain focused upon individual actors. Max Weber (1978) falls into this camp. He recognizes that the social world comprises various emergent phenomena as well as social actors and that social actors orient to such phenomena in their decisions and actions. However, such phenomena only affect social life in virtue of the choices and actions that individuals adopt towards them, from his perspective, and he therefore focuses upon those choices and actions.

The second approach, characterized by James Coleman (1990), amongst others (e.g. Laver 1997), adopts much the same stance but pushes the position further by seeking individual level explanations for emergent phenomena. Coleman accepts that human behavior is affected by norms, for example, but argues that sociology must explain the origin and maintenance of norms; a task which, he insists, entails a focus upon individual actors and their motivations. Individuals pre-exist the social world, from this point of view, and to explain the social world, which is the job of the sociologist, we must therefore begin with individuals (see also Laver 1997).

The individualist position is flawed on a number of grounds. Firstly, its tendency to abstract individuals from society, in some cases invoking a pre-social 'state of nature', in order to explain society is artificial and flies in the face of much evidence. In phylogenetic terms we know that our primate ancestors lived in groups and that group living was amongst the selection pressures which shaped our evolution into human beings. We were social, living with and in-relation-to others, before we were human and our biological evolution, qua humans, was shaped by this. No less importantly, however, ontogenetically our biology is only a starting point as far as 'the social actor' assumed in much sociological theory, including individualistic theories, is concerned. The human actor is an outcome of sexual relations; takes shape, biologically, within the womb of their mother; and then emerges into the world helpless and dependent upon others for many years. At birth they possess very few of the properties of 'the social actor' and they only acquire these properties as a consequence of interaction with others. Through social interaction the human organism acquires language and thereby a capacity for reflective thought; a sense of self/other and identity; tastes and preferences; a moral sense; and many of the 'body techniques' necessary for getting by, to name only the most obvious. It becomes a social actor and the process of becoming is unending. Actors are continually reshaped by the interactions and relations in which they participate. They are always active in such interactions and relations, from the very beginning, never mere passive recipients of a culture thrust upon them, but who and what they are is shaped and reshaped in interaction in ways often unintended by them. There is no social actor before or outside of the social world. The two emerge together.

This process of becoming is also a process of individuation in which the actor takes on a distinct identity and becomes aware of herself as a distinct and unique being. Consciousness of self arises against a backdrop of consciousness of 'not self'. And as Mead (1967) and Merleau-Ponty (1962), both important philosophers for relational sociology, argue, consciousness of self presupposes consciousness of the consciousness of the other. I become conscious of myself by becoming conscious of the other's consciousness of me. Furthermore, consciousness, in these philosophical traditions (which inform relational sociology), is conceived not as an 'inner realm', separate from the world, but rather as a tie connecting the individual to the world. To be conscious of something or someone is to connect with them.

The social actor, on this account, is an emergent property of social interaction and relations. We become who and what we are by way of our involvement in social worlds; that is, in networks, ties and interactions with others. And our capacity to engage in such interactions is rooted in our earlier history of interaction and its formative effects.

A further, no less serious problem with individualism is that it treats social actions as discrete, failing to give proper consideration to interaction and interdependency between actors. The social world is not an aggregate of individuals and their actions but rather arises from interaction, relations and the interdependence of human actions and thoughts.

Interestingly, some 'methodological individualists' acknowledge this point, incorporating interaction and interdependency in their work by way of game theory (which assumes that actors make decisions on the basis of how they observe and/or anticipate others will act and which, correspondingly, models the interdependence of individual decisions and its aggregate effects) and even, in some cases, social network analysis (which, like game theory, focuses upon interdependence) (Coleman 1990; Hedström 2005). In my view such thinkers are individualists in name only and have, in practice, crossed over to a relational perspective – albeit a fairly minimal relationalism which would benefit from further embellishment. Neither their ontological nor their methodological inventories are reducible to 'individuals', since they acknowledge, at both levels, the significance of interaction and, in some cases, ties and networks.

In what follows I elaborate upon the fundamental concepts of relational sociology: i.e. interaction, ties and networks. Before I do, however, I will briefly address a potential obstacle to the acceptance of relational thought in sociology: namely, a residual empiricism which resists the idea that relational phenomena are real. Empiricism identifies the real with the perceptible and this generally favors individualism. Human beings, qua bodies, can be seen, heard, touched etc. and their existence is therefore obvious. Relations, by contrast, cannot be directly perceived and, to the empiricist frame of mind, this renders their existence questionable. On a strictly empirical level the social world is an aggregate of biologically individuated beings and the popularity of individualism in social and political thought, I suggest, stems from this. Against such empiricism, however, we should remind ourselves of the role of 'unobservables' in other sciences (Keat and Urry 1975). Neither gravity nor electricity can be directly perceived, for example. We only perceive them indirectly, by way of their effects (e.g. falling bodies or illuminated light bulbs). However, nobody would dispute their existence or importance. If we can demonstrate the effect of relational phenomena, it follows, then it is legitimate to infer their existence, whether or not we can directly observe them. This is the task of relational sociology – to which I now turn.

9.3 Networks, Interactions and Ties

Human interaction is unobservable in strict empiricist terms. Actor *i* can be perceived to act. Likewise actor *j*. But the effect of each upon the other is not directly perceived unless it involves physical contact and causation, and even then empiricist conceptions of causality struggle with the idea of connection.[2] To 'observe' interaction is to infer that *i* acted as she did *in response to j*. Such inferences would not be contentious in most cases, however, and it is this mutual affecting that characterizes and allows us to speak of social interaction: *i* affects *j* and her actions; *j* affects *i* and her actions. Each is affected by and stimulates the other in an irreducible circuit which takes on a life of its own, drawing its participants along with it. Gadamer captures this with respect to conversation:

> The way one word follows another, with the conversation taking its own twists and reaching its own conclusion may be conducted in some way, but the partners conversing are far less the leaders of it than the led. No one knows what will come out of a conversation. (Gadamer 1989, 383)

[2] As critique of empiricist accounts of causation have noted, the tendency to conceptualize causation as a succession of two events (constant conjuncture) avoids reference to any connection between them (Keat and Urry 1975).

Likewise Merleau-Ponty:

> …my words and those of my interlocutor are called forth by the state of the discussion, and they are inserted into a shared operation of which neither of us is the creator … the objection which my interlocutor raises to what I say draws from me thoughts which [surprise me]. (Merleau-Ponty 1962: 353)

Interaction is a whole greater than the sum of the individual actors involved in it, a system, but in contrast to Parsonian and Althusserian systems, actors remain its central drivers. The direction which the interaction takes is entirely contingent upon the responses of those party to it but those party to it are transformed by it and can neither foresee nor control the direction which it takes. We cannot abstract the actor from interaction, as the individualist would like, nor the system from its actors, as the holist prefers. We must work relationally.

Note the processual nature of this conception. Interaction is a process and social life, as the culmination of interaction, is too therefore. The quotations from Gadamer and Merleau-Ponty suggest change and unpredictability. This is true of social life in some places, some of the time, but not everywhere and always. Interaction can reproduce patterns across time. Even where this is the case, however, 'the system' is still dynamic. There is no social world outside of interaction and whatever stability can be observed is an outcome of continuously on-going interaction.

Some interactions are 'one-shot'. Parties meet, having never met before and with little prospect of meeting again in the future. Many, however, including most of those which are personally and/or sociologically most important, are not. Actors engage on numerous occasions, building a shared history and entering interaction with the (often tacit) expectation that they will meet again. In such cases actors are tied. At its most basic *a social tie is a sedimented interaction history embellished by the anticipated likelihood of future interaction.*

Like interaction, ties are not empirically observable but can be inferred from their effects. Through repeated interaction actors co-produce shared, habitual interaction repertoires involving conventions, identities, understandings, trust etc., which afford them a rapport. What happens in interaction is affected by this sedimented collective history. They interact differently because they 'know' one another. Furthermore, knowing the effect which past has upon present, their anticipation of future interaction shapes their engagement in the present. Inappropriate behavior now, even if it cannot be punished now, might be punished in future interactions.

Ties and interactions are mutually affecting. Interactions, past and future, shape ties, and ties shape interaction. Furthermore, the actor assumes an identity, which may be specific to that tie, and the way in which they interact is shaped, in some part, by that identity. As actors move from one interaction to another they 'switch' identities, to borrow a term from Mische and White (1998), and their patterns of interaction change accordingly. Indeed, they may switch within what, from the outside, appears to be the same interaction: a boss-to-worker interaction becoming a father-to-son or friend-to-friend interaction, for example, with a consequent shift in the properties and dynamics of the interaction.

The conventions and identities which shape ties and interactions are not built from scratch in each case. They are carried across from previous relationships and vicariously, from the observed experiences of others. Indeed, actors enjoy access to a cultural stock of 'types' which they can employ, albeit often with a degree of individual tailoring, to make sense of new and unfamiliar encounters (Schutz 1972).

My conception of interaction is akin to what Dewey and Bentley (1949) call 'transaction', a concept which they contrast with 'interaction'. Parties to a 'transaction', as Dewey and Bentley conceptualize this distinction, are at least partly constituted by it whereas interaction occurs between otherwise independent entities. I prefer to stick with the term 'interaction', even though what I mean by it concurs with their 'transactions' because the term 'transaction' has a strong economic connotation, which is unhelpful, and because most other writers whom I draw upon do not make the distinction and, like me, use 'interaction' in a way which overlaps with what Dewey and Bentley call 'transaction'.

9.3.1 Interdependence and Power

In many cases actors' ties also involve interdependence. Goods and resources are exchanged and each comes to rely upon the other for those goods and resources. This may sound economistic but I see it as a means of recognizing the meaningfulness of ties and the attraction involved. Although some ties are involuntary actors generally select those with whom they repeatedly interact. The reasons for their selections may be cynical and economistic (e.g. 'because she's loaded and buys me things') but they often centre upon perceived personal qualities or qualities of a tie, built up over time, which make the other attractive: e.g. 'we have a laugh', 'we understand and value each other', 'we have shared interests to talk about'. These qualities are the goods to which I am referring, at least as much as material goods, and they are important because they make ties intelligible, furnishing a reason for the repeated contact between those involved.

Interdependence is important because it creates a balance of power (Elias 1978; Mohl 1997). Each needs the other and this affords the other a lever by which to affect their behavior, albeit perhaps sometimes unwittingly (Mohl 1997). From romantic relations, through employment, to the ties between a colonial power and its colony, the (often tacit) threat that desired goods could be withdrawn motivates compliance with the (perceived) wishes of the other, making social ties relations of power.

Levels of interdependence and (im)balance vary. The pleasant conversation afforded by a casual acquaintance can easily be found elsewhere, for example, making the mutual hold of acquaintances relatively weak. Financial dependence, by contrast, can create a strong hold. Likewise, where the exchange involved in casual acquaintance is often evenly balanced, each having the same hold over the other, financial exchanges are often imbalanced, with one party having more of a hold over the other. These variations are important and we are often only interested in power relations where they are strong and imbalanced. To reiterate, however, power balances are ubiquitous in social ties.

9.3.2 From Dyads to Triads and Networks

A focus upon dyadic ties, *i–j*, is, for many purposes, inadequate. Ties are usually embedded in wider networks which mediate their significance and effects. Actors enjoy multiple ties and, as Simmel's (1902) reflections upon 'the third' suggest, the pattern of ties within which any single tie is embedded will often modify its effect. Where different alters exert competing influence, for example, they may cancel one another out or inculcate a more cosmopolitan outlook on behalf of the actor, who learns to see the world from a variety of standpoints. Conversely, when singing from the same hymn sheet they may reinforce one another. To give another example, dependency in any one relation will be affected by other relations which potentially afford the actor access to the same goods or resources: *i*'s dependence upon *j* may be lessened by their tie to *k* if *k* affords them many of the same goods as *j*.

Furthermore, this is affected by ties (or their absence) between actors' alters. If *i* 'brokers' between *j* and *k* this puts him in a different position, with different opportunities and constraints, to a situation where each of the three knows the others (see Fig. 9.1). A broker is often rewarded for serving as a conduit of innovations and resources, for example (Burt 1992, 2005). In addition, as sexual health campaigns remind us, *i*'s relation with *j* is also an indirect tie to *j*'s alters, indirectly exposing her to whatever goods (or bads) *j*'s alters have. Rather than focus upon dyads, therefore, we need to focus upon networks, remembering of course that networks are always in-process as a consequence of the interactions between their nodes. New ties form. Old ties change and sometimes break etc.

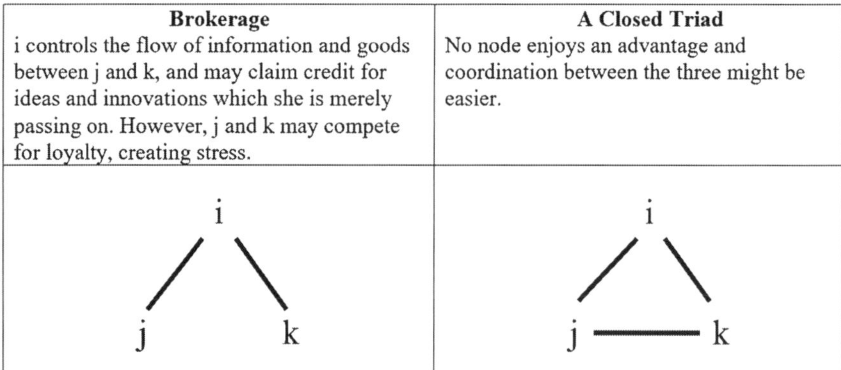

Fig. 9.1 Brokerage and closure

9.4 Social Worlds and the Social World

The social world, as conceived by the relational sociologist, is a vast and complex network; a network which is:

1. *Multiplex*: pairs of actors are tied in multiple different ways.
2. *Multi-Modal*: a network not only of human actors but also corporate actors (e.g. firms, governments etc.), places, events and other node types.
3. *Multi-Leveled*: certain nodes and networks are nested within others.
4. *Dynamic*: a network which is constantly evolving.

This begs questions of scale which I return to. Presently, however, note that, like most sociologists, relational sociologists recognize that *the* social world, writ large, is subdivided into smaller social worlds, centered upon particular shared foci of interest, and much analysis, in practice, is focused upon one or more of these worlds.

My chief concern in this chapter is with the network element of these worlds. It is important to note, however, that other elements are in play too. At the very least, social worlds are structured by:

1. *Conventions*: which are generated through interaction, diffuse through networks, evolve in subsequent interaction and which both facilitate coordination of the interactions constitutive of the world and serve to distinguish it from others worlds (where other conventions are in evidence).
2. *Resources*: which are mobilized and exchanged in interaction and unevenly distributed across networks, generating power imbalances and conflicts of interest.

9.5 Analyzing Networks

I suggested at the outset of this chapter that relational sociology is not only a theoretical but also a methodological program in sociology. Relational sociology requires relational methodologies. One such methodology is social network analysis (SNA). SNA affords a means of exploring patterns of ties empirically, studying actors-in-relation and capturing social worlds not as mere aggregates of actors but rather as relational 'wholes'. Furthermore, it allows us to empirically measure network properties and investigate their effects. This is not the place to offer a detailed introduction to SNA, nor to tackle the complex issues of multiplexity, multi-modality etc. referred to above. However, it would be

	John	Jane	Jake	Sue	Paul	Gill	Fred	Errol	Nina	Raj	Kirk	Billie	Nick	Frank	Nisha	Sarah	Martin	Charlie	Bud	Diana
John		1	1	1	1	0	0	0	0	0	0	0	0	0	0	0	0	0	0	0
Jane	1		1	1	1	0	0	0	0	0	0	0	0	0	0	0	0	0	0	0
Jake	1	1		1	1	0	0	0	0	0	0	0	0	0	0	0	0	0	0	0
Sue	1	1	1		1	0	0	0	0	0	0	0	0	0	0	0	0	0	0	0
Paul	1	1	1	1		0	0	0	0	0	0	0	0	0	0	0	0	0	0	0
Gill	0	0	0	0	0		1	1	1	1	0	0	0	0	0	0	0	0	1	0
Fred	0	0	0	0	0	1		0	0	0	0	0	0	0	0	0	0	1	0	0
Errol	0	0	0	0	0	1	0		0	1	0	0	0	0	0	0	0	1	0	0
Nina	0	0	0	0	0	1	0	0		0	0	0	0	0	0	1	0	0	0	0
Raj	0	0	0	0	0	1	0	1	0		0	0	0	0	0	0	1	0	0	0
Kirk	0	0	0	0	0	0	0	0	0	0		0	1	1	1	0	0	0	0	0
Billie	0	0	0	0	0	0	0	0	0	0	0		0	0	1	0	0	0	0	0
Nick	0	0	0	0	0	0	0	0	0	0	1	0		0	0	0	0	0	0	0
Frank	0	0	0	0	0	0	0	0	0	0	1	0	0		1	1	0	0	0	0
Nisha	0	0	0	0	0	0	0	0	0	0	1	1	0	1		0	0	0	0	0
Sarah	0	0	0	0	0	0	0	0	1	0	0	0	0	1	0		0	0	0	0
Martin	0	0	0	0	0	0	0	0	0	1	0	0	0	0	0	0		0	0	1
Charlie	0	0	0	0	0	0	1	1	0	0	0	0	0	0	0	0	0		0	0
Bud	0	0	0	0	0	1	0	0	0	0	0	0	0	0	0	0	0	0		0
Diana	0	0	0	0	0	0	0	0	0	0	0	0	0	0	0	0	1	0	0	

Fig. 9.2 An adjacency matrix

instructive to give a brief overview, showing how the approach might inform relational sociology.

I begin with two basic elements of the approach: graphs and adjacency matrices. The left-hand column of the matrix in Fig. 9.2 lists all of the actors involved in a particular context of interest. The top row repeats this list. Each actor, therefore, has both a row and column, and the presence of a tie between any two of them can be captured by placing a number in the cell where one's row meets the other's column. In the simple case a 1 represents the presence of a tie and a 0 its absence. If we have measured tie strength or counted the number of interactions between two actors, however, then we may use whatever range of values is required.

The matrix has two cells for each pair of actors, one on either side of the diagonal which runs from the top left to the bottom right of the matrix. There is a cell where John's row intersects Jane's column, for example, and one where her row intersects his column. This allows us to capture direction in ties. Perhaps we are interested in relations of liking and though John likes Jane she does not like him. If so we can put a 1 where his row intersects her column (indicating his liking for her) and a 0 where her row intersects his column (indicating the absence of any liking for him by her). Some relations are undirected, however, such that we would record the same information in each cell. If John plays tennis with Jane, for example, then Jane necessarily plays tennis with John, or rather *they* play tennis *together*. We might be interested in multiple types of tie or interaction, of course, in which case we can have multiple matrices, each capturing a different tie.

Note that I have left the diagonal of the matrix in Fig. 9.2, which captures a node's relation to itself, blank. For some purposes it may be meaningful to ask if a node enjoys a tie to their self (a reflexive tie), and SNA can allow for this. In many cases, however, it is not meaningful and we ignore the diagonal.

An adjacency matrix facilitates mathematical manipulation of relational data. The same information can be recorded in the form of a graph, however, where, in the simple case, actors are represented by shapes (vertices) and ties by connecting lines (edges) (see Fig. 9.3) (this graph has

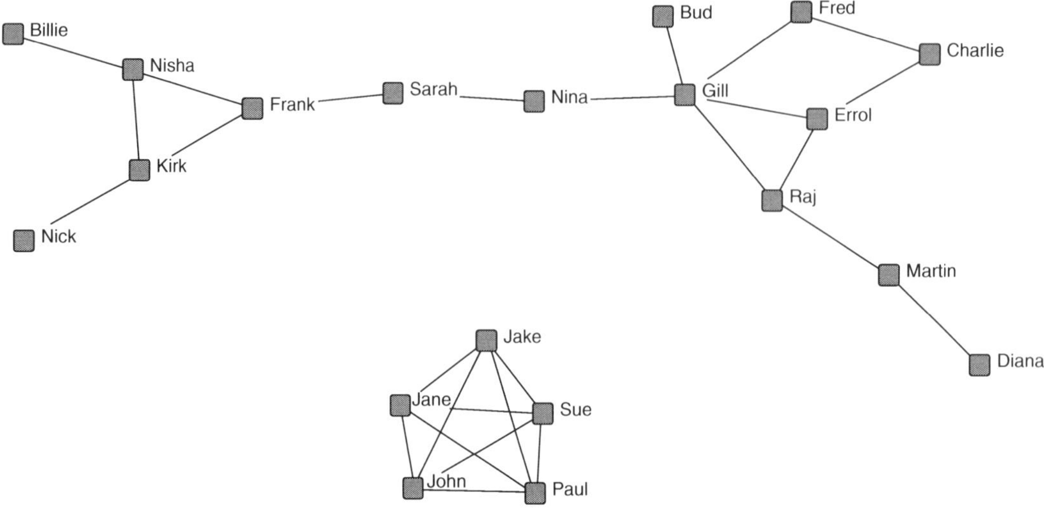

Fig. 9.3 A network graph (visualizing the relations recorded in Fig. 9.2)

been drawn and all network mesures derived using Ucinet software (Borgatti et al. 2002)). A graph makes both the structure of a network and the position of specific nodes within it more immediately apparent, and it affords a more intuitive way of explaining certain network properties (at least for smaller networks). In what follows I will briefly describe a number of these properties, for illustrative purposes, subdividing them into three levels: the whole network, subgroups and individual nodes.

9.5.1 The Whole Network

Looking firstly at the whole network we see immediately that there is a break in it, with a cluster of nodes to the bottom of the plot whose members each have a path connecting them to one another but no *path* connecting them to the rest of the network (all other nodes are connected to one another by a path). We express this by saying that the network comprises two *components* (some networks may have more than one component and some only one).

The existence of distinct components might be of interest to us if we are interested in the flow of goods or 'bads' (e.g. viruses) through a network because goods cannot flow where there is no path. Belonging to a discrete component therefore may afford a node safety from wider dangers. Conversely, it may cut them off from important resources, including new ideas, innovations and information. Similarly, if we were interested in collective action we would not expect any coordination or solidarity between members of discrete components because they lack the necessary contact. Furthermore, we would expect to find different emergent cultures across components as the relations of mutual influence generative of culture do not traverse them.

Even within the main component, however, and certainly for the network as a whole, we can see that only a fraction of the number of connections that could exist actually do. There are 20 nodes in this network and therefore $20 \times 19/2 = 190$ pairs of actors. Assuming that ties are undirected there are therefore 190 potential ties. Empirically, however, we only have 27 ties. This gives us a network *density* of $27/190 = 0.14$.

Density is important for various reasons. To return to the above examples: higher density has been shown both to speed up the rate at which goods/bads diffuse through a network (Valente 1995), and to cultivate trust, solidarity and incentive systems which, in turn, increase the likelihood of collective action (Coleman 1990; Crossley 2015a).

9.5.2 Subgroups

There are many different ways of identifying subgroups within a network, each based upon different principles and appropriate for different purposes. Components are one example but sometimes we find dense patches within a network whose members are not absolutely cut off and yet which form clear clusters. The discovery and verification of such clusters, which SNA techniques enable, may be important because the relatively high density of interaction and thus mutual influence within them and low density (and thus low influence) between them will encourage the formation of different emergent cultures. Moreover, the connections between them may encourage comparison and thereby the formation of distinct collective identities, competition, perhaps even conflict. Cohesive clustering in networks facilitates collective action and the formation of effective social groups.

Components and *density* are measures of cohesion. They allow us to measure how cohesive a network is and to identify *cohesive subgroups* within it. Another way of thinking about subgroups, however, is to focus upon nodes who occupy an equivalent position within a network, irrespective of cohesion. Middle managers in an organization may occupy a similar position, for example, mediating between the shop-floor and upper management, without necessarily enjoying any connection to one another. They are in a similar position but do not form a cohesive group. Such positions are important and interesting, sociologically, because they typically afford similar opportunities and constraints to all who occupy them, thereby shaping their interactions. SNA affords a number of methods for identifying these positions and analyzing the structure which they jointly form.

Another way of looking at subgroups in SNA is to focus upon attributes and identities which are exogenous to network structure but shape it. There is a great deal of evidence to suggest that actors are more likely to form ties to others of a similar status, such as race or social class ('status homophily'), for example, or to others who share salient values and/or tastes ('value homophily') (Lazarsfeld and Merton 1964; McPherson et al. 2001). It can be difficult to disentangle 'selection' from 'influence' in some cases; are our contacts similar to us because we have selected them on this basis or because our interactions have made us more alike? Both factors are in play much of the time but certain longitudinal methods in SNA allow us to capture their relative weighting in particular cases, and it can be instructive to explore whether such endogenous groupings as those discussed in the above paragraph map onto these exogenous divisions. Does ethnicity or income affect social mixing and consequent group formation, for example. Such issues have considerable significance beyond sociology and SNA affords means and measures for exploring them.

9.5.3 Node Level Properties

Beyond subgroups SNA also affords various measures for exploring the individual position of particular nodes within a network. There are, for example, a range of different methods for measuring and comparing the *centrality* of individual nodes within a network, each reflecting a different conception of what it is to be central and thus being more or less appropriate to different projects; and there are a range of methods for exploring the opportunities which particular nodes might enjoy for brokerage and the benefits it affords (Burt 1992, 2005). Several of these measures may be aggregated, moreover, in ways which afford us a perspective upon the whole network. For purposes of illustration consider *degree centrality*.

In this context 'degree' means the number of ties which any individual node has. In a friendship network a node who has three friends has a degree of 3, and the node with the most friends has the *highest degree*. They are the *most degree central* node in the network. This can be an advantage: having a lot of friends brings a lot of benefits. It involves costs and constraints, however, as maintaining ties requires time and energy, and friends will tend to ask favors (which are difficult to refuse) and make demands. Enjoying a high centrality is not always a benefit, therefore, but it exposes a node to different opportunities and constraints to less central nodes and we would expect this to make a difference. Furthermore, we may be interested in the impact of exogenous resources and statuses upon centrality. Are men, on average, more central than women in a particular network, for example, and therefore advantaged within it?

Building upon this, we can average degree for the whole network, thus enabling comparisons across networks (*average degree* is a closely related measure to *density*), and we can explore the distribution of degree in order to assess how (*degree*) *centralized* a network is. A skewed distribution in which a small number of nodes are involved in a high proportion of all ties reveals that the network is centered upon those nodes. This points to inequalities in the network but also perhaps to an enhanced opportunity for coordination of activities (Oliver and Marwell 1993), since the central nodes are in a position to centralize information and distribute orders.

As a final illustration of measurable network properties I will briefly discuss *geodesic distances*, a concept I return to later. Any two nodes within a component have a path (comprising ties and nodes) connecting them. In Fig. 9.3, for example, there is a path between Frank and Gill via Sarah, Nina and the three ties between them. Paths are measured in ties or 'degrees', as they are called in this context, so we say that Frank and Gill are at three degrees of separation. There are often several paths between the same two nodes. For example, Gill and Fred are directly connected (one degree) but there is also a more circuitous path between them via Errol and Charlie (three degrees). The shortest of these paths is referred to as the 'geodesic distance' between the nodes involved and it is this path-length, in particular, that is often of most interest in SNA because, all things being equal, it is the quickest route through which goods (and bads) can travel and involves the least likelihood of them being 'damaged' in transit.

Sometimes we may be interested in the geodesic distances between particular nodes or each individual node's total distance from all others in their component. Often, however, we are interested in the distribution of geodesic distances in a network or their average. Amongst other things, this tells us how likely it is that information and instructions will pass quickly through the network, facilitating coordination.

I have only scratched at the surface of SNA here. My intention has been to illustrate how the ties, interactions and networks which comprise the conceptual core of relational sociology can be methodologically incorporated and empirically explored. Many other measures, covering other properties, exist and, beyond these descriptive measures, there are many methods for both statistically modeling network structure (including dynamic changes over time) and exploring the significance of exogenous attributes and identities (both as factors which affect and factors which are affected by network patterns) (Borgatti et al. 2013; Lusher et al. 2013; Scott 2000; Snijders et al. 2010; Wasserman and Faust 1994). Furthermore, SNA is not the only relational method one might use and many studies will mix methods. The process of interaction might be analyzed by way of conversation analysis, for example, or indeed modeled by way of game theory, and the access to interaction and ties afforded by both participant observation and archival analysis often makes them good methods for relational-sociological research. SNA is an important relational method, however, and hopefully this brief introduction has been sufficient to give some inphenomena, however, and innumerable studiesdication of this. With that said I want to conclude this chapter by considering where relational sociology stands in relation to two thorny dualisms which have dogged sociology in recent years: (1) structure and agency, and (2) micro and macro.

9.6 Structure and Agency

The relational position involves both agency and structure. Network nodes are typically social actors, locked in relations and interactions with others which affect them, but also loci of decision and action and therefore agents all the same.

Structure figures by way of the conventions actors observe (and both co-create and modify in interaction), the uneven distribution of resources (including status) and power imbalances between them but more importantly, for present purposes, in the form of network structure which, I have suggested, generates both opportunities and constraints for those involved in it. The question of structure and agency, in this context, concerns the relative weight that we accord to each.

This is a live issue, as attested by a number of critiques of SNA published in recent years, both by network analysts themselves and others (Crossley 2010; Emirbayer and Goodwin 1994; Knox et al. 2006; Mische 2003). 'Old school' network analysis stands accused of positing a deterministic interpretation of networks which attributes fixed effects to particular network properties and suggests that incumbents of particular positions in a network are constrained to play certain roles within it. These criticisms are partly focused upon the neglect of culture in much SNA and also partly methodological. Network effects and dynamics are mediated by meanings, identities, actors' understandings and thus by culture, it is argued, none of which is necessarily captured in formal network analysis. The critics therefore call for a mixed method approach to SNA which brings qualitative data regarding these cultural elements to bear. The debate is also about agency, however. Meanings, identities, understandings etc. are negotiated in interaction, for example, as are opportunities and constraints. Actors can fail to take the opportunities which their network position affords them and might respond in different ways to the same constraints. Agents work within and around structure. It does not determine their action.

These criticisms are important and inform relational sociology. We must be attentive to culture, which, as shared, is itself relational (see Crossley 2015a, b), and we must avoid deterministic readings of the effect of network properties, recognizing the ways in which actors negotiate them. I am not convinced that there is a great deal more to be said, theoretically, about structure and agency, however, and would suggest that, beyond these general theoretical considerations, the issue is empirical. The structure/agency debate arose in some part from the theoretical divide between holists and individualists which I discussed above. Holists exclude actors and thus agency from their account. Individualists exclude structure. However, when a theory includes both agency and structure, as relational sociology does, and the question becomes one of relative weighting, we cannot answer that question in theory and cannot expect the same answer for every situation. Structure is more constraining in some contexts and at some times than others. Both structure and agency are important in every context but their relative weight will shift between contexts and it is the job of the sociologist to determine the weighting in the specific contexts they are researching.

9.7 Micro and Macro

There is yet another dualism that relational sociology is required to tackle, however; namely, the micro-macro divide. As I understand it, the micro-macro debate focuses upon scale. Sociology might focus upon the details of a few seconds of conversation between two people or upon matters of world history, begging the question of how such foci are linked and whether the principles governing one are relevant to the other. This is a potentially very complex issue and I cannot do complete justice to it here. It is important, however, to say something about context and something about scale. I begin with the former.

The link between micro and macro is not always as difficult to envisage as it initially sounds. The events which turn the wheels of world history, affecting large numbers of people, are sometimes, in themselves, relatively 'small'. As I write, for example, the Greek Parliament has just agreed, very reluctantly, to pass a number of 'austerity laws' demanded by the European Union in return for a (third) financial bailout, involving billions of Euros, in an effort to protect their country from economic disaster and possible exit from the Eurozone. This is an event of global significance with huge implications, especially in Greece but across Europe and, to some extent, the world. With the exception of the huge crowds of protestors who gathered outside the Greek Parliament when the decision was being made, and who I return to below, however, most of the decisions shaping and steering this situation were made in interactions between a relatively small number of people over a relatively short period of time. Greek politicians sat face-to-face and debated. Similarly, the demands of 'the European Union' were decided by a small number of European politicians over a few days, face-to-face in various committee rooms, and relayed directly to the Greek Prime Minister.

Any analysis of these interactions would have to understand their context: the various pressures upon those involved, the stakes involved, and so on. However, this moment in global history was decided through face-to-face interaction which, whatever its particularities, assumed much the same form as any other human interaction. This is not atypical. As the individualists recognize, it is actors who do things and make things happen in the social world. All sociological phenomena can and should be tracked back.

The Greek government is a corporate actor, involving irreducible mechanisms of decision making and implementation. Likewise the European Union. The decisions made by and between these corporate actors often affect millions of people. They are global in their reach; macro-cosmic. But they are interactions between actors all the same. The 'world system' or 'global social order' is not a mysterious force affecting our lives from without but rather a network, albeit a hugely complex network, involving millions of actors, both human and corporate, and the various (often unequal) ties between them, and as such it can be analyzed by way of SNA (Smith and White 1992; Snyder and Kick 1979). The social macro-cosm may involve 'bigger' actors and/or more actors (see below) but it is no different in kind to its constituent micro-cosms.

In the Greek example social movements and their protests also played a role. They put pressure on the Greek government and sent a signal to other European politicians. Social movements do not fit my definition of corporate actors because they generally have no means of making decisions or enforcing their own resolutions (Offe 1985), even if some of the 'social movement organizations' within them do. Movements are relational phenomena, however, and innumerable studies have pointed both to their network character and to the role of pre-existing networks in their formation and mobilization (Crossley 2007; Crossley and Krinsky 2015; Diani and McAdam 2003).

It isn't always possible to pin the twists and turns of history down to particular interactions. Certain trends and dynamics cannot be localized in this way. The relational approach is still the best way of making sense of such dynamics, however. Complexity theory in the natural sciences and the agent-based models employed therein provide a useful reference point for thinking about these issues (Watts 1999; Barabási 2003; Newman et al. 2006). In complex systems, which are usually conceived of as networks involving interaction between millions of nodes, the multiplication of interactions and intervention of cascade, feedback and other such mechanisms generate fascinating organizational forms and dynamics akin to those sometimes observed by sociologists. These dynamics and forms are often extremely impressive; everything happens 'as if' by grand design. Unlike the sociological holists discussed above, however, complexity scientists are able to show by way of their models that such emergent forms are indeed emergent, that is, generated from the bottom up by way of interactions and their concatenations, and not inevitable outcomes of history's grand plan. Complex systems are networks and their emergent organization can be analyzed as such. We might not be able to graph such networks very clearly, given their size, but we can analyze them using SNA and related methods. Interaction, ties and networks remain the bedrock of our understanding of what is going on.

The focus on networks in complexity theory has also led to an interesting exchange with social science. Emergent effects in complex systems are sometimes difficult to comprehend because it is difficult to imagine how order could emerge between such a large number of nodes (millions). Surely, complexity theorists puzzled, *geodesic distances* would be too long to facilitate any significant transfer of energy or information? In puzzling this question complexity theorists stumbled across work by social psychologist, Stanley Milgram (1967), which suggested that any two citizens picked at random from the US population, are, on average, separated by only six ties ('six degrees of separation'). This so-called 'small world' phenomena was intriguing to the complexity physicists because it rendered the idea of mutual influence between nodes in a network of millions far more plausible. Geodesics need not be very long even in huge networks; in which case, influence and coordination across such networks is plausible. This prompted complexity theorists both to conduct a variety of studies looking for 'small world' examples in the natural world, which they found in abundance, and to solve the mathematical problem posed by Milgram's work: namely, how can nodes in a network of millions be linked by such short geodesics? They came up with two possibilities, both of which work (mathematically), and have been demonstrated empirically and in simulations. More important for our purposes, however, is the support that it lends to my idea, introduced above, that the social world is a (multiplex, multi-modal, multi-leveled and dynamic) network. This idea sometimes attracts resistance because sociologists are inclined to believe that the scale of national and international societies is so big that 'something else', something other than interaction, ties and networks are at work. The work of the complexity theorists suggests that this need not be so and that a network model of society is plausible.

What the complexity theorists overlook in their use of Milgram, however, is his focus upon social division. Milgram conceived of social structure as a network. His research was focused, in some part, upon the basic properties of such networks, not least average geodesics. However, he was also interested in the impact of status differentials upon network structure. His work suggested that this could be considerable, particular in relation to race. His methodology involved asking people to mail a package to others whom they knew, with the ultimate aim of delivering the package to a target individual who was not directly known to those involved at the start of the experiment. The study suggested that packages often traversed geographical space with relative ease and speed but that, where they were required to cross a racial divide, the process often stalled. Participants enjoyed good relations with others of their own race across the country, in other words, but few such relations with members of other racial groups even in their own town. Ties were shaped by status and more especially ethnic homophily. I mention this here to demonstrate that and how relational sociology allows us to begin to think about and research such social divisions, on a macro-level. Social divisions, from a relational point of view, manifest in patterns of connection (and lack of connection) within a population and those patterns of connection are empirically analyzable using SNA (see also Blau 1974, 1977).

Status homophily is an example of what I described early as 'cohesive subgroups'. Actors who share a particular status tend to gravitate towards one another. Actors with different statuses do not. They may even actively avoid one another. As noted earlier, however, this is not the only way in which nodes might cluster. Nodes can be clustered where they occupy 'equivalent' positions in a network, as defined in SNA and measured by a number of dedicated clustering algorithms. A good example of this 'blockmodeling' in action is Peter Bearman's (1993) analysis of kinship networks and elite structures in Norfolk (England) prior to the (1642–1651) civil war. The details of the study are not strictly relevant here but it is important to note, firstly, that Bearman uses blockmodeling to render a very large network intelligible and to track both hierarchy and changes in hierarchy within English society; secondly, that he identifies changes in this network which played an important role in the precipitation of the civil war. Again here SNA proves a useful tool for exploring 'macro' processes and events, and again the keys to understanding those processes and events are shown to be networks, ties and interactions.

9.8 Conclusion

Sociological theory in the latter half of the twentieth century became caught in a dualism involving two equally problematic tendencies: a top down holism which removed social actors from consideration, treating 'society' and 'history' as greater than both their parts and the relations between those parts; and a form of individualism which effectively reduced society to an aggregate of self-contained social actors. Relational sociology is based upon a critique of these ideas and posits an alternative to them, focused upon the key concepts: interaction, ties and networks.

Relational sociology is not only a theory, however. Relational methodologies are necessary if a genuinely relational shift is to be achieved. This will involve methodological innovation but some relational methods do already exist and this chapter has focused upon social network analysis (SNA) in particular. SNA allows us to explore the properties of the networks in which all social actors are embedded, and in which they take shape, and it allows us to explore the importance of those properties.

Networks are structures and, as such, facilitate structural thinking and analysis in (relational) sociology. Structure is not 'above' or 'behind' actors, from this perspective, however. It lies *between* them. Furthermore, it does not determine action. How actors respond to situations depends upon cultural processes, including dialogue and debate; and structure, in any case, only affords opportunities and constraints which actors work around. There is both agency and structure in relational sociology. Quite how much agency and structure enter into any given situation depends upon the situation, however. The relational sociologist must look at the interplay and relative weighting of structure and agency in any particular situation.

Talk of interaction, ties and networks perhaps suggests a focus upon the social micro-cosm. Relational sociology is well-suited to analyze the micro-cosm but not only the micro-cosm. Macro-social life is open to relational analysis too. More to the point, it is a key claim of the relational sociologist that, whilst further mechanisms may be evident and a wide range of relational-analytic methods required, the dynamics and organization of the social macro-cosm are generated from the bottom up, through interaction, ties and networks, much as happens in the micro-cosm. Indeed, any distinction between micro and macro is unhelpful. It makes more sense to think of a continuum of scale along which different relational processes can be located.

References

Abbott, A. (1997). Of time and space. *Social Forces, 75*(4), 1149–1182.

Abbott, A. (2001). *Time matters*. Chicago: Chicago University Press.

Althusser, L. (1969). *For Marx*. London: Verso.

Althusser, L. (1971). *Ideology and the ideological state apparatus, in his essays on ideology* (pp. 1–60). London: Verso.

Axelrod, R. (1997). *The complexity of cooperation*. Princeton: Princeton University Press.

Barabási, A.-L. (2003). *Linked*. New York: Plume.

Bearman, P. (1993). *Relations into rhetorics*. New Brunswick: Rutgers University Press.

Billig, M. (1991). *Ideology and opinions*. London: Sage.

Blau, P. (1974). Parameters of social space. *American Sociological Review, 39*(5), 615–635.

Blau, P. (1977). A macrosociological theory of social structure. *American Journal of Sociology, 83*(1), 26–54.

Borgatti, S., Everett, M., & Freeman, L. (2002). *Ucinet 6 for windows: Software for social network analysis*. Harvard: Analytic Technologies.

Borgatti, S. P., Everett, M. G., & Johnson, J. (2013). *Analyzing social networks*. London: Sage.

Burt, R. (1992). *Structural holes*. Cambridge: Harvard University Press.

Burt, R. (2005). *Brokerage and closure*. Oxford: Oxford University Press.

Coleman, J. (1990). *Foundations of social theory*. Harvard: Belknap.

Crossley, N. (2007). Social networks and extra-parliamentary politics. *Sociology Compass, 1*(1), 222–236.

Crossley, N. (2010). The social world of the network: Qualitative aspects of network analysis. *Sociologica* (1). http://www.sociologica.mulino.it/main

Crossley, N. (2011). *Towards relational sociology*. London: Routledge.

Crossley, N. (2013). Interactions, juxtapositions and tastes. In F. Depelteau & C. Powell (Eds.), *Conceptualizing relational sociology*. London: Palgrave.

Crossley, N. (2015a). *Networks of sound, style and subversion: The punk and post-punk worlds of Manchester, London, Liverpool and Sheffield, 1975–1980*. Manchester: Manchester University Press.

Crossley, N. (2015b). Relational sociology and culture: A preliminary framework. *International Review of Sociology, 25*(1), 65–85.

Crossley, N., & Krinsky, J. (Eds.). (2015). *Social networks and social movements*. London: Routledge.

Depelteau, F., & Powell, C. (2013a). *Conceptualizing relational sociology*. London: Palgrave.

Depelteau, F., & Powell, C. (2013b). *Applying relational sociology*. London: Palgrave.

Dewey, J., & Bentley, A. (1949). *Knowing and the known*. Boston: Beacon.

Diani, M., & McAdam, D. (Eds.). (2003). *Social movements and networks*. Oxford: Oxford University Press.

Donati, P. (2011). *Relational sociology*. London: Routledge.

Elias, N. (1978). *What is sociology?* London: Hutchinson.

Emirbayer, M. (1997). Manifesto for a relational sociology. *American Journal of Sociology, 99*(6), 1411–1454.

Emirbayer, M., & Goodwin, J. (1994). Network analysis, culture and the problem of agency. *American Journal of Sociology, 99*, 1411–1454.

Gadamer, H.-G. (1989). *Truth and method*. London: Sheed and Ward.

Hedström, P. (2005). *Dissecting the social*. Cambridge: Cambridge University Press.

Hindess, B. (1988). *Choice, rationality and social theory*. London: Unwin-Hyman.

Hollis, M. (1994). *The philosophy of the social sciences*. Cambridge: Cambridge University Press.

Homans, G. (1973). Bringing men back. In A. Ryan (Ed.), *The philosophy of social explanation*. Oxford: Oxford University Press.

Keat, R., & Urry, J. (1975). *Social theory as science*. London: Routledge.

Knox, H., Savage, M., & Harvey, P. (2006). Social networks and the study of relations: Networks as method, metaphor and form. *Economy and Society, 35*(1), 113–140.

Laver, M. (1997). *Private desires, political action*. London: Sage.

Lazarsfeld, P., & Merton, R. (1964). Friendship as social process. In M. Berger, T. Abel, & C. Page (Eds.), *Freedom and control in modern society* (pp. 18–66). New York: Octagon Books.

Lusher, D., Koskinen, J., & Robins, G. (2013). *Exponential random graph models for social networks*. Cambridge: Cambridge University Press.

McPherson, M., Smith-Lovin, L., & Cook, J. (2001). Birds of a feather: Homophily in social networks. *Annual Review of Sociology, 27*, 415–444.

Mead, G. H. (1967). *Mind, self and society*. Chicago: Chicago University Press.

Merleau-Ponty, M. (1962). *The phenomenology of perception*. London: Routledge.

Merleau-Ponty, M. (1973). *Adventures of the dialectic*. Evanston: Northwestern University Press.

Merton, R. (1957). *Manifest and latent functions, in his social theory and social structure*. Glencoe: Free Press.

Milgram, S. (1967). The small world problem. In G. Carter (Ed.), *Empirical approaches to sociology* (pp. 111–118). Boston: Pearson.

Mische, A. (2003). Cross-talk in movements. In M. Diani & D. McAdam (Eds.), *Social movements and networks*. Oxford: Oxford University Press.

Mische, A. (2011). Relational sociology, culture and agency. In J. Scott & P. Carrington (Eds.), *The Sage handbook of social network analysis* (pp. 80–97). London: Sage.

Mische, A., & White, H. (1998). Between conversation and situation. *Social Research, 65*, 295–324.

Molm, L. (1997). *Coercive power in social exchange*. Cambridge, UK: Cambridge University Press.

Newman, M., Barabási, L., & Watts, D. (2006). *The structure and dynamics of networks*. Princeton: Princeton University Press.

Offe, C. (1985). New social movements. *Social Research, 52*(4), 817–868.

Oliver, P., & Marwell, G. (1993). *The critical mass in collective action*. Cambridge: Cambridge University Press.

Parsons, T. (1937). *The structure of social action*. New York: Free Press.

Parsons, T. (1951). *The social system*. New York: Free Press.

Popper, K. (2002). *The poverty of historicism*. London: Routledge.

Radcliffe-Brown, A. (1952). *Structure and function in primitive society*. London: Cohen and West.

Ryle, G. (1949). *The concept of mind*. Harmondsworth: Penguin.

Schutz, A. (1972). *The phenomenology of the social world*. Evanston: Northwestern University Press.

Scott, J. (2000). *Social network analysis: A handbook*. London: Sage.

Simmel, G. (1902). The number of members as determining the form of the group (I & II). *American Journal of Sociology, 8*(1), 1–46 & *8*(2), 158–196.

Smith, D., & White, D. (1992). Structure and dynamics of the global economy. *Social Forces, 70*(4), 857–893.

Snijders, T. A. B., van de Bunt, G. G., & Steglich, C. E. G. (2010). Introduction to stochastic actor-based models for network dynamics. *Social Networks, 32*(1), 44–60.

Snyder, D., & Kick, E. (1979). Structural position in the world system and economic growth. *American Journal of Sociology, 84*(5), 1096–1126.

Valente, T. (1995). *Network models of the diffusion of innovations*. New Jersey: Hampton.

Wasserman, S., & Faust, K. (1994). *Social network analysis*. Cambridge: Cambridge University Press.

Watts, D. (1999). *Small worlds*. Princeton: Princeton University Press.

Weber, M. (1978). *Economy and society*. New York: Bedminster Press.

Wrong, D. (1961). The oversocialized conception of man. *American Sociological Review, 26*(2), 183–193.

10 Varieties of Sociological Field Theory

Daniel N. Kluttz and Neil Fligstein

10.1 Introduction

The explanation of social action in sociological theory has traditionally focused on either macro- or micro-level analyses. Field theory offers an alternative view of social life. It is concerned with how a set of actors orienting their actions to one another do so in a meso-level social order. Field theory implies that there is something at stake in such an order, that there are rules governing the order, that actors have positions and resources, and that actors have an understanding of the order that allows them to interpret the actions of others and frame a response. Fields, once formed, are the arenas where the sociological game of jockeying for position constantly plays out.

Our purpose in this chapter is to review contemporary field theory as articulated in three major theoretical statements in sociology.[1] We begin with a brief description of the core tenets of any contemporary sociological field theory. We then discuss field theory's intellectual roots, paying particular attention to the influences of Max Weber and Kurt Lewin but also phenomenology and symbolic interactionism. We next provide an overview of three of the most developed elaborations of field theory from the last half-century – Pierre Bourdieu's theory of fields (1992), the neo-institutional approach to "organizational fields" (DiMaggio and Powell 1983), and the model of "strategic action fields" recently proposed by Fligstein and McAdam (2012). We follow these overviews with a more detailed examination of how each of these theories addresses two of the most fundamental problems in sociological theory: (1) how social fields emerge, reproduce, and change, and (2) how to conceive of agency and actors.

We spend the bulk of our essay discussing key differences between the three approaches on these issues. Although there are some commonalities across the varieties of field theory, there are also some clear differences of opinion. Drawing its model of social action from Berger and Luckmann (1967) and phenomenology, foundational neo-institutional theory downplays the exercise of power in fields and offers us a view of actors who tend towards habit and conformity in their actions and rely on cues from the field to legitimate their actions. In contrast, Bourdieu's theory emphasizes the role of power in field construction and focuses on how the structuring of the field gives more powerful actors the tools by which to consistently win the

[1] We only review theories that explicitly invoke the field concept. There are a great many perspectives in sociology that appear compatible with field theory, for example, network analysis (White 1992) and the institutional logics perspective (Thornton et al. 2012). But these perspectives eschew field as a central concept and are not discussed in this chapter.

D.N. Kluttz (✉) • N. Fligstein
University of California, Berkeley,
Berkeley, CA, USA
e-mail: dkluttz@berkeley.edu; fligst@berkeley.edu

S. Abrutyn (ed.), *Handbook of Contemporary Sociological Theory*,
Handbooks of Sociology and Social Research, DOI 10.1007/978-3-319-32250-6_10

game. He develops a sophisticated model of action predicated on "habitus," which is a concept to explain how people form cultural frames that inform their ability to interpret the actions of others. While there are clear affinities between the model of actors in Bourdieu and classic neo-institutional theory, Bourdieu's model focuses more on how actors use their existing cognitive frames to engage in strategic yet socially structured action.

On the questions of field emergence and change, Bourdieu and neo-institutional theory focus mostly on the reproducibility of field structure as the outcome of social action. Fligstein and McAdam (2012) theorize emergence and change more explicitly and offer the most fluid and political view of field dynamics. They suggest that even stable fields are constantly undergoing change, as contestation over all aspects of the field is part of the ongoing field project. Fligstein and McAdam advance the idea that fields are embedded in systems of fields that greatly influence the ability of actors to create and reproduce stable worlds. They also provide insight into field emergence and transformation by viewing these as situations in which all aspects of field formation are up for grabs. Finally, they develop the evocative concept of social skill to explain how actors influence, dominate, or cooperate with others to produce and sustain meso-level social order.

We clarify these differences of opinion to suggest two future lines of work. First, it is possible that each of these perspectives captures something plausible about how the world works. What is left unspecified is the scope conditions under which one or the other of these perspectives should be deployed. Second, it may turn out that one of these perspectives in fact offers a better empirical way to make sense of meso-level social orders. Establishing their differences allows scholars to construct tests by which the validity of one or the other of these perspectives can be established. The promise of field theory is its potential to explain interactions in a wide variety of social settings. It offers a set of conceptual tools that can be deployed for many of the most important sociological questions. Progress will be made only by sharpening our understanding of the differences in field theories in order to better understand how they can be profitably used.

10.2 Common Themes in Field Theories

The main idea in field theory is that most of social life occurs in arenas where actors take one another into account in their actions. These interactions occur where something is at stake. But fields also imply a stable order, one that allows for the reproduction of the actors and their social positions over time. This general formulation of a field is sometimes described as a meso-level social order. The term "meso" refers to the fact that actors are taking each other into account in framing actions within some theoretically or empirically defined social arena. This means that the explanation of social action is done in the context of the field. This does not mean that all actors are individuals. Instead, field theory conceives of actors as including individuals, groups, subunits of organizations, organizations, firms, and states. Examples of meso-level social orders made up of both individual and collective actors include groups of individuals who work in an office and cooperate over a task, subunits of organizations that vie for organizational resources, firms that compete with one another to dominate a market, and states that come together to negotiate treaties. The primary unit of analysis is neither a macro-social process that contains some underlying structural logic operating independently of actors (e.g., social class) nor is it a micro-social process that focuses on the idiosyncratic preferences and motivations of individual actors.

Field theorists share a spatial, relational approach to understanding how actors interact with one another. Actors are located in a social space (the field), which is a socially constructed arena in which actors are oriented toward one another over a common practice, institution, issue, or goal. Being oriented toward one another, field actors frame their actions and identities vis-à-vis one another (i.e., relationally). Actors within a field recognize (if not always follow) shared meanings, rules, and norms that guide their interactions. Fields structure actors' interests and influence them to think and act in accordance with the rules and expectations of the field. Nevertheless, field actors have the agentic capacity (again, to varying degrees depending on the version of the theory) to accumulate resources and/or seek advantages vis-à-vis others. Such resources and advantages can include legitimacy, the accumulation of various forms of capital in order to exert power over others, and the building of political coalitions to further collective interests.

Field theorists use the field construct to make sense of how and why social orders can be reproduced. But they have increasingly become interested in how fields emerge and are transformed. Underlying this formulation is the idea that a field is an ongoing game-like arena, where actors have to understand what others are doing in order to frame their action. This has caused field theorists to consider agency and action and to develop sociological views of how cognition works, focusing on issues of culture, framing, identity, habit, and socialization. Finally, while the role of actors varies across formulations of field theories, such theories explicitly reject rational actor models and instead rely on phenomenology and symbolic interactionism to understand what actors do under varying field conditions.

10.3 Classical Roots of Contemporary Sociological Field Theory

We trace the classical roots of contemporary sociological field theory to two primary influences, Max Weber and Kurt Lewin. Then we briefly discuss how phenomenology and symbolic interactionism have provided the foundations of field theories' models of action. We direct the reader to Mey (1972) and Martin (2003) for more detailed accounts of the classical foundations of field theory that draw from many more theoretical lines of inquiry. In particular, Martin (2003) provides a concise review of field theory's roots in the physical sciences (particularly classical electro-magnetism), the contributions of the Gestalt school of psychology apart from Lewin, and the contributions of other intellectual ancestors not discussed here, most notably Ernst Cassirer, Karl Mannheim, and Friedrich Fürstenberg.

Max Weber argued that social relationships require meaningful action between two or more actors whose actions are based on an awareness of and orientation to the other (Weber 1978: 28–30). Weber also took the position that social relationships can scale up to higher levels (e.g., organizations, associations, etc.) and become a social order that encompasses a multitude of actors. A social order can simultaneously be its own complex of meaning and part of a broader complex of meaning. Weber identified a small number of orders present in every society: legal, social, economic, political, and religious. He thought that something different is at stake in each order and the struggles over a particular order could only be interpreted from the perspective of groups vying for advantage in that order (1978). For example, honor or status is at stake in the social order, power in the political order, the saving of souls in the religious order, and economic advantage in the economic order. Weber argued that power in one order could bring about power in another. So, for example, economic success could spill over to social honor or esteem. However, Weber also thought that the relationship between orders was the product of history. For example, in a theocracy, the religious order could dominate the political and economic order. With his emphasis on the symbolic in addition to the material dimension of relations, Weber was of fundamental importance to field theorists' conceptions of fields as socially constructed arenas of action.

As a social psychologist with a background in Gestalt psychology, it was Kurt Lewin who most directly transferred the ideas of field theory from the physical sciences into the social sciences. Lewin applied Gestalt concepts of perception – that stimuli are not perceived as individual parts but by their relation to the whole field of perception – to social psychology and, in particular, human motivation and how social situations influence cognition (Mohr 2005). Lewin (1951: 240) also developed formal models to represent fields, which he defined as the "totality of coexisting facts which are conceived of as mutually interdependent," and the life space, defined as "the person and the psychological environment as it exists for him" (1951: 57).

For Lewin, the individual's phenomenological apprehension of the world could be simultaneously influenced by the field environment and his/her navigation of the life space. The life space is made up of regions of experience, the meaning of each being defined by its relations to other regions. And because one's apprehension of a field also influences the field itself, the effects of one on the other are reciprocal. Individual behavior, then, could be explained only by considering the totality of the interaction between the individual's navigation of the life space and the environment. Although Lewin has been criticized for, among other things, his ultimately unworkable topological formalizations (see Martin 2003: 18–19), his explicit use of the field metaphor and his emphasis on the co-constitution of fields and actors served as an important foundation on which contemporary sociological field theories were built.

Field theorists have used a variety of sources to construct their model of the actor. For example, Bourdieu's notion of habitus has many sources – some in philosophy like Husserl, Heidegger, and Merleau-Ponty as well as sociologists who were philosophically inclined and influenced by phenomenology, like Mauss and Elias.[2] Mauss (1973[1934]) defined habitus as those aspects of culture that are anchored in the body or daily practices of individuals, groups, societies, and nations. It includes the totality of learned habits, bodily skills, styles, tastes, and other forms of non-discursive knowledge that might be said to "go without saying" for a specific group. Elias used the habitus concept to make sense of the changes in personality he detailed in *The Civilizing Process* (1939).

Neo-institutionalists rely heavily on Berger and Luckmann's *The Social Construction of Reality* (1967) for their model of actors (Powell and DiMaggio 1991). Berger and Luckmann drew their inspiration from Alfred Schutz, a sociologist who was trained in phenomenology. Berger and Luckmann argued that the world is a social construction. It requires effort for this to emerge, effort that implied institutionalization and legitimation. Like the habitus for Bourdieu, an existing social world gets internalized via socialization.

Compared to the neo-institutional elaboration of organizational fields, Fligstein and McAdam (2012) draw more heavily on Mead's (1934) symbolic interactionism. Symbolic interactionism is a perspective grounded in American pragmatist philosophy (Menand 2001). It bears many resemblances to phenomenology, viewing the social world as a construction and socialization as the main way in which that world is inculcated in individuals. But Mead's symbolic interactionism also proposes that one of the main goals of social action is for actors to help shape and create their worlds. At the core of interaction is the idea that we have identities that we share with others. These identities provide the basis for our cooperation with others. Bourdieu also cites symbolic interaction as a source for his view of social action. Because he was interested in how power was actually experienced in interaction, he saw symbolic interaction as a way to frame how the less powerful accepted their fate in interaction with the more powerful.

10.4 Contemporary Elaborations of Sociological Field Theory

10.4.1 Bourdieu's Field Theory

Pierre Bourdieu is the contemporary sociologist most often associated with field theory. Bourdieu deployed the idea of field as part of a more com-

[2] Crossley (2004) provides a lengthy discussion of Merleau-Ponty's deep influences on Bourdieu's theoretical framework. Interestingly, it was also through Merleau-Ponty's work that Bourdieu first encountered Weber (Bourdieu et al. 2011: 112).

plex theoretical framework that included two other major concepts, capital and habitus (see generally Bourdieu 1977, 1986; Bourdieu and Wacquant 1992). For Bourdieu, social life takes place in fields. Fields are arenas of struggle, and Bourdieu frequently uses the game metaphor to describe how action takes place in fields. In fields, players occupy positions relative to one another but have a shared sense of the socially constructed, centralized framework of meaning, or what is at stake in the field. Bourdieu's fields are relatively autonomous, meaning each tends to have its own logic (or "rules of the game") and history. Players compete with one another for resources, status, and, most fundamentally, over the very definition of the "rules of the game" that govern field relations. Relations within Bourdieu's fields are mostly hierarchical, with dominant individuals or groups imposing their power over dominated groups as a result of their ability to control the field, what is at stake, and what counts as rules and resources.

The main source of power for dominant actors is the capital that they bring to the field. Actors within a field are endowed with physical (or economic), social, human, and cultural capital (Bourdieu 1986, 1989: 17).[3] One's position in a field is defined by the volume and form of capital one possesses. Those with similar volumes and forms of capital tend to cluster in similar positions in a field. Actors within a field wield capital in order to improve or maintain their field positions. A field is thus the site where actors carry out and reproduce power relations over others based on their capital endowments.

Habitus is the "strategy-generating principle" that enables actors to apprehend, navigate, and act in the social world (Bourdieu 1977: 78; see also Bourdieu 1990: 53).[4] It is subjective in that it represents the bundle of cognitive and evaluative capacities that make up one's perceptions, judgments, tastes, and strategies for actions. But habitus is not simply produced or employed subjectively. It is a highly structured system of dispositions. Strategies and actions generated by habitus are not products of motivations for future goals so much as products of past experience (Bourdieu 1977: 72). Habitus is internalized via (mostly early) socialization. But habitus is neither wholly static nor deterministic. It can change as one traverses the life course and interacts within different fields. Because an actor's habitus-generated perceptions and strategies lead to practices, they have real impacts on capital allocations and field structure. The habitus of actors is both constituted by and constitutive of the social structure of the field.

Bourdieu uses these concepts of field, capital, and habitus to understand why, in general, fields' structures of dominance tend to be reproduced. Given a field that contains a set of rules and players with fixed capital, the "game" will generally be rigged. Actors will perceive what others are doing and respond to their actions by deploying their capital in such a way as to preserve their current position as much as possible. In this way, both dominant and dominated actors play the game to the best of their abilities, but in doing so tend to reproduce their field positions. The reflexive field-capital-habitus relation gives Bourdieu powerful theoretical leverage to include both agency and structure in his explanation of social order. Bourdieu himself suggests that it gives him the ability to reject what he sees as false antimonies between objectivism and subjectivism (Bourdieu and Wacquant 1992).

10.4.2 Neo-institutional Theory of Fields

Scholars across disciplines, most notably sociology, political science, and economics, have developed substantial lines of inquiry, many sharing affinities with field-based approaches, under the broad umbrella of "new institutionalism" (for

[3] All of these forms of capital, when perceived or recognized by others as legitimate, confer symbolic capital (akin to prestige or honor) and thus the ability to exercise symbolic power over others (Bourdieu 1986, 1989).

[4] For an extended discussion of Bourdieu's habitus, see Lizardo (2004).

reviews, see Hall and Taylor 1996; Fligstein 2008). In order to avoid confusion, and in the interest of space, when we discuss "neo-institutional" theories of fields, we limit our discussions to neo-institutional theory in organizational sociology. Even within sociological neo-institutional organizational scholarship, there is considerable variation in approaches, emphases, and analytical techniques (Powell and DiMaggio 1991; Scott 2013). We focus here on classic neo-institutional formulations of organizational fields (DiMaggio and Powell 1983), first contextualizing when and why neo-institutional scholars developed the concept then explaining the essential characteristics of organizational fields.

During the late 1970s and early 1980s, neo-institutional sociologists began explicitly incorporating field-based principles to theorize the connection between organizations and their environments. Departing from organizational ecologists (e.g., Hannan and Freeman 1977a, b), whose fundamental motivating question was to examine why organizations within populations differ from one another, neo-institutional scholars asked why organizations within fields tend to exhibit similar forms, practices, or cultures. Although others employed similar constructs such as "institutional environment" (Meyer and Rowan 1977) and "societal sector" (Scott and Meyer 1983), "organizational field" (DiMaggio and Powell 1983) is the most widely accepted term used to denote an environment made up of organizations that interact around a given issue and affect one another via institutional processes.

DiMaggio and Powell (1983: 148) define an organizational field as "those organizations that, in the aggregate, constitute a recognized area of institutional life: key suppliers, resource and product consumers, regulatory agencies, and other organizations that produce similar services or products." Theirs is a broad definition of fields, encompassing "the totality of relevant actors" in an "institutionally defined" arena of organizations (DiMaggio and Powell 1983: 148). Their account of organizational fields draws primarily on phenomenology (Berger and Luckmann 1967), the structuration theory of Anthony Giddens (1979), and network-based ideas of connectedness (Laumann et al. 1978) and structural equivalence (White et al. 1976).

For DiMaggio and Powell (1983), the answer to the question of why organizations within fields tend to look the same is that organizations, once they are part of an organizational field, are usually driven more by institutional concerns (e.g., legitimacy) than by other factors, such as competition. Institutions, defined as "social patterns that, when chronically reproduced, owe their survival to relatively self-activating social processes (Jepperson 1991: 145)," confer legitimacy. Over the course of institutionalization, such self-sustaining patterns become more legitimate and stable, eliciting shared meanings and providing cultural models for organizing and acting (Zucker 1977; Suchman 1995; Berger and Luckmann 1967).

As a field undergoes structuration (see Giddens 1979), organizations within the field tend to become isomorphic, meaning that they become more similar. They do this because the imperative of an institutionalized field is to appear legitimate (Suchman 1995). For neoinstitutional scholars, legitimacy is "a generalized perception or assumption that the actions of an entity are desirable, proper or appropriate within some socially constructed system of norms, values, beliefs, and definitions" (Suchman 1995: 574). Mechanisms of isomorphism include coercive force from authorities or resource dependencies, normative sanctioning from experts or professional associations, and mimetic pressure to copy what others are doing, particularly during times of uncertainty (DiMaggio and Powell 1983; Scott 2013). Regardless of the mechanism, as something becomes increasingly institutionalized, it takes on an increasingly rule-like or taken-for-granted status. Thus, it becomes increasingly legitimate in the eyes of the field actors, which serves to reinforce and accelerate its being followed and reproduced by organizations in the field.

10.4.3 Strategic Action Fields

The most recent elaboration of field theory is the theory of strategic action fields proposed by Fligstein and McAdam (2012). Fligstein and

McAdam work to synthesize neo-institutionalist insights about fields as being driven by actors who live in murky worlds and seek legitimacy with Bourdieu's ideas about contestation within fields that reflect mainly the power of dominant actors. Fligstein and McAdam (2012: 9) thus define a "strategic action field" (hereinafter SAF) as "a constructed meso-level social order in which actors (who can be individual or collective) are attuned to and interact with one another on the basis of shared (which is not to say consensual) understandings about the purposes of the field, relationships to others in the field (including who has power and why), and the rules governing legitimate action in the field." As with the prior two versions of field theory discussed above, the theory of SAFs places utmost importance on understanding how actors, who occupy positions within a socially constructed order, relate to one another within that space.

SAFs are socially constructed in that (1) membership is based more on subjective than any objective criteria, (2) boundaries of the field can shift based on the definition of the situation and the issue at stake, and (3) fields turn on shared understandings fashioned over time by members of the field (Fligstein and McAdam 2012: 12–13). These shared understandings are of four kinds. First, actors share a sense of what is at stake in the field (a shared sense of what actors are vying for or the central issue around which the field revolves). Second, actors have a shared sense of the positions of others in the SAF (a recognition of which actors in the field have more or less power and who occupies which roles). Third, they have a shared understanding of the "rules" that guide what is considered legitimate action in the field. Finally, actors in certain positions within the field share interpretative frames (these frames vary within the field but are shared by actors in similar locations).

Importantly, Fligstein and McAdam propose that the degree of consensus and contention internal to a field is constantly changing. Bracketing a description of how SAFs themselves emerge and change for now (we discuss this in Sect. 10.6.3), the degree of consensus in a SAF depends on the degree to which a field is settled. Contrary to a neo-institutional account of highly institutionalized organizational fields, SAFs are rarely organized around a taken-for-granted "reality." Although there is more consensual perception of opportunities and constraints in highly settled SAFs, actors constantly jockey for position even in settled fields. Contention is highest when SAFs are unsettled, most often when a field is emerging or when a field undergoes crisis.

Similar to Bourdieu's fields, SAF membership is structured along incumbent/challenger dynamics, with actors possessing varying resource endowments and vying for advantage. Incumbents claim a disproportionate share of the material and symbolic resources in the field, and their interests and views tend to be disproportionately reflected in the rules and organization of the field. Challengers usually conform to the prevailing order of the field by taking what the system gives them, but they can also usually articulate an alternative vision of the field. Importantly, although SAFs have incumbents and challengers who always compete, SAFs are not necessarily marked by extreme hierarchy and conflict. SAFs can also have coalitions and cooperation. Fligstein and McAdam suggest that the higher the degree of inequality in the distribution of initial resources at field formation, the more likely the field will be organized hierarchically, with incumbents exerting their dominance over challengers.

Fligstein and McAdam introduce an important new actor to their fields – "internal governance units." These actors, often present within SAFs, generally serve to maintain order within the field. In practice, they usually serve to reinforce the position of the incumbents in the field, whether it be to stabilize a field settlement, respond to crises in order to produce stability, or act as a liaison to other fields (Fligstein and McAdam 2012: 94–96). Examples of internal governance units include certification boards set up by professional organizations in a newly formed SAF, the World Bank, which often disproportionately serves the interests of more developed economies, and a trade association that lobbies on an industry's behalf.

Fligstein and McAdam (2012: 34–56) also propose a novel micro-foundation of action based on collective meaning-making and belongingness. This foundation is what they term the "existential function of the social" – the profoundly human need to create meaningful social worlds and feelings of belongingness. In order to build political coalitions, forge identities, and fashion interests in service of that need, actors in SAFs use "social skill" (Fligstein 2001) to appeal to shared meanings and empathetically relate to others so as to induce cooperation and engage in collective action.

Another novel contribution of the theory of SAFs is its deep conceptualization of inter-field relations. Instead of attempting to explain only the internal dynamics of fields, Fligstein and McAdam (2012: 59) conceive of fields as embedded in complex, multi-dimensional webs of dependence with other fields. Such linkages most often result from resource dependencies or from formal legal or bureaucratic authority. These ties are also multi-dimensional. First, like a Russian doll, fields can be nested hierarchically within broader fields, meaning that the nested field is highly dependent on the broader field. Second, fields can also be linked via interdependencies, meaning that the fields are roughly equally dependent. Third, fields can be tied to any number of other fields. Of course, a field need not be connected to another field at all. The extent of dependency and quantity of ties can have implications for field emergence, stability, and change, which we discuss later in the chapter.

10.5 Agency and Actors

10.5.1 Bourdieu's Field Theory

Bourdieu's theoretical project has a complicated relationship with agency and actors. Although we are sympathetic to the difficulty of trying to account for structure and agency within social fields, we contend that Bourdieu's theory of fields is more deterministic than he was willing to admit. Ours is not an oversimplified, oft-repeated charge of determinism and, as we discuss below, Bourdieu's account of agency, via the habitus, is richer than classic statements in neo-institutional theory. (If we were to rank the three theories we discuss based on the agency they accord to field actors, we would place Bourdieu's actors somewhere between neo-institutional field actors on the low end and actors in SAFs on the high end.)

In Bourdieu's words, agents are "bearers of capitals and, depending on their trajectory and on the position they occupy on the field … they have a propensity to orient themselves actively either toward the preservation of the distribution of capital or toward the subversion of this distribution" (Bourdieu and Wacquant 1992: 108–109). Indeed, his field actors do have their own goals and do act to further their own interests vis-à-vis others in the field. Thus, actors in his fields do act strategically and engage in meaningful action.

Nevertheless, actors in Bourdieu's theory are not particularly reflective nor are they very capable of going against the constraining structural forces of the field. The "rules of the game" and what is at stake in the field are a product of social structure and are tacitly agreed upon by members of the field (what Bourdieu calls the *illusio*). Field actors' interests are defined by their position in the field (i.e., their capital endowment) and the historical trajectory that led them to the field (Bourdieu and Wacquant 1992: 117). Most field actors "know their place," and if they engage in competition with others, they are more likely to compete with those who are closest to them in social space than try to change the underlying social order (Bourdieu 1984).

Moreover, the habitus, which Bourdieu invokes to account for subjectivity and agency, is itself an *embodied, structured* set of dispositions that operates somewhere below the level of consciousness. It is socially structured as a function of one's field position, and it is passed on to subsequent generations through mostly nonconscious relations and processes of cultural transmission. Habitus tends to be durable and, if it does change, tends to align (or correspond) with one's field position and the field's particular logic.

True, Bourdieu's actors do have the ability to transpose their habitus to other fields, but even here, the habitus tends to correspond to that of homologous positions in other fields. Indeed, Bourdieu's individuals tend to become embedded within habitus classes, "the system of dispositions (partially) common to all products of the same structures" (Bourdieu 1977: 85). Thus, habitus, and as a consequence actors themselves, will usually operate to reproduce the very structures from which it arises (Bourdieu 1977: 78; Bourdieu and Wacquant 1992: 121–22).[5]

10.5.2 Neo-institutional Field Theory

Classic neo-institutional accounts of organizational fields provide a rich account of institutional persistence and constraint on actors, but they under-theorize how actors who are subject to institutional effects could nevertheless enact agency to affect those institutions. Neo-institutional scholars identified this problem relatively early on (see DiMaggio 1988; DiMaggio and Powell 1991). Others have termed it the 'paradox of embedded agency' inherent in neo-institutional theory. That is, if action in a field is constrained by the prescriptive, taken-for-granted scripts and rules of the institution in which actors are embedded, then how can actors conceive of, contest, and enact endogenous change to a field (see Battilana 2006)?

[5]This point should not be overstated. For Bourdieu, although habitus tends to align with the logic and expectations of the field, it is not necessarily a perfect alignment. The extent to which it does align is a matter of degree. Bourdieu's concept of "hysteresis," for example, accounts for situations in which one's habitus becomes mismatched or lags behind the logic of a field (Bourdieu 2000:160–161). This is exemplified in the character of Don Quixote, whose antiquated knightly disposition no longer fits in his contemporary world. However, other than a vague nod to crisis as a possible necessary condition (see our discussion of crisis below), Bourdieu does not systematically theorize the causes or consequences of such hysteresis. Why and when do some experience the disjuncture when others align? Why might some experience the disjuncture when, at other moments of field succession, they can align? Under what conditions does hysteresis lead to active efforts to hold on to the misaligned habitus? When might it lead to efforts to change the logic of a field rather than adapt the habitus to fit the different logic? For a similar critique, see Burawoy and Von Holdt (2012:38–39).

Responding to this criticism, a second wave of neo-institutionalists began to develop a literature on actors with the agency to initiate institutional change. The earliest and most developed idea of actors and agency within fields is the concept of institutional entrepreneurship (DiMaggio 1988, 1991). In general, an institutional entrepreneur is some actor (whether individual or collective) who initiates and participates in change to an institution.

Although DiMaggio (1988) is frequently cited as inspiration for the idea of institutional entrepreneurs, its main argument is that the neo-institutional theory of Meyer and Rowan (1977) and DiMaggio and Powell (1983) lacks an adequate theory of agency, power, and conflict. DiMaggio (1988) posits the idea of an institutional entrepreneur because he is trying to make sense of how a field comes into existence or experiences dramatic transformation. He suggests institutional entrepreneurship occurs when someone (or some group) comes along and figures out how to do something new and is able to convince others to go along with them. For DiMaggio (1988), institutional entrepreneurs are especially important early on in the institutionalization process, when organizational fields are being constructed. Then, as institutionalization takes hold, field participants usually settle down to playing their part as actors who operate mostly by habit or by watching and imitating others.

Scholarly interest in institutional entrepreneurship has grown considerably since DiMaggio's (1988) formulation, particularly among organizational sociologists and management scholars. Neoinstitutionalists have conducted numerous empirical studies across domains and made important theoretical advances on the concept (for recent reviews, see Garud et al.'s (2007) introduction to a journal issue on institutional entrepreneurship; Hardy and Maguire 2008; Battilana et al. 2009). However, we take the position that institutional entrepreneurship has become a concept so all-encompassing with regard to agency and change that it is not the most useful concept to employ to theorize agency within and across fields. As Suddaby (2010: 15) noted of the current state of the literature: "Any change, however slight, is now 'institutional' and any change agent is an 'institutional entrepreneur.'"

Indeed, as contemporary neoinstitutional scholars have pointed out (e.g., Powell and Colyvas 2008: 277; Lawrence et al. 2011: 52), the institutional entrepreneurship literature now tends to replace the actors of foundational neo-institutional theory – over-socialized and with relatively little reflexivity and agency – with actors who seem to have prescient views about new possible worlds, the motivation to contest institutional arrangements, and the power to enact change. In addition, institutional entrepreneurship's focus on divergent institutional change has resulted in a tendency to conflate agency with wholesale field-level change. Consequently, there is a selection bias in the institutional entrepreneurship literature of analyzing only situations in which contestation leads to change (Denrell and Kovács 2008). This produces a strange conception of institutional agency: actors are thought of as agentic only when they "successfully" form new fields or change existing ones, and only a few such actors really matter for field-level change. This idea flies in the face of common-sense experience, where we see people acting strategically all of the time.

Finally, institutional entrepreneurship's overly heroic view of actors tends to shift focus away from fields and avoid questions such as what alternative paths fields might take, why entrepreneurs choose the strategies of field contestation that they do, and what field-building projects are likely to win and lose. In essence, we submit that despite its substantial theoretical development over the last three decades, the concept of institutional entrepreneur lacks an adequate conceptualization of *fields* that would explain structural conditions enabling agency within and across different types of fields and during different stages of a field's existence.

10.5.3 Strategic Action Fields

Fligstein and McAdam's addition of "strategic action" to the term "fields" is an important theoretical development, as it incorporates Fligstein's (2001) concept of "social skill" into their theory of action and therefore provides a new, more systematic way to think about agency, actors, and field relations. Strategic action is "the attempt by social actors to create and maintain stable social worlds by securing the cooperation of others" (Fligstein and McAdam 2012: 17). The primary micro-level mechanism through which fields are constructed, transformed, and even maintained is "social skill," which is the cognitive capacity for reading people and environments, framing lines of action, and mobilizing people in the service of broader conceptions of the world and of themselves (Fligstein and McAdam 2012: 17). Some are endowed with greater social skill than others and are thus more likely than others, all else being equal (which of course, in reality, is hardly the case), to realize their interests and exert control vis-à-vis others in a field.[6]

This may beg the question of why social skill is so important as a driver of field relations. In other words, if social skill is the *mechanism* for stepping into the shoes of the other and mobilizing collective action, what is the *motivation* for doing so? Like Bourdieu, Fligstein and McAdam recognize that actors pursue their interests in the name of power. Indeed, SAFs are organized along incumbent/challenger dimensions and are sites of struggles for power and influence. However, their answer is not simply that actors draw on social skill in the pursuit of material self-interest.[7]

Fligstein and McAdam provide a second, deeper motivation that is deeply rooted in our evolutionary psychology – the basic human need to fashion a meaningful world for oneself and to engage in collective action. They call this the

[6] It remains an empirical question as to the distribution of social skill in given fields or across the population. Fligstein and McAdam (2012: 17) only offer an unsupported speculation that social skill could be distributed normally across the population.

[7] Here, they join Bourdieu in his critique of Marxist materialist conceptions of interaction. Like Bourdieu, they argue that interests themselves only have meaning because they are socially constructed and thus have symbolic meaning to field participants.

"existential function of the social." They argue that even the exercise of power and conflict with others are often manifestations of the more fundamental pursuit of collective meaning-making, identity, and belongingness. Innumerable examples of this abound. To list a few of the more extreme ones, the various religious crusades and wars waged throughout history were fundamentally about identity ("I am a Christian; I am a holy warrior.") and meaning-making and belongingness ("This is a battle between good (us) vs. evil (them)). However repulsive Nazism is from a moral standpoint to most in society, there is no question that Hitler was a supremely skilled social actor who could frame unambiguous "truths" in ways that valorized the lives of believers and serviced his interest in attaining power. Of course, the focus on intersubjectivity, collaborative meaning-making, identity, and collective mobilization does not mean that power relations, conflict, preferences, and the pursuit of those preferences (whether or not to the exclusion of others pursuing theirs) are not characteristic of SAFs. The point is that social skill is deployed for both kinds of pursuits.

The dual motivations in SAFs of the pursuit of material interests and the existential function of the social represent a key point of departure from neo-institutional and Bourdieu's explanations of what drives field relations. For neo-institutionalists, the basic driver of action within institutionalized organizational fields is the concern for legitimacy (Suchman 1995). Whether through coercive force, normative influence, or mimetic pressure to follow others in times of uncertainty, organizational field actors tend to act similarly in order to appear legitimate (DiMaggio and Powell 1983). Fligstein and McAdam agree with neo-institutional theorists that field actors tend to cohere in their actions, but instead of arguing that this is due to a mostly unreflective concern for legitimacy, they posit this is due to the existential function of the social. By combining symbolic interactionist approaches to empathetic understanding and identity (Mead 1934; Goffman 1974) with social movement theory's insights into framing processes as a path to collective action (e.g., Snow et al. 1986; Snow and Benford 1988), Fligstein and McAdam provide an answer to the 'paradox of embedded agency' that has plagued neo-institutional accounts while managing to avoid the overly heroic correctives proposed by theories of institutional entrepreneurship.

Importantly, however, Fligstein and McAdam (2012: 109–110) do not reject outright the idea of institutional entrepreneurs. Instead, they situate the role of institutional entrepreneur within the broader SAF environment and theorize that in the moment of field emergence or transformation when things are more or less up for grabs, such actors may emerge to help create a field. Institutional entrepreneur is thus a role that highly skilled social actors can play in unorganized social space to help produce a field. They do so by convincing others to accept their own cultural conception (via an appeal that resonates with others' identities or meaning), fashion political coalitions of disparate groups, and establish new institutions around which a field is ordered. If a field is in a more settled state, incumbents, who set the rules of the game and exert their power to reproduce the social order, are more likely to thwart attempts by an institutional entrepreneur to usurp the established field order. That said, actors even in settled SAFs are able to construct alternative understandings of the dominant field order and can act strategically to identify with others and engage in collective action.

The theory of SAFs also differs from Bourdieu's in its conception of actors and agency. For Bourdieu, fields are sites of conflict, striving, and the pursuit of one's interests over another's. True, Bourdieu recognizes that what one's interests are and how they are pursued are outcomes of social dynamics; they correspond to the one's position in the field, one's own habitus, and one's unique allocation of forms of capital. But the defining features of internal field relations for Bourdieu are no doubt conflict and domination. The theory of SAFs shares Bourdieu's conception of fields as sites of struggle between incumbents and challengers over resources and the ability to define the "rules of the game," but it goes further to make room for the crucial microfoundations of meaning, identity, cooperation, and collective action that are pursued by socially skilled actors. Actors can both engage in struggle and fashion cooperative coalitions. Fligstein and McAdam (2012) thus present a more agentic actor than the other two theories of fields discussed here.

Finally, the theory of SAFs differs from both neo-institutional and Bourdieusian accounts of field actors in that it explicitly accounts for individuals *and* collectivities as field actors and expressly theorizes each of their roles within their fields. Neo-institutional field theory, being born out of organizational theory, tends to focus on organizations as the actors within a field space. As such, neo-institutional accounts of organizational fields care very little about individuals' positions in fields and must abstract up to the organizational level when explaining an "actor's" subjective orientations, strategies for obtaining legitimacy, struggles for resources, etc. Although we take no issue with this abstraction (we very much view organizations as actors in social space), we recognize that it is less intuitive to think only of organizations as social actors in a field. Bourdieu's theory of fields, on the other hand, deals primarily with individuals as field actors and locates dispositions and practices primarily in individuals' trajectories through social space.[8] The consequences for the theory of SAF's flexibility in scaling up or down is non-trivial, as it forces Fligstein and McAdam (2012) to develop a more general, yet still workable, theory of relations between field actors, no matter whether they are individuals or organizations.

10.6 Field Emergence, Stability, and Change

We turn now to a discussion of how each theory deals with field-level emergence, stability, and change. In short, Fligstein and McAdam's theory of SAFs depicts fields as more changeable than neo-institutional field theory or Bourdieu's theory of fields. Moreover, we argue that, compared to the other accounts, the theory of SAFs provides the most comprehensive, systematic conceptualization of field emergence, stability, and change. As with the prior section, we develop these arguments by first analyzing how Bourdieu and neo-institutional theorists deal with the issue then juxtaposing those accounts against the theory of SAFs.

10.6.1 Bourdieu's Field Theory

Bourdieu's theory of fields is primarily one of social stability and reproduction. This is intentional, as it is Bourdieu's goal to understand and solve the agent-structure problem by positing how both actors (whether consciously or unconsciously) and structures correspond to one another and are complicit in the reproduction of social order. For Bourdieu, although fields are the sites of constant struggle and competition between the dominant and dominated, the social order ultimately tends to be reproduced. True, it is not uncommon for groups to succeed their prior equivalent group in terms of their place in the social order; this is what Bourdieu calls the "order of successions." (Bourdieu 1984: 163). The key here, however, is that relations between groups in a field (i.e., the social distance between them) remain mostly unchanged.

Bourdieu touches upon the conditions for how field logics could change when he mentions crisis as a necessary, but not sufficient, condition for the questioning of *doxa*. *Doxa* is the undiscussed, taken-for-granted aspect of the social world. Within it are those systems of classification, traditions, and rules for interaction that are so legitimate and ingrained that they are taken for granted as self-evident 'truths' about the world (Bourdieu 1977: 169).[9] Crisis can lead to the arbitrariness of the *doxa* being revealed to field actors' conscious-

[8] We acknowledge that Bourdieu did not *solely* study fields in which individuals were the primary participants. For example, he identifies firms as the key players in the economic field and speaks of the importance of their interactions with the state (Bourdieu 2005). He also links elite universities, corporations, and the state to the field of power (Bourdieu 1996a).

[9] We note the affinities between Bourdieu's doxa and a highly objectivated and internalized social reality, as defined by Berger and Luckmann (1967), or a highly institutionalized social institution (Meyer and Rowan 1977; Jepperson 1991).

ness and thereby finding its way into the universe of discourse, where orthodox and heterodox opinions can be expressed and contested. However, Bourdieu does not systematically theorize what brings about such moments of crisis, nor does he explicitly theorize the additional condition(s) besides crisis that result in a critical discourse.

Even when the *doxa* is brought into the universe of discourse, such questioning does not necessarily lead to challengers displacing the dominant class at the top of the field hierarchy. Indeed, challengers with heterodox views of the world rarely displace the dominant group, who work to preserve the "official" ways of thinking and speaking about the world and who aim to censor heterodox views. Finally, and most importantly, on the rare occasions that challengers *do* manage to displace incumbents as the dominant actors in a field (e.g., Bourdieu 1996b), they tend to do so by using, and therefore reproducing, the underlying "rules of the game" on which the field is based. For example, in Bourdieu's studies of the fields of cultural production (e.g., art, literature, theatre), one of the most fundamental principles of these fields, especially for the dominant, is an outward indifference to or disavowal of the profit motive. Not coincidentally, the best strategy for challenger groups to unseat the dominant cultural producers within the field is to disavow the commercial and promote their own activities and products as "purer" art than that of the dominant group. In doing so, however, the fundamental logic of the field only gets reinforced. "Thus," Bourdieu writes, "[challengers'] revolutions are only ever partial ones, which displace the censorships and transgress the conventions but do so in the name of the same underlying principles" (Bourdieu 1993: 83–84).

10.6.2 Neo-institutional Field Theory

Although recent efforts by institutional scholars have improved the situation, the neo-institutional theory of organizational fields continues to lack a well-developed and empirically tested theory of field emergence and change. The majority of neo-institutional research on organizational fields since DiMaggio and Powell's (1983) seminal article has pertained to how isomorphism among organizations occurs *after* an organizational field exists and, relatedly, how fields are stable and reproducible. In our view, then, the neo-institutional formulation of field theory has accounted for field stability and field reproduction quite well. However, from the outset, it lacked a systematic theory of field emergence and *divergent* field-level transformation.[10] A new generation of neo-institutional scholars has partly corrected for these limitations by proposing that institutional change can occur by way of institutional entrepreneurship, but, as we have argued, this is less a systematic theory of field change and more a thinly veiled "heroic man" theory of change that does not link entrepreneur-led change to broader field conditions.

The under-development of theories of field emergence and divergent change can be traced back to DiMaggio and Powell's (1983) all-too-brief discussion of the formation of an organizational field (or in their words, how it is that a set of organizations come to be "institutionally defined"). Using Giddens's (1979) terminology, they propose that a set of organizations comes to be a field through a process of "structuration:" (1) interaction among organizations involved in some area of social life increases, (2) hierarchies and coalitions develop, (3) the amount of information with which field members must contend increases, and (4) awareness among field members that they are involved in a common enterprise develops. However, the remaining focus of their article centers around institutional isomorphism in an already-existing organizational field and, as a corollary, how actors follow rules or scripts, either consciously by imitation or coercion or unconsciously by tacit agreement (Jepperson 1991).

Of course, we do not mean to say that neo-institutional literature has failed to elaborate any other concepts of field emergence and change after DiMaggio's (1988, 1991) seminal

[10] Neo-institutional scholars have provided a wealth of theoretical and empirical insights into convergent change (i.e., isomorphism) once a field exists.

works on institutional entrepreneurship. Indeed, since that time, several subfields within the neo-institutionalist literature have developed lines of inquiry that account for the possibility of institutional contestation and change. Examples include the continued development of the aforementioned institutional entrepreneurship literature as well as the institutional work (Lawrence et al. 2009) and institutional logics (Thornton et al. 2012) perspectives. There has also been a concurrent increase in empirical studies of institutional change (for reviews, see Clemens and Cook 1999; Schneiberg and Clemens 2006: 217–220). However, we maintain that a field theory of field emergence and divergent field change, cast specifically within the classic neo-institutionalist framework of organizational fields, is underdeveloped compared to its theories of field stability and isomorphic field change.

One particularly promising avenue for correcting this weakness, however, has been the integration of social movement theory with neo-institutional theories of organizations. A few sociologists have bridged social movements and organizational analysis for decades (Zald and Ash 1966; see Zald and McCarthy 1987). Moreover, some of the classic works in the social movement literature took field-like approaches even if they did not cite field theories at the time. For example, McCarthy and Zald (1973) developed a multi-leveled approach to social movement organizations and theorized meso-level "social movement industries" (McCarthy and Zald 1973), which are like fields of social movement organizations oriented to the same general social issue. Additionally, McAdam (1999) took a field-like analytic strategy by situating the American civil rights movement within the broader political and economic environments in which it was embedded and the institutions that fostered black protest.

Since the early 2000s, however, we have witnessed an increase in such scholarship (Davis et al. 2005). Because of that, what we may still label neo-institutional studies have increasingly incorporated ideas from social movement theory and have more directly linked *institutional* emergence to *field* emergence (Rao et al. 2000; Lounsbury et al. 2003; Morrill 2006). An exemplar of this line of scholarship is Morrill's (2006) analysis of the "interstitial emergence" of the court-based alternative dispute resolution field.[11] The key to the institutionalization of alternative dispute resolution was the innovation of practices, mobilization of resources, and championing of ideas by networks of actors who were located in overlapping fields. Their ideas and practices gained legitimacy because they resonated with different players across overlapping fields. As we discuss below, the importance of field linkages and borders to the emergence of new fields is an insight developed further in the theory of SAFs.

10.6.3 Strategic Action Fields

Of the three contemporary field theories discussed here, the theory of SAFs provides the clearest yet most nuanced conceptualization of field emergence, stability, and change (see Fligstein and McAdam 2012: 84–113; Fligstein 2013). Not only does it depict SAFs as sites of constant internal change due to conflict and jockeying for position (similar to Bourdieu's fields), it also sees entire field structures, especially at certain points in their evolution, as being more subject to change than the other two theories. We discuss each of these issues in this section.

SAFs emerge through a process akin to a social movement. An emerging field is a socially constructed arena in which two or more actors orient their actions toward one another but have not yet constructed a stable order with routinized patterns of relations and commonly shared rules for interaction. Similar to Morrill's (2006) interstitial emergence thesis, SAFs begin to form typically after some kind of exogenous change, more often than not in nearby proximate fields. This happens through "emergent mobilization," a social movement-like process in which actors begin fashioning new lines of interaction and shared understandings after (1) collectively

[11] Morrill borrows the term "interstitial emergence" from Mann (1986).

attributing a threat or opportunity, (2) appropriating organizational resources needed to mobilize and sustain resources, and (3) collectively engaging in innovative action that leads to sustained interaction in previously unorganized social space (McAdam 1999; McAdam et al. 2001).

As it is at every stage in the life of a SAF, social skill is vitally important here, as actors fashion the shared understandings that we discussed in our overview of the theory of SAFs. The state can also facilitate field emergence through processes such as licensing, passing/repealing laws, and the awarding of government contracts. Internal governance units, also discussed earlier, can further encourage stability. Actors organize the structure of their emerging field along a continuum of cooperation and coalition on one end and hierarchy and differences in power on the other. Whether an emerging field will become a stable, reproducible field depends, in part, on how it gets organized; as one moves toward either extreme of this continuum of field organization, the likelihood of stability increases because both extremes imply clear role structures for the actors.

A field becomes settled when its actors have a general consensus regarding field rules and cultural norms. Like highly institutionalized organizational fields, highly settled SAFs typically get reproduced. Because incumbents and challengers continue to engage in conflict even in settled SAFs, however, they share more similarities to Bourdieu's fields. Incumbents in such a settled field will have an interest in maintaining field stability. They will also have the resources to exercise power over challengers and will enjoy the benefit of the rules of the field, which they likely constructed, being slanted in their favor. Perhaps even more importantly, because actors in settled fields are more likely than those in unsettled fields to share common understandings and have similar conceptions of possible alternatives, even challengers in these fields usually will not mount serious challenges to the social order absent an exogenous shock to the field.

However, not all SAFs are highly settled. In the theory of SAFs, settlement is a matter of degree. As the degree of settlement decreases, SAFs become increasingly subject to change. SAFs are subject to two distinct kinds of field-level change: (1) continuous piecemeal change, the more common situation in which change is gradual and due to internal struggles and jockeying for position, and (2) revolutionary change, in which a new field emerges in unorganized social space and/or displaces another field. Both kinds of change occur, but under different conditions.

Change is constantly occurring within SAFs because actors constantly jockey for position within fields, whether through cooperation with allies or conflict with adversaries. Actors can occasionally shift strategies, forge subtle new alliances, and make small gains or losses in their position relative to others. However, from a field-wide perspective, these are usually piecemeal changes because incumbent field actors, who have access to relatively more resources and control the "rules of the game" in a SAF, can usually reinforce their positions and therefore reproduce the field order. Fligstein and McAdam (2012: 103) do note, however, that these gradual incremental changes, even if they usually result in overall field reproduction, can have aggregate effects. Eventually, they can undermine the social order to a 'tipping point' and begin the process of emergent mobilization discussed above or to 'episodes of contention,' in which the shared understandings on which fields are based become in flux and result in periods of sustained contentious interaction among field actors. Change is more possible in both situations than in settled fields.

The more common sources of transformative field change, however, come from outside of the field. First, fields may be transformed by invading groups that had not previously been active players in the focal field. These outsiders will not be as bound by the conventional rules and understandings of the field as challengers who had already been field players. The success of outsiders at altering the field order may depend on many factors, including their strength prior to invasion, the proximity (in social space) of their former field to the target field, and their social skill in forging allies and mobilizing defectors. Second, transformative change can be due to large-scale, macro-level events that disrupt numerous field linkages and lead to crises. These often, but not always, involve the state. Examples include economic depressions, wars, and regime change.

The third and final exogenous source of transformative change for SAFs emanates from Fligstein and McAdam's emphasis on inter-field linkages. The effects of a field's relations with other fields traditionally have been undertheorized, as field-level studies tend to examine only the internal dynamics of a focal field or else capture the structure of external field relations without developing a general theoretical framework for field interrelations. Bourdieu, for example, stated: "I believe indeed that there are no trans-historic laws of the relations between fields, that we must investigate each historical case separately" (Bourdieu and Wacquant 1992: 109) (emphasis in original). However, for Fligstein and McAdam (2012: 18, 59, 100–101), fields are not isolated social systems; they stand in relation to other fields in a broader social space. These relations play a key role in whether a field will change or remain stable. The authors conceptualize field-to-field linkages mostly based on the extent to which fields are dependent or interdependent with other fields in social space.

Because fields are often tied, via dependencies or interdependencies, to other fields, a destabilizing change in one field is "like a stone thrown in a still pond, sending ripples outward to all proximate fields" (Fligstein and McAdam 2011: 9). Usually, such a ripple is not so disruptive as to lead to an episode of contention within a field. But dependent field relationships yield unequal power relations and unidirectional influence by the dominant field, making a field particularly susceptible to change when there is rupture or crisis in the field on which it depends.[12]

In contrast to the idea of dependent field relations leading to change to a focal field, interdependent field relations can also buffer *against* change to the focal field (Fligstein and McAdam 2012: 59–61). This is because that field can count on the reciprocal legitimacy benefits and resource flows that it shares with related fields to resist change from within. Fligstein and McAdam (2012: 61) cite Bourdieu's (1996a) study of elite universities, corporations, and the state in France as an example of how fields depend on one another to reproduce their positions – elite universities depend on the state and elite corporations to hire their graduates into prestigious jobs, and the state and corporations depend on the credentialing process that elite universities provide. We note, however, that Bourdieu's interdependencies here ultimately serve to reproduce order in an even-higher, more abstract field (the "field of power"); his is not a direct account of interdependencies buffering against change within a focal field.

In conclusion, Fligstein and McAdam (2012) provide a more detailed, systematic account of field emergence and divergent change than neo-institutional theorists of organizational fields. They are also much clearer than Bourdieu on the conditions under which field change can occur. Whereas Bourdieu really only points to rare times of crisis, in which the *doxa* may be revealed and questioned by the dominated members of a field (as discussed above), Fligstein and McAdam (2012) elaborate a clearer and more elegant framework for the mechanisms of field stability and change.

10.7 Discussion and Conclusion

In this essay, we have pursued two goals. First, we have tried to show that a general notion of a field can be gleaned from the work of neo-institutionalists in organizational theory, Bourdieu, and Fligstein and McAdam's theory of SAFs. The consensus emphasizes the nature of fields as meso-level social orders populated with actors who take one another into account in their actions. Second, while these ideal-typical versions of field theories have many agreements, they differ markedly in terms of how they under-

[12] As we noted in our overview of the theory of SAFs, field dependencies can be based on legal or bureaucratic authority and on resource dependencies (Pfeffer and Salancik 1978).

stand the role of actors, power, consensus, and the dynamics of fields.

In order to make progress on understanding the significance of these disagreements, our basic message is that these differences should be confronted and explored not just theoretically, but empirically. Scholars should then be reflexive about how to revise theory in light of the differences. Instead of treating these ideas as separate schools of thought about fields, we should place them more directly in conversation with one another by examining which way of thinking about fields makes more sense in certain kinds of situations.

It is useful to consider how to proceed to adjudicate these differences of opinion. What should be done next is both conceptual and empirical. The concepts of field theory have been fleshed out in an abstract manner. The degree to which they differ needs to be made more explicit in order for them to be empirically useful. At the same time, while we have many studies that employ field theory in one form or another, we have very little general sense of how to produce measurement and comparability in observation in order to evaluate the conceptual disagreements. So, for example, Bourdieu's *Distinction* (1984) remains one of the few comprehensive field-level studies of social life. But the issues it raises have simply not been addressed consistently from a specifically field-theoretic point of view. Instead, scholars have picked and chosen aspects of Bourdieu's framework and ignored the general issue of the degree to which such a field of cultural production exists and how stable it may be across time and place (Sallaz and Zavisca 2007).

Moreover, scholars should clarify whether or not the disagreements between field theories is a matter of specifying more clearly the possible scope conditions of each of these perspectives or of their fundamental incompatibility. Again, this issue is both conceptual and empirical. From a conceptual point of view, it may be that there are conditions where one or the other perspective operates to make better sense of the world. Our ability to specify the mechanisms by which these concepts actually operate need to be clarified. This is certainly also an empirical question. So, for example, figuring out how to tell if a particular field is more driven by legitimacy, power and dominance, or identify and cooperation, is a difficult question that we have little experience attempting to answer empirically.

Field theory also can occupy an ambiguous epistemological status. On the one hand, field theorists may assume that fields are real, they can be measured, and their effects discerned. This would imply a more positivist or realist approach to fields that would emphasize common structures and mechanisms that researchers could look for and model across settings. But, one can also view field theory as a set of concepts, ideal types that help researchers make sense of some historical situation. Here, analysts deploy the sparse ideas of which field theory consists to help them put a structure onto empirical materials, be they historical, ethnographic, or quantitative. We are comfortable with either version of field theory. But some scholars will find it difficult to take seriously those who opt for one or the other view of fields.

Field theory also makes very general claims about its empirical scope. Given our view that one can observe fields in most of organized social life, it is necessary to consider what field theory does and does not apply to. Indeed, one can see field theory as a nascent attempt at a general theory of society. Although Bourdieu tried to maintain his perspective was not such a theory, it is difficult given the wide-ranging character of his work and the myriad topics he investigated not to see field theory in this way. The theory of SAFs is a useful model because it builds upon not only the other field theories discussed in this chapter but also incorporates other lines of inquiry like social movement theory, social psychology, and identity theory to create a novel and general theory of action and structure.

Another way to test the generalizability of field theory is to engage other perspectives that posit meso-level processes but do not use the field idea. We have only mentioned network analysis and the institutional logics perspectives. But there are others. For example, population ecology in organizational theory, with its conception of constructed organizational populations, shares affinities with field theory (see Haveman and Kluttz 2015). Additionally, much of the work done on policy domains and policy entrepreneurs in sociology and political science could also fit into the field perspective (e.g., Kingdon 1984; Laumann and Knoke 1987).

There are two logical possibilities here. First, field theory might aid other perspectives by providing them with a well-conceived concept of a meso-level social arena that would make such theories richer. Situating one's analysis of the social world at this meso-level has distinct advantages. To say that action and meaning occurs in fields – social orders made up of individual and collective actors in discernible social positions and centered around mutually recognized resources, issues, and/or goals – gives the theorist an orienting lens with which to test field-level hypotheses or explain social phenomena within a conceptually or empirically bounded arena. Such a meso-level framework recognizes the importance of both macro-level structural influences and micro-level exchange and meaning-making processes without favoring one to the exclusion of the other.

Alternatively, ideas from other theories might also enrich field theory. Take, for example, recent literature on institutional logics (see Thornton et al. 2012). A blind spot of field theory is how ideas move across fields. The role of ideas or institutional logics has been a focus of work in political science and organizational theory. But this literature tends to reify ideas or logics in a way that makes it difficult to tell what they are and how they are or are not transported into new arenas of action. Many of these discussions also underspecify the conditions under which this is likely to happen or not. Field theory, with its ideas about the institutionalization (or settlement) of social spaces and how they work, offers researchers social structures that can be used to identify when logics may or may not transfer across such spaces. It would be profitable to think through how field theory and the institutional logics perspective are complementary.

In conclusion, field theory is one of the most general theoretical accomplishments of the past 40 years in sociology. Although the complementarities between versions of field theories outnumber the differences, we should allow for recombination and synthesis in order to build on those complementarities and reconcile the differences. In doing so, we can avoid the theory fragmentation that has characterized sociological subfields over the last several decades and continue our path toward a comprehensive, contemporary theory of fields. As we hope we have shown, we are closer now to such a theory than ever before.

References

Battilana, J. (2006). Agency and institutions: The enabling role of Individuals' social position. *Organization, 13*(5), 653–676.

Battilana, J., Leca, B., & Boxenbaum, E. (2009). How actors change institutions: Towards a theory of institutional entrepreneurship. *Academy of Management Annals, 3*(1), 65–107.

Berger, P. L., & Luckmann, T. (1967). *The social construction of reality: A treatise in the sociology of knowledge*. Garden City: Doubleday/Anchor Books.

Bourdieu, P. (1977). *Outline of a theory of practice*. Cambridge, UK: Cambridge University Press.

Bourdieu, P. (1984). *Distinction: A social critique of the judgment of taste* (R. Nice, Trans.). Cambridge, MA: Harvard University Press.

Bourdieu, P. (1986). The forms of capital. In J. Richardson (Ed.), *Handbook of theory and research for the sociology of education* (pp. 241–258). New York: Greenwood.

Bourdieu, P. (1989). Social space and symbolic power. *Sociological Theory, 7*(1), 14–25.

Bourdieu, P. (1990). *The logic of practice*. (R. Nice, Trans). Stanford: Stanford University Press.

Bourdieu, P. (1993). *The field of cultural production: Essays on art and literature*. New York: Columbia University Press.

Bourdieu, P. (1996a). *The state nobility: Elite schools in the field of power*. Stanford: Stanford University Press.

Bourdieu, P. (1996b). *The rules of art: Genesis and structure of the literary field*. Stanford: Stanford University Press.

Bourdieu, P. (2000). *Pascalian meditations*. Stanford: Stanford University Press.

Bourdieu, P. (2005). Principles of an economic anthropology. In *The handbook of economic sociology* (pp. 75–89). Princeton: Princeton University Press.

Bourdieu, P., & Wacquant, L. (1992). *An invitation to reflexive sociology*. Chicago: University of Chicago Press.

Bourdieu, P., Schultheis, F., & Pfeuffer, A. (2011). With Weber against Weber: In conversation with Pierre

Bourdieu. In S. Susen & B. S. Turner (Eds.), *The legacy of Pierre Bourdieu: Critical essays* (pp. 111–124). London: Anthem Press.

Burawoy, M., & Von Holdt, K. (2012). *Conversations with Bourdieu: The Johannesburg moment*. Johannesburg: Wits University Press.

Clemens, E. S., & Cook, J. M. (1999). Politics and institutionalism: Explaining durability and change. *Annual Review of Sociology, 25*, 441–466.

Crossley, N. (2004). Phenomenology, structuralism and history: Merleau-Ponty's social theory. *Theoria: A Journal of Social and Political Theory, 103*, 88–121.

Davis, G. F., McAdam, D., Richard Scott, W., & Zald, M. N. (2005). *Social movements and organization theory*. Cambridge: Cambridge University Press.

Denrell, J., & Kovács, B. (2008). Selective sampling of empirical settings in organizational studies. *Administrative Science Quarterly, 53*, 109–144.

DiMaggio, P. (1988). Interest and agency in institutional theory. In L. G. Zucker (Ed.), *Institutional patterns and organizations: Culture and environment* (pp. 3–21). Cambridge, MA: Ballinger.

DiMaggio, P. (1991). Constructing an organizational field as a professional project: U.S. Art museums, 1920–1940. In W. Powell & P. DiMaggio (Eds.), *The new institutionalism in organizational analysis* (pp. 267–292). Chicago: University of Chicago Press.

DiMaggio, P., & Powell, W. (1983). The iron cage revisited: Institutional isomorphism and collective rationality in organizational fields. *American Sociological Review, 48*(2), 147–160.

DiMaggio, P., & Powell, W. (1991). Introduction. In W. Powell & P. DiMaggio (Eds.), *The new institutionalism in organizational analysis* (pp. 1–41). Chicago: University of Chicago Press.

Fligstein, N. (2001). Social skill and the theory of fields. *Sociological Theory, 19*(2), 105–125.

Fligstein, N. (2008). Fields, power and social skill: A critical analysis of the new institutionalisms. *International Public Management Review, 9*(1), 227–253.

Fligstein, N. (2013). Understanding stability and change in fields. *Research in Organizational Behavior, 33*, 39–51.

Fligstein, N., & McAdam, D. (2011). Toward a theory of strategic action fields. *Sociological Theory, 29*(1), 1–26.

Fligstein, N., & McAdam, D. (2012). *A theory of fields*. Oxford: Oxford University Press.

Garud, R., Hardy, C., & Maguire, S. (2007). Institutional entrepreneurship as embedded agency: An introduction to the special issue. *Organization Studies, 28*(7), 957–969.

Giddens, A. (1979). *Central problems in social theory: Action, structure, and contradiction in social analysis*. Berkeley: University of California Press.

Goffman, E. (1974). *Frame analysis: An essay on the organization of experience*. Cambridge, MA: Harvard University Press.

Hall, P. A., & Taylor, R. C. R. (1996). Political science and the three new institutionalisms. *Political Studies, 44*(5), 936–957.

Hannan, M. T., & Freeman, J. (1977a). The population ecology of organizations. *American Journal of Sociology, 82*, 929–964.

Hannan, M. T., & Freeman, J. (1977b). The population ecology of organizations. *American Journal of Sociology, 33*, 92–104.

Hardy, C., & Maguire, S. (2008). Institutional entrepreneurship. In R. Greenwood, C. Oliver, R. Suddaby, & K. Sahlin-Andersson (Eds.), *The SAGE handbook of organizational institutionalism* (pp. 198–218). London: Sage.

Haveman, H. A., & Kluttz, D. N. (2015). Organizational populations and fields. In R. A. Scott & S. M. Kosslyn (Eds.), *Emerging trends in the social and behavioral sciences* (pp. 1–15). Thousand Oaks: Wiley.

Jepperson, R. (1991). Institutions, institutional effects, and institutionalism. In W. W. Powell & P. J. DiMaggio (Eds.), *The new institutionalism in organizational analysis* (pp. 143–163). Chicago: University of Chicago Press.

Kingdon, J. W. (1984). *Agendas, alternatives, and public policies*. Boston: Little, Brown.

Laumann, E. O., & Knoke, D. (1987). *The organizational state: Social choice in national policy domains*. Madison: University of Wisconsin Press.

Laumann, E. O., Galaskieqicz, J., & Marsden, P. (1978). Community structure as interorganizational linkage. *Annual Review of Sociology, 4*, 455–484.

Lawrence, T. B., Suddaby, R., & Leca, B. (Eds.). (2009). *Institutional work: Actors and agency in institutional studies of organizations*. Cambridge: Cambridge University Press.

Lawrence, T., Suddaby, R., & Leca, B. (2011). Institutional work: Refocusing institutional studies of organization. *Journal of Management Inquiry, 20*(1), 52–58.

Lewin, K. (1951). *Field theory in social science*. New York: Harper & Row.

Lizardo, O. (2004). The cognitive origins of Bourdieu's habitus. *Journal for the Theory of Social Behaviour, 34*(4), 375–401.

Lounsbury, M., Ventresca, M., & Hirsch, P. (2003). Social movements, field frames and industry emergence: A cultural-political perspective on US recycling. *Socio-Economic Review, 1*, 71–104.

Mann, M. (1986). *The sources of social power, volume 1: A history of power from the beginning to A.D. 1760*. Cambridge, UK: Cambridge University of Press.

Martin, J. L. (2003). What is field theory? *American Journal of Sociology, 109*(1), 1–49.

Mauss, M. (1973) [1934]. Techniques of the body. *Economy and Society, 2*(1), 70–88.

McAdam, D. (1999). *Political Process and the Development of Black Insurgency, 1930–1970* (2nd ed.). Chicago: The University of Chicago Press.

McAdam, D., Tarrow, S., & Tilly, C. (2001). *Dynamics of Contention*. Cambridge: Cambridge University Press.

McCarthy, J., & Zald, M. (1973). *The trend of social movements in America: Professionalization and resource mobilization*. Morristown: General Learning Press.

Mead, G. H. (1934). *Mind, self, and society*. Chicago: University of Chicago Press.

Menand, L. (2001). *The metaphysics club*. New York: Farrar, Strauss, and Giroux.

Mey, H. (1972). *Field-theory: A study of its application in the social sciences*. New York: St. Martins Press.

Meyer, J. W., & Rowan, B. (1977). Institutionalized organizations: Formal structure as myth and ceremony. *American Journal of Sociology, 83*, 340–363.

Mohr, J. (2005). *Implicit terrains: Meaning, measurement, and spatial metaphors in organizational theory*. Unpublished manuscript, Dept. of Sociology, University of California, Santa Barbara. Accessed 1 July 2015.

Morrill, C. (2006). *Institutional change and interstitial emergence: The growth of alternative dispute resolution in American law, 1965–1995*. Working Paper, Center for the Study of Law and Society, University of California, Berkeley.

Pfeffer, J., & Salancik, G. R. (1978). *The external control of organizations: A resource dependence perspective*. Stanford: Stanford University Press.

Powell, W. W., & Colyvas, J. A. (2008). Microfoundations of institutional theory. In R. Greenwood, C. Oliver, K. Sahlin, & R. Suddaby (Eds.), *The SAGE handbook of organizational institutionalism* (pp. 276–298). London: Sage.

Powell, W. W., & DiMaggio, P. J. (1991). *The new institutionalism in organizational analysis*. Chicago: University of Chicago Press.

Rao, H., Morrill, C., & Zald, M. N. (2000). Power plays: How social movements and collective action create new organizational forms. *Research in Organizational Behavior, 22*, 237–281.

Sallaz, J., & Zavisca, J. (2007). Bourdieu in American sociology, 1980–2004. *Annual Review of Sociology, 33*, 21–41.

Schneiberg, M., & Clemens, E. S. (2006). The typical tools for the job: Research strategies in institutional analysis. *Sociological Theory, 24*, 195–227.

Scott, W. R. (2013). *Institutions and organizations: Ideas, interests, and identities* (4th ed.). Los Angeles: SAGE Publications.

Scott, W. R., & Meyer, J. W. (1983). The organization of societal sectors. In J. W. Meyer & W. Richard Scott (Eds.), *Organizational environments: Ritual and rationality* (pp. 129–153). Beverly Hills: Sage.

Snow, D., & Benford, R. (1988). Ideology, frame resonance, and participant mobilization. In B. Klandermans, H. Kriesi, & S. Tarrow (Eds.), *International social movement research: From structure to action* (pp. 197–218). Greenwich: JAI Press.

Snow, D. A., Burke Rochford, E., Jr., Worden, S. K., & Benford, R. D. (1986). Frame alignment processes, micromobilization, and movement participation. *American Sociological Review, 51*(4), 464–481.

Suchman, M. C. (1995). Managing legitimacy: Strategic and institutional approaches. *The Academy of Management Review, 20*(3), 571–610.

Suddaby, R. (2010). Challenges for institutional theory. *Journal of Management Inquiry, 19*(1), 14–20.

Thornton, P. H., Ocasio, W., & Lounsbury, M. (2012). *The institutional logics perspective: A new approach to culture, structure and process*. Oxford: Oxford University Press.

Weber, M. (1978). In G. Roth & C. Wittich (Eds.), *Economy and society: An outline of interpretative sociology*. Berkeley: University of California Press.

White, H. C. (1992). *Identity and control: A structural theory of social action*. Princeton: Princeton University Press.

White, H. C., Boorman, S. A., & Breiger, R. L. (1976). Social structure from multiple networks. I. Blockmodels of roles and positions. *American Journal of Sociology, 81*, 730–780.

Zald, M. N., & Ash, R. (1966). Social movement organizations: Growth, decay and change. *Social Forces, 44*(3), 327–341.

Zald, M. N., & McCarthy, J. D. (1987). *Social movements in an organizational society: Collected essays*. New Brunswick: Transaction Publishers.

Zucker, L. G. (1977). The role of institutionalization in cultural persistence. *American Sociological Review, 42*, 726–743.

Part III

A Coherent Social Universe

11 Institutional Spheres: The Macro-Structure and Culture of Social Life

Seth Abrutyn

11.1 Introduction

Since Parsons' grand theory fell in disrepute, sociologists have spilled much ink cautioning against reifying aspects of the social world that are invisible, macro, and perhaps invented by sociologists. Yet, as Fine notes, "People reify their life worlds, and do not, for the most part, think like interpretivist microsociologists" (1991:169). To be sure, Fine is thinking about collectives like the government or "big business" as the abstractions people assign exteriority to, and not larger, more abstract spheres of social reality. However, people routinely talk about "law," "religion," and the "economy" as things that act upon them and which others, especially elites, can act on (or use for their benefit). Indeed, even studies of small-scale societies demonstrate that nonliterate peoples cognitively distinguish between the beliefs and practices, underlying value-orientations and norms, and physical, temporal, social, and symbolic spaces of different spheres of reality like law and religion (Malinowski 1959). These spheres, or what I term *institutional spheres*, are the macro-level structural and cultural spheres that delineate the most central aspects of social life. Embedded within them are the various lower-level units of analysis other chapters in this handbook consider: the self (Chap. 17); corporate units like groups, organizations, and communities (Chaps. 13, 14, and 15); and congeries of corporate units, like fields (Chap. 10). *They do not act* in the Parsonsian sense of systems needing things and doing things. Rather, they are constructs that occupy real space and thus have real consequences. Moreover, spheres are not static, but processual; they vary in terms of their influence across time and space (Turner 2003); they have ecological dynamics associated with their level of autonomy and the degree to which an actor finds herself close to the institutional core (Abrutyn 2014b:68–98); but, ultimately, they shape the everyday reality of significant proportions of the population (1) cognitively as we develop identities embedded within relationships embedded within encounters embedded within corporate units that present actors with macro-level elements (see Chap. 6); (2) situationally when a person enters a courtroom for the first time in her life or when one goes to the mall on Black Friday; and (3) ritualistically when people anticipate and frequent religious services on a regular basis or when students take finals every year at the same time with the same preparatory lead up.

The following essay is organized as such: first, we explore the various usages of the term "institution" in sociology, arguing that there is both an historical basis for thinking about them as spheres

S. Abrutyn (✉)
Department of Sociology, University of Memphis, Memphis, TN, USA
e-mail: sbbrutyn@memphis.edu

S. Abrutyn (ed.), *Handbook of Contemporary Sociological Theory*, Handbooks of Sociology and Social Research, DOI 10.1007/978-3-319-32250-6_11

and practical reasons for doing so. Second, the major elements of institutions are elucidated, focusing particularly on the evolutionary, ecological, and entrepreneurial dynamics of institutional spheres. Third, and final, we consider the "frontiers" of institutional analysis. In particular, the temporal and symbolic spaces of institutional domains seem ripe for major advances, while the physical and social dimensions remain important and in need of further consideration.

11.2 The Many Varieties

I have commented elsewhere that the concept *institution* is one of the most commonly used concepts in sociology, yet is perhaps one of the vaguest and least precisely defined (Abrutyn 2009b, 2014b). An exhaustive review is not necessary, though it is worth noting the most common usages before moving on. Colloquially, an institution often refers to an enduring organization or association (e.g., Harvard; a research center), a long-standing member of said organization (e.g., a professor whose existence is synonymous with the department) or a formal position (e.g., the Presidency); it may also refer to an enduring custom (e.g., the handshake) or law. Early social scientists, and many today, used it to refer to enduring, patterned actions (e.g., marriage) or legal relations (e.g., private property), while those like Spencer used it both to refer to broader spheres of social structure like religion or law as well as the interrelated components that shaped social action. More recently, a loosely coupled group of scholars and scholarship, *new* or *neo-institutionalists*, use it in several divergent ways: cultural myths and patterns that generate isomorphism (Meyer and Rowan 1977; DiMaggio and Powell 1983); "rules of the game" that govern economic organizations (North 2005); forces of broad social control with varying levels of normative, regulative, and cognitive-cultural mechanisms (Scott 2001); or, broad organizational forms of modernity like "capitalism," "the State," or the "church" (Friedland and Alford 1991).

The number of uses—many of which stem from the new institutionalist school that is largely concerned with organizations (cf. Powell and DiMaggio 1991; Nee 2005)—is dizzying. That is, if the presidency, the handshake, Harvard, and sexism are all institutions (cf. Jepperson 1991:144), then one must logically ask what is not an institution? Or, perhaps the real question is, "are the differences in these phenomena more important than their similarities?" Besides the criticism surrounding the integration of colloquial vagaries with social scientific precision, we might raise several other issues with the new institutionalism. First, a close examination of the new institutionalist tradition reveals a focus on *organizations* with mostly taken for granted consideration of what the institution is, often pointing to an underexamined environment in which organizations do things (Sutton et al. 1994; Sutton and Dobbin 1996; Edelman and Suchman 1997). Second, like a lot of contemporary sociology, there is an ahistorical bias. Alford and Friedland's (1985) work, for example, is rooted in modernity and things like the "state" or "capitalism," which do not have one-to-one comparisons in other times, unless we take an overly simplistic Marxian view of polity or economy. Third, and closely related, neo-institutionalists have been criticized for overemphasizing convergence and isomorphism, while ignoring the tremendous variation in "state" or "capitalism." At times, the John Meyer "school" seems to assume rationality is *the* master process and all organizations, regardless of local custom or broader inequalities in the world-system, easily conform in lockstep to the basic pattern (Boli et al. 1985; Thomas et al. 1987). And thus it might be tempting to scrap the term itself, yet Durkheim (1895 [1982]:45) once described sociology as the "science of institutions," which both speaks to the centrality of the concept and the necessity in more precisely defining it.

However, rather than try and reinvent the wheel, or even challenge the status quo, this essay avoids the term institution to some degree, and its verb form *institutionalization*, for a more precise concept: *institutional sphere* or *domain*. Doing so affords us several ways to leverage greater swaths of sociological theory and research. First, it allows us to rescue aspects of functionalism and its close cousins (Shils 1975; Eisenstadt 1964, 1980; Turner 2003; Luhmann 2012) that may shed insights when consider in new light. Second, it moves us away from "system" language that overemphasizes similarities across levels of social reality so that we can talk about meaningful differences, as well as employ wide ranging explanatory frames like networks or social psychology. Third, and perhaps most importantly, we can move beyond the vague cultural theories of Parsons and functionalism (see Chap. 6) and offer a robust cultural theory to better balance the structural dimensions of institutions. This alone allows us to leverage the institutional logics perspective (Thornton et al. 2012) as well as revisit Weber's (1946) social psychological work on worldviews, ideas, and interests surrounding social orders. Fourth, we can introduce and embed the notion of history and evolutionary processes to underscore the ubiquity of institutional spheres, highlight some of the processes of change, and find the points of sociocultural and historic specificity that lend discrete texture to time and place.

11.3 Institutional Spheres

In essence, institutional spheres are the macro-level structural and cultural milieus in which most lower-order phenomena (e.g., fields; organizations; encounters) are organized and connected (Turner 2010). Though one can imagine a limitless number of potential spheres, ethnographic, historical, and sociological analyses point to a select set of domains that may be deemed institutions. In nearly every society, we find kinship (Fox 1967), political (Johnson and Earle 2000), religious (Radin 1937 [1957]), economic (Sahlins 1972), and legal spheres (Malinowski 1959); as well as, arguably, education (Turner 2003) and, perhaps, military (Collins 1986). In modern societies medicine (Starr 1982), science (Abrutyn 2009a), art (Luhmann 2000), and possibly media and/or sport (Abrutyn 2014b) join this list. Across time and space institutional spheres, and what may be called a society's *institutional complex* (or the total configuration of institutional spheres), vary in terms of their level of differentiation and, more importantly, autonomy (Abrutyn 2009b).

Differentiation occurs along four axes, the first three of which are common whereas the fourth is directly related to autonomy: physical, temporal, social, and symbolic. By physical, we are referring to the act of carving up geographic space and setting it aside for activities related to an institutional sphere; as well as stratifying access to these spaces. This may include buildings, monuments, statues, and the like. Temporal differentiation refers to the act of setting aside distinct time for activities, as well as hierarchicalizing how time shapes action, goals, and decisions. Temporal differentiation may resolve space limitations in so far as a space serves as an arena for two or more institutions, but only during certain times. Social differentiation involves the creation of new roles and status distinctions linked to the emergence of new groups, categories, and organizational units. The earliest form of this may be the growth of patri- and matrilines that signify a person's kinship position, descent, and inheritance (Levi-Strauss 1969). Finally, symbolic differentiation refers to the concomitant generalization and particularization of culture. On the one hand, generalization proceeds as space, time, and social relations grow complex and differentiated, as one mechanism of bringing all of these disparate pieces together (Alexander 1988). On the other hand, each disparate unit can come to "claim" a part of the broader culture as signifying something unique about it.

Thus, returning to institutional spheres, each sphere in a given society varies in terms of its level of physical, temporal, social, and symbolic differentiation. The greater is the degree to which each type of differentiation is higher, the greater is the degree to which the institutional sphere will be distinguishable by a significant proportion of the population vis-à-vis other institutions. Put another way, as polity becomes distinct from kinship around 5,000 years ago, the Palace and other public spaces become distinct from kinship buildings in size and scale—and, to some degree, function; public holidays and rituals are likewise distinct from local, familial rituals; kin relations and relations between subject and king become cognitively and materially consequential; and, finally, the polity usurps certain symbols that come to signify *power* and *force* as opposed to *loyalty* and *love* found in the family (Abrutyn 2015b). Differentiation, however, does not necessarily mean autonomy, as the Palace in Mesopotamian society was often conceptualized as a kinship domain, but one whose function mattered more than the ordinary house—e.g., the king's principal function was to uphold the secular and sacred order (Yoffee 2005). But autonomy cannot emerge without increasing levels of all four types of differentiation; especially symbolic.

By autonomy, we mean the process by which institutional spheres become discrete cultural spaces in so far as the physical, temporal, social, and symbolic elements come to orient most people's emotions, attitudes, and actions towards the institutional sphere's cultural system and source of authority (Abrutyn 2014b).[1] On your way to work, driving by a church, for instance, comes to signify a distinct set of actors, actions, attitudes and values, goals and preferences, and temporal dimensions. Even if an individual does not belong to the church or the broader religion, she can orient herself towards that building as if it is a microcosm of the religious sphere; and, as we shall see, the closer the actor is to the religious sphere, the more salient the meanings of the church will be when she drives past it. Hence, autonomy matters because institutional spheres come to *penetrate* the everyday lived experience of significant portions of the population such that they come to cognitively understand religion as separate—in the abstract and ideal—from polity or economy (Abrutyn 2014a); or, in the language of some institutional scholars, a unique *logic*, or symbols and practices that give "meaning to [actors] daily activity, organize time and space, and reproduce [actor's] lives and experiences" (Thornton et al. 2012:2), comes to mold the shape and texture of religion vis-à-vis kinship or economy. "How autonomous" is an empirical question revolving around historical factors, a given sphere's relationship to other spheres, and the ease with which resources (people, generalized media, etc.) flow across one sphere to the other signifying the circulation of intra-institutional meanings to other spheres. What matters, for now, is that societies are characterized by institutional spheres having greater or lesser autonomy; and which ones are more autonomous (as well as how many have become relatively autonomous) matters for understanding the underlying *ethos* of a given group of people as well as why cultural realities as expressed in micro-level processes like identities vary across time and space.

11.3.1 Evolutionary Institutionalism

An evolutionary analysis is essential to theorizing about institutional domains and their structural and cultural components; as well as what I call institutional *ecology* (see below). That is, institutions cannot be divorced from the long narrative of human history and the varieties of societal arrangements. Moreover, as Turner (2003) has asserted, neo-evolutionary thought provides us with the foundations for rehabilitating the functionalist trope of needs or requisites in ways that illuminate why humans construct macro-level spaces and why there are delimited numbers of institutional spheres (Abrutyn 2013a, b, 2015a). Thus, an evolutionary perspective sheds light on why the structure and culture of institutional spheres look the way they do.

In the following section, we consider what institutional evolution is by examining (a) the

[1] The concept of autonomy is borrowed from Niklas Luhmann's (2012) neo-system's theory. While Luhmann saw the system autonomy as tantamount to closure and, thus, a solution to the problem of differentiation, our conceptualization moves away from closure to a more Weberian, social phenomenological perspective: autonomy means spheres become *relatively* discrete cultural systems that increase the probability that an actor or set of actions will orient their emotions, attitudes, and actions when physically or cognitively near the institutional sphere. Hence why physical, temporal, social, and symbolic space matters: all four of these dimensions can make salient one institutional sphere's cultural reality vis-à-vis others.

material exigencies commonly driving societal evolution, (b) the universal human concerns that motivate humans, individually and collectively, try to solve problems around under the pressure of one or more of these material exigencies, and (c) the role institutional entrepreneurs play in evolution. Before exploring these three main topics, a brief elucidation of my view on sociocultural evolution is in order.

11.3.1.1 Sociocultural Evolution

Evolutionary thought and/or concepts have been a staple in sociology since Marx, Spencer, and Durkheim, as well as many other now-forgotten sociologists. Much of this thinking occurred before the modern synthesis of Darwinian natural selection and Mendelian genetics (cf. Mayr 2001), and before the types of empirical data necessary to draw good inferences were readily available. For many early sociologists, evolution implicitly or explicitly meant progressive gradual change that unfolded primarily at the macro-level in terms of time and space. It both fit the crude efforts at societal classification (e.g., savages-barbarians-civilized societies), and the growing social scientific efforts to understand colonized peoples. Hence, many of the criticisms of Eurocentrism were at least partially valid. In the 1960s, evolutionism returned in the form of stage models that sought to learn from the past (Bellah 1964; Lenski 1966; Parsons 1966). These too failed to use evolutionary principles and were more about discerning developmental stages and less about theorizing about sociocultural evolution (Blute 2010). In the last 25 years, neo-evolutionary theories have grown exponentially (for a review, see Chap. 24).

For our purposes, we are interested primarily in how institutions evolve, with autonomy being the principal dimension along which we can measure institutional evolution. Like libraries, institutional spheres become warehouses of material and symbolic elements which are sometimes combined into extant patterns that reflect past solutions, but remain capable of being recombined, forgotten and rediscovered, and manipulated in previously unforeseen ways. They are macro in so far as they contain large inventories of cultural elements that few, if any one person, can know or access. However, these libraries of culture are grafted onto physical, temporal, social, and symbolic spaces that are embodied in a series of encounters (more or less micro). Unlike libraries, institutional spheres are structural spaces with real positions reflective of power and authority, stratification patterns unique to the sphere and also indicative of broader societal patterns, and resource flows (Abrutyn 2014b:147–171). Thus, they do not serve as passive sites of storage, but also as arenas of competition and conflict that further fuel sociocultural evolution. If they are macro in that they contain numerous elements beyond the control of any one person, they are also macro in so far as they contain series of embedded sites of contestation—in many ways, like Fligstein and McAdam's (2011) notion of embedded fields of strategic action (see also Chap. 10)—as well as numerous structural connections like divisions of labor, patterns of exchange, and the like that tenuously link various levels of social reality as well as these embedded sites of contestation.

Because they are macro and collective and highly complex in their substance, institutions do not evolve based on Darwinian principles—though, like all things attached to the biotic world, institutions can be wiped out along with a society in the face of massive environmental change. To draw, then, from Turner (2010), institutional spheres reflect two of our very own theorists' models of evolution: *Spencerian* and *Durkheimian*. The gist of Spencer's model challenges purist Darwinian thinking because it does not rely on competition between species or traits or whatever is the unit of selection. Instead, he posited that societies were always at risk of collapse or conquest because environmental exigencies were not so much a constant, but an inherent risk of population growth and density; under "normal" conditions, existing structural (and I would argue cultural) solutions could be mobilized to resolve exigencies, but often times these were not sufficient and a society faced a "choice": either create new structural (and/or cultural) arrangements to resolve the problems or risk breaking down.[2] Spencerian evolutionary processes, then, operate by purposive, directed efforts of people in the face of real (and I would add, perceived) problems. As we shall see below, I believe Spencerian evolution also requires thinking about the link between macro-exigencies and micro-level exigencies, which often goes unexamined and assumed.

Durkheimian selection processes are more similar to Darwinian. In essence, Durkheim saw competition between individuals or groups for position and resources as the driving force of sociocultural evolution: some individuals or groups would prove more "fit" for a niche or position, while others would create new specializations, carve out new niches, or die. This model is more of an ecological evolutionism that has been developed extensively by human ecologists (Hawley 1986) and organizational ecologists (Hannan and Freeman 1977). Like Darwinian processes, competition over resources and specialization are key components; unlike Darwinian processes, Durkheim acknowledges that culture has the capacity to overcome the biotic world, expand resource bases, and reduce conflicts—and thus, like Spencer's model, humans can and do act purposively and creatively. Moreover, as strategic action field theorists (Fligstein and McAdams 2011)—who, admittedly, are not evolutionists—would add: competitions, their outcomes, and thereby potential evolutionary change, are not always blind and directionless from a Durkheimian perspective, but do involve strategizing, purposive actors working to improve their position, protect their power, destroy their opponents, and, under other circumstances, increase the collective's (or some segment of it) benefit (cf. Chaps. 25 and 26; also, Abrutyn and Van Ness 2015).

In short, evolutionary processes are real in sociology. Though our focus is on how and why institutions evolve, there are plenty of other levels of evolution under which other principles apply (Blute 2010). By moving towards Spencerian and Durkheimian processes, however, we gain several advantages to strict Darwinian accounts. First, we are freed from using biological concepts as metaphors for sociocultural evolution when they are not really one-to-one fits. Second, they open the door to thinking about who, that is what actual persons, are affecting evolution; as well as when, why, and how. Third, we can bury unidirectional and unilinear stage models for good, acknowledging that evolution is not necessary progressive in terms of growing complexity or differentiation, but in fact, evolution may mean different things across cases. While Bellah (1964), for instance, considers the Protestant reformation a moment of increasing complexity, I would characterize this transformative event as a moment of simplification when comparing the organizational, material, and symbolic elements of Protestantism to Catholicism. Likewise, institutional evolution may be the process by which one or more institutions grow in autonomy, or it may reflect the changing levels of autonomy across a series of institutions including the loss of autonomy in some cases. Finally, as Abrutyn and Lawrence (2010) have argued elsewhere, evolution though often gradual and slow, is sometimes rapid qualitative transformation; it often depends on the case, the historical scale one is interested in, and how we relativize temporality. We turn, now, to the basic material exigencies that seem ubiquitous to all societies.

11.3.1.2 The Material Exigencies

One of the principal critiques of structural-functionalism is that it relies too heavily on needs or requisites for societal equilibria (Parsons 1951); moreover, these needs are often conceptualized as *social* or *collective* needs, which imply a supra-consciousness. Herbert Spencer, for instance, famously argued that all societies had to deal with three basic adaptive problems (Turner 1985):

[2] First, by "choice" I do not believe Spencer literally saw societies as making choices. He was aware that supraorganisms, like societies, are not like organisms because they have myriad "central nervous system" and therefore choices require quotations. Second, Spencer was not naïve to think the process was as simple as create new structures and/or cultures or collapse. His model was recursive, and when solutions were not found or were unsuccessfully implemented, rather than collapse, exigencies likely became amplified or intensified or new exigencies emerged (Turner 2010).

operation (production of resources and reproduction of people); distribution; and, regulation (controlling and coordinating differentiated social units). While other functionalists would provide their own lists, the basic argument was the same: as societies grow larger, social equilibria are upset; in part, new structures with discrete functions emerge to deal with imbalance, but also cause new imbalances that are ultimately reduced by new integrative mechanisms. In short, structural differentiation is *always* the master process in functionalism, with emphasis either on the process of differentiation and its consequences (e.g., Spencer) or on the integrative mechanisms that bring differentiated society back into harmony (e.g., Durkheim).

Several problems emerge with structural-functional logic. First, there is a sense of inevitability and conservativism in most functionalisms. Durkheim, well aware of the competition and conflict found in modern, urban differentiated societies, incessantly searched for the lynchpin that balanced society; Parsons (1951), a worse offender, propagated a version of functionalism that led to studies legitimating inequality as "healthy" for society (Davis and Moore 1945). Second, most "solutions" to the problem of integration were weak or underdeveloped cultural solutions: for Durkheim, it was ritual and collective effervescence; Parsons settled on universal value-patterns; and for Merton, it was norms. In all of these cases, the outlines of a truly cultural solution to the problem of integration is present, yet in functionalism always put structure ahead of culture. Third, there is little room for multi-linear, multi-directional, contingent social change. Structural differentiation generally proceeds in a "progressive" direction (cf. Parsons 1966), whether from simple to compound (Spencer 1897), mechanical to organic (Durkheim 1893), or archaic to modern (Bellah 1964).

Yet, in spite of these criticisms, macro-level sociology must be able to explain and contend with macro-level material exigencies (Hawley 1986; Lenski 1966; Turner 2010). That is, we cannot turn a blind-eye to ubiquitous exigencies like population growth or density, resource scarcity, or heterogeneity that have relatively predictable outcomes. Nor can we adopt the functionalist perspective that often whitewashes (1) the purposive efforts to deal with these pressures—or, to deal with the secondary problems that people perceive like threats to a person or group's standard of living, (2) the proposed solutions that are sometimes beneficial to one group vis-à-vis others, and (3) the maladaptive consequences of short-sighted solutions. One solution Turner (2003) has offered is to focus, instead, on *selection pressures*, or the types of generic forces that, when present, press against a social unit's extant structure and culture in ways that lead to change; whether coerced, unintentional, or intentional. Though an exhaustive list of selection pressures would be preferable, for our purposes we can provide several exogenous and endogenous examples: population growth *or* rapid decline; population and social density; material, human, and/or symbolic resource scarcity; heterogeneity, stratification, and inequality; external threats or internal conflict; ecological degradation or climatic disasters. What links these examples together are several key aspects: (1) they all have the potential to threaten the survival of a given social unit; (2) they can appear, in variable size, scale, and magnitude, across all levels of social reality; (3) they all have short- and long-run structural and cultural solutions that are just as likely to fail or create new secondary pressures, as succeed; (4) more often than not, solutions include reconfiguring the physical, temporal, social, or symbolic spaces in directions of either greater or lesser differentiation.

11.3.1.3 Universal Human Concerns

Despite the importance of these exigencies in explaining sociocultural evolution and institutional change, it is far less common—especially before scientific inquiry became distinct from religious, legal, and philosophic epistemologies—for people to *feel* macro-level exigencies. That is, not many people conceptualize their discomfort and pursuit of individual or collective solutions as coming from, say, "too much population!" Rather, these macro-level exigencies tend to exacerbate concerns that appear to be ubiquitous to humans in both time and space (Abrutyn

2014b). Admittedly, sociologists tend to balk at lists that involve universals, but several caveats should put these fears in abeyance. First, by ubiquitous, I mean that any mentally, physically, and genetically "normal" human is *capable* of feeling these concerns are salient to their well-being. How they are made salient, however, is an empirical question: for instance, it could be a direct feeling, cultivated from the person's actual experiences just as much as it could be a feeling derived from a significant or prestigious other's influence. The point is that some concerns are *universal*, and under the right conditions can be made to feel problematic and in need of correction. Second, just because a concern is made salient does not mean individuals or groups will or can resolve the assumed problem. Technology or culture may not allow resolution; existing power structures may work in opposition to efforts to innovate; individuals or groups may fail to perceive the problem, or simply misperceived the problem or its solutions; finally, solutions have no guarantees over the short, medium, or long haul. Third, some ubiquitous concerns remain undifferentiated in many human societies, conflated or synthesized with other more "important" ones. That is, cultural variation is, in part, a product of the historical and sociocultural contingent nature of selection: one group may define *justice* as salient under the same exact pressures as another that defines *sacredness* and *loyalty* to be most relevant. How these concerns are grafted onto institutional spheres is what gives every society or social unit its unique texture and timbre.

That being said, there are a limited number of concerns and when these concerns become salient, and the production, distribution, and access to their solutions become monopolized by a specialized group, institutional spheres can become autonomous. That is, institutional spheres come to be the central locus for dealing with one or more human concerns. Table 11.1 offers a list of autonomous institutional spheres and the concerns often embedded within them. Of course, this fact does not necessarily lead to the functionalist or old evolutionary notion that structures and cultures are adaptive. Rather, institutional spheres are dominated by collectives who monopolize access to the goods and services associated with dealing with one or more concerns, and under most circumstances, these rights and privileges are unevenly distributed. An institution's autonomy, then, does not depend on objective adaptivity but instead on whether it penetrates the lives and experiences of a significant proportion of the population, while allowing the group and its cultural assemblage to persist over an indefinite period of time. The greater this penetration, (1) the greater the legitimacy granted to those monopolizing the institution's core, (2) the greater the subjective belief that the institution "correctly" distributes and produces solutions, and (3) the

Table 11.1 Ubiquitous human concerns and institutions often involved in their resolution

Biological reproduction	Kinship, polity
Cultural reproduction	Kinship, education, polity, religion, science
Security	Polity, kinship
Communication with the supernatural	Religion, polity, art
Conflict resolution/justice/fairness	Law, kinship, polity
Knowledge of the biotic/social world	Science, education, religion, polity, economy, art
Subsistence	Economy, polity, kinship, science, medicine
Transportation/communication tech.	Polity, economy, science, media
Distinction/status	Polity, economy, sport, religion, art, education
Moral order	Kinship, religion, law, polity
Socioemotional anchorage	Kinship, religion, art
Health	Medicine, kinship, religion

Note: This list is not definitive, but rather suggestive. Other concerns can become salient and, therefore, ubiquitous greater the likelihood that individuals and collectives will orient their emotions, attitudes, and actions—under the right conditions (which are elucidated in detail below)—towards the cultural and authority system(s) of the institutional core (and the specialists who are granted the right to impose a legitimate vision of reality). Note, some of these concerns are ubiquitous in so far as there are biological and, especially, neurological foundations for them. A strong sense of justice, for example, is found in both our primate kin and across *all* human brains (Gospic et al. 2011)—and, thereby, shapes the microdynamics constraining our everyday experience of social reality (Chap. 18). The specific cultural framework varies, to be sure, but the salience of justice as a human concern appears everywhere, with the earliest expression being in relatively distinct legal mechanisms (Hoebel 1973), but sometimes being grafted onto other concerns like *sacredness*, *loyalty*, and *power*.

A further note, whose full exploration is beyond the scope of this chapter, is the fact that widespread sense of salience is often historically phased (for more, see Abrutyn 2009a, 2014a, 2015a). Thus, while *power* is a concern across all social units across all times and places, its *institutionalization* and, therefore, widespread salience, only occurs when roles like chiefs become differentiated. Its scale and magnitude continues to increase as polity becomes autonomous. That is, when chiefs become kings seeking to *generalize power* across social units and monopolize its production and distribution within the political core—and thereby expropriating it from local kin relations—*power* becomes problematic more frequently and more complexly (Abrutyn 2013a). For instance, on a cognitive, micro/meso-level, political autonomy and the monopolization of *power* meant political goals become perceived as "different from other types of goals or from goals of other spheres [in so far as their] formation, pursuit, and implementation became largely independent of other groups, *and were governed mostly by political criteria and by consideration of political exigency*" (Eisenstadt 1963:19). The same point can be made about religion and the production and distribution of goods and services associated with concerns like *sacredness/piety* during the Axial Age (Abrutyn 2014a, 2015a); law and *conflict resolution/justice* during the Gregorian Reformation (Abrutyn 2009b); or, *health* and medicine during the early twentieth century (Starr 1982).

11.3.1.4 Institutional Entrepreneurship

Currently underexplored, a significant question that faces evolutionary accounts is how the macro-level processes are "translated" into the lived experience of people, motivating them to innovate and invent new organizational, symbolic, or technological elements of culture. One possible answer to this dilemma may derive from the transformation of exigencies into real or perceived threats to individual or groups of individuals' standards of living. That is, in the face of objective or subjective relative deprivation, actors are motivated to identify the source of threat and resolve it by eradicating the threat, adapting to it, stemming it, etc. However, this perspective avoids the possibility of purposive innovation where no perceived threat or exigency is present. Innovation for the sake of innovation as well as out of self-interest or collective benefit must be considered plausible sources of new cultural traits that, once present, can either spread by way of typical mechanisms such as propinquity, prestige-biases, or conformity (Abrutyn and Mueller 2014) or from being imposed from above by power elites (Abrutyn and Van Ness 2015). In both cases—reaction to threat or innovative agency—the primary driving force can be characterized as collective specialized actors who may best be called *institutional entrepreneurs*.

Entrepreneurs are Eisenstadt's (1964, 1980) interpretation of Weber's *charismatic carrier groups*. They are entrepreneurial in so far as they embark on high-risk/high-reward projects that can lead to, in the most extreme cases, their death. When truly successful, they are capable of reconfiguring the physical, temporal, social, and symbolic space and carving out distinct autonomous institutional spheres that encompass those differentiated dimensions of space (Abrutyn 2014b; Abrutyn and Van Ness 2015). From Weber,

Eisenstadt saw these groups as evolutionary when they are capable of convincing others that their project and the very grounds of their group's existence is rooted in the fundamental social, moral, and cosmic order (cf. introduction in Weber 1968). It was their charismatic "fervor" that became the force driving qualitative transformation. I (2014b) have added to this that the fundamental grounds were rooted not in vague notions of moral order, but rather linked to one or more human concerns in that they became the producers and distributors of goods and services associated with substantive or ultimate ends. As the purveyors of these goods and services, like priests dispensing grace or politicians transforming raw power into delimited authority, they are given the right to carve up institutional space. Bourdieu (1989), for instance, recognized the ability to appropriate social and symbolic space and differentiate it however one group sees fit as the ultimate form of symbolic power and violence. Groups, however, also carve up physical and temporal space. What makes entrepreneurship tricky, however, is the fact that entrepreneurial projects are often both self- and collectively-oriented; finding a balance between the two diametrically opposed goal structures matters for success, as too much of the former loses potential members and too much of the latter invites organizational and movement disasters.

Finally, there are different types of entrepreneurs and projects based on their own originating position. DiMaggio (1988), for instance, borrowed the term from Eisenstadt to discuss how existing organizational fields adapt or are modified by purposive innovation. A more Durkheimian, gradualist model of "reform" and quantitative growth underscores this model, as entrepreneurs work from within the existing institutional sphere. Eisenstadt (1964, 1980), conversely, pictured a different embedded entrepreneur: authorized by more powerful individuals to resolve pressing problems, they could leverage their success and monopoly over organizational, technological, and symbolic secrets to balance power differentials between their entrepreneurial unit and the extant power elite. To these two, I have added the "marginal" entrepreneurs, or those who begin to modify institutional reality from a distant position from the core; a process that seems to have occurred in some Axial Age (*c.* 1000–100 BCE) religio-cultural movements (Humphreys 1975; Abrutyn 2014a, 2015a); and, in addition, the *liaison*, or the entrepreneur whose position is at the overlap between two or more autonomous institutional spheres and can draw from both in new, creative ways (Abrutyn 2014b). More on these different types of entrepreneurs will be said shortly. For now, we turn to the ecological dynamics of institutions so that elucidating entrepreneurs and their positions will be anchored in something much more concrete.

11.3.2 Institutional Ecology and the Dynamics of Institutional Space

One of the oldest problems macrosociology has wrestled with is how macro level forces are translated into micro-level dynamics (for more, see Chaps. 7 and 8). Parsons (1951), for instance, posited a model (AGIL) that supposedly worked at all levels of reality, capturing the four basic needs individuals, groups, and societies were required to find structural solutions to. In this section we explore the way institutional domains organize ecological space and the ecological dynamics across levels of social reality. Conceptualizing ecological space allows us to move away from the abstraction present in Parsons or Luhmann, and take purchase of the way macro-reality, through *real physical, temporal, social, and symbolic* space comes to facilitate *and* constrain emotions, actions, and attitudes. Taking as my departure point, Shils' (1975) long-forgotten functionalist ecology, it is possible to visualize how institutional spheres become actualized in everyday reality without reducing the macro to the micro or vice versa. In addition, this strategy further bolsters the role of entrepreneurs who, as we shall see below, become the "fulcrum" between the macro and micro worlds; a strategy that Turner (2011) has long advocated for but which he has not fully elucidated in terms of actual groups doing real things.

11.3.2.1 Macro Ecology

In trying to think about the macro-micro link, Shils (1975) argued that societies have a "center" that penetrates, in varying degrees, the environment surrounding it. Inside the core are the principal institutions (polity; economy; cultural), authority system, and values, which emanated outward into the "mass" society. Besides the functionalist assumption of consensus and stability, Shils' model assumes a single core, offers only vague descriptions of what the center consists of, and has little explanation as to how and why the core form and whether it changes over time. However, I (2013c, 2014b) have made clear that this metaphor can work for understanding institutional autonomy, evolution, and macro-micro linkage.

We begin with a simple proposition: *the greater is the degree to which an institution is autonomous, the greater is the degree to which one (or more) discrete institutional cores form.*[3] The core is a physical and cognitive dimension of macro-reality. On the one hand, with greater autonomy comes the increasing likelihood that physical space—including buildings, pathways, and even people lodged temporarily or full-time in these spaces—will become distinguishable from other types of physical space. At first, physical space becomes differentiated temporally, such as the public "square" of a chiefdom serving as the daily meeting ground and, during the holiest of days, the sacred center once cleansed. Eventually, however, residential zones become bounded vis-à-vis politico-legal zones (e.g., downtown areas with courthouses, town halls, jails, and police stations); and, within a given institutional sphere, multiple cores can take up different or overlapping space such as an economic sphere subdividing into commercial and industrial zones. These spaces are *real* and macro in their totality, scale, size, and ability to impose cultural orientations on those passing through as well as those who spend much of their day working or acting within them. And, so, the core or cores become important not because they do not exist in abstract reality; rather we are embedded in the core when we enter a courthouse, a church, a college campus or building, or a home.

On the other hand, the core is not something only salient in physical reality. A lawyer can imagine and practice her courtroom role-performance at home, while chance encounters at a grocery store between a parishioner and his priest thrust both into an ephemeral religious encounter that is detached from the physical routine location(s). Hence, humans spend time in these places, can see them in real time *and* in their minds, and, as such, can reify religion or polity in ideal typical physical locations (e.g., Jerusalem or Washington D.C. respectively). These reifications and the actual "microcosms" we inhabit like houses or churches *extend*, cognitively, our orientation, encounters we engage in, and groups or other collectives we perform tasks within. By "extend," I mean they enlarge the circumference, in Kenneth Burke's (1989) terminology, or widen the frame, in Goffman's parlance, by which we label our self, sift through emotion/feeling rules, choose lines of action and order preferences, and define the situation.

In addition to these "locational" or "spatial" elements, an autonomous core also implies differentiated temporal, social, and symbolic space. For instance, working hours get split apart from family time; political holidays can be carved out vis-à-vis religious ones; and, decisions made in hierarchical space can shape the sequences of action in lower-order spaces. In addition, fields, organizations, groups, and role/status positions become increasingly distinct from each other. In the home, we expect people to be in kinship roles, even though work does not clearly end at the threshold of the doorway; when entering a courtroom, all other roles are temporally constrained, while we immediately assume a status far lower than the judge and, indeed, jurists and lawyers. Finally, symbolic markers emerge to carve up the physical, temporal, and social spaces and make them meaningfully discrete. Building architecture, for instance, stereotype the expectations,

[3] The "core" metaphor is preferable to center if only because a core does not assume centrality, but rather an essential space from which key elements of institutional domains are produced and distributed. Hence, there can be more than one core, and cores do not have to be harmoniously integrated or coupled.

activities, and attitudes inherent in a physical location; "totems" like a status of blind lady justice, a cross, or Latin phrasing cue appropriate role transitions; calendars and other means of demarcating time allow us to anticipate institutional rituals; and, various identity kits like white lab coats, tweed jackets with elbow patches, black robes, or business suits stereotype role expectations and obligations, as well as signify the social milieu in which a person has entered. Thus, the core is active in physical and temporal space, as well as social and symbolic space. More autonomy means more discreteness.

Likewise, surrounding any given institutional core is its environment. The environment and actors located throughout the environment are governed by the *rule of proximity*: the greater is the degree of institutional autonomy and the closer is the degree to which a person, group, of cluster of groups (e.g., field; niche; sector) is located vis-à-vis an institutional core, the greater is the degree to which the core exerts *centripetal* force—that is, draws actors into the orbit of the rules and resources and divisions of labor of the core (e.g., Fig. 11.1). The environment, like the core, is real. It is composed of the various meso-level spaces sociologists often study to avoid the abstraction of macrosociology: fields (Bourdieu 1993; Fligstein and McAdam 2011) or niches (Hannan and Freeman 1977). Some of these meso-level spaces are located within the core, but not all. Figure 11.1 presents an example of an autonomous institutional sphere, its core, and the surrounding environment. Here we see an autonomous legal sphere found in many urban spaces. The core is constituted by the federal and/or state courthouse that is often located in a downtown area. It is both real in the sense that it physically and symbolically marks the legal zone, and cognitive in the sense that it often blends stereotyped architecture (e.g., huge columns) with local flourishes that serve to both mark the generalized and specific elements of the core. Support and liaison actors pockmark the physical landscape near the courthouse. A police headquarters and local jail is often close, as are numerous law offices,

Fig. 11.1 Example of autonomous institutional sphere

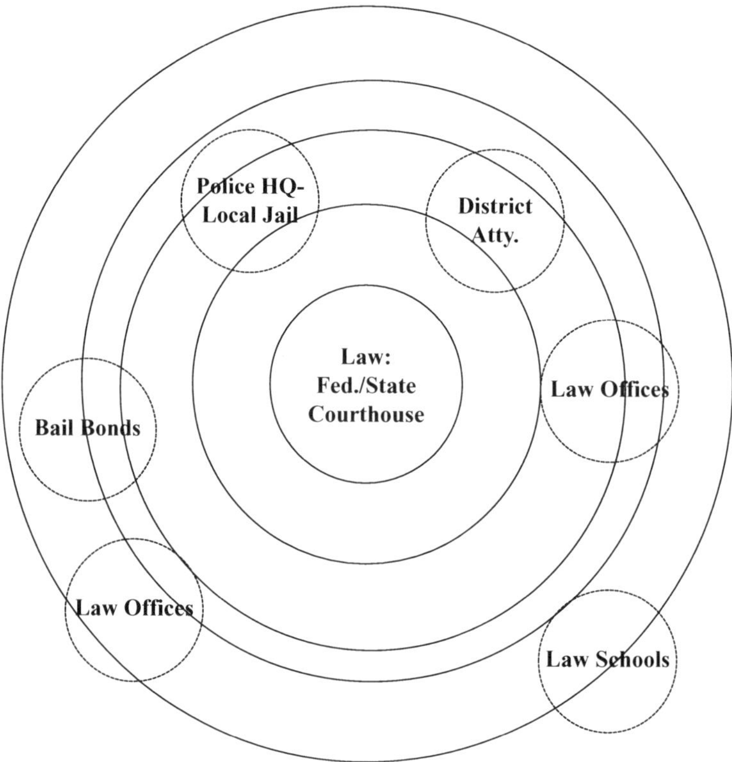

bailbondsmen, and, likely, a city hall or city office for the district attorney. Actors entering this zone are inundated with legal symbols cueing their actions and attitudes. And while there are numerous non-legal organizations like restaurants, cafes, convenient stores, apartments, and the like, these are invisible during legal hours as they are filled with legal actors talking "shop" or taking a temporary break from their official roles.

To be sure, no institutional space, no matter how autonomous, is an island unto itself. Figure 11.2 presents a complex, yet simplified, version of the legal example extended beyond its institutional boundaries. Beginning with the institutional core, we see double-sided arrows extending towards every space in the environment, denoting the flow of human, material, and symbolic (e.g., information) resources; additionally, many of these have their own connections with each other as resource flows across units. Some of these units, especially those on the top-right of the legal environment, have direct ties to the political sphere, including, in some cases, the core itself. The legal core, on the one hand, tests legislation, makes decisions that Congress must react to, and also has overlapping social relationships; conversely, on the other hand, legislation shapes court dockets, the President nominates judges that the Senate must approve, and some Congress persons were judges. Similar connections can be drawn between the police (who are an extension of the executive office), the district attorney (who work for the state or justice department), and law offices which are regulated by federal law and where many politicians come from or return to upon retirement or lost elections.

The rest of Fig. 11.2 is focused on the other institutional linkages. Bailbondsmen and lawyers act as *liaisons* between the legal sphere and the kinship sphere; helping shepherd normal people through the labyrinthine legal sphere; law offices,

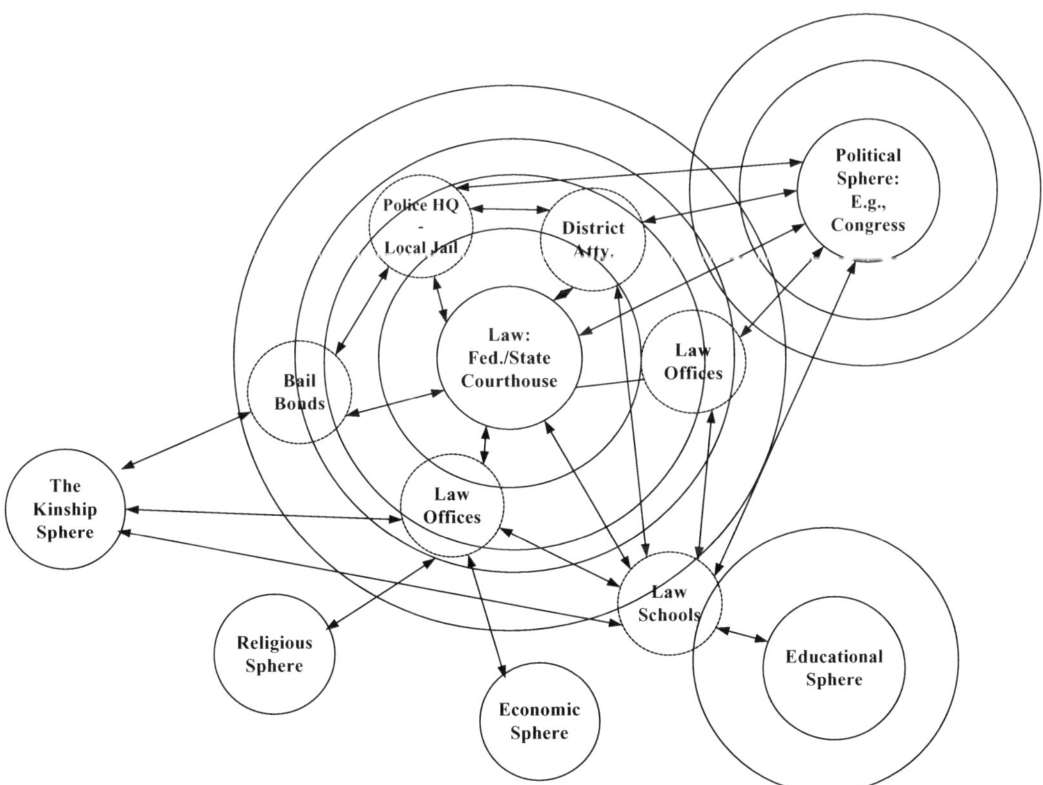

Fig. 11.2 Example of autonomous institutional sphere in institutional context

of course, also do the same for religious and economic actors, though in many cases, individual organizations have their own lawyers on retainer or entire legal departments devoted to interacting with the legal core. Law schools also act as liaisons, and key traffickers of human and symbolic resource mobility. Linking the educational sphere to the legal sphere, law schools produce lawyers for law offices and district attorneys; judges who have been professionalized within a legal sphere (who, like high profile lawyers, often return to their alma mater or some other prestigious school to teach later in their careers); and, of course, are shaped by federal laws for higher education, but also which produce clerks, campaign advisors, interns, and the like for politicians. To be sure, this model oversimplifies the much more complex social reality, and necessarily omits numerous "arrows" or resource flows for the sake of parsimony, while also highlighting the complex interplay between autonomous institutional spheres.

11.3.2.2 Micro Reality

At its most basic level, this briefest of ecological accounts matters at the micro-level. We can present several different propositions capturing how and why it manifests or translates into everyday, phenomenological reality (Abrutyn 2014b). First, being physically and/or cognitively closer to an autonomous institutional core means that actors are more likely to inhabit relationships, groups, and networks in which institution-specific roles and status positions will be routinely activated by intensive and/or extensive ties within institution-specific encounters; institution-specific resources act as means and ends of interaction patterns in said encounters; and, external mechanisms of control are visible, known, and easily administered. In short, the rule of proximity predicts probabilities with which actors will be repeatedly subject to the people, resources (as both things to pursue and things that are used in everyday life), and rules (both in terms of agents of control and sanctions) of a given institution and thus, their level of habituation, normative commitment, and the salience of their institutional identity.

Second, being closer and routinely subject to the institutional core's structural and cultural reality increases the likelihood that our feelings, thoughts, and actions will increasingly become aligned with those prescribed by entrepreneurs or the cultural system we internalize (Abrutyn 2014b; Abrutyn and Mueller 2015). At the social psychological level, this means that our self is more likely to merge with the role/status-position we find ourselves within the institutional sphere because of the intensive and extensive commitments, as well as the recurring rewards and punishments we earn (Turner 1978). As such, our institution-specific role-identity is more likely to be (a) *prominent* (McCall and Simmons 1978), (b) *salient* (Stryker 1980), (c) socioemotionally anchored to individuals, groups, and even systems (Chap. 8; also, Lawler et al. 2009), (d) restricted in its access to alternative institutional cores, (e) governed by institution-specific status beliefs (see Chap. 16) rooted in the institution-specific status hierarchy (Abrutyn 2014b), and, finally, (f) the central identity by which we measure our global self-esteem, efficacy, and worth (see Chap. 17).

Third, there is no need to turn to a Parsonsian (1951) view of the self and action that overemphasizes structure and underemphasizes culture. Indeed, the divisions of labor and other structural mechanisms of control are essential to understanding certain dynamics of core-environment ecology. Yet, I (2015b; also 2014b:121–146) have argued elsewhere that we can return to and rehabilitate the concept *generalized symbolic media* first present in Simmel's (1907) work on money and most prominent in Parsons' (1963) systems theory to explain how culture from the core comes to be an independent force in institutional life. Media are, in essence, the symbolic and material resources that denote institutional value and which constrain and facilitate feeling, thinking, and doing by acting as both means and ends deemed appropriate. Primarily, media manifest themselves in three ways: as (a) language and, more specifically, in the form of *themes of discourse* (Luhmann 2012) as well as the "forms" of actual talk (Abrutyn and Turner 2011) governing institutional communication; (b) the normative and cognitive-cultural framework and routines of social exchange—e.g., instrumental vs. moral; and (c) as external referents of value (Abrutyn 2015b), or the objects that signify to the possessor, user, pursuant, and audience the competence (Goffman 1967), authenticity (Alexander 2004), and status (Bourdieu 1991) institutionally prescribed. Taken together, these three axes allow for the embodiment of the macro-level into daily routines, mundane and ceremonial performances and rituals, and general encounters. Moreover, as Goffman's body of work suggests, as actors work to be better performers they increasingly become attached and committed to their roles as well as the situational spaces that allow them to "shine" the most. Hence, a professor who derives much of her self-esteem and worth from academic settings will be more likely to orient her emotions, attitudes, and actions to the educational-scientific spheres on a daily basis, while a legal actor will be more oriented towards the legal sphere. The more access to a particular generalized medium a person has access to, the more "fluent" and active he or she will be in the institution's cultural reality. Table 11.2 provides a list of common media and the institutional spheres they generally circulate within.

In many ways, this approach has strong parallels to the institutional logic perspective (Thornton et al. 2012), but we add several key wrinkles. First, while institutional logics remains rooted in the systems of modernity like capitalism, church, and state (Friedland and Alford 1991; Thornton et al. 2012), I take an evolutionary and historical view of economy, religion, and polity. Second, the model presented above remains committed to seeing institutions as real beyond just the beliefs and practices that folks adopt, conceptualizing their external presence in

Table 11.2 Generalized symbolic media of institutionalized domains

Kinship	**Love/loyalty**: language and external objects facilitating and constraining actions, exchanges, and communication rooted in positive affective states that build and denote commitments to others
Economy	**Money**: language and external objects related to actions, exchanges, and communication regarding the production and distribution of goods and services
Polity	**Power**: language and external objects facilitating and constraining actions, exchanges, and communication oriented towards making, enforcing, and securing assent for collective binding decisions and controlling emotions, actions, and attitudes of others
Law	**Justice/conflict resolution**: language and external objects facilitating and constraining actions, exchanges, and communication oriented towards mediating impersonal social relationships and invoking norms of fairness and morality
Religion	**Sacredness/piety**: language and external objects related to actions, exchanges, and communication with a non-observable supernatural realm
Education	**Learning/intelligence**: language and external objects related to actions, exchanges, and communication regarding the acquisition and transmission of material and cultural knowledge
Science	**Applied knowledge/truth**: language and external objects related to actions, exchanges, and communication founded on standards for gaining and using verified knowledge about all dimensions of the social, biotic, and physio-chemical universes
Medicine	**Health**: language and external objects related to actions, exchanges, and communication rooted in the concern about the commitment to sustaining the normal functioning of the body and mind
Sport	**Competitiveness**: language and external objects related to actions, exchanges, and communication embedded in regulated conflicts that produce winners and losers based on respective efforts of teams and players
Art	**Beauty**: language and external objects related to actions, exchanges, and communication founded on standards for gaining and using knowledge about beauty, affect, and pleasure

Note: These and other generalized symbolic media are employed in discourse among actors, in articulating themes, and in developing ideologies about what should and ought to transpire in an institutional domain. They tend to circulate within a domain, but all of the symbolic media can circulate in other domains, although some media are more likely to do so than others physical, temporal, social, and symbolic space. Third, as external referents or objects media allow us to recognize a very key aspect of culture: tangible things are as important as internalized values, embodied practices, or habituated norms because they are "out there" and can be touched, tasted, smelled, and seen. Humans are visual creatures and use objects to understand the universe. Culture externalized means culture that can be hoarded, pursued relentlessly, used deftly or clumsily, and sacralized into the totems Durkheim saw as so essential to group life.

11.3.3 Meso-Level Entrepreneurs

We are now in a position to return to the concept of entrepreneurship. Like most things in life, the macro and micro levels of social reality become realized in meso-level social units like groups, networks, and so forth. More specifically, it is at the meso-level within the ecological dynamics described above, that institutional change occurs. Some basic principles underscore this assertion. First, once autonomous, institutional spheres are subject to external and internal exigencies no different from any other group. While institutional spheres are by no means self-contained environments, the actors who derive the majority of their material and symbolic resources become subject to the same types of pressures associated with resource scarcity or challenges and threats to power and legitimacy. Entrepreneurs who carve out cores gain privilege and power and, like any interest group, work hard to protect and, in many cases, expand their influence over the institutional environment and across institutional boundaries (Abrutyn and Van Ness 2015). Second, while Weber's charismatic authority has been identified with individual traits, he (1968) was clear that the lasting consequences of an individual's impact on social structure and/or culture came not from the individual, but from the charismatic group charged with either propagating his ideas or succeeding him—see, for instance, Akhenaten's failed monotheistic revolution in the mid-second millennium BCE; institutional change, therefore, is driven by the routinization of charisma. Third, entrepreneurship does not come from nothing; it reflects relatively predictable patterns of ecological dynamics and how interests compete and conflict with each other based on positioning. Three particular sets of locations and entrepreneurs warrant our attention and deserve more systematic empirical elucidation.

11.3.3.1 Secondary Entrepreneurs

Weber's ideal type of bureaucracy rests on the tacit assumption of bounded rationality, stability, and taken for granted authority; characteristics reinforced by Michels' (1911 [1962]) "iron rule of oligarchy" and the tendency towards conservativism in bureaucracy and organization. Yet, contrary to these idyllic visions, history is littered with examples of "secondary" entrepreneurs, or actors close to the core—such as the district attorney's office in Fig. 11.1 above—whose primary function is to interact with non-core actors and core actors, facilitating the flow of resources both directions (Eisenstadt 1980). Thus, on the one hand these actors serve to support and reinforce the core and its entrepreneurs, yet on the other hand some fascinating institutional dynamics of contestation, conflict, and change are rooted in secondary elites.

Rueschemeyer (1986), for instance, cogently argued that most political change and instability came from secondary actors, as bureaucratic units do not always march in lockstep with their superiors; the latter of which come to depend on the former, and thus cede some power and authority. Moreover, secondary actors develop goals that transcend simple support: as a distinct corporate unit, they too become interested in survival as well as expansion of their influence. Hence, these ancillary goals are not always commensurate with efficiency or productivity. Furthermore, their unique position encourages the development of new worldviews, as well as positions them to resolve major or minor problems to further their interests (DiMaggio 1988), or because extant elites authorize them to resolve these problems and, therefore, increase their dependency on the secondary actors (Abrutyn 2014a).

11.3.3.2 Interstitial Liaisons

Arguably, the position with the greatest potential for future research is that of the *liaison*—see, for instance, lawyers and law schools in Figs. 11.1 and 11.2. In Luhmann's (2004) phenomenal work on the legal system, he argued that modern autonomous law resolved a key problem: by slowing down the adjudication of conflicts between parties, law used temporal differentiation to reduce the immediate passions on injustice and subject them to the rationalization found in procedural, formal justice. Reading this, I realized that lawyers were ideal types of liaisons. On the one hand, lawyers in autonomous legal spheres are professionalized and trained to be legal actors (Carlin 1980). As such, they "serve" the interest of the legal core in that they feel, think, and act in pursuit of *justice* and *conflict resolution* (Abrutyn 2009b). On the other hand, many lawyers serve the interests of non-legal actors, such as those who are either on retainer for particular religious or economic actors or, even more extreme, those who spend their careers serving a specific corporation (Dobbin and Sutton 1998). Hence, they are the actual collectives translating the problems and conflicts non-legal actors have into legal discourse in order to transform these religious or economic problems into legal problems that can be subjected to formal, procedural rationality and then they re-translate them into religious or economic language—that is, they explain the pragmatic impact judicial decisions have.

Liaisons, like secondary entrepreneurs, can become powerful forces of change or stasis. Because of their unique location, and ability to appeal to actors across varied institutional spheres, they can leverage their positions to innovate and carve out their own institutional space. Legal entrepreneurs during the Gregorian Reformation and leading up to the Protestant Reformation, played the Church and the various other classes (royal; aristocratic; urban; mercantile) against each other, and became an indispensable fulcrum with which these groups struggled against each other (Berman 1983). As such, they may be as responsible, if not more so, for the rise of the peculiar forms of western polity, religion, and economy that sociologists have spent so much time studying (Abrutyn 2009b, 2014b). Yet, they are also often stuck between two worlds, with little leverage, trying to protect their interests, and thus, acting conservatively. In Timmermans' (2006) ethnography of medical examiners, he brilliantly showed how the intersection of medicine (especially, the field deeply overlapping with science) and law constrained the decisions and thoughts of liaisons dealing with suspicious deaths.

11.3.3.3 Margins, Outsiders, and Radicalism

Though Eisenstadt (1984) rarely framed his thoughts on the Axial Age this way, he implied throughout his analysis that many of the religio-cultural entrepreneurs of the Axial Age emerged on the margins of existing cores (see also Humphreys 1975; Abrutyn 2014a, 2015a). In some cases, it was physical marginality, such as the Israelite prophets, priests, and scribes vis-à-vis the Assyrian, Babylonian, and Persian empires they were subjected to. Here, transportation and communication technologies limited the literal reach of each empire, despite political entrepreneurial strategies meant to mitigate these limitations. On the margins, monitoring and sanctioning is costly, and very often is the reason kings and empires collapse. In these relatively autonomous spaces, creativity is both an intrinsic activity born of fewer constraints as well as driven by threats from the distant core to restrict innovation and impose reality from without. But, Eisenstadt also shows how actors like the Confucian literati and the Buddhist-Brahmanic heterodoxy in India reflected *cognitive* marginality. That is, distance wasn't so much physical, but was far more about groups seeing the core as "alien" to a new set of organizational, symbolic, and normative frames of reality. In the modern world economy, we see these same types of marginal entrepreneurs in the various forms of religious radicalism across regions and across religions (Almond et al. 2003). In this case, the core is the modern world-system and it is a relatively autonomous polity and economy imposing "universal" culture and exploitative structure on local cultures in ways alien to traditional forms of kinship and religion. Hence, the dominant counter-ideologies, across cases, is a religio-kin traditionalism focused on particularism and fundamental values. Other examples of marginal actors can be found in Collins' (1981) geopolitical theory of "marcher" states or Chase-Dunn and Hall's (1997) similar idea of peripheral conquerors—both cases highlight the freedom to innovate militarily, organizationally, and symbolically in ways that make them swifter and stronger against city-states and empires that are too big to change rapidly.

11.4 Institutional Spheres in Four Dimensional Space

Besides further exploring and using entrepreneurs as means of introducing evolutionary accounts to historical methods, the cutting edge of institutional analysis finds itself in the four dimensional space—physical, temporal, social, and symbolic—that have become central to understanding how macro-level reality presents itself to people and affects their lives. Indeed, it is within each of these four dimensions that institutions make important cross-cutting linkages to other levels of analysis and substantive fields.

11.4.1 Physical Reality

Archaeologists have long recognized the importance of space and place, both in terms of size, scale, and differentiation; and place matters for political economy and, therefore, reverberates across other institutional spheres (Logan and Molotch 1988). Palaces were very often set upon a hill; built much larger and adorned with gaudier architecture than normal houses; surrounded by large courtyards to intensify the scale vis-à-vis the visitor; and, surrounded by walls that presented physical and cognitive barriers. Joyce (2000:71–2) remarks,

> By creating different kinds of space within sites, the continuing elaboration of monumental architecture served to create spatial arenas with restricted access, a constantly visible form of exclusivity [that had the double function of effecting] the patterns of habitual movement of all the inhabitants of the site, stratifying space and hence the people who were allowed access to different space, creating and marking centers and peripheries [and] permanently inscribed a small number of figures as actors linking the natural and supernatural world.

Physical space, then, becomes infused with meanings associated with patterns of behavior, role performances, temporal distinctions, activities and beliefs, and power/prestige differentials. To be sure, we often take for granted space, but it undoubtedly organizes reality for us, and often demarcates institutional space. This is especially clear when consider the physical construction of small towns where institutional space blurs together—e.g., city hall is next to the courthouse, the main church, and main street—and big cities where zones or districts emerge that differentiate the institutional activities (Abrutyn 2014b).

11.4.2 Temporal Reality

Sociologists have been slower to think about social structure in temporal terms, though clearly some have in abstract ways (Luhmann 2004). In short, temporality becomes important in three sorts of ways: (1) for compartmentalizing activities and orientations to reduce the complexity of role performances; (2) for sedimenting previous encounters into ritualized interactions that both reduce the need to produce culture completely anew and impose a sense of structure that guides interactions (Goffman 1967); and (3) as authoritative decisions made by one segment of institutional life reverberate and shape the reality of others. In each of these ways, time aids in the realization and manifestation of macro-level space. Sometimes it is in the cues that signal we are to reframe our identity performance to match the expectations of others, while other times it in the strain and conflicts that arise over the interstices of temporal institutional boundaries—e.g., when, not where, does the economic institution (e.g., work) end and the kinship institution begin? These are not individually based conflicts, though each person may experience them uniquely.

Rather, they become known sites of contestation, resistance, and struggle. Of the four dimensions, however, temporality demands the most future research.

11.4.3 Social Reality

Conversely, the institutional differentiation of social space has been well documented, ranging from research on role differentiation (Freidson 1962), group differentiation (Merton 1967), organizational differentiation (Blau 1970), and categoric differentiation (cf. Chap. 16 of this volume). Moreover, the division of labor is central to the classics. If there is any frontier here, is finding ways to empirically link the macro-level to the level of identity, self, and status. Social psychology assumes this link exists (; Fine 1991; Burke 2006), while some of my work on ecology explicitly highlights potential testable propositions that could bring the two into closer dialogue.

11.4.4 Symbolic Reality

One of the more exciting areas of institutional research is in the cultural and symbolic aspects of institutions that Parsons' left quite flat and unsatisfactory. The institutional logics perspective, for example, has worked to create ways of measuring specific logics, such as *love* and the way it shapes the practices and beliefs of real people (Friedland et al. 2014). The idea of a "logic," has its roots in the concept *generalized symbolic media*; a concept, unfortunately and unfairly, linked to Parsonsian (1963) functionalism. Its use, as noted above, predates Parsons in Simmel's (1907) work on *money* transforming the economy and economic relations and Mauss' (1967) and Levi-Strauss' (1969) respective work on non-economic media of exchange. As noted above (see Table 11.2), I have added numerous media to account for the number of autonomous institutional spheres. Like logics, media are vehicles of culture; unlike logics, media "circulate" along the many structural connections, are unevenly distributed like Bourdieuian capital, and are not merely "cognitive" things, but linguistic (themes; texts) (Luhmann 1995) *and* present in physical objects that act as referents of value (Abrutyn 2014b, 2015b). The latter is a major difference between the functionalist and the institutional logics program, and my own read on institutional spheres. In part, as value adheres in actual objects, the institution and commitment to the role-identity and status position one accesses the institution become powerful forces: objects are tangible, can be touched, hoarded, gazed longingly, monopolized, and provide sensual pleasure in their ownership and use. *Money* is not just a medium that regulates exchanges, then, it is also a language embedded in texts, themes of discourse, strategies mobilized in speech and performance *and* a set of objects—coins, cars, etc. It can be displayed or relegated to special places and rituals that reinforce its importance to the person's identity and, perhaps, global self. Same with *love*, *sacredness*, and *knowledge*—all of these media can be transformed into referents of value which are signs to the owner and the audience of the person's institutional self, their status, the expectations one might have of them, the obligations they have for themselves, and so forth.

11.5 Conclusion

The study of institutions has a long, rich history with sociology, and has become increasingly important to political science (Evans 1995) and economics (North 1990, 2005; Nee 2005). Yet, like culture (see Chap. 6 in this volume), it is one of the hardest concepts to nail down because it is used in so many different ways. While debatable, institutions were presented above as the major macro-level structural and cultural spheres of social reality such as polity, religion, or economy. They are constituted by meso-level social units like groups or organizations, micro-level units like encounters and identities, and cross-cut by global and situational stratification systems. While systems and subsystems, in the Parsonsian or Luhmannian traditions, are often overly abstract in their conceptualization, it was further argued above that institutional spheres, as they grow autonomous, carve up physical, temporal, social, and symbolic reality in ways that *impose*, external to the person, institutional reality. While individuals may not be fully conscious of this, the fact that ordinary people reify these spheres by talking about "the law," or "religion," or "economy," as entities that act collectively and beyond their control indicates just how powerful a force these spheres have on people's everyday reality.

A vibrant, and more empirically grounded, macrosociology becomes possible when we start to reconceptualize institutional spheres as such. Logics and media are created by elites, perpetuated by "canonical" texts, experts, routines, and the differentiation of those four dimensions of space, and, they circulate along structural connections that are infused with meaning by the pursuit, acquisition, and use of these media in linguistic, ideational, and physical forms. Institutional analysis, as Weber recognized under a different terminology, also offers much for an historical comparative sociology, as we can examine the synchronic or diachronic variation of a sphere or set of spheres, their autonomy, and the consequences across time and space. Either way, taking institutional spheres serious in sociological theory and research is important if we are to create the most robust and comprehensive conceptualization of the social world possible.

References

Abrutyn, S. (2009a). *A general theory of institutional autonomy.* Ph.D. dissertation, Department of Sociology, University of California, Riverside.

Abrutyn, S. (2009b). Toward a general theory of institutional autonomy. *Sociological Theory, 27*(4), 449–465.

Abrutyn, S. (2013a). Political evolution, entrepreneurship, and autonomy: Causes and consequences of an "Axial" moment. *Research in Political Sociology, 21*, 3–29.

Abrutyn, S. (2013b). Reconceptualizing religious evolution: Toward a general theory of macro-institutional change. *Social Evolution and History, 12*(2), 5–36.

Abrutyn, S. (2013c). Reconceptualizing the dynamics of religion as a macro-institutional domain. *Structure and Dynamics, 6*(3), 1–21.

Abrutyn, S. (2014a). Religious autonomy and religious entrepreneurship: An evolutionary-institutionalist's take on the axial age. *Comparative Sociology, 13*(2), 105–134.

Abrutyn, S. (2014b). *Revisiting institutionalism in sociology: Putting the "Institution" back in institutional analysis*. New York: Routledge.

Abrutyn, S. (2015a). The institutional evolution of religion: Innovation and entrepreneurship in ancient Israel. *Religion, 45*(4), 505–531.

Abrutyn, S. (2015b). Money, love, and sacredness: Generalized symbolic media and the production of instrumental, affectual, and moral reality. *Czech Sociological Review, 51*(3), 445–471.

Abrutyn, S., & Lawrence, K. (2010). From chiefdoms to states: Toward an integrative theory of the evolution of polity. *Sociological Perspectives, 53*(3), 419–442.

Abrutyn, S., & Mueller, A. S. (2014). Reconsidering Durkheim's assessment of tarde: Formalizing a tardian theory of imitation, contagion, and suicide suggestion. *Sociological Forum, 29*(3), 698–719.

Abrutyn, S., & Mueller, A. S. (2015). When Too much integration and regulation hurt: Re envisioning Durkheim's altruistic suicide. *Society and Mental Health*. doi:10.1177/2156869315604346.

Abrutyn, S., & Turner, J. H. (2011). The old institutionalism meets the new institutionalism. *Sociological Perspectives, 54*(3), 283–306.

Abrutyn, S., & Van Ness, J. (2015). The role of agency in sociocultural evolution: Institutional entrepreneurship as a force of structural and cultural transformation. *Thesis Eleven, 127*(1), 52–77.

Alexander, J. C. (1988). *Durkheimian sociology: Cultural studies*. Cambridge: Cambridge University Press.

Alexander, J. C. (2004). Cultural pragmatics: Social performance between ritual and strategy. *Sociological Theory, 22*(4), 527–573.

Alford, R. R., & Friedland, R. (1985). *Powers of theory: Capitalism, the state, and democracy*. Cambridge: Cambridge University Press.

Almond, G. A., Appleby, R. S., & Sivan, E. (2003). *Strong religion: The rise of fundamentalism around the world.* Chicago: University of Chicago Press.

Bellah, R. N. (1964). Religious evolution. *American Sociological Review, 29*(3), 358–374.

Berman, H. J. (1983). *Law and revolution: The formation of the western legal tradition*. Cambridge, MA: Harvard University Press.

Blau, P. M. (1970). A formal theory of differentiation in organizations. *American Sociological Review, 35*(2), 201–218.

Blute, M. (2010). *Darwinian sociocultural evolution: Solutions to dilemmas in cultural and social theory*. Cambridge: Cambridge University Press.

Boli, J., Ramirez, F., & Meyer, J. W. (1985). Explaining the origins and expansion of mass education. *Comparative Education Review, 29*(2), 145–170.

Bourdieu, P. (1989). Social space and symbolic power. *Sociological Theory, 7*(1), 14–25.

Bourdieu, P. (1991). *Language and symbolic power* (G. Raymond, & M. Adamson, Trans.). Cambridge, MA: Harvard University Press.

Bourdieu, P. (1993). *The field of cultural production: Essays on art and literature*. New York: Columbia University Press.

Burke, K. (1989). *On symbols and society*. Chicago: University of Chicago Press.

Burke, P. J. (Ed.). (2006). *Contemporary social psychological theories*. Stanford: Stanford University Press.

Carlin, J. E. (1980). Lawyers' ethics. In W. M. Evan (Ed.), *The sociology of Law: A social-structural perspective* (pp. 257–267). New York: The Free Press.

Chase-Dunn, C., & Hall, T. D. (1997). *Rise and demise: Comparing world-systems*. Boulder: Westview Press.

Collins, R. (1981). Long-term social change and the territorial power of states. In *Sociology since midcentury* (pp. 71–108). New York: Free Press.

Collins, R. (1986). *Weberian sociological theory*. Cambridge: Cambridge University Press.

Davis, K., & Moore, W. E. (1945). Some principles of social stratification. *American Sociological Review, 10*(2), 242–249.

DiMaggio, P. (1988). Interest and agency in institutional theory. In L. G. Zucker (Ed.), *Institutional patterns and organizations* (pp. 3–22). Cambridge, MA: Ballinger.

DiMaggio, P., & Powell, W. W. (1983). The iron cage revisited: Institutional isomorphism and collective rationality in organizational fields. *American Sociological Review, 48*(2), 147–160.

Dobbin, F., & Sutton, J. R. (1998). The strength of a weak state: The rights revolution and the rise of human resources management divisions. *American Journal of Sociology, 104*(2), 441–476.

Durkheim, E. (1893). *The division of labor in society* (W. D. Halls, Trans.). New York: The Free Press.

Durkheim, E. (1895 [1982]). *The rules of sociological method and selected texts on sociology and its method* (W. D. Halls, Trans., 1st American ed.). New York: Free Press.

Edelman, L. B., & Suchman, M. C. (1997). The legal environments of organizations. *Annual Review of Sociology, 23*, 479–515.

Eisenstadt, S. N. (1963). *The political system of empires: The rise and fall of the historical bureaucratic societies*. New York: Free Press.

Eisenstadt, S. N. (1964). Social change, differentiation and evolution. *American Sociological Review, 29*(3), 375–386.

Eisenstadt, S. N. (1980). Cultural orientations, institutional entrepreneurs, and social change: Comparative analysis of traditional civilizations. *American Journal of Sociology, 85*(4), 840–869.

Eisenstadt, S. N. (1984). Heterodoxies and dynamics of civilizations. *American Philosophical Society, 128*(2), 104–113.

Evans, P. (1995). *Embedded autonomy: States and industrial formation*. Princeton: Princeton University Press.

Fine, G. A. (1991). On the macrofoundations of microsociology: Constraint and the exterior reality of structure. *The Sociological Quarterly, 32*(2), 161–177.

Fligstein, N., & McAdam, D. (2011). Toward a general theory of strategic action fields. *Sociological Theory, 29*(1), 1–27.

Fox, R. (1967). *Kinship and marriage: An anthropological perspective*. London: Cambridge University Press.

Freidson, E. (1962). Dilemmas in doctor-patient relationships. In A. M. Rose (Ed.), *Human behavior and social processes* (pp. 207–224). Boston: Houghton Mifflin Company.

Friedland, R., & Alford, R. R. (1991). Bringing society back in: Symbols, practices, and institutional contradictions. In W. W. Powell & P. J. DiMaggio (Eds.), *The new institutionalism in organizational analysis* (pp. 232–266). Chicago: The University of Chicago Press.

Friedland, R., Mohr, J. W., Roose, H., & Gardinali, P. (2014). An institutional logic for love: Measuring intimate life. *Theory and Society, 43*(3–4), 333–370.

Goffman, E. (1967). *Interaction ritual: Essays on face-to-face behavior*. New York: Pantheon Books.

Gospic, K., Mohlin, E., Fransson, P., Petrovic, P., Johannesson, M., & Ingvar, M. (2011). Limbic justice – Amygdala involvement in immediate rejection in the ultimatum game. *PLoS Biology, 9*(5), e1001054. doi:10.1371/journal.pbio.1001054. doi:1001010.1001371/journal.pbio.1001054.

Hannan, M. T., & Freeman, J. (1977). The population ecology of organizations. *American Journal of Sociology, 82*(5), 929–964.

Hawley, A. H. (1986). *Human ecology: A theoretical essay*. Chicago: University of Chicago Press.

Hoebel, E. A. (1973). *The Law of primitive Man*. New York: Antheneum.

Humphreys, S. C. (1975). "Transcendence" and intellectual roles: The ancient Greek case. *Daedalus, 104*(2), 91–118.

Jepperson, R. L. (1991). Institutions, institutional effects, and institutionalism. In W. W. Powell & P. J. DiMaggio (Eds.), *The new institutionalism of organizational analysis* (pp. 143–163). Chicago: The University of Chicago Press.

Johnson, A. W., & Earle, T. (2000). *The evolution of human societies: From foraging groups to agrarian state*. Stanford: Stanford University Press.

Joyce, R. A. (2000). High culture, Mesoamerican civilization, and the classic Maya tradition. In J. Richards & M. Van Buren (Eds.), *Order, legitimacy, and wealth in ancient states* (pp. 64–76). Cambridge: Cambridge University Press.

Lawler, E. J., Thye, S., & Yoon, J. (2009). *Social commitments in a depersonalized world*. New York: Russell Sage.

Lenski, G. (1966). *Power and privilege: A theory of social stratification*. New York: McGraw-Hill.

Levi-Strauss, C. (1969). *The elementary structures of Kinship* (J. H. Bell, J. R. von Strumer, & R. Needhan, Trans.). Boston: Beacon Press.

Logan, J. R., & Molotch, H. L. (1988). *Urban fortunes: The political economy of place*. Berkeley: The University of California Press.
Luhmann, N. (1995). *Social systems* (J. Bednarz Jr., & D. Baecker, Trans.). Stanford: Stanford University Press.
Luhmann, N. (2000). *Art as a social system* (E. M. Knodt, Trans.). Stanford: Stanford University Press.
Luhmann, N. (2004). *Law as a social system* (K. A. Ziegert, Trans.). Oxford: Oxford University Press.
Luhmann, N. (2012). *Theory of society* (B. Rhodes, Trans., Vol. I). Stanford: Stanford University Press.
Malinowski, B. (1959). *Crime and custom in savage society*. Paterson: Littlefield, Adams, and Co.
Mauss, M. (1967). *The gift: Forms and functions of exchange in archaic societies*. New York: W. W. Norton.
Mayr, E. (2001). *What evolution is*. New York: Basic Books.
McCall, G. J., & Simmons, J. L. (1978). *Identities and interactions*. New York: Free Press.
Merton, R. K. (1967). *Social theory and social structure* (9th ed.). New York: Free Press.
Meyer, J. W., & Rowan, B. (1977). Institutionalized organizations: Formal structure as myth and ceremony. *American Journal of Sociology, 83*(2), 340–363.
Michels, R. (1911 [1962]). *Political parties: A sociological study of the oligarchical tendencies of modern democracy* (E. Paul, & C. Paul, Trans.). New York: Free Press.
Nee, V. (2005). The new institutionalisms in economics and sociology. In N. J. Smelser & R. Swedberg (Eds.), *The handbook of economic sociology* (2nd ed., pp. 49–74). Princeton: Princeton University Press.
North, D. C. (1990). *Institutions, institutional change, and economic performance*. Cambridge: Cambridge University Press.
North, D. C. (2005). Capitalism and economic growth. In V. Nee & R. Swedberg (Eds.), *The economic sociology of capitalism* (pp. 41–52). Princeton: Princeton University Press.
Parsons, T. (1951). *The social system*. Glencoe: Free Press.
Parsons, T. (1963). On the concept of political power. *Proceedings of the American Philosophical Society, 107*(3), 232–262.
Parsons, T. (1966). *Societies: Evolutionary and comparative perspectives*. Englewood Cliffs: Prentice-Hall.
Powell, W. W., & DiMaggio, P. J. (1991). *The new institutionalism in organizational analysis*. Chicago: The University of Chicago Press.
Radin, P. (1937 [1957]). *Primitive religion: Its nature and origin*. New York: Dover.
Rueschemeyer, D. (1986). *Power and the division of labour*. Stanford: Stanford University Press.
Sahlins, M. (1972). *Stone Age economics*. New York: Aldine.
Scott, W. R. (2001). *Institutions and organizations*. Thousand Oaks: Sage.
Shils, E. A. (1975). *Center and periphery: Essays in macrosociology*. Chicago: University of Chicago Press.
Simmel, G. (1907). *The philosophy of money*. Boston: Routledge & Kegan Paul.
Spencer, H. (1897). *The principles of sociology* (Vol. I–III). New York: Appleton.
Starr, P. (1982). *The social transformation of American medicine: The rise of the sovereign profession and the making of a vast industry*. New York: Basic Books.
Stryker, S. (1980). *Symbolic interactionism: A social structural version*. Menlo Park: The Benjamin Cummings Publishing Company.
Sutton, J. R., & Dobbin, F. (1996). The two faces of governance: Responses to legal uncertainty in U.S. Firms, 1955 to 1985. *American Sociological Review, 61*(5), 794–811.
Sutton, J., Dobbin, F., Meyer, J. W., & Scott, W. R. (1994). The legalization of the workplace. *American Journal of Sociology, 99*(4), 944–971.
Thomas, G. M., Meyer, J. W., Ramirez, F. O., & Boli, J. (1987). *Institutional structure: Constituting state, society, and the individual*. Newbury Park: Sage.
Thornton, P. H., Ocasio, W., & Lounsbury, M. (2012). *The institutional logics perspective: A New approach to culture, structure, and process*. New York: Oxford University Press.
Timmermans, S. (2006). *Postmortem: How medical examiners explain suspicious deaths*. Chicago: University of Chicago Press.
Turner, R. H. (1978). The role and the person. *American Journal of Sociology, 84*(1), 1–23.
Turner, J. H. (1985). *Herbert Spencer: A renewed appreciation*. Beverly Hills: Sage.
Turner, J. H. (2003). *Human institutions: A theory of societal evolution*. Lanham: Bowman & Littlefield Publishers.
Turner, J. H. (2010). *Theoretical principles of sociology, volume 1: Macrodynamics*. New York: Springer.
Turner, J. H. (2011). *Theoretical principles of sociology, volume 3: Mesodynamics*. New York: Springer.
Weber, M. (1946). Science as a vocation. In H. Gerth & C. W. Mills (Eds.), *From Max Weber: Essays in sociology* (pp. 129–156). New York: Oxford University Press.
Weber, M. (1968). *Max Weber on charisma and institution building*. Chicago: University of Chicago Press.
Yoffee, N. (2005). *Myths of the archaic state: Evolution of the earliest cities, states, and civilizations*. Cambridge: Cambridge University Press.

Stratification

12

Katja M. Guenther*, Matthew C. Mahutga*, and Panu Suppatkul

12.1 Introduction

The study of social inequalities has been central to the discipline of sociology since its beginnings. Sociology emerged after the Enlightenment era and during the upheavals of the industrial revolution in Europe and the United States, which together drew attention to social cleavages and the capacity to analyze them. Karl Marx and Max Weber, whose social theories were central to the emergence of sociology, were both deeply interested in class inequalities, and W. E. B. DuBois, one of the most influential early American sociologists, sought to draw attention to racial inequalities. Most generally, inequality and stratification refer to the unequal distribution of or access to resources or social goods in a society. Such goods most centrally include income and wealth, but also less tangible, yet also important, goods like power and status. Inequality directly affects every aspect of our lives: our health, educational opportunities, workplaces, families, and safety. It thus should be no surprise that the study of inequality continues to be so important to sociologists.

Some sociological conventions reserve the term "inequality" for explanations that evoke ascriptive social categories of people (e.g., race and gender) to explain unequal distributions of (or access to) resources. Other conventions similarly reserve the term "stratification" to describe explanations for unequal distributions that focus upon various notions of class, which includes studies of class hierarchy, inter-generational mobility, occupational prestige and wages, etc. It is increasingly apparent that contemporary sociological examinations are eroding this conceptual distinction between "inequality" and "stratification" by developing explanations at the intersection of class with race and gender inequalities. For example, the newer American Sociological Association section on *Inequality, Poverty and Mobility* includes members who focus on multiple and overlapping explanations that could include race, gender, and class, as well as organizational and institutional processes transcending each of these categories.

Theories of stratification can be categorized in many ways, but the most core difference between theories is whether a theory seeks to understand inequality at the macro level or at the micro level. In this chapter, we focus on macro theories—including theories of global inequality—while attending to how they inform our understanding of micro processes. We begin with a review of theories of stratification between and within countries. The between-country question asks

*Author contributed equally with all other contributors.

K.M. Guenther (✉) • M.C. Mahutga
P. Suppatkul
University of California, Riverside, Riverside, CA, USA
e-mail: katja.guenther@ucr.edu; matthew.mahutga@ucr.edu; psupp001@ucr.edu

S. Abrutyn (ed.), *Handbook of Contemporary Sociological Theory*, Handbooks of Sociology and Social Research, DOI 10.1007/978-3-319-32250-6_12

why some countries are so much richer than others, the answers to which vary from circumstantial differences in the timing of major technological advances to the enrichment of some nations at the expense of others through historically varying forms of coercion. The within-country question—the one most addressed by sociological approaches to stratification—instead asks why some *people* are rich, while others struggle to survive, given their national context. As we describe below, these answers vary from those that treat inequality as the outcome of political and economic processes to those that focus instead upon categorical attributes like class, gender, and race or the types of institutions that prevail in a given country.

We conclude by identifying what we see as key problems to be addressed in the sociology of stratification. First, there is a divide between those who contend that contemporary patterns of stratification are the result of the historical accumulation of patterned deprivations, and those who argue instead that stratification results from behavior that is patterned by discriminatory ideas. Second, we suggest that perhaps a grand sociological theory of stratification with endogenously determined macro and micro dynamics is both overly ambitious and unnecessary. Instead, sociologists may make better progress by focusing on the ways in which the stratifying effect of macro-level dynamics are conditional upon stratification processes at the micro level, and on the ways in which micro-level dynamics are in turn conditional on aggregate levels of material inequality.

12.2 The Wealth and Poverty of Nations

In the twenty-first century, the vast majority of all of the material (i.e., income) inequality in the world lies between countries. Studies examining data from the 1950s through the 1990s, for example, find that between country inequality accounts for somewhere in the range of 65–86% of all world income inequality, though these statistics are hotly contested (see Berry et al. 1991; Goesling 2001; Korzeniewicz and Moran 1997; Milanovic 2002; Schultz 1998; Theil 1979; Whalley 1979). From a historical perspective, however, large material inequalities across countries are relatively new. As recently as the early seventeenth century C.E, the difference in wealth between the "richest" and "poorest" countries of the world was probably no greater than 3:1 (Jolly 2006). However, beginning in the early 1800s, the world witnessed what has been referred to as the "great divergence"—the rapid expansion in material prosperity among a very small subset of the world's population.

The great divergence has been explained in two distinct ways: 1) the geographical concentration of technological advancements associated with the industrial revolution among a handful of Western European countries, and 2) the colonization of most of the non-European world by Western European powers. We consider each of these in turn, as these two explanations in some ways foreshadow theories of stratification more generally.

There is no denying that the timing of the great divergence coincides roughly with the industrial revolution. And there is little doubt that the industrial revolution mattered for the great divergence: if Great Britain doubles the productivity of its labor force and everyone else does not, *ceteris paribus*, Great Britain will grow faster than everyone else. That is, the industrial revolution contributed to the great divergence through technology that increased rapidly the productivity of economic activity in places where it occurred. Because these technological advancements were spatially concentrated, first in Great Britain, then in other parts of Western Europe, and only much later spread to European colonies, the European continent experienced an extended period of much more rapid economic growth.

To see how the aiding of labor with capital can dramatically boost productivity and thereby national income, consider the now classic "Cobb-Douglas" production function:

$$Y = AL^{\beta} K^{\alpha} \tag{12.1}$$

In (12.1), Yis national output, A is technology, K is capital and L is labor. β and α are "elasticity" coefficients (weights) determined by the sophistication of available technology. To see how this affects per capita national income (proxied by per worker output), we can manipulate (12.1) algebraically by dividing by labor throughout:

$$\frac{Y}{L} = \frac{A^{1-\beta}}{L} \frac{K^{\alpha-\beta}}{L} \quad (12.2)$$

What is clear from Eq. 12.2 is that, holding the supply of labor constant, per-worker national income increases multiplicatively with an increase in technology, and it does so by increasing the productivity of labor. Thus, the concentration of technology emerging from the industrial revolution in Western Europe can go a long way in explaining the great divergence.

However, we also know that industrialization did not occur in a vacuum. One of the earliest observers—and critics—of industrial capitalism in Great Britain, Karl Marx, argued that the British industrial capitalist must be understood not as a product of the slow accumulation of wealth through frugality and hard work (e.g., Weber 1930 [2001]), but rather as a benefactor of force and plunder:

> The discovery of gold and silver in America, the extirpation, enslavement and entombment in mines of the aboriginal population, the beginning of the conquest and looting of the East Indies, the turning of Africa into a warren for the commercial hunting of black-skins, signalised the rosy dawn of the era of capitalist production (Marx 1867 [1967]: 751).

Marx's point in this quote and in the chapter in which it appears is threefold. First, the capitalist mode of production would not have been possible absent an accumulation of capital that occurred before the capitalist mode of production. Second, the political success of industrial capitalism was financed by colonization. Third, historically, colonization expanded in lock step with the advance of industrial capitalism. Colonization thus matters for the great divergence in two important respects. First, colonization may have created a pre-existing level of wealth in Great Britain that made the industrial revolution possible, financed the political ascendance of the industrial capitalist in Great Britain, and, by facilitating the import of cheap intermediate inputs and expanding markets abroad, continued to boost the growth of Western Europe *at least* through the period of decolonization in the post WWII period.

Colonization also mattered for the great divergence in how it affected development among colonies and former colonies. Nevertheless, what matters from the large and rich literature on colonization for our discussion here is that colonization was an active form of stratification, insofar as the developmental trajectories of colonies were heavily influenced by the direct action of colonizers. The long list of deleterious effects of colonization includes mechanisms such as the establishment of outward-oriented economies (Bunker 1985; Chase-Dunn 1998), the inculcation of dependent trade relations between colonies and colonizers (Galtung 1971), the imposition of colonial institutions (Lange et al. 2006), cultural destruction, and the creation and maintenance of a native elite with interests tied to colonial administrators, among others. Processes such as these not only hindered the development of good governance institutions from within, but also represented forms of exploitation whereby economic relations between colonizer and colony enhanced the former at the expense of the latter (Hochschild 1999).

After the end of formal colonization, many suggest that Western states and capitalists engage in neo-colonialism by reasserting their control via indirect ways that include a disproportionate influence on transnational governance institutions like the International Monetary Fund (IMF), World Bank (WB) and the World Trade Organization (WTO) (Milanovic 2005), by engaging in foreign direct investment (Chase-Dunn 1975), and by military aggression. Early analysts of economic globalization very much analyzed it through the lens of neo-colonialism, but changes in the trajectory of between-country inequality have problematized that lens.

While between-country inequality remains "high" by historical standards, the last few decades have witnessed a *declining trend* in between-country inequality (Clark 2011; Firebaugh 2003; c.f. Milanovic 2005; Dowrick and Akmal 2005). While some point to this trend to draw inferences about the efficacy of international institutions (e.g., UN development goals) or the international dynamics of the world capitalist system (Korzienwicz and Moran 1997 c.f. Firebaugh 2000), the underlying driver of the declining trend belies such inferences. This is because measured levels of between-country inequality are driven by two components: average income differences between countries and population size. Two of the fastest growing countries over the last several decades are China and India, which together account for roughly 36 % of the world's population. Because the declining trend in between-country inequality is driven by China and India's rapid economic growth, and because China and India's rapid economic growth is exceptional vis-à-vis the rest of the less-developed world, one cannot draw much in the way of theoretical insight from the trend. Indeed, recent evidence suggests that if China and India maintain their trajectories of rapid economic growth, between-country inequality will rise again (Hung and Kucinskas 2011). Paralleling the declining trend in between-country inequality, however, is a rising trend in within country inequality, a subject to which we now turn.

12.3 Within Country Inequality

12.3.1 General Theories

If one begins with the thought experiment that all of the income inequality in the world can be decomposed into a component that lies between countries and a component that lies within countries, it's easy to see that most inequality in the world lies between countries. However, a transition occurred since the late twentieth century, namely a marked rise in within-country stratification. Particularly notable in some western industrialized nations, such as the United States, is the increasing concentration of wealth among a very small percentage of the population.

Societies divided into the "have a lots" and the "have nots" raise a number of important theoretical questions, including why income inequality is so persistent across generations, what the consequences of inequality are for individuals, groups, and societies, and what role, if any, states can play in reducing income inequalities. Figure 12.1 displays the Gini coefficient of income inequality among 14 advanced capitalist country from 1960 to 2010. The Gini coefficient is a statistical measure of income distribution within a country; a value of 0 indicates equality and a value of 1 complete inequality. As a basis for comparison, Fig. 12.1 also reports the average Gini for this group. These data come from Fred Solt's *Standardized World Income Inequality Database* (SWIID) (Solt 2009). What is clear from a casual inspection of Fig. 12.1 is both that income inequality generally began to rise during the 1980s after a period of decline, but also that the level of inequality is much higher in some countries than others.

In what follows, we consider explanations for both the rising trend in inequality commonly observed among advanced capitalist countries since the 1980s, as well as explanations for the large inequality differences that remain between these countries. That is, we consider inequality increasing processes that are common to all these countries, as well as inequality reducing processes that are more common in some of them than others.

12.3.2 Economic Development, the Kuznets Curve, and the "Great U-turn"

Perhaps the most well-known theory about the causes of income inequality within countries comes from work done by Simon Kuznets during the 1950s. Kuznets (1955) set out to theorize the relationship between income inequality and economic development. What was central to Kuznets' understanding was that labor force migrations from agriculture to industry over the course of development is the key driver of the level of inequality. In agrarian (i.e., less developed) societies, the majority of the labor force works in the agricultural sector, where wages are low and uniform. During the period of industrialization, however, the labor force gradually

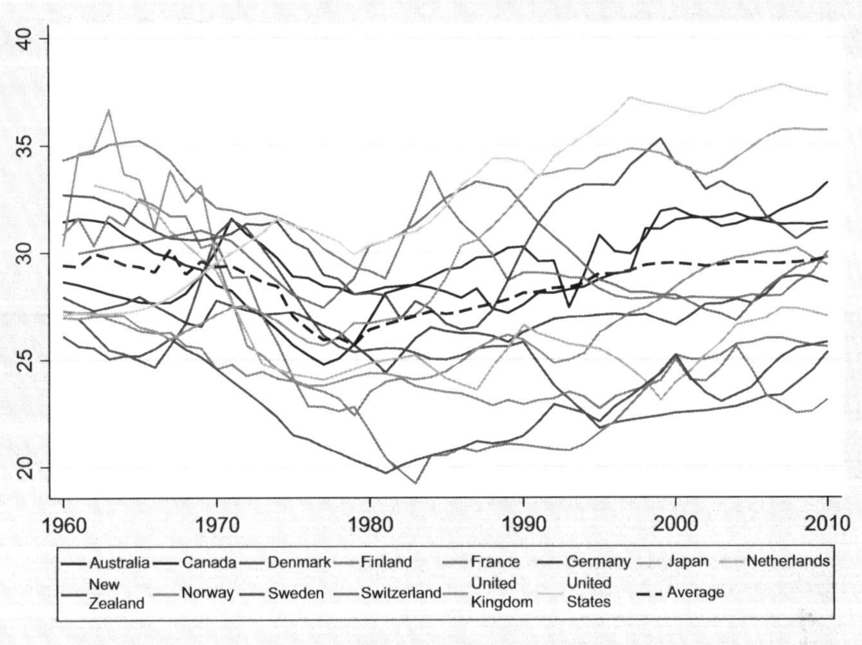

Fig. 12.1 Income inequality trends among advanced capitalist countries

migrates from agriculture to industry (or manufacturing), where wages are much higher. This creates a wage gap between the agricultural and industrial sectors that increases inequality proportionately to the share of the labor force in each sector. After a certain point, inequality begins to fall as the percentage of the population residing in the industrial sector becomes large enough that the wage gap between agriculture and industry contributes a dwindling amount of variation to the whole income distribution. The dynamic relationship between development and inequality hypothesized by Kuznets is displayed in Fig. 12.2, which depicts a rising and then falling inequality trend over the course of development.

Sociological inequality theorists have added two components to the basic Kuznets model. Beginning with Nielsen (1994), sociologists began to recognize that the demographic transition is also a prominent social change over the course of economic development. A combination of factors including low survival probabilities, declining death rates, high demand for household and agricultural labor, a low status for women, etc., combine to produce rapid population growth in less developed countries. In turn, rapid population growth expands the young, non-earning members of the population, who occupy the low end of the income distribution. As countries develop, the demand for household and agricultural labor declines, whereas the status of women, the proportion of the population living in cities, and access to contraception generally increase. In combination, these and other factors slow population growth and thereby shrink the proportion of the population occupying the low-end of the income distribution. The second added factor is the spread of education, which tends to reduce the wage premium for skilled workers. That is, as educational skills become less scarce, the financial rewards associated with skills decline.

There is much empirical support for this general theory of the relationship between income inequality and economic development. This includes the observation of a non-linear u shaped relationship between measures of economic development (e.g., GDP per capita) and income inequality, where middle-income countries have the highest level of inequality. This also includes cross-sectional and panel-levels studies showing

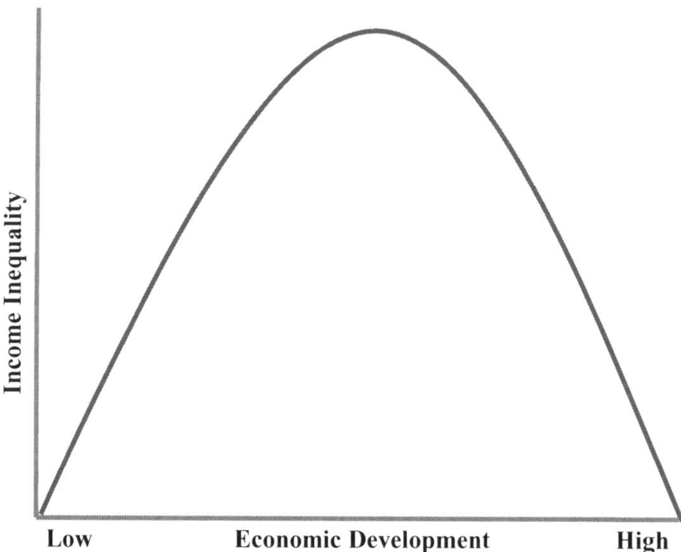

Fig. 12.2 The Kuznets curve

that the percent of the labor force in agriculture lowers income inequality, "sector dualism" (a measure of the dispersion of wages between the agriculture and manufacturing sectors) increases inequality, population growth increases inequality and secondary education enrollments reduce inequality (e.g., Nielsen 1994; Nielsen and Alderson 1997; Alderson and Nielsen 1999; c.f. Alderson and Nielsen 2002).

Thus, while this general theory of the relationship between economic development and income inequality is not without critics, the Kuznets curve created something of a paradox for scholars of inequality among advanced capitalist countries after the 1980s. Succinctly, if all of these countries had passed the developmental threshold at which income inequality should decline, why was inequality increasing in so many cases? While the answers are varied, several have received the bulk of scholarly attention.

12.3.3 Globalization, Skill Biased Technological Change, and Skill-Wage Premiums

One pair of (potentially competing) explanations place the changing fortunes of skilled and unskilled workers at the center of the analysis. The first draws from economic theories of international trade. Adrian Wood (1994) employed the Heckscher-Ohlin (H-O) model of trade to suggest that economic globalization should increase inequality in rich countries. The theory postulates that international trade reduces the price of economic inputs to that which prevails in countries for which the input is most abundant. Wood argued that this basic insight has implications for inequality because unskilled labor is relatively abundant in the global South, while high skill labor is abundant in the global North. Thus, if trade increases between the North and the South, one would expect the demand for unskilled labor to fall, and the demand for skilled labor to rise in the North (Wood 1994). The changing demand for skilled and unskilled labor will then manifest itself in changing wage premiums (declining for unskilled; rising for skilled), and thereby rising inequality.

The second theoretical perspective also suggests that the increasing within-country inequality is explicable in terms of inversely changing wage premiums to skilled and unskilled labor, but that rising trade between the North and the South is not the cause (or primary cause). Instead, this explanation suggests that skill-biased technological change—i.e., the introduction of technological fixes that reduce the demand for unskilled labor—has been the major driver of the changing fortunes of the skilled and unskilled (e.g., Katz and Autor 1999). In this formulation, low-skilled labor is not substituted by comparable labor from poorer countries, but rather by machinery and computing.

The relative importance of North/South trade and skill-biased technological change for the rise in income inequality among Northern countries has been particularly difficult to determine. First, it is clear that both processes are happening simultaneously, which creates identification problems for observational studies. Second, some suggest that the two processes are related. On one hand, labor-saving technological change and off-shoring are complimentary strategies by which to reduce the overall share of labor in output and thereby increase profitability. Theories of inequality for which antagonistic class relations reside at the center of the analysis view these as two sides of the same coin. On the other, some suggest at least some of the labor saving technological changes is caused by rising North/South trade. Here, labor-saving technological change is a competitive response by a subset of Northern manufacturing firms to the offshoring behavior of their rivals (Wood 1998).

12.3.4 The Accumulation of Wealth and the Ascendance of Finance Capital

While the twin theories of the globalization of production and labor-saving technological change focus on the distribution of income within the working class to explain the rise of income inequality since the 1980s, others focus on the distribution of income between labor and capital, or between the super-rich and the rest. In *Capital in the Twenty-First Century*, Thomas Picketty (2013) argues that rising inequality is an inherent feature of capitalism. While the thesis resonates with classic Marxism, it is much more informed by traditional economic thought than anything else. He suggests that it is incorrect to presume that income inequality follows a natural course. Rather, "institutions and policies that societies choose to adopt" determine whether inequality rise or falls (Picketty and Saez 2014: 842–843). The more rapid increase in income inequality in the United States than continental Europe despite comparable rates of technological change and educational expansion constitutes a puzzle in need of explanation. According to Picketty, what's unique about the US case is the exceptional rise in executive compensation, which he attributes to US tax policy and social norms about inequities that glorify the super-rich.

The other key explanation locating rising inequality in a growing rift between labor and capital is the ascendance of finance capital. Giovani Arrighi (1994) was among the first sociologists to theorize finance (also see Krippner 2011). His argument was that "financialization," defined as an increase in the returns to finance relative to the returns to fixed capital investment, is a repeating "signal crisis" in the historical development of capitalism. Economic expansions begin with (product or process) innovations in the core of the world-economy. As these innovations diffuse throughout the world-system, the rate of return on fixed capital investments begins to fall, which causes capital to shift into speculative endeavors.

Subsequent analyses focus upon the effect that financialization has on income inequality in the United States. In a series of papers, Ken-Hou Lin and Donald Tomaskovic-Devey argue that financialization matters for US income inequality because it erodes the reliance of capital on, and thereby the bargaining power of, labor in the United States. According to this perspective, the rise in income inequality in the United States is driven at least in part by the effect of financialization on the labor share of income (Lin and Tomaskovic-Devey 2013; Tomaskovic-Devey and Lin 2011).

12.4 Class, Gender, and Race

12.4.1 Class Inequality

Thus far, we've discussed theories of income inequality *within* countries that are "general" in so far as they explain inequality with systematic relationships among variables like skills, occupational characteristics, and structural changes to the economy without considering the extent to which the process by which citizens attain skills, occupy different occupational niches, or experience structural changes to the economy might vary systematically across subcategories. However, core sociological traditions hold that stratification occurs along three primary axes: class, gender, and race. Marx conceptualized social classes as defined by the relationships of groups to the means of economic production, and his emphasis on class conflict remains an important intellectual root of the conflict perspectives on class stratification. Weberian notions of social class treat groups of people with similar income, wealth, status, and levels of education as occupants of the same social class. In the US and other capitalist societies, social class, or socioeconomic status, is a key predictor of life chances, and the study of mobility—or the movement of people between classes, whether up or down—is the core area in contemporary stratification studies. The likelihood of significant upward mobility is quite small both within and across generations, even in wealthy nations.

Economic theories of income inequality hold that some jobs require specialized skills and are higher value positions, and therefore yield higher rates of remuneration. Some suggest that inequality can actually play a positive role in society, insofar as high-skill/high-status jobs provide incentives for individuals to complete necessary training and education and take on these important jobs (Davis and Moore 1945). Following this logic, for example, a heart surgeon earns more and has higher status than a restaurant server because the former occupation requires a higher level of skill and education. Conflict perspectives focus instead on which class an individual is born into as a key predictor of their education, occupation, and, ultimately, wealth attainment. Low socioeconomic class is associated with access to low quality schools and low educational attainment, for example. Someone born into a lower-income family and community with no experience applying to or attending college, let alone graduate school, is thus more likely to become a restaurant server than a heart surgeon. Thus, if skill acquisition is a major driver of income inequality, and is also patterned by the socio-economic status at birth, then we must look beyond economic theories of income inequality to fully understand the dynamics of income inequality within a society. That is, income inequality is not merely the outcome of economic processes, but is also inherently social.

Indeed, other conceptualizations of class consider cultural forms of class reproduction that are embedded in the social structure. Sociologists have long recognized that markers of social class—cultural tastes, social networks, institutional affiliations, etc.—are transmitted within classes over time through both formal processes (e.g., schooling, clubs and associations) and informal processes (e.g., cultural discrimination) (Bourdieu 1984). Thus, the type of cultural capital, or non-economic assets, members of a group possess shape life chances because cultural capital facilitates access to material forms of capital (Granovetter 1973). Those at the top of the power structure, who head government, cultural, and philanthropic organizations and whose contributions help fuel campaigns, are the power elite (C. W. Mills 2000 [1956]; Domhoff 2007 [1967]). They create mechanisms of exclusion to people from lower classes and develop ideologies supporting stratification to legitimate the social order (Gramsci 1971; Mahutga and Stepan-Norris 2015).

In the United States, the American Dream ideology—the belief that anyone can attain a higher class status than the one they were born in to if they only work hard enough—is a prime example of an ideology that supports stratification because it holds individuals, rather than the social structures they were born in to, responsible for their own outcomes. The reality is that lower class Americans are unlikely to achieve a class status higher than their parents, and people born in to the middle classes in the 2000s may even be at significant risk for experiencing downward mobility (Newman 1999; Neckerman and Torch 2007). At the micro level, processes of class-based inequality mean that individuals born into higher class households have better life chances than those born into lower class households.

Individuals encounter the mechanisms of class reproduction, including families, communities, and schools, at every turn, which limits possibilities for changing their class position.

12.4.2 Gender Inequality

Theorizing gender differences in wealth, income, power, and status are central areas in stratification studies. Joan Wallach Scott (1988) identifies two key dimensions of gender when she states that, "Gender is a constitutive element of social relationships based on perceived differences between the sexes…a primary way of signifying power" (42). Gender thus refers not only to the social relations that divide individuals and groups into differentiated gender statuses, but also to the consequences of those differences for a system of inequality. The most frequent consequence is that men enjoy a status superior to that of women and thus have greater access to power and resources.

Women's formal political rights and economic participation have swelled globally over the last century, yet substantial gender gaps exist in wealth and income, even in countries where women and men ostensibly enjoy similar rights. In the United States and globally, women are more likely to live in poverty than are men, are paid less, assume greater responsibility for household management and child care, and amass less wealth than men. Functionalist sociological theories and neoclassical economic theories both attempted to explain away these inequalities as the logical outcomes of sex differences, but these perspectives have been largely abandoned in favor of those that offer more nuanced understandings of gender stratification. Such nuance is necessary to untangle the complexities of why gender inequality remains so intractable; this is particularly perplexing in nations like the United States where women make up nearly half of the paid work force and graduate from college at higher rates than men.

Marxist feminist theories of gender stratification view women's subordinate social status as directly tied to the rise of capitalism and private property. Friedrich Engels (2010 [1884]) wrote about how the nuclear family emerged as a tool to promote men's control over women's reproductive capacities and their labor in the capitalist system, laying a groundwork for future feminist theories linking capitalism to women's exploitation. Later expansions of Marxist feminism retained an interest in the relationship between economic power, sexual politics, and women's political power and status (Blumberg 1984). Given the apparent linkages between women's economic exploitation and their low status in the household, sociological theory and research on gender inequality has especially focused on gender in the workplace.

Understanding the wage gap—which in turn helps explain women's overrepresentation among poor and low income people, as well as their more limited wealth accumulation—has been a core goal for stratification scholars interested in gender inequalities. Since the gap in wages contributes to the gender gap in wealth, status, and power, the wage gap may be an underlying problem. The primary group of theories that seek to explain the emergence and the persistence of the wage gap focus on occupational sex segregation, or the clustering of women and men into different occupations or into different jobs within the same occupations. Such theories generally fall into several overlapping categories. Social psychological and behavioral perspectives emphasize the status expectations and the internalization of social norms and gender stereotypes (including through gender socialization) as effecting women's and men's occupational preferences and behaviors (Ridgeway and Correll 2004). Men, for example, enjoy greater rewards in the workplace because their colleagues perceive them as more competent and committed. Institutional perspectives consider the implications of organizational practices for gender inequalities; such theories also sometimes incorporate cultural perspectives that focus on how cultural gender-typing of work and occupations shapes wages and workplace opportunities (Bielby 2000; Britton 2000). Such theories suggest that women and men are pushed into gender-typed occupations and work cultures reinforce boundaries, especially to keep women out of workplaces dominated by men, such as stockbrokers (Roth 2006; Williams 1995).

Feminist theories, which can cut across social psychological and institutional perspectives, view sex segregation and the wage gap as maintaining men's privilege over women (Acker 1992; Risman 2004; Williams 1992). That is, sex segregation and the mechanisms used to maintain it, such as the glass ceiling, hostile work environments, and other elements of gendered organizations, are tools that protect men's status and privilege. Recent research showing the workplace benefits of transmen's transitions support theories pointing to the importance of status as male for occupational success (Schilt 2006). Feminists are particularly concerned with women's economic equality for at least two key reasons. One is because feminist theories generally hold that money enhances power, such that women's status in the family will only improve as her economic power increases. A second is because of the reality that in industrialized nations, women are overrepresented among people living in poverty: in the United States, an estimated five million more women than men live in poverty. In the developing world, poverty strikes women and men more equally, but investments in women's education are particularly effective in reducing poverty.

Since the 1970s, feminist perspectives have significantly influenced the study of gender stratification, which have moved away from essentialist notions that women and men are simply fulfilling "natural" talents and toward social and structural explanations. Key theoretical insights that have emerged from this sea change include attention to gender stereotypes at both the level of individuals and institutions, recognition that unintentional discrimination is often central to maintaining occupational sex segregation and the wage gap, and a collective effort to develop theoretical and empirical works that offer possible pathways for reducing gender stratification. Feminists have also noted how the devaluing of feminized occupations points to the persistence of sexist ideologies about gender and work; that is, when a job that once was done mainly by men becomes one done mainly by women, the occupation loses status and compensation for the work shrinks (the inverse is also true) (England 1992; England et al. 2000, 2001; Levanon et al. 2009). Sexist belief systems also reinforce the idea that women and men are naturally better suited to some occupations, but the cross-national variation in the gender-typing of jobs reveals that occupational sex segregation is socially constructed (Charles and Grusky 2004).

12.4.3 Racial Inequality

Stratification also occurs along racial lines. Globally, those nations and regions with predominantly white populations tend to be wealthier and have better access to resources than those with predominantly non-white populations. In much of the industrialized world, racial inequalities are persistent, and, like gender inequalities, are slow to change even though racial and ethnic minorities have formal legal rights.

In the United States, African-Americans experience particularly pronounced disadvantage, especially when compared to whites. Empirical research consistently establishes yawning gaps between blacks and whites in the United States in terms of income, wealth, education, and health and longevity. Between 1980 and 2009, for example, blacks made a varying relative wage of 57.6–67.5 cents for every white dollar. Over the same period, the relative wage of Hispanic Americans varied from 63.9% to 75.5% of whites, and Asian Americans earned a relative wage varying from 114% to 127% of whites. After an increasing relative wage from 1980 to 2000, the trend for all three groups stalled in the 2000s, as did the average wage of whites (US Census Bureau 2012).

Historically-oriented perspectives recognize the legacies of slavery and the legal codification of discrimination in the United States (e.g., Oliver and Shapiro 2005 [1995]), which limited opportunities for black Americans through the 1960s, when civil rights legislation offered new protections against discrimination. Legal changes, however, have not afforded blacks the same opportunities as whites; African-Americans lag in the intergenerational transmission of wealth, are disproportionately clustered in the low-wage labor market, and most often live in racially segregated neighborhoods where schools are poor and where social networks and other resources that support upward mobility are absent.

In the mid-twentieth century, a "culture of poverty" theory dominated social science theorizing about racial inequalities. Championed across a range of academic disciplines and among policymakers (e.g., the Moynihan report of 1965), this theory held that poor communities respond to structural poverty and systemic exclusion by developing behaviors and norms that ultimately inhibit their ability to escape poverty. Widely criticized for blaming the poor for their disadvantage, competing theories alternately emphasize the structural obstacles to upward mobility for low income blacks, or focus on structural and individual racism as the primary explanation for the continued persistence of racial inequality in the US.

One key example of the structural approach is William Julius Wilson's controversial argument that poor blacks in the United States are disadvantaged by their social and economic isolation, which is itself an outcome of shifts in the labor market that have reduced opportunities for people with lower educational attainment to hold jobs that offer subsistence wages. Wilson's perspective thus ultimately asserts that class trumps race as an obstacle to upward mobility, a perspective captured in the title of his book *The Declining Significance of Race* (1980).

Split labor market theory also deemphasizes race-ethnicity in favor of other factors that contribute to wage differentials and inter-group antagonisms (Bonacich 1972). A split labor market contains at least two groups of workers whose price of labor differs for the same work, or would differ if they did the same work. However, Bonacich argues that the price of labor is not a response to the ethnicity of those entering the labor market per se. Instead, a price differential results from differences in resources and motives, which are often correlates of ethnicity. All else equal, employers will prefer the lower wage (i.e., non-white) workers, which then generates antagonism with the higher-wage white workers. The ensuing conflict tries to eliminate the split-labor market, as more powerful, higher-wage workers engage in exclusion movements (attempts to expel lower-priced workers from a fixed geographical space) or to erect a caste system (attempt to exclude lower-priced workers from a particular type of work). Thus, ethnic niches emerge at least in part as a consequence of limited opportunities, and become self-reinforcing over time.

Theories stressing the power of racism and discrimination counter that racially-specific barriers, including institutional mechanisms that restrict blacks from accessing equal opportunities and rewards, remain key for understanding the racial gap in income and wealth. Joe Feagin (1991) for example, holds that discrimination remains central to the lived experiences of African-Americans at the micro level, even as structural racism—configured as residential and occupational ghettoization—dominates the macro level. Sometimes micro-level discrimination is obscured by race-neutral language, such as employer emphasis on "soft skills," or interpersonal skills that are seen as particularly important in the service economy and which employers see blacks as less likely to possess than whites (Moss and Tilly 2001). Devah Pager and colleagues (2009), for example, have documented how black men seeking entry-level jobs experience a substantial race penalty; employers prefer to hire even whites with felony convictions before hiring blacks. Many employers are oblivious to their own racial bias, and/or use race-neutral language. However, rather than interpreting race-neutral language as evidence of an absence of racism, critical race theories argue that color-blind racism simply enables perpetrators of discrimination to deny their racist actions (Bonilla-Silva 2003; Moss and Tilly 2001).

Wealth inequalities are perpetuated through the gap in the intergenerational transmission in wealth (Oliver and Shapiro 2005 [1995]). Because African-American families historically were blocked from the major pathways to wealth accumulation, such as home ownership and well-paid jobs, they have yet to amass wealth that can be passed down generation to generation. The persistence of residential segregation, which pushes blacks into neighborhoods with lower property values, weaker public services, and constant contact with poorer blacks, also continues the cycle of the non-accumulation of wealth.

Racial inequalities persist, then, not just because of individual-level prejudices, but also because of how race structures all aspects of social life in the US. For blacks, the consequences include lower incomes and less wealth, residential segregation, and shorter life expectancies. For whites, the results are unearned advantages or privileges (McIntosh 1988). Lipsitz (1988) refers to the possessive investment in whiteness by which whites maintain a system that protects their assets (whether cultural or material) by limiting opportunities for upward mobility and resource accumulation among non-whites.

Race also operates in conjunction with class and gender to shape inequality. Intersectionality theory, first introduced conceptually by legal scholar Kimberle Crenshaw (1991) and later elaborated by sociologist Collins (1990), offers a powerful theoretical framework for understanding how race, class, and gender intersect to shape the experience of inequalities for individuals and groups in society. The intersectionality approach critiques additive approaches to oppression that conceptualize gender, race, and class as descriptive variables attached to individuals. Collins (2005) describes intersectionality theory as "two types of relationships: the interconnectedness of ideas and the social structures in which they occur, and the intersecting hierarchies of gender, race, economic, class, sexuality, and ethnicity" (p. 5). She argues that all groups possess varying amount of penalty and privilege in one historically created system. For example, white women are penalized by their gender but privileged by their race. To date, intersectionality theory has not been integrated into quantitative analyses of inequalities, other than through interaction variables (for an exception, see McCall 2005). However, ethnographers and qualitative sociologists have used intersectionality theory to illuminate the significance of multiple axes of inequality (e.g., Bettie 2002; Ferguson 2000). Intersectionality theory offers scholars of inequalities the opportunity to engage critically with how class, race, and gender intersect to shape life chances and life stories; future research will hopefully engage more deeply with intersectionality.

12.5 (De)stratifying Institutions

In this section, we review sociological theories of stratification in which institutions occupy the center of the analytical space. One of the most important institutions in this regard is the state. Theories of the welfare state seek to understand the causes and consequences of state interventions in social inequalities, including various forms of redistribution. Redistribution can take many forms, including social programs like unemployment insurance, retirement and health care benefits, family benefits, educational assistance, food stamps, and progressive tax systems. Because many of these social programs have progressive qualification requirements attached to them, they amount to a direct transfer income from wealthy to poorer individuals or families. In short, welfare states modify the effects of social or market forces on their citizens in order to achieve greater equality (Orloff 1996).

Early theories of the welfare state viewed welfare policy development as an outcome of industrialization: as nations industrialized and urbanized, welfare states emerged to protect citizens from the market. However, social scientists soon recognized the importance of political processes for shaping welfare policy, and began to focus on understanding variations across welfare states. Power resource theory emphasizes comparative welfare state studies, highlighting the market modifying force of welfare states and their capacity to mitigate class inequality (Esping-Andersen 1990). Power resource theory asserts that class alliances determine the expansion of modern welfare states. This perspective thus established politics—and political configurations of class power—as a major force behind welfare state evolution and policy-making. Furthermore, power resource theory introduced decommodification, or the degree to which social rights allow individuals to meet their living standards independent of pure market forces, as an analytic concept. Rather than viewing welfare state evolution as a by-product of industrialization and capitalist expansion, power-resource theory recognizes the importance of class configurations and politics in shaping welfare states, thereby combining elements of earlier non-Marxist political approaches and of structural Marxist approaches to the welfare state. Research using Power Resource theory to explain inequality is vibrant and ongoing (Huber and Stephens 2014).

Gøsta Esping-Andersen's (1990) *Three Worlds of Welfare Capitalism* has been an especially influential component of this perspective. Esping-Andersen advocates for a set of typologies that may be used to compare welfare regimes across types and which have been used to compare welfare regimes within types (O'Connor et al. 1999; Sainsbury 1999). Most simply, a welfare regime may be understood as "patterns across a number of policy areas," and within comparative welfare state studies usually includes the full range of domestic policy interventions as well as broader patterns of provisioning and regulation (O'Connor et al. 1999: 12).

Esping-Andersen's original typology classifies welfare regimes along three dimensions, namely relations between the state and the market, stratification, and social rights. Liberal welfare regimes seek to keep market forces sovereign. Such regimes tend to practice free-market liberalism, and are characterized by modest means-tested benefits and limited universal benefits and social insurance plans. Generally speaking, liberal welfare regimes offer their citizens few alternatives to relying on the market. The United States, the United Kingdom, and Australia are frequent examples of this type of welfare regime type. Conservative welfare regimes attach rights to class and status, and operate on the principle of subsidiarity, such that the state only intervenes with transfers and services when the family's ability to care for its members is exhausted. These regimes highlight the importance of the traditional two-parent family, as reflected in social policies that support marriage and women's reliance on a male breadwinner. Several continental European countries, such as Germany, Austria, and Italy, are identified as representing the conservative welfare regime type. Finally, social democratic regimes provide universal benefits that are intended to equalize the disparities between classes. Such states, which include the Scandinavian states, socialize family costs, and the state often serves as a substitute to a male breadwinner by providing high levels of support for single mothers.

Feminist scholars mobilized and modified Esping-Andersen's framework to consider the ways in which welfare regimes regulate gender via the state, the market, and the family (O'Connor et al. 1999). Including family in theories of the welfare state illuminates a core site of state regulation that has been a flash point for feminist state theory. Feminist state theory, pioneered by American and British Marxist feminists in the 1970s, views women as simultaneously oppressed by both capitalism and patriarchy (Hartmann 1979). With its strong emphasis on capitalism as the determining force behind the state's actions and policies, dual systems theory asserts that the state guides changes in the family and women's domestic behavior based on capitalism's needs. According to this perspective, women's labor, both inside and outside of the home, is manipulated by the state to serve capitalism's interests at a given historical point. Women thus became party to the social reproduction of both class and gender.

The state is implicated in the oppression of women because it supports a specific household structure, namely the two-parent or "nuclear" family, a structure that relies on male wages and female domestic labor (Eisenstein 1983). By keeping welfare payments low, and by limiting women's employment opportunities to low-wage jobs, the state in essence forces women to find a male breadwinner. The state is also implicated in the creation of public patriarchy. The state does not serve as the indirect oppressor of women via the nuclear family, but rather renders women dependent on the state itself. In line with this perspective, social welfare programs are analyzed for their tendency to make women dependent on men as collectively embodied in the state. In essence, the state takes on the role of a husband, both as provider and as controlling patriarch. As such, the state becomes the manager of women's dependence (Mink 1990).

Both power resource theory and feminist state theory draw attention to how welfare regimes can maintain and reproduce inequalities. That is, although the stated goal of welfare states is to protect citizens from the market and reduce stratification, welfare states also have hidden agendas that reinforce the status quo of inequality. Comparative research reveals that the reproduction of inequalities varies across welfare states, but is consistently present. Even as they purport to reduce inequalities, welfare states support the continuation of inequalities of class, gender, and race.

In addition to welfare states, there are other types of national institutions that matter for the distribution of income. Wage coordination among labor, capital and sometimes the state also stands out as prominent in this regard (Kenworthy 2001; Wallerstein 1999; Alderson and Nielsen 2002; Checchi and Garcia-Penalosa 2010; Mahler 2004). Examples of wage coordination include industry-level wage bargaining through formal relations between capital, peak labor confederations (Austria) or large unions from influential industries (Germany), between employer confederations and large firms (Japan and Switzerland), or by government imposition of wage schedules or freezes (e.g., Belgium, Denmark and the Netherlands) (Katzenstein 1985; Traxler 1999). On one hand, countries with strong corporatist, wage-setting institutions have strong labor unions, which tend to increase wages for both union and non-union members. Indeed, the declining rates of unionization in the United States have subjected workers to stagnant wages and limited workplace protections vis-à-vis workers in other developed countries, which in turn helps explain why the United States has the highest levels of income inequality among developed nations and the greatest rise in inequality (along with the UK) between 1975 and 2000 (Neckerman and Torche 2007).

Wage-coordination itself reduces inequality within the working class, as well as the income gap between labor and capital. In terms of the former, wage coordination dampens the link from wages to variance in the demands for particular sub-sets of workers because wages are determined through collective bargaining, which has been shown to benefit low-skill workers disproportionately (Wallerstein 1999). In terms of the income gap between labor and capital, wage-coordination shifts some workplace authority from capital to labor, and fosters collective identity among differentiated workers (Wallerstein 1999). Thus, it provides an institutional source of bargaining power that tends to increase the labor share of income in countries with strong corporatist institutions. As a product of both these mechanisms, a negative association between wage-coordination institutions and income inequality has been a persistent finding in the comparative political economy literature (Alderson and Nielsen 2002; Bradley et al. 2003; Checchi and Garcia-Peñalosa 2010; Pontusson et al. 2002; Wallerstein 1999).

12.6 Conclusions

Sociological theories of stratification have guided social scientists towards deeper and more nuanced understandings of social inequality. The topic remains gripping precisely because inequalities appear to be intractable, even as their form changes across historical periods. Given the complexity of inequalities, it is not surprising that many questions remain about both the causes and consequences of stratification, and we expect that theory and research on inequalities will continue to be central to the discipline of sociology. We hope that future theory and research on the consequences of inequalities include greater attention to the developing world, where inequalities have been taken for granted and understudied. These contexts may reveal dynamics different from those in industrialized capitalism economies.

Theorizing the institutional and societal consequences of inequality also requires consistent attention. Does between-nation inequality foment resentment and increase risk of conflict and, if so, through what mechanisms? Beyond social indicators of inequality, how is inequality reproduced through institutions and social practices, and how does it affect the ways in which individuals use institutions and social practices to monopolize resources (Neckerman and Torche 2007)? With the growth of the so-called precariat in the United States and other industrialized nations, theorists should also attend to the processes that lead to, and the consequences of, economic insecurity.

Over time, we might also develop better-articulated theories of stratification that elaborate how micro-level processes interact with macro-level structures, and vice versa. Focusing on the ways in which the stratifying effect of macro-level dynamics are conditional upon stratification processes at the micro level, and on the ways in which micro-level dynamics are in turn conditional on aggregate levels of material inequality, appears to be a fruitful path for future theory and research. For example, as articulated above, general theories of within-country inequality link stratification outcomes to the distribution of skills and occupations as they are impacted by changes in economic organization at the global and national levels, but are silent with respect to the sociological process by which skills and occupations are distributed; attending to this latter point will enrich our understanding of the reproduction of inequalities.

References

Acker, J. (1992). From sex roles to gendered institutions. *Contemporary Sociology, 21*(5), 565–569.

Alderson, A. S., & Nielsen, F. (1999). Income inequality, development, and dependence: A reconsideration. *American Sociological Review, 64*(4), 606–631.

Alderson, A. S., & Nielsen, F. (2002). Globalization and the great U-turn: Income inequality trends in 16 OECD countries. *American Journal of Sociology, 107*(5), 1244–1299.

Arrighi, G. (1994). *The long twentieth century*. London: Verso.

Berry, A., Bourguignon, F., & Morrison, C. (1991). Global economic inequality and its trends since 1950. In L. Osberg (Ed.), *Readings on economic inequality* (pp. 60–91). New York: M.E. Sharpe.

Bettie, J. (2002). *Women without class: Girls, race and identity*. Berkeley: University of California Press.

Bielby, W. T. (2000). Minimizing workplace gender and racial bias. *Contemporary Sociology, 29*(1), 120–129.

Blumberg, R. L. (1984). A general theory of gender stratification. *Sociological Theory, 2*, 23–101.

Bonacich, E. (1972). A theory of ethnic antagonism: The split labor market. *American Sociological Review, 37*(5), 547–559.

Bonilla-Silva, E. (2003). *Color-blind racism and the persistence of racial inequality in the united states*. New York: Rowman and Littlefield Publishers.

Bourdieu, P. (1984). *Distinction: A social critique of the judgement of taste*. London: Routledge & Kegan Paul.

Bradley, D., Huber, E., Moller, S., Nielsen, F., & Stephens, J. (2003). Distribution and redistribution in postindustrial democracies. *World Politics, 55*(4), 193–228.

Britton, D. M. (2000). The epistemology of the gendered organization. *Gender and Society, 14*(3), 418–434.

Bunker, S. G. (1985). *Underdeveloping the Amazon: Extraction, unequal exchange, and the failure of the modern state*. Chicago: University of Illinois Press.

Census Bureau, U. S. (2012). *Statistical abstract of the united states 2012*. Washington, DC: United States Census Bureau.

Charles, M., & Grusky, D. (2004). *Occupational ghettos: The worldwide segregation of women and men*. Stanford: Stanford University Press.

Chase-Dunn, C. (1975). The effects of international economic dependence on development and inequality: A cross-national study. *American Sociological Review, 40*(6), 720–738.

Chase-Dunn, C. (1998). *Global formation: Structures of the world-economy*. Lanhan: Rowman and Littlefield Publishers.

Checchi, D., & Garcia-Peñalosa, C. (2010). Labour market institutions and the personal distribution of income in the OECD. *Economica, 77*(307), 413–450.

Clark, R. (2011). World income inequality in the global Era: New estimates, 1990–2008. *Social Problems, 58*, 565–592.

Collins, P. H. (1990). *Black feminist thought*. New York: Nueva.

Collins, P. H. (2005). *Black sexual politics: African-Americans, gender, and New racism*. New York: Routledge.

Crenshaw, K. (1991). Mapping the margins: Intersectionality, identity politics, and violence against women of color. *Stanford Law Review, 43*(6), 1241–1299.

Davis, K., & Moore, W. E. (1945). Some principles of stratification. *American Sociological Review, 10*(2), 242–249.

Domhoff, G. W. (2007 [1967]). *Who rules America? The triumph of the corporate rich*. New York: McGraw Hill.

Dowrick, S., & Akmal, M. (2005). Contradictory trends in global income inequality: A tale of two biases. *Review of Income and Wealth, 51*(2), 201–229.

Eisenstein, E. L. (1983). *The printing revolution in early modern Europe*. New York: Cambridge University Press.

Engels, F. (2010 [1884]). *The origin of the family, private property, and the state*. New York: Penguin.

England, P. (1992). *Comparable worth: Theories and evidence*. New York: Aldine de Gruyter.

England, P., Hermsen, J. M., & Cotter, D. A. (2000). The devaluation of Women's work: A comment on Tam. *American Journal of Sociology, 105*(6), 1741–1760.

England, P., Thompson, J., & Aman, C. (2001). The sex gap in pay and comparable worth: An update. In I. Berg & A. Kalleberg (Eds.), *Sourcebook on labor markets: Evolving structures and processes* (pp. 551–556). New York: Plenum.

Esping-Andersen, G. (1990). *The three worlds of welfare capitalism*. Princeton: Princeton University.

Feagin, J. (1991). The continuing significance of race: Antiblack discrimination in public places. *American Sociological Review, 56*(1), 101–116.

Ferguson, A. A. (2000). *Bad boys: Public schools in the making of black masculinity*. Ann Arbor: University of Michigan Press.

Firebaugh, G. (2000). Observed trends in between-nation income inequality and two conjectures. *American Journal of Sociology, 106*(1), 215–221.

Firebaugh, G. (2003). *The new geography of global income inequality*. Cambridge, MA: Harvard University Press.

Galtung, J. (1971). A structural theory of imperialism. *Journal of Peace Research, 8*(2), 81–117.

Goesling, B. (2001). Changing income inequalities within and between nations: New evidence. *American Sociological Review, 66*(5), 745–776.

Gramsci, A. (1971). *Selections from the prison notebooks of Antonio Gramsci* (Q. Hoare, & G. N. Smith, Ed. and Trans.). New York: International Publishers.

Granovetter, M. S. (1973). The strength of weak ties. *American Journal of Sociology, 78*(6), 1360–1380.

Hartmann, H. I. (1979). The unhappy marriage of Marxism and feminism: Towards a more progressive union. *Capital and Class, 3*(2), 1–33.

Hochschild, A. (1999). *King Leopold's ghost: A story of greed, terror and heorism in Colonia Africa*. Boston: Houghton Mifflin.

Huber, E., & Stephens, J. D. (2014). Income inequality and redistribution in post-industrial democracies: Demographic, economic and political determinants. *Socio-Economic Review, 12*, 245–267.

Hung, H.-f., & Kucinskas, J. (2011). Globalization and global inequality: Assessing the impact of the rise of china and India, 1980–2005. *American Journal of Sociology, 116*(5), 1478–1513.

Jolly, R. (2006). *Inequality in historical perspective*. Research Paper, UNU-WIDER, United Nations University (UNU), No. 2006/32, ISBN 9291908002

Katz, L. F., & Autor, D. H. (1999). Changes in the wage structure and earnings inequality. In O. Ashenfelter & D. Card (Eds.), *Handbook of labor economics* (Vol. 3, pp. 1463–1555). Amsterdam: North Holland.

Katzenstein, P. J. (1985). *Small states in world markets: Industrial policy in Europe*. Ithaca: Cornell University Press.

Kenworthy, L. (2001). Wage-setting measures: A survey and assessment. *World Politics, 54*(1), 57–98.

Korzeniewicz, R. P., & Moran, T. P. (1997). World-economic trends in the distribution of income, 1965–1992. *American Journal of Sociology, 102*(4), 1000–1039.

Krippner, G. (2011). *Capitalizing on crisis: The political origins of the rise of finance*. Boston: Harvard University Press.

Kuznets, S. (1955). Economic growth and income inequality. *The American Economic Review, 45*(1), 1–28.

Lange, M., Mahoney, J., & vom Hau, M. (2006). Colonialism and development: A comparative analysis of Spanish and British colonies. *American Journal of Sociology, 111*(5), 1412–1462.

Levanon, A., England, P., & Alison, P. (2009). Occupational feminization and pay: Assessing causal dynamics using 1950–2000 U.S. Census data. *Social Forces, 88*(2), 865–891.

Lin, K.-H., & Tomaskovic-Devey, D. (2013). Financialization and US income inequality, 1970–2008. *American Journal of Sociology, 118*(5), 1284–1329.

Lipsitz, G. (1988). *The possessive investment in whiteness: How white people profit from identity politics*. Philadelphia: Temple University Press.

Mahler, V. A. (2004). Economic globalization, domestic politics, and income inequality in the developed countries: A cross-national study. *Comparative Politics Studies, 37*(9), 1025–1053.

Mahutga, M. C., & Stepan-Norris, J. (2015). Ideological hegemony. In G. Ritzer (Ed.), *Blackwell encyclopedia of sociology*. London: Blackwell Press. doi:10.1002/9781405165518.wbeos0202.

Marx, K. (1867 [1967]). *Capital, volume one*. New York: International Publishers.

McCall, L. (2005). The complexity of intersectionality. *Signs: Journal of Women in Culture and Society, 30*(31), 1771–1802.

McIntosh, P. (1988). *White privilege and male privilege: A personal account of coming to see correspondences through work in Women's studies*. Wellesley: Wellesley College Center for Research on Women.

Milanovic, B. (2002). True world income distribution, 1988 and 1993: First calculation based on household surveys alone. *The Economic Journal, 112*(476), 51–92.

Milanovic, B. (2005). Can we discern the effect of globalization on income distribution? Evidence from household surveys. *The World Bank Economic Review, 19*(1), 21–44.

Mills, C. W. (2000 [1956]). *The power elite*. Oxford: Oxford University Press.

Mink, G. (1990). The lady and the tramp: Gender, race, and the origins of the American welfare state. In L. Gordon (Ed.), *Women, the state and welfare* (pp. 92–122). Madison: University of Wisconsin Press.

Moss, P., & Tilly, C. (2001). *Stories employers tell: Race, skill, and hiring in America*. New York: Russell Sage Foundation.

Moynihan, D. P. (1965). *The negro family: The case for national action*. Washington, DC: Office of Policy Planning and Research, U.S. Department of Labor.

Neckerman, K. M., & Torche, F. (2007). Inequality: Causes and consequences. *Annual Review of Sociology, 33*, 335–357.

Newman, K. (1999). *Falling from grace: Downward mobility in the age of affluence*. Berkeley: University of California Press.

Nielsen, F. (1994). Income inequality and industrial development: Dualism revisited. *American Sociological Review, 59*(5), 654–677.

Nielsen, F., & Alderson, A. S. (1997). The Kuznets curve and the great U-turn: Income inequality in U.S. Countries, 1970 to 1990. *American Sociological Review, 62*(1), 12–33.

O'Connor, J. S., Orloff, A., & Shaver, S. (1999). *States, markets, families: Gender, liberalism and social policy in Australia, Canada, great Britain and the United States*. Cambridge: Cambridge University Press.

Oliver, M., & Shapiro, T. M. (2005 [1995]). *Black wealth/white wealth: A new perspective on racial inequality*. New York: Routledge.

Orloff, A. (1996). Gender in the welfare state. *Annual Review of Sociology, 22*, 51–78.

Pager, D., Western, B., & Bonokowski, B. (2009). Discrimination in a low-wage labor market: A field experiment. *American Sociological Review, 74*(5), 777–799.

Piketty, T. (2013). *Capital in the twenty-first century*. Cambridge, MA: Harvard University Press.

Piketty, T., & Saez, E. (2014). Inequality in the long run. *Science, 344*(6186), 838–843.

Pontusson, J., Rueda, D., & Way, C. R. (2002). Comparative political economy of wage distribution: The role of partisanship and labour market institutions. *British Journal of Industrial Relations, 32*, 281–308.

Ridgeway, C. L., & Correll, S. J. (2004). Unpacking the gender system: A theoretical perspective on gender beliefs and social relations. *Gender and Society, 18*(4), 510–531.

Risman, B. J. (2004). Gender as a social structure: Theory wrestiling with activism. *Gender and Society, 18*(4), 429–450.

Roth, L. M. (2006). *Selling women short: Gender and money on wall street*. Princeton: Princeton University Press.

Sainsbury, D. (1999). *Gender and welfare state regimes*. Oxford: Oxford University Press.

Schilt, K. (2006). Just one of the guys? How transmen make gender visible at work. *Gender and Society, 20*(4), 465–490.

Schultz, T. P. (1998). Inequality in the distribution of personal income in the world: How It is changing and why. *Journal of Population Economics, 11*(3), 307–344.

Scott, J. W. (1988). *Gender and the politics of history*. New York: Columbia University Press.

Solt, F. (2009). Standardizing the world income inequality database. *Social Science Quarterly, 9*, 231–242.

Theil, H. (1979). World income inequality and its components. *Economics Letters, 2*(1), 99–102.

Tomaskovic-Devey, D., & Lin, K.-H. (2011). Economic rents and the financialization of the US economy. *American Sociological Review, 76*(4), 538–559.

Traxler, F. (1999). Wage-setting institutions and European monetary union. In G. Huemer, M. Mesch, & F. Traxler (Eds.), *The role of employer associations and labour unions in the EMU* (pp. 115–135). Aldershot: Ashgate.

Wallerstein, M. (1999). Wage-setting and pay inequality in advanced industrial societies. *American Journal of Political Science, 43*(3), 649–680.

Weber, M. (1930 [2001]). *The protestant ethic and the spirit of capitalism* (T. Parsons, Trans.). London: Routledge.

Whalley, J. (1979). The worldwide income distribution: Some speculative calculations. *Review of Income and Wealth, 25*(3), 261–276.

Williams, C. (1992). The glass escalator: Hidden advantages for Men in the "Female" professions. *Social Problems, 39*(3), 253–267.

Williams, C. (1995). *Still a man's world*. Berkeley: University of California Press.

Wilson, W. J. (1980). *The declining significance of race: Blacks and changing American institutions*. Chicago: University of Chicago Press.

Wood, A. (1994). *North-south trade, employment and inequality: Changing fortunes in a skill-driven world*. Oxford: Clarendon Press.

Wood, A. (1998). Globalisation and the rise in labour market inequalities. *Economic Journal, 108*(450), 1463–1482.

13 The Concept of Community as Theoretical Ground: Contention and Compatibility Across Levels of Analysis and Standpoints of Social Processes

Michael D. Irwin

13.1 Introduction: Community as a Theoretical Linkage

Forty years ago community sociologists were widely expressing frustration with the concept of community. In summarizing 200 years of sociological work on the subject, in 1974 Bell and Newby seemed to have admitted defeat. "Yet out of community studies, there has never developed a theory of community, nor even a satisfactory definition of what community is" (Bell and Newby 2012, l. 795). Such a definition seemed unachievable "It should be apparent by now that it is impossible to give the sociological definition of community" (Bell and Newby 2012, l. 788). Likewise Cohen (1985) states "Over the years (community) has proved to be highly resistant to satisfactory definition in anthropology and sociology, perhaps for the simple reason that all definitions contain or imply theories, and the theory of community has been very contentious" (p. 8–9). Reflecting a generalized sentiment Stacey declared "It is doubtful whether the concept 'community' refers to a useful abstraction" and characterized the search for a cohesive theory of community as sociological ephemera (Stacey 2012, p. 13). Pahl (1966) describes the effort as a 'singularly fruitless exercise'. Stacey, Pahl and many others had come to see the promise of community studies as a sociological method and empirical endeavor rather than as a foundational movement to develop a theory of a sociological phenomenon (Bell and Newby 2012; Day 2006).

Within the community studies arena this failure seemed to undercut the foundation for theoretical discourse on community. "One of the main problems concerning the study of community is that it has little or no substantive sociological theory of its own. … Thus we cannot draw upon a body of theory of the community— rather we must fall back upon a list of individuals who have written about the concept of community itself" (Bell and Newby 2012, p. 3). If no definite theoretical body of work on community emerged during this time period, the list of individuals writing about community continued to accumulate. A practical regard for community as concept and as an object of analysis would remain the mainstay of sociological study in the latter twentieth century.

From that empirical literature a common constellation of characteristics emerged. According to Bruhn (2005) the concept of community involves (1) locality (2) a sense of place and (3) a sense of community. Similarly Flora and Flora (2013) situate the concept of community in locality but stress the importance of a locally bounded social system containing locally oriented organizations. Elias (2012) shifts the orientation from individuals to residence thus stressing the notions

M.D. Irwin (✉)
Duquesne University, Pittsburgh, PA, USA
e-mail: irwinm@duq.edu

S. Abrutyn (ed.), *Handbook of Contemporary Sociological Theory*,
Handbooks of Sociology and Social Research, DOI 10.1007/978-3-319-32250-6_13

of spatial proximity as a characteristic of community. Similarly McClay (2014) emphasizes both the tangible and intangible resources of place as well as the pervasive importance of community as place: "There is no evading the fact that we human beings have a profound need for 'thereness,' for visible and tangible things that persist and endure, and thereby serve to anchor our memories in something more substantial than our thoughts and emotions" (p. 2). Notably, despite very different basic theoretical assumptions, these definitions yield a common core of issues involving community. As Keller (2003) notes, despite major differences in basic theoretical assumptions there are constant elements that theorists use to describe community. "These include physical properties, such as land and boundaries, to cultural and social properties" (p. 266). Beyond agreements on these very general dimensions, however, the discipline had never coalesced around deeper theoretical issues. As Day (2006) states "At every level, it does appear community is contested, and contestable. There is disagreement about its essential meaning, and endless argument about what it signifies in terms of entitlements and responsibilities, and for whom" (p. 245). Bruhn (2005) echoes this assessment noting "The word 'community,' much like the word 'culture,' has been used so freely in the lay and scientific literature that it is often assumed that everyone understands it and is in agreement about its importance. Yet, while the definitions of both words can vary substantially, they seem to be as protected as if they were totems" (l. 469).

If community as a concept had limited common ground across perspectives, community as an important conceptual element permeated theoretical approaches in social science in the late 20th century. Technological developments in infrastructure and globalization of economic relations transformed the spatial limitations of interaction while shifts in the basis for affiliation among individuals created a new nexus of association that raised deep questions about the nature of community in the twenty-first century. Is the concept of community still meaningful in an age of transcendent individualism? Is there a role for space and place in community association? Has locality lost its associational force or has it simply been transformed? Contemporary works by Auge (2008), Bauman (2001, 2013), Bellah et al. (1992, 1996), Florida (2004, 2005), Fukuyama (1995, 1999), Putnam et al. (1993, 2000), and others concerned with the relationship between individuals and social life elevated the importance of community as concept and moved community theory to the center of sociological interest. Their works on social capital, civic engagement, trust and meaning were infused with discussions of community that recalled the 19th theoretical treatment of community by de Tocqueville, Tönnies, Durkheim, Marx, Simmel, and Weber. Why?

The concept of community has been used since Greek times to situate individuals in a larger social context. Linking the experiential world of the individual to the abstraction of society and culture has been an enduring analytic and theoretical problem in sociology and related disciplines (Cresswell 2015; Nisbet 1966; Keller 2003). Society, however influential on daily lives, is not readily perceived as an object or as context by individuals. And if these lines of influence lack experiential reality, then the processes by which individuals are integrated into society and culture are equally indefinite. The concept of community provides a theoretical counter to this ambiguity that is at once abstract and concrete.

However, theorizing community necessarily confronts two issues: the problem of locality and the problem of association. The problem of association includes the nature of association among individuals and the relationship of community both to individuals and to society at large. The nature of association has long been contrasted as either originating in social structure and culture or originating with individual recognition of common advantages and identity. This problem of association also involves the role that community plays in linking individuals to the broader social and cultural milieu. Here community may be seen as simply a microcosm of society or as a conceptually separate social form. The two aspects, community as a source or consequence of association, and the role of community as a mediator between individuals and society, are interrelated issues.

The problem of locality of community involves the degree to which community is bounded in space by either cultural or material factors. The social and physical character of community is used in social theories to refer to the tangible social and cultural milieu that is part of daily individual experience. Characterization of this community milieu is problematic. This problem of locality confronts the importance of spatial cohesion as opposed to social cohesion associated with community. This is often contrasted in terms of space vs. place and overlaps with positions on community's material character vs its symbolic character (Cresswell 2015, l. 1236–1237).

This chapter explores these two concepts, association and locality. It begins by tracing their history in formulations of community, from the Greeks through Medieval Christianity up to the Age of Enlightenment. Here community is variously formulated as contractual convenience or as organic whole; as territorially organized or culturally determined. Each approach implies a different relationship between community and society. Each has implications for the conception of communal association and the role of culture and of space. The traces of these ideas are identified in classic sociological treatises on community and tracked into early twentieth century sociology. In the latter half of the twentieth century significant divisions in sociology's conceptualization of community developed that resulted in the fragmentation of community as a theoretical object, as discussed above. In contemporary work theoretical diversity has continued to typify conceptions of community. Yet, synthesis has become emblematic of new approaches to community. In the early twenty-first century conceptualizations of community reconsider the relationships between organic and contractual elements of community and re-conceptualize connections between spatial forces and the culture of place. Here the problems of association and locality are being addressed in new ways, but these works also revisit enduring issues in the conceptualization of community.

13.2 Community, Association, and Locality: Historical Antecedents

13.2.1 Problems of Association: Individuals, Community, and Society

The nature of association and attachment in communities falls into two basic positions: individuals associate in communities because of common interests and individual association arises from the nature of community culture and structure (Kirkpatrick 2008; Keller 2003; Nisbet 1966, 2014; Gans 2015). The former notion is found in classic Greek formulations and also in the utilitarian theories of the Enlightenment. It views individuals as fundamentally atomistic, self-contained and separate entities that may come together or separate as circumstances dictate. It is founded on a premise of individual autonomy where social commonality is based on some form of enlightened self-interest. It is this commonality of interests that creates community (and society) through recognition of either personal gain or the achievement of communal ends through social association. This contractual association may be based on maximizing self-interest or it may be based upon transcendent interests beyond individual maximization. The former is found in the social philosophy of the utilitarians where boundaries on individual behavior are accepted in expectation that others will do the same. With this expected reciprocity individual interests are maximized. In this latter conception community association is a social contract, yet one not based upon expectations of reciprocity and the common good is the motivation for the social contract (Benn 1982). Characterized as an atomistic and contractual, this notion of community association runs through community theory from Plato through Putnam (Kirkpatrick 2008).

A second perspective stresses the existence of community as organic and holistic. Community creates individual attachments and, as it does, individual interests. This notion, found in early Christian theology (Augustine and Aquinas), in sociology (Hegelian/Marxian, Tönnies,

Durkheim, Cooley) and in philosophy (Hegel, Whitehead, systems theorists) (Kirkpatrick 2008). Where atomistic/contractual assumptions highlight individual autonomy, association in organically conceived notions of community tends toward the notion of individuals filling socially proscribed roles and behaviors (Benn 1982).

Nisbet proposes a very clear statement of community as an organic and holistic aspect of social organization. "Community is founded on man conceived in his wholeness rather than in one or another of the roles, taken separately, that he may hold in a social order … it achieves fulfillment in the submergence of individual will that is not possible in unions of mere convenience or rational assent" (1966, p. 46). Community is, in the organic view, the center of the communal. Here the basic unit is the social group, not the individual. The sum total of community structure and culture are taken to be cohesive. Remove any part and the communal glue weakens (Carroll 2014, l. 4779). For Nisbet and others in this vein, this is not to deny volitional aspects of individualism. Yet they do posit an essential tendency among individuals toward community engagement, for "the yearning for a feeling of participation, for a sense of belonging, for a cause larger than one's own individual purposes and a group to call one's own" (Douthat 2014, l. 59).

13.2.2 Greek Conception: Community for Common Good and Locality as Place

Keller (2003) argues that "It was the Greeks who were the first to work out the complex links between the individual and community" (p. 20) and in seeing community as an integrating force with the larger sociocultural system. The utilitarian conception of community as atomistic affiliation is often the foil of the more organic idea. However, the classic Greek conception of ideal community provided a somewhat different take on affiliated interests among individuals (Minar and Greer 1969). For the Greeks, the polis had a contractual basis of association, yet one based on communal rather than individual ends. Social integration lies most especially in the cultural ideals of community. Community, as an ideal, played two important integrating roles: linking an autonomous local people to a wider worldview – the cultural traditions, religion, and philosophical perspectives of a more extensive Greek cultural system and (b) forging collective bonds among individuals that moderate local tension between individual ambition and collective needs (Keller 2003). These wider cultural links were forged through religious ceremony, community festivals and other civic activity while individual affiliation was achieved through laws and norms. "[G]roup goals and loyalty to the totality were to be put above individual striving for wealth and fame. The highest honors were according to those who put the common good above individual gain" (Keller 2003, p. 20).

While linkages between the individual, community and society were clearly emphasized in the writings of Socrates, Plato, and Aristotle, it is community that plays the preeminent role (Cresswell 2015). Community is somewhat autonomous from larger culture and it is community that shapes the contractual connection among individuals on a daily basis (Keller 2003). Notably this contractual bonding was not simply an expression of enlightened self-interest, but a mechanism for enhancing individual natural faculties and common goals (Kirkpatrick 2008, p. 14). As Keller states "For Plato, virtue rather than happiness was the path to an integrated life and virtue was rooted in communal well-being (Keller 2003, p. 287).

In this sense community is the mechanism for individual self-actualization. The community provides a basis for individual rational and philosophical common interest. The shared commonality of this interest is of location, "Both 'politics' and 'ethics' go back to Greek words that signify place: polis and ethea, 'city-states' and 'habitats' respectively. The very word 'society' stems from socius, signifying 'sharing' – and sharing is done in a common place" (Casey 1997, p. xiv). It is for this reason that community as place predominates Greek thought. Society, like space, is everywhere, yet nowhere in particular. Community without spatial identity on the earth lacks commonality.

It is this spatial commonality of place that solidifies Greek culture and philosophy. Community of place becomes the basis of the contractual aspect of social organization. It had an individual centered and contractual formulation of individual relationship to community, albeit one immersed in culture and meaning. Individuals were immersed in community and through it society. Yet, community is an ongoing agreement among individuals. The weight of influence is from individuals up. The polis is only loosely coupled to larger culture. Community is the primary sociocultural mechanism linking individuals to larger society and affiliation among individuals is derived from notions of a common good. Community is contractual but not in the sense posited later by utilitarian thinkers. Delanty (2009) argues that this is the first of two modern ideas of community "the human order of the polis and the universal order of the cosmos. These traditions – one particularistic and the other universalistic – correspond approximately to the Greek and Christian traditions … Where the Greeks gave priority to the polis as the domain of community, Christian thought stressed the universal community as a communion with the sacred" (pp. 5–6).

13.2.3 Medieval Christian Conceptions: Community as Organic and Universal

The conceptual alternative to the polis is found in the monastic community and in the early writings of Augustine and Thomas Aquinas. Where the polis is local, territorial, concerned with the immediate and daily actions of its members, the monastic community is organic, holistic and embedded in a specific shared ideology. A position in space and territoriality is the least important dimension of community. Instead, the normative order transcends space and the connections binding individuals together transcend individual interests (Keller 2003). Augustine melds this ideal together with Cicero's concept of the economic commonwealth to a conception of a common spiritual good that transcends spatial boundaries and creates a community of the faithful (Keller 2003). Building on the Augustinian concept of a universal community, Aquinas argues that such communities rise based upon this common spiritual good and: "infused the notion of community as organism, an idea derived from Augustinian thought, added as an additional ingredient of community the pursuit of the common good" (Keller 2003, p. 38).

Individuals are mutually bound together by community although each person maintains identity and independent action. These bonds are not ones of self-interest but reflect "a notion of mutuality in which one person seeks out another and in some sense lives for it and not itself" (Kirkpatrick 2008, p. 105). It is the overarching spiritual principles that bind individuals to this universal community rather than the overlapping interests that emerge from the individuals themselves. In this, the ideal is the community that exists prior to and apart from the individuals. Communal cohesion among individuals is shaped by this universal recognition of a greater, trans-individual ideal.

The concept of community arising from the monastic conception of affiliations is organic, sui generis, deriving essential meaning as a mechanism linking individuals to the larger (religious) culture. The monastic notion of community is one based on the power of ideals and culture. This holistic notion of community would later return in early sociological writings of Comte, Durkheim and Cooley (among others), but with the advent of the Enlightenment, an organic conception would be set aside. The utilitarian basis of community was found in mutual self-interest (Minar and Greer 1969).

13.2.3.1 The Age of Enlightenment: Community as Contract for Individual Good

In this conception the basis of sociality lies exclusively in the protection of individual property. Community plays a minimal role in these formations (Keller 2003; Minar and Greer 1969). For Hobbes community is seen as largely an antiquated social convenience. Locke retains the notion of community but sees it as a regrettable local association for protection when general social law fails (Kirkpatrick 2008). Contractual and atomistic, this conception would provide a much more narrow idea of association than that of the polis. It is one based on individual good rather than common good. "Both [Locke] and Hobbes believed the purpose of society as such was to protect individual interest, primarily property. This seemed far more self-evident to them than any claim that persons entered in to society because it in any sense a fulfillment of their nature or because sociability is intrinsically enjoyable and an end in itself" (Kirkpatrick 2008, p. 28). Here utilitarian contractualism parts ways with the transcendent social contract of the Greeks. Community and society extend no further than individual self-interest dictates. This notion was extended to politics and law (Bentham), markets (Smith), and governance (Rousseau). The utilitarian social philosophers rejected the medieval organic model of community. Individual affiliation arises from individual self-interest. Largely, they also reject the premises of the community oriented affiliation of Greek thought.

De Tocqueville (1994) offers a singular exception. De Tocqueville clearly viewed association as atomistic and contractual (Kirkpatrick 2008). However, he painted a contrast between the self-interested aspect of this contract and transcendent common values linking individuals – self-interest rightly conceived. This contrast in social association is also a contrast between the role of community and of society. In American individualism he saw pecuniary self-interested motivation creating a trend away from community association for the common good. With this trend comes the ascendancy of larger society as the mechanism around which individual association was organized. However, with that ascendancy, the common goals linking individuals together would disappear. "What de Tocqueville feared was that this increasing isolation and sense of self-sufficiency would actually create the conditions for a more powerful and dominant state. Individualism might lead to the destruction of the virtue of public life and 'apathy toward the public weal'…" (Kirkpatrick 2008, pp. 35–36).

Community for de Tocqueville, especially as it creates cohesion, was the most critical issue in societal development. "Among the laws that rule human societies there is one which seems to be more precise and clear than all others. If men are to remain civilized or to become so, the art of associating together must grow and improve in the same ratio in which the equality of conditions is increased" (Vol 2, p. 110). This art of association lay with community, not society, if for no other reason than society was distant abstraction for most. "It is difficult to draw a man out of his own circle to interest him in the destiny of the state, because he does not clearly understand the influence the destiny of the state can have upon his own lot" (Vol 2, p. 104).

Community provided material and cultural immediacy that created cohesion. The issues of the local community engage the individual in an immediate recognition of common interests. "But if it is proposed to make a road cross the end of his estate, he will see at glance that there is a connection between his small public affairs and his greatest private affairs; and he will discover, without it being shown to him, the close ties that unites private to general interest" (Vol. 2, p. 104). In the local community de Tocqueville finds the utilitarian tendencies to be countered by transcendent interests in the common good. Here, what the Greeks found unproblematic about community, de Tocqueville highlights as a critical problem of community Self-interest may be rightly understood, or not. A contract of common purpose may triumph, or not.

This is "how an enlightened regard for themselves constantly prompts them to assist one another and inclines them willingly to sacrifice a portion of their time and property to the welfare of the state" (Vol. 2, p. 122). Yet de Tocqueville also places this transcendent interest in the cohesion brought about by the "constant habit of kindness and an established repudiation of disinterestedness." It is the local cultural identity "which leads a great number of citizens to value the affection of their neighbors and of their kindred, [and] perpetually brings men together and forces them to help one another in spite of the propensities that sever them" (Vol 2, 104). Common conditions and common affection are the contextual conditions forming contractual association, rather than pure self-interest. Critical to the formation of this mutuality among community members are the public associations that typify the local community.

De Tocqueville places the two types of contractual association in opposition to one another: society and individual self-interest vs. community and transcendent interests. This approach represents a break with the characterizations of association and community underlying utilitarian thought. Instead his formulation of community recalls the Greek notions of contractual association for higher purposes. This becomes de Tocqueville's analytic quest. Can community moderate society? Can the common weal triumph over self-interest? As Keller states of de Tocqueville "Crucial here is that individuals think it is to their interest to link themselves to others. But how to plant the same thought into a thousand minds at the same moment?" (Keller 2003, p. 230). De Tocqueville thought the answer lay in part in the local press but also in the proliferation of associations that created a shared identity in the community. For him, this was by no means an assured outcome. To the extent that community triumphed, individuals would find meaning in shared identity and in sharing common goals. To the extent that society triumphed individuals would isolate themselves and only associate according to the expedience of individual gain. This view of community association as a process would re-emerge with Tönnies (1887). However, for Tönnies this transition would be more profound. He would conceive this as a change in the essential nature of association, in the movement from the organic to the contractual.

13.3 Community, Association and Locality: Development in Sociology

13.3.1 Classic Sociology: From Community to Society

De Tocqueville aside, the reaction to the utilitarian concept of community sets the foundation of discussion for subsequent social science and philosophy (Kirkpatrick 2008; Keller 2003, Nisbet 1966). Nisbet in particular argues that the contemporary view of community and alienation is found in the philosophical conservative's view. They saw loss of institutional traditions as leading to alienation (Keller 2003; Nisbet 2014). Their response to the self-interested autonomy of the Enlightenment was to return to the organic, social individual of Augustine (Nisbet 1966). In part this reflects a nostalgia for the disappearing communities of the medieval age (Bell and Newby 1975), but it is also a reaction to the rise of political thought that prioritizes the national political state. "The idea of the abstract, impersonal, and purely legal state is challenged by the theories resting on the assumed priority of community, tradition, and status" (Nisbet 1966, p. 51). Social, moral, epistemological and metaphysical attacks in philosophy by Hegel, Bradley and Bergson mounted against the atomistic perspective, especially as it centered on self-interest. It is in this light that sociological treatises of the period should be understood (Kirkpatrick 2008; Keller 2003).

Using community as a central organizing concept, Durkheim rejected the notion that self-interest was the foundation of social cohesion, substituting common beliefs and sentiments – the collective conscience (Keller 2003). This conception parallels Comte's idea of the moral community (Nisbet 1966). Both see society simply as community written large. It is from both community and society that all phenomenon above the purely physiological is derived. The transition from mechanical to organic association in no way reflected a loss of the communal origins of attachment and affiliation. Rather this was a change from one type of community attachment; local, immediate, sentimental, to another type of attachment; less bounded by locality and similarity. In analyzing the shift to organic solidarity "Durkheim was gratified to conclude that, far from community disintegrating, society was becoming one big community" (Bell and Newby 1975, p. 23). His concern was that the emergence of organic solidarity might be threatened by a readiness to cooperate on behalf of common purposes (Day 2006). This could lead to greater anomie. However, this transition, for Durkheim, should not be mistaken for a shift to an atomistic character for association. Association in the organic society remains embedded in the common culture, the collective conscience of society (Keller 2003). The social system remains the force shaping individual attachment and association, not individual volition. This conception is holistic with individual behavior shaped conditions by the divisions of organic society rather than the communal mechanic solidarity of community. What does change is the role that community plays. Rather than the immediate mediator of larger culture, community is subsumed as a component of the larger division of labor. Community becomes society.

For Marx, community never differentiated from society. Like Durkheim, he rejects the utilitarian notions of association in favor of an organic conception (Kirkpatrick 2008). Individual association is shaped by society. Unlike Durkheim, community is relegated to a secondary role in shaping association. Both in his critique of pre-socialist society and in his prospective communist society, Marx turns away from localism in favor of a communal association at the societal level (Nisbet 1966). The importance of community lies in its historically specific role in mediating socioeconomic relationship. Community is simply the most local characterization of society (Nisbet 1966). Here community is simply a spatial node of larger society. Those elements of community association highlighted by his contemporaries, cooperation, mutuality and affection had little place in Marx's treatment of community (Kirkpatrick 2008). Those elements of association would not develop in community but ultimately they would in communist society.

Tönnies, unlike Marx, begins with the historical preeminence of community over society. Unlike Durkheim, he did see the transition from community to society as a fundamental shift from individuals as embedded social beings to individual autonomy, from the holistic to the atomistic. With this shift comes the loss of community as a mechanism for organizing association. Tönnies stresses *Gemeinschaft* as typified by cherished modes of community association (love, loyalty, honor, friendship) all of which are superseded by utilitarian 'society' the *Gesellschaft* of atomistic individualism and association based on divisions (Nisbet 1966). This is seen as a shift from a natural, organic character of local association, one based on shared history, traditions, and affective social connections to one of impersonal rationality. As Day (2006) characterizes Tönnies, "Community stands for real ties of interdependence and emotion between people who form part of an organic, bounded, entity, often linked to place or territory. 'Association' refers to exchanges among individuals who engage in essentially boundaryless, contractual relationships; the ties between them are merely convenient" (p. 6). Tönnies argues that modernization brings with it a shift to contractualism.

This shift is one from individual association embedded in community itself to one of association arising from the individual and based solely on mutual self-interest. In *Gemeinschaft* community binds individuals together through reciprocity, history, and shared culture. While Tönnies provided a central role for individual volition in this attachment, in community this volition is directed by the culture of place (*Wesenwille*) and is therefore of the community. In *Gesellschaft* society, that community is lost and with it the primacy of place. *Kurwille* (purposive-rational) volition predominates and is of the individual. Thus contractualism comes to characterize association in *Gesellschaft* society. Rudolf Heberle highlights this point in his preface to *Community and Society* (2002).

> Tönnies showed that Aristotle and Hobbes were both right. Each had focused on different aspects of social life: Man was indeed by his very nature a social being who would unfold his essence only by living in communities of kinship, space (neighborhood), and spirit, but who was also capable of forming and, at certain stages in history, compelled to form new kinds of associations by agreements – associations which could be understood as instruments for the attainment of certain ends – whereas those 'older' communities were taken as ends in themselves and therefore could not be understood by a utilitarian approach. (2002, p. *x*)

This point is echoed by Delanty (2009) "there is no doubt that Tönnies tended to polarize these terms, seeing community as encompassing tradition and society as modernity, and both interlocked in a 'tragic conflict'…" (p. 21). This theoretical synthesis is consequential, given that

Tönnies' typology continued to influence sociologists throughout the twentieth century. Rather than positing an essential character to association and community, Tönnies and subsequent work in this vein recognized the transitional nature of community and of association.

Tönnies, like Weber, treated community as typology although not in the empirical sense. For both, types of community represented types of association. This theme is picked up by Simmel (1971) and Weber (1958) (especially in his traditional vs rational types of authority, social action oriented to (1) interpersonal ends, (2) absolute value-ends, (3) emotional/affectual states, and (4) tradition and convention – as well as the transition from non-rational to rational society) and later by Cooley 2008) (in his primary vs secondary types of associations) and Durkheim (1964) (mechanical vs organic solidarity).

Notably these thinkers focus on a transition in general association rather than explicitly assigning the concept of 'community' to either. For Weber the communal is the antithesis of rational associative solidarity. With a shift to the rational associative comes an increase in atomistic isolation of the modern individual. In Durkheim however, this transition remains fundamentally determined by society. Here society operates through communal moral consensus and Durkheim, in his methodology, prioritizes community (in the sense of community of beliefs and sentiments) as the mechanism through which society influences individual behavior (Nisbet 1966).

Simmel parallels Durkheim's interest in institutions and associations, but at a micro level. A critique of utilitarian individualism, Simmel's view of society was one of individual contributions that aggregate up to society, although not necessarily on a contractual basis. Simmel puts autonomy into the forefront of sociological concern. "The deepest problems of modern life derive from-the claim of the individual to preserve the autonomy and individuality of his existence in the face of overwhelming social forces, of historical heritage, of external culture, and of the technique of life." His *Metropolis and Mental Life* is concerned with the transition from cohesive traditional community to de-socialized anonymous life (Nisbet 1966, 95–97).

By the end of the nineteenth century the concept of community was established in these two traditions. The organic notion viewed community as the ultimate cause of individual association through the influence of immediate norms, values and local goals. Community exists sui generis, as either the mediator between individuals and society (as with the monasitic vision), or as the immediate and primary mechanism shaping individual association (as with the Conservative reaction to the Enlightenment). However, in this conception, the immediate influences of community were being subsumed in organic society. Community may exist as a social entity but increasingly the character of community was dominated by the character of society. With this, the importance of community as place correspondingly is de-emphasized. Association no longer is seen as organized in space as communities of place. With that change, the organic bonding elements of association no longer have a particularly spatial identity. Society creates attachment and society is territorially pervasive.

Contractualist approaches viewed community as shaped by loosely amalgamated individual association aggregated up to form common mechanisms that either enhanced self-interest, as in the utilitarian approaches, or shared goals and ideals, as with the Greek classic notion of the polis. In the latter, locality reigned supreme in that the transmission of interests were local, face-to-face and immediate. Society and culture were filtered through community. For the utilitarians, such localism was simply the remnant of an earlier era. Contractual association was reorganized across commonalities that transcended locality. Neither ideals nor goals were contained within any particular community. Individual interests had universalized and the local community disappears as a recognizable theater of common interest.

Thus for both groups the foundational position of community's role in relation to association had shifted. The immediacy and proximity of social relations were of less importance. The universality of associations became the problem of interest. For Durkheim, Marx, Simmel and Weber, the importance of community gives way to society as the primary aspect of social organization linking individuals. As Day (2006) states "It is not necessarily the case that the classic sociologists wholeheartedly endorsed community as a value, or an end in itself. On the contrary, it can be argued that in general they welcomed social progress and development …" (p. 10). Certainly this is the case with early American theories of community and society.

13.3.2 Community and Theory in the Early Twentieth Century

Drawing from Durkheim and Simmel, Wirth and Cooley built their notions of community and association on an organic view of social relationships, "[T]he relation between society and the individual as an organic relation. That is, we see that the individual is not separable from the human whole… And, on the other hand, the social whole is in some degree dependent upon each individual, because each contributes something to the common life that no one else can contribute" (Cooley 2008, l. 527–531). Cooley rejected the atomistic notion of individuals, asserting that human develop led to an ever-widening association, based on primary group ideals, that would expand from the family to the local community, to the nation, and finally to the world community (Coser 1977). Likewise Wirth (1948) argued community association might not be limited by locality, but could be extended globally. Wirth and Cooley developed a notion of transcendent association based upon primary group ideals. These connections had their origins in the local community yet community was not a necessary element linking individuals together. The organic nature of social organization extended to society and societies. In this conception community association, in the sense of primary group affiliation, could create a global community. This approach retains the rejection of contractualism and the holistic notion of European sociology, yet excises the role of community (Kirkpatrick 2008). Here Tönnies' *Gemeinschaft* relations are extended to society at large. Society becomes community.

If some schools of American sociological thought treated changes in community association as a disappearing element in social life, others focused on the changing relationship between community and society. A concern with the relationship between community and society becomes one of the predominant interests whether of an organic or contractual orientation. This is seen early on in the works of MacIver (1917). While explicitly rejecting an organic view of community MacIver sees community and society as part of a continuum of the social interaction (Kirkpatrick 2008). He argues that society provide a vague and incoherent sense of one's association to others, "[It] is the small intense community within which the life of the ordinary individual is lived, a tiny nucleus of common life with a sometimes larger, sometimes smaller and always varying fringe" (p. 7). For MacIver there is a constant tension between community and society, with local community encompassing individuals' notions of shared fate and interdependence. It is community that links the individual to larger society. However MacIver thought that community itself is subordinate to the character of larger society (Minar and Greer 1969).

Human ecology builds a community centered theory, one that highlights the role that community plays in creating society. Drawing from both Durkheim and from biology, human ecologists developed an organic and holistic approach that parallels Cooley and Wirth. For them, however community becomes the focal point. It is the holistic, unit character of communities that Park, Burgess, McKenzie and others treat both society and community as a material whole, based on spatial and organization interdependence. This is not however a purely spatial notion of community and was concerned instead with the borders and boundaries of group processes, culture and association (Irwin 2015). It assumes that community proscribes the conditions for individual association "… for every individual, interdependence with other human beings is imperative. It is indispensable to life. … Interdependence is the irreducible connotation of sociality" (Hawley 1986, p. 6). Not that Hawley bases this interdependence on an assumption of rationality, like the utilitarians, but only as a material condition creating association. Community explains individual association. "The question to be asked in an ecological approach is not why persons do what they do, but under what conditions do given actions occur" (Hawley 1986, p. 6). This approach emphasized both the organic nature of community and social nature of individuals.

In this, human ecology rejected the utilitarian, contractual foundations human association instead applying sociological notions of cohesion and embeddedness in group processes (Irwin and Kasarda 1994). Community is both the building block for larger society and the boundary within which social life takes place (Gans 2015; Park et al. 1984; Hawley 1950, 1986; McKenzie 1967). With boundaries set by spatial constraints, by economic division of labor and by the demographic structures of cities, the ecological community was seen as setting the limits and possibilities for association. For the early Chicago school ecologists "One tendency was to see urbanization, industrialization and modernization as transforming the town into the city, creating new kinds of social relations and presenting new challenges for community" (Delanty 2009, p. 39).

One implication of this change was the separation of community as an ecological force binding together individuals towards a common material support, and community as attachments, sentiments and emotional commonality. As Delanty (2009) states "it might be said that these studies tend to see community as something preserved in the locality while being under threat in the wider city. An interpretation might be that the city has become absorbed into the *Gesellschaft* of society, while *Gemeinschaft* is preserved in the vestiges of locality" (p. 40). The ecological community contained many communities of attachment and shaped such communities. Much of the work of early human ecology was dedicated to the study of the relationship between these two types of communities.

From Wirth (1938) on, community studies in this vein focused on the relationship between material structures of the ecological community and cultural processes in these communities of attachment (Wirth 1928; Lynd and Lynd 1929; Park et al. 1984; Zorbaugh 1929; Whyte 1955; Redfield 1955; Frazier 1957; Warner and Lunt 1941; Hollingshead 1949). Here community attachment was considered to be an outcome of the organic whole of the ecological community. Individual attachment arose from the processes and interrelationships between the whole (the metropolitan community) and its parts (neighborhoods and local districts). Thus individual association was, in this view, shaped by the ecological community. Further, society was seen as constituted by the interrelationships among these ecological communities (McKenzie 1967; Hawley 1950).

13.4 The Post WWII Division in Community Sociology

In the post-WWII era, Chicago School scholarship split along these two lines, with the cultural elements of community attachment seen as a separate issue from the development of the ecological issues of community (Irwin 2015; Saunders 1986). With very few exceptions (Kasarda and Janowitz 1974) the whole/part relationships became of less importance and with that change, the role and theoretical orientation of community shifted. The two approaches came to be regarded as separate enterprises with neoclassical human ecology pursuing the structural aspects of community and the second Chicago School pursuing the processes and elements of community attachment (Gans 2015). This created a division between scholars that emphasized the material elements that constitute community as an object of study vs those who study the culture and ideology binding individuals together within community. More than a split in focus, this becomes a split between an organic and contractual conception of community.

For neoclassical human ecology individual attachment was relatively unproblematic and taken as a postulate of the organic nature of the ecological community (Hawley 1986). The role of place is conceptually straightforward.

Community is coterminous with the territory of community. Space, territory and place are inseparable concepts. The focus falls upon a) the social and spatial interrelationships among ecological communities and b) the implications of these macro relationships for societal processes (Hawley 1971).

In many ways society is viewed as arising from and built upon community. Work in this area focused on the communities themselves to the exclusion of micro-level social interaction. Association among individuals was derived from their position in the community, an organic formulation. The socio-spatial organization of community was studied as an integrated system. Scholarship in this approach pursued issues of community interdependence, social morphology, division of labor among communities and related issues (Berry and Kasarda 1977; Hauser and Schnore 1965; Schnore 1965; Zimmer and Hawley 1968; Frisbie and Poston 1978). The processes by which this took place at the micro-level were less emphasized than the macro-level structures which resulted.

For the second Chicago School (the intellectual extension of the Chicago community studies school) and for related work elsewhere in community studies, the focus was on people at the local community level, and the institutions, processes and patterns of attachment that create association. Without positing community as sui generis, their analyses shifted solely to the culture, history, institutions and local meaning that encourage affiliation. This line of work became associated with the careful explication of social interaction within communities. The focus highlighted people, not communities themselves (Gans 2015). Scholars in this vein explored types of local communities, differences in affiliation among these communities, individual attachment and meaning within communities and the social problems of these communities (Hunter 1953, 1974; Gans 1962, 1967; Wellman 1979; Suttles 1972; Bell and Newby 1975). These scholars emphasized community as a social contract although they rejected utilitarian notions of self-interest as the primary motivating factor in association. Here community was studied from the point of view of its members. Despite very distinctive approaches, both lines of scholarship retained the early human ecological notion that community was the critical linkage to society. This was seen either as a linking mechanism to broader society (as in the second Chicago School) or as the structural building blocks of society at large (as in neo-classical human ecology).

In the 1970s and 1980s scholars working in Marxian traditions focused on the ways that society created community. This new urban school reoriented this community centered understanding of places to one which situated community in larger society. Place is seen as a microcosm of larger social forces. The new urban approach retained the organic and materialist assumptions outlined by Marx. Society was a system which determined the character and nature of social association, of social institutions and especially of community. Impactful in sociology, geography and urban planning, the new urban approach highlighted the rise of global capitalism as the context in which places develop. Space more than place is conceptually ascendant in this point of view. Castells brings this issue front and center (Castells 1996, 2000; Susser 2002).

For Castells (1996) globalization and new technology gave rise to the reorganization of space. Noting that social flows always have a spatial component, Castells argues that society is reorganizing space, from a space of places to a space of flows. The space of flows is not based on propinquity but refers to the networks of finance, production, communication and power across the landscape. While these may come together in space, place and community are seen as epiphenomenal of these flows. "…[T]he space of flows does include a territorial dimension, as it requires a technological infrastructure that operates from certain locations, and as it connects functions and people located in specific places" (Castells 1996, p. 14). Place is a function of spatial organization, but one that shifts with the lines of power, production and technology. Place is always an outcome of spatially based networks, which are themselves products of society. Although Castells differs with Lefebvre on the importance of place, both see place and space as ultimately linked to society. In this sense, community is simply the local manifestation of society.

For Lefebvre (1991) place as a lived, tangible territory is the center of space as experienced in everyday life. Locality, as lived space, involves different experiences for individuals according to their position in society. That is, the experience of community is itself shaped by larger social forces. Thus the lived experience of place is also an experience of space as a product of capitalist society. For Lefebvre "ideas about regions, media images of cities and perceptions of 'good neighbourhoods' are other aspects of this space which is necessarily produced by each society" (Shields 2012, p. 284).

Building on the work of Lefebvre space, Soja (1989, 1996, 2010) explores the implications of space as the central dimension of capitalist society. Here he sees his work as linking Marxian and post-modern approaches. His concept of third spaces extends the idea of space as (1) a material condition and (2) as a symbolic construction. Third space is the expression of space as lived experience that combines the abstract and concrete dimensions into one (Latham 2012), implying that community is epiphenomenal of these other, more important elements, since the experience of community varies by all three dimensions. Thus in *Postmodern Geographies* (Soja 1989), different routes taken at different times through Los Angeles lead to distinct communities, such as the post-Fordist industrial metropolis, the globalized cosmopolis, the fractal city shattered by social divisions, and others, each occupying the same place.

The organization of space as intrinsic to capitalism (or any other social form) and the material implications of space as a social product are pervasive themes in new urban sociology. These are foundational concepts to the work of Logan & Molotch (1987), Harvey (1989), Massey (1994), Gottdiener (1985) and many others. The organic nature of society, especially in its capitalistic form, and the material implications of space as a social product parallel human ecology as both Hawley (1984) and Smith (1995) have noted. They find commonality in the material foundation of community, in the organic nature of macro social organization and in a rejection of contractual foundations for community organization. There are of course, many fundamental differences between the two approaches. Most pertinent here is that, unlike neoclassical ecology, the new urban sociology views community as a microcosm of society. Community is a consequence of forces of production and for contemporary community these are national and global forces. Although community may provide a basis for organization and resistance to these forces, ultimately the nature of community follows from the structure of society.

The commutarian approach, following the traditions of de Tocqueville and the ancient Greeks, sees communities arising from common goals, common purpose, and shared ideology (Bellah et al. 1992, 1996; Etzioni 1993, 1995, 1996). Community arises as a contractual obligation for the greater good. Commutarianism explicitly recalls de Tocqueville's contrast between self-interest and common interest as a basis for community association. Like de Tocqueville they clearly acknowledge community association can be typified by either form of contract. However, this work highlights the problems of self-interested individualism as opposed to the development of the common good. Community is the ground where this opposition is engaged.

Etzioni for instance contrasts the problems of persons acting as free agents as opposed to communal action based on common identities and purposes. As Bruhn (2005) typifies Etzioni "It is the challenge of communitarians to pull people together from the extremes of autonomy and antagonism to a middle zone of mutuality by relying on community pressure and individual morality. Communitarian thinking basically involves a return to 'we-ness' in our society, in our social institutions, and in our social relationships" (l. 673). Similarly Delanty (2009) says of Etzioni's work, "His advocation of community may be seen as an American reaction to the dominance of rational choice and neo-liberalism in the 1980s. ... Community entails voice – a 'moral voice' – and social responsibility rests on personal responsibility" (p. 68).

Bellah and colleagues (1992, 1996) also follow this neo-Tocquevillean theme however they highlight the importance of community based institutions and culture. For Bellah and colleagues the language of individualism and its impact on the nature of community association is especially important. They center their work on both the moral voice discussed by Etzioni and on the role that community plays in creating this voice. In their analysis they argue that in contemporary communities a culture of coherence, based on traditions, memory of place, and common identity is in contention with the a culture of separatism (Bellah et al. 1996). This is clearly a battle for contractual cohesion based on the greater good vs one based on limited individual self-interest. In exploring the nature of community cohesion, Bellah et al note "We found that it took a both a 'hard' utilitarian shape and a 'soft' expressive form. One focused on the bottom line, the other on feelings…" (p. viii). The choice between these two lies with their moral and social conception of community more than the material or structural conditions.

This distinguishes their approach from that later developed by Putnam. As Bellah typifies the central argument of *Habits of the Heart* "The argument for the decline in social capital was essentially a cultural analysis, more about language than behavior" (p. xvii). However they acknowledge the role the more institutional arguments put forward by Putnam. "We believe the culture and language of individualism influence these trends but there are also structural reasons for them…" (p. xvii). In this they situate community cultural changes in community institutional arrangements lauded by de Tocqueville and the loss of these arrangements lamented by Putnam (2000), Putnam et al. (1993, 2003).

Putnam's analysis focuses on the interrelationships among social institutions, civic engagement, and organizational performance. Some institutions, according to Putnam, promote "horizontal ties" that cut across diverse groups, link together isolated institutions (thereby enhancing their effectiveness) and foster trust and civic involvement in the local population. The collective elements of social capital, in this perspective, are found in the complex of community institutions acting together as a system. Local government, informal institutions, community associations, and economic enterprises interact to enhance civic welfare, and the benefits of this social capital accrue. In this sense benefits accrue to the system of institutions, not the institutions themselves. The beneficial outcomes too tend to be seen as public goods that are structural characteristics of community, such as decreased inequality, less poverty and other aggregate social welfare outcomes. In this social capital and its benefits are not reducible below the community level. The benefits of social capital (both economic and social welfare) accrue to communities. The benefits to social capital are collective gains. Better government, local economic growth and civic welfare are outcomes shared within the collectivity, not owned by individuals. However, individuals rightly understand that this general good is shared among individuals. It is a lesson that is founded in community and from there extends to society at large.

In the works of Putnam, Bellah and Etzioni, contractualism is moderated by a sense of community as sui generis. Pre-existing local institutions and a culture of civic engagement create collective local identity that is the foundation of the communitarian notion of community. It is also a perspective that looks at the interaction between the material and cultural elements of community. The cultural elements associated with community identity and the structural elements of social capital are, in practice, intertwined. Thus, while association is based upon contractualism for the public good, community has an organic quality to it that supersedes the individual contract. These elements are not strictly born from individual agreements, they also shape such agreements. The proliferation of civic organizations in a community creates a sense of community purpose and identity. At the same time general norms encouraging civic participation encourage the formation of civic organizations.

This intertwining of cultural and material bases of community is also found in phenomenological approaches albeit with an entirely different emphasis. Cresswell (2015) differentiates the phenomenological approach as one focused on the deeper elements of human association.

> This approach is not particularly interested in the unique attributes of particular places nor is it primarily concerned with the kinds of social forces that are involved in the construction of particular places. Rather it seeks to define the essence of human existence as one that is necessarily and importantly 'in-place.' This approach is less concerned with 'places' and more interested in 'Place' (l. 1439).

This work has an abiding concern on the internalization of community into individual's identity. Here the perception of space becomes as important as place in understanding community. As Tuan (2014) states "Human beings not only discern geometric patterns in nature and create abstract spaces in the mind, they also try to embody their feelings, images, and thoughts in tangible material" (p. 17).

Place becomes the meanings attached to space, especially in its symbols such as monuments, characteristics buildings and other icons of community. It is this meaning through the symbols of community that roots individuals to place. "Abstract space, lacking significance other than strangeness, becomes concrete place, filled with meaning" (p. 199). For Tuan, this phenomenology of place was of central importance. Yet his concern lay less in the implications of this phenomenology and more in "the emotional and intimate engagement of people, culture, environment and place" (Rodaway 2012, p. 427). This concern with meanings and attachment permeates most of the subsequent literature in the phenomenological approach to community.

Another recurring theme is the problem of hyper-individualism associated with the loss of place in a globalizing society. Auge's (2008) concept of 'non-place', those elements of space devoid of common culture, exemplifies this idea. "If a place can be defined as relational, historical, and concerned with identity, then a space which cannot be defined as relational, historical or concerned with identity will be a non-place" (p. 78). His non-places are spaces devoid of the traditional cultural characteristics of community that create meaningful and continuous social association (Merriman 2012). Instead they exist as spatial nodes of accumulation and consumption that are bondless and self-serving.

> A person entering the space of non-place is relieved of his usual determinants. He becomes no more than what he does or experiences in the role of passenger, customer, or driver … The space of non-place creates neither singular identity nor relations; only solitude, and similitude. There is no room for history unless it has been transformed into an element of spectacle, usually in allusive texts. (Auge 2008, p. 103)

Auge sees non-places in ascendancy and meaningful association among individuals in decline. Here Auge points to the loss of the social contractualism of community, much in the traditions of Töennies. However in his view, if identity becomes devoid of sociality, then even the minimal contractualism of the utilitarians is lost. "Place and non-place are rather like opposed polarities: the first is never completely erased, the second never totally completed… But non-places are the real measure of our time" (p. 79).

A similar concern is expressed by Certeau (1984). As Crang (2012) explains "he sees tactics transforming the places designed by hegemonic powers and envisioned as the neat and orderly realm of the concept city, into unruly spaces; that is, he sees practices as spatialising places" (p. 108). This loss of place in the midst of globalization is also a theme presented in Bauman (2001, 2013). Arguing that a global community is developing, place now becomes more associated with all of humanity, at least for those who are geo-mobile. Contrasting this 'glocalization' with localization, Bauman notes that failure to reorient to the global community leaves some caught in local space just as the foundations of association shift. Locality no longer is community. As Clarke (2012) says "Globalisation, Bauman maintains, is best thought of as glocalisation – which implies more than deterritorialisation and reterritorialisation occurring simultaneously, or the reassertion of place in the midst of space–time compression. It implies a worldwide restratification of society based on freedom of movement (or lack thereof)" (p. 51).

13.5 Reintegrating the Material and Ideal; Space and Place

One major issue in these foundational ideas lay in the relative importance of space vs. place. Locality is an ambivalent concept in the post WWII treatment of community. It is recognized as a critical factor in attachment, commonality and association, and yet its material existence in space provides theoretical discomfort. Space is often seen as devoid of culture and the territoriality of place often is seen as epiphenomenal of cultural attachments.

This is clearly seen in Gieryn's (2000) treatise, *A Space for Place in Sociology*. He argues that place has three necessary and sufficient conditions; geographic location, material form, and investment with meaning which he sees as inseparable elements (p. 463–466). His definition (following Soja 1989, 1996) brings together both the material and symbolic ideas arguing that "Places are doubly constructed: most are built or in some way physically carved out. They are also interpreted, narrated, perceived, felt, understood and imagined." Although rejecting a simple spatial measure of place he argues that the context of place is of overriding importance in shaping social life and in mediating between society/culture and the individual.

Gieryn argues that although community and place are not necessarily coterminous, the physical, cultural and material conditions of place set the foundations for community. "But is there a 'place effect' as well? … Enough studies suggest that the design and serial construction of places is at the same time the execution of community…" (p. 477). In this sense place is the necessary, if not sufficient basis for community formation and the continuation of community. He concludes that "… place matters for politics, and identity, history and futures, inequality and community" (p. 482). The important elements of community are all associated with place. Without place, community lacks social cohesion, without place community lacks identification, without place community lacks history. Not all places are communities yet most of what Gieryn finds important about place are elements we would commonly associate with community. Without community, place loses its essential impact. "Space is what place becomes when the unique gathering of things, meanings and value are sucked out … place is space filled up by people, practices, objects and representations" (p. 465). Gieryn does reject space as a factor creating community.

Logan's (2012) rejoinder, *A Place for Space*, rescues the spatial aspect critiqued in Gieryn. Logan points out that spatial relations are themselves social relations. Simply the socio-cultural patterns of place have spatial referents. "In fact, places are not only geographically located and material as Gieryn (2000) points out, but they are also spatial, and their spatiality gives rise to fruitful questions" (p. 509). Logan argues that "There is an implicit spatial reference in almost all studies of places" (p. 508). Logan notes that social relations have spatial locations and that the relative location of social activities of vital for understanding the causes and consequences of social activity. Distance and proximity, access and segregation, are all spatial referents that are cause and consequence of stratification and affiliation. Sometimes cause and sometimes consequence, these spatial patterns are inextricably bound to the character of social interaction.

This tension in the emphasis of place and space is not new. Casey (1993, 1997) outlines the philosophical history of space and place arguing that space was transcendent over place following Newton and Kant. He argues that contemporary postmodernism returns to the original Aristotelian formulation that place is the preeminent concept. He anchors this idea in the material conditions of individuals as inextricably place bound and the primacy of the experience of place in shaping human perception. The dialectic between place and perception makes individuals "not only in place but of place" (Casey 1997:322). Casey associates place with both meaning and location. "A place is more of an event than a thing to be assimilated to known categories. As an event, if it is unique, idiolocal. Its peculiarity calls not for assumption into the already known … but for the imaginative constitution for terms respecting idiolocality" (p. 329). Here community as place influences individuals and it also takes on the meanings and characteristics of its constituent population. This leads Casey to view culture and place as inextricably intertwined and propose to put culture back in place – to reunite the division between a behavioral/material view and a symbolic view.

Casey's assertion is that place re-emerges as a central philosophical concept following centuries relegation to a type of space. He argues that in the early modern era space is rethought as place and that this comes to fruition in post-modern thought. Bachelard reimagines place as a psychic, non-spatial entity; Foucault, Deleuze and Guattari rethink space as heterogeneous places of power and social differentiation; Derrida examines how building coverts space to places. The outcome is that these contemporary postmodern takes recapitulate the original Aristotelian view that space is not distinct from place. "... if place became increasingly lost in space after the demise of the classical era, in the twentieth century we stand witness to a third peripteia: space is now becoming absorbed into place..." (p. 340). Although Casey's interest is in the philosophical implications of place and space, his work is integrated in sociological literature by Kolb (2008).

Kolb synthesizes these ideas in both postmodern and Marxian theory to explore the territorial basis for community. Place is seen as the essence of community and is defined both by its normative character (recalling organic traditions) and by intentional unity (contractualism). That is, place exists independently of the individual by benefit of its location within spatially and normatively connected social organization: "to experience a place is to encounter an expanse of space as manifesting a web of social possibilities and norms" (p. 33). This notion of community then exists independently of any individual actor yet encompasses the mechanism (possibilities) for cooperative actions for any individual to achieve social action. "A place opens a landscape of action possibilities set in a spatial landscape" (p. 35).

In Kolb's formulation then, individual participation in community is an autonomous decision, but one required for effective action (p. 39). Community is the vehicle of action, but these vehicles come in many models. Each community has its own structures, culture, history, and therefore character for action. Individuals, in engaging in community, accept (or at least participate) in the mechanism of that place. Individual autonomy is limited by the social and spatial character of place. Here, as with the commutarian approaches, organic and contractual conceptions of community association are synthesized, as are material and symbolic bases of community. This is not to say that, in Kolb's view, places are autonomous from larger society.

> The structure of place never exists on its own: it results from larger social processes and decisions received into local processes of interpretation and embodiment. ... Local interpretation keeps normative and physical structures flexible, and it keeps larger causal and political processes from forcing every detail in a place. On the other hand, outside processes provide resources and keep local interpretive processes from closing in on themselves. (p. 45)

As with the new urban approaches, place/community links individuals to society. Place filters meaning from society and allows local variation yet links the local to the larger processes and culture of society.

Thus while community limits individual autonomy it allows heterogeneity of interpretation and social action. This strikes a balance between the social deterministic nature of individuals proposed by some of the classic theorists (Cooley, Marx, Durkheim) and the self-interested autonomy of the utilitarians but one not solely predicated on inter-individual commitment. Neither purely an aggregation of the individuals within it nor exclusively a microcosm of society, community becomes a normative and structural mechanism that mediates and attaches individual and society that exists in situ as place.

Kolb's analysis (drawing on Lefebvre 1991) also attempts to integrate spatial and symbolic aspects of community. In discussing his approach to place he lays out the relationship between spatially based concepts and place (which he takes to be the normative order associated with community). His typology of concepts is at once spatial and social. 'Areas' are expanses of space, 'locations' are events associated with area, 'locales' emerge when perceived meanings are associated with locations with perceived meanings. 'Places' bring these socio-spatial concepts together as a meaningful social unit. "Places in the sense I propose is an extended location consisting of one or more expanses of space where social norms of action define significant areas and transitions for activities. Places are permeated by social norms offering possibilities for action" (p. 32).

Kolb, like Lefebvre, highlights the spatial dimension shaping place though economic, environmental and technological connections to other places. These systematic linkages among places across space are the material causal constraints on place action and community normative order. "Lefebvre's discussion emphasizes how places, in the sense that I propose, come linked to one another and intertwined with causal systems that influence social norms. … Systematic effects constrain possibilities" (p. 39).

This recalls the integration of material space and culture that defined early human ecology, however, more full develops the normative order of place. Like the classical ecologists, the material spatial conditions set constraints on cultural possibilities. Also like the ecologists community (as place) becomes a vehicle for individuals to act. However, Kolb and Lefebvre include more room for elements of conflict and a greater role for norms in this process than an was ever made in ecological approaches. Describing how local normative order reinforce bias and make oppressive ideology seems natural, Kolb states "Places are not the single origin of oppression, but they spread it over space and people" (p. 39). Also unlike the ecologists, Kolb and Lefebvre take society as a social dimension that exists separately from community whereas ecologists treat the ecological community and interrelations among these communities as the foundation of society. On a phenomenological level, place mediates between culture and the individual. "… as places gather bodies in their midst in deeply enculturated ways, so cultures conjoin bodies in concrete circumstances of implacement" (p. 348).

Kolb's conception of community synthesizes much of the new urban sociology and phenomenological approaches to bring back interrelations between the material and normative aspects of community as well as the micro level processes of association in line with macrolevel community aspects of space and place. Incorporating these elements together requires a formulation of community as involving networks, connections and social fields that overlap. Unlike the more unidimensional concepts of place, community involves complexity. "By *complexity* I mean interacting multiplicities. A complex place will have multiple roles, forces, norms, processes, internal spatial divisions and external links to other places and to the processes that bring together multiple forces and systems" (p. 54). This conception of community involves both the phenomenology of personal awareness, linking individuals together within a community, and also larger structural forces that contain and shape this phenomenology. Here the macrolevel and microlevel integration of community forces are once again merged as was classical human ecology before its schism. Community is both action and structure, both emerging from persons and from social forces. However, the contemporary melding of these levels, of space and place, and of organic and contractual community solidarity comes as much from grounded empirical studies as theoretical tradition.

Social movements literature is one such arena for this blending of these elements. Not explicitly directed at community, work by Fligstein and McAdam (2011, 2012) nevertheless directly address these issues in their formulation of strategic action fields (see, also, Chap. 9). In applying their approach Irwin and Pischke (2016) argue "In their work, these authors have moved the study of social movements into the realm of networks and tied these networks to space, geography and community" (p. 205). Here, particular attention is paid to inter-areal interactions and the overlapping of institutional influences in space.

> First, the theory rests on a view that sees strategic action fields, which can be defined as mesolevel social orders, as the basic structural building block of modern political/organizational life in the economy, civil society, and the state. Second, we see any given field as embedded in a broader environment consisting of countless proximate or distal

> fields as well as states, which are themselves organized as intricate systems of strategic action fields. (McAdam and Fligstein 2012, p. 3)

Where these come together, communities have a greater capacity for grassroots based social action (McAdam and Boudet 2012). The approach highlights the coalescence of movements in space, much like the new urban school. Rather than conceiving these networks as emerging from society at large, however, they see this as a phenomenon generated by individual interests coming together in space. However they also incorporate elements of network and community structure, which they see as equally important factors shaping these social fields (p. 5). This synthesis integrates contractual and structural approaches (Diani 2003; Gould 2003). Working from different traditions, these conceptions of place parallel Kolb's notion of community as multilevel complexity. The notion of social fields situates the social movements literature directly in the central questions of community – the nature of association among individuals, the role that communities play in linking individuals to society, the spatial character of place and the cultural character of place.

13.6 Conclusion: Community as Theoretical Linkage in the Twenty-First Century

At the beginning of the twenty-first century the central questions of sociology orbit around the concept of community. The issues associated with community as a concept remain open, unresolved and reflective of different theoretical orientations and of the varieties of sociological issues. However, community as a concept has become more, rather than less important in studying these issues. Globalization, re-localization, the rise of hyper-individualism, the perpetuation of inequality, the emergence of new social divisions and the social actions that counter these trends have all incorporated community as a central organizing concept. This is because the concept of community is one that addresses the essential nature of association, of cultural cohesion, and of the territorial cohesion of individuals. As this chapter has outlined, social theory has long relied on the concept of community to link these issues together. What is new in the twenty-first century is the synthesis of once antithetical dimensions of community. Rather than positing an essential character to community, approaches are exploring the interrelationship between contractualism and organic elements of the communal, between material and cultural origins of association, between space and place and between society and community. In addressing the central questions of sociology, community has become a multilayered, complex, and nuanced concept, synthesizing previously disparate and separate theoretical elements.

References

Auge, M. (2008). *Non-places: An introduction to supermodernity* (2nd ed.). London: Verso.

Bauman, Z. (2001). *The individualized society*. Cambridge: Polity Press.

Bauman, Z. (2013). *Community: Seeking safety in an insecure world*. Wiley. Downloaded from Amazon.com

Bell, C., & Newby, H. (1975). *Community studies: An introduction to the sociology of local community* (2nd ed.). London: George Allen & Unwin LTD.

Bell, C., & Newby, H. (2012). *Sociology of community: A collection of readings*. Routledge.

Bellah, R. N., Madsen, R., Sullivan, W. M., Swidler, A., & Tipton, S. M. (1992). *The good society*. New York: Vintage Books.

Bellah, R. N., Madsen, R., Sullivan, W. M., Swidler, A., & Tipton, S. M. (1996). *Habits of the heart : individualism and commitment in American life* (Updated ed.). Berkeley: University of California Press.

Benn, S. I. (1982). Individuality, autonomy and community. In E. Kamenka (Ed.), *Community as a social ideal* (pp. 43–62). New York: St. Martin's Press.

Berry, B. J. L., & Kasarda, J. D. (1977). *Contemporary urban ecology*. New York: Macmillan.

Bruhn, J. G. (2005). *The sociology of community connections*. New York: Springer Science + Business Media.

Carroll, J. (2014). The state and fading community. In R. Nisbet (Ed.). *The quest for community: A study in the ethics of order and freedom* (Kindle ed., l. 4715–6619). Wilmington: Intercollegiate Studies Institute. Downloaded from Google Books.com.

Casey, E. S. (1993). *Getting back into place: Toward a renewed understanding of the place-world* (Studies in continental thought). Bloomington: Indiana University Press.

Casey, E. S. (1997). *The fate of place: A philosophical history*. Berkeley: University of California Press.

Castells, M. (1996). *The rise of the network society* (Information Age, Vol. 1). Cambridge, MA: Blackwell Publishers.

Castells, M. (2000). *The rise of the network society* (Information Age 2nd ed., Vol. 1). Oxford: Blackwell Publishers.

Certeau, M. d. (1984). *The practice of everyday life*. Berkeley: University of California Press.

Clarke, D. B. (2012). Zygmunt Bauman. In P. Hubbard, & R. Kitchin (Eds.), *Key thinkers on space and place* (Kindle ed., pp. 47–53). London: Sage. Downloaded from Amazon.com.

Cohen, A. P. (1985). *The symbolic structure of community* (2001 ed.). Taylor & Francis e-Library. Downloaded from Google Books.com.

Cooley, C. H. (2008). *Human nature and the social order* (Kindle ed.) Social Science Classics Series. Evergreen Review, Inc. Downloaded from Amazon.com.

Coser, L. A. (1977). *Masters of sociological thought: Ideas in historical and social context* (2nd ed.). New York: Harcourt Brace Jovanovich.

Crang, M. (2012). Michel de Certeau. In P. Hubbard, & R. Kitchin (Eds.), *Key thinkers on space and place* (Kindle ed., pp. 106–111). London: Sage. Downloaded from Amazon.com.

Cresswell. (2015). *Place: An introduction* (2nd ed., Kindle ed.). Wiley. Downloaded from Amazon.com.

Day, G. (2006). *Community and everyday life* (Kindle ed.). Taylor and Francis. Downloaded from Amazon.com.

Delanty, G. (2009). *Community: Key ideas* (2nd ed.). New York: Routledge.

Diani, M. (2003). Social movements, contentious actions, and social networks: 'From Metaphor to Substance'? In M. Diani & D. McAdam (Eds.), *Social movements and networks: Relational approaches to collective action* (pp. 1–18). Oxford: Oxford University Press.

Douthat, R. (2014). Introduction to the background edition. In *The quest for community: A study in the ethics of order and freedom. Robert Nisbet* (Kindle ed., pp. 39–169). Wilmington: Intercollegiate Studies Institute. Downloaded from Amazon.com.

Durkheim, E. (1964). *The division of labor in society*. London: Collier Macmillan; Free Press.

Elias, N. (2012). Toward a theory of community. In C. Bell, & H. Newby (Eds.), *Sociology of community: A collection of readings* (Kindle ed.). Taylor and Francis. Downloaded from Amazon.com.

Etzioni, A. (1993). *The spirit of community*. New York: Touchstone.

Etzioni, A. (1995). *New communitarian thinking: Persons, virtues, institutions, and communities* (Constitutionalism and democracy). Charlottesville: University Press of Virginia.

Etzioni, A. (1996). *The new golden rule: Community and morality in a democratic society* (1st ed.). New York: BasicBooks.

Fligstein, N., & McAdam, D. (2011). Toward a general theory of strategic action fields. *Sociological Theory, 29*(1), 1–26.

Fligstein, N., & McAdam, D. (2012). *A theory of fields*. New York: Oxford University Press.

Flora, C. B., & Flora, J. L. (2013). *Rural communities: Legacy and change* (4th ed.). Iowa State University, Perseus Books Group. Downloaded from Google Books.com.

Florida, R. L. (2004). *The rise of the creative class: And how it's transforming work, leisure, community and everyday life*. New York: Basic Books.

Florida, R. L. (2005). *Cities and the creative class*. New York: Routledge.

Frazier, E. F. (1957). *Black bourgeoisie*. Glencoe: Free Press.

Frisbie, W. P., & Poston, D. L. (1978). *Sustenance organization and migration in nonmetropolitan America* (Social organization of the community). Iowa City: University of Iowa Press.

Fukuyama, F. (1995). *Trust: The social virtues and the creation of prosperity*. New York: Free Press.

Fukuyama, F. (1999). *The great disruption: Human nature and the reconstitution of social order*. New York: Free Press.

Gans, H. J. (1962). *The urban villagers; group and class in the life of Italian-Americans*. New York: Free Press of Glencoe.

Gans, H. J. (1967). *The Levittowners; ways of life and politics in a new suburban community*. New York: Pantheon Books.

Gans, H. J. (2015). America's two urban sociologies. *City & Community, 14*(3), 239–241.

Gieryn, T. F. (2000). A space for place in sociology. *Annual Review of Sociology, 26*, 463–496.

Gottdiener, M. (1985). *The social production of urban space* (1st ed.). Austin: University of Texas Press.

Gould, R. (2003). In M. Diani & D. McAdam (Eds.), *Why do networks matter? Rationalist and structuralist interpretations* (pp. 233–257). Oxford: Oxford University Press.

Harvey, D. (1989). *The urban experience*. Baltimore: Johns Hopkins University Press.

Hauser, P. M., & Schnore, L. F. (1965). *The study of urbanization*. New York: Wiley.

Hawley, A. H. (1950). *Human ecology; a theory of community structure*. New York: Ronald Press Co.

Hawley, A. H. (1971). *Urban society; an ecological approach*. New York: Ronald Press Co.

Hawley, A. H. (1984). Human ecological and marxian theories. *American Journal of Sociology, 89*(4), 904–917.

Hawley, A. H. (1986). *Human ecology: A theoretical essay*. Chicago: University of Chicago Press.

Hollingshead, A. D. B. (1949). *Elmtown's youth: The impact of social classes on adolescents*. New York: Wiley.

Hunter, F. (1953). *Community power structure: A study of decision makers*. Chapel Hill: The University of North Carolina Press.

Hunter, A. (1974). *Symbolic communities: The persistence and change of Chicago's local communities*. Chicago: The University of Chicago Press.

Irwin, M. D. (2015). Evolving communities: Evolutionary analysis in classical and neoclassical human ecology. In J. H. Turner, R. Machalek, & A. Maryanski (Eds.), *Handbook on evolution and society: Toward an evolutionary social science* (pp. 316–332). Boulder: Paradigm.

Irwin, M. D., & Kasarda, J. D. (1994). Trade, transportation and spatial distribution. In N. J. Smelser & R. Swedberg (Eds.), *The handbook of economic sociology* (1st ed., pp. 342–367). Princeton: Princeton University Press & Russell Sage Foundation.

Irwin, M. D., & Pischke, E. C. (2016). Socio-spatial holes in the advocacy umbrella: The spatial diffusion of risk and network response among environmental organizations in the Marcellus hydro-fracturing region. In F. H. Howell, J. R. Porter, & S. A. Matthews (Eds.), *Recapturing space: New middle range theory in spatial demography* (pp. 199–233). New York: Springer.

Kasarda, J. D., & Janowitz, M. (1974). Community attachment in mass society. *American Sociological Review, 39*(3), 328–339.

Keller, S. (2003). *Community: Pursuing the dream, living the reality*. Princeton: Princeton University Press.

Kirkpatrick, F. G. (2008). *Community: A trinity of models*. Eugene: Wipf and Stock Publishers.

Kolb, D. (2008). *Sprawling places*. Athens: University of Georgia Press.

Latham, A. (2012). Edward W. Soja. In P. Hubbard, & R. Kitchen (Eds.), *Key thinkers on place and space* (Kindle ed., pp. 380–386). London: Sage. Downloaded from Amazon.com.

Lefebvre, H. (1991). *The production of space*. Oxford: Blackwell.

Logan, J. R. (2012). Making a place for space: Spatial thinking in social science. *Annual Review of Sociology, 38*, 507–524.

Logan, J. R., & Molotch, H. L. (1987). *Urban fortunes: The political economy of place*. Berkeley: University of California Press.

Lynd, R. S., & Lynd, H. M. (1929). *Middletown, a study in contemporary American culture*. New York: Harcourt.

MacIver, R. M. (1917). *Community: A sociological study; being an attempt to set out the nature and fundamental laws of social life* (3rd [1935] ed.). London: Macmillan.

Massey, D. B. (1994). *Space, place, and gender*. (pp. viii, 280 p). Minneapolis: University of Minnesota Press.

McAdam, D., & Boudet, H. S. (2012). *Putting social movements in their place: Explaining opposition to energy projects in the United States, 2000–2005*. Cambridge: Cambridge University Press.

McAdam, D., & Fligstein, N. (2012). *A theory of fields*. Oxford University Press. Kindle Edition. Downloaded from Amazon.com.

McClay, W. M. (2014). Introduction: Why place matters. In W. M. McClay & T. V. McAllister (Eds.), *Why place matters: Geography, identity, and civic life in modern America* (pp. 1–9). New York: New Atlantis Books, Encounter Books.

McKenzie, R. D. (1967). *The metropolitan community*. New York: Russell & Russell.

Merriman, P. (2012). Marc Auge. In P. Hubbard, & R. Kitchin (Eds.), *Key thinkers on space and place* (Kindle ed., pp. 26–32). London: Sage. Downloaded from Amazon.com.

Minar, D. W., & Greer, S. (Eds.). (1969). *The concept of community: Readings with interpretations*. New Brunswick: Aldine Transaction. Downloaded from Google Books.com.

Nisbet, R. A. (1966). *The sociological tradition*. New York: Basic Books.

Nisbet, R. A. (2014). *The quest for community* (Kindle ed.). Wilmington: Intercollegiate Studies Institute. Downloaded from Google Books.com.

Pahl, R. (1966). The rural urban continuum. *Sociologia Ruralis, 6*, 299–329.

Park, R. E., Burgess, E. W., & McKenzie, R. D. (1984). *The city* (The heritage of sociology). Chicago: University of Chicago Press.

Putnam, R. D. (2000). *Bowling alone: The collapse and revival of American community*. New York: Simon & Schuster.

Putnam, R. D., Leonardi, R., & Nanetti, R. (1993). *Making democracy work: Civic traditions in modern Italy*. Princeton: Princeton University Press.

Putnam, R. D., Feldstein, L. M., & Cohen, D. (2003). *Better together: Restoring the American community*. New York: Simon & Schuster.

Redfield, R. (1955). *The little community; viewpoints for the study of a human whole* (Comparative studies of cultures and civilizations). Chicago: University of Chicago Press.

Rodaway, P. (2012). Yi-Fu Tuan. In P. Hubbard, & R. Kitchin (Eds.), *Key thinkers on space and place* (Kindle ed., pp. 426–431). London: Sage. Downloaded from Amazon.com.

Saunders, P. (1986). *Social theory and the urban question* (2nd ed.). London: Hutchinson Education.

Schnore, L. F. (1965). *The urban scene; human ecology and demography*. New York: Free Press.

Shields, R. (2012). Henri Lefebvre. In P. Hubbard, & R. Kitchin (Eds.), *Key thinkers on space and place* (Kindle ed., pp. 279–285). London: Sage. Downloaded from Amazon.com.

Simmel, G. (1971). *On individuality and social forms; selected writings* (The heritage of sociology). Chicago: University of Chicago Press.

Smith, D. A. (1995). The new urban sociology meets the old: Rereading some classical human ecology. *Urban Affairs Review, 30*(3), 432–457.

Soja, E. W. (1989). *Postmodern geographies: The reassertion of space in critical social theory*. London: Verso.

Soja, E. W. (1996). *Thirdspace: Journeys to Los Angeles and other real-and-imagined places*. Cambridge, MA: Blackwell.

Soja, E. W. (2010). *Seeking spatial justice*. (Globalization and community series, pp. xviii, 256 p). Minneapolis: University of Minnesota Press.

Stacey, M. (2012). The myth of community studies. In C. Bell & R. Kitchin (Eds.), *Sociology of community: A collection of readings* (Kindle ed., pp. 13–26). New Sociology Library. Taylor and Francis. Downloaded from Amazon.com

Susser, I. (2002). *The Castells reader on cities and social theory*. Malden: Blackwell.

Suttles, G. D. (1972). *The social construction of communities*. Chicago: The University of Chicago Press.

Tocqueville, A. d. (1994). *Democracy in America*. New York: Alfred A. Knopf.

Tönnies, F. (1887). *Community and society*. Mineola: Dover Publications.

Tuan, Y.-f. (2014). *Space and place: The perspective of experience*. Minneapolis: University of Minnesota Press.

Warner, W. L., & Lunt, P. S. (1941). *The social life of a modern community* (Yankee City Series, Vol. 1). New Haven: Yale University Press & H. Milford, Oxford University Press.

Weber, M. (1958). *The city*. Glencoe: Free Press.

Wellman, B. (1979). The community question: The intimate networks of East Yorkers. *American Journal of Sociology, 8*(5), 1201–1231.

Whyte, W. F. (1955). *Street corner society; the social structure of an Italian slum* (Enl. 2d ed.). Chicago: University of Chicago Press.

Wirth, L. (1928). *The ghetto* (The University of Chicago sociological series). Chicago: The University of Chicago Press.

Wirth, L. (1938). Urbanism as a way of life. *American Journal of Sociology, 44*, 1–24.

Wirth, L. (1948). World community, world society, and world government. In Q. Wright (Ed.), *The world community* (pp. 9–20). Chicago: University of Chicago Press.

Zimmer, B. G., & Hawley, A. H. (1968). *Metropolitan area schools; resistance to district reorganization*. Beverly Hills: Sage Publications.

Zorbaugh, H. W. (1929). *The Gold Coast and the slum: A sociological study of Chicago's near North Side*. Chicago: University of Chicago Press.

Organizations as Sites and Drivers of Social Action

14

Walter W. Powell and Christof Brandtner

14.1 Introduction

Organizations generate power, employment, prestige, identity, contacts, and income. A person's life chances are shaped by the kinds of organizations he or she is associated with, and how well or poorly those organizations perform strongly affects the distribution of wealth in society. Friendships are formed in organizations, and biographies molded by organizational affiliations. Organizations are tools for shaping the world. And the gains that accrue from improving organizational performance and learning from successes can be enormous, just as the failures of organizations can damage lives and communities. Both success and failure change the probabilities that certain courses of action will occur.

Organizations are rarely powerful enough to simply dictate outcomes, in part because they are simultaneously both sites and drivers of action. As sites, organizations are the arena in which debates occur, struggles take place, and identities are formed. As drivers, organizations alter the odds that certain things get done. The leaders of organizations navigate particular paths, represent interests, and signal the importance of certain views. We use this dual imagery of sites and drivers to organize our discussion of the literature.

The sociology of organizations has a distinguished pedigree, tracing back to Max Weber and Robert Michels, and running through such luminaries as Peter Blau, Michel Crozier, Alvin Gouldner, Robert Merton, and Phillip Selznick. Collectively, these scholars produced touchstone portraits of twentieth-century organizational life. The 1970s and 1980s welcomed new theoretical perspectives with the writings of Michael Hannan, John Meyer, Charles Perrow, and Richard Scott. Today, however, the study of organizations has migrated out of sociology departments and into professional schools of business, government, education, and law. This development has brought ideas into a wider orbit and led to more engagement with the world of practice, but it also comes at a cost. Core areas of sociology have lost contact with, and enrichment by, an organizational perspective. Our goal in this chapter is to re-establish those links and re-connect with processes that shape and stamp the lives of people in organizations and reproduce larger patterns in society. We intend the chapter to be of interest to sociologists in general, and we hope that it stimulates organizations researchers to ask questions outside the confines of their subfields.

14.1.1 Sites and Drivers

We define an organization broadly as a purposeful collective of people, operating with formal

W.W. Powell (✉) • C. Brandtner
Stanford University, Stanford, CA, USA
e-mail: woodyp@stanford.edu; cbrandtner@stanford.ed

S. Abrutyn (ed.), *Handbook of Contemporary Sociological Theory*,
Handbooks of Sociology and Social Research, DOI 10.1007/978-3-319-32250-6_14

structures and perceived boundaries that both distinguish it and its members from the wider environment and draw a distinction between members and external stakeholders. Organizations are made up of individuals pursuing a common goal, such as producing a good or service or advocating for some cause. Organizations usually also display a certain level of formality, such as being registered with the government and having documented rules and regulations. In this sense, organizations form the social context in which people work, volunteer, or lead. This view of organizations underlies most economic and behavioral theories of firms, which are interested in understanding the day-to-day events of organizations, such as deciding between making or buying a component part of the final product, improving the motivation of employees, or determining what inhibits or stimulates careers.

Organizations can also be seen as discrete entities that are exposed to a social environment of their own; market institutions, the state, the professions, and society at large constrain and enable organizations in fulfilling their mission. From this 'open systems' point of view, the individual actions of people are less important than what they amount to on the organizational level. The open-systems view emphasizes different social processes: people are busy responding to and negotiating external pressures, as well as entering into transactions and collaborations with other organizations and individuals. Consequently, theories associated with organizations as an open system attempt to measure the implementation and diffusion of organizational practices, competition and collaboration between organizations, and the comparative status, power, and prestige of organizations.

As the boundaries between organizations and their environment, and sometimes even between two organizations, are often porous, a clear-cut distinction between the internal and external world of organizations is hard to make. Many organizational activities also cross the boundaries of the organization at some point. For instance, a press release is drafted, circulated, and authorized by people internally before eventually representing the organization to its external audiences. On the other hand, many products—from cars to medical drugs to apps—go through extensive market research with potential clients outside the organization before the assembly lines start moving. This feature of organizations is particularly evident in the following section on networks. Consequently, organizations have significance for sociological theory from both perspectives: as sites of social action and as drivers of it.

Our goal in this chapter is to illuminate the processes through which these recursive relations occur. To do so, we introduce important properties of organizations as nouns, and the processes and causal mechanisms of organizational life as verbs.

14.1.2 Verbs and Nouns

Most overview essays, as well as textbooks, on the sociology of organizations start with the viewpoint that it is a field typified by contrasting theories and lines of research. The 'theory-group' approach to surveying the literature has persisted for several decades. This pedagogical strategy has provided students of organizations with a good deal of insight, as well as notable texts by Charles Perrow (1972) and Richard Scott (2013). A number of handbook-type chapters also survey the field by making stops along the way at various theory communities.

We think the time is right to try a different approach. Rather than emphasize differences among rival theoretical perspectives, we want to stress commonalities. Moreover, in lieu of examining the literature at a high level of abstraction and discussing only disembodied things referred to as organizations, we want to bring the varied world of organizations to life. Contemporary studies have been conducted in hospitals, restaurants, social movements, biotech firms, investment banks, call centers, and factories. But this rich diversity is elided in most reviews, which focus only on particular theoretical approaches that deal with highly general statements about organizations.

Table 14.1 Organizations as sites and drivers of social action

Organizations as…	Mechanisms	Primary outcome	Organizations as sites of social action	Organizations as drivers of social action
Equalizers and stratifiers	Discrimination and formalization	Inequality	Rissing and Castilla (2014)	Kalev (2014)
			Castilla and Benard (2010)	Rivera (2012)
			Fernandez (2001)	
Standardizers and monuments	Institutionalization and imprinting	Persistence	Hallett (2010)	Phillips (2005)
			Turco (2012)	Johnson (2007)
			Espeland and Sauder (2016)	
			Sharkey and Bromley (2014)	
Movers and shakers	Socializing and mobilization	Change	McPherson and Sauder (2013)	Bidwell and Briscoe (2010)
			Bechky (2006)	Briscoe and Kellogg (2011)
			Okhuysen (2005)	Hwang and Powell (2009)
			Small (2009)	Chen (2009)
Networks and wirings	Learning and access	Embeddedness	Fernandez et al. (2000)	Whittington et al. (2009) and Owen-Smith and Powell (2004)
			Burt (1992) and (2004)	Fleming and Sorenson (2001)
			Kellogg (2010)	
			Macaulay (1963)	

Our attention is directed toward processes that occur in different kinds of organizations. We emphasize that organizations are the locus where many of the critical activities of modern society take place. Organizations compete, collaborate, create, coordinate, and control much of contemporary life. Consequently, it is not surprising that the sociology of organizations spills over into related subfields, including public administration, medicine and public health, education, industrial engineering, business history, and international business.

We posit a handful of critical processes, or mechanisms, that we argue are at the center of contemporary organizational research and are attended to by scholars of varied theoretical orientations. These include (1) discrimination and formalization, (2) institutionalization and imprinting, (3) socializing and mobilization, and (4) learning and access. Using these phenomena as the lens through which to view the field has several distinct advantages. One, we will show that these ideas come from multiple theories and that this attention unites rather than fractures the field. Two, we discuss the varied methods that have been used to study these phenomena and again highlight the complementarities of different approaches. Three, we describe the kinds of organizational settings in which these phenomena have been studied, illustrating the wide purchase of organizational research. We summarize the processes we cover in Table 14.1.

Our approach to reviewing the organizational theory literature was iterative. We started inductively by looking at the core themes of organizational theory articles published in major journals over the past 25 years, using methods from computational linguistics. The emerging themes reflected the field's conventional theoretical perspective, as well as the types of organizations studied.

These topic models, or linguistic clusters, were dominated by nouns and adjectives rather than verbs, and they obscured the mechanisms associated with the various perspectives. Following the recent turn in social theory to focus on mechanisms (Hedström 2005; Hedström and Bearman 2009; Padgett and Powell 2012), we chose to focus on processes that cut across research schools. Although each of the eight dynamics that are at the center of the chapter is useful for predicting multiple outcomes, we posit four primary outcomes associated with the mechanisms: inequality, persistence and order, change and disorder, and networks and relations. Because we see these attributes as central to sociological inquiry at large, we structured the chapter in accordance with the four outcomes. We are mindful of the theoretical origins of these mechanisms, but draw largely on recent, empirical research about a variety of organizational forms to illustrate the processes.

14.2 Organizations as Equalizers and Stratifiers

Organizations are often considered the great equalizers of modern civilization. Weber, one of the founding fathers of contemporary sociological theory, described the ideal-typical organizational form—bureaucracy—as a champion of both reliability and equality. By adhering to the rules of law and merit, corporate and public administrations could level social differences. Even though bureaucratic organizations are often complicated by informal relationships among colleagues (Blau 1955), influences that are often antagonistic to hierarchical structures (Dalton 1959), administrative arbitrariness is limited by both the primacy of expertise and the impersonality of the office. Despite the shortcomings of bureaucracy, equality is one of the core promises of complex organizations today. Many people regard universities as escalators to social mobility, see the armed services as a vehicle for upward mobility for racial and ethnic minorities, and perceive corporations as the manifestation of meritocracy. Thus Weberian bureaucracy, in theory, is the backbone of democracy and fairness.

That promise has often been belied by reality, however. Organizations are also the locus of various mechanisms of stratification. Firms, in particular, contribute to unequal income distribution and social hierarchy, through steps ranging from hiring to wage negotiations, gender and racial segregation of jobs, promotions, and firing.

Organizations reinforce gender and racial hierarchies, even when their clients are diverse, and such biases can inhibit the kinds of clients and employees that are subsequently attracted to companies. A 2015 survey by Page Mill Publishing of 257 US venture capital firms identified a total of only 403 women involved in the industry. Women are less likely to apply for jobs at venture firms with no female employees, and female entrepreneurs are less likely to approach all-male firms for funding. Similarly, a 2014 survey by the National Association for Law Placement revealed that only 5.6 % of US lawyers who hold top leadership positions at law firms are non-white. And fewer than 2 % of law firm partners are African-American. Black lawyers operate in a profession that is one of the country's least racially diverse (Rhode 2015), despite growing demands from clients to see more diversity.

Baron and Bielby (1980) depicted the organization of work as a primary mechanism of socioeconomic stratification, in both how workers are stratified inside organizations and how organizations are stratified in the market: "If firms are indeed 'where the action is,' then social scientists interested in the structure of social inequality should find the vast literature on complex organizations illuminating" (Baron and Bielby 1980, 748).

Contemporary empirical research has demonstrated that organizations from all walks of life, from daycare centers to research universities, contribute to the way society is stratified. Two particular organizational processes through which organizations shape societal outcomes are *formalization* and *discrimination*. Formalization (e.g., the introduction of written rules of conduct, normative codes of ethics, or policies) obviously has important implications for social outcomes. If hiring, for instance, is regulated by formal criteria and overseen by labor unions, organizations can be assumed to lead to a leveling of social hierarchies (Perrow 1972). Equal employment opportunity (EEO) legislation, for example, is meant to restrain discrimination in the labor market by targeting organizations (Dobbin 2009), and workplace policies aim to reduce work-life conflicts, for instance by improving employees' schedule control (Kelly et al. 2011).

Discrimination, in turn, may play out on the individual level. One example is racial discrimination among police, which has been shown to be a result of implicit biases against African-American men (Eberhardt et al. 2004; Saperstein et al. 2014). Another is the baseball field, where umpires favor white over black pitchers in spite of high levels of scrutiny from players, fans, and commentators (Kim and King 2014). But once sorting and exclusion become organizational practices, they can reproduce and persist regardless of the intent or interest of any of the individuals involved. In organizations, institutionalized discriminatory practices produce persistent and ever-increasing inequality through the process of accumulative advantage, which Merton (1968) famously described as the Matthew Effect: high-status actors stay on top because they are rewarded disproportionally for their good performance. As a result, those at the apex of a social order pull further away from those in the middle or at the bottom. Once a hierarchy—one of the constitutive elements of a bureaucracy—exists, the status order can exacerbate societal segregation. This is true for individuals in organizations as well as for organizations themselves. Sharkey (2014), for instance, shows that investors judge firms in higher-status industries less harshly than those of lower rank when the firms restate their earnings because of some form of wrongdoing.

14.2.1 Organizations as Sites of Inequality

Typically, organizational practices are not intended to introduce bias against particular groups of people, but they may have that unintended effect. As one illustration, Castilla and Benard (2010) find evidence for 'the paradox of meritocracy.' The authors asked MBA students to reward the performance of fictitious employees and then randomly manipulated the descriptions of the corporate setting. Study subjects who made decisions on behalf of firms with more meritocratic corporate values tended to distribute rewards based on gender rather than on talent and performance. The authors speculate that 'moral credentials' stemming from a formal commitment to meritocracy may have enabled prejudiced behavior. Their finding shows that "gender and racial inequality persist in spite of management's efforts to promote meritocracy or even because of such meritocratic efforts" (Castilla and Benard 2010: 544).

Biased behavior in organizations is by no means limited to salary, but can even affect where people can work. United States Department of Labor agents consistently discriminate against Latin American green card applicants and favor applicants of Asian descent (Rissing and Castilla 2014). The authors find that this bias is much smaller in a quasi-random set of audited cases, in which more performance information is available to the agents. This finding suggests that the bias against some applicant groups is not the result of the agents' own preferences regarding certain ethnicities, but more likely the outcome of statistical bias introduced by a lack of information. DoL agents, Rissing and Castilla conclude, unlawfully—but also unknowingly—use nationality as a proxy for performance in the absence of more detailed information. In this case, the organization of the application process gives rise to opportunities for discrimination that would be absent if agents had access to more detailed information. Rissing and Castilla's study is a good example of how larger societal trends such as prejudice against immigrants from certain nationalities, which are usually believed to operate at the individual level of analysis, shape social outcomes through organizations.

Sterling (2015) sought to understand how variation in social position can shape workplace opportunities. She studied the influence of individuals' social connections at the time of organizational entry on the subsequent formation of ties within the workplace. In a study of new business and law professionals, she found that individuals with an initial advantage in social ties formed more extensive networks post entry than those without such an advantage. But when there was clear evidence about the accomplishments of new hires, network formation was moderated by ability.

Another illustrative case is Fernandez's (2001) quasi-experimental study of a food processing firm before and after a retooling. The study investigates the black box of technological changes that underlie skill-based bias explanations of wage inequality (Autor et al. 1988; Card and DiNardo 2002). By studying one organization in unusual detail, Fernandez illuminates how an endogenous technological shift leads to wage inequality, rather than treating technological change as a residual variable that may be due to self-selection. Even though Fernandez links increases in wage inequality to the increased complexity of tasks, a result consistent with skill-based wage bias, he finds that the actual reason for increasing inequality is organizational turnover. There are significant wage differences between stayers and leavers: high-wage stayers (mostly electricians) received a wage increase, whereas low-wage leavers were replaced with even-lower-wage entrants. In this case, bureaucratic structures—unionization and a seniority-based pay scale—rendered the stayers better off.

14.2.2 Organizations as Drivers of Inequality

Particularism is not always purged through organizational structures; inequalities following from discrimination are a problem in hiring and firing alike. In some cases, such as Rivera's (2012, 2015) study of cultural matching in the hiring process in elite professional firms and Kalev's (2014) research on the effects of corporate downsizing on workforce diversity, managers are drivers of larger social inequity.

Rivera (2012) studied how employers made decisions about new hires based on fit; she conducted extensive interviews and observations in investment banks, law firms, and consulting firms. She finds that behind the closed doors of hiring committees, skills sorting—hiring based on competence—is frequently supplemented by cultural matching—hiring based on cultural similarity. Such homophily occurs not only because formal evaluation criteria emphasize fit between employee and company, but also because decision-makers evaluate performance through a cultural lens that they are familiar with and therefore prefer candidates from the same social backgrounds. Those doing the hiring establish an emotional connection with culturally similar applicants. "Whether someone rock climbs, plays the cello, or enjoys film noir may seem trivial to outsiders, but these leisure pursuits were crucial for assessing whether someone was a cultural fit" (Rivera 2012: 1009). Through homophily, even highly formalized hiring procedures can reproduce social segregation.

Organizational procedures and bureaucratic formalization are therefore not a guaranteed remedy for inequalities. Kalev (2014), in a mixed-methods study of 327 firms from 1980 to 2002, investigated how formal rules and managerial accountability affect gender and racial inequality in light of corporate downsizing. She finds that some forms of formalization—particularly restricting layoffs to people with certain lengths of tenure and in certain positions—in fact exacerbate the effects of downsizing on workforce diversity because recent hires are more likely to be women and minorities. In contrast, layoff rules that are based on performance evaluations improve the prospects of black and female managers. Moreover, both managerial discretion and reviews by an external attorney can offset the negative effect of formal rules on the diversity of employees. In short, "organizational structures and institutional dynamics, coupled with executives' accountability and agency, play an important part in shaping inequality" (Kalev 2014: 129).

14.3 Organizations as Standardizers and Monuments

The social forces that give rise to social arrangements are often different from those that hold them in place (Stinchcombe 1968). Yet organizational dynamics are important for both: as much as organizations can determine and create societal outcomes, they can solidify social relationships and standardize practices.

In fact, rigid organizations can be inadvertent anchors of the status quo. The role of organizations in the reproduction and stability of social settings and practices is particularly central to institutional theory. In that research program, the taken-for-grantedness of certain behaviors is seen as the source of persistence of culture and structure (DiMaggio and Powell 1983). Zucker (1977) cites "some sort of establishment of relative permanence of a distinctly social sort" as the primary characteristic of institutions; her view of institutionalization highlights that institutionalization is both a property variable (the fact that something is considered real) and a process (that meanings and taken-for-grantedness of actions change). Taken-for-granted norms are a strong form of conservation; for example, most people do not even consider questioning the fact that they have to go to work in the morning, and going to work requires no justification vis-à-vis others (Berger and Luckmann 1966; Colyvas and Powell 2006). But what is considered 'normal' also depends heavily on core sociological categories, such as class, race, or gender. For instance, women are evaluated less favorably when they take on stereotypically masculine jobs or work above-average hours because of prescriptive norms about how women ought to behave; and in some areas the working class might be expected to work two or even three jobs to make a living (Heilman 2001; Ely et al. 2011). Such norms limit people's range of action and create realities and routines that are difficult to disrupt.

At the same time, the rigidity of social hierarchies is directly linked to the fact that social structure can hold people and organizations in place. Organizations' limited ability to alter their realities arbitrarily is a fundamental assumption of the population ecology paradigm in organizational theory. For organizations, such inertia, or difficulty in changing, has internal as well as external causes (Hannan and Freeman 1984). Sunk costs, political contention, and habits restrict change inside organizations, and regulative and economic trade barriers as well as social norms lock whole industries within powerful constraints.

Inertial forces are particularly important for the reproduction of social orders because organizations are strongly influenced by the social context at the time of their founding. Society leaves deep marks on organizations. Through such imprinting, social arrangements can subsequently become extraordinarily persistent (Stinchcombe 1965). Stinchcombe illustrated his classic argument about the enduring influence of the social context at the time of an organization's founding by showing that the labor supply at the founding of various firms—from farms to construction companies—deeply affected how they were staffed much later. This observation applies equally to modern-day organizations such as Silicon Valley start-ups. In a study of 100 technology ventures in California, Baron et al. (1999) show that the founder's premises about employment relations are a better predictor of the current organizational model than the views of the current CEO, even after the founder's departure.

Taken together, *institutionalization* and *imprinting* are the fabric that weaves together and reproduces societal relations, for both good and ill. Organizations help to crystallize a status quo by copying wages, quotas, and policies from purportedly successful role models and relying on routines that invoke the authority of tradition. Organizations also create standards for what is considered normal, such as how much more a CEO can earn than his or her employees, or to the degree to which citizens can participate in the formation of public policies.

14.3.1 Organizations as Sites of Persistence

Institutionalization (and de-institutionalization) is not a uniquely organizational process, but it frequently becomes manifest in organizational practices and routines. Practices initially adopted out of contingent circumstances or for sensible political or economic reasons can enter the standard repertoire of organizations, regardless of their specific champions or function (Tolbert and Zucker 1983; Colyvas and Powell 2006). The idea of institutionalization—and especially decoupling of ceremonial structures and actual practices—may explain why many reforms hardly change the daily activities in organizations (Meyer and Rowan 1977; Bidwell 2001; Hallett 2010).

The similarity of structures across organizations and over time is not just a result of the invisible hand of culture: myths about what behavior is proper and rational can be reflected in such mundane things as people's professional education, the criteria of performance evaluation, codes of ethics, or even binding laws (Scott 2013). Institutionalized ideas can travel far and wide, despite (or because of) vague labels such as 'managerial reform', 'accountability', or 'sustainability' (Czarniawska-Joerges and Sevón 1996; Bromley and Meyer 2015). But empirical research has shown that institutional myths are not merely hot air. In various cases they can become manifest in organizations.

Institutionalized myths may constrain change by becoming incarnate in individuals and organizational culture. An apt example is Hallett's (2010) ethnographic study of teachers' compliance with accountability reforms at a public elementary school. Hallett (2010: 53) observes a dynamic that he calls recoupling, "creating tight couplings where loose couplings were once in place." Put simply, the ceremonial accountability structures that enhance public legitimacy can become manifest in the daily practices of the people inhabiting organizations. In this case, the hiring and managerial approach of a determined school principal transformed a previously ceremonial commitment to accountability into a new classroom reality. The disruption of teachers' autonomy and routines led to uncertainty, turmoil, and even political mobilization. By focusing on the local, micro-level dynamics of accountability reform in schools, Hallett shows that recoupling of institutionalized myths can create resistance and ultimately alter the legitimacy of reform endeavors. What began as reform momentum ended up in a morass of ambiguity and frustration.

Turco's ethnographic investigation into Motherhood Inc., a for-profit company that provides services to young mothers, illustrates that institutional processes also constrain change through organizational culture. As the firm's CEO put it, its business model was built on the fact that mothers' "stress is lucrative" (Turco 2012: 390). She also observes decoupling between commercial practices—the marketing and sales of products to a vulnerable target group—and the euphemistic discourse surrounding the business. By posing as the 'trusted advisor' to young mothers, Motherhood Inc. could gain public legitimacy for filling the supportive role of friends and family with 'child development professionals'—for a price. But the sugarcoating trickled down into organization culture and was co-opted by lower-level employees. In turn, this led to increasing resistance to the firm's perceived ruthless profit-making, surprisingly from the company's own employees. In one case, an employee even told a customer not to "waste money on [the company's] products" and to buy a swaddle blanket at a box store instead (Turco 2012: 397). Events like this one undercut the company's profitability and ultimately led to layoffs and business failure. Hallett's and Turco's studies show that institutional myths and discourse can constrain organizations and ultimately restrict societal change, be it the push for classroom accountability in education or market-taking services intruding into the personal realm of motherhood.

The power of institutional myths to create tangible constraints for organizations and ultimately lead to the standardization of structures and practices is apparent not only in micro-level studies. The phenomenon of rankings, ratings, and awards and how they standardize organizational behavior to fit institutionalized understandings of performance has been widely studied (Timmermans and Epstein 2010). Espeland and Sauder (2016), drawing on a series of interviews with officials in law schools throughout the United States, demonstrate that *U.S. News and World Report* rankings have introduced and materialized standards for law schools that have astonishing behavioral effects. Law school officials, despite widespread skepticism about the utility and methods of the rankings, react to evaluations by resorting to similar admission practices, pushing students to enter private practice over public service because of higher starting salaries, and re-classifying students to appear in a better light. Rankings alter how legal education is perceived through both coercion and seduction (Sauder and Espeland 2009). Bromley and Sharkey (2014), in a study of US firms' responses to ratings of environmental performance, find not only that rankings have direct effects on organizations; firms whose peers are ranked also tend to reduce their emissions of toxic pollutants in certain contexts. Firms in highly regulated industries decrease their emissions as more of their peers are rated, even if they are not evaluated themselves. These two studies, and a host of related research, suggest that rankings and ratings can have direct and indirect effects on the behavior of organizations, leading to new standards of environmental or educational management that are dictated neither by the law nor by market dynamics.

14.3.2 Organizations as Drivers of Persistence

As the studies above illustrate, social reform is often inhibited and shaped by how people and practices inside organizations represent larger social trends. A different perspective on the fixity of social orders sees organizations as carriers of practices through time and space instead. As Marquis and Tilcsik (2013) point out, organizations (as well as organizational collectives, building blocks of organizations, and individuals) can go through various sensitive periods that make them particularly susceptible to influences of the organizational environment. In light of the many inertial forces that prevent organizations from changing at the discretion of policy makers and managers, organizations can become monuments (or museums) of the past.

One insightful study of the tenacity of social relations is Phillips's ecological account of the genealogies of gender hierarchies in firms. Why does workplace discrimination—and inequality at large—change so little? Using longitudinal data on established law firms and their offspring 'progeny firms' in Silicon Valley, Phillips (2005) finds that many newly founded firms copy the gender hierarchy of existing firms. They do so as founders import workplace routines, including flexible work schedules and part-time employment, from their previous employers to their new companies. Such copying can be both positive and negative. For example, having worked alongside high-status women in previous positions tends to improve the views of new founders about the legitimacy of female leaders. Compared to newly founded firms, organizations with parental ties to Silicon Valley law firms with established female leadership are more likely to have women in partnership positions.

Johnson's (2007, 2008) analysis of the famous Paris Opera vividly illustrates the power of persistence. Johnson develops a theory of cultural entrepreneurship in order to unpack the mechanisms that underlie the observation that organizations reflect the social, economic, and technological context of their creation. Her argument highlights that this process of imprinting involves critically thinking people activating and recombining the resources available at the time. Her description of how the poet Pierre Perrin founded the Paris Opera in the seventeenth century illuminates the resilience of history. Drawing on organizational models available at the time of Louis XIV, Perrin was able to secure funding for the foundation of an opera modeled after the prestigious royal academies, with elements of a commercial theater. But the Opera also persisted after the French Revolution. Thus, as a second step, imprinting also includes the reproduction of historical elements at a later time, which implies that inertia and related dynamics can "reproduce the organizational status quo" (Johnson 2007: 121). The opera's properties of a commercial theater, for example, helped it survive the French revolution, when the royal academies were abolished. Throughout the process, the political goals of the authorities and stakeholders were as important for the outcome as the creative recombination of established organizational forms by the cultural entrepreneur, Perrin. This century-old mélange of zeitgeist and interests still shapes French culture and the panorama of Paris today, a reminder that social history undergirds contemporary society.

14.4 Organizations as Movers and Shakers

In the previous section, we argued that organizations often constrain societal change. But organizations can also be 'movers and shakers' of society. In myriad ways, organizations can enable social change and enhance people's life chances. On the micro- and meso-level, organizations help to perform tasks that invigorate and advance society. People in organizations coordinate the creation and enforcement of rules and regulation, be it under the roof of parliaments, the courts, or police departments (McPherson and Sauder 2013). Complex tasks exceeding the capability of any single person, from producing movies full of special effects to the creation of ever-smaller semi-conductors, are performed in organizations. On the macro-level, too, movement and fluidity characterize organizations. Ventures—both business start-ups and social enterprises—seek to disrupt the status quo and to create innovation and change. Countless organizations, especially though not exclusively nonprofits, are explicitly dedicated to improving social mobility and facilitating exchanges across nations, cultures, social classes, and generations.

Organizations can make the social manageable. In contrast to our previous discussion of formalization as a mechanism through which organizations can reproduce inequalities, changing society does not necessarily require the introduction of new bureaucratic rules or purposive structures. Chen (2009) provides a vivid account of an organization that manages to coordinate without creating order: the Burning Man organization (BMO) as an enabler of chaos. Burning Man is an arts festival with almost 50,000 annual guests in the Black Rock Desert in Nevada. Over the course of 10 years, Chen observed the growth and change of this volunteer organization that accomplishes the seemingly impossible. BMO manages an anti-commercial, quasi-anarchic festival and sells tickets for an event that operates strictly without monetary exchanges. The organization coordinates various complex tasks, from recruiting and training volunteers to dealing with permits, media inquiries, and the police, and leaves no trace once the festival is over. Organizations can also have unintended positive consequences on social life. Small's (2009) study of a childcare center in New York City illustrates the important ramifications of mundane tasks, ranging from children's birthday celebrations to field trips, on the creation of social capital. The encounters between parents, Small finds, lead to unexpected and rewarding social ties, and thus unanticipated network gains accrue from common experiences at schools and daycare centers.

In contrast to the rigidity of ideal-type bureaucracy, Small's and Chen's cases illustrate the versatility of organizations in catalyzing, supporting, and maintaining robust action in society. It would be misguided to portray organizations only as the guardians of the status quo. Societal progress is a frequent goal and regular outcome of action in and around organizations—whether intended or not. Organizations can act as catalysts of change on various levels of analysis. Within organizations, mundane social processes—such as socialization into roles and the routines of problem-solving—allow for the coordination of complex and difficult tasks (Rerup and Feldman 2011; Winter 2013). Organizational routines are both generative, in that they make complex activities possible, and performative, inasmuch as they enable responses to emergencies (Feldman and Pentland 2003). Consider the delicate interplay among surgical teams or in hospital emergency rooms; all these coordinated efforts are made possible because of *socialization* into routines (Edmondson et al. 2001). Nevertheless, fumbles with patient handoffs between medical shifts are, sadly, a leading cause of death in hospitals, and they indicate deficient routines (Cohen and Hilligoss 2010; Vogus and Hilligoss 2015).

Organizations are also involved in the *mobilization* of change. This is true not only in the important but exceptional cases of activists targeting and influencing firms with protests and boycotts (McDonnell et al. 2015; Bartley and Child 2014; King and Soule 2007). Social movement organizations create opportunities for the invention of new technologies and solutions to social problems, as illustrated in studies of the creation of consumer watchdogs (Rao 1998), cooperatives (Schneiberg et al. 2008), wind energy (Sine and Lee 2009), and soft drinks (Hiatt et al. 2009). On a more mundane level, the movement of people between organizations and the ideas they carry around in the course of their careers are a major source of change and its diffusion in society.

14.4.1 Organizations as Sites of Change

One important organizational process that enables action in organizations is coordination, that is, a set of interactions that allows the completion of a larger task (Okhuysen and Bechky 2009). Organizational theorists have long been preoccupied with coordination problems. Coase's (1937) famous essay on the nature of the firm contends that the very existence of bureaucracy is tied to the cost advantages of coordinating economic changes within firms rather than through the market. Chandler's (1977) seminal explanation of the rise of professional managers in the United States argued that technological change required more sophisticated coordination of tasks and people within capitalist enterprises. Organizational sociologists have criticized these arguments for their limited understanding of organizational environments, the role of bounded rationality, and social network effects (Granovetter 1985; Scott 2013). Nevertheless, sociologists concur that the coordination of social action is a central organizational task. Organizations and their participants can create order out of chaos and render difficult situations manageable, by providing rules and infrastructure for challenging situations and problems and by establishing a basis for members' socialization into specific roles.

Research on organizations as diverse as film crews and police teams vividly illustrates the social processes that enable the coordination of highly complex tasks. Bechky (2006: 4), in a comparative ethnography of four film sets, shows that temporary organizations can be structured through "enduring, structured role systems whose nuances are organized in situ." Even though the film crew works on a set for only a few days and does not necessarily undergo any formal training, the work gets done consistently and layoffs are rare. Bechky argues that roles, not swift trust or formal rules, allow coordinating complex tasks. Socialization into roles as diverse as electricians (called gaffers) and cameramen commonly occurs through everyday interactions, such as reinforcing appropriate behavior by saying thank you, making a joke to lower-status workers, and giving polite feedback.

Okhuysen (2005) studied Special Weapons and Tactics (SWAT) police teams and found that their professional, coordinated behavior is largely based on behavioral routines. SWAT teams are deployed in situations in which highly concerted action is required. For members of a special unit, organizational arrangements at various levels introduce "sets of actions by individuals that make up a larger unit of performance that repeats over time" (Okhuysen 2005: 140). Routines, such as how to enter a building dynamically, are introduced through a common 'basic school' training at the beginning of the career, adapted in the context of each specific SWAT group, and then continuously rehearsed in the group to refresh the core knowledge. In addition, specialized schools allow members to learn new practices, such as controlling crowds or handling explosives, to introduce them to the group. Okhuysen also observes that SWAT team members organize the routines in bundles of coherent practice and hierarchies of more or less preferred routines. His research highlights that the complex interrelated tasks that define coordination can be completed only if individuals learn a common core of routines and practice them collectively. But at the same time, for routines to really grease the wheels, "the group must also rely on individual members to use their experience to initiate change or to help maintain the repertoire as an ongoing activity" (Okhuysen 2005: 162).

There are obviously many other mechanisms through which organizations coordinate work, divide tasks, and allocate resources. The core insight of the Carnegie School (March and Simon 1958; Cyert and March 1963) is that through routines, standard operating procedures, and rules, organizations can accomplish complex actions and even respond "on the fly" to new situations and challenges. By managing coordination, organizations enable change as much as they constrain it; in so doing, they create social capital, facilitate and perform the law, and produce and curate culture.

14.4.2 Organizations as Drivers of Change

Change is by no means an endogenous process that occurs only inside organizations; social conflicts, power struggles, and technological innovations occur outside organizations as well. Debates on the external determinants of change in organizations are rich in both theoretical insights and empirical evidence. Among the often discussed mechanisms of change are learning from others (March 1991), the creation of resource dependencies (Pfeffer and Salancik 1978), the adoption of societally recognized templates (Meyer and Rowan 1977), and selection pressures stemming from competition for resources (Hannan and Freeman 1989).

These various theoretical traditions have generated a rich understanding of the trans- and inter-organizational dynamics that produce a heterogeneous landscape of organizations and lead to large-scale shifts in how society pursues its goals. Such macro-organizational research is sometimes difficult to connect with micro-sociological theories, in part because people's behaviors are treated as only secondary to that of organizations. As one illustration, a core feature of studies of institutional change is the travel of ideas: numerous empirical studies deal with the diffusion of organizational practices and structures (for an early review, see Strang and Soule 1998), the ensuing isomorphism of organizational form and content (Strang and Meyer 1993), and the variety that results from heterogeneous local translations and editing of global ideas (Sahlin and Wedlin 2008).

A related mechanism of change in and across organizations is the mobility of people throughout their careers (Stewman and Konda 1983; Rosenfeld 2003; O'Mahony and Bechky 2006). For studying social outcomes, organizations matter because of the simple fact that they employ all kinds of diverse people, who in turn move between organizations frequently. People move up and down career ladders inside and between organizations and bring along ideas and skills, transferring standards and practices; in so doing they can even generate novelty (Powell et al. 2012).

To understand the wide-ranging effects of careers on societal outcomes—at the individual as well as the organizational level—consider Bidwell and Briscoe's (2010) study of the careers of information technology workers. The authors investigate the way people move between jobs over the course of their lives. They find that the sequence of employers is life-changing: most people move from large, generalist organizations early in their careers to smaller workplaces that require more specialized knowledge. In other words, people do not arbitrarily move across jobs; their careers follow a structured progression, in which workers transpose the skills required in one position to other organizations that build on those skills. Inter-organizational career ladders thus have "important consequences for both firms and workers" (Bidwell and Briscoe 2010: 1034).

The effect on workers' life chances throughout their careers is a contested issue within organizational theory. In line with our discussion above about the constraints that organizations create, some jobs lock people into specific positions. For feature film actors, having a "simple, focused identity," that is, being renowned for appearing in a certain genre, can be beneficial for securing future work. But typecasting also limits actors' opportunities outside the genre they are known for and effectively constrains their career paths (Zuckerman et al. 2003). Another illustration is found in Briscoe and Kellogg's (2011) longitudinal study of family-friendly, reduced-hours programs in a law firm. The authors find that an initial assignment with a powerful supervisor makes it easier for workers later to use work-family programs and more generally improves their subsequent career outcomes.

Such career dynamics also have important implications for the industries and sectors in which organizations are situated. One the one hand, organizations can benefit economically from the skill and creativity of workers who join them, as brain drain can pose severe problems for management (Wang 2015). On the other hand, core sociological outcomes can be affected by workers' mobility. One example mentioned above is Fernandez's (2001) study of a plant retooling in which worker turnover was a major determinant of internal income inequality. Another case, from the nonprofit sector, involves managerial practices in public charities, which Hwang and Powell (2009) show are driven by the hiring of increasingly professional executives. Nonprofit leaders recently trained in professional schools are more likely to introduce rational methods—from strategic planning to quantitative performance evaluation—than long-tenured nonprofit executives or passionate activists (Hwang and Powell 2009; Suarez 2010). The managers exiting and entering charities thus contribute to transforming how civil society is coordinated. Through their roles in both structuring and managing careers, organizations embody and abet change in people's lives and social structures.

14.5 Organizations as Networks and Wirings

Networks are ubiquitous in organizations; they flow through and across organizations so extensively that efforts to classify their features have been challenging. Viewed in its most elemental form, a network is simply a node and a tie. Nodes can be persons, groups, organizations, or technological artifacts such as webpages, or even more abstract entities such as ideas or concepts. Ties are simply the relationships among the nodes. These relationships can take many forms, including friendship, advice, mentoring, or the exchange of resources or information. The social ties in and between organizations affect numerous outcomes of primary sociological significance, including the creation and distribution of ideas, resources, status, and power.

Researchers have developed numerous tools to try to capture the importance of networks and applied these both inside organizations and to inter-organizational relationships. Attempts at quantification reflect efforts to depict properties of both nodes and relationships; these include social processes such as influence, centrality, prestige, awareness, and leverage, as well as concepts including distance, centrality, cohesiveness, equivalence, and density. These various indicators portray how networks permeate organizational life and reflect our core contention that organizations are both venues for action and drivers of social and economic relations. When we analyze how networks influence organizations, the relationships can be portrayed at multiple levels. As sites of action, organizations host networks of people whose decisions are affected by their relations to people in other organizations. As drivers, organizations constitute and shape large inter-organizational networks that are usually perceived as communities—including industries, organizational fields, and cities.

14.5.1 Organizations as Sites of Social Relations

Organizations are rife with interpersonal networks; this realm of interaction reflects the informal life of organizations that is, at times, at odds with the formal hierarchy (Dalton 1959). Sometimes the formal and informal are aligned, for example in the case of mentoring networks. Friendship networks may even provide the fuel that makes the formal system run. But the formal and the informal can be misaligned, and they may then become a seedbed for discontent or resistance.

Inside organizations, networks influence hiring selection, perceptions of performance, and compensation and promotion. We have long known that employees often find jobs through acquaintances, the classic weak-tie network that was famously studied by Granovetter (1974) in his analysis of job-hunting by middle-class professionals in Newton, Mass. Indeed, weak-tie insights are now used by organizations in all manner of ways, from formal job-referral systems in which the referrers are paid bonuses, to automobile maker Tesla's use of referrals for new car sales and rewards to loyal early purchasers. Fernandez et al. (2000) analyzed employee referrals at a call center within a large bank and found that employee referrals not only were cost effective, but resulted in a richer applicant pool. Burt (1992) has shown that employees whose networks span disconnected parts of organizations—that is, "bridge a structural hole"—are promoted faster than those with more limited ties. In subsequent work, others have shown that such brokerage networks work differently for men and women and minority groups (Ibarra 1992). More generally, Burt (2004) has shown that employees who are located in positions that enable them to bridge ideas from different units can capitalize on their positions to propose better ideas.

Internally, organizations can be more or less porous. Some organizations have relational spaces where members from various ranks and departments can mix freely, undeterred by formal role differentiation (Kellogg 2010). Organizations can be structured more like a network than a hierarchy; this has long been a common practice in the construction, film, and fashion industries, where projects come together on a short-term, temporary basis. Many activities, from fashion to computers, are created in fast product cycles, where speed and timing are urgent concerns (Uzzi 1996). In such cases, a group of people act as the project organizers and work with others from the outside on teams of relatively short duration. The relationships may become repeated games, as has been shown in the case of particular genres of films where directors, writers, and actors come together on a project, disperse, and return to work with one another on a later project (Faulkner and Anderson 1987). Similarly, in the electronics sector, the model of contractors who design equipment but outsource the making of the parts is commonplace. There are also manufacturers, sometimes critically referred to as "box stuffers," who outsource many stages of the production process, performing only some high-level integration work (Sturgeon 2002). Dell Computer is a classic example. And recent efforts at open innovation have created new models, such as the confederacy represented by Wikipedia or crowd-funding forms such as Kickstarter (Von Krogh and Von Hippel 2006).

The social relations among people inside organizations not only shape professional mobility, they also enable and constrain organizational behavior. Classic research in organizational theory (Gouldner 1954) and a foundational work in economic sociology (Macaulay 1963) demonstrate that even highly purposive economic exchanges are enmeshed in and driven by social networks. Organizational and economic actions result from a complex lamination of motivations and meanings that participants draw from the various relations in which they participate.

In a study of auto dealers, Macaulay (1963) found that businessmen often disregard the legal rights and responsibilities inherent in contracts in favor of more social means of dealmaking and dispute resolution. Networks shaped how businessmen approached transactions. As one of his respondents commented, "You don't read legalistic contract clauses to each other if you ever want to do business again. One doesn't run to the lawyers if he wants to stay in business because one must behave decently" (Macaulay 1963: 61). Lawyers should be excluded, not because they are personal strangers, but because they view the same relationship through a different lens, which explains why they find the businessman's approach "startling." As Macaulay noted, where businessmen see orders that can legitimately be cancelled, lawyers view the violation of contracts as having strongly negative consequences.

The meaning of a relationship and the actions appropriate to it depend on the character of the parties to the tie *and* their broader professional milieus. Put differently, car dealerships promote a relational view suggesting that the parties will solve problems as they arise; lawyers, on the other hand, see their firms' role as drafting contracts that anticipate problems. The relational view, as opposed to a transactional one, eases the cost of doing business, enhances flexibility, and offers support during lean times (Dore 1983).

14.5.2 Organizations as Drivers and Constituents of Networks

Organizations are also connected through networks. Inter-organizational relations range from dyadic relations, such as research partnerships, supplier relations, and joint ventures, to multi-party research consortia and industry associations. Such linkages are particularly common in knowledge-intensive industries, where access to new ideas is critical and the sources of expertise are dispersed (Powell et al. 1996). Inter-organizational relations can also be linked to persons, as is the case with interlocking boards of directors (Palmer et al. 1986). Several decades of research have focused on the degree of linkage among corporate elites, asking how integrated are the large firms, such as the South Korean *chaebol*, that dominate the economies of their countries (Mizruchi 1996). It turns out that many organizational linkages are deeply dependent on personal relations; corporate executives are asked onto boards more because boards recruit individuals than they do the companies that the individuals represent. Leading executives find such positions both strategically valuable for the view of the business horizon they afford and highly remunerative (Useem 1984).

One application of inter-organizational networks is to the conception of networks as industrial districts—geographically concentrated regions in which relations among firms are so densely interwoven that the locus of innovation is found more in the overall network than in the individual constituents (Marshall 1890; Piore and Sabel 1984; Saxenian 1994).

To illustrate this phenomenon, we draw on prior work on the emergence of biotechnology districts in the United States (Owen-Smith and Powell 2004; Whittington et al. 2009). We discuss the Boston and San Francisco Bay Area biotech clusters, the two most densely populated scientific and commercial clusters in the United States. Both these two regional communities are highly productive, but one (Boston) is anchored in a network that grew from public-sector origins. The other community (SF Bay) is clustered around a network that emerged from venture capital initiatives. The different anchor tenants—the highly central organizations that have access to various other players and broker between them—in these two technical communities result in divergent approaches to innovation. Both clusters are successful, and networks are fundamental in both, but the types of success and the ways in which relations matter vary with the organizational form and mindsets of the respective participants.

Each region developed distinctive patterns of collaboration that stamped their trajectory of innovation. Where universities dominated, as in Boston, a focus on discovery that favored openness and information sharing prevailed, and membership alone sufficed to increase rates of innovation. In contrast, when for-profit organizations were core players in the network, more 'closed,' proprietary approaches dominated; thus a central network position was essential to extract benefits (Owen-Smith and Powell 2004). In addition to altering how organizations garner advantage from their networks, the different approaches associated with the disparate partners shaped strategies for innovation, the kinds of connections the organizations pursued, and the markets they sought to serve.

There are two notable differences between the Bay Area and Boston clusters. The former is larger, both organizationally and geographically, with many more biotech firms, several major universities, including Stanford and the Universities of California (UC) at Berkeley and at San Francisco (UCSF), and numerous venture capital firms. The Boston network, although denser and somewhat smaller and more geographically compact, had many more public research organizations, including MIT, Harvard, Massachusetts General Hospital, Dana Farber Cancer Center, and Brigham and Women's Hospital, among others. The Boston area had many fewer venture capital firms in the 1970s and 1980s; VCs arrived much later. Neither region housed a large multinational pharmaceutical corporation during the period from the 1970s through the 1990s, so both regions were free from the dominance of an "800-pound gorilla" (Padgett and Powell 2012: 439). Both clusters had structurally cohesive networks, but they differed in their organizational demography.

The Boston network grew from its origins in the public sector, and public science formed the anchor for subsequent commercial application (Owen-Smith and Powell 2004; Porter et al. 2005). Because the Boston biotechnology community was linked by initial connections to public research organizations, this cluster manifested an open trajectory. By contrast, the Bay Area was influenced by a host of factors: the prospecting and matchmaking work of venture capitalists, the multidisciplinary science of the UCSF medical school, and pioneering efforts at technology transfer at Stanford University (Colyvas and Powell 2006; Popp Berman 2012; Powell and Sandholtz 2012). The San Francisco Bay Area evolved out of a more entrepreneurial orientation than Boston's. Both the Boston and Bay Area clusters were catalyzed by a non-biotech organizational form, but these different forms left distinctive relational imprints on the respective clusters.

The two clusters also differed in how they produced knowledge and the products they developed. We compared the patent citation networks of biotech firms in the two clusters (Owen-Smith and Powell 2006). The results suggest that Boston biotechs more routinely engaged in exploratory search, which typically yields a few very-high-impact patents at the expense of numerous innovations with lower than average future effects (Fleming and Sorenson 2001). In contrast, the dominant Bay Area patenting strategy had a more directed 'exploitation' design, as one might expect of companies supported by investor networks that demand demonstrated progress. Companies that pursue exploitative strategies generally develop numerous related improvements on established components of their in-house research. Boston area companies were much more reliant on citations to prior art generated by universities and public research organizations than were Bay Area companies, which relied more on citations to their own prior art. As for medicines, many Boston-based firms have focused on orphan drugs, as one might have expected of companies that were enmeshed in networks dominated by universities and hospitals. In contrast, Bay Area biotech firms pursued medicines for larger markets in which the potential patient populations run into the millions, and for which there was likely to be stiff product competition. This high-risk, high-reward strategy reflected the imprint of the venture capital mindset.

This extended illustration underscores the dual effects of networks, both within and across organizations. Networks are constitutive in the sense that the people inside organizations are simultaneously embedded in both work and personal relations, sometimes to such an extent that it is difficult to disentangle the two. And organizations both *learn* and *access* resources and new knowledge through their inter-organizational relations. These sources of ideas and relationships also define what organizations do, as they are influenced by the actions of their peers. In so doing, networks shape how organizations come to regard themselves and conceive of their goals.

14.6 Implications

The studies reviewed in this chapter combine insights from a wide variety of recent research on different types of organizations across sectors, geography, and time periods. The authors we have discussed study schools, jazz producers, SWAT teams, maternity counselors, wind power, corporate foundations, art festivals, social movement organizations, drug courts, childcare centers, breweries, soft drink producers, environmental rating agencies, the film industry, the civil service, call centers, government bureaus, biotech firms, and law and investment firms.

14.6.1 Organizations Reflect and Remake Society

Organizations matter for the study of society in two fundamental ways. First, *organizations reflect social structure*. Society tailors organizations in many meaningful ways: the professions and the state, labor market structures, cultural fads, and political movements and ideologies all leave their mark on organizational practices and structures. Various processes, from imprinting to isomorphism, make organizations an effigy of society. In Perrow's (1972: 4) apt language, people "track all kinds of mud from the rest of their lives with them into the organization, and they have all kinds of interests that are independent of the organization." On the other hand, even though organizations are frequent sites of larger societal processes, *organizations also forge and remake society*. Once an organization has been founded that capably performs a certain task or represents some interest, structural dynamics such as inertia and institutionalization enable such interests and tasks to persist.

The effect that organizations—be they public agencies, business firms, or civil society groups—have on society is quite profound. They are responsible for hiring and firing people, for paying and promoting them, for giving them voice and instilling loyal membership, and even for provoking resistance. Organizations facilitate innovation, sort people through careers, reproduce stratification and solidify discrimination, and determine the reputation and power of certain individuals. Organizations matter because they are monuments of times past as well as sculptors of the future.

Indeed, extending Stinchcombe (1965), one might argue that generations and society are shaped by the kinds of organizations that are predominant in an era. Consider the post–World War II era, which some have termed *Pax Americana*, running from the 1950s to the 1980s. This period was characterized by the dominance of large corporations, with stable internal labor markets, and good middle-class and skilled blue-collar jobs. This era of US manufacturing dominance meant that employment futures were relatively secure for those who worked for such companies, and the larger society, from housing to shopping malls, was molded by these organizational dynamics.

The postwar organizational regime split apart at the seams in the face of global competition and the quest for cheap overseas labor, ushering in the end of long-term employment and creating a new period of downward mobility and rising inequality. In contrast, today we live in the age of the lean start-up, with work futures precarious and the distribution of rewards highly skewed. But the model of disruption that is the hallmark of Silicon Valley start-ups has become an enviable symbol worldwide for its innovative capabilities, even if its rewards do not generate stable employment for large numbers of workers. Thus one can view both social history and social change through the lens of organizational models.

Two luminaries of organizational research have made the argument that we live in an organizational society more succinctly. Nobel laureate Herbert Simon (1991: 42) averred that "the economies of modern industrialized society can more appropriately be labeled organizational economies than market economies," and organizational sociologist Charles Perrow (1972: vii) made the striking claim that "all important social processes either have their origin in formal organizations or are strongly mediated by them."

14.6.2 Organizational Dynamics at Multiple Levels of Analysis

Distinguishing among the different levels through which social relations shape organizational behavior and by which organizations alter social ties can be challenging. Networks spill over both within and across organizations, and an ostensibly internal relation can easily become an external affiliation as careers and organizations develop over time (Padgett and Powell 2012). Similarly, for inter-organizational relations, what makes for an attractive partner is an obvious question, and here having prior knowledge of and experience with a specific partnership eases external relations (Rosenkopf et al. 2001). The propensity to form an alliance, or create a regional cluster, depends on the parties sharing mutual interests. Such prior relations are more likely forged by individuals than by corporate entities.

Sorenson and Rogan (2014) argue that three factors enhance the likelihood that individuals are the key to inter-organizational affiliations: (1)

the extent to which the needed resources, such as tacit knowledge, belong to individuals rather than organizations; (2) the extent to which indebtedness and gratitude are owed to persons rather than formal organizations; and (3) the degree of emotional attachment associated with a linkage. Thus interpersonal relations are often the glue that binds inter-organizational relations. In this sense, organizations are the conduits through which interpersonal relations are actualized.

How society affects organizations and vice versa is also often a dynamic process. Viewing organizations as sites and drivers of social action does not imply that these two dimensions can, or should, always be separated. The relationship between organizations and society is rarely a one-way street.

Organizations may intervene in the regulation and structuring of their own institutional environment or resource space. Corporations, for instance, not only are influenced by public opinion, but can themselves alter public opinion by lobbying, contributing to electoral politics, or supporting grassroots efforts (Walker and Rea 2014). In her study of historically black colleges in the United States, Wooten (2015) shows that the organizational development and resource access of black colleges was constrained by American social and educational policy. One of her findings is that the legitimacy-building accreditation of the foundation-supported United Negro College Fund in the 1950s and 1960s favored organizational structures that maintained the discrimination against blacks in US society. Similarly, rankings and ratings are important touchstones for organizations ranging from law schools to companies, but how that information is implemented and used is subject to organizational involvement, as is the creation of rankings and ratings itself (Espeland and Sauder 2016).

Although organizational perspectives have many theoretical applications, their actual use may be limited. One problem is that data tend to be biased toward formal models of organization. Quantitative studies of civil society, for instance, are frequently limited to organizations formally registered as 501(c)(3)s, and studies of unemployment, crime, and inequality often rely on the comprehensiveness of administrative data. More informal arrangements—such as movements, casual groups, or temporary projects—are sometimes systematically excluded from organizational data.

Another limitation is that the importance of organizational dynamics is often revealed only in retrospect. Some exemplary studies of race, ethnicity, and culture applying an organizational lens are historical. One such study shows that organizational dynamics shape the politics of ethnic categories. Why, despite their different country of origin, skin color, and social class, did Puerto Ricans, Mexicans, and Cubans end up under the umbrella label of 'Hispanic'? Mora (2014) shows that it was neither a common language nor perceived cultural similarities that led to the emergence of the Latino category, as Spanish-speaking Haitians are left out whereas non-Spanish-speaking Mexicans are included. Instead, she finds that a field-spanning combination of pan-ethnicity activists, government bureaucrats, and media executives was responsible for creating a new identity category over the decades from the late 1960s to the 1990s.

Another compelling historical example of the influence of organizational context is Phillips's (2011, 2013) comprehensive study of the role of producers and places for predicting the success of jazz music. Why are some pieces of music, particularly those recorded in peripheral places and with elements hard to categorize, rerecorded many times in later years? Phillips argues that the appeal of 'authentic outsiders' explains the evolution of this cultural market. He finds that jazz from cities that were more disconnected from other jazz-producing cities was more likely to enter the jazz canon than jazz from cities central to the jazz music industry. The studies by Mora and Phillips illuminate how culture and ethnicity are shaped by organizations.

14.6.3 Conclusion

Many accounts of organizational performance, whether in schools, hospitals, or firms, are unable to explain why one unit has positive outcomes and another middling success. For example, why do hospitals vary in their rates of Caesarian births, even within the same county, or why do charter schools do better than public schools in low-income, non-white urban areas, but produce little difference in student performance in suburban school districts? Learning from the "bright spots" among hospitals, schools, manufacturing plants, or government bureaus, and understanding how these successes might be spread, could be immensely valuable, but researchers often struggle to explain variation, both within organizations and between organizations that are, roughly speaking, comparable.

The challenge for researchers who study schools, hospitals, or employee productivity is to understand how organizational factors dictate health, educational, and labor outcomes. Part of the difficulty is, of course, the familiar statistical problem of selection bias—that is, those who are chosen for 'treatment' differ in important ways from the larger population. But an equally vexing problem is determining the appropriate level of organizational analysis. For schooling, is it the classroom, the grade level, the school, the neighborhood, or the district? We contend that a number of subfields in sociology—medicine, education, law, and stratification, to name only the most obvious candidates, would greatly benefit from a deeper engagement with organizational sociology.

If organizations matter for society, does organizational theory matter for sociological theory? We think so, as the bidirectional relationship between organizations and a wide array of social institutions is reflected in the diverse empirical literature reviewed in this chapter. In some instances, organizational research draws heavily on core sociological theories (see the various essays in Adler (2009) for examples of how organizations scholars draw on a wide range of classical theorists). We do not want to be content with this distinguished pedigree; instead we want to urge scholars in other areas of mainstream research to re-engage with organizational analysis, as effects as varied as hospital mortality, people-processing in courts and bureaus, and learning in classrooms are fashioned by the organizational processes we have detailed here. We close with a nod to the father of organization studies, Max Weber, and invoke one of those delightfully indecipherable German terms, '*Querschnittsmaterie*', which describes a cross-sectional field that may apply across the board to a range of sub-disciplines. In our view, organizational sociology played this intellectual role throughout much of the twentieth century, and we hope that it resumes this position in the coming years.

References

Adler, P. S. (2009). *The Oxford handbook of sociology and organization studies*. New York: Oxford University Press.

Autor, D., Katz, L. F., & Krueger, A. B. (1988). Computing inequality: Have computers changed the labor market? *Quarterly Journal of Economics, 113*(4), 1169–1213.

Baron, J. N., & Bielby, W. T. (1980). Bringing the firms back in: Stratification, segmentation, and the organization of work. *American Sociological Review, 45*(5), 737–765.

Baron, J. N., Hannan, M. T., & Burton, M. D. (1999). Building the iron cage: Determinants of managerial intensity in the early years of organizations. *American Sociological Review, 64*(4), 527–547.

Bartley, T., & Child, C. (2014). Shaming the corporation: The social production of targets and the anti-sweatshop movement. *American Sociological Review, 79*(4), 653–679.

Bechky, B. A. (2006). Gaffers, gofers, and grips: Role-based coordination in temporary organizations. *Organization Science, 17*(1), 3–21.

Berger, P. L., & Luckmann, T. (1966). *The social construction of reality*. Garden City: Anchor Books.

Bidwell, C. E. (2001). Analyzing schools as organizations: Long-term permanence and short-term change. *Sociology of Education, 74*, 100–114.

Bidwell, M., & Briscoe, F. (2010). The dynamics of inter-organizational careers. *Organization Science, 21*(5), 1034–1053.

Blau, P. M. (1955). *The dynamics of bureaucracy: A study of interpersonal relations in two government agencies*. Chicago: University of Chicago Press.

Briscoe, F., & Kellogg, K. C. (2011). The initial assignment effect: Local employer practices and positive career outcomes for work-family program users. *American Sociological Review, 76*(2), 291–319.

Bromley, P., & Meyer, J. W. (2015). *Hyper-organization: Global organizational expansion*. New York: Oxford University Press.

Burt, R. S. (1992). *Structural holes: The social structure of competition*. Cambridge: Harvard University Press.

Burt, R. S. (2004). Structural holes and good ideas. *American Journal of Sociology, 110*(2), 349–399.
Card, D., & DiNardo, J. E. (2002). Skill biased technological change and rising wage inequality: Some problems and puzzles. *Journal of Labor Economics, 20*(4), 733–783.
Castilla, E. J., & Benard, S. (2010). The paradox of meritocracy in organizations. *Administrative Science Quarterly, 55*(4), 543–676.
Chandler, A. (1977). *The visible hand*. Cambridge: Harvard University Press.
Chen, K. K. (2009). *Enabling creative chaos*. Chicago: University of Chicago Press.
Coase, R. H. (1937). The nature of the firm. *Economica, 4*(16), 386–405.
Cohen, M. D., & Hilligoss, P. B. (2010). The published literature on handoffs in hospitals: Deficiencies identified in an extensive review. *BMJ Quality & Safety, 19*(6), 493–497.
Colyvas, J. A., & Powell, W. W. (2006). Roads to institutionalization: The remaking of boundaries between public and private science. *Research in Organizational Behavior, 27*, 305–353.
Cyert, R. M., & March, J. G. (1963). *A behavioral theory of the firm*. Englewood Cliffs: Prentice-Hall.
Czarniawska-Joerges, B., & Sevón, G. (1996). *Translating organizational change*. Berlin: Walter de Gruyter.
Dalton, M. (1959). *Men who manage*. New York: Wiley.
DiMaggio, P. J., & Powell, W. W. (1983). The iron cage revisited: Institutional isomorphism and collective rationality in organizational fields. *American Sociological Review, 48*(2), 147–160.
Dobbin, F. (2009). *Inventing equal opportunity*. Princeton: Princeton University Press.
Dore, R. (1983). Goodwill and the spirit of market capitalism. *British Journal of Sociology, 34*(4), 459–482.
Eberhardt, J. L., Goff, P. A., Purdie, V. J., & Davies, P. G. (2004). Seeing black: Race, crime, and visual processing. *Journal of Personality and Social Psychology, 87*(6), 876–893.
Edmondson, A. C., Bohmer, R. M., & Pisano, G. P. (2001). Disrupted routines: Team learning and new technology implementation in hospitals. *Administrative Science Quarterly, 46*(4), 685–716.
Ely, R. J., Ibarra, H., & Kolb, D. M. (2011). Taking gender into account: Theory and design for women's leadership development programs. *Academy of Management Learning & Education, 10*(3), 474–493.
Espeland, W. N., & Sauder, M. (2016). *Engines of anxiety: Academic rankings, reputation, and accountability*. New York: Russell Sage Foundation.
Faulkner, R. R., & Anderson, A. B. (1987). Short-term projects and emergent careers: Evidence from Hollywood. *American Journal of Sociology, 92*(4), 879–909.
Feldman, M. S., & Pentland, B. T. (2003). Reconceptualizing organizational routines as a source of flexibility and change. *Administrative Science Quarterly, 48*(1), 94–118.
Fernandez, R. M. (2001). Skill-biased technological change and wage inequality: Evidence from a plant retooling. *American Journal of Sociology, 107*(2), 273–320.
Fernandez, R. M., Castilla, E. J., & Moore, P. (2000). Social capital at work: Networks and employment at a phone center. *American Journal of Sociology, 105*(5), 1288–1356.
Fleming, L., & Sorenson, O. (2001). Technology as a complex adaptive system: Evidence from patent data. *Research Policy, 30*(7), 1019–1039.
Gouldner, A. W. (1954). *Patterns of industrial bureaucracy*. Glencoe: Free Press.
Granovetter, M. (1974). *Getting a job: A study of contacts and careers*. Chicago: University of Chicago Press.
Granovetter, M. (1985). Economic action and social structure: The problem of embeddedness. *American Journal of Sociology, 91*(3), 481–510.
Hallett, T. (2010). The myth incarnate recoupling processes, turmoil, and inhabited institutions in an urban elementary school. *American Sociological Review, 75*(1), 52–74.
Hannan, M. T., & Freeman, J. (1984). Structural inertia and organizational change. *American Sociological Review, 49*(2), 149–164.
Hannan, M. T., & Freeman, J. (1989). *Organization ecology*. Cambridge: Harvard University Press.
Hedström, P. (2005). *Dissecting the social: Social mechanisms and the principles of analytical sociology*. Cambridge: Cambridge University Press.
Hedström, P., & Bearman, P. (2009). *The Oxford handbook of analytical sociology*. Oxford: Oxford University Press.
Heilman, M. E. (2001). Description and prescription: How gender stereotypes prevent women's ascent up the organizational ladder. *Journal of Social Issues, 57*(4), 657–674.
Hiatt, S. R., Sine, W. D., & Tolbert, P. S. (2009). From Pabst to Pepsi: The deinstitutionalization of social practices and the creation of entrepreneurial opportunities. *Administrative Science Quarterly, 54*, 635–667.
Hwang, H., & Powell, W. W. (2009). The rationalization of charity: The influences of professionalism in the nonprofit sector. *Administrative Science Quarterly, 54*(2), 268–298.
Ibarra, H. (1992). Homophily and differential returns: Sex differences in network structure and access in an advertising firm. *Administrative Science Quarterly, 37*(3), 422–447.
Johnson, V. (2007). What is organizational imprinting? Cultural entrepreneurship in the founding of the Paris opera. *American Journal of Sociology, 113*(1), 97–127.
Johnson, V. (2008). *Backstage at the revolution: How the royal Paris opera survived the end of the old regime*. Chicago: University of Chicago Press.
Kalev, A. (2014). How you downsize is who you downsize biased formalization, accountability, and managerial diversity. *American Journal of Sociology, 79*(1), 109–135.
Kellogg, K. C. (2010). Operating room: Relational spaces and microinstitutional change in surgery. *American Journal of Sociology, 115*(3), 657–711.

Kelly, E. L., Moen, P., & Tranby, E. (2011). Changing workplaces to reduce work-family conflict: Schedule control in a white-collar organization. *American Sociological Review, 76*(2), 265–290.

Kim, J. W., & King, B. G. (2014). Seeing stars: Matthew effects and status bias in major league baseball umpiring. *Management Science, 60*(11), 2619–2644.

King, B. G., & Soule, S. A. (2007). Social movements as extra-institutional entrepreneurs: The effect of protests on stock price returns. *Administrative Science Quarterly, 52*(3), 413–442.

Macaulay, S. (1963). Non-contractual relations in business: A preliminary study. *American Sociological Review, 28*(1), 55–67.

March, J. G. (1991). Exploration and exploitation in organizational learning. *Organization Science, 2*(1), 71–87.

March, J. G., & Simon, H. A. (1958). *Organizations*. New York: Wiley.

Marquis, C., & Tilcsik, A. (2013). Imprinting: Toward a multilevel theory. *Academy of Management Annals, 7*(1), 195–245.

Marshall, A. (1890). *Principles of political economy*. London: Macmillan.

McDonnell, M.-H., King, B., & Soule, S. (2015). A dynamic process model of contentious politics: Activist targeting and corporate receptivity to social challenges. *American Sociological Review, 80*(3), 654–678.

McPherson, C. M., & Sauder, M. (2013). Logics in action managing institutional complexity in a drug court. *Administrative Science Quarterly, 58*(2), 165–196.

Merton, R. K. (1968). The Matthew effect in science. *Science, 159*(3810), 55–63.

Meyer, J. W., & Rowan, B. (1977). Institutionalized organizations: Formal structure as myth and ceremony. *American Journal of Sociology, 83*(2), 340–363.

Mizruchi, M. S. (1996). What do interlocks do? An analysis, critique, and assessment of research on interlocking directorates. *Annual Review of Sociology, 22*, 271–298.

Mora, G. C. (2014). *Making hispanics: How activists, bureaucrats, and media constructed a new American*. Chicago: Chicago University Press.

O'Mahony, S., & Bechky, B. A. (2006). Stretchwork: Managing the career progression paradox in external labor markets. *Academy of Management Journal, 49*(5), 918–941.

Okhuysen, G. A. (2005). Understanding group behavior: How a police SWAT team creates, changes, and manages group routines. In K. D. Elsbach (Ed.), *Qualitative organizational research* (pp. 139–168). Charlotte: Information Age Publishing.

Okhuysen, G. A., & Bechky, B. A. (2009). Coordination in organizations: An integrative perspective. *Academy of Management Annals, 3*(1), 463–502.

Owen-Smith, J., & Powell, W. W. (2004). Knowledge networks as channels and conduits: The effects of spillovers in the Boston biotechnology community. *Organization Science, 15*(1), 5–21.

Owen-Smith, J., & Powell, W. W. (2006). Accounting for emergence and novelty in Boston and Bay area biotechnology. In P. Braunerhjelm & M. Feldman (Eds.), *Cluster genesis: The emergence of technology clusters and their implication for government policies* (pp. 61–86). Oxford: Oxford University Press.

Padgett, J. F., & Powell, W. W. (2012). *The emergence of organizations and markets*. Princeton: Princeton University Press.

Palmer, D., Friedland, R., & Singh, J. V. (1986). The ties that bind: Organizational and class bases of stability in a corporate interlock network. *American Sociological Review, 51*(6), 781.

Perrow, C. (1972). *Complex organizations: A critical essay*. New York: McGraw-Hill Publishers.

Pfeffer, J., & Salancik, G. R. (1978). *The external control of organizations: A resource dependence perspective*. New York: Harper & Row.

Phillips, D. J. (2005). Organizational genealogies and the persistence of gender inequality: The case of silicon valley law firms. *Administrative Science Quarterly, 50*(3), 440–472.

Phillips, D. J. (2011). Jazz and the disconnected: City structural disconnectedness and the emergence of a jazz canon, 1897–19331. *American Journal of Sociology, 117*(2), 420–483.

Phillips, D. J. (2013). *Shaping jazz: Cities, labels, and the global*. Princeton: Princeton University Press.

Piore, M., & Sabel, C. (1984). *The second industrial divide*. New York: Basic Books.

Popp Berman, E. (2012). *Creating the market university: How academic science became an economic engine*. Princeton: Princeton University Press.

Porter, K., Whittington, K. B., & Powell, W. W. (2005). The institutional embeddedness of high-tech regions: Relational foundations of the Boston biotechnology community. In S. Breschi & F. Malerba (Eds.), *Clusters, networks, and innovation* (pp. 261–296). Oxford: Oxford University Press.

Powell, W. W., & Sandholtz, K. W. (2012). Amphibious entrepreneurs and the emergence of organizational forms. *Strategic Entrepreneurship Journal, 6*(2), 94–115.

Powell, W. W., Koput, K. W., & Smith-Doerr, L. (1996). Interorganizational collaboration and the locus of innovation: Networks of learning in biotechnology. *Administrative Science Quarterly, 41*(1), 116–145.

Powell, W. W., Packalen, K. A., & Whittington, K. B. (2012). Organizational and institutional genesis: The emergence of high-tech clusters in the life sciences. In *The emergence of organizations and markets* (pp. 434–465). Princeton: Princeton University Press.

Rao, H. (1998). Caveat emptor: The construction of nonprofit consumer watchdog organizations. *American Journal of Sociology, 103*(4), 912–961.

Rerup, C., & Feldman, M. S. (2011). Routines as a source of change in organizational schemata: The role of trial-and-error learning. *Academy of Management Journal, 54*(3), 577–610.

Rhode, D. L. (2015). *The trouble with lawyers*. New York: Oxford University Press.

Rissing, B. A., & Castilla, E. J. (2014). House of green cards: Statistical or preference-based inequality in the employment of foreign nationals. *American Sociological Review, 79*(6), 1226–1255.

Rivera, L. A. (2012). Hiring as cultural matching: The case of elite professional service firms. *American Sociological Review, 77*(6), 999–1022.

Rivera, L. A. (2015). *Pedigree: How elite students get elite jobs*. Princeton: Princeton University Press.

Rosenfeld, R. A. (2003). Job mobility and career processes. *Annual Review of Sociology, 18*(1), 39–61.

Rosenkopf, L., Metiu, A., & George, V. P. (2001). From the bottom up? Technical committee activity and alliance formation. *Administrative Science Quarterly, 46*(4), 748–772.

Sahlin, K., & Wedlin, L. (2008). Circulating ideas: imitation, translation and editing. In R. Greenwood, C. Oliver, R. Suddaby, & K. Sahlin-Andersson (Eds.), *The Sage handbook of organizational institutionalism* (pp. 218–242). Thousand Oaks: Sage.

Saperstein, A., Penner, A. M., & Kizer, J. M. (2014). The criminal justice system and the racialization of perceptions. *The ANNALS of the American Academy of Political and Social Science, 651*(1), 104–121.

Sauder, M., & Espeland, W. N. (2009). The discipline of rankings: Tight coupling and organizational change. *American Sociological Review, 74*(1), 63–82.

Saxenian, A. L. (1994). *Regional advantage*. Cambridge: Harvard University Press.

Schneiberg, M., King, M., & Smith, T. (2008). Social movements and organizational form: Cooperative alternatives to corporations in the American insurance, dairy, and grain industries. *American Sociological Review, 73*(4), 635–667.

Scott, W. R. (2013). *Institutions and organizations* (4th ed.). Thousand Oaks: Sage.

Sharkey, A. J. (2014). Categories and organizational status: The role of industry status in the response to organizational deviance. *American Journal of Sociology, 119*(5), 1380–1433.

Sharkey, A. J., & Bromley, P. (2014). Can ratings have indirect effects?: Evidence from the organizational response to peers' environmental ratings. *American Sociological Review, 80*(1), 63–91.

Simon, H. (1991). Organizations and markets. *Journal of Economic Perspectives, 5*(2), 25–44.

Sine, W. D., & Lee, B. H. (2009). Tilting at windmills? The environmental movement and the emergence of the US wind energy sector. *Administrative Science Quarterly, 54*(1), 123–155.

Small, M. L. (2009). *Unanticipated gains: Origins of network inequality in everyday life*. New York: Oxford University Press.

Sorenson, O., & Rogan, M. (2014). (When) do organizations have social capital? *Annual Review of Sociology, 40*, 261–280.

Sterling, A. D. (2015). Pre-entry contacts and the generation of nascent networks in organizations. *Organization Science, 26*(3), 650–667.

Stewman, S., & Konda, S. L. (1983). Careers and organizational labor markets: Demographic models of organizational behavior. *American Journal of Sociology, 88*(4), 637–685.

Stinchcombe, A. L. (1965). Social structure and organizations. In J. March (Ed.), *Handbook of organizations* (pp. 142–193). Chicago: Rand McNally.

Stinchcombe, A. L. (1968). *Constructing social theories*. Chicago: University of Chicago Press.

Strang, D., & Meyer, J. W. (1993). Institutional conditions for diffusion. *Theory and Society, 22*(4), 487–511.

Strang, D., & Soule, S. A. (1998). Diffusion in organizations and social movements: From hybrid corn to poison pills. *Annual Review of Sociology, 24*, 265–290.

Sturgeon, T. J. (2002). Modular production networks: A new American model of industrial organization. *Industrial and Corporate Change, 11*(3), 451–496.

Suarez, D. F. (2010). Street credentials and management backgrounds: Careers of nonprofit executives in an evolving sector. *Nonprofit and Voluntary Sector Quarterly, 39*(4), 696–716.

Timmermans, S., & Epstein, S. (2010). A world of standards but not a standard world: Toward a sociology of standards and standardization. *Annual Review of Sociology, 36*, 69–89.

Tolbert, P. S., & Zucker, L. G. (1983). Institutional sources of change in the formal structure of organizations: The diffusion of civil service reform, 1880–1935. *Administrative Science Quarterly, 28*(1), 22–39.

Turco, C. (2012). Difficult decoupling: Employee resistance to the commercialization of personal settings. *American Journal of Sociology, 118*(2), 380–419.

Useem, M. (1984). *The inner circle: Large corporations and the rise of business political activity in the US and UK*. Oxford/New York: Oxford University Press.

Uzzi, B. (1996). The sources and consequences of embeddedness for the economic performance of organizations: The network effect. *American Sociological Review, 61*(4), 674.

Vogus, T. J., & Hilligoss, B. (2015). The underappreciated role of habit in highly reliable healthcare. *BMJ quality & safety*, Published Online First: 14 December 2015.

von Krogh, G., & von Hippel, E. (2006). The promise of research on open source software. *Management Science, 52*(7), 975–983.

Walker, E. T., & Rea, C. M. (2014). The political mobilization of firms and industries. *Annual Review of Sociology, 40*(1), 281–304.

Wang, D. (2015). Activating cross-border brokerage interorganizational knowledge transfer through skilled return migration. *Administrative Science Quarterly, 60*(1), 133–176.

Whittington, K. B., Owen-Smith, J., & Powell, W. W. (2009). Networks, propinquity, and innovation in knowledge-intensive industries. *Administrative Science Quarterly, 54*(1), 90–122.

Winter, S. G. (2013). Habit, deliberation, and action: strengthening the microfoundations of routines and capabilities. *Academy of Management Perspectives, 27*(2), 120–137.

Wooten, M. E. (2015). *In the face of inequality: How back colleges adapt*. Albany: SUNY Press.

Zucker, L. G. (1977). The role of institutionalization in cultural persistence. *American Sociological Review, 42*(5), 726.

Zuckerman, E. W., Kim, T. Y., Ukanwa, K., & von Rittmann, J. (2003). Robust identities or nonentities? Typecasting in the feature-film labor market. *American Journal of Sociology, 108*(5), 1018–1074.

15 Small Groups: Reflections of and Building Blocks for Social Structure

Stephen Benard and Trenton D. Mize

15.1 Introduction

Our lives are tightly bound up in small groups. From our families, friends and peer groups, to athletic teams, voluntary associations, and work units, small groups constitute much of the fabric of our daily lives. In these groups we develop and shed identities, influence and are influenced by others, exercise power and are subject to the exercise of power, and shape and are shaped by the social norms and micro-cultures of these groups. Not surprisingly, small groups have long fascinated sociologists, psychologists, and other social scientists, and the literature is large enough to have been reviewed many times from a variety of perspectives (e.g. Burke 2006; Fine 2012; Kelly et al. 2013; Levine and Moreland 1990; McGrath et al. 2000). This interest peaked around mid-century (Steiner 1974), although substantial work on small groups continues (Burke 2006; Fine 2012; Levine and Moreland 1990). Like individuals or organizations, small groups are a unit of analysis that invite study from a broad range of perspectives, and have relevance for diverse substantive questions. As a result, there is no single theory of small groups. Instead, small groups can be thought of as a conceptual hub from which a number of theoretical spokes radiate.[1]

Our overarching argument is that small groups are important to the study of social life in part because they serve as building blocks of society, by offering settings in which rudimentary forms of social structure can emerge. Small groups serve as settings in which individuals learn to construct and interact in formal and informal hierarchies, create, follow, deviate from, and perhaps enforce social norms, develop group boundaries and learn to conceive of the group as a social object apart from its members, and where they develop and disseminate bits of culture. As such, we organize our chapter around five structure-producing social processes: status, power, identity, influence and social norms, and group cultures, and illustrate how these processes operate in small groups. Because the literature on small groups is so extensive, space constraints lead most reviews to concentrate on a particular dimension of this literature, and our review is no exception. In our focus on structure-producing mechanisms, we omit topics such as how groups form, what attracts members to groups, or the ecologies of groups (e.g. Levine and Moreland 1990). Our aim in this chapter is to provide an accurate discussion of key ideas and findings, rather than a comprehensive account of each sub-

S. Benard (✉) • T.D. Mize
Department of Sociology, Indiana University, Bloomington, IN, USA
e-mail: sbenard@indiana.edu; tmize@indiana.edu

[1] We thank John DeLamater and Seth Abrutyn for suggesting the "hub and spoke" metaphor.

S. Abrutyn (ed.), *Handbook of Contemporary Sociological Theory*, Handbooks of Sociology and Social Research, DOI 10.1007/978-3-319-32250-6_15

field; much excellent work was necessarily omitted. It is also important to note that most of the work we discuss here has been conducted in a western cultural context; researchers have suggested that some social psychological processes work differently in other cultural contexts (e.g. Zhong et al. 2006).

We focus in this chapter on the sociology of small groups, although we draw on research from other fields, including psychology, organizational behavior, and economics. Modern small groups research in sociology generally focuses on how social structure and culture influence group interaction and behavior, and in turn how these behaviors influence social structure (Thoits 1995). From a sociological perspective, many macro-level factors can be best understood by observing them at an interactional level. For instance, while race, gender, and socioeconomic status are structural factors, their effects on individuals take place in part through interpersonal and intergroup interaction (Cohen 1982; Ridgeway 1997). It is this emphasis on structural factors that distinguishes modern small groups research in sociology from the "psychological social psychology" research that House outlined almost 40 years ago (House 1977; Oishi et al. 2009; Stryker 1980). That said, these boundaries are porous and there is substantial overlap across disciplines. As a result, while we focus on the sociological literature, we draw on work in allied fields when it is relevant for understanding problems of interest to sociologists.

While definitions of the term "group" vary, many researchers agree that at a minimum, groups include three or more individuals "interacting with a common purpose" (Kelly et al. 2013: 413). This more minimal definition is common in the experimental literature, which often focuses on groups created in a lab and observed under controlled conditions (e.g. to see how individuals work together to solve problems). Other scholars, particularly those who study groups in the field, prefer more comprehensive definitions that specify a shared sense of culture, commitment, and identity among group members (Fine 2012). We include research taking a minimal as well as a more comprehensive view of groups in this chapter. This line is not always clear-cut: aspects of culture and identity emerge in initially minimal groups. We begin with a general overview of small groups as a source of structure, before moving on to discuss specific structure-producing mechanisms: status, power, identity, influence and social norms, and culture.

15.2 Small Groups as Self-Organizing, Emergent Structure

How do groups organize and accomplish desired goals? Why do some individuals attain positions of power and influence within groups, while other individuals find themselves on the margins? Questions such as these have been addressed by small groups researchers at least since the mid-twentieth century. Although small groups often reflect the structure of society, they also work to *create* structures. Robert Freed Bales and colleagues (1951) found that when small groups of individuals worked together on a task, consistent patterns emerged. In particular, certain individuals tended to dominate the group discussion while others largely remained silent. Interestingly, these patterns developed among groups of similar individuals (same sex, race, and education level). Therefore, even in the absence of easily observable cues about social status or ability, certain individuals gained greater influence and visibility in the group. Those who attained the highest ranks of the group tended to speak more and to address the whole group, while those of lowest rank tended to address only one individual at a time, usually the highest ranking individual.

The level of inequality within the groups was rather striking. Figure 15.1 displays the percent of the total number of remarks made to the group by each group member, for different size groups. For example, in a four-person group (middle figure in left column) we would expect each individual to contribute 25 % of the total remarks given complete equality. Instead, the highest ranking individual tends to make roughly 50 % of the total remarks for the entire group while the lowest ranking individual tends to provide only about 10 % of the remarks. In addition, the nature of the remarks varied based on one's status ranking. Those of higher rank gave more opin-

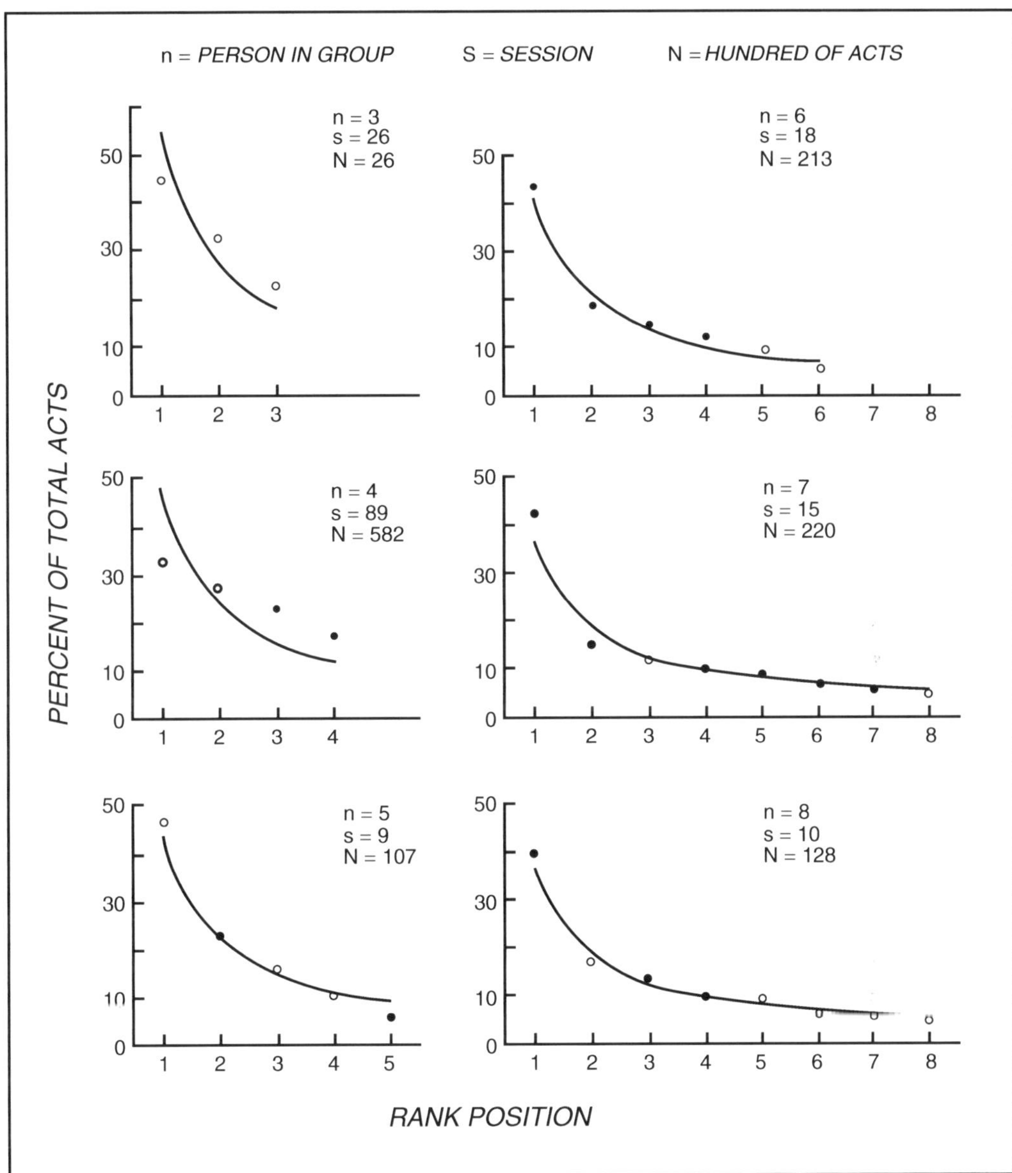

Fig. 15.1 Percent of the total number of remarks made to the group by each group member, by group size (Bales et al. 1951, Chart 1)

ions while those of lower rank agreed more often (Bales et al. 1951). Thus, even in groups of similar individuals, status hierarchies form and structure interaction.

Strodtbeck and colleagues (1957) built on the findings of Bales to examine how groups use observable characteristics of individuals to create status hierarchies. In observing mock jury deliberations, they found that status hierarchies formed that closely matched the status order of society. Specifically, men and those with higher status occupations dominated jury deliberations and were more likely to be selected as a jury foreman (Strodtbeck et al. 1957).

This tendency towards order, structure, and hierarchy appears to develop early in the life of groups. In his classic "Robber's Cave Experiment", Sherif and colleagues (1961) recruited well-adjusted middle-class boys to a summer camp. He then sorted the boys into two groups randomly. Almost immediately, leaders emerged in each group and clear hierarchies formed. This finding is similar to the findings of Bales: both illustrate that groups tend to have one or a few influential and outspoken individuals, with most others falling much lower in the status hierarchy and rarely being heard.

15.3 Status

As both Bales et al. (1951) and Sherif et al's (1961) studies demonstrate, groups tend to form status hierarchies quickly, with certain individuals attaining more influential positions that reflect their status within a group. These early studies led to a tremendous amount of work on the concept of status in groups. Sociologists define status as an individual's position in a group's hierarchy of "evaluation, influence, and participation" (Correll and Ridgeway 2003: 29) while psychologists define status similarly as "… an individual's prominence, respect, and influence in the eyes of others" (Anderson and Kilduff 2009b: 295).

Expectation states theory offered an early and still-influential explanation for these patterns. The theory argued that when group members see a need to work together ("collective orientation") in order to accomplish a particular task ("task orientation"), they will attempt to determine which group members are likely to have the most helpful contributions towards this goal. Those individuals who are seen to have more to contribute – because they are perceived to be more skilled, competent, or motivated to help the group – will attain greater status in the group. They will see their opinions given more weight, will be granted more opportunities to speak, participate more often in group discussions, and their contributions to the group will be viewed more positively than those of lower-status group members (Correll and Ridgeway 2003).

Berger and colleagues (1972) further argued that characteristics of individuals are partially responsible for the observed power and prestige orders that form in groups. Their theory of *status characteristics* proposed that certain states of an attribute – such as gender or race – sometimes carry different expectations for performance (see, also, Chap. 16). As a result, those who possess a more advantaged state of the attribute more easily attain status and influence in groups. For example, men are often expected to perform more competently than women on stereotypically male tasks, and accordingly groups are more likely to follow the suggestion of a man rather than a woman on such tasks, net of the actual competence of the man or woman on the task in question (e.g. Thomas-Hunt and Phillips 2004; Kalkhoff et al. 2008).

Two types of characteristics impact someone's status within a group: specific and diffuse. Specific status characteristics refer to attributes of an individual that carry specific and relevant assumptions of competence for the task at hand (Berger et al. 1972; Berger and Webster 2006). For example, someone's score on a standardized math test would influence their specific status for a group task involving math skills. In many ways, the link between specific status characteristics and status in groups are clear: it is not surprising that group members known to have scored well on a test of math ability are assumed to be better performers on math-related tasks. Diffuse status characteristics, in contrast, refer to characteristics that affect expectations for performance in a broad range of situations, regardless of their relevance to a specific task (Berger et al. 1972; Berger and Webster 2006). Race has been shown to affect interaction, with individuals often expecting minorities to perform worse in a broad range of situations, producing racial inequality in groups (Cohen 1982; Goar 2007; Goar and Sell 2005). Gender also acts a diffuse status characteristic, with women assumed to be generally less competent, regardless of gender's relevance to the task at hand (Correll and Ridgeway 2003; Ridgeway and Correll 2004; Pugh and Wahrman 1983; Smith-Lovin and Brody 1989; Thomas-Hunt and Phillips 2004).

Importantly, these status-based performance expectations derive from widespread cultural beliefs and are not necessarily associated with actual differences in competence or ability (Berger and Webster 2006). Status beliefs further operate at an unconscious level and affect individuals even if they do not consciously endorse them (Ridgeway et al. 1998; Correll and Ridgeway 2003). Years of experimental research has shown that individuals draw on these macro-level cultural beliefs in interaction, leading to disadvantages for racial minorities, women, less educated individuals, less attractive individuals, and sexual minorities to name a few (Cohen 1982; Goar and Sell 2005; Kalkhoff et al. 2008; Webster and Driskell 1983; Webster et al. 1998; Correll and Ridgeway 2003; Lucas and Phelan 2012).

These status hierarchies can be self-fulfilling: if someone is perceived as having little to offer the group, they will receive fewer opportunities to speak, and their opinions will be given less weight, reinforcing the perception that they have little to offer. Lower-status individuals are also often held to stricter standards, meaning that they must offer greater evidence of ability in order to be viewed as equally competent as higher-status individuals (Foschi et al. 1994; Foschi 1996; Wenneras and Wold 1997; see Foschi 2000 for a review). Similarly, individuals may shift the standards of evaluation to match the qualifications of a preferred individual, rather than using consistent standards (Norton et al. 2004).

15.3.1 Overcoming Disadvantaging Status Beliefs

An individual's status in a group reflects not only their actual performance, but also perceptions of their performance, potentially filtered through stereotypes and other cognitive distortions. As a result, status imperfectly reflects actual competence and can disadvantage otherwise deserving individuals. These errors in status judgments can also impair group performance, by leading groups to overweight the input of less competent group members and underweight the input of more-competent group members (Thomas-Hunt and Phillips 2004). Correcting misperceptions of competence is therefore beneficial for both groups and individuals.

Several types of interventions have been shown to effectively reduce status effects, particularly in regards to gender discrimination. Women can attain relatively high status positions in groups when they demonstrate group-oriented motivation; but not when they demonstrate more self-centered motivations. In contrast, men can attain high status regardless of their motivation (Ridgeway 1982). Settings in which women are known to succeed can also reduce status effects. Lucas (2003) shows that creating an organizational setting where women were known to be successful leaders led to women leaders being given equal influence to men leaders. Goar and Sell (2005) find that task groups show less racial inequality in participation when they believe they are trying to solve a complex task for which no one group member is likely to have a complete solution. Importantly, these interventions should apply to any disadvantaging status characteristic. That is, the examples are not limited to gender or race, but the interventions instead help overcome *status* disadvantages, regardless of their source.

Other research shows that increased motivation to avoid stereotyping can help decrease stereotyped judgments of groups such as women and minorities (e.g. Devine et al. 2002). That is, when individuals put greater effort and care into thinking through their decisions, they are less likely to rely on stereotypical judgments that disadvantage lower status groups. Correspondingly, individuals rely on stereotypes to a greater extent when they lack the motivation to examine their thoughts or behaviors closely, such as when they are angry (Bodenhausen et al. 1994), tired (Bodenhausen 1990), or when their self-view has been threatened by criticism (Sinclair and Kunda 2000). Similarly, settings that encourage individuals to think through their decisions more carefully – such as when individuals expect they will have to explain their judgments to others – reduce stereotyping (e.g. Foschi 1996; see Lerner and Tetlock 1999 for a review). Further, asking individuals to commit to a specific, transparent standard of evaluation limits the likelihood that individuals will apply different standards to different group members (Norton et al. 2004).

15.3.2 Status Construction Theory

How do status beliefs develop? Ridgeway (2006) proposes that we attach diffuse status beliefs to particular categories (e.g. gender and race) when it is easy to observe the different resources held by members of these groups, but difficult to observe the processes and behaviors through which these resources were acquired. For example, in many organizations men disproportionately hold high status positions. These high status men's gender is easily observable, while the circumstances that led to them obtaining these positions are harder to ascertain. Over time, individuals attach status value to those higher in the status hierarchy, and attribute their differential position to the characteristics of the individuals (Ridgeway 2006). Thus, in situations where high status individuals such as men enact more high status behaviors (e.g., assertiveness) and are given more deference, individuals attribute greater status value to the category of "men" as their gender is easily observable, while men's structurally advantaged positions are more likely to go unnoticed. Empirical tests of status construction theory have generally supported its basic propositions. Both men and women treat others unequally on the basis of established status distinctions. However, men are more likely to act on emerging status distinctions – with women more cautious about using new distinctions as reasons to guide their behavior (Ridgeway et al. 2009; see also Brashears 2008 for a cross-national test in support of the theory).

15.3.3 Further Developments in Status Research

In recent years, status research has continued to develop in new directions. Although status characteristics theory developed within sociology, much new work in psychology and organizational behavior contributes to this body of work by drawing on and extending sociological theories and conceptions of status. This work has identified a number of factors that increase or decrease an individual's status in groups, including confidence (Kennedy et al. 2013), extraversion (Anderson et al. 2001), trait dominance (Anderson and Kilduff 2009a); generosity (Flynn 2003; Flynn et al. 2006), sharing expertise (Cheng et al. 2013), and self-sacrifice for the group (Willer 2009).

Although those of higher status receive more respect and influence, not all individuals are able to claim or even desire higher status. Anderson and colleagues (2006) find that people dislike individuals who do not accurately perceive their own status. In particular, those that overestimate their own status (have overly-flattering views of themselves) are disliked compared to individuals who accurately perceive their own status. In contrast, those who are self-effacing (view themselves as lower in status than they truly are) are particularly well liked by others.

Berger and colleagues' (1972) original formulation of status characteristics theory referred to status as the "power and prestige order" while Anderson emphasizes the "...prominence, respect, and influence" an individual has in a group (Anderson et al. 2006, Anderson and Kilduff 2009b). In an empirical test, Anderson and colleagues (2012) show that what sociologists generally refer to as status has both a rank and a respect dimension. All individuals desire respect and would like to be valued; however not all individuals desire high rank within a group's hierarchy. Put in status characteristics theory terms: not all individuals appear to want the "power" part of status, but all individuals desire the "prestige" aspect.

15.4 Power

Although status characteristics theory occasionally uses the term "power" to refer to one's place in a status hierarchy, for the most part sociologists use the terms "power" and "status" to refer to different aspects of how people relate to one another in groups. While status underlies situations in which we *choose* to follow another person because we respect their competence or motivation to help the group, power underlies situations in which we *have* to follow another person because they can compel us to do so. In this section, we discuss the sources of power as well as the experience of power – how having or lacking power shapes our thoughts, feelings, and behavior.

Many sociologists study power from the perspective of exchange theory (e.g. Homans 1951 [1992]; Blau 1964; Emerson 1976; see Cook and Rice 2003 for a review). Exchange theory argues that in a wide range of social interactions, people exchange material and non-material resources in an effort to reach their goals (e.g. money, gratitude, social status, see Blau 1964). This process is obvious in formal negotiations over cars, houses, or an employment contracts, but also occurs informally in many settings. Couples explicitly or implicitly negotiate where to eat for dinner, who does the housework, and whose career receives priority. Social exchange is not always negotiated; indeed, people often reciprocally exchange resources with no explicit promise of repayment (Molm 2010). For example, friends might give each other birthday gifts, rides to the airport, or social support as needed. The concept of power helps us understand why social exchanges sometimes favor one party over another, and how these imbalances shape our thoughts, feelings, and behavior. Research on power also helps us understand the quality of our interpersonal relationships: while exchange in unequal-power relationships can be exploitative, exchange in equal-power relationships tends to produce trust, commitment, and solidarity.

15.4.1 Dependence and Power

Informally, we can think of power as one person's capacity to get what they want in a social exchange, regardless of the wishes of the other person. Emerson (1962: 32) offered a more formal definition: "[t]he power of actor A over actor B is the amount of resistance on the part of B which can be potentially overcome by A." This definition forms the starting point for Emerson's *power-dependence theory*, which has played an important role in shaping sociological research on power, particular within the group process and small group traditions (e.g. Emerson 1962, 1964, 1976; see Cook et al. 2006 for a review).

The key insight of power-dependence theory is that power is relational. This means that no individual is inherently powerful; instead, individuals are powerful to the extent that they hold power over others. Emerson argued that power stems from dependence, such that A has influence over B to the extent that B is dependent on A in order to reach goals that are important to B. In turn, dependence stems from two sources. The first of these is the availability of alternative means of reaching one's goals. To the extent that B can find other individuals who will help her or him reach a valued goal, B is less dependent on A, and A will have less influence over B. For example, workers are less likely to put up with abusive supervisors when they plan to change jobs in the near future, while those who do not expect to be able to leave their job tend to tolerate more abuse (Tepper et al. 2009).

The second source of dependence is motivational investment. To the extent that B is motivationally invested, or in other words strongly cares about a goal that A can help B to reach, A will hold more influence over B. This is sometimes referred to as the "principle of least interest"; in romantic relationships, the partner with less emotional attachment to the relationship tends to have more power (Sprecher et al. 2006).

Emerson's conception of dependence as a source of power leads to a number of interesting insights. One is that the distribution of power across exchange partners predicts the likelihood that they will develop a cohesive, trusting, committed relationship. The distribution of power in a relationship is not necessarily zero-sum: relationships can be high or low in *total power*. When A and B are equally and highly dependent on one another, the relationship is high in total power; when neither depends on the other, the relationship is low in total power. High total power relationships are expected to be cohesive, because both partners depend on one another and should be less likely to leave the relationship. Accordingly, experimental work finds lower levels of conflict in high total power relationships than unequal power relationships (Lawler et al.

1988). Further, work on the theory of relational cohesion finds that individuals in high total power relationships tend to see their relationships as more cohesive and to be more committed to those relationships (see Chap. 8; also, Lawler and Yoon 1993, 1996, 1998; Lawler et al. 2000). Similarly, a field study of car dealers and their suppliers found that the partnerships that were highly and equally interdependent had more committed relationships than those that were not (Kumar et al. 1995).

Within equal power relationships, a number of other factors affect the partners' levels of trust, cohesion, and commitment. These include the form of exchange (i.e. negotiated, reciprocal, generalized, or productive; Lawler et al. 2008; Molm et al. 2007) and the extent to which the relationship is perceived as competitive versus cooperative (Kuwabara 2011). At least one study finds greater cohesion in triads than dyads, perhaps due to lower levels of uncertainty and conflict in triads (Yoon et al. 2013). Rational choice theories also predict that, as individuals are more dependent on the group, they will accept more extensive obligations on behalf of the group and will be less likely to exit (Hechter 1988).

A second set of insights from power-dependence theory concerns how individuals can balance power in a network (Emerson 1962). Individuals often find low power positions uncomfortable and seek to tilt the power imbalance more to their favor. By identifying dependence as the source of power, the theory provides a road map to equalizing power relations. Because power is based in part on the availability of alternatives, one can equalize power by increasing their own alternatives or limiting their partner's alternatives. A dissatisfied employee may apply for other jobs, broadening their range of alternatives (Tepper 2009), and weaker parties in many settings form coalitions to prevent higher power actors from using a "divide and conquer" strategy (Emerson 1964; Simpson and Macy 2001). In addition, because power is also based on one's motivational investment in a goal, one can balance power by reducing one's own motivational investment, or by increasing their partner's motivational investment. Emerson (1962) suggests that low power individuals can increase a higher-power partner's motivational investment by treating that person with respect and deference. The logic is that the high status person enjoys being treated in this way, and is thus less likely to take steps that would end the relationship. Individuals can also be constrained in their use of power by their commitment to the relationship, or by social norms prescribing fairness (Cook and Emerson 1978).

The insight that power derives from dependence has motivated decades of systematic research to map out precisely how power and dependence are related. This has led to the development of a family of *network exchange theories*, which take Emerson's insights and examine how they operate in increasingly complex social networks (e.g. Bienenstock and Bonacich 1992; Cook and Emerson 1978; Cook and Yamagishi 1992; Friedkin 1992; Heckathorn 1983; Markovsky et al. 1988; Markovsky 1992). These theories differ in their formal or mathematical methods for predicting when and how individuals will use power, and substantial debate has occurred around the best method for predicting power in networks (e.g. Willer 1992). Nevertheless, these research programs concur on Emerson's primary argument that power derives from dependence. This body of work consistently finds that our location in a social network – including the number of alternative exchange partners we have, and the value of those relationships to us – shapes our dependence on others and correspondingly shapes how much power we hold. This extends beyond our direct connections: individuals with the same number of alternative exchange partners may not be equally powerful if the partners to whom they are connected differ in power (Cook and Emerson 1978).

To illustrate, Fig. 15.2 shows two exchange networks based on those studied in Cook and Emerson (1978), but simplified for this example. In this figure, the lettered boxes represent individuals, and the lines represent connections indicating that those actors can exchange with one another. This could represent, for example, a network of acquaintances who trade help and information. In both networks, the central actor is

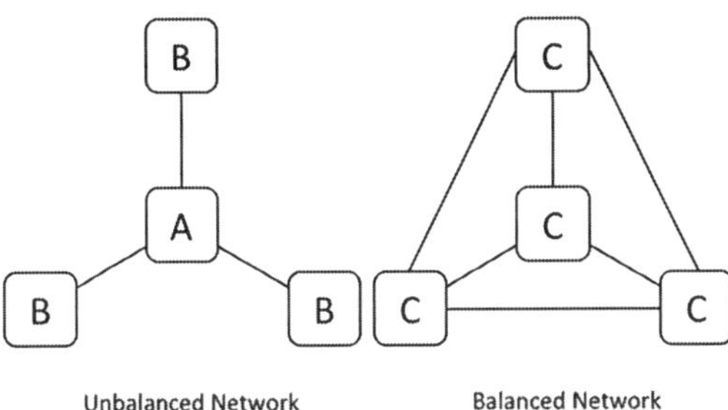

Fig. 15.2 Unbalanced and balanced exchange networks – simplified figure based on Fig. 15.2 in Cook and Emerson (1978)

connected to three other actors. But in the unbalanced network (left panel), each B has only A to rely on for help or information, while A can rely on three individuals. In this network, the Bs depend on A more than the reverse, and so A is more powerful than the Bs. In contrast, in the balanced network (right panel), each person has three potential exchange partners, and so all actors are equally dependent. These processes become increasingly subtle in more complex networks.

15.4.2 The Experience of Power

People have long speculated about how power affects the person wielding it. It is easy to find anecdotal examples in support of Lord Acton's famous aphorism that "power corrupts, and absolute power corrupts absolutely." However, research suggests the truth is more nuanced. And indeed, one can think of anecdotal examples in which powerful individuals were not corrupted, but instead served the greater good. So how does power actually affect the person who holds it?

Rather than having a universally corrupting influence, it appears that holding power or feeling powerful increases "action orientation", or goal-seeking behavior (Anderson and Berdahl 2002; Galinsky et al. 2003; see Keltner et al. 2003 for a review). Because powerful individuals face fewer consequences for taking action, they tend to be less wary and more assertive in pursuit of their goals. As a result, individuals who feel powerful are more direct with strangers, more flirtatious, and more likely to take action even when it is unclear if that action is allowed (Galinsky et al. 2003). Similarly, powerful individuals may feel less constrained to follow social norms (Bargh et al. 1995). As a result, holding power can magnify an individual's existing tendencies, such that communally-oriented individuals behave in more prosocial ways when they hold power, but self-interested individuals behave in more selfish ways (Chen et al. 2001).

Nevertheless, much research suggests that power can lead individuals in groups to behave in ways that fellow group members may find off-putting, abrasive, or exploitative. High power individuals tend to be less concerned with having a "smooth and pleasant" working relationship, compared to their low power partners (Copeland 1994: 273). Powerful group members are more likely to express their true feelings (Anderson and Berdahl 2002), to see their partners as means to an end (Gruenfeld et al. 2008), and to focus on their own versus their partner's perspective (Galinsky et al. 2006). Perhaps not surprisingly, powerful individuals overestimate their partner's positive emotions, while more cautious low power individuals overestimate their partner's negative emotions (Anderson and Berdahl 2002). Further, group leaders sometimes withhold useful information from the group or exaggerate external threats to suppress competition for their position (Barclay and Benard 2013; Maner and Mead 2010).

15.4.3 Power and Other Dimensions of Small Group Interaction

In addition to studying how power shapes small group dynamics, social scientists have examined how power intersects with other group processes. One area of research examines when groups will voluntarily cede power to leaders (i.e., create legitimate or recognized authorities, see Zelditch 2001 for a review). Some evidence suggests that groups dislike having leaders, and tend to prefer democratic voting over allowing a leader to have control over the group (Rutte and Wilkie 1985). However, groups do turn to leaders to help them deal with crises, such as when the group is at risk of overusing a scarce resource (Messick et al. 1983).

A number of studies investigate how power and status are related. Thye (2000) finds that the resources owned by high status actors tend to be valued more than those owned by low status actors. For example, a car owned by a celebrity can sell for more than a similar car owned by a non-celebrity. This can serve as a source of power when the resources of a high status person offer more leverage in negotiation. Other work finds that status moderates the behavior of those in power, such that powerful actors who lack status (e.g. are not respected) are more likely to treat interaction partners in demeaning ways (Fast et al. 2012). Powerful individuals can gain status through generosity or philanthropy, which may offset the often negative perception of powerful individuals as selfish or exploitative (Willer et al. 2012).

15.5 Social Norms and Influence

When we are part of a group, we often take our cues from the behavior or expectations of other group members. Students hesitate to raise their hands in class if no one else does, and many people choose which movie to watch or which restaurant to visit based on what their friends do. Not surprisingly, sociologists and social psychologists have devoted considerable attention to understanding how social influence works. As early as the 1930s, studies found that people tend to rely on the opinions of other group members when making judgments about ambiguous stimuli, such as how much a point of light appears to be moving in a dark room (Sherif 1937). Many people are familiar with the famous Asch (1951) conformity studies, which found that participants were more likely to agree with a clearly incorrect statement about the relative length of several lines when other group members unanimously supported this statement.

More broadly, social psychologists have identified two processes by which groups influence their members: *normative* and *informational* influence (Deustch and Gerard 1955). Normative influence occurs when people conform to the perceived expectations of other group members in order to gain social rewards (acceptance, approval) or avoid social punishments (embarrassment, disapproval) from others. Normative influence is at work when people don't voice their true opinion for fear of criticism, laugh at a joke they don't understand to avoid appearing humorless, or buy articles of clothing because they hope others will approve of them. In contrast, informational influence occurs when people conform to the behavior of their peers because they believe this behavior provides useful and accurate information that will improve the quality if their decisions. Informational influence is at work when people choose to eat at a busy restaurant because they believe the busyness reflects its quality, or when lost individuals follow a crowd because they believe the crowd must be headed to the same destination.

Sociologists have had a particular fascination with social norms and normative influence since the early days of the field (Hechter and Opp 2001), and often rely on social norms to explain particular phenomena (Horne 2001; Wrong 1961). There are a number of reasons for this interest in norms. Broadly, groups often use social norms to define their rules and boundaries (Durkheim [1894] 1988; Erikson 1966; Mead 1918). In small groups, social norms can sustain and encourage group cohesion, and serve as the building blocks of more complex social structures and forms of social organization (Hechter 1988; Hechter and Opp 2001). Social norms are transmitted across generations (Sherif 1936), helping groups maintain an existence independent of particular group members, because group traditions continue even as membership changes. Norms also help explain how human groups worked together effectively before the advent of legal systems to forestall exploitative or harmful behavior (Ellis 1971; de Quervain et al. 2004). Even today, individuals often rely on social norms to resolve disputes informally, without turning to the law (e.g. Ellickson 1994).

This interest in norms has led sociologists to focus on different questions than psychological studies of influence. While psychologists often create a norm in the laboratory to understand the circumstances under which people conform, sociologists have more often been interested in the conditions under which norms will arise. This is a trend rather than an absolute distinction: sociologists have conducted intriguing studies on how social influence contributes to unpredictability in online markets (Salganik et al. 2006), or how the social status of majority and minority group members shapes conformity when groups fail to reach unanimity (Melamed and Savage 2013). For this reason, our discussion of social norms and influence will tend towards emphasizing normative over informational influence. In addition, because the voluminous work on the Asch study and related paradigms and debates mainly occur in psychology, and have been subject to extensive reviews and meta-analyses (e.g. Bond and Smith 1996; Bond 2005; Wood et al. 1994) we do not review them here.

15.5.1 How Do Social Norms Arise?

While there is no universally agreed-upon definition of social norms, many scholars conceptualize norms as rules for behavior, consensually held by group members, and supported by rewards or punishments (Horne 2001). Under this definition, norms exist to the extent that individuals are willing to spend time and effort enforcing them (Hechter 1988; Oliver 1980). A team working to complete a group project may hold the norm that group members should work hard to help the group succeed, rather than free-ride and create more work for their peers or endanger the group's success. Those that conform to this rule receive praise or other forms of social approval from their peers, while those who deviate experience disapproval or criticism. Scholars disagree about the extent to which such norms are generally clear and observed by group members, or instead continually shifting and renegotiated (Hechter and Opp 2001).

Early discussions of social norms suggested that they arise through social interaction (Homans [1951] 1992). A key problem in understanding how this happens is explaining why individuals are willing to enforce group norms, given that doing so is often costly. For example, criticizing a free-riding member of a work team might encourage them to change their behavior and help the group, but it might also be uncomfortable, and provoke resentment or even retaliation. As a result, individuals sometimes hesitate to enforce group norms, even when doing so benefits the individual and the group (Horne 2009; Oliver 1980).

To answer this question, small groups researchers often use experiments in which they create groups in the laboratory, and ask the groups to engage in a public goods or social dilemma task (e.g. Kollock 1998; Komorita and Parks 1994). These group tasks give participants a choice between acting in a self-interested way or in a way that helps that group. Individuals fare better when they make the self-interested choice, but if everyone behaves in a self-interested manner, the group as a whole fares more poorly than if individuals had opted to help the group. For example, individuals on a project team might be tempted to free-ride and let others complete the project for them, thus allowing the free-rider to succeed with minimal effort. However, if everyone chooses to free-ride, the group fails and all members are worse off than if they had all opted to work hard. In these studies, researchers give participants the option to enforce norms – often by allowing participants to spend some of the money that they are being paid to take part in the experiment to penalize free-riders or reward those who do contribute to the group's success.

The overarching pattern is that people are willing to enforce norms of contribution to the group, even when doing so is personally costly (e.g. Fehr and Gachter 2002; Horne 2009; Ostrom et al. 1992; Yamagishi 1986). A number of factors moderate this tendency. Individuals are more likely to enforce norms of group cooperation when the costs of enforcing norms are lower (Horne and Cutlip 2002), when they don't trust other group members to cooperate (Yamagishi 1986, 1988a), when the risks faced by the group are serious (Yamagishi 1988b), or when the group is threatened by a competing outgroup

(Benard 2012; Sherif 1966). Individuals also appear to be more receptive to norm enforcement from a democratically elected versus a randomly assigned leader (Grossman and Baldassari 2012).

This willingness to enforce norms despite the cost seems in part driven by anger at non-contributors (Fehr and Gächter 2002); one study using PET scans found that punishing non-contributing group members appears to be rewarding at the neural level (de Quervain et al. 2004). Individuals may also enforce norms as a way of signaling that they are committed to the group, which in turn encourages valuable exchanges with other group members (Homans [1951] 1992; Horne 2004). Those who enforce group norms tend to be rewarded by other group members, and are rewarded more as the cost of enforcing norms increases (Horne and Cutlip 2002) and as the direct and indirect benefits of exchanging with other group members increase (Horne 2004). Individuals who enforce group norms are also seen as more worthy of respect and trust than those who do not, as long as they are perceived to enforce norms fairly (Barclay 2006).

15.5.2 The "Dark Side" of Social Norms

The tendency of groups to enforce norms by punishing low-contributing group members or rewarding high-contributors can help groups to achieve their goals, by reducing the level of free-riding in the group (e.g. Gürerk et al. 2006). Indeed, because willingness to contribute to or sacrifice for one's group is often viewed as a behavioral indicator of group solidarity, norms can be an important mechanism for maintaining solidarity (Hechter 1988). However, the use of rewards and punishments to encourage solidarity can have negative consequences as well. When groups depend on rewards and punishments to maintain order, they may undermine the development of trust because individuals do not know if their peers behave cooperatively because they are motivated to help the group, or because they fear being sanctioned by other group members. Members of groups that rely on both punishments (Mulder et al. 2005) and rewards (Irwin et al. 2014) to maintain order tend to have lower levels of trust in one another, compared to groups that do not rely on rewards and punishments.

Further, groups do not always restrict themselves to punishing free-riders. Research has documented "antisocial punishment", in which group members punish those who contribute to the group at a high rate (Herrman et al. 2008; Homans [1951] 1992; Parks and Stone 2010). This may occur because high contributors are seen as atypical (Irwin and Horne 2013) or because they are seen as "rate-busters" who make others look bad (Homans [1951] 1992).

In especially puzzling cases, groups maintain norms that *harm* the group. Some college students publicly endorse binge drinking, while privately holding reservations about it (Prentice and Miller 1993), and some disadvantaged groups hold "leveling norms" that discourage their members from attaining economic success beyond that of other group members (Portes 1998). Historically, social norms have encouraged dueling and other dangerous activities (Axelrod 1986). One possible explanation for these "bad" norms is that individuals may enforce them to signal their commitment to the group (Centola et al. 2005; Willer et al. 2009). Under this explanation, those who publically conform to a norm that they privately oppose fear that their insincerity will be discovered. To compensate, they make a special effort to criticize those who do not conform to the norm, under the logic that publicly defending the norm will convince others of their sincerity. Willer et al. (2009) found that people who conformed to an incorrect majority group opinion in a wine-tasting study – by agreeing that two wines differed greatly in quality when they were actually poured from the same bottle – were publically critical of the wine-tasting ability of an individual who accurately described the wines as identical, while privately agreeing with that individual. Because individuals in these cases misrepresent their true feelings, this can lead group members to mistakenly overestimate support for norms that most group members disagree with.

15.6 Identity

How do we come to identify with groups? How do the groups we belong to and the roles we have within them define us? Two theories help answer these questions: identity theory and social identity theory. Identity theory helps explain how *social roles* – including roles tied to group membership – shape our behavior and identities. Social identity theory focuses on how membership in *social categories* influences our views of and behavior towards ourselves and others. To date, identity theory has focused on the implications of social roles for individual rather than group behavior, but identity theory shares important ideas with other theories of small groups, and the identities that stem from small group membership should be an important determinant of behavior and views of the self. In contrast, social identity theory has primarily focused on intra- and intergroup behavior; we discuss both theories in this section.

15.6.1 Identity Theory

Identity theory is a sociological theory based on symbolic interactionist principles. Symbolic interactionists propose that we define and evaluate ourselves through the eyes of others, in response to their real and imagined perceptions of us (Cooley 1902). From this perspective, our sense of self develops through interaction with others, and our ability to view ourselves through the eyes of others is part of what makes us human (Dewey [1922] 2002; Mead 1934). Thus, we develop a sense of identity and determine who we are largely by the things we do and the way others view us. The self is not made up of a single concept, but instead consists of multiple aspects and selves (later, referred to as identities).

While early theorists such as Mead provided many of the central principles underlying symbolic interactionism, the ideas represented a framework and not a testable theory (Stryker 2008). In order to codify symbolic interactionism's core ideas and principles into a testable theory, Stryker presented his version of "structural symbolic interactionism" and identity theory (1980). Stryker drew on role theory to propose that our social roles are primary determinants of our sense of self, or identity. Roles are the expectations and behaviors that are associated with positions in the social structure (Merton 1957; Stryker 1980). For example, individuals may be an employee, a mother, a boyfriend, a teammate, or a volunteer, among many other roles. Individuals take a sense of identity and meaning from these positions in the social structure and their roles in groups, which are referred to as role-identities (McCall and Simmons 1966). Roles help us learn who we are and also give us a sense of behavioral guidance, or ideas about the appropriate behavior necessary to fulfill our role responsibilities (Stryker 1980; Thoits 2011).

Individuals often hold multiple roles and are members of multiple groups which provide them with a variety of individual. These multiple role-identities are arranged in a hierarchy with higher ranking roles more likely to be invoked and acted upon in a wide range of situations (Stryker 1980). Stryker (1980) defines identity salience as an identity's place within this hierarchy. For example, someone who is married, a mother, and an executive will use one of these three identities most often in interaction with others. Put another way, the role that someone would use to describe themselves when being introduced to someone is likely their most salient role (e.g., "I'm an executive at..." vs. "I'm a mother of two...").

Thoits (1992, 2012) defines identity salience differently, viewing it as the importance of a role to an individual, drawing on what McCall and Simmons (1966) defined as prominence. Therefore, in Thoits' conception, the identity that you consider most important and central to your self is the most salient. Callero (1985) proposes that identity salience, however defined, should impact the effect of an identity on self-esteem. Identities that are more important (or more likely to be invoked) should be more intricately tied to our self-concept and self-esteem.

Membership in small groups confers additional identities, which help individuals define themselves and guide their behavior (e.g. "group member", "chapter president"). The salience of an identity for an individual is further determined by the number of social ties that stem from a role. Individuals are more committed to role identities that involve important connections and ties to others, resulting in those particular identities becoming more salient (Stryker 1980, 2008). Thus, to the extent that small groups provide individuals with roles, and connect them with others who know them in the context of that role, they generate and maintain identities.

Why do role-identities matter? Thoits argues that role-identities give individuals purpose and meaning in life and behavioral guidance, which leads to a stable sense of our selves and positive mental and physical health outcomes (Thoits 1983, 2011, 2012). Although early theorists suggested that holding multiple roles may be stressful or bad for health due to the conflicting demands of balancing multiple responsibilities (Merton 1957; Goode 1960), Thoits (1983, 1986, 2003) instead argues for and finds consistent evidence that holding multiple roles has positive influences on mental and physical health. Therefore, membership in more groups and thus more role-identities appears beneficial for health – largely due to the intrapersonal rewards that come from occupying social roles.

Burke's (1991) more micro-oriented *identity control theory* argues that individuals are motivated to confirm their identity in interaction. If their identity is not confirmed, they feel distress and are motivated to act to restore their identity. Identities are not seen as fixed, but as a continuous process that is played out in interaction (Burke and Stets 2009; Stets and Serpe 2013). For example, a group member may consider themselves to be a high-status leader. If this identity is challenged, perhaps by learning that other group members view them as occupying a low-status subordinate role, the individual should feel distress, which will motivate them to restore their original identity as a high-status leader. It is through their behavior in interaction that individuals can alleviate the distress they feel and re-establish their original identity. A recent experimental study found support for identity control theory's propositions in regards to gender identity. Willer and colleagues (2013) show that when men's masculine identity is threatened, they react with compensatory behavior that reasserts their masculinity – and thus restores their original identity. Specifically, men whose masculinity was threatened compensated by espousing more homophobic views, showing higher support for war, and expressing greater belief in male superiority (all of which were shown to be associated with masculinity by the study population).

Research has both supported and challenged identity control theory's proposition that individuals attempt to confirm their identities in interaction. However, although individuals strive to confirm their identities, it is not always possible to do so. One experimental test showed male leaders faced such high expectations that they were unable to meet them, and thus unable to confirm their leadership identity (Burke et al. 2007). Another interesting test showed that individuals strive to maintain their identity even when that identity is negative. That is, individuals will chose to maintain a negative identity over a positive identity, if the positive identity is incongruent with how they see themselves (Robinson and Smith-Lovin 1992).

More recent work has attempted to connect identity theory with other theories, both within and outside of the identity tradition. Stryker and Burke (2000) work integrate identity and identity control theory, arguing that Stryker's structural identity theory explains how social roles and positions in the social structure shape identities and the self. Once these identities are established, Burke's identity control theory explains how behavior in interactions confirms and stabilizes these identities over time.[2] Stryker (2008) has further argued that identity theory shares many underpinnings with theories of status in sociology, in particular status characteristics theory. In both theories, individuals determine what to expect from themselves and from others based on consensual expectations and meanings placed on characteristics and identities. For instance, a person interacting with a doctor has a sense of how

[2] See Burke and Stets (2009) and Stets and Serpe (2013) for integrated versions of the two identity theories.

the interaction should play out based on expectations that derive from cultural meanings attached to the role of doctor. This means that identities may play an important role in structuring small group interaction, by moderating – or being moderated by – how individuals respond to status cues and other information about social position within groups. If one's identity is strongly predicated on the belief that men are more competent than women, how will such individuals respond to information indicating that women in their group are highly competent (Stryker 2008)? Such individuals might be less receptive to this information, or alternatively may revise their identities.

15.6.2 Social Identity, Realistic Group Conflict, and Group Position

Identities not only stem from the roles we hold in groups, but also from the social categories we belong to. Sociologists and psychologists have distinguished between identities individuals hold based on their social roles (as reviewed above), and from identities that derive from social categories: an individual's race, ethnicity, nationality, religious affiliation, and others. The delineation between the two types of identities is not always clear, and some roles and groups likely provide a sense of both types of identities (see Hogg et al. (1995) and Deaux and Burke (2010) for a discussion of the similarities and differences between the two types of identities). Below, we review three additional perspectives on group membership and identity that describe the impacts that groups have on our beliefs and behavior beyond the influence of role occupancy: realistic group conflict theory, the group position model, and social identity theory.

Group membership – regardless of its source – promotes cognitive, emotional, and behavioral identification with the group, which are important sources of positive outcomes such as group bonding and attachment (Dimmock et al. 2005; Henry et al. 1999). At the same time, ingroup identification is closely bound up with intergroup competition and conflict (Coser 1956; Sherif 1966; Simmel [1908] 1955; Sumner [1906] 1960; see Benard and Doan 2011; Stein 1976 for reviews). Early work on identity and intergroup conflict led to the development of Muzafer Sherif's *realistic group conflict theory* (Sherif 1966; see Jackson [1993] for a review). Sherif's theory argues that when two groups share incompatible goals – for example both seeking to possess the same resource – the groups tend to become more internally cohesive and externally competitive. Individuals develop more positive attitudes, stereotypes, and emotions towards their ingroup members, and more negative attitudes, stereotypes, and emotions towards outgroup members. Thus, while conflict may begin from a rational basis, such as contesting ownership of a resource, the ensuing stereotypes and emotional attachments that develop around group identities can lead the conflict to escalate out of proportion to the original dispute. This argument finds support in Sherif's field studies on conflict, conducted in summer camps in the late 1940s and early 1950s (Sherif 1966), as well as later studies using different settings (Blake et al. 1964; Struch and Schwartz 1989).

Blumer's (1958) *group position model* views intergroup conflict as rooted not simply in competing goals, but in the response of a dominant group to the perception that they are losing ground to a subordinate group. Proponents of the group position model argue that it is compatible with, but more comprehensive than, realistic group conflict theory (Bobo 1999). Under the group position model, intergroup prejudice arises when a dominant group, which feels superior to and entitled to greater rights and privileges than a subordinate group, perceives the subordinate group to be threatening its longstanding advantage. This implies that individuals take changes in their group's position seriously, even when their own individual position is unchanged. Blumer developed the theory to explain white attitudes in the midst of the civil rights movement in the United States, but later empirical work has found support in the contemporary US (Bobo 1999; Bobo and Hutchings 1996) and internationally (Minescue and Poppe 2011).

Tajfel and Turner's (1979, 1986) *social identity theory* challenged realistic group conflict theory by showing that groups often show ingroup favoritism and out-group hostility even in the absence of conflicting goals. Experiments in the "minimal group paradigm" tradition found that even small, inconsequential distinctions – such as a preference for the painter Klee versus Kandinsky – cause individuals to favor those in their own group. Even "the mere perception of belonging to two distinct groups…" triggers ingroup favoritism and out-group discrimination (Tajfel and Turner 1986, p. 81). Empirical tests of this idea show that trivial and even explicitly random distinctions suffice to form groups and influence differential attitudes toward in-group and out-group members (Tajfel et al. 1971; Tajfel and Turner 1979, 1986).

In-group favoritism is motivated by self-enhancement: we desire to view ourselves and our groups positively (Tajfel et al. 1971; Tajfel and Turner 1979, 1986; Hogg 2006). The close tie between ingroup and self-evaluation leads individuals to be more extreme in their evaluations of ingroup members than outgroup members: likable ingroup members are rated more highly than likable outgroup members, but unlikable ingroup members are rated lower than unlikable outgroup members (Markovsky et al. 1988). Similarly, people often judge ingroup deviants more harshly than outgroup deviants (Marques et al. 1998), especially when ingroup members deviate in ways that lead them to be more similar to the outgroup (Abrams et al. 2000).

Most people belong to a large number of groups, but a particular group affiliation may seem more relevant in a given situation and will correspondingly do more to determine our behavior in that situation. For example, one's American identity might be most important at a fourth of July parade, while their soccer allegiance might matter most when attending a soccer match. In support of this, Levine et al. (2005) found that when British study participants were primed to think of their favorite soccer team, they were more likely to help the victim of a staged accident if the victim was wearing a t-shirt signaling loyalty to their favorite team, compared to a plain t-shirt or a shirt signaling loyalty to a rival team. In a subsequent study, they primed individuals to think of themselves as soccer fans more broadly. When the study participants' "soccer fan" identity was salient, they were more likely to help those wearing a t-shirt supporting either their favorite team *or* its rival; they were less likely to help those in a plain t-shirt. Identity thus leads us to demonstrate ingroup favoritism, but the particular identity that we favor may shift with the situation. This situational nature of social identities is in contrast to Stryker's (1980, 2008) identity theory, which describes role-identities as relatively stable across various situations.

15.6.3 Optimal Distinctiveness

While social identity theory focuses on group identification as a source of self-esteem, Brewer (1991; see also Pickett and Brewer 2001) proposes that individuals strive for "optimal distinctiveness" when joining social groups. She argues that individuals have a human need to be similar to and validated by others, but also a simultaneous need to be unique and individual. Groups must facilitate affiliation and belonging within a group, but must also maintain boundaries that differentiate them from other groups. For example, youth cohorts often look and dress like each other, which allows them to form a group identity. However, youth fashions often look quite different from those of other age groups, which allows them to distinguish themselves as unique (Brewer 1991). The basic tenants of optimal distinctiveness have been supported, with individual's using both a need for assimilation and a need for differentiation as motivations for their views of their own groups and of out-groups (Pickett and Brewer 2001).

The basic ideas underlying Brewer's theory share many aspects with some early sociological theory. Specifically, Simmel ([1908] 1971) argued that modern life led to increased individualization of individuals. As societies and groups expand and become more diverse, the individual members become more individuated and distinguished. Simmel further argued that individuals have a "dualistic drive" or "a need within us both for individuation and for its opposite…" (Simmel [1908] 1971, p. 259). That is, individuals strive to be seen as unique and individual, but also simultaneously strive to belong.

15.7 Group Culture

While culture is often thought of as a property of society at large, small groups also develop cultures of their own. These "idiocultures" or "microcultures" arise through social interaction, as groups accumulate "…a system of knowledge, beliefs, behaviors, and customs shared by members of an interacting group to which members can refer and employ as the basis of further interaction" (Fine 1979). These local cultures play a key role in patterning social life. In this section, we highlight three important aspects of culture in small groups (noted in Fine 2012, see that paper for a more extensive review). First, small groups are a key location in which individuals learn, modify, create, and diffuse culture. Second, by defining local contexts and shared meanings for individuals, culture shapes group members' behavior, either through scripting appropriate actions for group members in particular situations (Goffman 1959, 1983; Fine 2012) or providing a "toolkit" of strategies for approaching particular situations (Swidler 1986). Third, culture plays an important role in group members' efforts to demarcate and police the boundaries of the group, define group identity, and build group cohesion.

15.7.1 Learning and Creating Culture

Although culture exists at the level of society as a whole, people's day-to-day experience with culture occurs on a smaller scale (Fine 2012). People absorb much of what they know about culture through interaction in small groups, often beginning with families, and continuing with peer groups, teams, coworkers, and others. In addition to learning culture in groups, individuals also create novel bits of culture through their interactions, either by modifying previously-known aspects of mainstream culture, or by inventing new beliefs, behaviors, and customs.

Children learn culture from adults, but also interpretively create their own peer cultures (Corsaro and Eder 1990). In Sherif et al's (1961) Robber's Cave study, groups of young boys created symbols such as group names, logos, and flags that demarcated their group as unique. They also collectively developed shared histories in the form of discussions about meaningful events in the group's recent past. Fine (1979) reports that little league teams generate nicknames, norms, and even taboos through interaction. Fine argues that the emergence and longevity of these new cultural practices depend on a number of factors, including how well they support the group's status structure and functional needs, how well they relate to mainstream cultural reference points familiar to the group, whether they are consistent with existing group practices, and whether they are triggered by key events that occur in the course of group life.

In organizations, informal cultures often emerge that are "decoupled" from the official, formal practices of the organization (Meyer and Rowan 1977). This may occur when workers discover that two formal rules conflict, and must informally negotiate a solution. Similarly, when organizational rules are vague or abstract, individuals and groups within the organization have wide latitude to interpret them and develop their own practices, leading to local cultures that differ widely. When "re-coupling" occurs – that is, when individuals come under pressure to make their informal practices correspond to formal requirements – intra-organizational conflict often ensues (Hallett 2010). For example, Hallett (2010) finds that when teachers who had previously been free to implement their own approaches to accomplish their educational mission were held to more rigid, uniform standards, many became frustrated and distressed.

At times, groups create cultures that depart quite substantially from the mainstream cultures in which they are embedded. For example, peer groups sometimes embrace "oppositional" cultures that reject mainstream emphasis on institutions such as school, work, and family (e.g. Anderson 2000; MacLeod 1987; Shibutani 1978). Such cultures are often thought to arise when traditional routes to success are blocked, prompting individuals to find new ways to establish a sense of identity and self-respect (Bourgois 1995; Portes 1998). Despite their oppositional stance, such groups have their own hierarchies of power and status, and their own norms for appropriate behavior, which at times can be quite rigid (Becker 1963).

The novel bits of culture created by small groups can diffuse outwards to other groups, occasionally becoming part of mainstream culture. For example, hip-hop culture began among a small group of adolescents in the Bronx in the 1970s, before becoming a tremendously influential global phenomenon (Chang 2005). While this process is in part driven by mass media and other macro-level phenomena, interpersonal influence also plays a role Strang and Soule 1998). This occurs when individuals bow to conformity pressures or imitate prestigious individuals (Henrich 2001), when individuals adopt cultural practices in use by those who are similar to themselves in other dimensions (Mark 2003), or are influenced by "opinion leaders" in their personal networks (Katz 1957).

15.7.2 Group Culture Shapes Individual Action

Small groups – especially ongoing groups with a history and a sense of collective identity – play an important role in shaping individuals' behavior, because they create "[a] local context, or set of shared understandings arising from continuing interaction…" (Fine 2012: 160). As Goffman (1959) notes, a set of shared understandings or a common "definition of the situation" is necessary for people to understand how to act in a given setting. These shared understandings signal to individuals what their role in a given situation is, and what the roles of others are. To illustrate, Goffman (1983) uses the example of a person approached by a stranger. To determine if the stranger is friendly or dangerous, people rely on culturally relevant cues such as manner of dress and self-presentation and choose their subsequent course of action accordingly.

Studies of interpersonal aggression provide an example of how group culture shapes individual action. While early research saw aggression as a product of social learning or frustration, much work in recent decades has focused on aggression as a form of impression management (Felson 1978; Gould 2003). According to this work, individuals use aggression as a way of negotiating their identities and social standing within a group. For example, if two individuals in conversation come to a disagreement, their subsequent actions may depend on whether they interpret this disagreement as a simple difference of opinions, or instead an attack on their intelligence or competence. In the latter case, individuals may feel pressure to re-assert themselves initially through verbal means, but if they fail, to resort to violence (Felson 1978).

Many components of such interactions – interpretating a remark as a grave insult, subsequently needing to assert one's social status, the acceptability of violence as a means of doing so – vary substantially by context. In some local cultures, escalating a verbal argument to violence is viewed as natural, in others, as absurd. For example, Anderson's (2000) ethnography of a Philadelphia neighborhood distinguishes between "decent" and "street" subcultures. The "street" subculture places a premium on toughness, and members of this subculture believe that failure to demonstrate toughness can lead them to be labeled as a victim or an easy target. As a result, they are highly sensitive to perceived slights and insults that may undermine their social standing. Similarly, work comparing the northern and southern United States finds that southerners are more likely to emphasize the importance of personal reputation and honor, and more likely to respond aggressively to perceived affronts (Nisbett and Cohen 1996). One study, for example, found that southerners tended to be angered by an insult from a stranger, while northerners tended to find it amusing (Cohen et al. 1996). Thus, local cultures can produce differing interpretations of the same event, and correspondingly lead to different behaviors.

Culture also shapes behavior within small groups by providing a "toolkit" of strategies that individuals use in their daily life (Harrington and Fine 2000; Swidler 1986). This toolkit consists of various "symbols, stories, rituals, and world-views" that inform individuals' daily habits and interpersonal styles, and that they draw on for solving everyday problems (Swidler 1986: 273). For example, Lareau (2011) finds that middle-class children are raised with a stronger sense of entitlement, and encouraged to use self-advocacy as a strategy for interacting with authority figures to a greater extent than working-class children. Similarly, Calarco (2014) finds that middle-class and working-class children tend to take different approaches when having difficulty with their schoolwork, with middle class children more likely to ask a teacher for help, and working class children more likely to persist in working on the problems alone. These results can have implications for social stratification, as middle-class students subsequently receive more help and attention from teachers. More generally, these patterns illustrate how small groups serve as the setting in which individuals experience and express larger social realities. In this case, while social class is a macro level-phenomenon with deep roots in institutions – such as the labor market, the education system, and the welfare state – these roots are not salient to individuals in their daily lives. Instead, they experience these macro-level phenomena in their everyday interactions with parents, teachers, and friends.

15.7.3 Culture and Group Boundaries

Individuals draw on culture to define and adjust group boundaries (Fine 2012; Lamont and Molnàr 2002). Such boundaries help to define what it means to be a group member, and to generate cohesion and solidarity within groups (Durkheim [1894] 1988; Erikson 1966; Mead 1918; Sherif et al. 1961). Both ingroup and outgroup members rely on cultural signals of group membership when deciding how to interact with strangers. These interactions may be positive, neutral, or negative, but the fact that they center around symbols of group membership serves to strengthen perceived group boundaries and group identities. For example, Tavory (2010) observes that for Orthodox Jewish men in Los Angeles, their religious attire – especially yarmulkes – leads strangers to interact with them primarily on the basis of their Jewish identity. This ranged from requests for advice on how to prepare kosher foods to verbal abuse. In contrast, the Orthodox men were so used to wearing yarmulkes that they rarely thought about them, except in these types of interactions. This led their Orthodox Jewish identity to be more salient to them than it might have been otherwise.

Even groups of children create social boundaries, often along gender lines (Thorne 1993). Gender can persist as a social boundary into adulthood, for example, when groups develop norms about which kinds of jobs are considered appropriate for men and women (e.g. Pierce 1995). Individuals also rely on a variety of other factors to define group boundaries, ranging from ethnicity to patterns of cultural consumption (Lamont and Molnàr 2002). Becker's classic (1951) study of jazz musicians found that they drew distinctions between groups (e.g. musicians versus an audience of non-musician "squares"), and within the ingroup (financially successful but artistically compromised "commercial" musicians versus true "jazz" musicians). Such distinctions helped musicians maintain positive self-views in the face of their frustrating dependence on "square" audience members for income. Indeed, groups often support social boundaries by developing negative stereotypes about outgroups and positive stereotypes about outgroups, which can serve as a source of group cohesion (Blumer 1958; Sherif 1966), or by employing relational means of social exclusion such as gossip (Eder 1985).

15.8 Conclusion

Sociologists aim to understand social structure – the institutions, networks, hierarchies, roles, and other extra-individual factors that make up the complex web of society. Structure fascinates sociologists in part because it shapes individual behavior and choices. The same person born today versus a century ago, or in Spain versus Japan, would face a somewhat different set of constraints and options. Social structure also fascinates sociologists because, even while it constrains people's choices, people can modify, build, and disseminate new forms of social structure. Much of sociology thus revolves around the puzzle of how people simultaneously create and are constrained by the social world in which they live.

Small groups play an important role in solving this puzzle, existing in an intermediate "meso-level" space between individuals and larger social systems (Fine 2012: 160). Small groups' shared history, identity, structure, and culture make them more than simply the sum of their individual members (Simmel 1898). Small groups serve as a key setting through which people feel the constraints of social structure – such as family obligations, team rules, coworker expectations – as well as a key setting for creating social structure. As we have discussed, small groups provide an important setting in which status, power, identity, norms, and culture develop, organize behavior, and are transmitted to other groups. They thus provide a useful setting for sociologists to observe how people create and respond to small-scale social structures.

Despite the utility of small groups as a setting for the study of social structure, most reviews of the literature note that interest in this area peaked in the middle of the twentieth century and has since declined. This may reflect the fact that sociologists have more options for studying social life: the quality and availability of nationally-representative survey data has improved, as has the availability of data and tools for studying social networks or constructing simulation models. It may also reflect the "cognitive revolution" in psychology, which some psychologists argue has moved the field too far from studying behavior, in favor of understanding cognitive mechanisms (Baumeister et al. 2007: 398; Cialdini 2009).

We have noted the "hub and spoke" nature of of small groups research, in which the central concept of small groups animates a range of theoretical and empirical approaches. In general, this is beneficial for small groups researchers because it provides a wealth of perspectives and findings to build on. At the same time, the sheer size and diversity of the literature can make it challenging to navigate and synthesize these findings. In our view, there is much to be gained from building bridges between these spokes, both within and across disciplines and subfields. Moving forward, we suggest three broad ways in which small groups researchers can connect the spokes to further develop the small groups literature and contribute to sociology. These include (1) reconnecting with other disciplines, especially psychology, (2) bridging the small groups literature with other subfields within sociology, and (3) continuing to synthesize areas of research within the small groups literature.

The first point – reconnecting with other disciplines – might on the face of it seem unnecessary, since the study of small groups has traditionally been an interdisciplinary field on the boundary of sociology and psychology. Over time, however, sociological and psychological social psychology have moved further apart, and genuine engagement between the two fields is less common (Thoits 1995; Oishi et al. 2009). This may stem, as noted, because psychologists are increasingly interested in cognitive mechanisms while sociologists primarily focus on structural factors. But structural factors often moderate cognitive processes, and cognitive processes in turn often mediate the effects of structural factors. To the extent that both fields work separately, we are less likely to have a complete picture of how small groups work, particularly if there are cross-level interactions between the structural factors emphasized by sociologists and the cognitive processes often examined by psychologists. For example, Anderson and colleagues (2012) fruitfully examined a range of both micro-level (e.g. individual personality measures) and more meso-level factors (e.g. group expectations) to build a better understanding of why individuals sometimes prefer to occupy low-status positions in groups.

A second area for future work is building additional bridges between small groups and other areas of research in sociology. For example, Bobo and Hutchings (1996) bridged social psychology and work on race and ethnicity to productively extend Blumer's group position model – formulated to understand the relationships between dominant and subordinate groups – to the study of a complex multiracial society. Useful bridging could also occur between the areas of social networks and small groups – both function as meso-level connections between individuals and larger social structures, but in different ways. Networks can link far-flung individuals, but do not necessarily impart a sense of shared identity or community – indeed, one of the fascinating aspects of social networks is that we may be structurally connected to other individuals without being aware of it (Watts 1999). One example of bridging these areas is Lawler's (2002) work on micro-social orders, which helps explain how a network of individuals may begin to develop a sense of themselves as a group. Fine (2012) also suggests examining connections between networks of small groups, which may help explain how ideas and other aspects of culture diffuse across groups.

A third approach is to build bridges within small groups research, further linking work on status, power, identity, influence, and culture. There has been much promising work linking the concepts of power and status (e.g. Fast et al. 2012; Thye 2000; Willer et al. 2012), status and influence (Melamed and Savage 2013), identity and social identity (Hogg et al. 1995; Stets and Burke 2000), and status and identity (Burke et al. 2007). There are many ways to profitably continue in this vein. For example, as a theory of the self, identity theory has been less focused on group interaction than work in other areas of sociological social psychology. While all social roles individuals occupy should provide them with a sense of identity – including those stemming from membership in groups – we know less about how these identity processes interact with other intragroup processes such as status or power dynamics. Given that few studies drawing on identity theory examine small groups, this could be a fruitful avenue for future research. As a second example, more work could link social identity theory to other areas. For example, Yamagishi et al. (1999) argue that the ingroup favoritism reported in studies of social identity is not driven by psychological identification with the group, but instead by a rational expectation that group members will reciprocate the favoritism in the future. This suggests that what appears to be a social identity process could be a form of exchange, similar to those documented in work on power. Yamagishi et al. (1999) provide some evidence in favor of this argument, but as far as we are aware there has not been a great deal of additional work addressing this question. Further research exploring the link between identity and exchange could help elucidate this relationship.

To offer a final example, perhaps some of the largest gains to be made are in linking work on culture with the other areas. While work on power, status, identity, and influence often uses laboratory experiments and surveys, much work on culture employs ethnography and open-ended interviews (although some work takes a quantitative approach, e.g. Vaisey 2009; Fishman and Lizardo 2013). The methods preferred in the two areas yield different, but complementary types of knowledge. For example, experimental work often examines short-lived groups that offer a high degree of control and allow researchers to make causal inferences – but provide little evidence as to how groups change and develop over time (McGrath et al. 2000). The qualitative approaches more common in studies of culture are excellent for abductively generating hypotheses and theories (Timmermans and Tavory 2012), and examining groups over longer periods of time. However, these methods don't offer the same degree of control or causal inference found in experimental work. That is, while these methods both contain limitations, together they have high potential to generate holistic inferences about the social processes present in small groups when considered in tandem. We believe that future work could benefit by considering creative new ideas that broker links between the two methods (e.g. Burt 2004; Jick 1979). Others have emphasized the value of bridging social psychology and culture (see, e.g. the special issue of *Social Psychology Quarterly* and the introductory article by Collett and Lizardo 2014; Dimaggio 1997), but there remains much room for further development.

For sociologists, small groups have moved from being a relatively central to a relatively peripheral part of the field. For most of us, however, small groups have always been an integral part of our daily lives. Small groups provide the settings in which we learn about our social world, and where abstract concepts such as status, power, and identity become real for us. They are also the setting in which most people play a role in shaping their social world, whether inventing a nickname for a friend, or launching a movement with global implications. In the end, it is this centrality to our daily lives that keeps the study of small groups crucial for sociologists.

References

Abrams, D., Marques, J. M., Bown, N., & Henson, M. (2000). Pro-norm and anti-norm deviance within and between groups. *Journal of Personality and Social Psychology, 78*(5), 906–912.

Anderson, E. (2000). *Code of the street: Decency, violence, and the moral life of the inner city*. New York: WW Norton & Company.

Anderson, C., & Berdahl, J. L. (2002). The experience of power: Examining the effects of power on approach and inhibition tendencies. *Journal of Personality and Social Psychology, 83*(6), 1362–1377.

Anderson, C., & Kilduff, G. J. (2009a). Why do dominant personalities attain influence in face-to-face groups? The competence-signaling effects of trait dominance. *Journal of Personality and Social Psychology, 96*(2), 491–503.

Anderson, C., & Kilduff, G. J. (2009b). The pursuit of status in social groups. *Current Directions in Psychological Science, 18*(5), 295–298.

Anderson, C., John, O. P., Keltner, D., & Kring, A. M. (2001). Who attains social status? Effects of personality and physical attractiveness in social groups. *Journal of Personality and Social Psychology, 81*(1), 116–132.

Anderson, C., Srivastava, S., Beer, J. S., Spataro, S. E., & Chatman, J. A. (2006). Knowing your place: Self-perceptions of status in face-to-face groups. *Journal of Personality and Social Psychology, 91*(6), 1094–1110.

Anderson, C., Willer, R., Kilduff, G. J., & Brown, C. E. (2012). The origins of deference: When do people prefer lower status? *Journal of Personality and Social Psychology, 102*(5), 1077–1088.

Asch, S.E. (1951). Effects of group pressure upon the modification and distortion of judgments. *Groups, Leadership, and Men*. pp. 222–236.

Axelrod, R. (1986). An evolutionary approach to norms. *American Political Science Review, 80*(04), 1095–1111.

Bales, R. F., Strodtbeck, F. L., Mills, T. M., & Roseborough, M. E. (1951). Channels of communication in small groups. *American Sociological Review, 16*(4), 461–468.

Barclay, P. (2006). Reputational benefits for altruistic punishment. *Evolution and Human Behavior, 27*(5), 325–344.

Barclay, P., & Benard, S. (2013). Who cries wolf, and when: Manipulation of perceived threats to preserve rank in cooperative groups. *PLoS ONE, 8*(9), e73863.

Bargh, J. A., Raymond, P., Pryor, J. B., & Strack, F. (1995). Attractiveness of the underling: An automatic power→ sex association and its consequences for sexual harassment and aggression. *Journal of Personality and Social Psychology, 68*(5), 768–781.

Baumeister, R. F., Vohs, K. D., & Funder, D. C. (2007). Psychology as the science of self-reports and finger movements: Whatever happened to actual behavior? *Perspectives on Psychological Science, 2*(4), 396–403.

Becker, H. S. (1951). The professional dance musician and his audience. *American Journal of Sociology, 57*(2), 136–144.

Becker, H. (1963). *Outsiders: Studies in the sociology of deviance. The Free Press of Glencoe*. New York: The Free Press.

Benard, S. (2012). Cohesion from conflict does intergroup conflict motivate intragroup norm enforcement and support for centralized leadership? *Social Psychology Quarterly, 75*(2), 107–130.

Benard, S., & Doan, L. (2011). The conflict-cohesion hypothesis: Past, present, and possible futures. *Advances in Group Process, 28*, 189–224.

Berger, J., & Webster, M., Jr. (2006). Expectations, status, and behavior. In P. J. Burke (Ed.), *Contemporary social psychological theories* (pp. 268–300). Stanford: Stanford University Press.

Berger, J., Cohen, B. P., & Zelditch, M., Jr. (1972). Status characteristics and social interaction. *American Sociological Review, 37*(3), 241–255.

Bienenstock, E. J., & Bonacich, P. (1992). The core as a solution to exclusionary networks. *Social Networks, 14*(3), 231–243.

Blake, R. R., Shepard, H. A., & Mouton, J. S. (1964). *Managing intergroup conflict in industry*. Houston: Gulf Publishing Company.

Blau, P. M. (1964). *Exchange and power in social life*. New Brunswick: Transaction Publishers.

Blumer, H. (1958). Race prejudice as a sense of group position. *Pacific Sociological Review, 1*(1), 3–7.

Bobo, L. D. (1999). Prejudice as group position: Microfoundations of a sociological approach to racism and race relations. *Journal of Social Issues, 55*(3), 445–472.

Bobo, L., & Hutchings, V. L. (1996). Perceptions of racial group competition: Extending Blumer's theory of group position to a multiracial social context. *American Sociological Review, 61*(6), 951–972.

Bodenhausen, G. V. (1990). Stereotypes as judgmental heuristics: Evidence of circadian variations in discrimination. *Psychological Science, 1*(5), 319–322.

Bodenhausen, G. V., Sheppard, L. A., & Kramer, G. P. (1994). Negative affect and social judgment: The differential impact of anger and sadness. *European Journal of Social Psychology, 24*(1), 45–62.

Bond, R. (2005). Group size and conformity. *Group Processes & Intergroup Relations, 8*(4), 31–354.

Bond, R., & Smith, P. B. (1996). Culture and conformity: A meta-analysis of studies using Asch's (1952b, 1956) line judgment task. *Psychological Bulletin, 119*(1), 111.

Bourgois, P. (1995). *In search of respect: Selling crack in El Barrio* (Vol. 10). Cambridge, UK: Cambridge University Press.

Brashears, M. E. (2008). Sex, society, and association: A cross-national examination of status construction theory. *Social Psychology Quarterly, 71*(1), 72–85.

Brewer, M. B. (1991). The social self: On being the same and different at the same time. *Personality and Social Psychology Bulletin, 17*(5), 475–482.

Burke, P. J. (1991). Identity processes and social stress. *American Sociological Review, 56*(6), 836–849.

Burke, P. J. (2006). Interaction in small groups. In J. DeLamater (Ed.), *Handbook of social psychology* (pp. 363–387): New York: Springer.

Burke, P. J., & Stets, J. E. (2009). *Identity theory.* New York: Oxford University Press.

Burke, P. J., Stets, J. E., & Cerven, C. (2007). Gender, legitimation, and identity verification in groups. *Social Psychology Quarterly, 70*(1), 27–42.

Burt, R. S. (2004). Structural holes and good ideas. *American Journal of Sociology, 110*(2), 349–399.

Calarco, J. M. (2014). The inconsistent curriculum cultural tool kits and student interpretations of ambiguous expectations. *Social Psychology Quarterly, 77*(2), 185–209.

Callero, P. L. (1985). Role-identity salience. *Social Psychology Quarterly, 48*(3), 203–215.

Centola, D., Willer, R., & Macy, M. (2005). The Emperor's dilemma: A computational model of self-enforcing norms. *American Journal of Sociology, 110*(4), 1009–1040.

Chang, J. (2005). *Can't stop won't stop: A history of the hip-hop generation.* New York: Macmillan.

Chen, S., Lee-Chai, A. Y., & Bargh, J. A. (2001). Relationship orientation as a moderator of the effects of social power. *Journal of Personality and Social Psychology, 80*(2), 173.

Cheng, J. T., Tracy, J. L., Foulsham, T., Kingstone, A., & Henrich, J. (2013). Two ways to the top: Evidence that dominance and prestige are distinct yet viable avenues to social rank and influence. *Journal of Personality and Social Psychology, 104*(1), 103.

Cialdini, R. B. (2009). We have to break up. *Perspectives on Psychological Science, 4*(1), 5–6.

Cohen, E. G. (1982). Expectation states and interracial interaction in school settings. *Annual Review of Sociology, 8*, 209–235.

Cohen, D., Nisbett, R. E., Bowdle, B. F., & Schwarz, N. (1996). Insult, aggression, and the southern culture of honor: An "experimental ethnography". *Journal of Personality and Social Psychology, 70*(5), 945.

Collett, J. L., & Lizardo, O. (2014). Localizing cultural phenomena by specifying social psychological mechanisms introduction to the special issue. *Social Psychology Quarterly, 77*(2), 95–99.

Cook, K. S., & Emerson, R. M. (1978). Power equity and commitment in exchange networks. *American Sociological Review, 43*(5), 721–739.

Cook, K., & Rice, E. R. W. (2003). Social exchange theory. In J. DeLamater (Ed.), *Handbook of social psychology* (pp. 53–76). New York: Kluwer Academic/ Plenum Publishers.

Cook, K. S., & Yamagishi, T. (1992). Power in exchange networks: A power-dependence formulation. *Social Networks, 14*(3), 245–265.

Cook, K. S., Cheshire, C., & Gerbasi, A. (2006). Power, dependence, and social exchange. In P. J. Burke (Ed.), *Contemporary social psychological theories* (pp. 194–216). Stanford: Stanford University Press.

Cooley, C. H. (1902). *Human nature and the social order.* New York: Charles Scribner's Sons.

Copeland, J. T. (1994). Prophecies of power: Motivational implications of social power for behavioral confirmation. *Journal of Personality and Social Psychology, 67*(2), 264.

Correll, S. J., & Ridgeway, C. L. (2003). Expectation states theory. In L. De John (Ed.), *Handbook of social psychology* (pp. 29–51). New York: Springer.

Corsaro, W. A., & Eder, D. (1990). Children's peer cultures. *Annual Review of Sociology, 16*, 197–220.

Coser, L. A. (1956). *The functions of social conflict* (Vol. 9). London: Routledge.

De Quervain, D. J. F., Fischbacher, U., Treyer, V., & Schellhammer, M. (2004). The neural basis of altruistic punishment. *Science, 305*(5688), 1254.

Deaux, K., & Burke, P. (2010). Bridging identities. *Social Psychology Quarterly, 73*(4), 315–320.

Deutsch, M., & Gerard, H. B. (1955). A study of normative and informational social influences upon individual judgment. *The Journal of Abnormal and Social Psychology, 51*(3), 629.

Devine, P. G., Plant, E. A., Amodio, D. M., Harmon-Jones, E., & Vance, S. L. (2002). The regulation of explicit and implicit race bias: The role of motivations to respond without prejudice. *Journal of Personality and Social Psychology, 82*(5), 835.

Dewey, J. ([1922] 2002). *Human nature and conduct.* Mineola, New York: Dover.

DiMaggio, P. (1997). Culture and cognition. *Annual Review of Sociology, 23*, 263–287.

Dimmock, J. A., Grove, J. R., & Eklund, R. C. (2005). Reconceptualizing team identification: New dimensions and their relationship to intergroup bias. *Group Dynamics: Theory, Research, and Practice, 9*(2), 75–86.

Durkheim, E. ([1894] 1988). *The rules of sociological method*. Chicago: University of Chicago Press.

Eder, D. (1985). The cycle of popularity: Interpersonal relations among female adolescents. *Sociology of Education, 58*(3), 154–165.

Ellickson, R. C. (1994). *Order without law: How neighbors settle disputes*. Cambridge, MA: Harvard University Press.

Ellis, D. P. (1971). The Hobbesian problem of order: A critical appraisal of the normative solution. *American Sociological Review, 36*(4), 692–703.

Emerson, R. M. (1962). Power-dependence relations. *American Sociological Review, 27*(1), 31–41.

Emerson, R. M. (1964). Power-dependence relations: Two experiments. *Sociometry, 27*(3), 282–298.

Emerson, R. M. (1976). Social exchange theory. *Annual Review of Sociology, 2*, 335–362.

Erikson, K. T. (1966). *Wayward puritans: A study in the sociology of deviance*. New York: Wiley.

Fast, N. J., Halevy, N., & Galinsky, A. D. (2012). The destructive nature of power without status. *Journal of Experimental Social Psychology, 48*(1), 391–394.

Fehr, E., & Gächter, S. (2002). Altruistic punishment in humans. *Nature, 415*(6868), 137–140.

Felson, R. B. (1978). Aggression as impression management. *Social Psychology, 41*(3), 205–213.

Fine, G. A. (1979). Small groups and culture creation: The idioculture of little league baseball teams. *American Sociological Review, 44*(5), 733–745.

Fine, G. A. (2012). Group culture and the interaction order: Local sociology on the meso-level. *Annual Review of Sociology, 38*, 159–179.

Fishman, R. M., & Lizardo, O. (2013). How macro-historical change shapes cultural taste legacies of democratization in Spain and Portugal. *American Sociological Review, 78*(2), 213–239.

Flynn, F. J. (2003). How much should I give and how often? The effects of generosity and frequency of favor exchange on social status and productivity. *Academy of Management Journal, 46*(5), 539–553.

Flynn, F. J., Reagans, R. E., Amanatullah, E. T., & Ames, D. R. (2006). Helping one's way to the top: Self-monitors achieve status by helping others and knowing who helps whom. *Journal of Personality and Social Psychology, 91*(6), 1123.

Foschi, M. (1996). Double standards in the evaluation of men and women. *Social Psychology Quarterly, 59*(3), 237–254.

Foschi, M. (2000). Double standards for competence: Theory and research. *Annual Review of Sociology, 26*, 21–42.

Foschi, M., Lai, L., & Sigerson, K. (1994). Gender and double standards in the assessment of job applicants. *Social Psychology Quarterly, 57*(4), 326–339.

Friedkin, N. E. (1992). An expected value model of social power: Predictions for selected exchange networks. *Social Networks, 14*(3), 213–229.

Galinsky, A. D., Gruenfeld, D. H., & Magee, J. C. (2003). From power to action. *Journal of Personality and Social Psychology, 85*(3), 453–466.

Galinsky, A. D., Magee, J. C., Inesi, M. E., & Gruenfeld, D. H. (2006). Power and perspectives not taken. *Psychological Science, 17*(12), 1068–1074.

Goar, C. D. (2007). Social identity theory and the reduction of inequality: Can cross-cutting categorization reduce inequality in mixed-race groups? *Social Behavior and Personality: An International Journal, 35*(4), 537–550.

Goar, C., & Sell, J. (2005). Using task definition to modify racial inequality within task groups. *The Sociological Quarterly, 46*(3), 525–543.

Goffman, E. (1959). *The presentation of self in everyday life*. New York: Anchor Books.

Goffman, E. (1983). The interaction order: American Sociological Association, 1982 presidential address. *American Sociological Review, 48*(1), 1–17.

Goode, W. J. (1960). A theory of role strain. *American Sociological Review, 25*(4), 483–496.

Gould, R. V. (2003). *Collision of wills: How ambiguity about social rank breeds conflict*. Chicago: University of Chicago Press.

Grossman, G., & Baldassarri, D. (2012). The impact of elections on cooperation: Evidence from a lab-in-the-field experiment in Uganda. *American Journal of Political Science, 56*(4), 964–985.

Gruenfeld, D. H., Inesi, M. E., Magee, J. C., & Galinsky, A. D. (2008). Power and the objectification of social targets. *Journal of Personality and Social Psychology, 95*(1), 111.

Gürerk, Ö., Irlenbusch, B., & Rockenbach, B. (2006). The competitive advantage of sanctioning institutions. *Science, 312*(5770), 108–111.

Hallett, T. (2010). The myth incarnate recoupling processes, turmoil, and inhabited institutions in an urban elementary school. *American Sociological Review, 75*(1), 52–74.

Harrington, B., & Fine, G. A. (2000). Opening the "black box": Small groups and twenty-first-century sociology. *Social Psychology Quarterly, 63*(4), 312–323.

Hechter, M. (1988). *Principles of group solidarity* (Vol. 11). Berkeley: Univ of California Press.

Hechter, M., & Opp, K.-D. (2001). *Social norms*. New York: Russell Sage.

Heckathorn, D. D. (1983). Extensions of power-dependence theory: The concept of resistance. *Social Forces, 61*(4), 1206–1231.

Henrich, J. (2001). Cultural transmission and the diffusion of innovations: Adoption dynamics indicate that biased cultural transmission is the predominate force in behavioral change. *American Anthropologist, 103*(4), 992–1013.

Henry, K. B., Arrow, H., & Carini, B. (1999). A tripartite model of group identification theory and measurement. *Small Group Research, 30*(5), 558–581.

Herrmann, B., Thöni, C., & Gächter, S. (2008). Antisocial punishment across societies. *Science, 319*(5868), 1362–1367.

Hogg, M. A. (2006). Social identity theory. *Contemporary Social Psychological Theories, 13*, 111–1369.

Hogg, M. A., Terry, D. J., & White, K. M. (1995). A tale of two theories: A critical comparison of identity theory with social identity theory. *Social Psychology Quarterly, 58*(4), 255–269.

Homans, G. C. ([1951] 1992). *The human group*. New York: Harcourt, Brace.

Horne, C. (2001). Sociological perspectives on the emergence of social norms. In M. Hechter & K.-D. Opp (Eds.), *Social norms* (pp. 3–34). New York: Russell Sage.

Horne, C. (2004). Collective benefits, exchange interests, and norm enforcement. *Social Forces, 82*(3), 1037–1062.

Horne, C. (2009). *The rewards of punishment: A relational theory of norm enforcement*. Palo Alto: Stanford University Press.

Horne, C., & Cutlip, A. (2002). Sanctioning costs and norm enforcement an experimental test. *Rationality and Society, 14*(3), 285–307.

House, J. S. (1977). The three faces of social psychology. *Sociometry, 40*(2), 161–177.

Irwin, K., & Horne, C. (2013). A normative explanation of antisocial punishment. *Social Science Research, 42*(2), 562–570.

Irwin, K., Mulder, L., & Simpson, B. (2014). The detrimental effects of sanctions on intragroup trust comparing punishments and rewards. *Social Psychology Quarterly, 77*(3), 253–272.

Jackson, J. W. (1993). Record. *The Psychological Record, 43*(3), 395–413.

Jick, T. D. (1979). Mixing qualitative and quantitative methods: Triangulation in action. *Administrative Science Quarterly, 24*(4), 602–611.

Kalkhoff, W., Younts, C. W., & Troyer, L. (2008). Facts & artifacts in research: The case of communication medium, gender, and influence. *Social Science Research, 37*(3), 1008–1021.

Katz, E. (1957). The two-step flow of communication: An up-to-date report on an hypothesis. *Public Opinion Quarterly, 21*(1), 61–78.

Kelly, J. R., McCarty, M. K., & Iannone, N. E. (2013). Interaction in small groups. In *Handbook of social psychology* (pp. 413–438). New York: Springer.

Keltner, D., Gruenfeld, D. H., & Anderson, C. (2003). Power, approach, and inhibition. *Psychological Review, 110*(2), 265.

Kennedy, J. A., Anderson, C., & Moore, D. A. (2013). When overconfidence is revealed to others: Testing the status-enhancement theory of overconfidence. *Organizational Behavior and Human Decision Processes, 122*(2), 266–279.

Kollock, P. (1998). Social dilemmas: The anatomy of cooperation. *Annual Review of Sociology, 24*, 183–214.

Komorita, S. S., & Parks, C. D. (1994). *Social dilemmas*. Boulder: Westview Press.

Kumar, N., Scheer, L. K., & Steenkamp, J.-B. E. M. (1995). The effects of perceived interdependence on dealer attitudes. *Journal of Marketing Research, 32*(3), 348–356.

Kuwabara, K. (2011). Cohesion, cooperation, and the value of doing things together how economic exchange creates relational bonds. *American Sociological Review, 76*(4), 560–580.

Lamont, M., & Molnár, V. (2002). The study of boundaries in the social sciences. *Annual Review of Sociology, 28*, 167–195.

Lareau, A. (2011). *Unequal childhoods: Class, race, and family life*. Berkeley: University of California Press.

Lawler, E. J. (2002). Micro social orders. *Social Psychology Quarterly, 65*(1), 4–17.

Lawler, E. J., & Yoon, J. (1993). Power and the emergence of commitment behavior in negotiated exchange. *American Sociological Review, 58*(4), 465–481.

Lawler, E. J., & Yoon, J. (1996). Commitment in exchange relations: Test of a theory of relational cohesion. *American Sociological Review, 61*(1), 89–108.

Lawler, E. J., & Yoon, J. (1998). Network structure and emotion in exchange relations. *American Sociological Review, 63*(6), 871–894.

Lawler, E. J., Ford, R. S., & Blegen, M. A. (1988). Coercive capability in conflict: A test of bilateral deterrence versus conflict spiral theory. *Social Psychology Quarterly, 51*(2), 93–107.

Lawler, E. J., Thye, S. R., & Yoon, J. (2000). Emotion and group cohesion in productive exchange1. *American Journal of Sociology, 106*(3), 616–657.

Lawler, E. J., Thye, S. R., & Yoon, J. (2008). Social exchange and micro social order. *American Sociological Review, 73*(4), 519–542.

Lerner, J. S., & Tetlock, P. E. (1999). Accounting for the effects of accountability. *Psychological Bulletin, 125*(2), 255.

Levine, J. M., & Moreland, R. L. (1990). Progress in small group research. *Annual Review of Psychology, 41*(1), 585–634.

Levine, M., Prosser, A., Evans, D., & Reicher, S. (2005). Identity and emergency intervention: How social group membership and inclusiveness of group boundaries shape helping behavior. *Personality and Social Psychology Bulletin, 31*(4), 443–453.

Lucas, J. W. (2003). Status processes and the institutionalization of women as leaders. *American Sociological Review, 68*(3), 464–480.

Lucas, J. W., & Phelan, J. C. (2012). Stigma and status the interrelation of two theoretical perspectives. *Social Psychology Quarterly, 75*(4), 310–333.

MacLeod, J. (1987). *Ain't no makin' it: Leveled aspirations in a low-income neighborhood*. Boulder: Westview.

Maner, J. K., & Mead, N. L. (2010). The essential tension between leadership and power: When leaders sacrifice group goals for the sake of self-interest. *Journal of Personality and Social Psychology, 99*(3), 482.

Mark, N. P. (2003). Culture and competition: Homophily and distancing explanations for cultural niches. *American Sociological Review, 68*(3), 319–345.

Markovsky, B. (1992). Network exchange outcomes: Limits of predictability. *Social Networks, 14*(3), 267–286.

Markovsky, B., Willer, D., & Patton, T. (1988). Power relations in exchange networks. *American Sociological Review, 53*(2), 220–236.

Marques, J., Abrams, D., & Serôdio, R.G. (2001). Being Better by Being Right: Subjective Group Dynamics and Derogation of In-Group Deviants When Generic Norms are Undermined. *Journal of Personality and Social Psychology 81*(3), 436–447.

McCall, G. J., & Simmons, J. L. (1966). *Identities and interactions*. New York: Free Press.

McGrath, J. E., Arrow, H., & Berdahl, J. L. (2000). The study of groups: Past, present, and future. *Personality and Social Psychology Review, 4*(1), 95–105.

Mead, G. H. (1918). The psychology of punitive justice. *The American Journal of Sociology, 23*(5), 577–602.

Mead, G. H. (1934). *Mind, self, and society from the standpoint of a behaviorist*. Chicago: University of Chicago Press.

Melamed, D., & Savage, S. V. (2013). Status, numbers and influence. *Social Forces, 91*, 1085–1104. sos194.

Merton, R. K. (1957). The role-set: Problems in sociological theory. *British Journal of Sociology, 8*(2), 106–120.

Messick, D. M., Wilke, H., Brewer, M. B., Kramer, R. M., Zemke, P. E., & Lui, L. (1983). Individual adaptations and structural change as solutions to social dilemmas. *Journal of Personality and Social Psychology, 44*(2), 294.

Meyer, J. W., & Rowan, B. (1977). Institutionalized organizations: Formal structure as myth and ceremony. *American Journal of Sociology, 83*(2), 340–363.

Minescu, A., & Poppe, E. (2011). Intergroup conflict in Russia testing the group position model. *Social Psychology Quarterly, 74*(2), 166–191.

Molm, L. D. (2010). The structure of reciprocity. *Social Psychology Quarterly, 73*(2), 119–131.

Molm, L. D., Collett, J. L., & Schaefer, D. R. (2007). Building solidarity through generalized exchange: A theory of reciprocity 1. *American Journal of Sociology, 113*(1), 205–242.

Mulder, L. B., Van Dijk, E., Wilke, H. A. M., & De Cremer, D. (2005). The effect of feedback on support for a sanctioning system in a social dilemma: The difference between installing and maintaining the sanction. *Journal of Economic Psychology, 26*(3), 443–458.

Nisbett, R. E., & Cohen, D. (1996). *Culture of honor: The psychology of violence in the south*. Boulder: Westview Press.

Norton, M. I., Vandello, J. A., & Darley, J. M. (2004). Casuistry and social category bias. *Journal of Personality and Social Psychology, 87*(6), 817.

Oishi, S., Kesebir, S., & Snyder, B. H. (2009). Sociology: A lost connection in social psychology. *Personality and Social Psychology Review, 13*(4), 334–353.

Oliver, P. (1980). Rewards and punishments as selective incentives for collective action: Theoretical investigations. *American Journal of Sociology, 85*(6), 1356–1375.

Ostrom, E., Walker, J., & Gardner, R. (1992). Covenants with and without a sword: Self-governance is possible. *American Political Science Review, 86*(02), 404–417.

Parks, C. D., & Stone, A. B. (2010). The desire to expel unselfish members from the group. *Journal of Personality and Social Psychology, 99*(2), 303.

Pickett, C. L., & Brewer, M. B. (2001). Assimilation and differentiation needs as motivational determinants of perceived in-group and out-group homogeneity. *Journal of Experimental Social Psychology, 37*(4), 341–348.

Pierce, J. (1995). *Gender trials: Emotional lives in contemporary law firms*. Berkeley: University of California Press.

Portes, A. (1998). Social capital: Its origins and applications in modern sociology. *Annual Review of Sociology, 24*, 1–24.

Prentice, D. A., & Miller, D. T. (1993). Pluralistic ignorance and alcohol use on campus: Some consequences of misperceiving the social norm. *Journal of Personality and Social Psychology, 64*(2), 243.

Pugh, M. D., & Wahrman, R. (1983). Neutralizing sexism in mixed-sex groups: Do women have to be better than men? *American Journal of Sociology, 88*(4), 746–762.

Ridgeway, C. L. (1982). Status in groups: The importance of motivation. *American Sociological Review, 47*(1), 76–88.

Ridgeway, C. L. (1997). Interaction and the conservation of gender inequality: Considering employment. *American Sociological Review, 62*(2), 218–235.

Ridgeway, C. L. (2006). Status construction theory. In P. J. Burke (Ed.), *Contemporary social psychological theories* (pp. 301–323). Stanford: Stanford University Press.

Ridgeway, C. L., & Correll, S. J. (2004). Unpacking the gender system a theoretical perspective on gender beliefs and social relations. *Gender & Society, 18*(4), 510–531.

Ridgeway, C. L., Boyle, E. H., Kuipers, K. J., & Robinson, D. T. (1998). How do status beliefs develop? The role of resources and interactional experience. *American Sociological Review, 63*(3), 331–350.

Ridgeway, C. L., Backor, K., Li, Y. E., Tinkler, J. E., & Erickson, K. G. (2009). How easily does a social difference become a status distinction? Gender matters. *American Sociological Review, 74*(1), 44–62.

Robinson, D. T., & Smith-Lovin, L. (1992). Selective interaction as a strategy for identity maintenance: An affect control model. *Social Psychology Quarterly, 55*(1), 12–28.

Rutte, C. G., & Wilke, H. A. M. (1985). Preference for decision structures in a social dilemma situation. *European Journal of Social Psychology, 15*(3), 367–370.

Salganik, M. J., Dodds, P. S., & Watts, D. J. (2006). Experimental study of inequality and unpredictability in an artificial cultural market. *Science, 311*(5762), 854–856.

Sherif, M. (1936). *The psychology of social norms*. United States of America: Harper & Brothers.

Sherif, M. (1937). An experimental approach to the study of attitudes. *Sociometry, 1*(1/2), 90–98.

Sherif, M. (1966). *In common predicament: Social psychology of intergroup conflict and cooperation*. Boston: Houghton Mifflin.

Sherif, M., Harvey, O. J., White, B. J., Hood, W. R., & Sherif, C. W. (1961). *Intergroup conflict and cooperation: The Robbers Cave experiment* (Vol. 10). Norman: University Book Exchange.

Shibutani, T. (1978). *The derelicts of Company K: A sociological study of demoralization*. Berkeley: University of California Press.

Simmel, G. (1898). The persistence of social groups. *The American Journal of Sociology, 3*(5), 662–698.

Simmel, G. ([1908] 1955). *Conflict and the web of group affiliations* (trans: Wolff, K., & Bendix, R.). New York: Free Press.

Simmel, G. ([1908] 1971). *Georg Simmel on individuality and social forms*. Chicago: University of Chicago Press.

Simpson, B., & Macy, M. W. (2001). Collective action and power inequality: Coalitions in exchange networks. *Social Psychology Quarterly, 64*(1), 88–100.

Sinclair, L., & Kunda, Z. (2000). Motivated stereotyping of women: She's fine if she praised me but incompetent if she criticized me. *Personality and Social Psychology Bulletin, 26*(11), 1329–1342.

Smith-Lovin, L., & Brody, C. (1989). Interruptions in group discussions: The effects of gender and group composition. *American Sociological Review, 54*(3), 424–435.

Sprecher, S., Schmeeckle, M., & Felmlee, D. (2006). The principle of least interest inequality in emotional involvement in romantic relationships. *Journal of Family Issues, 27*(9), 1255–1280.

Stein, A. A. (1976). Conflict and cohesion a review of the literature. *Journal of Conflict Resolution, 20*(1), 143–172.

Steiner, I. D. (1974). Whatever happened to the group in social psychology? *Journal of Experimental Social Psychology, 10*(1), 94–108.

Stets, J. E., & Burke, P. J. (2000). Identity theory and social identity theory. *Social Psychology Quarterly, 63*(3), 224–237.

Stets, J. E., & Serpe, R. T. (2013). *Identity theory*. New York: Springer.

Strang, D., & Soule, S. A. (1998). Diffusion in organizations and social movements: From hybrid corn to poison pills. *Annual Review of Sociology, 24*, 265–290.

Strodtbeck, F. L., James, R. M., & Hawkins, C. (1957). Social status in jury deliberations. *American Sociological Review, 22*(6), 713–719.

Struch, N., & Schwartz, S. H. (1989). Intergroup aggression: Its predictors and distinctness from in-group bias. *Journal of Personality and Social Psychology, 56*(3), 364.

Stryker, S. (1980). *Symbolic interactionism: A social structural approach*. Menlo Park: Benjamin & Cummings.

Stryker, S. (2008). From mead to a structural symbolic interactionism and beyond. *Annual Review of Sociology, 34*, 15–31.

Stryker, S., & Burke, P. J. (2000). The past, present, and future of an identity theory. *Social Psychology Quarterly, 63*(4), 284–297.

Sumner, W. G. (1906). *Folkways: A study of the sociological importance of usages, manners, customs, mores, and morals*. Boston: Ginn.

Swidler, A. (1986). Culture in action: Symbols and strategies. *American Sociological Review, 51*(2), 273–286.

Tajfel, H., & Turner, J. C. (1979). An integrative theory of intergroup conflict. *The Social Psychology of Intergroup Relations, 33*(47), 74.

Tajfel, H., & Turner, J. C. (1986). The social identity theory of intergroup behavior. In S. Worchel & W. G. Austin (Eds.), *Psychology of intergroup relations* (2nd ed., pp. 73–98). Chicago: Nelson-Hall.

Tajfel, H., Billig, M. G., Bundy, R. P., & Flament, C. (1971). Social categorization and intergroup behaviour. *European Journal of Social Psychology, 1*(2), 149–178.

Tavory, I. (2010). Of yarmulkes and categories: Delegating boundaries and the phenomenology of interactional expectation. *Theory and Society, 39*(1), 49–68.

Tepper, B. J., Carr, J. C., Breaux, D. M., Geider, S., Hu, C., & Hua, W. (2009). Abusive supervision, intentions to quit, and employees' workplace deviance: A power/dependence analysis. *Organizational Behavior and Human Decision Processes, 109*(2), 156–167.

Thoits, P. A. (1983). Multiple identities and psychological well-being: A reformulation and test of the social isolation hypothesis. *American Sociological Review, 48*(2), 174–187.

Thoits, P. A. (1986). Multiple identities: Examining gender and marital status differences in distress. *American Sociological Review, 51*(2), 259–272.

Thoits, P. A. (1992). Identity structures and psychological well-being: Gender and marital status comparisons. *Social Psychology Quarterly, 55*(3), 236–256.

Thoits, P. A. (1995). Social psychology: The interplay between sociology and psychology. *Social Forces, 73*(4), 1231–1243.

Thoits, P. A. (2003). Personal agency in the accumulation of multiple role-identities. In *Advances in identity theory and research* (pp. 179–194). New York: Springer.

Thoits, P. A. (2011). Mechanisms linking social ties and support to physical and mental health. *Journal of Health and Social Behavior, 52*(2), 145–161.

Thoits, P. A. (2012). Role-identity salience, purpose and meaning in life, and well-being among volunteers. *Social Psychology Quarterly, 75*(4), 360–384.

Thomas-Hunt, M. C., & Phillips, K. W. (2004). When what you know is not enough: Expertise and gender dynamics in task groups. *Personality and Social Psychology Bulletin, 30*(12), 1585–1598.

Thorne, B. (1993). *Gender play: Girls and boys in school.* New Brunswick: Rutgers University Press.

Thye, S. R. (2000). A status value theory of power in exchange relations. *American Sociological Review, 65*(3), 407–432.

Timmermans, S., & Tavory, I. (2012). Theory construction in qualitative research from grounded theory to abductive analysis. *Sociological Theory, 30*(3), 167–186.

Vaisey, S. (2009). Motivation and justification: A dual-process model of culture in action 1. *American Journal of Sociology, 114*(6), 1675–1715.

Watts, D. J. (1999). Networks, dynamics, and the small-world phenomenon 1. *American Journal of Sociology, 105*(2), 493–527.

Webster, M., Jr., & Driskell, J. E., Jr. (1983). Beauty as status. *American Journal of Sociology, 89*(1), 140–165.

Webster, M., Jr., Hysom, S. J., & Fullmer, E. M. (1998). Sexual orientation and occupation as status. *Advances in Group Processes, 15*, 1–21.

Wenneras, C., & Wold, A. (1997). Nepotism and sexism in peer-review. Nature 387, 341–343.

Willer, D. (1992). Predicting power in exchange networks: A brief history and introduction to the issues. *Social Networks, 14*(3), 187–211.

Willer, R. (2009). Groups reward individual sacrifice: The status solution to the collective action problem. *American Sociological Review, 74*(1), 23–43.

Willer, R., Kuwabara, K., & Macy, M. W. (2009). The false enforcement of unpopular norms 1. *American Journal of Sociology, 115*(2), 451–490.

Willer, R., Youngreen, R., Troyer, L., & Lovaglia, M. J. (2012). How do the powerful attain status? The roots of legitimate power inequalities. *Managerial and Decision Economics, 33*(5–6), 355–367.

Willer, R., Rogalin, C. L., Conlon, B., & Wojnowicz, M. T. (2013). Overdoing gender: A test of the masculine overcompensation thesis. *American Journal of Sociology, 118*(4), 980–1022.

Wood, W., Lundgren, S., Ouellette, J. A., Busceme, S., & Blackstone, T. (1994). Minority influence: A meta-analytic review of social influence processes. *Psychological Bulletin, 115*(3), 323.

Wrong, D. H. (1961). The oversocialized conception of man in modern sociology. *American Sociological Review, 26*(2), 183–193.

Yamagishi, T. (1986). The provision of a sanctioning system as a public good. *Journal of Personality and Social Psychology, 51*(1), 110.

Yamagishi, T. (1988a). The provision of a sanctioning system in the United States and Japan. *Social Psychology Quarterly, 51*(3), 265–271.

Yamagishi, T. (1988b). Seriousness of social dilemmas and the provision of a sanctioning system. *Social Psychology Quarterly, 51*(1), 32–42.

Yamagishi, T., Jin, N., & Kiyonari, T. (1999). Bounded generalized reciprocity: Ingroup boasting and ingroup favoritism. *Advances in Group Processes, 16*(1), 161–197.

Yoon, J., Thye, S. R., & Lawler, E. J. (2013). Exchange and cohesion in dyads and triads: A test of Simmel's hypothesis. *Social Science Research, 42*(6), 1457–1466.

Zelditch, M. (2001). Processes of legitimation: Recent developments and new directions. *Social Psychology Quarterly, 64*(1), 4–17.

Zhong, C., Magee, J. C., Maddux, W. W., & Galinsky, A. D. (2006). Power, culture, and action: Considerations in the expression and enactment of power in East Asian and Western societies. *Research on Managing in Teams and Groups, 9*, 53–73.

The Theories of Status Characteristics and Expectation States

16

Murray Webster Jr. and Lisa Slattery Walker

16.1 Overview and Background

Status Characteristics and Expectation States names a family of interrelated theories, along with research settings devised to help develop the theories and bodies of empirical tests and practical applications. While we mostly describe the theories and their structures, we will mention empirical work and applications as they are significant for theory development.

These theories all involve various sorts of social inequality, from the smallest social settings, face to face interaction, through institutional settings including the family and business organizations, to entire social systems, nations and cultures. We begin with the theories' analyses of how inequality develops and is maintained or changed in small, face to face task groups. Task groups are ubiquitous in all societies. They include committees and task forces in business, sports teams, juries, military units, classroom group activities, and many others.

Two of the best established findings in face-to-face social interaction are:

1. If members of a task group begin meeting with some noticeable social status inequality differentiating them (for instance, on juries where occupation and education differentiate members), *that status inequality will create a recognized inequality* among group members.
2. If members of a task group begin meeting as equals (for instance workers at the same level in a business organization or college students working on a group project) *the interaction process will create a recognized inequality* among group members.

In the next two sections we will develop theoretical explanations for those two findings. Following that, we describe further development of the theories for other theoretical questions and some applications of the work. Issues of inequality at the interpersonal level, such as in groups, and at the level of society long have been central to sociological theorizing. Although all of the theories in this chapter cannot be said to have developed out of a particular older theory, some of the concerns of older theorists appear in topics of the theories in this chapter.

Status—consisting of respect, prestige, and social advantages and disadvantages—has been studied and theorized from many different viewpoints. Early in the twentieth century, status was important in the writing of the American economist Thorstein Veblen (1857–1929). In an essay that also identifies "conspicuous consumption,"

M. Webster Jr. (✉) • L.S. Walker
Department of Sociology, University of North Carolina, Charlotte, Charlotte, NC, USA
e-mail: mawebste@uncc.edu; lisa.walker@uncc.edu

S. Abrutyn (ed.), *Handbook of Contemporary Sociological Theory*,
Handbooks of Sociology and Social Research, DOI 10.1007/978-3-319-32250-6_16

Veblen (1899/1953) analyzed the importance of status value of objects. Status value impresses others without conferring any utilitarian value. For instance, an expensive new car in the driveway can impress the neighbors but it offers very little practical value above what could be gotten from a secondhand economy car. The German philosopher and social theorist Georg Simmel (1858–1918) wrote that "The first condition of having to deal with somebody… is to know with whom one has to deal" ([1908] 1950: 307). Presumably, knowing the status position of a person is important social information for knowing how to deal with him or her. More recently, Erving Goffman (1922–1982) wrote about self-presentation, efforts to control the impressions that one makes during interaction (1959, 1970). Goffman's writing often focuses on techniques to convey a high-status image, presumably for the interaction and other advantages that it can confer. Veblen and Goffman treat status as desirable and something that people seek. Simmel treated status as only one part of an overall identity, and was silent about whether people expend energy seeking status. As we will see later in this chapter, the contemporary view is that, while status confers some advantages it also entails costs including responsibility, and thus whether it is desirable rests on other concerns and conditions. Under all conditions, status differences are related to social inequalities.

Talcott Parsons (1902–1979), influenced by early theorists, primarily Emile Durkheim (1858–1917), developed a conception of social systems that dominated sociological thought for at least a quarter century after the end of World War II in 1945. In Parsons' view, all social systems, whether entire societies or small groups such as a family, faced the same four problems, called "functional prerequisites," for effective functioning and even for survival (Parsons 1937, 1951). To fulfill the functional prerequisites, groups organize and develop patterned interaction. Often the organization is what Durkheim (1893 [1933]) had called "organic solidarity," a division of labor such that some subsets of a group emphasize solving one prerequisite and other subsets emphasize other prerequisites.

Robert Freed Bales (1916–2004), who worked with Parsons (Parsons et al. 1953), studied small discussion groups in a laboratory and focused on how the nature of interaction develops during the course of a meeting.[1] To study interaction patterns, Bales developed a famous 12-category system, Interaction Process Analysis, (Bales 1950, 1999; Bales et al. 1951) for classifying every speech and other communicative action, such as gestures, in the group.[2]

A Bales group comprises approximately 2–20 members, the upper limit determined by the number of people that we can interact with as individuals. (Beyond 20, the situation becomes a speaker and an undifferentiated audience, and participation is mostly one-way rather than interactive.) Bales recruited individuals, often college students, to join a problem-solving group and at the end of discussion, the group must settle on a single "best answer" to the group problem. The problem-solving task must be reasonably interesting to facilitate participation, and its outcome has to be somewhat ambiguous so that people can express different views and offer different contributions. An arithmetic problem would not be suitable since it has a clear-cut answer; a question of how best to handle a case of juvenile misdemeanor would be perfect.

It is worth pointing out that terms sometimes applied to theories—whether they refer to *macro* phenomena, *meso* phenomena, or *micro* phenomena—do not really fit here. The theories in this

[1] In Bales' view, early interaction emphasized defining the problem—remember, these are task groups—and collecting information. Later phases evaluated and synthesized information and reached conclusions, and towards the end of the meeting, individuals turned to planning how to implement the conclusions (Bales and Strodtbeck (1951).

[2] Many people are unaware how many innovations from Bales' research have become accepted parts of our culture. A one-way mirror is essential equipment for every cop show on TV; Bales was the first to equip a laboratory with one-way mirrors so that observers were removed from the interaction. Marketing research relies on focus groups to assess potential new products and even plotlines in movies; those are modifications of the research design that Bales developed. Many leadership training courses adapt the idea of phases in group problem-solving that were first studied by Bales and his students. And the distinction of "pro-active" and "reactive" styles of speech traces to Bales' reports of group interactions.

chapter, and many other theories as well, span the range of sizes. As will be seen, expectation states and interaction involve individuals and face to face interaction. Status characteristics are features of larger society, e.g., the social definitions of the characteristics *gender*, *race*, *occupation*, *education*, and *age*. Theories in this section apply to the smallest units, individuals and dyads; they also apply to groups and larger social structures; and they explain how societal social beliefs and definitions affect interaction and group structure, and how status beliefs themselves form and become established.

We begin, in the next section, with development of a theory explaining how face to face interaction can create *expectation states*, which are roughly comparable to ideas of task skill. We show how expectation states affect individuals' awareness and behavior, change the nature of interaction, and create group structure. Subsequent sections address larger social settings within which interacting groups exist.

16.2 Performance Expectations and Behavior

Theories include scope conditions, descriptions of the kinds of situations to which they apply, and by exclusion, situations where the theories cannot predict. The scope conditions for theories in this chapter are more precise definitions of the kinds of groups we have been discussing as "task groups." Two scope conditions are crucial for all the theories in this chapter, *task focus* and *collective orientation*.

Task focus means that the primary reason for meeting is to solve a problem or set of problems. Another feature of task focus is that the outcome can be evaluated by extra-systemic standards. That simply means that someone doesn't have to be a member of the group to judge whether it did a good job; the standards for evaluation are not different for different people or for different groups. While many groups are task focused, others are process focused; that is, the members' main concern is the interaction itself rather than producing a product or a right answer. Friendship groups, therapy groups, and social events such as parties are mainly process oriented. An outsider cannot really judge whether a party or a therapy group was successful because that depends on subjective experiences of those who were there.

Collective orientation means that the task is a group task. It is legitimate and necessary to take everyone's ideas into account. A soccer team is collectively oriented; most coaches like to say "There is no 'I' in 'team'." In contrast, a classroom of students taking a test are individually oriented if it is not legitimate to share ideas and everyone can come up with different right or wrong solutions. A jury, which must reach a unanimous verdict, must be a collectively oriented group.

Let us return to our illustrative Bales group, composed of volunteer students who will discuss a group problem for 50 min or so, and at the end they will produce a single group answer. They will then complete confidential post-session questionnaires asking who had the best ideas, who seemed to understand the problem best, who showed leadership, who exerted influence, and other measures of inequality among the members.[3] During interaction, observers behind a one-way mirror will code every speech act during discussion. Here we focus on how often each person speaks and how often each person is spoken to.

16.2.1 Interaction Regularities

Four regularities in speaking are virtually certain to appear in task focused collectively oriented groups:

1. *Inequality*. The members will differ in how much of the group's time each of them controls. Some people speak frequently, some infrequently, and some participate hardly at all. Inequality is clear even in groups as small as three or even two members.

[3] To avoid normative answers such as "Everyone showed great leadership," participants are asked to rank all members of the group, including themselves, on most of the questions.

2. *Reciprocity*. If you rank group members from the highest interactor to the lowest, you also will have ranked them in order of receipt of interaction. People who speak most are those who are most often spoken to.

Let us pause to consider these two regularities.

The first shows the inequality that we said is characteristic of task focused collectively oriented groups. Furthermore, as groups get larger, the amount of inequality increases. In a three-person Bales group, the highest interactor controls about 43 % of the group's time; the second, about 30 %; and the third, about 23 %. In a six-person group, the numbers are about 43 %, 19 %, 14 %, 11 %, 8 % and 5 %. The trend is that as the group gets larger, the top interactor controls about 45–50 % of the group's time, and the remaining 50 % or 55 % is spread more and more thinly across everyone else. By the time we get to a 12-person group such as a jury, there will be some members who hardly contribute at all.

The second regularity shows that, in task focused, collectively oriented groups, participation rates are socially controlled. People speak frequently *because* they are spoken to frequently, and not otherwise. It is not true that someone runs on and on without social permission. Group members usually are very effective at controlling each other through appearing interested or bored, asking questions or telling someone to let others speak. Why do they do that? The reason is task focus; they have to solve the group's problem, and time is limited. Even in a jury, which has no official time limit, people still want to finish their work and go home. Nobody wants to waste time while someone goes talks on without helping to solve the problem; or worse, gives bad ideas that could mislead the group. And on the other side, if it looks as though someone can help solve the problem, that is a powerful reason to encourage that person to participate more.

3. *Consistency*. On the confidential questionnaires, group members show high agreement with each other on the various rankings. There is consensus on who had good ideas, understood the problem, showed leadership, exerted influence, etc. If the observers also have rated group members, observers' ratings concur with those of group members. And the questionnaire measures correlate highly with initiation rates. In other words, a person speaks frequently *because* others have decided that he has good ideas. This means that the behavior and questionnaire measures reflect a single *power and prestige structure* which we discuss in more detail below.
4. *Persistence*. The inequality structure that can be seen after the first few minutes is the inequality at the end of the meeting. If the same group returns to discuss a different task (even if one or two members have been replaced), the inequality that developed in the first meeting tends to persist through subsequent meetings. This suggests that a semi-permanent mechanism has been created during interaction that tends to maintain the particular inequality structure that emerged.

16.2.2 Abstract Conception of Interaction

Joseph Berger, a student of Bales, became interested in the inequality and the four regularities that we have just discussed. However, Berger was concerned with understanding abstract general patterns rather than particular features of each group. He sought general patterns, and more importantly, he sought an explanation for the patterns. This led him to formulate the first theory of performance expectations and behavior.

All of the four regularities can be explained by an underlying structure of *performance expectation states* that develop during interaction and then creates and maintain the power and prestige structure. This concept—expectation states—is key to all of the theory development and empirical research described throughout this chapter, and we describe it in some detail.

Expectations are anticipations of the quality of future performances. They are specific to particular actors and particular tasks, as in "I think she understands this task better than I do." Thus expectations are not quite the same as common usage such as "I think she's really smart" because what matters here is: "*Relative to the task at hand* and *relative to other people in the group*, I expect that she will perform better at this task than some specific other person (possibly myself)."

Furthermore, although it is sometimes possible to bring expectations into conscious awareness through careful interviewing and in other ways, most of the time expectations operate below the conscious level. People in a task group do not often state, even to themselves, just where they feel everyone's task ability stands. Instead, they act *as if* they thought about relative expectations before acting. We measure expectations through some of their behavioral effects, such as participation rates or influence. The theory predicts behavior; it does not predict what people are thinking when they act.[4]

Berger's approach was to develop a theory explaining the development and maintenance of inequality using the mechanism of expectation states. The interaction process creates expectations for each group member, and once those expectations exist, they affect all components of the power and prestige structure of the group. So group members participate at a high rate *because* they hold relative high self-expectations. Other group members let those people participate at a high rate *because* they hold high expectations for their performances.

16.2.3 Building a General Theory

To construct a theory describing the processes of expectation formation and maintenance, Berger (1958) first developed an abstract conceptualization of task focused interaction. This is a simplified model of task interaction. Omitting pleasantries, jokes, irrelevant talk and other kinds of social-emotional speech, task focused interaction can be seen as having the following four components, in sequence:

1. *Action opportunities*, or socially distributed chances to perform. In a discussion, group, someone might say "Do you have a suggestion for how to do this task?"
2. *Performance outputs*, or attempts to move the group towards problem solution. For instance, "I suggest we begin by listing all possible options." A performance is likely, although not certain, to follow a given action opportunity.
3. *Unit evaluations* of performance outputs. For instance "That's a good (or a bad) idea." A unit evaluation follows every performance output, although it might be formed privately rather than expressed openly.
4. *Influence* when two or more performance outputs or expressed evaluations disagree. For instance, "I guess you were right and I was wrong."

We can think of interaction as composed of series of these sequences. Why does everyone make private unit evaluations of every performance output, even if they are not going to voice them? Because group members are highly task focused; they need to know who is helping reach the group's goal and who is not. Why must every disagreement be resolved through accepting or rejecting influence? Because the group members are collectively oriented and they cannot just "agree to disagree." That would mean not reaching a conclusion to the group task.

Unit evaluations are crucial to forming performance expectation states. An expectation state forms after a series of unit evaluations. If someone thinks "She's right" "good idea," "she's right," "good idea," etc., at some point that generalizes into "I think she knows how to do this." That shows formation of high expectations for that person. In the same way, people form self-expectations through unit evaluations, and a task

[4]An expectation state is a *theoretical construct*; a term used for things that are not directly observable, but that produce effects that can be observed. *Gravity* is a familiar theoretical construct. We cannot see gravity or touch it, but we can see its effects and predict the effects with great accuracy. In everyday usage, *a conscience* is another theoretical construct. We cannot observe a conscience directly, but if we believe that someone has a well-developed conscience, we can use that belief to make predictions of his or her likely behavior. Andreas (2013) describes theoretical constructs more fully.

group fairly quickly becomes structured in terms of the unequal distribution of expectations attached to its members.

Once expectations form, they will affect all components of interaction and other elements of power and prestige in the group. The higher the expectations associated with a given individual, the more likely is he or she to receive action opportunities; the more likely is that individual to accept an action opportunity and make a performance output; also, the more likely is any performance output to receive a positive unit evaluation; and if disagreement arises, the more likely is that person to reject influence attempts.

Expectations, once they have formed, tend to persist. Why don't they change? The main reason is that expectations affect the very conditions that created them; that is, the unit evaluations of performances. A performance coming from a person linked to high expectations "just sounds better" than a similar performance coming from a person associated with low expectations.[5] Unless they are powerfully contradicted, once expectations form, they tend to persist. Expectation states produce effects that could be considered self-fulfilling prophecies.

Besides affecting the interaction sequence, differentiated expectations will account for questionnaire measures of ability, leadership, etc., and will also explain actual choices for leadership positions and other positions of honor. The theory describes the following sequence shown in Fig. 16.1 for formation of expectation states through interaction in task groups.

[5] Most of us can remember a time in school when a child who was generally considered to be smart—that is, a child for whom other students and the teacher held high expectations—gave an answer that was less than stellar, but the teacher said "good." The opposite happens with perfectly good answers from a child thought to be dumb. Expectations affect unit evaluations of performances, which usually makes expectations stable.

16.2.4 Explaining the Interaction Regularities

We now have a theoretical explanation for the four regularities noted earlier.

1. *Inequality*. The fact that participation is unequal is caused by the formation of performance expectations that get associated with every group member.
2. *Reciprocity*. The correlation of initiation and receipt of interaction is produced by the fact that both elements are produced by the same underlying structure of expectations.
3. *Consistency*. Interaction, perceptions of ability and leadership, and behavioral outcomes including influence and leadership choices all are produced by the structure of expectations.
4. *Persistence*. The stability of inequality, once it emerges, is produced by the stability of expectation states.

16.3 Status Characteristics and Expectations States

To this point, we have described how task focused interaction will create expectations and a structured group inequality in a group of people who begin interaction as equals. The Harvard students who made up the groups that Bales studied were about as homogeneous as you could find, reflecting the Harvard student body in the 1950s. All were white males who had done well in high school, their family incomes were high, they were all about the same ages, and they dressed similarly. That initial homogeneity is what made the inequality that formed in Bales groups so striking to observers.

Most natural task groups are composed of members who are differentiated on many characteristics. Consider a jury. Its members differ on gender, occupational prestige, income, educational level, race, age, and many other social characteristics. How does interaction differ in a heterogeneous group?

Initially homogeneous and initially heterogeneous task groups are alike in one way: they both display inequalities of power and prestige. However the inequality develops differently in the two kinds of groups. Rather than developing over a few minutes as in Bales groups, heterogeneous groups usually are differentiated from the outset of interaction. Another difference is that homogeneous Bales groups often pass through an initial period of contentiousness as several members vie to dominate the discussion. Heterogeneous groups, in contrast, very seldom go through a struggle for control; the power and prestige structure is evident from the very beginning of the interaction.

Those similarities and differences would all be explainable if people in differentiated groups formed expectations for everyone at the very outset, before any interaction takes place. In fact, that is what happens. People use socially evaluated characteristics to infer performance expectations. Then expectations determine interaction patterns and the group's power and prestige structure, as we have already seen. The inequality in the outside society is "imported" to the task group so that group structure is consistent with social inequalities. This is the process of *status generalization* illustrated in Fig. 16.2. This process adds an additional way that expectation states can form to the process shown in Fig. 16.1 earlier. We turn to constructing a more rigorous theoretical explanation of the process.

16.3.1 Defined Terms

To begin, we use precise definitions of the types of characteristics that will function in status generalization. There are two types, *specific status characteristics* and *diffuse status characteristics*, denoted respectively by C and D.

A characteristic C is a *specific status characteristic* ≡

1. C has two or more states that are differentially evaluated in the culture; and
2. Each state of C (C+ and C−), is associated with the similarly valued state of specific expectations.

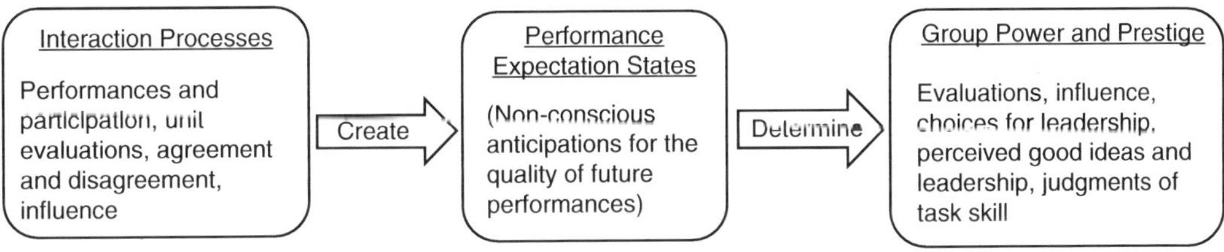

Fig. 16.1 Interaction, expectation states, and power and prestige

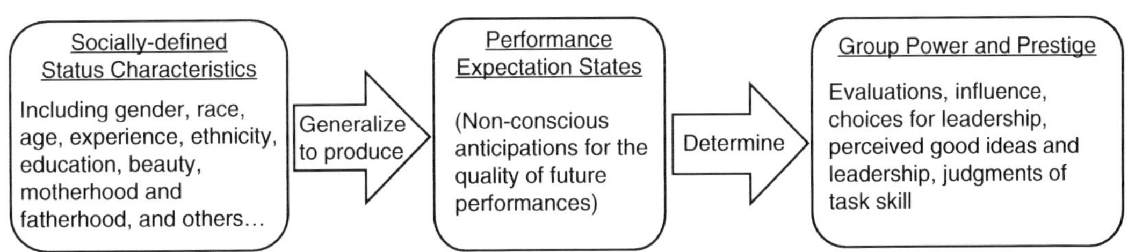

Fig. 16.2 Status, expectation states, and power and prestige

A specific status characteristic has limited scope. It conveys advantages and disadvantages in certain situations and only in those situations. Being a champion or an incompetent weight lifter, winning a spelling bee or being unable to spell most three-syllable words, and being an ace or a beginner at Sudoku are specific status characteristics. It is preferable to have one state than the other; that is, the states have esteem associated with them; this fulfills part (1) of the definition. And (2) people expect that someone possessing the high state of the characteristic can do something better than someone else who has the low state. But not everything. We do not ordinarily expect a champion weight lifter to excel at Sudoku, or vice-versa.

A characteristic D is a *diffuse status characteristic* ≡

1. D has two or more states that are differentially evaluated in the culture; and
2. Each state of D (D+ and D−), is associated with the similarly valued state of specific expectations; and
3. Each state of D is associated with the similarly valued state of general expectations of unknown or unspecified limits.

Diffuse status characteristics are much broader than specific characteristics because of part (3) of their definition. They can create expectations for virtually any task, with one limitation that we will note below. If, for instance, we live in a society in which people believe that (1) it is advantageous, preferable, better to be male than female; (2) that males are better at doing math problems than are females; and (3) that males are stronger, more rational, more logical, better at gambling, more mechanical, better programmers, etc., than women, then gender is a diffuse status characteristic in our society. It is the "etc." in part (3) of the definition that makes gender a diffuse status characteristic. Race, age, educational level, and other characteristics also meet the definition in our society.

Notice that this theory does *not* predict that gender, race, age, or any other characteristic will be a status characteristic. That depends on social definitions, how the culture defines characteristics. What the theory says is that *if* something is a specific or diffuse status characteristic in a particular culture, *then* certain power and prestige consequences follow. Societies differ in just which characteristics they ascribe status beliefs to, and characteristics can acquire or lose status value as times change. Some of the further developments that we review below describe processes by which an initially unevaluated characteristic can gain status value, how status beliefs diffuse in a society, and how a characteristic can lose status value.

Now we can develop a theoretical explanation that covers what happens in heterogeneous groups where one or more status characteristics are salient. The theory uses the same scope conditions as did the theory of expectations and behavior: task focus and collectively orientation. It adds the definitions of specific and diffuse status characteristics. The full theoretical explanation uses five general propositions, shown in Table 16.1.

16.3.2 Theoretical Propositions

Assuming a task group of people who are differentiated by one or more diffuse or specific status characteristics, group inequality is created by the following process.

1. *Salience.* All differentiating status information, and any status information that is already linked to the task by cultural beliefs, becomes *salient.*
2. *Burden of Proof.* Unless interactants believe for certain that a salient status characteristic is irrelevant to the task, they will treat it as relevant and will form task-specific expectations consistent with the states of the characteristic.
3. *Sequencing.* If interactants enter or leave the group, or if the task changes, expectations already created by processes in (1) and (2) will transfer, with attenuation, to the new task situation.

Table 16.1 Status characteristics and expectation states

Assumption 1 (Salience). Any specific or diffuse status characteristic that differentiates actors, and any characteristic already believed to be relevant to the group task will become *salient*; that is, it will become a significant social fact that affects interaction
Assumption 2 (Burden of Proof). Unless an interactant believes that a particular status element is irrelevant to the task, he or she will treat it as relevant for performance expectations for every actor. All salient characteristics will affect performance expectations, as follows
Diffuse characteristics will become linked to states of Γ (general performance expectations) having the same + or − sign as the characteristic. States of Γ will link to similarly signed states of C*, the specific ability to complete the task. States of C* will link to similarly signed states of T, task success (T+) and task failure (T−)
Specific characteristics will become linked to states of τ (specific performance expectations) having the same + or − sign as the characteristic. States of τ will link to similarly signed states of ϒ (general task ability). States of ϒ will link to similarly signed states of T, task success (T+) or task failure (T−)
Assumption 3 (Sequencing). The status generalization process will continue as described in Assumptions 1 and 2 until all interactants are linked to states of T by all possible paths. If a new actor enters the situation, the salience and burden of proof processes will connect that actor to paths of T in the same manner. If an actor leaves the situation after paths have formed, existing connections will remain
Assumption 4 (Combining Status Information). All salient status information functions to connect all actors to states of C*, the specific task ability. Aggregate expectations form according to these functions:
$e_{p+} = \left[1-\left((1-f(i))\ldots(1-f(n))\right)\right]$;
$e_{p-} = -\left[1-\left((1-f(i))\ldots(1-f(n))\right)\right]$;
and $e_p = e_{p+} + e_{p-}$.
e_p is aggregate expectations for actor p, $f(i)$ is a function of the length of path i connecting an interactant to outcome states of the task T through intervening status elements
The expectation advantage of actor p, which may be positive or negative, is:
$e_p - e_o$.

4. *Combining*. All salient status information functions in the status generalization process; none is ignored.
5. *Power and Prestige*. Once aggregate expectations form for all interactants, every person's relative position in the group power and prestige structure is a direct function of their expectation advantages and disadvantages.

This completes the development of the core theory.

16.4 Some Instances of Status Generalization

16.4.1 Juries and Sports Teams

Before considering further theoretical developments, we pause to study some cases that illustrate the basic process of status generalization. All of these illustrate how the status inequalities in a society get "imported" to small task groups, where they organize the group's power and prestige structure and interaction patterns among group members.

In our society (and in many others), all of the following carry status information: gender, race and ethnicity, age, educational level, and occupation. The basic process of status generalization, illustrated in Fig. 16.2 above, is that status information becomes salient when interactants notice that they possess different states of a status characteristic. Remember also that status generalization occurs when certain scope conditions obtain; both task focus and collective orientation are crucial before status generalization is likely to take place.

A very common instance of status generalization can be seen in mixed-gender groups. In our society, males have status advantages. The status inequality produces differential performance expectations; group members form higher expectations for males than for females, whether or not the group task is related to gender. The differentiated performance expectations affect all elements of power and prestige in the group. Men get to participate more and are more influential; they are thought to be "doing better" at the group task and to be more valuable group members, and are more likely to be chosen for leadership positions.[6]

As we noted, a jury is a 12-person or a 6-person task focused, collectively oriented discussion group quite similar to the Bales groups described above. While it is usually impossible to study actual jury deliberations (juries work in seclusion), we can see some status effects from public data and other effects from conducting simulated juries and observing them.

Feller (2010) reported that a foreperson is most often:

- Male. Only about 20 % of women are chosen as foreperson (despite the gender neutral term that replaced "foreman" some years ago).
- Old. Only about half of jurors age 18–35 become foreperson; a person between 45 and 65 is about twice as likely to become foreperson compared to the number of jurors in that age group.
- Educated. Two-year and 4-year college graduates are over-represented as foreperson; people whose education ended before college are under-represented.
- Experienced. Someone who has previously served as a foreperson is more likely to be selected again than someone without jury experience.

Once deliberation begins, the foreperson usually is the highest interactor, controlling about 25–31 % of the time in the group. (If participation were equally distributed in a 12-person jury, each member would speak about 8 % of the time.)

All of those findings are accounted for when we note that gender, age, and education are *diffuse status characteristics* in our society. The theoretical process is that jurors form expectations from status generalization, and then select as leader the person with a status and expectation advantage. The foreperson not only speaks more than others, but he or she also is more influential over the verdict.

What about the effect of experience? Experience is a *specific status characteristic* indicating some skill at working on a jury. Status generalization works with both diffuse and specific status characteristics, in both instances affecting performance expectations.

A striking fact about foreperson selection is that it takes place *before* any actual deliberation. In other words, jurors are asked to select a leader before they have any evidence about skill, knowledge, interest, or anything else. They have very little basis for choosing their leader other than that provided by status generalization.

A sports team is very different from a jury in terms of concrete details such as what they do and what their goal is; interaction is physical rather than verbal, and the main goal is to win games. A team definitely is a task focused collectively oriented group, and thus see status effects appear in interaction processes.

Some years ago, two scholars in Israel (Yuchtman-Yaar and Semyonov 1976) studied effects of status generalization from ethnicity—Sephardic or Ashkenazi ancestry—among Israeli soccer teams. This case is interesting because the ethnicity characteristic studied here is one that most Americans wouldn't recognize, although it is important and easily recognized in Israel. This illustrates the point above that what constitutes a status characteristic is determined by the society, what that society invests with advantages and disadvantages.

The finding is that, as players progress through the ranks, the proportions of players from the two ethnicities changes dramatically. Table 16.2 shows the proportions.

The challenge is to account for the changing proportions of Sephardic and Ashkenazi players. At the outset, in high school, 46 % of players are Sephardic; at the highest level National Team, fewer than 10 % are Sephardic. This cannot be accounted for by players' wishes, for twice as many Sephardic players said they had "a strong desire" to become professional.

[6]Remember that this theory does not justify gender inequality or any other sort of inequality. The theory describes how things work, not how they ought to work, what we might wish, or even what is natural. To the contrary, if you want to promote gender equality in task groups, the first step is to understand what's producing the inequality—performance expectations formed from status generalization—and then use that analysis to design interventions. We will mention some effective interventions later in this chapter.

Table 16.2 Proportions of Sephardic and Ashkenazi soccer players, and desire to become professional

Group	% Sephardic	% Ashkenazi
All high school boys	46	54
Junior league players	69	31
Senior league players	59	41
Among senior league players, having "a strong desire" to become a professional	68	32
Promotion to second league (professional) player	71	32
Promotion to first league (professional) player	19	31
Promotion to national team (professional) player	9.4	37.2

From Yuchtman-Yaar and Semyonov (1979)

To understand how status generalization can produce that effect, think about how players progress through the ranks. Being picked for a promotion in level depends on coaches' unit evaluations of performances. Coaches see players making a very large number of performance outputs, attempts to help their teams attain success: kicking, passing, blocking, and all the other kinds of action. Coaches evaluate those performances, and those evaluations generalize into performance expectations that coaches attach to players. When it comes time to recommend a player for promotion to the next rank, those expectations are very influential; coaches recommend promotion for players for whom they have come to hold high performance expectations.

Status generalization will affect unit evaluations of performances, which will (probably very slightly) bias evaluations upwards for Ashkenazi players and downwards for Sephardic. The bias can be small because there will be so many performances and evaluations. The cumulative effect makes Ashkenazi players seem a little better than they would by a purely objective measure, and Sephardic players seem a little worse.

Notice that we are NOT saying that the coaches favor Ashkenazi players because of "prejudice" or liking them better, or any of the common arguments. A coach is fundamentally concerned with winning games. Whether he likes a particular player or wants to favor an ethnicity is virtually out of the picture. A coach will choose and promote any player who seems to perform highly. But the status generalization process is quite subtle and mostly unconscious; it makes the Ashkenazi players just seem to be performing a little better, on average.

16.4.2 Using the Theory

Could someone use the theoretical understanding of status processes to make himself or herself leader of a task group? The answer is yes, but a more interesting question is: Do people want to occupy high status positions? Certainly there are pleasant aspects. One is listened to and influential and enjoys enhanced evaluations from others. What is sometimes overlooked, however, is that group leaders bear more responsibility for group actions than do ordinary members. Not everyone would want to be foreperson of a jury in a murder case. That might entail dooming a defendant—or it might entail blocking justice for a victim. Being team leader in a business organization certainly carries some perks, but if the team does not succeed, the leader is going to get much of the blame. Power and prestige usually bring responsibility, and each person has to decide whether to strive to be leader.

16.4.3 Status or Dominance?

It is important to understand that processes of status generalization are consensual. In a jury, men are elected foreperson by both women and men; it is not as though the men seize control or suppress the women. Status generalization processes affect everyone, both those who are advantaged by it and those who are disadvantaged. Power and prestige inequality, when it is produced by status generalization, is usually peacefully arrived at. The ordering seems right to the interactants.

Dominance processes are quite different. They create inequality through intimidation, threats, and bullying, and they are conflictual rather than consensual. Someone can seize control to his or her advantage, but others will probably resent that and when an opportunity presents itself, they will retaliate. Many years ago, Max Weber (Chap. 3) distinguished *power* from *authority*. Authority marks legitimate inequality, whereas inequality based on raw power is not seen as legitimate. If a structure of inequality is not legitimate, it will be unstable.

An experimental study by Cecilia L. Ridgeway (1987) composed three-person groups of women in which one person was instructed to display either status cues (evidence of task skill) or dominance cues (giving commands, interrupting, pointing, or shouting). There were four conditions, defined by how the pre-instructed person acted: high task, low task, high dominance, low dominance. Results showed that high task behavior made the focal person quite influential in the group, and low task behavior reduced her influence. She also was seen as more competent on post-session questionnaires. However when she displayed high dominance behaviors, she was no more influential and seen as no more competent than when she displayed low dominance. She was, however, more disliked.

A second experiment (Ridgeway and Diekema 1989) studied effects of dominance behaviors in four-person groups of either men or women. Here, two members of each group were pre-instructed how to act. One displayed either dominance attempts (threatening behavior) or neutral behavior towards the second, who did not react to either kind of behavior. Again, dominance attempts were unsuccessful at increasing the person's influence or perceived competence, and in these groups, the two bystander members usually intervened to support the person who was the target of the dominance attempts. All-female and all-male groups displayed the same effects, though the level of retaliatory behaviors was higher in the male groups.

We might ask why the dominance attempts were so unsuccessful at achieving a high position in the groups' inequality structures, since in other settings dominance sometimes works. The answer seems to be that we are dealing here with highly task focused groups and dominance usually threatens successful task completion. The members really want to do a good job of whatever their task is, so they want influence and group structure to help further that goal. If people are not task focused, dominance attempts might well be successful, and if the threat is sufficiently large, bystander intervention also may be inhibited.

16.4.4 Complexity and Simplification

The theory of status characteristics and expectation states in Table 16.1, like all sound theories, is stated precisely. Consider Assumption 4, which contains functions describing how multiple items of status function to affect expectations. This assumption is needed to describe expectations attached to someone when multiple status characteristics are salient—including gender, age, educational level, race, and others that may function in a particular case.

Assumption 4 claims that status information will be separated into positive and negative sets. The first contains all items of status that advantage a person, and the second contains all items that disadvantage the person. Within sets, items are combined with declining importance. For instance, the first positive item gives a large boost to expectations for that person. A second positive item will increase expectations, but not so much as the first status item. And so on. The same process applies to items of negative status information. Finally, the positive and negative sets are added together to yield aggregate or overall expectations for a person.

If status items were combined consciously, nobody would be able to perform the operations in those functions in his or her head. What the theory claims is that they act *as if* they did that. In other words, the theorist's job is to predict how people will act. We do not believe that people perform advanced numerical calculations before acting, only that we can predict behavior accurately using those functions. The theory presumes more complicated calculations than are apparent to people whose behavior we want to predict.

In another way, the theory simplifies reality in describing status positions. It treats status characteristics as dichotomous, either positive or negative, without degrees. This means, for instance, that if a college student interacts with a high school student or with a middle school student, the college student will treat either of them as giving him or her the same status advantage on education. The theory does not distinguish grades of status characteristics. It predicts that a college student treats a high school student or a middle school student equivalently when it comes to power and prestige.

Of course we know that is a simplification and reality is more comple16. But the question is not whether people *could* make fine status distinctions; of course they could. The question is whether they *do* make fine distinctions when interacting in task focused groups. The evidence shows that they do not. Balkwell (2001) analyzed a large amount of data relevant to the issue of graded characteristics. He found that the basic theory of status characteristics better predicted behavior than any alternate theory using graded characteristics. He noted that in task groups, people's primary interest is in solving the group's problem, not in assessing fine distinctions of status. "It may be comforting to believe that people process finely graded social information so as to use its full richness, but this assumption consistently has been shown wanting (2001: 112)."

Furthermore, the theory treats all status characteristics as equal in effect on expectations; no status is more important than another, all carry equal weight. This means that age, gender, race, and all other characteristics contribute equally to performance expectations; no salient characteristic is ignored, and no characteristic is so important that it overwhelms everything else. This theoretical view is much simpler than some alternate views of how people use status information. For instance, some might think that people attend mostly to status characteristics on which they have an advantage and ignore or downplay those on which they do not. Or perhaps people treat certain statuses—gender and race are often mentioned—as so important that they make any other status information irrelevant. Or perhaps people simply add up all the positive and negative statuses rather than combine them according to the functions in Assumption 4.

Berger et al. (1992) conducted an elaborate experimental test of alternate models of status processing. Results of all those experimental tests were much closer to predictions from the theory as stated than they were to any of the alternate models. The evidence shows that under the conditions of task focus and collective orientation, this theory describes behavior very well and better than alternatives that have been considered.

16.5 Two Prominent Status Characteristics

16.5.1 Beauty

Folklore and reality television tell us it is fortunate to be beautiful and unfortunate to be ugly. Almost a century ago, Perrin (1921) showed that attractiveness was important for popularity among college students, and numerous studies since then have documented many positive consequences of physical attractiveness. Many, though not all, of those studies involve performance skills. Essays said to have been written by attractive students received better grades than did the same essays when the purported authors were unattractive (Landy and Sigall 1974), and many subsequent studies have found that attractive students of all ages are judged more favorably by teachers (e.g., Ritts et al. 1992). Attractive defendants in swindling cases are seen as more dangerous and given longer sentences (Sigall and Ostrove 1975). So whether the task is admirable (doing well in school) or despicable (swindling), attractive people are thought to be better at it. Frevert and Walker (2014) reviewed a large number of studies that show advantages include: hiring and promotions in organizations, wages, success in civil lawsuits, and marketing. Those findings are all explained by the theory of status characteristics and expectation states if beauty fits the definition of a status characteristic, given above.

Webster and Driskell (1983) showed respondents photos of college students previously rated as highly attractive or highly unattractive by other students. To measure general expectations, they asked respondents to estimate, among other things, reading ability, grade point average, and ability at "things that you think count in this world." To measure specific expectations, respondents estimated success of the targets at the FAA exam for private pilots. Results showed, as predicted, that respondents estimated higher specific and general expectations for the attractive people pictured. An additional finding is that gender of raters did not affect their judgments. In other words, they were responding to status rather than to sexual or romantic attraction.

16.5.2 Motherhood and Fatherhood

Many studies of employment by sociologists and economists show that mothers experience disadvantages in hiring and salaries when compared with comparable women who do not have dependent children. Ridgeway and Correll (2004) reviewed the literature to see whether those disadvantages might have status aspects; that is, whether motherhood carries status disadvantages. They found that motherhood indeed leads to attributions of lower competence and lower job commitment. Those factors, of course, could account for the hiring and salary discrepancies.

Correll et al. (2007) conducted direct tests of the analysis with experiments and an audit study of actual employers. The experiments confirmed status disadvantages connected with motherhood. Those effects were found for both male and female raters, showing that the status significance of motherhood appears among both women and men. In the audit studies, the researchers answered actual job announcements with resumes including either childfree or motherhood as characteristics of applicants. Childfree resumes generated over twice as many callbacks (offers of an interview) from potential employers.

At the same time, Correll et al. (2007) found what might be called a "fatherhood premium," though that effect is less pronounced. In the experiments, men who were described as fathers were seen as more competent and committed, and were recommended for higher starting salaries. Audit studies here did not show a difference in callbacks, perhaps due to a weaker effect or to having fairly small sample sizes. Killewald (2013) analyzed other data to show that fatherhood seems to be an advantage when the man is in a "standard situation;" that is, married, the biological parent, and living with the children. Without that situation, Killewald found no fatherhood premium. Overall, motherhood carries status disadvantages, while fatherhood does not.

16.6 Status Interventions

Of course, several important status characteristics have been documented besides the ones just described. Here we turn to using the theoretical understandings to devise interventions to overcome effects of our society's status advantages and disadvantages. Effective interventions of three kinds have been developed. First are those that intervene in power and prestige aspects of interaction processes. Second are interventions that use Assumptions 3 and 4 on how status affects expectations. Third are interventions using task definition.

16.6.1 Interaction in Schools

Classrooms, at least for the first 12 grades, are task focused situations where teachers distribute action opportunities (such as asking "Who knows the answer to this question?"), students offer performance attempts (such as raising hands and answering), and teachers (and sometimes also other students) distribute unit evaluations ("Right" or "Wrong"). The unit evaluations lead to teachers and students forming performance expectations. Those performance expectations then affect future interaction, such as the likelihoods that a given child will offer a performance output, and that any future performance will receive a positive evaluation in class and on a grade sheet.

Entwisle and Webster (1978) conducted several experimental studies in classrooms in which they showed that giving children positive evaluations would indeed raise their self-expectations, and those raised expectations led to a change in behavior known to affect learning, participation rates.

Entwisle et al. (1997) studied effects of parents' expectations for their children. On the first day of first grade, the researchers asked parents to tell their most realistic expectations for their children's school performance. Parents' expectations were positively associated with desirable outcomes later—teachers' marks and standardized test scores—and were negatively associated with negative outcomes—bad conduct reports, being held back a year. Most impressively, those effects persisted through fifth grade. While parents' reported expectations probably are connected to many different ways that parents interact with their children, this research shows the importance of expectations in school settings.

16.6.2 Using Assumptions 3 and 4

Elizabeth G. Cohen and Rachel Lotan (1997) modified expectation effects by assigning roles. They selected children with a visible ethnic status disadvantage (Hispanic children in majority-Anglo classes), showed them how to make objects (e.g., a simple radio receiver) and then gave them the role of "teacher" to show other children, "learners," how to do it. This approach overcomes the ethnic status disadvantage and equalizes interaction by adding status advantages based on knowledge and role.

Lisa Walker et al. (2014) conducted laboratory studies of groups of three adult women, one African American and two white. In the control condition, without any experimental treatment, white women participated more in discussion and exerted greater influence over the group decision. In an experimental condition, a computer distributed action opportunities—telling each person when to participate—and raised the number of action opportunities given the African American women. This change in participation rates, simply inviting them to speak more often, equalized their influence over group decisions. This intervention is potentially quite useful, for it can occur unobtrusively and is at least partly under control of the interactants.

16.6.3 Task Definition

Status generalization works most powerfully in simple situations. Any sort of complexity is likely to increase variability and add additional sources of information to expectation formation. Another intervention developed by Cohen and Lotan (1997) and used with groups of children of different ethnicities, stressed task definition. These studies counteracted a common misconception among children (and some adults) that school ability is unitary; either one is good at school or one is not. But a more accurate representation is that school and most tasks in life require multiple abilities and that most of the time someone who is good at one part of the task is less skillful at other parts of the task. This is what Cohen and Lotan showed the students. They described a group task that required multiple abilities—defining the task, making suggestions, organizing ideas, synthesizing ideas to a useful action, implementation, evaluation, etc. They told children that success required many different abilities, and that it is reasonable to expect that some people will be good at one part, and others, at other parts. In technical terms, they defined the task as complex, not unitary. Thus expectations for each part of the task are likely to be different.

Among the questions for Cohen and Lotan was whether task complexity would lead students to conclude that, on average, each person is likely to contribute about the same to group success. They did. The task complexity instruction equalized interaction and influence among the children in mixed-ethnic groups.

Carla Goar and Jane Sell (2005) adapted the task complexity intervention for use among adults. They composed three-person groups of college women, one African American and two white, and asked them to develop a group decision. (This is the situation that Walker et al. (2014) later adapted for the interaction study described above.) In the control condition, status generalization created expectation advantages from race and the white women participated more and exerted greater influence. In the experimental condition, Goar and Sell's instructions emphasized the complexity of the group task, as Cohen and Lotan had done. Results were very similar. Goar and Sell succeeded in equalizing interaction and influence using this simple intervention.

In summary, the theory gives many ways to intervene in situations where it is desirable to affect status generalization processes. New ways suggested by the theory await implementation. Most of the intervention studies to date have aimed at reducing unwanted status generalization, such as that from gender or race/ethnicity. However there are other instances where one might wish to enhance effects of status generalization. For instance, if status accurately reflects task ability (as in a well-functioning bureaucracy such as a business organization or the military), and if prompt acceptance of influence is needed, it would be desirable to enhance status and interaction advantages. Interventions to strengthen status effects would use the same theoretical principles as interventions to lessen or overcome those effects, but of course with direction of the influence reversed.

16.7 Theoretical Extensions

Extensions build on a core theory to address new questions. In this section we consider two recent extensions that explain how descriptive terms can be transformed into diffuse status characteristics. Following those theories, we briefly describe other theoretical extensions, with references for additional information.

16.7.1 Creating Status Characteristics

If certain diffuse status characteristics, including gender and race, simply named groups without implying evaluative beliefs and ideas of abilities, many societal problems would disappear. Recall that whether a characteristic is a *status* characteristic depends on cultural beliefs and there is no inherent reason why any particular characteristic must carry those beliefs. But once the beliefs spread in a society, they can have profound consequences for interaction, social structure, and people's lives. Where did those beliefs come from? Two recent theoretical extensions explain ways in which an unevaluated nominal characteristic can acquire status beliefs making it into a diffuse status characteristic.

16.7.1.1 The Theory of Status Construction

In this theory, status construction proceeds from other types of inequality, particularly of possessions or other resources (Ridgeway 1991; Ridgeway and Erickson 2000). First, two (or more) groups may control different amounts of wealth and other status-valued objects. Suppose, for instance, that an observer notices that the group "male" controls more wealth or more social esteem than the group "female." If the difference between the groups is regular so that someone is more likely to encounter a rich male than a rich female, there is a tendency to reason that "there must be a reason for it." Then it is a short step to granting more social esteem and to inferring differential competence. This is the creation of status beliefs and attaching them to different states of the characteristic gender. For that observer, gender has become a status characteristic.

The second condition is interaction of the observer with members of the two groups; this will spread the beliefs among a society. Suppose the observer is male and encounters a woman who at this point does not hold any status beliefs for gender. The man, however, sees a status difference between them, and so he acts as a status superior towards her: he interacts at a high rate, tries to exert influence, etc. Since people tend to align their actions, the woman adopts complementary low status behaviors. If that happens repeatedly, she begins to associate low status with being female; interaction includes "training" for status beliefs. And of course a comparable process can train new men into status beliefs regarding gender.

16.7.1.2 The Theory of Spread of Status Value

A second mechanism is that status beliefs can spread from existing status characteristics to new, initially unevaluated characteristics (Berger and Fisek 2006). For instance, if new immigrants from Country X are low on education and occupational prestige, the low status value from those characteristics can spread to attach low status to the group of X-ers. Thus immigrants can acquire low status value. Comparable processes can spread positive status value to other groups. Experimental tests (Walker et al. 2011) confirmed that process. So we have two theories of how status characteristics get created: (1) through differences in possessions and interaction patterns, and (2) through spread of status value from established status characteristics. The two theories have minor differences in scope of applicability, and they also have much overlap.

Notice also that both theories predict ways that status value can decline or vanish. One way in both theories is inconsistency. If people encounter wealth and gender groups inconsistently linked—one is as likely to encounter a rich female as a rich male—then the conditions for creating and maintaining status beliefs no longer exist. Similarly, if people encounter immigrants from country X who have high education and high occupational status as often as the opposite case, then spread of status value will equal out and the ethnicity X will no longer carry status beliefs. And of course status value could be reversed by processes similar to the ones that create it. Status beliefs can be altered through deliberate intervention, using predictions derived from the theories. In addition, historical changes might well produce conditions for the decline of status value of certain characteristics. Equal opportunity programs and laws and regulations might break up the regular association of wealth and some characteristics. Changing status value of an existing characteristic will require overcoming existing status beliefs and then replacing them with beliefs in equality.

16.7.2 Other Extensions, Variants, and Elaborations

In addition to research programs on creating status characteristics, a number of different theories have been developed to address specific topics regarding social structures and interpersonal behavior. In this section we review five of these; Berger et al. (2014) describe several other developments related to theories of status processes.

All of these developments use the core concepts of expectation states and status characteristics that we have been working with, adding concepts and conditions to explain a much wider range of phenomena. Recall that we began this survey by noting the ubiquity of inequality in groups and group structures. These theories address different sorts of inequality and structural conditions, but it is easier to understand them by keeping in mind the overall concern with sources, forms, and consequences of inequality.

16.7.2.1 Double Standards

Martha Foschi and her collaborators (Foschi 1989, 1996, 2000; Foschi and Valenzuela 2015) have developed a longstanding research program on ways that double standards—demanding different performance levels—can affect inequality. In general terms, the theory explains when and how *interpretations* of performance levels can maintain existing status distinctions. Individuals having high status may be judged by more lenient standards than other individuals having low status. This can occur even among people showing the same objective performance levels. Standards are invoked to decide whether a particular performance level is "good enough;" that is, whether it meets the requirements for adequacy or excellence. The double standards process has greatest effect when the objective performance scores are intermediate; their operation is harder to see when objective performance is extremely high or extremely low.

A typical application of this theory is to hiring recommendations. Suppose that members of a hiring committee review folders of two candidates for a job. Both are recent college graduates and they have comparable GPAs in relevant courses—not outstanding grades, but above the threshold set for hiring. If the candidates differ on gender status (one is female and one is male), the status difference is sufficient to trigger the double standards process. The woman is judged by a more stringent standard and so the man is more likely to receive hiring recommendations. Foschi and her collaborators have conducted a large number of studies that repeatedly demonstrate the basic process, and also have studied additional processes, one of which we describe below, that affect double standards.

16.7.2.2 Race and Interaction

All of Foschi's work to date has studied gender status. Sharon Doerer (2013) studied the same processes, but with a different status characteristics, race. In Doerer's study, both job candidates were identified as male, but one was African American and the other was white. The same process took place; the white candidate was more often recommended for hiring, despite the equal qualifications of the two candidates.

Both Foschi and Doerer also studied the effect of responsibility, having to write justifications for the hiring recommendations. (In the basic studies, respondents only had to recommend a candidate, without explaining their choices.) Simply adding a requirement for responsibility greatly reduced the use of double standards, both for gender and for race. Why should that be the case? Because status processes operate below the level of conscious awareness. They alter specified types of behavior, but generally without awareness that is occurring, at least during the interaction situation. Having to justify hiring recommendations apparently focuses respondents more sharply on what they are doing and the job requirements. In other words, conscious processes—in this case, choosing the more qualified candidate—take over and the subconscious effects of double standards become less significant. Introducing a requirement of justification is a simple change in procedure, but one with important consequences.

16.7.3 Emotions, Sentiments, and Status Processes

Emotions are generally defined as temporary feeling states, subject to social conditions. They are only partly under one's control (e.g., it usually doesn't do much good to tell someone "Don't be angry.), and while an emotion exists it affects both thoughts and behavior.

A theoretical paper by Ridgeway and Johnson (1990) describes some effects of one's position in a group structure on emotions. Suppose two people, one in a high status position and the other in low status, disagree about something they both consider important. That is likely to generate different emotions for the two of them, such as anger and guilt or depression. The high status individual is more likely to attribute the emotion to the other person ("He is annoying me"), while the low status person is likely to attribute it to himself ("I may have done something wrong."). Besides the experience of emotion, the social structure also affects the likelihood of expressing it. Norms generally discourage expressing negative emotions and encourage expressing positive. However high status individuals are freer to express anger, and thus negative expressions tend to move downwards in the structure, while positive expressions tend to move upwards.

Despite popular beliefs about inherent differences between males and females in emotionality, most research shows a more complex relationship. Gender, of course, is a diffuse status characteristic, so in mixed-gender groups, it is a marker of status inequality. Two studies on emotions help fill in the picture of how gender and emotion interrelate. Simon and Nath (2004) analyzed a nationally representative sample of adults and found no difference in the frequency of experiencing emotion between men and women.

However status advantages (being male and/or earning more money) is associated with experiencing more positive emotions. For the often-studied emotion anger, again women and men experience it about equally often, though their ways of dealing with it differ. Women are more likely to talk about it with friends or co-workers and to pray, and men are more likely to mask it with alcohol and other psychoactive drugs. Overall, this study and many others (described in greater detail in Webster and Walker 2014) show the importance of social structures in generating emotions and in people's expression of them.

Sentiments, enduring positive and negative emotions, are extremely common in interpersonal situations. Do they affect expectations? For instance, if I dislike someone, does that lower my performance expectations for that person? Perhaps a more familiar case is positive sentiment. When a parent strongly loves a child, does that love bias the parent's view of how capable the child is? Casual observation in both instances might make it seem that sentiments do affect expectations, but some careful experimental studies disconfirm that. The relations of sentiment and status are a bit more complex than they might appear at first.

The first question, whether sentiments affect expectations, was addressed in a four-condition experiment by Driskell and Webster (1997). In condition 1 of the experiment they created a status difference, showing participants that their partners were highly skillful at the group task, and measured the partner's influence during interaction. As expected, influence of the highly skilled partner was quite high. In condition 2, they added dislike, showing participants that the partner disagreed with their values on several significant issues. That lowered the influence of the partner, which of course would also happen if expectations for the partner were lowered.

However, if liking and disliking are a separate process from status and expectations, then as the task becomes more important, the effect of liking will decrease. If sentiment affects expectations, task importance will have no effect. Conditions 3 and 4 of the experiment were comparable to conditions 1 and 2, but with payment added for task success to increase the value of good problem solution. With payment, effect of disliking was greatly reduced; participants attended mostly to expectations for the partner, as they did in condition 1. This experiment showed that sentiment is a separate social process from status and expectations. Bianchi (2004) replicated that experiment with better controls and results showed the same conclusion.

In discussion groups, sentiment has an indirect effect on expectations. Shelly (1993, 2001), Shelly and Webster (1997), and Lovaglia and Houser (1996) discovered how sentiment can indirectly affect expectations. Sentiment affects the interaction process in open interaction. For instance, liking someone can make us more likely to give that person action opportunities, leading to his or her greater participation. Also, liking makes us less likely to express negative unit evaluations even if we believe the person is wrong, and more likely to express any positive evaluations. That too will affect the target person's self-expectations, and of course those expectations will affect interaction process and the group's power and prestige structure.

Other elaborations apply ideas of status and expectations to understand *fairness*, how certain kinds of relations between individual characteristics and outcomes can come to seem fair. For instance, it is widely thought that it is "fair" for a college graduate to be paid more than a high school graduate, even for jobs that do not need abilities beyond those that a high school graduate has. The same process operates for undesirable outcomes: we form beliefs about how much punishment is "fair" for different sorts of crimes. These theories and some empirical tests are available in Berger et al. (1972), Webster (1984), and Webster and Smith (1978), among other places.

16.7.4 Creating Legitimate Authority Structures

Legitimation, the process by which a group inequality structure comes to be seen as right and proper, is crucial to authority structures in businesses and in the military. If the structure is seen as legitimate, authority is accepted, its members are satisfied, and the organization functions efficiently. Of course when authority is not seen as legitimate, significant problems follow. (Readers who are conversant with classical theory will recognize that a concern with how structures gain and lose legitimacy was a main concern for Max Weber. It is an enduring, highly important topic.) Status and legitimacy are dealt with in papers by Berger et al. (1998), Kalkhoff (2005), Ridgeway and Berger (1986), and others.

16.8 Summary

Task groups of all sorts, including discussion groups, juries, athletic teams, and work groups in organizations generate performance expectations or accept them from outside the group or from status generalization. Those expectations then determine most features of inequality in interaction and group structure. Understanding the sources and consequences of performance expectations is crucial for understanding how groups structure themselves and how individuals act in such groups.

Status generalization is a process of forming performance expectations, not from observations of performance, but rather from importing society's inequalities and thus allowing them to affect task group structures and interaction patterns. In many cases, but not all, status generalization can produce undesirable effects, such as: unfairly reducing a low status individual's chances to perform, depriving the group of contributions from low status but competent individuals, making less than optimal choices for leadership positions, and generally distributing power and prestige on basis other than merit.

In many other situations, status generalization produces desirable effects, augmenting the influence and authority of a leader who actually does possess high ability. Dangerous situations such as can occur during widespread fires or in the military, may require quick obedience to commands. When a group leader truly does have high competence, dangerous situations make quick following of orders important and even life preserving. Status generalization is neither good nor bad by itself; that depends on other features of situations in which it occurs. The important thing is to understand conditions under which it is likely to occur and its effects when it does.

In this entry we have reviewed status processes as related to some everyday characteristics. We also considered interventions, deliberately using theoretical knowledge about status processes to advance desirable outcomes. This research program has developed a great deal of information on the operation of expectation state and status processes in the past 50 years. There are currently more than a dozen research traditions under this large classification, and new theory and evidence are accumulating rapidly.

Taken as a whole, the theories in this chapter demonstrate powerful effects of small differences in face-to-face interaction in producing social inequality. Once characteristics have acquired status value, they serve to drive much of what happens when interactants work together on tasks. Many arenas of social life, from the criminal justice system to the classroom to the work team, illustrate the importance of having a clear theoretical understanding of the inequalities that occur in our day-to-day lives.

References

Andreas, H. (2013). Theoretical terms in science. In E. N. Zalta (Ed.), *The Stanford encyclopedia of philosophy* (Summer 2013 Edition). Palo Alto: Stanford University Press.

Bales, R. F. (1950). *Interaction process analysis*. Reading: Addison-Wesley.

Bales, R. F. (1999). *Social interaction systems: Theory and measurement*. New Brunswick: Transaction.

Bales, R. F., & Strodtbeck, F. (1951). Phases in group problem solving. *Journal of Abnormal and Social Psychology, 46*, 485–495.

Bales, R. F., Strodtbeck, F. L., Mills, T. M., & Roseborough, M. E. (1951). Channels of communication in small groups. *American Sociological Review, 16*, 461–468.

Balkwell, J. W. (2001). How do actors in task-oriented situations process finely graded differences in ability? *Sociological Focus, 34*, 97–115.

Berger, J. (1958). *Relations between performance, rewards, and action-opportunities in small groups*.

Unpublished doctoral dissertation, Harvard University, Boston.

Berger, J., & Hamit Fisek, M. (2006). Diffuse status characteristics and the spread of status value: A formal theory. *The American Journal of Sociology, 111*, 1038–1079.

Berger, J., Cohen, B. P., & Zelditch, M., Jr. (1972). Status characteristics and social interaction. *American Sociological Review*, 37, 241–255.

Berger, J., Norman, R. Z., Balkwell, J., & Smith, R. F. (1992). Status inconsistency in task situations: A test of four status processing principles. *American Sociological Review, 57*, 843–855.

Berger, J., Hamit Fisek, M., & Norman, R. Z. (1998). The legitimation and de-legitimation of power and prestige orders. *American Sociological Review, 63*, 379–405.

Berger, J., Wagner, D. G., & Webster, M., Jr. (2014). Expectation states theory: Growth, opportunities, and challenges. In S. R. Thye & E. J. Lawler (Eds.), *Advances in group processes* (Vol. 31, pp. 19–55). Bingley: Emerald Publishing.

Bianchi, A. J. (2004). Rejecting others' influence: Negative sentiment in task groups. *Sociological Perspectives, 47*, 339–355.

Cohen, E. G., & Lotan, R. (1997). *Working for equity in heterogeneous classrooms: Sociological theory in practice*. New York: Teachers College Press.

Correll, S. J., Benard, S., & Paik, I. (2007). Getting a job: Is there a motherhood penalty? *The American Journal of Sociology, 112*, 1297–1339.

Doerer, S. C. (2013). Double standards and selection. Unpublished doctoral Dissertation, University of North Carolina, Charlotte.

Driskell, J. E., & Webster, M., Jr. (1997). Status and sentiment in task groups. In J. Szmatka, J. Skvoretz, & J. Berger (Eds.), *Status, network, and organization* (pp. 179–200). Stanford: Stanford University Press.

Durkheim, E. (1893 [1933]). *The division of labor in society*. New York: Free Press of Glencoe.

Entwisle, D. R., & Webster, M., Jr. (1978). Raising expectations indirectly. *Social Forces, 57*, 257–264.

Entwisle, D. R., Alexander, K. L., & Olson, L. S. (1997). *Children, schools, & inequality*. Boulder: Westview.

Feller, T. (2010). What the literature tells us about the Jury Foreperson. *The Jury Expert, 22*, 42–51.

Foschi, M. (1989). Status characteristics, standards, and attributions. In B. Joseph, M. Zelditch Jr., & A. Bo (Eds.), *Sociological theories in progress: New formulations* (pp. 58–72). Newbury Park: Sage.

Foschi, M. (1996). Double standards in the evaluation of men and women. *Social Psychology Quarterly, 59*, 237–254.

Foschi, M. (2000). Double standards for competence: Theory and research. *Annual Review of Sociology, 26*, 21–42.

Foschi, M., & Valenzuela, J. (2015). Choosing between two semi-finalists: On academic performance gap, sex category, and decision question. *Social Science Research, 54*, 195–208.

Frevert, T. K., & Walker, L. S. (2014). Physical attractiveness and social status. *Sociology Compass, 8*, 313–323.

Goar, C., & Sell, J. (2005). Using task definition to modify racial inequality within task groups. *The Sociological Quarterly, 46*, 525–543.

Goffman, E. (1959). *The presentation of self in everyday interaction*. New York: Anchor Books. rev. ed.

Goffman, E. (1970). *Strategic interaction*. Oxford: Blackwell.

Kalkhoff, W. (2005). Collective validation in multi-actor task groups. *Social Psychology Quarterly, 68*, 57–74.

Killewald, A. (2013). A reconsideration of the fatherhood premium: Marriage, coresidence, biology, and Fathers' wages. *American Sociological Review, 78*, 96–118.

Landy, D., & Sigall, H. (1974). Beauty is talent: Task evaluation as a function of the performer's physical attractiveness. *Journal of Personality and Social Psychology, 29*, 299–304.

Lovaglia, M. J., & Houser, J. (1996). Emotional reactions and status in groups. *American Sociological Review, 61*, 867–883.

Parsons, T. (1937). *The structure of social action*. New York: McGraw-Hill.

Parsons, T. (1951). *The social system*. New York: Free Press.

Parsons, T., Bales, R. F., & Shils, E. A. (1953). *Working papers in the theory of action*. Glencoe: Free Press.

Perrin, F. A. C. (1921). Physical attractiveness and repulsiveness. *Journal of Experimental Psychology, 4*, 203–217.

Ridgeway, C. L. (1987). Nonverbal behavior, dominance, and status in task groups. *American Sociological Review, 52*, 683–694.

Ridgeway, C. L. (1991). The social construction of status value: Gender and other nominal characteristics. *Social Forces, 70*, 367–386.

Ridgeway, C. L., & Balkwell, J. W. (1997). Group processes and the diffusion of status beliefs. *Social Psychology Quarterly, 60*, 14–31.

Ridgeway, C. L., & Berger, J. (1986). Expectations, legitimation, and dominance behavior in task groups. *American Sociological Review, 51*, 603–617.

Ridgeway, C. L., & Correll, S. (2004). Motherhood as a status characteristic. *Journal of Social Issues, 60*, 683–700.

Ridgeway, C. L., & Diekema, D. (1989). Dominance and collective hierarchy formation in male and female task groups. *American Sociological Review, 54*, 79–93.

Ridgeway, C. L., & Erickson, K. G. (2000). Creating and spreading status beliefs. *The American Journal of Sociology, 106*, 579–615.

Ridgeway, C. L., & Johnson, C. (1990). What is the relationship between socioemotional behavior and status in task groups? *The American Journal of Sociology, 95*, 1189–1212.

Ritts, V., Patterson, M. L., & Tubbs, M. E. (1992). Expectations, impressions, and judgments of physically attractive students: A review. *Review of Educational Research, 62*, 413–426.

Shelly, R. K. (1993). How sentiments organize interaction. In E. J. Lawler (Ed.), *Advances in group processes* (pp. 113–132). Greenwich: JAI Press.

Shelly, R. K. (2001). How performance expectations arise from sentiments. *Social Psychology Quarterly, 64*, 72–87.

Shelly, R. K., & Webster, M., Jr. (1997). How formal status, liking, and ability status structure interaction: Three theoretical principles and a test. *Sociological Perspectives, 40*, 81–107.

Sigall, H., & Ostrove, N. (1975). Beautiful but dangerous: Effects of offender attractiveness and nature of the crime on juridic judgment. *Journal of Personality and Social Psychology, 31*, 410–414.

Simmel, G. (1908 [1950]). The secret and the secret society. In (trans: Wolff, K. H.), *The sociology of Georg Simmel* (pp. 305–376). Glencoe: The Free Press.

Simon, R. W., & Nath, L. E. (2004). Gender and emotion in the United States: Do men and women differ in self-reports of feelings and expressive behavior? *The American Journal of Sociology, 109*, 1137–1176.

Veblen, T. (1953 [1899]). *The theory of the leisure class: An economic study of institutions* (Rev. ed). New American Library.

Walker, L. S., Webster, M., Jr., & Bianchi, A. J. (2011). Testing the spread of status value theory. *Social Science Research, 40*, 1652–1663.

Walker, L. S., Doerer, S. C., & Webster, M., Jr. (2014). Status, participation, and influence in task groups. *Sociological Perspectives, 57*, 364–381.

Webster, M., Jr. (1984). Social structures and the sense of justice. In E. J. Lawler & S. Bachrach (Eds.), *Research in the sociology of organizations* (Vol. 3, pp. 59–94). Greenwich: JAI Press.

Webster, M., Jr., & Smith, R. F. (1978). Justice and revolutionary coalitions: A test of two theories. *The American Journal of Sociology, 84*, 267–292.

Webster, M., Jr., & Driskell, J. E. (1983). Beauty as status. *The American Journal of Sociology, 89*, 140–165.

Webster, M., Jr., & Walker, L. S. (2014). Emotions in expectation states theory. In J. E. Stets & J. H. Turner (Eds.), *Handbook of the sociology of emotions* (Vol. 2, pp. 127–153). New York/London/Heidelberg: Springer Dordrecht.

Yuchtman-Yaar, E., & Semyonov, M. (1979). Ethnic inequality in Israeli schools and sports: an expectation states approach. *The American Journal of Sociology, 85*, 576–590.

The Self

17

Alicia D. Cast and Jan E. Stets

17.1 Introduction

The concept of *self* is ubiquitous; it has been written about in a variety of disciplines such as philosophy, sociology, psychology, and political science. Clearly, the self has utility for understanding questions about the human experience. Unfortunately, given its ubiquity, conceptual confusion emerges on what is the self (Schwalbe 1988). A discussion that would cover how the self is viewed from different areas would be a difficult undertaking. Our approach is simply an overview of the theoretical and empirical research on the self from a sociological perspective.

After introducing current sociological conceptions of the self, we organize the remaining chapter into three major areas: *Self in Interaction*, *Self in Groups and Social Categories*, and *Self in Society and Cross-Culturally*. These three areas have a close affinity to understanding all sociological processes at the micro, meso, and macro levels (Turner 2010a, b, 2012).

A.D. Cast (✉)
Department of Sociology, University of California, Santa Barbara, Santa Barbara, CA, USA
e-mail: acast@soc.ucsb.edu

J.E. Stets
Department of Sociology, University of California, Riverside, Riverside, CA, USA
e-mail: jan.stets@ucr.edu

Self in Interaction conceptualizes the micro realm as involving the encounter or interaction between individuals (Turner 2010b). The focus is on the positions that persons occupy in the situation, and the role-related behaviors associated with those positions. Included in this level of analysis are the presentation strategies that individuals employ to manage their own and others' identities. In this section, we also discuss the identity verification process, which is a major way that people obtain support in interaction.

Self in Groups and Social Categories focuses on the self at the meso level, which is comprised of corporate and categoric units (Turner 2012). The corporate unit reflects individuals' embeddedness in proximal groups of varying sizes and organizational structures such as work organizations, schools, and families. The categoric unit is a social distinction that places individuals into distinct social categories as in being a member of a particular gender, race, class, and sexual orientation. Given individuals' involvement in corporate groups and their membership in particular categorical units within those groups, a distinct set of experiences emerges for the self. For instance, membership as a woman (in the gender category) will influence her experiences within particular (corporate) groups such as the family or work, and these experiences will differ from those whose categoric membership is a man. Because of space limitations, we will organize our discussion around categoric units (gender, race, and class), but we

S. Abrutyn (ed.), *Handbook of Contemporary Sociological Theory*,
Handbooks of Sociology and Social Research, DOI 10.1007/978-3-319-32250-6_17

will highlight the way that categoric units influence the self through corporate groups.

Self in Society and Cross-Culturally discusses the self at the macro level by examining how the organization of society facilitates the development of particular selves, beginning with the distinction between *institutional* and *impulsive* selves (Turner 1976). The distinction between one's real self as having an institutional locus (the real self is revealed in adherence to normative standards and is in control of his/her behaviors) or impulsive locus (the real self is something to be discovered and is revealed when inhibitions are lowered) has facilitated an analysis of the role of modernity in theorizing about the self. We briefly will discuss how modernity has influenced conceptualizations of self.

More generally, society and culture help construct particular kinds of selves, and cross-cultural research reveals this. Indeed, in Western societies, the self is defined as more independent and autonomous while in Eastern societies, it is defined as more interdependent and relational (Markus and Kitayama 1991). Thus, we discuss the different self-orientations that have appeared in cross-cultural work. Finally, we identify how a society's particular morals and values shape the self. Here we address emerging research on the moral identity (Stets and Carter 2012).

We conclude the chapter with some thoughts about future directions in the study of the self from the micro, meso, and macro levels. At the micro level, an area that has been garnering attention is the self in neuroscience. Early neuroscientists (Damasio 1994; LeDoux 1996) created a good foundation in which sociological social psychologists are now thinking about the self (Franks 2010). At the meso level, there is a growing interest in investigating how the self is experienced differently when individuals stand at the intersection of different groups in society. The way in which a white, middle class, heterosexual man experiences his work or home life is likely to be very different from a nonwhite, lower class, lesbian woman. At the macro level, we see globalization as impacting the self as reflected in wider social networks and increasing exposure to different cultures.

17.2 Conceptualizing the Self

17.2.1 The Early Thinkers

William James (1890) is credited as the first person who provided a serious treatment on the self. He conceptualized the self as the sum total of all that individuals could lay claim to or call their own. He discussed four kinds of self: the *material self*, the *spiritual self*, the *social self*, and the *pure ego*. His social self has been central to the development of contemporary symbolic interactionism (Stryker 2002 [1980]). Through his analysis of the social self, we learn that individuals are complex, having as many social selves as there are individuals who recognize them and carry an image of them in their heads. For instance, an individual might be known to her children as "mom," to her husband as "wife," to her peers as "friend," and to her employees as "boss." Each image has a set of meanings and expectations that individuals internalize, and which guide their behavior. Thus, the self is located in the minds of others, and among the multiple selves that exist, each reflects a different image others have of the self.

Not long after James's seminal work, Charles Horton Cooley (1902) extended James' ideas on the social self in his now classic *looking glass self*. As in a mirror, people see themselves, but they also see the reactions of others reflected back to themselves. As Cooley indicated, individuals imagine how they appear to others, they imagine how others judge that appearance of them, and they have an emotional reaction to that judgment that is either positive, in form of pride, or negative, in the form of shame.[1] A person might think that others see her as intelligent, she might think that others will judge intelligence as good or positive given that being intelligent is valued in our society, and she will feel proud as a result.

[1]Our reflection as to the reactions others' have to us, in contemporary terms, are called *reflected appraisals*. Reflected appraisals or how we *think* others see us is one of the main ways we come to understand who we are in identity theory (Burke and Stets 2009).

Like Cooley, George Herbert Mead emphasized the social self, underscoring the intimate connection because self and society in a series of lectures that were eventually published in *Mind, Self, and Society* (Mead 1934). Similarly to Cooley, Mead envisioned the self as a product of society. As Cooley conceptualized individuals' views of themselves as a series of imaginations about how individuals believed others saw them, Mead saw the social self as derived from individuals getting outside of themselves and taking the standpoint or role of the other and seeing who they were through the lens of others. Through repetition and over time, individuals would come to share others' understanding as to who they were, they would anticipate the reactions of others to their actions, and the meaning of the self would become a shared meaning.

For Mead, the social self was revealed when individuals engaged in *reflexivity*. Indeed, reflexivity is the hallmark of selfhood; humans have the ability to reflect back on themselves and take themselves as an object. Reflexivity, selfhood, and the development of a social self is seen in Mead's classic discussion of the internal conversation between the *I* and the *Me* that emerges within individuals and in and across situations.

The *I* is the self-as-subject. It is the self that initiates action in a situation to bring about a particular outcome. It represents that part of the self that is responsible for agency and creativity. The *Me* is the self-as-object. It is the self that looks at the action (of the *I*), the environment, and the relationship between the two in order to guide the *I* to its intended outcome. The *Me* also contains the views of society or culture or what Mead labeled the *generalized other*. The *Me* acquires this perspective through the process of role-taking where individuals attempt to perceive the situation from the view of others. Thus, the *Me* is the self that is social because it embodies the perceptions and understandings from the standpoint of others. However, the *Me* is also individual because it attempts to help the *I* satisfy its goal. In this way, the *Me* is reflexive because it is able to take the self into account that is distinct from others, while at the same time it locates the self in a community of others.

Aside from developing the social aspect of the self, Mead also develops the cognitive aspect of the self. In Cooley's looking-glass self, we see how thinking about how others see oneself influences the way the person feels. But Mead is more explicit about minded activity. In *Mind, Self, and Society*, he opens with a discussion of the mind. For Mead, the self originates in the mind of individuals. The mind develops and arises out of social interaction. Mentality comes when individuals are able to point out to themselves and to others objects in situations and the meanings associated with those objects. These meanings are communicated through signs and symbols (language). Identifying these meanings gives humans some control in the situation and allows for the coordination of activity.

To the extent that the self is an object like any other object that humans point out in situations, individuals attempt to control the meanings that are associated with who they are in order to sustain themselves. The control of self-meanings is social: how individuals see themselves comes from the standpoint of others. Individuals respond to themselves as others would respond to them, the meanings of the self are shared, and there is a merger of perspectives of the self and others becoming one.

17.2.2 Contemporary Thinkers

Over time, as individuals point out who they are to themselves and to others, they come to develop an understanding of who they are; this is their *self-concept*. The self-concept is the sum total of individuals' thoughts, feelings, and imaginations on themselves (Rosenberg 1979). Following Mead's approach to understanding the self in terms of the mind, researchers during the twentieth century expanded on the cognitive aspect of the self by studying the content and the structure of the self, that is, one's self-concept. The content of the self is understood as having cognitive components such as one's identities and emotional components such as one's self-esteem.

The cognitive component of one's *identity* refers to the set of meanings about the self that defines him/her as a particular kind of person (person identities), as a role occupant (role identities), or as a member of a group/category (group/social identities) (Burke and Stets 2009). Meanings are individuals' responses when then reflect upon themselves in a person, role, or group/social identity. More specifically, they are the way people describe or characterize themselves in an identity. For instance, one may have the meaning of being "caring" when she thinks of how moral she is, "hardworking" when she thinks of herself as a student, and "cooperative" when she thinks of herself as a member of her neighborhood watch group. Caring, hardworking, and cooperative, help define her in her moral person identity, student role identity, and neighborhood group identity, respectively.

Identities guide one's behavior in interaction. Looked at another way, individuals should behave in ways consistent, in meaning, with the meanings in their identities. Thus, if a person saw herself as hardworking in the student role identity, then we could expect that in the student role, she would be highly motivated to attend her classes, participate in class discussion, do her homework, and take her exams. In this way, people's behavior is a window into the self-meanings tied to their identities.

The emotional component of *self-esteem* is the degree to which individuals evaluate themselves in positive or negative terms. Individuals are taking themselves as an object and reflecting upon who they are in evaluative terms of goodness or badness. Self-esteem can be traced back to the early writing of James (1890) who understood it to be a function of achievements as well as aspirations as expressed in the formula: self-esteem = successes/pretensions. How individuals feel about themselves is the result of their accomplishments (successes) relative to their goals (pretensions). Thus, individuals could have low self-esteem even if their accomplishments were high because their goals could be higher. Alternatively, persons could have high self-esteem if their successes were modest and their goals were even more modest.

Contemporary thinkers have had a tendency to see self-esteem in terms of self-worth, that is, the degree to which individuals feel that they are valued, accepted, and respected (Rosenberg et al. 1995). However, recently, it is argued that there may be two other components of self-esteem: being efficacious and being authentic (Stets and Burke 2014b). We will have more to say about this later.

17.2.3 Self as Cognitive and Emotional

Historically, the cognitive and emotional aspects of the self were seen as opposing forces with cognition synonymous with rationality and emotion synonymous with irrationality (Turner and Stets 2005). Cooley more than Mead incorporated emotions into his analysis of the self in social interaction given his looking glass self and individuals' emotional reactions of pride or mortification to how they thought others evaluated them. Mead did not ignore emotions altogether, but he was less interested in the emotion, itself, and he was more interested in the display of emotions such as moving one's top lip upward to show disgust or shedding tears to show sadness or grief (Ward and Throop 1992). What was important was that the emotional display called forth a response in others, operating as a social cue. The display of disgust would cue to others to stay away from whatever was the object of the person's attention; the tears might signal that the person needed comfort thereby activating social support from others.

It wasn't until the latter part of the twentieth century that the self as an emotional entity became the focus of attention for sociological research (Turner and Stets 2005). We now have a wide array of theories that help us understand why and when individuals will experience particular emotions. We know that the culture influences whether these emotions will be expressed, or whether individuals will engage in emotion management. And, we know that one's position in the status structure encourages the expression of some emotions over others.

Advances in neuroscience have made it clear that cognition and emotion should no longer be seen as polar opposites. The early work of Damasio (1994) was critical in showing the intimate connection between emotions and reason. He revealed how, when the cortical region of the brain (where cognitive functioning occurs) is disconnected from the subcortical region of the brain (where emotions are located), individuals have difficulty making good decisions; in fact, their decisions are irrational. Emotions serve as an important guide for choosing between alternatives, and the choices that are made have consequences for the emotions that are experienced. Today, the cognitive and emotional aspects of the self are seen as inextricably connected.

17.2.4 Self and Social Structure

A hallmark of a sociological approach to the self is to recognize that self and society mutually influence each other (Stryker 2002 [1980]). Society creates opportunities for the development and organization of the self, and it provides a set of meanings through language that allows for the self to interact with others. In turn, when individuals interact in groups and within institutions using shared meanings, they recreate the very social structures that are represented by those meanings. Thus, social structure arises from the actions of individuals. However, because of the reflexive nature of the self, there is always the potential for creativity and a change to the social structure.

Recognizing the influence of the self on society and society on the self is expressed in the idea that the self is a *social force* as well as a *social product* (Rosenberg 1981). As a social force, the self can be seen as motivated to bring about particular outcomes or accomplish specific goals. Action is intentional, monitored, and regulated with the commitment to bring about one's goals despite disturbances in the environment. If one's goals are consistent with structural arrangements, they reinforce not only the person, but also the interaction within which the action emerged, and the structure within which the interaction is embedded. If the goals are in opposition to social structural arrangements, interaction may become disrupted and destabilize existing structures.

As a social product, the self is shaped by the social structure through interactions with others. This begins at birth and continues throughout the life cycle. While social structures impose constraints on individuals in terms of their actions, it also provides resources and opportunity structures for the self. For example, while we see the intergenerational transmission of class position, the unexpected also occurs as when we witness upwardly mobile actors. Considering the influence of the social structure makes one aware that a person's outcomes are not completely orchestrated by his/her own or even others' actions. Structural arrangements persist according to their own principles and intrude into interaction, constraining the actions of individuals. Indeed, every situation has an implicit status hierarchy, a distribution of resources, and a set of norms that shape and guide interaction, and this may constrain what individuals can accomplish.

Another way to conceptualize the self and society interplay is to view the self as embedded in social networks (Stryker 2002 [1980]). Embeddedness both reflects the number of social ties within a network (referred to as extensive commitment) and the emotional ties to the network (referred to as affective commitment). Therefore, we can think of a social network as embedding individuals in a circle of others to whom one feels connected. Access to particular networks is based on people's positions in the social structure and the roles they enact, with ties to others based on self and others enacting the same roles. A student, for instance, will be more likely to have a network of others comprised of students than non-students. When people's ties to others depend upon them enacting a particular identity, then that identity will be salient to them. Increasing commitment to that identity is based on being emotionally close to others in the social network based on that identity and having a large compared to small social network that is based on that identity. The greater the commitment to an identity, the higher the salience of the identity (Stryker and Serpe 1982). Thus, we see how the self is understood in terms of its embeddedness in the social structure.

Recently, researchers have gone beyond the role of social networks in characterizing the social structure, and they have differentiated large, intermediate, and proximate social structures (Stryker et al. 2005). Large social structures reflect the stratification system along such lines as race, class, and gender. Ties to the social structure along these lines provide individuals with different social identities that reflect their membership in these groups. Intermediate social structures are more local networks such as an organization or neighborhood that provides social boundaries for the probability of particular social relationships forming. Proximate social structures are those associations and interactions that are more personal to individuals such as ties to one's family, one's school, or one's immediate department in an organization (Serpe and Stryker 2011; Stryker et al. 2005). In proximate social structures, role identities and person identities have the opportunity to be developed. Taken together, social structures both influence and constrain the development of a particular kind of self and the corresponding identities associated with it.

17.3 Self in Interaction

When we think about the self in interaction, we cannot think of the whole person communicating with others, but only a part of the self, depending upon what *position* the person is occupying in the situation, the corresponding *role* (behavioral expectations) associated with the position that is played out, and the *identity* attached to the role (the meanings associated with who one is in that role). An illustration of this might be if a person occupies the position of professor in a classroom. There are cultural expectations attached to this position such as lecturing, answering questions from students, testing students' knowledge, and rendering an evaluation on their performance. What lies behind these behaviors are the meanings about who one is when these actions are performed. This is the professor identity. The professor identity may carry meanings of being intelligent and critical, and these meanings will correspond to the meanings that are "given off" when the professor lectures, answers students' queries, and provides grades at the end of the term. Corresponding to the professor is a counter-position, counter-role, and counter-identity to which the professor is related and that characterizes another person in the situation. This counter-position would be student, the role expectations might include listening attentively, taking notes, asking questions, and taking exams, and the identity meanings implied by the role expectations and that may be associated with the student identity may include being logical, hard-working, and curious.

Notice that in the above illustration, what gets activated for each set of actors is only one aspect of who they are (either professor or student). Clearly a professor has other positions/roles/identities that could be claimed such as friend, spouse, and or parent. Similarly, the student has other aspects that characterize who s/he is such as son/daughter, boyfriend/girlfriend, and/or worker. Each person in the situation does not have immediate access to all other aspects of another in the situation, but one does not have to have access to know that these other aspects exist.

17.3.1 Role-Taking

What makes for successful interaction among actors is taking the role of the other or seeing a situation from the other's vantage point. This process is an extension of what occurs in the development of the self. Over time, who we come to be is influenced by taking the role of significant others such as family and friends in situations, envisioning how they see us, and using that as a guide for how we see ourselves and how we behave (Kinch 1963; Mead 1934; Schwalbe 1988; Turner 1962). Looked at another way, role-taking is the appraisals of others that are reflected back on us, and that influence how we see ourselves and how we behave.

Role-taking may be conceptualized along the dimensions of accuracy, range, and depth (Schwalbe 1988). Accuracy is correctly identifying how another sees oneself. More sensitive individuals may be better at accurately reading the views of others than less sensitive persons. Range is the degree to which one can identify various different views on oneself. Those who have contact with a diverse set of others may be exposed to more varying views of oneself. Depth is how much one can see the full range or total view that another has on oneself. More intimate, long-term relationships reveal a more in-depth view as to how another sees oneself.

Individuals are born with the capacity to role-take, and it develops over time through their interactions with others (Mead 1934). Mead's distinction between the *play* and *game* stage is an account of how individuals develop this ability. The initial development occurs through children acting out the role of specific actors that they encounter such as "mom," "the store cashier," "the mail carrier," and "the daycare teacher." While the child role-takes the position of specific others, the child has not yet developed an understanding that these specific others have others who they relate to in the form of counter-roles such as the store cashier responding to the requests of the store manager. The child also does not understand that these specific others occupy several other positions within society; mom might also be a doctor at the hospital, and a friend to another.

It is not until children enter team sports, Mead's game stage, that children learn about roles and counter-roles, and how individuals take on the perspective of several other viewpoints simultaneously when they act. In the same way that a pitcher on a baseball team plays his/her position effectively by coordinating his/her actions with all other players in the infield and outfield, children come to learn how roles in society are related to counter-roles, and how goals are reached through cooperation. Through repetitive involvement in organized activities, children learn that organized groups expect certain things of them. When children take these expectations into account in team sports, they are rehearsing taking the role of the generalized other or imagining what they think society demands of them when they act. As children age, they increasingly take the role of the generalized other, internalizing the expectations of society. This helps them abide by the norms of society.

Some have suggested that rather than individuals taking the perspective of society at large when acting, they take into account the views of significant others such as family and friends (Rosenberg 1990) or reference groups (Shibutani 1955). Therefore, individuals are likely to have a sense not only of what the members of society at large expect but also what specific individuals expect. More generally, the ability to take the role of the other is what makes a biological being into a truly social being. By individuals taking the views of others into account when they act, coordinated activity is possible. Without the ability to anticipate the reactions of others, actors are unable to fit their actions to the actions of others. It is what makes group life possible.

Role-taking would appear to be inherently conformist given that individuals adopt the perspective of others and behave accordingly. However, individuals also role-make in interaction (Turner 1962). They not only imagine the perspective of others and take that into account, but they also creatively construct their own role given their goals. A conception of interaction as having a certain amount of role-taking and role-making means that individuals both conform to others' expectations as well as create some of their own expectations.

Some have questioned how central role-taking is for self-development since individuals' self-concept is not highly correlated with how others actually see them. Instead, the self-concept appears to be filtered through perceptions and resembles how people *think* that others see them (Shrauger and Schoeneman 1979). Thus, individuals may not be very accurate in judging what others think of them. This inaccuracy may be partly due to others being reticent in revealing their views, or if they reveal their views, they may reveal primarily favorable views rather than both favorable and unfavorable views (Felson 1993).

When sociologists have empirically investigated role-taking in interaction, they have studied how one's membership in the stratification system influences who is more likely to shape their view of themselves and who is more likely to role-take. We find, for example, that in newly married couples, spouses with higher status (more education, a higher occupation, and more income) in the marriage are more likely to not only influence their partner's self-views but also the partner's views of these higher status spouses (Cast et al. 1999). Lower status spouses have less influence on the self-views' of their higher status counterparts, or on how their higher status counterparts view them.

Those of lower status appear to role-take more than those of higher status (Thomas et al. 1972). Powerful, higher status individuals, given their greater influence, may see no reason to be sensitive to others' views in a situation and take those views into account. Their structurally advantaged position is enough to maintain control over others. Alternatively, given the structurally disadvantaged position of less powerful individuals, role-taking is a way to meet the needs of the more powerful. Research reveals that women are more likely to role-take and role-take more accurately (Love and Davis 2014). However, since women have lower status in society, gender is confounded with status. When the two are disentangled, we find that status rather than gender predicts role-taking accuracy (Love and Davis 2014).

17.3.2 Self-Presentation

Self-presentation refers to a set of activities people use to control an image as to who they are in the eyes of others. While self-presentation often evokes the image of people conveying a positive view that advantages them in terms of obtaining power, wealth, friends, and/or self-esteem, self-presentation may also involve an image that accurately or authentically represents them (Schlenker 2012). These different goals are analogous to the different self-motives that underlie human behavior. Either people want to be seen favorably, or they want to be seen in ways that are consistent with how they see themselves. From the former has developed self-enhancement theory; from the latter has developed self-verification theory (Kwang and Swann 2010).

Self-presentation is a central process within Goffman's dramaturgical approach (Goffman 1959). Using the analogy of a theater's front and back stage, self-presentations are carried out in the front region or "on stage," and individuals may employ a variety of behaviors, props, words, and gestures to convey a particular person in the situation. The back region or "off stage" is largely inaccessible to audience members, so individuals can behave in ways that contradict front stage performances.

Performances must be believable otherwise they risk being negatively sanctioned (Goffman 1959). While people may exaggerate their abilities or accomplishments, this is more likely to occur if their claims cannot be verified. When their claims can be verified, and if negative information is revealed as to who they are, they may exaggerate abilities or accomplishments on dimensions that reflect more positively about themselves (Schlenker 2012). Sometimes, individuals may discredit their own self-presentations as when they fail to show evidence of a skill they claim to have. Embarrassment is experienced, which is the uncomfortable feeling of being exposed (Goffman 1959). To restore face, one may apologize or provide an excuse. If that is ineffective, audience members may help to restore a person's face by ignoring the misstep or providing an account that the person had not offered.

The proliferation of social media communication such as Facebook and Twitter provides new venues for self-presentation. While some people tend to create a self-image that is positive and flattering online, it could be discredited to the extent that viewers see these self-images as contradicting offline performances. Others, however, seek to present an authentic view as to who they are. Interestingly, psychological well-being both predicts authentic self-presentations on social media, and well-being is enhanced when one is authentic. However, this is especially the case when it is a positive authentic self-presentation or people present a positive but honest view of themselves (Reinecke and Trepte 2014). The positivity norm of social media thus creates some tension between the motive to verify the self and the motive to enhance the self.

The front and back stage regions of social media are somewhat different than Goffman's stage metaphor where individuals are directly communicating with their audience. In one sense, the front stage in social media is akin to the performances given off when television captures a person's performance, or when film follows one's daily activities such as a reality show. The viewer can return to this performance by revisiting the archive, or in social media, return to the original posting. The presenter does not see the audience, and the audience can be broad in scope. And, because as discussed earlier, individuals have as many social selves as there are individuals who recognize them and carry an image of them in their heads, a self-presentation may confirm one social self but disconfirm another social self because the social networks that were ordinarily distinct in interaction now overlap.

But, there are some differences between the self that is presented in interaction or in television and the self that is presented over social media. The self-presentations over social media may be frequent as one posts daily accounts of experiences and events. Others may help in a person's presentation as they post to a person's site through "tagged" information. Audience members can provide feedback on a person's presentation through text and images of their own, which can be easily transmitted to other audience members. And, that feedback can be immediate, or it can be delayed. Such audience involvement suggests that they have a closer hand in the creation of a person's self-presentation than is ordinarily the case in other communication channels.

The back stage region of social media involves the preparation of content that eventually gets posted over social media (the front stage region) such as carefully composing one's thoughts, crafting status updates, and fine-tuning photos for one's audience (Davis 2016). This careful crafting of one's self-image reduces the likelihood of a faux pas emerging and creating embarrassment, although embarrassment can arise when one's social network members present images on oneself that were not authorized for viewing.

More generally, as communication with others increasingly becomes digitally mediated, researchers need to examine how social actors' performances take a new form so that they can continue to be positively viewed and verified. People are networked in ways they have never been before, and the overlapping networks create challenges to successful self-presentations to diverse networks. As the self becomes connected to more and more individuals and groups, there is an increasing number of people to whom the self is held accountable for successful self-presentations (Gergen 1991).

17.3.3 Identity Verification

Aside from role-taking and self-presentation, identity verification is a third process in interaction that we want to highlight. Identity verification occurs when individuals perceive that others in an interaction see them in the same way that they see themselves (Burke and Stets 2009). Essentially, people observe the feedback that they receive from others, and they interpret this feedback in terms of how they *think* that others see them.

More specifically, individuals enter an interaction with self-meanings, that is, characterizations or descriptions as to who they are, for example, "I am caring and fair," "I am strong-willed and confident," or "I am competitive and unemotional" that are associated with the different identities that they claim. These self-meanings comprise the *identity standard* for each of their identities: "caring and fair" may be the identity standard for the moral identity, "strong-willed and confident" may be the standard for the control identity, and "competitive and unemotional" may be the standard for the gender identity. A particular set of identity meanings gets activated in a situation to the extent that the identity meanings are aligned with the meanings in the situation, making the identity *relevant* in the situation

(Stets and Burke 2014a; Stets and Carter 2012). It is this relevant identity that is important in the identity verification process. For instance, if the meanings in the situation call forth moral behavior such as helping an elderly person cross an intersection, the moral identity (as opposed to some other identity such as the identity of "artist" or "golfer") will be activated to guide the prosocial act. If the person thinks that given her helpful act, others see her as moral in a way that matches her self-view as a moral person, identity verification has occurred.

While situational meanings can "activate" a particular identity that corresponds to the situational meanings, it is also possible for people to call up or activate a salient identity regardless of situational meanings. Here, the individual would construct a set of meanings in the situation that would correspond to the meanings in the salient identity. If the parent identity, for example, is particularly salient for individuals, they may call up this identity at work and construct meanings that correspond to it such as talking about their children to their co-workers, showing pictures of their children, texting their children at work, and bringing their children to work. Identity verification of the parent identity would occur to the extent that co-workers evaluate the person in the parent identity in the same way that the individual evaluates herself in this identity with all of this taking place in the workplace rather than the home setting.

The outcome of identity verification is positive feelings for the individual (Burke and Harrod 2005; Stets and Burke 2014a; Stets and Carter 2011, 2012; Stets and Harrod 2004). Individuals feel good when they experience identity verification because it helps foster the view that their world is predictable and controllable. It also provides a feeling of support: that others know who one is. These positive feelings may be revealed in positive emotions such as happiness or positive self-evaluations such as increased self-esteem.

Recent research theorizes and finds that the verification of different bases of identities (*group/social*, *role*, and *person identities*) influence different self-esteem outcomes (*self-worth*, *self-efficacy*, and *authenticity*, respectively) (Burke and Stets 2009; Stets and Burke 2014b). While group identities are the self-meanings that emerge in interaction with a specific set of others such as family or work group, social identities are the meanings associated with an individual's identification with a social category such as one's gender, race, or social class. When individual's group and social identities are verified, they experience a sense of social belongingness and integration including being accepted and valued. This is the self-worth dimension of self-esteem.

Role identities are the self-meanings associated with a role that individuals play out such as the role of student, worker, friend, or spouse. The roles require specific performances that should be consistent with one's role identity meanings. As an illustration, if one perceives another playing out the role of friend by routinely coming to the aid of friends when they are upset or need financial help, we might assume that for this person, the friend identity involves self-meanings of being "reliable" and "supportive." Enacting performances in accordance with one's role identity is about agency and accomplishing one's goals. Thus, when people experience verification of role identity, it increases feelings of self-efficacy, a second dimension of self-esteem.

Finally, person identities are the meanings that individuals attribute to themselves as unique individuals that set them apart from others. These self-meanings may be core to the individual and include one's values (Hitlin 2003) or morals (Stets and Carter 2012), but they also include characterizations of individuals such as the degree to which they are controlling (Stets 1995) or outgoing (Stets and Cast 2007). Since the person identity identifies what is central to the person, when person identities are verified, people should see that their "real" self is being affirmed. This is the authenticity dimension of self-esteem. Thus, while group/social identities are about social acceptance (self-worth esteem), role identities are about whether one's roles performance is effective (self-efficacy esteem), and person identities are about whether one's true self is revealed (authenticity self-esteem).

While identity verification fosters good feelings, identity non-verification leads to negative feelings. These negative feelings emerge not only when individuals think that others see them more negatively than how they see ourselves, but also when they think that others see them more positively than how they see themselves (Burke and Stets 2009). Further, there is a stronger negative response as the magnitude of the discrepancy increases. Either a positive or negative direction in the discrepancy is upsetting because it is not verifying. Even when individuals think that others are over-rating them, it is still upsetting because it may set up expectations to meet a higher standard – a standard they are not prepared to meet.

When identity non-verification occurs, the negative emotion creates a pressure or drive within individuals to reduce the discrepancy between how they see themselves and how they think others view them. They may reduce this discrepancy through behavioral strategies such as doing something different in the situation so that the behavior signals different meanings that others may see as more consistent with their identity standard meanings. Alternatively, cognitive strategies may be enacted such as ignoring the discrepant views of others or seeing more consistency in others' views than actually exists. Still yet, individuals could slowly change the self-meanings associated with their identity so that they are more consistent with others' meanings of them. In extreme circumstances, individuals might simply abandon interactions with non-verifying others. Regardless of the strategy chosen, individuals strive to move from a state of non-verification to a state of verification.

To avoid the work associated with responding to non-verifying situations, it would be easier to reside in situations where the discrepancies between self and others' views are small or non-existent and positive feelings are typical. Indeed, some may gravitate to family and friends because they provide a verifying context. Support is felt. When this is not possible, individuals may actively construct such contexts, which have been labeled *opportunity structures* (Swann 1983). Swann indicates three ways that individuals create their own opportunity structures.

First, individuals may "give off" a particular *appearance* that conveys meanings as to who they are. They may dress a certain way or use objects such as the car they drive, the home they live in, or the artwork that hangs on their walls to signal specific self-meanings. This appearance announces to others how they anticipate they will be seen and treated. Second, people may *selectively interact* with those who they know will verify them and avoid those who they know will not verify them. Finally, people may use *interpersonal prompts* to get others to see them in a way that they see themselves. This is done partly through appearance as suggested above. However, it also occurs by behaving in a particular manner that is consistent with one's identity or, alternatively, treating others is a manner that facilitates verification of one's own identity. The latter is what has been otherwise labeled *altercasting* (Weinstein and Deutschberger 1963). Individuals cast others into particular roles or identities such that it encourages them to think and act in ways that verifies those who do the casting. For example, if a person seeks verification of the parent identity, the individual might treat another as a child, casting the other into a dependent role.

Identity verification takes two people: one who needs verification and one who does the verifying. However, in interaction, individuals can build a mutually verifying set of behaviors and identity standards such that what emerges is a *mutual verification context* (Burke and Stets 1999). This is a situation where two or more individuals mutually support each other by not only verifying their own identities, but in doing so, support the verification of others' identities in the situation. This is common in close relationships. Research shows that when this occurs, it can create a stable relationship where positive feelings are felt, and trust and commitment is experienced between individuals (Burke and Stets 1999).

17.4 Self in Groups and Social Categories

The self is not only involved in different interactional processes as discussed above, but it is also a product of interactions within proximate groups of varying sizes and organizational structures. Here, the self is a member of corporate and categoric units (Turner 2010a). The categoric unit is a social distinction that places individuals into distinct social categories such as gender or race/ethnicity. Being defined as a member of a categorical unit results in a distinctive set of socialization experiences and outcomes such as the development of one's identity, self-esteem, and self-efficacy in families, schools, and work organizations. Furthermore, categorization carries with it the implication that some groups are more valuable and have more power than others (Callero 2014).

Due to space limitations, we will be brief in our discussion of the role of corporate groups in understanding the self. We will primarily focus on the categoric units of gender, race, and class, but we will also illustrate how categoric units shape and are shaped by interactions within corporate groups. First, we briefly discuss the mechanism that fosters internalization of categoric unit meanings: the socialization process.

Through socialization, individuals learn the "norms, values, beliefs, attitudes, language characteristics, and roles appropriate to their social groups" (Lutfey and Mortimer 2003). Through interaction in groups such as the family, school, one's peer group, religious group, and work group, individuals learn the positions they occupy in the social structure and the expectations associated with those positions. In the process, the self takes shape. Cooley (1909) alluded to the importance of *primary groups* such as the family in self-formation. In primary groups where there is intimate and frequent face-to-face interaction and individuals are valued and seen as unique and irreplaceable actors, Cooley suggested a "fusion" of the individual with the group resulting in a feeling of "we-ness."

Secondary groups are less influential in self-formation. Here, individuals are largely understood in terms of the position they occupy in organizations, and these positions can have interchangeable actors such as a teacher in a school, a leader of a congregation, or a CEO of a company. The distinction between socialization in primary and secondary groups reflects somewhat the distinction between socialization during childhood and adulthood. Socialization in childhood tends to take place in primary groups and is focused on teaching children broad principles for behavior. Socialization during adulthood involves interaction in primary and especially secondary groups where individuals adopt positions within the workplace and broader community and learn the roles associated with these positions (Preves and Mortimer 2013). Since socialization in childhood serves as the foundation for self-development, we discuss gender, race/ethnicity, and class socialization during childhood.

17.4.1 Gender

Research on gender socialization reveals that boys and girls are treated differently from birth given the stereotypes associated with sex and gender categories. Gender socialization occurs with a variety of different agents and in a variety of contexts. Families tend to be the primary context, but gender socialization also occurs at school and with peers. Through social learning, boys and girls learn the norms for femininity and masculinity. These norms become internalized in the form of one's gender identity, which is the set of meanings individuals associate with themselves as male or female in society (Burke and Stets 2009).

Most children develop the ability to label themselves and others with the label of "boy" or "girl" by the age of 2 (Zosuls et al. 2009). They are first labeled by others who tend to respond to them in sex-typed ways, shaping children's understanding of gender and of themselves as "gendered selves" (Howard and Hollandar 2000). Because initial categorization and internalization begins so early, gender identity becomes an important component of the self-concept. Some argue that it is the first category that children learn and thus the first identity they recognize in themselves and in others (Ridgeway 2011). While socialization occurs throughout the life course, we focus on gender socialization in families because it is here that a gendered self is established.

There are several learning mechanisms that facilitate the development of a child's gender identity: imitation, praise and discouragement, and self-socialization (Maccoby and Jacklin 1974). Parents treat boys and girls differently, and children imitate their parents thereby reproducing gender differences in thought, feeling, and action. For example, mothers see girls as more delicate, passive, and cooperative compared to the view of boys as more sturdy, active, and competitive. Mothers are more attentive and responsive to girls than boys, and they foster the development of girls' emotional worlds and the expression of it compared to boys. Mothers also encourage girls to stay in close proximity while boys are encouraged to be adventurous and explore. Gender differences persist in how girls and boys are clothed, what toys are appropriate for them, what home chores are expected of them, and the décor of their bedrooms. Essentially, we impose a "gendered lens" on the world that presumes difference, ignoring the role of stereotypes as the source of many differences (Bem 1993). The result is that girls and boys develop in ways that help sustain a gendered social order.

Gendered expectations extend to school activity. One area of concern in recent years is the differential involvement of males and females in science, technology, engineering, and mathematics (STEM) because these fields offer comparatively higher salaries and prestige than others fields. As early as elementary school, children have internalized the gender stereotype that math is for boys and not girls (Cvencek et al. 2011). By high school, girls have significantly less motivation to pursue both mathematics and science compared to boys (Catsambis 1994).

In a study of talented high school students enrolled in a science, mathematics, and engineering (SME) summer camp, Lee (1998) examined students' internalized meanings, and their interest in science-related fields. He found that girls tended to see themselves as more different than other science students compared to the boys enrolled in the program. Girls whose self-views were similar to those they associated with the career of engineer, physicist, and mathematician expressed greater interest in those careers than did girls whose self-views differed from those with such careers. Lee (1998: 214) concluded that one of the ways to increasing women's participation in STEM fields would entail "closing the gaps between gendered self-concepts and perceptions of SME disciplines."

17.4.2 Race

Some of the earliest work on racial socialization was conducted by two psychologists who became concerned about Black self-hatred when they found that Black children showed a preference for white dolls (Clark and Clark 1947). This led to extensive work on Black children's self-image, identity adjustment, self-esteem and more. The idea was that because Black children were victims of prejudice, exhibited poor performance in school relative to their White peers, and interpreted their low status as reflecting a personal failure, they internalized the prejudice, and it led to negative self-views such as low self-esteem (Rosenberg 1981).

Over the ensuing decades, little support was found for these expectations. Researchers anticipated Black children would use the broader society and its racist views to define them without considering children's reliance on proximal interactions with individuals of their own race (Rosenberg 1981). Specifically, the source of one's self-views were most likely to come from those in one's immediate social environment such as one's parents, teachers, and friends, all of whom were more likely to be Black than White. Similarly, when considering school performance, black children were more likely to compare themselves to those with whom they were primarily interacting – other Black children. Finally, since one's status was ascribed rather than achieved, children were less inclined to attribute their position to personal failure. Together, these findings led to the idea that Black children's self-esteem was not as vulnerable as previously anticipated.

Parents can play an important role in offsetting many of the harmful effects of prejudice and discrimination and foster a positive identity. Toward this end, they may adopt different strategies such as teaching children about their racial/

ethnic heritage and customs, and promoting pride; creating an awareness of discrimination and the ways to cope; teaching children to be cautious and distrustful of interracial interactions; and encouraging children to value their individual characteristics over their group membership and avoid discussions on race (Hughes et al. 2006). Such studies illustrate how macro-level systems of inequality influence micro-levels interactions that, in turn, reproduce macro-level structures of inequality.

17.4.3 Social Class

Kohn (1977) was one of the first to emphasize how one's social class as reflected in one's occupation shaped individuals' values. He argued that occupations varied according to how much self-direction, complexity, and autonomy was required on the job. High status occupations were more self-directed, complex, and autonomous compared to low status occupations where there was more conformity to authority, jobs were simple, routinized and repetitive, and there was a great deal of supervision. When individuals were rewarded for behaviors consistent with the level of self-direction or conformity expected in the workplace, they came to value these qualities and foster them at home through their parenting style.

The consequence of the above is that children from different classes are reared in different ways given their parents' work experiences. Children from higher classes are taught such values as independence and creativity, and children from lower classes are taught obedience to authority and following societal norms. As they mature and choose careers of their own, they have a tendency to select occupations in which they are expected to behave in ways consistent with how they were raised. Thus, children come to value what their parents' value, and they gravitate toward occupations similar to those chosen by their parents, facilitating the intergenerational transmission of class values and jobs. A provocative amount of work over the years and cross-culturally has supported the reciprocal relationship between occupation and personal values.

In more contemporary work, Lareau (2002) studied social class and childrearing in middle and working-class white and black families. Similar to Kohn's argument, she argued that parents differed in their childrearing practices. Middle-class parents tended to employ a "cultural logic" of what she referred to as "concerted cultivation" (Lareau 2002: 748). This involved engaging children in activities such as music and dance lessons, sports, scouts, and other cultural activities. Discipline involved reasoning and talking with their children, and as a result, children spent a great deal of time in the company of adults. This produced an emerging sense of entitlement when interacting with others in various institutional contexts such as educational and medical systems.

Lower class parents tended to adopt what Lareau referred to as "the accomplishment of natural growth" (Lareau 2002: 748). Children were involved in fewer activities, and parents believed that if they provided the basic necessities, their children would thrive. Discipline was less likely to involve reasoning and more likely to involve an authoritarian, punishing style. Interactions with institutions tended to be characterized by distrust and fear. Similar to Kohn's work, Lareau's two cultural logics related to parents' occupational experiences. Middle-class parents found their work to be challenging and exciting and wanted to develop in their children the skills necessary to be successful in the workforce. Working class parents tended to find their work lives as drudgery, and they wanted to protect their children from life's pains by just letting "kids be kids."

In later work, Weininger and Lareau (2009) found support for Kohn's assertion that middle class parents valued self-direction in their children more than lower class parents. However, the value of self-direction was not well represented in their actual parenting behavior. Middle class parents often employed practices that reduced the amount of self-direction in their children. For example, in the interest of developing valuable skills and interests in their children, middle class parents asserted high levels of control over their activities. In contrast, the parenting practices of lower class parents who presumably valued more conformity than middle-class parents actually allowed children to assert a great deal of control over their activities given that much of their time was spent away from the physical presence of adults. Thus, while adult occupational experiences shaped parental values, the strategies by which they instilled these values in their children seemed less direct.

17.5 Self in Society and Cross-Culturally

17.5.1 Self in Society

The idea that there is an intimate connection between self and society, that the self reflects society and vice versa, can be traced to the early thinkers such as Mead and Cooley as well as more contemporary theorists such as Stryker and Rosenberg. In this section, we broadly examine how the organization of society and its culture shape the particular kinds of selves that are possible and available to individuals. It is at the macro level that fundamental connections between social organization, culture, and self can be seen.

One issue is how the self has responded to postmodern times. Early theorizing on this comes from Turner's (1976) distinction between the self as anchored in *institutions* and the self as anchored in *impulse*. A stronger adherence to social norms and conventions is expected of individuals with institutionally defined selves. In contrast, impulsive selves are defined more in terms of individual preferences and self-discovery. Here, the "true self" is discovered and achieved rather than prescribed by the institution. The immediate access to multiple worlds created by technological advances only intensifies this movement towards an impulsive self by weakening bonds to traditional institutions such as the family and other immediate communities (Gergen 1991).

Writing in the mid-1970s, Turner speculated on a shift in the self from an institutional to an impulsive emphasis. He saw this as emerging, in part, from the political process during his time as revealed in social movements such as the student demonstration movement and the women's movement of the 1960s. Additionally, he noted a greater acceptance of expressing one's impulses – one's spontaneous thoughts and feelings – in literary writings (e.g. Nietzsche), psychology, (e.g. Freud), and child-rearing. But Turner took a step back from these more recent patterns to indicate some general trends over time that might provide an explanation as to the shift from an institutional anchorage to an impulsive anchorage.

One trend he discussed was the cultural changes that occurred in the nineteenth and twentieth centuries where cultural diversity challenged a consensual world view such that institutional frameworks were seen as relativistic rather than absolute, thereby weakening institutional allegiances. Another trend was the movement from a producing society to a consuming society where group life and disciplined work habits became more tenuous, and achievement and interpersonal bonds appeared as less credible clues to a real person. Still another trend was the Freudian dynamic that inhibiting one's impulse caused a preoccupation with the blocked tendency, making it more real and important.

To a certain extent, postmodernist scholars also have commented on a general shift away from defining the self in institutional terms. Essentially, societal advancement influences a destabilization of institutional practices and cultural assumptions. Giddens (1991) argues that in the postmodern world, increasing individualism and the growing complexity of society creates the possibility and potential for any number of "selves" to be constructed by the individual. Gergen (1991: 61) discusses how technological advances have "saturated the self." Our ability to communicate instantly through a variety of different technologies anywhere in the world creates a "swirling set of social relations" such that individuals come to have the potential to possess a variety of different identities within an ever-increasing number of social relationships. This creates challenges for constructing a coherent self.

Others emphasize the self as a site of political controversy; through the specific historical systems of discourse, individuals are controlled and dominated (Thomas et al. 1972). Agency is an illusion. While some have argued that within such historically specific systems of domination the possession of a true self is not possible (Love and Davis 2014), others have argued that the centrality of reflexivity within symbolic interactionst theorizing allows for the retention of a self that is constructed and constituted within systems of power while still retaining the possibility of emancipation (Schlenker 2012).

Other evidence of a movement away from the self in institutional terms has emerged in the argument of a loss of the communal self and a focus on the individual as revealed in the work of Bellah and his colleagues (1985) and Putnam (2000). Analyses such as these are not without controversy including the recent analysis by Fischer (2011) that reveals that the bonds with family and friends are alive and strong. Individuals adjust to a changing society, but it is not at the sacrifice of personal relationships.

17.5.2 Self Cross-Culturally

Culture is characterized by a set of shared values and ideas that are revealed in institutional practices, customs, and artifacts within a particular community. Individuals may not always endorse the values and ideas, but they generally are aware of their existence, and they often inform their behavior. Culture is both internal and external to the individual. Internally, it may be seen in individuals' understandings of how they appear to others in their community (the reflected appraisals process); externally, it may be seen in the patterns of individuals' interactions in groups and organizations and in the underlying logic of social institutions (Reinecke and Trepte 2014). A view of culture that emphasizes both the internal and external components is analogous to our conceptualization of the self at the micro, meso, and macro levels. Culture not only shapes the internal dynamics of the self but also the identities enacted within proximal and larger social institutions.

Cross-cultural research on the self conceptualizes the self as a social construction. Individuals are socialized into different cultures (and in different positions within those cultures), thus they have different selves or *self-construals*. Self-construal is "how individuals define and make meaning of the self" (Cross et al. 2011: 143). Cross and her colleagues point out that self-construal has become synonymous with the distinction between *independence* and *interdependence* or how people see themselves in relation to others. This distinction was originally identified by Markus and Kitayama (1991) who found Westerners (Europeans and Americans) and Easterners (Japanese) showed differences in self orientations. Westerners construe the self as separate from others. The question "Who am I?" is answered in terms of internal traits that set the person apart from others.[2] Interpersonal relationships are important to the extent that they benefit the self in terms of providing support or esteem. In contrast, Easterners construe the self as connected to others. "Who am I?" is answered with reference to important relationships (such as being a wife/husband, or a parent/son or daughter) or group memberships (church member or Latino). Fitting in is an important basis of self-esteem. Social comparisons are used to determine whether individuals are fulfilling their obligations within their relationships, and there is a concern with how they benefit the groups to which they belong (Cross et al. 2011).

While individuals possess both independent and interdependent characteristics, culture influences the development of one self-construal more than the other. Independent self-construals generally correspond to individualistic cultures and interdependent self-construals correspond to collectivistic cultures. In individualistic cultures, priority is given to personal goals over collective goals; in collectivistic cultures, the emphasis is on collective goals (Miyamoto and Eggen 2013). While the dimension of individualism-collectivism describes cultures (Triandis et al. 1989), independent-interdependent self-construals

[2] Early research in this area began by simply asking individuals to list their identities using the Twenty-Statements Test (TST) that asked the question "Who am I?" (Kuhn and McPartland 1954).

describe individuals, thus the two refer to different levels of analysis (Cross et al. 2011). Independent and interdependent self-construals are only one dimension of individualistic and collectivistic cultures. Another dimension of such cultures is the degree to which behavior is guided by individual attitudes (more so in individualistic cultures) compared to social norms (more likely in collectivistic cultures) (Triandis 1995).

More recently, a third type of self-construal has been distinguished: the *relational self-construal* (Kashima et al. 1995). This is a self that is defined in terms of close relationships (e.g. family and friends) rather than a self that is connected to others through proximal social groups as characterized by an interdependent self-construal. Kashima and colleagues were not only the first to identify relational self-construal as distinct from an interdependent self-construal, but they also argued that this relational dimension could distinguish between men and women across cultures.

Others went on to use the relational self-construal dimension to differentiate men and women in Western cultures (Cross and Madson 1997). Women were more likely to create self-views that focused on connection in social relationships, and men were more likely to see themselves as independent and distinct from social relationships. However, other research revealed that while women were more likely to see themselves in relational terms, men were more likely to see themselves in terms of the group or the collective (Gabriel and Gardner 1999). Thus, interdependence had relational and collective aspects. Essentially, being connected to others is core to human existence. It just gets expressed differently for men and women.

Most research has investigated the consequences of having an independent compared to interdependent self-construal. A useful review of this research reveals some of the following patterns (Cross et al. 2011). An independent self-construal is associated with greater positive emotions such as happiness and less negative emotions such as unhappiness, depression, and social anxiety; an interdependent self-construal is associated with greater negative emotions. Part of this difference may be due to the mediating role of social anxiety, which interdependent persons are more likely to feel than independent persons as they are more concerned with appropriate behavior in relationships. Indeed, when social anxiety is controlled for in analyses, the difference in depression disappears.

Still another distinction is how individuals exercise control over themselves to attain their goals. Two self-regulatory foci have been identified: a focus on *promotion* or the motivation to approach one's goal state, and a focus on *prevention* or the motivation to avoid undesired goals (Higgins 1999). Those with an independent self-construal are more inclined to engage in promotion as they seek to reach their desired end state. Because those with an interdependent self-construal want to fit in, maintain harmony in their relationships, and fulfill others' expectations, they are more sensitive to the harm that potential failures could create. Thus, they are more oriented to preventive self-regulation. Consistent with these patterns, we also find that those with an independent self-construal are more likely to engage in primary control (manipulate the environment to meet their needs), while those with an interdependent self-construal are more likely to rely on secondary control (modify their own thoughts and feelings to fit into the environment).

It is assumed that individuals possess all three (and possibly other) self-construals but to varying degrees. For our purposes, we see much affinity between conceptions of the self at the micro, meso, and macro levels with these three dominant self-construals. As identity theorists note, individuals define themselves as unique individuals in terms of individual characteristics (person identities); this is similar to the individual self-construal. Individuals also define themselves as members of larger social groups (group/social identities), and this is similar to having an interdependent self-construal in that the self is defined in relation to larger collectivities. Finally, individuals define themselves in terms of role identities and the counter role identities to which they are related as in the parent role identity and child counter-role identity, teacher role identity and student counter-role identity, and the employer role identity and the employee counter-role identity. This shares an affinity to the relational self-construal. Sociological research on the self could benefit from understanding both intra-cultural and inter-cultural contexts that make different self-construals and the identities potentially attached to them more or less relevant in particular situations.

17.5.3 Morals and Values Cross-Culturally

Another important area where cross-cultural studies have been important is in the study of people's morals and values. Here, we examine the degree to which individuals are oriented to the "good" and the "desirable," and how this varies across the globe. A shared sense of morality and values within a given culture creates social integration and cohesion among members while simultaneously creating the potential for conflict between cultures.

As defined elsewhere, morality is the "evaluative cultural codes that specify what is right or wrong, good or bad, acceptable to unacceptable" in a society (Turner and Stets 2006: 544). At the level of the self, individuals internalize meanings as to who they are along the good-bad dimension. This is their moral identity. While many psychologists argue that having a moral identity means that being moral is at the core of the self, it is the essence of who they are, sociologists would argue that having a moral identity does not necessarily mean that it is core to the self, but rather that it is one among a host of identities that individuals may claim (Stets 2010). What psychologists and sociologists agree on is that self-views along the moral dimension, the moral identity, influence behavior in situations.

When the moral identity has been studied, two underlying meaning dimensions typically have been operationalized: a justice and rights dimension and a care and relationship dimension (e.g. Stets and Carter 2011, 2012). This is consistent with earlier discussions regarding the basis of morality (Gilligan 1982; Kohlberg 1981). Additionally, it is consistent with Western compared to Eastern conceptions of morality in which the fundamental unit of moral value is the individual, and the person's autonomy and welfare are to be protected (Haidt and Graham 2009).

The *individualizing* approach to morality that characterizes Western countries does omit a *binding* approach that may describe many non-Western countries (Haidt 2008). For example, an in-depth analysis of India revealed that there are three bases of morality: an ethic of autonomy, community, and divinity (Shweder et al. 1997). The emphasis on community highlights the collective, and the emphasis on the divine incorporates societal members focus on the sacred. Others have developed Shweder and his colleagues work further by offering not three but five bases of morality cross-culturally (Graham et al. 2011). These include the individualizing foundations of fairness/reciprocity and harm/care, and three communal foundations: in-group/loyalty, authority/respect, and purity/sanctity.

Values are beliefs about what is desirable that guides behavior and transcend situations (Gecas 2000; Hitlin and Piliavin 2004). Some see values as core to one's personal identity (Hitlin 2003). More specifically, Hitlin sees the personal identity as "produced through value commitments" (Hitlin 2003: 121). Identity theorists would agree that values may be meanings that make up the person identity, but there also are other meanings that make up the person identity and that characterize one as distinctive or unique compared to others, which is a defining feature of person identities (Burke and Stets 2009). Empirical work would be needed to examine whether values are more likely to be linked to person identities then role identities or group/social identities.

In a slightly different conceptualization, Gecas (2000) maintains that people have *value-identities*, that is, they define themselves in terms of the values they hold. Value identities can refer to desired personal qualities such being honest or brave as compared to value identities that refer to social conditions such as freedom or equality (Gecas 2000). Values that refer to personal qualities Gecas labels one's "character identity." Here, we begin to see an overlap with the moral identity as discussed above. Gecas discusses the relationship between values and morality by maintaining that the relationship is tighter when one's moral orientation is justice-oriented vs. care-oriented. In the former, values and principles are more likely to guide moral behavior compared to the latter, which is more likely to be guided by situational circumstances and interpersonal concerns. This is analogous to the independent vs. interdependent self-construals discussed earlier. Those with an independent self-construal are more likely to have their value identities guide their moral behavior compared to those with an interdependent self-construal.

How values are represented cross-culturally is evidenced in Schwartz's (1992, 1994) research, although the findings primarily exists in literate or developed countries. He reveals that individuals across societies endorse ten values that have two broader value dimensions. One dimension is *openness to change* vs. *conservation*, which includes the values of self-direction, stimulation, and hedonism vs. tradition, conformity and security. A second dimension is *self-transcendence* vs. *self-enhancement*, which includes the values of universalism and benevolence vs. achievement and power. Generally, those who endorse one dimension, such as openness to change, have a tendency not to endorse its opposite – conservation. Interestingly, a recent cross-cultural analysis reveals that Schwartz's model of values does a better job of predicting value priorities across countries than within countries, thereby refuting the strong claim that culture determines individual values (Fischer and Schwartz 2011). Only the value of conformity such as honoring one's parents, politeness, and obedience appear to garner within country consensus. Recently, the ten values have been expanded to 19 values with data from ten countries (Schwatz et al. 2012).

17.6 Future Micro, Meso and Macro Directions

At the micro level, in the last 20 years, research in neurosociology has generated important insights into how self-related processes are associated with the activation of particular regions in the brain including but not limited to self-reflection and taking the role of the other. In this regard, two functionally related areas of the brain are important: the default mode network (DMN) and the mirror neuron system (MNS) (Molnar-Szakacs and Uddin 2013). The DMN is associated with the processing of self-related information such as how individuals think about themselves, while the MNS is associated with taking the role of the other and reflecting on the behaviors and emotions of others, reproducing those same actions and feelings within the person. Because the MNS is activated when individuals act as well as when they observe the actions of others, the MNS apparently facilitates the development of shared meanings in interaction (Molnar-Szakacs and Uddin 2013). Further, while the DMN and MNS have different functions, they are interrelated. In the same way that when the self is formed, it is always in relation to others, the DMN and MNS interact to allow for an integrated self-representation, reminding us of Cooley's dictum that self and society are "twin born."

The potential for resolving issues in the area of self and identity using neurosociology is a rich and fruitful line of further work. For example, given the centrality of role-taking in understanding the self, and given that lower status actors are more likely to role-take than higher status actors, neuroimaging might be able to map changes in the flow of blood to particular areas of the brain in response to situational shifts in status and power (Franks 2013).

As another illustration, because activating different kinds of memory (episodic, semantic, and semantic autobiographical) stimulates different parts of the brain, linking the conventional and idiosyncratic self-meanings of an identity to semantic and episodic memories, respectively, would allow us to study how individuals employ conventional and idiosyncratic identity meanings in different situations (Niemeyer 2013). Situations that are informed by cultural norms may activate more conventional meanings of an identity, thereby linking identities and normative behavior. Conversely, situations that are less controlled by normative imperatives may stimulate idiosyncratic identity meanings, allowing for more novel ways in which an identity is enacted.

At the meso level, future research on the self could more systematically address issues of intersectionality that are pervasive in feminist literatures. James' early idea that people possess as many selves as there are individuals to whom they relate to shores up the idea of intersectionality in contemporary work. Individuals are members of multiple social categories and multiple groups, creating a unique set of experiences. Research on the self can be advanced by examining how intersectionality provides insights into how to understand multiple identities that individuals claim within and across situations. For instance, in the family group identity, there are certain expectations attached to the parent role identity that vary across the categorical identities of being male and female, white and non-white, and heterosexual and homosexual. Further, as meanings in one identity change, they create the potential for a change in meanings in other identities (Burke and Cast 1997). Thus, the unique experiences associated with any one intersectional profile may be rooted in compromises that are made along the way to reach a set of non-conflicting meanings that individuals can manage in interaction.

At the macro level, researchers may want to study the self in relation to globalization. The process of globalization and the increasing connectedness in the world includes but is not limited to transnational migrations, international business interests, world tourism, and the existence of technology and media, all of which create the potential for individuals to have instant access to information from around the world. The ability to interact with a variety of individuals from around the world and in a variety of cultures has the potential for the colonization of the self (Callero 2008).

The colonization of the self refers to the idea that globalization is primarily fueled by capitalist markets and a Western consumerist culture. The proliferation of Western businesses and global media conglomerates throughout the world creates a self that is uniform in terms of its cultural content. According to Callero, selves are reconstructed in a way that traditional roles disappear, are redefined, and novel roles potentially emerge that are inconsistent with traditional cultural practices but consistent with global economic conglomerates.

One new shape that the self may take is in the development of a new identity given the mixing of cultures. Another is the development of a multicultural identity in which individuals adopt multiple identities that represent identification with a variety of cultures. Alternatively, people might develop a defensive stance toward encroaching cultural influences.

Finally, Callero suggests that globalization can create the potential for radical social change. The rapid-fire communication networks that on the one hand have the potential to constrain the self to hegemonic cultural ideals also have the potential to resist cultural hegemony. One example of this is the use of Facebook to organize protests locally and globally on a variety of social issues including climate change and human rights.

Globalization carries with it the potential to not only allow for greater individual choice in the construction of the self but also constrain the self (Callero 2008). One fruitful line of research would seek to understand the conditions that allow for multicultural identities to emerge and the conditions that limit their development. Another possible line of research would be to examine the different cultural contexts in which identities are managed. Are multicultural identities easier to claim and maintain in culturally diverse than culturally homogenous contexts? More generally, increasing exposure to different cultures can broaden the self, perhaps leading to greater adaptability across space and time.

References

Bellah, R. N., Madsen, R., Sullivan, W. M., Swidler, A., & Tipton, S. M. (1985). *Habits of the heart*. Berkeley: University of California Press.

Bem, S. L. (1993). *The lenses of gender*. New Haven: Yale University Press.

Burke, P. J., & Cast, A. D. (1997). Stability and change in the gender identities of newly married couples. *Social Psychology Quarterly, 60*, 277–290.

Burke, P. J., & Harrod, M. M. (2005). Too much of a good thing? *Social Psychology Quarterly, 68*, 359–374.

Burke, P. J., & Stets, J. E. (1999). Trust and commitment through self-verification. *Social Psychology Quarterly, 62*, 347–366.

Burke, P. J., & Stets, J. E. (2009). *Identity theory*. New York: Oxford University Press.

Callero, P. L. (2008). The globalization of the self: Role and identity transformation from above and below. *Sociology Compass, 2*, 1972–1988.

Callero, P. L. (2014). Self, identity, and social inequality. In J. D. McLeod, E. J. Lawler, & M. Schwalbe (Eds.), *Handbook of the social psychology of inequality* (pp. 273–294). New York: Springer.

Cast, A. D., Stets, J. E., & Burke, P. J. (1999). Does the self conform to the views of others? *Social Psychology Quarterly, 62*, 68–82.

Catsambis, S. (1994). The path to math: Gender and racial-ethnic differences in mathematics participation from middle school to high school. *Sociology of Education, 67*, 199–215.

Clark, K. B., & Clark, M. P. (1947). Racial identification and preference among negro children. In E. L. Hartley & T. M. Newcomb (Eds.), *Readings in social psychology* (pp. 169–178). New York: Holt, Rinehart, and Winston.

Cooley, C. H. (1902). *Human nature and social order*. New York: Scribner's.

Cooley, C. H. (1909). *Social organization*. New York: Scribner.

Cross, S. E., & Madson, L. (1997). Models of the self: Self-construals and gender. *Psychological Bulletin, 122*, 5–37.

Cross, S. E., Hardin, E. E., & Gercek-Swing, B. (2011). The what, how, why, and where of self-construal. *Personality and Social Psychology Review, 15*, 142–179.

Cvencek, D., Mtltzoff, A. N., & Greenwald, A. G. (2011). Math-gender stereotypes in elementary school children. *Child Development, 82*, 766–779.

Damasio, A. R. (1994). *Descartes' error: Emotion, reason, and the human brain*. New York: Putnam.

Davis, J. L. (2016). Identity theory in a digital age. In J. E. Stets & R. T. Serpe (Eds.), *New directions in identity theory and research*. New York: Oxford.

Felson, R. B. (1993). The (somewhat) social self: How others affect self-appraisals. In J. M. Suls (Ed.), *The self in social perspective* (Vol. 4, pp. 1–26). Hillsdale: Lawrence Erlbaum Associates.

Fischer, C. S. (2011). *Still connected: Family and friends in America since 1970*. New York: Russell Sage.

Fischer, R., & Schwartz, S. (2011). Whence differences in value priorities? Individual, cultural, or artifactual sources. *Journal of Cross-Cultural Psychology, 42*, 1127–1144.

Franks, D. D. (2010). *Neurosociology: The nexus between neuroscience and social psychology*. New York: Springer.

Franks, D. D. (2013). Why we need neurosociology as well as social neuroscience: Or – Why role-taking and theory of mind are different concepts. In D. D. Franks & J. H. Turner (Eds.), *Handbook of neurosociology* (pp. 27–32). Dordrecht: Springer.

Gabriel, S., & Gardner, W. L. (1999). Are there "his" and "hers" types of interdependence? The implications of gender differences in collective versus relational interdependence for affect, behavior, and cognition. *Journal of Personality and Social Psychology, 77*, 642–655.

Gecas, V. (2000). Value identities, self-motives, and social movements. In S. Stryker, T. J. Owens, & R. W. White (Eds.), *Self, identity, and social movements* (pp. 93–109). Minneapolis: University of Minnesota Press.

Gergen, K. J. (1991). *The saturated self: Dilemmas of identity in contemporary life*. New York: Basic Books.

Giddens, A. (1991). *Modernity and self-identity*. Cambridge: Polity.

Gilligan, C. (1982). *In a different voice: Psychological theory and women's development*. Cambridge, MA: Harvard University Press.

Goffman, E. (1959). *The presentation of self in everyday life*. Garden City: Doubleday.

Graham, J., Nosek, B. A., Haidt, J., Iyer, R., Koleva, S., & Ditto, P. H. (2011). Mapping the moral domain. *Journal of Personality and Social Psychology, 101*, 366–385.

Haidt, J. (2008). Morality. *Perspectives on Psychological Science, 3*, 65–72.

Haidt, J., & Graham, J. (2009). Planet of the Durkheimians: Where community, authority, and sacredness are foundations of morality. In J. T. Jost, A. C. Kay, & H. Thorisdottir (Eds.), *Social and psychological bases of ideology and system justification* (pp. 371–401). New York: Oxford.

Higgins, E. T. (1999). Beyond pleasure and pain. *American Psychologist, 52*, 1280–1300.

Hitlin, S. (2003). Values as the core of personal identity: Drawing links between two theories of self. *Social Psychology Quarterly, 66*, 118–137.

Hitlin, S., & Piliavin, J. A. (2004). Values: Reviving a dormant concept. *Annual Review of Sociology, 30*, 359–393.

Howard, J. A., & Hollandar, J. (2000). *Gendered situations, gendered selves*. Walnut Creek: AltaMira.

Hughes, D., Rodriguez, J., Smith, E. P., Johnson, D. J., Stevenson, H. C., & Spicer, P. (2006). Parents' ethnic-racial socialization practices: A review of research and directions for future study. *Developmental Psychology, 42*, 747–770.

James, W. (1890). *Principles of psychology*. New York: Holt Rinehart and Winston.

Kashima, Y., Yamaguchi, S., Kim, U., Choi, S.-C., Gelfand, M. J., & Yuki, M. (1995). Culture, gender, and self: A perspective from individualism-collectivism research. *Journal of Personality and Social Psychology, 69*, 925–937.

Kinch, J. W. (1963). A formalized theory of the self-concept. *American Journal of Sociology, 68*, 481–486.

Kohlberg, L. (1981). *The philosophy of moral development*. San Francisco: Harper and Row.
Kohn, M. L. (1977). *Class and conformity*. Chicago: University of Chicago Press.
Kuhn, M. H., & McPartland, T. S. (1954). An empirical investigation of self-attitudes. *American Sociological Review, 19*, 68–76.
Kwang, T., & Swann, W. B. (2010). Do people embrace praise even when they feel unworthy? A review of critical tests of self-enhancement versus self-verification. *Personality and Social Psychology Review, 14*(3), 263–280.
Lareau, A. (2002). Invisible inequality: Social class and childrearing in black families and white families. *American Sociological Review, 67*, 747–776.
LeDoux, J. E. (1996). *The emotional brain: The mysterious underpinnings of emotional life*. New York: Simon and Schuster.
Lee, J. D. (1998). Which kids can "become" scientists? Effects of gender, self-concepts, and perceptions of scientists. *Social Psychology Quarterly, 61*, 199–219.
Love, T. P., & Davis, J. L. (2014). The effect of status on role-taking accuracy. *American Sociological Review, 79*, 848–865.
Lutfey, K., & Mortimer, J. T. (2003). Development and socialization through the adult life course. In J. DeLamater (Ed.), *Handbook of social psychology* (pp. 183–202). New York: Academic/Plenum.
Maccoby, E. E., & Jacklin, C. N. (1974). *The psychology of sex differences*. Stanford: Stanford University Press.
Markus, H. R., & Kitayama, S. (1991). Culture and the self: Implications for cognition, emotion, and motivation. *Psychological Review, 98*, 234–253.
Mead, G. H. (1934). *Mind, self, and society*. Chicago: University of Chicago Press.
Miyamoto, Y., & Eggen, A. (2013). Cultural perspectives. In J. D. DeLamater & A. Ward (Eds.), *Handbook of social psychology* (pp. 595–624). New York: Springer.
Molnar-Szakacs, I., & Uddin, L. Q. (2013). The emergent self: How distributed neural networks support self-representation. In D. D. Franks (Ed.), *Handbook of neurosociology* (pp. 167–182). Dordrecht: Springer.
Niemeyer, R. E. (2013). What are the neurological foundations of identities and identity-related processes? An examination of how the default mode network relates to identity theory. In D. D. Franks & J. H. Turner (Eds.), *Handbook of neurosociology* (pp. 149–165). Dordrecht: Springer.
Preves, S. E., & Mortimer, J. T. (2013). Socialization for primary, intimae, and work relationships in the adult life course. In J. DeLamater & A. Ward (Eds.), *Handbook of social psychology* (pp. 151–187). Dordrecht: Springer.
Putnam, R. D. (2000). *Bowling alone: The collapse and revival of American community*. New York: Simon and Schuster.
Reinecke, L., & Trepte, S. (2014). Authenticity and well-being on social network sites: A two-wave longitudinal study on the effects of online authenticity and the positive bias in SNS communication. *Computers in Human Behavior, 30*, 95–102.
Ridgeway, C. L. (2011). *Framed by gender: How gender inequality persists in the modern world*. New York: Oxford University Press.
Rosenberg, M. (1979). *Conceiving the self*. New York: Basic Books.
Rosenberg, M. (1981). The self-concept: Social product and social force. In M. Rosenberg & R. H. Turner (Eds.), *Social psychology: Sociological perspectives* (pp. 593–624). New York: Basic Books.
Rosenberg, M. (1990). The self-concept: Social product and social force. In M. Rosenberg & R. H. Turner (Eds.), *Social psychology: Sociological perspectives* (pp. 593–624). New Brunswick: Transaction Publishers.
Rosenberg, M., Schooler, C., Schoenbach, C., & Rosenberg, F. (1995). Global self-esteem and specific self-esteem: Different concepts, different outcomes. *American Sociological Review, 60*, 141–156.
Schlenker, B. R. (2012). Self-presentation. In M. R. Leary & J. P. Tangney (Eds.), *Handbook of self and identity* (pp. 542–570). New York: The Guilford Pres.
Schwalbe, M. L. (1988). Role taking reconsidered: Linking competence and performance to social structure. *Journal for the Theory of Social Behavior, 18*, 411–436.
Schwartz, S. H. (1992). Universals in the content and structure of values: Theoretical advances and empirical tests in 20 countries. In M. P. Zanna (Ed.), *Advances in experimental social psychology* (pp. 1–65). San Diego: Academic.
Schwartz, S. H. (1994). Are there universal aspects in the structure and content of human values? *Journal of Social Issues, 50*, 19–45.
Schwatz, S. H., Cieciuch, J., Vecchione, M., Davidov, E., Fischer, R., Beierlein, C., & Konty, M. (2012). Refining the theory of basic individual values. *Journal of Personality and Social Psychology, 103*, 663–688.
Serpe, R. T., & Stryker, S. (2011). The symbolic interactionist perspective and identity theory. In S. Schwartz, K. Luyckx, & V. Vignoles (Eds.), *Handbook of identity theory and research* (pp. 225–248). New York: Springer.
Shibutani, T. (1955). Reference groups as perspectives. *American Journal of Sociology, 60*, 562–569.
Shrauger, J. S., & Schoeneman, T. J. (1979). Symbolic interactionist view of self-concept: Through the looking glass darkly. *Psychological Bulletin, 86*, 549–573.
Shweder, R. A., Much, N. C., Mahapatra, M., & Park, L. (1997). The big "three" of morality (autonomy, community, and divinity), and the big "three" explanations of suffering. In A. Brandt & P. Rozin (Eds.), *Morality and health* (pp. 119–169). New York: Routledge.
Stets, J. E. (1995). Role identities and person identities: Gender identity, mastery identity, and controlling one's partner. *Sociological Perspectives, 38*, 129–150.
Stets, J. E. (2010). The social psychology of the moral identity. In S. Hitlin & S. Vaisey (Eds.), *Handbook of*

the sociology of morality (pp. 385–409). New York: Springer.
Stets, J. E., & Burke, P. J. (2014a). Emotions and identity non-verification. *Social Psychology Quarterly, 77*, 387–410.
Stets, J. E., & Burke, P. J. (2014b). Self-esteem and identities. *Sociological Perspectives, 57*, 1–25.
Stets, J. E., & Carter, M. J. (2011). The moral self: Applying identity theory. *Social Psychology Quarterly, 74*, 192–215.
Stets, J. E., & Carter, M. J. (2012). A theory of the self for the sociology of morality. *American Sociological Review, 77*, 120–140.
Stets, J. E., & Cast, A. D. (2007). Resources and identity verification from an identity theory perspective. *Sociological Perspectives, 50*, 517–543.
Stets, J. E., & Harrod, M. M. (2004). Verification across multiple identities: The role of status. *Social Psychology Quarterly, 67*, 155–171.
Stryker, S. (2002 [1980]). *Symbolic interactionism: A social structural version*. Caldwell: The Blackburn Press.
Stryker, S., & Serpe, R. T. (1982). Commitment, identity salience, and role behavior: A theory and research example. In W. Ickes & E. S. Knowles (Eds.), *Personality, roles, and social behavior* (pp. 199–218). New York: Springer.
Stryker, S., Serpe, R. T., & Hunt, M. O. (2005). Making good on a promise: The impact of larger social structures on commitments. *Advances in Group Processes, 22*, 93–123.
Swann, W. B., Jr. (1983). Self-verification: Bringing social reality into harmony with the self. In J. Suls & A. Greenwald (Eds.), *Psychological perspectives on the self* (pp. 33–66). Hillsdale: Erlbaum.
Thomas, D. L., Franks, D. D., & Calonico, J. (1972). Role-taking and power in social psychology. *American Sociological Review, 37*, 605–614.
Triandis, H. C. (1995). *Individualism and collectivism*. Boulder: Westview.
Triandis, H. C., Bontempo, R., & Villareal, M. J. (1989). Individualism and collectivism: Cross-cultural perspectives on self-ingroup relationships. *Journal of Personality and Social Psychology, 54*, 323–338.
Turner, R. H. (1962). Role-taking: Process versus conformity. In A. M. Rose (Ed.), *Human behavior and social processes* (pp. 20–40). Boston: Houghton Mifflin.
Turner, R. H. (1976). The real self: From institution to impulse. *American Journal of Sociology, 81*, 989–1016.
Turner, J. H. (2010a). *Theoretical principles of sociology, volume 1: Macrodynamics*. New York: Springer.
Turner, J. H. (2010b). *Theoretical principles of sociology, volume 2: Microdynamics*. New York: Springer.
Turner, J. H. (2012). *Theoretical principles of sociology, volume 3: Mesodynamics*. New York: Springer.
Turner, J. H., & Stets, J. E. (2005). *The sociology of emotions*. New York: Cambridge University Press.
Turner, J. H., & Stets, J. E. (2006). Moral emotions. In J. E. Stets & J. H. Turner (Eds.), *Handbook of the sociology of emotions* (pp. 544–566). New York: Springer.
Ward, L. G., & Throop, R. (1992). Emotional experience in Dewey and Mead: Notes for the social psychology of emotion. In D. D. Franks & V. Gecas (Eds.), *Social perspectives on emotion* (pp. 61–94). Greenwich: JAI Press.
Weininger, E. B., & Lareau, A. (2009). Paradoxical pathways: An ethnographic extension of Kohn's findings on class and childrearing. *Journal of Marriage and the Family, 71*, 680–695.
Weinstein, E. A., & Deutschberger, P. (1963). Some dimensions of altercasting. *Sociometry, 26*, 454–466.
Zosuls, K. M., Ruble, D. N., Tamis-LeMonda, C. S., & Shrout, P. E. (2009). The acquisition of gender labels in infancy: Implications for sex-typed play. *Developmental Psychology, 45*, 688–701.

Part IV

Constraints on Experience

Microsociologies: Social Exchange, Trust, Justice, and Legitimacy

18

Michael J. Carter

18.1 Introduction

The past decades have witnessed the growth and development of various sociological theories that address micro-level social phenomena. The "micro realm" of social reality encompasses intra- and interpersonal processes that influence social interaction. Microsociological theories address dyads, triads, and small groups—the everyday social structures that influence (and constrain) experience (Turner 2010).

This chapter surveys contemporary sociological theories and research that address four micro-level processes: *social exchange*, *trust*, *justice*, and *legitimacy*. These four processes are central in social life; they are common themes that are diffuse and active in virtually all social interactions. Whether experiences are novel or routine, attitudes and behaviors are greatly influenced by social norms that represent what is right and proper. Knowing how individuals (and groups) determine what is right and proper—and why social interactions often go smoothly—requires an understanding of how actors exchange resources, how they come to trust (and distrust) others, how they attribute actions and experiences as just or unjust, and how they endorse (or do not endorse) power differentials between self and others.

M.J. Carter (✉)
Sociology Department, California State University, Northridge, Northridge, CA, USA
e-mail: michael.carter@csun.edu

The plan of this chapter is as follows: I first discuss how social exchange, trust, justice, and legitimacy operate as specific dimensions of social comparison. I then address each process individually, summarizing their basic elements and illustrating each. In each summary section I survey the recent literature that has advanced our understanding of how the processes operate to influence interactions in social life. Finally, I discuss recent research that has examined interrelations of exchange, trust, justice, and legitimacy—work that has addressed some combination of these processes.

In the literature, social exchange, trust, justice, and legitimacy are often treated as analytically distinct. Across the social sciences, there are thoroughly developed research programs that address each—to some degree—in relative isolation. Examining them together makes sense however, as each is a specific dimension of a greater abstract process: *social comparison*.

Comparisons are central in social life. There is ample evidence that individuals compare themselves to others in the social structure on multiple dimensions, beginning early in the life-course and continuing throughout life (Jensen et al. 2015; Hoorens and Van Damme 2012; Boissicat et al. 2012). For instance, from early on we compare what we look like to what others look like,

S. Abrutyn (ed.), *Handbook of Contemporary Sociological Theory*,
Handbooks of Sociology and Social Research, DOI 10.1007/978-3-319-32250-6_18

and what we have to what others have. We also compare how we are treated, and what we receive compared to what others receive. Perceptions based on social comparisons influence many important behavioral and emotional outcomes, such as motivation, self-esteem, and self-efficacy. Theories that examine how social exchange, trust, justice, and legitimacy operate as comparison processes attempt to understand how individuals make evaluative determinations about the relative status, power, dependability, entitlement, and properness of others in society (and oneself), and how individuals act based on those determinations.

To illustrate how social exchange, trust, justice, and legitimacy operate in social life let us consider the example of an individual who is stopped by a police officer for speeding on a freeway. Such occurrences are relatively common, especially in metropolitan areas, and the interaction between the police officer and the individual caught speeding in this example might be considered somewhat predictable: The police officer would likely approach the perpetrator from behind, flash the lights of her police car to signify that the speeder should pull to the side of the road, and approach the individual on foot after both cars had come to a stop. The interchange between the police officer and the speeder may then take various forms, depending on a variety of factors, such as the prevailing cultural norms that define acceptable behavior, personality traits/dispositions of each actor in the situation, each actor's experience in previous situations that are similar to the present situation, meanings of the present context (time of day, others present in the situation, etc.), and each actor's personal biography. A predictable script in this example would be the police officer informing the driver that they were speeding, the police officer asking the driver for their license and proof of insurance, a ticket being written and administered, and both actors going on with their day.

The situation described above seems commonplace and not particularly novel, but what makes such an example so commonplace? What basic social processes are active in the situation that account for the behavior of each actor? What accounts for variations in real-life situations such as this? For instance, why do some people comply in such situations, listening to and following the orders of the police officer as the situation unfolds, whereas others do not comply, arguing with the police officer, becoming disruptive and uncooperative? How do some people persuade authority figures to give them a warning rather than a ticket in such situations? And why do some people attribute the situation of being stopped for a traffic infraction as caused by external factors (e.g., the perception that the law regarding the speed limit is unfairly slow) rather than due to their own actions (e.g., speeding because one wanted to get a good parking spot at work)? How can we understand these different courses of action, none of which are uncommon? Answers to these questions require us to understand basic social processes that commonly occur in social situations, such as the how individuals exchange resources, defer to authority, trust and predict courses of action, and strive to behave in expected, normative ways.

In the above example, it is evident that social exchange, trust, justice, and legitimacy are all in operation. The police officer is depending on the speeder to respect her authority, and comply with her demands; the respect of authority is a *legitimation* process. The interaction between the officer and the speeder is also influenced by *procedural justice* processes; the speeder perceives whether the officer acts within the bounds of what is fair (and lawful), and in line with how an authority figure should behave. *Trust* is evident as well (or the *lack* of trust); because if the police officer is unfamiliar with the perpetrator she would likely approach the car cautiously, perhaps with her hand on her gun in case something goes awry during the interaction. Without a previous history of interactions neither the officer nor the speeder will have high feelings of trust for one another, and such perceptions will likely affect the manner in which each talk to one another, and what each expects the other to do. And, if the speeder tries to talk the officer out of receiving a ticket it is likely that some form of *social exchange* process would be invoked, e.g., either an ingratiation tactic or perhaps even monetary bribery. It is clear that even in the most routine micro-level encounters, social comparison processes such as exchange, trust, justice, and legitimacy can operate to influence how people interact.

There are myriad theories in sociology that address the manner in which individuals compare themselves to others. Let us now examine contemporary theoretical frameworks that have developed regarding social exchange, trust, justice, and legitimacy.

18.2 Social Exchange Theory

Of all the processes that involve social comparisons, social exchange has been a central focus in sociology and psychology (see Cook et al. (2013), Emerson (1981) and Molm and Cook (1995) for detailed summaries of exchange theory as an evolving, cumulative research program). Classic ideas on the nature of social exchange were developed by George C. Homans (1958, 1961), John Thibaut and Harold Kelley (1959), and Peter Blau (1964). Richard Emerson (1962, 1976) then furthered understanding of social exchange by incorporating power and dependence in classic models of social exchange, providing a more complete understand of exchange relations (see Chap. 15 in this volume for a detailed discussion of Emerson's power-dependence theory). The work of Homans, Thibaut and Kelley, Blau, and Emerson have inspired many contemporary sociologists, who together have established a strong and thorough research program over the past half-century (Molm 1997; Chesire et al. 2010; Cook and Emerson 1978).

The exchange tradition in sociology began with Homans' (1961) belief that all social behavior is *exchange* behavior: it involves two actors who exchange some resource, and all social behavior involves the reinforcement or punishment of one individual upon the other. This basic orientation to social life provided the foundation for all future work on social exchange. While many now see Homans' work as simplistic and reductionist (he focused mostly on dyadic exchange), his five propositions of social exchange still resonate and apply to contemporary exchange theories. Based on the notion that all social behavior is influenced by perceived rewards and punishments that one receives while interacting with others, Homans' (1961) propositions for social exchange include: (1) *The stimulus proposition* (the idea that past behavior that has been rewarded is likely to be performed in future encounters), (2) *the success proposition* (the idea that behavior that leads to positive outcomes is likely to be enacted in future encounters), (3) *the value proposition* (the idea that the more valuable an outcome of an action is, the more likely the action will be performed in the future), (4) *the deprivation-satiation proposition* (the idea that accumulated rewards have a utility of diminished marginal returns—the more of a resource one receives, the less valuable additional units become), and (5) *the frustration-aggression proposition* (the idea that actors become agitated when they are withheld a resource in which they anticipate receiving or feel entitled to have).

Generally, social exchange theory examines the *benefits* people gain from interacting with others and the *opportunity structures* and interdependencies that influence and constrain those exchanges (Emerson 1981; Molm 2006; Molm and Cook 1995). Let us examine the relationship between benefits and opportunity structures by summarizing the basic concepts of social exchange, to better understand how individuals exchange resources in social life.

18.2.1 Elements of Social Exchange

Social exchange involves the "exchange of activity, tangible or intangible, and more or less rewarding or costly, between at least two persons" (Homans 1961). All forms of social exchange contain three elements: *actors*, *resources*, and *exchange structures* (Molm 2006). An "actor" in an exchange relation is a general term that can represent various entities, including both individuals and groups (i.e., when group members behave in solidarity as a singular unit).

"Resources" are skills or things one possesses that have value for others. Resources can be material (i.e., *tangible*) such as money or goods, or immaterial (i.e., *intangible*), such as love or affection.

Exchanges between actors do not occur outside a specific social context; various factors influence and determine the nature of an exchange, such as the number of actors involved in an exchange, and the setting in which an exchange occurs. These varying factors are known as *exchange structures* (Emerson 1972), which can take the form of *direct*, *generalized*, or *productive* exchange (Molm 2006). A direct exchange is a situation where (usually) two actors' outcome in an exchange relation is directly dependent on one another's actions. For example, purchasing an iPod from the Apple Store is an example of direct exchange; a customer pays a specific amount of money to a clerk for the good—the transaction is singular (though direct exchanges can also be repeated over time), immediate, and direct between the exchanging units.

A generalized exchange is an exchange among three or more actors, where the reciprocal dependence among all actors in the exchange is indirect rather than direct. For instance, in a generalized exchange actor A provides actor B with some resource, but actor B does not reciprocate and provide A with a resource in return. After A provides the resource to B, B in turn provides some resource to actor C, and actor C then provides some resource to A. Generalized exchange is circular rather than direct. Universities provide a good example of generalized exchange. Students pay tuition to take classes from professors; professors are paid for their expertise and teaching service. However, students and professors are not directly involved in an exchange relation. Rather, a student (actor A) pays tuition to a university (Actor B); the university then pays the professor (actor C), and the then professor renders their service to the student (by teaching the student).

In a productive exchange two or more actors work together to produce some valued commodity or outcome that benefits all members in the exchange. Team sports provide good examples of productive exchange. For instance, all members on a football team work together, exchanging individual efforts to the team concept (i.e., everyone role-plays) so that the team can win. All members of the team realize that in order for everyone to accomplish the common goal, all must exchange and sacrifice individually; the reward (winning) is accomplished through productive exchange.

18.2.2 The Exchange Process

In addition to defining the elements of social exchange, exchange theory also addresses the *process* by which exchanges occur within exchange structures. The process of social exchange involves four components: *exchange opportunities*, *initiations*, *transactions*, and *exchange relations*. An exchange opportunity refers to an actor's opportunity to initiate an exchange. When an initiated exchange is reciprocated by another it is called a transaction. Transactions are mutual exchanges of benefits between two or more actors. When multiple transactions occur between or among actors, it is known as an exchange relation (Molm 2006).

When actors develop an exchange relationship, the relationship takes the form of being a *negotiated* exchange relation or a *reciprocal* exchange relation (Emerson 1981; Molm et al. 1999, 2000; Lawler 2001). Negotiated exchanges occur when actors engage in a joint decision making process and reach an agreement about the terms of the exchange. Negotiated exchanges are discrete and singular; generally, actors involved in negotiated exchanges are not considering the effect of the exchange relation on future interactions or exchanges. An example of negotiated exchange would be the purchasing of a home. Both the buyer (actor A) and the seller (actor B) negotiate an acceptable price and then complete the transaction, in a one-time deal.

Reciprocal exchanges, on the other hand, occur when an actor provides a resource to another actor without the expectation that a resource will be immediately returned (or without the absolute knowledge that a resource indeed *will* be returned at a future date). Reciprocal transactions are generally the most interesting to sociologists. While negotiated exchanges are often economic transactions, reciprocal exchanges are inherently social (and not economic). Reciprocal exchanges imply that exchange behaviors between actors are multiple rather than singular; the exchange carries forth across transactions, not solely within a single transaction. Therefore, exchange theorists treat the sequence or series of transactions between actors as the unit of analysis in reciprocal exchange, rather than one specific exchange transaction. The classic example of a common reciprocal exchange is that of helping a friend move. In helping a friend move one provides a service to another without knowing when (or even if) the friend will reciprocate the favor. Reciprocal exchanges involve a complex set of psychological and sociological processes, including social integration and trust. The crucial difference between negotiated and reciprocal exchanges are that in negotiated exchange actor A's benefits to actor B are contingent on B's benefits to A, where as in reciprocal exchange benefits provided and received in previous exchanges between actor A and actor B affect A's future behavior toward actor B (Molm 2006).

18.2.3 General Assumptions and Propositions of Social Exchange

While theories of social exchange have different emphases, all share a few common assumptions and make similar predictions. Exchange theory makes assumptions about the structure in which *exchange relations* occur, the manner in which actors will *behave* in social structures, the way that actors will *interact* within social structures, and the classes (or types) of *resources* exchanged between actors in social structures (Molm and Cook 1995). More specifically, exchange theory involves four core assumptions: (1) Exchange relations develop within existing structures of mutual dependence between actors, (2) actors behave in ways to increase outcomes they positively value and decrease outcomes they negatively value, (3) actors engage in recurring, mutually contingent exchanges with specific partners over time, and (4) all outcomes of value obey a principle of satiation (in psychological terms) or diminishing marginal utility (in economic terms) (Molm and Cook 1995).

18.2.4 Recent Research on Social Exchange

Recent applications of exchange theory have addressed a wide variety of processes. For instance, some have addressed the structure of reciprocity—the giving of benefits to another in return for something received—arguing that reciprocity is structured and variable across different forms of exchange, and that variations in the structure of reciprocity have profound effects on the emergence of integrative bonds of trust and solidarity (Molm 2010).

A network exchange approach has also been employed to understand social exchange. Some have examined how exchange patterns of commitment and inequality are affected when negotiated exchanges are combined with reciprocal exchanges in more complex relationships of embeddedness (Molm et al. 2013), showing that embedding negotiated exchanges in a relationship of reciprocal exchange increases the strength of behavioral commitments and reduces the effects of structural power differences on inequality.

Others have examined the development of commitments in structurally enabled and structurally induced (constraining) exchange relations, revealing that a structurally enabled relation generates a greater sense of control, more positive emotions, greater perceived cohesion, and more commitment behavior than a structurally induced relation (Lawler et al. 2006). Studies such as these show the importance for understanding both enabling and constraining features of network structures and how they impact cohesion and commitment in relations within such structures.

And, some have examined how groups form in competitive exchange networks, specifically how and when small networks of self-interested agents generate group ties at the network level, revealing that group affiliations are formed when actors perceive themselves as members of a group and share resources with each other (despite an underlying competitive structure in which actors may be embedded) (Thye et al. 2011).

18.3 Theories on Trust

Theory and research on trust is found in both sociology and psychology (Lewis and Weigert 2012). In sociology, most scientific investigations of trust as a social process are found in the social exchange literature (Cook et al. 2009). Work in this vein examines how trust and confidence in others influences social exchange relationships, specifically how uncertainty affects cooperative relationships. Similar to social psychological examinations of trust in sociology, research in economics has examined how trust and the fear of betrayal motivate individuals when they participate in negotiated (economic) exchanges (Bohnet and Zeckhauser 2004). Regardless of disciplinary emphasis, most contemporary perspectives on trust see it as a foundational interpersonal process that involves cognition, behavior, and emotions (Weber and Carter 2002).

Much of the work on trust is found in psychology, influenced by the work of Morton Deutsch, who defines trust as the confidence that an individual will find what is desired from another rather than what is feared (Deutsch 1973). While work on trust is often psychological in nature, most contemporary scholars believe that trust is an objective social reality, not reducible to psychological factors alone (Lewis and Weigert 2012; Kasperson et al. 2005). Research has shown that trust plays a central role in social life, not only in maintaining successful interpersonal relationships, but in developing as a healthy human being over time (Miller and Rempel 2004; Cook and Cooper 2003).

Theories on trust are generally classified three ways, addressing either *ultimate causation*, *ontogeny*, or *proximate causation* (Sherman 1988; Tinbergen 1963; Simpson 2007). Theories on trust that are centered on ultimate causation focus on evolutionary and cultural origins of traits that are associated with trusting behavior; theories of trust centered on ontogeny address environmental, experiential, and socialization factors that influence how trusting behavior becomes a valued orientation for individuals in society; theories that address proximate causal mechanisms of trust examine stimuli or events that activate, maintain, or regulate trusting behavior in populations. Let us examine these three theoretical perspectives on trust more closely.

18.3.1 Ultimate Causal Theories of Trust

Ultimate causal theories of trust cite a plethora of historical factors that together provide evidence for trust evolving in the human species as a survival mechanism (Cosmides and Tooby 1992; Brewer and Caporael 1990). For instance, some theorists conceive trust (and altruistic behavior) as an evolutionary byproduct that emerged in human civilizations due to the need for humans to hunt cooperatively (Kurzban 2003). Popular theoretical orientations on trust in this tradition link the emergence of trust in humans to their tendency and ability to mutually sanction one another for transgressions; the idea being that without mutual sanctioning, trust in the norms and social institutions of contemporary society—and the tendency for individuals to regulate trustworthiness in one another—would not have evolved as it has (Simpson 2007; Henrich and Boyd 2001; Gintis 2003).

Ultimate causal theories of trust often cite genetics as determinants of trusting behavior, emphasizing that trust is a trait that was selected during evolution. Here, gene-centered evolutionary models of selection such as inclusive fitness theory (Hamilton 1964) and reciprocal altruism theory (Trivers 1971) have been applied to understand the development of trust. These models see trust as an evolutionary trait that is passed down through generations; altruistic behavior emerged when individuals showed preferences toward helping biological relatives. These early, mostly biological explanations for the development of trust evolved to more sociological perspectives, which noted that altruistic behavior is not rooted solely in primary groups or in-groups—that trusting and self-sacrificial behavior is extended outward among inhabitants of a community, as a mechanism of social integration and social control. More recent, gene-cultural co-evolutionary models emphasize that humans developed trust via their tendency toward "strong reciprocity," which occurs when individuals enforce social norms and keep others in check to ensure that cheaters do not destroy the cooperative mechanisms that exist within groups (Fehr and Fischbacher 2003).

18.3.2 Ontogenetic Theories of Trust

Early ontogenetic theories of trust were influenced by Erikson (1963), who emphasized that trust develops early in life-course socialization, from conflicts that children must deal with as they mature across stages of development (Simpson 2007). Erikson noted that trust vs. mistrust is one of the first conflicts for children. Feelings of trust toward others are influenced by how attentive or neglectful primary group members are regarding early psycho-social needs. Children who have needs met by significant caregivers come to expect—and trust—that such needs will be met in the future, while children whose needs are not met come to doubt and distrust that their needs will be met.

Subsequent ontogenetic theories of trust were developed by Bowlby (1969, 1973, 1980), whose attachment theory showed that children develop trust when they learn that they can turn to support systems in times of distress, and by Bowen (1978), whose family systems theory links trust to the development of a differentiated self-concept, representing an individual's ability to feel both attachment to and independence from others. Bowlby and Bowen's ontogenetic theories show that those with differentiated self-concepts find it easier to develop trusting relationships with others as they progress through their life-course; the differentiation in attachment and independence allows for individuals to trust others and rely on them in times of need while not over-identifying with others and relying solely on them.

More recent ontogenetic, life-history theories of trust state that early childhood experiences provide children with diagnostic information about the situations and environments they are likely to experience as adults. For example, stressful situations and family dissension in early childhood can influence children to develop negative conceptions of themselves and others, which leads a child to have more insecure attachment patterns later in life (Belsky et al. 1991; Chisolm 1993). Early life experiences such as these can lead one to adopt short-term expectations for future relationships, based on a level of distrust and belief that such relationships are ephemeral rather than long-lasting.

18.3.3 Proximate Causal Theories of Trust

Many of the proximate causal theories of trust have emerged in the past few decades, in the work of Kelley et al. (2003), Holmes and Rempel (1989), and Wieselquist et al. (1999). Deutsch (1973) provided one of the original proximate causal theories of trust. These theories emphasize situational factors that influence the development of trust between individuals. For instance, Kelley et al. (2003; Kelley and Thibaut 1978) and others see trust emerging when high levels of *interdependence* exist between social units, when individuals need to *coordinate* activities to achieve goals, and when individuals are involved in *exchange relationships* where positive outcomes are needed for one or both exchanging partners. The model of trust proposed by Kelley et al. sees interdependence, coordination, and exchange being largely influenced by fear (Simpson 2007).

Additional proximate theories of trust focus on the normative development of relationships, specifically how trust develops based on *predictability* and *uncertainty reduction* (Holmes and Rempel 1989). Trust emerges between individuals when they come to expect and predict others' behavior. For instance, two individuals who meet likely have idealized expectations for what the other is and should be. These idealized expectations are vague and generalized in the initial stages of a relationship, but become more specific as interdependency forms between the individuals over time. As individuals form a dependency, doubt, fear, and concern of rejection can emerge, causing anxiety. Actors diminish their anxiety by reciprocating trusting actions toward one another. This "reciprocal assurance" reveals that each individual remains attached and committed to the other. Trust elevates when such reciprocated action takes the form of making sacrifices, taking risks, or placing oneself in a vulnerable position in relation to the other (Simpson 2007; Pruitt 1965).

18.3.4 Recent Research on Trust

Classic research on trust found that trust violations during interactions tend to be more harmful when they occur early on rather than later during interactions (Komorita and Mechling 1967). Recent research has addressed this phenomenon by examining the operation of trust cross-culturally, in high-trust vs. low-trust cultures. In an examination of trust behaviors in the United States (a society defined by high-trust) and Japan (a society defined by low-trust), Kuwabara et al. (2014) discovered that during interactions early trust violations are more harmful than late trust violations (but only in high-trust societies). They also found that generalized trust is not only lower but also less important in low-trust cultures. This research advances our understanding of how culture affects the development of solidarity in exchange relations.

Recent studies have examined whether reward systems generate the same positive effects as punishment systems (increased cooperation) without negative side effects (decreased interpersonal trust), or whether reward systems also lead to detrimental effects on trust, finding that while reward systems can generate the same positive effects as punishment systems, they also generate the same negative side effects (Irwin et al. 2014).

Classical sociological ideas on trust has been revisited as well; Frederiksen (2012) has applied Simmel (1971) to better understand how trust operates differently in various types of social relations. Contemporary research on trust spans various disciplines and is both qualitative and quantitative in nature. Recent qualitative studies on trust have examined the distrust people feel toward healthcare systems (Meyer 2015) and how trust influences doctor-patient relationships (Skirbekk et al. 2011). Recent quantitative studies have shown that the possession of high status leads individuals to trust others more (Lount and Petit 2012). Game-theory has also been used to understand how trust influences investments and returns in social networks (Frey et al. 2015).

18.4 Justice Theories

Theories of justice seek to understand how people assess the allocation of resources amongst self and others, particularly whether resources are distributed equitably (Hegtvedt 2006; Jasso 2001, 1980). Justice represents one's notion that resources, procedures, and/or outcomes of social relationships are administered or distributed fairly. Justice is a fundamental social comparison process; one does not need to look far to see examples of individuals evaluating self and others in terms of justice orientations. A young child may react negatively when they perceive that they do not receive as many cookies as another child; adults protest when they feel they are overcharged during a monetary transaction—justice processes are ubiquitous in social life. Much of the theory and research on justice is sociological (Hegtvedt and Markovsky 1995; Hegtvedt and Scheuerman 2010; Jasso 2007b), though it is commonly examined across the social sciences (Young 2011; Sen 2009).

18.4.1 The Elements of Justice

The process of justice involves a combination of both individual and situational factors, which involve *perceivers*, *receivers*, and *evaluations*

(Hegtvedt 2006). Perceivers are individuals who assess the outcome of some procedure or distributed resource. Receivers are recipients of outcomes or targets of a procedure. Justice evaluations are determinations made regarding expected outcomes or procedures, or whether a distributed resource or procedure was properly conducted.

Three personal factors influence how a perceiver assesses whether an outcome or procedure is just: The first regards an individual's *characteristics*, such as status (e.g., one's gender or age) (Hegtvedt and Cook 2001) and identity meanings (based on in-group favoritism and the tendency for individuals to devalue out-groups) (Clay-Warner 2001). Second, one's *beliefs* can influence perceptions of justice. For example, if one believes that gambling is immoral one would likely not feel as sympathetic for someone who lost money gambling. Third, personal *motivations* can influence whether one sees an outcome as just or unjust (for example, if one behaves altruistically toward another they may not expect resources in return, whereas if one's motivations were self-interested a resource may be expected after some helping behavior).

In addition to personal factors, situational factors are also important to consider in justice evaluations. Generally, individuals will behave more justly when they are in situations that increase their level of self-awareness; also, decisions made in groups are often perceived as more just than decisions made by individuals alone (Hegtvedt and Markovsky 1995). Additionally, justice outcomes can be interpreted differently depending on whether such outcomes exist between friends or strangers (individuals generally prefer more equitable distributions between friends than with strangers) (Hegtvedt and Cook 2001; Tyler and Dawes 1993).

Justice evaluations are determined based on the previous personal and situational factors, and are influenced by both *cognitive* (Cohen 1982; Van den Bos et al. 1999) and *comparison* processes (Hegtvedt 2006). Social cognition comes into play when an individual makes an attribution regarding a source of injustice. For instance, research has shown that being under-rewarded is likely to be perceived as more unjust than being over-rewarded, and that people tend to perceive situations as more just when attributions of injustice are internal rather than external (Utne and Kidd 1980). Social comparison processes operate to determine one's evaluation of justice as well, illustrated by Adams' (1965) formula of justice determination:

$$O_A / I_A = O_B / I_B$$

Where "O" represents an actor's outcomes, "I" indicates an actor's inputs, and "A" and "B" represent two different individuals in a situation. The comparison equation reveals an unjust situation when actor A or B believe that their outcomes compared to their inputs are not commensurate with one another. Drawing on cognitive dissonance theory, Adams noted that an imbalance in the formula of justice determination causes distress in an actor whose outputs do not equate their inputs, in comparison to another. In these situations actors will seek to reduce their discomfort and restore balance to the equation, by either: (1) Altering inputs, (2) altering outcomes, (3) cognitively distorting inputs or outcomes, (4) exiting the situation, (5) cognitively distorting inputs or outcomes of the other, or (6) changing the object of comparison (Hegtvedt and Markovsky 1995; Adams 1965).

When an individual determines that something is unjust, it causes a reaction, taking the form of an emotion, cognition, or behavior (Hegtvedt 2006). Regarding emotional outcomes of justice evaluations, individuals often feel guilt when they assess that they are over-rewarded some resource or when a procedure or outcome goes in their favor unfairly, and they feel anger when they are under-rewarded or when procedures or outcomes are deemed unfair. Regarding cognitive outcomes of justice evaluations, individuals are likely to alter their attitude or belief about another who has contributed to their injustice. And, individuals are likely to behave toward another differently based on whether one attributes a justice evaluation as contingent on another's motives or actions. For example, one may behave aggressively toward another if one perceives that the other person is responsible for an outcome that is unjust.

18.4.2 Distributive Justice and Procedural Justice

Past research has examined various dimensions of justice. Two main areas of emphasis in the justice literature include theories of *distributive justice* and *procedural justice*. Theories on distributive justice address how resources are distributed among individuals, noting that one's perception of distributive justice is influenced by *equality* (the idea that recipients of resources should receive equal shares of distributed outcomes), *equity* (the idea that resources should be commensurate to contributions), and *need* (the idea that resources should be distributed based on recipients' needs) (Hegtvedt 2006). Theories of procedural justice address the fairness of processes by which resources are distributed. Classic work on procedural justice examined legalities of resource allocation and conflict resolution (Thibaut and Walker 1975; Lind and Tyler 1988) and situational and consistent decision making in organizational settings (Leventhal et al. 1980; Folger 1977). Generally, scholars of procedural justice have found that individuals prefer procedural rules that fulfil important situational goals (Hegtvedt and Markovsky 1995; Leventhal et al. 1980); thus, individuals' perceptions of procedural justice are influenced by: (1) Consistency of procedures across individuals and across time, (2) the suppression of bias in procedures, (3) the accuracy of information regarding a procedural decision, (4) Mechanisms to correct bad decisions, (5) representativeness of the participants to a decision, and (6) The ethicality of standards.

Another area of focus in the justice literature regards *authoritative justice* (Hegtvedt 2006; Tyler and Lind 1992), which addresses how individuals defer to and obey authority, revealing that individuals defer to authority figure based on an authority figure's *standing* (one's relative status and degree of respect and treatment shown), *neutrality* (an authority figure's equal treatment of subordinates), and *trust* (an authority figure's intentions of fairness).

Justice evaluations take many forms, and have varying degrees of significance and intensity regarding the outcomes they influence. Social interactions are often affected by justice processes; they are a fundamental comparison process that defines the structure of people's experience in society. Hegtvedt (2006) summarizes the three main assumptions implicit in justice processes, based on previous theory and research on justice (Adams 1965; Berger et al. 1972; Leventhal et al. 1980; Lind and Tyler 1988; Walster et al. 1978; Van den Bos et al. 2001): (1) Individuals attempt to make sense of their social experiences and are likely to assess the justice of their expectations, (2) evaluations of injustice produce unpleasant sensations of distress and tension, and (3) individuals are motivated to eliminate distress by restoring justice for themselves (and, if applicable, for others).

18.4.3 Recent Research on Justice

Recent research on justice processes has examined how individual-level and contextual factors combine to affect one's perception of justice. For instance, Parris et al. (2014) examined college students' perceptions of justice with regards to the environment, showing that one's environmental identity and perception that one's university encourages sustainability enhances perceptions of procedural, distributive, and ecological injustice regarding the environment. Clay-Warner et al. (2005) examined how procedural and distributive justice impact worker attitudes differently, showing that each type of justice predicts different levels of commitment to an organization for workers who are victims or survivors of downsizing (results showed that procedural justice is a more important predictor of organizational commitment for survivors and unaffected workers of downsizing than for victims of downsizing, while distributive justice is more important for victims than for either survivors or unaffected workers).

Additional research on justice includes work by Melamed et al. (2014) that examines distributive justice and referent networks, and Hegtvedt and Isom's (2014) summary on the relationship between justice and inequality. Methodology in justice studies has also been addressed, with scholars providing criticism and recommendations for how to improve research designs that address justice and social comparison processes (Jasso 2012; Markovsky and Eriksson 2012). Social psychologists have examined the relationship between justice and identity, revealing how one's moral identity (based on meanings of justice and care) operates to motivate behavior and emotions across social situations (Carter 2013; Stets and Carter 2011, 2012). And, some have examined the relationship between justice and emotions (Jasso 2007a).

18.5 Legitimacy Theory

Legitimacy theory is a theory of social comparison that examines whether things in society (such as authority figures) are right and proper, and in accord with how they ought to be (Zelditch 2006). Legitimacy theory is a theory of perception, seeking to explain how power is defined, respected, and obeyed—i.e., legitimized—among individuals in society. In legitimacy theory, power is one's ability to control and allocate resources; or more simply, power is the ability to reward or penalize others. Generally, legitimacy theory seeks to understand how power becomes legitimated in social groups and in greater society, and the causes and consequences of the legitimation of power (Zelditch 2006; Zelditch et al. 1983; Walker et al. 1991).

18.5.1 The Elements of Legitimacy

Central to legitimacy theory is the notion that once power becomes legitimated it takes the form of *authority*. Authority represents an individual's ability to regulate others' behavior by invoking rights that are vested in a social role. But once authority is established, not everyone complies with it. Legitimacy theory seeks to understand the situational contexts that are present when an individual voluntarily complies (or does not comply) to an authority figure. To understand how and why people comply with authority, a better understanding of power is needed. In legitimacy theory, power takes two forms: *pure power*, and *legitimate power* (Zelditch 2006).

Pure power is power that is overt and coercive, such as direct physical aggression. Pure power is difficult to wield effectively, especially over time, because it is often not respected, costly, and unstable. Military regimes that have had difficulty garrisoning borders or coercing large populations of people provide examples of pure power being ineffective; the continuing need to display and enact power through coercion makes it unstable and difficult to maintain. Legitimate power is authority that is generally respected and obeyed willingly, making it the much more effective and stable form of maintaining order.

Legitimacy theory differentiates the meaning of power at different levels of analysis. At the micro (individual) level, legitimacy is *propriety*. At the macro (group) level, legitimacy is *validity* (Zelditch 2006; Dornbusch and Scott 1975; Weber 1968 [1918]). When an individual treats another as a legitimate authority figure, that person has propriety. When an individual accepts the existence of a normative order and complies with general expectations for behavior as defined by sources of power in the greater social structure, the individual sees the normative order as valid.

Legitimacy theory also distinguishes the levels of the hierarchy of authority that supports a legitimate entity. When an authority figure (or an entity that has authority) receives support from peers or superiors, it is the *authorization* of their power. When subordinates act in deference to authority, they *endorse* the authority figure's power as legitimate. A main concern of legitimacy theory is the manner in which validity, propriety, authorization, and endorsement interrelate to influence stable authority structures and the normative regulation of power (Zelditch 2006).

Previous work in legitimacy theory has revealed that legitimation is a function of four elements (Zelditch and Walker 2003): *consensus*, *impartiality*, *objectification*, and *consonance*. These four elements represent the notions that:

(1) Generally, an authority's claim to legitimacy will not be successful unless a consensus exists between authority figures and subordinates regarding norms, values, beliefs, purposes, practices, or and procedures that are aligned with the use of power, (2) additionally, authority will not be considered legitimate unless it is fair and impartial—that benefits gained by the authority figure benefit the common good or have some universal applicability, (3) beliefs in which an authority figure appeals must be based on objective facts, and (4) there must be an agreement between values, norms, beliefs, purposes, or procedures, and the nature, conditions, and consequences of the structure of the authority that is legitimated (Zelditch 2006). Myriad empirical studies have validated these prior conditions of legitimacy as central to the process of authority and subordinate relationships (Massey et al. 1997; Zelditch and Floyd 1998; Zelditch and Walker 2000).

18.5.2 Recent Research on Legitimacy

One of the most common applications of legitimacy theory is to law enforcement. Scholars have used legitimacy theory to understand how police and civilians interact, and how power is wielded by those in positions of authority. One example of such research is provided by Long et al. (2013), who examined how legitimacy and fairness processes influence whether or not police officers report acts of misconduct perpetrated by fellow officers. This research found that the perceived seriousness of an offense and legitimacy (endorsement) are consistently strong predictors of officers' intentions to report misconduct. Legitimacy theory has also been applied to understand how modern sexist viewpoints are endorsed (legitimized) by men and women, showing that females are relatively disinclined to recognize expressions of modern sexism as prejudicial, and positing that modern forms of prejudice may be perilous because they remain unchallenged (Barreto and Ellemers 2005).

Legitimacy theory has also been used to understand identity verification processes, specifically how individuals verify their "leader identity" in a task-oriented group (Burke et al. 2007). Findings of this work revealed that verification of one's leader identity is influenced by both gender and legitimation processes: Legitimated female leaders and non-legitimated males find it easier to verify identities in task-oriented groups. In addition, legitimated male leaders tend to be over-evaluated in the amount of their leadership relative to their own identity standards, while non-legitimated female leaders' leadership behavior tends to be under-evaluated relative to their own identity standards.

Legitimacy theory has also been expanded and applied to marketing research. A recent study by Wang et al. (2014) has shown that individuals perceive the worth and legitimacy of products differently depending on the country in which the product is produced. And, some have examined how annual reports and financial statements of organizations create a sense of legitimacy, showing how fledging companies carve out legitimate reputations over time in a competitive market (Irvine and Fortune 2015, forthcoming). A review of the literature that incorporates some facet of legitimacy theory shows how central notions of authority and subordination are in social interactions.

18.6 Interrelations Among Social Exchange, Trust, Justice, and Legitimacy

So far we have covered four main areas of inquiry in microsociological theory: social exchange, trust, justice, and legitimacy. While these subjects have been presented in discrete sections, it is important that their commonalities be addressed. After all, these social processes do not operate in isolation; each operates reflexively, often simultaneously with corresponding processes. For example, trust, justice, and legitimacy often influence how individuals exchange resources with one another. When an individual makes a justice assessment regarding how resources are allocated, the legitimacy of the involved actors often influences perceptions of equity and fairness. And, an individual's feelings of trust toward another are sometimes affected by the perception that they abuse a position of authority, or do not treat others in a just manner. It is more likely that these processes operate in concert rather than in isolation. With that notion in mind, let us investigate recent research that has examined interconnections among social exchange, trust, justice, and legitimacy.

Past research applied knowledge of social exchange and trust to understand what affects individuals' trust toward managers in organizational settings (Whitener et al. 1998). More recent work has examined the reciprocal relations between trust and perceived justice, using neuroscientific evidence that suggests that trust can develop between actors without conscious deliberation; this shows that contrary to previous notions that trust develops slowly between workers and management, trust can also form rapidly, exerting a significant influence on employee perceptions of justice (Holtz 2013). Exchange theory and theories of procedural justice have been applied to management, specifically to understand how firms are managed differently depending on whether firms are populated by family or non-family managers (Barnett et al. 2012).

Using a more sociological lens, Hegdvedt (2015) summarized the interrelated roles of justice and trust, showing how social identity-models and resource-based models of justice processes facilitate the creation of legitimacy, and revealing how justice and trust are influenced by power and leadership, intergroup processes, situational factors, and emotions. In addition, Max Weber's conceptions of legitimate and charismatic authority have been applied to understand how trust develops in online worlds, when people collaborate to accomplish a task together (O'Neil 2014).

In research examining the relationship between justice and legitimacy, Bottoms and Tankebe (2012) examined how legitimacy operates in the criminal justice system, proposing that a dialogic model that includes both power-holder legitimacy and audience legitimacy must be considered to understand legitimacy processes in the criminal justice field. This work advances previous work that focuses mostly on compliance to the law to address justifications of the claims to legitimacy made by power-holders, and how legitimacy changes over time. In a similar vein, Murphy (2005) examined relationships among procedural justice, legitimacy, and tax non-compliance, showing that attempts to coerce and threaten taxpayers into compliance can undermine the legitimacy of a tax office's authority, which in turn can affect taxpayers' subsequent compliance behavior.

Some have applied theories of justice and legitimacy and examined the collectivity-generated legitimacy of reward procedures and individual-level justice perceptions about reward distributions, finding that collectivity sources of validity (authorization and endorsement) exert positive effects on individual-level justice perceptions (as predicted by Hegtvedt and Johnson (2000)), but that the influence is entirely indirect through an individual's perception of procedural justice (Mueller and Landsman 2004).

Trust has also been examined in the context of social exchange. For instance, the relationship between uncertainty and trust in exogenous shifts in modes of social exchange has been addressed (exchanges that are not initiated by individuals in a given exchange system) (Colquitt et al. 2012). Results in these studies have shown that trust declines when the uncertainty created by the mode of exchange decreases, if cooperation rates between exchange partners are high before and after a change occurs in the mode of exchange (Chesire et al. 2010). Others have examined how power, trust, and social exchange combine to determine how a community supports tourism, finding that communities are more likely to support tourism when residents trust in their government officials and when they trust that that benefits will be realized by increased tourism (Nunkoo 2012).

There are many other examples of recent research that has examined some relationship among exchange, trust, justice, and legitimacy (Gillham and Edwards 2011; Schilke et al. 2015; Mazerolle et al. 2013). One can see how broadly these four processes have been applied in recent years. While most work on each originated in sociology or psychology, scholars from across the disciplines have applied theories of exchange, trust, justice, and legitimacy to understand areas of social life.

18.7 Conclusion

One of the great conundrums in sociology is to understand how free-willed individuals are constrained by greater social forces that they themselves create. Reconciling this somewhat paradoxical duality has been a charge for sociologists since the discipline's inception. Understanding social exchange, trust, justice, and legitimacy as core social processes that connect individuals to others in the social structure helps us detangle the mystery of social organization. Scholars who have generated theories on and researched these processes have moved us toward answering the questions that have commonly plagued sociology; by understanding how people exchange resources, trust in others, perceive things as just, or legitimize the use of power, we begin to conceive how ephemeral micro-level encounters connect to stable macro-level social structures. In many ways, social exchange, trust, justice, and legitimacy are bridges that link the micro- and macro-realms.

Of course, these four processes are not the only mechanisms by which individuals create and maintain the social structure. But, they are ubiquitous elements of social life, active to some degree in virtually all encounters. As dimensions of social comparison, these processes greatly influence attitudes and behaviors of individuals in society. And, these processes are also crucial dimensions of social integration and social regulation—perhaps the two most central sociological processes.

As with all areas of inquiry in sociology, more work is to be done. Future research is needed to further understand the four social processes addressed in this chapter. The fact that there is a legion of scholars (and students) oriented toward studying exchange, trust, justice, and legitimacy provides confidence that their respective research programs will be carried forward. Social scientists will also continue to investigate the interrelations among exchange, trust, justice, and legitimacy, and even more work will be aimed toward revealing how each process connects to other core social processes, such as self and identity, status, and deviance.

References

Adams, J. S. (1965). Inequity in social exchange. In L. Berkowitz (Ed.), *Advances in experimental social psychology* (pp. 267–299). New York: Academic.

Barnett, T., Long, R. G., & Marler, L. E. (2012). Vision and exchange in intra-family succession: Effects on procedural justice climate among nonfamily managers. *Entrepreneurship: Theory and Practice, 36*(6), 1207–1225. doi:10.1111/j.1540-6520.2012.00546.x.

Barreto, M., & Ellemers, N. (2005). The perils of political correctness: Men's and women's responses to old-fashioned and modern sexist views. *Social Psychology Quarterly, 68*(1), 75–88.

Belsky, J., Steinberg, L., & Draper, P. (1991). Childhood experience, interpersonal development, and reproductive strategy: An evolutionary theory of socialization. *Child Development, 62*, 647–670.

Berger, J., Zelditch, M. J., Anderson, B., & Cohen, B. P. (1972). Structural aspects of distributive justice: A status value formation. In J. Berger, M. J. Zelditch, & B. Anderson (Eds.), *Sociological theories in progress* (pp. 119–146). Boston: Houghton-Mifflin.

Blau, P. M. (1964). *Exchange and power in social life*. New York: Wiley.

Bohnet, I., & Zeckhauser, R. (2004). Trust, risk, and betrayal. *Journal of Economic Behavior and Organization, 55*, 467–484.

Boissicat, N., Pansu, P., Bouffard, T., & Cottin, F. (2012). Relation between perceived scholastic competence and social comparison mechanisms among elementary school children. *Social Psychology of Education, 15*(4), 603–614.

Bottoms, A., & Tankebe, J. (2012). Beyond procedural justice: A dialogic approach to legitimacy in criminal justice. *Journal of Criminal Law and Criminology, 102*(1), 119–170.

Bowen, M. (1978). *Family therapy in clinical practice*. New York: Jason Aronson.

Bowlby, J. (1969). *Attachment and loss: Volume 1: Attachment*. New York: Basic Books.

Bowlby, J. (1973). *Attachment and loss: Volume 2: Separation: Anxiety and anger*. New York: Basic Books.

Bowlby, J. (1980). *Attachment and loss: Volume 3: Loss*. New York: Basic Books.

Brewer, M. B., & Caporael, L. R. (1990). Selfish genes vs. selfish people: Sociobiology as origin myth. *Motivation and Emotion, 14*, 237–243.

Burke, P. J., Stets, J. E., & Cerven, C. (2007). Gender, legitimation, and identity verification in groups. *Social Psychology Quarterly, 70*, 27–42.

Carter, M. J. (2013). Advancing identity theory: Examining the relationship between activated identities and behavior in different social contexts. *Social Psychology Quarterly, 76*, 203–223. doi:10.1177/0190272513493095.

Chesire, C., Gerbasi, A., & Cook, K. S. (2010). Trust and transitions in modes of exchange. *Social Psychology Quarterly, 73*, 176–195.

Chisolm, J. S. (1993). Death, hope, and sex: Life-history theory and the development of reproductive strategies. *Current Anthropology, 34*, 1–24.

Clay-Warner, J. (2001). Perceiving procedural injustice: The effects of group membership and status. *Social Psychology Quarterly, 64*(3), 224–238.

Clay-Warner, J., Hegdvedt, K. A., & Roman, P. (2005). Procedural justice, distributive justice: How experiences with downsizing condition their impact on organizational commitment. *Social Psychology Quarterly, 68*(1), 89–102.

Cohen, R. L. (1982). Perceiving justice: An attributional perspective. In J. Greenberg & R. L. Cohen (Eds.), *Equity and justice in social behavior* (pp. 119–160). New York: Academic.

Colquitt, J. A., LePine, J. A., Piccolo, R. F., Zapata, C. P., & Rich, B. L. (2012). Explaining the justice–performance relationship: Trust as exchange deepener or trust as uncertainty reducer? *Journal of Applied Psychology, 97*(1), 1–15. doi:10.1037/a0025208.

Cook, K. S., & Cooper, R. M. (2003). Experimental studies of cooperation, trust, and social exchange. In E. Ostrom & J. Walker (Eds.), *Trust and reciprocity: Interdisciplinary lessons form experimental research* (pp. 209–244). New York: Russell Sage.

Cook, K. S., & Emerson, R. M. (1978). Power, equity and commitment in exchange networks. *American Sociological Review, 43*(5), 721–739.

Cook, K. S., Levi, M., & Hardin, R. (2009). *Whom can we trust? How groups, networks and institutions make trust possible*. New York: Russell Sage Foundation Publications.

Cook, K. S., Chesire, C., Rice, E. R. W., & Nakagawa, S. (2013). Social exchange theory. In J. D. DeLamater & A. Ward (Eds.), *Handbook of social psychology* (2nd ed., pp. 61–88). New York: Springer Science + Business Media.

Cosmides, L., & Tooby, J. (1992). Cognitive adaptations for social exchange. In J. Barkow, L. Cosmides, & J. Tooby (Eds.), *The adapted mind* (pp. 163–228). New York: Oxford University Press.

Deutsch, M. (1973). *The resolution of conflict*. New Haven: Yale University Press.

Dornbusch, S. M., & Scott, W. R. (1975). *Evaluation and the exercise of authority*. San Francisco: Jossey-Bass.

Emerson, R. M. (1962). Power-dependence relations. *American Sociological Review, 27*, 31–40.

Emerson, R. M. (1972). Exchange theory, part 2: Exchange relations and networks. In J. Berger, M. Zelditch Jr., & B. Anderson (Eds.), *Sociological theories in progress* (Vol. 2, pp. 61–83). Boston: Houghton-Mifflin.

Emerson, R. M. (1976). Social exchange theory. *Annual Review of Sociology, 2*, 335–362.

Emerson, R. M. (1981). Social exchange theory. In M. Rosenberg & R. H. Turner (Eds.), *Social psychology: Sociological perspectives* (pp. 30–65). New York: Basic Books.

Erikson, E. (1963). *Childhood and society*. New York: Norton.

Fehr, E., & Fischbacher, U. (2003). The nature of human altruism. *Nature, 425*, 785–791.

Folger, R. (1977). Distributive and procedural justice: Combined impact of 'Voice' and improvement on experienced inequity. *Journal of Personality and Social Psychology, 35*, 108–119.

Frederiksen, M. (2012). Dimensions of trust: An empirical revisit to Simmel's formal sociology of intersubjective trust. *Current Sociology, 60*(6), 733–750.

Frey, V., Buskens, V., & Raub, W. (2015). Embedding trust: A game-theoretic model for investments in and returns on network embeddedness. *The Journal of Mathematical Sociology, 39*(1), 39–72. doi:10.1080/0022250X.2014.897947.

Gillham, P. F., & Edwards, B. (2011). Legitimacy management, preservation of exchange relationships, and the dissolution of the mobilization for global justice coalition. *Social Problems, 58*(3), 433–460. doi:10.1525/sp.2011.58.3.433.

Gintis, H. (2003). The hitchhiker's guide to altruism: Gene-culture co-evolution and the internalization of norms. *Journal of Theoretical Biology, 220*, 407–418.

Hamilton, W. D. (1964). The genetic evolution of social behavior. *Journal of Theoretical Biology, 7*, 1–52.

Hegtvedt, K. A. (2006). Justice frameworks. In P. J. Burke (Ed.), *Contemporary social psychological theories* (pp. 46–69). Palo Alto: Stanford University Press.

Hegdvedt, K. A. (2015). Creating legitimacy: The interrelated roles of justice and trust. In A. J. Borstein & A. J. Tomkins (Eds.), *Motivating cooperation and compliance with authority* (Vol. 62, pp. 55–80). Cham: Springer.

Hegtvedt, K. A., & Cook, K. S. (2001). Distributive justice: Recent theoretical developments and applications. In J. Sanders & V. L. Hamilton (Eds.), *Handbook of justice research in law* (pp. 93–132). New York: Kluwer Academic/Plenum Publishers.

Hegtvedt, K. A., & Isom, D. (2014). Inequality: A matter of justice. In J. D. McLeod, E. J. Lawler, & M. Schwalbe (Eds.), *Handbook of the social psychology of inequality* (pp. 65–94). Dordrecht: Springer.

Hegtvedt, K. A., & Johnson, C. (2000). Justice beyond the individual: A future with legitimation. *Social Psychology Quarterly, 63*(4), 298–311.

Hegtvedt, K. A., & Markovsky, B. (1995). Justice and injustice. In K. S. Cook, G. A. Fine, & J. House (Eds.), *Sociological perspectives on social psychology* (pp. 257–280). Boston: Allyn Bacon.

Hegtvedt, K. A., & Scheuerman, H. L. (2010). The justice/morality link: Implied, then ignored, yet inevitable. In S. Hitlin & S. Vaisey (Eds.), *Handbook of the sociology of morality* (pp. 331–360). New York: Springer.

Henrich, J., & Boyd, R. (2001). Why people punish defectors: Weak conformist transmission can stabilize costly enforcement of norms in cooperative dilemmas. *Journal of Theoretical Biology, 208*, 78–89.

Holmes, J. G., & Rempel, J. K. (1989). Trust in close relationships. In C. Hendrick (Ed.), *Close relationships* (pp. 187–220). Newbury Park: Sage.

Holtz, B. C. (2013). Trust primacy: A model of the reciprocal relations between trust and percieved justice. *Journal of Management, 39*, 1891–1923. doi:10.1177/0149206312471392.

Homans, G. C. (1958). Social behavior as exchange. *American Journal of Sociology, 62*, 597–606.

Homans, G. C. (1961). *Social behavior: Its elementary forms*. New York: Harcourt Brace and World Inc.

Hoorens, V., & Van Damme, C. (2012). What do people infer from social comparisons? Bridges between social comparison and person perception. *Social and Personality Psychology Compass, 6*(8), 607–618. doi:10.1111/j.1751-9004.2012.00451.x.

Irvine, H. J., & Fortune, M. (2016). The first 25 years of the Queensland Rugby Football League: Claims to legitimacy in annual reports. *Accounting History, 21*(1), 48–74. doi:10.1177/1032373215614116.

Irwin, K., Mulder, L., & Brent, S. (2014). The detrimental effects of sanctions of intragroup trust: Comparing punishments and rewards. *Social Psychology Quarterly, 77*(3), 253–272. doi:10.1177/0190272513518803.

Jasso, G. (1980). A new theory of distributive justice. *American Sociological Review, 45*(1), 3–32.

Jasso, G. (2001). Comparison theory. In J. H. Turner (Ed.), *Handbook of sociological theory* (pp. 669–698). New York: Kluwer Academic/Plenum Publishers.

Jasso, G. (2007a). Emotion in justice processes. In J. E. Stets & J. H. Turner (Eds.), *Handbook of the sociology of emotions* (pp. 321–346). New York: Springer.

Jasso, G. (2007b). Theoretical unification in justice and beyond. *Social Justice Research, 20*, 336–371.

Jasso, G. (2012). Safeguarding justice research. *Sociological Methods and Research, 41*(1), 217–239.

Jensen, A. C., Pond, A. M., & Padilla-Walker, L. M. (2015). Why can't I be more like my brother? The role and correlates of sibling social comparison orientation. *Journal of Youth Adolescence, 44*(11), 2067–2078.

Kasperson, R. E., Golding, D., & Tuler, S. (2005). Social distrust as a factor in siting hazardous facilities. In J. X. Kasperson & R. E. Kasperson (Eds.), *The social contours of risk: Vol. 1, publics, risk communication and social amplification of risk* (pp. 29–50). Trowbridge: Cromwell Press Ltd.

Kelley, H. H., & Thibaut, J. W. (1978). *Interpersonal relationships: A theory of interdependence*. New York: Wiley.

Kelley, H. H., Holmes, J. G., Kerr, N. L., Reis, H. T., Rusbult, C. E., & Van Lange, P. A. M. (2003). *An atlas of interpersonal situations*. New York: Cambridge University Press.

Komorita, S. S., & Mechling, J. (1967). Betrayal and reconciliation in a two-person game. *Journal of Personality and Social Psychology, 6*(3), 349–353.

Kurzban, R. (2003). Biological foundations of reciprocity. In E. Ostrom & J. Walker (Eds.), *Trust and reciprocity: Interdisciplinary lessons from experimental research* (pp. 105–127). New York: Russell Sage.

Kuwabara, K., Vogt, S., Watabe, M., & Komiya, A. (2014). Trust, cohesion, and cooperation after early versus late trust violations in two-person exchange: The role of generalized trust in the United States and Japan. *Social Psychology Quarterly, 77*(4), 344–360. doi:10.1177/0190272514546757.

Lawler, E. J. (2001). An affect theory of social exchange. *American Journal of Sociology, 107*, 321–352.

Lawler, E. J., Thye, S. R., & Yoon, J. (2006). Committment in structurally enabled and induced exchange relations. *Social Psychology Quarterly, 69*(2), 183–200.

Leventhal, G. S., Karuza, J., Jr., & Fry, W. R. (1980). Beyond fairness: A theory of allocation preferences. In G. Mikula (Ed.), *Justice and social interaction* (pp. 167–218). New York: Springer.

Lewis, J. D., & Weigert, A. J. (2012). The social dynamics of trust: Theoretical and empirical research, 1985–2012. *Social Forces, 91*(1), 25–31.

Lind, E. A., & Tyler, T. R. (1988). *The social psychology of procedural justice*. New York: Plenum.

Long, M. A., Cross, J. E., Shelley, T. O. C., & Ivkovic, S. K. (2013). The normative order of reporting police misconduct: Examining the roles of offense seriousness, legitimacy, and fairness. *Social Psychology Quarterly, 76*(3), 242–267. doi:10.1177/0190272513493094.

Lount, R. B., Jr., & Petit, N. C. (2012). The social context of trust: The role of status. *Organizational Behavior and Human Decision Processes, 117*(1), 15–23. doi:10.1016/j.obhdp.2011.07.005.

Markovsky, B., & Eriksson, K. (2012). Comparing direct and indirect measures of just rewards. *Sociological Methods and Research, 41*(1), 199–216.

Massey, K., Freeman, S., & Zelditch, M., Jr. (1997). Status, power and accounts. *Social Psychology Quarterly, 60*(3), 238–251.

Mazerolle, L., Antrobus, E., Bennett, S., & Tyler, T. R. (2013). Shaping citizen perceptions of police legitimacy: A randomized field trial of procedural justice. *Criminology, 51*(1), 33–63. doi:10.1111/j.1745-9125.2012.00289.x.

Melamed, D., Park, H., Zhong, J., & Liu, Y. (2014). Referent networks and distributive justice. *Advances in Group Processes, 31*, 241–262.

Meyer, S. B. (2015). Investigations of trust in public and private healthcare in Australia: A qualitative study of patients with heart disease. *Journal of Sociology, 51*(2), 221–235. doi:10.1177/1440783313500855.

Miller, P. J. E., & Rempel, J. K. (2004). Trust and partner-enhancing attributions in close relationships. *Personality and Social Psychology Bulletin, 30*, 695–705.

Molm, L. D. (1997). *Coercive power in exchange*. Cambridge: Cambridge University Press.

Molm, L. D. (2006). The social exchange framework. In P. J. Burke (Ed.), *Contemporary social psychological theories*. Palo Alto: Stanford University Press.

Molm, L. (2010). The structure of reciprocity. *Social Psychology Quarterly, 73*(2), 119–131. doi:10.1177/0190272510369079.

Molm, L. D., & Cook, K. S. (1995). Social exchange and exchange networks. In K. S. Cook, G. A. Fine, & J. S. House (Eds.), *Sociological perspectives on social psychology* (pp. 209–235). Needham Heights: Allyn and Bacon.

Molm, L. D., Peterson, G., & Takahashi, N. (1999). Power in negotiated and reciprocal exchange. *American Sociological Review, 64*(6), 876–890.

Molm, L. D., Takahashi, N., & Peterson, G. (2000). Risk and trust in social exchange: An experimental test of a classical proposition. *American Journal of Sociology, 105*(5), 1396–1427.

Molm, L. D., Melamed, D., & Whitman, M. M. (2013). Behavioral consequences of embeddedness: Effects of the underlying forms of exchange. *Social Psychology Quarterly, 76*(1), 73–97. doi:10.1177/0190272512468284.

Mueller, C. W., & Landsman, M. J. (2004). Legitimacy and justice perceptions. *Social Psychology Quarterly, 67*(2), 189–202.

Murphy, K. (2005). Regulating more effectively: The relationship between procedural justice, legitimacy, and tax non-compliance. *Journal of Law and Society, 32*(4), 562–589. doi:10.1111/j.1467-6478.2005.00338.x.

Nunkoo, R. (2012). Power, trust, social exchange, and community support. *Annals of Tourism Research, 39*(2), 997–1023. doi:10.1016/j.annals.2011.11.017.

O'Neil, M. (2014). Hacking Weber: Legitimacy, critique, and trust in peer production. *Information, Communication and Society, 17*(7), 872–888. doi:10.1080/1369118X.2013.850525.

Parris, C. L., Hegtvedt, K. A., Watson, L. A., & Johnson, C. (2014). Justice for all? Factors affecting perceptions of environmental and ecological injustice. *Social Justice Research, 27*, 67–98.

Pruitt, D. G. (1965). Definition of the situation as a determinant of international action. In H. C. Kelman (Ed.), *International behavior* (pp. 393–432). New York: Holt, Rinehart, and Winston.

Schilke, O., Reimann, M., & Cook, K. S. (2015). Power decreases trust in social exchange. *Proceedings of the National Academy of Sciences of the United States of America, 112*(42), 12950–12955.

Sen, A. (2009). *The idea of justice*. Cambridge, MA: Harvard University Press.

Sherman, P. W. (1988). The levels of analysis. *Animal Behavior, 36*, 616–619.

Simmel, G. (1971). *On individuality and social forms*. Chicago: University of Chicago Press.

Simpson, J. A. (2007). Foundations of interpersonal trust. In A. W. Kruglanski & E. T. Higgins (Eds.), *Social psychology: Handbook of basic principles* (2nd ed., pp. 587–607). New York: The Guilford Press.

Skirbekk, H., Middelthon, A.-L., Hjortdahl, P., & Finset, A. (2011). Mandates of trust in the doctor-patient relationship. *Qualitative Health Research, 21*(9), 1182–1190. doi:10.1177/1049732311405685.

Stets, J. E., & Carter, M. J. (2011). The moral self: Applying identity theory. *Social Psychology Quarterly, 74*, 192–215.

Stets, J. E., & Carter, M. J. (2012). A theory of the self for the sociology of morality. *American Sociological Review, 77*, 120–140.

Thibaut, J. W., & Kelley, H. H. (1959). *The social psychology of groups*. New York: Wiley.

Thibaut, J., & Walker, L. (1975). *Procedural justice: A psychological analysis*. Hillsdale: Erlbaum.

Thye, S. R., Lawler, E. J., & Yoon, J. (2011). The emergence of embedded relations and group formation in networks of competition. *Social Psychology Quarterly, 74*(4), 387–413. doi:10.1177/0190272511415553.

Tinbergen, N. (1963). On the aims and methods of ethology. *Zeitschrift für Tierpsychologie, 20*, 410–433.

Trivers, R. (1971). The evolution of reciprocal altruism. *Quarterly Review of Biology, 46*, 35–57.

Turner, J. H. (2010). *Theoretical principles of sociology, volume 2: Microdynamics*. New York: Springer.

Tyler, T. R., & Dawes, R. (1993). Fairness in groups: Comparing the self-interest and social identity perspectives. In B. A. Mellers & J. Baron (Eds.), *Psychological perspectives on justice: Theory and application* (pp. 87–108). London: Cambridge University Press.

Tyler, T. R., & Lind, E. A. (1992). A relational model of authority in groups. *Advances in Experimental Social Psychology, 25*, 115–191.

Utne, M. K., & Kidd, R. F. (1980). Equity and attribution. In G. Mikula (Ed.), *Justice and social interaction* (pp. 63–93). New York: Springer.

Van den Bos, K., Bruins, J., Wilke, H. A. M., & Dronkert, E. (1999). Sometimes unfair procedures have nice aspects: On the psychology of the fair process effect. *Journal of Personality and Social Psychology, 77*, 324–336.

Van den Bos, K., Lind, E. A., & Wilke, H. A. M. (2001). The psychology of procedural and distributive justice viewed from the perspective of fairness heuristic theory. In R. Cropanzano (Ed.), *Justice in the workplace* (pp. 49–66). Mahwah: Erlbaum.

Walker, H. A., Rogers, L., Thomas, G. M., & Zelditch, M. J. (1991). Legitimating collective action: Theory and experimental results. *Research in Political Sociology, 5*, 1–25.

Walster, E. G., Walster, W., & Berschied, E. (1978). *Equity: Theory and research*. Needham Heights: Allyn and Bacon.

Wang, T., Zhou, L., Mou, Y., & Zhao, J. (2014). Study of country-of-origin image from legitimacy theory perspective: Evidence from the USA and India. *Industrial Marketing Management, 43*(5), 769–776. doi:10.1016/j.indmarman.2014.04.003.

Weber, M. (1968 [1918]). *Economy and society*. Berkeley: University of California Press.

Weber, L. R., & Carter, A. I. (2002). *The social construction of trust*. New York: Springer.

Whitener, E. M., Brodt, S. E., Kosgaard, M. A., & Werner, J. M. (1998). Managers as initiators of trust: An exchange relationship framework for understanding managerial trustworthy behavior. *Academy of Management Review, 23*(3), 513–530. doi:10.5465/AMR.1998.926624.

Wieselquist, J., Rusbult, C. E., Foster, C. A., & Agnew, C. R. (1999). Committment, prorelationship behavior, and trust in close relationships. *Journal of Personality and Social Psychology, 77*, 942–966.

Young, I. M. (2011). *Justice and the politics of difference*. Princeton: Princeton University Press.

Zelditch, M., Jr. (2006). Legitimacy theory. In P. J. Burke (Ed.), *Contemporary social psychological theories* (pp. 324–352). Stanford: Stanford University Press.

Zelditch, M., Jr., & Floyd, A. S. (1998). Consensus, dissensus, and justification. In J. Berger & M. Zelditch Jr. (Eds.), *Status, power, and legitimacy* (pp. 339–368). New Brunswick: Transaction Publishers.

Zelditch, M., Jr., & Walker, H. A. (2000). The normative regulation of power. *Advances in Group Processes, 17*, 155–178.

Zelditch, M., Jr., & Walker, H. A. (2003). The legitimacy of regimes. *Advances in Group Processes, 20*, 217–249.

Zelditch, M., Jr., Harris, W., Thomas, G. M., & Walker, H. A. (1983). Decisions, nondecisions, and metadecisions. *Research in Social Movements, Conflicts and Change, 5*, 1–32.

Ethnomethodology and Social Phenomenology

19

Jason Turowetz, Matthew M. Hollander, and Douglas W. Maynard

19.1 Introduction

"Ethnomethodology," a term coined by the American sociologist Harold Garfinkel (1917–2011) in the 1950s (Garfinkel 1967: 11), represents a theoretical paradigm that emerged out of his thinking from the 1940s onward. From its inception, ethnomethodology was influenced by and in dialogue with the philosophy of phenomenology, particularly the social phenomenology developed by Alfred Schütz and later popularized by his students. To understand and appreciate the core precepts of ethnomethodology, then, familiarity with the basic features of phenomenology is necessary. At the same time, in tracing the evolution of ethnomethodology and its relationship with phenomenology, we can also see how ethnomethodologists advanced the theories of phenomenologists by grounding many of their fundamental insights in empirical results and "re-specifying" key concepts. As we will see, such re-specification (Garfinkel 1991) entails (re)-describing social phenomena in terms of the observable, concrete, and concerted practices of society's members, or what Garfinkel calls "members' methods."

This chapter has two principal aims. First, it provides a comprehensive overview of classic and contemporary research in ethnomethodology. In this we proceed chronologically, beginning with Garfinkel's earliest work and then tracking its development, by both Garfinkel and his students, in the latter part of the twentieth century through to contemporary theoretical and empirical projects in the ethnomethodological tradition. Second, we emphasize the ongoing dialogue and reciprocity between ethnomethodology and social phenomenology. Thus, while our major focus is ethnomethodology, we also review key developments in philosophical and social phenomenology, particularly with respect to their influence on Garfinkel and their re-specification by ethnomethodologists. Accordingly, the chapter starts with a discussion of phenomenology's origins and evolution, its development by Schütz in a sociological direction, and its further development and popularization by his students, most notably Peter Berger and Thomas Luckmann (1966). Further, as the chapter proceeds, we address contemporary ideas and advances in social phenomenology as these become relevant to our exposition. It is worth noting from the outset, though, that by the 1990s, social phenomenology had largely merged with other micro-sociological paradigms in a kind of "theoretical syncretism" (Flaherty 2009) that variously mixed phenomenology with elements of symbolic interactionism, Goffmanian micro-structuralism, and

J. Turowetz (✉) • M.M. Hollander • D.W. Maynard
Department of Sociology, University of Wisconsin-Madison, Madison, WI, USA
e-mail: jturowet@ssc.wisc.edu; mholland@ssc.wisc.edu; maynard@ssc.wisc.edu

S. Abrutyn (ed.), *Handbook of Contemporary Sociological Theory*, Handbooks of Sociology and Social Research, DOI 10.1007/978-3-319-32250-6_19

ethnomethodology. Therefore, when referring to recent developments in social phenomenology, we are not dealing with a coherent paradigm per se, but rather a syncretic hybrid of which phenomenology forms a more or less prominent part. Finally, we evaluate ethnomethodology's position in the contemporary field of sociological theories and propose avenues for dialogue with other paradigms, while also proposing future research agendas.

19.2 Phenomenology: Origins of Social Phenomenology and Ethnomethodology

Phenomenology is a philosophical tradition with origins in systematic efforts to anchor classical Western claims about knowledge and reality, particularly those of natural science, logic, and mathematics, in universal structures of human consciousness. Founded by German philosopher Edmund Husserl (1859–1938), phenomenology sought to methodically investigate and lay bare the most basic elements of conscious perception. In Husserl's philosophy, this took the form of establishing the relationship between *noesis*—the act by which consciousness constitutes reality—and *noema*, the reality so constituted. As in Kant's transcendental idealism (a major influence on Husserl), perception of objects is regarded as an activity with distinct stages, and their existence for an ego-subject is "an accomplishment of consciousness" (Moran 2005: 53). Mediating this fundamental relationship is *intentionality*, "the manner in which objects disclose themselves to awareness as transcending the act of awareness itself" (*ibid*). Put differently, for Husserl consciousness is always consciousness *of* something. The method of phenomenological analysis, accordingly, entailed describing how the intentionality of consciousness constitutes objects of perception and experience. Phenomenological description requires the "bracketing" of our ordinary experience of the world via a series of phenomenological "reductions." This disciplined and rigorous suspension of the *natural attitude* of everyday life—which takes for granted that things in the world are generally as they appear—reveals how acts of consciousness are ceaselessly producing the apparent naturalness of the world.

Husserl's goal was to ground knowledge in general, and scientific knowledge in particular, in propositions about consciousness that were necessarily and certainly true. He thought of the history of the sciences in terms of perennial crisis, a situation in which what was required was a systematic transcendental philosophy. Phenomenology would establish indubitable truths about the conditions of the possibility of our everyday experience and knowledge of ordinary worldly objects, which would then provide a universal basis for the more specific knowledge claims of the sciences.[1]

Starting in the 1910s, Husserl's program was taken up and developed by a series of students, some of whom departed in brilliant and original ways from his own developing vision of phenomenology. Those of his disciples with the most relevance to ethnomethodology and social phenomenology include Martin Heidegger, Aron Gurwitsch, and (although not personally working with him) Alfred Schütz and Maurice Merleau-Ponty. Heidegger, generally regarded as Husserl's single most influential student, also has the distinction of being his most radical critic. Trained in medieval philosophy, Heidegger was primarily concerned with the history of ontology and how it had seemingly trivialized "the question of being" (Heidegger 1996: 1). He thus combined an awareness of modern philosophy with the ontological concerns of medieval Scholastic and ancient Greek philosophers. In his lecture courses of the 1920s, culminating in the classic treatise *Being and Time* (1927), he transformed Husserl's epistemological and Kantian understanding of intentionality (consciousness is always correlated with an object of consciousness) into an original ontological view (being is always the being of something). The distinctive way of existing of

[1] Husserl was initially a student of mathematics, and his concern for system and certain knowledge reflects this background. Though a "continental" philosopher, his ideas stemmed from some of the same sources (e.g., Frege) that inspired Russell, Moore, Wittgenstein, and the first generation of "analytic" philosophers in Britain.

human beings (*Dasein*: literally "being there") is seen as necessarily situated and engaged with worldly activities, with theoretical consciousness emerging as only one among many ways of human "being-in-the-world" (Dreyfus 1991).

The contrast of Husserl and Heidegger is particularly instructive for our later discussion of Garfinkel's relationship with much of the sociology of his time (see below). Whereas Husserl held that conscious, intentional mental states provide a primordial foundation for our engagement with the world, Heidegger developed a "phenomenology of 'mindless' everyday coping skills" (Dreyfus 1991: 3), or pre-conceptual practices by which people make themselves at home in the world, rendering worldly phenomena intelligible and familiar. Such commonsensical practices both precede and make possible the adoption of various theoretical perspectives on the world, including Husserlian phenomenological analysis. Consider, for example, the ordinary, everyday activity of opening a door. It is not necessary to perceive or understand doors theoretically—as wooden artifacts with certain colors, textures, and geometric dimensions—in order to competently interact with them. Rather, opening doors is a commonsensical cultural skill that we acquire during socialization as young children; only later do we come to regard doors as possible objects of theoretical inquiry. Indeed, Heidegger argues that this intellectual stance typically only arises when our normal non-conceptual relationships to worldly objects is disrupted in some way.[2] The door as an "ontological" entity embedded in the flow of lived experience then shows up for us in a different mode, as an "ontic" one with abstract attributes that can be contemplated independently of any particular door. By conflating ontic and ontological modes of being, argues Heidegger, the Western philosophical tradition has overlooked the transcendental conditions of the possibility of any determinate way of human being-in-the-world.

Another of Husserl's students, Aron Gurwitsch, took his philosophy in a different direction, producing a phenomenological psychology. Gurwitsch was critical of Husserl's notion that consciousness constitutes objects out of discrete, unconnected elements, arguing instead that we always confront objects in the world that are already constituted as wholes, or *gestalts*. Rather than asking how consciousness unifies discrete elements of experience into coherent objects, Gurwitsch's gestalt theory posits the pre-intentional appearing of phenomena as cohesive totalities. Objects appear to us as wholes, rather than collections of parts; indeed, the parts that comprise an object appear as individual parts only secondarily, against the background of the whole. This would suggest, *pace* Husserl, that a complete reduction of the elements of reality to atomistic elements (as constituted by individual acts of consciousness) is impossible.

A third student, the French phenomenologist Maurice Merleau-Ponty, also begins from the premise that a complete reduction of the phenomenal world to individual acts of consciousness is impossible; also, like Gurwitsch, he had a keen interest in psychology, and held that philosophy can make crucial contributions to that science. In contrast with Gurwitsch, however, Merleau-Ponty's analysis of perception is grounded more in embodiment than cognition. More precisely, he insists on the irreducible role of the body in cognition, and refuses to consider mental processes apart from their embodiment. In this, he is closer to Heidegger, whose work influenced Merleau-Ponty's classic study *Phenomenology of Perception* (1962)—although, in contrast to Heidegger, he explicitly accords the body a central place in his analysis of being-in-the-world.

Merleau-Ponty thus challenges the assumptions of traditional European philosophies, and the psychologies that arose from them, that mind and body are distinct kinds of reality; that mind is the seat of human volition and takes ontological precedence over body; and that the body is a mere instrument through which mind acquires impressions of the world, which it then

[2] Heidegger's view of mind and thinking is thus broadly parallel with that of the classical pragmatists Dewey and Mead.

synthesizes independently of the body—a position that received its classic statement in Descartes' dictum *cogito ergo sum* (I think, therefore I am). In effect, Merleau-Ponty turns the cogito on its head, reformulating it as "I am, therefore I think" (Dreyfus 1991). As in Heidegger, being-in-the-world precedes, and makes possible, any conceptual reflections that take the world as an object of inquiry. In place of the Cartesian intellectualized body, Merleau-Ponty posits the "phenomenal body" whose primordial, pre-representational practices disclose the existential horizons that make rational thought and action possible.

The work of these classical phenomenologists, particularly as interpreted by Alfred Schütz (see below), laid the groundwork for interpretivist and interactionist phenomenological variants of sociological theory. As we will see, the earliest formulations of social phenomenology followed Husserl in according primacy to mental constructs—most notably the idealizations and typifying schemas posited by Schütz—in their analyses of the social world. Early social phenomenology, in turn, inspired Garfinkel in his creation of ethnomethodology, which originated in part as a critique of Schütz's emphasis on concepts at the expense of actual bodily practices. Garfinkel's relationship to Schütz, then, paralleled that of Heidegger and Merleau-Ponty to Husserl. In both cases, dissatisfaction with the cognitivist aspects of the work of an influential mentor led to an original and non-cognitivist vision of the structures of experience and how people make sense of the world.

19.2.1 Social Phenomenology

In the 1920s, Alfred Schütz (1899–1959) was one of the first (with Max Scheler) to make connections between sociological theory, particularly that of Max Weber, and Husserlian phenomenology. His reasons for doing this were analogous to those of Husserl, but in the context of the social sciences rather than of philosophy. Specifically, Schütz held that, like the natural sciences, the social sciences need a phenomenological grounding in what Husserl termed the *Lebenswelt* ("life-world"); without such foundations, the findings of any sociological theory of social action will perforce be incomplete (Schütz 1962). Especially after his emigration to New York in the 1930s, Schütz was in dialogue with other influential philosophers of science such as John Dewey and Carl Hempel, and with sociological theorists such as Talcott Parsons (and, starting in the late 1940s, with Garfinkel, who was Parsons' student at Harvard).

In his mature statement of social phenomenology, Schütz highlights the role of common sense thinking and knowledge in social action and social scientific theorizing. Following Weber, Schütz posited that we act with awareness that others are acting; from this precept, he developed a theory of how mutually coordinated social action is possible.[3] To this end, he argues that by way of socialization, we assimilate idealizations that structure our perception of the world. Central among these idealizations are (1) the *reciprocity of perspectives*, which assumes that standpoints are interchangeable, such that if person A stands in person B's position, they'll see the same object, X, in the same way; and (2) the *congruency of relevances*, or that any way of perceiving X stemming from biographical differences will not affect its objective empirical identity. Further, A assumes B imputes these idealizations to her, and assumes B assumes that A does the same. Together, (1) and (2) illustrate "the general thesis of reciprocal perspectives." This allows us to (re)-construct the other's subjective point of view

[3] Schütz follows Weber in defining social action in terms of (actual or intended) interaction with other persons. According to Weber, "Social action…can be oriented to the past, present, or future anticipated behavior of others" (Whimster 2004: 327). The stipulation that action is social "only when one's own behavior is sensibly oriented to that of others" (ibid: 328) implies that conduct oriented to non-human objects is asocial, "a mere event" or occurrence (ibid). As we argue later in the chapter, this conception of the social is unnecessarily narrow, and recent developments in ethnomethodology (anticipated to some degree in the philosophical phenomenology of Merleau-Ponty and others) point to "acting alone" (i.e., with non-human entities) as a viable domain for sociological analysis.

in an intelligible way. It is on this foundation that the typified constructs of common sense are based (Schütz 1962: 12–13). Typifications, in turn, are formulated preeminently through the medium of language, enabling the transmission of knowledge within and between generations.

Although prominent American philosophers of science knew of Schütz, his work being published in prestigious academic journals, he did not achieve wide recognition as a sociological theorist until after his death in 1959. Two of his former students at the New School, Peter Berger and Thomas Luckmann, went on to develop and popularize his ideas in their highly influential book *The Social Construction of Reality* (1966). This classic statement of social phenomenology launched numerous sociological variants of what soon became known as "social constructionism." Though conducting original and important studies of their own, their basic philosophy of social science derived from Schütz. For example, they argue that it is only in and through human interaction that social reality emerges, such that the social world is continually produced and enacted through social interaction. More specifically, building on a scheme Berger also articulated in an influential study of religion (1967), he and Luckmann posit that social reality consists of three dialectically interrelated moments: (1) *externalization*, whereby subjective attitudes are made available to other members of a society, primarily through the medium of language, (2) *objectivation*, or the concretization of externalized phenomena in the form of routines and institutions, and (3) *internalization*, whereby individuals are socialized into the norms and practices embedded in these structures. This phenomenological conception of social reality contrasted with the positivist orthodoxy pervading the philosophy of social science in the 1960s, and for this reason was regarded as revolutionary. Social constructionism especially resonated with symbolic interactionists, resulting in an alliance that reinvigorated that paradigm (Fine 1993). It also influenced sociologists with a Marxist bent, who saw parallels between social phenomenology and the humanistic philosophy of the young Marx (circa 1843–1844). It was in this intellectual context of the late 1960s that ethnomethodology first became a household word among sociologists.

19.3 Garfinkel and the Development of Ethnomethodology

Like social phenomenology, ethnomethodology was significantly influenced by classical phenomenology. Born in 1917, Garfinkel developed a strong interest in sociology as a young man, attending the University of North Carolina, where he received his Master's degree in 1942, and then Harvard, where he earned a PhD in 1951. Although it is well known that he was a student of Talcott Parsons, whose concern with the problem of social order and theory of social action became central to Garfinkel's own project, it is less often noted that during his time in North Carolina, he closely studied (under Howard Odum) the works of the early Chicago School ethnographers, especially Florian Znaniecki (Rawls 2002). As Emirbayer and Maynard (2011) have noted, this represents an early engagement on Garfinkel's part with classical American pragmatism, although the writings of the pragmatists had less of a direct influence on his formative ideas than those of the phenomenologists, particularly Husserl and, several years later, Schütz and Gurwitsch.

Like his teacher Parsons, Garfinkel's touchstone question (sometimes referred to as the "Hobbesian problem of order") was, "How is social order possible?" But rather than pursuing this question by moving away from the details of life as it is lived and experienced, as Parsons did in the 1940s and 1950s, Garfinkel followed both the Chicago school ethnographers and the phenomenologists in striving to keep the details of concrete action in the forefront of his sociological lens. During his years in Cambridge, he also began reading, and then personally meeting with, Schütz, periodically taking the train to New York to discuss phenomenology and sociology with him. He also had fruitful discussions with

Gurwitsch, who was also living in Cambridge as a lecturer at Harvard (Rawls 2006).

By the early 1950s, Schütz had developed a mature version of his social phenomenology and was publishing his ideas in leading American sociology journals (e.g. Schütz 1945). In many ways, Garfinkel's work began at the point at which Schütz's ended. Although a kindred spirit in many respects, even at this early stage of his development Garfinkel differed from Schütz (as noted earlier) in his interest in the *empirical observation* of people acting in actual, everyday situations. For Garfinkel, this is the sine qua non of any adequate theory of social action: it must do justice to actual human activities in their concrete and detailed orderliness (Heritage 1984; Garfinkel and Rawls 2006). In contrast, Schütz remained a philosopher to the end, content to theorize about action in the abstract without observing it in real time (also characteristic of Berger and Luckmann). It is perhaps ironic that, despite their many differences, Schütz shared a number of traits with Parsons and other positivistic theorists of action and philosophers of science. Both sought to model the foundation of society with conceptual structures, thereby relying on unexamined assumptions—unscientific, commonsensical notions—of what commonsense knowledge actually consists of. Whereas for Parsons this approach culminated in formalistic typologies (e.g., AGIL diagrams), for Schütz it led to universal structures of common-sense knowledge (e.g., "in-order-to-" and "because-motives," "stocks of knowledge," and "we-orientations" that collectively comprised the fabric of the life-world).[4]

Garfinkel, however, was dissatisfied with abstract sociological typologies of any sort, whether those of Parsons or of Schütz. Though Schütz came closer to the domain of human beings' *actual* sense-making practices, he nevertheless stopped short of the observable and reportable activities in and by which social actors produce a shared, mutually intelligible world. According to Garfinkel, these practices, which he came to call "ethnomethods," were not located primarily in the private cognitions of actors—the contents of their minds—but rather in the lived, recognizable, and accountable actions that individuals concertedly exhibited in interaction. It was not that consciousness and intentionality do not matter for ethnomethodology; but rather, that these features of human life are always already embedded in shared practices, which precede them and provide for their intelligibility. Garfinkel was not the first to have this overall insight: G.H. Mead (1934), for example, had argued that mental activity was a phase of social interaction, rather than its antecedent (see also Joas 1996; Emirbayer and Maynard (2011). And as we saw above, Heidegger and Merleau-Ponty criticized Husserl's privileging of conscious intentionality, instead emphasizing the background conditions for its emergence. However, Garfinkel went farther than these predecessors in his efforts to *empirically* demonstrate and specify the practices that constituted the seen-but-unnoticed background against which social action becomes visible and possible. Thus, in his early work (see below), Garfinkel offered experimental demonstrations of Schütz's abstract theses (e.g. about the thesis of reciprocal perspectives) and, in the process, detailed how the natural attitude—the mundane, common-sense perception of the life-world—is in fact an ongoing *preconceptual* achievement of social actors.

In their overview of the varieties of ethnomethodology, Maynard and Clayman (1991) suggest three basic concerns shared by ethnomethodology and phenomenology. First, they share a focus on **gestalt contextures**, or the constitutive features of everyday settings that make up the life-world. To explain how these contextures are achieved in interaction, Garfinkel proposed that people make use of the *documentary method of interpretation*, an ethno-method by which underlying patterns are ascribed to local phenomena. As Garfinkel puts it, "The method consists of treating an actual appearance as a 'the

[4] Both thinkers also drew extensively on empirical psychology to explain the motives shaping social action. Whereas Parsons drew on Freud, Schütz drew on William James and phenomenological psychologists such as Gurwitsch.

document of', as 'pointing to', as 'standing on behalf of', a presupposed underlying pattern. Not only is the underlying pattern derived from its individual documentary evidences, but the individual documentary evidences, in their turn, are interpreted on the basis of 'what is known' about the underlying pattern. Each is used to elaborate the other" (Garfinkel 1967: 78). Second, ethnomethodology treats **rules as resources** that actors use to accomplish situated activities, rather than abstract algorithms that predetermine behavior. That is, a rule is not an exogenous force that causes us to act in one way or another; nor does it have a determinate sense apart from the occasions of its use. Rather, members use rules as resources in performing various actions, such as justifying, exculpating, sanctioning, categorizing, etc. Moreover, since no rule can ever exhaustively specify all conditions of its application, members must continually manage the discrepancy between rules and their referents; we continually bring our actions into alignment with rules, which requires practical competences not encoded in the rules themselves. Just as contracts have a non-contractual basis, per Durkheim's (1964 [1893]) well-known formulation, so too do rule following and usage have a basis that is not stated in the contents per se. Third, ethnomethodology highlights the **accomplished character of the world**, delineating the idealizations that support our shared belief in and orientation to an objective reality. Rather than presuppose the existence of the natural attitude, or ascribe it to a vague mechanism such as "socialization," Garfinkel treats it as a topic of inquiry in its own right and demonstrates how, through mutual adherence to the basic constitutive rules of daily life, we continually (re)-produce the commonsensical fabric of the everyday world.

A reading of Garfinkel's classic *Studies in Ethnomethodology* (1967), which constituted the culmination of his thinking by the late 1960s, reveals all of these convergences between ethnomethodology and phenomenology. At the same time, it indicates some crucial differences. As intimated earlier, the most basic difference was Garfinkel's insistence that theories of social action be empirically grounded in people's actual activities, in their details. This, in turn, led to a reciprocal engagement between his analytical vocabulary for documenting members' practices (ethnomethods) on the one hand, and his empirical findings, on the other. The best-known, and arguably most important, concepts in this vocabulary are (1) indexical expressions, (2) accountability, and (3) reflexivity.

1. *Indexical expressions* are utterances that are understood according to their deep embeddedness in the social context of their production and understanding. Such expressions have posed problems for traditional linguists and philosophers, who have spent much effort incorporating certain classes of statements (e.g. deictic references, performative speech acts, etc.) into formal theories of language use. To paraphrase Garfinkel and Sacks (1970), the mission of the social sciences, traditionally speaking, has involved repeated attempts to substitute objective expressions, which are putatively context-independent, for indexical ones, which are susceptible to endless (re)-specifications relative to their spatio-temporal location in particular situations. Rather than trying to tame indexical expressions in the sense of regarding them as targets of remedy or repair, Garfinkel effectively radicalizes them by making them subject to inquiry, and positing that *all* speech (and embodied action) is irremediably and inherently indexical—including any and all formal treatments of such expressions, as in social scientific theorizing.

   Garfinkel's famous breaching experiments (1963, 1967), wherein his confederates (mostly students) intentionally violated social expectations to reveal their taken-for-granted features, illustrate the pervasiveness of indexical expressions. For example, Garfinkel describes an episode where a wife continually asks her husband to elaborate on what he means by the statement "I'm tired" (1967: 43), asking if he means "physically, mentally, or just bored"; thus, when he replies "physically, mainly" she requests further clarification ("You mean your muscles ache or your bones?"). The fact that endless clarification/

elaboration like this is not requested in ordinary conversation is due to the use of tacit practices whereby members "fill in the gaps" surrounding such expressions and hold one another *accountable* for doing so (see below).

2. *Accountability*: The accountable character of situated social life has two dimensions. First, when participants or members are engaged with one another, there are accounting practices used to make their remarks to one another both intelligible and warranted. Those practices are constantly, and without remediation or time out, conferring meaning on what we say and do. For example, participants accord meaning to deictic terms in talk (such as pronouns) by way of practices for relating such terms to some referent in previous talk, the person using the expression, or an aspect of the environment in which it is spoken. Garfinkel's fundamental insight was that all expressions are like deictic ones in that they acquire their meaning through participants' methods of contextualizing them. Second, members use of practices and methods have an inherently moral dimension in the sense that we take it for granted, and assume others take for granted, that practices and methods indeed will be conjoined with our talk to render what we say meaningful. Garfinkel refers to this mutuality of assumptions as a kind of *trust*. In other words, we ordinarily do not have to explain ourselves in so many words and do not hold others to such a requirement, which would only result in the chaos of an infinite regress of such explanations if we did.

   When that kind of trust is violated, i.e. we encounter someone acting in culturally inept ways, that causes a breakdown in our sense of reality unless we can rationalize it, for example by coming to regard the person as incompetent (Garfinkel 1963). As shown by the breaching experiments, people do not simply let breaches stand, but take swift action to restore a sense of normality and predictability. For instance, in the discussion between wife and husband described above, the husband reprimands his wife, admonishing her, "Don't be so technical"; indeed, later in the conversation, after further prompts for clarification ("What do you mean"), he lashes out, saying "You know what I mean! Drop dead!" (1967: 43). Here, the husband's directives (don't be technical) and subsequent expletive treat his wife as deliberately violating social expectations. In other cases, a member may decide the other party is joking around, being evasive, or even showing signs of mental illness. As Garfinkel puts it, "…activities whereby members produce and manage settings of organized everyday affairs are identical with members' procedures for making those settings account-able" (1967: 1). That is, acting accountably is a ubiquitous concern of society's members; it is a condition of displaying one's competence.

3. *Reflexivity*: since its introduction into the vocabulary of the social sciences, reflexivity has taken on varied, and sometimes incommensurable, meanings. When Garfinkel coined the term, he had in mind a very specific meaning: that everything members say and do is a constitutive feature of the setting in which it's said or done, and that each next-action feeds back into the intelligibility of that setting. To concretize this, consider again the wife-husband conversation above: the husband's directive (don't be so technical) treats the wife's actions as pedantic, and thereby constitutes the situation as one where she is being difficult; by continuing to solicit clarifications, she may be seen to not comply with the directive, which would in turn reinforce the husband's definition of the situation. Suppose, though, that the husband were to laugh at his wife, treating the whole matter as a joke. This would result in a very different understanding by the participants of "what's going on here." The situation is now (re)-defined as humorous; a definition which the wife could then affirm or challenge in her next turn at talk. The point is that each one of the participants' actions evinces an understanding of what's currently happening, such that each next-action does not simply respond to the situation, but continually (re)-constitutes it. Further, there is "no time out" (Garfinkel)

from this process; even if one were to leave the situation entirely, that, too, would occasion an account ("did you leave because you were angry?" "Was it because you were bored?" "Did you have to go to the washroom?" etc.), that would then reflexively feed back into the situation's definition.

In addition to the aforementioned breaching experiments (also known as "tutorial demonstrations"), Garfinkel empirically illustrates and analyzes indexical expressions, accountability, reflexivity, documentary method, and other phenomena ("ad hocing," "the etcetera clause") in studies of jury deliberations, determining causes-of-death (at a suicide prevention center), data coding, clinical record making (and keeping), patient selection at a psychiatric clinic, and the ongoing accomplishment and demonstration of femininity by an inter-sexed person (in his famous investigation of "Agnes"). Garfinkel's early followers supplied further investigations of ethnomethodological themes, to which we now briefly turn.

19.3.1 Other Classic Ethnomethodological Investigations

Garfinkel's early ideas and writings inspired a number of colleagues and students to investigate ethnomethodology's topics by undertaking their own research. These scholars collectively co-created the genre of ethnomethodological ethnography, which pays particular attention to the details of members' practices for achieving the intelligibility of their actions. Their studies show how the precepts central to Garfinkel's program are operative in a range of everyday and institutional settings. Classic exponents of this form of ethnography include Egon Bittner (1967a, b), Lawrence Wieder (1974), Don Zimmerman (1969a, b), David Sudnow (1965, 1967), and Aaron Cicourel (1964). In what follows, we review three now-canonical contributions from this early group of ethnomethodologists—those of Bittner, Zimmerman, and Wieder—paying particular attention to how they investigated and developed key concepts originated by Garfinkel.[5]

Bittner's (1967a, b) investigations of policing on skid row have become classic examples of how members use rules as resources to solve practical problems. In contrast with traditional approaches to law and social action, which treat laws as exogenous rules that structure conduct in a deterministic way, Bittner examines how they are drawn upon in specific situations to accomplish local tasks. One of his central findings concerns the amount of discretion police display in applying the letter of the law to particular cases. For example, police use laws to achieve objectives like "keeping the peace," the definition of which depends on what is considered normal or routine for a given setting. A panhandler on a street corner who is part of the routine goings-on in that context may not be cited or arrested, as the law may prescribe; however, were that same panhandler discovered in a different (atypical) location, he could face legal consequences. This is one way of further specifying what Garfinkel's notion of commonsense knowledge of social structures could mean in the context of policing. In addition to rules-as-resources, the analysis also illustrates the phenomena of indexical expressions, in that the panhandler's actions take on different meanings and significances depending on their context, to which they are reflexively connected.

Another classic demonstration of rules-as-resources is Zimmerman (1969a, b) study of how welfare officers apply bureaucratic regulations. Previous studies of bureaucratic organizations largely accepted the Weberian model of bureaucracy, whereby formal, codified rules prescribe best practices for most efficiently achieving

[5] Other classic studies include Sudnow's (1965) ethnography of a public defender's office, in which he documents how a range of criminal acts are (re)-interpreted as "normal crimes" committed in usual ways for reasons typical of a given class of offenders; Cicourel's (1964) critical analysis of measurement in the social sciences; Pollner's (1975) explication of "reality disjunctures"; and Harvey Sacks' (1963) early research on descriptive categories that eventually evolved into conversation analysis, which will be addressed later in the chapter.

organizational ends. The more closely members of the organization adhere to these rules (the more they conform to the ideal-type of legal rationality), the more effectively they perform their work. What Zimmerman found, in contrast, is that in many instances, welfare officers handled difficult situations in ways not prescribed by the rules in order to make the agency function smoothly. That is, there is a gap between blueprints for how the organization is to run and the actual situations encountered by members; members' practices and routines are indispensible for bridging that gap and rendering it unproblematic (and perhaps even "uninteresting" per Garfinkel 1967).

A third classic study in this tradition is Wieder's (1974) ethnomethodological ethnography of a halfway house for paroled drug offenders, which has become a classic example of ethnomethodology's take on the relation between rules and action. The first half of the study presents a fairly traditional ethnography of Wieder's experiences learning about the "convict code," a name given to the informal rules of conduct by which residents regulated their own and others' behavior. For example, the rules prohibited snitching on fellow residents and "copping out" (i.e., confessing to illegal activities) and sharing information with staff members. He also showed how staff and residents accounted for the overall failure of the reform program in terms of the code—for instance, residents would invoke it to justify not sharing information with staff, who then used it, in turn, to account for why the reform program was failing (the majority of residents were rearrested or jumped parole).

The second half of the study is an ethnomethodological "re-specification" of the ethnographic first half. Wieder argues that the reflexive, accountable, and indexical features or properties of the code are exemplified in the setting of the halfway house. The code was not merely a normative guide to conduct; instead, it constituted the very conduct that it regulated. Wieder (1974: 169–70) presents the example of a resident refusing to answer a staff member's question, saying, "I can't answer that; you know I won't snitch." Besides accounting for his refusal to answer in terms of the code, the resident also frames the situation as one in which the staff person is fishing for information; he thereby reflexively constitutes the ongoing conversation as one where staff are trying to make him slip up. By invoking the code to make sense of situations and motives, residents and staff simultaneously constitute these as instances to which the code applies; indeed, the code receives its definiteness solely in terms of such instances. Accordingly, though staff and residents oriented to the code as an external, objective constraint on their behavior—a social fact—this objectivity was only achieved in and through the work of applying it—work that quickly becomes invisible even as it is being done.

19.4 The Evolution of Ethnomethodology (Post-1967)

Like Husserl, Garfinkel was a thinker in constant motion; he regularly revised, and occasionally even rejected, his own previous analyses (Lieberman 2013). Accordingly, despite its overall continuity, any sharply drawn characterization of his work will be somewhat misleading. Nonetheless, for expository purposes a useful distinction may be drawn between his earlier thinking through 1967, and his later output. Reviewing Garfinkel's work in the 1970s and beyond, two key developments can be identified: (1) the emergence of a clearer, more programmatic commitment to non-cognitivism, or the rejection of theories that accord causal primacy to private mental states in explaining human behavior; and (2) an increasing interest in what Garfinkel termed "ethnomethodology's topics": particularly studies of science and work, as well as natural language (Garfinkel and Sacks 1970). During this period there was also confusion and debate about ethnomethodology's relationship to other types of sociology, a matter which Garfinkel and his students made numerous attempts to clarify. Their efforts would result in ongoing and occasionally polemical exchanges between ethnomethodologists and their critics. In what follows, we first discuss these exchanges, and then turn to the two aforementioned developments in Garfinkel's post-1967 work.

19.4.1 Controversy and Clarification

When ethnomethodology entered the common vocabulary of sociology in the 1960s, there was uncertainty about its aims. To some, it seemed like a radical critique of the very possibility of producing sociological knowledge. Accordingly, it appeared to some that Garfinkel was trying to subvert the discipline, replacing it with a relativisitic, "anything goes" ethos (Coser 1975).[6] Others were more sympathetic, but appropriated ethnomethodology in ways that Garfinkel would come to take issue with. In this group we can place Aaron Cicourel (1964) and Dorothy Smith (1987), as well as certain figures in symbolic interaction (e.g. Denzin 1969). As a result, Garfinkel increasingly lost control over the meaning of "ethnomethodology"; these proliferating interpretations continue to influence the way many non-specialists understand ethnomethodology to this day (e.g. Collins 2004).

How, then, did Garfinkel conceive of ethnomethodology's relationship to sociology? In a paper with Harvey Sacks (Garfinkel and Sacks 1970), Garfinkel distinguishes between *constructive analysis* and *ethnomethodology*. This early distinction later evolved into one between Formal Analysis (FA) and ethnomethodology (EM), or what Garfinkel would come to call ethnomethodology's "asymmetric alternates" (Garfinkel 2002). Formal analysis adopts a theoretical stance toward the world, transforming it into an object of disinterested inquiry. This attitude is characteristic of conventional social science, and of the academic disciplines more broadly. Ethnomethodology, by contrast, is concerned with the very conditions under which worldly phenomena can be made into research objects in the first place. EM and FA are asymmetric alternates because a precondition for doing formal analysis is glossing over, or concealing, the practices through which theoretical objects are produced; one cannot do both simultaneously, though one (FA) begets the other (EM). Accordingly, the EM-FA relationship is not one of antagonism or subversion, but complementarity, in the sense that all attempts at FA invariably conceal their preconditions, which then become EM's topics.

Thus, in response to critics who accused him of undermining the discipline, Garfinkel made it clear that he intended no such thing. Rather, his intention was, and always had been, to ground the formal analytic claims of sociology in an understanding of the preconditions for their articulation. Inspired by the phenomenologists who influenced him in his formative years, particularly Husserl, Garfinkel sought to delineate the taken-for-granted background procedures and practices that give rise to the phenomena of the social sciences (see Psathas 1989). That is, just as Husserl sought to "ground" the particular sciences by means of phenomenological analysis without thereby claiming to criticize or revise their findings, so Garfinkel sought to discover the roots of the various topics studied by sociologists in actual human activities.

Garfinkel would later frame the FA-EM distinction in terms of "Durkheim's aphorism," or the dictum that, "The objective reality of social facts is sociology's fundamental principle" (Garfinkel 1991, 2002). Whereas FA is concerned to enumerate, categorize, and analyze objective social facts, EM seeks to understand how these facts are generated in and as the concerted actions of social actors. In order to accomplish this, EM needs to remain separate from FA; for, otherwise, EM would just become another branch of FA and treat its phenomena as given, rather than being

[6]As Maynard (1986) observed, from its outset, ethnomethodology was regularly characterized in starkly contrasting ways: methodologically, as a method without substance vs. lacking any methodology whatsoever; theoretically, too subjective and embedded in philosophical idealism vs. radically empirical and neo-positivistic; politically conservative (with its seeming avoidance of history and social structure), vs. liberal because of its focus on freedom of action and intention, vs. radical in uncovering the tacit procedures for reproducing reality and its capacity to demystify social reifications, vs. apolitical because any political perspective could "use" it.

constituted in and through the practices of ordinary members of society.[7] In other words, they are and must remain "asymmetric." This, then, is Garfinkel's mature response to sympathetic thinkers who appropriated EM to do constructive/formal analysis, namely, that they reduced EM to just another variant of FA.

19.4.2 Ethnomethodology and Non-cognitivism

To return to the new directions in Garfinkel's thinking, during the 1970s and 1980s, he became increasingly critical of *cognitivism* and concerned to argue that ethnomethodology had always been a non-cognitivist enterprise. Although there are many different varieties of "cognitivism," it is a general theoretical approach taken by many social scientific, psychological, and philosophical explanations of mentality, language, and behavior. Cognitivist explanations tend to share the view that mental states play a paramount role in explaining human behavior. The relationship is typically presented as causal: antecedent mental states cause social actions, such that in order to explain actions, we must determine the intention behind them. By contrast, non-cognitivist approaches, represented in philosophy by Ludwig Wittgenstein (2010) and Gilbert Ryle (1984 [1949]), as well as certain strains in phenomenology (e.g. Merleau-Ponty and Heidegger; see Dreyfus 1991) and pragmatism (see Emirbayer and Maynard 2011) view mental states, along with rules and norms, not as causal forces, but resources with which to account for and describe actions. Minded action, then, is itself a phenomenon for members (Coulter 1989). Mind does not cause actions, but rather emerges in the course of action, particularly when a problematic or perplexing (Dewey 1910) situation arises—e.g., when our habitual ways of acting encounter obstacles or aporia. Accordingly, mentality is not an omnipresent feature of social action, but rather is a special feature of certain of its cases.

For many thinkers of the 1960s and 1970s, the only alternative to cognitivism was behaviorism, as classically articulated by John Watson and B.F. Skinner. Cognitivism, having become ascendant in the 1960s with Noam Chomsky's revolutionary work on computational linguistics and generative grammar, posited mental activity as the basis for our relationship to the world. To this extent, it drew on established Western philosophical traditions in prioritizing the theoretical and mental. Any human activity should be understood as caused by the mind, or our rational mental faculties. Regardless of what we're doing, our mind is always engaged. Behaviorism, by contrast, treats mind as an epiphenomenon that has no scientific validity, as it is not directly observable. Thus, the focus should be entirely on visible behavior, and all descriptions ought to be in behavioral terms.

Ethnomethodology, with its unique conception of mentality-in-action, and as it evolved in the hands of Garfinkel and a younger generation that he influenced—especially Jeff Coulter (1979)—represented a third way that pointed beyond the impasse between cognitivism and behaviorism. Coulter worked out a coherent social philosophy of mind that combines ethnomethodology with the later philosophy of Wittgenstein, terming the resultant approach "epistemic sociology" (Coulter 1979). Coulter conceives of mind as a publically observable feature of certain human activities; it follows that we commit a "category mistake" (Ryle 1949) when we reify mind and treat it as a distinct type of reality. Mind is a way of doing things, and is not located in either a spatio-temporal locus (i.e. a module(s) in the brain, as argued by cognitive scientists and philosophers [e.g. Fodor 1983]) or

[7] Garfinkel's position on this matter recalls Heidegger's (1996) insistence on the fundamental, radical distinction between beings, or empirical entities and objects in the world, and Being (Dasein), as the irreducible, ineffable background against which beings appear. Any attempt to articulate a formal analytic conception of Being reduces it to a particular being, thereby concealing what it meant to reveal. By the same token, efforts to translate EM into formal analytic terms would reduce it to another branch of FA, and thereby lose the phenomena that are EM's topics.

a second type of immaterial reality. Beyond philosophical materialism and dualism, third ways of understanding mentality are possible.

Many of the discussions and debates over the relationship of ethnomethodology to the rest of sociology, including social phenomenology, hinge on the question of cognition, and its place in an analysis of members' methods for constituting social phenomena. Husserl's phenomenology was decidedly concerned with cognition, consciousness, and the role of intentionality in constituting phenomena. As we saw, this was the version of phenomenology that Schütz transformed into a social phenomenology that was developed and popularized by Berger and Luckmann. It was also the version to which certain scholars tried to assimilate ethnomethodology in the 1970s and 1980s, including Denzin (1969) and Psathas (1989).

Psathas in particular sought to articulate a distinctively phenomenological ethnomethodology, which involved arguing that the two enterprises were basically pursing the same objectives, such that ethnomethodology provided an empirical extension and grounding of phenomenology's theoretical concepts. Thus, Psathas compares the phenomenologist's eidetic reduction, or suspension of belief in the natural attitude in order to study its preconditions, to the "ethnomethodological attitude" which similarly "suspends belief in society as an objective reality, *except* as it appears and is 'accomplished' in and through the ordinary everyday activities of members themselves. That is, [it] does not suspend belief in members' beliefs or in their practices as being themselves in the world of everyday life" (Psathas 1989: 82–3).

Psathas rightly points out that ethnomethodology involves transcending and bracketing the natural attitude to investigate its essential constituents. At the same time, however, Psathas' formulation proposes that our fundamental relation to society is one of *belief*. Here, he runs into the same difficulties that Merleau-Ponty and Heidegger identified in Husserl. In particular, the most basic relation of humans to each other and the world is not a matter of consciousness or conscious states like believing or knowing; rather, it is constituted through shared actions and practices, or what Wittgenstein called shared "forms of life." Accordingly, the attitude ethnomethodology takes up, beyond a "suspension of belief," is one that highlights what Garfinkel (1967) called the "seen-but-unnoticed" features of human actions.

19.4.3 Ethnomethodological Studies of Work

The second of Garfinkel's post-1967 preoccupations was with "work," particularly scientific work, and the uniquely adequate procedures needed to accomplish it. Early reflections of this interest can be found in Garfinkel's studies of jury deliberations, outpatient psychiatric clinics, and suicide prevention centers (1967). Later, in a paper written with Michael Lynch and Eric Livingston, he examined the discovery of a scientific object—a pulsar—by workers in an astronomical observatory (Garfinkel, Lynch, and Livingston 1981). Garfinkel and his collaborators treat the discovered object as inextricably bound up with the process of its discovery; it is constituted through the very embodied practices, or members' methods, that provide for its manifestation, rather that somehow existing outside of or apart from them. That is, they were interested in the "*particular occasions* as of which the object's production—the *object*—consists, only and entirely" (ibid: 139, *italics in original*).

Already in 1967, Garfinkel had challenged the conventional distinction between scientific and everyday ("lay") rationalities. Rather than posit a sharp difference between the disciplined inquiry of the scientist and the undisciplined reasoning of the layperson, Garfinkel instead proposes that, in fact, scientific activities depend on and adapt practices of commonsense reasoning to the constitution and investigation of scientific objects.

As he developed his thinking about work and the professions, Garfinkel (1986) conceived of "hybrid studies" in which researchers immerse themselves in a work setting—the classroom, factory, laboratory, etc.—and learn the practices necessary to become competent practitioners there. In the process, students of the workplace become hybrid worker-researchers who can reflexively articulate the *just-thisness*, and phenomenal properties, of professional practice. Working on this level of detail provides fine-grained insights into the *shop floor problem*, which essentially concerns the actual making of coherent, worldly things (Garfinkel 2002: 109). Like his earlier demonstrations of the inexhaustibility of descriptions, which are indefinitely extendible (i.e. indexical), the shop floor problem denotes the ever-present discrepancy between blueprints and the practices through which they are realized; or, as Suchman (1987) puts it, between "plans and situated actions."

In addition to his own research (Garfinkel 1986, 2002), Garfinkel's students and colleagues published a number of influential hybrid studies. Among the better known of these are Lynch's (1985) investigation of neurobiological laboratory work—which, along with Latour and Woolgar (1979) and Knorr-Cetina (1981), was among the earliest and most influential lab ethnographies in the field of science and technology studies; Suchman's (1987) research on human-machine interaction, and its implications for cognitive science (1988); and Livingston's (1987) analysis of mathematical reasoning.

19.4.4 Natural Language in Interaction: Conversation Analysis

Another important event in the 1960s and 1970s was the development of conversation analysis (CA), which emerged out of and in dialogue with ethnomethodology. As already noted, from the 1970s onward Garfinkel became increasingly interested in natural language in interaction, and collaborated with CA founder Harvey Sacks on a seminal paper (Garfinkel and Sacks 1970) in which they analyzed language use as a members' method for accomplishing social actions. While CA has become more autonomous from ethnomethodology over time, the mainstream view of CA is that its theoretical commitments are similar to those of ethnomethodology.[8] These include, but are not limited to, preserving the phenomenon being analyzed; warranting analyses of talk-in-interaction through members' own displayed orientations and actions (rather than those of the analyst); and a reflexive sense that concrete social interaction is "a primordial site" of human sociality (Schegloff 1986).[9]

CA, emerging from the collaborative work of Harvey Sacks with Emanuel Schegloff and Gail Jefferson in the 1960s and 1970s, examines naturally occurring talk and embodied conduct in interaction, with the aim of identifying procedures that members deploy to co-produce the intelligibility of everyday and institutional actions. CA works with audio and, more recently, video data, which the analyst transcribes according to a set of conventions developed by Jefferson (1974) that are meant to capture the details of speech and gesture in social conduct. While CA as an autonomous research tradition is outside the scope of this paper (see Clayman and Gill (2004), for a comprehensive overview, and Maynard (2013) for CA's relationship to EM and cognate disciplines), many of the scholars who advanced both ethnomethodology and conversation analysis work in both traditions, effectively doing ethnomethodological CA. Accordingly, their work will be presented below.

---

[8] Some ethnomethodologists have been critical of what they deem CA's pretensions to formal analysis. Lynch (1997), for example, charges that CA practices a "molecular sociology" that risks losing its phenomena by assimilating them to a uniform analytic apparatus.

[9] There are also affinities between the phenomenologist's method of eidetic reduction—bracketing all assumptions about and knowledge of phenomena in order to analyze just how they present themselves to consciousness—and the disciplined commitment of CA to remaining agnostic about actors' mental and psychic states and motives in order to attend to the granularity of members' practices. That is, the analyst tries, to the extent possible, to bracket "commonsensical" intuitions about *why* members do certain things and to attend instead to *how* they do what they do—how, that is, they collaboratively produce intelligible, recognizable social phenomena in and through their interactional practices.

19.5 Current and Future Directions

In this section, we review recent and ongoing developments in ethnomethodology, explore their points of convergence (and divergence) with contemporary practice-theoretic approaches to sociology—especially social phenomenology—and project lines of development for future ethnomethodological scholarship. We concentrate on the following four areas: (1) social praxis—specifically in the realms of culture and morality, (2) embodied action, (3) acting alone (or solitary action), and (4) the interaction order.

19.5.1 Social Praxis

In recent decades, there have been many attempts, both in sociology and the philosophy of the social sciences, to theorize how social structures and categories are embodied in the practices and corporeal experiences of individuals and groups. Prominent exponents of such theories, which can be grouped under the (admittedly broad) umbrella of *social praxis* or "practice theory" (Vom Lehn 2014), include Pierre Bourdieu, Anthony Giddens, Theodore Schatzki, and Ann Swidler, to name a few. One of the key questions addressed by these thinkers is the relationship between cognition and action, and how it plays out in various social domains.

A recent wave of theorizing has proposed cognitivist or psychologistic answers to these questions. A representative example can be found in the work of Vaisey (2009) who, in comparing subjects' responses to interview questions about their moral values with their answers to survey questions, discovered that the latter predicted future behavior, whereas the former did not. Since the interview questions were explicitly about morality, while the survey question was not, he concluded that participants were acting on motives of which they were not consciously aware (here, he draws on a distinction in cognitive psychology between type one processing, which is unconscious/automatic, and type two processing, which involves reflection). Further, he argues that if actions are conditioned by implicit, unconscious motives, those motives may be said to effectively *cause* the actions; this challenges Mills' (1940) position that motives are anticipatory and post-hoc justifications for actions, rather than causal forces per se, along with that of scholars in the Millsian tradition (for a lively debate on this topic, see the exchange between Vaisey (2008) and Swidler (2008)).

What might ethnomethodology contribute to this conversation? To begin with, the concepts at issue would need to be re-specified in terms of members' observable and reportable practices. Further, these practices would need to be observed in situ and as they unfold in real time, rather than as reported retrospectively (e.g. via survey or interview). To concretize our discussion, we will concentrate on two substantive areas that have been of considerable interest to practice-theoretic researchers of various stripes: culture and morality.

19.5.1.1 Culture

The relationship between culture and social action is complex, and sociologists have long been concerned to explain how cultural discourses affect praxis. That is, by what mechanism(s) does culture translate into action, and vice-versa? A number of influential mechanisms have been proposed, including habitus (Bourdieu 1984), culture as tool-kit (Swidler 1986, drawing on Mills 1940), rational choice (Coleman 1994), the *dispositifs* of power (Foucault 1977), performance (Alexander 2004), and ritual (Collins 2004). The distinctive feature of ethnomethodology's approach to culture is its re-specification of cultural phenomena in terms of members' practices. In what follows, we provide two examples that illustrate this mode of analysis. The first shows how biomedical models of self and disorder are reproduced through practices for diagnosing autism; the second, how legitimacy and authority were negotiated in an (in)famous situation of social interaction, the Milgram "Obedience" Experiment.

Autism is a developmental disorder of childhood characterized by impairments in communication and social interaction, and repetitive, stereotyped behaviors. No biomarkers have been established for autism, and clinicians rely on a combination observation, interviewing, testing, and third-party reports to make a diagnosis. Recent studies by Turowetz (2015a, b) examine how clinicians identify children's potentially symptomatic behaviors, particularly in the context of reporting on their interactions with a particular child to colleagues during diagnostic discussions. For example, key figures in the assessment process, including the child, clinician, and test instrument, are represented in ways that foreground the child's conduct—by way of a practice called *citation*—while eliding the interactional context where it appeared (2015a). While this practice comports with the requirement of standardized assessment that other agents (clinician, test instrument) not contribute to the child's performance, it has the effect of individualizing children's symptoms, which it locates primarily inside the child, rather than the environment in which s/he is embedded. In so doing, it reproduces reductionist tenets of modern biomedicine, which tends to treat patients as self-contained monads divorced from the social world. Further, it encourages interventions aimed principally at the child, leaving the environment largely unchanged.

By fitting their reports to standardized assessment protocols, clinicians demonstrate that results were achieved in a warrantable and accountable way. Indeed, such reports do not simply document standardization, but help constitute it as an established fact. In the process, however, clinicians also reproduce the medicocultural assumptions that standardized protocols encode.

A second example concerns the negotiation of legitimate authority in the Milgram "Obedience" Experiment of 1961–1962. In one of the most famous and controversial series of experiments in twentieth century social psychology, Stanley Milgram (1933–1984) found that randomly selected residents in Connecticut would deliver what they thought were increasingly powerful electroshocks to another ordinary citizen, simply on the say-so of a research psychologist. In 24 experimental conditions, Milgram tested a variety of situational variables, some of which dramatically raised or lowered rates of obedience to the psychologist (e.g., proximity to the man receiving shocks, placement in a chain of command, proximity of the authority figure). Despite the seeming importance of these findings (the question of Milgram's research ethics notwithstanding), social psychologists have experienced great difficulty over the years in arriving at a consensus as to how they are best interpreted. In "obedience to authority," did Milgram discover a coherent social psychological process at work in a wide variety of real-world situations, ranging from everyday authority-subordinate relations at work and school to cases of genocide such as the Holocaust? Is "obedience to authority" in fact the process at work in the experiments, or is some other description of action more apt?

Recently, Hollander (2015) has addressed such questions from the perspective of ethnomethodology and conversation analysis, re-specifying "obedience to authority" in terms of directive-response conversational sequences. Whereas most literature on Milgram has focused on obedience, Hollander highlights the role resistance to continuation played in the experiments. Specifically, he finds that resistance to the Experimenter's directives to continue shocking the Learner is a typologically and sequentially organized phenomenon of social interaction. By "typologically," he means that six types of resistance to the directives recur amongst both outcome groups (the "obedient" research participants who fully complied, and the "defiant" ones who successfully stopped the experiment). By "sequentially," he indicates that resistance takes place against a background of organized conversational sequencing. Conversation analysis can show how Milgram's research participants find themselves in a situation of competing and opposed relevant next actions—whereas the Experimenter directs them to continue (directive-response sequencing), the Learner complains about the shocks and demands for the experiment to be discontinued (complaint-remedy sequencing). This research thus takes a classic topic of social psychology—obedience to authority—and rethinks it, examining the Milgramesque situation at the level of detailed structures of social interaction.

19.5.1.2 Morality

Some of the liveliest debates about cognition and practice have concerned morality and moral behavior. On one side of this debate are scholars like Vaisey, who view (implicit) values as causes of action; on the other are those who, like Swidler, defend a version of Mills' pragmatist conception of values, construing them as tools for justifying and accounting for actions (for another classic statement of this perspective, see Scott and Lyman 1968).

On the territory of this debate, ethnomethodology is certainly closer to Mills' side of the terrain. However, whereas those in the Millsian tradition have conventionally used actors' responses to interview and survey questions (or vignettes; see Swidler 2013) to investigate their moral orientations, ethnomethodologists examine their situated practices, increasingly with the assistance of video technology (see below), to identify morality-in-action. As Rawls (2006) points out, interviews and surveys are different from the social contexts in which the asked-about behavior actually occurs (also Jerolmack and Khan 2014); at best, they provide ex post facto accounts of actions from the perspective of an interviewee, rather than the situated rationalities evinced as these actions were performed. Since an action's meaning is inseparable from the sequence of talk-based and embodied moves in which it's located, it is to that sequential context that ethnomethodologists would recommend turning our attention.[10]

In many ways, morality is at the center of the ethnomethodological perspective (Turowetz and Maynard 2010). Garfinkel always stressed that the social order was a moral order founded on mutual trust that others will act as expected. Following his lead, Garfinkel's students have interrogated the socio-logic of moral concepts (Coulter 1989) as well as their use-in-practice (Turowetz and Maynard 2010). Moral reasoning and accountability are observable, reportable, and analyzable in such everyday activities as agreeing and disagreeing with others' assessments (Pomerantz 1984), aligning and/or affiliating with others' actions (Heritage and Stivers 2013), turn-taking (Sacks et al. 1974), complaining (Drew 1998), blaming (Pomerantz 1978), arguing (Antaki 1994; Reynolds 2011), or delivering or receiving bad or good news (Maynard 2003), as well institutional activities that proceed in such venues as courtrooms (Atkinson and Drew 1979; Maynard 1984), doctor's offices (Heritage and Maynard 2006), and social scientific experiments (Hollander 2015). Accordingly, any attempt to predict moral behavior would first need to specify just what that behavior is, in its details, and how it looks in practice. Among other things, such specifications have the potential to open a fruitful dialogue between EMCA and other approaches to moral praxis.

19.5.2 Embodied Action

Recent research in ethnomethodology and conversation analysis has stressed the embodied, multimodal character of social action. Multimodality refers to the synchronized use of speech, gesture, gaze, and bodily comportment to coordinate and accomplish everyday activities. This line of work has been greatly enhanced by the use of video recordings (Vom Lehn 2014), which allow researchers to repeatedly examine the concerted, moment-by-moment performance of social actions at a level of detail and granularity that would otherwise be unavailable. Social phenomenologists, too, have begun to make use of video technology to analyze the lived, embodied production of social actions. Katz (1996, 2001), for example, analyzes video-recordings of fun-house visitors, demonstrating how patrons combine various practices to construct fractured (and sometimes grotesque) mirror images of themselves and others as humorous.

[10] For a different take for ethnomethodology's relation to the survey interview—wherein the interview is treated as an interactional domain for investigation along the lines of studies of work, see Maynard and Schaeffer (2000). On ethnomethodological studies of work, see below.

Within ethnomethodology and conversation analysis, video research was pioneered by Charles Goodwin (1981) who developed a notation system to accompany Jefferson's (1974) conventions for transcribing speech, and by Christian Heath (1986, 1989) who used video data to analyze doctor-patient interactions. These studies, in turn, built on the pioneering work of Kendon (1990) and Goffman (e.g. 1963). Since the corpus of EMCA research employing video data to analyze multimodal action is much too broad to cover here, we will restrict ourselves to a few illustrative examples and substantive areas.

Beginning with Goodwin's (1981) studies of the relationship between gaze and turn allocation, there emerged a substantial literature on embodied conduct and turn taking and construction. In contrast to other disciplines, such as cognitive science, that sought to locate the coordination of gaze and talk in cognitive processes, early conversation analysts found that actors construct their turns to accomplish interactional tasks—for example, interrupting a turn-in-progress to secure a recipient's gaze (Heath and Luff 2013: 286). Subsequent research suggests a more complex, nuanced relation between speech and gaze, with Rossano et al. (2009: 188) finding, on the basis of a cross-cultural study, that gaze is not directly connected to turn-taking per se, but rather is used "to coordinate the development and closure of sequences and courses of action, to pressure for responses and pursue them, [and] to indicate special states of recipiency." Alongside this research on focused interaction (Goffman 1961) involving parties in an already constituted interactional space, recent work has examined how multimodal practices may be used in unfocused situations—such as passing through public spaces—to initiate and stabilize focused encounters (Heath and Luff 2013: 307). For example, in her analysis of video footage of researchers approaching strangers for directions in public places, Mondada (2009) shows how actors transform an unfocused encounter (being in proximity to another in an anonymous setting) into a focused one by way of "a range of multimodal resources: walking trajectories, body positions, body postures, unilateral glances, mutual gaze, [and] vocal and verbal materials designing turn pre-beginnings, beginnings, and completions" (2009: 1994). Indeed, on close inspection, the apparent simplicity of these encounters turns out to conceal a range of skillful, finely orchestrated practices: categorizing strangers as approachable persons (or not), coordinating walking trajectories in space and time (e.g., pacing, rhythm), establishing contact (often via joint gaze or a turn pre-beginning particle like "euh" to secure the target's attention), transitioning from walking to standing together—and thereby establishing a stable, shared interactional space; and initiating a question-answer sequence about directions (ibid). Relatedly, Vom Lehn et al. (2001) examine video recordings of actors in a public, but institutional, space—museums—to determine how they interact with exhibits in the presence of known (companions) and unknown (strangers) others; and with a view to explicating how "the physical environment and material realities affect conduct and interaction and are constituted through conduct and interaction" (2001: 208). They show how, among other things, the sequential order in which exhibits are viewed matters for how they are seen; how patrons achieve a joint focus of attention; and how their bodily comportment affects not just their own experience of an exhibit, but also whether their fellows look at it, and for how long (ibid: 207).

Video data has also played a critical role in workplace studies (Heath and Luff 2000). In addition to studies of medical consultations (see Heritage and Maynard (2006) and Gill and Roberts (2013), for a comprehensive overview) and diagnostic practices (Gill 1998; Heath 1992; Maynard 1992; Perakyla 1998; Turowetz 2015a, b), workplace researchers have examined railway conductors (Heath and Luff 1991), auctioneers (Heath 2012), the news media (Clayman and Heritage 2002), computer-mediated action and interaction (Suchman 1987; Heath and Luff 2000), the use and production of clinical (Heath and Luff 1996) and legal (Suchman 2000) documents, and command-control centers (Goodwin and Goodwin 1996)—to name just a few areas of inquiry. These studies resonate with cognate research in the actor-network tradition (Latour

2005) and practice-theoretic paradigms (e.g. Pickering 1995) in their conception of technology as not just an instrument for human use, but a kind of agent (or, in the parlance of actor-network theory, *actant*) in its own right that variously constrains, enables, and mediates action.

19.5.3 Acting Alone (and with Objects)

Traditionally, sociologists have defined social action in terms of interaction with other human beings. This approach, which can be traced to Weber and was adopted by Schütz, views human interactions with non-human entities as basically asocial. On this view, there is a dichotomy between actions involving the use of objects, on the one hand, and interactions with other humans, on the other, with only the latter qualifying as social. In recent decades, this division has been challenged and problematized on various fronts: for example, post-humanist theories (e.g. Haraway 2013) posit that as with other dichotomies inherited from the Enlightenment (e.g. nature/culture, mind/body), the social and non-social are always already entangled, such that sharp distinctions between human (social) and non-human (animals, objects, environmental ecologies) cannot stand up to critical scrutiny; similar arguments have been made by actor-network theorists (e.g. Latour 2005), for whom "the social" consists of more or less stable assemblages of human and non-human actants.

Recent work in ethnomethodology similarly expands the scope of social action to include non-human objects, treating these as actors in their own right. In addition to a growing body of research on human-animal interaction (e.g. Solomon 2015) and the human-machine interfacing examined in workplace studies (see above), ethnomethodologists have also begun to explore solitary action, or action on one's own. Among other things, such studies demonstrate that we are never truly "alone" or "asocial" in that we are always using socially learned practices to engage with objects embedded in a web of practical significances. This resonates with the arguments of classical phenomenologists (Heidegger, Merleau-Ponty) and pragmatists (Dewey, Mead) that the individual self does not end with the epidermis; rather, the soma is extended, so to speak, in and through objects in the immediate environment, to which we have habitual, pre-reflective ways of relating. These habits, and the modes of practical, situated reasoning they entail, can be investigated through close observation of one's own behaviors, either extemporaneously or with the aid of video technologies. Livingston (2008), for example, carefully reflects on his efforts to assemble tangrams and jigsaw puzzles (among other objects), enumerating the (usually tacit) practices involved in and disclosed by this work. Besides demonstrating the domain-specific character of the skill and reasoning required for these projects, his results point to the social, and socialized, nature of his activities, such as the ability to recognize patterns and gestalts (e.g. to see puzzle pieces as parts of a whole image). Other studies in this vein include an investigation, also by Livingston (1987), of the reasoning involved in proving mathematical theorems, Sudnow's (1978) phenomenological account of learning to play jazz piano, and Bjelic's (1996) extemporaneous analysis of replicating a classic experiment (Galileo's pendulum).

Given the prevalence of machines and other artificial media in post-modern life, ethnomethodological and cognate (e.g. actor-network theory) re-specifications of social action, and corollary investigations thereof, are both timely and potentially far-reaching in their implications.

19.5.4 Mapping the Interaction Order

The final focus for current and future research encompasses the previous three but also extends beyond them. Goffman's (1983) notion of an interaction order, defined as a sui generis domain of face-to-face interaction that is relatively autonomous from other orders of society (markets, states, etc.) and governed by its own endogenous "rules of traffic," has been influential among ethnomethodologists, and conversation analysts in particular (see Kendon et al. 1988). Indeed, the procedures for concertedly producing recognizable social actions, including turn-taking, repair, preference organization, etc., identified by conversation analysts can be viewed as invariant features of the interaction order of society. These practices have their roots in ordinary conversation; when modified, however, they can be adapted to more circumscribed interaction orders—for example, courtrooms prescribe specific rules for the allocation of turns, repairing misunderstandings, question-answer sequences, etc. (Atkinson and Drew 1979); doctor's offices have their characteristic interactional structures (Heritage and Maynard 2006); and so forth.

Rawls (1987) has written extensively on the interaction order from an ethnomethodological perspective, particularly with regard to how it organizes and sustains self-presentation, and its attendant obligations and entitlements, in everyday interactions. The interaction order is both a social and moral order, in that it forms the basis for mutual intelligibility and self-presentation. Different expectations about the interaction order can reflect and (re)-produce divisions among groups, effectively creating separate interaction orders with disparate moral commitments and values (Rawls 2000: 247). This, in turn, can create conflict. For example, Rawls (2000) finds that interactional troubles between white and black Americans result from the two groups' divergent expectations about social conduct and communication, such that "persons are not able to recognize one another's conversational moves" (2000: 241). Members treat these perceived breaches as accountable, and the accounts they produce often draw upon and reproduce racial stereotypes, which in turn contributes to the perpetuation of social inequality.[11]

Rawls provides an empirical illustration of her argument by analyzing differences in the greeting and introductory talk practices of African Americans and White Americans. She shows that whereas White Americans prioritize information seeking by way of category-questions (e.g. about occupation, residence, etc.), African Americans tend to focus on displaying solidarity—which, among other things, involves not placing interlocutors in hierarchical categories; further, where African Americans generally prefer to volunteer personal information, whites expect to be asked (249). These conflicting expectations can lead to misunderstandings and resentment, with African Americans viewing whites as prying and intrusive and whites perceiving African Americans as rude or ignorant (255).

Another recent investigation of race and inequality that takes an ethnomethodological approach to interaction orders is Duck's (2015) ethnographic study of a poor, predominantly African American neighborhood in an urban area. In the tradition of ethnomethodological ethnography pioneered by Garfinkel, Wieder, and Bittner (see above), Duck documents the practices and expectations whereby residents constitute their neighborhood as a community. Whereas outsiders view the neighborhood as chaotic and disorderly, and plagued by drugs and violence, Duck demonstrates that for residents, the community is both orderly and organized; and, to the extent that outsiders—from the media to policymakers—misconstrue the neighborhood as a disorganized space, this is due to a failure to understand the dynamics of the local interaction order and how it provides for the intelligibility and accountability of everyday happenings.

The work of Rawls and Duck represents, and exemplifies, the potential of the interaction order, specified in terms of members' concerted practices and perspectives, to illuminate the interactional bases of phenomena ranging from microaggression and conversational misunderstandings to large-scale social-structural inequalities.

19.6 Concluding Remarks

When Garfinkel died in 2011 at the age of 93, he left a vast legacy to sociological theory: through his scholarly efforts, he created one field, ethnomethodology, and contributed to the creation of another, conversation analysis. The aims of this

[11] Building on Du Bois' (1903) notion of double consciousness, Rawls (2000: 247) argues that the African American self is simultaneously accountable to both interaction orders—white and black—whereas the white self can safely ignore the latter and orient only to the former.

chapter have been to expound ethnomethodology's core precepts, as Garfinkel conceived of them; to enumerate key points of convergence and divergence between Garfinkelian ethnomethodology and other theoretical traditions, particularly social phenomenology, and thereby encourage dialogue among exponents of these perspectives; and to give some indication of how ongoing scholarship in EM and CA continues to address prominent themes, topics, and challenges in contemporary sociological theory.

As we have shown, ethnomethodologists remain committed to the basic impulse behind both classical and social phenomenology. Like phenomenology, ethnomethodology is concerned with the ways in which members concertedly create a shared, mutually intelligible reality that, in turn, serves as a foundation for the various projects and acts of meaning-making they undertake in their daily lives. However, whereas phenomenologists locate the wellspring of this achievement in the private cognitions of individuals, ethnomethodologists emphasize instead a set of shared practices, or ethnomethods, that are discoverable in the observable and reportable behavior of the society's members. The present chapter has reviewed several of these ethnomethods as documented in the early work of Garfinkel and his students (e.g. indexical expressions, reflexivity) and in more recent research concerning social praxis, embodied action, acting alone, and the interaction order. Moreover, we have emphasized how EM re-specifies canonical theoretical concepts in terms of these ethnomethods. Although these re-specifications have sometimes been considered subversive, critique of other forms of sociology has not been central to ethnomethodology, as this chapter hopefully makes clear. Rather, the aim has always been to ask "what more" is left out of formal analytic glosses of worldly phenomena, and to recover such phenomena by way of ethnomethodological inquiry and critique; to always return to the phenomena themselves, as they reveal themselves in and through and for members of the society.

As our review of current research in EM (and CA) indicates, ethnomethodology continues to be a vibrant paradigm in contemporary sociological theory. Further, given its grounding in an empirical program of research, EM is constantly confronted with novel phenomena which, in turn, provide for its ongoing evolution, and continued relevance, as a theoretical approach. Indeed, as advances in audio and video technology make the accomplishment of social life available for analysis at ever-finer levels of detail, and as EM explores new domains of action (e.g. acting alone), it promises to continue to discover the "what more" of social order, yielding novel insights while also providing a constant reminder of the near-infinite richness of what Garfinkel memorably termed "Immortal Ordinary Society" (Garfinkel 2002).

References

Alexander, J. C. (2004). Cultural pragmatics: Social performance between ritual and strategy. *Sociological Theory, 22*, 527–573.

Antaki, C. (1994). *Explaining and arguing: The social organization of accounts*. London: Sage.

Atkinson, J. M., & Drew, P. (1979). *Order in court*. New York: Macmillan.

Berger, P. (1967). *The sacred canopy: Elements of a sociological theory of religion*. Garden City: Anchor Doubleday.

Berger, P., & Luckmann, T. (1966). *The social construction of reality: A treatise in the sociology of knowledge*. Garden City: Anchor Books.

Bittner, E. (1967a). The police on skid-row: A study of peace keeping. *American Sociological Review, 32*, 699–715.

Bittner, E. (1967b). Police discretion in emergency apprehension of mentally ill persons. *Social Problems, 14*, 278–292.

Bjelic, D. (1996). Lebenswelt structures of Galilean physics: The case of Galileo's pendulum. *Human Studies, 19*, 409–432.

Bourdieu, P. (1984). *Distinction: A social critique of the judgment of taste*. Cambridge, MA: Harvard University Press.

Cicourel, A. V. (1964). *Method and measurement in sociology*. Oxford: Free Press.

Clayman, S., & Heritage, J. (2002). *The news interview: Journalists and public figures on the air*. Cambridge: Cambridge University Press.

Clayman, S., & Gill, V. (2004). Conversation analysis. In A. Bryman & M. Hardy (Eds.), *Handbook of data analysis* (pp. 589–606). London: Sage.

Coleman, J. S. (1994). *Foundations of social theory*. Cambridge, MA: Harvard University Press.

Collins, R. (2004). *Interaction ritual chains*. Princeton: Princeton University Press.
Coser, L. (1975). Presidential address: Two methods in search of a substance. *American Sociological Review, 40*, 691–700.
Coulter, J. (1979). *The social construction of mind: Studies in ethnomethodology and linguistic philosophy*. London: MacMillan.
Coulter, J. (1989). *Mind in action*. Atlantic Higlands: Humanities Press International.
Denzin, N. (1969). Symbolic interactionism and ethnomethodology: A proposed synthesis. *American Sociological Review, 34*, 922–934.
Dewey, J. (1910). *How we think*. Lexington: Heath.
Drew, P. (1998). Complaints about transgressions and misconduct. *Research on Language & Social Interaction, 31*(3–4), 295–325.
Dreyfus, H. (1991). *Being-in-the-world: A commentary on Heidegger's being and time, division I*. MA: MIT Press.
Du Bois, W. E. B. (1903). *The souls of Black Folk*. London: Oxford University Press.
Duck, W. (2015). *No way out: Precarious living in the shadow of poverty*. Chicago: University of Chicago Press.
Durkheim, E. (1964 [1893]). *The division of labor in society*. New York: Free Press.
Emirbayer, M., & Maynard, D. W. (2011). Pragmatism and ethnomethodology. *Qualitative Sociology, 34*, 221–261.
Fine, G. A. (1993). The sad demise, mysterious disappearance, and glorious triumph of symbolic interactionism. *Annual Review of Sociology, 19*, 61–87.
Flaherty, M. (2009). Phenomenology. In B. S. Turner (Ed.), *The new Blackwell companion to social theory* (pp. 218–234). New York: Wiley.
Fodor, J. (1983). *The modularity of mind: An essay on faculty psychology*. MA: MIT Press.
Foucault, M. (1977). *Discipline and punish: The birth of the prison*. New York: Vintage.
Garfinkel, H. (1963). A conception of, and experiments with, "Trust" as a condition of stable concerted actions. In O. J. Harvey (Ed.), *Motivation and social interaction* (pp. 187–238). New York: Free Press.
Garfinkel, H. (1967). *Studies in ethnomethodology*. Englewood Heights: Palgrave.
Garfinkel, H. (1986). *Ethnomethodological studies of work*. London: Routledge & Kegan Paul.
Garfinkel, H. (1991). Respecification: Evidence for locally produced, naturally accountable phenomena of order, logic, reason, meaning, method, etc. in and as of the essential haecceity of immortal ordinary society (I)—an announcement of studies. In G. Button (Ed.), *Ethnomethodology and the human sciences* (pp. 10–19). Cambridge: Cambridge University Press.
Garfinkel, H. (2002). *Ethnomethodology's program: Working out Durkheim's aphorism*. Lanham: Rowan & Littlefield Publishers.
Garfinkel, H., & Rawls, A. W. (2006). *Seeing sociologically: The routine grounds of social action*. Boudler: Paradigm.
Garfinkel, H., & Sacks, H. (1970). On formal structures of practical actions. In J. C. McKinney & E. A. Tiryakian (Eds.), *Theoretical sociology: Perspectives and development* (pp. 337–366). New York: Appleton–Century–Crofts.
Garfinkel, H., Lynch, M., & Livingston, E. (1981). The work of a discovering science construed with materials from the optically discovered pulsar. *Philosophy of the Social Sciences, 11*, 131–158.
Gill, V. (1998). Doing attributions in medical interaction: Patients' explanations for illness and doctors' responses. *Social Psychology Quarterly, 61*(4), 342–360.
Gill, V. T., & Roberts, F. (2013). Conversation analysis in medicine. In J. Sidnell & T. Stivers (Eds.), *The handbook of conversation analysis* (pp. 575–592). New York: Wiley.
Goffman, E. (1961). *Encounters: Two studies in the sociology of interaction*. Oxford: Bobbs-Merrill.
Goffman, E. (1963). *Behavior in public places: Notes on the social organization of gatherings*. New York: Free Press.
Goffman, E. (1983). The interaction order: American Sociological Association, 1982 presidential address. *American Sociological Review, 48*, 1–17.
Goodwin, C. (1981). *Conversational organization: Interaction between speakers and hearers*. New York: Academic.
Goodwin, C., & Goodwin, M. H. (1996). Seeing as situated activity: Formulating planes. In Y. Engström & D. Middleton (Eds.), *Cognition and communication at work* (pp. 61–95). Cambridge: Cambridge University Press.
Haraway, D. (2013). *Simians, cyborgs, and women: The reinvention of nature*. London: Routledge.
Heath, C. (1986). *Body movement and speech in medical interaction*. Cambridge: Cambridge University Press.
Heath, C. (1989). Pain talk: The expression of suffering in the medical consultation. *Social Psychology Quarterly, 52*, 113–125.
Heath, C. (1992). Diagnosis and assessment in the medical consultation. In P. Drew & J. Heritage (Eds.), *Talk at work* (pp. 235–267). Cambridge: Cambridge University Press.
Heath, C. (2012). *The dynamics of auction: Social interaction and the sale of fine art and antiques*. Cambridge: Cambridge University Press.
Heath, C., & Luff, P. (1991). Collaborative activity and technological design: Task coordination in London underground control rooms. In L. Bannon, M. Robinson, & K. Schmidt (Eds.), *Proceedings of the second European conference on computer-supported cooperative work* (pp. 65–80). Amsterdam: Springer.
Heath, C., & Luff, P. (1996). Documents and professional practice: 'Bad' organizational reasons for 'Good'

clinical records. In L. Bannon, G. De Michelis, & P. Soergaard (Eds.), *Proceedings of the 1996 ACM conference on computer supported cooperative work* (pp. 354–363). New York: ACM

Heath, C., & Luff, P. (2000). *Technology in action*. Cambridge: Cambridge University Press.

Heath, C., & Luff, P. (2013). Embodied action and organizational activity. In J. Sidnell & T. Stivers (Eds.), *The handbook of conversation analysis* (pp. 281–307). New York: Wiley.

Heidegger, M. (1996). *Being and time*. New York: SUNY Press.

Heritage, J. (1984). *Garfinkel and ethnomethodology*. Malden: Polity Press.

Heritage, J., & Maynard, D. W. (2006). *Communication in medical care: Interaction between primary care physicians and patients*. Cambridge: Cambridge University Press.

Heritage, J., & Stivers, T. (2013). Conversation analysis and sociology. In J. Sidnell & T. Stivers (Eds.), *The handbook of conversation analysis* (pp. 657–673). New York: Wiley.

Hollander, M. (2015). The repertoire of resistance: Non-compliance with directives in Milgram's 'Obedience' experiments. *British Journal of Social Psychology*. doi:10.1111/bjso.12099.

Jefferson, G. (1974). Error correction as an interactional resource. *Language in Society, 3*, 181–199.

Jerolmack, C., & Khan, S. (2014). Talk is cheap ethnography and the attitudinal fallacy. *Sociological Methods & Research, 43*, 178–209.

Joas, H. (1996). *The creativity of action*. Chicago: University of Chicago Press.

Katz, J. (1996). Families and funny mirrors: A study of the social construction and personal embodiment of humor. *American Journal of Sociology, 101*, 1194–1237.

Katz, J. (2001). *How emotions work*. Chicago: University of Chicago Press.

Kendon, A. (1990). *Conducting interaction: Patterns of behavior in focused encounters*. Cambridge/New York: Cambridge University Press.

Kendon, A., Drew, P., & Wootton, A. (1988). *Erving Goffman: Exploring the interaction order*. Boston: Polity Press.

Knorr-Cetina, K. (1981). *The manufacture of knowledge*. Oxford: Pergamon.

Latour, B. (2005). *Reassembling the social: An introduction to actor-network-theory*. London: Oxford University Press.

Latour, B., & Woolgar, S. (1979). *Laboratory life: The social construction of scientific facts*. Beverly Hills: Sage.

Lieberman, K. (2013). *More studies in ethnomethodology*. New York: SUNY Press.

Livingston, E. (1987). *Making sense of ethnomethodology*. New York: Taylor & Francis.

Livingston, E. (2008). *Ethnographies of reason*. London: Ashgate Publishing.

Lynch, M. (1985). *Art and artifact in laboratory science*. London: Routledge and Kegan & Paul.

Lynch, M. (1997). *Scientific practice and ordinary action: Ethnomethodology and social studies of science*. Cambridge: Cambridge University Press.

Maynard, D. W. (1984). *Inside plea bargaining*. New York: Springer US.

Maynard, D. W. (1986). New treatment for an old itch. *Contemporary Sociology, 15*, 346–349.

Maynard, D. W. (1992). On clinicians co-implicating recipients' perspective in the delivery of diagnostic news. In P. Drew & J. Heritage (Eds.), *Talk at work: Social interaction in institutional settings* (pp. 331–358). Cambridge: Cambridge University Press.

Maynard, D. W. (2003). *Bad news, good news: Conversational order in everyday talk and clinical settings*. Chicago: University of Chicago Press.

Maynard, D. W. (2013). Everyone and no one to turn to: Intellectual roots and contexts for conversation analysis. In J. Sidnell & T. Stivers (Eds.), *The handbook of conversation analysis* (pp. 9–31). New York: Wiley.

Maynard, D. W., & Clayman, S. E. (1991). The diversity of ethnomethodology. *Annual Review of Sociology, 17*, 385–418.

Maynard, D. W., & Schaeffer, N. C. (2000). Toward a sociology of social scientific knowledge: Survey research and ethnomethodology's asymmetric alternates. *Social Studies of Science, 30*, 264–312.

Mead, G. H. (1934). *Mind, self and society form the standpoint of a social behaviorist*. Chicago: University of Chicago Press.

Merleau-Ponty, M. M. (1962). *Phenomenology of perception*. London: Routledge & Keegan Paul.

Mills, C. W. (1940). Situated actions and vocabularies of motive. *American Sociological Review, 5*, 904–913.

Mondada, L. (2009). Emergent focused interactions in public places: A systematic analysis of the multimodal achievement of a common interactional space. *Journal of Pragmatics, 41*, 1977–1997.

Moran, D. (2005). *Edmund Husserl: Founder of phenomenology*. London: Polity Press.

Perakyla, A. (1998). Authority and accountability: The delivery of diagnosis in primary health care. *Social Psychology Quarterly, 61*, 301–320.

Pickering, A. (1995). *The mangle of practice: Time, agency, and science*. Chicago: University of Chicago Press.

Pollner, M. (1975). 'The Very Coinage of Your Brain': The anatomy of reality disjunctures. *Philosophy of the Social Sciences, 5*, 411–430.

Pomerantz, A. (1978). Attributions of responsibility: Blamings. *Sociology, 12*, 115–121.

Pomerantz, A. (1984). Agreeing and disagreeing with assessments: Some features of preferred/dispreferred turn shaped. In J. M. Atkinson & J. Heritage (Eds.), *Structures of social action* (pp. 57–101). Cambridge: University Press.

Psathas, G. (1989). *Phenomenology and sociology: Theory and research*. Boston: University Press of America.

Rawls, A. (1987). The interaction order Sui Generis: Goffman's contribution to social theory. *Sociological Theory, 5*, 136–149.

Rawls, A. (2000). "Race" as an interaction order phenomenon: Web Du Bois's "Double Consciousness" thesis revisited. *Sociological Theory, 18*, 241–274.

Rawls, A. (2002). Introduction. In A. Rawls (Ed.), *Ethnomethodology's program: Working out Durkheim's aphorism*. Lanham: Rowan and Littlefield.

Rawls, A. (2006). Respecifying the study of social order—Garfinkel's transition from theoretical conceptualization to practices in details. In A. Rawls (Ed.), *Seeing sociologically* (pp. 1–97). Boulder: Paradigm Publishing.

Reynolds, E. (2011). Enticing a challengeable in arguments: Sequence, epistemics and preference organization. *Pragmatics, 21*, 411–430.

Rossano, F., Brown, P., & Levinson, S. C. (2009). Gaze, questioning and culture. In J. Sidnell (Ed.), *Conversation analysis: Comparative perspectives* (pp. 187–249). Cambridge: Cambridge University Press.

Ryle, G. (1984 [1949]). *The concept of mind*. London: Hutchinson.

Sacks, H. (1963). Sociological description. *Berkeley Journal of Sociology, 8*, 1–16.

Sacks, H., Schegloff, E. A., & Jefferson, G. (1974). A simplest systematics for the organization of turn-taking for conversation. *Language, 50*, 696–735.

Schegloff, E. A. (1986). The routine as achievement. *Human Studies, 9*(2–3), 111–151.

Schütz, A. (1945). On multiple realities. *Philosophy and Phenomenological Research, 5*, 533–576.

Schütz, A. (1962). *Collected papers* (Vol. 3). The Hague: Martinus Nijhoff.

Scott, M. B., & Lyman, S. M. (1968). Accounts. *American Sociological Review, 33*, 46–62.

Smith, D. (1987). *The everyday world as problematic: A feminist sociology*. Toronto: University of Toronto Press.

Solomon, O. (2015). "But-He'll Fall!": Children with autism, interspecies intersubjectivity, and the problem of 'Being Social'. *Culture, Medicine and Psychiatry, 1*, 1–22.

Suchman, L. (1987). *Plans and situated actions: The problem of human-machine communication*. Cambridge: Cambridge University Press.

Suchman, L. (1988). Representing practice in cognitive science. *Human Studies, 11*(2–3), 305–325.

Suchman, L. (2000). Making a case: 'Knowledge' and 'Routine' work in document production. In P. Luff, B. Hindmarsh, & C. Heath (Eds.), *Workplace studies: Recovering work practice and informing system design* (pp. 29–45). Cambridge: Cambridge University Press.

Sudnow, D. (1965). Normal crimes: Sociological features of the penal code in a public defender office. *Social Problems, 12*, 255–276.

Sudnow, D. (1967). Passing on: The social organization of dying. *Nursing Research, 17*(1), 81.

Sudnow, D. (1978). *Ways of the hand: The organization of improvised conduct*. Cambridge, MA: MIT Press.

Swidler, A. (1986). Culture in action: Symbols and strategies. *American Sociological Review, 51*, 273–286.

Swidler, A. (2008). Comment on Stephen Vaisey's "Socrates, Skinner, and Aristotle: Three Ways of Thinking About Culture" in Action. *Sociological Forum, 23* 614–618.

Swidler, A. (2013). *Talk of love: How culture matters*. Chicago: University of Chicago Press.

Turowetz, J. (2015a). Citing conduct, individualizing symptoms: Accomplishing autism diagnosis in clinical case conferences. *Social Science & Medicine, 142*, 214–222.

Turowetz, J. (2015b). The interactional production of a clinical fact in a case of autism. *Qualitative Sociology, 38*, 57–78.

Turowetz, J., & Maynard, D. W. (2010). Morality in the social interactional and discursive world of everyday life. In S. Hitlin & S. Vaisey (Eds.), *Handbook of the sociology of morality* (pp. 503–526). New York: Springer.

Vaisey, S. (2008). Socrates, Skinner, and Aristotle: Three ways of thinking about culture in action. *Sociological Forum, 23*, 603–613.

Vaisey, S. (2009). Motivation and justification: A dual-process model of culture in action. *American Journal of Sociology, 114*, 1675–1715.

Vom Lehn, D. (2014). *Harold Garfinkel: The creation and development of ethnomethodology*.Walnut Creek: Left Coast Press.

Vom Lehn, D., Heath, C., & Hindmarsh, J. (2001). Exhibiting interaction: Conduct and collaboration in museums and galleries. *Symbolic Interaction, 24*, 189–216.

Whimster, S. (2004). *The essential Weber: A reader*. London: Routledge.

Wieder, L. (1974). *Language and social reality: The case of telling the convict code*. The Hague: Mouton.

Wittgenstein, L. (2010). *Philosophical investigations*. New York: Wiley.

Zimmerman, D. (1969a). Record keeping and the intake process in a public welfare organization. In S. Wheeler (Ed.), *On record* (pp. 319–354). New York: Russel Sage Foundation.

Zimmerman, D. (1969b). Tasks and troubles: The practical bases of work activities in a public assistance agency. In D. Hansen (Ed.), *Explorations in sociology and counselling* (pp. 237–266). New York: Houghton Mifflin.

Theory in Sociology of Emotions 20

Emi A. Weed and Lynn Smith-Lovin

20.1 Introduction

For over 100 years, the study of emotions played a minor role in sociology. Emotions were conceptualized as antithetical to rationality. As an apparently individual, ephemeral phenomenon, emotions seemed more suited for study in psychology and the interpretative humanities, rather than in the struggling new social science. Even early sociologists who focused on micro-level processing, the thinkers that we now call symbolic interactionists, emphasized cognitive processing and ignored emotional response as theoretically in significant.

That situation changed dramatically in the late 1970s and early 1980s. Several major works brought emotions to the fore of sociological thinking (e.g., Denzin 1985; Heise 1974; Hochschild 1979, 1983; Kemper 1978). These scholars theorized that cognition and emotion were inextricably tied. Over the past 40 years, the importance of culture in shaping both emotional experience and expression have become increasingly clear. In modern sociology, emotions play a central role in the way that the discipline views how we, as people, interact with our social environment. Theory in sociology of emotions seeks to better understand the role of emotions in people's social lives at the individual, small group, and societal levels.

There are actually two literatures that could be termed sociologies of emotion. Most central is the scholarly tradition that grew out of a group of primarily qualitative researchers, including Hochschild (1979, 1983), Shott (1979), Thoits (1984), and Clark (1987), among many others. As investigators of a previously ignored phenomenon, these researchers used inductive methods to develop new concepts and describe how social forces shaped emotional experience. These researchers drew on dramaturgical and symbolic interactionist perspectives to argue for the social nature of emotions. The second sociology of emotions developed more directly from work in social psychology. Kemper published *A Social Interactional Theory of Emotions* (1978) around the same time as Hochschild's work (1979), as an attempt to develop a traditional, hypothetical-deductive framework within which emotions could be explored. Consistent with his goals, many sociological social psychologists drew on Kemper's work and began to incorporate emotions into their theoretical work on identity, status, exchange and justice. In this chapter, we summarize theoretical developments within both of these "sociologies" of emotion. We concentrate first on the former, qualitative tradition, since it is seldom treated elsewhere and is centered more exclusively on emotion. We then

E.A. Weed (✉) • L. Smith-Lovin
Department of Sociology, Duke University, Durham, NC, USA
e-mail: eaw42@duke.edu; smithlov@ssc.duke.edu

S. Abrutyn (ed.), *Handbook of Contemporary Sociological Theory*, Handbooks of Sociology and Social Research, DOI 10.1007/978-3-319-32250-6_20

review the latter, more structural, approach, because it contains many important developments in sociological understanding of emotion. Though researchers in these two theoretical traditions use very different approaches, as we detail below, they occasionally share a vocabulary, and regularly arrive at findings that are consistent with one another.

Both literatures on emotion within sociology use a variety of terms to refer to their phenomena of study – emotion, affect, sentiment, mood, etc. These terms have different meanings within different theoretical traditions and have evolved over time even within specific strands of research. Rather than try to define the terms in general here, we discuss specific definitions that are relevant to the traditions that we describe below. However, we will concentrate this review on what are typically called feelings and emotions. *Feelings* are physical sensations that are subject to cognitive interpretation. *Emotions* are states of feeling that can include the initial physical sensation, the cognitive appraisal of that sensation, the continued rumination on that feeling as it passes through consciousness, and the physical manifestation of that cognitive appraisal or the display. We treat more trans-situational, long-term phenomena like moods, affect, sentiments, and so on, only as they are relevant for theoretical traditions that also involve feelings and emotions. In this chapter, we selectively review the contributions of three traditions in sociology – the dramaturgical approach, symbolic interactionism, and group processes – to current theory in sociology of emotion. Along the way, we recount the evolution of the field, tying the development of theory to recent empirical research and method. We end by providing our hopes for the future of emotion theory in sociology.

20.2 Dramaturgy and Culture

Our first section centers around dramaturgical theory, as first stated by Erving Goffman, and developed by many others since, including Arlie Hochschild, Peggy Thoits, and Candace Clark. Emotion theory in the dramaturgical tradition generally lays out abstract understandings of how emotions are used in social interaction, focusing less on how emotional arousal is experienced. Work in this tradition is largely qualitative, exploring emotions across a wide variety of contexts. Dramaturgical researchers have developed new ways to classify emotion by studying it as a tool used to perform roles and manage others' impressions.

20.2.1 Erving Goffman's Dramaturgy

The dramaturgical approach developed out of the insights put forth by Erving Goffman in his seminal work *The Presentation of Self in Everyday Life* (1959). Goffman's work was among the first to study the sociological importance of face-to-face interaction. He proposed that social scientists could gain a better understanding of society and social structure by imagining individuals as actors on a stage, wearing masks and putting on performances to manage the expectations and impressions of valued others. The focus of dramaturgical analysis, then, is not on an individual's personal thoughts or feelings, but rather on their performance, and how it is perceived. Goffman's work provided a foundation for important research into emotional display, beginning with Arlie Hochschild's work in emotion management in the early 1980s, and continuing through the present day with Candace Clark's sympathy margins.

In keeping with Goffman's metaphor of the actor on a stage, researchers in the dramaturgical tradition generally share his original language, examining and labeling social life in terms of frontstage and backstage, scripts, roles, scenes, acts, and audience. Individuals perform on the *frontstage*, where they display and interact. While in the frontstage, people perform their *roles* by communicating in *scripts* and performing *acts* that consist of sequences of behavior and interaction. All performances unfold in a particular context or setting, the *scene*, for a particular *audience*. Of course, no individual can present their public face every moment of every day. Following a performance, the *actors* retire once again to the *backstage* to relax, evaluate the success of their performance, and prepare for their next public appearance. This extensive metaphor forms the common language with which dramaturgical researchers analyze the social world.

20.2.2 Arlie Hochschild's Emotion Management

The rise of emotion studies within sociology represents a divergence from previous research emphasizing the rational concerns and appraisals that motivate human action. The limited theorizing on emotion that existed prior to the 1970s generally contrasted the affective with the rational. This distinction has since been disproved; in fact, rationality without emotion is now thought to be impossible (Damasio 1995). However, in 1983, Arlie Hochschild broke new ground in sociological theory and emotion research by combining rational, culturally–informed action with automatic emotional response in her work *The Managed Heart: The Commercialization of Human Feeling* (1983).

In *The Managed Heart*, Hochschild studies the day–to–day interaction of Delta flight attendants with their superiors, peers, and passengers. She finds that the flight attendants perform emotion management, also called emotion work, to bend their emotional responses to fit their context and smooth the rough edges in social interactions that occur at 30,000 feet. She further notes that their emotions are managed in one of three ways: cognitively, bodily, and expressively. Because emotion management is a mandatory part of the attendants' jobs, Hochschild terms this work emotional labor. Hochschild theorized that through emotion management, individuals bring their emotional responses into line with culturally–shared emotional ideologies, feeling rules, and display rules by engaging in either surface acting or deep acting.

In Hochschild's framework, emotion management and emotional labor are guided by feeling rules, prescriptions of what we ought to feel and how we ought to show it (1979). We all learn feeling rules throughout our lives. In childhood, these rules are often quite explicit, such as "Big boys don't cry." In adulthood, these may take more nuanced forms, and may be instead disguised as statements of shared assumptions or as questions, such as "Aren't you psyched to ride that new roller coaster!?" In this case, it is entirely possible that you are terrified of roller coasters and would rather fight a bear than be anywhere near one, but your social interaction will be much smoother if you embrace and share your friend's understanding that riding roller coasters is cause for happiness and excitement.

If you decide to manage your fear of roller coasters, you have two options: deep acting and surface acting. In surface acting, you maintain your emotion, but display another. You take your place as an actor on the stage and don a mask of excitement while internally, your fear is unabated. In deep acting, you work to turn the socially problematic emotion into something more appropriate. You might, for example, work to slow your breathing, or tell yourself that very few people die on rollercoasters and think about the whole experience as a fun adventure instead of a ride to your inevitable death. No matter what strategy you use, your aim in employing deep acting is to change the underlying emotion in order to change your performance or display to match shared emotion norms.

Consider this passage from *The Managed Heart* where a flight attendant describes how she deals with problem passengers:

> If I pretend I'm feeling really up, sometimes I actually get into it. The passenger responds to me as though I were friendly, and then more of me responds back. [*surface acting*] Sometimes I purposely take some deep breaths. I try to relax my neck muscles. [*deep acting with the body*] . . . I try to remember that if he's drinking too much, he's probably scared of flying. I think to myself, "he's like a little child." [*cognition*] Really, that's what he is. And when I see him that way, I don't get mad that he's yelling at me. He's like a child yelling at me then. [*deep acting*][1]

This interaction demonstrates Hochschild's core concepts, and makes clear use of the

[1] Descriptions in brackets altered from original (Hochschild 1983, p. 55)

dramaturgical analogy. The scene is an airplane cabin. This setting and her employment limits the attendant's ability to leave a difficult situation. Instead, she must stay on the frontstage and in character as the flight attendant for the majority of the long flight. Her role as flight attendant, hired by an airline that does little to protect its employees from angry passengers, severely limits her personal agency. In fact, during training, she has been taught several scripted methods for dealing with passengers. These scripts ensure that all employees will be successful in managing their emotions. Here, the attendant describes a successful performance for a particularly tough audience. Through surface and deep acting, she successfully maintains the interaction and handles the drunken passenger without displaying any of her own negative emotions. Though not described here, she is supported by the cast of other flight attendants, who assist her in her efforts at emotion management, and may even intervene to allow her to recover backstage before heading back to the frontstage to perform some more.

Although managing her own emotions and the emotions of others may make the interaction easier for the attendant, there is significant emotional cost to being frontstage for so long (see a similar point by Wharton 2009). Further, because she is hired and directed by the airline, most of the value of her acting accrues to her employer. Her emotion management, then, has a paid value, and is more appropriately referred to as emotional labor.

Importantly, the kinds of feeling rules to which people are subject depend on the social position they occupy. Imagine you are watching a football game and one of the wide receivers fumbles the ball and the opposing team runs it back. Angrily, he stamps his feet and throws his helmet on the ground shouting expletives. Now imagine you are in an office meeting and the new intern flubs his presentation and begins throwing a similar tantrum. While we expect impassioned display from athletes on the field, we do not expect the same from the office intern – to display intense anger would be inconsistent with his role. Next, imagine the intern flubs his presentation and is angrily and loudly rebuked by his older, white, male supervisor. In this case, the supervisor will probably not be censured for his behavior – he has enough status to overcome this inappropriate display. Lastly, imagine that instead of being older, white, and male, the angry supervisor is young, black, and female. Instead of accepting her criticism, the intern may report her for inappropriate behavior, evaluate her more poorly as a supervisor, or she may be labeled in the office as "the angry black woman." People experience different rules and different consequences for violating the rules based on their roles, their relative status in the context of the interaction, and personal characteristics that are tied to stereotypes or shared beliefs about what kind of person they are. For this reason, as Hochschild found, even within the same role as flight attendants, men and women can have very different experiences of emotional labor because of different status and the different expectations for social engagement that are tied to their gender. Hochschild does not develop her discussion of the effect of social position on emotion into an explicit framework. Still, her discussion is strongly consistent with Kemper's theorization of status and power as part of his social interactional theory of emotion (1978), outlined in the final section of this chapter on group processes.

20.2.2.1 Advances in Emotion Management Theory: The Intersection of Race and Gender

Consistent with Hochschild's early findings, work in the emotion management tradition shares a focus on the inequalities inherent in emotion management, and how the gendered, classed, and racialized socialization of emotion can reaffirm differences in status and contribute to overarching inequality. Roxanna Harlow investigated the impact of occupying an intersectional minority status on emotion management and emotion labor in her (2003) article "'Race Doesn't Matter, But…': The Effect of Race on Professors' Experiences and Emotion Management in the Undergraduate College Classroom." Because black professors are seen by students as lower status, and even out of place in the classroom environment, they are not afforded the same respect and deference as their white colleagues. Of Harlow's interviewees, just 7 % of the white professors felt that students called their qualifications into question, compared with 76 % of black professors (2003, p. 353), and a greater proportion of black professors felt as if their authority in the classroom had been challenged. Their subordinate social position requires black professors to engage in more emotion management and to more strictly enact the perfect professor role than white professors, in order to be taken seriously and to be considered good at their jobs.

Harlow combines emotional labor and management with approaches from identity theory and affect control theory (both presented in greater detail later). Harlow draws on work by Stryker, Burke, and Heise, among others, and argues that while individuals have multiple important identities, the more salient or relevant identity for her interviewees in the classroom is that of professor. When black professors enact the professor identity by teaching, they are met by students who instead treat them as if their most salient identity were their race. Black professors must then do emotion work to manage their negative feelings in response to these macro– and micro–aggressions, and do identity work to reaffirm their identity as professors by going to extra lengths to successfully enact their professor roles, despite doubt and criticism. Here, identity, emotion work, and emotional labor are intimately tied.

In response to doubt about their ability and more blatant disrespect, black professors work to reassert their identity in the professor role while downplaying the importance of race as a factor. To remain professional and successfully enact the professor role, they must manage the negative emotions that result from any disrespect, such as anger, frustration, annoyance, and hurt or sadness. Black women, Harlow notes, must negotiate a dually devalued status in terms of both race and gender. Black female professors were more likely to be officially evaluated by students as mean, cold, or intimidating. This is because black women face the overlap of two potentially injurious stereotypes: the angry black woman, and the overly–emotional, nurturing, matronly, obedient mammy (2003, p. 360). In the words of one black female faculty member:

> I'm just so aware of this whole black woman as, you know, angry person kind of myth. Somehow that we're like 70 percent attitude [. . .] I think they don't allow me the room to be serious, and I really do think that's about the "angry black woman with so much attitude" myth, you know? ... I do feel like some students expect that I'm gonna be more maternal, and if I don't live up to that, then the only place that's familiar to them that they can go in terms of judgments is "Oh, then she must have an attitude." So I'm not like "Oh come here, honey, let me hug you, feel my bosom" kind of thing, right ... but I really do feel like I don't have options. That there are these sort of two caricatures of black womanhood that they're familiar with, and that somehow I have to work within those.[2]

By not being overly nurturing in ways that would not be expected of white male professors, black women are cast as the angry black woman; their teaching is evaluated negatively as a result. Thus, for these women, like Hochschild's flight attendants, emotional labor is required for them to be good at their jobs, while it is not required of white men.

Through her work, Harlow demonstrates how racialized culture and structure shape individuals' experiences of emotion management and emotional labor. Although most black professors in her sample were cognizant of the impact of race, it was only by devaluing and ignoring the salience of race that they were able to manage their emotions. They had to prevent negative classroom experiences from negatively affecting their self–identities and their effectiveness as professors. Others have since investigated differences in black/white feeling rules in professional environments (Wingfield 2010), and for black women (Durr and Wingfield 2011).

As the study of emotion management has expanded, research on emotional labor has grown into a vast literature in its own right. In the absence of a clear, testable theoretical framework, many researchers have contributed to the literature on emotional labor by cataloguing

[2] Shortened from original length (Harlow 2003, p. 357)

unique workplaces and the differences between them (e.g., Kang 2010; Smith 2008; Smith and Kleinman 1989). As a result of this tendency to emphasize difference, most articles in this theoretical tradition replicate Hochschild's original findings with a twist, but do not contribute to theory or to a clearer model of emotion in the workplace.

20.2.2.2 Advances in Emotion Management Theory: Interpersonal Emotion Management

One notable exception to this tendency is Jennifer Lois' (2003) book, *Heroic Efforts: The Emotional Culture of Search and Rescue Workers*. In this book, Lois spends 6 years volunteering as part of a search and rescue team, documenting her own experience of the emotional culture. Through in–depth interviews and participant observation, Lois finds evidence for separating out two new types of emotion management: tight and loose.

Although most of the discussion up to now has primarily focused on how individuals manage their own emotions as part of successful interaction, emotion management can also be interpersonal: that is, individuals can manage others' emotions, aiding others in their performance (Thoits 1995), also called "collaborative emotion management" (Staske 1996). Building on the idea of interpersonal emotion management, Lois differentiated between "tight" and "loose" interpersonal emotion management.

Rescue workers employed tight emotion management when they needed victims to quickly follow directions that might be emotionally difficult for them. Lois recalls the story of a woman who fell into the water and was badly beaten by the river. When she finally made it to a small island in the middle of the river, her rescuers decided to evacuate her back through the water to safety, but the woman was terrified of going back into the water. She described her experience after:

> When I began to cry, he took me gently by the shoulders and told me I could not do that right now, he needed me there with him… They were very clear with their directions… They held me tight and made me feel safe… (Lois 2003, p. 126)

Here, the rescuer asserts control over the victim's feelings, telling her she cannot cry, in order to ensure that she can be evacuated safely. By changing her body sensation and reorienting the focus of the interaction, the rescuer manages the victim's fear, doing the deep acting for her, replacing the petrifying fear with emotions more conducive to her rescue. Because male rescue workers tended to be on the frontlines and in charge, tight emotion management more commonly fell to the men.

Rescue workers employed loose emotion management to manage victim's families' emotions. As families struggled to come to terms with the possible and, in some cases, eventual loss of a loved one, rescue volunteers worked with them, empathizing, expressing sympathy, and practicing active listening. This task was primarily assigned to women, who were said to have better skill in handling delicate emotions. Lois described these interactions as compressed intimacy. Through this process of being managed by the rescue workers, many of the families developed deep bonds with the members of the rescue team assigned to be family liaisons, though these bonds varied in strength after the rescue effort was complete. With few exceptions, these deep bonds ended just after the rescue effort did, often with a letter of thanks or a donation.

Like other emotion management researchers, Lois details the status and gender differences associated with different types of emotion management. In doing so, however, she also contributes to a more refined typology of emotion management and sociological understanding of the ongoing social construction of personally experienced emotion.

20.2.3 Peggy Thoits' Emotional Deviance

While work in emotion management has shed light on the social process of emotion management, it has generally given less attention to the question "How is emotion management achieved?" Studies in emotion management often provide deep descriptions of the cognitive strategies that people use, such as Harlow's conclusion that black professors downplay the importance of race in order to manage their emotions and identity. They frequently fall short, however, of systematically addressing how individuals go about changing the emotion itself. In 1984, Peggy Thoits expanded Schacter's two–factor theory of emotion, which described emotion as having two components: bodily sensation or arousal, and situational cues that prompt a cognitive appraisal of the arousal (Schachter and Singer 1962). Thoits called instead for a four–factor theory of emotion, including: physiological arousal, cognition, labeling the experience, and expression of the emotion (1984). In 1990, Thoits further developed her four–factor model to include emotion management techniques. This model includes four foci: situation, emotion and physiology, gesture and expression, and label. Individuals can use either behavioral or cognitive strategies to change any of these focuses. For example, one might change the situation by either leaving it (behavioral) or reinterpreting it (cognitive), but either strategy would change the associated emotion.

Thoits argued that individuals could intervene to alter their own emotions or the emotions of others at any of these key points. These four factors are also interdependent, so a change in one can prompt a change in the others. Recall the experience of the young woman trapped on the island in the middle of the cold river in Lois' *Heroic Efforts*. Being physically held by the rescuer changes her physiological experience – she may feel warmer and stop shaking – and this causes her to feel safe, mitigating her fear. At the same time, her rescuer works on her cognition by refocusing her attention, and relabels the situation as safe. With her emotion managed, she is able to successfully keep herself together long enough to get across the river to safety. People naturally rely on this interdependence of factors to change their experience of the world. Athletes breathe quickly and hop from foot to foot to psych themselves up before a big race, and parents inform their children that roads are not fun, but rather dangerous and deadly, relabeling the situation to inspire fear that keeps their children from running out into traffic.

Both Hochschild and Thoits have contributed to our understanding of what happens when there is discrepancy between felt emotions and feeling rules that define what is appropriate in a given situation. However, where the literature on emotion management has tended to focus primarily on how individuals successfully manage their emotions, Thoits' contribution to emotion theory has been more focused on emotional deviance and what happens when individuals are unable to manage their own emotions and thus behave in ways that are considered abnormal or inappropriate by the other people in the interaction.

Thoits suggests that individuals engage in more noticeable emotional deviance when they: (1) occupy multiple, generally contradictory, roles; (2) belong to two or more competing or contradictory subcultures; (3) undergo a major role transition due to personal or structural factors; or (4) are subject to especially rigid emotional constraints (1990). Individuals who publicly engage in deviant emotion risk being labeled deviant and/or mentally ill, either by themselves or others. Thoits' explicit discussion of emotional deviance and its ties to labeling theory has been widely used in the literature on mental health and stigmatized identities.

Martha Copp's (1998) article "When Emotion Work is Doomed to Fail: Ideological and Structural Constraints on Emotion Management" ties together Hochschild's emotion management with Thoits' work in emotional deviance and labeling theory. In this work, Copp investigates the constraints placed on workers' emotion management and emotional labor by examining the experiences of instructors and managers at a social service agency that provides vocational training and 'sheltered employment' to people with developmental disabilities. Though instructors aspire to cultivate a friendly, supportive environment in which to teach developmentally disabled people how to work, the work environment is difficult and repetitive, and the job doesn't pay well. Under these conditions, Copp asserts, instructors move from gentle, cooperative interpersonal emotion management to coercion and confrontation, often losing control all together.

As described by Hochschild (1983) and Thoits (1984, 1990), Copp's instructors engaged in cognitive emotion management strategies to manage their emotions, reframing their experiences in a positive light and working to find the positive parts of their work and to emphasize these experiences (1998). Instructors often had help in this management from their peers, who engaged in backstage teamwork, validating and managing each other's emotions on breaks away from the disabled employees, relaxing together after long shifts on the frontstage. As Hochschild found, however, the relief provided by these backstage support sessions was only temporary. Too much time in the job resulted in burnout, and instructors became largely unsuccessful at continuing to manage their own emotions and those of their disabled employees. When the amount of emotion management and emotional labor are unrealistic, employees have little choice but to breach the norms or to leave the situation. Instructors' breaching of the emotion norms of their workplace is an important example of emotional deviance as described by Thoits (1990). Copp contributes to emotion theory by differentiating emotional deviance by domain – occupational and personal – similar to Hochschild's distinction between emotion management and emotional labor. Copp's work also shows just how intertwined emotion management and emotional deviance are. Both the emotion management and emotional deviance traditions rely heavily on the idea of feeling rules, but there is relatively little theory around feeling rules in and of themselves. Candace Clark's work, presented in the next section, is an exception.

20.2.4 Candace Clark's Theory of Sympathy Margins

The work of emotions scholars relies heavily on the concept of feeling rules, or shared understandings of what emotions are appropriate for certain settings and how they ought to be expressed. Despite this, sociology of emotions scholars have generally taken an "I'll know it when I see it" approach, addressing particular feeling rules that become obvious in the course of research, but putting little effort toward developing a comprehensive theory of how feeling rules function or what the content of these feeling rules is. One exception to this gap in emotion theory is Candace Clark's work on sympathy margin (see Clark 1997 for an overview).

Clark's theory of sympathy margin integrates past work on social margin with emotion theory. Consistent with research in emotional deviance, very few singular acts of emotional deviance are severe enough to result in the person being labeled as deviant. Instead, most transgressions are slight and pass quickly. This is because most people possess enough social margin (i.e. social ties, material resources, and an established identity) to overcome slight slips. Clark's work draws on our understanding of social margin to illustrate how sympathy, a social emotion, is negotiated through interaction.Clark argues that there are four general rules of sympathy etiquette.

1. Do not make unwarranted claims to sympathy.
2. Do not claim too much sympathy or accept it too readily.
3. Claim and accept some sympathy to keep sympathy accounts open.
4. Repay sympathy with gratitude, sympathy, or both.

(Clark 1987, p. 290)

These rules are always in place, and people draw on the same sympathy margin across time. Thus someone who in the past claimed sympathy when others judged them underserving of it (a fraudulent claim) may find it harder to claim sympathy in the future, even if a new circumstance might have drawn sympathy otherwise (a valid claim). Clark describes people who follow these rules well enough as having acceptable sympathy biographies: they are likely to be able to draw upon their sympathy margin and exercise their right to sympathy should an appropriate situation arise.

Clark argues that sympathy, then, is traded through micro-interaction, resulting in a kind of relationship politics. When an individual is provided sympathy, she or she is in a lower status position compared to the provider of the sympathy, who occupies a higher status position. This is because sympathy both benefits the recipient and obligates him or her to repay it. By offering sympathy, individuals can knowingly or unknowingly place the recipient of the sympathy in a lower social position. As such, attempts to offer sympathy to higher status individuals by lower status group members may cause the high status member to refuse the offer of sympathy. At the same time, those who always refuse sympathy and always avoid the lower status position may be seen as not playing fair and not valuing the relationship. To maintain balance, individuals generally must swap sympathy. Relationships in which one person gives all the sympathy are unbalanced, and this imbalance may complicate social interaction, even to the point of moving one person to dissolve the relationship.

As an emotion, sympathy can also be subject to emotion management. As Clark notes, Hochschild's flight attendants sometimes cultivated sympathy for their passengers to counteract feelings of anger. Clark further argues that sympathy can be manipulated to counter fear, hatred, and anger. Feeling sorry for someone may feel like a much stronger position than being angry at someone, especially when a display of anger would be unacceptable. Emotion management also becomes necessary for those who have exhausted their sympathy margins. Clark notes that people recognize these limitations on others' sympathy, as demonstrated in her interview with this middle–aged man:

> That month when I had three deaths in the family and my car broke down and my mother–in–law needed constant care and the kids were sick, well, it was too unbelievable. I was embarrassed to even tell people what was happening. I didn't bring up the details. (Clark 1987, p. 306)

Those who have no sympathy margin left must limit their display of negative emotion, avoiding drawing attention to their negative feelings and unpleasant circumstances. Drawing on depleted sympathy margins can result in censure, exclusion, and further decreased margins. As a result, these people may choose to manage their own negative emotions without the help of a supportive cast of interaction partners. This can prove exceedingly difficult and emotionally exhausting.

Clark's work on the rules of sympathy is intimately tied to emotion management theory and research on identity work (presented in the next section). Kenneth Kolb ties these themes together in his recent article "Sympathy Work: Identity and Emotion Management Among Victim–Advocates and Counselors" (2011). In this work, Kolb describes how victim–advocates use emotion management to muster up sympathy for those who have violated sympathy rules. Although many clients are cooperative and enjoyable to work with, a few clients continually engage in problematic behaviors – illegal drug use, returning to abusers, accusing advocates of coercion – that interfere with advocates' abilities to feel sympathy for them. By turning anger and frustration into sympathy, advocates reinforce their identities as good, kindhearted helpers and are more successful in their jobs providing support for victims.

Goffman's metaphor of the actor on a stage provided fertile ground for a wide variety of work that has shed light on the nature of emotion. While the dramaturgical metaphor has allowed new understandings of how people cognitively manage their emotions in response to social pressure, this literature focuses more on general cultural rules for emotion and behavior that shape individuals' lives. The individual as a person with a singular self that enacts roles or identities is discussed primarily as the recipient of these cultural rules. The next section focuses on work that ties emotion to interaction and identity, consisting largely of theories that lay out blueprints for testing hypotheses about the emotional and social world. In contrast to dramaturgical theories, then, interactionist theories tend to use quantitative analysis and survey or experimental methods to provide insight into how emotions are personally experienced and the role they play in interaction.

20.3 Symbolic Interactionism and Identity

Our second section centers around research on identity, in the tradition of symbolic interactionists such as Cooley, Mead, and Blumer. Though emotion is not their focus, identity theories developed in this tradition by Stryker, Burke, and Heise, among others, have significantly influenced how emotion is understood today. Similar to the dramaturgical tradition, emotion theory in the symbolic interactionist tradition generally centers around the experience of emotion in interaction, but differs in its attention to self-structure and internalized identities. Symbolic interactionism focuses on how people form their identities, label their world, and reflect on the judgments of themselves and others. Identity theories address identity from either an individual or a structural perspective, keeping the role of culture in mind throughout. Work in this tradition is largely quantitative, using hypothetical-deductive theories to create predictions about the social world, and statistical analyses to test them.

20.3.1 Cooley and Mead

Symbolic interactionism in the twentieth century begins with Charles Horton Cooley and his concept of the looking–glass self. The looking–glass self is the process by which individuals imagine how they appear to others, then how those others judge or perceive them. They then experience an affective response to that imagined judgment (1902). Cooley noted that very powerful emotions are attached to an individual's sense of self. Further, emotions themselves are not only made up of physical responses; they are socially constructed through the process of reflexivity (1964).

George Herbert Mead expanded on this idea of the self as formed through interaction. He stressed the importance of *significant symbols* – words, gestures, and actions that people use to call forth in others the same meanings that they themselves understand (1934). For example, you might smile at a friend to indicate that you are happy with them, assuming that they will understand your smile as a sign of warmth and goodwill because that is what you think when someone smiles at you. While there is a possibility that they will not understand your smile in the same way that you do, this possibility is remote. As members of the same culture, you generally share the same meanings of the significant symbols that constitute everyday interaction.

Mead reasserted the importance of the generalized other – the people an individual imagines when thinking about how they appear to others. He argued that the generalized other is fundamental to social control because it causes individuals to police their own thoughts, emotions, and actions (1934). Shame, for example, stems from the perception that one's group members are disappointed in, angry with, or disgusted by the individual's self. This negative emotion serves as an impetus to stop or make amends for behaviors that are deemed inappropriate by the group. In the reverse, an individual feels pride when he or she takes the role of the other interaction partners and perceives positive evaluations of the self (also see Cooley 1964).

Much research in the symbolic interactionist tradition points to the centrality of emotion in shaping how people understand the world, the kinds of behaviors in which they choose to engage, and even how they think about themselves. Like research in the dramaturgical tradition, symbolic interactionist research relies, often implicitly, on the notion of feeling rules, the social guidelines for how we ought to feel in a given situation. While research in the dramaturgical tradition has focused more on how individuals navigate emotion, however, for symbolic interactionists, the social act is the primary unit of analysis, as it is through repeated interaction that individuals become human and a society is formed. As a result, researchers and theorists in this tradition tend to use statistical research to aggregate people's definitions of situations and circumstances.

20.3.2 Identity Theory

The term *identity* is so widely used that it has developed many different meanings within sociology. For the purpose of discussing identity in the context of the two identity theories presented in this section, identity refers to the meanings attached to the roles that people play. In identity theories, each individual can be said to have multiple selves, each tied to a group of people with whom they interact and a role that they play. You may be a graduate student at school, a musician when you play an instrument in a band, and a tutor or mentor when you teach someone else to play like you do. Each of these roles – graduate student, musician, and tutor – and the meanings and social ties attached to them are identities. Together, these overlapping and different identities make up your self. You learn, develop, confirm, and legitimize your identities through interaction with others, who provide affirmation for successful performances and censure for mistakes. Identities theories seek to understand why, when people have agency and freedom to choose, people behave in one way instead of another. Identity theories explain why people make the decisions they do by tying the behaviors in which people engage to the roles they occupy.

20.3.2.1 Sheldon Stryker's Identity Theory

Sheldon Stryker's work comes from the tradition of structural symbolic interactionism, focusing on how social structure affects the organization and content of the self, and how this self in turn affects social behavior (2000). In Stryker's conception, similar to that of identity theories as a whole and drawing directly on the work of Mead, identities are the internalized meanings attached to roles. The self is made up of multiple identities, which are organized in a salience hierarchy, some identities being more important and enacted more frequently than others (2004). The ordering of identities is based on what Stryker calls *commitment*: how strong a person's social ties are to the network that activates a particular role and its associated identity (2001, 2004). Clearly, then Stryker's theory is primarily a theory of identity and not emotion. In keeping with the work of Cooley, however, Stryker recognizes the importance of emotion as a force that shapes and motivates behavioral choices, believing as Hochschild does, that emotions act as a liaison between the self and the outside world (Hochschild 1983; Stryker 2004).

Stryker argues that the strength of emotional reactions helps to signal the importance of a particular identity, ordering and reordering identities in an individual's salience hierarchy, and affecting their commitment to different identities (2004). Imagine you enroll in graduate school, and you expect to enact the role of graduate student. Instead, you find upon starting your new career as a graduate student, you are treated more like a gofer, and you have very few opportunities to properly enact your graduate student role and receive praise for doing so. This is likely to cause an intensely negative emotional response, and it may lead you to reevaluate whether you really are a graduate student and how important it is to you to be a graduate student. Having been consistently disconfirmed, and feeling very negatively about your ability to enact the graduate student role, you are likely to change your self and take on a new identity that you can enact. You might, for example, prioritize a new identity – perhaps that of gofer – or move to a new network and take on a new identity – perhaps that of a researcher in industry. In either case, you will experience more positive, less intense emotion once you are able to successfully enact your most valued identities.

Stryker's instincts about the centrality of emotion are made more concrete in Peter Burke's work in identity control theory, and even more so in David Heise's affect control theory. Because of its ambiguity surrounding the integration of emotion, cognition, and interaction, few researchers use Stryker's theory of emotion and identity in isolation. Instead, it is frequently paired with work by Peter Burke and Jan Stets..

20.3.2.2 Burke's Identity Control Theory

Where Stryker's identity theory focuses on how structure influences identity (Stryker and Burke

2000), Burke's identity control theory, first delineated in the early 1990s, focuses on how individuals process their roles in relation to their context, and how this process shapes their social behavior (Burke 1991). Identity in identity control theory has four components: identity standard – what it means to be oneself in a particular situation; input – how one sees oneself in the situation based on feedback from others; comparator – a comparison between the input and the standard; and output – the difference between the ideal identity enactment and the individual's perception of others' judgment of their identity enactment (Burke and Stets 2009). When the discrepancy between ideal and perceived is small or decreasing, identity control theory predicts people will feel positive emotions. When the discrepancy is large or increasing, they will feel negative emotions. In accordance with these emotional prompts, individuals will make efforts to decrease this discrepancy and avoid the associated negative emotions (Burke and Harrod 2005). In 2004, Stryker expanded his theory, presenting several hypotheses, most of which are consistent with Burke's earlier discussion. A few articles have attempted to demonstrate the validity of the theoretical prediction that discrepancy between identity standard and input, or output, predicts emotional experience. The most commonly cited of these articles is by Burke and Michael Harrod, entitled "Too Much of a Good Thing?" (2005).

In their paper, Burke and Harrod compare two types of identity theories: self-discrepancy theories and self-enhancement theories (2005). Self-discrepancy theories, like identity control theory, assert that people experience negative emotions when they are either over- or under-evaluated, and that they are motivated to avoid either case. Self-enhancement theories assert instead that people seek out, and respond positively to, over-evaluations but negatively toward under-evaluations. Burke and Harrod test these conflicting predictions using longitudinal data of married couples, from newly-wed to their third year of marriage. Each participant was asked to rate themselves on intelligence, physical appearance, likeability, friendliness, and how understanding they are. They were then asked to rate their partner. The discrepancy between a person's own rating and their partner's rating of them was used as a measure of self-evaluation discrepancy. One issue to note is that identity control theory makes predictions about one's self and one's perception of how others see the self, while this study design collects information on how one sees oneself and how one's partner sees oneself. To equate a partner's evaluation with input is to assume perfect information and interpretation, unlikely under even the best conditions. Therefore, self-evaluation discrepancy is not equal to the theoretical concept of output. Despite this, Burke and Harrod find that people feel worse about themselves, in terms of their self-worth, self-efficacy, and experience more depression, anger, and distress when their partners over- or under-evaluate them.

Two issues are worth noting, however. Firstly, depression, self-worth, and self-efficacy are not emotions as defined by most sociologists of emotion. Secondly, most people feel pretty good about themselves. Those who rate themselves poorly enough that their spouses can rate them higher than they do themselves are likely to be more negative in general than their positively-rating counterparts. As a result, they may be more likely to evaluate their self-worth and -efficacy negatively and to experience more negative emotions than those who rate themselves more positively. Most research studying identity control theory and emotion has been done using this same data set, rendering the findings about emotion similarly inconclusive. More research is needed to ascertain whether over-evaluation leads to positive or negative emotion. This debate is taken up by the affect control theory literature, which makes very different predictions about emotion.

20.3.3 Heise's Affect Control Theory

An alternative model of identity and emotion is provided by David Heise, developed in the 1970s (see Heise 2007 for a complete overview). Affect control theory is tied more concretely to emotion than either Stryker's work before or Burke's work after. Under affect control theory, members of a culture share meanings about roles, objects, and behaviors. Members of the same culture share these understandings, whether they agree with them or not. In affect control theory, actors, behaviors, and objects are conceptualized in three dimensions: evaluation – good to bad; potency – powerful to powerless, or big to little; and activity – slow to fast, quiet to noisy, or inactive to active (EPA, hereafter). Every identity (mother, banker, prisoner) and behavior (run, talk to, hit) has an EPA value, a point in a three-dimensional space that describes how good, powerful, and active that concept is. Emotions are also rated on the same EPA scales.

Affect control theory asserts that members of a culture share these understandings. For example, most Americans think of mothers as quite good, somewhat powerful, and somewhat active. Even if our own mother is not this way, or we see a mother behaving badly in the news, we share an understanding of what the prototypical mother ought to be. Thus, when we see a mother doing something relatively good and powerful like hugging another good but less powerful actor, like a baby, we feel that things are as they should be. On the other hand, when we hear news of a mother abusing a baby, we probably think this is a very surprising and disconcerting event. Affect control theory uses a mathematical model to analyze these events, made up of an actor (role/identity), behavior (action), and an object (role/identity). When people interact, they may have different conceptions of the situation. Returning to an earlier example, as a graduate student in conversation with your professor, you might cognitively label the situation graduate student talks with professor. If the professor instead sees the situation as gofer talks with professor, then there is a calculable discrepancy between the EPA values for graduate student and gofer. Gofers are less good (lower E) and less powerful (lower P) than graduate students. Affect control theory predicts that this discrepancy, called *deflection*, will cause an emotion, *and* push you to action or cause you to re-label part of the situation. Individuals can be negatively deflected, as when someone refers to the graduate student as a gofer, or positively deflected, as when someone refers to the graduate student as a genius.

Affect control theory is situated in between self-enhancement and self-discrepancy theories, in that it predicts that (1) individuals will feel positive emotions when positively deflected and negative emotions when negatively deflected (self-enhancement consistent), but (2) individuals are driven to confirm their identities and conform to culturally shared understandings in order to facilitate social interaction, and (3) when individuals confirm their identities, they feel emotions fitting with that identity (Heise 2007; MacKinnon 1994). Picture a funeral. As suits the setting, most of the people there are probably mourners. In one corner, two people are conversing, and one laughs loudly at a joke that was told. They both probably feel happy, an emotion with a similar EPA rating to the identity of friend. Unfortunately, while the conversing pair was probably defining themselves as friend talks to friend and friend laughs with friend, the other mourners probably expected the pair to be a mourner whispering to a mourner. The laugh disrupted the understanding of the situation as mourner whispers to mourner, causing a great deal of deflection: mourners are very different from friends and whispering is very different from laughing. This difference between expectation and perceived reality may cause the mourners to shush the pair or glare at them. In response, the chastened pair may make a gesture to restore their identities to something close to mourner and socially appropriate, perhaps by apologizing or beseeching the other attendees for their forgiveness and feeling ashamed. Once the people are firmly back in the identity of mourner, affect control theory predicts that they will feel emotions consistent with being a mourner, including sadness and anguish.

Importantly, though these examples make intuitive sense, they actually originate from the formal math of the model, which uses EPA ratings and a set of equations that calculate deflection between events to predict what emotions people will feel as a result of participating in an event, how people can cognitively re-label parts of events, and how people act to change events.

In this way, affect control theory is consistent with Hochschild's research in emotion management and Thoits' four-factor theory of emotion. Affect control theory independently predicts that Hochschild's stewardesses would relabel a belligerent man as a fearful child because fearful child yells at stewardess is a lower deflection event than man yells at stewardess. Affect control theory is also consistent with other emotion theory. Like Thoits' work in labeling theory, affect control theory relies on the assumption that labels have significant implications for our orientations and actions. Recent research using affect control theory has also found support for the symbolic interactionist assumption that labels have real effects on how people think about, feel about, and act toward, situations (for example, see Boyle and McKinzie 2015).

Despite this strength, the emotion predictions of the affect control theory model are its weakest part. It is currently unclear what exactly the emotions predicted by the mathematical model indicate. As an example, consider the event mother hits baby. Affect control theory predicts that the mother feels angry and the baby feels sad. Though the math is the same for calculating the appropriate emotion for the mother (actor) and the baby (object), the model appears to predict emotions that prompt actors to action, while predicting emotions that objects of actions feel following the event. In this case, an angry mother would hit a baby, but a baby would feel sad only once he or she has been hit. The emotions predicted, then, have different meanings depending on where a person is in the sequence of the event. More research is needed to clarify and test the emotional hypotheses of affect control theory.

One recent advance in emotion theory comes directly from affect control theory. In their (2004) analysis, *Sociological Realms of Emotional Experience*, Kathryn Lively and David Heise developed a model of emotional experience that integrates work in affect control theory and emotion management, explicitly and clearly tying identity to emotional transitions. Using EPA ratings of emotions collected for work in affect control theory as their starting point, Lively and Heise applied shortest path analysis to correlations between pairs of emotions in order to create a measure of relative distance between emotions. The authors demonstrate that the distance between distress and tranquility can be reduced by segueing through anger and fear.

As described previously, in affect control theory, emotions are tied to consonant identities: when confirmed in their identities, mourners feel sad and friends feel happy. As such, individuals should be able to change their emotions by transitioning to new identities, and vice versa. This model is consistent with qualitative research in the dramaturgical tradition on emotions in therapy, in which mental health care providers have been found to redefine patients' identities in order to manage their emotions (Francis 1997). By transitioning bereaved spouses from victims to mourners to widow[er]s to survivors, mental health professionals change their patients' emotions from sad and distressed to happy and tranquil. Lively later expanded on this model in examining how men and women experience emotional transitions differently, finding that women tend to have a longer, more complicated series of emotional segues than do men, with more positive and less powerful emotions than their male counterparts (2008).

Though not initially focused on emotion, identity theories have provided new models of describing individuals' emotional experience. While identity theories have made great strides in situating the individual in a cultural context, concrete theory in this tradition focuses on dyadic interactions. In its focus on individual identities, identity theory has largely neglected empathetic and sympathetic emotion. The next section focuses on work that investigates emotion in the context of the group, particularly as emotion is used to negotiate and affirm social hierarchies. In contrast to interactionist theories, then, work in group processes seeks more information about *how* individuals interact to negotiate status and power, and theorizes the impact of exchange interactions on larger group order. Group processes researchers generally rely on experiments to describe the creation and reification of power and status differences on a broad scale.

20.4 Group Processes: Social Exchange, Status, Legitimacy, and Justice

Our third and final section centers around research on status, power, and justice in social exchange, in the tradition of Bales and Kemper. Exchange theories developed in this tradition by Berger, Ridgeway, Lawler, and others have contributed greatly to sociology of emotions by calling attention to how emotions shape, and are shaped by, social and structural arrangement. Social structure, in the form of status and power hierarchies, is the focus of analysis. Despite this dramatic difference in focus, emotion theory in the group processes tradition shares several assumptions with the literature in both the dramaturgical and symbolic interactionist traditions. Work in this tradition is largely quantitative, using primarily experimental methods, though the use of survey measures has grown in recent years.

20.4.1 Kemper's Social Interactional Theory of Emotion

In the late 1970s, Theodore Kemper established status and power as two important features of social interaction (1978). For the purposes of discussing his work and the work of others who have come after, *status* refers to voluntary deference, while *power* refers to deference gained by coercion. Kemper suggested that emotions emerged from these two key aspects of interaction. Under his paradigm, different emotions are associated with different levels of power and status, and changes in power or status cause correspondent changes in emotion. Kemper's work served as a foundation for later scholars in this tradition, who relied on his conjectures on the importance of status and power.

20.4.2 Expectation States Theories

Expectation states theory is a research program for the study of status hierarchies, most concisely laid out in Joseph Berger and colleagues' 1974 treatise, Expectation States Theory: A Theoretical Research Program (Berger et al. 1974). Drawing on Robert Bales' work on affect and behavior in small groups (1950), Berger asserted that much of small group behavior can be explained in terms of power and prestige (1974). Under expectation states theory, members of a group develop expectations for their own and others' behavior in comparison with other group members. These *performance expectations* are an individual's best guess for how others expect them to behave, and are generally unspoken and may be unconscious. Much like Burke's identity control theory model, individuals form these expectations through interaction with others, interpreting other group member's actions to situate themselves appropriately within the group. Research using the status characteristics branch of this theory has emphasized the importance of differences in salient social and demographic attributes – such as age, race, and gender – that influence the expectations a group has for an individual's prestige, participation, and influence in a group (for a review, see Ridgeway 2001).

20.4.2.1 Joseph Berger's Affect Expectation Theory

In 1988, Berger expanded on expectation states theory to develop the closely-related affect expectation theory (1988). In a chapter about the future of expectation states theory, Berger describes four stages of emotional reaction. In the first stage, some stimulus leads an individual to experience affect. In the second, this affect is exchanged between the individuals of the group. This exchange process prompts individuals to form or reform their expectations for affect in the group. In the third stage, the affect becomes more stable and more consistently influences group members' behavior and orientations toward each other. In the fourth and final stage, affect becomes a part of personality, and expectations for affect are made more concrete.

To place these stages in the context of a real life situation, imagine you are running late to a lunch meeting when you join your colleagues at the table. Although lunch was promised, there were not quite enough meals, and since you were late, there is no lunch for you. You might feel frustrated and angry about this, and make your displeasure known by speaking harshly to the person who ordered lunch. They, in turn, calmly and evenly rebut your criticism, making you even angrier as you sit there watching everyone else eat with your stomach growling. As you continue through the meeting with a gruff tone, a furrowed brow, and red face, other members of the group may decide that anger is a stable characteristic of yours. As a result, they act toward you expecting you to respond negatively and angrily in return. If this happens enough, your anger may be seen as part of who you are. Unfortunately, your anger may not end with you. If, at this meeting, you are representing social psychologists and enacting the role of social psychologist as your primary role, others at the meeting may come to believe that all social psychologists are angry – applying your personality trait to the entire group you represent (Ridgeway 1991).

20.4.2.2 Cecelia Ridgeway's Theory of Socioemotional Behavior and Status

Cecelia Ridgeway, in collaboration with Cathryn Johnson, drew upon Kemper and Berger's theories to develop a new theory that ties together the dramaturgical tradition with work in group processes (for a review, see Ridgeway 2006). Ridgeway's theory of socioemotional behavior and status is founded on the understanding that every situation has norms for behavior that are shared among members of the group, called *blueprint rules* (Ridgeway and Johnson 1990). Ridgeway and Johnson argue that these blueprint rules include feeling rules, consistent with work by Hochschild in the emotion management literature (Hochschild 1979). Thus, in an extension of Berger's model (1974), Ridgeway and Johnson draw on Kemper's insights into status and power (1978) to argue that the flow of affect within a group is affected by the status of the members in the group (1990). Emotion is structured by status hierarchies in that individuals are subject to different blueprint rules, and more specifically, feeling rules, based on their status in the group (Ridgeway 2006). Empirical tests of this theory have shown that low-status individuals are expected to manage their negative emotions in interaction with higher-status individuals. High-status individuals do not face the same constraints (Ridgeway and Johnson 1990).

To return to the example of voicing anger in an office meeting, some people have more social leeway to voice their negative emotions, like anger, without facing harsh sanctions or social rebuke. If you were an older, white, male with a seat on the board, for example, few would argue when you began yelling. Indeed, your lower-status group members would probably defer to you and look properly guilty and ashamed for not saving a lunch for you. If, however, you are a young, black, female who has just started at the company, for you to voice your anger to your higher-status group members would be seen as an affront, and rather than being met with ashamed faces, other group members might instead sanction you for failing to follow the emotion norms commensurate with your status and discredit your emotions by attributing your anger to your characteristics. This insight from group processes literature parallels findings by Harlow (2003) and other researchers (Durr and Wingfield 2011; Wingfield 2010) in the dramaturgical literature. In Harlow's case, black, female professors were constrained in their behavior and emotional display for fear of being labeled the stereotypical angry black woman. These often unspoken assumptions about what emotions are appropriate for different people reaffirm stereotypes and reinforce status hierarchies. Enforcing these norms can amount to symbolic violence, as the enforcement of status-based emotion norms acts is a form of social and cultural domination (Bourdieu 1979).

Further research has expanded on this theory to demonstrate that, consistent with affect control theory, members of the same culture have a shared understanding of certain emotions (Lively and Heise 2004) as being more or less acceptable for low- or high-status individuals (Tiedens et al. 2000). In their article, "Sentimental Stereotypes: Emotional Expectations for High- and Low-Status Group Members," Tiedens et al. conduct a series of vignette studies to examine emotional stereotypes of high and low status individuals (2000). They find that in negative situations, participants expect high-status individuals to feel angry, in contrast to low-status individuals, who are expected to feel more sad and guilty. In positive situations, high-status individuals were expected to feel more pride, while low-status individuals were expected to feel appreciation.

In an extension of Berger and Ridgeway's work, Tiedens and colleagues used another vignette to test whether emotions could be used to infer social status: a reversal of most previous literature (Tiedens et al. 2000). In the vignette, the authors present two characters: "X" and "Y." They varied which of the two characters – X or Y – was described as sad and guilty, or angry, and then asked which of the characters was an executive and which was an assistant. The authors found that when Y was described as feeling angry, and X was described as feeling sad and guilty, respondents more frequently inferred that Y was the executive and X was the assistant. That is, people may use information about others' emotions to infer social status. A similar pattern was found by Robinson et al. in the context of affect control theory (1994). While these vignette studies contribute greatly to furthering the literature, they leave open the question of interactions between status and emotion, and race and gender. Future research in this literature may have important implications for understanding how inequality develops and persists in small groups and larger society.

20.4.3 Edward Lawler's Affect Theory of Social Exchange

Researchers in the Bales and Kemper traditions have primarily focused on theorizing specific emotions and distinguishing between positive and negative emotional situations, rather than developing general theories of emotion. In his affect theory of social exchange, Edward Lawler distinguishes between emotions as more global feelings toward a situation, in comparison with sentiments, which in his paradigm are affective responses directed at specific others (Lawler 2001). Under this theory, then, the object of a sentiment can be used to predict the type of emotion. In Lawler's paradigm, emotions can be attributed to the task at hand, the self, another social actor, or the social unit as a whole. When emotions are attributed to each of these four social objects, the following is expected.

1. The positive emotion felt toward a task is pleasantness; the negative is unpleasantness.
2. The positive emotion felt toward the self is pride; the negative is shame.
3. The positive emotion felt toward another social actor is gratitude; the negative is anger.
4. The positive emotion felt toward the social unit as a whole is affective attachment; the negative is affective detachment.

(Lawler 2001, p. 332)

Lawler notes, however, that based on work by Bernard Weiner (1986), individuals are more likely to attribute positive feelings to themselves and negative feelings to outside factors (Lawler 2001). To better understand how individuals move past this bias in order to attribute positive emotion toward outside factors, Lawler looks to two key factors of social exchange: the type of exchange, and the extent to which a person's contribution to the task can be isolated from the contributions of others.

While Lawler's affect theory of social exchange is the most emotion-focused, there are several variations of exchange theory that provide predictions or make assumptions about the role of emotion in social exchange or interaction. Taken together, the affect theory of social exchange (Lawler 2001), relational cohesion theory (Lawler and Yoon 1996), and the theory of social commitments (Lawler et al. 2009) all predict or assume that people who believe they are in equal and just social exchanges experience more positive emotion, which can increase their affective commitment to, and participation in, the group.

20.4.4 Justice and Equity Theory

Like other group processes theories, the literatures of equity and justice have detailed the reciprocal relationship between emotion and social structure. These parallel literatures theorize emotion primarily as a response to inequity and injustice. Although there are many possible objective ways to measure how fair a situation is from the outside, understanding objective fairness is not a focus of either literature. As noted to varying degrees by other theories previously discussed – including affect control theory, identity control theory and emotion management – emotion is a personal response to a stimulus *as that stimulus is perceived* by an individual. Further, perception is consistently more predictive of behavior and emotional response than more objective measures (Merton 1995). What is fair to one person is not always fair to another. Thus, these literatures generally evaluate *perceptions* of equality and justice in relation to emotions.

20.4.4.1 Justice Theory

Justice theory study of emotion generally centers around two types of justice: *distributive* and *procedural*. Distributive justice assesses the extent to which outcomes are allocated according to equity or equality (Hegtvedt 2006). If everyone gets the same thing, then the distribution is equal. If everyone is given enough to have the same outcome, then the distribution is less equal, but more equitable, since it is based on need. Procedural justice, by contrast, is concerned with the process by which outcomes are distributed (2006). Members of a group can agree that a process (e.g. pulling names from a hat) is agreed-upon and procedurally just, even when the distributive outcome (only one person is selected) is quite unjust.

Generally, people feel more positive emotions when both procedural justice and distributive justice are high, and experience more negative emotions when procedures and outcomes are perceived as unfair (Hegtvedt and Parris 2014). This is true whether a person is thinking about what is just for his or herself or another. Because justice has at least two parts, there is an interaction between distribution and procedure. Even when people get less than they believe they should, if they believe that the way the decision was made was fair (Hegtvedt and Killian 1999), or that the person who made the decision had the right to do so (Clay-Warner 2006), they will feel less negative emotion than if both distribution and procedure were perceived to be unjust. While most justice literature continues to focus on the direction (positive or negative) and intensity of emotion, as opposed to the theorization of discrete emotions, such as anger, joy, or sadness (see Guillermina 2007 for examples), equity literature has recently moved toward more distinct classifications of emotion.

20.4.4.2 Equity Theory

Exchange interactions are *equitable* not when all individuals contribute or gain equally from the interaction, but rather when all individuals involved in the group or task have roughly the same ratio of perceived contributions to benefits. Under equity theory, negative emotions follow inequity while positive emotions follow equity. As a result, individuals are motivated to maintain equitable situations. Notably, both over-benefiting and over-contributing are predicted to cause negative emotions for all individuals involved (Adams 1965). Over time, this relatively uniform notion of negative emotion or distress was differentiated into more specific emotions. Tests of the theory showed that anger is more likely when individuals over-contribute, while guilt or shame is more likely when individuals over-benefit (Walster et al. 1975). Research in this literature has investigated many contexts in which people may experience inequity [e.g. stem cell transplants (Beattie and Lebel 2011), expression of white privilege (Branscombe et al. 2007), impression management in communication with journalists (Westphal et al. 2012)]. Although most equity researchers who focus on emotion have used experiments, a few have approached the issue through surveys to investigate longer-term inequity than can be simulated in experiments.

In their 2010 article, "Equity, Emotion, and Household Division of Labor," Kathryn Lively, Lala Carr Steelman, and Brian Powell use the

General Social Survey and the National Survey of Family and Households to examine inequity in the household division of labor and its impact on emotions within couples. Lively and colleagues start with the equity theory finding that over-benefiting and over-contributing lead to guilt and anger, respectively (Walster et al. 1975). The authors then draw on Kemper's social interactional theory and his notions of power and status (1978), as well as research from affect control theory on role-consistent emotions (Heise 2007) to further develop how emotions interact with consistent inequalities in long-term relationships (Lively et al. 2010). Lively and colleagues find that, in the case of household labor, men are more likely to report feeling anger or rage when they perceive that they are under-benefitting, while women are more likely than men to report feeling fear and mild guilt/shame when they perceive they have under-contributed.

As the authors point out, their findings suggest that women may be willing to do more housework than their male partners, both to minimize their own guilt and their partner's anger. Consistent with work in emotion management by Hochschild (1979) and Thoits (1990), doing more housework may allow women to manage their own emotions and their partners' emotions. This inequality in household labor and emotion work is exacerbated by the fact that men overestimate their work in the household to a greater extent than do women, meaning that male partners are quicker to perceive that they are over-contributing and to respond with anger (Coltrane 1996). While emotion management may help couples cooperate and maintain their relationships, it does little to change the conditions that underlie perceptions of inequity, and may even operate to disguise what inequity does exist.

Work in group processes has demonstrated quite conclusively the importance of emotion in the negotiation of power and status. This literature has also made the greatest contribution to theorizing emotions beyond the individual level, developing new models that describe how emotion is involved in the creation of society-wide inequalities and stereotypes. Because of the complexity of establishing a mechanism between individual's emotion, dyadic interaction, group-level emotions, and widespread inequalities, more work is needed to test this theoretical framework.

20.4.5 Ritual Theories

A similar process to that described in the group processes literature is *ritual*. In the early 1900s, Durkheim theorized that culture exerts a common pull on individual people through emotionally arousing rituals (Durkheim 2001). He described the result of shared rituals as effervescence, in which emotions are heightened and group membership becomes more central.

20.4.5.1 Interaction Ritual Chains and Emotional Energy

Randall Collins developed Durkheim's initial theorization about rituals to describe interaction ritual chains. According to Collins, emotions are aroused when individuals meet and interact, as well as throughout the course of interaction (2004). When individuals reference their group, positive feelings are aroused, and this phenomenon reinforces group culture. Individuals move through many single rituals, making ritual chains. Emotional energy is positive when these rituals succeed, and negative when they do not. Collins' draws on Kemper's notions of status and power to suggest that individuals with high power and status have a greater capacity to create positive emotional energy and are motivated to reaffirm group culture (1990). As a result, positive emotional energy lifts high status individuals and helps them retain their higher status. This understanding of the important of differential social position in interaction ritual is in accordance with findings in the literatures on emotion management, expectation states, and equity theory, reviewed above.

Erika Summers-Effler's work offers an extension of ritual theory. Summers-Effler has theorized that when circumstances prevent individuals from leaving an interaction or group, they develop strategies to minimize negative emotional energy (2004b). Her recent research represents an important start to integrating theory of self and identity into ritual theory (Summers-Effler 2004a), but more work is needed to concretely tie emotional experience to ritual.

20.5 Avenues for Future Research and Concluding Thoughts

Theory in sociology of emotions seeks to understand an experience that is often ephemeral, fleeting, and deeply personal, as a shared, social phenomenon. In this chapter, we have detailed the contributions of three traditions within sociology of emotion: dramaturgical, symbolic interactionist, and group processes. In 40 years, sociology has moved the concept of emotion from an unfortunate complication of rationality to a fundamental, shared experience that shapes and is shaped by society at every level of interaction. Despite these advances, however, there is much room for further growth. Though there are areas of almost perfect overlap, emotion theory in the dramaturgical tradition remains quite distinct from work in symbolic interactionism and group processes, creating parallel literatures that fail to draw on each other's successes, though they reside in the same academic discipline. Two points of disagreement make integration difficult. These are: what an emotion is, and what a useful theory of emotion contains.

There are over 20 typologies of emotion within sociology (Turner 2000). Despite this vast array from which to choose, most emotion scholars neglect to pick one, instead settling for their own typology of emotion that fits a particular study or dataset. This practice has resulted in almost as many conceptualizations of emotion as there are sociological emotion scholars. Scholars in the dramaturgical tradition generally focus on one of four emotions or their variants: happiness, fear, anger, and sadness. Identity theory, by contrast, considers a broad array of concepts in testing their hypotheses about emotion. This array includes these four emotions, but also includes states such as depression, general distress (Burke and Harrod 2005), apathy, compassion, lustfulness, regret, and grief (Heise 1997). By most definitions in the dramaturgical tradition and the literature in psychological social psychology, none of these states is an emotion. Instead, they represent moods, and even behavioral impulses or identity labels, but not emotions or variants thereof. Emotion research is still ongoing, but it may be most useful for scholars who seek to discuss and theorize emotion to start with the four emotions that are shared between sociology and psychology: happiness/joy, anger, fear, and sadness/upset. These emotions are experienced and displayed in similar ways across cultures (see Turner 2000 for an overview) and could represent a common point of departure for emotions scholars.

Having established commonality around what an emotion is, the issue of theory remains. Hochschild's work provided a unique look at emotion and valuable insight into the workings of emotion management. Her central concepts – emotion management, feeling rules, and surface and deep acting – have served as a foundation for much of the work in emotion since. Unfortunately, she neglected to enumerate a testable framework, and the research that has followed has done the same. The literature of emotion management has remained a collection of examples, with each new piece of research offering little new theoretical insight. At the same time, researchers in the identity theory and group processes literatures have advanced theories of emotion, but these theories are either underspecified, or largely untested. For example, Burke's identity control theory lays out specific hypotheses about emotion, but the theory focuses on the simplified contrast between positive and negative emotions, and research remains mixed, especially about the effects of over-reward. Similarly, Heise's affect control theory leaves emotion relatively undertheorized, in stark contrast with the rest of the model.

Thoits' 1984 work on her four-factor model of emotion offers insight into a possible common approach. In developing her theory, Thoits draws on previous work across disciplines to present a clear, testable hypothesis about what makes up an emotion, and tests these hypotheses across several case studies in mental health and gender. Her theory is also testable using experimental and survey methods, and has clear implications for work in identity and group processes that have yet to be picked up.

The integration of emotion management theories with identity and group processes theories is still under development, but represents a unique opportunity to unite three essentially separate traditions – dramaturgy and culture, symbolic interactionist, and group processes – over their common interest: sociology of emotion. One particularly salient place of commonality across theories appears to be the importance of status and power in shaping emotional responses, and the reciprocal significance of emotion as a marker of differences in social position. Adopting status and power as common intellectual ground may help to prevent scholars from talking past and around each other. Alongside a common topic, the best way to integrate these theories is to develop a language that is common to emotion theorists. Individual researchers can work toward this integration by being clear about the emotions they are studying; by stating why they are classifying those emotions as emotions and under what typology; by using research not only to describe the world, but to advance and test theory; and by ensuring that theory reflects the most recent empirical research available within the entire sociology of emotions subfield and across disciplines in psychology and neuroscience.

References

Adams, J. S. (1965). Inequity in social exchange. *Advances in Experimental Social Psychology, 2*, 267–299.

Bales, R. F. (1950). *Interaction process analysis: A method for the study of small groups*. Cambridge, MA: Addison-Wesley Publishing Company.

Beattie, S., & Lebel, S. (2011). The experience of caregivers of hematological cancer patients undergoing a hematopoietic stem cell transplant: A comprehensive literature review. *Psycho-Oncology, 20*, 1137–1150.

Berger, J. (1988). Directions in expectation states research. In *Status generalization: New theory and research* (pp. 450–474). Stanford: Stanford University Press.

Berger, J., Conner, T. L., & Fisek, M. H. (Eds.). (1974). *Expectation states theory: A theoretical research program*. Cambridge, MA: Winthrop Publishers.

Bourdieu, P. (1979). *Distinction: A social critique of the judgement of taste*. Cambridge, MA: Harvard University Press.

Boyle, K. M., & McKinzie, A. E. (2015). Resolving negative affect and restoring meaning: Responses to deflection produced by unwanted sexual experiences. *Social Psychology Quarterly, 10*(5), 1–22.

Branscombe, N. R., Schmitt, M. T., & Schiffhauer, K. (2007). Racial attitudes in response to thoughts of white privilege. *European Journal of Social Psychology, 37*(2), 203–215.

Burke, P. J. (1991). Identity processes and social stress. *American Sociological Review, 56*(6), 836–849.

Burke, P. J., & Harrod, M. M. (2005). Too much of a good thing…. *Social Psychology Quarterly, 68*(4), 359–374.

Burke, P. J., & Stets, J. E. (2009). *Identity theory*. New York: Oxford University Press.

Clark, C. (1987). Sympathy biography and sympathy margin. *American Journal of Sociology, 93*(2), 290–321.

Clark, C. (1997). *Misery and company: Sympathy in everyday life*. Chicago: University of Chicago Press.

Clay-Warner, J. (2006). Procedural justice and legitimacy: Predicting negative emotional reactions to workplace injustice. In *Advances in group processes* (Vol. 23, pp. 207–227). Bingley: Emerald Books.

Collins, R. (1990). Stratification, emotional energy, and the transient emotions. In *Research agendas in the sociology of emotions* (pp. 27–57). Albany: State University of New York Press.

Collins, R. (2004). *Interaction ritual chains*. Princeton: Princeton University Press.

Coltrane, S. (1996). *Family man: Fatherhood, housework, and gender equity*. New York: Oxford Press.

Cooley, C. H. (1902). *Human nature and the social order* (1st ed.). New York: Charles Scribner's Sons.

Cooley, C. H. (1964). *Human nature and the social order*. New York: Schocken Books.

Copp, M. (1998). When emotion work is doomed to fail: Ideological and structural constraints on emotion management. *Symbolic Interaction, 21*(3), 299–328.

Damasio, A. R. (1995). In colder blood. In *Descartes' error: Emotion reason, and the human brain* (pp. 127–164). New York: Avon Books.

Denzin, N. K. (1985). Emotion as lived experience. *Symbolic Interaction, 8*(2), 223–240.

Durkheim, E. (2001). *The elementary forms of religious life: A new translation by Carol Cosman*. (C. Cosman, trans., M. S. Cladis, Ed.) New York: Oxford University Press.

Durr, M., & Wingfield, A. H. (2011). "Keep Your 'N' In Check!" African American women and the interactive effects of etiquette and emotional labor. *Critical Sociology, 37*(5), 557–571.

Francis, L. E. (1997). Ideology and interpersonal emotion management: Redefining identity in two support groups. *Social Psychology Quarterly, 60*(2), 153–171.

Goffman, E. (1959). *The presentation of self in everyday life*. Garden City: Doubleday Anchor Books.

Guillermina, J. (2007). Emotion in justice processes. In J. Stets & J. H. Turner (Eds.), *Handbook of the sociology of emotions* (Vol. I, pp. 321–347). New York: Springer.

Harlow, R. (2003). "Race Doesn't Matter, But…': The effect of race on professors' experiences and emotion management in the undergraduate college classroom. *Social Psychology Quarterly, 66*(4), 348–363.

Hegtvedt, K. A. (2006). Justice frameworks. In P. J. Burke (Ed.), *Contemporary social psychological theories* (pp. 46–69). Stanford: Stanford University Press.

Hegtvedt, K. A., & Killian, C. (1999). Fairness and emotions: Reactions to the process and outcomes of negotiations. *Social Forces, 78*(1), 269–302.

Hegtvedt, K. A., & Parris, C. L. (2014). Justice theory and emotions. In J. E. Stets & J. H. Turner (Eds.), *Handbook of the sociology of emotions* (Vol. II). New York: Springer.

Heise, D. R. (1979). *Understanding events: Affect and the construction of social action*. New York: Cambridge University Press.

Heise, D. R. (1997). INTERACT: Introduction and software. Retrieved from http://www.indiana.edu/~socpsy/ACT/interact.htm

Heise, D. R. (2007). *Expressive order: Confirming sentiments in social actions*. New York: Springer.

Hochschild, A. R. (1979). Emotion work, feeling rules, and social structure. *American Journal of Sociology, 85*(3), 551–575.

Hochschild, A. R. (1983). *The managed heart: Commercialization of human feeling*. Berkeley: University of California Press.

Kang, M. (2010). *The managed hand: Race, gender, and the body in beauty service work*. Berkeley: University of California Press.

Kemper, T. D. (1978). *A social interactional theory of emotions*. New York: Wiley.

Kolb, K. H. (2011). Sympathy work: Identity and emotion management among victim-advocates and counselors. *Qualitative Sociology, 34*(1), 101–119.

Lawler, E. J. (2001). An affect theory of social exchange. *American Journal of Sociology, 107*(2), 321–352.

Lawler, E. J., & Yoon, J. (1996). Commitment in exchange relations: Test of a theory of relational cohesion. *American Sociological Review, 61*(1), 89–108.

Lawler, E. J., Thye, S. R., & Yoon, J. (2009). *Social commitments in a derpsonalized world*. New York: Russell Sage Foundation.

Lively, K. J. (2008). Emotional segues and the management of emotion by women and men. *Social Forces, 87*(2), 911–936.

Lively, K. J., & Heise, D. R. (2004). Sociological realms of emotional experience. *American Journal of Sociology, 109*(5), 1109–1136.

Lively, K. J., Steelman, L. C., & Powell, B. (2010). Equity, emotion, and household division of labor. *Social Psychology Quarterly, 73*(4), 358–379.

Lois, J. (2003). *Heroic efforts: The emotional culture of search and rescue volunteers*. New York: New York University Press.

MacKinnon, N. J. (1994). *Symbolic interactionism as affect control*. Albany: State University of New York Press.

Mead, G. H. (1934). In C. W. Morris (Ed.), *Mind, self, and society from the standpoint of a social behaviorist*. Chicago: University of Chicago Press.

Merton, R. K. (1995). The Thomas theorem and the Mathew effect. *Social Forces, 74*(2), 379–424.

Ridgeway, C. L. (1991). The social construction of status value: Gender and other nominal characteristics. *Social Forces, 70*(2), 367–386.

Ridgeway, C. L. (2001). Social status and group structure. In M. A. Hogg & S. Tindale (Eds.), *Blackwell handbook of social psychology: Group processes* (pp. 352–375). Maulden: Blackwell Publishing.

Ridgeway, C. L. (2006). Expectation states theory and emotion. In J. E. Stets & J. H. Turner (Eds.), *Handbook of the sociology of emotions* (pp. 347–367). New York: Springer.

Ridgeway, C. L., & Johnson, C. (1990). What is the relationship between socioemotional behavior and status in task groups? *American Journal of Sociology, 95*(5), 1189–1212.

Robinson, D. T., Smith-Lovin, L., & Tsoudis, O. (1994). Heinous crime or unfortunate accident: Emotion displays and reactions to vignettes of criminal confessions. *Social Forces, 73*, 175–190.

Schachter, S., & Singer, J. E. (1962). Cognitive, social, and physiological determinants of emotional state. *Psychological Review, 69*(5), 379–399.

Shott, S. (1979). Emotion and social life: A symbolic interactionist analysis. *American Journal of Sociology, 84*(6), 1317–1334.

Smith, R. T. (2008). Passion work: The joint production of emotional labor in professional wrestling. *Social Psychology Quarterly, 71*(2), 157–176.

Smith, A. C., I, & Kleinman, S. (1989). Managing emotions in medical school: Students' contacts with the living and the dead. *Social Psychology Quarterly, 52*(1), 56–59.

Staske, S. A. (1996). Talking feelings: The collaborative construction of emotion in talk between close relational partners. *Symbolic Interaction, 19*(2), 111–142.

Stryker, S. (2001). Traditional symbolic interactionism, role theory, and structural symbolic interactionism: The road to identity theory. In J. H. Turner (Ed.), *Handbook of sociological theory* (pp. 211–231). New York: Kluwer Academic/Plenum Publishers.

Stryker, S. (2004). Integrating emotion into identity theory. In *Theory and research on human emotions* (Vol. 21, pp. 1–24). Boston: Elsevier.

Stryker, S., & Burke, P. J. (2000). The past, present, and future of an identity theory. *Social Psychology Quarterly, 63*(4), 284–297.

Summers-Effler, E. (2004a). A theory of the self, emotion, and culture. In *Advances in group processes* (Vol. 21, pp. 273–308). Bingley: Emerald Books.

Summers-Effler, E. (2004b). Defensive strategies: The formation and social implications of patterned self-destructive behavior. In *Advances in group processes* (Vol. 21, pp. 309–325). Bingley: Emerald Books.

Thoits, P. A. (1984). Coping, social support, and psychological outcomes: The central role of emotion. *Review of Personality and Social Psychology, 5*, 219–238.

Thoits, P. A. (1990). Emotional deviance: Research agendas. In T. D. Kemper (Ed.), *Research agendas in the sociology of emotions* (pp. 180–203). Albany: State University of New York Press.

Thoits, P. A. (1995). Stress, coping, and social support processes: Where are we? What next? *Journal of Health and Social Behavior, 35*(Extra Issue), 53–79.

Tiedens, L. Z., Ellsworth, P. C., & Mesquita, B. (2000). Sentimental stereotypes: Emotional expectations for high-and low-status group members. *Personality and Social Psychology Bulletin, 26*(5), 560–575.

Turner, J. H. (2000). *On the origins of human emotions: A sociological inquiry into the evolution of human affect*. Stanford: Stanford University Press.

Walster, E. H., Berscheid, E., & Walster, G. W. (1975). New directions in equity research. In *Advances in experimental social psychology* (Vol. 9). New York: Academic.

Weiner, B. (1986). *An attributional theory of motivation and emotion*. New York: Springer.

Westphal, J. D., Park, S. H., McDonald, M. L., & Hayward, M. L. A. (2012). Helping other CEOs avoid bad press: Social exchange and impression management support among CEOs in communications with journalists. *Administrative Science Quarterly, 57*(2), 217–268.

Wharton, A. S. (2009). The sociology of emotional labor. *Annual Review of Sociology, 35*, 147–165.

Wingfield, A. H. (2010). Are some emotions marked "Whites Only"? Racialized feeling rules in professional workplaces. *Social Problems, 57*(2), 251–268.

Sociology as the Study of Morality 21

Kevin McCaffree

21.1 Introduction

The sociology of morality has had a rocky history. Explicitly sociological studies of morality rose in prominence in the mid-to-late nineteenth and early twentieth centuries. From its inception, sociology was justified in moral language—Auguste Comte, considered the French founder of the discipline, introduced the term "altruism" into the scientific literature. His reluctant intellectual heir, Emile Durkheim, directly equated societal stability ("solidarity") with morality (Smith and Sorrell 2014). Spencer in England and Pareto in Italy and Northern Europe spoke of the ethics of individualism and the irrationality/emotionality of moral judgments, respectively.

In more recent years, with the slow erosion of Parson's theoretical hegemony throughout the 1970s, 1980s and 1990s, "issue-based" moral rhetoric has emerged forcefully in sociology (Turner and Turner 1990). These "issue-based" morally-laden research programs have not been formally about what *morality* is, but rather about what *immorality* might be understood as in various areas of human life. Though immorality was studied prolifically in sociology after the mid-twentieth century (i.e., qualitative and quantitative studies of inequalities, prejudicial attitudes and violence associated with race, gender and social class/income, homophobia and transphobia, nationalistic ethnocentrism, policing/imprisonment/conviction), the frequencies with which authors used the terms "moral," "morals," and "morality," in sociology journals declined precipitously from the years 1950 to 2010 (Hitlin and Vaisey 2013; Brueggemann 2014).

The study of morality, as such, had gone underground in sociological theory beginning in the 1950s. The study of morality ceased being the dispassionate, theoretical, concern of naive intellectuals, interested in the tools of dissection and analysis, and became the luminescent passion of the workers, women and cultural minorities who understood instances of immorality more precisely, and who were as a result too emotionally impatient to bother with mere observation and armchair theory. The academic shift was profound. Sociology went from a positive inquiry into the content of morality to a critical inquiry into the nature (and prevalence) of immorality. The sociology of morality became expressly—manifestly—political and critical.

An over-focus on the documentation and understanding of immorality obscures inquiry into what morality *is* in the *positive* sense of what something we call "morality" substantively constitutes. This dialogue is inclusive of all of the acts and attitudes that are immoral, it merely directs its attention to the positive,

K. McCaffree (✉)
Department of Sociology, Indiana-Purdue University, Fort Wayne, IN, USA
e-mail: kmcca007@ucr.edu

S. Abrutyn (ed.), *Handbook of Contemporary Sociological Theory*,
Handbooks of Sociology and Social Research, DOI 10.1007/978-3-319-32250-6_21

interdisciplinary contents of what the term "morality" means for sociologists. A sociological study of morality cannot exist without a documentation and investigation into injustice. But, it also cannot exist without a definition of what morality (as opposed to immorality) *is*, in other words, without an inquiry into the social and physiological mechanisms of solidarity and bonding.

Some contemporary general theorists are openly critical of the contemporary sociology of (im)morality. Donald Black, for example, argues,

> [Sociologists] side with blacks and other minorities against whites, women against men, and anyone else with power or other social status against those with more. ...much of what they call sociology is little more than the promotion of liberal or otherwise left-wing ideology, (Black 2013, pp. 764).

Other contemporary theorists of the sociology of (im)morality, often the younger ones, say something a bit more diplomatic,

> [Sociologists of morality work] in many domains, including...the Vietnam War, and 9/11, fights over the contents of school curricula, abortion politics, food politics, animal rights, protest movements, and the development of welfare policy, to name a few areas of research. What unites these diverse studies as part of the sociology of morality is not a shared substantive focus, but the recognition that moral evaluations and categorizations are an essential part of struggles in 'social fields,' (Hitlin and Vaisey 2013, pp. 59).

The sociology of morality is a rapidly growing area, despite the potential biases Black points out or the admitted lack of a substantive focus mentioned by Hitlin and Vaisey. In this essay, I will attempt to organize the primary areas of research. After reviewing these popular topics in the field, I will point out some critical disciplinary disputes and, lastly, provide an integrative, positive, theoretical framework for the sociology of morality.

21.2 Sociological Definitions of Morality

Several theorists of morality within sociology have recently attempted to provide substantive definitions of morality. Stephen Vaisey and Andrew Miles, for example, suggest that morality has two meanings, and that one meaning addresses "a priori, universal standards of harm, rights, and justice," while the other meaning addresses "questions of good and bad or right and wrong that might vary between individuals or collectivities," (2014, pp. 312).

Gabriel Abend (2011, 2013) has defined the sociology of morality, in part, in terms of the study of "thick" and "thin" morality. Thin morality involves relatively simple, decontextualized judgments or attitudes about what is right as opposed to wrong or good as opposed to bad. The kinds of experiments conducted by neuroscientists, that involve subjects having their brain scanned in an MRI machine while making snap judgments during abstract thought experiments, are examples of "thin morality".[1]

If examples of "thin" moral judgments are "right vs wrong" and "good vs bad," than examples of "thick" morality include judgments about "dignity, decency, integrity, piety, responsibility, tolerance, moderation, fanaticism, extremism, despotism, chauvinism, rudeness, uptightness, misery, exploitation, oppression, humanness, hospitality, courage, cruelty, chastity, perversion, obscenity, lewdness, and so on and so forth," (Abend 2011, pp. 150). Thick morality, as opposed to thin morality, involves description *and* evaluation. When you make thin moral judgments, you only describe an act, policy or person as good or bad, right or wrong. With thick morality, however, description and evaluation occur simultaneously. Calling a father cruel for beating his children provides a condemnation of an act (beating children is wrong/bad), while simultane-

[1] See Abend (2011) for a review of the relevant arguments against viewing artificially/philosophically constructed moral judgements as entirely, sufficiently, constitutive of morality.

ously describing an element of the nature of that act (cruelness is a certain way of acting/behaving, in addition to being wrong or bad). Courage, on the other hand, is a moral good, in most cases. But, in addition to being good, courage is also a certain kind of behavior. In this way, judging something as courageous both describes an act (as a certain type of behavior—courageous behavior) and evaluates that act (as morally good) simultaneously. Abend argues that thick morality, moreso than thin morality, is culturally embedded. Thick morality is therefore more in the purview of sociology than of neuroscience or cognitive psychology.

Abend, in his more recent work, argues for three levels of analysis within the sociology of morality (Abend 2011). He suggests we should consider (a) the behavior and practices that people call "moral," (b) the moralistic judgments, attitudes and beliefs that people hold and, lastly, (c) what he calls the "moral background," or cultural milieu, that frames behavior and cognition generally. The moral background of a culture defines the behaviors and attitudes of individuals in terms of thick morality. That is, the moral background of a culture provides definitions of behaviors and attitudes as cruel, rude, hospitable, perverse, chaste and so on. These three levels of analysis interact and reciprocally form one another—they are the constitutive, substantive "stuff" of morality that sociologists should consider.

The closest approximation I can make to a current substantive sociological definition of a "morality" would be something like, *the universal mechanisms of social bonding* (i.e., *emotion, entrainment, exchange relationships*, etc.) *as shaped by localized, cultural bonding styles/patterns* (i.e., *normative behaviors, attitudes, identities, values and worldviews*). This definition is overbearing, perhaps, and may not be quite exhaustive. Nevertheless, it captures the tensions as well as the topics, of the current state of the discipline.

Substantive definitions of morality are bound to be complex, but the contemporary sociology of morality has something of an identity crisis—a crisis of priority between description and explanation, between effecting social change and searching for mechanisms of stability, and between studying zoologically universal or culturally relative aspects of morality. I think these conflicts are inherent to sociological inquiry, but I think they can be satisfyingly addressed. I will show this as the essay progresses, but next I describe the current state of scientific knowledge in the sociology of morality.

21.3 Social Psychological Aspects of Morality

From a social-psychological standpoint, emotions (e.g., anger, guilt and shame), reputational concerns, and self-conceptions (or identities) drive moral behavior. Emotions motivate us to conform to normative expectations and to condemn normative transgressions, reputational concerns direct our attention to how others perceive our behaviors, and our moral identities guide our actions in morally relevant situations. In this section, I will briefly review research in the areas of moral emotions, reputational concern and the moral identity.

21.3.1 Moral Emotions

Emotion research has a long and storied pedigree within the sociology of morality (Harkness and Hitlin 2014). Recognition for the importance of emotions in social solidarity and social coordination goes back at least to Durkheim in France, and no doubt even earlier to Islamic sociologist Ibn Kaldun in the fourteenth century. In Durkheim's ([1912] 1976) understanding, positive emotional energy circulated between people when they had self and group-affirming interactions. When people congregate, ritualistically and habitually, a sort of energy builds up which feels externally pressuring due to the crystallization of expectations into norms and rules. This congregating originally happened in large tribal festivals among hunter gatherers, but the interactional accumulation of emotional energy can, in principle, be measured within and compared across a variety of more modern institutional domains—occupational, economic, familial, religious, political, and educational (Collins 2004; Turner 2007, 2010a).

Emotions scholarship in the sociology of morality is also driven by a structural, Goffmanian line of research that comes from Identity Theory (Stryker 1980, 2004; Stryker and Burke 2000; Burke and Stets 2009). In Identity Theory, self-views, dramaturgically created and re-created in interaction, are the units of analysis when speaking of emotional energy. When our identities as parents, workers or community members are verified by others in interactions, the emotions felt are positive and motivating. On the other hand, when our situational performances fail to elicit the expected approval from others, the emotions we feel are very negative and potentially de-motivating.

If modern inquiry into the emotional aspects of social bonds and identities owes its license to Kaldun, Durkheim, and Goffman, contemporary inquiries into the emotional aspects of values and worldviews (e.g., Vaisey and Miles 2014; Miles 2014; Hitlin and Pinkston 2013) owe their sociological roots to Weber. Weber denied that ideal, moral, values could be determined by scientific inquiry, and saw value systems fluctuating between historical epochs more or less randomly (Weber [1919] 2004). Values, attitudes and worldviews were nevertheless emotionally influential for Weber, at least once they were diffused among populations in large numbers. He famously argued that nascent industrial capitalism grew so quickly in Europe precisely because the logic of hard labor and accumulation had found emotional justification in a previous historical epoch's worldview of puritan ascetic devotion (Weber [1920] 2002).

More recent scholarship has suggested that the moral emotions people experience may be influenced by psychological attribution mechanisms. When individuals feel fearful or threatened, they begin to make attributions about the causes of these emotions. In many cases, the causes of these emotions are attributed to something the self has done wrong—a broken rule, tradition or expectation. When one blames self for violating a moral transgression, one may additionally feel a sense of shame, embarrassment or guilt. Conversely, however, if one attributes the perception of threat and fear to the actions of another, the emotions felt include contempt, anger and disgust. These are sets of moral emotions in that shame, embarrassment and guilt motivate individuals to conform to social expectations, while contempt, anger and disgust motivates individuals to punish rule and norm violators.

The psychologist Paul Rozin has been influential in this area of research, and has attempted to show how each set of moral emotions emerge from specific social contexts (Rozin et al. 1999; Brandt and Rozin 2013). Appealing to anthropologist Richard Shweder's (Shweder et al. 1997) three "ethics" of morality, Rozin suggests that violations of communal norms by others lead to feelings of contempt, arbitrary violations by others of one's own freedom/autonomy lead to the experience of anger, and violations of bodily purity/health or ideological purity by others lead to the feeling of disgust.

The experience of moral emotions is also driven by status differences between individuals. It is often assumed in sociology that high-status individuals tend to experience a greater freedom of emotional expression within the family and workplace (Hochschild [1983] 2003). This greater freedom of emotional expression sometimes, in turn, enables the expression of aggression and anger towards those who are perceived to be lower in status. Due to the higher status individual's relatively greater access to power, rewards and resources, the potential social costs and consequences associated with displays of anger or frustration are fewer than they would be for a lower-status actor (in any given situation).

In an important study, Jessica Collett and Omar Lizardo (2010) provide evidence to show that the experience of anger is common among both high and low status actors, depending on the context. Collett and Lizardo test two general hypotheses against one another with regard to the experience of anger—do higher status individuals experience more anger because of a tendency to attribute failures to others, instead of the self? Recall, as discussed above, that when blame for negative emotions is directed towards self, shame, guilt and embarrassment result, but when blame for negative emotions is attributed to the actions of another, anger and disgust result. Thus, could it be that higher status individuals are more likely to experience and express anger because they are more likely to blame others for their failures and indiscretions? Or, alternatively, are higher status individuals *less* likely to experience and express anger precisely because of their high status (i.e., relatively greater access to power and resources)? After all, low-status parties are, by definition, in a power and resource-disadvantaged position. People who are perceived as low status, in numerous areas of their life, may actually be the ones accumulating anger, frustration and negative emotionality more generally (Turner 2010a).

Collett and Lizardo (2010) show that both hypotheses can be supported, with scope conditions. That is, lower status individuals do, indeed, feel more anger associated with the sense of a "loss of control" that results from occupying resource and power-disadvantaged positions in society. However, under certain circumstances, high status actors are also likely to experience and express anger—specifically, when they begin blaming unfamiliar, lower-status others in formal settings such as the workplace. Lower-status individuals, however, tend to make more self-attributions for personal failures, are more likely to experience a sense of losing control in their lives, and consequently, are more likely to feel guilt and shame (Turner 2010a). When lower-status individuals do express anger, it tends to be anger directed towards the self, which may be experienced as shame (Turner 2007). Higher-status actors appear to disproportionately use their positions of power to externalize anger (and blame) for frustrations onto subordinate others, while lower-status parties may be more likely to internalize their anger and feel a sense of shame.

It appears, then, that moral emotions like anger, shame and guilt may be differentially experienced by individuals depending on the status positions they occupy vis a vis others across institutional domains, due to the patterns of attributions they make regarding the negative emotional states they experience.

21.3.2 Reputational Maintenance

In addition to the emotional dimensions of morality, concerns over reputation also influence how individuals act towards one another. Historically, foraging bands of hunter-gatherers maintained a pluralistic social cohesion by constantly scrutinizing one another's reputation. Foragers make and maintain strong, emotionally rich social ties with under 150 people, and usually fewer than 50 (Turner and Maryanski 2008; Apicella et al. 2012). These "families" of genetic and fictive kin hunt, play, worship, gather materials, raise children and go to war together. One's reputation is their greatest resource—their greatest form of capital—because of the dense, supervisory networks that foragers depend on for survival. Cooperators choose to interact with others who cooperate, so that both achieve collective goals (food, shelter, protection) more quickly.

Anthropologist Christopher Boehm (2012) has drawn on the work of evolutionary biologist Richard Alexander, in addition to his own ethnographic work on contemporary hunter-gather societies, in order to craft a theory of social cohesion in hunter-gatherer bands. Reputation, he concludes, is a primary force driving the earliest of humanity's moral bonds—small supervisory networks do a lot of gossiping and, as a result, have a lot of power to rescind tribal membership to deviant individuals. Tribal deviants and bullies—say, those who put in little effort during the hunt, sleep with someone else's partner, repeatedly lie about something or arbitrarily instigate someone—are often dealt with ruthlessly, though typically democratically. Social ostracism is a typical punishment pluralistically agreed upon by other band members. Repeat and chronic offenders, however, are sometimes abandoned entirely.

Given that foragers depend on their tribe—their society—for their clothes, shelter, food (hunting success is mercurial), and protection, abandonment by the tribe is tantamount to death. Establishing a good reputation, therefore, is every bit as important as avoiding a negative one. The notion that one might strive for and maintain a good reputation—that is, a form of social capital accrued merely by virtue of the kindness and helpfulness one offers—provided emotional/motivational encouragement to follow rules and contribute fairly to the maintenance of the band, while simultaneously providing the social legitimacy to force others to do so as well.

Sociologists Brent Simpson and Robb Willer have contributed critical insights into the moral dynamics of reputations (e.g., Simpson and Willer 2008, 2015; Willer et al. 2012). Among other things, their laboratory research has revealed that self-interested actors behave altruistically (i.e., contribute more resources in a public goods game) when others have the opportunity to witness their actions and form judgments about their behaviors. When individuals motivated by self-interest conduct their affairs in private, or are somehow obscured from full transparency, they begin to behave much less altruistically. Public perceptions of reputation-relevant behavior therefore, appear to turn self-interested psychological motivations into socially cooperative behaviors.

Most everyone should have a motivation to forge and maintain a positive reputation to the degree that they perceive themselves to be socially/emotionally or financially dependent on co-present others. However, when avenues for the creation of a reputation are blocked (as when one acts anonymously or in a context of low supervision), selfish motivations become more powerful. To be a bit blunt, "watched people are nice people," (Norenzayan 2013).

Once individuals are visible and accountable to others, positive reputations accrue, in part, from acts of deference and kindness. This is especially true when an individual occupies a position of power—Robb Willer and colleagues (2012) find in a study that powerful individuals (i.e., those with greater degrees of material resources) are perceived as having better reputations by observers to the degree that they withhold from accepting maximal rewards during exchange opportunities, or elect to donate to charity. Confirming the research from the anthropological record on foraging societies described above, it appears that kindness is socially advantageous, even if one already occupies a position of power, as perceptions of power legitimacy appear to covary with visible displays of kindness and fairness.

This is a general principle of morality that is now underscored by numerous lines of separate research from different scientific fields. In a recent summarization of the social science literature, Simpson and Willer conclude that those with good (that is, pro-social) reputations, "are trusted more, are respected more, are cooperated with more, have more influence, and are disproportionately selected as exchange partners and group leaders," (Simpson and Willer 2015, pp 10.7).

21.3.3 The Moral Identity

In addition to research on the moral dynamics of emotions and reputations, research on moral self-perceptions or "identities," continues to grow in sociology. The central dynamic here involves the degree to which some people view themselves as moral (vs immoral) and the influence that this self-conception has on behavior. It is not only the desire for a good reputation that is morally motivating, but also a desire for cognitive consistency. Thus, if an individual understands themselves to be an "honest, "fair" or "helpful" person, let's say, than this individual will generally behave in a way consistent with this self-understanding, all else equal, in order to achieve a comforting sense of psychological stability and control (Carver and Scheier 1982). Though one's identity as a certain type of moral actor will change throughout the life-course, the psychological desire to perceive trans-situational stability within the self will be a constant motivator of behavior.

As for what *counts* as a moral identity, Jan Stets and Michael Carter (2012), have argued that the most substantive meanings that comprise the moral identity include meanings related to *justice* and *care* as these meanings are regarded as moral universals in human and primate societies (e.g., Newman 1976; Brown 1991, 2004; Shweder et al. 1997; Boehm 1999; De Waal 2009; Haidt 2012). Stets and Carter subsequently specify—and factor load—a number of self-meanings that might reasonably be associated with holding a view of oneself as a *just* or *caring* person. These meanings included perceiving oneself as honest, kind, fair, helpful, generous, compassionate, truthful, hardworking, friendly, selfless, or principled. They find that study participants with higher moral meanings within their moral identity—that is, with higher scores (1–5) on meanings measures like fair, helpful or generous—acted more ethically than those with lower average scores. In Stets and Carter's study, ethical behaviors involved not copying on tests, not driving drunk, not stealing, and other behaviors of specific relevance to college students who, of course, comprised the study sample.

Theoretically, the moral identity should drive the objective display of moralistic behaviors, due to an emotional motivation to maintain cognitive consistency. It is not only identities that drive behaviors, of course, behaviors also drive identity processes. Research shows that making moralistic judgments about others, or even just watching others engaging in moralistic judging behaviors, may increase the strength of meanings within peoples' own moral identities (Simpson et al. 2013).

Research into moral identities has proven to be practically useful. Consider a pair of recent examples in criminology and environmentalism. Drawing on Wikstrom's (2010) Situated Action Theory, Hitlin and Kramer (2014) suggest a path to identity change for delinquent adolescents. In their model, they show that arrest and conviction, to the degree that it produces shame in the individual (i.e., a self-attribution regarding felt negative emotions), provides an emotional opportunity for a re-appraisal of self. This re-appraisal of self might involve changing the strength of the meanings within the moral identity. Assuming the individual holds some degree of legitimacy for the criminal justice system, and assuming the individual has a remaining reservoir of self-esteem, experiencing shame may provide an emotional and psychological incentive for identity change.

Research into environmentalism has been equally intriguing. Stets and Biga (2003) find that views about oneself as being part of, in cooperation with, or dependent on, the environment better predict participants' self-reported environmentalist behavior than political attitudes about social policy and environmental protection. Put another way, self-meanings, moreso than attitudes about objects (i.e., the environment, in this case) better predict self-reported behaviors. Further research has underscored this finding. A recent study showed that participants who identified themselves as environmentalist were also more likely to have donated money to or volunteer with an environmentalist organization (Farrell 2014). Moreover, holding a self-conception as an "environmentalist" predicted charity donations and volunteered time before and after the BP gulf oil spill better than prior civic engagement or political affiliation.

Before concluding, I would like to point out a very important caveat. Typically, in studies of the moral identity, respondents report high levels (consistently above the midpoint on a given response scale) of moral self-views. This tendency to self-enhance is well documented in psychology—people tend to think they are more trustworthy, more honest, more responsible, more kind and more fair than the average person (Gilovich 1991). A problem, however, arises when theorists *also* assume a tendency towards cognitive consistency among respondents. If people tend to see themselves as more moral than the average person, *and* people also strive to maintain consistent self-views (i.e., as a moral person), than how can identity dynamics explain immorality? Why would anyone ever act unethically if they view themselves as moral and seek—always—to gain confirming feedback from others? Clearly, there is a theoretical gap here. The solution to this conundrum, which requires copious future research, is that attentional allocation can be diverted based on situational dynamics. Thus, people may tend to view themselves as more moral than the average person, and they may also seek cognitive consistency, but certain situational characteristics (e.g., a person is under pressure to perform, as when business leaders engage in price-fixing in order to meet profit goals) may reduce individuals' allocation of attention to moralistic self-views.

21.4 Structure and Culture

Comte, Durkheim, Marx, and Weber all feared, in their own ways, the encroachment of a market-based, differentiated, metropolitan, irreligious modernity (Hodgkiss 2013). Comte and Durkheim worried about how and whether atheists could create a secular, civil form of social solidarity, while Weber and Marx concerned themselves with how power relationships in capitalist culture and economy were driving people to form exploitive, disenchanted relationships and ideologies. This section addresses these, still relevant, moral concerns about modernity. Specifically, I review here some of the central debates surrounding the moral significance of religion and capitalist economies, before discussing the moral import of cultural values more generally.

21.4.1 Capitalism

The above mentioned study by Justin Farrell (2014) on environmentalism and self-identity also highlights an interesting point about disasters—corporate-caused human disasters may be harder for people to understand compared to other forms of deviance (like street crime), and therefore, may be harder to address from a humanitarian and financial standpoint. Corporate-caused human disasters may not be concentrated in any specific geographical/community location, and may cause harm over long stretches of time, leading to relatively few immediate deaths. Unlike a murder or a natural disaster, where death follows immediately from a localized behavior or meteorological event, violations of laws on fossil fuel emissions, for example, may elevate cancer rates in an area over 30 years. Farrell cites each of these reasons in noting how comparatively little money Americans donated to the BP relief fund after the oil spill compared to how much was donated after Hurricane Katrina (only 4 million dollars 42 days after the spill compared to 580 million dollars only 8 days after Hurricane Katrina).

Market-driven corporate competition may drive certain organizations to avoid, for example, addressing regulatory increases, or consistent maintenance. Regardless of the reasons for corporate malfeasance and corporate crime, it may be harder for individuals to perceive corporate deviance because it is (a) more likely to occur in remote areas, (b) oftentimes not immediately physically visible in its damaging effects and (c) responsibility for action is distributed among hundreds, if not thousands, of employees. It is possible that, for the above reasons, corporate crime is also less likely to be reported on in media. These, and other, perceptual barriers may prevent individuals from experiencing the same kinds of emotional responses as they often do with more perceptually proximate street crimes like robbery, burglary, and murder. Perhaps as a result of these obstructions to public perception, government estimates of the cost in dollars and human lives of corporate crimes are 50–100 times greater than street crime (Iadicola 2014).

Capitalism, as a general economic system, has also been critiqued as distributively and contributively unjust (e.g., Sayer 2011). At least since the work of Marx and Engels, the ruthless side of capitalism has been a major focus of sociologists who study moral problems (e.g., Marx [1857] 2008; Anderson 1999; Wright 2010). The sense in which capitalist economies are considered to be *distributively unjust* is the sense in which occupational prestige hierarchies (rooted in cultural practice and tradition) unfairly (that is, extremely inequitably) distribute valued social (i.e., respect, influence, power) and material (i.e., income, healthcare and retirement programs) resources. The sense in which capitalist economies are considered to be *contributively unjust* is the sense in which under-employment and micro-management in the workforce prevent people from realizing their own personal potential as creative contributors to the economic system (Sayer 2011).

Women (and especially non-white women), for example, are both more likely to work in jobs low in the occupational prestige hierarchy (e.g., hospice care, childcare, secretarial office work, nannies) and paid less income over their lifetimes compared to white men (Ridgeway 2007, 2009, 2011). Black and Hispanic men, meanwhile, are both more likely to be arrested (or even contacted by the criminal justice system) and more likely to be unemployed and live in poverty compared to the rates for white men (Rios 2009; Peterson and Krivo 2010; Krivo et al. 2013; Wagmiller and Lee 2014).

Work by others has also established a strong, empirically verified, connection between social class and health (Link and Phelan 1995; Phelan et al. 2004, 2010). Poverty is not often thought of as a health risk, but it is. Prolonged poverty may lead to depression and a lack of social support that, combined with chronic stress and uncertainty, leads to a higher rate of disease. Bruce Link and other researchers have disentangled the complicated empirical web of when poor health leads to poverty and vice versa. Subsequent research confirms some pretty horrific conclusions. Rates of infant morality, heart disease, diabetes, obesity, cancer and other diseases are all higher among racial minorities in the United States, and especially among African Americans (Schnittker and Mcleod 2005). Poverty, un/under-employment, healthcare and housing discrimination have mutually conspired to produce these outcomes (see also Marmot 2006).

Empirical observations like these motivate many sociologists to take a critical stance towards capitalist economies, and this is a rich literature that sociologists of morality will need to engage with more directly moving forward. The moral consequences of market-driven corporate malfeasance, or of class structure and health are significantly more complicated than I can do justice to here. I only wish to point out that moral critique of market competition among corporations, and the economic system of capitalism more generally, continues to be a central focus of many sociologists.

Although some studies simply involve narrated counts of the immoral aspects of market-based societies (i.e., harsh working conditions, exploitation, workaholism, overscheduling, divorce, debt, tax loopholes, lobbying and so on—see e.g., Brueggemann 2014), other studies address the comparative benefits of capitalist societies compared to agrarian or horticultural societies and their respective feudalistic and monarchical economies (e.g., Lenski 2005; Turner and Maryanski 2008). Still others dissect the variation within capitalist economies. A recent study, for example, found that people in the "professional" class who make over 125,000 dollars per year (in the US) were more generous (using a dictator game experimental paradigm) when their perceptions of income inequality were lower. Perceptions of higher income inequality actually reduced the generosity of donors (Côté et al. 2015).

Critique and analysis of capitalist democracies is crucial and important both practically and theoretically. However, such critique and analysis cannot therefore conclude that capitalist democracies are the *worst possible* form of economy/government.

This would be very, very difficult to show, let alone defend. And, if capitalist democracies are not the *worst possible* form of societal economy/governance, then some subset of scholars should also focus on the relative improvements or benefits that have accrued to human beings by virtue of shifts from widespread slavery or monarchal/ideological dictatorship to a (relatively) more open, democratic, market economy. This research on the benefits of capitalism (i.e., higher per capita income) should occur alongside, and in dialogue with, those revealing the inequalities and injustices of capitalist democracies.

21.4.2 Religion

Many sociologists of morality have considered the importance of religion and religious belonging for human values and social solidarity (Durkheim [1912] 1976; Weber ([1920] 2002), Emerson and Smith 2000; Bader and Finke 2010; Lee 2014). Research in this vein often discusses the social psychology of belonging to a religious community, and about the ways in which religion can motivate altruism or compassion.

There does appear to be some good data on religion and charitable donation that shows religious individuals to be more giving (e.g., Brooks 2006). This work is often criticized, however, as it is typically based upon *self-reported* giving behavior, and religious individuals often self-report being more generous than they actually are in laboratory studies of their behavior (Norenzayan and Shariff 2008; Galen 2012). Also, to the degree that religious individuals donate to charities which promote their specific religion, it is unclear how this constitutes "charity." Political psychologists have, moreover, shown religious fundamentalism to correlate strongly with political conservatism, and both have been positively associated with racial (and general out-group) prejudice, authoritarianism, generalized perceptions of threat, death anxiety, and intolerance of ambiguity (Jost et al. 2003; Jost 2006; Amodio et al. 2007; Carney et al. 2008; Johnson et al. 2010, 2012). Even more damning for the religion-compassion thesis, the most secular (that is, least religious) nations on Earth are also the greatest disseminators of social welfare and assistance to the poor, elderly, and those struggling with drug addiction and other health problems (Paul 2005; Zuckerman 2008).

There nevertheless appears to be a pop-culture equivocation of religion with moral behavior, at least in the United States (Edgell et al. 2006; Gervais et al. 2011). This equivocation of religion and morality in popular culture seems to be processed at a subliminal level for many Americans. Priming studies, for example, have shown that when participants are subliminally flashed with religious concepts on a computer screen, asked to unscramble words denoting religious terminology, or even just asked to write down religious rules (e.g., the Ten Commandments), they subsequently act more pro-socially. This pro-sociality ranges widely, from cheating less on tests to donating more money to charity (see Bloom 2012, for a review). People appear to make subliminal associations between religious terminology and situational expectations for moral behavior. These studies suggest that the socio-cultural development of individuals in the US contains numerous narratives about the supposed link between religious belief and morality.

It is possible, but incredibly unlikely, that moral beliefs and values come from (that is, have their ultimate origin in) religious beliefs. There are mountains of ethnographic and laboratory examples of mammals (with, of course, no religion) displaying ethical behavior, and there are good theoretical and empirical reasons to believe that the neural mechanisms that underlie parent-infant bonding, in general, are the ultimate, phylogenetic, origins of moral concern (e.g., De Waal 2009; Churchland 2011; Preston 2013; McCaffree 2015).

Even if religions cannot be considered the origin of human values, religious commitments and religious beliefs do, of course, influence the moral beliefs and behaviors that people express during the course of their practical, everyday life. For example, religious institutions tend to address sexual behavior and drug use, moreso than other institutions in Western society, and as a result, sociologists have speculated that moral attitudes about these issues are most likely to be influenced by religious commitment (e.g., Desmond and Kraus 2014). However, as other scholars have insisted, most prominently, Rodney Stark, any influence religion has on behavior will only hold for those who truly believe in the holy doctrine and the strength of god, and who have friends that do as well (Bainbridge 1992). Casual, "cafeteria Christians," who self-identify as Christian (or whatever religion) but who engage in few religious behaviors and rituals (e.g., church attendance, prayer, fasting, volunteering) will likely not be influenced by the moral proscriptions advocated by religious institutions (Bruce 2011).

21.4.3 Values

Several prominent sociologists of morality have recently followed social psychologists Shalom Schwartz and Jonathan Haidt in operationalizing the term "values" (e.g., Hitlin and Pinkston 2013;

Vaisey and Miles 2014). Values, for Schwartz are a list of ten "concepts or beliefs, about desirable end states or behaviors, that transcend specific situations, guide selection or evaluation of behavior or events and are ordered by relative importance," (Schwartz and Bilsky 1987:551 quoted from Hitlin and Pinkston 2013). Schwartz's ten universal values included conformity, tradition, benevolence, achievement, hedonism, security, universalism, self-direction, stimulation, and power.

Jonathan Haidt's (2001, 2012; Haidt and Bjorklund 2007) work has been even more influential within the contemporary sociology of morality. Haidt cites anthropology and philosophy in formulating his five moral foundations that, he says, explain and underlie all of the variation in human value systems. Morality for Haidt is "intuitionist" in that we are rarely aware of the emotional influences behind our moral judgments. We can, and often do, however, use our education and reflection in order to justify the moral judgments we come to for emotional reasons. Haidt uses the metaphor of the rational mind as the rider of an unruly elephant. The erratic elephant, who no doubt dictates when and where the rider goes despite the rider's rational protestations, represents our emotions and feelings in any given context. For Haidt, our emotional intuitions drive our moral judgments and these emotional intuitions have five manifestations—concerns for *care*, *fairness*, *loyalty*, *respect for authority*, and *purity/sanctity*.[2]

Using these definitions of moral values, Miles (2014) in an analysis of a sample of over 2,000 Americans, finds that, for example, women are more likely to emphasize the value of benevolence, and of having a moral identity, whereas men were more likely to value power and achievement. Also of interest is his finding that, compared to those with no religious identity, those who were religiously affiliated had a stronger moral identity and were more likely to value conformity and tradition.

[2]Elsewhere, Haidt has flirted with adding additional moral foundations to his list. Here I discuss only his original "foundations".

This emerging literature on values within the sociology of morality has its true roots in the work of Alan Fiske (1992), Fiske and Haslam (2005), Richard Shweder et al. (1997), Robert Bellah and colleagues ([1985] 2008), Ronald Inglehart (1977, 1997), and James Hunter (1992). Shweder and Fiske both argue in favor of their respective cross-cultural typologies of values. Bellah, Inglehart and Hunter, on the other hand, focus on the modernization of values in terms of people in the West becoming more expressive, progressive and individualistic. Though not every theorist mentioned above expressly uses the term "values," for their inquiry, a discussion of their approaches is relevant to this subject matter.

Anthropologists Shweder and Fiske both presented summarized "ideal-type" models of the cross-cultural variation in human value systems. For Shweder, human values can be organized into three basic types—values relating to autonomy, community and divinity. Roughly, these three "ethics" represent the universal cultural tendencies of individuals to find value in the integrity of the individual, the importance of the family and collective, and the purity/sacredness of the soul/heart/mind/god. What is interesting about Shweder's scheme is that each of his three ethical value sets can be emphasized differently depending on the society in which they are found. This therefore constitutes an example of moral universalism with relativist scope conditions relating to the idiosyncratic history and traditions of each society.

Fiske takes a similar approach to crafting broad ideal-types of value categories from historical and anthropological data. He refers to his categories of values as the "relational models" of "communal sharing, "authority ranking," "equality matching," and "market pricing" (Fiske 1992). Each of Fiske's four basic relational models of values has their own logic of materialism, work, distribution, reciprocation, decision making, motivation, aggression and so on.

"Community sharing" includes a set of values oriented towards treating every member (of the ingroup) of society fairly and integratively. Secondly, "authority ranking" involves values associated with people loyally, dutifully, and honorably serving in their roles as workers, protestors, parents, religious adherents, students and so on.

Thirdly, Fiske defines the relational model of "equality matching" as a set of values about balanced fairness and reciprocity. Values related to equality matching are values that deal with balancing the allocation of contributions and rewards, and just desserts. Lastly, values in the "market pricing" category include highly rationalized, utilitarian moral calculations. Market pricing values are those that are invoked by large multinational corporations that wish to create actuaries of the risk of death and illness in order to make decisions about whether to recall deficient car models, or offer healthcare or life insurance plans to people. Though these business decisions may appear cold and calculated, they are, for Fiske, merely more rationalized, abstract, and financialized moral values compared to those values underlying other relational models. Other, more altruistic examples of the market pricing set of values might be given—consider the values of entrepreneurialism, thrift, efficiency, managerial compassion, and attention to financial detail that would be required to make a non-profit philanthropic organization thrive.

Bellah and colleagues ([1985] 2008), Inglehart (1977, 1997), and Hunter (1992), moreso than Shweder and Fiske, focus on the recent trends of the last 50 or so years of cultural change. Bellah and colleagues rely largely on analyses of qualitative interviews and ideal-typical social generalizations in order to conclude that American values are shifting slowly away from biblical and nationalist concerns and increasingly more toward individual achievement and individual expression. This trend is analogous to Inglehart's contention that, as societies increase their wealth through market capitalism, people will increasingly assert the value of human rights, equality and self-expression primarily because they have the material resources to access the educational and political avenues necessary to do so. Where poverty is extreme and political instability or corruption is very high, individuals tend to endorse values that emphasize order, safety and stability. This is because individuals in this deprived context lack the avenues for political visibility and support, and so they cling—orderly and dogmatically—to the modicum of living and self-actualization that is available.

Thus, it is not that citizens of Western democracies are somehow more innately individualistic or self-expressive—rather, it is that market systems, in concert with technological sophistication and dissemination, have provided political, occupational and educational outlets for self-expression and self-improvement. In further consonance, James Hunter suggests that peoples' value structures in the US (and in the West) are becoming more progressive (relativistic, local, skeptical, individually tailored, non-traditional) and less orthodox (universal, transcendental, pious, communally embedded, traditional).

Amidst all of this interesting work into the shifting nature of moral values, Jonathan Haidt's "Moral Foundation Theory" stands as the most currently influential. Haidt (2012) and Haidt and Kesebir (2010) argues that all humans experience intuitive emotional states that result from adaptations to social situations that are common to mammals in general, primates in particular and humans especially. Mammals, primates and people care for their young, hunt cooperatively, maintain fairly strict status hierarchies, and try to avoid biological pathogens (i.e., viruses and bacteria) and social threats (ostracization, gossip). The result of long-term adaptations to these common social problems, is that human beings, the world over, supposedly emphasize (more or less, depending on the person and social context): care, fairness, loyalty, respect for authority, and purity/sanctity (of the body or of ideology).

Haidt has argued that social science has historically used too narrow a definition of morality. Though eighteenth and nineteenth century liberal enlightenment philosophers may have emphasized care and fairness in their critiques of monarchy and religion, according to Haidt, they failed to pay equally good attention to the moral values of loyalty, respect and purity. As a result, according to Haidt, the largely liberal academic social science tradition over-emphasizes the largely liberal moral values of harm and care. This bias in academia has not only produced inadequate research into the group-binding values of loyalty, respect for authority and purity/sanctity, it has also discriminated against conservative students and scholars (Haidt 2012).

Haidt's theory has widely been used to explain differences between political liberals (who value care and fairness especially) and political conservatives (who tend to value loyalty, respect and purity moreso). Statistical models that control for all five of Haidt's moral foundations—not just harm and care—are good predictors of political affiliations, as well as voting behavior and attitudes toward contentious social issues like gun control, stem cell research, immigration, or same-sex marriage (Graham et al. 2009; Koleva et al. 2012; Johnson et al. 2014). It appears descriptively true that political liberals and conservatives emphasize different value systems or "moral foundations", and that these different foundations further predict peoples' individual social attitudes.

In a piece of theory that unifies the work of Haidt with the cultural predictions of Bellah et al. ([1985] 2008), Eriksson and Strimling (2015) suggest that liberals will canalize the political nature of future cultural trends because they emphasize fewer moral foundations. Since both conservatives *and* liberals emphasize values related to care and fairness, but only conservatives tend to *also* emphasize respect, loyalty and purity/sanctity, liberal arguments will seem more persuasive to conservatives, over time, than the alternative. Put differently, it is easier to win over a conservative, than it is a liberal, because conservatives have a broader base of moral values or foundations. The implication is that, since 1950, conservatives have been changing their minds to embrace liberal positions at a faster *rate* than liberals have been changing their mind to embrace conservative positions.

There is more to the story of Haidt's moral foundations than this, however. The values/foundations of loyalty, respect for authority and sanctity/purity may be a result of *motivated cognition*. Cultural liberals and conservatives may only appear different because those who are emphasizing loyalty, respect and purity are actively recruiting psychological and emotional resources in order to do so. At least one study has shown that when conservatives are tired from engaging in self-regulation, or fatigued from using their working memory, they begin to self-report moral values similarly to liberals (Wright and Baril 2011).

Recent research by Florian van Leeuwen and Park (2009, 2012) and van Leeuwen et al. (2014) establishes a robust empirical and theoretical relationship between historical and cross-sectional perceptions of biological and social threats and endorsement of collectivist moral values in general, including Haidt's binding values. In an analysis of over 100,000 respondents from over 65 countries, historical and contemporary levels of global pathogen and parasite stress levels positively predicted Haidt's binding values of loyalty, authority and purity. Further research has confirmed this relationship between perceptions of social or biological threat and moral values emphasizing tradition, respect for authority, and purity/sanctity (e.g., Oxley et al. 2008; Dodd et al. 2012; Hibbing et al. 2014, 2015).

The reason, of course, why values that underlie group-bonding become more prevalent in a population when perceptions of threat rise is because in-groups can protect people from the fatal consequences of disease and social persecution. Perceptually, people assume that pathogen and parasite transmission can be reduced to the degree that they become discriminatory about who they interact with, and to the degree that they follow old, familiar rituals and behaviors, as opposed to new, less understood ones. The same is true for individuals who desire to reduce the perception of social threats emanating from rapid technological, cultural, or political changes. Sticking with the old ways of behaving, and the old hierarchies of leadership, appear safer than adopting new behaviors and new hierarchies that are both less understood and, by definition, less experienced. This is why individual and group differences in the perception of stress and threat appear related to the endorsement of more conservative, collectivist value-orientations.

21.5 Contemporary Debates in the Field

Almost no general theory exists in the modern sociology of morality (with some exceptions, e.g., Black (2011). I contend that this is because of the persistence of several unresolved theoretical issues. These issues are various, but they conspire to make the sociology of morality a very treacherous and exciting field to navigate. These issues are: disagreements about the primacy of structure over culture, dual-process models of culture-in-action, and whether moral realism or moral relativism is the proper meta-theoretical position for sociologists of morality to take. Let me say just a bit about each.

21.5.1 Structure Versus Culture

There are countless thorny debates in sociology and anthropology about the relationship between social structure and culture that I will not have time to address here (e.g., Durkheim and Mauss [1903] 1963; Levi-Strauss 1966; Giddens 1984; Harris 1989). More recently, sociologists of morality have insisted theoretically and demonstrated empirically that moral values and beliefs are better predictors of behavior than network structure, previous behavior or demographic category membership alone (Vaisey 2007; Vaisey and Lizardo 2010; Miles and Vaisey 2015). Location in social structure—as, say, a woman, Muslim, student or homosexual—actually tells researchers *less* about who people will interact with or about how they will behave than does an examination of who shares and does not share moral identities, values and attitudes. Individuals who share their moralities in common, according to this view, are more likely to interact with one another and to share behaviors.

The sociology of morality has recently tended to emphasize the importance of this shared moral culture in rates of interaction and subsequent behavioral outcomes. Researchers might, just as easily, however, study how the structure of interactions influence the formation of shared moral identities, values and attitudes. Ed Lawler and colleagues (2009), for example, show that cooperative exchange contexts, and other forms of exchange with a high rate and duration of interaction and mutuality of attentional focus, produce, over time, shared goals, identities and values. Moral identities and attitudes are produced by structures of interaction and exchange, while simultaneously serving as the basis for the formation of shared beliefs and the adoption of shared behaviors. Once these shared moral beliefs and behaviors emerge, they now serve as their own, higher-order, dynamic influencing individual selection of future network ties and future exchange relationships. The generation of culture may have its origins in networks and exchange structures, but culture becomes causally autonomous once it emerges. Structure produces culture and this emergent culture subsequently canalizes future structures.

All of this is to say that there is no inherent conflict between the structure and culture of morality. Cross-sectionally and longitudinally, researchers are free to either study (a) how shared conceptions of moral values, attitudes and identities lead to new network ties and the adoption of new behaviors or (b) how extant network ties and shared behaviors enable and constrain the development of new moral values, attitudes or identities.

21.5.2 Cognition and Culture as Dual Processes

The second issue facing the sociology of morality is the need to integrate dual-process models of culture into current theory and research. In an influential article, Vaisey (2009) integrates recent research from cognitive neuroscience and suggests that people enact culture in two ways—as subliminally habituated behavior (one's day-to-day routines—see Bourdieu 1990; Ignatow 2009) or by employing various, highly cognitive, ideological "tools" or strategies (when confronting especially complex or novel problems). He calls these the "practice" and "culture-as-toolkit" models of culture.

The advantage of Vaisey's approach is that it updates sociological theory to be current and consistent with neuroscientific data showing the brain to be, at times, a rapid, habituated, subliminal processor of information and, at other times, a deliberative, reflective, effortful processor. Oftentimes, according to Haidt's (2001) "social intuitionism," people cannot be expected to articulate or understand the subliminal emotional motivations underlying their moral beliefs and behaviors. Consistent with this view, Vaisey (2009) finds that individuals' moral worldviews (part of their "cultural toolkit"), regardless of their ability to articulate them, later predict behavior.

An important emerging area of research for the sociology of morality involves specifying what practical, daily aspects of morality occur relatively effortlessly, ritualistically and subconsciously and what practical, daily, aspects of morality require more directed attention and focus. Preliminary research suggests that people will be *more likely* to effortfully/consciously/reflectively use their cultural ideologies when addressing moral issues where (a) self-presentational concerns are not especially salient in the situation, (b) the self is not very emotionally invested, (c) the self perceives the moral identity, attitude or value at issue to be commonplace, typical or banal (Hitlin and Pinkston 2013).

That is, when situational concerns with self-presentation are greater, emotional arousal is higher, or the context is uncomfortable/unfamiliar, people may respond more habitually/subliminally. When the brain is taxed with higher processing burdens (i.e., greater situational attentional allocation), fewer cognitive resources (i.e., circulating blood glucose levels in the brain) remain to suppress habitual responding (see Baumeister et al. 2007). Individuals, thus, are most capable of responding carefully, reflectively and abstractly when they are in situations that require lower levels of situational attentional allocation. As situations become more self-relevant, more emotional, or more atypical, the neural resources recruited to increase attentional allocation prevents the suppression of habituated responses. Conversely, when situations are less self-relevant, less emotional or more typical, situational attentional allocation is lower, and available cognitive resources can be recruited for more reflective/abstract thought and behavior.

These remain, largely, theoretical speculations in need of further research. That the brain is a dual processor, responding in both habitual and reflective ways, is beyond dispute. However, the situational dynamics driving more habitual versus more reflective responses remain empirically under-explored.

21.5.3 The Ontology of Morality

A final disciplinary debate within the sociology of morality that I wish to highlight involves a metatheoretical debate. The debate over moral realism and moral relativism is a debate over what morality, itself, *is*. Is morality an objective phenomenon, something that individuals and cultures can have more or less of? Or, is morality entirely a social construction—just the arbitrary cultural expression of status hierarchies, religions, legal systems and traditions?

In principle, this is a very important issue for sociologists of morality to resolve. In practice, however, sociologists of morality have mostly ignored it. Most sociologists are methodologically relativist and philosophically and ontologically agnostic about morality (Lukes 2008; Abend 2008, 2010; Goode and Ben-Yehuda [1994] 2009; Black 2013; Smith 2013).

Tavory's (2011) effort to theorize moral action is a representative example of such metatheoretical moral agnosticism. He claims that moral realism is false because it supposes, a priori, that morality is a universal human phenomenon and not a culturally-relative one, and that, in essence, this presumptuous claim is presumptuous. Moral relativist arguments, he adds, are equally problematic because they preclude comparisons of moral dynamics between societies and between historical epochs. His solution is to suggest that the moral relevancy of a subject matter should be determined by *whether or not individual and collective self-conceptions are emotionally impacted by the behavior of others*, *trans-situationally and over-time*. This is an incredibly broad, albeit ingenious, attempt to characterize what should count as "moral" to scholars in this area. Still, it teeters on being too broad to satisfyingly be called morality. And, as I want to suggest, sociologists of morality would be far more substantively satisfied with an interdisciplinary, moral realist definition of morality.

If sociologists will generally admit that facts are value-laden, why won't they admit that values are also fact-laden (Gorski 2013)? Moral relativism is a flawed metatheoretical position because certain objective states of consciousness are universally better than/preferable to others (Harris 2010). Consequently, some social policies and aspects of traditions will be—empirically—more or less conducive to the moment to moment wellbeing of individuals.[3] For example, high rates of poverty and chronic stress are objectively harmful to health and psychological efficacy. Social policies that produce lower rates of poverty and chronic stress (invariably concentrated among women and minorities) are universally, cross-culturally, objectively, better than policies that contribute to higher rates. Social structures and contexts of interaction can be substantively critiqued with regard to their capacity to contribute to the resources and opportunities that individuals need to build communities and express themselves.

Moral relativism is mistaken because it makes the old Weberian assumption that people differ irrationally and endlessly in their moral needs and expectations for treatment. On the contrary, humans are united by phylogenetically mammalian concerns for group belonging, care for infants, fairness in the distribution of resources and loyalty in exchange for protection (Turner 2014; McCaffree 2015). Peoples' behaviors and attitudes are structured by their preferences and their preferences share an ancient, mammalian set of expectations for fairly re-distributive, caring treatment. The sociology of morality is therefore intrinsically evaluative. Though descriptive accounts of the societal distribution of moral identities, attitudes and values are critically important, so too are empirically supported, clinical, evaluations of how formal policy and informal tradition impact the wellbeing of individuals. Andrew Sayer (2011) argues,

> [There is] the common idea that social scientific discourses regarding what *is* are simply incommensurable with normative discourse regarding what *ought* to be...However, this is an unhelpful polarization...Critique is...implicit in our descriptions of social life, rather than a separate activity involving stepping into a separate realm of 'values'....If one doesn't know that suffering or racism are *bad*, then one doesn't understand what they *are* ...a description of an abused child which did not acknowledge that it was suffering would fail not merely as an evaluation but as an adequate description of its state of being, (Sayer 2011, pp 8–9, italics in original).

21.6 A Proposed Theoretical Unification

I have recently advanced a synthetic theory of morality that integrates the work of Emile Durkheim ([1912] 1976, [1893] 1997), Jonathan Turner (2010b), Turner and Maryanski (2008), Turner (2014), Jan Stets and Peter Burke (Stets and Carter 2012; Stets and McCaffree 2014), and Randall Collins (1981, 2004), in addition to large bodies of work in psychology, zoology and biology (e.g., Epley and Gilovich 2006; Panksepp and Panksepp 2013; Decety 2011; Decety and Svetlova 2012; Decety 2014). By way of concluding, I will briefly show how this synthetic theory of morality (McCaffree 2015) may be helpful to integrating the diverse and divergent issues discussed throughout this chapter.

Moral beliefs and behaviors, in this scheme, are conceived of as resulting from *perceptual overlap*, or the degree to which two animals or groups of animals view themselves as physically similar, familiar or competent. The physiological mechanisms of perceptual overlap include mirror neurons and executive cognitive functioning at the neural level and oxytocin, dopamine and

[3] I am defining wellbeing in a psychological and social sense—wellbeing involves cognition that is not overly taxed with stress and fear, and it also involves the networks, opportunities and resources (power, respect, influence, capital) people need to pursue valued cultural goals.

serotonin at the hormonal level. From an evolutionary standpoint, these physiological mechanisms evolved alongside mammalian reproductive strategies emphasizing mother-offspring social bonds (Churchland 2011). The cognitive and hormonal hardware that enables mammalian mothers to extensively care for their infants, also underlies the pro-social motivations unrelated, but familiar or similar conspecifics have for each other.

Perceptual overlap—that is, perceptions of familiarity, physical similarity and competence—is created through long and frequent bouts of co-presence. During such bouts of co-presence, individuals will spontaneously begin mimicking (i.e., matching) the posture and emotional expressions of others, in addition to synchronizing (i.e., coordinating) vocalizations, heart rates, breathing rates, gestures and other behaviors. When this physiological and emotional entrainment occurs between human beings, as opposed to non-human animals, peoples' identities bubble up to the surface via symbolic language. Once people have an understanding of one another's identities, they can begin searching for *symbolic* (in addition to purely physical) similarities to self.

Co-presence does not necessarily lead to perceptual overlap, of course. Theoretically, there are three mediating variables that threaten to reduce the flow of perceptual overlap between individuals: (1) exchange contexts, (2) proximity contexts, and (3) status contexts. These three contexts harbor the causes of immorality.

Exchange contexts influence the absolute rate and duration of co-presence, in addition to the distribution of resources. Within sociological exchange theory (e.g., Molm 2003; Lawler et al. 2009), four ideal-typical forms of exchange relationships are outlined: cooperative exchange, negotiated exchange, reciprocal exchange and generalized exchange. Each of these exchange relationships differ by their characteristic rate and duration of interaction, along with their degree of shared intentionality.

Cooperative exchanges, for example, are characterized by a high rate and duration of interaction oriented toward the accomplishment of a shared goal. Negotiated exchanges, on the other hand, are not necessarily oriented toward a shared goal, though each party is obligated to provide some form of service or resource to other parties in the exchange. Each form of exchange is important for determining the rate, duration, and degree of shared intentionality among interacting parties. When the rate and duration of interaction, along with shared intentionality, are low among interacting parties, perceptual overlap between interacting parties will lessen and displays of empathy will be less common.

Proximity contexts include where people are arranged in geographic and cultural space. When individuals or groups are separated by geographic distance, the expected rate and duration of interaction will obviously be lower than in contexts where people live close in proximity. However, cultural distance also critically influences the likelihood of interaction. People with shared cultural characteristics are more likely to interact regardless of geographic distance, a phenomenon known as the "homophily bias," (McPherson and Ranger-Moore 1991; McPherson et al. 2001). Someone living next door to a person of a different religion or ethnicity might, despite being in close geographic proximity, avoid interaction due to lower perceived physical or symbolic similarity. Thus, geographic proximity is important for predicting co-presence and perceptual overlap, but so too is cultural proximity or "social distance," (Park 1924).

Status contexts, lastly, influence perceptual overlap between individuals and groups by casting some parties as more competent than others. Research from both zoology and psychology indicates that mammals, including human children and adults, preferentially mimic and synchronize body language, emotion and vocalizations with higher-status others (Over and Carpenter 2012; see also McCaffree 2015). Status considerations canalize entrainment because perceived competence is a general source of prestige in mammalian hierarchies. Even when perceived status is illegitimately rooted in historical discrimination—as when men are, on average, assumed to be more competent as task leaders than women (see Ridgeway 2011)—this status may still serve to direct the situational mimicry and synchrony of behaviors and emotion.

This theory of perceptual overlap—that physiological entrainment and perceptions of symbolic (i.e., identity) similarity drive empathy and that this entrainment and perceived symbolic similarity is mediated by exchange, proximity and status contexts—is sufficiently robust to explain many of the above-mentioned empirical observations within the sociology of morality. Consider, as an example, how the forces of perceptual overlap might be used to theoretically interpret some of the empirical findings on the moral significance of reputations.

21.6.1 Applying the Principles of Perceptual Overlap: The Example of Reputational Maintenance

To demonstrate the usefulness of this theory of morality, allow me to discuss the forces of perceptual overlap in the context of the research on reputation discussed above. Reputational concerns might be theoretically understood as attempts to mitigate the perceptual partitioning that accrues from constant evaluations of greater competence associated with social status. That is, when a person or group is presumed to be more competent by virtue of their (potentially arbitrary) higher status in a given institutional domain, the potential of that person or group to be unfair or uncaring in exchange relationships rises. Higher status actors tend to have greater access to resources (material or social) and to also be in positions to disseminate these resources to lower status others. Higher status parties, therefore, tend to have greater power in exchange relationships. This power (rooted in justified or unjustified perceptions of competence) provides greater freedom to aggress and discriminate.

The accumulation of status has the potential to reduce perceptions of similarity and familiarity. To the degree that higher status parties consequently perceive themselves to be less similar to or familiar with lower status others, they will act increasingly selfish, malicious and unfair. Though higher status parties may canalize entrainment initially, unfair or malicious behavior (when perceived by lower status others) may reduce lower status actors' perceptions of physical or symbolic similarity or familiarity with higher status actors. In order to maintain status, then, individuals must concern themselves with their reputations as fair or caring. As a corollary, when individuals use their status to greedily accrue resources and power, perceptual overlap with surrounding others will begin to decline—to the degree that their malevolent behaviors are perceived—and rebellion or revolt becomes more probable in that specific exchange relationship.

In short, *social status increases empathy in an exchange network to the degree that it hierarchically directs entrainment from low to high status actors, but social status will also decrease empathy to the degree that accumulated status produces perceptions of dissimilarity or unfamiliarity among interacting parties*. An appreciation of the principles of perceptual overlap shows the phenomenon of "reputation maintenance," as just one example, to be rooted in the status dynamics that potentially enhance or degrade entrainment.

References

Abend, G. (2008). Two main problems in the sociology of morality. *Theory and Society, 37*, 87–125.

Abend, G. (2010). What's new and what's old about the new sociology of morality. In S. Vaisey & S. Hitlin (Eds.), *Handbook of the sociology of morality* (pp. 561–584). New York: Springer.

Abend, G. (2011). Thick concepts and the moral brain. *European Journal of Sociology, 52*, 143–172.

Abend, G. (2013). What the science of morality doesn't say about morality. *Philosophy of the Social Sciences, 43*, 157–200.

Amodio, D., Jost, J. T., Master, S. L., & Yee, C. (2007). Neurocognitive correlates of liberalism and conservatism. *Nature Neuroscience, 10*, 1246–1247.

Anderson, E. (1999). *Code of the street: Decency, violence, and the moral life of the inner city*. New York: WW Norton & Company.

Apicella, C. L., Marlowe, F. W., Fowler, J. H., & Christakis, N. A. (2012). Social networks and cooperation in hunter-gatherers. *Nature, 481*, 497–501.

Bader, C. D., & Finke, R. (2010). What does God require? Understanding religious context and morality. In

S. Hitlin & S. Vaisey (Eds.), *Handbook of the sociology of morality* (pp. 241–254). New York: Springer.

Bainbridge, W. S. (1992). Crime, delinquency, and religion. In J. F. Shumaker (Ed.), *Religion and mental health* (pp. 119–210). New York: Oxford.

Baumeister, R. F., Vohs, K. D., & Tice, D. M. (2007). The strength model of self-control. *Current Directions in Psychological Science, 16*, 351–355.

Bellah, R. N., Madsen, R., Sullivan, W. M., Swidler, A., & Tipton, S. M. ([1985] 2008). *Habits of the heart: Individualism and commitment in American life.* Berkeley: University of California Press.

Black, D. (1993). *The social structure of right and wrong.* Cambridge: Academic.

Black, D. (2011). *Moral time.* New York: Oxford University Press.

Black, D. (2013). On the almost inconceivable misunderstandings concerning the subject of value-free social science. *The British Journal of Sociology, 64*, 763–780.

Bloom, P. (2012). Religion, morality, evolution. *Annual Review of Psychology, 63*, 179–199.

Boehm, C. (1999). *Hierarchy in the forest: The evolution of egalitarian behavior.* Cambridge, MA: Harvard University Press.

Boehm, C. (2012). *Moral origins: The evolution of virtue, altruism, and shame.* New York: Basic Books.

Bourdieu, P. (1990). *The logic of practice.* Palo Alto: Stanford University Press.

Brandt, A. M., & Rozin, P. (2013). *Morality and health.* New York: Routledge.

Brooks, A. C. (2006). *Who really cares: The surprising truth about compassionate conservatism.* New York: Basic Books.

Brown, D. E. (1991). *Human universals.* New York: McGraw-Hill.

Brown, D. E. (2004). Human universals. *Daedalus, 133*, 47–54.

Bruce, S. (2011). *Secularization: In defense of an unfashionable theory.* New York: Oxford University Press.

Brueggemann, J. (2014). Morality, sociological discourse, and public engagement. *Social Currents, 1*, 211–219.

Burke, P., & Stets, J. E. (2009). *Identity theory.* Oxford: New York.

Carney, D. R., Jost, J. T., Gosling, S. D., & Potter, J. (2008). The secret lives of liberals and conservatives: Personality profiles, interaction styles, and the things they leave behind. *Political Psychology, 29*, 807–840.

Carver, C. S., & Scheier, M. F. (1982). Control theory: A useful conceptual framework for personality–social, clinical, and health psychology. *Psychological Bulletin, 92*, 111–135.

Churchland, P. S. (2011). *Braintrust: What neuroscience tells us about morality.* New Jersey: Princeton University Press.

Collett, J. L., & Lizardo, O. (2010). Occupational status and the experience of anger. *Social Forces, 88*, 2079–2104.

Collins, R. (1981). On the micro-foundations of macrosociology. *American Journal of Sociology, 86*, 984–1014.

Collins, R. (2004). *Interaction ritual chains.* Princeton: Princeton University Press.

Côté, S., House, J., & Willer, R. (2015). High economic inequality leads higher-income individuals to be less generous. *Proceedings of the National Academy of Sciences, 112*, 15838–15843.

De Waal, F. (2009). *Primates and philosophers: How morality evolved: How morality evolved.* Princeton: Princeton University Press.

Decety, J. (2011). The neuroevolution of empathy. *Annals of the New York Academy of Sciences, 1231*, 35–45.

Decety, J. (2014). The neuroevolution of empathy and caring for others: Why it matters for morality. In J. Decety & Y. Christen (Eds.), *New frontiers in social neuroscience* (pp. 127–151). New York: Springer.

Decety, J., & Svetlova, M. (2012). Putting together phylogenetic and ontogenetic perspectives on empathy. *Developmental Cognitive Neuroscience, 2*, 1–24.

Desmond, S. A., & Kraus, R. (2014). The effects of importance of religion and church attendance on adolescents' moral beliefs. *Sociological Focus, 47*, 11–31.

Dodd, M. D., Balzer, A., Jacobs, C. M., Gruszczynski, M. W., Smith, K. B., & Hibbing, J. R. (2012). The political left rolls with the good and the political right confronts the bad: Connecting physiology and cognition to preferences. *Philosophical Transactions of the Royal Society: Biological Sciences, 367*, 640–649.

Durkheim, E. (1893 [1997]). *The division of labor in society.* New York: Free Press.

Durkheim, E. (1912 [1976]). *The elementary forms of the religious life.* New York: Routledge.

Durkheim, E., & Mauss, M. (1903 [1963]). *Primitive classification.* Chicago: University of Chicago.

Edgell, P., Gerteis, J., & Hartmann, D. (2006). Atheists as "Other": Moral boundaries and cultural membership in American society. *American Sociological Review, 71*, 211–234.

Emerson, M. O., & Smith, C. (2000). *Divided by faith: Evangelical religion and the problem of race in America.* New York: Oxford University Press.

Epley, N., & Gilovich, T. (2006). The anchoring-and-adjustment heuristic: Why the adjustments are insufficient. *Psychological Science, 17*, 311–318.

Eriksson, K., & Strimling, P. (2015). Group differences in broadness of values may drive dynamics of public opinion on moral issues. *Mathematical Social Sciences, 77*, 1–8.

Farrell, J. (2014). Moral outpouring: Shock and generosity in the aftermath of the BP oil spill. *Social Problems, 61*, 482–506.

Fiske, A. P. (1992). The four elementary forms of sociality: Framework for a unified theory of social relations. *Psychological Review, 99*, 689–723.

Fiske, A. P., & Haslam, N. (2005). The four basic social bonds: Structures for coordinating interaction. In

M. W. Baldwin (Ed.), *Interpersonal cognition* (pp. 267–298). New York: Guilford Press.

Galen, L. W. (2012). Does religious belief promote prosociality? A critical examination. *Psychological Bulletin, 138*, 876–906.

Gervais, W. M., Shariff, A. F., & Norenzayan, A. (2011). Do you believe in atheists? Distrust is central to anti-atheist prejudice. *Journal of Personality and Social Psychology, 101*, 1189–1206.

Giddens, A. (1984). *The constitution of society: Outline of the theory of structuration*. Berkeley: University of California Press.

Gilovich, T. (1991). *How we know what isn't so: The fallibility of human reason in everyday life*. New York: Free Press.

Goode, E., & Ben-Yehuda, N. (1994 [2009]). *Moral panics: The social construction of deviance*. New York: Wiley.

Gorski, P. S. (2013). Beyond the fact/value distinction: Ethical naturalism and the social sciences. *Society, 50*, 543–553.

Graham, J., Haidt, J., & Nosek, B. A. (2009). Liberals and conservatives rely on different sets of moral foundations. *Journal of Personality and Social Psychology, 96*, 1029–1046.

Haidt, J. (2001). The emotional dog and its rational tail: A social intuitionist approach to moral judgment. *Psychological Review, 108*, 814–834.

Haidt, J. (2012). *The righteous mind: Why good people are divided by politics and religion*. New York: Vintage.

Haidt, J., & Bjorklund, F. (2007). Social intuitionists answer six questions about morality. In W. Sinnott Armstron (Ed.), *Moral psychology volume 2: The cognitive science of morality* (pp. 181–217). Cambridge: MIT Press.

Haidt, J., & Kesebir, S. (2010). Morality. In S. T. Fisek, D. T. Gilbert, & G. H. Lindzey (Eds.), *Handbook of social psychology* (5th ed., pp. 797–832). Hoboken: Wiley.

Harkness, S. K., & Hitlin, S. (2014). Morality and emotions. In *Handbook of the sociology of emotions: Volume II* (pp. 451–471). New York: Springer.

Harris, M. (1989). *Cows, pigs, wars, and witches: The riddles of culture*. New York: Vintage.

Harris, S. (2010). *The moral landscape: How science can determine human values*. New York: Basic Books.

Hibbing, J. R., Smith, K. B., Peterson, J. C., & Feher, B. (2014). The deeper sources of political conflict: Evidence from the psychological, cognitive, and neuro-sciences. *Trends in Cognitive Sciences, 18*, 111–113.

Hibbing, J. R., Smith, K. B., & Alford, J. R. (2015). Liberals and conservatives: Non-convertible currencies. *Behavioral and Brain Sciences, 38*, 27–28.

Hitlin, S., & Kramer, K. W. (2014). Intentions and institutions: Turning points and adolescents' moral threshold. *Advances in Life Course Research, 20*, 16–27.

Hitlin, S., & Pinkston, K. (2013). Values, attitudes, and ideologies: Explicit and implicit constructs shaping perception and action. In J. DeLamater (Ed.), *Handbook of social psychology* (pp. 319–339). New York: Springer.

Hitlin, S., & Vaisey, S. (2013). The new sociology of morality. *Annual Review of Sociology, 39*, 51–68.

Hochschild, A. R. (1983 [2003]). *The managed heart: The commercialization of human feeling*. Berkeley: University of California Press.

Hodgkiss, P. (2013). A moral vision: Human dignity in the eyes of the founders of sociology. *The Sociological Review, 61*, 417–439.

Hunter, J. D. (1992). *Culture wars: The struggle to control the family, art, education, law, and politics in America*. New York: Basic Books.

Iadicola, P. (2014). Economic crime: The challenges of regulation and control. *Economic Forum, 531*, 158–163.

Ignatow, G. (2009). Why the sociology of morality needs Bourdieu's habitus. *Sociological Inquiry, 79*, 98–114.

Inglehart, R. (1977 [2015]). *The silent revolution: Changing values and political styles among western publics*. Princeton: Princeton University Press.

Inglehart, R. (1997). *Modernization and postmodernization: Cultural, economic, and political change in 43 societies*. Princeton: Princeton University Press.

Johnson, M., Rowatt, W., & LaBouff, J. (2010). Priming christian religious concepts increases racial prejudice. *Social Psychological and Personality Science, 1*, 119–126.

Johnson, M., Rowatt, W., & LaBouff, J. (2012). Religiosity and prejudice revisited: In-group favoritism, out-group derogation, or both? *Psychology of Religion and Spirituality, 4*, 154–168.

Johnson, K. M., Iyer, R., Wojcik, S., Vaisey, S., Miles, A., Chu, V., & Graham, J. (2014). Ideology-specific patterns of moral indifference predict intentions not to vote. *Analyses of Social Issues and Public Policy, 14*, 61–77.

Jost, J. T. (2006). The end of the end of ideology. *American Psychologist, 61*, 651–670.

Jost, J. T., Glaser, J., Kruglanski, A., & Sulloway, F. (2003). Political conservatism as motivated social cognition. *Psychological Bulletin, 129*, 339–375.

Koleva, S. P., Graham, J., Iyer, R., Ditto, P. H., & Haidt, J. (2012). Tracing the threads: How five moral concerns (especially Purity) help explain culture war attitudes. *Journal of Research in Personality, 46*, 184–194.

Krivo, L. J., Washington, H. M., Peterson, R. D., Browning, C. R., Calder, C. A., & Kwan, M.-P. (2013). Social isolation of disadvantage and advantage: The reproduction of inequality in urban space. *Social Forces, 92*, 141–164.

Lawler, E. J., Thye, S. R., & JeongkooYoon, J. (2009). *Social commitments in a depersonalized world*. New York: Russell Sage Foundation.

Lee, M. T. (2014). The essential interconnections among altruism, morality, and social solidarity: The case of religious altruism. In V. Jeffries (Ed.), *The Palgrave handbook of altruism, morality, and social solidarity: Formulating a field of study* (pp. 311–332). New York: Palgrave Macmillan.

Lenski, G. E. (2005). *Ecological-evolutionary theory: Principles and applications*. Colorado: Paradigm Publishers.

Levi-Strauss, C. (1966). *The savage mind*. Chicago: University of Chicago Press.

Link, B. G., & Phelan, J. (1995). Social conditions as fundamental causes of disease. *Journal of Health and Social Behavior, 35*, 80–94.

Lukes, S. (2008). *Moral relativism*. New York: Palgrave Macmillan.

Marmot, M. G. (2006). Status syndrome: A challenge to medicine. *Journal of the American Medical Association, 11*, 1304–1307.

Marx, K. (1857 [2008]). Condition of factory laborers. In J. Ledbetter (Ed.), *Dispatches for the New York tribune: Selected journalism of Karl Marx* (pp. 189–191). New York: Penguin.

McCaffree, K. (2015). *What morality means: An interdisciplinary synthesis for the social sciences*. New York: Palgrave Macmillan.

McPherson, J. M., & Ranger-Moore, J. R. (1991). Evolution on a dancing landscape: Organizations and networks in dynamic blau space. *Social Forces, 70*, 19–42.

McPherson, M., Smith-Lovin, L., & Cook, J. M. (2001). Birds of a feather: Homophily in social networks. *Annual Review of Sociology, 27*, 415–444.

Miles, A. (2014). Demographic correlates of moral differences in the contemporary United States. *Poetics, 46*, 75–88.

Miles, A., & Vaisey, S. (2015). Morality and politics: Comparing alternate theories. *Social Science Research, 53*, 252–269.

Molm, L. D. (2003). Theoretical comparisons of forms of exchange. *Sociological Theory, 21*, 1–17.

Newman, G. (1976). *Comparative deviance: Law and perception in six cultures*. New York: Elsevier.

Norenzayan, A. (2013). *Big gods: How religion transformed cooperation and conflict*. New Jersey: Princeton University Press.

Norenzayan, A., & Shariff, A. (2008). The origin and evolution of religious prosociality. *Science, 322*, 58–62.

Norenzayan, A. (2012). *Big gods: How religion transformed cooperation and conflict*. New Jersey: Princeton University Press.

Over, H., & Carpenter, M. (2012). Putting the social into social learning: Explaining both selectivity and fidelity in children's copying behavior. *Journal of Comparative Psychology, 126*, 182–192.

Oxley, D. R., Smith, K. B., Alford, J. R., Hibbing, M. V., Miller, J. L., Scalora, M., Hatemi, P. K., & Hibbing, J. R. (2008). Political attitudes vary with physiological traits. *Science, 321*, 1667–1670.

Panksepp, J., & Panksepp, J. B. (2013). Toward a cross-species understanding of empathy. *Trends in Neurosciences, 36*, 489–496.

Park, R. E. (1924). The concept of social distance. *Journal of Applied Sociology, 8*, 339–344.

Paul, G. F. (2005). Cross-national correlations of quantifiable societal health with popular religiosity and secularism in the prosperous democracies: A first look. *Journal of Religion and Society, 7*, 1–17.

Peterson, R. D., & Krivo, L. J. (2010). *Divergent social worlds: Neighborhood crime and the racial-spatial divide*. New York: Russell Sage Foundation.

Phelan, J. C., Link, B. G., Diez-Roux, A., Kawachi, I., & Levin, B. (2004). "Fundamental Causes" of social inequalities in mortality: A test of the theory. *Journal of Health and Social Behavior, 45*, 265–285.

Phelan, J. C., Link, B. G., & Tehranifar, P. (2010). Social conditions as fundamental causes of health inequalities theory, evidence, and policy implications. *Journal of Health and Social Behavior, 51*, 28–40.

Preston, S. D. (2013). The origins of altruism in offspring care. *Psychological Bulletin, 139*(6), 1305.

Ridgeway, C. L. (2007). Gender as a group process: Implications for the persistence of inequality. *Advances in Group Processes, 24*, 311–333.

Ridgeway, C. L. (2009). Framed before we know it: How gender shapes social relations. *Gender and Society, 23*, 145–160.

Ridgeway, C. (2011). *Framed by gender: How gender inequality persists in the modern world*. New York: Oxford University Press.

Rios, V. M. (2009). The consequences of the criminal justice pipeline on black and latino masculinity. *The Annals of the American Academy of Political and Social Science, 623*, 150–162.

Rozin, P., Lowery, L., Imada, S., & Haidt, J. (1999). The CAD triad hypothesis: A mapping between three moral emotions (contempt, anger, disgust) and three moral codes (community, autonomy, divinity). *Journal of Personality and Social Psychology, 76*, 574–586.

Schnittker, J., & McLeod, J. D. (2005). The social psychology of health disparities. *Annual Review of Sociology, 31*, 75–103.

Schwartz, S. H., & Bilsky, W. (1987). Toward a theory of the universal content and structure of values: Extensions and cross-cultural replications. *Journal of Personality and Social Psychology, 58*, 878–891.

Shweder, R., Much, N., Mahapatra, M., & Park, L. (1997). The big 'Three' of morality (autonomy, community, and divinity) and the big 'Three' explanations of suffering. In A. Brandt & P. Rozin (Eds.), *Morality and health* (pp. 119–169). New York: Routledge.

Simpson, B., & Willer, R. (2008). Altruism and indirect reciprocity: The interaction of person and situation in prosocial behavior. *Social Psychology Quarterly, 71*, 37–52.

Simpson, B., & Willer, R. (2015). Beyond altruism: Sociological foundations of cooperation and prosocial behavior. *Annual Review of Sociology, 441*, 1–21.

Simpson, B., Harrell, A., & Willer, R. (2013). Hidden paths from morality to cooperation: Moral judgments promote trust and trustworthiness. *Social Forces, 91*, 1529–1548.

Smith, C. (2013). Comparing ethical naturalism and 'Public Sociology'. *Society, 50*, 598–601.

Smith, C., & Sorrell, K. (2014). On social solidarity. In V. Jeffries (Ed.), *The Palgrave handbook of altruism, morality, and social solidarity: Formulating a field of study* (pp. 219–248). New York: Palgrave Macmillan.

Stets, J. E., & Biga, C. (2003). Bringing identity theory into environmental sociology. *Sociological Theory, 21*, 398–423.

Stets, J. E., & Carter, M. J. (2012). A theory of the self for the sociology of morality. *American Sociological Review, 77*, 120–140.

Stets, J. E., & McCaffree, K. (2014). Linking morality, altruism, and social solidarity using identity theory. In V. Jeffries (Ed.), *The Palgrave handbook of altruism, morality, and social solidarity* (pp. 333–351). New York: Palgrave Macmillan.

Stryker, S. (1980). *Symbolic interactionism: A social structural version*. California: Benjamin-Cummings Publishing Company.

Stryker, S. (2004). Integrating emotion into identity theory. In J. H. Turner (Ed.), *Theory and research on human emotions* (pp. 1–23). New York: Emerald Group Publishing Limited.

Stryker, S., & Burke, P. J. (2000). The past, present, and future of an identity theory. *Social Psychology Quarterly, 63*, 284–297.

Sayer, A. (2011). Habitus, work and contributive justice. *Sociology, 45*, 7–21.

Tavory, I. (2011). The question of moral action: A formalist position. *Sociological Theory, 29*, 272–293.

Turner, J. H. (2007). *Human emotions: A sociological theory*. New York: Taylor & Francis.

Turner, J. H. (2010a). The stratification of emotions: Some preliminary generalizations. *Sociological Inquiry, 80*(2), 168–199.

Turner, J. H. (2010b). Natural selection and the evolution of morality in human societies. In S. Hitlin & S. Vaisey (Eds.), *Handbook of the sociology of morality* (pp. 125–145). New York: Springer.

Turner, J. H. (2014). The evolution of affect, sociality, altruism and conscience in humans. In V. Jeffries (Ed.), *The Palgrave handbook of altruism, morality and social solidarity: Formulating a field* (pp. 275–302). New York: Palgrave Macmillan.

Turner, J. H., & Maryanski, A. (2008). *On the origin of societies by natural selection*. New York: Routledge.

Turner, S. P., & Turner, J. H. (1990). *The impossible science: An institutional analysis of American sociology*. New York: Russell Sage.

Vaisey, S. (2007). Structure, culture, and community: The search for belonging in 50 urban communes. *American Sociological Review, 72*, 851–873.

Vaisey, S. (2009). Motivation and justification: A dual-process model of culture in action. *American Journal of Sociology, 114*, 1675–1715.

Vaisey, S., & Lizardo, O. (2010). Can cultural worldviews influence network composition? *Social Forces, 88*, 1595–1618.

Vaisey, S., & Miles, A. (2014). Tools from moral psychology for measuring personal moral culture. *Theory and Society, 43*, 311–332.

Van Leeuwen, F., & Park, J. H. (2009). Perceptions of social dangers, moral foundations, and political orientation. *Personality and Individual Differences, 47*, 169–173.

Van Leeuwen, F., Park, J. H., Koenig, B., & Graham, J. (2012). Regional variation in pathogen prevalence predicts endorsement of group-focused moral concerns. *Evolution and Human Behavior, 33*, 429–437.

Van Leeuwen, F., Koenig, B., Graham, J., & Park, J. H. (2014). Moral concerns across the United States: Associations with life-history variables, pathogen prevalence, urbanization, cognitive ability, and social class. *Evolution and Human Behavior, 35*, 464–471.

Wikström, P. O. H. (2010). Explaining crime as moral actions. In S. Vaisey & S. Hitlin (Eds.), *Handbook of the sociology of morality* (pp. 211–239). New York: Springer.

Wagmiller, R. L., Jr., & Lee, K. (2014). Are contemporary patterns of black male joblessness unique? Cohort replacement, intracohort change, and the diverging structures of black and white men's employment. *Social Problems, 61*, 305–327.

Weber, M. (1919 [2004]). The vocation of science. In S. Whimster (Ed.), *The essential weber: A reader* (pp. 270–287). New York: Routledge.

Weber, M. (1920 [2002]). The protestant ethic and the 'Spirit' of Capitalism. In *The protestant ethic and the spirit of capitalism: And other writings* (pp. 1–201). New York: Penguin.

Willer, R., Youngreen, R., Troyer, L., & Lovaglia, M. (2012). How do the powerful attain status? The roots of legitimate power inequalities. *Managerial and Decision Economics, 33*, 355–367.

Wright, E. O. (2010). *Envisioning real utopias*. London: Verso.

Wright, J. C., & Baril, G. (2011). The role of cognitive resources in determining our moral intuitions: Are we all liberals at heart? *Journal of Experimental Social Psychology, 47*, 1007–1012.

Zuckerman, P. (2008). *Society without god: What the least religious nations can tell us about contentment*. New York: New York University Press.

22 Forgetting to Remember: The Present Neglect and Future Prospects of Collective Memory in Sociological Theory

Christina Simko

22.1 The Classical Roots of Collective Memory

Memory is rarely considered one of the core subjects of sociological theory. Yet a concern with memory—and indeed an understanding of memory as integral to the heart and soul of collective life—has been inscribed in the sociological tradition from the beginning. In *The Elementary Forms of Religious Life*, Émile Durkheim captured the social power of commemorative rites. These rituals, he argued, "serve only to sustain the vitality" of the beliefs that comprise a group's mythology, "to keep them from being effaced from memory and, in sum, to revivify the most essential elements of the collective consciousness" (Durkheim [1912] 1915:375). In reminding group members of cherished mythology, commemoration "renews the sentiment which [a group] has of itself and of its unity," and links "the present to the past or the individual to the group" (ibid.:375, 378). Commemoration is thus a crucial wellspring for social solidarity, common identity, and collective effervescence.

Carrying forward this line of thinking—and expanding it from a few powerfully suggestive lines to a more fully developed theory—Durkheim's student, Maurice Halbwachs, elaborated the concept of *collective memory*.[1] Halbwachs veered somewhat from an orthodox Durkheimian view, emphasizing *collective consciences* in the plural—"the multiplicity," as he put it, "of collective memor*ies*" (Halbwachs [1950] 2011:146, emphasis added) developed within group contexts, including families, religions, and social classes rather than in 'Society' writ large. Nevertheless, Halbwachs argued forcefully that memory is a fundamentally *social* phenomenon: in order to understand memory, we should not search for where memories are stored in the brain, but instead look to the social contexts within which people "acquire their memories" as well as "recall, recognize, and localize their memories" (Halbwachs [1925] 1992:38). Social groups give shape and form to our past, and our parents, siblings, and friends, among others, spur us on as we remember, providing social cues that guide *what* we remember as well as *how* and *when*. Indeed, understanding memory requires attention to group dynamics in and of themselves: "It is not sufficient," Halbwachs (ibid.:40) argued, "to show that individuals always use social frameworks when they remember. It is necessary to place oneself in the perspective of the group or groups" within which the

C. Simko (✉)
Department of Anthropology and Sociology, Williams College, Williamstown, MA, USA
e-mail: Christina.Simko@williams.edu

[1]Halbwachs was not the first to use the term "collective memory," but he imbued it with "a theoretical weight previously unknown" and outlined a set of ideas that continue to be remarkably generative (Olick et al. 2011:16).

S. Abrutyn (ed.), *Handbook of Contemporary Sociological Theory*, Handbooks of Sociology and Social Research, DOI 10.1007/978-3-319-32250-6_22

individual's memories take on shape and meaning.

In a similar vein, Halbwachs argued that the act of remembering is not fundamentally 'about' recalling the past as it happened or somehow recovering history 'intact.' Instead, it is oriented toward the needs of the present, the demands of our immediate social milieu: "collective memory," he argued, "adapts the image of ancient facts to the beliefs and spiritual needs of the present" (quoted in Schwartz 1982:376). Writing in a different context, George Herbert Mead advanced a remarkably similar argument. Much like Halbwachs, he understood the past as a tool for addressing present dilemmas: "reality," Mead wrote, "is always that of a present," and "the past…is as hypothetical as the future" (1932:235, 12). Again, memory is a social phenomenon, amenable to continuous reconstruction, and must therefore be understood using distinctively sociological tools.

Over the past few decades, the insights these figures have bequeathed to us have been brought to bear in reviving a vibrant discourse on collective memory, within sociology and beyond. In sociology, however, this revival has had a relatively delimited impact. At present, the sociology of memory is largely understood not as a broad concern for sociological theory, but as a special interest—a sub-subfield within cultural sociology, composed of scholars with particular interests in history or commemoration. Yet this assumption obscures the profound ways in which the sociology of memory addresses central questions in contemporary theory. For as Durkheim, Halbwachs, and Mead all recognized in their own ways, memory belongs at the core of our understanding of the social. It is the tissue that binds collectivities—from families to religions to nations—together. It is not merely a way of preserving bygone history, but a source of both power and meaning in the present. In the pages that follow, then, I argue for re-centering the sociology of memory, for moving it from the periphery to the core of pressing theoretical debates. Specifically, I argue that the scholarship on memory can move forward two major projects in contemporary theory: first, the project of theorizing the nature of the epoch in which we live—making sense of the moment that theorists have termed "late," "high," "reflexive," "liquid," or "post" modernity (e.g., Giddens 1990; Beck 1992; Bauman 2000)—and second, the project of theorizing the meaning of "culture," a term that has simultaneously captivated and perplexed recent generations of sociologists.

Today, as I alluded above, the study of collective memory is a vibrant interdisciplinary enterprise.[2] Especially for scholars well versed in this enterprise, it is worth clarifying my purposes here. There are now numerous review essays (e.g., Olick and Robbins 1998; Conway 2010b), survey texts (e.g., Misztal 2003; Erll 2011), handbooks (e.g., Erll and Nünning 2008), and readers (e.g., Olick et al. 2011) that synthesize the field, often taking into account—and even thematizing—the conversations and tensions that exist between and across disciplines. Here, my focus is more delimited: to provide a broad sense for the relationship between sociological work on memory in particular and some of the overriding concerns in contemporary theory. My aim, then, is not to provide a comprehensive review of the memory literature, but to highlight the themes most pertinent to sociological theorizing, and to sensitize a broader community of theorists to the (perhaps surprising) relevance that collective memory might hold in addressing their concerns. First, however, I set the stage with a brief account of collective memory's reemergence as an

[2]Indeed, the classic sociological texts on memory have become core references in the interdisciplinary field of "memory studies," which has—over the past few decades—brought together scholars from across the humanities and social sciences in a vigorous dialogue about the nature of memory and its place in human social life (for recent overviews, see Erll 2011; Olick et al. 2011). The field now has its own journals (e.g., *Memory Studies*), book series (e.g., Palgrave Macmillian's "Memory Studies" and Stanford's "Cultural Memory in the Present"), and conference circuit, among other markers of its institutionalization.

explicit analytic framework in sociology during the 1980s and 1990s.

22.2 Recovering "Collective Memory"

For several decades following his death, Halbwachs had little influence in the English-speaking world. The concern with memory did not disappear—perhaps most notably, W. Lloyd Warner's (1959:278) *The Living and the Dead* turned a Durkheimian lens on the commemorative rituals of "Yankee City," highlighting the integrative powers of Memorial Day rites and arguing that they constituted "a modern cult of the dead" that conformed "to Durkheim's definition of sacred collective representations." Yet the specific language of collective memory remained notably absent from Warner's discussions. By the early 1980s, however, sociologists had begun to revive Halbwachs' legacy and renovate his idea of collective memory for contemporary sociology, creating an organized field of inquiry around the concept.[3]

The first English translation of selections from Halbwachs' writings on collective memory—a series of programmatic essays that his admirers had published 30 years prior—appeared in 1980 under the title *The Collective Memory*, with an introduction by Mary Douglas. Though the book quickly went out of print, Lewis Coser's translation of key selections from Halbwachs' 1925 work *The Social Frameworks of Memory* as well as a brief excerpt from his 1941 work *The Legendary Topography of the Gospels in the Holy Land* appeared in 1992, and has had much greater staying power. Influential as it would be, however, Halbwachs' work "did not cause the present current of collective memory research" but was "rather swept into it" (Schwartz 1996a:276). Indeed, throughout the 1960s and 1970s, broad intellectual, cultural, and political factors created conditions for a renewed concern with the past, including such issues as memory, tradition, and heritage. Reflecting on the reemergence of collective memory from the vantage of the mid-1990s, Barry Schwartz (ibid.:277–278)—who was perhaps the preeminent architect behind the contemporary sociology of memory—pointed to the rise of multiculturalism, postmodernism, and hegemony theory as the links between the 1960s and 1970s "cultural revolution" and the scholarly interest in the (re)construction of the past that solidified throughout the 1980s. Specifically, all three of these perspectives challenged taken-for-granted images of, and narratives about, the past, underscoring how they excluded women, minorities, and working classes. They thus heightened both sensitivity to and interest in the social construction—and the possibilities for *re*construction—of the past.

The reemergence of "collective memory" as an organizing principle for a field of inquiry thus resonated with wider intellectual currents that sensitized sociologists to the role of the past in the present. On the one hand, scholars highlighted, and even celebrated, the continued power of the past in providing meaning and orientation in the late modern world: Edward Shils' (1981) *Tradition* argued that the sharp boundaries the classical theorists drew between tradition and modernity in fact obscured the enduring relevance of the past in providing moral guidance; in *Habits of the Heart*, Robert Bellah and his colleagues ([1985] 1996:152–155) wrote powerfully about "communities of memory," bound together by a sense of shared history. On the other hand, Eric Hobsbawm and Terence Ranger (1983) dismantled and desacralized the "invented traditions" that modern nation-states elaborated in the effort to shore up their legitimacy, uncovering the centrality of the past—or rather, highly fabricated *images* of the past—in securing and maintaining political power. Here, in keeping with the cultural transformations mentioned above, memory was less a source of solidarity and group identity and more a tool for elites to manipulate the masses. Ultimately, the language of collective memory provided a rubric for synthesizing these kinds of concerns—for systematically examining the

[3]For a discussion of other relevant scholarship in the years between Halbwachs' death in 1945 and the revival of his work in the Anglophone world during the 1980s, see Olick et al. (2011:25–29).

interplay between past and present and for making this relationship an explicit object of concern for social theory.

A series of works by Schwartz reappropriating, renovating, and reformulating the concept of collective memory paved the way for a vibrant sociological discourse on the subject—one whose theoretical relevance is still underappreciated today. Schwartz's early work situated collective memory squarely within the Durkheimian tradition. In a 1982 article examining the events and persons commemorated in the United States Capitol—a study that can retrospectively be understood as the starting point for this new tradition of inquiry—Schwartz (1982:374) pointed out that "[f]ew contemporary sociologists have systematically studied how the past, as a 'collective representation,' is affected by the organization and needs of social groups." Yet this, he pointed out, was precisely Halbwachs' concern in his writings on collective memory: Halbwachs, Schwartz (ibid.:375) explained, concluded "that changes in our knowledge of the past correspond to changing organization needs and to transformations in the structure of society." Grappling with this conclusion, Schwartz simultaneously introduced Halbwachs to American sociologists and laid the groundwork for the theoretical debate that would propel the contemporary sociology of memory into being: namely, the debate over the malleability of memory.

22.2.1 The Malleability of Memory

As I noted above, one of the core claims in Halbwachs' sociology of memory—a claim that also found support in Mead—was that our understanding of the past is the product of our interests and needs in the present. Indeed, Halbwachs went so far as to claim that "a knowledge of the origin of these facts [about the past] must be secondary, if not altogether useless, for the reality of the past is no longer *in* the past" (quoted in Schwartz 1982:376). In keeping with this "presentist" view, Schwartz (1982:395–396) found that the demands of the present bore powerfully on the commemorative symbolism displayed in the U.S. Capitol: prior to the Civil War, Capitol iconography featured "founding heroes" whose memory underwrote unity for the fledgling nation. Following the Civil War—with the federal union secured—the commemorative symbolism in the Capitol expanded significantly. American leaders rediscovered post-revolutionary events that once would have provoked conflict; they established the National Statuary Hall as a forum for commemorating regional heroes whose inclusion would have been too threatening when national unity was still problematic; and they began to commission busts and portraits according to incumbency rather than perceived achievement—honoring individuals for their offices rather than their personal qualities. In short, as the nation's needs transformed, so, too, did its commemorative symbolism—just as Halbwachs would have anticipated.

Yet Schwartz qualified Halbwachs' presentism in important ways, and in doing so established the foundation for the broad debate about the malleability of memory. Certainly, Schwartz acknowledged, recollections are called forth and shaped by present circumstances. But even as circumstances change, the new symbolism that emerges to address them does not *supplant* earlier commemorations; it is instead *superimposed* upon them (1982:396).[4] Earlier symbolism thus endures—and presumably confers its legacy—within the ever-shifting present, apart from (and perhaps even in spite of) the exigencies of the moment.

The revived tradition of collective memory research took up the questions Schwartz opened in this study. To what extent can the past be reimagined and reformulated to suit present interests? Is the past more of a mechanism for gaining and sustaining power, or a source of collective identity, solidarity, and moral guidance? When and how does the past constrain social actors in the present, limiting what they can do or say? Presentism, as Jeffrey Olick and Joyce Robbins

[4]Schwartz (1982:396) argues that this "pattern conforms to Durkheim's observations that organic solidarity does not negate the mechanical kind but rather presupposes it and is welded on to it."

(1998:128) point out, can "emphasize either instrumental or meaning dimensions of memory." For instance, while Hobsbawm and Ranger's (1983) landmark work stressed the instrumental dimensions of tradition, Schwartz and his colleagues' study on the recovery of Masada among Palestinian Jews—which drew heavily on Mead's legacy as well as Halbwachs'—stressed the role of the past in fulfilling a subsequent desire for meaning and orientation: Masada's function, they explained, was "not instrumental...but semiotic," and it provided "a symbolic structure in which the reality of the community's inner life could be rendered more explicit and more comprehensible than it would have been otherwise" (Schwartz et al. 1986:160). The past can serve present needs not only by feeding the quest for power or domination, but also by filling an existential void.

By and large, however, memory sociologists worked to forge *via media* between presentist views—whether instrumentalist or cultural—and a more objectivist view of the past as durable and unchanging. Arising alongside the "cultural turn" and now integral to cultural sociology, the early discourse on collective memory was particularly concerned with countering strictly instrumentalist views of the past. Building on Schwartz's argument that fresh reconstructions of the past are superimposed upon their predecessors, other scholars elaborated the specific factors that limit or constrain the malleability of the past. Michael Schudson (1989) identified three such limitations: the structure of pasts available in a given social context, the structure of individual choice, and the structure of social conflicts over the past. Actors thus cannot simply "invent" pasts out of thin air to serve their needs in the present, but instead must work with the materials available to them, and within a structure imposed by their social and historical context. And importantly, these materials and structure may or may not serve their present desires and aspirations—an insight brought vividly to life in Schudson's (1992) study of Watergate in American memory.

In a similar vein, Olick and Daniel Levy (1997) argue that the past constrains present actors in different ways depending on the cultural logic attached to it: *mythic* or *rational*. Mythic constraints are "[m]oral, constitutive, endogenous, projective, [and] definitional," and take the form of either *taboos* (proscriptions) or *duties* (prescriptions), while rational constraints are "[c] alculative, interested, exogenously caused, mundane, [and] strategic," taking the form of either *prohibitions* (proscriptions) or *requirements* (prescriptions) (ibid.:925). The prevailing logic applied to a particular past, however, can change over time. For instance, successful appeals to rationality can, at times, transform a taboo into a prohibition that can be dealt with calmly and calculatively, having lost its mythic power (ibid.:931–933).

Observing such transformations, Olick and Levy (ibid.:934) go one step further to outline a processual approach to collective memory that overcomes the dichotomy between presentist and objectivist views of the past: collective memory, they argue, *is itself* the "continuous negotiation between past and present...rather than pure constraint by, or contemporary strategic manipulation of, the past." Collective memory, in other words, is a dynamic *process*, not a static thing—"an active process of sense-making through time" (ibid.:922)—and conceptualizing it as such captures the constant tension between malleability and constraint. Subsequently, Olick (1999b, forthcoming) specified the mechanism for this ongoing negotiation: namely, dialogue. Fresh representations of the past, he argues, are not just *superimposed* upon earlier images—discrete moments in a series of representations—but instead emerge in conversation with them; the *memory of commemoration* thus intervenes in the interplay between past and present.

Though there of course remain tensions over the malleability of memory, the prevailing wisdom is that the relationship between past and present is a complex and variable one. Largely embracing these *via media*, recent scholarship has continued the effort to specify the mechanisms of path-dependency (e.g., Saito 2006; Jansen 2007), or to clarify the nexus of cultural and institutional factors that shape commemorative trajectories (e.g., Vinitzky-Seroussi 2002; Simko 2012; Steidl 2013), refining the conceptual toolkit for grasping mnemonic processes.

22.2.2 New Directions

As a body of research on collective memory has solidified, of course, new issues have come to the fore. In the pages that follow, I focus in depth on two lines of inquiry that speak especially powerfully to broad questions in sociological theory. But it is worth pausing for a moment here to highlight salient debates and tensions that space considerations preclude me from fully elaborating here.

For one, sociologists have debated the relative primacy of collective representations sui generis—monuments, memorials, museums, public addresses, textbooks, and the like—and aggregated individual memories, accessed primarily through interviews or survey research. Olick (1999a) characterizes these two competing "cultures" as *collective* and *collected* memory, respectively. While early studies generally approached collective memories as collective representations in the Durkheimian sense—and Halbwachs was, after all, inspired and informed by his mentor's work—Halbwachs' legacy is indeed multiple, stressing both the representations of the past embodied in broadly shared symbolism *and* the social frameworks that filter individual memory. In particular, Howard Schuman, Barry Schwartz, and their collaborators have called for memory scholars to "bring people back in" through surveys that capture how "individuals process historical and commemorative statements," arguing that "individuals… alone, as creators and recipients, ascribe meaning to historical and commemorative objects" (Schwartz and Schuman 2005:183, 186, 198; see also Schuman et al. 2005; Schuman and Corning 2011). Here, Schwartz expands upon his earlier Durkheimian approach by examining the interplay between collective representations and individual interpretations. While Schuman, Schwartz, and their colleagues emphasize survey research as a complement to the analysis of public symbolism, in a related strain of research and theorizing, other scholars have used in-depth interviews and ethnographic observation to examine collective memory from the micro level—asking, for instance, how individuals deploy collective memories to make sense of present problems or challenges (e.g., Teeger 2014), or how people draw on collective representations to organize their autobiographical narratives, linking past and present in meaningful ways in order to create a sense of coherence over time (e.g., Vinitzky-Seroussi 1998; DeGloma 2010).[5]

At the other end of the spectrum, sociologists have criticized the focus on *national* memories specifically—not because they obscure individual experience or the multiplicity of memories but because they fail to recognize that in modern consumer societies "an increasing number of people…no longer define themselves (exclusively) through the nation" (Levy and Sznaider 2006:2). Increasingly, these scholars suggest, people understand themselves as part of wider communities that transcend ethnic and/or territorial boundaries. As such, collective memory now takes on *transnational* or *cosmopolitan* forms, cracking the "container of the nation state" (ibid.) in ways that call for analytic attention. The Holocaust, for instance, has increasingly become a global emblem of evil (Alexander 2002) and a catalyst for a cosmopolitan human rights culture (Levy and Sznaider 2006). Though I take up this argument in a different context below, it is worth underscoring here the concern with the units of analysis most appropriate for understanding collective memory in the present moment—sociologists call for attention to both the micro (autobiographical memories) and the radically macro (global frameworks of memory).

Indeed, the latter critique is bound up with a broader transformation in substantive focus that has profound—and, I argue, underappreciated—relevance for contemporary social theory: what we might characterize as a "melancholic turn" in collective memory itself, and a corresponding

[5]Micro and macro approaches need not be seen in opposition, of course. For instance, Thomas DeGloma (2015:158, 161) examines how mnemonic agents deploy autobiographical narratives in their struggles to gain "mnemonic authority" within the public sphere—a particularly crucial strategy given the "new ethic of autobiographical storytelling" that influences public debates. "Collected" memories in Olick's (1999a) sense are thus deployed to legitimate particular claims about "collective" memory.

shift in the subjects of memory research. The shift identified in the collective memory literature—from heroism and triumph to victimhood and atrocity—is not merely about the subjects of commemoration, however. Rather, the subjects of commemoration embody broad epochal transformations that we can understand when we afford memory a more central place in our theories of modernity. Here, the sociology of memory intersects with, and speaks to, much more general concerns.

22.3 Memory, Melancholy, and Modernity

On the face of it, the transformation that now preoccupies many sociologists of memory is deceptively simple. Collective memory once centered upon the heroic: national celebrations (e.g., Spillman 1997), national idols (e.g., Schwartz 1991b, 1998, 2000, 2008), and the stuff of triumph. Today, commemorative symbolism is increasingly preoccupied with much darker subjects, including both suffering inflicted *upon* collectivities and the atrocities perpetrated *by* them. For one, "victims assume the position that, before, was the place of heroes" at the center of collective identities (Giesen 2004:3). For another, political legitimacy increasingly hinges on acknowledging and atoning for misdeeds rather than celebrating past glories and present greatness (Olick 2007b:122). Not surprisingly, this transformation has shaped the core questions of contemporary memory research. How do collectivities come to terms with "difficult pasts" and find languages for memorializing suffering, misdeeds, and/or dissent, and how do these differ from the languages used to memorialize triumph, heroism, and unity? Perhaps even more profoundly, *why* have victims supplanted heroes as the linchpin of collective narratives, and *why* is it now incumbent upon collectivities to grapple explicitly and publicly with pasts that are difficult, ugly, and shameful? Suffering and atrocity are themselves nothing new, but their centrality to the political agenda certainly is. And answering these questions takes us to the very heart of sociology's effort to theorize the modern.

22.3.1 Collective Identity in a Melancholic Age

Once again, the founding questions for this line of inquiry emerged out of a dialogue with Durkheim. As Robin Wagner-Pacifici and Schwartz (1991:379) summarize—and as I noted above—for Durkheim, commemorative rituals "preserve and celebrate traditional beliefs," integrating "the glory of a society's past into its present concerns and aspirations." Accordingly, a strict Durkheimian perspective assumes that "the events or individuals selected for commemoration are necessarily heroic, or at least untainted," allowing for "a unified, positive image of the past" (ibid.). Even the piacular rites that Durkheim ([1912] 1915:494) described—"rites which are celebrated by those in a state of uneasiness or sadness"—arouse common emotions and in doing so reconstitute the social body. Here, too, "collective sentiments are renewed which then lead men to seek one another and to assemble together," and indeed "[s]ince they weep together...the group is not weakened, in spite of the blow which has fallen upon it" (ibid.:507, 510).[6]

Yet modern commemorations take shape in deeply pluralistic contexts, and frequently under the shadow of divisive debates over the meaning of the past. How, then, do collectivities construct representations of episodes that evoke conflict and dissensus rather than unity, shame and regret rather than pride? Examining the development of the Vietnam Veterans Memorial on the U.S. National Mall in Washington, D.C., Wagner-Pacifici and Schwartz (1991) argue that Maya Lin's design addressed this powerful commemorative dilemma through its multivocality:

[6]Putting Durkheim in conversation with more contemporary treatments of emotion, Schwartz argues that piacular rites impose "feeling rules" (Hochschild 1979) indicating "what sort of affect is to be displayed on a given occasion" (Schwartz 1991a:354); common emotion thus regenerates the group's sense of solidarity.

the black granite walls, inscribed with the names of over 58,000 dead, allow people to project their own sentiments and interpretations onto the memorial, providing contemplative space that visitors can share even in the absence of a common narrative.

Building on this foundational case study, sociologists have theorized how collectivities commemorate difficult pasts under varying social conditions. Vered Vinitzky-Seroussi (2002) identifies factors that support *multivocal* commemorations such as the Vietnam Veterans Memorial: a relatively consensual political culture, a past that is not highly relevant to the contemporary political agenda, and a circumstance where nonstate agents of memory possess relatively little power. The commemorations of Yitzhak Rabin in Israel, she argues, took shape under very different circumstances: the political culture was deeply conflictual; the past remained highly relevant; and nonstate agents of memory possessed significant power. Here, commemorations assumed a *fragmented* form: they took place across multiple (separate) spaces, each with its own distinct commemorative discourse and audience. And examining the memory of the May 4, 1970, shootings at Kent State University, Christina Steidl (2013:19) traces how commemorations can shift dynamically between forms, theorizing a third, *integrated* commemorative type that "allows for the expression of divergent narratives and the maintenance of separate commemorative spaces (like a fragmented memorial) and enhances social solidarity through shared meta-narratives stressing overarching values" like a multivocal memorial.

This strand of research and theorizing has wide implications, examining the complex symbolism that emerges in commemorative rituals Durkheim could not have anticipated—commemorations that not only center on painful episodes, but also grapple overtly with mnemonic conflict and its ramifications for collective identity. With this transformation in the core subjects of collective memory has come a steady stream of books and articles addressing how "difficult pasts" have reverberated among both "victims" and "perpetrators" (while also illuminating the contestation that often emerges over this very boundary): the Nazi past in postwar Germany (Olick 2005, forthcoming); the atomic bombing of Hiroshima and its legacies in both the United States (Zolberg 1998) and Japan (Saito 2006); apartheid in South Africa (Teeger and Vinitzky-Seroussi 2007; Teeger 2014); and Bloody Sunday in Northern Ireland (Conway 2010a), among many others. More broadly, others have addressed the array of mnemonic practices that have developed to deal with these weighty legacies, including political apologies (Celermajer 2009), reparations politics (Torpey 2006), and truth commissions (Jelin 2003; Posel 2008), as well as the phenomena of silence and denial (Cohen 2001; Zerubavel 2006; Vinitzky-Seroussi and Teeger 2010) that—even in an era of acknowledgment—are often integral in the trajectory of difficult pasts.[7] Our age is different from Durkheim's, and—while there is still crucial guidance to be found in his treatment of commemoration—grasping the sources of collective identity and social solidarity in contemporary society also requires new theoretical tools.[8]

22.3.2 Memory and the Modern

Even more, understanding this transformation can provide a window onto modernity itself. What does the preoccupation with these darker

[7]As Vinitzky-Seroussi and Teeger (2010) point out, however, silence can be a vehicle for memory and commemoration, not only for forgetting: for instance, the "moments of silence" that are now a ubiquitous part of commemorative rituals interrupt the ordinary flow of time to provide space for contemplating the past, *facilitating* memory rather than undermining it.

[8]In a related line of theorizing, Gary Alan Fine has examined "difficult" or "negative" reputations. While memories of evil and villainy (e.g., Ducharme and Fine 1995)—like the memories of greatness that Schwartz emphasizes—serve to reinforce a society's moral boundaries (and thus underwrite consensus), memories of failure and incompetence are generated through "discursive rivalry," tension and debate among competing "reputational entrepreneur[s]" (Fine 1996:1160, 1162). Fine's approach thus expands upon the Durkheimian view of memory, emphasizing the "intense battle for control" that often takes place before a symbol comes to represent society for its members (ibid.:1160).

narratives say about the epoch in which we live? Can a focus on memory illuminate modernity in new ways? For a number of sociologists, the answer is yes, and sites of memory become windows onto the conditions of late modern life broadly conceived. Here, I consider four perspectives arising out of or in dialogue with the sociology of memory that offer particularly rich insights for this line of inquiry.

22.3.2.1 The Post-Heroic Era

Schwartz (2008), for one, theorizes an inverse relationship between a society's investment in equality and its reverence for heroes. The very developments that fueled renewed intellectual interest in collective memory—multiculturalism, postmodernism, hegemony theory, and the like—have also given rise to a cultural moment in which the power of the past to orient and inspire has severely diminished. Focusing particularly on the U.S. case, but also drawing comparisons (e.g., Schwartz and Heinrich 2004), Schwartz (2008:187) argues that ours is "a post-heroic" era, in which "the very notion of greatness has eroded." Figures such as Abraham Lincoln and George Washington, once perceived as godlike, are now understood in more complicated terms, as a mélange of good and evil, strength and weakness. As the boundary between ordinary people and their heroes has eroded, the qualities associated with each are visible in the other.

For Schwartz, this is part of the disenchantment process outlined by Max Weber—though he is careful to note that the transformation is not total; reverence for heroes *diminishes* rather than disappearing altogether. In this way, Schwartz challenges postmodernist theories that posit a more radical disintegration of the national memories that once provided a sense of collective identity (e.g., Nora 1989): the post-heroic age is not a fundamentally new epoch, but a shift that—in keeping with his earlier accounts of commemoration—is superimposed upon what came before. With this assessment, Schwartz seeks to draw attention to what he perceives as the tradeoffs that come with equality and inclusivity. While he makes clear that "[e]quality and distrust of authority"—which "[lead] to the rupturing of the tissue connecting past and present"—are in his view "benign conditions to be maintained, not pathologies to be deplored and abolished" (Schwartz 2008:218), he also argues that something has been lost in the process. Equality and inclusivity are bound up with "the fraying fabric of American nationhood and self-esteem" (ibid.:267), leaving citizens without the sources of inspiration and orientation that once sustained their predecessors. Whatever one thinks of Schwartz's normative take on these developments—and many contemporary sociologists no doubt view them through a different ideological lens—Schwartz maps a profound transformation in the relationship between past and present, with significant implications for collective life: certainly, the declining power of heroes contributes to the sense of unmooring captured in the discourse on "liquid" (Bauman 2000) or "reflexive" (Beck 1992) modernity.

22.3.2.2 The Politics of Regret

Even more explicit in its contribution to epochal theories is Olick's account of the contemporary "politics of regret." Though they have long been omitted from this tradition of theorizing, Olick (2007b:130) argues that "memory and regret" in fact belong "at the center" of our "sociological account of modernity." Observing that political legitimation increasingly relies on "'learning the lessons' of history more than...fulfilling its promises or remaining faithful to its legacy" (ibid.:122), he shows that attention to *temporality* can illuminate the contemporary preoccupation with regret and indeed the very emergence and development of the modern.

Familiar theories of modernity capture crucial background factors that help explain the contemporary preoccupation with regret. Durkheim ([1893] 1984) and, subsequently, Elias ([1939] 2000) captured the process of *differentiation* that creates conditions for regret: collective memory itself arises to fill the gap that opens between individual and collective experience in increasingly complex urban environments, while "the dense networks of relations" that emerge "give any single action a wide and unforeseeable circle of implication" (Olick 2007b:131), generating an intensified sense of both personal and collective responsibility. Rationalization, as Weber described it, produces the conditions of possibility for an *ethic of responsibility* (Weber [1919] 1946), which presumes both a sense that values are relative—and thus that value conflicts are ultimately inescapable—and an ability to distinguish means from ends.[9] And the emergence of universalistic principles of justice that Jürgen Habermas (1996) traces also paves the way for the contemporary politics of regret. According to Olick (2007b:136), however, these standard accounts miss "the most important…feature of modernity's trajectory"—namely, *temporality*.

In this view, the transformation in our experience of time is the hallmark of modernity: as Reinhardt Koselleck (1985), Lutz Niethammer (1992), and Benedict Anderson (1991) have argued, cyclical temporality—supported by both the rhythms of rural life and church eschatology—gave way to progressive linear temporality. And the "historical consciousness" that arose as a result is the primary force behind modern regret (Olick 2007b:136). With the rise of linear temporality came the grand narratives of modernity—narratives of ascent and progress, with the nation-state as their "dominant purveyor" (ibid.:188). Uninterrupted progress, however, never materialized in the way these narratives anticipated: instead, the triumphant march forward was interrupted by a series of atrocities, culminating in a century that some observers (e.g., Hobsbawm 1994) have characterized as unprecedented in its brutality. And because these violent interruptions cannot be assimilated into a narrative that moves inexorably forward, they undermine linear temporality. In doing so, they alter our relationship to the past, to history. No longer is the past strictly a source of glorious triumphs that foreshadow an even more promising future. It is also a source of painful episodes that haunt us in the present—episodes that in some sense *demand* to be reckoned with, interpreted, and understood, even as they resist narrativization.

22.3.2.3 Cultural Trauma

Within this context has also arisen an influential sociological discourse on "cultural trauma." Bringing it into conversation with reflections on regret and temporality can enhance our understanding of the present epoch in productive ways. A trauma is precisely an interruption to progressive temporality (Olick 2007b:164): an event is so painful that it cannot be absorbed into existing narratives—and so it does not pass away, but instead returns, as if of its own accord, against the sufferer's will (Caruth 1995:4–5). While the psychological discourse on trauma refers to pasts that cannot be assimilated at the individual level—ultimately codified in the diagnosis of "post-traumatic stress disorder" (Hacking 1995; Young 1995)—the more recent sociological theorizing on cultural trauma refers to a breach in a *collective* narrative.[10] Cultural traumas—Jeffrey Alexander, Ron Eyerman, and their colleagues argue—are events that create "wounds to social identity" (Alexander 2012:2), setting off "a deep-going public discourse" that questions and interrogates the very foundations of that identity (Eyerman 2011:xv). Ultimately, cultural traumas—like psychological traumas—are understood as leaving indelible wounds, "marking [a collectivity's] memories forever and changing [its] future identity in fundamental and irrevocable ways" (Alexander 2004:1).

Countering "naturalistic" perspectives, Alexander and his colleagues emphasize that cultural trauma inheres not in an event itself, but in its interpretation: "cultural traumas are for the most part historically made, not born" (Smelser 2004:37), and they come into being when "[c]ollective actors 'decide' to represent social pain as a fundamental threat to their sense of who

[9]Weber ([1919] 1946), of course, contrasted this ethic of responsibility with an *ethic of conviction*, which pursues "ultimate ends"—general ethical principles—without regard for their consequences.

[10]The psychological understanding of trauma is itself a metaphor. Originally, trauma referred to a physical wound, and indeed the term still carries that meaning—as in the "trauma center" of a hospital. The concept of cultural trauma, then, takes the metaphor one step further.

they are, where they came from, and where they want to go" (Alexander 2004:10). It is *carrier groups*—in Weber's sense of the term—who construct events as traumatic, as indelible wounds to a social group or body politic. Indeed, this constructivist approach to cultural trauma has been applied across a vast—and ever-growing—array of cases, from slavery in the United States (Eyerman 2001), to World War II in Germany (Giesen 2004) and Japan (Hashimoto 2015), to political assassinations in the United States, Sweden, and the Netherlands (Eyerman 2011).

Contemporary approaches to cultural trauma explicitly revive the link between emotions and memory evident in Durkheim's foundational treatments of commemoration and piacular rites. As Hiro Saito (2006:358) points out, cultural trauma "has an emotional and therefore psychological dimension, which cannot be reduced to discursive construction." In Japan, he argues, the atomic bombing of Hiroshima came to be understood as a cultural trauma only after the fallout from a hydrogen bomb test near Bikini Atoll struck a Japanese fishing boat in March 1954. Almost a decade after Hiroshima, the overarching "structure of feeling" (see Williams 1977) transformed from "pity" for "distant suffering" to "sympathy" and an understanding of the Japanese nation as "a community of wounded actors" (Saito 2006:354) affected profoundly by the suffering in Hiroshima. More recently, Seth Abrutyn (2015) has both expanded the historical reach of the trauma concept and further illuminated the intricate relationship between memory and emotion. Collective traumas, he suggests, were "the core framework and motivating force undergirding the evolution of Israelite religion and contemporary Judaism's adaptive success" (ibid.:131). Interpreting communal suffering through a pollution narrative (see Alexander 1988), elite entrepreneurs "impos[ed] daily, weekly and annual purification rituals" that served as a "true shield against the outside," resulting in "a strongly solidarious community, anchored socioemotionally and morally to a multilayered center that had to be protected" (Abrutyn 2015:125). Collective suffering thus generated rituals that sustained—and in some cases continue to sustain—memory and community.[11]

Though the trauma metaphor has been fruitfully extended beyond the modern epoch as an analytic tool, it is also worth noting that the language of trauma itself emerged and gained traction under the peculiar set of social and cultural conditions outlined above. And trauma's emergence as a rubric for coming to terms with *modern* suffering, whether individual or collective, is no accident. To be traumatized, again, is to be unable to move forward in a narrative, to be caught unwillingly in a past that will not pass away. The experience of trauma, then, interrupts the modern sense of time as linear, the assumption that one will move continuously ahead (Olick 2007b). Cultural trauma thus not only involves the stories that carrier groups actively *construct* out of the troublesome past, but also the force of "what the past does *to* us" (Olick 2007a:21)—an interplay between an event (that disrupts or undermines a received narrative) and a broad historical context (that arguably makes the very experience of trauma possible, or at least increasingly probable). Indeed, the concept of trauma resonates powerfully in the present moment; it is not only a psychiatric diagnosis and a cultural metaphor, but it has also "infiltrate[d] social discourse" (Fassin and Rechtman 2009:22) and become a pervasive frame for characterizing the confrontation with suffering (see also Davis 2005; Illouz 2007). Transformations in the experience of time heighten the potential for trauma, and help to explain why it has become such a hallmark feature of the present age.

[11]As the anthropologist Paul Connerton (1989:102)—a seminal figure in the interdisciplinary field of memory studies—underscores, collective memory is not only *inscribed* through language, but also *incorporated* in the body: "the past," he writes, "can be kept in mind by habitual memory sedimented in the body." Expanding on this argument, Rafael Narvaez (2006:52, 56, 57) points out that the past is carried forward through "practices that work 'below' and beyond consciousness"—an idea with roots in Durkheim's accounts of "effervescent—thus highly bodily—collective rituals" that lead to "the social construction of affect and the affective construction of social meaning."

22.3.2.4 Cosmopolitan Memory

As I alluded above, the melancholic turn in memory is bound up with the decline of the nation-state as a source of identity and orientation in a globalizing world (Nora 1989): the traumas and atrocities that interrupt progressive narratives also undermine the state's legitimacy. In this milieu, sociologists have theorized the emergence of new, more encompassing identities and forms of solidarity—as well as new *transcultural* or *cosmopolitan* memories that support them.

Representations of the Holocaust, Levy and Natan Sznaider (2006) theorize, have been at the foundation of these new memoryscapes. Initially met with silence, then subsequently brought to public awareness and transformed into the subject of national memories, the Holocaust—they suggest—has become a globally recognizable representation of evil (see also Alexander 2002). Because its meaning is so widely shared, memories of the Holocaust have underwritten the emergence of a pervasive concern for "distant suffering" (Boltanski 1999), fostering social action on behalf of victims across the globe. After the fall of the Berlin Wall—and in the midst of what Ulrich Beck terms Second Modernity, modernity that "has become reflexive, directed at itself"—the Holocaust has become a source of "moral certainty," specifically by providing the foundation for "moral consensus about human rights," making this issue "politically relevant to all who share this new form of memory" (Levy and Sznaider 2006:6, 18, 20, 132; see also Beck 2000). According to this view, then, even in a time of deep uncertainty and 'liquidity' (Bauman 2000)—following the demise of modernity's master narrative—collective memory, albeit in new forms, provides an anchor, a source of connective tissue and social solidarity that transcends enormous geographic distance.

22.4 Memory and Culture, Memory as Culture

The assumption that memory is a special interest—a framework useful for a small cadre of scholars inclined toward both culture and history, or, even more limiting, a perspective pertinent only to those who study commemorations and memorials—has also led sociologists to underestimate its relevance for addressing core theoretical questions in the sociology of culture. Re-emerging in a robust way around the same time as "collective memory," culture is now central to the broad disciplinary conversation. The culture section is one of the largest in the American Sociological Association, and sociologists have developed a cultural perspective on a dizzying array of substantive issues (see Chap. 6). Even more important in the present context, parsing the relationships between "material" and "ideal," "culture" and "structure," is one of the core questions reverberating through the canon of sociological theory.

Despite the widespread interest in culture—or perhaps because of it—sociologists still struggle to define the very concept that motivates their work. Is culture largely discursive and public, the stuff of collective representations and shared symbolism (e.g., Alexander and Smith 1993; Alexander 2003), or is it cognitive and practical, consisting of everyday habits and routines (e.g., Lizardo and Strand 2010)? Is culture largely implicit and even inarticulable—the things we "just know" (e.g., Lizardo and Strand 2010; Martin 2010)—or is it the accounts, justifications, and repertoires we deploy consciously as we make decisions, define and navigate social situations, and draw social boundaries (Swidler 1986; Lamont 1992; Boltanski and Thévenot 1999)? Is culture the process of arranging and re-arranging fundamental and unchanging structures—binary codes, generic forms, narrative templates (e.g., Alexander and Smith 1993; Alexander 2010)—or are symbols, genres, and narratives themselves always in motion (Townsley 2001; Sewell 2005; Olick 2007b, forthcoming)? The sociology of memory cannot resolve *all* of these questions. But it *can* shed new light on the question of what culture is, how it is comes into being, and how it helps to shape and direct social and political processes, playing the constitutive—even causal—role in social life that leading culture scholars (e.g., Alexander 2003, 2010; Wagner-Pacifici 2010; Reed 2011) have claimed for it.

22.4.1 Cultural Claims in the Sociology of Memory

Schwartz's body of work has been duly recognized for bringing memory back into sociological discourse. What is less commonly noticed, however, is that these works address not only memory specifically, but also culture writ large, and the crucial place of memory within it. In his series of books and articles on Abraham Lincoln, Schwartz (1996b, 2000, 2008) develops the twin concepts of "keying" and "framing" to capture how memory serves as both a model *of* society—a "mirror" of what we *are*—and a model *for* society—a "lamp" for what we might become. For Schwartz (2000:252), memory's primary function is "semiotic"—it illuminates the values that undergird and motivate collective action. It does so by linking past with present—not merely through analogies, but through the more profound mechanism of *keying*, which places the present "against the background of an appropriate symbol" from the past (Schwartz 2008:xi) that then provides a *frame* "for the perception and comprehension of current events" (Schwartz 1996b:911). For instance, in the U.S., the suffering and bloodshed of World War II took on shape and meaning with reference to Abraham Lincoln and the Civil War. In the 1940s, it was memory that provided orientation and hope. Following Clifford Geertz (1973), then, memory is a *cultural system*, "an organization of symbolic patterns on which people rely to make sense of their experience" (Schwartz 1996b:909).

Schwartz (ibid.:924–925) suggests that, in the present post-heroic age, memory's power as a cultural system is in decline: "Americans," he observes, "now look less often to the past as a model *for* the present than ever before," recognizing "that their nation's history can be seen as a source of shame rather than direction and inspiration." Yet we should not be too quick to dismiss the power of memory as a cultural system even when it does not serve as an *explicit* source of inspiration. As Olick's (1999b, 2005, forthcoming) work on postwar German memory demonstrates, the past powerfully structures what can be said in the present as public officials grapple with the toxic legacies of the Nazi past. This is not necessarily because speakers are explicitly referencing earlier commemorations, as were those who held up Abraham Lincoln as a symbol during World War II. But because their responses to enduring commemorative dilemmas are moments in an ongoing dialogue, they are part of *memory genres* that inevitably contain residues of earlier claims and frames. Here, memory is not exactly a lamp, but it nevertheless remains a powerful cultural structure, often operating beneath the level of conscious awareness.

Indeed, it is perhaps *because* memory's influence is often so subtle that it has largely been omitted from our broad theories of culture. Certainly, even in a post-heroic age, there are still moments when the past once again becomes a lamp, a source of guidance and a wellspring for social solidarity. In the days following September 11, 2001, for instance, memories of Abraham Lincoln once again provided consolation, orientation, and hope—and memories of Franklin Roosevelt, Winston Churchill, and World War II more generally took their place alongside these references to Lincoln (Simko 2015). Even when the past is not overtly on the agenda, however, the symbolic materials we deploy to come to terms with the unfolding present are "historical accretions," containing "memory traces" of what came before (Olick 1999b:383). In this sense, "[a]ll memory is cultural, and all culture is historical" (Olick 2008:16).

22.4.2 Cultural Memory

Capturing the fullest implications of this perspective requires a brief detour outside sociology, though we remain in direct dialogue with the sociological tradition. Indeed, this detour brings us back full circle to Halbwachs. We turn, specifically, to the German Egyptologist Jan Assmann, whose critical reading of Halbwachs led him to coin the term *cultural memory*.[12] Assmann (2006:8) praises Halbwachs for over-

[12] See also Olick's (2007a, 2008) discussions of Assmann and cultural memory, to which I am indebted here.

coming solipsism, for leading the study of memory outside "the internal world of the subject." Yet he argues that Halbwachs failed to elaborate the most radical implications of the collective memory concept: much as he recognized "the social and emotional preconditions of memory," Assmann (ibid.) claims that Halbwachs "refused to go so far as to accept the need for symbolic and cultural frameworks."[13] Halbwachs, that is, focused on what Assmann (ibid.) terms *communicative* memory—"lived, embodied memory" that spans about three generations. Yet Assmann (1995:132) points out that collective memory is transmitted more subtly, and over much longer timespans, through "that body of reusable texts, images, and rituals specific to each society in each epoch, whose 'cultivation' serves to stabilize and convey that society's self-image." This is what Assmann refers to as *cultural memory*—the signs and symbols inherited from the past to which we turn, often implicitly and unthinkingly, for meaning in the present. The signs and symbols that comprise cultural memory inevitably contain residues from the past—including the very distant and largely forgotten past that is no longer part of "communicative" memory. Such residues of the past influence the present even if those who deploy these symbols are unaware of their trajectories.

Building on Assmann, Astrid Erll (2009) develops a pair of sensitizing concepts that help to capture the dynamics of cultural memory: remediation and premediation. First, *remediation* captures how the past is re-presented, and thus in some sense reconstructed or reinterpreted, in new, and sometimes quite disparate, contexts. Remediation is perhaps the dominant subject in the sociology of memory: how is the past refashioned in the present, how much can it be transformed to serve present purposes, and how do we adapt when the past is especially problematic, conflictual, or burdensome? Second, *premediation* captures how symbolic frameworks inherited from the past impinge upon our understanding of the present even as it unfolds. "[E]xistent media which circulate in a given society," Erll (ibid.:111) explains, "provide schemata for new experience and its representation," giving shape and meaning to fresh events from the first. In many ways, this conceptual pair resembles Schwartz's keying and framing: when the present is linked to the past, the past provides orientation, a framework through which new experience is filtered and understood. Yet Erll (ibid.:114) stresses the implicit and even unconscious dimensions of this process: her discussion of premediation underscores the ways in which the past infuses and structures the present "inconspicuously," as we turn reflexively to familiar frames to impose order upon fresh events.

So, we may indeed turn less and less to heroic ideals as the idols of the past—the Washingtons and Lincolns—diminish in prestige. But the past is no less influential in the present, because cultural memory—that storehouse of symbols—confers the only tools we possess in making sense of our world, even as we transform these tools in turn. As Philip Abrams (1982:8) put it, "the past is not just the womb of the present but the only raw material out of which the present can be constructed." Again, culture is laden with memory, and memory is the lifeblood of culture (see also Olick 2008:16). And theories of cultural memory offer analytic tools for capturing the construction of the present *out of* the past.

To illustrate, consider one brief anecdote from my own work. When I began a project on the political discourse surrounding the events of September 11, 2001, in the United States, I was struck by the presence of the past: references to Lincoln and Roosevelt, Valley Forge and Gettysburg, Pearl Harbor and Iwo Jima—both implicit and explicit—provided consolation and meaning in the midst of collective suffering and uncertainty about the future. But one reference to the past was more subtle and perplexing—namely, the term "ground zero," which was quickly adopted as the nomenclature for the site

[13]As Olick and his colleagues point out, Assmann's interpretation understates the extent to which Halbwachs in fact acknowledged the power of collective representations in his discussion of *historical memory*, which he understood as "residues of events by virtue of which groups claim a continuous identity through time," even if none of their members have autobiographical memories of these events (Olick et al. 2011:19).

in lower Manhattan where the Twin Towers once stood. Today, this usage is so widely accepted that it is often rendered as a proper noun: "Ground Zero." Politicians, journalists, and even scholars have readily adopted it. What perplexed me was that the term "ground zero" originally referred to the site directly beneath a detonated atomic bomb. It was initially used in the U.S. Strategic Bombing Survey, commissioned by the Truman administration to assess the impact of the atomic weapons that U.S. forces dropped on the Japanese cities of Hiroshima and Nagasaki in 1945. How, then, did this term that originated to describe an act of American violence come to stand for American victimhood, and indeed even American nationhood?

Theories of cultural memory provide a language for understanding the connection between these two disparate events. In some subtle and implicit way, Hiroshima and Nagasaki *premediated* the events of September 11, 2001: they provided one of the key symbols through which this disorienting series of occurrences was understood from the first. But why was this symbolism so readily available? In fact, there is a long tradition of envisioning an "American ground zero" that emerged quite rapidly in the months and years following the August 1945 bombings. The U.S. Strategic Bombing survey itself contemplated this possibility, calculating the damage that an atomic explosion would cause in American city centers, including Washington, D.C. and New York. What would an American "ground zero" look like? Subsequently, popular magazines and national newspapers published detailed descriptions of the suffering and devastation an atomic attack on American soil could cause, often accompanied by vivid visual images that depicted these imagined attacks. Again, these projections frequently focused on the very spaces where the violence of September 11, 2001, unfolded, selecting landmarks in Manhattan and Washington as the epicenter—"ground zero."

At a theoretical level, the transformation of ground zero reveals that culture is indeed memory-laden. Memory, therefore, is not only the stuff of commemorations and memorials. It is not a special interest but instead the central constituent of the tools and tropes, repertoires and schemas, signs and symbols that cultural analysts identify. It influences our interpretation of new events even when we do not turn to it explicitly, because it infuses the only frameworks available to us to find orientation, to gain a foothold in the face of the unfolding present. And the specific case of "ground zero" illuminates the payoff of this historical understanding of culture—the view of symbols as containing residues of the past—in a particularly powerful way. The connection between Hiroshima and Nagasaki in 1945 and lower Manhattan in 2001 is rarely recognized and articulated, let alone discussed or grappled with explicitly. But what would it mean for Americans to understand that the ground zero designation—which now evokes sorrow, respect, and even reverence—is a borrowed term? And even more, that it originally referred to a site where *American* forces unleashed an unprecedented act of violence, ushering in a new era in global politics? Understanding the power of the past—especially when it remains implicit, even invisible to most observers—is a crucial part of grasping the constitutive force of culture. As meanings exert their influence in larger social and political processes, they carry with them the weight of the past, residues that ideas of "collective" and "cultural" memory enable us to identify and illuminate in new ways.

22.5 The Future Prospects of Collective Memory

Despite the revitalization of collective memory in sociology, much of the discipline has nevertheless forgotten to remember. Not only have we failed to integrate collective memory into our theories, however. We have also in many ways forgotten the guiding questions that captivated the classical figures whose meditations on the modern gave birth to the tradition we have inherited. Yet the answers to these questions have been magnificently generative. Classical theorists' efforts to come to terms with industrial modernity, to comprehend a new epoch even as it came into being, bequeathed to us concepts and frames—from anomie and alienation, to rationalization and legitimation, to differentiation and disenchantment—that continue to illuminate and enlighten, that guide us as we work make sense of our own milieu. And thus it seems that reconnecting with these questions is an especially worthwhile endeavor for contemporary theorists.

The vibrant conversations taking place around collective memory provide a powerful framework for rejuvenating this tradition of theorizing. For the core questions of collective memory aim precisely to understand the powerful social transformations that shape the present epoch—transformations that once again alter the foundations for collective life, raising questions about the future prospects for solidarity, community, and the pursuit of unifying aspirations. Why do public debates so frequently hinge on the legacies of the past rather than the possibilities and promises of the future? Is it possible to maintain compelling collective identities after the demise of modern metanarratives and the progressive temporality that animated them? What moral, cultural, and political ties will bind us together in our increasingly interconnected global society? There are certainly many narratives that can be told about the emergence of the sociological tradition, but as we survey the landscape of contemporary theory, it seems especially important to recall the pressing impulse to theorize the nature of modernity, and to reconnect with that impulse as we formulate conceptual frameworks for understanding our own time.

Collective memory is not only a means for reviving enduring questions and addressing them in new ways, however. It also cuts to the core of lively contemporary debates concerning the meaning of "culture" and its significance in social life. For culture is, after all, composed of frameworks inherited from the past—frameworks that bear the marks of their histories even as they guide our understanding of the unfolding present, the fresh realities we face with each new day. While Durkheim's brief reflections on commemoration suggested long ago that memory—the interplay between past and present—is at the very core of the social, there remains much work to be done to understand how the past reverberates, how it shapes the tools and tropes available to us for making sense of our world, how it implicitly infuses every act of meaning. Even if the world we inhabit is profoundly different from the one that Durkheim observed, memory is no less critical in our ongoing effort to understand it.

References

Abrams, P. (1982). *Historical sociology*. Ithaca: Cornell University Press.

Abrutyn, S. (2015). Pollution–purification rituals, cultural memory and the evolution of religion: How collective trauma shaped ancient Israel. *American Journal of Cultural Sociology, 3*, 123–155.

Alexander, J. C. (1988). Culture and political crisis: 'Watergate' and Durkheimian sociology. In J. C. Alexander (Ed.), *Durkheimian sociology: Cultural studies* (pp. 187–224). New York: Cambridge University Press.

Alexander, J. C. (2002). On the social construction of moral universals: The 'Holocaust' from war crime to trauma drama. *European Journal of Social Theory, 5*, 5–85.

Alexander, J. C. (2003). *The meanings of social life: A cultural sociology*. New York: Oxford University Press.

Alexander, J. C. (2004). Toward a theory of cultural trauma. In J. C. Alexander, R. Eyerman, B. Giesen, N. J. Smelser, & P. Sztompka, *Cultural trauma and collective identity* (pp. 1–30). Berkeley: University of California Press.

Alexander, J. C. (2010). *The performance of politics: Obama's victory and the democratic struggle for power*. New York: Oxford University Press.

Alexander, J. C. (2012). *Trauma: A social theory*. Malden: Polity Press.

Alexander, J. C., & Smith, P. (1993). The discourse of American civil society: A new proposal for cultural studies. *Theory and Society, 22*, 151–207.

Anderson, B. (1991). *Imagined communities: Reflections on the origin and spread of nationalism*, revised edition. New York: Verso.

Assmann, J. (1995). Collective memory and cultural identity (trans: Zaplicka, J.). *New German Critique, 65*, 125–133.

Assmann, J. (2006). *Religion and cultural memory: Ten studies* (trans: Livingstone, R.). Stanford: Stanford University Press.

Bauman, Z. (2000). *Liquid modernity*. Malden: Blackwell.

Beck, U. (1992). *Risk society: Towards a new modernity* (trans: Ritter, M.). Newbury Park: Sage Publications.

Beck, U. (2000). The cosmopolitan perspective: The sociology of the second age of modernity. *British Journal of Sociology, 51*, 79–105.

Bellah, R. N., Madsen, R., Sullivan, W. M., Swidler, A., & Tipton, S. M. ([1985] 1996). *Habits of the heart: Individualism and commitment in American life*, updated edition. Berkeley: University of California Press.

Boltanski, L. (1999). *Distant suffering: Morality, media and politics* (trans: Burchell, G.). New York: Cambridge University Press.

Boltanski, L., & Thévenot, L. (1999). The sociology of critical capacity. *European Journal of Social Theory, 2*, 359–377.

Caruth, C. (Ed.). (1995). *Trauma: Explorations in memory*. Baltimore: Johns Hopkins University Press.

Celermajer, D. (2009). *The sins of the nation and the ritual of apologies*. New York: Cambridge University Press.

Cohen, S. (2001). *States of denial: Knowing about atrocities and suffering*. Malden: Blackwell.

Connerton, P. (1989). *How societies remember*. New York: Cambridge University Press.

Conway, B. (2010a). *Commemoration and Bloody Sunday: Pathways of memory*. New York: Palgrave Macmillan.

Conway, B. (2010b). New directions in the sociology of collective memory and commemoration. *Sociology Compass, 4*, 442–453.

Davis, J. E. (2005). *Accounts of innocence: Sexual abuse, trauma, and the self*. Chicago: University of Chicago Press.

DeGloma, T. (2010). Awakenings: Autobiography, memory, and the social logic of personal discovery. *Sociological Forum, 25*, 519–540.

DeGloma, T. (2015). The strategies of mnemonic battle: On the alignment of autobiographical and collective memories in conflicts over the past. *American Journal of Cultural Sociology, 3*, 156–190.

Ducharme, L. J., & Fine, G. A. (1995). The construction of nonpersonhood and demonization: Commemorating the traitorous reputation of Benedict Arnold. *Social Forces, 73*, 1309–1331.

Durkheim, É. ([1893] 1984). *The division of labor in society* (trans: Halls, W. D.). New York: Free Press.

Durkheim, É. ([1912] 1915). *The elementary forms of religious life* (trans: Swain, J. W.). London: George Allen and Unwin.

Elias, N. ([1939] 2000). *The civilizing process: Sociogenetic and psychogenetic investigations*, revised edition (trans: Jephcott, E.). Malden: Blackwell.

Erll, A. (2009). Remembering across time, space, and cultures: Premediation, remediation and the 'Indian Mutiny'. In A. Erll & A. Rigney (Eds.), *Mediation, remediation, and the dynamics of cultural memory* (pp. 109–138). Berlin: Walter de Gruyter.

Erll, A. (2011). *Memory in culture* (trans: Young, S. B.). New York: Palgrave Macmillan.

Erll, A., & Nünning, A. (Eds.). (2008). *Cultural memory studies: An international and interdisciplinary handbook*. Berlin: Walter de Gruyter.

Eyerman, R. (2001). *Cultural trauma: Slavery and the formation of African American identity*. New York: Cambridge University Press.

Eyerman, R. (2011). *The cultural sociology of political assassination: From MLK and RFK to Fortuyn and Van Gogh*. New York: Palgrave Macmillan.

Fassin, D., & Rechtman, R. (2009). *The empire of trauma: An inquiry into the condition of victimhood* (trans: Gomme, R.). Princeton: Princeton University Press.

Fine, G. A. (1996). Reputational entrepreneurs and the memory of incompetence: Melting supporters, partisan warriors, and images of President Harding. *American Journal of Sociology, 101*, 1159–1193.

Geertz, C. (1973). *The interpretation of cultures: Selected essays*. New York: Basic Books.

Giddens, A. (1990). *The consequences of modernity*. Stanford: Stanford University Press.

Giesen, B. (2004). *Triumph and trauma*. Boulder: Paradigm Publishers.

Habermas, J. (1996). *Between facts and norms: Contributions to a discourse theory of law and democracy* (trans: Rehg, W.). Cambridge, MA: MIT Press.

Hacking, I. (1995). *Rewriting the soul: Multiple personality and the sciences of memory*. Princeton: Princeton University Press.

Halbwachs, M. ([1925] 1992). *The social frameworks of memory*. In L. Coser (Ed.), *On collective memory* (pp. 37–189). Chicago: University of Chicago Press.

Halbwachs, M. ([1950] 2011). From "*The collective memory*" (excerpt). In J. K. Olick, V. Vinitzky-Seroussi, & D. Levy (Eds.), *The collective memory reader* (pp. 139–149). New York: Oxford University Press.

Hashimoto, A. (2015). *The long defeat: Cultural trauma, memory, and identity in Japan*. New York: Oxford University Press.

Hobsbawm, E. (1994). *The age of extremes: A history of the world, 1914–1991*. New York: Pantheon Books.

Hobsbawm, E., & Ranger, T. (Eds.). (1983). *The invention of tradition*. New York: Cambridge University Press.

Hochschild, A. R. (1979). Emotion work, feeling rules, and social structure. *American Journal of Sociology, 85*, 551–575.

Illouz, E. (2007). *Cold intimacies: The making of emotional capitalism*. Malden: Polity Press.

Jansen, R. S. (2007). Resurrection and appropriation: Reputational trajectories, memory work, and the political use of historical figures. *American Journal of Sociology, 112*, 953–1007.

Jelin, E. (2003). *State repression and the labors of memory* (trans: Rein, J. & Godoy-Anativia, M.). Minneapolis: University of Minnesota Press.

Koselleck, R. (1985). *Futures past: On the semantics of historical time* (trans: Tribe, K.). Cambridge, MA: MIT Press.

Lamont, M. (1992). *Money, morals, and manners: The culture of the French and American upper-middle class*. Chicago: University of Chicago Press.

Levy, D., & Sznaider, N. (2006). *The holocaust and memory in the global age* (trans: Oksiloff, A.). Philadelphia: Temple University Press.

Lizardo, O., & Strand, M. (2010). Skills, toolkits, contexts and institutions: Clarifying the relationship between different approaches to cognition in cultural sociology. *Poetics, 38*, 205–228.

Martin, J. L. (2010). Life's a beach but you're an ant, and other unwelcome news for the sociology of culture. *Poetics, 38*, 229–244.

Mead, G. H. (1932). *The philosophy of the present*. LaSalle: Open Court Press.

Misztal, B. A. (2003). *Theories of social remembering*. Philadelphia: Open University Press.

Narvaez, R. F. (2006). Embodiment, collective memory and time. *Body & Society, 12*, 51–73.

Niethammer, L. (1992). *Posthistoire: Has history come to an end?* (trans: Camiller, P.). London: Verso.

Nora, P. (1989). Between memory and history: *Les lieux de mémoire*. *Representations, 26*, 7–24.

Olick, J. K. (1999a). Collective memory: The two cultures. *Sociological Theory, 17*, 333–348.

Olick, J. K. (1999b). Genre memories and memory genres: A dialogical analysis of May 8, 1945 commemorations in the Federal Republic of Germany. *American Sociological Review, 64*, 381–402.

Olick, J. K. (2005). *In the house of the hangman: The agonies of German defeat, 1943–1949*. Chicago: University of Chicago Press.

Olick, J. K. (2007a). From usable pasts to the return of the repressed. *Hedgehog Review, 9*, 19–31.

Olick, J. K. (2007b). *The politics of regret: On collective memory and historical responsibility*. New York: Routledge.

Olick, J. K. (2008). The ciphered transits of collective memory: Neo-Freudian impressions. *Social Research, 75*, 1–22.

Olick, J. K. (Forthcoming). *The sins of the fathers: Germany, memory, method*. Chicago: University of Chicago Press.

Olick, J. K., & Levy, D. (1997). Collective memory and cultural constraint: Holocaust myth and rationality in German politics. *American Sociological Review, 62*, 921–936.

Olick, J. K., & Robbins, J. (1998). Social memory studies: From 'collective memory' to the historical sociology of mnemonic practices. *Annual Review of Sociology, 24*, 105–140.

Olick, J. K., Vinitzky-Seroussi, V., & Levy, D. (Eds.). (2011). *The collective memory reader*. New York: Oxford University Press.

Posel, D. (2008). History as confession: The case of the South African truth and reconciliation commission. *Public Culture, 20*, 119–141.

Reed, I. A. (2011). *Interpretation and social knowledge: On the use of theory in the human sciences*. Chicago: University of Chicago Press.

Saito, H. (2006). Reiterated commemoration: Hiroshima as national trauma. *Sociological Theory, 24*, 353–376.

Schudson, M. (1989). The past in the present versus the present in the past. *Communication, 11*, 105–113.

Schudson, M. (1992). *Watergate in American memory: How we remember, forget, and reconstruct the past*. New York: Basic Books.

Schuman, H., & Corning, A. (2011). The roots of collective memory: Public knowledge of Sally Hemings and Thomas Jefferson. *Memory Studies, 4*, 134–153.

Schuman, H., Schwartz, B., & d'Arcy, H. (2005). Elite revisionists and popular beliefs: Christopher Columbus, hero or villain? *Public Opinion Quarterly, 69*, 2–29.

Schwartz, B. (1982). The social context of commemoration: A study in collective memory. *Social Forces, 61*, 374–402.

Schwartz, B. (1991a). Mourning and the making of a sacred symbol: Durkheim and the Lincoln assassination. *Social Forces, 70*, 343–364.

Schwartz, B. (1991b). Social change and collective memory: The democratization of George Washington. *American Sociological Review, 56*, 221–236.

Schwartz, B. (1996a). Introduction: The expanding past. *Qualitative Sociology, 19*, 275–282.

Schwartz, B. (1996b). Memory as a cultural system: Abraham Lincoln in World War II. *American Sociological Review, 61*, 908–927.

Schwartz, B. (1998). Postmodernity and historical reputation: Abraham Lincoln in late twentieth-century American memory. *Social Forces, 77*, 63–103.

Schwartz, B. (2000). *Abraham Lincoln and the forge of national memory*. Chicago: University of Chicago Press.

Schwartz, B. (2008). *Abraham Lincoln in the post-heroic era: History and memory in late twentieth-century America*. Chicago: University of Chicago Press.

Schwartz, B., & Heinrich, H.-A. (2004). Shadings of regret: America and Germany. In K. R. Phillips (Ed.), *Framing public memory* (pp. 115–144). Tuscaloosa: University of Alabama Press.

Schwartz, B., & Schuman, H. (2005). History, commemoration, and belief: Abraham Lincoln in American memory, 1945–2001. *American Sociological Review, 70*, 183–203.

Schwartz, B., Zerubavel, Y., & Barnett, B. M. (1986). The recovery of Masada: A study in collective memory. *The Sociological Quarterly, 27*, 147–164.

Sewell, W. H., Jr. (2005). *Logics of history: Social theory and social transformation*. Chicago: University of Chicago Press.

Shils, E. (1981). *Tradition*. Chicago: University of Chicago Press.

Simko, C. (2012). Rhetorics of suffering: September 11 commemorations as theodicy. *American Sociological Review, 77*, 880–902.

Simko, C. (2015). *The politics of consolation: Memory and the meaning of September 11*. New York: Oxford University Press.

Smelser, N. (2004). Psychological and cultural trauma. In J. C. Alexander, R. Eyerman, B. Giesen, N. J. Smelser, & P. Sztompka, *Cultural trauma and collective identity* (pp. 31–59). Berkeley: University of California Press.

Spillman, L. (1997). *Nation and commemoration: Creating national identities in the United States and Australia*. New York: Cambridge University Press.

Steidl, C. R. (2013). Remembering May 4, 1970: Integrating the commemorative field at Kent State. *American Sociological Review, 78*, 749–772.

Swidler, A. (1986). Culture in action: Symbols and strategies. *American Sociological Review, 51*, 273–286.

Teeger, C. (2014). Collective memory and collective fear: How South Africans use the past to explain crime. *Qualitative Sociology, 37*, 69–92.

Teeger, C., & Vinitzky-Seroussi, V. (2007). Controlling for consensus: Commemorating apartheid in South Africa. *Symbolic Interaction, 30*, 57–78.

Torpey, J. (2006). *Making whole what has been smashed: On reparations politics*. Cambridge, MA: Harvard University Press.

Townsley, E. (2001). 'The sixties' trope. *Theory, Culture & Society, 18*, 99–123.

Vinitzky-Seroussi, V. (1998). *After pomp and circumstance: High school reunion as an autobiographical occasion*. Chicago: University of Chicago Press.

Vinitzky-Seroussi, V. (2002). Commemorating a difficult past: Yitzhak Rabin's memorials. *American Sociological Review, 67*, 30–51.

Vinitzky-Seroussi, V., & Teeger, C. (2010). Unpacking the unspoken: Silence in collective memory and forgetting. *Social Forces, 88*, 1103–1122.

Wagner-Pacifici, R. (2010). Theorizing the restlessness of events. *American Journal of Sociology, 115*, 1351–1386.

Wagner-Pacifici, R., & Schwartz, B. (1991). The Vietnam Veterans Memorial: Commemorating a difficult past. *American Journal of Sociology, 97*, 376–420.

Warner, W. L. (1959). *The living and the dead: A study of the symbolic life of Americans*. New Haven: Yale University Press.

Weber, M. ([1919] 1946). *Politics as a vocation* (H. H. Gerth & C. W. Mills, Eds., pp. 77–128). New York: Oxford University Press.

Williams, R. (1977). *Marxism and literature*. Oxford: Oxford University Press.

Young, A. (1995). *The harmony of illusions: Inventing post-traumatic stress disorder*. Princeton: Princeton University Press.

Zerubavel, E. (2006). *The elephant in the room: Silence and denial in everyday life*. New York: Oxford University Press.

Zolberg, V. (1998). Contested remembrance: The Hiroshima exhibit controversy. *Theory and Society, 27*, 565–590.

Intersectionality 23

Zandria Felice Robinson

23.1 Introduction

The term "intersectionality," the epistemological, theoretical, and methodological ground it covers, and the lived experiences it captures were once very much on the conceptual margins of the discipline of sociology proper. Although it had been a central feature of black women's intellectual work in history (Barnett 1993; Davis 1998), fiction, women's and gender studies (Springer 2002; Andersen 2005; Johnson 2005; Moore 2006), and critical legal studies (Roberts 1997), particularly since the 1980s, sociology was slower to canonically adopt the theory than other fields of inquiry. Yet, over the course of the 25 years from the coining of the term to its mainstreaming as a household theory, intersectionality has moved in, through, and beyond sociology while remaining central to some of the field's most pressing questions about the workings of power. Building on the intellectual labor of generations of black women before them, black feminist sociologists positioned intersectionality in the center of stratification research in the field, which subsequently began to parse the theoretical purchase and empirical conundrums of the theory (Collins 1989, 1990; King 1988). In concert with the emergence of social media, intersectionality moved definitively outside of the academy as black women social media users refined and expanded the theory's emphasis and critiqued mainstream feminism's racial blindspots (Jarmon 2013). By 2015, *The Washington Post* had published a symposium on the term and the theory, reflecting and signaling its mainstream import and including an essay by critical legal scholar Kimberlé Crenshaw, who coined the term in 1989.

Across the social sciences, the term and the multilayered practices it constitutes have caused theoretical, methodological, and empirical conundrums, which black feminist scholar Patricia Hill Collins has called intersectionality's "definitional dilemma" (Collins 2015; Cho et al. 2013; MacKinnon 2013; Choo and Ferree 2010; McCall 2005). Certainly, intersectionality has been adapted by several disciplines, including psychology, political science, and anthropology, towards disciplinary-specific ends. Yet, beyond its current and varied disciplinary uses, intersectionality's enduring dilemma is one best articulated through an intellectual history of intersectionality as an idea. Specifically, attention to the tension between its origins in black women's theorizations of their experiences and social structures and its current use as shorthand for co-occurring and intersecting disadvantaged positions reveals two somewhat divergent, and in some cases contradictory, paths for the theory. This chapter attends to the black feminist origins

Z.F. Robinson (✉)
Rhodes College, Memphis, TN, USA
e-mail: robinsonz@rhodes.edu

S. Abrutyn (ed.), *Handbook of Contemporary Sociological Theory*,
Handbooks of Sociology and Social Research, DOI 10.1007/978-3-319-32250-6_23

of intersectionality, highlighting how black women's theory shaped intersectional thought (Smith 1984; hooks [1984] 2000; Guy-Sheftall 1995; Taylor 2001).

At its core, intersectionality is concerned with how multiple systems of oppression—racism, classism, sexism, heterosexism, cissexism, and ableism in particular—simultaneously reinforce and constitute one another to maintain existing stratification hierarchies across categories. Rather than focusing on oppression as an additive phenomenon, e.g., black + woman = more oppressed than white + woman, intersectionality highlights the "multiplicative" effect of interlocking systems of oppression, or the "multiple jeopardy" faced by black women, who, because of the intersections of racism and sexism, are often economically disadvantaged (King 1988; Hancock 2007). In this vein, intersectionality theorists in general reject the notion that race *or* gender *or* class are the primary axis on which inequality is based, thereby diverging from early race men and Marxist theorists, and even from some Marxist feminisms.

From a theoretical perspective, there are three tenets of intersectionality: (1) its analytical critique of labor and capital, as well as other social institutions like family and health, vis-à-vis black women's experiences; (2) its epistemological critique of the positivist claims of social scientific research; (3) and its accounts of resistive praxis through descriptions of black women's everyday organizing and community-based social justice initiatives. Analyses often emerge from black women's critiques of labor and capital, and their place in a system that exploits their physical and reproductive labor to, in effect, enrich the nation and maintain white supremacy (Murray 1970; Davis 1983; Brewer 1993, Jones 1985; Glenn 2009); include critiques of how black women are represented in the media and other sites in the public sphere to delegitimize their claims of and simultaneously justify their oppression (Ladner 1971; Pough 2004); and consider how black women's sexuality is policed in concert with the goals of capital (Collins 2005). Whereas the positivist core of social science, and sociology in particular, essentially dismisses individual or group knowledge claims as disruptive to the integrity of scientific inquiry, intersectionality theorists offer an important and radical rejection of this claim on two fronts—the fallacy and impossibility of objectivity and value-neutrality as well as the idea that a social science must draw on lived experience as empirical evidence that guides question development, theory building, and interpretation. Intersectionality's engagement with epistemology is often conceptualized as a form of identity politics; but for these theorists, identity is an outcome of processes of stratification, rather than a starting point. Standpoint theory, then—which insists that any science or knowledge claim emerges from a particular standpoint, or lived experience, that is often obscured or deemed irrelevant when the knower is white and male (Harding 2003)—works to make visible the producers of knowledge and compels us to consider how their place in the "matrix of domination" affects their scientific inquiries and conclusions.

Intersectionality is the sociological theory that is perhaps the most exemplary of praxis. It is, in fact, through the action of navigating an unequal society that the theory's structure and import become apparent. Thus, this chapter both narrates the theorizing and resistance strategies that constitute the contours of intersectionality and assesses the theory as sociologists have deployed it towards various substantive ends. It traces the history of intersectionality through two parallel and sometimes intersecting histories of the idea—that of black feminist and womanist thinkers and that of sociologists, two usually, but certainly not always, mutually distinct groups. Black feminist organizing and theorizing extended to analyses of labor and capital, as well as other social institutions, like marriage; of the epistemology that undergirded inequality research and movement organizing; and of representations and identities. In sociology, late nineteenth and early twentieth century black sociologists, including Anna Julia Cooper, Ida B. Wells, and W. E. B. Du Bois, laid the groundwork for the theory's sociological importance and offered important contributions to its foundations, although intersectionality would not be canonized in the field until nearly a century later. The chapter then considers intersectionality's quarter century in the discipline of sociology, beginning with the publication of Patricia Hill Collins' *Black Feminist Thought* in 1990, assessing the methodological and theoretical challenges of the theory and the field's transformation of the theory into a scientific enterprise. Finally, this chapter discusses the implications of continued black feminist theorizing that calls for fresh theoretical language with which to describe interlocking systems of oppression for the discipline of sociology.

23.2 Intersectionality, Inequality, and the Black Feminist Tradition

From slavery to the present, the black feminist tradition in the U.S. has concerned itself with highlighting the importance of an intersectional perspective, variously situating intersectionality as a moral claim, then as a claim for political equality, and more recently as an epistemological claim and a claim for inclusion and social justice. Although the tradition is often communicated through the writings of formally educated women, black feminist academics recognize that most black feminist theorizing, and therefore most of the black feminist tradition, occurs outside of the academy in the intellectual culture work of black women comedians, singers, artists, and other kinds of culture workers taking up questions of race, class, gender, and sexuality. At the center of the tradition is a critique of the specific arrangements of inequality that disproportionately affect black women in U.S. society and a call for an epistemic shift in how we conceptualize both race and gender as interlocking oppressions.

23.2.1 Black Women, Enslavement, and Theory

Intersectionality is rooted in theorizations of U.S. nineteenth century enslaved and free women in speeches and writings they generated on abolition, race, and the woman question. Beyond these narratives of women who had more access to the public sphere than most enslaved women, black feminist historians have uncovered the lived experiences of enslaved black women to understand more about these women's everyday lives and how they theorized labor, capital, and resistance in antebellum America (Davis 1983; Hine and Thompson 1999; White 1999). These historians' research demonstrates how the lived experiences of enslaved women gave them a distinct space through which to evaluate and critique the structure and hierarchies of race, gender, and capital as they were being shaped by a shifting slavery context. Enslaved women recognized that they were a source of capital as childbearers, as laborers, and as reproductive laborers in the plantation economy. They also were aware that their status as black and property relegated them to particular kinds of labor that would not have been fitting for a "woman" or a "lady," including fieldwork and cooking (Fox-Genovese 1988). Women and ladies were free, white, and often wealthy and slave holding, circumscribed in a sphere of power and domesticity to which enslaved women did not have access. Further, enslaved women were especially aware of how their status as black women and property rendered them vulnerable to sexual violence that regulated and constrained their economic choices as well as contributed directly to the plantation economy. Using their critical understanding of the intersecting systems of gender and race inequality in the plantation economy, these women developed resistance strategies to protect themselves and undermine the power structure. It is in these women's resistance strategies, in addition to the arguments made by enslaved and formerly enslaved women in slave narratives, that the origins of black feminist theorizing can be found.

The narratives of women who had been enslaved, like Harriet Jacobs' ([1861] 2009) *Incidents in the Life of a Slave Girl*, plainly delineated the perils of being both enslaved and a woman. Like Sojourner Truth's ([1851] 1995) famous "ain't I a woman?," Jacobs' narrative is indicative of black women's use of intersectional epistemologies as a moral claim, appealing to white women and abolitionists to understand how enslavement, as a function of race, prevented enslaved women having agency over moral choices about sexual behavior and domestic power over childrearing. Indeed, this was a rhetorical strategy meant to appeal to the milieu, but it is an important strategy in that it rests on the intended audiences' acknowledgement of the uniquely disadvantaging intersection of race and gender in the lives of enslaved women. Using this argument, enslaved and free women advocated for the abolition of slavery, presuming that the absence of an unequal structural context—the plantation economy—would decrease the power of race as a determinant of black women's lives. As such, black women would have access to the moral and social protections of womanhood. However, this kind of discursive appeal also required its intended audiences to believe that black women were, in fact, women and therefore deserving of the protections afforded wealthy white women. Although this moral argument about the intersection of race and gender gained some traction in abolitionist discourse, it was ultimately broader considerations of morality that overshadowed these in the push for freedom. Still, the groundwork had been laid for organizing around a disadvantaged social location, epistemic position, and set of lived experiences.

23.2.2 Intersectionality and Feminist Fissures from Suffrage to Jim Crow

The battle for suffrage was the first national political moment when black women were discursively trapped between the "woman question" and the "Negro problem." White women actively campaigned against black suffrage, which would have only been extended to men, but women's suffrage would ultimately have only been extended to white women given the nature of race prejudice in the South. Black women, including Ida B. Wells-Barnett in Chicago, established their own suffrage organizations, again recognizing that their status as both women and black situated them outside of the political discourse (Higginbotham 1993; Giddings 2009). During the struggle for suffrage, black women made both moral and political intersectional claims to suffrage, drawing on still prevalent discourses about the role of women in elevating the race as well as discourses of political equality and representation for all citizens, regardless of their place in the social structure. Advocating for black women as central political agents in a bourgeoning post-slavery American democracy, theorist Anna Julia Cooper argued that "only the BLACK WOMAN can say when and where I enter, in the quiet, undisputed dignity of my womanhood, without violence and without suing or special patronage, then and there the whole Negro race enters with me" (Cooper 1892: 31). However, this discursive epistemological strategy did not overcome entrenched white supremacy. In fact, in the following years, black women's status as non-women and non-citizens as a result of their race and gender positions was reinforced by the systematic lack of response to crimes committed against them by whites.

After the outcome of the suffrage battle solidified black women's political place as partial citizens and non-women because of their race and gender, racialized and gendered Jim Crow violence reinforced black women's status on the outside of the legal protections of the law and the social protections of womanhood. Throughout the South, as well as other regions of the country, including the Midwest, white men raped black women with impunity, often arguing that the victim was a prostitute or otherwise enticed the men into sex (Hine 1989; McGuire 2011). Even in cases where victims were not accused of being paid for sex, black women's unequal race, gender, and citizen statuses meant that investigations and prosecutions were rare. Still, organizing around moral and political claims as women and citizens, black women demanded their grievances be recognized on both fronts. The denial of black women's womanhood on the basis of race became a point of organizing and resistance for black communities, and public spaces where black women were most vulnerable, like buses, became targets for boycotts. Thus, drawing on a moral claim to the protections of womanhood and a political claim to the protections of citizenship, black women led the charge to disrupt the workings of capital in order to bolster their claims to protection. Here, both race and gender are centered in black women's lived experiences of inequality and strategies of resistance. The struggle against sexual assault reflected black feminists' refusal to put either race or gender first, but to instead lay moral and political claim to the privileges afforded both (white) women and (black and white) men by situating their strategy firmly within the theoretical and epistemic premise of intersectionality.

In addition to critiquing and resisting the gendered and racialized sexual violence that they experienced, black women critiqued the labor conditions to which they were relegated in the South, and domestic labor in particular. They wrote to public officials, and even to sitting presidents, asking for relief from the low wages, the lack of work protections, and the lack of access to a variety of employment opportunities they faced (Sharpless 2010). Again, here, black women understood that it was intersection of race and gender that was disadvantaging them, tying labor discrimination to the sexual violence they experienced and appealing to the government for their rights as women, citizens, and mothers to work for decent wages, control their work conditions, and support their families without the threat of violence (Jones 1949).

23.2.3 Movement Politics and the Emergence of Modern Black Feminist Thought

Modern intersectional thought is built on the acknowledgement of this legacy of resistance at the nexus of interlocking systems of oppression. It is also a response to the continued ignoring of intersectionality in movement politics by black men in the civil rights and Black Power movements and by white women in the women's liberation movement (Hull et al. 1982). In their April 1977 declarative, "A Black Feminist Statement," the Combahee River Collective, a group of black women thinkers and organizers, argued that they were "actively committed to struggling against racial, sexual, heterosexual, and class oppression and see as our particular task the development of integrated analysis and practice based upon the fact that the major systems of oppression are interlocking" (CRC 1977: 232). In concert with black feminist thinkers that came before them, they offered sophisticated institutional critiques of the social structures that contributed to black women's labor, sexual, and race oppression. The Combahee River Collective's statement is foundational for modern intersectionality because of its deliberate and centering integration of black women's sexuality into black feminist analyses. Consisting of black lesbian thinkers, the CRC represented a break from moral appeals—which often applied to married women, black women who could be considered "ladies" in black communities because of their education or access to capital—to definitively political and social justice-based demands for reprieve from oppression.

As the Combahee River Collective was meeting, organizing, and preparing to craft its foundational statement, black women workers at General Motors were suing the company for discrimination on the basis of race and gender. The gender and race division of labor opportunities at General Motors excluded black women entirely from participation—only men, which included black men, were allowed to work on the factory floor; and only whites, which included white women, were allowed to work administrative positions. Thus, all the jobs were for black men or white women, but not black women. As Kimberlé Crenshaw (1989) points out in her analysis of the case as a galvanizing moment for the importance of intersectionality in the modern moment, the court's ruling—that the black women could only claim discrimination based on one of their statuses, race or gender, and not on the intersection of both—was a legal dismissal of the lived experiences of black women whose lives occurred at the nexus of multiple oppressions. Reflecting on how this case led to her articulation of intersectionality, Crenshaw (2015) writes,

> I wanted to define this profound invisibility in relation to the law. Racial and gender discrimination overlapped not only in the workplace but in other arenas of life; equally significant, these burdens were almost completely absent from feminist and anti-racist advocacy. Intersectionality, then, was my attempt to make feminist, anti-racist activism, and anti-discrimination law do what I thought they should—highlight the multiple avenues through which racial and gender oppression were experienced so that the problems would be easier to discuss and understand.

Crenshaw's argument, as well as that of the Combahee River Collective, was built on a personal-is-political, theory-as-praxis black feminist tradition that began with the experiences of black women in various structural configurations—the plantation economy, Jim Crow domestic labor, and the industrial economy. From these positions in an unequal economic system, black feminist thinkers theorized how racial, gender, and sexuality oppression intersected to compound and reflect economic marginalization. They developed sophisticated analyses of how various forms of violence were used to reinforce this societal disadvantage, but also highlighted how black women's understanding of their place in the social structure influenced their development of resistance strategies that simultaneously addressed multiple systems of oppression and the mechanisms of those systems.

Intersectionality is now shorthand for this tradition of black feminist thought, organizing, critique, and activism, and this fact is due in part to the work of sociologist and black feminist scholar Patricia Hill Collins (1990). However, intersectionality is not the whole of black feminist thinking (Cooper 2015). Ironically, its acceptance in the wider field of sociological theory and research largely divorced it from the considerations of social critique based on lived experiences in which it was once rooted. Its portability beyond this initial, broad context rested on its ability to be extricated from its theoretical and epistemological origins. This portability has been useful in highlighting the nature and shape of the "multiple jeopardy" experienced by a variety of racial and ethnic minority groups simultaneously occupying several disadvantaged positions. However, the excising of intersectionality from these origins has also created methodological, theoretical, and epistemological challenges (McCall 2005; Davis 2008). In social scientific and popular deployments of intersectionality, the fundamental aspects of black women's arguments are obscured, compromising the scientific enterprise and our ability to understand how institutions work together to disadvantage specific groups.

23.3 Classical Black Sociology and Intersectional Thought

American sociology began as a multicultural enterprise that built on the work of European thinkers and generated new theoretical foundations for the U.S. context to interrogate community life, social problems, industrialization, and other issues of modernity. From its inception, the field was comprised of two distinct epistemic foundations—one white (and thus at best epistemologically misguided and at worst outright racist) and one black. Despite limited access to institutions, academic and otherwise, black sociologists developed a tradition of investigating the place of newly freed African Americans in America's evolving democracy and offering distinct theoretical and methodological contributions to the discipline of sociology—contributions that were later erased in historiographies of the field—in the process (Wright 2016; Young and Deskins 2001). These contributions are central to recovering the theoretical origins of intersectionality in sociology.

Only recently have the three pioneering scholars of the first period of African American sociological thought—Anna Julia Cooper, W.E.B. Du Bois, and Ida B. Wells-Barnett—been recognized as founding thinkers, theorists, and scholars in the field. In the case of Du Bois, despite the canonization of his work in American sociology through the naming of awards and attention to scholarship that recovers his contributions, the field has still been slow to broadly incorporate his multiple contributions to the field's methodological and theoretical interventions beyond his theory of double consciousness (Morris 2015;

Wright 2016). Yet, to understand the sociological origins of intersectionality, these thinkers must be situated as contributing to a distinct early *black* sociology that challenged the racist undertones of the emerging field of American sociology while producing theoretical, methodological, and empirical innovations (Young and Deskins 2001). These thinkers took up and shaped the culture/structure dualism with attention to how social institutions reinforced inequality and disadvantaged black populations at multiple intersections.

Anna Julia Cooper's work is pioneering in both black feminism and sociology. Earning the PhD from the Sorbonne, Cooper's work spoke fundamentally to questions of race, gender, and region that were central to early American sociological thought and research. Her book, *A Voice from the South, By a Black Woman of the South* (1892), is the first black feminist text that theorizes the intersections of race and gender simultaneously in the lives of black women. Writing on the eve of the Chicago World's Columbian Exhibition, Cooper (1892) said, "The colored woman of to-day occupies, one may say, a unique position in this country. In a period of itself transitional and unsettled, her status seems one of the least ascertainable and definitive of all the forces which make for our civilization. She is confronted by both a woman question and a race problem, and is as yet an unknown or an unacknowledged factor in both" (Cooper, 45). Cooper here acknowledges the distinctiveness of black women in American democracy, and in this case formerly enslaved women as well as women coming of age in the early years of freedom. She quickly points out their social location as central to both the "race problem" and the "woman question" has not been sufficiently theorized. Still, she highlights the important role black women were already playing in American politics through their organizations and through the shaping of men's political behavior. Further, she considers the special knowledge that black women bring to multiple institutions—education, politics, criminal justice, and healthcare—and calls in particular on black men to recognize black women's import in reforming those institutions. *A Voice from the South* is the first book-length text to explicitly advocate for black women's unique epistemological perspectives as both a moral and political imperative for American democracy, and to analyze black women's relationship to the nation's growing global sensibility.

Class was a central, though sometimes implicit, feature in Cooper's analysis of black women's position vis-à-vis social institutions. She was aware, however, like many of her antebellum abolitionist predecessors, of the distinct economic disadvantages that black women experienced as a result of their intersecting race and class positions. She advocated for black women to have access to education and other economic resources and frequently criticized black men on this account, declaring that on questions of other matters pertinent to the race they were especially vocal but were strangely silent on issues that would improve the status of women. She was also especially critical of the institution of marriage as a site in and through which women were economically subjugated and unable to reach their full potential as contributors to improving the nation. As such, Cooper brought forth an analysis of race, class, and gender in a moment where class for African Americans had transitioned from the dichotomous categories of enslaved or free.

Whereas Cooper's work shaped sociological theory through a focus on the lived experiences and epistemology of black women, Du Bois's work on the simultaneity of institutions of oppression were largely a critique of structure. As such, although Du Bois rarely considered the simultaneity of race *and* class *and* gender, like Cooper and other black women writers did, race and class or race and gender were central to his understanding of the racialized structure of American inequality. As Du Bois scholar Ange-Marie Hancock (2005) notes, Du Bois's work contains allusions to either a "theory of *multiple* yet mutually exclusive identities and oppressions, or toward a theory of *intersecting* and mutually constitutive identities and oppressions" (2005:74). Writing about the experiences of black women, Du Bois, like Cooper, is concerned with how the woman question and the Negro question can be simultaneously considered. Similarly, writing about the experiences of poor black people in Philadelphia's Seventh Ward, Du Bois (1899) actively considers how racial disadvantage co-occurs and intersects with economic disadvantage, theorizing the two as mutually constitutive and reinforcing forms of oppression that uniquely affected black people in an anti-black society. Du Bois, thus, applies theories of intersecting oppressions to his findings in the field, and it is this theoretical perspective that undergirds his analyses in the studies produced through the Atlanta Sociological Laboratory (Wright 2016).

Journalist Ida B. Wells-Barnett is also central to founding theories of intersectionality in early black sociology, applying intersecting theories of race, class, and gender to her analyses of lynchings in the South (Wells-Barnett 1959). Wells-Barnett's analysis is rooted in lived in experiences but is simultaneously critical of the social structures that shape lived experience. As such, Wells-Barnett's work is perhaps the most similar to modern black feminist analyses. It takes on a particular problem—the national problem of lynching—and examines the phenomenon from multiple institutional perspectives, uncovering the economic, sexual, and social control motivations for the persistent and unpunished violence. She roundly critiques a criminal justice system that gestured towards civility but was, in fact, overtaken by a spirit of lawlessness and an "unwritten law" of lynching. Engaging in one of the first known uses of content analysis in sociology, Wells combed newspaper accounts of lynchings, creating a statistical record of lynching and what she called its "alleged causes," which she compiled in the pamphlet *A Red Record*, published in 1895 with a preface from Frederick Douglass. In a 1900 follow-up essay to her original analysis, Wells writes, "instead of lynchings being caused by assaults upon women, the statistics show that not one-third of the victims of lynchings are even charged with such crimes" (Wells-Barnett, 73). She highlights, instead, the significant number of unpunished rapes endured by black women at the hands of white men compared to the dearth of such crimes, alleged or actual, perpetrated by black men against white women. Here, then, Wells-Barnett uses methodological innovations—content and statistical analyses—to substantiate her epistemological claims about anti-black racism, lynching, economic inequality, and sexual violence in the South and beyond (Royster 1997).

In addition to these contributions on the intersection of race, labor, and capital as explanatory factors in lynchings, Wells-Barnett made significant theoretical contributions to how black feminism would later more explicitly incorporate sex and sexuality into analyses of economic and racial inequality. Offering up a discursive analysis of what Patricia Hill Collins would call "controlling images," Wells-Barnett critiqued the myth of the black male rapist and the black female prostitute, both narratives constructed in the public discourse and media as justifications for lynching. She deconstructed these narratives and demonstrated their relationship to economic competition in a South where whites were determined to maintain complete political and economic control through whatever means. It was this plain deconstructive analysis that led to the burning of her paper, *The Free Speech and Headlight of Memphis*, and her inability to return to the city. In an editorial she wrote in the paper on May 21, 1892, a couple of months after three of her friends were murdered by a lynch mob for running an economically profitable grocery, Wells-Barnett declared: "Nobody in this section of the country believes the old threadbare lie that Negro men rape white women. If Southern white men are not careful, they will over-reach themselves and public sentiment will have a reaction; a conclusion will then be reached which will be very damaging to the moral reputation of their women." Here, Wells-Barnett provides a sophisticated analysis of the discourse about race and moral superiority that supported the institution of lynch law in the American South in the late nineteenth and early twentieth century. Later, scholars working in the black feminist tradition would apply similar discursive analyses to constructions of "welfare queens" and "baby mamas," deconstructing how these discourses were designed to obscure unequal economic relationships.

Intersectionality was central to these thinkers' critical analyses of the social world as they worked to bridge empiricism and epistemology. For Cooper in particular, the experiences of black women were a starting point from which to assess the political landscape and theorize new possibilities for freedom with black women at the helm of addressing society's ills. For Wells and Du Bois, the experiences of black people in their interactions with the social structure, particularly the economy, were the beginning point of theory-generation about the intersections of race and class or race and gender. Wells and Cooper offered epistemological critiques that privileged black women's unique standpoint, while Du Bois uncovered how economic inequality and racial inequality created structurally unequal outcomes. Wells and Du Bois provided important methodological interventions based on their understanding of intersectionality, and from these methods discovered new ways of thinking about how the intersection of social locations and social institutions worked together to disadvantage black people in general and black women in particular. Although they were working firmly within the structure of a discipline that, as Young and Deskins (2001) argue, drew on "the same paradigms, language, and logic employed by the creators of not just racialist, but racist American social thought," they nonetheless improved upon and created new theory and methods that prefigure the institutionalization of intersectionality. Their work is indeed the groundwork of sociological theories of intersectionality, foreshadowing how black feminist epistemologies are central to the development of methodological innovation in intersectionality research.

23.4 Black Feminist Organizing and Modern Black Feminism

Black feminist work, rooted in activist responses to conditions specific to black women's lives in the context of American inequality, continued after this classical period, still carving out space in the public discourse for black women to author and theorize their own experiences. After the suffrage struggle underscored the identity, analytic, and epistemological fissures that excluded black women from visions of freedom in a changing nation, black women increasingly formed spaces to theorize their particular experiences, whether in the Jim Crow South or in Diasporic contexts. Some of the most significant work that served as the basis for intersectional theory and practice emerged from the organizing work of black women in the anti-imperialist, civil rights, and women's rights movements in postwar era. Imperialist expansion, sexual violence against black women, degenerating conditions in black communities, an oppressive welfare state that frustrated black women's ability to choose how and when they formed families, lack of access to equal healthcare, and persistent racial inequality were among the many manifestations of oppression that black women's consciousness raising and liberation groups organized to address.

23.4.1 Black Feminist Theorizing on the Margins of Movements

As with the classical period, black women's post-suffrage organizing is central to understanding the development of black feminist thought in general and theorizations of intersectionality in particular. Although black feminist theorizing vis-à-vis communism and radicalism in the interwar and immediate postwar periods is understudied, black women's analyses of communist texts and ideologies shaped The Left and the African American intellectual enterprise. In one of her most widely cited essays, "An End to the Neglect of the Problems of the Negro Woman!" prominent radical thinker Claudia Jones (1949) implores labor unions to take up the cause of advocating for domestic workers to have the same labor protections as other workers to relieve their economic disenfranchisement. Highlighting what she dubbed the "double exploitation" of women as gender and class minorities, Jones contended that "negro women—as workers, as Negroes, and as women—are the most oppressed stratum of the whole population" (109). She described what she called the "superexploitation" of black working class women, and drawing on U.S. Department of Labor statistics, she connected black women's economic status to their place in movement politics and ideology. Perhaps most significant to one of the key interventions of black feminism, Jones analyzed how the denial of labor and property rights affected black women's ability to protect their bodies from white sexual violence. She calls out white women's complicity in a system that lynched black men to avenge white women's allegedly violated womanhood while simultaneously subjecting black women to "daily insults…in public places, no matter what their class, status, or position" (119). Sexual violence affected black women across class, but also was a result of their broad economic marginalization, rooted in an institutionalized anti-black misogyny that imagined all black women as disposable laborers and disposable bodies. Although Jones' political biographer (Davies 2007) notes that she frequently returned to the party line—that an anti-capitalist and anti-imperialist victory would alleviate if not eradicate black women's marginalization—Jones' theorizations of sexual violence against black women indicate her understanding of the specific intersections of oppression for black women. They also underscore some of black people's, and black women's in particular, frustrations with the radical Left in this particular historical moment.

In the height of the civil rights and Black Power eras, black women worked diligently in a wide range of organizations, from civil rights organizations like the Southern Christian Leadership Conference to the Black Panther Party to the National Organization for Women. Some prominent black feminists straddled multiple organizations, like attorney Florynce Kennedy who helped found NOW and worked diligently in the Black Power Movement (Kennedy 1976; Randolph 2015). These women's labor often went unseen and exploited in these organizational contexts, and their experiences were often marginalized in movement goals. In organizing for their liberation, black women found themselves again trapped by a discursive and policy erasure of their lives and experiences of inequality. For instance, advocating for reprieve from and punishment for domestic violence meant relying on police who were often hostile to the interests of black men and women. Also, while some white women advocated for the right to control their fertility, including the right to be sterilized whenever they chose without the consent of their partners or physicians' restrictions, black women and other women of color were still facing forced sterilizations, performed without their knowledge and often at the behest of government organizations. These women, who were forming the basis for the reproductive justice movement, were excluded from considerations and protections for which white women, and white middle class women especially, were striving. Socialist and other anti-capitalist movements too often subsumed practices of inequality that disproportionately affected certain groups under an umbrella that would supposedly resolve itself when labor triumphed over capital. At every turn, the dominant narratives of most large-scale movement organizations ignored, or at least downplayed, the experiences of black women and the histories of anti-black misogyny that undergirded all systems of oppression. Yet, out of this praxis came further refinement and expansion of black feminist theorizing on race, gender, and class oppression as systems, as well as specific intersectional analyses of social institutions—family, health, the labor market and economy, religion, politics, and education.

The intersection of race and gender, and specifically disadvantaged positions in those two systems, remained central to black feminist conceptions of the structure of inequality in America. Analyzing black women's economic lives as enslaved and later as relegated to the worst paying jobs in the labor force, intersectionality theorists carefully delineated how black women's distinct economic subjugation was rooted in anti-black misogyny. Writing in 1970, lawyer and scholar Pauli Murray argued that "the economic disabilities of women generally are aggravated in the case of black women," highlighting how a significant proportion of working women of color were then employed as domestic laborers with no labor protections (195). The denial of labor protections for this class of workers was an explicit denial of labor rights to black women. Black feminist historians have noted how domestic labor was framed as black women's work, continuing slavery-era discourse about black women's "special talents" as wet nurses, nannies, and cooks during slavery (Sharpless 2010; Wallace-Sanders 2009). These discourses reflected and reinforced black women's economic disempowerment but also underscored their particular vulnerability as unprotected and undervalued laborers. Their working conditions rendered them subject to sexual violence and physical abuse while earning low wages that were often withheld by employers. Black feminist theorists connected this subjugation to the maintenance of white racial supremacy and capitalism domestically and internationally.

23.4.2 Theorizing Sexual Violence

Black women also organized against sexual, reproductive, and heterosexist oppression in the United States and in the communities of color in the developing world. These systems were conceptualized as intersecting and were analyzed for how they contributed to economic disadvantage while simultaneously compounding racial disadvantage. While all women—across class and marital status—were disadvantaged by patriarchal power that governed sex, black women experienced a racialized sexual oppression that meant that anyone could lay claim to their bodies and they would have little to no recourse. Constant assaults against black women constrained their labor choices, further exposing them to economic disadvantage. Thus, their organizing also recognized the economic underpinnings of unchecked sexual violence. This work laid the foundation for Joan Little, a woman tried for defending herself against an assailant, to be acquitted in 1974 (McGuire 2011). This verdict, widely seen as a victory of a multiracial movement coalition, helped change how the law treated rape and opened the door for marital rape to be punished. Black women's decades of resistance to sexual violence, and their strivings to protect themselves, helped win broad victories for women in general.

Black feminist theorists saw sexual violence as tied to reproductive oppression, writing eloquently about practices of forced birth control and sterilization of people of color in the U.S. and abroad. Because access to welfare benefits was often predicated upon visits to specific clinics or doctors, women of color were forced to exchange their reproductive liberty, usually without their knowledge, for meager economic resources in a society that designed and profited from their impoverishment and low wages. After surgical sterilizations abated, long-acting reversible contraception was often forced on black women, especially when those women were receiving welfare benefits. Yet, in cases where women wanted to access birth control, costs were often prohibitively high to enable them to do so. In addition to bodily reproductive oppression through forced sterilization, black women organized in concert with several other movements, including the environmental movement, to highlight how the conditions in which black women found themselves were often not conducive to reproduction. Government disinvestment in black communities, lack of protection from violence, environmental hazards, and low wages all created circumstances in which black women could not choose to give life.

In their critique of the system of patriarchy that enabled sexual violence against black women and the restriction of their reproductive choices based on their economic status, black women—and black lesbian women in particular (CRC 1977; Lorde 1984a, b)—also launched a critique of heterosexism, which they argued was integral to the deployment of racial, economic, and gender inequality. Writing in *This Bridge Called My Back*, published on the Kitchen Table: Women of Color Press started by Barbara Smith, Cheryl Clarke (1983 [1995]) contended that, "while the black man may consider racism his primary oppression, he is hard put to recognize that sexism is inextricably bound up with the racism the black woman must suffer, nor can he see that no women (or men for that matter) will be liberated from the original "master-slave" relationship, viz., that between men and women, until we are all liberated from the false premise of heterosexual superiority" (246). Black lesbian women struggled against heterosexism in movement organizations and dismal economic outcomes that were a product of their intersecting race, gender, and sexuality statuses. They were also central to a radical broadening of the foci of black feminist praxis to more definitively include attention to global oppressions, sexuality oppressions, trans* oppression, and the intersection of race, gender, and disability studies.

23.4.3 From Parallels to Intersections

As part of the turn towards new language in the theorization of black women's experience, black feminist intellectuals began to more explicitly resist the parallelism in the juxtaposition of analyses of racism and sexism. Whereas aligning the two had been a moral and rhetorical strategy used by women abolitionists to advocate for the end of slavery, describing slavery's ills as something that burdened black enslaved women and white mistresses equally was neither accurate or aligned with achieving justice. After slavery, describing the race problem as akin to the problem of women's suffrage or other forms of inequality yielded friction between black and white women suffragists. Black women's employment in dangerous and grossly underpaid domestic labor in the homes of white women, even those white women who were not wealthy, further highlighted the distinctions in outcomes between black and white women. Further, these inequities could not be explained away with merely an analysis of class inequality. Black feminist theorists therefore emphasized that sexism and racism were inextricably linked with the mechanisms of capitalism, rather than operating as mere derivative outcomes of capitalism.

Although a few theorists continued to analyze the parallels between racism and sexism in the 1960s and into the 1970s, this kind of theorizing fell out of favor as black women intellectuals worked to more accurately articulate how multiple systems of oppression interacted with one another to produce differential outcomes based on one's position in the structure of power. Rather than "twin evils," then, racism and sexism were increasingly theorized as interdependent and mutually constitutive systems of oppression. Building on previous generations' analyses of the "double slavery" or "double burden" of the woman question and the Negro question, black feminists in the 1960s increasingly began elaborating on the simultaneous outcomes of racism and sexism in mathematical terms. Drawing on Marxist critiques of women's place in a capitalist society, activists like Frances Beale focused on how black women, as "the slave of slaves," were exposed to "double jeopardy" as they were exploited in labor markets that constrained them both on the basis of race and gender. But this double jeopardy implied more than the addition of one system to another (and therefore the ability to subtract one system from the other and altogether absent its effects from existence); rather it signified a multiplying and reinforcing condition in which these respective systems do not exist without, and in fact enable, one another.

It is this theorization of the gendered and racialized exploitation of black women, rooted in black feminist economic analyses since slavery, that heightened differences between black women's and white women's respective movements for liberation. Beale (1970) argued that, "if the white groups do not realize that they are in fact fighting capitalism and racism, we do not have common bonds" (153), therefore requiring an anti-racist struggle that also recognized economic inequities and an anti-capitalist struggle that understood how eradicating racism was necessary for eliminating capitalism. In tandem with these analyses, black feminist activists elaborated on how sexism functioned to disadvantage black women in and outside of black communities, as well as how sexism and heterosexism within black communities reflected and reinforced both racism and capitalism. They critiqued the tendency to place the restoration of black men's masculinity via patriarchy ahead of race and gender liberation for black women. They also deconstructed resurgent discourses about black people's unfitness for the middle class family model, including notions of "pathology," black "matriarchy," and the supposed inferiority of woman-headed households.

Black women's organizing in resistance to rape, economic oppression, sexual and reproductive oppression, and racism forms the fundamental backbone of intersectionality theorizing. It is in and through mobilization for self-preservation and survival that this aspect of black feminist theorizing emerged as a significant marker of black women's experiences. This organizing, and the hard-fought gains won from black feminist activism since WWII, co-occurred with theory-building and the institutionalization that contributed to the expansion of black feminist theory in the academy beginning in the 1980s.

23.5 Black Feminist Theory and the Expansion of Intersectionality

The expansion of racial, ethnic, and women's studies departments in American institutions in the 1960s and 1970s provided the first broad-scale opportunity for the institutionalization of black women's studies, and by the 1980s, black feminist intellectuals had formed a recognizable field, historiographical practice, and theoretical enterprise (Guy-Sheftall 1992). This field compelled a reimagining of black studies and women's studies, in addition to the core of various humanities and social science disciplines. Documenting and archiving of black women's work as central to the American intellectual and activist enterprise, black women academics, intellectuals, and activists aimed to rewrite American history and the history of contemporary movements—women's liberation and civil rights. This task included the development of new language to capture and theorize black women's experiences, a reformulation of coalition politics to maximize the possibilities for justice, and the recovery of a range of black women's experiences into formally recognized aspects of the black feminist movement and black feminist thought.

As part of this expansion, and in tandem with movement organizing, black women scholars in and outside of the academy wrote corrective, descriptive, and theoretical scholarship about their experiences and the structure of inequality in the U.S. and globally. They fundamentally rewrote American history, recovering the role black women played in shaping not only race, gender, and sexuality politics but also national politics. Highlighting the "racist, sexist, and class biases [that] are perpetuated in American historiography" (Scott 1982:87), they emphasized the importance of an intersectional focus in the grand narrative of American history, from slavery, to suffrage, to labor, to anti-war activism, to the civil rights, women's rights, and LGBT movements. Just as movement activists had done in the 1960s and 1970s, black feminist scholar-activists theorized race, class, gender, sexuality, gender presentation, ability, and nationality as part of a structural system of domination that influenced individual and group outcomes, privileging those on the chosen end of those status spectra and disadvantaging those on the oppressed end. They consistently emphasized that the contemporary arrangement and structure of inequality was rooted in America's capital origins in slavery. Yet, rather than recast slavery as solely an economic system that simply arranged an unequal system in service of itself, black feminists contended that in fact racism, anti-black misogyny, and suppression of labor worked in tandem to maintain white supremacy and capitalism simultaneously. Proceeding from slavery, black feminist scholars critiqued the epistemic underpinnings of much work about black women, which towards the end of the civil rights era was influenced by the arguments of the Moynihan report and notions of a pathological black "matriarchy."

Black feminists also began intensive projects of anthologizing and canonizing black women's work. Beginning with Hull et al. (1982) *But Some of Us Are Brave*, anthologies of black feminist writing, either by a sole author or a collection of writers, increasingly defined the field and the theoretical grounds on which intersectionality would take hold. *Brave* was, at its core, a black feminist disciplinary intervention, covering women's studies, black studies, and the humanities and social sciences. Angela Davis anthologized a set of her previously published essays in *Women, Race, and Class* in 1983. That same year, Barbara Smith's edited volume, *Home Girls: A Black Feminist Anthology*, was published on Kitchen Table: Women of Color Press. Smith's volume was disciplinarily expansive, including humanistic, social scientific, and aesthetic works, and was also the most explicitly dedicated to highlighting the distinctive voices of black lesbian feminists in movement politics and aesthetic practice. In 1984, black feminist scholar bell hooks published a collection of essays on feminist theory. Ultimately, these and other anthologies and edited volumes rendered the contours of black feminist theorizing visible in academic contexts.

Major theoretical formulations emerged from this work, as black feminists reflexively assessed their positions in the radical, women's liberation, and civil rights movements as well as assessed their current economic positions. For black women scholars and activists, gender and sexuality oppression were not secondary forms of inequality that would fall away after capitalism or racism. In a discursive shift, Smith (1985) writes that "a black feminist perspective has no use for ranking oppressions, but instead demonstrates the *simultaneity* of oppressions as they affect Third World women's lives" (6, emphasis added). This notion of a "simultaneity" of oppression reflected a shift in movement politics from single-issue to multi-issue organizing in some of the mainstream organizations. Although black women had always been compelled to, in many ways, serve two or more movements, this new emphasis on coalition building, spurred on by Third World and indigenous feminist theorizing and activism, held major groups accountable for rethinking movement action.

Simultaneity was inherently more complex than double-ness; even though the latter required a sense of simultaneity, it did not necessarily encapsulate the multiple oppressions black women were organizing against. Building on W. E. B. Du Bois' "double consciousness" of the turn of the century and Frances Beale's (1970) "double jeopardy" nearly two decades previous, sociologist Deborah King (1988) offered "multiple jeopardy" and "multiple consciousness" to describe the context of black feminist theorizing and organizing, as well as the structure of inequality. Recognizing that the widespread use of race-sex parallelism in social theory was largely due to its legibility and portability—"the race-sex correspondence has been used successfully because the race model was a well-established and effective pedagogical tool for both the theoretical conceptualization of and the political resistance to sexual inequality" (44)—King contended that this "race-sex correspondence" could not stand because within it, "all the women are white and all the blacks are men." Further, in underscoring the limits of "double" and "triple" jeopardy, King highlights that "racism, sexism, and classism constitute three, *interdependent* control systems" (emphasis added, 47) for which an "interactive model" (Smith and Stewart 1983) is necessary. Importantly, King uses historical and contemporary instances of movement organizing to elaborate this interactive model, demonstrating the continued significance of experiences of organizing against oppression to developing and refining black feminist theory in general, and intersectionality in particular.

Other language emerged to capture the move beyond additive models of oppression. In addition to multiple jeopardy/consciousness, Smith and Stewart's (1983) notion of a "contextual interactive model/perspective" and Jeffries and Ransford's (1980) "ethnogender" were exemplary of language shifts intended to recognize the multiplicity, simultaneity, and interdependence of systems of inequality. Yet, Kimberlé Crenshaw's (1989) "intersectionality"—which stood for ideas that had been theorized for more than a century under different names and through different forms—became canonical language and later shorthand for difference, diversity, and inclusion. Crenshaw elaborated the concept in two practical cases: a legal case of black women against General Motors (1989) and the case of women's organizing against gendered violence

(1991). These two works exemplified the idea of an intersecting, interactive model of oppression that was interested in how interdependent systems of oppression operated to erase the experiences of certain groups. Moreover, these papers, like other black feminist work emerging in the 1980s, argued for a recognition of the vast intraracial diversity amongst black people and black women. This language was taken up in the work of critical race theorists and critical legal theorists, in some black feminist scholarly and activist circles, and later would become common language in feminist movement politics.

It was in this expansion period of intersectionality theory in the 1980s that two disciplinary fissures—one epistemological and one methodological—emerged. Social science, in the inherently racist and sexist biases in its language, was often times ill-equipped to appropriately theorize about black women's lives, experiences, and outcomes. Black social scientists in the 1970s and 1980s, like the classical black sociologists, found themselves up against a set of methods that were based on faulty assumptions (Ladner 1973; Aldridge 2008). They consequently attempted to both build on these methods and devise new ones to appropriately address black women's lives. While the humanities provided a more expansive lens through which to conceptualize black women's experiences, this created an empirical conundrum in enumerating inequality. Further, the rise of critical theory and post-structural and post-modern theories pushed scholars to move further from their subjects, an epistemic position anathema to the organizing-bases of black feminist theory. Black feminist theorists, notably Barbara Christian, were critical of this particular theoretical turn because of how it functioned to devalue, erase, and exclude black women's work just as the process of formalizing black feminist theory was underway in the academy. On the rise of theory as commodity in the 1980s, Christian (1987) argued that "people of color have always theorized—but in forms quite different from the Western form of abstract logic. And I am inclined to say that our theorizing (and I intentionally use the verb rather than the noun) is often in narrative forms, in the stories we create, in riddles and proverbs, in the play with language, since dynamic rather than fixed ideas seem more to our liking" (52). How to reconcile the knowledge that arose from lived experiences, one's standpoint, as it were, with the knowledge that came from assessing categorical aggregate distributions of privilege and disadvantage became central to the course of intersectionality's reassertion in sociology.

23.6 Sociology and the Science of Intersectionality

23.6.1 Black Feminist Thought and the Institutionalization of Intersectionality

The sociologist Patricia Hill Collins is the black feminist scholar most frequently tied to the advent of intersectionality in the field. Her seminal monograph in this area, *Black Feminist Thought* ([1990] 2000), chronicled and built upon black women's studies across disciplines, representing the first historiography of U.S. black feminist theory. It offered important new language to solidify the turn from parallelism to simultaneity and multiplicity. Describing how intersectionality related to the work she sought to undertake in *Black Feminist Thought*, Collins wrote: "Intersectional paradigms remind us that oppression cannot be reduced to one fundamental type, and that oppressions work together in producing injustice. In contrast, the matrix of domination refers to how these intersecting oppressions are actually organized. Regardless of the particular intersections involved, structural, disciplinary, hegemonic, and interpersonal domains of power reappear across quite different forms of oppression" (18). Collins retools standpoint theory via a black feminist lens, and thus creates a threefold approach to black feminist theory and methodology. (1) Intersectionality, in her analysis, operated on a meta-level to capture the simultaneity of oppressions in the lives of groups and individuals; (2) standpoint theory was the individual, epistemic ground on which black feminist thought was built and conceived on the micro-level, as it had been since slavery; and (3) the matrix of domination was a macro-structural description of how these multiple oppressions were organized. These levels were at once co-occuring and interacting, as were the multiple systems of oppression. This sociological intervention, then, accounted for a long history of black feminist theorizing in the U.S., developed and refine language with which to better research inequality in the U.S., and highlighted the importance of black feminist epistemologies to theorizing about a range of institutional inequities—family, labor, religion, politics, and education amongst others.

After the initial publication of *Black Feminist Thought*, black feminist theory and language were rapidly integrated into analyses of stratification. Rather than assuming gender meant white women and race meant black men, inequality scholars began to more consistently examine the "four categories"—black men, white men, black women, white women. While these categories continued to be extraordinarily limited in their recognition of intragroup diversity or racial and ethnic groups beyond black and white, the mainstream move from two categories of analysis to four or more significantly expanded the rigor and usefulness of inequality research, illuminating precisely how inequality affected groups in multiple locations in the matrix of domination.

Black feminist theory was also institutionalized in the discipline in various ways, including the founding of *Race, Gender, and Class* journal in 1993[1] and the establishment of the Race, Gender, and Class section of the American Sociological Association in 1996. These formal academic channels, established by people who had been working in the bourgeoning field of "race, class, gender studies" for several years, provided a space for intersectional scholarship to be published, debated, and recognized. Still, competing ideas about what constituted race, class, and gender research, particularly in the context of which research was taken up and recognized beyond the boundaries of the section, shaped both the institutionalization of intersectionality and how the theory would be expressed in the discipline. These priorities reflected the disciplinary rift evidenced in the 1980s between humanities and social scientific approaches to theorizing about inequality and black women's experiences in particular.

23.6.2 The Rise of Intersectionality Research in Sociology

The 1990s marked the beginning of an explosion of intersectionality and intersectionality-inspired research—that is research that used the word "intersectionality" to describe its methods, theory, or epistemology; that explicitly drew on a race, class, gender paradigm to account for inequality; that analyzed race, gender, class, and another system of oppression or difference, like sexuality; and/or that acknowledged the researcher's location in the matrix of domination to contextualize the research and its findings. This proliferation occurred simultaneously with intersectionality's institutionalization in the discipline, the rise of the reflexive turn in postmodern theory, and sociology's reinvigorated commitment to documenting inequality as a distinguishing disciplinary feature. The theory's institutionalization yielded a large and broad field of work unified chiefly by its insistence on considering the simultaneity of oppressions, both as experienced by individuals and groups and as arranged in the matrix of domination. This expansive and diverse field yielded some of the most important sociological work on the nature of inequality in the post-civil rights era. However, its breadth yielded methodological and theoretical challenges in the field.

This work can be divided analytically into three distinct but interrelated branches: (1) empirical, (2) theoretical, and (3) methodological. The empirical branch of this work was interested in how race, class, and gender interacted to affect a number of outcomes, from family formation, maintenance, and parenting strategies (Dill 1988; Jacobs 1994; McDonald 1997; Battle 1999; Dillaway and Broman 2001), hiring prac-

[1] The journal's original title was *Race, Sex, and Class* and was changed to *Race, Gender, and Class* in 1995.

tices (Bertrand and Mullainathan 2004; Pager and Quillian 2005), occupational segregation (Glenn 1992, 2009; Romero 1995; Wingfield 2009), housing (Massey and Lundy 2001), organizations (Acker 2000), political ideologies (Simien 2005), policy (Deitch 1993; Haney 1996; Roberts 1996; Mink 1999; Mink et al. 2003; Lovell 2002) and education (Bettie 2002; Stoll 2013). This research also more explicitly treated sexuality as a category of analysis and lived experience, bringing theories of sexuality and queer theory into intersectional research (Gamson and Moon 2004; Moore 2008; Hunter 2010).

The theoretical and methodological branches of this work both built on empirical intersectionality research by assessing and refining its methods and theoretical assumptions as well as continued in theory-building in ways somewhat separate from the developing body of empirical research. In an early sociological evaluation of the relationship of Marxist and neo-Marxist theories to the claims of intersectionality theory, Belkhir (1996) carefully analyzes the respective relationships between Marxism and feminism and Marxism and race theory, concluding that Marxist theory nor class analysis alone are useful to understanding the fractured, rather than strictly hierarchical, nature of domination in the U.S. and globally. As with most theoretical analyses of intersectionality, Belkhir utilized a theoretical case study—hers was the case of domestic laborers and their employers—to demonstrate how and intersectional perspective might be used and why it, to the exclusion of other forms of analysis that did not take these intersections into account, should be used.

Scholars consistently acknowledged the complexity of theorizing, researching, and writing about these interactive systems of domination. West and Fenstermaker (1995) proposed "doing difference" as a new way to think about these systems, contending that the mathematical metaphors that had been used and critiqued since early black feminist thought—double, triple, intersecting, simultaneous, multiplicative, additive. In a symposium of responses to West and Fenstermaker's article, several scholars expressed reservations with the authors' apparent elision of power and oppression for the language of "doing" difference. In her response, Collins (1995) offered a classic critique of postmodernism, contending that social constructions of "difference" had erased the very real systems of racism, patriarchy, and capitalism. She reviewed the field of race, class, and gender studies up to that point to rearticulate some of the key theoretical claims in her work and the work of activists and theorists working in the black feminist tradition. Describing the existing language, Collins wrote, "...the notion of interlocking oppressions refers to the macro level connections linking systems of oppression such as race, class, and gender. This is the model describing the social structures that create social positions. Second, the notion of intersectionality describes micro level processes—namely how each individual and group occupies a social position within interlocking structures of oppression described by the metaphor of intersectionality. Together they shape oppression" (492). This response and other similar responses revealed the theoretical tensions in the postmodern turn in critical theory and the lived experiences of people of color and other marginalized groups and their theorizations of those experiences.

The West and Fenstermaker symposium also underscored ongoing epistemological concerns in intersectionality research, both as a result of the erasure of black feminist activism and theory as well as exogenous forces, like the rise of postmodern theory, from outside of the discipline. Still, working in the tradition of black feminist thought, several race, class, and gender sociologists highlighted the importance of the scholarship in black women's studies and moreover the voices of black women as key to understanding inequality and to theoretical innovations in sociology (Barnett et al. 1999). Jewish, Latina, and Asian women scholars also contributed to theorizing on intersectionality, drawing on standpoint theory and the history of women of color organizing separately and in coalitions with black women (Chow 1987; Blea 1992; Martinez 1996; Greenebaum 1999; Bettie 2002; Wilkins 2004).

If the epistemological question, a source of tension in the evolution of intersectionality, was not fully addressed during this period in intersectionality's development in sociology, the related questions of methodology were amplified. Sociologists working in the area of race, class, and gender and in adjacent areas of inquiry have been chiefly concerned with how to deploy intersectionality methodologically (Cuadraz and Uttal 1999; McCall 2005; Bowleg 2008; Choo and Ferree 2010). The wide emphasis on issues of method could at once be seen as the disciplinary requirements for sound and precise methodology and as an attempt to nullify or at least muddy the findings of intersectionality research. Critics expressed concern about the lack of a uniform method and skepticism about measuring the interactive effects of discrete systems of power on individual and group outcomes. Moreover, assessing and measuring such complex dynamics so that findings might be considered definitive, authoritative, or significant often necessitated leaving certain variables or categories out altogether. Researchers thus needed to account methodologically for these absences, even as it was evident that these absences mattered for outcomes.

23.6.3 Intersectionality's Methodological and Epistemological Complexities

After over a decade of increased intersectionality research in sociology, sociologist Leslie McCall (2005), writing primarily about women's studies but implicitly to sociology as well, surveyed the methodological approaches of intersectional research. Providing a typology of intersectional research that is now widely used across humanities and social science disciplines, McCall attempts to construct a bridge between interdisciplinary fields, like gender and sexuality studies, and disciplinary fields, like sociology. The distinctions she draws between typologies are as much about the theoretical assumptions that undergird scholars' methodologies—"the philosophical underpinnings of methods and the kinds of substantive knowledge that are produced in the application of methods" (1774)—as they are about precisely *how* scholars investigate their subjects. Imagining these approaches on a continuum of the conceptualization of categories, McCall describes the (1) "anticategorical" approach, which rejects categories given the fluidity of social identities and structures and resembles the ethnomethodological approach of "doing difference"; (2) the "intracategorical" approach, which recognizes the slippage of categorical boundaries while also holding those categories constant, particularly in terms of structures of oppression; and (3) the intercategorical approach, which accepts categories based largely on how they are created by hegemonic structures in order to measure and assess inequalities, while implicitly recognizing (outside of the context of the research) the shifting nature of these boundaries. The intercategorical approach is one McCall described as applicable to her own research on the structural intersections of race, class, and gender inequality across social institutions, and employment in particular. Although these kinds of large-scale quantitative analysis that account for inequities between groups at multiple intersections were and are sometimes cast as irrevocably complex, they nevertheless have, in the years since the publication of McCall's work, increased significantly.

Developing along quantitative and qualitative lines within the discipline, intersectionality research described the precise nature of inequality across groups, space, and place; illustrated how categories of race, class, gender, and sexuality were made and re-made by state and individual actors (Moore 2008; Hunter 2010); accounted for how individuals and groups made sense of categories of identity and instances of domination within place and space contexts (Garcia 2012; Robinson 2014); and attended to unaccounted for social locations (Chun 2011; Moore 2011). This scholarship both generated empirical research and built on existing research, expanding intersectionality's scope to include a wide range of study types that were focused on uncovering the relational nature of social inequality and oppression, how groups navigated equality vis-à-vis their social locations, and how overarching social structures reinforced the inequality order.

Through this scholarship, the discipline carved out the scientific boundaries of intersectionality research in sociology, even as approaches to and uses of intersectionality in the field remained varied. On the whole, sociology bracketed the more "complicated" aspects of theory, particularly as they had been articulated by black feminist and black queer theorists, in favor of a theoretical approach that could be more easily integrated into existing paradigms in stratification and inequality research. Intersectionality's main theoretical assumptions were widely portable—systems of oppression are interlocking and the effects of this should be assessed at micro, meso, and macro levels. In the process, methodological consistency and replicability became essential to transforming intersectionality into a disciplinarily legible science. Because methodology and theory are often created and refined in a dialectical process, this methodological work of trimming intersectionality into a sociological science simply demonstrated the various conceptions of science and approaches to analyses that undergird sociological scholarship.

23.7 Black Feminist Theorizing and the Legacy of Intersectionality

As a robust and diverse assessment of interlocking systems of oppression with attention to empirical data, sociology's engagement with intersectionality has transformed sociological research on stratification. Through the use of qualitative and quantitative empirical data, and theorizing that has emerged from these research findings, sociologists have been able to empirically confirm and theoretically complement the major tenets of intersectionality that black feminist scholars have articulated since slavery. This work theorizes the mechanisms of inequality largely as they affect groups at different social locations, e.g., black lesbian women or working class white men, as well as how social structures of inequality interlock to create disadvantage. It has become increasingly influential in how non-profit organizations, philanthropic groups, and public policy scholars think about inequality.

Yet, as part of a broader range of black feminist theorizing, intersectionality has not yet been fully integrated into sociological knowledge production practices. There is a disjuncture between the black feminist origins of intersectionality and the deployment of intersectionality in sociology. Sociology tacitly recognizes that people experience the world as their simultaneous embodiments and social locations in the matrix of domination, and therefore and cannot be neatly subdivided into categories. Yet, by taking categories as the enduring unit of analysis, even solely for purposes of creating a general narrative about inequality, the specific mechanisms of inequality for people at the most marginalized social locations are obscured. Further, the workings of oppression—the fundamental questions of power—are often inadvertently obscured in social scientific research. Conversely, black feminist theorists strove tirelessly to interrogate and make visible these systems of power, and not solely how the systems manifested in people's lives. The discipline thus lacks a key historiographical consciousness about the development of intersectionality within the context of a long history of black feminist theorizing and black women's organizing and activism. As a result, its epistemological blindspots and insistence on a certain kind of empiricism continue to ensure that most new intersectionality theorizing happens outside of the discipline.

With the popularization of intersectionality in the academy and the public discourse, there have been multiple calls for scholars to "move beyond" the concept, even as it has been divorced from its epistemic origins and thus shorn of its original potential as a methodological and theoretical intervention in traditional disciplinary forms of knowledge. Collins (2015) acknowledges this shift, arguing that "intersectionality now garners its share of self-proclaimed experts and critics of its ideas and potential, many of whom demonstrate unsettling degrees of amnesia and/or ignorance concerning the scope of intersectional knowledge projects writ large" (11). In her assessment of black feminist theorizing and the function of shorthand concepts like "the politics of respectability," "standpoint," and "intersectionality," black feminist historian Brittney Cooper (2015) encouraged black feminist theorists across disciplines to finish covering the theoretical ground of black feminist thought. This pushback against intersectionality in and beyond the discipline reflects a broad fatigue with the idea and its prominence, our various disciplinary needs to be in constant search of new theories, and an unwillingness to reckon how the theoretical shortcuts we have taken to arrive at our respective versions of intersectionality have compromised our ability to fully appreciate the concept.

The popularity of intersectionality in the 2010s grew as a result of a proliferation of black feminist work on social media (Jarmon 2013), a reinvigoration of feminist movement politics in response to America's rape culture, an expanded recognition of the experience of trans* people, and increased constraints on women's reproductive rights. Further, in response to the murder of Michael Brown in August 2014, the founding of Black Lives Matter by community organizers Patrisse Cullors, Alicia Garza, and Opal Tometi also thrust intersectionality into the public discourse. Black feminist activists in particular have been especially vocal about the importance of intersectionality in the Black Lives Matter movement, highlighting the victimization of black women by the state, via extrajudicial violence, and through domestic violence in black communities. This resurgence of attention to black feminist organizing created a new opportunity for black feminist theorizing, returning to the origins of intersectionality to refine how twenty-first century movement politics affect theory-building and vice versa.

The two broad tracts of intersectionality research—the theoretical and discursive analysis in humanities and the empirical data focus in the social sciences—continue to shape the development of the theory, albeit in different directions and to somewhat divergent ends. Academic work occurs in tandem and sometimes in cooperation with organizing work. Increased attention to the radical potential of conversations about organizing and scholarship might theoretically inform more than just the inequality literature, but also the social movements literature as well (Cohen 2004). From its inception, black feminist theory has suggested that inquiry should begin with lived experience and help refine and drive theory-building and empirical investigations. Black feminist scholars have continued to hold this theoretical tenet as central to their intersectional investigations, recognizing the dialectical relationship between theory and practice. By engaging more directly with black feminist theories of intersectionality outside of the discipline, as well as the intersectionality theory developed within the field of sociology since the classical period, sociologists can strengthen the robustness of intersectionality by not avoiding or bracketing some of its more reflexive and critical theoretical histories. This more comprehensive engagement would illuminate how the macro-structural contours of the matrix of domination, the lived experiences of identity at multiple social locations, and coalition-based social movements function simultaneously to shape outcomes, theory, methods, and practice.

References

Acker, J. (2000). Revisiting class: Thinking from gender, race, and organizations. *Social Politics: International Studies in Gender, State & Society, 7*(2), 192–214.

Aldridge, D. P. (2008). *Imagine a world: Pioneering black women sociologists*. University Press of America.

Andersen, M. (2005). Thinking about women: A quarter century's view. *Gender & Society, 19*(4), 437–455.

Barnett, B. M. (1993). Invisible southern black women leaders in the civil rights movement: The triple constraints of gender, race, and class. *Gender and Society, 7*(2), 162–182.

Barnett, B. M., Brewer, R. M., & Kuumba, M. B. (1999). New directions in race, gender and class studies: African American experiences. *Race, Gender & Class, 6*(2), 7–28.

Battle, J. (1999). How the boyz really made it out of the hood: Educational outcomes for African American boys in father-only versus mother-only households. *Race, Gender & Class, 6*(2), 130–146.

Beale, F. M. (1970). *Double jeopardy: To be female and black. Words of fire: An anthology of black feminist thought*. New York: Signet.

Belkhir, J. A. A. (1996). Social inequality and race, gender, class: A working class intellectual perspective. *Race, Gender & Class, 4*(1), 167–194.

Bertrand, M., & Mullainathan, S. (2004). Are Emily and Greg more employable than Lakisha and Jamal? A field experiment on labor market discrimination. *The American Economic Review, 94*(4), 991–1013.

Bettie, J. (2002). Exceptions to the rule upwardly mobile white and Mexican American high school girls. *Gender & Society, 16*(3), 403–422.

Blea, I. I. (1992). *La chicana and the intersection of race, class, and gender*. Westport: Praeger Publishers.

Bowleg, L. (2008). When black+ lesbian+ woman≠ black lesbian woman: The methodological challenges of qualitative and quantitative intersectionality research. *Sex Roles, 59*(5–6), 312–325.

Brewer, R. M. (1993). Theorizing race, class and gender: The New scholarship of black feminist intellectuals and black women's labor. In S. M. James & A. P. A. Busia (Eds.), *Theorizing black feminisms: The visionary pragmatism of black women* (pp. 13–30). New York: Routledge.

Cho, S., Crenshaw, K. W., & McCall, L. (2013). Toward a field of intersectionality studies: Theory, applications, and praxis. *Signs, 38*(4), 785–810.

Choo, H. Y., & Ferree, M. M. (2010). Practicing intersectionality in sociological research: A critical analysis of inclusions, interactions, and institutions in the study of inequalities. *Sociological Theory, 28*(2), 129–149.

Chow, E. N. L. (1987). The development of feminist consciousness among Asian American women. *Gender & Society, 1*(3), 284–299.

Christian, B. (1987). The race for theory. *Cultural Critique, 6*, 51–63.

Chun, J. J. (2011). *Organizing at the margins: The symbolic politics of labor in south Korea and the united states*. Ithaca: Cornell University Press.

Clarke, C. ([1983] 1995). Lesbianism: Act of resistance. In B. Guy-Sheftall (Ed.), *Words of fire: An anthology of African-American feminist thought* (pp. 242–251). New York: Signet.

Cohen, C. (2004). Deviance as resistance: A new research agenda for the study of black politics. *Du Bois Review, 1*(1), 27–45.

Collins, P. H. (1990). *Black feminist thought: Knowledge, consciousness, and the politics of empowerment*. New York: Routledge.

Collins, P. H. (1995). Symposium on West and Fenstermaker's doing difference. *Gender & Society, 4*(9), 491–494.

Collins, P. H. (2005). *Black sexual politics: African Americans, gender, and the new racism*. New York: Routledge.

Collins, P. H. (2015). Intersetionality's definitional dilemmas. *Annual Review of Sociology, 41*, 1–20.

Combahee River Collective (CRC). (1977). A black feminist statement. In G.-S. Beverly (Ed.), *Words of fire: An anthology of African-American feminist thought* (pp. 231–240). New York: The New Press.

Cooper, A. J. (1892). *A voice from the South: By a black woman of the South*. Chapel Hill: North Carolina Collection, University of North Carolina Chapel Hill.

Cooper, B. C. (2015). Love no limit: Towards a black feminist future (in theory). *The Black Scholar, 45*(4), 7–21.

Crenshaw, K. (1989). Demarginalizing the intersection of race and sex: A black feminist critique of antidiscrimination doctrine, feminist theory and antiracist politics. *University of Chicago Legal Forum* (pp. 139–167).

Crenshaw, K. (1991). Mapping the margins: Intersectionality, identity politics, and violence against women of color. *Stanford Law Review, 43*(6), 1241–1299.

Crenshaw, K. (2015, September 24). Why intersectionality can't wait. *The Washington Post*. Available at: https://www.washingtonpost.com/news/in-theory/wp/2015/09/24/why-intersectionality-cant-wait/

Cuadraz, G. H., & Uttal, L. (1999). Intersectionality and in-depth interviews: Methodological strategies for analyzing race, class, and gender. *Race, Gender & Class, 6*(3), 156–186.

Davies, C. B. (2007). *Left of Karl Marx: The political life of black communist Claudia Jones*. Durham: Duke University Press.

Davis, A. Y. (1983). *Women, race, and class*. New York: Vintage.

Davis, A. Y. (1998). *Blues legacies and black feminism: Gertrude "Ma" Rainey, Bessie Smith, and Billie holiday*. New York: Pantheon Books.

Davis, K. (2008). Intersectionality as buzzword: A sociology of science perspective on what makes a feminist theory successful. *Feminist Theory, 9*(1), 67–85.

Deitch, C. (1993). Gender, race, and class politics and the inclusion of women in title VII of the 1964 civil rights act. *Gender & Society, 7*(2), 183–203.

Dill, B. T. (1988). Our mothers' grief: Racial ethnic women and the maintenance of families. *Journal of Family History, 13*(4), 415–431.

Dillaway, H., & Broman, C. (2001). Race, class, and gender difference in marital satisfaction and divisions of household labor among dual-earner couples: A case for intersectional analysis. *Journal of Family Issues, 22*, 309–327.

Du Bois, W. E. B. (1899). *The Philadelphia negro: A social study (No. 14)*. Philadelphia: University of Pennsylvania Press.

Fogg-Davis, H. G. (2006). Theorizing black lesbians within black feminism: A critique of same-race street harassment. *Politics & Gender, 2*(1), 57–76.

Fox-Genovese, E. (1988). *Within the plantation household: Black and white women of the old south*. Chapel Hill: University of North Carolina Press.

Gamson, J., & Moon, D. (2004). The sociology of sexualities: Queer and beyond. *Annual Review of Sociology, 30*, 47–64.

Garcia, L. (2012). *Respect yourself, protect yourself: Latina girls and sexual identity*. New York: New York University Press.

Giddings, P. J. (2009). *Ida: A sword among lions*. New York: Harper Collins.

Glenn, E. N. (1992). From servitude to service work: Historical continuities in the racial division of paid reproductive labor. *Signs, 18*(1), 1–43.

Glenn, E. N. (2009). *Unequal freedom: How race and gender shaped American citizenship and labor*. Cambridge, MA: Harvard University Press.

Greenebaum, J. (1999). Placing Jewish women into the intersectionality of race, class and gender. *Race, Gender & Class, 6*(4), 41–60.

Guy-Sheftall, B. (1992). Black women's studies: The interface of women's studies and black studies. *Phylon, 49*(1–2), 33–41.

Guy-Sheftall, B. (1995). *Words of fire: An anthology of African-American feminist thought*. New York: The New Press.

Hancock, A. M. (2005). W. E. B. Du Bois: Intellectual forefather of intersectionality? *Souls, 7*(3), 74–84.

Hancock, A. M. (2007). When multiplication doesn't equal quick addition: Examining intersectionality as a research paradigm. *Perspectives on Politics, 5*(1), 63–79.

Haney, L. (1996). Homeboys, babies, men in suits: The state and the reproduction of male dominance. *American Sociological Review, 61*(5), 759–778.

Harding, S. G. (2003). *The feminist standpoint theory reader: Intellectual and political controversies*. New York: Routledge Press.

Higginbotham, E. B. (1993). The politics of respectability. In *Righteous discontent: The women's movement in the black Baptist church, 1880–1920* (pp. 185–229). Cambridge: Harvard University Press.

Hine, D. C. (1989). Rape and the inner lives of black women in the Middle West. *Signs, 14*(4), 912–920.

Hine, D. C., & Thompson, K. (1999). *A shining thread of hope: The history of black women in America*. New York: Broadway.

Hooks, B. (2000 [1984]). *Feminist theory: From margin to center*. New York: South End Press.

Hull, G. T., Scott, P. B., & Smith, B. (Eds.). (1982). *But some of us are brave: Black men's studies*. New York: Feminist Press at CUNY.

Hunter, M. A. (2010). All the gays are white and all the blacks are straight: Black gay men, identity, and community. *Sexuality Research and Social Policy, 7*(2), 81–92.

Jacobs, J. L. (1994). Gender, race, class, and the trend towards early motherhood: A feminist analysis of teen mothers in contemporary society. *Journal of Contemporary Ethnography, 22*(4), 442–462.

Jacobs, H. A., Jacobs, J. S., & Yellin, J. F. (2009). *Incidents in the life of a slave girl: Written by herself* (Vol. 119). Cambridge, MA: Harvard University Press.

Jarmon, R. (2013). *Black girls are from the future: Essays on race, digital creativity, and pop culture*. Jarmon Media.

Jeffries, V., & Ransford, H. E. (1980). *Social stratification: A multiple hierarchy approach*. Boston: Allyn & Bacon.

Johnson, P. E. (2005). 'Quare' studies, or (almost) everything I know about queer studies I learned from my grandmother. In E. P. Johnson & M. G. Henderson (Eds.), *Black queer studies: A critical anthology* (pp. 124–157). Durham: Duke University Press.

Jones, C. C. (1949). An end to the neglect of the problems of the Negro Woman. In B. Guy-Sheftall (Ed.), *Words of fire: An anthology of African-American feminist thought* (pp. 108–123). New York: The New Press.

Jones, J. (1985). *Labor of love, labor of sorrow: Black women, work, and the family, from slavery to present*. New York: Random House.

Kennedy, F. (1976). *Color Me Flo: My hard life and good times*. New York: Prentice Hall.

King, D. (1988). Multiple jeopardy, multiple consciousness: The context of a black feminist ideology. *Signs, 14*(1), 42–72.

Ladner, J. A. (1971). *Tomorrow's tomorrow: The black woman* (Vol. 839). Lincoln: University of Nebraska Press.

Ladner, J. A. (1973). *The death of white sociology: Essays on race and culture*. Baltimore: Black Classic Press.

Lorde, A. (1984). *Sister outsider: Essays and speeches*. Crossing Press.

Lorde, A. (1984b). *Sister outsider: Essays and speeches*. Berkeley: University of California Press.

Lovell, V. (2002). Constructing social citizenship: The exclusion of African American women from employment insurance in the U.S. *Feminist Economics, 8*(2), 191–197.

MacKinnon, C. A. (2013). Intersectionality as method: A note. *Signs, 38*(4), 1019–1030.

Martinez, T. A. (1996). Toward a Chicana feminist epistemological standpoint: Theory at the intersection of race, class, and gender. *Race, Gender & Class, 3*(3), 107–128.

Massey, D. S., & Lundy, G. (2001). Use of black English and racial discrimination in urban housing markets new methods and findings. *Urban Affairs Review, 36*(4), 452–469.

McCall, L. (2005). The complexity of intersectionality. *Signs, 30*(3), 1771–1800.

McDonald, K. B. (1997). Black activist mothering: A historical intersection of race. *Gender, and Class Gender and Society, 11*(6), 773–795.

McGuire, D. L. (2011). *At the dark end of the street: Black women, rape, and resistance-a new history of the civil rights movement from Rosa parks to the rise of black power*. New York: Vintage.

Mink, G. (Ed.). (1999). *Whose welfare?* Ithaca: Cornell University Press.

Mink, G., et al. (2003). Feminist policy scholars intervene in the welfare debate. *Social Justice, 30*(4), 107–134.

Moore, M. (2006). Lipstick or timberlands? Meanings of gender presentation in black lesbian communities. *Signs, 32*(1), 113–139.

Moore, M. (2008). Gendered power relations among women: A study of household decision making in black, lesbian stepfamilies. *American Sociological Review, 73*, 335–356.

Moore, M. (2011). *Invisible families: Gay identities, relationships, and motherhood among black women*. Berkeley: University of California Press.

Moraga, C., & Anzaldúa, G. (Eds.). (1981 [2015]). *This bridge called my back: Writings by radical women of color*. Albany: SUNY Press.

Morris, A. (2015). *The scholar denied: WEB DuBois and the birth of American sociology*. Berkeley: University of California Press.

Murray, P. (1970). The liberation of black women. In B. Guy-Sheftall (Ed.), *Words of fire: An anthology of African-American feminist thought* (pp. 186–197). New York: The New Press.

Pager, D., & Quillian, L. (2005). Walking the talk? What employers say versus what they do. *American Sociological Review, 70*(3), 355–380.

Pough, G. (2004). *Check it while I wreck it: Black womanhood, hip-hop culture, and the public sphere*. Lebanon: Northeastern University Press.

Randolph, S. M. (2015). *Florynce "Flo" Kennedy: The life of a black feminist radical*. Chapel Hill: University of North Carolina Press.

Reid, L. W., Adelman, R. M., & Jaret, C. (2007). Women, race, and ethnicity: Exploring earnings differentials in metropolitan America. *City and Community, 6*(2), 137–156.

Roberts, D. (1997). *Killing the black body: Race, reproduction, and the meaning of liberty*. New York: Vintage.

Roberts, D. (1999). Welfare's ban on poor motherhood. In G. Mink (Ed.), *Whose welfare?* (pp. 152–167). Ithaca: Cornell University Press.

Roberts, D. E. (1996). Meaning of Blacks' fidelity to the constitution. *Fordham Law Review, 65*, 1761.

Robinson, Z. (2014). *This ain't Chicago: Race, class, and regional identity in the post-soul South*. Chapel Hill: University of North Carolina Press.

Romero, M. (1995). Life as the Maid's daughter: An exploration of the everyday boundaries of race, class, and gender. In M. Romero & P. Hondagneu-Sotelo (Eds.), *Challenging fronteras: Structuring Latina and Latino lives in the U.S.: An anthology of readings* (pp. 195–209). New York: Routledge.

Royster, J. J. (Ed.). (1997). *Southern horrors and other writings: The anti-lynching campaign of Ida B. Wells, 1892–1900*. Boston: Bedford Books.

Scott, P. B. (1982). Debunking Sapphire: Toward a non-racist and non-sexist social science. In G. T. Hull, P. B. Scott, & B. Smith (Eds.) *All the women are white, all the blacks are men, but some of us are brave* (pp. 85–92). New York: The Feminist Press.

Sharpless, R. (2010). *Cooking in other Women's kitchens: Domestic workers in the south, 1865–1960*. Chapel Hill: University of North Carolina Press.

Simien, E. M. (2005). Race, gender, and linked fate. *Journal of Black Studies, 35*(5), 529–550.

Smith, B. (1984). *Home girls: A black feminist anthology*. New Brunswick: Rutgers University Press.

Smith, B. (1985). Some home truths on the contemporary black feminist movement. *The Black Scholar, 16*(2), 4–13.

Smith, A., & Stewart, A. J. (1983). Approaches to studying racism and sexism in black women's lives. *Journal of Social Issues, 39*(3), 1–15.

Springer, K. (2002). Third wave black feminism. *Signs, 27*(4), 1059–1082.

Stoll, L. C. (2013). *Race and gender in the classroom: Teachers, privilege, and enduring social inequalities*. Lanham: Lexington Books.

Taylor, U. Y. (2001). The theory and practice of black feminism. *The Black Scholar, 28*(2), 18–28.

Truth, S. (1995 [1851]). Woman's rights. In B. Guy-Sheftall (Ed.), *Words of fire* (36). New York: The New Press.

Wallace-Sanders, K. (2009). *Mammy: A century of race, gender, and southern memory*. Ann Arbor: University of Michigan Press.

Wells-Barnett, I. (1959). Law in America. In B. Guy-Sheftall (Ed.), *Words of fire: An anthology of African-American feminist thought* (pp. 70–76). New York: The New Press.

West, C., & Fenstermaker, S. (1995). Doing difference. *Gender & society, 9*(1), 8–37.

White, D. G. (1999). *Ar'n't I a woman?: Female slaves in the plantation south*. New York: WW Norton & Company.

Wilkins, A. C. (2004). Puerto Rican wannabes sexual spectacle and the marking of race, class, and gender boundaries. *Gender & Society, 18*(1), 103–121.

Wingfield, A. H. (2009). Racializing the glass elevator: Reconsidering men's experiences with women's work. *Gender & Society, 23*(1), 5–26.

Wright, E., II. (2016). *W. E. B. Du bois and the Atlanta sociological laboratory: The first American school of sociology*. London: Ashgate Publishing Company.

Young, A. A., Jr., & Deskins, D. R., Jr. (2001). Early traditions of African-American sociological thought. *Annual Review of Sociology, 27*, 445–477.

Part V

Modes of Change

24 Social Evolution

Richard Machalek and Michael W. Martin

24.1 Introduction

In common usage, including that employed by social scientists, the term *evolution* typically refers to change that is both gradual and long-term. Social change has been described by western thinkers as evolutionary at least as early as the writings of Kant (Degler 1991), and some of the earliest social scientists framed their thinking in evolutionary terms (e.g., Herbert Spencer, Emile Durkheim, Edward A. Ross, Charles Ellwood, Franklin Giddings, Charles Horton Cooley, Lester Frank Ward, William Graham Sumner). There is, however, considerable variation with regard to specific phenomena that can be said to undergo evolutionary change. For example, early sociological theorists often described various social structures such as groups or institutions, and even entire societies or social systems, as subject to evolutionary change (e.g., Spencer 1885; Durkheim 1947). With the rise of Darwin's theory of evolution, entire species came to be viewed as subject to transformation by the evolutionary processes comprising "natural selection" (Darwin 1859). In Darwin's view, evolutionary change is manifest over generational time in populations of individuals, and such change entails modifications in their morphological and physiological traits. When such traits promote the survival and reproductive prospects of individuals, they are said to be adaptations. Until recently, the term evolution in the social sciences has been used less frequently to describe changes in individual organisms and more frequently to describe changes in society and its constituent parts. In contemporary sociology, considerations of evolutionary changes in the human organism have attracted the attention of sociologists only during the last 40 years or so, prompted in large part by the publication of Edward O. Wilson's book *Sociobiology: The New Synthesis* (1975) and the extensive scientific developments to which it has given rise.

This chapter provides an overview of evolutionary thinking in sociological theory from the nineteenth century to the present. Particular attention is devoted to the emergence and development of theoretical ideas and empirical research that have been stimulated by the "second Darwinian revolution," which is the application of neo-Darwinian theory (the integration of Darwin's theory of natural selection with Mendelian genetics) to the study of human social behavior. The 1975 publication of Wilson's *Sociobiology* can be said to have signified the dawning of the second Darwinian revolution.

R. Machalek (✉)
University of Wyoming, Laramie, WY, USA
e-mail: machalek@uwyo.edu

M.W. Martin
Adams State University, Alamosa, CO, USA
e-mail: mwmartin@adams.edu

S. Abrutyn (ed.), *Handbook of Contemporary Sociological Theory*,
Handbooks of Sociology and Social Research, DOI 10.1007/978-3-319-32250-6_24

Two primary branches of behavioral biology, sociobiology and behavioral ecology, have been most influential in guiding efforts to apply insights derived from the second Darwinian revolution to the study of human social behavior. More recently, sociologists have begun to turn to the neurosciences as well in order to gain purchase on how natural selection has shaped the evolution of human social behavior (Turner 2000, 2012, 2015; Franks 2010, 2015).

Thus, a perusal of the history of evolutionary thinking in sociology reveals two primary foci: (1) a traditional focus on changes in the structure of society and its various components, and (2) a more recent focus on the evolved features of the human brain and mind and how these features help shape human social behavior. Elements of both foci can be found in a growing body of sociological thought and inquiry that is being called "evolutionary sociology" (Maryanski 1998; Turner and Maryanski 2008; Runciman 2015). In recent years, much of evolutionary thinking in sociology has begun to converge. But various conceptual and theoretical divergences persist, and a strong consensus about exactly what a unified evolutionary perspective in sociology should entail remains elusive. This situation is not unique to evolutionary sociology. In fact, significant differences prevail even today among biologists regarding fundamental issues in evolutionary theory and research. One of the foremost and most contentious of such issues is the recent debate over levels of selection in social evolution (Wilson and Wilson 2007; West et al. 2011). Given continuing debate among evolutionary biologists themselves about fundamental issues in evolutionary theory, it is hardly surprising that evolutionary-minded sociologists are not of one mind about how to develop and apply evolutionary thinking to the study of human social behavior. The purpose of this chapter is to review key issues and recent developments in theoretical thinking produced by evolutionary sociologists and to summarize and consolidate basic insights that are emerging among those engaged in a pursuit of an evolutionary understanding of human social behavior.

24.2 Fundamental Issues in Conceptualizing Evolution

The notion of evolution in the history of social thought ranges from very casual conceptions such as "long-term, gradual change" to more formal and technical conceptions that derive from current work being conducted in scientific disciplines such as evolutionary biology, population and molecular genetics, behavioral ecology, and the cognitive neurosciences. In that regard, we will briefly review basic issues entailed in viewing social change as an evolutionary process.

Although the rate and degree of change that can be regarded as evolutionary in nature vary, most traditional conceptualizations of evolution, including social evolution, connote change that is both gradual and incremental. In organic evolution, natural selection occurs over intergenerational time, from reproductive cycle to reproductive cycle. Recent conceptualizations of sociocultural evolution posit that evolutionary change also can occur intragenerationally, within an individual's lifetime. The evolutionary sociologist Jonathan H. Turner has posited three forms of selection that can occur in sociocultural evolution: "Darwinian selection," "Durkheimian selection," and "Spencerian selection" (Turner 2010). Durkheimian selection and Spencerian selection will be discussed later.

In classical, Darwinian evolutionary theory, evolution means intergenerational changes in the distribution of traits within populations of individuals. These traits are the product of gene-environment interactions that produce phenotypes, some of which constitute evolved adaptations. An adaptation is a genetically-based trait that enhances an individual's chances of survival and reproductive success within a particular environment. Adaptations comprise morphological, physiological, and behavioral traits. In theories of sociocultural evolution, individuals are sometimes the focus of evolutionary analysis, but most traditional sociological theories of evolution focus on changes in the structure of society or its corporate components (groups, organizations, institutions, or stratification systems). Such changes can occur either within or across generations.

Both organic and sociocultural evolution depend upon the influence of informational media that produce evolved adaptations (phenotypic traits). In organic evolution, the informational medium is genetic. In sociocultural evolution the medium is culture. However, culture can also be conceptualized as an environment that interacts with genes to produce evolved adaptations. The study of how genes and culture interact to produce traits at both the individual and collective level is called gene-culture coevolution (Boyd and Richerson 1985; Lumsden and Wilson 1981). Evolutionary changes in the distribution of either individual or societal traits are understood to represent adjustments to conditions presented by environments. Such adjustments may constitute modifications that are responses to stable features of environments, or they may entail modifications that are responses to changing environmental conditions.

In classical organic evolutionary theory, phenotypic changes produced by the interaction between genes and their environments are the result of random, non-purposive (non-teleological) changes in genes whose products are subject to non-random, but equally non-purposive environmental forces of selection. That is, organic evolution is not directed by goals or informed by foresight. It is a purely mechanical process entailing gene-environment interaction that has been described metaphorically as the work of a "blind watchmaker" (Dawkins 1986). By way of contrast, sociocultural evolution can, but need not be, powered by purposive, goal-oriented human conduct that is informed by foresight and directed by planning. In other words, sociocultural evolution can be shaped by teleological processes while, simultaneously, remaining subject to purely mechanical, non-purposive forces as well.

Almost all versions of evolutionary explanation imply that either individual or collective adjustments to features of environments confer advantages of some sort. In classical organic evolutionary theory, such advantages constitute elevated prospects for survival and reproduction by individuals (and sometimes, kin groups) and are summarized by the expressions "fitness" or "reproductive success." Accordingly, the measure of evolutionary success is not captured by a literal interpretation of the phrase *survival* of the fittest. Instead, survival matters only if it yields the consequence of reproductive success of either individuals, which is labeled individual or Darwinian fitness, or the reproductive success of members of kin groups, which is labeled inclusive fitness (Hamilton 1964). In sociocultural evolution, the notion that evolutionary change confers advantages extends beyond the survival and reproductive success of individuals. Instead, fitness (success in sociocultural evolution) is commonly construed to mean "the ability of sociocultural units to *sustain themselves in their environments*" (Turner 2010:30). Thus, fitness in sociocultural evolution (the enhanced ability of a society or a corporate structure to persist) may or may not contribute to biological fitness (reproductive success of individuals). In fact, the maintenance of a sociocultural system that is stressed in terms of resources needed to sustain its population may be enhanced by reduced biological fitness (fertility rates) among members of that population, because this will reduce demand for resources such as food. While sociocultural fitness and biological fitness may be mutually enhancing in certain environmental contexts, they may work at cross-purposes in others.

Among evolutionary theorists, a long debated question is the level at which adaptations evolve. Does natural selection produce traits that enhance the survival and reproductive success of individuals alone, or does it produce traits that are fitness-enhancing for groups, populations, or even species as well? This is commonly discussed as the "group selection" (or "levels of selection") problem. Most of the discussion pertains to behavior that is mediated by genes rather than culture. Accordingly, the levels of selection debate is more contentious among biologists studying organic evolution than it has been among sociologists studying sociocultural evolution. In simplified terms, the basic question is this: Does natural selection produce traits for the "good of the individual" or for the "good of the group?"

Though sociocultural evolution arguably entails phenomena of greater complexity than does organic evolution, the question of group selection is, ironically, more easily resolved in the minds of sociologists rather than biologists. In conventional organic evolutionary theory, the forces of selection act directly on individuals and indirectly on the genes that produce them. Since only individual bodies, not groups, actually house genes and transmit them to individual offspring, the "target of selection" is the individual. However, when describing and analyzing patterns of sociocultural evolution, sociologists view various sorts of collectivities as "superorganisms" that are also "potential units subject to selection," and such superorganisms include groups, organizations, communities, institutional domains, entire societies, or even intersocietal systems (Turner and Maryanski 2015:103). Like the physical phenotypes of individual organisms, "sociocultural phenotypes" are seen as "survivor (sic) machines" that buffer the forces of selection which emanate from the environments in which populations of individuals live (Turner and Maryanski 2015:103–106). In sociocultural evolution, the targets of selection are complex and multi-layered forms of culture and social structure, not merely the physical phenotypic traits of individual organisms. Over time, some sociocultural phenotypes succumb to various forces of selection, while others exhibit higher "fitness," which is defined in terms of length of time that a sociocultural system exists or its ability to exist and endure in a range of environments (Turner and Maryanski 2015:95).

An example of this sort of thinking about sociocultural evolution and group selection is available in historical analyses of the survival of a sociocultural system that has been targeted by some of the most severe selection forces to which any human population has been subjected, the people of Israel and their religion (Abrutyn 2015a, b). By integrating elements of cultural sociological analysis with principles derived from theories of sociocultural evolution, Abrutyn explains how "institutional entrepreneurs" acting over long periods of historical time crafted "cultural assemblages" that contributed significantly to the survival of Israelite religion and the population that bore it (2015b). Particularly significant were pollution-purification rituals that were performed annually, weekly, and even daily, and these rituals integrated the salvation of the individual with the well-being and endurance of the community, thereby functioning as a group-selection mechanism that helps explain the survival of the Jewish people and their religion for over two millennia (Abrutyn 2014, 2015b).

As conceptualized by evolutionary sociologists such as Lenski (2005), Turner (2010), Blute (2010), and Abrutyn (2014), the history of sociocultural evolution presents unassailable evidence of the existence of group selection, a complex set of processes by means of which diverse sociocultural phenotypes evolve among different groups and populations. Consequently, in the view of at least two evolutionary sociologists, "it is so obvious that selection is working on social structures and their cultures organizing individual organisms that it is difficult to see what the controversy (about group selection) is all about in biology" (Turner and Maryanski 2015:104). The question of why the issue of group selection is more hotly disputed among evolutionary biologists than among evolutionary sociologists becomes clearer when differences in the way group selection is viewed by these "two cultures" of evolutionary thinkers are understood.

In simplest terms, evolutionary biologists approach the levels of selection (including group selection) issue in terms of the genetic, not cultural, forces that underpin social evolution. In mainstream, evolutionary biological theory, natural selection favors any genetically-based trait that increases the survival and reproductive success of an individual bearing that trait, not other members of groups to which that individual might belong. In organic evolutionary theory, the idea of group selection means that natural selection would somehow favor genes that would *reduce* the survival and reproductive chances of any individual that bore them, but simultaneously, *increase* the survival and reproductive success of the population of the group as a whole. Put casually, group selection would mean that natural selection would favor genes that are "good for the group" at the expense of genes that are "good for the individual." In this conception of group selection, the adaptive consequences of a trait are always measured using the metric of "gene-counting," not the persistence or demise of a collectivity organized and regulated by the "sociocultural phenotypes." Thus, the case of the variable success and failure of automobile companies as an example of group selection in sociocultural evolution fails to address the central issue around which the debate over group selection in organic evolution revolves (Turner and Maryanski 2015:104). Unless, and *only* unless, the survival or demise of automobile companies could be shown to be linked somehow to genetic variability among individuals who comprise the populations of those companies, the issue of group selection as conceptualized in *organic evolution* is not even addressed in this example.

It is not surprising that confusion persists about what is at issue in notions of group selection in sociocultural evolution versus organic evolution. In fact, debate about the levels of selection issue is even more extensive, and probably rancorous, among evolutionary biologists than it is between social scientists and biologists. A recent article written by three evolutionary biologists identifying 16 misconceptions about the evolution of cooperation among humans provides insight into the complexity of this issue (West et al. 2011). Of the 16 misconceptions, almost one-third (five) pertain to the issue of group selection. Efforts to determine if group selection actually occurs in organic evolution are made more challenging by the fact that the concept of group selection has at least four different meanings (West et al. 2011:246–249). Though most of their discussion pertains to group selection in organic evolution alone, the authors briefly address "cultural group selection," and conclude that "while it is often argued that the group is a fundamental unit of cultural evolution, or that cultural evolution is a group-level process (Boyd and Richerson 1985), there is no formal basis for this" (West et al. 2011:248). As is clear from this brief discussion of group selection, the levels of selection issue is complex and multifaceted in the context of both organic and sociocultural evolution, and it does not resolve itself easily to the satisfaction of all participants. As more dialogue develops between social scientists and evolutionary biologists, prospects increase for the advancement of scientific understanding of this important aspect of social evolution.

In summary, the very existence of sociocultural systems and sociocultural evolution depends ultimately on processes of organic evolution, because the existence of culture depends on the evolved cognitive capabilities of a species that has a brain that can produce and process symbols. The trajectory of organic evolution, however, can be and is shaped by processes of sociocultural evolution, as is illustrated by biological fitness-reducing meanings (e.g., celibacy norms in certain religious groups) and technologies (effective contraceptive technologies). Thus, the relationship between organic evolution and sociocultural evolution represents an important topic in evolutionary inquiry in general.

24.3 Evolutionary Sociological Theory Before the Second Darwinian Revolution

In the broad, most general sense of the term, evolution in traditional sociological thought commonly referred to long-term, gradual changes in the overall organization of society or certain parts of it. Evolutionary change was frequently characterized as entailing a sequence of stages. In almost all such conceptions of evolutionary change, each stage was viewed as an "advancement" of some sort, and the overall course of evolution was commonly understood to represent "progress" (Blute 2010:3–7, 183). Eventually, Darwin's theory of evolution by natural selection largely replaced teleological and orthogenetic conceptions of change in which evolution was viewed as a process directed toward a predetermined outcome.

24.3.1 Evolutionary Thought in Classical Sociological Theory

The two classical sociological theorists whose writings were most heavily infused with biological ideas were Herbert Spencer and Emile Durkheim. Of the two, Spencer's theoretical thinking was more fully developed in evolutionary terms. Though Durkheim relied heavily on biological metaphors to propose a structural-functional analysis of society, Spencer's theories provided a more complete and nuanced account of processes implicated in societal evolution. A number of key ideas were shared by both thinkers, including the notion that (1) populations of human societies exhibit a long-term trend toward growth, (2) population growth leads to increasing complexity and structural differentiation within societies, (3) increasing societal complexity alters the nature of integration/solidarity within societies, (4) all of these changes typically enhance the ability of societies to adjust more successfully to their environments, and (5) all of these changes are amenable to systematic, empirical investigation. Another key feature shared by the writings of both thinkers, also influenced by biology, was their advocacy of interpreting the "structures" of sociocultural systems in terms of the "functions" those structures performed for the survival and maintenance of those systems. Subsequently, both Spencer and Durkheim became associated with the theoretical perspective of "functionalism," or "structural-functionalism" which dominated western sociology through the first half of the twentieth century, and slightly beyond.

Because of his role in the development of extensive data sets on many societies, Spencer's theories were heavily informed by empirical evidence (Turner 1985). As a result, his evolutionary analysis is perhaps the most detailed and empirically-informed of that among any of his contemporaries and most of his successors in western classical sociological theory. The organizing theme of all of his evolutionary analyses was the empirical tendency for human societies to exhibit a near-universal transition from structural simplicity to complexity, a development that was echoed in the work of a number of his successors in classical sociological theory, including Durkheim, Marx, Simmel, Tönnies, and Veblen, among others. The work of all of these theorists placed heavy emphasis on the evolutionary trend toward greater structural differentiation within societies, which, in turn, was often described as a series of evolutionary stages through which societies evolved.

Spencer was perhaps the first classical theorist to assert that, inasmuch as human societies are "superorganisms," their analysis requires concepts and explanatory principles beyond those that are sufficient for studying organic systems. Yet, there is considerable isomorphism in the conceptual apparatus that Spencer used to analyze sociocultural evolution and that used to analyze organic evolution. In fact, as has been commonly observed, Darwin expressed a debt of gratitude to Spencer (as well as to Adam Smith and Thomas Malthus) for insights about organic evolution, including Spencer's now-famous phrase, "the survival of the fittest."

According to Spencer, the fundamental force that drives the evolution of the transition of societies from simplicity to complexity is growth in population size, a development which itself became the focus of explanatory efforts among later evolutionary thinkers. According to Spencer, the survival of all human societies depends on their ability to solve three basic problems that he labeled operation (the production of resources and the reproduction of populations and social structures), regulation (the coordination and control of activities of members of a population), and distribution (the allocation of information and resources among members of a population, and the movement of those people) (Spencer 1885). In Spencer's view, these three problems constitute adaptive challenges in response to which adaptive structures such as human institutions evolved.

Spencer's scheme for specifying how societal complexity, or differentiation, evolves merits brief description as both a framework for conducting comparative analysis among societies as well as a map of stages through which he contended that societies tend to evolve. Foreshadowing the kind of thinking that eventually developed into the full-blown theoretical school known as "functionalism," Spencer contended that, as populations grow, they evolve increasingly specialized structures that achieve the societal mandates of operation, regulation, and distribution. Some of this growth occurs by means of amalgamation, whereby previously distinct societies become conjoined, while normal demographic processes of migration and fertility contribute further to larger population sizes. Spencer used the term "compounding" to denote the trend toward greater differentiation within societies, and this, in turn, led to his designating stages of societal evolution as comprising simple (with and without heads) societies, compound societies, doubly compound societies, and trebly compound societies (Spencer 1885). Informed by systematic, detailed cross-cultural data sets, Spencer's scheme for classifying societies at different stages of evolution was the most sophisticated and empirically informed of his time (Turner 1985, 2013).

Though far-less conceptually and theoretically detailed than Spencer's scheme, Durkheim also contributed to a stage-model conceptualization of societal evolution which, in many ways, closely parallels that of Spencer (Durkheim 1947). Like Spencer, Durkheim tried to explain the nature and course of the long-term trend of increasing structural complexity commonly evident in human societies. And like Spencer, Durkheim focused on increasing population size as the driving force behind this trend. For Durkheim, greater structural differentiation was most sociologically significant in the form of the division of labor and its consequences for the mechanisms by means of which societies achieved (or failed to achieve) solidarity, or integration. In Durkheim's view, the evolution of increasingly complex societies constituted a long-term evolutionary trend that could be described in terms of a transition from a form of societal cohesion based on shared culture (mechanical solidarity) to a form of cohesion based on specialization and the interdependence that it necessitated (organic solidarity). Like Spencer, Durkheim's work was highly influential both in stimulating subsequent stage-model thinking among sociological theorists and in laying a foundation for the development of functionalism.

Though less fully developed than the work of Spencer and even Durkheim as a distinct theoretical perspective, evolutionary ideas populate aspects of the writings of other classical sociological theorists as well. Like Spencer and Durkheim, Georg Simmel attributed considerable sociological significance to increasing structural differentiation (Turner 2013:172–176, 192–203). Similarly, by tracing the rise of capitalism through a sequence of eras distinguished by their modes of production, Marx's writing provided another stage model of societal evolution, one which later became influential in informing the more explicitly evolutionary theory of Gerhard Lenski (2005). Adopting L. H. Morgan's labels of "savagery," "barbarism," and "civilization, Thorstein Veblen described and analyzed long-term changes in human societies. The characteristics of his societal stages correspond surprisingly closely to contemporary models which feature hunting-gathering, horticultural, agricultural, and industrial stages of societal evolution found commonly in contemporary anthropological and sociological analyses. And though most closely associated with his contributions to the development of micro-sociology and social psychology, evolutionary insights constituted foundational principles on the basis of which George Herbert Mead constructed his theory of self and society.

The work of the sociological theorists discussed above represented attempts to characterize and explain societal-level changes in social structure in evolutionary terms. Another group of classical sociologists, some of whom were associated with the intellectual misadventure of Social Darwinism, focused more directly on the evolution of human nature. Interestingly, however, they were not all of one mind. While some contributed directly to the development of Social Darwinism, including racist conceptions of human variation, others explicitly rejected ideas on which Social Darwinism was based. For example, eschewing the notion that the idea of the survival of the fittest necessarily led to the conclusion that natural selection is driven by a ruthless war of "all against all," both L. F. Ward and E. A. Ross attributed to evolution the existence of "social instincts" that make humans concerned with the welfare of others and in possession of both "human sympathies" and a sense of "the corporate self" (Degler 1991:12–14). Ward, in fact, viewed evolution as a powerful, progressive force that installed extraordinary, innate potential in human nature that was all-too-often thwarted by environmental circumstances.

Nevertheless, both racist and sexist conceptions of human nature that prevailed in the late nineteenth and early twentieth centuries clearly helped shape the thought and writings of other sociologists as well as anthropologists, economists, and psychologists (Degler 1991:13–31). As the twentieth century progressed, however, hereditarian conceptions of human nature waned, and the concept of culture became the primary notion informing explanations of human behavior in both the social and behavioral sciences. It was not until the mid- to latter part of the twentieth century that ideas and information from evolutionary biology prompted a re-examination of the possibility that an evolved human nature manifests itself in human social behavior.

24.3.2 Evolutionary Thought in Sociological Theory Before 1975

The survival and development of evolutionary thinking in sociology during most of the second half of the twentieth century was limited largely to the further development of stage-models of evolution represented by the work of theorists such as Talcott Parsons, Gerhard and Jean Lenski, Patrick Nolan, and Jonathan H. Turner, among others. Prior to the onset of the second Darwinian revolution, roughly 1975, Lenski (1966) and Parsons (1966) produced the most influential stage models in evolutionary sociological theory. Like Spencer and Durkheim before them, Lenski and his colleagues traced the long-term evolution of human societies from the hunting-gathering era to the industrial and post-industrial eras. They placed primary emphasis on the role of subsistence technologies as the primary driving force of societal evolution, and they mapped the consequences of changes in subsistence technology on economic activity, the development of surplus, and the evolution of systems of social stratification (Lenski 1966; Lenski and Lenski 1970; Nolan and Lenski 2015). As did Spencer and Durkheim before them, Lenski and his colleagues emphasized the long-term trend toward greater structural differentiation within societies and accompanying developments in both societies' institutions and corporate structures. Societal evolution was characterized as consisting of process of variation and selection within environmental contexts, including the contexts created by other societies. The analogue to genetic variation in their models was cultural innovation, and the social structural products of cultural information were patterns of social structure, the sociocultural analogue to phenotypes in organic evolution. Subsistence technology was the feature of culture to which Lenski and his colleagues attributed greatest influence in shaping societal evolution.

About the same time that Lenski (1966) was developing his "ecological-evolutionary" model of societal evolution, Parsons also produced a theory of societal evolution (1966). As did Spencer and Durkheim before him, Parsons focused on the long-term evolutionary trends toward increasing societal size and greater cultural and social structural differentiation. Framing his evolutionary thinking in functionalist terms, Parsons addressed the question of how increasing societal complexity affects the problem of "integration" and yields "adaptive upgrading" which better enables societies to cope both with new, internal societal developments as well as novel environmental conditions.

Sociologists often equate evolution and development, but biologists distinguish between these two processes. Development occurs in individuals, while evolution occurs in populations. Reflecting on this distinction, Marion Blute explains that stage models of societal change are better regarded as developmental than evolutionary in nature (2010:3–7). Blute concludes that the theories of social change produced by Spencer, Durkheim, and even Parsons better characterize processes of biological development than they do evolution. And since the process of development can be described as a sequence of stages that ends in a largely predetermined outcome (e.g., and infant matures into an adult), early social thinkers tended to think about change as representing "progress" (Blute 2010). As will become evident later, contemporary stage-theories of evolution rarely imply developmental trajectories that are somehow predetermined in the process of social change itself. Though stage-model thinking can still be found in sociological theory, this tradition of sociological thought is being succeeded by newer versions of evolutionary theory, which will be discussed later.

During the 1960s and 1970s, significant developments occurred in evolutionary biology which eventually led to the threshold of what is now called the "second Darwinian revolution" (Machalek and Martin 2004). The most influential of those developments was the publication of *Sociobiology: The New Synthesis* (Wilson 1975), and it launched a new era of evolutionary thinking not only in behavioral biology (ethology, behavioral ecology), but eventually, in the social and behavioral sciences as well. The remainder of this chapter reviews key developments within sociobiology and associated fields of evolutionary inquiry and their eventual impact on the rise of a new "evolutionary sociology."

24.4 Evolutionary Sociological Theory After the Second Darwinian Revolution

24.4.1 The Rise and Influence of Sociobiology

Sociobiology is a branch of evolutionary biology devoted to the scientific study of the biological bases of social behavior among animals, including humans. Preceded by older branches of behavioral biology such as ethology and comparative psychology, sociobiology coalesced into a new and distinct branch of behavioral biology in 1975 with the publication of Wilson's tome. As Wilson describes it, sociobiology is simply the study of how social behavior and societies evolve by natural selection. The explanatory logic of sociobiology was developed for the study of non-human animals, but Wilson expanded it to include the study of human social behavior and societies as well.

In evolutionary theory, if a trait produced by natural selection contributes to an organism's chances of survival and reproductive success, it is called an adaptation. Adaptations consist of morphological (anatomical) traits, physiological traits, and behavioral traits, including social behaviors. Sociobiological research entails efforts to identify and analyze patterns of social behavior as possible evolved adaptations. For example, sociobiologists are interested in exploring how the allocation of parenting responsibilities, which they call "parental investment," might entail evolved adaptations for assuring that offspring survive to reproductive age (Trivers 1972). Categories of social behavior that sociobiologists have identified as possibly influenced by evolved adaptations include parenting, mating and mate selection, cooperation, competition, conflict, communication, altruism, reciprocity and exchange, aggression and violence, parent-offspring conflict, sibling competition, and status competition, among others.

Natural selection favors traits which, within the environmental contexts in which they exist, maximize an individual's *fitness*, or its genetic representation in the next generation. Sociobiological theory distinguishes between *individual fitness* (also called "Darwinian" fitness), and *inclusive fitness.* Individual fitness refers to the success of an individual in contributing its genes to the next generation by reproduction, and inclusive fitness refers to the sum of an individual's fitness plus that individual's contribution to the fitness of its relatives other than direct descendants. Inclusive fitness is increased by the process of *kin selection*, whereby social behaviors have adaptive consequences for members of kin groups, not just individuals.

Sociobiological theory traces the evolution of basic forms of cooperation among individuals in groups to the processes of kin selection, which can be supplemented by other evolutionary mechanisms such as "mutualism" (interaction with consequences that benefit all participants, regardless of their degree or relatedness) or "reciprocal altruism" (reciprocity among non-kin).

The idea that genetic kinship is the foundation on which cooperative social life first evolved was influenced strongly by research on the eusocial insects, which are ants, bees, wasps and termites. Ants, bees, and wasps (but not termites) feature an unusual genetic system known as "haplodiploidy" whereby sisters within a colony are more closely genetically related to each other than they are to their mothers. The genetic "hyper-relatedness" among full sisters means that they share, on average, 75 % of their genes with each other in contrast to full siblings in diploid species, which share, on average, only 50 % of their genes. Consequently, kin selection favors high levels of cooperation among the eusocial insects, commonly giving rise to colonies with very large populations and colony-level complex systems of social organization (Hölldobler and Wilson 1990). One of the most notable features of such colonies is the phenomenon of "reproductive altruism" whereby as few as one female (the "queen") in the colony monopolizes all egg-laying activity and is supported by all of the other females. It might be said that the queen occupies the status of "designated reproducer" for the entire colony, and all of the other females labor in support of her reproductive effort. The colony itself, sometimes described as a "superorganism," is like an individual, a reproductive unit, and the extraordinary degree of cooperation and sacrifice exhibited by colony members inspired evolutionary biologists to investigate the extent to which genetic kinship comprises the foundation of cooperative social life among other taxa as well, including vertebrates, thereby launching a now 50-year long program of sociobiological research (Hölldobler and Wilson 2009).

It is important to understand that sociobiology, when applied to humans, does not entail studying a non-human species and then extrapolating to humans what has been first learned about the non-human species. For example, a sociobiologist would never claim that the existence of "altruistic suicide" among bees and ants explains "altruistic suicide" among human soldiers. Rather, sociobiological research on non-human animals can lead to the discovery of *general evolutionary processes and mechanisms* that can inform explanations of social behavior across species lines. Simply put, though general evolutionary processes such as kin selection are expressed among many social species, this does not mean that a particular behavior found in two species means that the behavior was inherited by one species from the other. Consequently, early objections by critics of sociobiology that it is futile to try to explain the causes of human social behavior by studying ants (or, for that matter, any other non-human species) reveals a failure to understand the logic of evolutionary theory in general and sociobiological theory in particular.

Efforts to explain human social behavior on the basis of what has been learned by studying non-human social species precede the emergence of sociobiology. The anthropologists Lionel Tiger and Robin Fox advocated the adoption of a zoological perspective in social science almost a decade before the publication of *Sociobiology* (Tiger and Fox 1966). Similarly, the sociologist Pierre van den Berghe's advocacy of the development of a "biosocial" approach to the study of human social behavior also preceded the publication of Wilson's tome (van den Berghe 1973, 1974). Not long after the publication of *Sociobiology,* another sociologist, Joseph Lopreato, was pioneering the application of sociobiological theory to the study of human society and social behavior (Lopreato 1984). The work of van den Berghe and Lopreato represent early, "first-generation" sociological efforts to apply sociobiological principles to the study of human social behavior.

Though all organisms have kin, only humans clearly have a concept of kinship. Accordingly, it is plausible in terms of sociobiological theory to hypothesize that evolved psychological mechanisms that support nepotism (favoritism directed toward kin-group members) could also constitute a platform upon which kin-*like* groups could be constructed. Van den Berghe takes the idea that preferential association and cooperation among kin group members could be extended somehow to non-kin and become the basis of group affiliation among individuals who are not close kin and uses it to explain the existence of and cooperation within ethnic groups (van den Berghe 1981). In van den Berghe's view, ethnic groups can be thought of as "fictive" kin groups, the members of which are united not by genetic kinship but by cultural identity. Van den Berghe coined the term "ethny" for such groups, and he analyzes relations within and between ethnys using concepts derived from sociobiology, including kin selection, inclusive fitness, and reciprocal altruism (van den Berghe 1981). Though true genetic relatedness among members of an ethnic group dissipates as group size increases, processes of reciprocity and mutualism and cultural labels can create a *sense* of kinship among group members who are "genetic strangers" to each other. Thus, psychological mechanisms that evolved in support of cooperation based on genetic kinship can be extended to enable the formation and maintenance of cooperative groups based on cultural "kinship."

In addition to his analysis of ethnic groups, van den Berghe also uses sociobiological concepts and theory in analyzing patterns of marriage and mating among humans (1990). Specifically, like sociobiologists, van den Berghe looks at variation in systems of marriage (monogamy, polygamy, polygyny, hypergamy, etc.) as evolved strategies for maximizing fitness. As has long-been observed, human mating systems (marriage) are highly variable and thus might not seem tractable to sociobiological interpretation because of their variability. However, following sociobiological reasoning, van den Berghe interprets such variability as adaptive variation to variable environmental contexts, variation that has been designed by natural selection to be fitness-maximizing for its participants. For van den Berghe, instead of constituting evidence for the lack of biological influence on patterns of human mate-selection and mating, the variability of human mating strategies represents evolved sensitivities to the opportunities and threats posed by variation of dimensions of environments in which humans live and strive (almost always unconsciously) to maximize inclusive fitness.

About the same time that van den Berghe was developing new sociological explanations of kinship and ethnic relations based on sociobiological theory and research, Lopreato was re-framing established topics of sociological research in sociobiological terms and exploring the compatibility between sociobiological theory and strains of classical sociological theory (1984). Lopreato contended that sociobiology provides sociologists with an opportunity to develop new and more powerful explanations of numerous topics of traditional sociological interest including incest, gender relations, marriage and family patterns, relations of domination and subordination, cultural evolution, relations of reciprocity and exchange, and even fertility-mortality patterns (Lopreato 1984, 1989; Carey and Lopreato 1995). Lopreato argued that sociology had close ties to evolutionary thinking in classical sociological theory, especially in theoretical work of Vilfredo Pareto (Lopreato 1984). Lopreato also proposed a modified "maximization principle" on the basis of which sociobiological theory could be used to guide sociological inquiry. While embracing the sociobiological premise that organisms evolve traits that maximize their inclusive fitness, Lopreato argued that the maximization principle must be modified somewhat to accommodate the unique evolved attributes of *Homo sapiens* (Lopreato 1989). Specifically, Lopreato contended that an evolved human nature manifests a tendency to maximize inclusive fitness, but some elements of this nature are far from fitness-maximizing, and there is significant variation among individuals with regard to the extent to which they adopt fitness-enhancing, much less maximizing, behaviors. Furthermore, culture, itself a product of natural selection, often produces fitness-reducing behaviors, such as contraceptive technology, and humans appear predisposed to try to satisfy their needs and wants in a manner that may or may not yield fitness-enhancing results. Thus, culture and evolved psychological attributes of human nature may work at cross-purpose to adaptations that evolved in archaic environments to maximize human inclusive fitness.

Sociobiology places primary emphasis on trying to determine if, and to what extent, patterns of social behavior constitute evolved adaptations for maximizing inclusive fitness. By the late 1980s, an emerging cadre of psychologists was developing an alternative approach for analyzing human behavior in evolutionary terms. Instead of trying to determine if currently observable patterns of human behavior are adaptive in contemporary environments, the new evolutionary psychologists pursued research designed to discover evidence of evolved mental mechanisms that may have produced adaptive behaviors in the archaic environments in which they evolved, especially the Pleistocene era (Barkow et al. 1992), but may or may not be adaptive in contemporary environments. Furthermore, evolutionary psychologists place little, if any, emphasis in trying to ascertain the fitness consequences of contemporary human behavior, including social behavior. Thus, evolutionary psychology developed primarily as an effort to identify and explain the nature and origins of evolved human "cognitive algorithms," the sum of which might be seen as constituting a universal, species-specific human nature that is the product of 2 million years of hominin evolution.

24.4.2 The Rise and Influence of Evolutionary Psychology

By about 1940 or so, biological explanations of human social behavior had all but disappeared in the western social science canon, and the concept of culture became central to virtually all social science analysis. A new orthodoxy about human nature and behavior emerged which later came to be described as the "Standard Social Science Model" (Tooby and Cosmides 1992). Key elements of this model include the basic notions that (1) environmental factors and experience, not heritable traits, determine human behavior, (2) there is insufficient variability in the human genome to account for the almost infinite variability within and among human cultures, (3) learning, not instinct, determines human behavior, and (4) the human mind is, at birth, virtually devoid of content that specifies behavior, especially social behavior, and such content must be acquired by experience, including social learning (Tooby and Cosmides 1992). The fourth notion is commonly characterized as the *tabula rasa*, or blank slate, assumption about the nature of the human brain and mind (Pinker 2002).

By the mid- to late-1980s, a growing number of psychologists were questioning the blank slate assumption about human nature, and they had begun to pursue inquiries that were guided by theory and research derived from evolutionary biology. One of the earliest and most influential of such efforts was the work of Martin Daly and Margo Wilson on homicide (1988). Guided by the sociobiological principle that the expression of violence among humans will be influenced by the degree of genetic relatedness between attackers and victims, Daly and Wilson reviewed data about patterns of homicide to see if they conformed to predictions derived from sociobiological theory. They were successful in demonstrating that sociobiological principles, especially kin selection, provided predictions about the incidence of homicide that could not be derived from other theoretical perspectives in the behavioral and social sciences. Consequently, their work helped launch a rapidly growing branch of psychology now known as "evolutionary psychology" (Buss 2008).

Evolutionary psychologists replaced the blank slate conception of the human mind with a new model that they called the "adapted mind" (Barkow et al. 1992). The adapted mind is said to have evolved during the Pleistocene era, and it consists of specialized "cognitive algorithms" that represent mental adaptations for solving the challenges posed routinely by the environments in which humans evolved. These cognitive algorithms resemble closely what sociobiologists have called "epigenetic rules" (Lumsden and Wilson 1981) and sociologists have called "behavioral predispositions" (Lopreato 1984; Lopreato and Crippen 1999) or "behavioral propensities" (Turner 2015). The full complement of evolved cognitive algorithms that constitute the adapted mind are said to have evolved in the "environment of evolutionary adaptedness" (the EEA) and can be thought of as the defining components of a universal, species-specific human nature (Bowlby 1969; Tooby and Cosmides 1990).

It is erroneous to think of the adapted mind as the "nature" version of a "nature versus nurture" model of the human brain and mind. In the classical, stereotypic "nature" conception of the human mind, learning is absent, and heritable, inalterable "instincts" govern human behavior. By way of contrast, the adapted mind model incorporates what psychologists call "prepared" or "biased" learning (Garcia and Koelling 1966; Seligman 1971; Seligman and Hager 1972). In this view, the human brain features learning biases that enable humans to learn more quickly, easily, and reliably from experiences that are adaptively relevant. Put differently, the adapted mind is said to possess innate "aptitudes" for acquiring information and behavioral strategies for coping with circumstances that are highly salient to prospects for survival and reproductive success. For example, Wilson asserts that the human mind is likely to possess a special learning bias regarding the threat posed by snakes, an archaic and near-universal threat to humans in environments the world-over (Wilson 1998:79). An innate propensity to be especially vigilant for serpentine forms and a behavioral inclination to behave very cautiously when they are detected represents a highly adaptive learning bias from which ancestral (as well as many contemporary) humans have benefitted.

The notion of the adapted mind is most relevant to sociological theorists when considering the possibility that humans may possess innate cognitive algorithms for coping with threats and opportunities created by social living. In that regard, a number of pioneering experiments conducted by John Tooby and Leda Cosmides provide an example of one such mental adaptation that appears designed specifically for group life. A defining sociological feature of group life among humans, in both ancestral and contemporary contexts, is the existence of systems of reciprocity and exchange. The development of exchange theory within sociology testifies to the fundamental importance of these processes (e.g., Homans 1961; Blau 1964; Emerson 1972). To the extent that a social relationship depends on reliable and stable reciprocity among participants in a system of exchange, instances wherein one party fails to uphold a contractual obligation to another party constitute a threat to the durability of the relationship. Conceptualized as "defection" or "cheating" by evolutionary game theorists (Axelrod 1984; Maynard Smith 1982), such behavior threatens participants who might fail to detect such contractual violations. Accordingly, Cosmides and Tooby conducted a series of controlled experiments designed to determine if humans have an innate aptitude for detecting instances of non-reciprocity in relations of social exchange (Cosmides and Tooby 1992). Their experiments provided evidence of the existence of an innate "cheating-detection mechanism" which Cosmides and Tooby interpret as an evolved, mental adaptation for coping with the threat of non-reciprocity in social relations comprising cooperation based on social exchange.

Following the lead provided by Cosmides and Tooby, evolutionary psychologists are now engaged in systematic searches for other cognitive algorithms that may have evolved to enable the establishment and maintenance of stable patterns of cooperation on the basis of which societal life is made possible. Consequently, the tabula rasa assumption about human nature has been discarded by sociological theorists whose work is informed by contemporary evolutionary sciences, including sociobiology and evolutionary psychology. And though, as will be discussed later, some evolutionary sociologists take exception to the model of the adapted mind proposed by Cosmides and Tooby and other evolutionary psychologists, none embrace the tabula rasa model which has dominated the social sciences for most of the twentieth century.

24.4.3 Evolutionary Sociology

After decades of near total quiescence in sociology, evolutionary thinking has re-emerged in sociological theory, and it has assumed diverse forms and has addressed a growing range of topics. What is now being characterized as "evolutionary sociology" features work that can be classified roughly into four basic variants, each of which addresses different aspects of human social evolution: (1) sociocultural evolution, (2) the adapted mind, (3) neurosocial evolution, and (4) cross-species analysis. Each variant will be discussed in turn.

24.4.3.1 Sociocultural Evolution

Several sociologists including Gerhard Lenski, Jonathan Turner, Marion Blute, and Christopher Chase-Dunn have developed new variants of sociocultural evolutionary theory that are informed by neo-Darwinian evolutionary theory in biology. However, all of these theorists adopt the position that explaining sociocultural evolution requires an explanatory approach that takes into account emergent, unique properties of human societies and thus requires the use of additional concepts and explanatory principles that are unavailable in sociobiology and evolutionary psychology alone. Accordingly, these sociological theorists develop new theoretical ideas designed specifically for analyzing the emergent properties of human societies and the processes by means of which they evolve.

Building on his earlier version of ecological-evolutionary theory, Lenski advocates the pursuit of a "new evolutionary theory in the social sciences" (2005:3). Parting company with most sociological theorists who subscribe to the Standard Social Science Model, Lenski asserts the necessity of acknowledging that humans possess an evolved human nature that is genetically based and manifests itself in the "neurological information" that produces human social behavior (2005:45–50). In Lenski's theory of sociocultural evolution, human societies are "adaptive mechanisms that mediate relations between a population and its environment" (2005:60). The goal of his ecological-evolutionary theory is to help develop a comprehensive science for analyzing human societies at three levels: (1) individual societies, (2) sets of societies, and (3) the global system of societies. Social relations within and among human societies are the product of five sets of forces that comprise three types of information (genetic, neurological, and cultural) and two kinds of environments (biophysical and sociocultural). Like the early stage theorists who preceded him, Lenski's ecological-evolutionary theory is designed for macro-level and comparative sociological analysis, a project largely abandoned when sociologists abandoned structural-functional analysis (2005:15).

In Lenski's view, the key to explaining the evolution of human societies is to understand that evolution fundamentally entails the "cumulation of information," and in sociocultural evolution, the fundamental driving force of societal evolution is technological information, especially subsistence technology (2005:63–68). Subsistence technologies represent an extension of the human genetic heritage, and while they are not narrowly deterministic of human social behavior and human societies, Lenski describes them as the "critical interface between the biophysical environment and all the other components of sociocultural systems" (2005:62). Consequently, Lenski maps the basic types of societies produced by humanity in terms of the relationship between subsistence technology and environments. This yields a taxonomy of seven major "sets" of societies which are hunting-gathering, fishing, horticultural, herding, agrarian, maritime, and industrial societies (Lenski 2005:84). Ecological-evolutionary theory provides a framework for analyzing the nature and evolution of each societal set, its relations to other societal sets, and the global network of relations among these sets. It provides a comprehensive vantage point for analyzing the universe of human societies and patterns of continuity and change therein.

A more recent variant of evolutionary theory designed for analyzing sociocultural evolution has been produced by Turner (2010). Like Lenski, Turner builds his theory on the established theoretical principles and empirical findings of the evolutionary life-sciences. However, Turner rejects the premise that fields such as sociobiology or evolutionary psychology alone are adequate for analyzing and explaining patterns of sociocultural evolution (Turner and Maryanski 2015). Rather, emergent properties of human societies that derive from the production and use of symbols (and culture) require additional, as well as novel, concepts and principles for explaining the evolution of human sociocultural systems. Accordingly, Turner sets about to resurrect the tradition of "grand theory" in sociology based on well-established (as well as novel) principles in evolutionary theory. In Turner's view, contemporary sociological theory is remiss in its neglect of macro-level phenomena including stratification systems and societies themselves as distinctive macro-level units of analysis (2013:434–435). Similarly, Abrutyn (2014) and Abrutyn and Turner (2011) point to the surprising irony that, despite its centrality and pervasiveness in conventional sociological thought, sociological explication of the macrodynamics of societal institutions suffers surprising vagueness and neglect. Both Abrutyn and Turner contend that the full potential and analytical value of the long-venerated but surprisingly under-theorized sociological concept of institutions can best be realized by subjecting it to evolutionary theoretical scrutiny.

Turner built his theory from information derived from stage-models of societal evolution, and his goal is to identify the common social dynamics that operate at "any stage" of societal evolution and in all types of societies (2010). Toward that end, he develops a theory comprising 23 abstract propositions about the macrodynamics of human society that can be used to analyze any human social system (Turner 2010:323–344). Turner contends that focusing on *selection* processes in sociocultural evolution can revive the project of grand theorizing that characterized structural-functionalism but avoid the shortcomings of functional analysis that eventually led to its near-total abandonment by sociologists.

In order to extend evolutionary thinking beyond its biological origins, Turner identifies two forms of selection besides Darwinian selection that operate in sociocultural systems: "Durkheimian selection" refers to competition among actors that drives them to find resources in new niches, and "Spencerian selection" refers to the process by means of which actors innovate and produce entirely new adaptations for coping with selection pressures (2010:24–27). Spencerian selection acknowledges the almost-certainly unique human trait of foresight, the ability to imagine future conditions, envision novel ways of behaving in response to future conditions, and adopt novel strategies in an effort to cope with these conditions. In Turner's theory, changes in five fundamental properties of human societies can act as selection forces, and they are population, production, regulation, distribution, and reproduction (2010:41–103). Like numerous evolutionary theorists before him, Turner identifies *integration* as a basic focal point of his analysis. Specifically, Turner asks how social structure and culture are integrated by means of both cultural and structural mechanisms that operate in response to various selection pressures. Only by resurrecting the project of grand theory and framing it in evolutionary terms does Turner believe that sociological theorists can produce macro-level theories that are adequate to the task of explaining the behavior of entire societies.

Other contemporary sociologists have adopted evolutionary thinking to explain fundamental processes of sociocultural change and stability. For example, Marion Blute distinguishes among gene-based, social learning (meme-based), and dual inheritance (coevolutionary) Darwinian theories of change (2010:7). Like Turner, Blute contends that a satisfactory explanation of sociocultural evolution is not available in sociobiological or evolutionary psychological theory alone. Rather, in order to explain processes of sociocultural evolution, attention must be devoted to (1) the unique properties of culture and social learning, (2) memes as units of cultural inheritance and transmission, (3) the role of human agency in producing and guiding human social behavior, (4) human subjectivity and the processes by means of which humans construct and are constructed by niches, and (5) the role of both ecological complexity (more kinds) and individual complexity (more complex kinds) in sociocultural evolution (Blute 2010). While Blute acknowledges and appreciates both gene-based and dual inheritance evolutionary theories, she makes the case for the necessity of developing a Darwinian theory of sociocultural evolution that places primary emphasis on processes of human social learning and meme-based information systems.

Though, as Turner notes, macro-level theorizing declined significantly with the demise of grand theory in general and functionalism in particular, contemporary sociology has exhibited high levels of activity about global or "world-system" level societal change (2013:434). Recently, theorists of sociocultural evolution have contributed to these efforts at global-level, intersocietal analysis (Lenski 2005; Chase-Dunn 2015). Lenski's ecological-evolutionary theory is designed to provide a framework for understanding the nature of the "global system of societies," how it came into existence, and its sociocultural evolution (2005:111–124). In a recent effort to account for the emergence of global level, sociocultural complexity, Chase-Dunn has integrated world-systems theory with ideas derived from evolutionary theory (2015). In his analysis of the sociocultural evolution of world-systems, Chase-Dunn assigns primary significance to phenomena such as semiperipheral development, waves of trade globalization and deglobalization, and crises of the contemporary world-system and its possible futures (2015:270–282).

24.4.3.2 The Adapted Mind

Most contemporary sociological theory is based on the tabula rasa assumption about the human brain and mind, a core component of the Standard Social Science model. At best, most sociologists will concede only that the newborn human infant is in possession of a few inborn "reflexes," such as rooting and suckling, swallowing, the Moro (startle) reflex, the Palmar grasp (grasping an object placed in the palm of the hand), and the Babinski reflex (extension of the big toe and fanning of other toes). It is very uncommon to find in contemporary sociological theory a view of the human brain and mind as instantiated, at birth, with an extensive suite of innate behavioral predispositions for producing complex behaviors, including social behaviors. Rather, the brain is typically viewed as a powerful, complex information processing machine that captures, stores, organizes, and expresses information that is acquired by personal experience or cultural transmission. And it is by means of symbolic media that such information is processed. The emergence of sociobiology and later, evolutionary psychology, has posed a direct and formidable threat to this traditional view of human mental life and social behavior.

In *Sociobiology,* Wilson identified a range of social behaviors displayed by numerous taxa that he analyzed as genetically-based, evolved adaptations produced by natural selection (1975). However, Wilson said little in *Sociobiology* about mental processes by means of which such adaptations might be organized and operate in the human mind. In response to those who criticized him for this omission, he and Charles Lumsden published *Genes, Mind, and Culture: The Coevolutionary Process* (1981) in an effort to identify and explicate the psychological processes that comprise the "ontogenetic development of mental activity and behavior" and how such processes evolved by natural selection (1981:ix). The development of various mental activities and the behaviors they produce are described by Lumsden and Wilson as entailing "epigenetic rules," especially "secondary epigenetic rules" (1981:53–98). Epigenetic rules channel and direct the development of anatomical, physiological, and cognitive traits. They can be thought of as "rules of thumb" that provide responses to environmental stimuli so as to yield adaptive outcomes. Thus, a brain supplied with a repertoire of epigenetic rules is far from a blank slate, but rather, a complex information processing machine that is richly supplied with adaptively-relevant information for producing adaptive behavior in response to environmental challenges and opportunities.

Evolutionary theorists have used additional terms to characterize epigenetic rules including "behavioral predispositions" (Lopreato 1984), "cognitive algorithms" (Cosmides and Tooby 1992) and "behavioral propensities" (Turner

2015). A growing number of sociologists have begun exploring the possibility that the human mind contains specialized, evolved cognitive mechanisms that constitute the platform on which behavioral adaptations can develop. For example, rejecting the long-standing orthodoxy that the human mind is a tabula rasa, generalized information-processing machine, Rosemary Hopcroft proposes, instead, the notion of an "evolved actor" that is in possession of an entire suite of evolved, innate behavioral predispositions including an innate aptitude for learning social norms above other kinds of rules, an innate preoccupation with fairness and altruism when interacting with genetic strangers, behavioral predispositions toward religious sentiments, a predisposition to form social hierarchies, and a predisposition to be preferentially loyal to close kin (2009b). Hopcroft also applies the notion of behavioral predispositions in her analyses of evolved gender differences (2009a, 2002, 2006).

The sociologist (and evolutionary psychologist) Satoshi Kanazawa also offers evolutionary explanations of evolved cognitive adaptations possessed by humans regarding phenomena such as intelligence (2004a, 2010), risk-taking and crime (Kanazawa and Still 2000), gender differences in preferences for different types of social capital (Savage and Kanazawa 2002), and human decision-making in the context of prisoner's dilemma and public choice contexts (2004a). Much of Kanazawa's theorizing about these and other phenomena is informed by his "Savanna-IQ Interaction Hypothesis" which states that the human mind is equipped with both specialized, domain-specific algorithms for coping with archaic and recurrent challenges that all humans confront, as well as a second, "generalized intelligence" that enables humans to reason about and cope with problems that are adaptively relevant but appear only in novel environments (2010). Thus, the human brain and mind enable humans to cope quickly, and largely unreflectively, with challenges that have been present in virtually all environments in which humans have evolved and currently live, as well as with unprecedented challenges presented by newly-developed environments that feature novel demographic, technological, cultural, and sociological traits. According to Kanazawa, we can expect more variability among humans in terms of their generalized intelligence, and less variability in their specialized mental adaptations for coping with the archaic and near-universal challenges confronted by ancestral humans in the EEA (2010).

An important concept on the basis of which the notion of the adapted human mind rests is the psychological phenomenon of "prepared" or "biased" or "directed" learning (Garcia and Koelling 1966; Rachman and Seligman 1976; Seligman 1971, 1993; Seligman and Hager 1972). The idea of prepared learning stands in contrast to the long-standing misconception that a behavior must be the consequence of either instinct or learning. The Standard Social Science Model represents the human brain as a general, equipotential, all-purpose information processing machine, and almost all behavior is attributed to learning and not instinct (Tooby and Cosmides 1992). In contrast, evolutionary theory suggests that the brain is predisposed to learn and retain certain types of information over others, and that the adaptive relevance of the information is what causes the brain to preferentially acquire and process it.

An example of how biased learning occurs is provided by what psychologists call "ophidiophobia," the development of an extreme fear of snakes (Wilson 1998:79). Snakes have long represented a serious source of mortality in many human populations, so evolutionary reasoning would predict that natural selection would favor the evolution of a cognitive algorithm in the brain that makes humans highly vigilant about possible encounters with snakes. A fear of snakes must be learned, but the brain appears to learn to fear snakes much more easily than it learns to fear novel and more recent threats such as fast-moving automobiles, which are currently a much greater source of human mortality. Automobiles, however, were not a feature of ancestral human environments. Accordingly, automobiles, however deadly, are rarely the target of phobias. The notion of prepared learning means that it is theoretically plausible that natural selection would have supplied the human brain with suites of cognitive algorithms for coping with highly adaptively relevant threats and opportunities that were presented by the environments in which humans evolved. Part of those environments are social environments, thus, social structures and processes themselves are likely to have functioned as selection forces, equipping the human mind with learning biases that enable them to recognize and process effectively any information about social scenarios that is highly adaptively relevant.

One such scenario that has been the investigated by experimental research is the work of Cosmides and Tooby on cognitive adaptations for social exchange (1992). Well over a century of sociological theorizing and research has documented the importance of relations of reciprocity and exchange in human social systems (e.g., Smith 1776 [1805]; Lévi-Strauss 1969; Homans 1961; Blau 1964; Emerson 1972). More recently, sociobiologists have also explored the nature and incidence of systems of reciprocity in non-human societies (Trivers 1971; Clutton-Brock 2009). A serious threat to any participant in an exchange relationship is that alter will fail to provide a resource that s/he owes ego in repayment for a resource that s/he received from ego. In the game theoretic model of the prisoner's dilemma, this is known as the threat of defection. If ego is unable to recognize and respond effectively to acts of defection by alter, then s/he faces a serious, adaptively-relevant threat within this system of reciprocity and exchange. Thus, evolutionary reasoning would lead to the hypothesis that humans may possess an evolved, specialized cognitive algorithm to protect against this selection force.

In a series of ingenious controlled experiments designed to determine how competent humans are at detecting instances of non-reciprocity in a prisoner's dilemma scenario, Cosmides and Tooby adduced evidence in support of their hypothesis that humans appear to have a strong aptitude for detecting instances of cheating in relations of social exchange, and they characterize this specialized aptitude, or cognitive algorithm, as a "cheating detection mechanism" (1992).

One of the most interesting lines of inquiry that has been prompted by theory-building and empirical research about the adapted mind is the possibility that the human brain/mind may be densely supplied with specialized cognitive algorithms that represent evolved adaptations to selection forces presented by the structures and processes of group life itself. In short, it is now plausible to use evolutionary theory to pursue new avenues inquiry that might lead to the discovery of other types of cognitive adaptations that evolved to enable humans to cope with the challenges and opportunities presented by the social environments in which they live and have evolved.

24.4.3.3 Neurosocial Evolution

Until recently, it would not have been indefensible to describe sociology as an "acerebral science." To most sociologists, the brain is relevant to sociological explanation only as a recorder and processor of personal experience and culture. In terms of specifying and generating social behavior, the brain is viewed as virtually empty of informational content. Put more casually, sociologists commonly regard the human brain as devoid of "social instincts," therefore, there is little if anything to be learned about the nature, causes, or consequences of social behavior by studying the brain itself. Contemporary evolutionary theory and research make this an increasingly untenable position for sociologists to embrace.

One of the earliest, and most thorough, theoretical developments in evolutionary sociology to focus attention on the evolved properties of the human brain is the work of Turner on the evolution of human emotions and their role in social behavior (1996, 1999, 2000, 2007). In Turner's view, the adapted mind consists of complex arrays of neural systems that are "diffuse and complex sub-assemblages" which are distributed across the neo-cortex and sub-cortex and function as "bioprogrammers for group living" (2015:177). Disproportionately large, even for a primate, the neo-cortex has been regarded as especially important in explaining complex behavior because of its ability to support reasoning and other sophisticated cognitive activities. Turner, however, credits the limbic systems of the brain, also disproportionately large, with comparable significance in promoting the evolution of human sociality (2000). The limbic systems enhance the emotional repertoire of humans, thereby enabling the formation of strong social ties and complex patterns of social interaction (Turner and Maryanski (2008). The work of Turner and Maryanski represents an important new direction in an effort to synthesize the neurosciences with sociological, ecological, anthropological, and psychological perspectives toward the development of a comprehensive, evolutionary theory of the evolution of human societies.

Another recent contribution to the development of a neurosociology is the work of David Franks (2010, 2015) and Franks and his colleague Jeff Davis (2012). Franks provides an account of the phylogeny of the human brain and the ecological and evolutionary forces that shaped its development into an organ with specialized features that support the existence of complex patterns of social organization and interaction. Reviewing hominin phylogeny, Franks explains how changing ecological forces led to selection for brain structures that favored a shift from olfaction to vision as a primary sensory modality, enhanced memory, and enhanced capabilities for abstract thought which, in turn, strongly predisposed the evolution of human language (2015). Reviewing the evolution of these neural systems, Franks concludes that the human brain is highly social by nature, a determination that has significant implications for the future development of sociological theory (2015:294).

Other developments in the nascent area of neurosociology provide additional examples of how the integration of sociological inquiry with the neurosciences can promote the development of a robust evolutionary sociology. For example, Leveto and Kalkhoff show how a neurosociological perspective can provide insight about how brain function pertaining to the processing of paralanguage and biosocial interaction are implicated in Autism Spectrum Disorders (2012). Similarly, Firat and Hitlin demonstrate how integrating neuroscientific and sociological thinking can shed new light on the scientific study of morality and its bearing on the formation of groups and interactional dynamics among them (2012). Finally, and perhaps surprisingly to traditional sociological theorists, the phenomenon of intersubjectivity, a concept central to theoretical perspectives in sociology such as phenomenology, may be tractable to neurosociological analysis. Franks and Davis review neuroscientific studies of "mirror neurons," and they conclude that their activity may be foundational to key social interactive processes like imitation, role-taking, ritual, cooperation, self-control, and other sociological phenomena that generate social cohesion (solidarity) which, in the words of Franks and Davis, constitutes the "glue" of social life (2012).

24.4.3.4 Cross-Species Analyses

Historically, sociology has been a "single-species science," devoted almost exclusively to the study of human social behavior alone. The uniqueness of human beings, attributed basically to the human capacity for symbol production and use (culture), has justified in the minds of many sociologists an assumption that humans are essentially exempt from most of the biological forces that shape the social behavior of other species. This is a position that has come under direct criticism recently by evolutionary behavioral and social scientists (e.g., Kanazawa 2004b). However, a number of sociologists see value in extending the scope of sociological theory and research beyond humans to include some of the thousands of other social species as well. Two rationales are advanced to justify this extension in the scope of sociological analysis: (1) integrating biological methodologies like cladistics analysis with sociological approaches like social network analysis can provide insight about the origins of human nature and how it shapes group life among humans, and (2) comparing basic forms of social organization, like dominance hierarchies or macrosocieties, across species lines can help identify and explain the fundamental processes by means of which all societies are assembled and function.

The work of Maryanski (and Maryanski and Turner) provides a good example of how comparisons between humans and other primates can provide insights about how natural selection has shaped the constitutive elements of human nature and how this nature has influenced the evolution of human social life (Maryanski 1992; Maryanski and Turner 1992; Turner and Maryanski 2008). By comparing the phylogenies of humans to other apes and to monkeys, Maryanski has provided new theoretical insights and empirical evidence in support of her claim that humans are, by nature, less highly-social than long-believed (Maryanski 1992; Maryanski and Turner 1992). Like other apes, early humans were unlikely to have been predisposed to forming strong social ties, and it was only when natural selection modified the human brain to expand the palette of emotions that humans now possess that they became a "strong tie" primate (Maryanski 1992). In fact, Maryanski concludes that natural selection has produced a human nature that is predisposed in part toward sociality, but equally predisposed toward individuality, and these two propensities co-exist in a sort of uneasy tension that is evident in human group life.

An early example of extending the sociological study of social structure and social dynamics to include nonhuman animals is the work of Ivan Chase (1974, 1980; Chase et al. 2002). Chase reviews two models designed to explain the development of dominance hierarchies among both human and nonhuman social species. The first model predicts position in dominance hierarchies on the basis of individual trait differences, and the second predicts dominance position as the product of iterated social interactions. Experimental work he conducted on how dominance hierarchies develop in chickens supports the social interaction explanation (1980). In this regard, Chase's work suggests that there is merit in pursuing a Simmelian-type analysis of "social forms" across species lines. That is, regardless of the species in which a particular social form is found, there may be features that are common to that form and the processes by which it develops and operates, whatever the species that expresses it.

More recently, Machalek (1992) and Cohen and Machalek (1988) also advocate the development of a "new comparative sociology" that explores how forms of social organization evolve among diverse social species and how these forms are expressed by animals as different as eusocial insects (ants, bees, wasps, and termites) and humans (Machalek 1992). Noting that a "form of sociation" that he calls "macrosociality" occurs only among modern humans (10,000 years ago to present) and the eusocial insects, Machalek identifies the organismic, ecological, cost-benefit, and sociological constraints that have to be overcome if macrosociality is to evolve in any species (1992:39–59). A macrosociety consists of a very large population that is organized into a complex division of labor executed by members of distinct social categories. Only the eusocial insects and modern humans have overcome these constraints to produce and live in macrosocities, and theoretical principles developed for a cross-species version of comparative sociology offer promise for explaining how and why this occurs (Machalek 1992:59–61). Finally, another example of how evolutionary thinking makes possible cross-species analyses of sociological phenomena is provided by the work of Cohen and Machalek on "expropriative crime" (1988). Using basic concepts and explanatory principles derived from sociobiology and behavioral ecology, Cohen and Machalek offer an account of how the incidence of expropriative behaviors (called "social parasitism" by behavioral biologists), is either enabled or inhibited by routine patterns of social organization and processes of social interaction. When expropriative behaviors violate laws, as occurs only in humans, they are called crimes. However, forms of expropriation occur in nonhuman societies as well, and Cohen and Machalek identify properties of any social system, human or nonhuman, that are conducive to the incidence of expropriation.

24.5 Conclusion: A Future for Evolutionary Theory in Sociology

Evolutionary thinking flourished in much of the work of the founders of sociology. However, the misadventure of Social Darwinism and the rise of cultural explanations of human social behavior eventually consigned evolutionary thought to obscurity for much of the twentieth century. By the mid-1960s, new variants of stage models of social change were being developed, but it was not until the 1970s that a new wave of evolutionary analysis began to proliferate in the social and behavioral sciences. The major impetus behind this newly resurgent interest in evolutionary analyses of human social behavior was the publication of Wilson's *Sociobiology: The New Synthesis* (1975).

Despite initial and widespread fears of a reappearance of Social Darwinism and a reintroduction of long-discredited positions of naïve reductionism, genetic determinism, and new ideological agendas designed to support sexism and racism, more and more social and behavioral scientists became drawn to the evolutionary life-sciences. Eventually, the growing receptivity among social scientists to evolutionary theory and research led to the development of new fields such as evolutionary anthropology, evolutionary economics, evolutionary psychology, and evolutionary sociology. All of these new ventures share a common premise: the tabula rasa model of the human brain and mind is no longer tenable, and it must be replaced by a conception of an adapted mind that is the product of evolution by natural selection. As previously discussed, evolutionary social and behavioral scientists are not of one mind about the nature of the adapted mind and how it functions. However, they all share a common interest in exploring its features and how they influence complex processes such as the generation and transmission of culture, the role of prepared learning in the development of social behaviors, the manner in which genetic and memetic (cultural) information interact, and the influences of an evolved mind on the development of the emergent properties of human groups and societies.

When Wilson speculated about how sociology, and the other social sciences, appeared destined to be transformed by new developments in sociobiology, behavioral ecology, and the neurosciences, many social and behavioral scientists reacted with alarm (Wilson 1975:574–575; Segerstråle 2000). Many expressed apprehension about what they perceived as an imperial intellectual agenda in Wilson's work. Four decades later, however, these fears and apprehensions have not been realized. Even in light of the "triumph of sociobiology," as Alcock puts it (2001), and the increasing colonization of the social and behavioral sciences by evolutionary ideas, none of these disciplines, including sociology, have been dissolved in the corrosive solvents of biological reductionism or genetic determinism. In fact, as some sociologists have become knowledgeable about the evolutionary life-sciences, they have discovered opportunities to apply fundamental sociological principles in the study of nonhuman social species and their patterns of social interaction. For example, the emergent nature of group structures and even societal-level social organization has been documented in *sociological* analyses of species ranging from ants (Machalek 1992, 1999) to chickens (Chase 1974, 1980). Thus, instead of posing a threat to conventional sociological analysis, a dialogue between sociologists and evolutionary biologists can result in potentially fertile and mutually enriching relations of intellectual reciprocity.

As has been discussed, a four decades-long dialogue between evolutionary biologists and a growing number of sociologists has led to the development of new areas of theoretical inquiry in sociology. New theories of sociocultural evolution have emerged which are informed by neo-Darwinian theory and research but are not burdened by indefensible assumptions or premises of a dogmatic reductionist or determinist nature. Instead, these new theories of sociocultural evolution can build on an increasingly sophisticated understanding of the adapted mind and, simultaneously, provide new insight about the emergent structures and processes by means of which social systems function within the ecosystems in which they develop. Similarly, as the nascent field of neurosociology provides greater depth of understanding about the evolved properties of the social mind, sociological theorists will be in a better position to understand the forces by means of which phenomena such as social solidarity develop and function. And as the scope of sociological inquiry expands beyond the study of *Homo sapiens* alone to include any of the tens of thousands of nonhuman social species, entirely new kinds of opportunities for the development of sociological theory and research will emerge.

Twenty-first century sociological theory appears poised to be energized by the development of a stronger and closer association with the evolutionary life sciences. And, in turn, it offers promise to stimulate new types of theoretical inquiry and empirical research among behavioral scientists who study nonhuman social species and their social lives.

References

Abrutyn, S. (2014). *Revisiting institutionalism in sociology: Putting the "institution" back in institutional analysis*. New York: Routledge Taylor & Francis Group.

Abrutyn, S. (2015a). Pollution-purification rituals, collective memory, and the evolution of religion: How cultural trauma shaped ancient Israel. *American Journal of Cultural Sociology, 3*(1), 123–155.

Abrutyn, S. (2015b). The institutional evolution of religion: Innovation and entrepreneurship in ancient Israel. *Religion, 45*(4), 505–531.

Abrutyn, S., & Turner, J. (2011). The old institutionalism meets the new institutionalism. *Sociological Perspectives, 54*(3), 283–306.

Alcock, J. (2001). *The triumph of sociobiology*. New York: Oxford University Press.

Axelrod, R. (1984). *The evolution of cooperation*. New York: Basic Books.

Barkow, J. H., Cosmides, L., & Tooby, J. (Eds.). (1992). *The adapted mind: Evolutionary psychology and the generation of culture*. New York: Oxford University Press.

Blau, P. M. (1964). *Exchange and power in social life*. New York: Wiley.

Blute, M. (2010). *Darwinian sociocultural evolution: Solutions to dilemmas in cultural and social theory*. New York: Cambridge University Press.

Bowlby, J. (1969). *Attachment and loss. Volume I: Attachment*. New York: Basic Books.

Boyd, R., & Richerson, P. (1985). *Culture and the evolutionary process*. Chicago: University of Chicago Press.

Buss, D. M. (2008). *Evolutionary psychology: The new science of the mind* (3rd ed.). Boston: Pearson and Allyn & Bacon.

Carey, A. D., & Lopreato, J. (1995). The evolutionary demography of the fertility-mortality quasi-equilibrium. *Population and Development Review, 21*, 726–736.

Chase, I. D. (1974). Models of hierarchy formation in animal societies. *Behavioral Science, 19*(6), 374–382.

Chase, I. D. (1980). Social process and hierarchy formation in small groups: A comparative perspective. *American Sociological Review, 45*(6), 905–924.

Chase, I. D., Tovey, C., Spangler-Martin, D., & Manfredonia, M. (2002). Individual differences versus social dynamics in the formation of animal dominance hierarchies. *Proceedings of the National Academy of Sciences of the United States of America, 99*(8), 5744–5749.

Chase-Dunn, C. (2015). The sociocultural evolution of world-systems. In J. H. Turner, R. Machalek, & A. Maryanski (Eds.), *Handbook on evolution and society: Toward an evolutionary social science* (pp. 267–284). Boulder: Paradigm Publishers.

Clutton-Brock, T. (2009). Cooperation between non-kin in animal societies. *Nature, 462*, 51–57.

Cohen, L. E., & Machalek, R. (1988). A general theory of expropriative crime: An evolutionary ecological approach. *American Journal of Sociology, 94*, 465–501.

Cosmides, L., & Tooby, J. (1992). Cognitive adaptations for social exchange. In J. H. Barkow, L. Cosmides, & J. Tooby (Eds.), *The adapted mind: Evolutionary psychology and the generation of culture* (pp. 162–228). New York: Oxford University Press.

Daly, M., & Wilson, M. (1988). *Homicide*. Hawthorne: Aldine De Gruyter.

Darwin, C. (1859). *The origin of species by means of natural selection or the preservation of favored races in the struggle for life and the descent of man and selection in relation to sex*. New York: Modern Library.

Dawkins, R. (1986). *The blind watchmaker: Why the evidence of evolution reveals a universe without design*. New York: W. W. Norton & Company.

Degler, C. N. (1991). *In search of human nature: The decline and revival of Darwinism in American social thought*. New York: Oxford University Press.

Durkheim, E. (1947). *The division of labor in society*. New York: Free Press.

Emerson, R. M. (1972). Exchange theory, part I: A psychological basis for social exchange; exchange theory, part II: Exchange relations and network structures. In J. Berger, M. Zelditch, & B. Anderson (Eds.), *Sociological theories in progress* (pp. 38–87). New York: Houghton-Mifflin.

Firtat, R., & Hitlin, S. (2012). Morally bonded and bounded: A sociological introduction to neurology. In W. Kalkhoff, S. R. Thye, & E. J. Lawler (Eds.), *Advances in group processes: Biosociology and neurosociology* (pp. 165–199). Bingley: Emerald.

Franks, D. D. (2010). *Neurosociology: The nexus between neuroscience and social psychology*. New York: Springer.

Franks, D. D. (2015). The evolution of the human brain. In J. H. Turner, R. Machalek, & A. Maryanski (Eds.), *Handbook on evolution and society: Toward an evolutionary social science* (pp. 285–294). Boulder: Paradigm Publishers.

Franks, D. D., & Davis, J. (2012). Critique and refinement of the neurosociology of mirror neurons. In W. Kalkhoff, S. R. Thye, & E. J. Lawler (Eds.), *Advances in group processes: Biosociology and neurosociology* (pp. 77–117). Bingley: Emerald.

Garcia, J., & Koelling, R. (1966). Relation of cue to consequence in avoidance learning. *Psychonomic Science, 4*, 123–124.

Hamilton, W. D. (1964). The genetical evolution of social behavior, I and II. *Journal of Theoretical Biology, 7*, 1–52.

Hölldobler, B., & Wilson, E. O. (1990). *The ants*. Cambridge, MA: The Belknap Press of Harvard University Press.

Hölldobler, B., & Wilson, E. O. (2009). *The superorganism: The beauty, elegance, and strangeness of insect societies*. New York: W. W. Norton & Company.

Homans, G. H. (1961). *Social behavior: Its elementary forms*. New York: Harcourt Brace Jovanovich.

Hopcroft, R. (2002). The evolution of sex discrimination. *Psychology, Evolution & Gender, 4*(1), 43–67.

Hopcroft, R. (2006). Status characteristics among older individuals: The diminished significance of gender. *The Sociological Quarterly, 47*, 361–374.

Hopcroft, R. (2009a). Gender inequality interaction: An evolutionary account. *Social Forces, 87*(4), 1845–1872.

Hopcroft, R. (2009b). The evolved actor in sociology. *Sociological Theory, 27*(4), 390–406.

Kanazawa, S. (2004a). The Savanna principle. *Managerial and Decision Economics, 25*, 41–54.

Kanazawa, S. (2004b). Social sciences are branches of biology. *Socio-Economic Review, 2*(3), 371–390.

Kanazawa, S. (2010). Evolutionary psychology and intelligence research. *American Psychologist, 65*(4), 279–289.

Kanazawa, S., & Still, M. (2000). Why men commit crimes (and why they desist). *Sociological Theory, 18*(3), 434–447.

Lenski, G. (1966). *Power and privilege*. New York: McGraw-Hill.

Lenski, G. (2005). *Ecological-evolutionary theory: Principles and applications*. Boulder: Paradigm Publishers.

Lenski, G., & Lenski, J. (1970). *Human societies: An introduction to macrosociology*. New-York: McGraw-Hill.

Leveto, J. A., & Kalkhoff, W. (2012). Biosocial interaction rituals of autism spectrum disorders: A research agenda for neurosociology. In W. Kalkhoff, S. R. Thye, & E. J. Lawler (Eds.), *Advances in group processes: Biosociology and neurosociology* (pp. 119–138). Bingley: Emerald.

Lévi-Strauss, C. (1969). *The elementary structures of kinship*. Rev. ed. Boston: Beacon

Lopreato, J. (1984). *Human nature and biocultural evolution*. Winchester: Allen & Unwin.

Lopreato, J. (1989). The maximization principle: A cause in search of conditions. In R. W. Bell & N. J. Bell (Eds.), *Sociobiology and the social sciences* (pp. 119–130). Lubbock: Texas Tech University Press.

Lopreato, J., & Crippen, T. (1999). *Crisis in sociology: The need for Darwin*. London: Transaction.

Lumsden, C. J., & Wilson, E. O. (1981). *Genes, mind and culture: The coevolutionary process*. Cambridge, MA: Harvard University Press.

Machalek, R. (1992). The evolution of macrosociety: Why are large societies rare? *Advances in Human Ecology, 1*, 33–64.

Machalek, R. (1999). Elementary social facts: Emergence in nonhuman societies. *Advances in Human Ecology, 8*, 33–64.

Machalek, R., & Martin, M. W. (2004). Sociology and the second Darwinian revolution: A metatheoretical analysis. *Sociological Theory, 22*, 455–476.

Maryanski, A. (1992). The last ancestor: An ecological-network model on the origins of human sociality. *Advances in Human Ecology, 2*, 1–32.

Maryanski, A. (1998). Evolutionary sociology. *Advances in Human Ecology, 7*, 1–56.

Maryanski, A., & Turner, J. H. (1992). *The social cage: Human nature and the evolution of society*. Stanford: Stanford University Press.

Maynard Smith, J. (1982). *Evolution and the theory of games*. Cambridge: Cambridge University Press.

Nolan, P., & Lenski, G. (2015). *Human societies: An introduction to macrosociology*. New York: Oxford University Press.

Parsons, T. (1966). *Societies: Evolutionary and comparative perspectives*. Englewood Cliffs: Prentice-Hall.

Pinker, S. (2002). *The blank slate: The modern denial of human nature*. New York: Penguin.

Rachman, S. J., & Seligman, M. E. P. (1976). Unprepared phobias: Be prepared. *Behaviour Research and Therapy, 14*, 333–338.

Runciman, W. G. (2015). Evolutionary sociology. In J. H. Turner, R. Machalek, & A. Maryanski (Eds.), *Handbook on evolution and society: Toward an evolutionary social science* (pp. 194–214). Boulder: Paradigm Publishers.

Savage, J., & Kanazawa, S. (2002). Social capital, crime, and human nature. *Journal of Contemporary Criminal Justice, 18*, 188–211.

Segerstråle, U. (2000). *Defenders of the truth: The battle for science in the sociobiology debate and beyond*. Oxford: Oxford University Press.

Seligman, M. E. P. (1971). Preparedness and phobias. *Behavior Therapy, 2*, 307–320.

Seligman, M. E. P. (1993). *What you can change and what you can't*. New York: Fawcett Columbine.

Seligman, M. E. P., & Hager, J. L. (1972). *Biological boundaries of learning*. New York: Meredith.

Smith, A. (1776 [1805]). *An inquiry into the nature and causes of the wealth of nations*. London: Davis.

Spencer, H. (1885). *The principles of sociology. (3 volumes)*. New York: Appleton-Century-Crofts.

Tiger, L., & Fox, R. (1966). The zoological perspective in social science. *Man, 1*, 75–81.

Tooby, J., & Cosmides, L. (1990). The past explains the present: Emotional adaptations and the structure of ancestral environments. *Ethology and Sociobiology, 11*, 375–424.

Tooby, J., & Cosmides, L. (1992). The psychological foundations of culture. In J. H. Barkow, L. Cosmides, & J. Tooby (Eds.), *The adapted mind: Evolutionary psychology and the generation of culture* (pp. 19–136). New York: Oxford University Press.

Trivers, R. L. (1971). The evolution of reciprocal altruism. *Quarterly Review of Biology, 46*, 35–57.

Trivers, R. L. (1972). Parental investment and sexual selection. *American Zoologist, 14*(1), 249–264.

Turner, J. H. (1985). *Herbert Spencer: An appreciation*. Beverly Hills: Sage Publications.

Turner, J. H. (1996). The evolution of emotions in humans: A Darwinian-Durkheimian analysis. *Journal for the Theory of Social Behavior, 26*, 1–34.

Turner, J. H. (1999). Toward a general sociological theory of emotions. *Journal for the Theory of Social Behavior, 29*, 133–162.

Turner, J. H. (2000). *On the origins of human emotions: A sociological inquiry into the evolution of human affect*. Stanford: Stanford University Press.

Turner, J. H. (2007). *Human emotions: A sociological theory*. Oxford: Routledge.

Turner, J. H. (2010). *Theoretical principles of sociology, vol. 1: Macrodynamics*. New York: Springer.

Turner, J. H. (2012). The biology and neurology of group processes. *Advances in Group Processes, 29*, 1–38.

Turner, J. H. (2013). *Theoretical sociology: 1830 to the present*. Los Angeles: Sage.

Turner, J. H. (2015). The evolution of the social mind: The limits of evolutionary psychology. In J. H. Turner, R. Machalek, & A. Maryanski (Eds.), *Handbook on evolution and society: Toward an evolutionary social science* (pp. 177–191). Boulder: Paradigm Publishers.

Turner, J. H., & Maryanski, A. (2008). *On the origin of the societies by natural selection*. Boulder: Paradigm Publishers.

Turner, J. H., & Maryanski, A. (2015). The prospects and limitations of evolutionary theorizing in the social sciences. In J. H. Turner, R. Machalek, & A. Maryanski (Eds.), *Handbook on evolution and society: Toward an evolutionary social science* (pp. 92–111). Boulder: Paradigm Publishers.

van den Berghe, P. (1973). *Age and sex in human societies: A biosocial perspective*. Belmont: Wadsworth.

van den Berghe, P. (1974). Bringing beasts back in: Toward a biosocial theory of aggression. *American Sociological Review, 39*, 777–788.

van den Berghe, P. (1981). *The ethnic phenomenon*. New York: Elsevier.

van den Berghe, P. (1990). *Human family systems*. Prospect Heights: Waveland.

West, S. A., El Moulden, C., & Gardner, A. (2011). Sixteen common misconceptions about the evolution of cooperation in humans. *Evolution and Human Behavior, 32*, 231–262.

Wilson, E. O. (1975). *Sociobiology: The new synthesis*. Cambridge, MA: Belknap.

Wilson, E. O. (1998). *Consilience: The unity of knowledge*. New York: Alfred A. Knopf.

Wilson, D. S., & Wilson, E. O. (2007). Rethinking the theoretical foundation of sociobiology. *Quarterly Review of Biology, 82*, 327–348.

Reimagining Collective Behavior 25

Justin Van Ness and Erika Summers-Effler

25.1 Introduction

From religion, recreation, and city-life, to emergency response, social movements, and revolutions, people come together in time and space to engage in the business of social life. They seek each other to define situations, to create order during crisis, and to drive social, cultural, and political change. In all of its forms, collective behavior is alive and well. However, can the same be said about collective behavior *theory*?

The 1960s witnessed a dismissal of collective behavior theory as it was supplanted in favor of rational choice explanations in the burgeoning field of social movements. Early theories of motivation, emotionality, and the effects of groups on individuals were often without systematically collected empirical data and thus became labeled as conjecture and promptly rejected. Activists turned academics issued in an era of portraying the rational protestor (see Morris and Herring 1987). Decades of social movement research followed suit, leaving long-lasting consequences to theory development. Though case studies of collective behavior have continued, general collective behavior *theory* has withered.

Over the past 20 years, the study of culture, emotions, and cognition have undergone substantial theoretical and methodological innovation. Increasingly, theories of collective action are treating culture, emotions, and social psychological processes seriously (e.g., Abrutyn 2014; Abrutyn and Van Ness 2015; Abrutyn et al. 2017; Collins 2009; Gould 2009; Jasper 1997; Klandermans 1997; Polletta 2008; Polletta and Jasper 2001; Summers-Effler 2010; Summers-Effler and Kwak 2015). In fact, many argue that explanations of social behavior not integrating these dynamics remain undertheorized and leave much to be desired (Jasper 2011; Scheff 1990). With new tools to explain individual, interactional, and situational dynamics, and the thriving interdisciplinary field of cognitive social science, it is time to make use of theoretical and methodological advances to revisit and rebuild the field of collective behavior. In this chapter, we contribute to this revitalization movement by reviewing what the past got right and wrong, and using new findings and theory to pave a way forward. Specifically, we argue the field of collective behavior has been trapped in old ways of thinking in spite of theoretical and empirical advances and when we turn towards these advances we find that early collective behavior theory had more right than we tend to credit.

This chapter will continue in four parts. In the first, we review the major approaches to categorizing the study of collective behavior. Following, we trace the history of major theoretical contributions and perspectives while also discussing

J. Van Ness (✉) • E. Summers-Effler
University of Notre Dame, Notre Dame, IN, USA
e-mail: jvanness@nd.edu; erika.m.effler.1@nd.edu

S. Abrutyn (ed.), *Handbook of Contemporary Sociological Theory*,
Handbooks of Sociology and Social Research, DOI 10.1007/978-3-319-32250-6_25

the rationalist's turn away from early theory. Next, we revisit the prematurely dismissed theories in light of recent advances in cognitive social science with an emphasis on emotion, cognition, and action. Finally, we end the chapter with fruitful paths for the future of collective behavior. This includes not only a suggestion for where our theoretical attention can be focused but also a methodological approach which we believe affords great potential for creativity and theoretical innovation.

25.2 Defining Collective Behavior

The study of collective behavior has referred to wide ranging phenomena. Some scholars have used the term for the study of crowds, mobs, panics. Crazes, fads, manias and other spontaneous acts also fall within this scope. Others have used the term for the study of riots and behavior during crises. Collective behavior can also describe rather mundane events that take place when two or more people come together in time and space. These may include waiting in line, marching, singing in church, rooting for sports teams, victory celebrations, or mosh-pits at a concert. To account for such a wide range, Clark McPhail defines collective behavior as "two or more persons engaged in one or more behaviors (e.g., locomotion, orientation, vocalization, verbalization, gesticulation, and/or manipulation) judged common or concerted on one or more dimensions (e.g., direction, velocity, tempo, or substantive content)" (1991: 159). As if McPhail's definition wasn't all encompassing, Park and Burgress (1921) even went so far as to claim the entire field of sociology as "the science of collective behavior". To a fault, when theories begin to "explain" everything, they lose their power to anticipate specific dynamics. This is part of the reason the theoretical baby was thrown out with the underspecified empirical bath water.

Another approach to the study of collective behavior focuses on a collectivity creating social, political, and cultural change (e.g., Blumer 1969 [1939]; Marwell and Oliver 1993; Marx and Wood 1975; Oliver 1989). Many in this perspective tend to use "collective action" interchangeably with collective behavior to attempt to emphasize rationality and purpose behind actions. This change-oriented perspective emerges when "usual conventions cease to guide social action and people collectively transcend… established institutional patterns and structures" (Turner and Killian 1987). Snow and Oliver (1995) define this as "extrainstitutional" behavior aimed at problem solving. Broadly conceived, these events tend to be temporary gatherings and less organizationally based than social movement campaigns and protest events. They tend to arise during moments of newly available opportunities or when established conventions cease to guide action. Scholars contributing to this perspective often heavily contribute to the field of social movements as well.

American sociology often fuses collective behavior and social movements together. McCarthy (1991) states "scholars…have insisted on wedding the study of crowds and social movements…A distinctively American marriage, it was one not consummated in Europe" (xii). While all social movements are a form of collective behavior, not all collective behavior takes the form of an organizationally based social movement. Despite this, the distinction has been less defined because most developments in the study of collective behavior have come from the study of protest events or from disaster research. Consequently, the breadth of cases with systematic research is rather limited. Additionally, what contributions have come from these two specializations have also been hindered by their own methodological biases. Protest event research, for instance, largely relies on newspaper records which limit the ability to record and theorize the individual and interactional processes in naturalistic contexts (e.g., Amenta et al. 2009; Andrews and Caren 2010; Earl et al. 2004; Oliver and Meyer 1999).

Generally, early collective behavior developed with an explicit attention to psychological processes, both through psychological and sociological standpoints. The former tended to focus on the influence of crowds and group behavior on the individual's cognition, behavior, and emotions. The sociological approach tends to focus on processes facilitating the emergence of collective behavior, the interactional processes, and the consequences of action. These two approaches should be viewed as complementary rather than contrasting. The distinctions are less visible than they were during the developments of early collective behavior theory and sociologists often integrate psychological research into their work (Thoits 1995).

Increasingly, scholars are integrating theories across specializations and disciplines in order to provide the most well-informed explanations of behavior (e.g., Abrutyn and Mueller 2015; Collett and Lizardo 2014; Summers-Effler et al. 2015). The field of collective behavior is particularly well suited for integration; Marx and McAdam agree, stating "the eclectic nature of the field of collective behavior…is an ideal area within which to examine basic, and unfortunately often unrelated, theoretical perspectives" (1994: 4). Thus, whether one chooses to focus on the emotions of crowds, the potential for change, emerging interaction orders, stability through crises, or the conditions and consequences of collective action, the field of collective behavior is ripe with potential for theoretical innovation (see Summers-Effler 2007).

25.3 Collective Behavior Theory

Eighteenth and nineteenth century crowd psychology birthed early collective behavior theory. During this time period, scholars were trying to explain the radical social, economic, and political upheaval of urban Europe. Violent strikes, riots, conflicts, and repression painted the social scene. Society was rapidly changing. Attempting to explain this assault upon the status quo, scholars honed their attention onto crowds. Many believed that by understanding the mechanisms and processes of crowds, they could better educate and assist the government's ability to control the masses. This historical period, perspective, and intent filtered the theoretical lens through which early theory developed (see Borch 2012). In this section, we review the major theoretical strands in the field of collective behavior.

25.3.1 Transformation

Arguably, LeBon's *The Crowd* has been the most influential work in the early study of collective behavior. LeBon believed that when people came together, no matter their individual characteristics, the nature of being together transforms individuals into a crowd and induces within them a collective mind (1895). A "mental unity" is born. This new state of mind leads individuals to feel, think, and act differently than they would if they were in isolation. Consequently, he argued, this transformation lead to the disappearance of critical reasoning skills, placing the crowd in a position "perpetually hovering on the borderland of unconsciousness" (LeBon 1895: 14). He also believed that the anonymity of the crowd would lead one to believe that they were unaccountable for their behaviors; that is, there is a sense of "invincibility" when acting within a crowd. Together, this would lead to otherwise normal individuals acting in extraordinary ways. This transformation became all the more dangerous as the crowd increases "suggestibility" in individuals, making them more vulnerable to the influence and potential manipulations of leaders.

LeBon's ideas were most directly introduced to American sociology through Robert E. Park (1904; Park and Burgess 1921), while also influencing French sociologists (e.g., Tarde 1901) and American psychologists (e.g., Freud 1921; Martin 1920). Park is often credited with founding the field of collective behavior within sociology (Turner and Killian 1987: 2). He argued that crowds and collective behavior played pivotal roles in social change. They were "forces which dealt the final blow to old existing institutions… and introduced the new spirit of new ones" (Park 1972: 48). Park added that the crowd transformation takes place within the context of "social unrest". During these tense moments of unrest, a mutual contagion – what he called "circular reaction" – creates a shared mood and a common impulse to act. Interaction, communication, and circular reaction then create unanimity within the crowd and afford the potential to achieve common ends.

Herbert Blumer, a student of Robert Park and George Herbert Mead, continued with an emphasis on interaction and the communication processes through which people construct and share worldviews. Blumer argued that "social unrest" emerges from the disruption of routine activities or the onslaught of new impulses or dispositions which the social order cannot accommodate. People respond to this lack of accommodation with a feeling of restlessness act aimlessly, erratically, excited, and are vulnerable to rumors.

Blumer argued that crowds come to act through five steps. First, an exciting event captures the attention of the crowd. People then begin milling about by walking around, exchanging rumors, and focusing on the event. This is when circular reactions "make the individuals more sensitive and responsible to one another" (Blumer 1969 [1939]: 174). The crowd becomes more cohesive as a group. Third, a common object of attention gives the group a shared orientation and mutual excitement. This furthers conformity. As the group shares a common heightened mood and orientation, the fourth step is the stimulation of shared impulses. Finally, the crowd acts upon impulse in a way they would not have acted if alone.

The transformation hypothesis developed through LeBon, Park, and Blumer portrays crowd behavior as irrational and strongly influenced by group emotions. From a distance, the crowd is treated as a collective whole with universal characteristics. Some argue that this is an oversimplification for the potential diversity of emotions, motives, roles, and actions within groups. Couch (1968) argues that behaviors such as protesting and rioting become described as irrational because they challenge the normative expectations from the analyst's cultural expectations – not because they are actually irrational. The transformation thesis remained the dominant collective behavior theory into the 1960s. The idea of a "group mentality" was especially influential in popular culture, though some claim it has not withstood empirical scrutiny (Allport 1924b; McPhail 1991; Norris 1988). Interestingly enough, emerging work is supporting of some LeBon, Park, and Blumer's theories which had been dismissed long ago. We will return to this later in the chapter.

25.3.2 Predisposition and Deprivation

Another thesis views crowds as composed of individuals with common predispositions, inner impulses, and unmet needs (Hoffer 1951; Lasswell 1930; Martin 1920). The predisposition explanation argues there is nothing unique about crowds or crowd behavior. There is no "transformation" or "mob mentality" when people come together. Rather, behavior is simply the result of actors converging with similar interests towards releasing tension. Some in this perspective even believed crowd participants converge to act out narcissism and latent homosexuality (cf. Lasswell 1930).

Floyd Allport (1924a, b), one of the first major critics of the transformation hypothesis, argued that innate and learned tendencies predispose people to crowd participation. These tendencies compelled people to converge in common locations in order to satisfy drives or overcome barriers to rewards; any action would be the result of shared predispositions being triggered by a situational stimulus. This activation could come from a leader's suggestion or from the crowd modeling behavior. To the extent that individuals influence one another, they are intensifying and activating latent impulses rather than generating new ones.

Allport continued the assumption that crowd behaviors are driven by strong emotional responses with tendencies towards violence (1924b). In contrast to crowds, "common group behaviors" were non-emotional and means-ends oriented. Similar to Blumer's "circular reaction," Allport's "social facilitation" was a reciprocal process wherein actors model, suggest, and activate behaviors within one another. The circular process may strengthen when spatial arrangements and other mediating ecological factors increase crowd density, thus bringing nearness to potential activating stimuli.

This thesis has been critiqued as a sleight of hand, simply taking the transformation view from the group level and positioning it at the individual level (McPhail 1991). Questions of motivation also became problematic as actions were used post-hoc to explain driving factors. For instance, those participating in dancing manias were believed to be victims of devil possession and people in lynch mobs were argued to be driven by religious fanaticism. These assumptions lie beyond the limits of our knowledge; thus, this speculation is often a better reflection of the theorist than the phenomena which being studied. However, there are benefits to breaking down types of emergent crowd behavior; we can think of the differentiation as analogous to different types of individual behavior. Cognitively, we can see this as sometimes acting out of the highly reflexive cerebral cortex, other times the emotional amygdala, and other times the fight, flight, or freeze of the brain stem.

Miller and Dollard (1941) developed the *deprivation* thesis through the use of learning theory which views behaviors as a result of learned tendencies in response to rewards. An inability to attain rewards through behaviors which have previously been successful creates a sense of frustration. This eventually leads to action in order to remove what is perceived as the blockade when previous behavior-reward pathways become problematic. Thus, they argued that aggressive action always indicates the existence of prior frustration and collective behavior emerges as a solution to overcome reward-barriers.

Ted Gurr (1970) built on the deprivation thesis by arguing that *relative* deprivation emerges with an actor's perception of the discrepancy between what one deserves and what one is capable of attaining and keeping. A point of reference may come from history, an abstract ideal, a leader's vision, or a comparison group. The relative deprivation thesis was largely used to explain urban riots of the 1960s and 1970s. Arguments were made about perceived injustice, anger, and frustration because of the rioters' position in society. The more extreme the negative affect, the greater the intensity of relative deprivation. Gurr states "one innate response to perceived deprivation is discontent or anger, and the anger is a motivation state for which aggression is an inherently satisfying response" (1968: 1105). Others have argued that *absolute* deprivation is also a precipitating factor for collective behavior (e.g., Toch 1965). For instance, Rude (1964) argues rising food prices and worsening conditions threatening minimum human survival motivated France's revolutionary crowds.

25.3.3 Emergent Norms

Ralph H. Turner and Lewis Killian, both students of Herbert Blumer, posited the emergent norm theory of collective behavior. This interactionist approach diverged from the early work of LeBon, Park, and Blumer by rejecting the "illusion of unanimity" premise. In contrast, Turner and Killian believed that crowds were composed of individuals with varying motives, emotions, and behaviors. Wherein day-to-day life is governed by routine social norms, Turner and Kilian described collective behavior as "extraordinary social behavior" which operates outside of habitual norms and is the product of a negotiated emergent norm particular to that situation in time and space. In these moments, an opening emerges where actors within the situation have greater ability to shape the attitudes of others.

Crowds and gatherings emerge in response to a condition or event that generates extraordinary circumstances. These circumstances may emerge from the physical world, such as tsunamis, earthquakes, and wildfires, or from chemical spills or nuclear accidents. Events may also emerge from social problems in the normative order, social structure, or communication channels. For instance, sudden repression and censorship may motivate collective behavior. Alternatively, in conditions that were previously repressive, new opportunities for free speech and assembly may also facilitate gatherings. Across situations, people utilize existing channels of communication to exchange rumor in response to the changing conditions; the growing literature on social networks has broadened our understanding and increased our ability to predict and explain these mechanisms and processes (e.g., Beyerlein and Hipp 2006; Beyerlein and Sikkink 2008; Gould 1991; McAdam and Paulsen 1993; Snow et al. 1980).

Unlike previous conceptions of rumor, Turner and Killian did not assume that rumor was the perpetuation of inaccurate information. Rather, in alignment with the symbolic interactionist perspective, it was a form of communication to construct a definition of the problematic situation in order to guide future lines of action. This information could be spread through face-to-face interactions or various forms of mass media. It may also precede or emerge concomitantly with convergence in a common location. Rumor tends to develop in reaction to the exciting event. In different degrees, actors provide suggestions for what has happened, what is happening, and what should happen next. Others may be concerned with leadership and who is going to act first. After an exciting event and the rumoring and milling process, a common mood and imagery emerges as the new definition of the situation and lines of action develop (Turner and Killian 1987: 4).

Questions of motivation lead Turner and Killian to posit five roles in collective behavior situations. The first were "ego-involved" who tended to have direct relationships to the extraordinary event. "Concerned" participants were those with personal relationships but a lesser degree of involvement. "Insecure" persons sought out crowds for the direct satisfaction of participation and security that stems from the emergence of definitions that make sense of extraordinary conditions. "Spectators" can also be found, motivated by curiosity and intrigue. Lastly, "exploiters" are present to capitalize on the concentration of people in a common location for self-interested gains. Breaking down crowds into types is generally a useful theoretical move.

In addition to arguing for a variation in motives and emerging norms in crowd situations, Turner and Killian's second edition of Collective Behavior (1972) argues ecology, social control, and shared symbols may also facilitate or inhibit collective behavior. While still a theoretically and empirically underdeveloped insight, more recently, ecology is central to Zhao's (1998) research on the 1989 Beijing student movement. He argues the university campuses had a unique spatial distribution with high density of students in small areas which nurtured close knit student networks. The layout of the dorms facilitated quick transmission of dissident ideas, created predictable patterns of interactions, and made communication between campuses easy. The campus density also directly exposed students to a collective action environment once crowds formed, thus facilitating recruitment. Since the campuses were surrounded by a brick wall, students were afforded protection from social control agents, creating a low-risk mobilization environment.

Exposure to emotionally powerful cultural symbols can also facilitate the rumor and milling process as people seek to construct a definition of the situation. For example, in 2009, when anti-abortion activists protested President Barack Obama's commencement speech by flying a plane with a banner in tow of an aborted fetus over the University of Notre Dame, they were inciting a rumor and milling process. It was an attempt to make salient the supposed conflict in values between President Obama's pro-choice stance and the Catholic Church's anti-choice position. Other examples may be more reactive situations where culturally powerful symbols are introduced less consciously into situations where they are not expected. That is, crowds may emerge in reaction to a cultural symbol which may have conflicting meanings or has been integrated into a situation where it is deemed inappropriate.

25.3.4 Life Course

Clark McPhail contends that too often scholars conflate the study of crowds with the study of collective behavior (McPhail 1991; McPhail and Miller 1973). This leads to an overemphasis on theories being developed about what happens when a large group of people are already congregated. He argues that not only does an emphasis on the crowd narrow the range of sociological phenomena within the study of collective behavior, but the notion of crowds implies homogeneity of motivations and behaviors. To counter, McPhail (1991) draws from Goffman (1963), suggesting collective behavior be studied in a life-course perspective with an analytic focus on *gatherings*.

When two or more people come together, a gathering is created which creates the *opportunity* for collective behavior, though it does not guarantee it (Goffman 1963; McPhail 1991). Gatherings tend to be temporary and undergo three stages: the assembling process, the assembled gathering, and the dispersal process. The assembling process refers to the forces which bring groups of people together, such as exciting events. The assembled gathering is the moment when people are in a similar space and time with the potential for collective action.[1] Dispersals are often unproblematic though they can also take the form of emergency dispersals, such as exiting a burning building, or through coercion, as when the police intervene. By differentiating the various stages of collective behavior, theories can be developed with greater specificity and not misstep by creating too general of arguments. Similar to Turner and Killian's move to differentiate roles within collective behavior situations, differentiating stages in time is also a useful move.

Oliver (1989) argues that *prior* to assembling processes there are often "occasions" where actors engage in calculation and planning. During occasions, people communicate and signal to one another their intentions to act or not under future conditions. Feelings of injustice and indignation motivate future action and future successes build a sense of efficacy in collective action. Through occasions, tactics become loosely structured and are open to modification when they are deployed in collective action situations. Oliver also argues that behind some crowd events is a social movement downplaying an organizational role because of the "odd cultural belief" that spontaneous crowds are more legitimate than calculated and organized crowd events. Some of these organizational decisions may be choosing the time and place and even planning for social control measures to prevent "true" spontaneous crowd formation.

Spontaneity has also returned to the study of collective behavior and social movements. An insight present in Turner and Killian's *Collective Behavior* (1987), Snow and Moss (2014) revisit the concept and posit conditions when spontaneity becomes likely to emerge and consequential to organization and collective action outcomes. They argue nonhierarchical movements encourage openness, innovation, and experimental forms of collective action. These dynamics increase the likelihood for unplanned action and spontaneity. They also argue that behavioral and emotional priming creates sensitivity to stimuli prior to experiences and increases the probability of directing future emotions and lines of actions. Priming becomes particularly influential during moments of ambiguity and situational breakdown. Finally, they too argue spontaneity is influenced by the ecological arrangements in situations. Not only can ecology facilitate crowd formation and mobilization, but it also may increase the likelihood of unplanned action and confrontation from social control agents and exacerbate effects of ambiguity and priming.

McPhail and Miller (1973) differentiate the assembling process between periodic assembly and non-periodic assembly. Periodic assemblies tend to have recurring participants who establish schedules to converge at the same time-space locations. For instance, churches, which have services at the same time and place every week, or classes, which announce their schedules semesters at a time. Non-periodic assemblies seldom have completely sustained membership across events and often have differing motivating forces. Communication channels can also lead to differing assembly processes and can be distinguished between short range communication (e.g., face-to-face interaction) and long range communication (e.g., social media). Nearness to

[1] For a complete discussion on how to systematically record data during collective gatherings see *The Collective Action Observation Primer* (McPhail et al. 1997).

events, such as a fire or a protest, may explain variation in who enters into non-periodic assemblies. Thus, for non-routine gatherings, theories about ecology, population density, communication, and afforded interactions, can be theorized in distinctly different ways than those that are more deeply rooted in personal and institutional histories. Non-routine dispersals, such as those coerced by social control agents, also focus on similar intervening variables.

25.3.5 Repression

Research on the effects of social control on collective behavior has produced mixed and even contradictory findings. Rational choice explanations argue that repression depresses resistance because it increases the costs of participation (e.g., Opp and Roehl 1990; Snyder and Tilly 1972; Tilly 1978), while others argue the opposite claiming repression *increases* mobilization (Khwaja 1993; Rasler 1996). Gurr (1970) argues the greatest magnitude of violence and resistance emerges at medium levels of repression. Some argue for a various non-linear relationship between repression and resistance (De Nardo 1985; Muller and Weede 1990).

Zimmermann (1980) claims there to be arguments for all conceivable relationships between repression and mobilization, except for the claim that there is no relationship. Indeed, this seems to be the case. Koopmans (1997) states this disagreement exists because of poor methodology, data, and theory. Most models use static, cross-sectional data, despite the fact that repression is *dynamic* (see Maher 2010) and varies across situations and time. Snyder (1976) has similarly critiqued the field for a lack of differentiation between forms and timing of coercion.

Despite the mixed findings, the field is ripe with case studies that afford potential for innovation. One such article is Khwaja (1993) response to Snyder's critique. He uses data from the Palestinian West Bank from 1976 to 1985 to address both shifts in form and level of repression and the effects on collective action. Because the Israeli military uses various countermeasures of coercion to suppress resistance, he says it allows insight into various strategies used by the state. Of the 14 forms of repression measured, all forms of repression *increased* collective action except for one: home searches. This implies that generally repression reinforces resistance regardless of costs (also see: De Nardo 1985; McAdam [1982] 1999). However, this also suggests that repression at the group or crowd level (e.g., curfews) may create mixed results compared to repression at the individual level (e.g., invading a family's home).

In addition to motivating increased resistance, Khawaja argues repression can also strengthen collective identity, provide a sense of belonging to a group, and can operate as a symbolic reminder of a group's shared circumstances vis-à-vis authorities. Perhaps one of Khawaja's most interesting, yet arguably under-theorized, findings is the notion that during acts of repression, authorities are likely to violate moral standards which may further draw in bystanders who were previously unengaged. This insight can be integrated with Thomas Scheff's theory shame/rage spirals (1990). Scheff argues for a dynamic understanding of shame and anger which can rise both between interactants and within actors, manifesting as explosive outbursts or enduring tones, and may operate at varying levels along the micro-macro continuum. Enduring tones of shame and rage can give way to outbursts through group conflict. A historical and cultural analysis of the group's histories, with a particular attention to emotions of shame and rage, can help explain reactions to particular triggers of conflict.

Koopmans (1997) finds a lack of consistency by repressive forces may also generate moral outrage among public sympathizers; that is, tolerating a protest tactic 1 day and then repressing it the next is likely to anger and motivate participation. From violation of consistency, repression comes to "embod[y] the very message that [protestors] seek to convey…a repressive political system that is in need of revolutionary change" (Koopmans 1995: 32). Differentiating between institutional repression (e.g., bans, trials, raids) and situational repression (e.g., tear gas, arrests), he finds situational repression escalating tensions while institutional repression comparatively lessening levels of protests. In Smith's (1996) research with the Central America Peace Movement, the government used institutional repression by relabeling Nicargua as a high-risk destination, consequently making travel difficult, while also requiring burdensome tax audits, tapping protestors phones, and going to great lengths to intimidate and discredit protestors, sympathetic journalists, and academics. He finds varying effects on mobilization from discouragement, ineffectiveness, and even re-motivating protestors. Generally, he argues when repression generates fear activism tends to be lessened; feelings of anger, however, tended to increase commitment and investment. With a similar attention to perception and emotions, Maher (2010) finds that in highly repressive environments, collective action may emerge when the absence of group action is perceived as posing a greater threat than the potential response to resistance.

25.3.6 Structure

Three main macro concepts have received the most theoretical attention and development: *strain*, *breakdown*, and, *quotidian-disruption*. Neil Smelser, a student of Talcott Parsons, argues that collective behavior emerges in response to "strain" in the social structure (Smelser 1962). This strain emerges when environmental conditions create impairments in the structural relations among components of society. As structure breaks down, actors begin to feel tension and a feeling of uncertainty. In a post-hoc explanation, Smelser argues that the nature of collective action is proof of the existence of structural strain.

While some advocated for the merit of strain theory (Marx and Wood 1975), the Tilly's (1975) supplanted the strain metaphor with a distinction between "breakdown" and "solidaristic" theories of collective action. The central tenet of breakdown theories is that underlying all forms of collective action is rapid social change and disintegration. Crises weaken the regulative and integrative functions in society, thereby threatening social cohesion. Consequently, these strains in the sociopolitical order incite frustration which motivates collective action. To a fault, this approach perpetuates the assumption that society can actually achieve a harmonious, perfectly integrated and regulated state. Like strain theory, it has not fared well to empirical tests. Tilly et al. (1975) found little support for the breakdown thesis. Rather, they found it was new forms of organization, with new bonds of solidarity, which incited collective action. Thus, they posited the "solidaristic" approach as opposed to supporting breakdown theories. Broadly conceived, these theories can be viewed as push and pull theories of collective action whereas breakdown pushes and solidarity pulls. One of the main tenets in the "push" hypothesis from strain theory which social movement research has rejected is the notion that collective behavior is incited by socially isolated actors. In fact, one of the most well supported findings in the study of social movements confirms that participants are often embedded in social networks and organizations which draw one into participation (Gould 1991, 1993; McAdam and Paulsen 1993; Snow et al. 1980).

Useem's (1985) research on the 1980 New Mexico prison riots suggests that breakdown processes can contribute to at least some instances of collective action. The brutal prison riots were a product of the termination of inmate programs, crowding, idleness, poor administration, and bad living conditions. Over the course of 5 years, living conditions in the prison gradually worsened. This incited feelings of deprivation and frustration which eventually amounted into a bloody prison riot. Useem's findings challenge both the Tilly's (1975) solidaristic model and social movement theory's resource mobilization thesis. Collective action did not arise because of an increase in solidarity amongst inmates nor the infusion of new resources – quite the opposite, in fact. The processes of disorganization and the fragmenting of bonds among inmates contributed to the weak and chaotic leadership structures. Even though inmates were in prison, prisoners set standards by which how much deprivation can be tolerated. It was the violation of these standards that created the frustration which fueled the response.

Another perspective focuses on the routine in day-to-day life. Snow et al. (1998) utilize cognitive psychology's prospect theory to argue the key relationship between breakdown and collective action emergence resides in the "quotidian" and its actual or threatened disruption. Prospect theory argues that actors will be more likely endure risk in order to protect what they already have rather than take on the same level of risk in order to gain something new. Thus, when one's everyday life – their quotidian – is disrupted, actors are more likely to respond in order to restore life conditions than they are to attempt to improve them. Quotidian's can become disrupted by: (1) an increase in claimants or demand for resources, yet no change in resource availability; (2) a decrease in available resources but constant claimants and demand; (3) crises which disrupt or threaten a community's daily routines; (4) actual or threatened intrusions on privacy and safety. The quotidian-disruption approach appears most useful as it gives attention to individual perception, resource disparities, population pressures, and other structural phenomena which may threaten the true or perceived conditions in one's daily life. It also demonstrates how the politically rich get richer and other forms of inequality become exacerbated in addition to why resistance does *not* emerge despite conditions which one would expect to motivate action (see Della Fave 1980).

25.3.7 Testing the Myths

Some empirical research claims to have dispelled many of the early collective behavior "myths" (see McPhail 1991). Disaster research, for instance, has argued that even in moments of crisis, people in crowds do not suffer from irrationality or cognitive deficiencies (Bryan 1982; Cantor 1980; Johnston and Johnson 1989). For example, Tierney (2002) describes the emergency evacuations in the World Trade Center on September 11th, 2001 as prosocial, orderly, and "with a virtual absence of panic". This emphasis on rationality is also present in much social movement research, particularly within the rationalist and resource mobilization tradition (Klandermans and Oegema 1987; McCarthy and Zald 1977; Walsh and Warland 1983). Many theorists who have made this move continue to perpetuate the false dichotomy between emotionality and rationality. As we explain in the next section of this chapter, this contrast is no longer empirically supportable. Thus, theorizing which assumes that action driven through emotions is reflective of a "cognitive deficiency" is inherently problematic.

In addition to research challenging the "irrationality" of actors, the myth of the anonymous and violent crowd has also been critiqued with much greater success. Despite popular conceptions, crowds are not typically violent (Collins 2009; Eisinger 1973; McPhail 1994). Violence is often carried out by small groups within a crowd or by state authorities (Couch 1968; Marx and McAdam 1994; Stott and Reicher 1998). Collins (2009) provides a thorough account of processes and pathways creating violent situations. By all measures, violence is a rare phenomenon and it is a more useful theoretical move to consider the conditions when *situations* become violent, rather than emphasizing violent *individuals*. Collins argues violent situations create an emotional field of tension and fear. Within these fields, actual violence happens when one side of the confrontation turns emotional tension into emotional energy, becomes more attuned to the situation's audience in order to assert dominance, or when one side has a fracture in solidarity and shows weakness.

The evolving histories of collective behavior theories suggests not that some are completely wrong and others are right, but that it would behoove us to understand how and when different causes and conditions create variation in outcomes. Certainly, the history of collective behavior has provided important pieces of the puzzle. The most pressing work is finding a common foundation and putting them all together. In the next section, we work towards this endeavor by drawing from interdisciplinary cognitive social science to begin to salvage theories which were prematurely dismissed in order to recover some of our puzzle pieces.

25.4 Collective Behavior Theory Redux

Thus far, we have covered the first two movements within the field of collective behavior. The first movement focused on theories of how individuals are changed by a result of their participation in crowds, as well as the nature, causes, and consequences of collective behavior. The second movement was marked by the emergence of the social movement field (see Chap. 26) and coinciding rationalist turn in collective behavior (McPhail 1991; McPhail and Miller 1973; McPhail et al. 1997). The rationalist turn quickly became the dominant approach to collective behavior and often scholars continue to set up their contributions in reaction to the theories of LeBon, Blumer, and Turner and Killian.

If one were to ignore developments outside of sociology, or work from the more recent emotions turn within sociology, one would likely be content with where the field of collective behavior and social movements is currently positioned vis-à-vis the early theories. However, when one looks outside of sociology and into the interdisciplinary field of cognitive social science, as many in the emotions turn tend to do (Collins 2001; Gould 2009; Jasper 2011; Summers-Effler 2010), one would likely be surprised by recent finding's resemblance to early collective behavior theories.

In this section, we draw from recent advancements in interdisciplinary field of cognitive social science to discuss the implications for collective behavior theory with a specific focus on how emotions and cognitions influence and are influenced by collective behavior. Specifically, we utilize research on dual process models, mirror neurons, and embodied cognition to re-center the body and to revisit theories of emotionality, cognition, and action. In so doing, we contribute to the revitalization of collective behavior now emerging with, what we believe, is the third movement within collective behavior (e.g., Snow and Moss 2014; Van Dyke and Soule 2002). Recent research returning to the first movement reveals that the early theorists had more right than what the rationalist turn gave credit for.

25.4.1 Dual Process

Research in cognitive science, neuropsychology, and social psychology have uncovered that humans possess two memory systems which has been developed under the "dual process framework" (Brewer 1988; Gawronksi and Bodenhausen 2006; Haidt 2001; Smith and DeCoster 2000). Within the dual process framework, there are dual process models which describe the implications for the enculturation process, culture in thinking, storage, and culture in action (see Lizardo et al. unpublished). Of the varying models, those focused on culture in storage and action differentiate between schematic, *associative* memory processes and symbolically-mediated, *rule-based* processes (see Kahneman 2011; Smith and DeCoster 2000). Research in this area has uncovered how and under what conditions actors tend to use one type of memory over another. Both memory systems influence perception, judgments, affective states, and lines of action in distinct ways (e.g., Hunzaker 2014; Lizardo and Strand 2010; Vaisey 2009).

Schematic memory records information through a slow, incremental patterning of experiences which develop into general, stable expectations. Once created, schemas help "fill in" missing information pre-consciously in day-to-day life by automatically relating the current situation to expected information and affective reactions from similar situation's in one's history (Strauss and Quinn 1997). When situations are predictable and stable, actions tend to flow automatically (Strack and Deustch 2004). Fast-binding, symbolically-mediated "*rule-based*" processes encode episodic experiences and contexts. This system constructs new representations which bind together disparate information from an immediate context and can often be constructed, directed, and controlled strategically by others within the situation (Smith and DeCoster

2000: 112). Fast learning systems particularly attend to details of events which are novel and interesting, with a specific focus on the *unexpected* and *unpredicted*. That is, one is more likely to encode and act through rule-based processes in atypical moments as opposed to relying on deeply engrained schemas and habits. Understanding that conditions influence which type of cognitive processes drive action reveals why some theorists see situations of radical moments full of creativity while others see situations of "rationality," stability, and habit.

LeBon, Park, and Blumer all centered their analyses within conditions of social unrest. Turner and Killian described collective behavior as being precipitated by an "exciting event" and "extraordinary circumstances". All agreed these were atypical moments which afforded potential for creativity and significant change. Specifying the context for the behavior being theorized is important because humans utilize differing memory systems depending upon the novelty, stability, or predictability of a situation (also see Harvey 2010). Thus, to understand variation in lines of action, we must make the microsociological move towards the situation (Collins 2004, 2009; Goffman 1974). By doing this, the analyst observes how the *situation* evokes varying emotions, motives, and actions rather than presuming that individuals are constant across situations. It is problematic to assume that theories of action in abnormal situations can be "disproven" by developing theories in mundane situations because *variation in the situation evokes variation in cognitive and emotive processes.*

Here we discover the importance of specifying situational conditions. Atypical situations are likely to shift one out of associative, schematic processing and into rule-based symbolically-mediated processing and action (Smith and DeCoster 2000). Conditions of social unrest evoke cognitive and emotive processes qualitatively different than those evoked during comparatively stable conditions. Such situational conditions afford opportunities for the creative development of lines of action not afforded in comparatively stable, predictable situations. Thus, when LeBon spoke of "suggestibility" and Blumer of "susceptibility to rumor," their concepts emphasize where an actor's attention lies and the potential the situation affords. Susceptibility to rumors can be understood as susceptibility to prioritizing emerging understandings over historical ones because they are utilizing symbolically mediated rule-based processing instead of schematic associations. One does not have increased suggestibility because they are a "dope," but rather because in unexpected situations actors hone their attention towards processes in the immediate present and are more open for the construction of novel lines of action.

LeBon's fixation with the unequal influence of leaders during "suggestible" situations can be understood as an actor's ability to influence the emerging definition of the situation and lines of action. Inequality of attention within situations is not a contested notion; the unequal distribution of attention and emotional resources is a structural property of situations, not a property of individuals (Collins 2004). Thus, when certain situational conditions encourage rule-based processing, there is an increased opportunity for the transmission of emergent meanings and lines of action which may be influenced in unequal ways dependent upon the distribution of attention within the situation.

Turner and Killian's theory of emergent norms has also found its support from the dual process framework. In situations where emergent meanings are in tension with one's historical understanding, conformity towards the emergent develops through the perception of situational group consensus (Smolensky 1988). When lines of action are articulated through explicit, conscious thought, actors are more likely to assume proposals are valid (Mackie and Skelly 1994). Once perceived as valid, actors are more likely to attribute emergent meanings as objectively true and become less likely to assume they are an artifact of possible interpretive errors or misrepresentations (Smith and DeCoster 2000: 112). The notion that actors may align themselves to emergent meanings, despite the possibility that they may be in conflict with one's historic understandings, aligns with Turner and Killian's suggestion that norms may emerge within situations and align actions even though co-present actors may hold varying motives and dispositions. Such an attention to situational conditions, and the corresponding perceptual, emotive, and cognitive effects, also reveals the power of a skilled frame articulator and a successful frame alignment process; alignment processes are more complex and situationally contingent than simply broadening, bridging, or transforming symbolically-mediated meanings – an insight underdeveloped within the extensive framing literature (see Snow et al. 2014).

25.4.2 Contagion

Many early collective behavior theorists described processes of conformity. LeBon described a "mental unity," both Park and Blumer spoke of a "circular reaction," and Allport emphasized "social facilitation". While Allport might disagree with how LeBon, Park, and Blumer chose to emphasize the circular nature to contagion, even Allport argued that co-presence facilitates the activation of inner impulses. These insights can broadly be referred to as *contagion*. Contagion is the process where members imitate the emotions, action states, and behaviors of others. Interestingly enough, and perhaps to the surprise of many, neuropsychology has decades of research supporting contagion theories (Gallese and Sinigaglia 2011; Hatfield et al. 1994, 2009; Knoblich and Flach 2003; Rizzolatti and Sinigaglia 2007). Indeed, actors *do* influence the emotions and readiness for action in other individuals in pre-conscious ways (for a list of contagion mechanisms, see Hatfield et al. 2009).

One major mechanism facilitating contagion is through the activation of mirror neurons. Research has found that human brains are biologically wired to be social. Mirror neurons link perception and motor action directly, affording the potential for perceived sights and sounds to activate embodied simulation (Gallese and Sinigaglia 2011; Iacoboni 2008; Rizzolatti and Sinigaglia 2007). This simulation alters the bodily and emotional states in the perceiver, creating a "resonance" which "is the functional outcome of attunement that allows us to feel what is felt by another person" (Siegel 2007: 166). Co-presence initiates this attunement as mirror neurons are particularly receptive to face-to-face interactions, responding to even the most micro of gestures such as facial expressions (Christakis and Fowler 2009; Iacoboni 2008), in addition to other synchronization processes which respond to body posturing (Bernieri et al. 1988) and voice tones (Hatfield et al. 1995). Importantly, mirror neuron activation does *not* require explicit, deliberate recognition of the information being simulated; rather, it is an "*effortless*, automatic, and unconscious inner mirroring" (Iacoboni 2008: 120).

Research within the dual process framework also finds that moods can influence the types of memory systems driving action. Actors are more likely to rely on schematic processes during positive moods, while negative moods tend to increase a reliance on emergent meanings (Smith and Decoster 2000: 117). Aligning this insight with mirror neuron research, we know that emotions can spread contagiously, often in preconscious ways when co-present. The tone of the emotions being spread influences whether greater weight is placed on the present situation or on historical meanings. When co-presence facilitates the contagion of negative emotions, actors are more likely to rely on symbolically-mediated rule based processing, just as they are when embedded within novel situations. In addition to the interactional contagion of negative moods, an inability to rely on historical dispositions may also give rise to a sense of frustration. This insight is shared with the pragmatists who suggest that engaging in an unpredictable and novel situation may force attention towards the immediate present because of the inability to rely on historical understandings (Dewey 1922; James 1890 [2007]; Mead 1934). Contagion research supports the insights of the early theorists who believed there to be emergent processes which arise when groups of people come together in time and space.

25.4.3 Rationality and Emotionality

Finally, the fallacy that emotionality and rationality are at odds has long been dispelled – though this belief unfortunately continues to linger in Sociology. Frequently, sociologists perpetuate this misconception because of the false assumption that individual reflexive thought is the seat of all rationality. As discussed, reflexive thought is only a portion of cognition and much which drives action happens through pre-conscious habitual associations linking situations to expected cognitions and affective states. When emotions are accounted for, they're often associated with intuition, as if emotions do not influence both reflexive reasoning and intuition (Haidt 2001). Turning this misconception on its head, research in neuroscience suggests rational thinking requires emotional attunement (Damasio 1994). The human amygdala, for instance, has been found to link emotional cues to other cognitive systems underlying cognition and action (see Phelps 2006; Whalen 1998). In fact, when the prefrontal lobe becomes separated from the subcortical emotion stem, individuals have a difficult time making decisions and often engage in actions which one may classify as irrational (Damasio 2003). Again, this demonstrates that emotionality is a requisite for rational thinking.

Early collective behavior theory was well attuned to emotional dynamics in group situations. Granted, many of these theorists relied on the perception of emotionality as an indication of a group's irrationality. Despite this, it is surprising that it took decades for the study of emotions to return to theories of collective behavior (Jasper 2011). The decades-long extraction of all emotional dynamics from theories of collective behavior and social movements actually perpetuated this antagonism between emotionality and rationality rather than challenge and critique such an assumption. Fortunately, those who treat emotions seriously have begun to rebuild theories of collective action and a growing body of literature has emerged (e.g., Collins 2009; Goodwin et al. 2001; Gould 2009; Summers-Effler 2002, 2010; Turner and Stets 2005). Among other salvageable components of early theories, there is still great potential for revisiting and rebuilding emotional dynamics in collective behavior.

25.5 Future Directions

In this section, we focus primarily on three areas where we believe collective behavior theory can develop. First, we emphasize a methodological approach which re-centers the body. Second, we believe questions of time and space should be revisited with the methodological approach advocated, particularly with an attention towards emotional dynamics. Finally, we argue that questions of motivation, which are rising to the surface in recent theories of collective action, should be developed with an awareness of cognitive social science's contributions.

25.5.1 Re-centering the Body

The eclectic nature of collective behavior is reflected in the diversity of methods scholars have employed. Despite wide variation and the creative combination of multiple approaches (e.g., Collins 2009), detailed ethnographic accounts of collective behavior are in short supply. With some exceptions, much of what is classified as ethnographic research is simply a form of interviewing in naturalistic contexts. This creates a tendency to privilege discourse over emotive processes and habitual behaviors which may fall outside of discursive awareness (see Summers-Effler et al. 2015). It also makes theorizing processes of time and space more difficult when the researcher's data is limited by the cognitive constraints of the interviewee (see Baddeley 1986).

A particularly fruitful method which may help address this bias in data collection comes from Summers-Effler's (2010) comparative ethnography. Her multisensory approach utilizes the Self as a form of social propioception in order to account for how one's social position and the role of the body, timing, and emotions influence processes of social organization (see Summers-Effler 2010: 203–212). This approach affords researchers the potential to purposefully align oneself in relational fields so as to take up varying positions in order to develop a multidimensional theory. It also encourages reflexivity of one's research role in relation to the phenomena being explained which helps reveal why some scholars distant from the field tend towards viewing action as rooted in more rational motivations while those more embedded tend to see the emotional and cultural motivations. Ethnographers who adopt an active research role have produced compelling ethnographic research (e.g., Desmond 2007; Pagis 2009; Tavory 2009; Wacquant 2004) and Summers-Effler's approach lends itself well for creative theorizing of collective behavior.

25.5.2 Space and Time

By re-centering the body, dynamics of space and time can be more directly and creatively theorized. Indeed, spatial and temporal dynamics are often implicit and, in some cases, explicit, in both early and contemporary collect behavior theories. At its core, collective behavior developed as a way to make sense of radical change. Thus, when an analyst seeks to make sense of how change evolves through space and time, she finds herself in the realm of *rhythmanalysis* (Lefebvre 2014 [2004]). Such theorizing fits well with Summers-Effler's approach to ethnography, as Lefebvre states "the theory of rhythms is founded on the experience and knowledge of the body… the rhythmnanalyst calls on all of his [sic] senses" (Lefebvre 2014 [2004]: 31). With the Self as a resource, rhythm becomes a tool for analysis rather than simply an object of study. As a novel way of seeing, the analyst unveils that which rhythms make apparent and that which they conceal. For instance, one may make perceptible patterns of stability and change by varying temporal constraints or positions of perception. By doing so, analysts will reveal how collective action leaves imprints on the social, cultural, and political fabric of an era.

To aid future research, the microsociological unit of analysis – *situations* – is due resurgence in the field of collective behavior. Researchers should situate themselves within collective behavior situations and record how material and social conditions constrain or encourage particular meanings, emotions, and actions. In this respect, J.J. Gibson's (1979) theory of affordances becomes particularly useful and can be integrated with the pragmatists emphasis on history in order to understand how and when history enables or constrains moments of change (Dewey 1922; James 1912; Mead 1934). Situations afford particular emotions, meanings, and interactions which may become constrained or enabled by perceptual and material conditions. An embedded analyst can purposefully problematize components of situations in order to theorize variation in affordances (e.g., McDonnell 2016). This may include an attention towards potential cultural, political, and emotional meanings of places (e.g., Fuss 2004; Gieryn 2000, 2002; Mukerji 1994), ecological conditions facilitating or inhibiting group formation (e.g., Haffner 2013; Lefebvre 1991; Scott 1998; Zhao 1998), or the way material conditions interact with an actor's perceptual capabilities (e.g., Griswold et al. 2013; Klett 2014; McDonnell 2010).

25.5.3 Motivation

Finally, in light of recent advancements in cognitive science and the study of emotions, questions of motivation and theories of action are rising to the surface in studies of social movements and collective behavior (Jasper 2010). More often than not, scholars leave implicit their assumptions about human motivation or they simply fall back on utilitarian rational-choice assumptions. It is important to realize that the rationalist approach *is* an assumption of motivation – but it is not the only perspective. Future research can intentionally cycle through alternative theories of motivation to uncover novel insights. For instance, one could substitute utilitarian approaches for assumptions of self-consistency (Robinson and Smith-Lovin 1992), solidarity (Durkheim 1912), or self-expansion (Summers-Effler 2004). Creativity will emerge as theorists combat seemingly incompatible findings by engaging in theoretical and methodological innovations (Summers-Effler 2007).

25.6 Conclusion

In this chapter, we revisited and reimagined early collective behavior theories through the lens of recent cognitive social science. We began by illustrating the wide variation in how scholars conceptualize collective behavior and then we focused on the major theoretical contributions to the field. Following, we revisited major theories with a renewed understanding of emotion and cognition. We then suggested areas where the future of collective behavior can continue to develop. This included a methodological approach, a renewed focus on space and time, and an attention to motivation and action. Moreover, we've argued that cognitive social science provides the foundation from which the future of collective behavior theory can and should be built. This foundation also affords the potential for novel methodological developments, ways of seeing, and an opportunity for new understandings of past contributions. All said, the future of collective behavior theory looks promising.

References

Abrutyn, S. (2014). *Revisiting institutionalism in sociology: Putting the "Institution" back in institutional analysis*. New York: Routledge.

Abrutyn, S., & Mueller, A. S. (2015). When too much integration and regulation hurts: Reenvisioning Durkheim's altruistic suicide. *Society and Mental Health*. doi:10.1177/2156869315604346.

Abrutyn, S., & Van Ness, J. (2015). The role of agency in sociocultural evolution: Institutional entrepreneurship as a force of structural and cultural transformation. *Thesis Eleven, 127*(1), 52–77.

Abrutyn, S., Van Ness, J., & Taylor, M. A. (2017). Collective acton and cultural change: Revisiting Eisenstadt's evolutionary theory. *Journal of Classical Sociology 17*(1).

Allport, F. H. (1924a). The group fallacy in relation to social science. *Journal of Abnormal and Social Psychology, 19*, 60–73.

Allport, G. (1924b). *Social psychology*. Boston: Houghton Mifflin.

Amenta, E., Caren, N., Olasky, S. J., & Stobaugh, J. E. (2009). All the movements fit to print: Who, what, when, where, and why SMO families appeared in the "New York Times" in the twentieth century. *American Sociological Review, 74*(4), 636–656.

Andrews, K. T., & Caren, N. (2010). Making the news: Movement organizations, media attention, and the public agenda. *American Sociological Review, 75*(6), 841–866.

Baddeley, A. (1986). *Working memory*. New York: Oxford University Press.

Bernieri, F. J., Reznick, J. S., & Rosenthal, R. (1988). Synchrony, psuedosynchrony, and dissynchrony: Measuring the entrainment process in mother-infant interactions. *Journal of Personality and Social Psychology, 54*, 243–253.

Beyerlein, K., & Hipp, J. R. (2006). A two-stage model for a two-stage process: How biographical availability matters for social movement mobilization. *Mobilization, 11*(3), 219–240.

Beyerlein, K., & Sikkink, D. (2008). Sorrow and solidarity: Why Americans volunteered for 9/11 relief efforts. *Social Problems, 55*(2), 190–215.

Blumer, H. (1969 [1939]). Collective behavior. In Lee, A. M. (Ed.), *Principles of sociology* (pp. 67–121). New York: Barnes and Noble.

Borch, C. (2012). *The politics of crowds: An alternative history of sociology*. Cambridge: Cambridge University Press.

Brewer, M. B. (1988). A dual process model of impression formation. In T. K. Srull & R. S. Wyer (Eds.), *Advances in social cognition* (pp. 1–36). Hillsdale: Erlbaum.

Bryan, J. (1982). *An examinaiton and analysis of the dynamics of human behavior in the MGM Grand Hotel fire: Clark Couny, Nevada November 21, 1980*. Washington, DC: National Fire Protection Association.

Cantor, D. (1980). An overview of human behavior in fires. In D. Cantor (Ed.), *Fires and human behavior*. New York: Wiley.

Christakis, N. A., & Fowler, J. H. (2009). *Connected: The surprising power of our social networks and how they shape our lives*. New York: Back Bay Books.

Collett, J. L., & Lizardo, O. (2014). Localizing cultural phenomena by specifying social psychological mechanisms: Introduction to the special issue. *Social Psychology Quarterly, 77*(2), 95–99.

Collins, R. (2001). Social movements and the focus of emotional attention. In J. Goodwin, J. M. Jasper, & F. Polletta (Eds.), *Passionate politics: Emotions and social movements* (pp. 27–44). Chicago: University of Chicago Press.

Collins, R. (2004). *Interaction ritual chains*. Princeton: Princeton University Press.

Collins, R. (2009). *Violence: A micro-sociological theory*. Princeton: Princeton University Press.

Couch, C. J. (1968). Collective behavior: An examination of some stereotypes. *Social Problems, 15*, 310–322.

Damasio, A. R. (1994). *Descartes' error: Emotion, reason, and the human being*. New York: Putnam.

Damasio, A. R. (2003). *Looking for Spinoza: Joy, sorrow, and the feeling brain*. Orlando: Harcourt Inc.

De Nardo, J. (1985). *Power in numbers: The political strategy of protest and rebellion*. Princeton: Princeton University Press.

Della Fave, R. L. (1980). The meek shall not inherit the earth: Self-evaluation and the legitimacy of stratification. *American Sociological Review, 45*(6), 955–971.

Desmond, M. (2007). *On the fireline: Living and dying with wildland firefighters*. Chicago: University of Chicago Press.

Dewey, J. (1922). *The nature of human conduct*. Carbondale: Southern Illinois University Press.

Durkheim, E. (1912). *The elementary forms of religious life*. Oxford: Oxford University Press.

Earl, J., Martin, A., McCarthy, J. D., & Soule, S. A. (2004). The use of newspaper data in the study of collective action. *Annual Review of Sociology, 30*, 65–80.

Eisinger, P. (1973). The conditions of protest behavior in American cities. *American Political Science Review, 67*, 11–28.

Freud, S. (1921). *Group psychology and analysis of the Ego*. London: International Psychoanalytical Press.

Fuss, D. (2004). *The sense of an interior: Four writers and the rooms that shaped them*. New York: Routledge.

Gallese, V., & Sinigaglia, C. (2011). What is so special about embodied simulation? *Trends in Cognitive Sciences, 15*(11), 512–519.

Gawronksi, B., & Bodenhausen, G. V. (2006). Associative and propositional processes in evaluation: An integrative review of implicit and explicit attitude change. *Psychological Bulletin, 132*, 692–731.

Gibson, J. J. (1979). *The ecological approach to visual perception*. Hillsdale: Erlbaum.

Gieryn, T. F. (2000). A space for place in sociology. *Annual Review of Sociology, 26*, 463–496.

Gieryn, T. F. (2002). What buildings do. *Theory and Society, 31*, 35–74.

Goffman, E. (1963). *Behavior in public places*. New York: The Free Press.

Goffman, E. (1974). *Frame analysis: An essay on the organization of experience*. Boston: Northeastern University Press.

Goodwin, J., Jasper, J. M., & Polletta, F. (2001). Why emotions matter. In J. Goodwin, J. M. Jasper, & F. Polletta (Eds.), *Passionate politics* (pp. 1–24). Chicago: University of Chicago Press.

Gould, R. V. (1991). Multiple networks and mobilization in the Paris commune, 1871. *American Sociological Review, 56*(6), 716–729.

Gould, R. V. (1993). Collective action and network structure. *American Sociological Review, 58*(2), 182–196.

Gould, D. B. (2009). *Moving politics: Emotion and ACT UP's fight against AIDS*. Chicago: University of Chicago Press.

Griswold, W., Mangione, G., & McDonnell, T. E. (2013). Objects, words, and bodies in space: Bringing materiality into cultural analysis. *Qualitative Sociology, 36*, 343–364.

Gurr, T. R. (1968). A causal model of vicil strife: A comparative analysis using new indices. *American Political Science Review, 67*, 1104–1124.

Gurr, T. R. (1970). *Why men rebel*. Princeton: Princeton University Press.

Haffner, J. (2013). *The view from above: The science of social space*. Cambridge, MA: MIT Press.

Haidt, J. (2001). The emotional dog and its rational tail: A social institutionist approach to moral judgment. *Psychological Review, 108*(4), 814–834.

Harvey, D. C. (2010). The space for culture and cognition. *Poetics, 38*(2), 185–204.

Hatfield, E., Cacioppo, J., & Rapson, R. (1994). *Emotional contagion: Studies in emotion and social interaction*. Cambridge: Cambridge University Press.

Hatfield, E., Hsee, C. K., Costello, J., Weisman, M. S., & Denny, C. (1995). The impact of vocal feedback on emotional experience and expression. *Journal of Social Behavior and Personality, 10*, 293–312.

Hatfield, E., Rapson, R., & Le, Y. L. (2009). Emotional contagion and empathy. In J. Decety & W. Ickes (Eds.), *The social neuroscience of empathy* (pp. 19–30). Boston: MIT Press.

Hoffer, E. (1951). *The true believer: Thoughts on the nature of mass movements*. New York: Harper Collins.

Hunzaker, M. B. F. (2014). Making sense of misfortune: Cultural schemas, victim redefinition, and the perpetuation of stereotypes. *Social Psychology Quarterly, 77*(2), 166–184.

Iacoboni, M. (2008). *Mirroring people: The new science of how we connect with others*. New York: Farrar, Straus and Giroux.

James, W. (1890 [2007]). *The principles of psychology*. New York: H. Holt.

James, W. (1912). *Essays in radical empiricism*. New York: Dover Publications.

Jasper, J. M. (1997). *The art of moral protest*. Chicago: University of Chicago Press.

Jasper, J. M. (2010). Social movement theory today: Toward a theory of action? *Sociology Compass, 4*(11), 965–976.

Jasper, J. M. (2011). Emotions and social movements: Twenty years of theory and research. *Annual Review of Sociology, 37*(1), 285–303.

Johnston, D. M., & Johnson, N. R. (1989). Role extension in disaster: Employee behavior at the Beverly Hills Supper Club Fire. *Sociological Focus, 22*(1), 39–51.

Kahneman, D. (2011). *Thinking, fast and slow*. New York: Farrar, Strauss, Giroux.

Khwaja, M. (1993). Repression and popular collective action: Evidence from the West Bank. *Sociological Forum, 8*(1), 47–71.

Klandermans, B. (1997). *The social psychology of protest*. Cambridge, MA: Blackwell.

Klandermans, B., & Oegema, D. (1987). Potentials, networks, motivations, and barriers: Steps towards participation in social movements. *American Sociological Review, 52*(4), 519–531.

Klett, J. (2014). Sound on sound: Situating interaction in sonic object-settings. *Sociological Theory, 32*(2), 147–161.

Knoblich, G., & Flach, R. (2003). Action identity: Evidence from self-recognition, prediction, and coordination. *Consciousness and Cognition, 12*(4), 620–632.

Koopmans, R. (1995). *Democracy from below. New social movements and the political system in west Germany*. Boulder: Westview.

Koopmans, R. (1997). Dynamics of repression and mobilization: The German extreme right in the 1990s. *Mobilization: An International Journal, 2*(2), 149–164.

Lasswell, H. D. (1930). *Psychopathology and politics*. Chicago: University of Chicago Press.

LeBon, G. (1895). *The psychology of the crowd*. New York: Viking.

Lefebvre, H. (1991). *The production of space*. Malden: Blackwell.

Lefebvre, H. (2014 [2004]). *Rhythmanalysis: Space, time and everyday life*. London: Bloomsbury.

Lizardo, O., & Strand, M. (2010). Skills, toolkits, contexts and institutions: Clarifying the relationship between different approaches to cognition in cultural sociology. *Poetics, 38*(2), 205–228.

Lizardo, O., Mowry, R., Sepulvado, B., Stoltz, D. S., Taylor, M. A., Van Ness, J., & Wood, M. What are dual process models? Implications for cultural analysis in sociology. Unpublished manuscript.

Mackie, D. M. & Skelly, J. J. (1994). The social cognition analysis of social influence: Contributions to the understanding of persuasion and conformity. In Devine, P. L., Hamilton, D. L., & Ostrom, T. M. (Eds.), *Social cognition: Impact on social psychology* (pp. 259–291). Academic.

Maher, T. V. (2010). Threat, resistance, and collective action: The cases of Sobibor, Treblinka, and Auschwitz. *American Sociological Review, 75*(2), 252–272.

Martin, E. D. (1920). *The behavior of crowds: A psychological study*. New York: Harper and Brothers.

Marwell, G., & Oliver, P. (1993). *The critical mass in collective action: A micro-social theory*. Cambridge: Cambridge University Press.

Marx, G. T., & McAdam, D. (1994). *Collective behavior and social movements: Process and structure*. Englewood Cliffs: Prentice-Hall.

Marx, G. T., & Wood, J. L. (1975). Strands of theory and research in collective behavior. *Annual Review of Sociology, 1*, 363–428.

McAdam, D. ([1982] 1999). *Political process and the development of black insurgency, 1930–1970*. Chicago: University of Chicago.

McAdam, D., & Paulsen, R. (1993). Specifying the relationship between social ties and activism. *American Journal of Sociology, 99*(3), 640–667.

McCarthy, J. D. (1991). Foreword. In *The myth of the madding crowd* (pp. xi–xviii). New York: Aldine De Gruyter.

McCarthy, J. D., & Zald, M. N. (1977). Resource mobilization and social movements: A partial theory. *American Journal of Sociology, 82*(6), 1212–1241.

McDonnell, T. E. (2010). Cultural objects as objects: Materiality, urban space, and the interpretation of AIDS campaigns in Accra, Ghana. *American Journal of Sociology, 115*(6), 1800–1852.

McDonnell, T. E. (2016). *Best laid plans: Cultural entropy and the unraveling of AIDS media campaigns*. Chicago: University of Chicago Press.

McPhail, C. (1991). *The myth of the madding crowd*. New York: Aldine De Gruyter.

McPhail, C. (1994). The dark side of purpose: Individual and collecitve purpose in riots. *The Sociological Quarterly, 35*(1), 1–32.

McPhail, C., & Miller, D. (1973). The assembling process: A theroetical and empirical examination. *American Sociological Review, 38*(6), 721–735.

McPhail, C., Schweingruber, D., & Berns, N. (1997). *The collective action observation primer*. Urbana: University of Illinois.

Mead, G. H. (1934). *Mind, self, and society from the standpoint of social behaviorist*. Chicago: University of Chicago Press.

Miller, N., & Dollard, J. (1941). *Social learning and imitation*. New Haven: Yale University Press.

Morris, A., & Herring, C. (1987). Theory and research in social movements: A critical review. *Annual Review of Political Science, 2*, 137–198.

Mukerji, C. (1994). The political mobilization of nature in seventeenth century French formal gardens. *Theory and Society, 23*, 651–677.

Muller, E. N., & Weede, E. (1990). Cross-national variation in political violence: A rational approach. *Journal of Conflict Resolution, 34*, 624–651.

Norris, J. (1988). Fire in a crowded theater. *International Journal of Mass Emergencies and Disasters, 6*, 7–26.

Oliver, P. (1989). Bringing the crowd back in: The nonorganizational elements of social movements. *Research in Social Movements, Conflicts and Change, 11*, 1–130.

Oliver, P. E., & Meyer, D. J. (1999). How events enter the public sphere: Conflict, location, and sponsorship in local newspaper coverage of public events. *American Journal of Sociology, 105*(1), 38–87.

Opp, K.-D., & Roehl, W. (1990). Repression, micromobilization, and political protest. *Social Forces, 69*, 521–547.

Pagis, M. (2009). Embodied self-reflexivity. *Social Psychology Quarterly, 72*(3), 265–283.

Park, R. E. (1904). *The crowd and the public*. Chicago: University of Chicago Press.

Park, R. E. (1972). *The crowd and the public and other essays*. Chicago: University of Chicago Press.

Park, R. E., & Burgess, E. W. (1921). *Introduction to the science of sociology*. Chicago: University of Chicago Press.

Phelps, E. A. (2006). Emotion and cognition: Insights from studies of the human amygdala. *Annual Review of Psychology, 57*, 27–53.

Polletta, F. (2008). Culture and social movements. *The Annals of the American Academy of Political and Social Science, 619*(78).

Polletta, F., & Jasper, J. M. (2001). Collective identity and social movements. *Annual Review of Sociology, 27*(1), 283–305.

Rasler, K. (1996). Concessions, repression and political protest in the Iranian revolution. *American Sociological Review, 61*, 132–152.

Rizzolatti, G., & Sinigaglia, C. (2007). Mirror neurons and motor intentionality. *Functional Neurology, 22*(4), 205–210.

Robinson, D. T., & Smith-Lovin, L. (1992). Selective interaction as a strategy for identity maintenance: An affect control model. *Social Psychology Quarterly, 55*(1), 12–28.

Rude, G. (1964). *The crowd in history, 1730–1848*. New York: Wiley.

Scheff, T. J. (1990). *Microsociology: Discourse, emotion, and social structure*. Chicago: University of Chicago Press.

Scott, J. C. (1998). *Seeing like a state: How certain schemes to improve the human condition have failed*. New Haven: Yale University Press.

Siegel, D. (2007). *The mindful brain: Reflection and attunement in the cultivation of well-being*. New York: W.W. Norton.

Smelser, N. J. (1962). *Theory of collective behavior*. New York: Free Press.

Smith, C. (1996). *Resisting Reagan: The U.S. Central American peace movement*. Chicago: The University of Chicago Press.

Smith, E. R., & DeCoster, J. (2000). Dual-process models in social and cognitive psychology: Conceptual integration and links to underlying memory systems. *Personality and Social Psychological Review, 4*(2), 108–131.

Smolensky, P. (1988). On the proper treatment of connectionism. *Behavioral and Brain Sciences, 11*, 1–74.

Snow, D. A., & Moss, D. M. (2014). Protest on the fly: Toward a theory of spontaneity in the dynamics of protest and social movements. *American Sociological Review, 79*(6), 1122–1143.

Snow, D. A., & Oliver, P. (1995). Social movements and collective behavior: Social psychological dimensions and considerations. In K. S. Cook, G. A. Fine, & J. S. House (Eds.), *Sociological perspectives on social psychology*. Boston: Allyn and Bacon.

Snow, D. A., Zurcher, L. A., Jr., & Ekland-Olson, S. (1980). Social networks and social movements: A microstructural approach to differential recruitment. *American Sociological Review, 45*(5), 787–801.

Snow, D. A., Cress, D. M., Downey, L., & Jones, A. W. (1998). Disrupting the "quotidian": Reconceptualizing the relationship between breakdown and the emergence of collective action. *Mobilization, 3*, 1–22.

Snow, D. A., Benford, R. D., McCammon, H. J., Hewitt, L., & Fitzgerald, S. (2014). The emergence, development, and future of the framing perspective: 25+ years since "frame alignment". *Mobilization: An International Journal, 19*(1), 23–45.

Snyder, D. (1976). Theoretical and methodological problems in the analysis of governmental coercion and collective violence. *Journal of Political and Military Sociology, 4*, 277–293.

Snyder, D., & Tilly, C. (1972). Hardship and collective violence in France, 1830 to 1960. *American Sociological Review, 37*, 520–532.

Stott, C., & Reicher, S. (1998). Crowd action as intergroup process: Introducing the police perspective. *European Journal of Social Psychology, 28*, 508–529.

Strack, F., & Duetsch, R. (2004). Reflective and impulsive determinants of social behavior. *Personality and Social Psychology Review, 8*(3), 220–247.

Strauss, C., & Quinn, N. (1997). *A cognitive theory of cultural meaning*. New York: Cambridge University Press.

Summers-Effler, E. (2002). The micro potential for social change: Emotion, consciousness, and social movement formation. *Sociological Theory, 20*(1), 41–60.

Summers-Effler, E. (2004). A theory of the self, emotion, and culture. *Advances in Group Processes, 21*, 273–308.

Summers-Effler, E. (2007). Vortexes of involvement: Social systems as turbulent flow. *Philosophy of the Social Sciences, 37*(4), 433–448.

Summers-Effler, E. (2010). *Laughing saints and righteous heroes: Emotional rhythms in social movement groups*. Chicago: University of Chicago Press.

Summers-Effler, E., & Kwak, D. (2015). Weber's missing mystics: Inner-worldly mystical practices and the micro potential for social change. *Theory and Society, 44*, 251–282.

Summers-Effler, E., Van Ness, J., & Hausmann, C. (2015). Peeking in the black box: Studying, theorizing, and representing the micro-foundations of day-to-day interactions. *Journal of Contemporary Ethnography, 44*(4), 450–479.

Tarde, G. (1901). Opinion and the crowd. In T. Clark (Ed.), *Gabriel Tarde: On communication and social influence*. Chicago: University of Chicago Press.

Tavory, I. (2009). Of yarmulkes and categories: Delegating boundaries and the phenomenology of interactional expectation. *Theory and Society, 39*(1), 49–68.

Thoits, P. A. (1995). Social psychology: The interplay between sociology and psychology. *Social Forces, 73*, 1231–1243.

Tierney, K. (2002). Strength of a City: A disaster research perspective on the world trade center attack. *Social Science Research Council*.

Tilly, C. (1978). *From mobilization to revolution*. Reading: Addison-Wesley.

Tilly, C., Tilly, L., & Tilly, R. (1975). *The Rebellious Century, 1830–1930*. Cambridge: Harvard University Press.

Toch, H. (1965). *The psychology of social movements*. Indianapolis: Bobbs-Merrill Co.

Turner, R. H., & Killian, L. M. (1972). *Collective behavior* (2nd ed.). New York: Prentice-Hall.

Turner, R. H., & Killian, L. M. (1987). *Collective behavior* (3rd ed.). New York: Prentice Hall.

Turner, J. H., & Stets, J. E. (2005). *The sociology of emotions*. Cambridge: Cambridge University Press.

Useem, B. (1985). Disorganization and the New Mexico prison riot of 1980. *American Sociological Review, 50*(5), 677–688.

Vaisey, S. (2009). Motivation and justification: A dual-process model of culture in action. *American Journal of Sociology, 114*(6), 1675–16715.

Van Dyke, N., & Soule, S. A. (2002). Structural social change and the mobilizing effect of threat: Explaining levels of patriot and militia organizing in the United States. *Social Problems, 49*(2), 497–520.

Wacquant, L. (2004). *Body and soul: Ethnographic notebooks of an apprentice-boxer*. New York: Oxford University Press.

Walsh, E. J., & Warland, R. H. (1983). Social movement involvement in the wake of a nuclear accident: Activists and free riders in the TMI area. *American Sociological Review, 48*(6), 764–780.

Whalen, P. J. (1998). Fear, vigilance, and ambiguity: Initial neuroimaging studies of the human amygdala. *Current Directions in Psychological Science, 7*, 177–188.

Zhao, D. (1998). Ecologies of social movements: Student mobilization during the 1989 prodemocracy movement in Beijing. *American Journal of Sociology, 103*(6), 1493–1529.

Zimmerman, E. (1980). Macro-comparative research on political protest. In Gurr, T. R. (Ed), *Handbook of political conflict: Theory and research* (pp. 167–237). New York: The Free Press.

Theorizing Social Movements

26

Dana M. Moss and David A. Snow

26.1 The Importance of and Warrants for Social Movement Theory

The analysis and theorization of social movements is central to the study of social life, state-society relations, and social change, and comprises one of the most vibrant areas of sociological inquiry today. From the proletarian revolutions envisioned by Marx, to the Protestant Reformation theorized by Weber, to the civic associations described by de Tocqueville, the examination of collective action has long been central to the sociological enterprise. In addition to its central place in classical theory, the emergence, dynamics, and outcomes of social movements have grown to encompass much of the study of contemporary politics and culture. For as long as there have been social problems creating systemic inequality based on class, ethnicity, race, gender, or religion, there has also been subversion and dissent, and rarely does there exist an important social issue about which there is no contentious collective debate and organized resistance on one side or the other. Theories of social movements aim to understand the factors and conditions producing such organized, collective action dedicated to producing or resisting change across time and place and the consequences of those struggles.

From the rise of Christianity to the Arab Spring revolutions, challenges to entrenched power structures and formalized systems of social control comprise some of the most formative and well-recognized events in human history. For this reason, social movements are often conceived of as collectivities, ranging from informal groups to formal organizations, that launch campaigns challenging governing structures and the elites who run them. Because governments and regimes have considerable advantages that others lack, including a monopoly over the use of force in a given territory (Weber 1978), social movements are often distinguished by their extra-institutional character and exclusion from the polity (Gamson [1975]1990; Tilly 1978). This conceptualization distinguishes actors who seek to initiate or prevent change through means of normative politics from those who are engaged in what McAdam et al. (2001) call "transgressive contention." Social movements, therefore, do not rely primarily or solely on institutionalized mechanisms, such as casting votes, as a means with which to lodge claims and induce or prevent social change. Instead, movements are often characterized by their extra-institutional character

D.M. Moss (✉)
University of Pittsburgh, Pennsylvania, PA, USA
e-mail: dmmoss@uci.edu

D.A. Snow
University of California, Irvine, CA, USA
e-mail: dsnow@uci.edu

S. Abrutyn (ed.), *Handbook of Contemporary Sociological Theory*,
Handbooks of Sociology and Social Research, DOI 10.1007/978-3-319-32250-6_26

and tactics. Because social movements challenge powerholders on unequal terms, a guiding concern driving theories of mobilization is how movements lacking the authority, legitimacy, capacity, and the means of social control possessed by states come into being, sustain their campaigns, and sometimes win in spite of their systemic disadvantages.

Social movements are not only those collectivities seeking to challenge, reform, or replace state authorities, however. Instead, they may also be conceived more broadly as collective challenges to systems or structures of authority writ large (Snow 2004b). An authority is any center of decision-making, regulation, or procedure that influences the lives of individuals and social groups. This perspective recognizes that the relevance and targets of social movements extend beyond the state to other types of institutions, systems of beliefs, socio-cultural practices, identities, and social groups. Collective actors may, for example, call the values, beliefs, and interpretations that undergird and legitimate social structures into question and aim to reconfigure relationships of entities within those structures. Social movements sometimes seek to change the cultural and legal relations between persons in everyday life—such as those between children and adults, husbands and wives, or persons of different racial or ethnic categories—or the relationship of persons to non-persons, such as that of people to animals or the environment. Movements may also challenge socio-cultural and legal systems of authority by working to bestow recognition and dignity on subordinated groups, from slave-caste groups to the transgendered; appropriate and reconfigure social institutions, such as marriage; and define actions and behaviors as more or less moral and legitimate, from littering to abortion. Social movements also arise in opposition to other extra-institutional actors and the causes and authorities that they represent, producing counter-movements. Furthermore, rather than emerging outside of a given authority structure, members of organizations often challenge normative cultural practices and meanings within hierarchical or patriarchal institutions through more or less obtrusive means of contention (Katzenstein 1990; Kucinskas 2014). In addition, as we discuss further below, movements may also launch challenges by exiting from institutions and by withdrawing from society more generally (Hirschman 1970; see Snow and Soule 2010).

Whether movements are conceptualized as being opposed to states or to other kinds of authorities, both views are mutually conducive to understanding the course and character of movements and their outcomes. As such, we define social movements broadly as *collectivities that seek to challenge or defend institutional and/or cultural systems of authority and their associated practices and representatives* in order to account for the fact that social movements take a range of forms, employ a variety of more- or less-transgressive tactics, may last for a matter of days or decades, and may be embedded in the social structures they seek to challenge to varying degrees, such as state institutions. They can also arise in opposition to other movements and collectivities, elites, and objects that are perceived as representing unwanted systems of authority, such as other social movements, the display of the Ten Commandments in public places, or Muslim women's headscarves.

Importantly, we also distinguish between what social movements *are* and what social movement theory can help to *explain*. Though social movements are often defined as extra-institutional to some degree, this does not mean that theories explaining their emergence, dynamics, and outcomes are limited to cases of protest movements or radical groups. On the contrary, theories of collective action may be useful in explaining the mobilization of institutional group dynamics, such as those occurring within and between political parties, the various institutions comprising the military, religious organizations, and interest groups, as well as changes in organizational fields, such as those that take place among domestic and international non-governmental organizations or educational systems. Furthermore, in societies in which demonstrations and civic organizing are permitted and not inherently transgressive, the distinction between extra-institutional mobilization and institutionalized politics has become increasingly fuzzy

(Meyer and Tarrow 1998). We therefore submit that social movement theory may be applied to a wide variety of cases and collective actions across different venues, historical periods, and places.

26.2 Theorizing the Emergence of Social Movements

The factors and conditions producing social movements' emergence are arguably at the core of the study of social movements and associated collective actions, such as demonstrations, strikes, sit-ins, boycotts, and rebellions. Indeed, few topics in the field have generated such a range of theorization and research, with the possible exception of the study of recruitment and participation in collective action.[1] As we outline below, a range of theories are currently employed by social scientists to explain how, why, where, and when individuals come together and the conditions prompting and sustaining their mobilization.

26.2.1 Social Strain and Breakdown

Theories of mobilization were first derived by classical theorists who emphasized the role of social strains in the emergence of collective action. Strains are the conditions, trends, or events—such as economic hardship or violence—that create the mobilizing grievances motivating disruptive collective action. Emile Durkheim, for example, argues that because society is characterized by social integration, strains that disrupt the functioning and integration of normative social life produce grievances and correspondingly deviant behavior. In addition, Karl Marx and Friedrich Engels argue in the *Manifesto of the Communist Party* that capitalism produces and depends on the increased exploitation and alienation of the proletariat, which in turn produce shared interests among workers and lead to the mobilization of class-based social movements. Additionally, theorists writing in the years following the genocidal violence and disruptions of World War II likewise argued that mobilizing grievances arise from the disintegration of social life (Kornhauser 1959), and that structural strains are one of several necessary conditions for individuals to participate in collective protest (Smelser 1962).

Subsequent studies published in the 1970s argued against strain theory, finding little evidence of breakdown as a precipitating factor of protest and rebellions (Tilly et al. 1975; Rule and Tilly 1972). These studies also refuted earlier social psychological and functionalist approaches to protest that viewed rebellion as anomic or irrational (see Hoffer 1951; LeBon 1897). In response to the emergence of the Civil Rights Movement and other rights-oriented movements taking place across the U.S. in the 1960s, social movements came to be understood as rational responses to injustice by educated individuals and integrated social groups (McAdam [1982] 1999). Furthermore, rather than viewing action-driving grievances as the outcome of acute socio-economic downturns or political upheavals, scholars instead argued that grievances arising from structural conditions are often long-term, ubiquitous phenomena. Because African Americans had been facing systemic repression and violence for decades after emancipation in the U.S., the existence of strain-induced grievances did little to explain why the movement for civil and political rights emerged where and when it did. In order to address these shortcomings, subsequent perspectives began to theorize alternatives, and social strain was largely discarded in the theoretical canon for several decades (see Buechler 2004).

[1] Since the topics of differential recruitment and participation have received considerable attention in recent years (see, for example, Corrigall-Brown et al. 2009; Diani 2004; Klandermans 2004; Rohlinger and Snow 2003; Snow and Soule 2010), we devote less attention to the topic throughout the chapter.

26.2.2 Resource Mobilization

The turn away from strain theory was marked in part by the founding of the resource mobilization approach to movement emergence, spear-headed by John McCarthy and Mayer Zald (1973, 1977). This perspective argues that social movements are distinct from collective behavior writ large because they have organized and institutionalized characteristics that allow them to launch and sustain action-oriented campaigns. Because social movement organizations (SMOs) are like other kinds of organizations in society, they are therefore likely to emerge when resources are available to sustain them. This perspective acknowledges that SMOs do not have the complete freedom of choice in how they organize and what they do, but maintains that the greater the pool of resources available to fuel a given issue—including the labor of volunteers, the expertise of professional advisors and full-time staff, and the support of conscience constituents—the more likely that SMOs will proliferate in order to compete for these resources and engage in collective actions (Edwards and McCarthy 2004). Although critiqued in part for being overly-rationalistic (Ferree 1992), the resource mobilization approach has remained an integral "partial theory" with which to which understand movement emergence (McCarthy and Zald 1977).

26.2.3 Political Process and Opportunity Theory

A second influential post-1970 genre of theorization draws attention to how changes in movements' political contexts and relations with elites influence their emergence across place and time (Kriesi 2004). This line of theorization was heavily influenced by Michael Lipsky's *Protest in City Politics* (1970), which called for increasing attention as to how facilitative political conditions for protest fluctuate over time, as well as Peter Eisinger's (1973) hallmark study of riots. Eisinger found that disruptive events were most likely to occur in cities exhibiting both "open" and "closed" features, i.e., in places where local authorities were tolerant enough to allow people to mobilize, but closed off to negotiation with marginalized groups. These formative studies gave rise to the "political process" model of movement emergence (McAdam [1982] 1999; Tarrow 1994; Tilly 1978, 1995). The political process approach argues that the key to explaining movement emergence resides primarily in relation to their political context, which sets the baseline rules of dissent and determines their opportunities for protest. In addition to how liberal or intolerant a polity is, studies of political opportunity generally focus on four factors denoting what kinds of opportunities can facilitate movement emergence. These include (1) increased access to political authorities, (2) divisions between power-holders, (3) the presence of allies to the movement among elites, and (4) a relative decrease in state repression (McAdam 1996; Meyer 2004). Such opportunities may be generated at different levels, including at the local, national, and extra-national level (McAdam 1998) and by elites with varying degrees of authority and control. Further complicating the "opportunity structure" are the presence and actions of counter-movements (Meyer and Staggenborg 1996; Mottl 1980), as well as changes in public opinion that may occur independently of movements. Critiques of this perspective as unwieldy and potentially tautological notwithstanding (see Goodwin and Jasper 1999), the core of the paradigm, which asserts that social movements' political environments are greatly determinative of their emergence and character, continues to drive much of the study of emergence.

26.2.4 Advancing Theories of Emergence

Since the rise and dominance of the political process perspective, theory has developed in two general directions. The first has been to revitalize discarded theories, such as social strain and breakdown, to demonstrate their utility in explaining mobilization, as well as to refine and modify structural theories of emergence, such as that of political opportunity. The second has been to expand explanations of emergence by bringing in neglected concepts, such as emotions, networks, ecological factors, and culture and identity to its theorization. We elaborate on these in turn below.

26.2.4.1 Revitalizing Theories of Strain and Breakdown

Recent studies have reintroduced social strain into the discussion of emergence by demonstrating how structural conditions, such as relatively high levels of inequality and economic decline, generate oppositional frameworks that can produce high levels of extra-institutional behavior (McVeigh 2006). For instance, the emergence of protests by homeless populations has been shown to be more likely in cities experiencing a rising cost of living and a decline in manufacturing jobs (Snow et al. 2005). Van Dyke and Soule (2002) also explain the emergence of radical movements by showing that economic restructuring, indicated by the loss of manufacturing jobs and family farms, are highly correlated with white patriot and militia organizing. Furthermore, while the causes of the Arab Spring revolutions that swept across the Middle East in 2011 will remain the subject of heated debate in the years to come, the rising disparity between the number of university-educated youths and unemployment in places such as Tunisia and Egypt is a probable factor in creating the grievances necessary for high-risk collective action (see Goldstone 2014). As such, social strains can play a role in movement emergence and may be a necessary condition, albeit not a sufficient one, for mobilization—particularly for movements that form despite significant resource shortages and a relative lack of political opportunities.

In an effort to better specify the effects of social disruptions on mobilization, Snow and his colleagues (1998) also argue that *breakdown*, an acute variant of social strain, can also play an important role in the emergence of movements, but in a different way than classically theorized. They argue that collective action is often the product of actual or threatened disruption of the "quotidian," or the taken-for-granted routines and attitudes of everyday life. Such breakdowns in the normative social order include: (1) accidents that disrupt routines and threaten a community's survival; (2) an actual or threatened intrusion that decreases the collective sense of safety, privacy or sense of control; (3) alterations in subsistence routines, such as the means by which people attain food and shelter; and (4) dramatic changes in the structures and implementation of social control. These factors have been at play in collective movements ranging from prison riots (Useem 1985), to "Not In My Backyard" movements (Snow and Anderson 1983), to women's activism in Argentina (Borland and Sutton 2007). Because individuals are adverse to loss, as argued by prospect theory (Kahneman and Tversky 1979), they are more likely to engage in collective action in order to preserve what they already have, as opposed to mobilizing in order to gain something new. This finding complements studies of the effects of state repression on mobilization. Violent quotidian disruptions instigated by authorities often spur a backlash because severe escalations in violence violate normative expectations about how authorities should act, whether inside of prisons or in authoritarian states (Almeida 2003; Einwohner 2003; Goodwin 2001; Hess and Martin 2006; Kurzman 2004; Loveman 1998; Moss 2014; Moore 1978; Useem and Kimball 1989; White 1989). As such, changes in the quotidian can spur mobilization and participation under repressive conditions.

26.2.4.2 Refining Political Opportunity

Scholars have also refined theories of political opportunities by testing its assumptions against alternative cases and specifying how opportunities should be delimited (Meyer 2004). For example, Eisinger's (1973) curvilinear model of movement emergence has been challenged by studies analyzing non-Western movements in authoritarian or democratizing states. De la Luz Inclán's (2008) study of Zapatista mobilization in Mexico finds that protest activity emerged in localities that were closed and repressive and decreased in more democratic zones. Almeida (2003) also demonstrates that strains and threats prompted heightened protest waves in El Salvador by examining the effects of economic strains, land access, bank closures, and the general erosion of rights and state repression on public dissent. Other scholars have also called for increased attention as to how collective actors' perceptions of political opportunities and threats shape their mobilization dynamics, since grievances and corresponding actions are dependent on subjectively-understood and interpretive processes (Kurzman 1996; see also Khadivar 2013).

26.2.4.3 The Role of Emotions

Relatedly, scholars have also brought renewed attention to the role of emotions in movement emergence (Goodwin et al. 2001; Jasper 2011), as when feelings anger and shock produce collective responses that impact the course and character of mobilization. Smith (1996), for example, argues that moral outrage prompted mobilization against the Reagan administration's deportation of refugees from Central America in the 1980s. In an analysis of the emergence of the Montgomery Bus Boycott, Shultziner (2013) demonstrates that this landmark civil rights-era protest movement emerged as a result of the escalation in the abuse and humiliation of African-American passengers by white bus drivers. Furthermore, movements are often produced and sustained by sentiments of altruism, compassion, and empathy. As Randal Collins' (2004) theory of interaction ritual chains argues, emotional energies can produce and reinforce solidarities necessary for collective action (see also Fantasia 1988). Activists therefore often work strategically to amplify and sustain outrage or empathy among members and to foster sympathy among observers to bolster their campaigns (Nepstad 2004; Summers-Effler 2010).

26.2.4.4 Networks

Scholars have also paid increased attention to how networks facilitate the emergence of, and members' participation in, social movements. This line of research demonstrates how actors' embeddedness in particular social arrangements and relationships make individuals more or less susceptible to collective action (Diani and McAdam 2003; Fernandez and McAdam 1988; Gould 1991; McAdam and Paulsen 1993; Passy 2003). As Diani (2013) writes, social movements may draw in prospective participants through both recruitment efforts and personal networks, neither of which are mutually exclusive (Snow et al. 1980). Participation in movements is dependent, at least in part, on the absence of blockages (Kitts 2000). The anchoring effects of immediate family, for example, significantly shape the likelihood of participation in protest and high-risk activism (Viterna 2006). Potential participants also consider the reactions of people with whom they have strong ties when deciding to participate in risky collective actions (McAdam 1986). But further complicating these dynamics is the fact that individuals are embedded in multiple relationships that expose her or him to conflicting pressures (McAdam and Paulsen 1993: 641). Relationships are "multivalent" in that they can exert positive and negative effects (Kitts 2000), and the effects of social ties may change over the course of a conflict, rather than be static forces that either block or facilitate mobilization (Viterna 2006).

26.2.4.5 Ecological Factors

The focus on relations between individuals has also brought attention to the importance of ecological factors in shaping possibilities for protest (Sewell 2001). Such theories harken back to the arguments of Tilly et al. (1975) that capitalists "unwittingly afforded the proletariat ideal settings within which to mobilize" by concentrating workers in urban dwellings (McAdam and Boudet 2012: 19). Ecological structures can also foster spontaneous protest events, which refer to actions not planned or organized in advance, such as riots and sit-in movements (Snow and Moss 2014). For example, Zhao's (2001) study of movement emergence during the 1989 "Beijing Spring" demonstrates that the unique spatial distribution of students on university campuses created the conditions necessary for the occupation of Tiananmen Square. Important ecological factors prompting the emergence of the student movement included the closeness of various university campuses to one another; the separation and protection of students by campus security and high walls; the dense living conditions; the "total institution" characteristics of the campuses; and the walking and biking routes taken by students.

Free spaces, or small-scale settings insulated from the repressive intrusion of authorities, are also important incubators of mobilizing ideas and plans for action (Snow and Soule 2010). Free spaces do more than provide a physical structure for nascent collective action; they also foster relationships that produce oppositional ideas and cultures (Polletta 1999). Morris' (1981) study of Black colleges and churches, for example, argues that these institutions served as important resources, both ecologically and culturally, for dissident ideas and emergent solidarities in the Civil Rights Movement. Futrell and Simi (2004) further demonstrate how white power activism requires different types of ecological spaces in order to facilitate networks and solidarity and to shield the Aryan movement from repression. Likewise, Johnston and Snow (1998) find that in Estonia under Soviet rule, accommodative subcultures emerged that hid dissident opinions within adversarial talk, songs and poetry. These cultures were an important factor in prompting above-ground resistance and nationalist solidarity when the political context changed and mobilization broke above-ground.

26.2.4.6 Culture and Identity

Relatedly, scholars have also increasingly turned to cultural explanations in examining emergence processes, which has shed light on how beliefs, identities, and solidarities emerge and motivate collective action. The role of culture in movement emergence draws attention to how collective behavior is contingent upon how events and environments take on meanings that are not inherent to them, but are instead "assigned or imputed through interpretive processes" (Snow 2003: 818). Collective actors may be inspired by more than the prospect of some utilitarian gain, mobilizing instead to assert a particular way of life, a set of values, and the production of culture and knowledge. Moral and cultural resources are also important for emergence processes and may spark changes in collective consciousness. Such resources may be "out there," but must be harnessed and framed to motivate participation, as is discussed later in this chapter (Snow et al. 1986, 2013). Movements focused on "identity politics," for example, seek recognition for their identities and lifestyles in ways that overlap with politically-oriented goals, such as with gay, lesbian, bisexual, and transgender rights movements (Polletta and Jasper 2001; Taylor et al. 2009).

26.2.5 Challenges to Understanding Emergence

While all of the aforementioned perspectives have done a great deal to refine theories of emergence, we note that identifying when and how movements are born is conceptually tricky. As Taylor (1989) argues, literatures tend to assume that movements are "birthed," rather than the outcome of continuous mobilization processes that may be less visible to researchers. Further complicating matters is that movements give rise to other movements, particularly within the context of a "social movement society" where protest has become a routine feature of civic life (Meyer and Tarrow 1998). As we discuss in more detail below, movements may diffuse through spillover effects (Meyer and Whittier 1994), in reaction to other movements (Meyer and Staggenborg 1996), and as later generations of founding movements, such as the various "generations" of feminist thought and activism. The Civil Rights Movement, for example, had mobilizing effects and influences on women's, environmental, ethnic, and peace movements, but was itself also influenced by independence movements against colonialism and preceded by abolitionist movements, the formation of the National Association for the Advancement of Colored People, and lesser known forms of collective resistance by African Americans. Furthermore, the eruption of transgression and protest in the streets is not always a reliable marker of movement emergence. As Johnston (2006) argues, protest is often just one tactic that signifies the presence of a new or revitalized movement and may be the end result of mobilization processes, rather than marking the beginning of a new social movement or set of collective actors.

26.3 Theorizing Movements' Dynamics

Theories of social movement dynamics draw attention to what movements do and how they change over time in light of their revolutionary or reform-oriented goals. Explanations take into account movements' tactics and strategies; their claims-making processes; their organizational forms and the cultures that undergird activist collectivities; and the relational processes taking place within movements and with their allies or opponents, including counter-movements.

26.3.1 Revolutionary Versus Reform-Oriented Movements

Discussions of social movement dynamics, whether implicitly or explicitly, often cast social movements as either revolutionary or reform-oriented. Reformist movements seek to gain concessions within existing social structures, such as changes in the law, increased material benefits, shifts in public opinion, or adjustments in individuals' consumption habits. As such, their calls for change address a specific area of social life. Revolutionary movements, on the other hand, seek more sweeping and disruptive changes, often by circumventing routinized means of social change because those means are perceived as futile or illegitimate. Because revolutionaries call social arrangements and culture into question more than their reformist counterparts, their rationales often require greater elaboration (Williams 2004). These collectivities may work to overthrow governing authorities by force or through disruptive social actions or seek to exit from existing authority structures altogether.

Revolutionary and reformist are relative terms, and are labels to be applied in light of movements' socio-political contexts, since how radical a set of grievances, claims, and demands are depends on the degree of change demanded, the status quo at play, and the interpretive or labeling powers of the institutionalized authorities or targets. While movements can exhibit a combination of radical and reformist tendencies and lie on a continuum between these two ideal types, revolutionary and reformist views are not easily reconciled. As such, disagreement over how revolutionary or reform-oriented a social movement should be among participants is likely to be a source of factionalization within and between movement groups. Additionally, the conditions under which movements transform from one type to the other, as when reformers become radicalized, or when insurgents become institutionalized, remains an important topic of study in understanding mobilization and social conflict. As we discuss below, the potential efficacy of reformers and revolutionaries in achieving social change goals informs much of the debate over movements' strategies and tactics, forms, and ideologies.

26.3.2 Strategies and Tactics

Movements are largely characterized by their strategies and tactics. Strategies[2] are broad plans for attaining goals, and tactics are the specific means and methods by which strategies are enacted. Groups of previously unorganized or unrecognized actors often use forbidden tactics in an effort to produce "negative inducements to bargaining" (Lipsky 1970; McAdam 1983; Wilson 1961). In other words, some movements launch tactics with the intention of creating disruptions in the normative order of everyday life and in authorities' social control. These tactics are designed to attract publicity and attention through the media (Gamson 2004; Gamson and Wolfsfeld 1993; Wisler and Giugni 1999), and to provoke authorities into reacting in ways that damage their legitimacy (McAdam 1983). This process offsets the relative disadvantage facing movements by placing pressure on authorities to

[2]For a more theorized and detailed assessment of strategy, see Jasper (2004, 2013), Meyer (2015), and Turner (1970).

respond favorably by intervening on behalf of, or negotiating with, social movements (see also Schattschneider 1960). In certain times and places, disruptive tactics characterize insurgencies and revolutionary movement goals (Jenkins and Eckert 1986). Yet, no tactic is inherently transgressive. How disruptive a given protest or boycott is, for example, depends on a number of factors, including the socio-historical context in which movements operate, local and national-level laws regulating the expression of dissent, the relations of movements to existing institutions and political entities, and the degree of repression wielded by authorities against challengers. That said, even when public demonstrations are not transgressive, they can still serve to demonstrate movements' worthiness, unity, numbers, and solidarity to authorities and the public (Tilly and Tarrow 2007).

While public rallies, marches, protests, and violence largely dominate the study of movements' tactics, often because these events are easier to count in data sources such as newspapers, movements may engage in a variety of other tactics to promote or prevent social change. As mentioned above, members may seek to withdraw or exit from authority structures as a form of protest (Tierney 2013). Commune and "cult" movements of the 1960s and 1970s, for example, were initiated as a result of dissatisfaction with larger and more amorphous authority structures perceived as illegitimate or harmful, including mainstream religions and capitalism. Movements may also seek to exit from authorities by contesting powerholders' monopoly and jurisdiction over territory, violence, or the means of economic production. This includes labor movements that have reinstated jobs and instituted boss-less systems of production by reclaiming shuttered factories through nonviolence resistance, for example. Secessionist movements seek to withdraw from existing authority structures by claiming territory and establishing their own states. Violent tactics, such as mass murders and suicide bombings, also serve to target states indirectly by attacking symbols of state power or illegitimate institutions, punishing bystanders, and bringing international attention to movements' grievances and demands. Radical movements sometimes also target other non-state actors that threaten their worldview and systems of belief, as in the case of Taliban attacks against women's rights organizations and activists in Afghanistan and Pakistan (Jafar 2007).

Movements are dynamic social entities, however, and are likely to draw on a range of tactics to pursue their goals. As Snow (2003: 817) writes, a social movement is "engaged in a highly interactive relationship with various publics and collectivities that constitute its environment of operation, and this ongoing dialectic" prompts movements to engage in a range of "anticipatory strategic action[s]." Relatedly, McAdam's (1983) study of the tactical interactions between the Civil Rights Movement and repressive authorities highlights how movements are engaged in a dynamic process of contention with their opponents. Movements work to innovate their tactics in order to evade repression or create leverage, and movement opponents engage in tactical adaptations that seek to neutralize the effects of movements' innovations and reassert social control. As a result, challengers involved in resistance against highly repressive state systems must continuously engage in a process of tactical modification and change in order to be effective. And yet, movements do not innovate their tactics out of thin air. Instead, they rely on tactical repertoires that are shaped and constrained, at least in part, by broader social structures (Tilly 1995). As Snow and Soule (2010: 179) posit, "the occurrence of peasant revolts and food riots in agrarian society, labor strikes in capitalist societies, and public demonstrations in democratic societies" suggest that dominant political and economic arrangements shape and constrain the tactical repertoires of challengers and their opponents. Movements' tactical choices are also shaped by their worldviews and ideologies, such as principles of nonviolence, and best practices are typically the subject of great debate within movements. A change in tactics is likely when activists view that the costs of a given tactic outweigh prospective gains, when they perceive that bargaining or negotiating with authorities is no longer a viable option, or when they gain access to new resources or technological innovations

(Snow and Soule 2010; see also Colomy 1998 on organizational entrepreneurs).

The literature on movement dynamics has also pointed to the importance of understanding the conditions under which movements engage in strategic accommodations in response to their broader environments. In order to shore up legitimacy and respectability in the eyes of the communities in which they are embedded, movement actors may deploy specific strategies to try to "fit in" and achieve a degree of acceptance while simultaneously pursuing social change goals and enacting alternative or non-normative rituals and lifestyles (Snow 1979). Strategies of accommodation by movements' targets are also an important part of the tactical interactions that unfold between collective actors and their opponents, as when movements gain concessions and are permitted to demonstrate in public spaces, for example, or have a portion of their demands granted by authorities. Though strategies of accommodation on either side may be perceived as giving in or a form of cooptation, how movements strive to accommodate external audiences, as well as how they are accommodated at times by their opponents, is an important aspect of understanding how tactical interactions unfold in a dynamic fashion, as well as how both sides attempt to accrue legitimacy in the eyes of broader publics.

26.3.3 Cultural and Discursive Dynamics

In addition to more radical and visible forms of resistance, movements are also characterized by their cultural and discursive dynamics, including everyday forms of resistance (Scott 1985) and contentious talk and oppositional speech (Johnston 2005, 2006; Johnston and Mueller 2001). These include meaning-making activities that David Snow and his colleagues brought to the fore with the introduction of the framing processes perspective of collective action. Building from Goffman's 1974 essay on *Frame Analysis*, their theory argues that meanings do not automatically arise in a given situation, but instead come about through interactive and interpretive processes (Benford and Snow 2000; Snow et al. 1986, 2014). Framing calls attention to how grievances are understood and strategically transformed by collective actors into injustices that warrant mobilization, as well as how collective actors serve as signifying agents by bringing certain issues in frame while discarding others. Frames diagnose social problems, describe what is to be done through prognostic frames, and motivate participation. They are derived in part from the culture in which social movements are embedded, but may also challenge that culture and frame the status quo as contestable (Snow 2004a). This perspective differentiates frames from ideologies, which are typically conceptualized as a relatively stable set of values or beliefs. While frames and ideologies may overlap, frames do not just stem automatically from ideology, but are debated, negotiated, and deployed strategically by collective actors (see Oliver and Johnston 2000; Snow 2004a).

26.3.4 Organizational Forms

In addition to understanding what movements do, scholars have also paid a great deal of attention to movements' organizational forms, which range from "loosely networked groups… to highly bureaucratic and formal social movement organizations" (Snow and Soule 2010: 150–151). The benefits and drawbacks of various organizational types comprise a longstanding theoretical debate in the literature. The bureaucratization and professionalization of movements has been controversial because, as argued by Michels' ([1915] 1962) "iron law of oligarchy," organizations often come to value their own survival and interests over those of their members and conservatize the movement's tactics. The very process of organization, Michels argues, enforces a separation between leaders and their members and an abandonment of revolutionary or radical social change goals. The fact that professionalized SMOs tend to be run by members of the middle class and are funded by resourced patrons, often without members, has been interpreted as an elitist shift in advocacy more generally (Skocpol 2003).

Institutionalized movements have also been accused of forfeiting the ability to utilize extra-institutional and disruptive tactics on behalf of society's most marginalized members (Piven and Cloward 1979). For example, Jenkins and Eckhert's study of the Civil Rights Movement (1986) argues that the most effective branch of the Black insurgency acted as an indigenous organization, relying primarily on volunteer labor by the intended beneficiaries of the movement. After the movement was "channeled" by elite patrons into professionalized SMOs with a paid staff and a formalized leadership, the movement lost its leverage. Private foundations, Jenkins and Eckhert (1986: 819) argue, are "institutionalized agencies of the capitalist class and, as such, will generally be politically cautious in their support for social reform." Elite patrons, including government agencies and private foundations, tend to support moderates, and in so doing, they undermine the "radical flank" (Haines 2013). In this view, social movements require sustained indigenous and disruptive mobilization in order to produce meaningful change, whereas reformist organizations are a hindrance to that change.

In response to the bifurcation of movements into coopted/reformist/institutionalized versus militant/radical/volunteerist variations, subsequent scholarship has painted a more complex picture of movements' organizational forms and their effects (Clemens and Minkoff 2004). For example, Meyer's (1990) study on the nuclear freeze movement demonstrates that the institutionalization of anti-nuclear proliferation movements left behind an extensive advocacy network, making anti-nuclear advocacy a relatively stable fixture of the political landscape. Professionalized movements may also provide a foundation for future incarnations of protest and sustain activism during periods of abeyance (Taylor 1989) when political opportunities for protest diminish. It is therefore useful to conceptualize professionalization and institutionalization as more than a process of self-interested, inefficient bureaucratization. In addition, having both member and non-member advocacy organizations work on a particular issue may foster a productive division of labor that helps to strengthen activists' aggregate capacity to lobby on a behalf of a given cause (Walker et al. 2011). Nor do formal organizations always trade in their radical methods for moderate and non-disruptive approaches (Rucht 1999). Movement organizations thought to be hopelessly ineffective and oligarchical may also experience revitalizations. As Voss and Sherman's (2000) study of labor unions demonstrates, movements may break out of bureaucratic conservatism under certain conditions in spite of contracting political opportunities and resources.

Important addendums to these organizational debates have further demonstrated that "bottom-up" grassroots and deliberative movements have their own sets of limitations. While informal and leaderless organizations may seek to practice what they preach by working to equalize relations between members and defending their organizations from elite cooptation, no movement is fully egalitarian (Robnett 1996). In addition, organizations seeking to remain separated, both pragmatically and ideologically, from institutionalized politics may limit their influence and input on policy (see Blee and Currier 2006). Participatory democratic organizations are inherently fragile and susceptible to internal conflicts (Blee 2012; della Porta 2005; Polletta 2012). Leaderless movements also face hurdles to mobilization when their members come to be more focused on democratic deliberation than on implementing strategies through collective action (Polletta 2005). For example, while participants in the Occupy Movement that emerged across U.S. cities in 2011 engaged in reflexive rituals to promote inclusiveness and egalitarianism, the movement as a whole may have been subsumed more by its focus on internal inclusion and self-expression than by concrete, outward-looking change-oriented goals. While future studies are likely to find that Occupy movements had varying dynamics and consequences by city, this example highlights the limitations of deliberative democracy in action. In sum, no one organizational form can or should be uniformly equated with efficacy or "true" social change.

26.3.5 Movement Diffusion and Spillover

Theories of mobilization dynamics have also raised important questions about how social movements influence one another (Oliver and Myers 2003; Soule 1997). In addition to the fact that certain structural conditions make specific types of movements more or less likely (Oberschall 1973; Pinard 1971), movements may also diffuse across time and place through specific mechanisms. Tactical innovations, ideas, or practices spread through direct and indirect ties, innovations in communication, organizational and network infrastructures, or cultural "caches" of best practices, for instance. Soule (2004) suggests that tactics are likely to diffuse when they are perceived by receiving movements as effective, cost-friendly, and compatible with the values and needs of activists. Meyer and Whittier's (1994) study of "spillover" from the women's movement to the peace movement suggests that cross-movement influence occurs under specific conditions, including the formation of movement coalitions, shared communities of support and activist personnel, and facilitative changes in movements' external environments. This research brings important attention to the ways in which a set of actors in a given "strategic action field" (Fligstein and McAdam 2012) shape one another and produce effects that can outlast the life of a given campaign or social movement organization.

26.4 Theorizing Movement's Outcomes and Consequences

Because movements articulate claims against authorities, studies of social movement outcomes generally focus on whether or not movements gained concessions or received a desired response from third-parties in pursuit of their goals. The consequences can vary temporally and in scope, and it is usually up to the researcher to delimit what an outcome means for a given case. If movements are conceived of as challenging the state, regime change or policy modifications are likely to be the outcomes under scrutiny (e.g., Amenta et al. 1992, 2005; McAdam and Su 2002). Movement consequences also include how their mobilization dynamics influence subsequent episodes of contention (McAdam et al. 2001), as well as how they produce transformations in cultures, consciousness, and identities among movement members and among wider publics (Morris 1992). However, the distinction between political and cultural outcomes should not be drawn too sharply, as we will argue below.

26.4.1 Assessing Movement Success

Theories of movement success, originally posited by William Gamson ([1975] 1990) include the acceptance of movements by elites and the gaining of new advantages. Conceptualizing movement success as win-or-lose can be analytically useful when a movement has a delimited goal, such as changing a specific law or raising the minimum wage to a set amount. However, what success looks like may be difficult to discern in light of the fact that movements may have publicly-stated goals that differ from their private goals (Andrews 2004) and that these goals are subject to change over time. In addition, after a movement suffers a defeat or setback, activists may shift their aims or revert to clandestine actions. Furthermore, even when movements do not get exactly what they want (which they rarely, if ever, do) they may still achieve some degree of favorable policy change or collective good for their constituents, whether material or immaterial (Amenta 2006).

26.4.2 Movement's Unintended Consequences

The actions of collective actors can also have unintended consequences that harm the realization of a movement's ambitions or damage their influence in the political process. For example, McVeigh et al.'s (2004) study of the Ku Klux Klan in Indiana demonstrates that the framing processes effective in promoting grassroots mobilization hindered access to and influence over presidential candidates in the 1924 election. As such, tactics that produce favorable outcomes in a given context may not translate effectively to other arenas, thus potentially contributing to movement decline. Furthermore, unintended movement outcomes may include schisms and civil wars, as well as repression and counter-mobilization by third-parties (Snow and Soule 2010: 208). As such, the actions of social movements may draw in third parties into their spheres of contention that subvert movements' aims. For example, when the Egyptian military defected on behalf of protesters calling for the end to Hosni Mubarak's autocratic reign in 2011, this was initially viewed as a movement success. However, the Supreme Council of Armed Forces later launched a coup in 2013 against president-elect Mohamed Morsi and subsequently assumed the governance of Egypt. To date, this has produced a retrenchment of the military elite in the executive branch of government, the release of deposed dictator Hosni Mubarak from prison, the imprisonment and court-ordered death sentence of Morsi, and severe violent repression against Muslim Brotherhood members and leftists alike. Cycles of contention, therefore, can produce a variety of gains and setbacks for social movements.

26.4.3 Clarifying Movement Outcomes

Because social movement consequences can vary dramatically, scholars have increasingly called for clarification of their outcomes by level of analysis and over time. At the macro-level, for example, SMO action could lead to the extension of democratic and civil rights. At the intermediate level, movements may push for policy creation, modification, extension, or enforcement. They may also spur the establishment or institutionalization of new collective identities that foster the labeling of certain social groups as worthy of concessions or as moral and deserving social groups (Skrentny 2006). Political representation and resources, whether for the movement itself or for its beneficiary groups, and relief are also important outcomes sought by movements (Amenta 2006; Cress and Snow 2000). Another related outcome is that SMO actors in a given "policy monopoly" field may come to be perceived as legitimate representatives of a wider constituency (Meyer 2005). This is likely to determine which social movements will incur attention and resources in a given field, as well as what issues are deemed to be worthy recipients of governmental attention, access, and influence. The institutionalization of a given issue may also comprise an important consequence of social movement activity. Baumgartner and Mahoney (2005), for example, demonstrate that there is a growing correlation over time between congressional hearings and particular interest issues after the emergence and growth of a movement family. However, while governmental attention to an issue of relevance to social movements may grow over time, such attention may also court the efforts of counter-movements. An increase in congressional hearings on women's issues, for example, could have as much to do with some movements' mobilization against women's use of contraception as it does with their access to legal abortions.

How tightly the grievances and demands of social movements "fit" with the agenda of elites also matters for their outcomes (Skocpol 1992). If the frames espoused by the movement mirror the agendas of bureaucracies or the political regime, then their movement is more likely to be accommodated by state actors, and less assertive action will be required (Amenta 2006). This process is not solely the result of coincidental movement-state compatibility. Movements can improve the fit between their demands and the agendas of elites through strategic action and framing and accommodative tactics, referenced above (McCammon et al. 2008). However, the fit of movement frames at one level may foster adversarial conditions at another (McVeigh et al. 2004). The outcome of movements' tactical interactions with counter-mobilized groups and political elites have also been shown to produce specific outcomes. In his study on the civil rights movement, for example, Andrews (2004) examines how SMO infrastructures and strategies, in combination with the degree of white countermobilization and federal intervention, produced a localized legacy of civil rights activism in Mississippi. More attention is needed to understand how conflict is patterned by these interactions and what the enduring consequences of those conflicts are in history.

26.4.4 Cultural and Biographical Outcomes

Social movements also matter in shaping culture and biography. As Earl (2004) describes, cultural outcomes may include changes in values, opinions, and beliefs; cultural production and practices, including language and fashion; and broader, more encompassing worldviews and beliefs that lie outside of what is in people's heads, such as the rise of an international human rights regime. While tying the actions of specific social movements and their organizations to sweeping changes in public opinion or practice is empirically challenging, Earl (2004) suggests that scholars consider the cultural impact of movements as a matter of degree, rather than as a zero-sum dependent variable. For example, even if movements fail to achieve policy change, the act of participating in a movement may have notable consequences on the belief systems and practices of its members. Studies of movements' biographical consequences have shown that participation in collective action may shape members' worldviews and actions in important ways over the life course (Fernandez and McAdam 1988; Klatch 1999; Giugni 2004; Corrigall-Brown 2012). Likewise, outcomes for participants in religious movements can include significant changes in lifestyle and beliefs, as well as a radical configuration of everyday life and activists' orientations toward authority, their family members, and fellow participants.

Cultural consequences may be influenced by movement action through a variety of mechanisms, such as through framing processes, their networks, and the ways in which movement leaders and organizations serve as cultural brokers with other audiences and movements (Diani 1997; McAdam 1994). Snow and his colleagues (2013) suggest, for example, that movements can spur cultural revitalization and fabrication through framing mechanisms that connect and accent specific events and ideas in a strategic fashion. Movements may, for instance, select artifacts of history, including written materials, identities, and symbols, to legitimize their ideas and to promote their worldviews and agendas. The use of the swastika by the Nazi regime or the appropriation of Nordic iconography by contemporary white supremacists, for example, illustrates how movements use culture and revitalize cultural elements selectively for their purposes (Snow et al. 2013), but also change what cultural symbols and artifacts come to mean. While more research is needed to link the actions of social movements to cultural outcomes, we again caution scholars from drawing too fine a line between political and cultural consequences. Amenta's (2006) study of the Townsend Plan, for example, addresses both how the movement influenced welfare policy and cultural understandings of the "aged" as an identity group warranting rights and protections (see also Skocpol 1992). When movements produce long-term changes in identity and behavior, such as political party affiliation (McVeigh et al. 2014), or changes in how people perceive and respond to injustice (McVeigh et al. 2003), these outcomes also signify normative changes in society-wide practices and values as much as in the political realm.

26.5 Developing Theory

The study and theorization of social movements has produced an expansive research agenda in sociology that will continue to shed light on critical historical and contemporary social problems, events, and conflicts. As outlined above, young scholars of today are likely to acknowledge that a multitude of factors, including political contexts, resources and mobilizing structures, framing processes, social networks and ecological structures, culture, emotions, and identities, all impact mobilization processes. As Snow (2013: 1201) writes, "one does not have to choose one emphasis or focus over another so long as it is recognized that each conceptualization accents a particular dimension or aspect of social movements, much like the case of the storied description of an elephant rendered by six blind men on the basis of the part they touched: all parts were important features of the elephant but alone could not provide a complete picture." So where is the discipline to go from here? In closing, we draw on recent innovations in the field and suggest ways to refine, elaborate, and expand the existing theoretical repertoire.

26.5.1 Collective Behavior and Social Psychology

First, we suggest that scholars incorporate theories of collective behavior and social psychology in the study of movements (Oliver 1989). While older theories associating collective protest with irrationality certainly warranted criticism and reformulation, scholars should attend to the relatively unplanned, uncoordinated, and spontaneous dynamics that take place in crowds and during organized or SMO-sponsored protest events (Snow and Moss 2014). While social movements are largely rational enterprises, not all social movement-related occurrences are preplanned or strategized in advance of their occurrence. Drawing on theories of breakdown, ecological factors, and emotions, this perspective accounts for the fact that spontaneous interactions and occurrences can shape the course and character of social movements and related protest events. Such occurrences may also produce the riots and violence that inspired the study of collective behavior in the first place. Social movements' trajectories or collective revolts often evolve in ways that appear puzzling or irrational if scholars only look at "objective" criteria, such as changes in fungible resources or political opportunities. By taking into account the perspectives, emotions, and relational dynamics of social movements and protest events, we can better understand the conditions shaping the dynamics of mobilization and how contention unfolds over time.

26.5.2 Analyzing Movements Within Their Fields of Contention

Second, we support recent calls by McAdam and Boudet (2012) and Fligstein and McAdam (2012) for scholars to better understand how social movements emerge and mobilize within broader fields of contention. As McAdam and Boudet argue (2012: 21), social movement theorists should not be limited to investigating processes and dynamics internal to those of social movements. In order to remedy what some scholars perceive as a narrowing of social movement theory and its application, scholars may find it useful to adopt a wider lens to understanding movements' embeddedness in and relation to larger social systems (see also Goldstone 2004). This includes, for example, how episodes of contention are impacted by political economies, such as capitalist systems of production (Paige 1975), the crises and recessions produced within the world system (Smith and Weist 2012), and the relations between social movements and global conflicts and wars (Chaudhary and Guarnizo 2016; Tarrow 2015). Furthermore, additional theorization is needed as to how cases of "domestic" mobilization are impacted by extra-national events, transnational cultural and ideational trends, and foreign regimes. This includes, for example, relationship between the American civil rights movement and anti-colonialist movements (see McAdam 1998) and the repression or sponsorship of domestic collective actors by foreign states (Moss 2015). Further theorization is needed as to how social movements become transnational (Tarrow 2005), including the conditions under which movements scale up and across borders to link with extra-national actors and institutions (Ayoub 2013; Bob 2005; Smith 2004; von Bülow 2010). A comparative, transnational perspective will help scholars to understand why movements with similar goals and tactics have arisen simultaneously across the globe and the trends in movements' political orientations in history (Mannheim [1936] 2013; Turner 1969; Walder 2009).

Third, while we know a great deal about the factors producing movement emergence, increased attention is needed as to understanding their trajectories and transformations over time (Zald and Ash 1966). How and why movements succumb to infighting and factionalization, repression, or end up purging their own constituents matters greatly for understanding the rise and demise of movements and their related forms (Davenport 2014; Kretschmer 2013). Additionally, greater specification of the actors operating in a given field is needed. Disaggregating the state, for example, is theoretically necessary in order to understand its varying methods of social control, the state's varying capacities for accommodation and repression, and officials' differential relations with activists (Loveman 1998; Moss 2014; Su and He 2010). This calls attention to the importance of understanding regime types as existing on a range between democratic and authoritarian, and variations in the degrees to which state authority and coercion are applied by social movement, population, and place (Cunningham 2004). Extra-institutional and revolutionary activists may, for example, engage in routine interactions and dialogues with state officials or work to persuade state institutions, such as militaries or foreign regimes, to take the movement's side. The benefits of problematizing the people-versus-the-regime archetype will undoubtedly lead to innovation in theorizing processes of contention.

26.5.3 Attending to Neglected Movement Types

Fourth, we suggest that scholars attend to certain types of social movements that remain on the periphery of movement studies despite their centrality and importance in history and contemporary social life, such as formative pre-modern movements and the study of religious movements, including sects and cults (but see Kniss and Burns 2004). Despite the fact that religious movements were at the forefront of classical theories of society and change (Wuthnow 1986), their study has been more recently neglected in case studies of social movements and in the theoretical development of the field (Snow 2015). Additionally, studies rarely incorporate social movement theory into the study of collective action that produces political violence, mass killings, and genocide (see della Porta 2008; Luft 2015; Olzak 2004; Owens et al. 2013). Movement theorists also neglect to address how religion and violence intersect, despite the prominence of violent religious movements in some of the most contentious and consequential events in recent memory (Almond et al. 2003; Hall 2000, 2003; Juergensmeyer 2000). For reasons unclear to us, the study of these movements has been largely relegated to the field of international relations, despite the pervasive existence and threat of domestic violent extremism and the transnational operation and effects of extra-national radical movements.

Relatedly, we lack theorization as to what role religion plays in such movements. Questions remain about whether violent non-state actors, such as the so-called "Islamic State" (ISIS) or Christian anti-abortion activists, are "really" religious and represent permutations of that religion, or are just "using" religion. In either case, far more empirically-grounded theorization is needed as to how waves of religious extremism arise across different belief systems and how religious authorities incite collective action and violence. Furthermore, understanding how extremist movements are produced and supported by broader communities of sympathy—or are not supported (Acevedo and Chaudhary 2015)—will enhance our understanding of how cultural and political conditions shape social movements, and in turn, how those movements shape broader conflicts in history (Jurgensmeyer 2000). This line of inquiry complements the work of resource mobilization and framing scholars in that it draws attention to how religion is used as an ideological and material resource by movements, as well as how movements can shape religious ideas, offshoots, and organizations (Williams 1996).

26.5.4 Changes in Activists' Tools

Lastly, because theoretical trends in any discipline are themselves embedded in the historical contexts in which scientists work, it will be useful for scholars to consider how protest and counter-protest has changed by venue and medium over time. This includes what the rise and evolution of information communication technologies mean for social movements, such as those made available through the internet and on cell phones. As Jennifer Earl, Katrina Kimport, and their colleagues have demonstrated, social movements use the internet as a means of sharing information, garnering support and participation, and as a medium to organize protests (Earl and Kimport 2011). While the role of internet-based technologies and their importance varies by case, the potential for activists to connect—as well as for countermovements and regimes to repress—through these relational networks have real-life consequences for social movements, as activist bloggers, "Tweeps", and journalists end up in prison or experience worse fates across the globe. At the same time, while states' increased used of surveillance technologies may signify growth in the means of social control, activists are also savvy and inventive in their use of those technologies as a way to document abuses, pursue their claims, and shed light into dark places. Whether internet-based activism is merely a form of "clicktivism" or something more remains an important topic of debate and further empirical inquiry (Carty 2015), but we submit that scholars would do well to understand whether what happens online facilitates or hinders the face-to-face interactions between movements and their participants and the potential for social change.

References

Acevedo, G., & Chaudhary, A. R. (2015). Islam and suicide bombings: Religion, cultural clash and Muslim American attitudes towards politically motivated violence. *The Journal for the Scientific Study of Religion, 54*(2), 242–260.

Almeida, P. D. (2003). Opportunity organizations and threat-induced contention: Protest waves in authoritarian settings. *American Journal of Sociology, 109*(2), 345–400.

Almond, G. A., Scott Appleby, R., & Sivan, E. (2003). *Strong religion: The rise of fundamentalism around the world*. Chicago: University of Chicago Press.

Amenta, E. (2006). *When movements matter: The Townsend Plan and the rise of social security*. Princeton: Princeton University Press.

Amenta, E., Carruthers, B. G., & Zyland, Y. (1992). A hero for the aged? The Townsend movement, the political mediation model, and U.S. old-age policy, 1934–1950. *American Journal of Sociology, 98*(2), 308–339.

Amenta, E., Caren, N., & Olasky, S. J. (2005). Age for leisure? Political mediation and the impact of the pension movement on U.S. old-age policy. *American Sociological Review, 70*(3), 516–538.

Andrews, K. T. (2004). *Freedom is a constant struggle: The Mississippi civil rights movement and its legacy*. Chicago: University of Chicago Press.

Ayoub, P. M. (2013). Cooperative transnationalism in contemporary Europe: Europeanization and political opportunities for LGBT mobilization in the European Union. *European Political Science Review, 5*(2), 279–310.

Baumgartner, F. R., & Mahoney, C. (2005). Social movements, the rise of new issues, and the public agenda. In D. S. Meyer, V. Jenness, & H. Ingram (Eds.), *Routing the opposition: Social movements, public policy, and democracy* (pp. 65–86). Minneapolis: University of Minnesota Press.

Benford, R. D., & Snow, D. A. (2000). Framing processes and social movements: An overview and assessment. *Annual Review of Sociology, 26*, 611–639.

Blee, K. M. (2012). *Democracy in the making: How activist groups form*. New York: Oxford University Press.

Blee, K. M., & Currier, A. (2006). How local social movement groups handle a presidential election. *Qualitative Sociology, 29*(3), 261–280.

Bob, C. (2005). *The marketing of rebellion: Insurgents, media, and international activism*. New York: Cambridge University Press.

Borland, E., & Sutton, B. (2007). Quotidian disruption and women's activism in times of crisis, Argentina 2002–2003. *Gender & Society, 21*(5), 700–722.

Buechler, S. M. (2004). The strange career of strain and breakdown theories of collective action. In D. A. Snow, S. A. Soule, & H. Kriesi (Eds.), *The Blackwell companion to social movements* (pp. 47–66). Malden: Blackwell.

Carty, V. (2015). *Social movements and new technology*. Boulder: Westview.

Chaudhary, A. R., & Guarnizo, L. E. (2016). Pakistani organizational spaces in Toronto and New York City. *Journal of Ethnic and Migration Studies, 42*(6), 1013-1035.

Clemens, E. S., & Minkoff, D. C. (2004). Beyond the iron law: Rethinking the place of organizations in social movement research. In D. A. Snow, S. A. Soule, &

H. Kriesi (Eds.), *The Blackwell companion to social movements* (pp. 155–170). Malden: Blackwell.

Collins, R. (2004). *Interaction ritual chains*. Princeton: Princeton University Press.

Colomy, P. (1998). Neofunctionalism and neoinstitutionalism: Human agency and interest in institutional change. *Sociological Forum, 13*(2), 265–300.

Corrigall-Brown, C. (2012). *Patterns of protest: Trajectories of participation in social movements*. Palo Alto: Stanford University Press.

Corrigall-Brown, C., Snow, D. A., Quist, T., & Smith, K. (2009). Explaining the puzzle of homeless mobilization: An examination of differential participation. *Sociological Perspectives, 52*(3), 309–335.

Cress, D. M., & Snow, D. A. (2000). The outcomes of homeless mobilization: The influence of organization, disruption, political mediation, and framing. *American Journal of Sociology, 105*(4), 1063–1104.

Cunningham, D. (2004). *There's something happening here: The new left, the Klan, and FBI counterintelligence*. Los Angeles: University of California Press.

Davenport, C. (2014). *How social movements die: Repression and demobilization of the Republic of New Africa*. New York: Cambridge University Press.

de la Luz Inclán, M. (2008). From the ¡Ya Basta! to the Caracoles: Zapatista mobilization under transitional conditions. *American Journal of Sociology, 113*(5), 1316–1350.

della Porta, D. (2005). Deliberation in movement: Why and how to study deliberative democracy and social movements. *Acta Politica, 40*(3), 336–350.

della Porta, D. (2008). Research on social movements and political violence. *Qualitative Sociology, 31*(3), 221–230.

Diani, M. (1997). Social movements and social capital: A network perspective on movement outcomes. *Mobilization: An International Quarterly, 2*(2), 129–147.

Diani, D. (2004). Networks and participation. In D. A. Snow, S. A. Soule, & H. Kriesi (Eds.), *The Blackwell companion to social movements* (pp. 339–359). Malden: Blackwell.

Diani, M. (2013). Networks and social movements. In D. A. Snow, D. della Porta, B. Klandermans, & D. McAdam (Eds.), *The Wiley-Blackwell encyclopedia of social and political movements* (pp. 835–840). Malden: Blackwell Publishing.

Diani, M., & McAdam, D. (2003). *Social movements and relational networks: Relational approaches to collective action*. New York: Oxford University Press.

Earl, J. (2004). The cultural consequences of social movements. In D. A. Snow, S. A. Soule, & H. Kriesi (Eds.), *The Blackwell companion to social movements* (pp. 508–530). Malden: Blackwell.

Earl, J., & Kimport, K. (2011). *Digitally enabled social change: Activism in the internet age*. Cambridge, MA: MIT Press.

Edwards, B., & McCarthy, J. D. (2004). Resources and social movement mobilization. In D. A. Snow, S. A. Soule, & H. Kriesi (Eds.), *The Blackwell companion to social movements* (pp. 116–152). Malden: Blackwell.

Einwohner, R. L. (2003). Opportunity, honor, and action in the Warsaw ghetto uprising of 1943. *American Journal of Sociology, 109*(3), 650–675.

Eisinger, P. (1973). The conditions of protest behavior in American cities. *American Political Science Review, 67*(1), 11–28.

Fantasia, R. (1988). *Cultures of solidarity: Consciousness, action and contemporary American workers*. Berkeley: University of California Press.

Fernandez, R. M., & McAdam, D. (1988). Social networks and social movements: Multiorganizational fields and recruitment to Mississippi Freedom Summer. *Sociological Forum, 3*(3), 357–382.

Ferree, M. M. (1992). The political context of rationality: Rational choice theory and resource mobilization. In A. Morris & C. Mueller (Eds.), *Frontiers of social movement theory* (pp. 29–52). New Haven: Yale University Press.

Fligstein, N., & McAdam, D. (2012). *A theory of fields*. New York: Oxford University Press.

Futrell, R., & Simi, P. (2004). Free spaces, collective identity, and the persistence of U.S. white power activism. *Social Problems, 51*(1), 16–42.

Gamson, W. A. (1975 [1990]). *The strategy of social protest*. Homewood: Dorsey.

Gamson, W. A. (2004). Bystanders, public opinion, and the media. In D. A. Snow, S. A. Soule, & H. Kriesi (Eds.), *The Blackwell companion to social movements* (pp. 242–261). Malden: Blackwell.

Gamson, W. A., & Wolfsfeld, G. (1993). Movements and media as interacting systems. *Annals of the American Academy of Political and Social Science, 528*, 114–125.

Giugni, M. (2004). Personal and biographical consequences. In D. A. Snow, S. A. Soule, & H. Kriesi (Eds.), *The Blackwell companion to social movements* (pp. 489–507). Malden: Blackwell.

Goldstone, J. A. (2004). More social movements or fewer? Beyond political opportunity structures to relational fields. *Theory and Society, 33*(3), 333–365.

Goldstone, J. A. (2014). *Revolutions: A very short introduction*. New York: Oxford University Press.

Goodwin, J. (2001). *No other way out: States and revolutionary movements, 1945–1991*. New York: Cambridge University Press.

Goodwin, J., & Jasper, J. M. (1999). Caught in a winding, snarling vine: The structural bias of political process theory. *Sociological Forum, 14*(1), 27–54.

Goodwin, J., Jasper, J. M., & Polletta, F. (2001). *Passionate politics: Emotions and social movements*. Chicago: University of Chicago Press.

Gould, R. V. (1991). Multiple networks and mobilization in the Paris commune, 1871. *American Sociological Review, 56*(5), 716–729.

Haines, H. H. (2013). Radical flank effects. In D. A. Snow, D. della Porta, B. Klandermans, & D. McAdam

(Eds.), *The Wiley-Blackwell encyclopedia of social and political movements*. Malden: Blackwell Publishing.

Hall, J. R. (2000). *Apocalypse observed: Religious movements and violence in north America, Europe, and Japan*. London: Routledge.

Hall, J. R. (2003). Religion and violence: Social processes in comparative perspective. In M. Dillon (Ed.), *Handbook of the sociology of religion* (pp. 359–384). Cambridge: Cambridge University Press.

Hess, D., & Martin, B. (2006). Repression, backfire, and the theory of transformative events. *Mobilization: An International Quarterly, 11*(2), 249–267.

Hirschman, A. O. (1970). Exit, voice, and the state. *World Politics, 31*(1), 90–107.

Hoffer, E. (1951). *The true believer: Thoughts on the nature of mass movements*. New York: The New American Library.

Jafar, A. (2007). Engaging fundamentalism: The case of women's NGOs in Pakistan. *Social Problems, 54*(3), 256–273.

Jasper, J. M. (2004). A strategic approach to collective action: Looking for agency in social movement choices. *Mobilization, 9*, 1–16.

Jasper, J. M. (2011). Emotions and social movements: Twenty years of theory and research. *Annual Review of Sociology, 37*, 1–19.

Jasper, J. M. (2013). Strategy. In D. A. Snow, D. della Porta, B. Klandermans, & D. McAdam (Eds.), *The Wiley-Blackwell encyclopedia of social and political movements* (pp. 1262–1267). Malden: Blackwell Publishing.

Jenkins, J. C., & Eckert, C. M. (1986). Channeling Black insurgency: Elite patronage and professional social movement organizations in the development of the Black movement. *American Sociological Review, 51*(6), 812–829.

Johnston, H. (2005). Talking the walk: Speech acts and resistance in authoritarian regimes. In C. Davenport, J. Johnston, & C. Mueller (Eds.), *Repression and mobilization* (pp. 108–137). Minneapolis: University of Minnesota Press.

Johnston, H. (2006). "Let's get small": The dynamics of (small) contention in repressive states. *Mobilization: An International Quarterly, 11*(2), 195–212.

Johnston, H., & Mueller, C. (2001). Unobtrusive practices of contention in Leninist regimes. *Sociological Perspectives, 44*(3), 351–375.

Johnston, H., & Snow, D. A. (1998). Subcultures and the emergence of the Estonian nationalist opposition, 1945–1990. *Sociological Perspectives, 41*(3), 473–497.

Juergensmeyer, M. (2000). *Terror in the mind of God: The global rise of religious violence* (3rd ed.). Los Angeles: University of California Press.

Kadivar, M. A. (2013). Alliances and perception profiles in the Iranian reform movement, 1997 to 2005. *American Sociological Review, 78*(6), 1063–1086.

Kahneman, D., & Tversky, A. (1979). Prospect theory: An analysis of decision under risk. *Econometrica, 47*(2), 263–291.

Katzenstein, M. F. (1990). Feminism within American institutions: Unobtrusive mobilization in the 1980s. *Signs: Journal of Women in Culture and Society, 16*(1), 27–54.

Kitts, J. A. (2000). Mobilizing in black boxes: Social networks and participation in social movement organizations. *Mobilization: An International Quarterly, 5*(2), 241–257.

Klandermans, B. (2004). The demand and supply side of participation: Social-psychological correlates of participation in social movements. In D. A. Snow, S. A. Soule, & H. Kriesi (Eds.), *The Blackwell companion to social movements* (pp. 360–379). Malden: Blackwell.

Klatch, R. E. (1999). *A generation divided: The new left, the new right, and the 1960s*. Berkeley: University of California Press.

Kniss, F., & Burns, G. (2004). Religious movements. In D. A. Snow, S. A. Soule, & H. Kreisi (Eds.), *The Blackwell companion to social movements* (pp. 694–716). Malden: Blackwell Publishing.

Kornhauser, W. (1959). *The politics of mass society*. New York: The Free Press.

Kretschmer, K. (2013). Factions/factionalism. In D. A. Snow, D. della Porta, B. Klandermans, & D. McAdam (Eds.), *The Wiley-Blackwell encyclopedia of social and political movements* (pp. 443–446). Malden: Blackwell Publishing.

Kriesi, H. (2004). Political context and opportunity. In D. A. Snow, S. A. Soule, & H. Kriesi (Eds.), *The Blackwell companion to social movements* (pp. 67–90). Malden: Blackwell.

Kucinskas, J. (2014). The unobtrusive tactics of religious movements. *Sociology of Religion, 75*(4), 537–550.

Kurzman, C. (1996). Structural opportunity and perceived opportunity in social movement theory: The Iranian revolution of 1979. *American Sociological Review, 61*(1), 153–170.

Kurzman, C. (2004). *The unthinkable revolution in Iran*. Cambridge: Harvard University Press.

LeBon, G. (1897 [1960]). *The crowd: A study of the popular mind*. New York: Viking Press.

Lipsky, M. (1970). *Protest in city politics*. Chicago: Rand-McNally.

Loveman, M. (1998). High-risk collective action: Defending human rights in Chile, Uruguay, and Argentina. *American Journal of Sociology, 104*(2), 477–525.

Luft, A. (2015). Genocide as contentious politics. *Sociology Compass, 9*(10), 897–909.

Mannheim, K. ([1936] 2013). *Ideology and utopia: Collected works of Karl Mannheim* (Vol. 1). New York: Routledge.

McAdam, D. ([1982] 1999). *Political process and the development of Black insurgency, 1930–1970*, 2nd edn. Chicago: University of Chicago Press.

McAdam, D. (1983). Tactical innovation and the pace of insurgency. *American Sociological Review, 48*(6), 735–754.

McAdam, D. (1986). Recruitment to high-risk activism: The case of Freedom Summer. *American Journal of Sociology, 92*(1), 64–90.

McAdam, D. (1994). Culture and social movements. In J. R. Gusfield (Ed.), *New social movements: From ideology to identity* (pp. 36–57). Philadelphia: Temple University Press.

McAdam, D. (1996). Political opportunities: Conceptual origins, current problems, future directions. In D. McAdam, J. D. McCarthy, & M. N. Zald (Eds.), *Comparative perspectives on social movements* (pp. 23–40). New York: Cambridge University Press.

McAdam, D. (1998). On the international origins of domestic political opportunities. In A. N. Costain & A. S. McFarland (Eds.), *Social movements and American political institutions* (pp. 252–267). Lanham: Rowman & Littlefield.

McAdam, D., & Boudet, H. S. (2012). *Putting social movements in their place: Explaining opposition to energy projects in the United States, 2000–2005*. New York: Cambridge University Press.

McAdam, D., & Paulsen, R. (1993). Specifying the relationship between social ties and activism. *American Journal of Sociology, 99*(3), 640–667.

McAdam, D., Tarrow, S., & Tilly, C. (2001). *Dynamics of contention*. New York: Cambridge University Press.

McAdam, D., & Su, Y. (2002). The war at home: Antiwar protests and congressional voting, 1965 to 1973. *American Sociological Review, 67*(5), 696–721.

McCammon, H. J., Chaudhuri, S., Hewitt, L., Muse, C. S., Newman, H. D., Smith, C. L., & Terrell, T. M. (2008). Becoming full citizens: The U.S. women's jury rights campaigns, the pace of reform, and strategic adaptation. *American Journal of Sociology, 113*(4), 1104–1147.

McCarthy, N. D., & Zald, M. N. (1973). *The trend of social movements in America: Professionalization and resource mobilization*. Morristown: General Learning.

McCarthy, J. D., & Zald, M. N. (1977). Resource mobilization and social movements: A partial theory. *American Journal of Sociology, 82*(6), 1212–1241.

McVeigh, R. (2006). Structural influences on activism and crime: Identifying the social structure of discontent. *American Journal of Sociology, 112*(2), 510–566.

McVeigh, R., Welch, M. R., & Bjarnason, T. (2003). Hate crime reporting as a successful social movement outcome. *American Sociological Review, 68*(6), 843–867.

McVeigh, R., Myers, D. J., & Sikkink, D. (2004). Corn, Klansmen, and Coolidge: Structure and framing in social movements. *Social Forces, 83*(2), 653–690.

McVeigh, R., Cunningham, D., & Farrell, J. (2014). Political polarization as a social movement outcome: 1960s Klan activism and its enduring impact on political realignment in southern counties, 1960 to 2000. *American Sociological Review, 79*(6), 1144–1171.

Meyer, D. S. (1990). *A winter of discontent: The nuclear freeze and American politics*. New York: Praeger.

Meyer, D. S. (2004). Protest and political opportunities. *Annual Review of Sociology, 30*, 125–145.

Meyer, D. S. (2005). Social movements and public policy: Eggs, chicken, and theory. In D. S. Meyer, V. Jenness, & H. Ingram (Eds.), *Routing the opposition: Social movements, public policy, and democracy* (pp. 1–16). Minneapolis: University of Minnesota Press.

Meyer, D. S. (2015). *The politics of protest: Social movements in America* (2nd ed.). New York: Oxford University Press.

Meyer, D. S., & Staggenborg, S. (1996). Movements, countermovements, and the structure of political opportunity. *American Journal of Sociology, 101*(6), 1628–1660.

Meyer, D. S., & Tarrow, S. (1998). *The social movement society: Contentious politics for a new century*. Boulder: Rowman & Littlefield.

Meyer, D. S., & Whittier, N. (1994). Social movement spillover. *Social Problems, 41*(2), 277–298.

Michels, R. (1915 [1962]). *Political parties: A sociological study of the oligarchical tendencies of modern democracy*. New York: Dover.

Moore, B., Jr. (1978). *Injustice: The social bases of obedience and revolt*. White Plains: M. E. Sharpe.

Morris, A. D. (1981). Black southern student sit-in movement: An analysis of internal organization. *American Sociological Review, 46*(6), 744–767.

Morris, A. D. (1992). Political consciousness and collective action. In A. D. Morris & C. M. Mueller (Eds.), *Frontiers in social movement theory* (pp. 351–373). New Haven: Yale University Press.

Moss, D. M. (2014). Repression, response, and contained escalation under 'liberalized' authoritarianism in Jordan. *Mobilization: An International Quarterly, 19*(3), 489–514.

Moss, D. M. (2015). Transnational repression and diaspora mobilization. *Conference paper, the American Sociological Association's annual meeting*. Chicago, August 24.

Mottl, T. L. (1980). The analysis of countermovements. *Social Problems, 27*(5), 620–635.

Nepstad, S. E. (2004). Persistent resistance: Commitment and community in the plowshares movement. *Social Problems, 51*(1), 43–60.

Oberschall, A. (1973). *Social conflict and social movements*. Englewood Cliffs: Prentice-Hall.

Oliver, P. E. (1989). Bringing the crowd back in: The nonorganizational elements of social movements. *Research in Social Movements, Conflicts and Change, 11*, 1–30.

Oliver, P. E., & Johnston, H. (2000). What a good idea! Ideologies and frames in social movement research. *Mobilization: An International Quarterly, 5*(1), 37–54.

Oliver, P. E., & Myers, D. J. (2003). The coevolution of social movements. *Mobilization: An International Quarterly, 8*(1), 1–25.

Olzak, S. (2004). Ethnic and nationalist social movements. In D. A. Snow, S. A. Soule, & H. Kriesi (Eds.), *The Blackwell companion to social movements* (pp. 666–693). Malden: Blackwell.

Owens, P. B., Su, Y., & Snow, D. A. (2013). Social scientific inquiry into genocide and mass killing. *Annual Review of Sociology, 39*, 69–84.

Paige, J. M. (1975). *Agrarian revolution*. New York: Free Press.

Passy, F. (2003). Social movements matter. But how? In M. Diani & D. McAdam (Eds.), *Social movements and relational networks: Relational approaches to collective action* (pp. 22–48). New York: Oxford University Press.

Pinard, M. (1971). *The rise of a third party: A study in crisis politics*. Englewood Cliffs: Prentice-Hall.

Piven, F. F., & Cloward, R. A. (1979). *Poor people's movements*. New York: Vintage Books.

Polletta, P. (1999). "Free spaces" in collective action. *Theory and Society, 28*, 1–38.

Polletta, P. (2005). How participatory democracy became white: Culture and organizational choice. *Mobilization: An International Quarterly, 10*(2), 271–288.

Polletta, F. (2012). *Freedom is an endless meeting: Democracy in American social movements*. Chicago: University of Chicago Press.

Polletta, F., & Jasper, J. M. (2001). Collective identity and social movements. *Annual Review of Sociology, 27*, 283–305.

Robnett, B. (1996). African-American women in the civil rights movement, 1954–1965: Gender, leadership, and micromobilization. *The American Journal of Sociology, 101*(6), 1661–1693.

Rohlinger, D., & Snow, D. A. (2003). Social psychological perspectives on crowds and social movements. In J. Delamater (Ed.), *Handbook of social psychology* (pp. 503–527). New York: Kluwer Academic/Plenum Publishers.

Rucht, D. (1999). Linking organization and mobilization: Michels's iron law of oligarchy reconsidered. *Mobilization: An International Quarterly, 4*(2), 151–169.

Rule, J., & Tilly, C. (1972). 1830 and the unnatural history of revolution. *Journal of Social Issues, 28*(1), 49–76.

Schattschneider, E. E. (1960). *The semisovereign people: A realist's view of democracy in America*. New York: Thomson Learning.

Scott, J. C. (1985). *Weapons of the weak: Everyday forms of peasant resistance*. New Haven: Yale University Press.

Sewell, W. H., Jr. (2001). Space in contentious politics. In R. R. Aminzade, J. A. Goldstone, D. McAdam, E. J. Perry, W. H. Sewell Jr., S. Tarrow, & C. Tilly (Eds.), *Silence and violence in the study of contentious politics* (pp. 51–88). New York: Cambridge University Press.

Shultziner, D. (2013). The social-psychological origins of the Montgomery bus boycott: Social interaction and humiliation in the emergence of social movements. *Mobilization: An International Quarterly, 18*(2), 117–142.

Skocpol, T. (1992). *Protecting soldiers and mothers: The political origins of social policy in the United States*. Cambridge: Harvard University Press.

Skocpol, T. (2003). *Diminished democracy: From membership to management in American civic life*. Oklahoma City: University of Oklahoma Press.

Skrentny, J. D. (2006). Policy-elite perceptions and social movement success: Understanding variations in group inclusion in affirmative action. *American Journal of Sociology, 111*(6), 1762–1815.

Smelser, N. J. (1962). *Theory of collective behavior*. New York: The Free Press.

Smith, C. (1996). *Resisting Reagan: The U.S. Central America peace movement*. Chicago: University of Chicago Press.

Smith, J. (2004). Transnational processes and movements. In D. A. Snow, S. A. Soule, & H. Kreisi (Eds.), *The Blackwell companion to social movements* (pp. 311–336). Malden: Blackwell Publishing.

Smith, J., & Weist, D. (2012). *Social movements in the world-system: The politics of crisis and transformation*. New York: Russell Sage.

Snow, D. A. (1979). A dramaturgical analysis of movement accommodation: Building idiosyncrasy credit as a movement mobilization strategy. *Symbolic Interaction, 2*(2), 23–44.

Snow, D. A. (2003). Social movements. In L. T. Renolds & N. J. Herman-Kinney (Eds.), *Handbook of symbolic interactionism* (pp. 811–833). Walnut Creek: Rowman & Littlefield Publishers.

Snow, D. A. (2004a). Framing processes, ideology, and discursive fields. In D. A. Snow, S. A. Soule, & H. Kriesi (Eds.), *The Blackwell companion to social movements* (pp. 380–412). Malden: Blackwell.

Snow, D. A. (2004b). Social movements as challenges to authority: Resistance to an emerging conceptual hegemony. *Research in Social Movements, Conflicts and Change, 25*, 3–25.

Snow, D. A. (2013). Social movements. In D. A. Snow, D. della Porta, B. Klandermans, & D. McAdam (Eds.), *The Wiley-Blackwell encyclopedia of social and political movements* (pp. 1201–1205). Malden: Blackwell Publishing.

Snow, D. A. (2015). Bringing the study of religion and social movements together: Toward an analytically productive intersection. Unpublished manuscript.

Snow, D. A., & Anderson, L. (1983). *Down on their luck: A study of homeless street people*. Berkeley: University of California Press.

Snow, D. A., & Moss, D. M. (2014). Protest on the fly: Toward a theory of spontaneity in the dynamics of protest and social movements. *American Sociological Review, 79*(6), 1122–1143.

Snow, D. A., & Soule, S. A. (2010). *A primer on social movements*. New York: W. W. Norton.

Snow, D. A., Zurcher, L. A., Jr., & Ekland-Olson, S. (1980). Social networks and social movements: A microstructural approach to differential recruitment. *American Sociological Review, 45*(5), 787–801.

Snow, D. A., Rochford, E. B., Jr., Worden, S. K., & Benford, R. D. (1986). Frame alignment processes, micromobilization, and movement participation. *American Sociological Review, 51*(4), 464–481.

Snow, D. A., Cress, D. M., Downey, L., & Jones, A. W. (1998). Disrupting the "quotidian": Reconceptualizing the relationship between breakdown and the emergence of collective action. *Mobilization: An International Quarterly, 3*(1), 1–22.

Snow, D. A., Soule, S. A., & Cress, D. M. (2005). Identifying the precipitants of homeless protest across 17 U.S. Cities, 1980 to 1990. *Social Forces, 83*(3), 1183–1210.

Snow, D. A., Tan, A., & Owens, P. (2013). Social movements, framing processes, and cultural revitalization and fabrication. *Mobilization: An International Quarterly, 18*(3), 225–242.

Snow, D. A., Benford, R., McCammon, H., Hewitt, L., & Fitzgerald, S. (2014). The emergence, development, and future of the framing perspective: 25+ years since "frame alignment". *Mobilization: An International Quarterly, 19*(1), 489–512.

Soule, S. A. (1997). The student divestment movement in the United States and tactical diffusion: The shantytown protest. *Social Forces, 75*(3), 855–882.

Soule, S. A. (2004). Diffusion processes within and across movements. In D. A. Snow, S. A. Soule, & H. Kriesi (Eds.), *The Blackwell companion to social movements* (pp. 294–310). Malden: Blackwell.

Su, Y., & He, X. (2010). Street as courtroom: State accommodation of labor protest in South China. *Law & Society Review, 44*(1), 157–184.

Summers-Effler, E. (2010). *Laughing saints and righteous heroes: Emotional rhythms in social movement groups*. Chicago: University of Chicago Press.

Tarrow, S. (1994). *Power in movement: Social movements, collective action and politics*. New York: Cambridge University Press.

Tarrow, S. (2005). *The new transnational activism*. New York: Cambridge University Press.

Tarrow, S. (2015). *War, states, & contention: A comparative historical study*. Ithaca: Cornell University Press.

Taylor, V. (1989). Social movement continuity: The women's movement in abeyance. *American Sociological Review, 54*(5), 761–775.

Taylor, V., Kimport, K., Van Dyke, N., & Andersen, E. A. (2009). Culture and mobilization: Tactical repertoires, same-sex weddings, and the impact on gay activism. *American Sociological Review, 74*(6), 865–890.

Tierney, A. C. (2013). System exiting and social movements. In D. A. Snow, D. della Porta, B. Klandermans, & D. McAdam (Eds.), *The Wiley-Blackwell encyclopedia of social and political movements* (pp. 1310–1312). Malden: Blackwell Publishing.

Tilly, C. (1978). *From mobilization to revolution*. Reading: Addison-Wesley.

Tilly, C. (1995). *Popular contention in Great Britain, 1758–1834*. Cambridge: Harvard University Press.

Tilly, C., & Tarrow, S. (2007). *Contentious politics*. Boulder: Paradigm.

Tilly, C., Tilly, L., & Tilly, R. (1975). *The rebellious century, 1830–1930*. Cambridge, MA: Harvard University Press.

Turner, R. H. (1969). The theme of contemporary social movements. *British Journal of Sociology, 20*(4), 390–405.

Turner, R. H. (1970). Determinants of social movement strategies. In T. Shibutani (Ed.), *Human nature and collective behavior: Papers in honor of Herbert Blumer* (pp. 145–164). Brunswick: Transaction Books.

Useem, B. (1985). Disorganization and the New Mexico prison riot of 1980. *American Sociological Review, 50*(5), 677–688.

Useem, B., & Kimball, P. (1989). *States of Siege: U.S. prison riots, 1971–1986*. New York: Oxford University Press.

Van Dyke, N., & Soule, S. A. (2002). Structural social change and the mobilizing effect of threat: Explaining levels of patriot and militia organizing in the United States. *Social Problems, 49*(4), 497–520.

Viterna, J. S. (2006). Pulled, pushed, and persuaded: Explaining women's mobilization into the Salvadoran guerrilla army. *American Journal of Sociology, 112*(1), 1–45.

von Bülow, M. (2010). *Building transnational networks: Civil society and the politics of trade in the Americas*. New York: Cambridge University Press.

Voss, K., & Sherman, R. (2000). Breaking the iron law of oligarchy: Union revitalization in the American labor movement. *American Journal of Sociology, 106*(2), 303–349.

Walder, A. G. (2009). Political sociology and social movements. *Annual Review of Sociology, 35*, 393–412.

Walker, E. T., McCarthy, J. D., & Baumgartner, F. (2011). Replacing members with managers? Mutualism among membership and nonmembership advocacy organizations in the United States. *American Journal of Sociology, 116*(4), 1284–1337.

Weber, M. (1978). In G. Roth & C. Wittich (Eds.), *Economy and society: An outline of interpretive sociology*. Berkeley: University of California Press.

White, R. W. (1989). From peaceful protest to guerrilla war: Micromobilization of the Provisional Irish Republican Army. *The American Journal of Sociology, 94*(6), 1277–1302.

Williams, R. H. (1996). Religion as a political resource: Culture or ideology? *Journal for the Scientific Study of Religion, 35*(4), 368–378.

Williams, R. H. (2004). The cultural contexts of collective action: Constraints, opportunities, and the symbolic life of social movements. In D. A. Snow, S. A. Soule, & H. Kriesi (Eds.), *The Blackwell companion to social movements* (pp. 91–115). Malden: Blackwell.

Wilson, J. Q. (1961). The strategy of protest: Problems of negro civic action. *Journal of Conflict Resolution, 5*(3), 291–303.

Wisler, D., & Giugni, M. (1999). Under the spotlight: The impact of media attention on protest policing. *Mobilization: An International Quarterly, 2*(2), 171–187.

Wuthnow, R. (1986). Religious movements and counter-movements in North America. In J. A. Beckford (Ed.), *New religious movements and rapid social change* (pp. 1–28). Newbury Park: Sage.

Zald, M. N., & Ash, R. (1966). Social movement organizations: Growth, decay and change. *Social Forces, 44*(3), 327–341.

Zhao, D. (2001). *The power of Tiananmen: State-society relations and the 1989 Beijing student movement.* Chicago: University of Chicago Press.

Index

S. Abrutyn (ed.), *Handbook of Contemporary Sociological Theory*, Handbooks of Sociology and Social Research, DOI 10.1007/978-3-319-32250-6

U

V

W

Druck

Canon Deutschland Business Services GmbH
Ferdinand-Jühlke-Str. 7
99095 Erfurt